CASUALTY CLAIM PRACTICE

The Irwin Series in Insurance and Economic Security
Davis W. Gregg   Consulting Editor

CASUALTY
CLAIM
PRACTICE

JAMES H. DONALDSON, LL.B., LL.M.
of the New York and New Jersey Bar

1984 Fourth Edition

RICHARD D. IRWIN, INC. Homewood, Illinois 60430

ISBN 0-256-02822-2
Library of Congress Catalog Card No. 84–80443
Printed in the United States of America

7 8 9 0 MP 1 0 9

To My Mother

Who, like all mothers the world over,
always had more confidence in her son
than he could ever justify in himself,
this volume is affectionately dedicated.

Preface

In recent years, we have seen increased public awareness in certain areas of the social impact caused by the application of current rules of law to the disposition of claims. This is especially true in cases arising out of the manufacture and use of automobiles, the disposition of hazardous waste, the use of hazardous materials in construction, the manufacture and sale of hazardous drugs, and the failure of the medical profession to render satisfactory health care.

The legislative response has been the enactment of new laws, such as no fault automobile laws and the adoption of comparative negligence rules. This places a burden on the claim department to amend its procedures of investigation and settlement to conform to the new rules. Since this legislative activity is a continuing one, an additional burden is placed on the claims representative, who must remain alert to the new laws and amendments that will affect his activity. Even as this book goes to press, there may be pending legislation that will affect claim handling.

In this volume, we have tried to include all the changes that have been made and to suggest amendments in claim procedure to conform with the new legislation. The purpose of this volume remains the same as that of previous editions: to present the basic knowledge that every claims representative should have, to suggest investigation and settlement procedures, to provide a ready reference for the experienced claims representative, and to provide a starting point for those whose duty it is to research various phases of applicable law.

The author gratefully acknowledges the helpful suggestions received from claims representatives everywhere. The suggestions have received careful attention, contributing in large measure to the final result. The errors and omissions are, as usual, the author's own.

James H. Donaldson

Contents

IV.   Tort doctrines   81

V.   Statutory modifications of the law of torts   139

VI.   Judicial modifications of the law of torts   155

VII.   Law of contracts   175

VIII. Law of agency and contractors 211

IX. Law of bailments, innkeepers, and carriers 234

X. Law of products 253

XI.   Professional liability   326

XII.   Law of automobiles   368

XIII.   Federal jurisdiction and authority   436

XIV.   Law of admiralty   458

XV.   Law of evidence   509

XVI.   Liability insurance contracts   543

XXII.   Trial preparation and litigation   885

XXIII.   Employers' liability and workmen's compensation   906

CHAPTER I

Casualty claims and the claims representative

100 Casualty claims defined

A claim is the assertion of an alleged legal right, which carries with it a demand for appropriate relief. The legal right asserted may involve any right in the legal spectrum, and the relief demanded may be any one or more of the forms of relief afforded by the courts.

A casualty claim, for the purposes of this work, is one which arises out of, or is the subject matter of, an insurance contract of indemnification, in which the promises of the insurance carrier hold the insured harmless against financial loss from an unknown or contingent event. The relief which may be demanded in a casualty claim is the payment of money or its equivalent.

The promise of indemnification may involve either or both of the following types of losses:

1. Losses sustained directly by the policyholder.
2. Losses sustained by others to whom the policyholder is legally liable.

1. *Losses sustained by the policyholder.* This type of promise is one whereby the policyholder obtains protection from financial loss which he would otherwise have to bear because of damage to, or destruction of, property which he owns or in which he has an interest, or because of injury to his person. Since there are only two parties to this contract—the policyholder, the first party, and the insurance carrier, the second party—the insurance afforded is referred to as *first-party coverage,* and the losses thereunder as *first-party claims,* since the loss is suffered by the first party to the contract.

2. *Losses sustained by others.* The second type of promise is one whereby the policyholder obtains protection against the loss which he would be legally obligated to pay as damages to others because of bodily injury, sickness or disease, or death, or because of the injury to or destruction of their property, including damages for loss of use.

There are three parties involved in this situation: (1) the policyholder, or first party, (2) the insurance carrier, or second party, and (3) the party who

1

has been injured or whose property has been damaged, the third party. Thus a promise of indemnification referring to this type of situation is called *third-party coverage,* and the claims are referred to as *third-party claims,* since the person asserting the alleged legal right against the insured is the third party.

101   The claims representative

A claims representative[1] is one who represents an insurance carrier in the investigation, adjustment, negotiation, and trial preparation of claims arising under the policies of insurance written by the company which is represented. Various other titles are used to describe this position, such as an adjuster, investigator, claim auditor, or claim agent. The claims representative may be employed (1) directly by the insurance company; (2) by an independent adjuster; or (3) by a company-owned adjustment bureau.

1. *Direct employment by the insurance company.* A salaried claims representative, employed directly by the insurance company devotes the entire working time to the exclusive handling of claims made against the company and its insureds. Some companies use the terms of staff adjuster or staff claims representative to describe this type of employment.

2. *Independent adjuster.* This term refers to a person, firm, or corporation which is held out to the insurance industry for employment in the handling of claims for more than one insurance company; does not work exclusively for one insurance company; and is paid in each case for the time devoted to the handling of the claim plus the expenses incurred. The claims representative may be the principal owner of the business or may be an employee of a person, firm or corporation of this type.

3. *Company-owned adjustment bureau.* This term refers to a corporation whose stock is owned entirely and exclusively by one or more insurance companies. The claims representative employed by such a corporation handles the claims of the stockholder companies and of any other insurance companies to whom the directors of the corporation make its services available, payment for such service being made on an individual fee basis for each case, or by means of an overall assessment.

102   Responsibilities of the claims representative

The responsibilities of the claims representative to the company he or she represents are the same whether the claims representative is employed by the company or undertakes to represent the company while employed by an adjusting organization. The claims representative is a fiduciary agent. The relationship is one in which the company, as the principal, places special trust

---

[1] Women as well as men are active in all branches of insurance including casualty claims, and the terms *claims representative* and the more traditional *claimsman,* which are used interchangeably throughout this book, should be understood to include both men and women. Similarly, the common pronoun *he,* when not identifying a particular individual who happens to be male, refers to persons of either sex and is not intended to be masculine or feminine but simply human.

and confidence in the claims representative and a relationship which requires that the representative maintain a high degree of fidelity and loyalty to the interests of the principal. Thus the claims representative must treat the affairs, the money or other property of the principal with a high degree of care at all times.

It is fundamental that a fiduciary agent cannot serve two masters in the same transaction. He or she cannot on the one hand act as agent for the principal and at the same time deal with himself or herself as an individual. Should this type of transaction be undertaken without the knowledge or consent of the principal, the transaction is in law conclusively presumed to be fraudulent, regardless of whether the claims representative personally profited from the transaction or not. For example, if a stolen car is recovered after payment therefor has been made by the insurance company, the claims representative may be instructed to sell the car to the highest bidder. If the claims representative made a bid on the car, which bid is the highest amount offered, permission must be secured from the principal before the sale is made at the figure offered in the bid. The claims representative must honestly and fairly disclose the amounts of the other bids, and the sources from which they were received. It must appear that bids were invited from a representative group of salvage buyers. Should there be a failure on the part of the claims representative to disclose the full facts of the bid which he or she made on the car (no matter how honestly the bid was made), the transaction is conclusively presumed to be fraudulent and may be set aside or voided at the option of the insurance company.

The fiduciary agent may not in any way deal with the principal's property with motives of self-interest. If, in the previous example, the claims representative did not bid on the salvage but solicited a friend to make the bid on his or her behalf, the failure of the claims representative to disclose to the company the fact that the bid was made under these circumstances, the result would be the same. The transaction is fraudulent. The claims representative may not represent interests which are adverse to those of the principal. Using the above example, if the claims representative should disclose to a salvage buyer the amounts of the bids already received so that he or she could bid accordingly, the claims representative would be serving an interest which is adverse to that of the principal, and this transaction is a breach of trust.

Likewise, if an independent adjuster or an employee of a company-owned adjustment bureau should accept an assignment from one company involving an accident, no other claim arising under the same transaction can be accepted unless both companies involved are made aware of the facts and give their permission to the dual representation. The acceptance of the later assignment and the failure to make full disclosure to the companies involved, with the representation of the adverse interests amounts to a breach of trust against both companies. For such breach of trust the claims representative is liable in damages to the company whose interests are adversely affected.

Finally, a claims representative may never profit from an outside source as a consequence of actions and dealings taken for and in behalf of the principal. Surely, the claims representative may accept the salary or the fees agreed upon with the principal, but may not accept any gift, service, or other emolument from persons who provide services in connection with the claims handled. Should such gifts be accepted, it constitutes a breach of trust, even though the principal's interests are not adversely affected by the gift.

103   Functions of the claims representative

The general functions of the claims representative are to investigate, negotiate, evaluate, or prepare claims for trial and to keep the company's file on the claim up to date so that it will reflect all of the actions taken by the claims representative and will also indicate the present status of the claim whether it be in a preliminary, investigating, or negotiating stage. This latter duty of the claims representative is of vital importance to the company, since its business records and its decisions with respect to the claim are fashioned from the information in the file. Among the decisions to be made are questions of coverage, the amount of the reserve to be carried on the file, and, more importantly to the claims representative, the amount of the settlement authorization which will be given.

A decision is no better than the information on which it is based. Therefore, if there is evidence which has not been transmitted to the file or if the claims representative has information which has not been reported to the file, the decision based on only what is in the file may be faulty. If this should happen, the claims representative is to blame and not the person who was required to make the decision with insufficient information.

The reports to the file should be clear, concise, and as brief as they can be made, but should contain all of the available information and evidence. In making the reports, the claims representative should confine the information transmitted to the file to the facts as supported by the available evidence. The claims representative should refrain from transmitting to the file unnecessary characterizations or opinions concerning the claimant and any other persons involved in the claim, and should be especially wary of making derogatory statements which are not supported by the evidence. In some instances, company files are seen by others, as when they are subpoenaed in court proceedings or reviewed by insurance examiners from various states. The reports should be such that they reflect the fairness with which both the company and the claims representative view the evidence and there should be nothing in the file which could possibly form a basis for an action against either the company or the claims representative for defamation.

104   Duties of the claims representative

The overall duty of the claims representative is to dispose of claims. This may be accomplished by payment of the full amount demanded, settlement on a negotiated basis, or an outright denial of liability. The ultimate objective is accomplished in three steps, as follows:

1. Investigation.
2. Evaluation.
3. Termination.

1. *Investigation.* This consists of a reasonable inquiry into the facts of the accident or occurrence. Since the claims representative seldom, if ever, is an eyewitness to the accident, reliance must be placed upon secondary evidence in the form of statements from others who were present at the scene as well as the physical facts, such as skid marks, debris and other evidences of the accident, and the extent of the damage to the vehicles and the injuries sustained by the persons involved. In cases other than automobile, the investigation might include statements from eyewitnesses, a survey of the premises or an examination of the offending instrumentality, if any.

Every investigation starts out with some known evidence. This usually is in the form of a report of accident from the insured, giving his or her version of what occurred. The inquiry will start by verifying the known evidence and by establishing or uncovering whatever other evidence there may be. The extent of the inquiry will be dictated by the amount of believable evidence available, and the severity of the injuries claimed or the value of the property damage allegedly caused. In some cases much of this evidence can be secured by telephone without the necessity of making an inquiry in the field.

Among the first items of inquiry is the question of whether or not the accident or occurrence comes within the scope of the insurance contract. In some cases this will be established with the minimum of effort, and in others it will not. If the inquiry discloses any question as to whether or not the claim comes within the coverage afforded, the company must make a decision at that moment as to what position it will take in regard to coverage. If the accident is not covered because of its location, or because it did not occur within the policy period or if there has been a breach of a condition of the policy contract by the insured, the company cannot consistently continue with the investigation and at the same time deny coverage. Therefore, when the claim representative is aware that there is a coverage question, the claims representative must STOP the investigation and seek advice from the company as to what further activity should be undertaken. By continuing the investigation with the knowledge of the fact that the claim is not within the terms of the contract, the company may waive its right to deny coverage.

The form that the investigative inquiry will take will be conditioned by the evidence which is needed to reach a conclusion as to the possible liability of the insured and the probabilities of the claim. The claims representative must be informed of the applicable law and the statutes in the state which have a bearing on the possible liability of the insured.

2. *Evaluation.* Having gathered a sufficient amount of evidence, the amount of damage claimed, and the specific details, consisting of out-of-pocket expenses, the claimed loss of earning capacity, and the injuries sustained or the property damage involved, the claims representative will make some approximation of the value, or the lack of it, of the claim. Some companies give the claims representative blanket authority for settlement, subject to a maximum amount. In that area, the claims representative may exercise judgment as to settlement valuations, seeking advice from the supervisor where necessary. As to values above the settlement authorization, the claims representative will make recommendations as to value to the company, supporting the conclusion reached with evidence of the injuries, details of the expenses claimed, and an evaluation of the applicable law. The claims representative will then proceed as instructed, whether the instructions be directed toward further investigation, denial of the claim, or for further negotiation of a settlement within the limits authorized.

3. Termination.   This is the ultimate objective of all claims handling. The two preliminary steps were taken solely to bring the claim to this stage. To dispose of the case, the claims representative may take one of the following three actions:

1. Acceptance.
2. Rejection.
3. Compromise.

1. *Acceptance.*   This means that the claimant's demand is considered to be reasonable and it will be paid in full, or that it is in the company's best interest to dispose of the claim on that basis.

2. *Rejection.*   This means that the claims representative will turn down the claim if it is being actively pressed, or if it is not being pressed, no action will be taken and no contact will be made with the claimant. In either case, there is no guarantee that the claim will be abandoned. The best that can be said is that by the rejection of the claim or the lack of action in contacting the claimant the initiative has been transferred to the claimant. If he or she presses the claim, the claims representative should be prepared to offer sufficient evidence to defeat it, or to have sufficient evidence available to effectuate an attractive compromise. If the claimant takes no action and abandons the claim, the rejection has effectively terminated it.

3. *Compromise.*   This action refers to negotiating a settlement of the claim for an amount which is consistent with its merits and in accordance with and subject to the settlement authorization. Whether or not the claims representative will utilize the entire settlement authorization, or something less, will be a matter that must be decided as the negotiations progress.

Not all cases in which a compromise is attempted will result in a settlement. Where the claimant is unwilling to accept the top offer and the company is unwilling to meet the claimant's lowest demand, there will be a rejection of both offer and demand, and the same principles would apply here as where the company has rejected the claim from the outset. When this impasse is reached and the company refuses to increase its offer and the claimant has refused to decrease his or her demand, the initiative passes to the claimant and the next move is up to him or her. The claimant may engage counsel and bring the case to trial; may continue to try negotiation; or may finally accept the company's highest offer. On the other hand, with the passage of time, the company may be induced to increase its offer, especially if further investigation reveals facts which are not conducive to a successful defense.

105   Required knowledge

The duties of the claims representative do not require admission to the bar or a complete legal education. They do require some knowledge of the basic rules of law which are applicable to the insurance claims industry, some knowledge of medicine to the extent of being able to evaluate the periods of disability which will follow the infliction of a particular injury together with the costs and the type of treatment needed. In addition, specific knowledge of the terms of the insurance policies written in the first- and third-party areas is necessary. The claims representative will also have to develop personal skills in investigation and claims negotiation.

Knowledge can be acquired; and it is the purpose of this volume to provide an insight into the basic principles and to point the way toward the development of the necessary skills.

CHAPTER II

Common law and equity

200 Common law defined

The common law of England, upon which the jurisprudence of most of our states is based, consists of a body of principles and rules of action which relate to the government and security of persons or property and which derive their authority solely from usages and customs, or from judgments and decrees of the courts which recognize, affirm, and enforce such usages and customs. It is unwritten law in the sense that it has never been codified or enacted into statute law. It can be found only by referring to the various decisions of the courts.

Statute law, as distinguished from common law, is written law. It is the written will of the legislature solemnly expressed according to the forms necessary to constitute it the law of the state. Thus, statute law represents the will of the people as expressed by their elected representatives, whereas the common law is reflective of the will of the people as expressed by the establishment of usages and customs, which are interpreted and enforced by the courts.

The colonists brought the common law of England to this country, and during colonial days it was the rule of decision in all the courts. After the Revolution, the existing common law was adopted by the several states and has developed through the decisions of the courts of the states from that time forward.

201 Early concepts

The jurisdiction originally assumed by the courts and the judges was that of a criminal nature. They heard and determined cases involving unreasonable or unlawful conduct in violation of the law and assessed punishment. They made no distinction between a violation which involved the public as a whole and one which involved only one individual or group of individuals. Thus, if a

8

man committed larceny, assault, or murder, he was punished as a criminal. If a man negligently injured his neighbor, he likewise was punished as a criminal. Gradually, the courts made a distinction between the two classes of cases. Acts which were offensive to the community and the public as a whole, such as larceny, assault, and murder, were classified as crimes and were punished accordingly. Acts which were not offensive to the public in general but which caused injury to another because of socially unreasonable conduct were classified as *torts* and were considered to involve only the parties thereto. These acts were punished only by an award of money damages in favor of the injured party and against the wrongdoer.

In addition to the determination of rights arising out of the social relationships, the courts also assumed jurisdiction over contractual relationships into which the parties entered. Where there was a breach of contract, the common-law courts would award damages.

202   Common-law rights

The common-law courts adopted as a fundamental concept that each individual was endowed with certain rights which the law was bound to protect. These are the right to liberty; security of person, property, and reputation; and the services of a wife, unemancipated child, and bounden servant. Any wrongful deprivation or diminution of the enjoyment of these rights gave rise to an action at law for damages against the wrongdoer.

While all individuals were possessed of these rights, there were certain classes of individuals who could not assert them except through a guardian. These persons were infants, idiots, insane persons, habitual drunkards, and married women. This common-law disability of married women has been removed by the statute law of all of our states, and today a married woman may sue and be sued as if she were a single woman. As to the other classes of persons, the common-law disability still remains, and they may sue or be sued only through a guardian.

203   Common-law duties

In its use in law, the word *duty* is also correlative of a right. For example, whenever a person has a right, there is a corresponding duty upon some other person or upon all persons generally. The common law imposes duties of performance, care, or observance in matters arising out of the social relationships of an individual in favor of (1) the *community* at large and (2) *other individuals*.

As to the community at large, the common law recognized that individual members of the community were obligated to regulate their conduct in such a way so as to be in conformity with the law, both human and divine. Any act done in violation of those duties which the individual owed to the community was a crime for which the individual was answerable to the community. The common law took the view that any acts which offended the community and which, if repeated, would undermine the peace and harmony of the community were violations of the duty owed to the community. Therefore, such acts as larceny, robbery, burglary, atrocious assault, mayhem, and homicide were regarded as offensive to the peace and dignity of the community and punishable by the community as crimes.

As for the individual, the common law imposed a duty on others to regulate their conduct with due care so as to avoid an infringement of the basic rights recognized by the law. Failure to exercise just, proper, and sufficient care which results in the invasion of the legal rights of another is called a tort. The consequences of a tort, as we have said, are "private" in nature in the sense that they affect only the individual. A crime, on the other hand, involves public consequences because it affects the community generally.

An act, or omission, may be both a crime and a tort. It may be an offense against the peace and dignity of the community at large, and it also may invade the rights of an individual. In such a case, the offender is subject to both criminal and civil liability. He is answerable to the public for his violation of his public duty and will be punished according to the penal law; he is also answerable to the individual for damages sustained as a result of his wrongful invasion of the individual's private right. These are separate and distinct liabilities as far as the offender is concerned, and the disposition of one will have no effect upon the disposition of the other.

A fairly common example of this situation is the automobile accident case where the death of an individual was caused by the culpably negligent operation of the vehicle. Under those circumstances, the driver would be answerable in damages to the estate of the victim, but he could also be indicted for automobile homicide or manslaughter and subjected to criminal liability if convicted. The fact that he settled the private claim of the deceased's estate will not relieve him of criminal liability, nor will his conviction or acquittal on the criminal charges relieve him of his liability in tort.

A tort is based on the rights and duties arising from social relationships which are recognized by law and ordinarily are not voluntarily acquired or assumed. A contract is a voluntary agreement between parties which creates rights and duties on the part of each. These rights and duties are enforceable by the courts. The individual can avoid the obligations imposed by a contract by not making one.

204   Law reports

Since the common law consists of the sum total of all the judicial decisions, there had to be some means available to lawyers and judges whereby prior decisions could be located and reviewed in order to determine applicability to common-law rule. Originally, the court reporter undertook this duty, collecting the decisions of the court and issuing a printed volume from time to time containing the decisions. Each volume was designated by number and was identified by the name of the reporter.

The use of the reporter's name, however, was found to be unsatisfactory, so that at the present time these volumes are part of the reporter system of the state and are identified by the name of the state and numbered in sequence. When referring to a case, the court or the attorney will indicate the location of the decision by identifying the number of the volume together with the page on which the decision is to be found. The volume number is given first, then the state name, and finally the page number. Thus, if the case of *Jones* v. *Smith* is cited as 232 N.Y. 25, this would mean that the decision is found in volume 232 of the New York Reports on page 25.

Each state has its own reporter system, identified by the name of the state. However, the lawbook publishers found that there was a need for a collection of the reports of more than one state in one volume. Therefore, they divided the United States into areas and published the reports of the states, according to area, in separate volumes. For example, the *Atlantic Reporter* covers New England, Maryland, and Pennsylvania (and excludes Massachusetts and New York). The *Northeastern Reporter* covers New York and Massachusetts, plus Ohio and Indiana. The *Southeastern, Southern, Southwestern, Northwestern,* and *Pacific Reporters* cover the states in these areas. Because of this additional system, cases are sometimes cited with both the location in the state reports and the national reporter system. Thus *Jones* v. *Smith,* 232 N.Y. 25 and 120 N.E. 16, gives both locations.

The opinions of the Supreme Court of the United States are recorded in the *United States Reports,* and as in other citations, the volume number and the page number are given in order to locate the decision: as 300 U.S. 25. The opinions of the inferior federal courts are collected in the *Federal Reporter* and the *Federal Supplement.*

Rather than have the volume numbers reach large figures, most systems have begun a second series beginning with volume number one. Thus a case cited which is located in the second series of law reports will be designated as 25 N.Y. 2d 150. This means that the decision is located in volume 25 of the second series, on page 150.

205 *Stare decisis*

This doctrine refers to a policy adopted by the courts that where the court has once laid down a principle of law as applicable to a certain state of facts, it will adhere to that principle and apply it to all future cases where the facts are substantially the same. The doctrine is grounded on the theory that security and certainty require that an accepted and established legal principle, under which rights may accrue, be recognized and followed. The doctrine is subject to the exception that the court may in its discretion modify or overrule a legal principle where public policy requires it or where the reason for the rule no longer exists. For example, the original common-law view with respect to the ownership of land contemplated that the owner of the property owned the land to the center of the earth and to the heavens above. Anyone who invaded any portion of this area was a trespasser. An aircraft, flying over the owner's property, committed a trespass.

In the light of modern conditions and public necessity, the rule has been modified to the extent that the ownership of the land either upward or downward is limited to that portion of the land which has been reduced to possession by occupancy, plus the area needed for the enjoyment of that occupancy. Thus, if a man built a building 100 stories high, he then would have reduced to possession by occupancy the space from the ground to the top of the building. An intrusion by an aircraft into that area would be a trespass.

In addition, some courts hold that he not only owns the area reduced to possession, but also the surrounding airspace needed for the peaceful enjoyment of his property. In any case, where an aircraft is flown at a high altitude and does not interfere with the owner's right of possession or enjoyment, there is no trespass.

206   Statutory modifications of the common law

Statute law, as enacted by the legislature, can alter, amend, or abrogate any principle of the common law and can also create new causes of action which were not recognized by the common law. The rule is, however, that any legislation which is contrary to or "in derogation of" the common law is strictly construed, and the legislation changes the common law only in those areas where the statute specifically says it does. As an example of such a change, the common-law view was that a man ceased his legal existence at death. Therefore, he could not make a will which would call for the performance of an act after death, namely, the distribution of his property—nor could he sue or be sued. The theory was that since the man had ceased to exist, he could neither perform nor be held accountable for any earthly actions. But as a result of legislative enactment, a man may now make a will which will effectively dispose of his property after his death in accordance with his wishes, and he may sue for damages through his personal representative to recover for injuries suffered prior to his death—and he may also be sued, by means of an action brought against his personal representative, after his death.

At common law, an employee could recover damages for bodily injury from his employer only if the employer had failed in one of his common-law duties to the employee. Workmen's compensation laws represent legislation which completely abrogates the common-law principles applicable to the relationship of master and servant, and substitutes a new remedy which was completely unknown to the common law.

207   The common law in the United States

As a result of the Revolutionary War, the Thirteen Colonies became separate sovereignties. They exercise all of the rights of sovereignty to this very day, with the exception of the rights which they specifically delegated to the federal government by means of the Constitution of the United States. One of the inherent rights of sovereignty which was not delegated to the federal government was the right to make its own laws applicable within its jurisdiction, as well as the maintenance of courts for the purpose of interpreting and applying the law to matters within the same jurisdiction.

As to the common law, the states adopted the English common law as it existed at the time of the Revolution, and the courts of each state in turn, from that time forward, developed common law in response to the prevalent customs and usages.

Thus the highest court of each state has the supreme authority to declare what constitutes the common law of the state and what is applicable to all matters occurring within its borders. It is not bound by the decisions of the courts of other states as to applicable common law. It may be persuaded by those other decisions, but each state supreme court has the authority and duty to declare the common law of the state. As a result, what might be the common law in one state is not necessarily the common law of another, and the best way this situation can be expressed is to say that the common law of each state is what the supreme court of the particular state says it is. The common law might be the same as in some other states, and it might differ completely. Where there is some uniformity, and a large group of states has adopted certain common-law principles as a rule of decision, this view is generally referred to as the *majority view*, as opposed to the *minority view* held by a smaller group.

When we acquired what is now the state of Louisiana, part of the Louisiana Purchase, the courts of that area were applying the French civil law—which had its origins in the Roman civil law set forth in the compilations of Justinian. French civil law was applied until the adoption of the Civil Code of Louisiana, but even at the present time Louisiana applies common-law principles to most of the matters with which we are concerned.

The Constitution of the United States authorizes the establishment of federal courts in the various states for the purpose of hearing and determining certain matters within their jurisdiction. In each case, the federal district courts apply the common law of the state in which they sit, so that it is quite possible to find one federal court (applying the common law of one state) reaching a conclusion entirely different from the decision of another federal court.

208 Lex loci *and* lex fori

Lex loci literally translated means the "law of the place." Generally, the substantive rights of the parties are governed by the *lex loci*, or the law of the place where the rights were acquired or the liabilities incurred. Substantive law is that part of the law which creates, defines, and regulates the rights of the parties, whereas adjective law prescribes the method of enforcing the rights so created or obtaining redress for their invasion.

Lex loci contractus refers to the substantive law applicable to contracts. Where there is no agreement to the contrary, it usually refers to the law of the place where the contract is made. The parties may agree that the rights of the parties will be governed by the law of another state, rather than the state in which the contract was actually made.

Lex loci delecti refers to the law of the place where the crime or wrong took place. In tort cases as a general rule, the substantive rights of the parties are determined by the law of the place where the wrongful act was committed, regardless of whether suit was actually brought and tried in another jurisdiction. There are some exceptions to this rule. (See Section 605, Center-of-Gravity Rule, below.)

Lex fori means the law of the forum, or the procedural law of the court in which the action is brought. All contract and tort actions are transitory, in the sense that the action may be brought in any state where the court has jurisdiction of the parties. The *lex fori* will govern the procedure by which the moving party seeks to obtain a remedy. The *lex loci* will be applied by the court to decide the rights of the parties against each other. For example, let us assume that an automobile accident occurred in Massachusetts, involving a negligent New Jersey driver and a Massachusetts citizen. It results in the death of the Massachusetts party. Action for wrongful death is brought in the Superior Court of New Jersey. Recovery under the Massachusetts Wrongful Death Statute is limited to $50,000, whereas the New Jersey statute has no limitation on the amount of recovery for wrongful death. The Rules of Court of New Jersey will govern the procedure to be followed (*lex fori*), but the court will apply the substantive law of Massachusetts (*lex loci*) in determining the remedy available. Thus, the plaintiff would be limited to the maximum amount allowed by the Massachusetts law, or $50,000.

209   Restatement of the law

As we have seen, the common law consists of the sum total of all the decided cases with no particular codification or actual index. The legal profession thought that there should be an orderly statement of the common law, rather than to continue to rely on the "growing indigestible mass of decisions." It was for this purpose that the American Law Institute was formed in 1923. Its membership included outstanding lawyers, judges, and law professors. Its purpose was to make a statement of the law based on the mass of decisions which constituted the common law. The result of their labors is called the "Restatement of the Law." It deals with various branches of the law, notably Agency, Conflict of Laws, Contracts, Restitution, and Torts.

The common law applicable in each state is what the Supreme Court of that state says it is. We took the English common law and added to it our own decisions. These were made by the various state courts, and unfortunately the decisions are not all the same. In some areas there is a hopeless conflict. Therefore in such situations, the Restatement recommends a rule to be applied. While the Restatement is not binding on any court, many of them have been persuaded to adopt the Restatement rule as their own, or to accept the Restatement rule with some exceptions. Others have rejected certain Restatement rules. Therefore, we can regard the Restatement as being persuasive of what the American Law Institute thinks the law should be. A check of the decisions of the court in the state under consideration should be made to determine whether they have adopted, adopted with reservations, or rejected the Restatement rule.

Having completed the original Restatement, the American Law Institute undertook a complete revision. The revised Restatement is referred to as the second series. Thus, in citing the revised edition, we will refer to the subject followed by the word, "second." For example, when citing the Restatement rule applicable to Torts as revised, we will refer to it as "Restatement, Torts, Second."

210   Corpus juris

Corpus juris means "body of the law." This term is used to signify a book comprehending several collections of the law. *Corpus juris canonici* refers to a body of canon law, consisting of a compilation of the canon law, comprising the decrees and canons of the Roman Catholic Church and constituting the body of ecclesiastical law of that church. *Corpus juris civilis* refers to a body of civil law under the system of Roman jurisprudence, compiled and codified under the direction of the Emperor Justinian in A.D. 528–534.

The term, *corpus juris*, also refers to an encyclopedic statement of the principles of Anglo-American law. It consists of a series of books—approximately 100—in which the subjects are each analyzed according to their legal significance and relationship. The original work has been updated and is in a second series, called *Corpus Juris Secundum*, cited as CJS. In referring to this work, the citation will refer to the volume number, the subject matter, and the section number. Thus 65 CJS Navigable Waters 11 will identify the volume, the subject and the section.

The work is kept current by yearly "pocket parts" which are added to each volume and which amplify the existing material and also cite the latest decided cases. These additions are placed in the back of each volume so that the user can read the text and then check the pocket part to ascertain the current state of the law on any given subject.

211   Origin of equity

The English common-law courts had only the power to award money damages or to deny them. They could not avert a threatened injury, nor could they compel the performance of a contract. They could not look behind a written contract to determine if it represented the agreement of the parties, or whether or not the contract was induced through fraud. They could and did award money damages after the injury had been sustained or the contract had been breached. In a large number of cases, the award of money damages was a satisfactory solution, but there were some cases where the award of money damages was inadequate and others where the award of damages would be unjust. For example, if a person maintained a nuisance in the form of a slaughterhouse in a residential neighborhood and the noxious fumes permeated the home of a neighbor, endangering his health and impairing his enjoyment of his property, the common law gave him a right to bring an action for damages against the slaughterhouse operator for each intrusion of noxious fumes.

Clearly, the award of damages would not enable the neighbor to enjoy his home, and for that reason the common-law remedy was inadequate. If an action were brought for breach of a written contract, and through a scrivener's error the contract did not conform to the agreement of the parties, the common law would award damages for the breach on the basis of the written terms of the instrument without regard to the intention of the parties. Also, where a contract came to suit and it was alleged that the contract was signed by mistake, or that the defendant signed it thinking that it was another type of instrument, the common law would again enforce the contract in accordance with its terms.

Because of such cases the practice arose of appealing to the king for the relief which the common-law courts were unable to give. If the king determined that the common-law remedy was inadequate, he would hear the evidence and take whatever action his conscience dictated. He might command the slaughterhouse operator to cease and discontinue his operations (*injunction*) ; he might order that the contract be rewritten so as to conform to the agreement of the parties (*reformation*) ; or he might command that the contract in the last instance be delivered up and destroyed (*rescission*). It should be emphasized that the king had no desire to impair the authority of his courts, and he would act only in those instances where there was no adequate remedy at law available.

As cases became more numerous, the king delegated the decision-making authority to the chancellor. Since all of the cases were appeals to the king's conscience, it seemed fitting to turn over this duty to the chancellor, who was known as the "keeper of the king's conscience." The chancellor soon established other courts presided over by his vice-chancellors, and these courts came to be known as chancery or equity courts. They functioned in the same area as did the king, in that their jurisdiction was confined to cases in which there was no adequate remedy at law.

The chancery or equity courts functioned as a separate system, independent of the common-law courts, until the last century. By degrees, each state consolidated the functions of the law and equity courts into one legal system, accomplishing this result either by constitutional amendment or by legislation. A certain division still remains in that the courts are divided into law and chancery divisions, or reference is made to the trial term or the special term of court. *Trial term* refers to law causes, and *special term* refers to equity.

212   Equitable remedies

The remedies which the king delegated to the chancellor consisted of those types of cases wherein there was no adequate remedy at law, and even though the courts of equity could award damages under certain circumstances, the remedies with which we will be concerned consist of the following:

1. Injunction. Defined as a prohibitive writ issued by a court of equity at the suit of a party complainant, directed to a party defendant in the action, or a party made defendant for that purpose, forbidding the latter to do some act, or to permit his servants or agents to do some act, which he is threatening or attempting to commit, or restraining him in the continuance thereof; such act being unjust and inequitable, injurious to the complainant, and not such as can be adequately redressed by an action at law. For example, a man operates a dog kennel in a residential neighborhood and the residents are disturbed by the barking of the dogs at night. Upon petition and answer, the court could issue an injunction, or order, compelling the kennel owner to cease his operations and to remove the dogs from the neighborhood. In such a case, it is clear that a judgment for money damages would not be an adequate remedy since the neighbors wanted to be free from the disturbing noise, rather than to receive money in payment for the continued inconvenience.

2. Reformation. The power of a court of equity to reform or rewrite a contract to conform to the intent of the parties. It is a remedy afforded by the courts of equity to parties to a written instrument which imports a legal obligation, to reform or rectify such an instrument whenever it fails through fraud or mutual mistake to express the real intention of the parties. For example, a man's house is partially destroyed by fire on March 10. He has no insurance, but his loss convinces him of the necessity for fire insurance. He promptly applies for such insurance on March 11 and an insurance contract is issued. Through a scrivener's mistake, the inception date of the policy was incorrectly noted as March 1 instead of March 11 as agreed. The man makes a claim for the fire damage which occurred on March 10. The insurance company may petition a court of equity to reform the policy so as to reflect the intentions of the parties; namely, that the inception date of the policy was to be March 11 and not March 1 as written.

3. Rescission. This refers to the power of a court of equity to abrogate, annul, void, or cancel a contract upon a showing of fraud, either in the inducement or making thereof. For example, if an adjuster induced a claimant to sign a general release on the representation that, in spite of the language contained therein, it was only a partial receipt and that other and further payments would be made to him. On those facts, the court of equity could set aside the release and order that it be destroyed. This is an example of fraud in the inducement in that the claimant was induced to sign the release solely as a result of the adjuster's fraudulent statements. In another case, the claimant has lost his glasses and cannot read without them. The adjuster asks him to sign a receipt for a certain amount of money, which the claimant does, not knowing that the paper he signed was a general release. On these facts, there is fraud in the factum on in the making of the contract. A court of equity has the power to void the instrument.

213 Maxims of equity

The courts of equity early established certain principles in the form of maxims or conclusions of reason that they applied as the rule of decision in cases coming before them. A few of these maxims follow:

1. Equity follows the law.
2. Equity considers that as done which ought to have been done.

3. He who seeks equity must do equity.
4. He who comes into a court of equity must come with clean hands.
5. Where equities are equal, the law must prevail.

1. *Equity follows the law.* Equity adopts and follows the rules of law in all cases to which these rules may be applicable. Thus, equity in dealing with its cases adopts and follows the analogies furnished by the rules of law.

2. *Equity considers that as done which ought to have been done.* Equity will treat the subject matter, as to collateral consequences and incidents in the same manner as if the final acts contemplated by the parties had been executed exactly as they should have been and not as the parties might have executed them.

3. *He who seeks equity must do equity.* This maxim means that the party asking the aid of an equity court must stand in a conscientious relation toward his adversary and the transaction from which his claim arises must be fair and just and the relief demanded must not be harsh and oppressive on the defendant. The court will not confer equitable relief on a party seeking its aid, unless he has acknowledged and conceded, or will admit and provide for all equitable rights, claims and demands justly belonging to the adverse party and growing out of or involved in the subject matter of the controversy.

4. *He who comes into a court of equity must come with clean hands.* Equity will not aid a suitor who himself has been guilty of fraud, overreaching conduct, or unconscionable behavior.

5. *Where the equities are equal, the law must prevail.* This means that equity will not intervene in a case where both parties are equally entitled to equitable relief one against the other. In such a case, the matter will be decided strictly on the law without resort to equity.

214   Appellate courts

The establishment of law and chancery courts did not entirely insulate the king from other and further appeals. An aggrieved litigant in the law or chancery courts would still appeal to the king on the theory that there were some errors committed by the trial judge or the chancellor, or that the judges acted in excess of their powers. These appeals became so numerous that the king finally established an appellate or appeals court consisting usually of from three to five judges, whose duty it was to hear and determine appeals from the lower courts. The king still remained the supreme judicial authority and those who were still aggrieved after the decision was made in the appellate court, could still appeal to the king. With the establishment of the constitutional monarchy in England, the king was divested of all judicial power, and today the highest court in England is the Law Committee of the House of Lords.

In America, each colony had a judicial system comparable to that of England. With the coming of independence, each colony established a Supreme Court, as the highest judicial authority in the state. The Constitution of the

United States established a federal judicial system within the limits prescribed by the Constitution, which also created the Supreme Court of the United States. (See Chapter XIII, "Federal Jurisdiction and Authority.")

215 Legal terminology

There are certain legal terms which are commonly used in the opinions of the courts. Therefore, an understanding of these terms will be helpful in understanding both the text and the opinions of the courts which are cited. The following are such terms:

Ab initio. From the beginning.

Acknowledgment. Formal declaration before an authorized official (such as a notary public) by a person who executed (signed) an instrument that it is his free act and deed. The affiant likewise declares under oath that the information contained in the affidavit is true. If it is untrue the affiant may be subject to perjury.

Action. A legal demand of one's right to remove from another person or party made before a court; a lawsuit.

Action ex contractu. Action for damages for the breach of a promise set forth in a contract, express or implied.

Action ex delicto. An action for damages sustained as a result of a breach of duty on the part of the defendant; action in tort.

Affirmed. In the practice of the appellate courts, to affirm a judgment, decree or order, is to declare that it is valid and right, and must stand as rendered below (in the lower court); to concur in its correctness.

Reversed. The action of the appellate court in annulling or making void a judgment rendered in the court below.

Affiant. A person who makes or subscribes to an affidavit.

Affidavit. A written or printed declaration or statement of fact made voluntarily and confirmed by the oath or affirmation of the party, who makes it, and taken before an officer having authority to administer such oath.

Annul. To make or declare void or invalid; nullify or cancel as to invalidate a contract of marriage.

Appeal. The right of a party who has received an adverse decision to take the case to a higher court for review.

Appellant. The person taking the appeal.

Appellee. The person against whom the appeal is taken. Also referred to as the respondent.

Appellate. Usually refers to the higher court to which an appeal is taken for a review of the decision of the lower court.

Assumpsit. Lat;, he promised. In practice, it refers to a form of action for damages for the nonperformance of a contract.

Bill. A formal declaration, complaint, or statement of particular things in writing.

Bill in equity. A formal written complaint, in the nature of a petition, addressed by the suitor in chancery (equity) to the chancellor or to a court of equity, or a court having equitable jurisdiction, showing the names of the parties, stating the facts which make up the case and the complainant's allegations, averring the facts disclosed are contrary to equity, and praying for process and specific relief, or such relief as the circumstances demand.

Bill of exceptions. A formal statement in writing of the objections or exceptions taken by a party during the trial of a cause to the decisions, rulings, or instructions of the trial judge, stating the objection, with the facts and circumstances on which it is founded, and, in order to attest to its accuracy, signed and sealed by the judge; the object being to put the controverted rulings or decisions upon the record for the information of the reviewing court.

Declaration. In practice, it is the first pleading on the part of the plaintiff in an action at law, being a formal and methodical specification of the facts and circumstances constituting the cause of action. Also called the Narr (narrative) or complaint.

Demurrer. The formal pleading to dispute the sufficiency in law of the pleading of the other side. In effect, it is an allegation that, even if the facts as stated by the adverse party in his pleading are true, there is no assertible cause of action against the demurring party.

Error. A mistaken judgment or incorrect belief as to the existence or effect of matters of fact, or a false or mistaken conception of the application of the law. On appeal, the appellant alleges that the lower court judge has committed error or errors in his rulings on the law.

Et seq. Abbreviation for *et sequentes* or *et sequentia* meaning "and the following one."

Infra and supra. Infra means below or following, whereas supra means above or preceding.

Nonsuit. A term broadly applied to a variety of terminations of an action which do not adjudicate issues on the merits. Judgment of nonsuit is of two kinds— voluntary and involuntary. When the plaintiff abandons his case and consents to have the judgment go against him for costs, it is voluntary. But where he, being called, neglects to appear, or when he has given no evidence on which a jury could find a verdict, the judgment of the court dismissing the case is called an involuntary nonsuit.

Reversal. A changing or setting aside of lower court decisions by a higher court, and, in most cases, remanding it or sending it back to the lower court for further action.

CHAPTER III

Law of torts

300   Tort defined

While a completely satisfactory definition of a tort is yet to be devised, we may define the term for the purposes of our work, as follows:

A tort is a wrongful act or omission, arising in the course of social relationships other than contracts, which violates a person's legally protected right, and for which the law provides a remedy in the form of an action for damages.

This definition contemplates that for an act or omission to constitute a tort all three of the following elements must be present:

1. A legally protected right.
2. A wrongful invasion of that right.
3. Damages as a proximate result of that invasion.

   1. *The existence of a legally protected right.*   The English common law recognized certain rights which were legally protected, such as the right of the individual to liberty; security of person, property, and reputation; and the services of a wife and an unemancipated child. Under our present system, these rights are still legally protected, but we have added others, either by statute or by further development of the common law. Among the added rights are the right of privacy, the right to vote, the right to earn a living, and the right to an education. In some states the common-law rights have been extended to include matters which were never contemplated before. As an example, some states recognize that the members of the family have a "property" right in the body of a deceased member and allow recovery for the mishandling or the mutilation of the body.

All rights are not legally protected, and those which are not will not form the basis of tort liability. For example, a customer offers to buy a certain article from a store owner and tenders the purchase price. The owner refuses to sell. The right to purchase is not a legally protected right, and therefore there is no tort liability involved.

2. *A wrongful invasion of that right.* This contemplates not only an act which is either intentional or careless and negligent but also acts which subject the actor to liability even though they are neither intentional nor negligent. This latter classification includes the possession and maintenance of dangerous instrumentalities as well as the conducting of ultrahazardous operations, both of which expose others to unreasonable risks of harm.

The invasion must be wrongful. Merely because a legally protected right is invaded does not in and of itself create tort liability. For example, the right to liberty is a legally protected right. If a police officer with a warrant arrests an individual, the right to liberty has been invaded. The invasion, however, is legal and not wrongful. On the other hand, if the police officer made the arrest without having reasonable and probable cause for believing that the individual had committed a crime, or without a warrant, then the invasion would be wrongful and the police officer would be answerable in damages.

3. *Damages as a proximate result thereof.* Theoretically, if the first two elements are established, a tort has been committed, but in the absence of actual damages sustained as a proximate result, the plaintiff would be entitled only to nominal damages (usually 6 cents). Where damages are alleged, it must be established that they were sustained as a direct result of the tort committed and that there is a direct chain of causation running from the tortious act to the injury claimed.

The person charged with the commission of the tort is referred to as the *wrongdoer* or the *tort-feasor.* Where two or more persons commit the tort, they are referred to as joint tort-feasors.

Tort and contract distinguished. The liability in tort arises out of social relationships. Members of society are entitled to rights and are subject to liability solely because of their status as members of the community. The rights and liabilities of the members of the community are involuntarily assumed and no member can waive his rights or avoid his responsibilities. On the other hand, the obligations of contract are voluntarily assumed as a consequence of an agreement. A person can avoid the obligations of a contract by not making one.

Tort and crime distinguished. The common law required that each member of the community regulate his or her conduct in such a way that none of his acts were offensive to the community at large. If an act was committed which was offensive to the community, the person would, upon conviction, be subject to criminal liability. Such acts would include assault and battery, larceny, burglary, mayhem, and homocide. Criminal liability would subject the person to punishment in the form of a fine, imprisonment or, in extreme cases, execution. This criminal liability is often referred to as the "public consequences" of his act. Penal statutes have been enacted defining the elements of these crimes and, in some states, fix the amount of punishment which is to be imposed.

The same act may have "private consequences" as well, and in such a case the injured person will have the right to bring a civil action for damages. For example, *A* assaults *B* with a deadly weapon, causing serious injuries. *A* is indicted, tried, and convicted of assault with a deadly weapon, and is sentenced to a term of imprisonment. These are the "public consequences" of his act. However, *B* has sustained injuries, which are "private consequences" and *A* is subject to civil liability for the injuries which his action has caused. Thus, *A* is subject to criminal liability for his act, but also civil liability as well.

301　Classification of torts

Torts may be divided into three groups as to their nature and origin, according to whether they involve:

1. Intention.
2. Negligence.
3. Liability without fault.

1. Intention. An intentional tort is an act which is done with the intention of bringing about injury to the person or property of another. It contemplates a state of mind either prior to or concurrent with the commission of the act, where the tort-feasor deliberately determines to do the act which produces the injury. This state of mind can usually be established by the nature of the act itself.

Thus, if a man strikes another with his fist inflicting physical injury, such action is deemed an assault and battery. Since a man is deemed to have intended the reasonable consequences of his acts, mere proof of the occurrence will be sufficient to create an inference of the tort-feasor's intent. But the words spoken immediately preceding the act and the surrounding circumstances may change the character of the act. If *A* and *B* decide to engage in a boxing bout and, during the encounter, *A* strikes *B*, no tort has been committed. B gave up his right to the security of his person and voluntarily assumed the risk of injury which would arise as a result of the boxing bout. Therefore *A* has not invaded the right of *B*. However, *B* relinquished his right to security of person only for the limited purpose of boxing, and he assumed only the risk of being struck by the boxing gloves on *A*'s hands. If during the bout *A* became infuriated and struck *B* with an axe which was near at hand, such would be a tortious act and subject *A* to liability.

The intended victim is not the only person who can claim damages for an intentional tort. Suppose *A* discharges a pistol into a crowd of people, intending to injure *B*. His aim is poor and the bullet hits *C*. Although *A* had no intention of injuring *C*, the law will transfer his intent to injure *B* to *C*, making *A* guilty of an assault and battery on *C*. This is called the doctrine of *transferred intent*, and *A* is liable to *C*.

In addition to assault and battery, which we have considered, intentional torts include malicious prosecution (prosecution begun with evil intent and without probable cause to believe the charges can be sustained), *malicious abuse of legal process* (willfully misapplying court process to obtain an object not intended by law), *false imprisonment* (wrongfully depriving a person of his right to liberty), *defamation*, or *libel and slander* (injuring a person's character, fame, or reputation by false and malicious statements), and *conversion* (the wrongful taking of the property of another).

2. Negligence. Negligent torts refer to those which arise as a result of the failure to meet the duty to exercise care. The invasion of a legally protected right may come about without any intention of so doing, but because of carelessness, neglect, or indifference. The person who fails to exercise due care so as to avoid invading the rights of others, is answerable for any injury or damage caused by his lack of care.

3. *Liability without fault*. These torts refer to situations where a person is held to a strict and absolute liability regardless of any negligent act, fault, or intent. They can be divided into two classes as to their origin: (1) those created by the common law and (2) those created by statute.

Torts created by the common law. The common-law rule applicable in most jurisdictions is that where the owner or occupier of property makes such unnatural or abnormal use of his property so as to expose the community to a greater risk of harm than normal, he is absolutely liable for any injury or loss occasioned by his unnatural use. The abnormal use might consist of the storage of explosives or inflammable liquids, or the unnatural collection of water in a dangerous place, or the keeping of wild animals dangerous to man, lions, tigers, etc. Likewise, abnormal activities on the land which will subject the community to an unreasonable risk of harm are also within the area of these torts. Such activities could consist of blasting, fumigating a building with cyanide gas, or a dangerous excavation which removed the lateral support from adjoining land.

Torts created by statute. The legislature has the power to enact statutes which impose absolute liability regardless of any negligent act, fault, or intent, and they have done so in a number of areas. For example, under the Uniform Aeronautics Law, adopted in some of the states, absolute liability is imposed upon the owner of an aircraft for injuries to persons or property on land caused by the ascent, descent, or flight of the aircraft, or the dropping or falling of any object therefrom. This means that regardless of fault, mere proof of the happening of the event will be sufficient to impose liability upon the owner, even though the event occurred as a consequence of an act of God, or from a cause which human foresight could not have anticipated or prevented.

At common law an employee could recover of the employer for bodily injury only where the injuries were sustained as a result of the negligence of the employer. By the enactment of workmen's compensation laws, the common-law rule of liability has been eliminated, and an employer is liable, regardless of negligence, if an employee is injured in an accident which arises out of and in the course of employment.

302　Negligence

Negligence is the failure to exercise that degree of care which the law requires to protect others from an unreasonable risk of harm. This contemplates a legally protected right, a duty owed to the person possessing the right, conduct which falls below the standard required by law to meet that duty, and injury as a result of the failure to meet that standard. In a tort cause of action based on negligence, the following elements must be established by the person asserting the claim:

1. A legal duty owed.
2. Failure to comply with the standard required by law to meet the duty.
3. A causal relationship between the failure to meet the standard and the resulting injury.
4. Damages as a proximate result.

1. *A legal duty owed.* A duty is an obligation recognized by law to conform to a certain standard of conduct for the protection of others. It arises from the social relationships of the parties, and in the absence of such a social relationship, which creates the duty, there is no obligation. For example, the owner of a motor vehicle is required to maintain his vehicle in reasonably safe condition for the protection of others using the highway, but his car has faulty brakes. It is stolen by a thief who is injured in an accident caused by the failure of the brakes to function. There is no social relationship between the car owner and the thief from which a duty of care on the part of the owner could arise for the benefit of the thief.

The same situation would obtain where a burglar or trespasser made illegal use of an owner's premises and was injured because of negligent maintenance. No duty of care is owed to either by the owner. An old English case sums up the relationship of duty and negligence as follows:

The question of liability for negligence cannot arise at all until it is established that the man who has been negligent owed some duty to the person who seeks to make him liable for his negligence. . . . A man is entitled to be as negligent as he pleases toward the whole world if he owes no duty to them. (*LeLievre* v. *Gould,* 1 Q.B. 491.)

The duties which the law recognizes as arising out of social relationships have their origin in one of the following three sources:

1. The common law.
2. A statute.
3. A voluntary act.

1. *The common law.*   Among the duties recognized by the common law is the duty of the owner or occupier of land to maintain his premises in a reasonably safe condition for the safety of those who are lawfully on the premises by invitation or license. The duty is owed only to those persons who are within the class designated, namely, those who are lawfully on the premises by invitation or license. The duty does not exist in relation to anyone not in the designated class. An automobile driver has a duty of reasonable care in the maintenance of his vehicle and in its operation. He owes this duty of care for the safety of the person and property of others lawfully using the highway or situated at or near the highway. Thus the driver owes this duty to his own passengers, the drivers and passengers in other cars, pedestrians, the owner of property lawfully on the highway, and the owner of property adjoining or adjacent to the highway.

2. *A statute.*   All statutes or ordinances do not create duties. There are some which require that an act be done, or an act not be done, for the safety of certain classes of persons. When a statute sets up a requirement for the safety of a certain class of persons, a duty arises, but only to that particular class of persons.

For example, where a statute required that every three-story tenement house have either fire escapes directly accessible to each apartment or two independent stairways not adjacent to each other, the owner of the tenement house was held liable for the deaths of tenants when a fire broke out in the hallway and prevented the tenants from escaping because of the absence of either fire escapes or two independent stairways. [*Soles et al.* v. *Franz-Blau et al.*, 352 Fed. 2d 47 (New Jersey).] In some cities, there are local ordinances which require that the stairways in public buildings be provided with handrails. If a person is injured because of the absence of handrails, or his injury could have been prevented if handrails had been provided, the owner of the building is liable for the injury. In both of these cases, the injury was sustained by a person for whose safety the statute was enacted, and in each case the statute created a duty on the part of the owner to provide the necessary equipment.

On the other hand, if the person injured is not within the class of persons for whose safety the statute was enacted, there is no duty owing to that person. For example, a local ordinance prohibited the washing of cars on a public street. The statute was enacted for the traveling public for the purpose of expediting travel. *A* washes his car on the street in violation of the statute. The water he used for washing his car collects in the gutter and freezes during the night. The next morning *B* slips on the ice thus formed and breaks his leg.

A is not liable to *B*. The purpose of the ordinance was to expedite travel and not to prevent the water from collecting in the gutter or freezing. The class of persons for whose benefit the statute was passed was the class traveling on the highway. *B* was not within the class of persons for whose benefit the statute was passed, and therefore the statute created no duty on the part of *A* to *B*.

In another case, let us assume that a local blue law prohibits the driving of motor vehicles on Sunday except for matters of necessity. *A* drives his car for pleasure in violation of the ordinance and collides with a vehicle driven by *B*, a local physician making his rounds. *A* is not liable to *B* solely because of *A*'s violation of the ordinance. The ordinance was not passed for the protection of those lawfully using the highway on Sunday, and therefore it created no duty on the part of *A* to *B*.

3. *A voluntary act.* The law does not require anyone to aid another person in distress. This is true even though a man is a physician and he sees another person in dire need of medical treatment. In no case is there any duty imposed by law to give aid and assistance to an injured person, even though common decency would seem to require it. Where one does come to the aid of a person in distress, he has assumed a duty of reasonable care in the performance of the assistance, and he will be answerable in damages if he fails to exercise due care and the victim sustains further injury as a result.

For example, a man is trapped in a burning automobile. His rescuer, in the course of removing him from the vehicle, carelessly drops him to the ground. The rescuer will be held answerable in damages for the injury sustained as a result of the fall to the ground. This is true even though the victim might have been burned to death had the rescuer not intervened.

More common occurrences involved physicians. A physician, on a pleasure trip or on vacation, comes upon an injured or sick person whose condition is such that an immediate operation is necessary to save his life. The physician does not have any surgical instruments with him, nor are any available. The physician operates with whatever instruments are available and saves the victim's life. If there are any unsatisfactory results of the operation, the physician is liable in damages to the patient, the liability being based on the physician's failure to exercise reasonable care in operating. The failure to use proper surgical instruments is evidence of a lack of reasonable care, and the physician is liable, even though if he did not act the patient would have lost his life.

The same concept has been applied to situations where no emergency existed but where there was a voluntary assumption of a duty not required by law. For example, a railroad might have no duty to station a flagman at a grade crossing, but it does so. The flagman is present for a long period of time, and the public became accustomed to relying on the warning which he gave every time a train approached. Should the railroad remove the flagman, or discontinue the service he gave without notice to the people using the crossing, the railroad could be held responsible for any accident which might occur due to the absence of the flagman. Having assumed the duty of supplying a flagman, the railroad is under a duty of exercising reasonable care in the performance of such duties.

2. *Failure to comply with the standard.* The courts require that where there is a duty owed that the person owing the duty exercise reasonable or due care in performing the duty. Clearly, the amount of care which must be exercised will vary with the circumstances and the degree of danger involved. Therefore, the common-law courts applied the *reasonably prudent man standard*, which means that the defendant's conduct will be judged by comparing it with what the reasonably prudent man would or would not do under similar circumstances. If the conduct of the defendant falls below the standard thus invoked, the defendant is charged with negligence.

The conduct of the defendant may involve an act or a failure to act. If an act is one which the reasonably prudent man would not have done, then the act is one of *commission* and constitutes negligence. If the duty required the doing of an act which the reasonably prudent man would have done in the exercise of due care, and the defendant failed to act, then the failure to act is referred to as an *omission,* and is also negligence.

For example, the reasonably prudent man will obey the traffic regulations with respect to the use of his vehicle; he will obey the rules of the road, the posted speed limits, and the traffic control signs displayed on the highway. If the defendant's conduct differed from that of the prudent man in exceeding the speed limit (an act of commission) or in failing to obey a traffic control sign (an act of omission), his conduct is negligent.

The reasonably prudent man standard is applied to all persons irrespective of intellect or education, with the exception of children and, possibly, aged persons. As to children, the law requires that they exercise a degree of care and caution commensurate with their age and intelligence. This standard will vary with the age and intellectual attainments of the child. Some courts have applied the measure of the criminal law to the effect that a child of seven or under is incapable of a criminal intent and is therefore not chargeable with negligence. From 7 to 14 a child is chargeable with negligence if it can be proved that he has the intelligence and capacity to exercise care. Over 14, the child is treated as an adult. But states applying this rule are in the minority.

Moreover, in all states where an infant is qualified to obtain an automobile driver's license, the infant so licensed is held to the same degree of care in driving the vehicle as an adult. The same ruling would seem to follow in other cases where the infant is engaged in operating a dangerous instrumentality. For example, in *Dellwo* v. *Pearson* [107 N.W. 2d 859 (Minnesota)], the plaintiff was injured as a result of the negligent operation of a boat with an outboard motor driven by a 12-year-old boy. In finding for the plaintiff, the court said:

To give legal sanction to the operation of automobiles by teenagers with less than ordinary care for the safety of others is impractical today, to say the least. We must take judicial notice of the hazards of automobile traffic, the frequency of accidents, the often catastrophic results of accidents, and the fact that immature individuals are no less prone to accidents than adults. While minors are entitled to be judged by standards commensurate with age, experience and wisdom, it would be unfair to the public to public to permit a minor in the operation of a motor vehicle to observe any other standard of care and conduct than those expected of others. A person observing children at play with toys, throwing balls, operating tricycles or velocipedes, or engaged in other childhood activities may anticipate conduct that does not reach an adult standard of care and prudence. However, one cannot know whether the operator of an approaching automobile, airplane or powerboat is a minor or an adult, and usually cannot protect himself against youthful imprudence even if warned. Accordingly, we hold that in the operation of an automobile, airplane or power boat, a minor is held to the same standard of care as an adult.

Therefore, where the minor engages in an adult activity, it can be concluded that he would be held to the same degree of care as an adult. In other areas, his conduct is judged by his age, experience, and understanding. In some cases his infancy might be a complete defense. As to aged persons, there are very few cases, but there is a suggestion in some cases in which opinions have been rendered that an aged person, like a child, is to be held to only a degree of care which is commensurate with his age, condition, and mental capacity. Obviously if he does engage in the operation of a dangerous instrumentality, such as an automobile or airplane, he would be liable if he fails to exercise the care required of all other persons so engaged. As to the exact age when a person can be regarded as "aged," the cases do not set up any standard; so that if it is urged that a person is "aged" the question of whether he is or is not would seem to be a jury question.

3. Causal relationship. In some cases, it is quite possible that there was a duty owed and that conduct fell below the required standard—but that there was no chain of causation running from the duty, and the failure to meet it, to the event which occurred. In such a case, there is no actionable negligence. For a recovery to be had, there must be a relationship as to causation between the duty, the failure to meet it, and the event. This is usually referred to as the requirement of *proximate cause*. (See Section 308.)

4. Damages. In a negligence cause of action, damages are never presumed. They must be pleaded and proved by the plaintiff, and it must be shown that all of the damages claimed were sustained as a direct result of the negligence of the defendant and from no other cause.

303　Imputed negligence

Imputed or vicarious negligence is negligence which is not directly attributable to the person himself but which is the negligence of a person who is in privity with him and with whose fault he is chargeable. At common law it contemplates an actual or fictional relationship of master and servant, or principal and agent, where the master has control of the servant's behavior and thus becomes responsible for the negligence of the servant in relation to third persons as if the negligence were his own. Imputed negligence may arise from the following relationships and situations:

1. Servant.
2. Independent contractor.
3. Joint enterprise.

1. *Servant.*   The negligence of a servant is imputed to the master when his negligent act is within the scope of his employment. The original concept was that where the servant was on a frolic or a detour of his own that the master was not liable. However, this concept has been limited in its application in the more recent cases. These cases hold that where the master could reasonably expect a deviation, he is still liable.

In some situations, the common law has created a fictional relationship of master and servant. As an example, the Family Purpose doctrine (see Section 1226) creates a fictional relationship of master and servant between the father-owner of an automobile, which he has supplied for family use, and the member of the family driving the vehicle.

2. *Independent contractor.*   Generally the master is not responsible for the negligence of an independent contractor over whom he exercises no control, except

1. Where the work involves a duty of the master which is by law nondelegable.
2. Where the subject matter of the work involves an inherently dangerous or ultrahazardous operation.

If the master continues to control the work, the contractor is not independent and is regarded as a servant. A contractor is independent only when he represents the owner or master as to the results to be accomplished and not as to the methods and means of doing the work.

3. *Joint enterprise.*   This is similar to a partnership where the negligence of one partner is imputed to the other with respect to injuries sustained by a third person. It is a situation where two or more persons engage in a joint undertaking with a common purpose and mutual rights of control. Imputed negligence is involved only with respect to the liability of the members of the joint enterprise to third persons and is not applicable to actions between the parties against each other.

Some statutes create a vicarious liability by imputing the negligence of one person to another. For example, some motor vehicle statutes create a fictional relationship of master and servant between the owner of a motor vehicle and another person driving the car with the owner's permission. Other statutes make the owner liable for the negligence of anyone driving the car with the owner's permission, with no attempt being made to create a relationship of master and servant, fictional or otherwise.

The question of imputed negligence also arises in family relationships, such as parent and child, and husband and wife. The general rule, subject to few exceptions, is that the negligence of one in this relationship is not imputed to the other.

Parent and child. The English common-law rule was that the negligence of the parent was imputed to the child. Thus, where a child was in the custody of a parent (or grandparent), and the child wandered into the street where it was injured, the negligence of the parent in failing to keep the child in a safe place was imputed to the infant and barred a recovery. This rule has been overruled in almost all of the American states (in New York and Massachusetts by specific statutes); the exceptions are Maryland [*Graham* v. *Western Maryland Dairy*, 81 Atl. 2d 457], and Maine [*Wood* v. *Balzano*, 15 Atl. 2d 188].

On the other hand, the negligence of an infant has never been imputed to the parent solely because of the relationship of parent and child. The infant or minor child is responsible for his own torts, whether the negligence of the child resulted in bodily injury or property damage or both, and the relationship of parent and child imposes no liability on the parent for the torts of the child. This common-law rule applies not only to natural parents but also to anyone standing *in loco parentis* (in place of a parent) to the child, be he a stepparent, adopting parent, or a guardian. The exceptions to this rule under which the parent may be liable are:

1. When the child's act is done as the parent's agent or servant,
2. Where the parent's negligence makes the injury possible, or
3. Where the parent participates in the child's tortious act by consenting to it.

1. *Agency.* Where the parent authorizes or commands the child to act as his agent and to do a certain act, the parent will be liable for the negligence of the child within the scope of the authorization or command thus given. This liability does not arise out of the relationship of parent and child but rather from the relationship of principal and agent and is merely an application of the fundamental principle of agency that where a principal does an act through another under his control, he does it himself. Therefore, in this situation, the vicarious liability of the parent is based on the rules relating to principal and agent.

2. *Negligence of the parent.* The majority of the cases involving exceptions to the common-law rule of nonliability on the part of parents are found in this particular area. Generally, the parent is required to exercise reasonable care in controlling the actions of his child for the safety of others. This does not mean that the parent is liable if he fails to maintain strict control over the actions of the child. He must reasonably foresee the risks of harm to others which might arise under unusual circumstances, such as placing a gun in the hands of a child unfamiliar with its use or making such an instrumentality available to the child by failing to take adequate measures to store the gun out of the reach of the child. If the parent fails to take such steps as are necessary to avoid these risks of harm to others, he will be charged with negligence.

Likewise, where the child has exhibited vicious tendencies toward other children, adults, or animals, and such characteristics were known to the parent, the parent is himself negligent if he fails to adopt reasonable means for the protection of others who may be injured as a result. The extent of the protective measures which the parent must take will be measured by the extent of the danger to others. In addition, where such characteristics are known to the parent, he might be under a duty to disclose the existence of these characteristics to persons who might be injured thereby, such as a baby-sitter, private tutor, or any other person who has temporary custody of the child. It must be emphasized that the liability of the parent herein arises not from the negligent or tortious act of the child, but from the parent's own negligence in failing to warn the injured person of the dangerous characteristics of the child, thus failing to meet the duty which the law imposes upon him.

Also the parent would be held liable in a case where the parent, either in violation of an ordinance or statute or in failing to foresee the risks of injury to others, provides the child with a dangerous instrumentality, the parent would be guilty of negligence and answerable therefor. For example, in *Faith* v. *Massengill* (121 S.E. 2d 657), an eight-year-old child was provided with an air rifle by his father. The plaintiff was struck in the eye by a pellet from the gun which ricocheted off the concrete sidewalk. There was a local ordinance which made it unlawful for a parent having custody of a child under the age of 12 years to permit the child to have possession of an air rifle within the corporate limits of the city. Under the circumstances, the father was held to be negligent in providing the child with an air rifle in the face of the statutory prohibition. The ordinance was enacted for the safety of others and did set forth the standard of care which was to be exercised by a parent with regard to the use and possession of an air rifle. The court observed that even if there were no statute, an air rifle in the hands of an eight-year-old was a dangerous instrumentality and that the parent who had provided the instrument was answerable in damages to others who were injured as a result.

An air rifle in the hands of an older child, who is familiar with its use would not be a dangerous instrumentality, and the parent providing the child with one would not be considered negligent. Therefore, the question of whether or not an object is a dangerous instrumentality will depend not only upon the inherent nature of the article but also upon the age of the child to whom it is entrusted. Thus, where a parent provides an automobile for his 17-year-old son, who is a licensed driver and who has a satisfactory driving record, the parent is not negligent. However, should the parent permit a 15-year-old unlicensed driver to use the automobile, the parent is negligent. An automobile in the hands of such an immature, inexperienced driver becomes a dangerous instrumentality and exposes others to an unreasonable risk of harm. The parent thus would be answerable in damages for any injuries which may occur.

On the other hand, where the parent provides ordinary toys or sports equipment which are normally used by children, he is not accountable if the child should use the article for a purpose for which it was not intended. Thus, if a child should use a baseball bat, a hockey stick or other similar article as a weapon, the parent would not be chargeable with negligence solely because he provided the child with it.

3. *Participation.* Where a parent actively participates in the commission of a tort together with his child, the parent then becomes a joint tort-feasor and is liable as such. Participation may also consist of a failure to act when there is a duty to do so. For example, in *Langford* v. *Shu* [128 S.E. 2d 210 (North Carolina)], the plaintiff was a visitor in the defendant's home. The defendant's sons exhibited a box which carried a label which read as follows: "Danger, African Mongoose Live Snake Eater." The defendant assured the plaintiff that the box did in fact contain such a wild animal, whereas the box contained only a foxtail. One of the boys released a spring in the box and the foxtail flew out. The plaintiff, terror-stricken, started to run and in so doing she struck a lounge chair and a brick wall injuring herself. The court allowed a recovery on the theory that the defendant had participated in the so-called joke and was therefore liable. The court felt that Mrs. Shu intended to enjoy the joke on her neighbor as much as the children and that she participated in the act with them.

Statutory modifications. In most of the states, statutes have been enacted which in substance provide that the parent is liable for the malicious and willful acts of his child resulting in property damage to others. These statutes are subject to a limited amount of recovery. Originally these laws were enacted at the request of the state highway departments and were intended to provide a means whereby some recovery could be made from the parents of children who removed highway signs and other directional markers from the highway. All states included within the persons or organizations benefited by the legislation municipal corporations, county, city, village, school district or person, partnership, corporation, association, or religious organization. Some statutes also include bodily injuries caused by the child, but in most instances the recovery is limited to the medical and hospital expense. A list of the present state statutes and their limitations is shown in the table.

As to the states which are not included in this list, there is no similar legislation.

It should be emphasized that the liability created by these statutes is in addition to any other liability which is imposed by law. The common-law liability of the child is still in existence and the liability of the parent for the acts of the child under certain circumstances may still be enforced. A settlement under the statute will not absolve either the child or the parent from liability in tort, although payments under the statute will be taken into account in the event of a tort judgment.

The acts of the child for which the parent is liable under the statute are those which can be characterized as "willful and malicious." This means that the child must have had an intent to do the act and also that such intent was evil and with malice. At common law, a child under the age of seven years is incapable of forming an intent. Therefore, where a child of that age or

State	Property Damage (dollars)	Bodily Injury (If Included) (dollars)
Alabama	$ 500	
Alaska	2,500	
Arizona	500	$ 500
Arkansas	300	
California	2,000	2,000 (Medical expense only.)
Colorado	1,000	
Connecticut	1,500	1,500
Delaware	1,000	
Florida	1,000	
Georgia	Unlimited	Unlimited
Idaho	300	
Illinois	500	500 (Medical, dental, and hospital services only.)
Indiana	750	
Iowa	1,000 (For one act and not more than $2,000 payable to the same claimant for two or more acts.)	
Kansas	1,000 (If a malicious or willful act of the minor is the result of parental neglect, there is no limit.)	
Kentucky	500	
Louisiana	No limit	No limit
Maine	250	
Maryland	1,000	1,000
Massachusetts	300 (Additional $300 allowed for attorney's fees for representing the minor.)	
Michigan	1,500	1,500
Minnesota	100	
Mississippi	300	
Missouri	300	
Montana	300	
Nebraska	1,000	1,000 (Medical expense only.)
Nevada	2,000	
New Hampshire	500	500
New Jersey	250	
New Mexico	1,000	1,000
New York	500	
North Carolina	500	
North Dakota	300	
Ohio	2,000	2,000
Oklahoma	1,500	
Oregon	300	
Pennsylvania	1,000	1,000
Puerto Rico	No limit (Liability ceases when liable persons shall prove that they employed the diligence of a father to preclude the damage.)	
Rhode Island	250	

State	Property Damage (dollars)	Bodily Injury (If Included) (dollars)
South Carolina	1,000 (Shall not limit the application of the family purpose doctrine.)	
South Dakota	300 (Not applicable to motor vehicle damage.)	
Tennessee	2,500 (No recovery shall be had if parent or guardian shows due care and diligence in his care and supervision of such minor child.)	
Texas	5,000 (If due to negligent failure of parent or guardian, or, if child is over 12, due to the willful and malicious conduct of the child.)	
Vermont	250	
Virginia	200	
Washington	1,000	
West Virginia	300	
Wisconsin	1,000	1,000
Wyoming	300	

younger is involved, no evidence of willful or evil intent can be introduced. In cases of older children, the burden of proving the intention of the child is on the person asserting the claim. In most cases the facts of the case will be such that the jury can infer the intent.

Husband and wife. With the emancipation of married women, the wife is considered as an individual, capable of acting independently without any coercion or direction from her husband. She can sue or be sued in her own name. She is not the agent of her husband in all matters nor is he hers. With few exceptions the negligence of one spouse is not imputed to the other solely because of the marital relationship. The exceptions are found in some of the states where community property laws are in effect. In such states any recovery obtained would become part of the community property owned by both husband and wife. In those states the negligence of the husband is imputed to the wife and may be an effective bar to her recovery. For example, where the husband is driving the car and the wife is a passenger, an accident occurs in which the negligence of the husband and that of the adverse driver causes the accident. The contributory negligence of the husband is imputed to the wife, thus barring her recovery from the adverse driver. The theory behind this is that if the wife were permitted to recover, any money which she might receive would become part of their community property in which the husband had a one-half interest. Therefore, if a recovery were allowed, the contributorily negligent husband would indirectly benefit from an accident which was caused partly by his own negligence. Thus, the wife may not recover. The application of this rule is called the Community Purpose Doctrine. The following states have adopted this rule: Arizona (*Pacific Constr. Co.* v. *Cochran*, 243 Pac. 405), California (*Solko* v. *Jones*, 3 Pac. 2d 1028) and Texas (*Dallas Ry.* v. *High*, 103 S.W. 2d 735).

304   Negligence per se

This is negligence in itself or negligence as a matter of law. It is conduct, whether an action or omission, which may be declared and treated as negligence without any argument or proof of the surrounding circumstances because it is so palpably opposed to the dictates of common prudence that it can be said without hesitation or doubt that no careful person would have been guilty of it. Whether or not certain actions or lack of action constitute negligence per se is a question for the court and not for the jury. Where the court decides the question affirmatively, it will direct the jury to assume that negligence has been established as a matter of law. For example, if the evidence indicated that the defendant drove his automobile at a speed of 100 miles per hour in a congested area where the posted speed limit was 20 miles per hour, reasonable minds could not differ as to whether or not he was negligent. Therefore, the court would rule that the defendant was chargeable with negligence as a matter of law since there was in fact no question for the jury to decide.

Where there is a duty to the public created by a statute and the person injured is one of the class of persons intended to be protected by the statute, the majority of the courts which have passed on the question hold that the violation of the statute is negligence per se. The theory is that the legislature has fixed the standard of conduct which must be observed and the jury would have no right to overrule the legislative objective. In a minority of states they treat the violation of a statute as creating a presumption of negligence which can be overcome by evidence in the form of an explanation of his conduct by the defendant. Still others hold that the violation of a statute is merely evidence of negligence and nothing more.

As to the plaintiff the general rule is that his violation of a statute which involves his injury constitutes contributory negligence per se and is therefore a complete defense to his cause of action.

305   Degrees of care

Some cases refer to degrees of negligence, although what they actually discuss are degrees of care. The courts sometimes characterize an act in terms of negligence rather than in terms of the amount of care which is exercised. Expressed in terms of the care which the defendant failed to exercise, the negligence terms are as follows:

1. Slight negligence: failure to exercise great care.
2. Ordinary negligence: failure to exercise reasonable care.
3. Gross negligence: failure to use slight care.

1. *Slight negligence.* This term is referable to cases where the defendant is under a duty to exercise a high degree of care. For example, a common carrier of passengers is under a duty to exercise a high degree of care for their safety. If it fails to exercise great care or, conversely, is chargeable with slight negligence which results in an injury to a passenger, the common carrier is answerable in damages. Also, a high degree of care is required of motorists who take some action which is contrary to the normal flow of traffic, such as making U turns or backing. The failure to exercise great care under these circumstances constitutes actionable negligence.

2. *Ordinary negligence.* This refers to situations where the duty owed is one of reasonable care, as measured by the reasonably prudent man standard. If the defendant's conduct falls below the standard, he is chargeable with ordinary negligence.

3. *Gross negligence.* Basically, this connotes a more aggravated form of carelessness than ordinary negligence. It is discussed in detail in the following paragraph.

306 Gross negligence

This term is defined in cases involving gratuitous bailments, automobile guest statutes, and comparative negligence statues. All of the cases agree that it means conduct more culpable than ordinary negligence, but when it comes to fixing the dividing line between ordinary and gross negligence, the cases are in hopeless confusion. At one extreme are the cases which define gross negligence as a complete lack of care, or a complete lack of regard for the safety or the rights of others, characterized as an intentional failure to perform a manifest duty in reckless disregard of the consequences. Supporting this view, in *McDonald* v. *Railroad Co.* (21 S.W. 775), the court said:

In the law of torts (and especially with reference to personal injury cases) the term (gross negligence) means such negligence as evidences a reckless disregard of human life, or the safety of persons exposed to its dangerous effects, or that entire want of care which would raise the presumption of a conscious indifference to the rights of others which is equivalent to an intentional violation of them.

At the other extreme are the cases which hold that gross negligence is the same as ordinary negligence except that it is carelessness of a more exaggerated form, not necessarily involving recklessness. The trend of the more recent cases seems to be toward this view rather than the first extreme.

It must be recognized that if the burden is on the plaintiff to establish the gross negligence of the defendant, the burden would be much more onerous under the first definition than the second and that there would be fewer recoveries possible under the first view than the second.

307 Willful, wanton, or reckless misconduct

These terms have been subject to various definitions by the courts which have had occasion to consider them. They were originally used to describe conduct on the part of the defendant which was so outrageous as to support an award of punitive damages as punishment, but more recently the terms have found their way into automobile guest statutes. Some of these statutes preclude a recovery by a gratuitous passenger against the host unless the host is guilty of willful and wanton misconduct; willful, wanton, and reckless misconduct; or willful and wanton negligence.

These terms would all seem to be alike, but in the interpretation of what they mean, there are apparently two schools of thought among the courts. Both schools agree that the terms mean something more than mere ordinary negligence, but they part company when it comes to deciding where ordinary negligence ends and willful and wanton negligence begins. The first, or what can be characterized as the extreme school, compares willful and wanton negligence with gross negligence, holding that if the legislature had gross negligence in mind, they would have said so; in using the terminology *willful and wanton* they meant something more culpable than gross negligence. The courts reasoned that since gross negligence was a complete lack of care, then willful and wanton negligence referred to a complete want of care, plus a willful intention to exercise no care at all.

The opposing school makes no attempt whatsoever to compare willful and wanton negligence with gross negligence, but takes the position that it is more than ordinary negligence and that the use of the word *willful* defines conduct which is more culpable than negligence, which is the result of inattention, inadvertence, or mistake.

308   Proximate cause

Proximate cause is the connecting link between the defendant's breach of a duty and the injuries sustained by the plaintiff. To prevail, the plaintiff must establish that the defendant's negligent act was the responsible cause of the injury sustained. The mere fact that the defendant's conduct was negligent will not sustain the claim unless it can be shown that there was an unbroken chain of causation from the negligent act to the infliction of the damage. When this chain is established, it is said that the defendant's negligence is the proximate cause of the damage.

Proximate cause has been defined by the courts as that which in a natural and continuous sequence, unbroken by any efficient intervening cause, produces the injury, and without which the result would not have occurred. To determine whether or not the defendant's negligent act was or was not the proximate cause of the injury, the courts applied the "but for" or *sine qua non* test: Could it be said that the damage would not have been sustained *but for* the defendant's negligent act?

If the damage would have been sustained *without* the negligent act of the defendant, then the defendant's act is not the proximate cause of the damage. On the other hand, if no damage would have been sustained but for the defendant's negligent act, then the negligence of the defendant is the proximate or responsible cause of the damage. If the defendant's negligent act were to be eliminated, would there have been any damage sustained? If there would have been, then the negligence of the defendant was not the proximate cause, whereas if no damage would have been sustained but for the defendant's negligent act, then the negligence of the defendant is the proximate cause of the damage.

For example, if the defendant's vehicle struck a pedestrian on the sidewalk, the proximate cause of the pedestrian's injuries would be the negligent operation of the defendant's vehicle. If the negligent operation of the vehicle was eliminated, then the pedestrian would have sustained no injury. Therefore, but for the negligent operation of the vehicle, the injury would not have been sustained.

The classic example illustrating the rule of proximate cause is the *Squib* case [*Scott* v. *Shepherd* (1772), 2 W. B. 1892, 96 Eng. Rep. 525]. The defendant threw a lighted squib, which appears to be an ancient version of our modern day firecracker, into a crowded marketplace. In the instinct of self-preservation, several persons in the crowd successively took the squib and threw it away from themselves. It ultimately exploded and caused injury to the plaintiff.

Clearly, the original act of the defendant in throwing the lighted squib into the marketplace was wrongful, but the question before the court was whether or not this act was the proximate cause of the plaintiff's injury. The defendant contended that if the squib had exploded at the place where he threw it originally, some distance from where the plaintiff was standing, the plaintiff would not have been injured, and therefore the negligent or intentional wrongful act was not the proximate cause of the plaintiff's injuries. The court ruled that the defendant should have reasonably foreseen the action of others endangered by the lighted squib, and therefore ruled that there was an unbroken chain of causation running from the negligent act to the injury. Applying the "but for" test, the court reasoned that if the defendant's act was eliminated, the injury would not have occurred. Therefore the throwing of the lighted squib was the proximate cause of the plaintiff's injuries.

The application of the "but for" test was found to produce a satisfactory solution to most of the cases, but as time went on the courts were confronted with situations where there was more difficulty in applying it. For example, automobiles driven negligently by *A* and *B* collide at an intersection, and as a result *A*'s vehicle is forced onto the sidewalk where it hits *C*, a pedestrian. It is clear that both drivers are to blame for *C*'s injuries, but the application of the "but for" rule would lead to a conclusion that the negligence of neither driver was the proximate cause.

If we eliminate *A*'s negligent act, then the accident would not have happened but for the negligence of *B*; therefore, *A*'s negligence is not the proximate cause of *C*'s injuries. Applying the same reasoning to *B*'s negligence, the accident would not have happened but for the negligence of *A*, and *B*'s negligence is not the proximate cause either. With this result, *C*, the innocent party, would be without a remedy against either *A* or *B*.

To avoid such an unconscionable result, the courts adopted the *substantial factor* rule as being applicable to situations of this kind. The rule is that the defendant's conduct is a cause of the event if it was a "material element and a substantial factor in bringing it about." Applying this test to the preceding situation, the proximate cause of *C*'s injuries was the negligence of *both A* and *B*, and both are answerable. The negligence of either *A* or *B*, when examined separately, was a material element and substantial factor in the causation of the event.

The rule of proximate cause applies not only to the happening of the event but also to the events which follow as a natural consequence of the event itself. For example, if *A*'s automobile, negligently driven, damages a fence belonging to *B*, with the result that *B*'s cattle wander off, *A* is liable not only for the damage to the fence but also for the expense of rounding up the cattle—as well as any damage which might be caused by the escape of the cattle.

In another case, *A* negligently stalls the passenger bus he is driving on a railroad crossing. A train is approaching at a fast rate of speed. *B*, a passenger on the bus, jumps through the window and fractures his ankle. *A*'s negligence is the proximate cause of *B*'s injury. This is true even though *A* is able to get the bus started and clears the track before the train arrives.

Proximate cause has also been applied to complications and events following the infliction of a bodily injury. There are three situations which may be involved.

1. Complications of the injury itself.
2. Complications as a result of the medical treatment.
3. Consequential injuries.

1. *The injury itself.* The tort-feasor is answerable for the injury which he inflicted, together with any other physical conditions which unavoidably arise therefrom. Therefore, if the injured person sustains lacerations which subsequently become infected, even though prompt and proper medical treatment is instituted, the tort-feasor is answerable not only for the lacerations but for the results of the infection as well.

Another such example is that of a claimant, suffering from a preexisting heart condition, who, as a result of the accident and injuries he sustains, requires an immediate operation to save his life. During the operation the claimant dies as a result of surgical shock superimposed upon an already weakened heart. The tort-feasor is liable for the claimant's death; there is a direct chain of causation from the infliction of the injury to the death of the claimant. Were it not for the accident, the operation would not have been required. And since the operation was required solely as a result of the injury, the tort-feasor is liable for the result of the operation, whatever it may be.

Where the injured person refuses medication, refuses to follow the advice of his physician, or removes a bandage or a plaster cast, all with the result that his disability is prolonged, the proximate cause of his increased disability is not the injury but his own acts, and the tort-feasor therefore is not responsible for the increase in disability or any medical costs which are incurred as a result of the injured's own failure to cure and relieve himself.

2. *Complications as a result of the medical treatment.* The tort-feasor is answerable for any normal complications which could result from the treatment rendered by a physician chosen with reasonable care by the injured person. If, for example, the injured was allergic to tetanus antitoxin and this fact was unknown to the injured or his physician, and the patient suffered a severe reaction when such antitoxin was administered in the course of treatment, the tort-feasor is answerable for this result.

Where the complications are the result of the malpractice of the physician, the tort-feasor is still liable for the entire damage, since this was a foreseeable risk of harm to which the tort-feasor's negligent act exposed the victim. The physician is himself responsible as a joint tort-feasor for his malpractice and may be joined as a codefendant by the injured, but the physician is liable only for the effects of his malpractice and not for the entire injury. In no case will the malpractice of a physician insulate the tort-feasor from liability for the entire injury, since the risk of improper diagnosis or negligent treatment is a risk inherent in all medical service.

When an event which is entirely unrelated to the original accident takes place in the course of treatment, the tort-feasor is not answerable for the result. For example, if while in the hospital recovering from his injuries, *A* makes an improper advance to a nurse and she hits him on the head with a chair, causing severe head injuries, the original tort-feasor is not liable for the head injuries so sustained.

3. *Consequential injuries.* The rule of proximate cause has been applied to subsequent injuries alleged to have been sustained as a result of the original injury. If there is an unbroken chain of causation from the original injury to the cause of the second, recovery will be allowed; otherwise not. For example, *A* sustains a badly fractured leg as a result of *B's* negligence. While in the hospital, *A* is supplied with walking caliper and is told to begin weight-bearing. While trying to walk, *A's* leg gives way, and he sustains a fracture of the other leg. *B* is liable for both fractures.

Now let us assume the same facts, but add that *A* has been discharged from the hospital and given a prescription for medications he must take. On the way to the drugstore, *A* slips on the ice, or is struck by an automobile, sustaining a fracture of the other leg. *B* is not liable for the second fracture, even though the trip to the drugstore was required as a result of the original injury. The second occurrence was too remote from the chain of causation to be a part of it.

309 Intervening cause

There are situations where another act or cause comes in between the original negligent act of the tort-feasor and the resulting injury. If this act or cause is in concert with the original wrongful act, it does not break the chain of causation and does not absolve the original wrongdoer from liability. Again the "but for" rule; if it can be said that but for the intervening cause the accident would not have happened, then the intervening cause becomes a superseding, independent cause and a proximate cause of the injury.

For example, if a driver is operating an automobile at a speed of 80 miles per hour, in excess of the speed limit and an excessive speed under the driving conditions, and a passenger grabs the wheel to turn the car away from an oncoming vehicle with the result that the car goes out of control and rolls over, injuring the passenger and the driver, the original act of negligence—driving at an excessive speed—has been superseded by another cause, the action of the passenger. It cannot be established that the excessive speed would have caused an accident; the driver could have slowed down or could have controlled the vehicle so as to have avoided an accident. Therefore, there is no evidence that an accident would have happened had the passenger not intervened. The action of the passenger relieved the driver of the responsibility arising from the excessive speed. The condition created by the driver was merely a circumstance of the accident and not its proximate cause.

The negligence of the operator of a motor vehicle in obstructing the highway may be a proximate cause of an injury to others, even though the negligence of the operator of another vehicle is an active and later cause in contributing to the final result. One cannot excuse himself from liability arising from his own negligent conduct merely because the later negligence of another concurs to cause an injury, if the later act was legally foreseeable. A later event, or second act, will break the chain of causation only where under no rational interpretation of the evidence the later act of negligence could have been reasonably foreseen.

If an automobile breaks down on the traveled portion of the highway, and the owner does not remove it, or does not provide for some means of warning oncoming traffic of the obstruction, either by flares, lanterns, flags, or other devices, the conduct of the owner is negligent. It is reasonably foreseeable that oncoming traffic might not be able to avoid the obstruction where no warning of its presence has been given. But if a car carrying passengers runs into the disabled vehicle, it could be claimed that the negligence of the driver of the oncoming car, in not having it under control, was the proximate cause of the accident; the circumstances do not absolve the second driver from responsibility to his passengers. It may well be that the negligence of the driver, as between himself and the owner of the disabled vehicle, would be considered as contributory negligence so as to defeat the driver's recovery. The passengers are not chargeable with their own driver's negligence, and since the negligence of their driver was foreseeable by the owner of the disabled vehicle, both the owner and the driver are liable to the passengers as joint tort-feasors. The negligence of both were material elements and substantial factors in causing injuries to the passengers.

Let us assume the same facts—except that the owner of the disabled vehicle moved it onto the shoulder of the highway but did not set any flares or other warning devices to give notice of its presence to oncoming traffic. An oncoming car, traveling on the shoulder, runs into it. Since the second act of negligence was not foreseeable, it becomes the sole proximate cause of the accident, even though the owner of the disabled vehicle failed to give notice of its presence on the shoulder.

The theory of intervening cause can also be applied to the injuries sustained. As we have seen, the action of a patient in interfering with the work of the physician by removing bandages or plaster casts is an intervening cause in the sense that it is itself the proximate cause of any disability occasioned thereby. But a more perplexing question is presented where the injured person commits suicide during the period of medical treatment. If it can be established that the motive for the suicide was causally related to the original injury, then the act of the injured person in destroying himself is not an intervening cause. On the other hand, if there is no connection between the original injury and the motive for the suicide, then the injured person's action is an intervening cause, absolving the original tort-feasor from liability.

For example, if the evidence established that the injured person suffered such excruciating pain that it affected his mind to the extent that it drove him to suicide, or if it was established that the injured person had been told that he would never work again, or that his life-span had been shortened by the injury, and he destroyed himself rather than become a burden on his family or on society, then there is a direct chain of causation running from the injury to the suicide, and the act of the injured person is not an independent, intervening cause of his death. On the other hand, if the evidence established that the injured person had other personal motives for the commission of the act, such as the breaking of an engagement, a divorce from his wife, or the death of a close family member, and his injury had nothing to do with the motive for suicide, then his act of destruction is an intervening cause of his death which relieves the tort-feasor from liability.

310   Joint tort-feasors

Where two or more persons owe the same duty to another, and by their common neglect, the other is injured, they are joint tort-feasors. All tort-feasors are responsible for the legal consequences of their wrongful acts, but where the causation of the injury is complicated by the introduction of other wrongful acts in the chain of causation, the extent to which the individual tort-feasor is answerable will depend upon the relationship which his particular wrongful act bears to the causation and result. His negligent act will partake of one of the following causative qualities:

1. Concurrent.
2. Successive.
3. A combination of both.

1. *Concurrent.* Where the negligent acts of two or more persons, although independent of each other, combine to produce a single event or a single injury, they are classified as concurrent, and the tort-feasors are jointly and severally liable to the injured person for the entire damage. For example, two automobiles negligently driven by *A* and *B* collide at an intersection, and *B*'s car goes out of control and strikes *C*, a pedestrian on the sidewalk. *C* may recover for his entire injury from either *A*, or *B*, or both. The fact that *B*'s car struck *C*, and *A*'s did not, will not in any way alter the situation. The negligence of both *A* and *B* combined to produce the event and the injury to *C*. Nor would the fact that one driver's negligence was more culpable than the other's change the situation in any way. If *A* was driving 10 miles over the speed limit and *B* was driving 30 miles over the speed limit, both are still liable for the causation of the event.

In the foregoing example, the joint negligence of *A* and *B* produced a single indivisible result, the injury to *C*. But suppose some facts were added and, with the additional facts, we were able to separate *C*'s injuries into two parts: those caused by *A* and those caused by *B*. Would these additional facts change the responsibilities of the parties? Suppose that after the initial impact, *B*'s car struck *C* first, causing a fractured leg, and immediately thereafter *A*'s car struck *C*, causing a fractured skull. Could it be said that *B* is liable only for the fractured leg and that *A* is liable only for the fractured skull? The answer to the question is in the negative. The transaction was a single event and under the circumstances the courts will not apportion responsibility between *A* and *B* but will hold both jointly and severally liable for the entire damage.

C may, at his election, sue either *A* or *B*, or both, for his entire injury. Should he decide to sue one and not the other, his recovery from one will extinguish his cause of action for the reason that *C* is entitled to only one satisfaction for one injury. Therefore, the practical effect of a recovery from one will be to discharge the other. Where *C* elects to sue one of the joint tort-feasors and not the other, his motivation for so doing is not an issue, and he is not required to offer an explanation as to why he made the decision. He may have been persuaded by the fact that one is a rich man and the other poor, one is insured and the other is not, or that one is his friend and the other is not. In any case, he is not required to explain. From a tactical standpoint, however, if he sues only one and not the other, it gives the defendant an opportunity to claim that the event was caused solely by the negligence of the other who has not been joined as a defendant. The practice followed by most plaintiffs' lawyers is to include all parties who have a possible responsibility as defendants in the action.

2. Successive. Where the negligent acts of two or more tort-feasors do not combine to produce the event, but do combine to produce the injury, the general rule is that each is responsible for the effects of his own act, whether the injury sustained is a single indivisible injury or multiple injuries which can be separated.

For example, *C* is injured through the negligence of *A*, and sustains a fractured right leg. While lying on the sidewalk, awaiting an ambulance, *C* is struck by an automobile negligently driven by *B* and sustains a further injury in the form of a fractured skull. *A* is liable for the fractured leg, and *B* is liable for the fractured skull; the damages are apportioned against each by the jury under instructions from the court.

If we change the facts to the extent that *C* sustained a fractured right leg in the first accident, and the same leg is further damaged by the second accident, we would have a single indivisible injury. There would be no evidence as to how badly fractured the leg was prior to the second accident, or exactly what physical injury was caused by the second impact. Under those circumstances the jury would be instructed to apportion the damages between *A* and *B* on the basis of whatever evidence was produced.

C has the right to sue *A* and *B* in separate actions or to combine both claims in one action against both. If he brings separate actions, a recovery in one action will not extinguish his cause of action against the other tort-feasor. Again, the usual practice of the plaintiff's attorney would be to sue both in one action for the entire injury.

3. *Combination of both.* It is possible for the negligent acts of two tort-feasors to be concurrent with respect to a part of the claimant's injuries and to be successive as to the remainder. For example, *C* is injured through the negligence of *A*, sustaining a fractured skull. While lying in the roadway, *C* is again struck by an automobile, this time negligently operated by *B*, and he sustains a fractured right leg as a result of the second impact. The negligence of *A* caused the fractured skull—and also placed *C* in a position of danger where it was reasonably foreseeable that he might be further injured by other motorists. Therefore *A* is liable for both injuries.

As for *B*, his negligence did not cause the fractured skull, and he is liable only for the injuries which he did cause, namely, the fractured right leg. Therefore, as to the fractured skull, *A* alone is responsible. As to the fractured leg, *A* and *B* are concurrent joint tort-feasors and are jointly and severally liable.

In the foregoing example, the injuries are separable, and the relative responsibilities of the tort-feasors are capable of ascertainment. Complications develop in this type of situation where the injuries are of such a nature that they constitute one single indivisible result. For example, if *C* was lying in the roadway in a dying condition as a result of *A*'s negligence, and was then struck by *B*'s car, which kills him outright, what is the extent of *B*'s responsibility? If *C* was going to die anyway, it would appear that *B*'s responsibility would be limited to the value of what life *C* had left—or to the outside possibility of a recovery.

The extent of *B*'s responsibility is a jury question. On the other hand, if *C* was already dead when *B* struck him, then *B* would not be liable for any bodily injury but might be liable for "property" damage if the law of the state in which the accident happened recognized such a right.

The same problems arise in cases where further injury is caused by the malpractice of a physician treating the case. The original tort-feasor is liable for the entire injury, including that sustained as a result of the physician's malpractice. The physician's liability is limited to the injury caused by his malpractice alone.

Where the claimant sues the original tort-feasor, who is liable for the entire injury, and recovers, such recovery extinguishes his cause of action. He has obtained complete satisfaction for his entire injury and he is entitled to no more. The effect of the recovery will be also to extinguish the liability of the successive joint tort-feasor. A recovery against the successive joint tort-feasor (*B* in the first example and the physician in the second) would exonerate the original tort-feasor from the responsibility for the second accident, but he would still remain liable for his original negligence and the damages sustained as a result thereof. This latter situation is extremely rare and highly unlikely, since the practice would be to sue all tort-feasors in the one action, and if there is to be a choice between them, the "better" defendant would be the one who is liable for the entire injury rather than one who is liable for only a part.

311   Release-of-one rule

The English common-law rule, to which a number of our courts are still committed, is that the release of one or more joint tort-feasors releases all of them. This rule is based on the theory that there can be but one satisfaction for one injury. Some of our courts have relaxed the rule to the extent that they hold that a release of one joint tort-feasor does not release the other unless the release was so intended or unless the consideration which was given constituted full satisfaction of the claim. These pose factual situations which are within the province of the jury to determine. Where it is held that the release constituted only partial satisfaction of the claim, the holding is that the claim is satisfied to the extent (*pro tanto*) of the payment made. The courts holding these views are in the minority.

Some states have changed the rule by statute. For example, in New York the General Obligations Law, Section 15–108 provides (*a*) that a release given to one or more joint tort-feasors, unless specified to the contrary, releases that tort-feasor only. It also provides that a release reduces the plaintiff's recovery from the other tort-feasors by the amount of damages attributable to the released tort-feasor. (*b*) It further provides that the released tort-feasor is free from any liability to any other tort-feasor for contribution, provided that a good faith release was given by the injured party. (*c*) In any case the tort-feasor who procures his own release waives his right to contribution from any other tort-feasor. This legislation is designed to encourage settlements which will ultimately reduce the calendar congestion in the courts. It is possible that other states may take similar action.

The majority of American courts still hold to the common-law rule that a release to one or more, but less than all, concurrent tort-feasors is a complete surrender of the entire cause of action, without regard to the sufficiency of the compensation so received. This rule is followed even though there is an agreement between the parties that it shall be only a partial release or the agreement is in writing and made part of the release itself. A small minority of the courts give effect to a *restrictive* release where there is language inserted in the instrument to the effect that it is to be construed as a release of one tort-feasor only and is not intended to be a release of the entire cause of action. Other states have accomplished this same result by statute.

Even in those states where the rule is strictly applied, the courts have allowed the parties to circumvent the rule by the use of an agreement called a *covenant not to sue* in which the claim is not released at all: in consideration of the payment by one tort-feasor, the injured party agrees not to sue him, and if the injured party actually sues the tort-feasor, he agrees to make himself liable for an amount equivalent to the amount of the recovery.

312   Contribution and indemnity

Contribution contemplates only a situation where there are two or more joint tort-feasors whose combined active negligence produced the injury and who are therefore equally responsible for the resulting accident. It refers to the right of one of the joint tort-feasors, who has paid more than his share of the settlement or judgment, to recover the excess over his proportionate share from the others equally liable. For example, *A* is a passenger in a car driven by *B*. *B* collides with a car driven by *C*, and the accident is caused by the joint negligence of *B* and *C*. *A* sues *C* and recovers a judgment of $10,000, which *C* pays. *C* is entitled to recover $5,000 from *B*, since this represents the excess over *C*'s proportionate share.

The common-law courts never recognized the right of contribution as an enforceable right. They reasoned that since both were wrongdoers, the courts would not aid one tort-feasor against another because no one should be permitted to found a cause of action upon his own wrong. This common-law rule has been modified by statute in a number of states so as to permit claims for contribution.

Indemnity also involves joint tort-feasors, but it is implied only where the joint tort-feasors are not equally culpable, and where one joint tort-feasor is held liable because of his relationship to the accident, which was due to the active negligence of another. In *Herrero* v. *Atkinson* (227 Cal. App. 2d 69, 8 ALR 3d 629) in defining indemnity, the court said:

As a general rule an implied right of indemnity does not exist among tortfeasors where the parties are *in pari delicto*, that is, when the fault of each is of equal grade and similar in character. . . . Nevertheless, the right to implied indemnity has been recognized and allowed in many cases and in varying fact situations where considerations require the right to be recognized. Numerous theories have been advanced to support the allowance of indemnity in particular cases, among them distinctions between primary and secondary liability, constructive liability, derivative liability, a difference in the respective duties owed by the tortfeasors, active and passive negligence, and even the doctrine of the last clear chance.

The duty to indemnify may arise, and indemnity may be allowed in those fact situations where in equity and good conscience the burden of the judgment should be shifted from the shoulders of the person seeking indemnity to the one from whom indemnity is sought. The right depends upon the principle that everyone is responsible for the consequences of his own wrong, and if others have been compelled to pay damages which ought to have been paid by the wrongdoer, they may recover from him. Thus, the determination of whether or not indemnity should be allowed must of necessity depend upon the facts of each case.

The court went on to say that no one theory or explanation appears to cover all cases. The general rule seems to be that where we have a nonnegligent joint tort-feasor, or a passively negligent joint tort-feasor (one who is not guilty of any act of commission), who is compelled to respond in damages because of his relationship either to the other joint tort-feasor or the event, he will be allowed indemnity from the joint tort-feasor whose active negligence caused the accident. This would mean that the passively negligent joint tort-feasor be reimbursed for his payment, whatever it was, and the full payment would have to be made by the active tort-feasor. It should be noted that the distinction between indemnity and contribution is that indemnity seeks to transfer the entire loss imposed on one tort-feasor to another, who in justice and equity should bear it, whereas contribution distributes the loss equally among the tort-feasors, each bearing his pro rata share.

The active-passive negligence theory has been under critical attack by legal scholars for many years. It was argued that the application of this principle resulted in an unfair distribution of the loss and that the actively negligent party suffered the entire loss while the passively negligent party came out scot-free and unpunished for his participation. It was submitted that a better rule would require each party to contribute to the loss in proportion to the part that his negligence played in the causation of the loss. In *Dole* v. *Dow Chemical Company* (282 N.E 2d 288), the New York Court of Appeals (highest state court) abandoned the active-passive negligence concept and adopted the rule that there must be an apportionment of the responsibility between the parties. The court noted the widespread dissatisfaction with the old rule together with the inequitable results which were produced together with the extreme difficulty of its application. In departing from the old active-passive concept, the court established new guidelines. The court said:

The conclusion reached is that where a third party is found to have been responsible for a part, but not all, of the negligence for which a defendant is cast in damages, the responsibility for that part is recoverable by the prime defendant against the third parties. To reach that end there must necessarily be an apportionment of responsibility in negligence between those parties.

The later cases have illustrated the difficulty in applying this new rule. For example, in *Sanchez* v. *Hertz Rental Corp.* (70 Misc. 2d 449), Victor Sanchez was the owner and operator of an automobile which was involved in a collision with the defendant's vehicle. He brought suit individually and as administrator of the estate of his deceased son, Javier. The defendants made a motion for leave to serve an amended answer which included a cross complaint against the plaintiff Sanchez. In granting the motion, the court said:

. . . the court must perforce grant the defendants' application so as to permit them to cross-complain against Victor M. Sanchez as a co-tortfeasor. While it may be argued that he is already in the case as a plaintiff, it is nevertheless necessary to spell out a new role in the case of Victor M. Sanchez, viz. "defendant" so that the rights of the original defendants may be preserved.

*   *   *   *   *

Admittedly, complications at the trial may possibly occur as it was noted in the Dole case, by the advent of new defendants and new issues, but these may be controlled by the trial court by separate hearings at the verdict.

Under the present law the contributory negligence of the parents may not be imputed to his child to bar the child's cause of action. This court also adds, that if an infant sues a car driver, the defendant may implead the child's parent if the parent was negligent in any sense. This meets the circumstances in this case exactly since the father was the driver of the vehicle in which the infants were passengers. He may be shown to have been negligent in one action, to the end that all liability may be determined simultaneously, a most cogent reason for permitting the cross-complaint.

The New York Court of Appeals again considered the question of apportionment against joint tort-feasors in *Kelly* v. *Long Island Lighting Co.* (31 N.Y. 2d 25). The court clarified the intent of *Dole* v. *Dow* as follows:

Prior to our recent decision in *Dole* v. *Dow Chemical Co.*, it had been held to be the rule that a defendant found guilty of "active" negligence could not recover over against another guilty of "active" tort negligence. The rule as stated in Dole now permits apportionment of damages among joint or concurrent tortfeasors regardless of the nature of the concurring fault. We believe a new rule of apportionment to be pragmatically sound, as well as realistically fair. To require a joint tortfeasor who is, for instance, 10% causally negligent to pay the same amount as a co-tortfeasor who is 90% causally negligent seems inequitable and unjust. The fairer rule, be believe, is to distribute the loss in proportion to the allocable concurring fault.

In this case the court was dealing with two defendants, both of whom were guilty of active negligence, holding that the same rule as enunciated in Dole should apply. Under the old rule if one defendant, guilty of active negligence were sued, he could not bring in another defendant who was also guilty of active negligence, nor could he compel contribution from such other defendant. The common-law view was that since both were wrongdoers, the court would do nothing to assist either one. Under the new rule in New York, one defendant may bring in another as a codefendant if the other defendant is guilty of either active or passive negligence, and can compel contribution.

Thus, we have in effect two rules regarding joint tort-feasor whether they are both guilty of active negligence or whether one is guilty of active negligence and the other guilty of passive negligence. Under the New York rule, both defendants may be sued, or brought in by means of a cross complaint, and both will be liable in proportion to the extent that their negligence contributed to the loss. In other states where the common-law rule prevails, the defendant guilty of passive negligence has no ultimate liability for the payment for the loss. If he is sued and a judgment rendered, he has a cause of action against the defendant guilty of active negligence and may recover indemnity for the entire verdict. If the defendant guilty of active negligence is sued, there is no way that he can implead the defendant guilty only of passive negligence.

It will be interesting to see how many of the courts will adopt the New York rule and how many will retain the old common-law principle.

Among the more common situations involving indemnity are the liabilities arising out of the relationship of principal and agent and that of owner and independent contractor. Consideration of both will be illustrative of the application of these principles.

Principal and agent.   Let us assume that *A* is driving *B*'s car at the direction of *B* and on *B*'s business. *A* negligently injures *C*, a pedestrian. *C* recovers a judgment against *B*, whose liability is based upon the application of the doctrine of *Respondeat Superior*. Clearly, there was nothing that *B* could have done to have prevented the accident, and the event was due solely to the negligence of *A*. *B* is entitled to indemnity from *A*, and may recover the entire amount of the judgment. Thus, the negligent tort-feasor is compelled to assume the entire loss.

It is also quite possible that a principal be liable to the agent on the theory of implied indemnity. For example, *B* instructs *A*, his employee, to demolish a small building which *B* believes to be located on his property. *A* does as he is instructed. Unknown to both *B* and *A*, the building is owned by *C* and is located on *C*'s property. *C* recovers a judgment against *A*. *A* is entitled to indemnity from *B*. *B*'s negligence consists of his failure to verify that the building was located on his property. *A* was not negligent at all. He was under no duty to ascertain the ownership of the building and he was entitled to rely on *B*'s instructions.

Owner and independent contractor.   *B*, a carpenter, installs a cornice on *A*'s house in such a negligent manner that it falls and strikes *C*, a business visitor. *C* recovers damages from *A* on the allegation that *A* was negligent in failing to maintain his premises in reasonably safe condition for his safety, and further because *A* had failed to make inspection to determine the presence of an unsafe condition. As to *C*, both *A* and *B* are joint tort-feasors in the sense that they both owed *C* a duty of care. *C* chose to sue *A*. Independent of his duty to *C*, *B* owed *A* the duty of reasonable care in the installation of the cornice as well as the duty to do the job in a workmanlike manner. As a result of the breach of *B*'s duty to him, *A* has been compelled to respond in damages to *C*, since if *B* had properly installed the cornice, *A* would not have sustained any loss. *B* was guilty of active negligence while *A*'s negligence was passive in the sense that he did not commit any act whatsoever.

Under the common-law rule, *A* is entitled to indemnity for the entire loss from *B*. Under the New York Dole rule, both would be liable for the loss in proportion to the degree of culpability involved in the causation of the accident. Thus, *A* would not be entitled to full indemnity but since his negligence in failing to inspect and repair if necessary the dangerous cornice, he would be entitled to something less, depending upon the percentage of culpability which the jury or the court would assess against him.

For a discussion of the liability of a manufacturer to a retailer who has been compelled to pay a judgment obtained by a customer, see Chapter X.

313 Contributory negligence

The common-law rule which is applied in the majority of our states is that if the conduct of the injured person falls below the standard of care which he is required to exercise for his own safety, and if such conduct was a contributing cause of the event, the injured person may not recover. Therefore, if the injured person's lack of care for his own safety contributed in the slightest degree to the happening of the event, the verdict must be for the defendant. This is true even though the negligence of the defendant is great and that of the injured person is slight. Contributory negligence on the part of the injured person is a defense against all causes of action based on negligence—but it is not a recognized defense against actions where the conduct of the defendant is intentional or where the defendant's conduct is willful, wanton, and reckless.

The individual is required to exercise reasonable care for his own safety. His conduct will be measured by the reasonably prudent man standard, and if it falls below that standard, it will be characterized as negligent. The standard is a variable one and will depend upon the surrounding circumstances. For example, the reasonably prudent man would not run in front of a speeding train, but he might feel compelled to do so if it was necessary to save the life of a child who was in the path of the train. It might be contributory negligence to run in front of the train with no other surrounding circumstances, but where it is necessary to do so to save a child, the chances are that the jury would view the same act as not constituting contributory negligence. The standard by which the injured person's conduct is judged is what the reasonably prudent man would have done—or would not have done—under the same or similar circumstances.

In cases involving a claim for damages arising out of the intentional infliction of injuries, or willful and wanton misconduct amounting to an intentional infliction of injuries, contributory negligence is not a defense. Thus, if a man walked down a dark street in the dead of night and was assaulted, the fact that a reasonably prudent man would not have walked on that street at that hour is not a defense to an action brought against the wrongdoer for damages arising out of the bodily injuries sustained.

Imputed contributory negligence. Just as in negligence, contributory negligence may be imputed from one person to another where there is a relationship between them which makes one responsible for the acts of the other. This situation usually comes about where there is a right of control on the part of the one over the actions of the other, as in the relationship of principal and agent and master and servant. Thus, where the agent or servant of the owner of a motor vehicle is involved in an accident caused by the joint negligence of the servant and another person, the contributory negligence of the servant is imputed to the owner and may be interposed as a defense to his action against the other person for the damage to the owner's vehicle. This has come to be known as the "Both Ways" Rule in the sense that the negligence of the driver-agent is imputed to the principal-owner, regardless of whether the action is one by the other person for damages or an action by the owner-principal for the damage to his vehicle, or to his person. For an extended discussion of this rule, see Section 1225.

On the other hand, the contributory negligence of the bailee-driver is not imputed to the bailor-owner, since the element of control is lacking. It is only where the owner has the right to control, whether he exercises it or not, that the negligence of the driver is imputed to him.

314   Assumption of risk

A person who knowingly exposes himself to the danger of injury is said to have assumed the risk of such injury. This means that, under the circumstances, the injured person cannot recover, even though the injuries were sustained through no fault of his own but through the fault of someone else. The legal maxim used to describe this situation is *volenti non fit inuria:* that to which a person assents is not in law actionable.

In order to invoke the defense of assumption of risk, two elements must be present:

1. Knowledge or awareness of the existence of the risk, with a corresponding appreciation of the extent of the danger.
2. A voluntary exposure to the danger.

Suppose A has a learner's permit, B, knowing this, agrees to teach A how to drive an automobile, and therefore in entering the car assumes all risks incident to riding in a car operated by such a driver. If an accident should occur as a result of a lack of skill on the part of A, and B is injured, B cannot recover. Both of the necessary elements of assumption of risk are present. B knew that A was inexperienced and knowingly exposed himself to the risk of A's inexperience. Therefore he cannot recover.

Suppose A has a learner's permit, or no license at all, but assures B that he has a driver's license and that he has driven cars for several years. B, unaware of A's lack of driving experience, enters the car and is injured as a result of A's incompetent driving. B may recover from A, both elements of assumption of risk being lacking in this case. B did not know of the risk to which he was being exposed in riding with A; therefore B could not possibly have voluntarily assumed a risk of which he was not aware.

ILLUSTRATIONS

Baseball games

When spectators at baseball games sit in areas without a protective screen they voluntarily assume the risk of being struck by batted balls. The risk is open and obvious, and if the plaintiff does not wish to assume such a risk he can secure a seat behind a protective screen or refrain from going to the ball game altogether. In the case of injury in the open area, the defense of assumption of risk can be successfully interposed. The spectator is charged with the knowledge of the danger, and in sitting in an unprotected area voluntarily exposes himself to the danger.

If a spectator secures a seat behind a protective screen, he has assumed no risk at all as far as batted balls are concerned. The defense of assumption of risk would not be available. Should a ball go through the protective screen and strike the plaintiff, he would be entitled to recover.

A spectator at a baseball game does not assume all the risks of injury, and especially those of which he could have no knowlege. For example, the operator of the baseball stadium has the duty of maintaining order and in the exercise of this duty must assign personnel to each area in sufficient numbers to reasonably meet this obligation. In a recent case the plaintiff, a 69-year-old paying patron, was seated in a box without a protective screen located between home plate and third base. A foul ball was struck high in the air, landing two rows in front of the plaintiff's chair. A crowd of 10 or 12 customers, scrambling for the ball, converged on her from all directions. She was dislodged from her chair into the aisle and trampled upon, suffering personal injuries.

The evidence showed that a capacity crowd was on hand and that one usher was assigned to each box section, which seated 176 to 200 people. The usher assigned to the plaintiff's box was usually stationed in the aisle about 8 to 10 feet to the rear of the plaintiff's chair. At the time the human stampede overran the plaintiff's chair in pursuit of the foul ball, the usher so assigned had gone to another area to perform some other duties. As a result, he was in no position to protect the plaintiff at the time of the accident.

If the plaintiff had been struck by the foul ball itself, and there were no other injuries, the defense of the assumption of risk could have been maintained. However, here the baseball club failed to take reasonable steps to protect the plaintiff from harm by the acts of other spectators, and she did not assume the risk of being injured as a result of the scramble for a foul ball. The essential element of knowledge or awareness of the danger was absent, and for that reason the court refused to apply the doctrine of assumption of risk. [*Lee* v. *National League Baseball Club of Milwaukee*, 89 N.W. 2d 811.]

The same rule applies to all other sporting events. The spectators assume the risk of injury from open and obvious dangers which are common to the particular sport that is being witnessed. The spectator, however, does not assume any risks which are occasioned by the improper maintenance of the arena, the seats, or the failure of the operator to maintain order.

Theaters

The patron of a theater assumes the risk of injury which is occasioned as a result of darkness within the theater and other conditions which the patron normally expects to find and to watch he voluntarily exposes himself. The theater owner has the duty of maintaining the premises in a safe condition and the duty of maintaining order in his establishment. The patron does not assume the risk of injury as a result of the breach of either of these duties by the theater owner.

Amusement parks

The same rules apply to patrons of an amusement park and those who participate in the use of amusement devices. The patron will be considered to have assumed the risk of injury in any situation where the risk is open, obvious, and foreseeable. The owner of the amusement device is responsible for its proper maintenance and is required to take all possible measures for the safety of those using the device.

Reasonable inspection of all moving parts, straps, gates, and other equipment must be made, and where an injury is caused by a breach of the duty of proper maintenance, the defense of assumption of risk will not be available. This is true even though many amusement parks post signs in conspicuous places that the use of the equipment is "at your own risk." The posting of these signs does not absolve the park or the operator of the equipment from the duty of proper and careful maintenance.

315   Unavoidable accident

This has been defined as an inevitable accident, or one which could not have been foreseen or prevented by using ordinary diligence, and resulting without fault. It is not necessarily an accident which was physically impossible, in the nature of things, for the person to have prevented, but one not occasioned by any degree, either remotely or directly, by the want of such care or skill the law holds every man bound to exercise. Therefore, it is an accident which could not be prevented by the exercise of ordinary care and prudence.

For example, an automobile driver who had no prior knowledge or history of heart disease suffers a fatal heart attack while driving his automobile, and as a result thereof his car crashes into another, causing personal injuries and property damage. Here the driver had no notice of his heart condition and, in the exercise of reasonable prudence, he could not possibly be expected to submit himself to repeated physical examinations, since he had no previous physical manifestations of the disease. This is an unavoidable accident, and no recovery can be had against the estate of the deceased automobile driver.

Let us add one fact to the previous situation; let us assume that the automobile driver had been physically examined, had been told that he had a serious heart ailment, and had been warned not to subject himself to any stress or strain, including the driving of an automobile. Despite this warning he drove the car, with the same unfortunate result. The accident could not be considered unavoidable, and certainly the exercise of reasonable prudence could have prevented it. Therefore, it is not an unavoidable accident and recovery may be had.

The defense is sometimes offered that an insect, usually a bee or a wasp, entered the automobile and stung, bit, or otherwise deprived the driver of his ability to control the vehicle. Since the presence of the insect is not something that reasonable prudence could have prevented, the accident then is unavoidable. Since this defense can be easily fabricated, a great deal will depend upon whether or not the fact can be established by clear and convincing evidence. As in other matters of fact, the jury is the final arbiter as to whether the fact exists or not. If the jury finds that the insect so distracted or deprived the driver of his ability to control the vehicle, they can find that the accident was unavoidable.

An unavoidable accident may be used as a defense in a case where an irresponsible party is actually guilty of a wrongful act. Infants of tender years are not chargeable with negligence, nor are people of unsound minds, or those with no minds at all. If one of these individuals dashes into the street in the path of an oncoming automobile and is struck by the automobile, without any negligent act on the part of the driver, this occurrence is termed an unavoidable accident. The fault, if there was any, is on the person who dashed into the street. Legally, fault cannot be ascribed to the injured person, and therefore the accident is deemed to be unavoidable.

The defense of inevitable accident is frequently interposed in automobile cases where, without any previous notice of the condition, a car is suddenly enveloped in smoke from a railroad train, a fire nearby, an unanticipated fog, or where the driver is confronted with an unanticipated patch of ice or water on the highway. If the driver were driving his car at a proper speed, maintaining control, and being able to stop within the range of his vision, he cannot be charged with negligence if one of these unusual and unforeseeable conditions arises and he strikes another car or object.

Some courts take the position that the defense of unavoidable accident is simply a denial of negligence and proximate causation, and refuse to give such an instruction as to unavoidable accident except in the clearest cases (such as the heart attack suffered by a driver noted above). The leading case on this subject is *Butigan* v. *Yellow Cab Co.* [320 Pac. 2d 500 (California)], wherein the court said:

The so-called defense of inevitable accident is nothing more than a denial by the defendant of negligence, or a contention that his negligence, if any, was not the proximate cause of the injury. . . . Since the ordinary instructions on negligence and proximate cause sufficiently show that the plaintiff must sustain his burden of proof on these issues in order to recover, the instruction of unavoidable accident serves no useful purpose.

This view has been adopted in four states: Arkansas (*Houston* v. *Adams,* 389 S.W. 2d 872), Colorado (*Lewis* v. *Buckskin Joe's,* 396 Pac. 2d 933), New Jersey (*Vespe* v. *DiMarco,* 204 Atl. 2d 874), and Oregon (*Fenton* v. *Aleshire,* 393 Pac. 2d 217). On the other hand, five states have refused to follow the *Butigan* case. These are Delaware (*Dietz* v. *Mead,* 160 Atl. 2d 372), Idaho (*Lallatin* v. *Terry,* 340 Pac. 2d 112), Montana (*Rodoni* v. *Hoskin,* 355 Pac.

2d 296), New Mexico (*Lucero* v. *Torres*, 350 Pac. 2d 1028), and Utah (*Porter* v. *Price*, 355 Pac. 2d 66).

316   Act of God

This is defined as any accident, misadventure, or casualty when it happens by the direct, immediate, and exclusive operation of the forces of nature, uncontrolled or uninfluenced by the power of man, and without intervention, and is of such a character that it could not have been prevented or escaped from by any amount of foresight or prudence, or by any reasonable degree of care or diligence, or by the aid of any appliances which the situation of the party might reasonably require him to use. Where damage occurs solely as a consequence of an act of God, no liability is imposed upon anyone, whereas if human agency or negligence concurs *with* an act of God, the person injured or suffering damage because of the occurrence may recover.

The classic example of the application of these principles involves a case where the owner of land constructs a dam across a stream running through his property. The dam will withstand the normal pressure exerted against it by the water as well as the extra pressure created by an ordinary rainfall. An unprecedented cloudburst occurs, however, which so increases the pressure against the dam that it crumbles under the impact and the water thus released inundates the land of his neighbor. This is an act of God, and the dam owner is not liable to his neighbor for the damage caused by the water. Nor is the owner of the dam bound to anticipate and guard against all of the possibilities of damage that the forces of nature might create. But he is bound to anticipate the ordinary course of nature. Therefore, under these circumstances, the owner of the dam would be responsible if the dam crumbled under the impact of ordinary rainfall.

In another case, the owner of a business establishment suspends a large electric sign on the outside of his premises. The sign is so anchored that it will withstand ordinary rainfall and the pressure of ordinary wind. A tornado strikes the area, and the sign is torn loose from its moorings and crashes into a building, causing property damage and personal injuries to the persons inside. This again is an act of God, and the owner of the sign is not answerable for the damage or for the personal injuries. On the other hand, if the sign should fall as a result of the impact of wind which is ordinarily present in the neighborhood at certain times of the year, the owner of the sign is liable for any loss or damage caused as a result thereof.

Let us assume that a painter left a ladder standing against the building. Ordinary wind would blow it over. There is a tornado or an unprecedented amount of wind created by the forces of nature, and the ladder is blown over, causing personal injuries to persons nearby. Under those circumstances, the painter is liable to the persons injured. He is bound to anticipate the normal forces of nature, and the normal forces of nature would have caused the accident. Therefore, the excessive amount of wind has no bearing on the causation of the accident, and since the painter has failed in his primary duty to anticipate the normal forces of nature, he is liable for the damage.

The application of these principles poses questions of fact for the jury. The jury will decide, as a matter of fact, whether or not the cloudburst is unprecedented, the wind is unusual, and whether or not the owner of the dam, the sign, or the ladder should have anticipated the possibilities of injury from the forces of nature. In deciding the question of fact, the jury will be guided by weather reports of previous years, the testimony of persons who have lived in the area for a long period of time, as well as by evidence with respect to other damage in the vicinity caused as a consequence of the same forces of nature.

317   Duties of the possessor of land

The possessor of land, for the purposes of determining the duties owed, is the person in control of the premises. He could be the owner of the property or he could be a tenant to whom the owner has transferred the incidents of ownership for a period of time. The transfer could involve the entire premises, leased to one tenant, or several tenants, or it could involve a transfer of part of the premises to one or more tenants with the owner reserving some part of the premises to himself. In either case, the responsible party will be the one who has the right of occupancy and control of that portion of the premises from which the duty of care arises.

The owner or occupier of land must exercise reasonable care in the maintenance and use of his premises so as to avoid any interference with the rights of others as well as to avoid exposing others to unreasonable risks of harm. The persons to whom he owes these duties will come within one of two classes:

1. Those outside the premises.
2. Those on the premises.

1. *Those outside the premises.* These will include all who are in the vicinity, either neighbors or those using the public streets and sidewalks. To his neighbors the owner owes the duty of making reasonable use of his premises so as not to interfere with the neighbors' property and his peaceful enjoyment thereof. He may not change the natural drainage of his land so as to deposit excess water on his neighbor's land. He must exercise reasonable care in the erection of buildings and other structures on his land (as well as in the digging of excavations) so as not to interfere with the neighbor's use of his property or the neighbor's right to lateral support for his land and buildings. Also, the possessor of land is required to exercise reasonable care in the inspection of his premises and to keep them in repair so that no part of the buildings will collapse and injure the neighbor or his property.

He has no duty of care with respect to natural conditions on his land, either to his neighbor or anyone else. Thus he is not required to remedy a swampy condition, fence in a lake or pond, or to prevent weeds from spreading to the neighborhood. Local ordinances may create a duty with respect to these conditions, but in the absence of such statutes, the owner has no responsibility to others for natural conditions.

As to the public streets and sidewalks, the abutting owner has no responsibility for their maintenance, but he is liable for any conditions which he creates, such as the deposit of excess water on the street which collects in a pool and freezes or damage to the street or sidewalk by his actions. He is also responsible for the safe maintenance of coal holes, sidewalk elevators within his control, and objects overhanging the street and sidewalk from his property. He is not responsible for the accumulation of snow and ice or water on the street and sidewalk, which are natural incidents and not ones he worsened or created. (See Responsibility for Streets and Sidewalks.) He is, however, responsible for the safe maintenance of objects on his premises which can be seen from the highway and which are attractive to children of tender years. (See Attractive Nuisance Doctrine.)

2. *Those on the premises.* To those who are on the premises, by invitation or license, the owner has a duty of maintaining the premises in a reasonably safe condition, the extent of the duty depending upon the relationship of the parties. In addition, there are some duties arising out of the presence of a person on the premises without either invitation or license. These persons are classified as trespassers, licensees, social guests, and business invitees. The responsibilities of the owner as to each class will be discussed in the following paragraphs.

318   Trespassers

The owner or occupier of land has a legally protected right to the exclusive use of his property, and no one may enter on his premises without his consent. A trespasser is a person who is on the premises without the consent of the owner and therefore is invading a legally protected right. The trespasser is liable to the owner for any damage which his unlawful use of the property may cause. The owner owes no duty of care to the trespasser either as to the maintenance of the premises or his own activities thereon. He is under no duty to inspect his premises to discover the presence of a trespasser, but if the owner has knowledge of the trespasser's presence on his premises, he may not take action which is designed to injure him beyond the use of such force as is necessary to expel the trespasser from the premises. In addition, the owner may not set traps or other devices calculated solely to injure the trespasser. This duty of refraining from committing an assault on the trespasser, and from maintaining traps and other devices designed only to injure him, is sometimes referred to as the duty of *slight care*.

319   Licensees

A licensee is a person who enters or remains on the premises with the owner or occupier's consent, express or implied, for his own personal benefit, convenience, or pleasure. To the licensee, the owner or occupier owes practically no duty at all. The general rule is that the licensee voluntarily exposes himself to the same conditions and the same dangers to which the owner or occupier himself is exposed. Thus the licensee takes the premises as he finds them, and he may not expect that the owner or occupier will take any steps to prepare for his coming nor will he make any inspection of the premises to discover the presence of unsafe conditions. The owner or occupier is required to warn the licensee of any unsafe condition which is not open and apparent, but once the licensee has knowledge of the unsafe condition, there is no duty to repeat the warning. This duty to warn is limited in that it applies only to those portions of the premises which the owner or occupier may reasonably expect the licensee to use. This would refer to the normal and usual access ways to the premises and would not refer to the premises as a whole. For example, if a licensee entered the premises over the back fence and proceeded across the backyard, the owner or occupier would be under no duty to warn him of the presence of an unsafe condition in the backyard.

Both the licensee and the trespasser enter the premises for their own purposes and not for the purpose of conferring any benefit on the owner, but the distinction between the two lies in the presence or absence of the owner's consent, which may be manifested in several ways. He may expressly invite the person to enter the premises, or in the absence of any notice, his consent may be implied from local customs and usages. Thus, in a community where it is customary to issue licenses to door-to-door salesmen, canvassers, and solicitors of charitable contributions, the owner will be held to have given his implied consent to the custom in the absence of a fence or sign excluding such persons. Where it is a local custom for persons to take a shortcut across the owner's land, and the owner has made no effort to exclude them and has not erected any signs, fences, or other barriers, his consent will be implied from his lack of protest and lack of action.

The same principle will be applied in the case of the owner of a building where people are inclined to loiter, use the building in order to come in out of the weather, or to post a letter in the mailbox maintained for the use of tenants only. The failure of the owner to exclude these people, by fences, barriers, or signs, is generally construed as an implied consent. The same thing is true with reference to persons who enter the premises for the purpose of visiting the owner's employees. Consent to their presence will be implied from the absence of rules enforced by the owner forbidding such visits.

320   Social guests

Social guests are licensees, and the duty of the owner to them is the same as to any other licensees. This is true no matter how cordial the invitation is and no matter how formal the party to which they are invited happens to be. The common-law view, which is still the view today, is that the social guest comes as a quasi member of the family, that he takes the premises as he finds them, and is subject to the same conditions as other members of the family.

321   Invitees

An invitee is a business visitor whose presence on the premises is encouraged either by the use to which the premises are put or by an express or implied invitation. The business which is the subject matter of his visit must be for the advantage of the owner, even though it might be to the advantage of the business visitor as well. This characteristic distinguishes the invitee from the licensee. To the invitee, the owner owes the following duties. He must:

1. Exercise reasonable care in the maintenance of the premises for his safety.
2. Warn him of any dangerous conditions which are not open and obvious, and of which the owner has knowledge.
3. Make reasonable inspections of the premises and remedy any dangerous conditions which the inspection revealed.

The duties owed to an invitee are the same as those owed to a licensee, but there is an additional duty of inspection and repair, and whether the inspection is made or not, the owner is chargeable with the knowledge which a reasonable inspection would have revealed. What would constitute a reasonable inspection will depend upon the type of premises involved and the use to which they are put.

For example, if the owner is operating a fruit and vegetable store where water and vegetable debris will accumulate on the floor, the exercise of reasonable inspections and the correction of unsafe conditions might require an inspection every 30 minutes during the business day. If the owner is conducting a millinery store, reasonable inspections might consist of one inspection per day.

The courts have been extremely liberal as to the qualifications which create the legal status of invitee. The general requirement is that there be some business advantage to the owner of the premises, but this has been extended to matters where the advantage is extremely obscure and in some cases difficult to find. For example, friends who visit the guests of a hotel are invitees with relation to the hotel; people who meet incoming passengers at a railroad depot are invitees in relation to the railroad; persons attending free public lectures, church services, and even the opening of stores where free gifts are given are all invitees as to the owners of such premises. With respect to federal, state, and municipal services, those who utilize public parks, playgrounds, libraries, comfort stations, and community centers are invitees as to the authority operating these services.

With respect to stores open to the public, any customer, prospective or otherwise, who enters that portion of the store which is devoted to the sale of the owner's goods is an invitee whether the customer actually makes a purchase or not. The store offers an implied invitation to all to enter, examine the goods, and make a purchase if the goods meet their requirements. The area of invitation also includes others who may accompany the prospective customer, and these are invitees as well. This could include a friend who comes with the customer, or a child or children brought into the store by the customer. Persons who use the store as a shortcut to somewhere else and persons who come in out of the weather, both without protest from the owner, have been held to be invitees on the theory that there was always a possibility that such persons might be attracted by the merchandise and make a purchase, thus supplying the business advantage element to the status.

Salesmen and solicitors who enter the premises without special invitation are licensees, but where the owner specifically invites them to demonstrate a particular product, or to estimate the cost of repairs, they become invitees, since they are business visitors for the business advantage of the owner.

Applicants for employment who appear looking for work without invitation are usually licensees. However, where they appear in response to an advertisement inviting applications for employment, they are invitees. Also, in industries where the customs are such that there is a continuing need for employees and applications are accepted on a daily basis, such applicants are business invitees on the theory that the owner impliedly invites such persons to make application because of the custom and usage of the particular business in which he is engaged.

As owner, maintaining a private home, is considered to be in the "business" of maintaining a place of abode. Persons who enter the premises for the purpose of rendering some service in connection with the business of living therein are invitees. Thus, in this category would come delivery men of all kinds, meter readers employed by gas, electric, or water companies, milkmen, and public employees such as the postman, safety, sanitary inspectors, garbage collectors, and even tax appraisers and collectors.

322 Area of invitation or license

It is possible for a person to be a licensee or an invitee as to one portion of the premises and a trespasser as to another. It is also possible for a person to be a licensee or an invitee at one time of the day and a trespasser at another. The extent of the license or invitation given by the owner will determine the limitations of his consent. For example, a meter reader is normally an invitee, but only as to those portions of the owner's premises which must be traversed in order to read the meter. Should the meter reader go into the backyard and use the owner's swimming pool, he is a trespasser. In addition, such invitation is limited to those times during the day when the meter can conveniently be read. If the meter reader called in the early hours of the morning, he would be a trespasser on the premises. On the other hand, if a milkman made his delivery at the same hour, he would be an invitee, since this is a customary time for such delivery to be made. Therefore, the question will turn on the area of invitation. In the case of the meter reader, it is limited by time and area, and the same is true with respect to the milkman, but the hours are different since the area of invitation differs.

Where a store owner invites the public to enter his premises, no one would seriously argue that the area of invitation included anything more than an invitation to enter the store during the usual hours of business. Therefore, if a customer entered the store at an early hour of the morning, even though the door was open, the customer would be a trespasser and not an invitee. Also, the customer is normally limited to those portions of the store set aside for the purpose of exposing merchandise for sale. Unless there is an express invitation, if the customer enters other parts of the premises not set aside for the display of merchandise, such as the workrooms, receiving or shipping rooms, executive offices, and the like, he is a trespasser, or at best a bare licensee.

323   Revocation of invitation or license

The owner or occupier of the land is not required to extend the invitation or license indefinitely. He may revoke the invitation or license at any time. He may ask the person to leave the premises, and the person must leave. If he remains, he is a trespasser from that point forward. He is, however, an invitee or licensee, as the case may be, up to the time that the invitation or license is revoked.

A person may enter the premises as an invitee or a licensee, but because of his conduct, which amounts to a breach of the peace, become a trespasser *ab initio* (from the beginning). This is an ancient rule of the common law, first enunciated in the *Six Carpenters'* case [77 *English Reporter* 695 (1610)]. The case holds that if a person comes upon the property of another by license or invitation, and commits thereon an affirmative act of wrongdoing, and hence abuses the privilege given him, the same shall render the actor a trespasser from the beginning, and so to subject the actor to liability both for the wrongful act and for trespass, even though the original entry upon the land was not wrongful. The effect of the case is that the wrongdoer not only endangers his status, as well as the obligation of the owner to him, but also makes himself liable for any damage which his presence on the premises caused from the very beginning.

324   Policemen and firemen in the line of duty

Policemen and firemen do not readily fit the categories of licensees or invitees. They are in a special class. Both licensee and invitee enter upon the premises with the consent of the owner; one is tolerated and the other solicited. In the case of policemen and firemen, the owner's consent is irrelevant. It makes no difference if their entrance is permitted or invited, since if conditions calling for their entry exist, they enter the premises as a matter of right. The landowner is not free to give or to withhold his consent, nor are policemen and firemen in a position to make a choice as to whether they will enter or refrain from entering the premises. They act neither by permission nor invitation but by command of the governmental authority by whom they are employed.

Since the consent of the owner is not required, the owner cannot revoke or rescind an invitation or license. The owner has no right to bar their entry or in any way to impede them in the performance of their duties. For example, the owner decides to demolish a building which is on his property. There is no insurance. The building catches fire in some unknown fashion. As far as the owner is concerned, he would save money if the building were consumed by fire, because demolition costs are high. He may not prevent the firemen from extinguishing the fire. They may enter the premises and extinguish the fire, or do whatever else is necessary, in the line of their duty.

A policeman may enter upon any portion of the owner's property for the purpose of apprehending a criminal. This includes any room in the house, the roof, the outbuildings, or any part of the premises. The owner may not impede the policeman in the execution of his duty. His duty might even consist of arresting the owner. Again, the owner cannot prevent the policeman's entry upon his land even for a purpose which is hostile to the interests of the owner.

As to firemen and policemen, the owner is obligated to use reasonable care in keeping those portions of the premises which are utilized as the ordinary means of access for all persons entering therein in a safe condition. The owner is not required to keep all portions of his premises in a safe condition, but only those portions which are ordinarily used for access. For example, if a policeman is chasing a fugitive and in such pursuit he finds it necessary to climb the owner's fence, which gives way under his weight, the owner has no liability, since he is under no duty to keep his fence in such repair so as to withstand the weight of anyone who decides to climb over it. As a matter of fact, the purpose of a fence is to prevent access. The same thing would be true if the policeman pursued a fugitive over the roof of the owner's house or garage and the roof gave way under his weight. These situations do not involve the liability of the owner, even though the owner may have requested the presence of the policeman on his premises. The owner has no duty to safeguard those parts of his property not ordinarily utilized for passage through the premises or to make any inspection in order to discover potential dangers therein.

If the owner knows of the presence of policemen or firemen on his premises, and is cognizant of a dangerous condition thereon which he has reason to believe is not open and obvious so that the policeman or fireman would be unaware of it, he is under a duty to warn them of the risks involved. He is not under a duty to inspect the premises, nor is he chargeable with any unsafe conditions which are unknown to him but which a reasonable inspection would have revealed. Therefore, at least as to one phase of his duty, a policeman and fireman are comparable to licensees.

In some cities there are municipal ordinances which require that certain precautions be taken by the owner for the safety of firemen in fighting fires which may arise. For example, in New York City the owner of the premises is required to mark by appropriate signs any windows which enter into a shaftway. The purpose of the statute is to give notice to firemen who might enter the premises through these windows that there is no floor on the other side of the window. If the owner failed in his duty and a fireman were injured as a consequence of the failure, the owner would be required to respond in damages, since his failure to comply with the ordinance enacted for the safety of firemen resulted in injury.

The same rule would apply where the ordinance required the erection and maintenance of fire doors, sprinkler systems, and other appliances designed to control the fire and prevent injury to firemen. The owner's duty in these respects would be different if the building was on fire during the course of construction so that the owner had no opportunity to comply with the fire ordinances, or if the building was in the course of demolition. In either of these cases, the firemen would know the condition of the building and would not rely on the owner's compliance with the local ordinances.

As to fires caused by the negligence of the owner, either by specific negligent act or failure to maintain the premises in condition to prevent the inception of a fire, most jurisdictions hold that if a fireman is injured in fighting such a fire there is no liability to him on the part of the owner. This would be true even though the owner himself turned in the alarm and was responsible for the presence of the firemen on the premises. The theory on which this view is based is that the fireman, by his calling, assumes all the risks which are incidental to fighting a fire, irrespective of the cause thereof.

It might be added that in the case of a negligent fire the liability of the owner of the premises to his neighbor (should the neighbor's premises or business suffer as a result of a fire) is the common-law responsibility of ordinary care. The owner is liable to the neighbor for damages as a result of a negligent fire, whereas the owner would not have a similar responsibility toward the firemen attempting to extinguish the fire.

There are some exceptions to the general rule with respect to the owner's liability to firemen on account of injury sustained in fighting a negligent fire. A fireman who is employed by private persons, or who responds to such a call as a volunteer, has been held to be an invitee or business visitor to whom the landowner owed a duty of reasonable care to keep the premises safe. The difference seems to be that the person undertaking to act as a fireman is not so employed by a governmental agency and therefore does not assume the risk of injury as part of his employment. In addition, these firemen, apparently, have the right to make an attempt to extinguish the fire or to make no attempt at all—at their option. Thus, in the following cases the person attempting to extinguish the fire, while privately employed, was held to be an invitee to whom the owner owed a high degree of care. [*Clink Sales* v. *Mundkoski*, 79 Fed. 2d 562 (Oklahoma); *Zuercher* v. *Northern Jobbing Co.*, 66 N.W. 2d 892 (Minnesota); *Buckeye Cotton Oil Co.* v. *Campagna*, 242 S.W. 646 (Tennessee).]

The Supreme Court of Illinois has imposed the duty of reasonable care in the maintenance of the premises upon the landowner with respect to injuries to municipally employed firemen resulting from an attempt to extinguish a fire on the premises [*Dini* v. *Naidich*, 170 N.E. 2d 881]. The court specifically held that the fireman was in the category of a business invitee on the theory that the benefit to the landowner was the decisive factor and so constituted the fireman as a business invitee for the benefit of the landowner. Therefore, the landowner was held to a high degree of care, as to the fireman, and responsible for any condition which could have been reasonably foreseen as a cause of fire or of injury. The majority rule is to the contrary.

325   Modifications of occupiers' liability

In 1968, the California Supreme Court was called upon to reexamine the status of a social guest and the liability of the host toward him. In *Rowland* v. *Christian* (70 Cal. Rptr. 97), the plaintiff, a guest, was injured when the defective knob of a bathroom faucet broke in his hand and he sustained very serious lacerations. Ordinarily, the guest would take the premises as he finds them and there would be no liability on the part of the host, but in this case the court decided that there was no legal justification for the exceptions from liability on the part of a social guest or even a trespasser. The court said that: "Everyone is responsible for an injury occasioned to another by his want of ordinary care or skill in the management of his property." The court refused to follow the rigid classifications of licensee, invitee, and trespasser, and substituted instead the following:

The proper test to be applied to the liability of the possessor of land . . . is whether in the management of his property he has acted as a reasonable man in view of the probability of injury to others, and although the plaintiff's status as a trespasser, or as a licensee or invitee may in the light of the facts giving rise to such status have some bearing on the question of liability, the status is not decisive.

In 1975, the Supreme Court of Rhode Island in *Mariorenzi* v. *Joseph DiPonte, Inc.* (333 Atl. 2d 127) decided to follow the reasoning of the California court. The case involved an infant trespasser. In abandoning the classifications of trespasser, licensee, and invitee, the court said:

As we assign the trichotomy to the historical past, we substitute in its place the basic tort test of reasonableness. Hereafter, the common-law status of an entrant onto the land of another will no longer be determinative of the degree of care owed by the owner, but rather the question to be resolved will be whether the owner has used reasonable care for the safety of all persons reasonbly expected to be upon his premises. Evidence of the status of the invitee may have some relevance to the question of liability but it no longer will be conclusive. The traditional tort question of foreseeability will become important.

Both of these cases apparently have reference to the status of a trespasser, even though the last case refers to an infant trespasser attracted to the premises. In applying the rule enunciated by both cases, the occupier must exercise care for the safety of all persons reasonably expected to be on the premises. As to invitees and licensees, it is easy to apply, but in the case of a trespasser it is difficult to imagine a situation where the presence of a trespasser on the premises is to be "reasonably expected." Cases in other jurisdictions which in some aspects follow the *Rowland* case restrict the application of the rule of reasonable care to all *lawful* entrants. The following cases have abolished the distinction between invitee and licensee and have adopted the rule of reasonable care:

Colorado	*Mile High Fence Co.* v. *Radovich,* 489 Pac. 2d 308.
District of Columbia	*Smith* v. *Arbaugh's Rest,* 469 Fed. 2d 97.
Hawaii	*Pickard* v. *City of Honolulu,* 452 Pac. 2d 445.
Louisiana	*Alexander* v. *General Ins. Co.,* 98 So. 2d 730.
Massachusetts	*Mounsey* v. *Ellard,* 297 N.E. 2d 43.
Michigan	*Genessee Bank* v. *Payne,* 148 N.W. 2d 503. Aff'd 161 N.W. 2d 17.
Minnesota	*Peterson* v. *Balach,* 199 N.W. 2d 639.
New York	*Basso* v. *Miller,* 386 NYS 2d 564

Connecticut has by statute abolished the distinction between invitees and licensees substituting the rule of reasonable care for their safety. (Conn. Gen. Stat. Ann. 52–557a.)

With the exception of California and possibly Rhode Island, the duty owed to a trespasser would seem to remain the same. The trespasser is making illegal use of the occupier's premises and therefore the only duty of care which is imposed on the occupier is a negative one in that he need only to refrain from willful, wanton, and intentional misconduct which is calculated to injure the trespasser. Other than that, it would seem that the occupier of land would owe no further duty to a burglar or other person illegally on the premises. However, in California, the Supreme Court did find an exception in *Mark* v. *Pacific Gas & Elec. Co.* (496 Pac. 2d 1276). In that case an adult, a college student, was electrocuted when he reached out of his apartment window to unscrew a street light bulb which was throwing glaring light into his apartment. He had previously unscrewed the light for the same purpose. The court held that the complaint covering those facts stated a cause of action on the theory that the duty of the defendant was to exercise reasonable care under the circumstances in line with the court's ruling in the *Rowland* case.

No other cases involving trespassers have been found so that in those states strictly following the *Rowland* decision, there is some doubt as to the ruling. As to the states which have limited the application of the *Rowland* case to legal entrants, the rule with respect to trespassers would seem to remain the same.

326   Liability of infants

An infant is liable for his own torts and may be sued, through a guardian, in exactly the same manner as an adult. The parents of the infant, in the absence of a statute, are not liable for the torts of the child, nor is the negligence of the child imputed to his parents. The parents, however, are liable for their own negligence, as in a case where the parents make firearms available to an infant who is unfamiliar with their use.

At common law a child under the age of seven is conclusively presumed to be incapable of committing a crime, forming a malicious intent, or of being guilty of negligence. Thus, as to intentional torts, where a malicious intent is one of the elements which must be established, the conclusive presumption will prevent the court from receiving evidence of malicious intent. The same thing would be true with respect to negligence. The child under the age of seven is incapable of negligence and since this is a conclusive presumption, no evidence is admissible to establish the child's negligence or contributory negligence.

As to torts committed by infants over the age of seven, the question of the infant's responsibility will turn on his actual age and his mental capacity for apprehending whether or not his action is wrongful. The intelligence of the infant will be taken into account in determining whether or not the infant was capable of exercising due care. These considerations apply equally to contributory negligence. An infant under the age of seven who is incapable of being negligent, could not be guilty of contributory negligence in failing to exercise care for his own safety. An infant over the age of seven will be chargeable with contributory negligence only if his age and intelligence are such that he should have been able to apprehend the danger and then failed to take reasonable precautions for his own safety.

As to infants who are licensed to drive automobiles, they are held to the same degree of care which is required of an adult driving an automobile.

327   Liability of insane persons

There are few cases reported concerning insane persons—either as to the duties owed to them by others or the duties owed by them. This is undoubtedly due to our social policy of confining or placing under restraint those whose disease of mind is such that they cannot care for themselves. In the few cases available, the general rule seems to be that insane persons are held to the same duty of care which would be required of a sane person, whether that duty of care be owed to others or be required for his safety. It has been argued that the duty of care required of an insane person should be the same as required of an infant, and the intelligence and strength of mind of the insane person should be taken into account in determining whether or not he could respond to the duty of care required of him.

While the question seems to be an open one at this time, it would open a wide field of discussion and decision if this contention were ever sustained. If an insane person were to drive an automobile, would he be subject to the same duties of care as required of a sane person? If we apply the same rule that is applicable to infants, the insane person would be held to the same duty of care while driving an automobile as is required of a sane person. If the insane person owned real property, would he be subject to a lesser duty of care for the safety of his tenants and invitees than that required of a sane landlord? If we apply a different standard of care to this situation than we do to the driving of an automobile, the justification for such a double standard would be difficult to sustain. In any case, the question is an open one, and it will be interesting to observe the methods used by the courts in disposing of these problems.

328   Landlord and tenant

The owner of real property may transfer to another all of the incidents of ownership and use of the property, or of a part of it, for a period of time in return for a consideration called the *rent.* The contract by means of which this transfer is accomplished is the *lease.* Like any other contract, the rights of the parties may be modified, limited, or extended by the insertion of various terms in the contract. Therefore, the consideration of any claims arising in connection with the relationship of landlord and tenant must begin with an examination of the lease.

Under a "bare" lease which contemplates only the transfer of possession and the incidents of ownership to the tenant for a term of years, the general rule is that the landlord is under no obligation to keep the premises in repair, nor is he responsible either to the tenant or others for conditions which develop after the transfer of possession, whether arising from the premises themselves or from the activities conducted thereon by the tenant. The general rule also is that the tenant takes the premises as he finds them and assumes the responsibility for any damages which may arise from dangerous conditions on the premises, whether they are open and obvious or hidden and concealed. This rule has been modified to the extent that the landlord is obligated to reveal to the tenant any hidden dangerous conditions of which he has actual knowledge and is responsible for his failure to do so, but the cases hold that the obligation of the landlord refers only to conditions concerning which he has actual knowledge and that he is not required to make an inspection to determine the existence of conditions not known to him.

In the absence of an agreement to the contrary in the lease, the tenant generally is responsible for the condition of the premises and is required to make necessary repairs to keep them in reasonably safe condition. The rule has been modified by statute in a number of states by requiring the landlord to maintain in safe condition certain types of premises, such as multiple dwellings and tenement houses, and creating a liability on his part for his failure to do so.

The cases have developed another exception to the general rule with respect to premises which are leased for the purpose of admitting the general public, such as stores, theatres, amusement parks, beaches, hotels, and stadium grandstands. In those cases, the landlord is under a duty to inspect and to repair any dangerous conditions existing prior to the transfer of possession, and agreement by the tenant to make these repairs will not relieve the landlord of his duty to do so. Clearly, the obligation of the landlord would be limited to those portions of the premises which would normally be open to the public and would also be limited to the persons who would normally be invited to use the premises for the purposes for which they are leased.

The tenant is liable to his invitee for injuries sustained on the premises as a result of a failure to maintain them in a reasonably safe condition. If the condition which caused an injury existed at the time of the transfer of possession, the invitee will have an additional cause of action against the landlord, which he may or may not assert, at his election. Where he does not, the Rules of Court in most states will allow the tenant to bring the landlord in as an additional defendant on the theory that the tenant is entitled to indemnity from the landlord. Adding the landlord as an additional defendant in the same action will obviate the necessity of another suit covering substantially the same subject matter.

In many cases, the landlord will transfer possession of only part of the premises to the tenant, retaining part of the building himself. This condition is usually met in cases of multiple dwellings, such as apartment houses, tenement houses, and duplexes. The landlord will retain the common access ways, the elevators, stairways, and other parts of the building, and will transfer possession to the tenant of an apartment. As to the apartment, the tenant has the same rights and is subject to the same rules of responsibility as would be the case if the entire building were in his possession. He is responsible for repairs and is liable to others if he fails to keep his apartment in a reasonably safe condition.

Usually, the landlord has no right to enter the leased portion of the premises during the period of the lease without the consent of the tenant. As to the portions of the premises reserved to himself, the landlord is under a duty to maintain them in a reasonably safe condition, and he is liable for his failure to do so. The parts of the premises reserved include not only the access ways mentioned above but also such parts of the premises as the tenant is invited to use, such as a laundry room, a recreation room—or an outside swimming pool or recreational area. In addition, the landlord is responsible for the safe maintenance of other parts of the premises, reserved but not physically accessible to the tenant, such as the roof, water pipes, gas and electric conduits, sewer pipes, and heating vents. Failure to maintain these parts of the premises in reasonably safe condition, which results in injury to the tenant, will require the landlord to respond in damages.

As to the portions of the premises retained by the landlord, the relationship of the tenant to the landlord is that of an invitee. His presence on the premises is to the business advantage of the landlord, and therefore the tenant is entitled to all of the rights of an invitee. This relationship also applies to the members of the tenant's family, his employees, his social guests, and his business invitees. All of these people are invitees as to the landlord, since they produce a business advantage to the landlord in the sense that he would not be able to rent his premises if he excluded them.

The tenant is required to maintain the premises of which he has possession in a reasonably safe condition. Therefore, he is liable to those entering his premises in the same manner and to the same extent as any other landowner. His social guests are licensees as to him, and his employees and business visitors are invitees as to him.

The parties to the lease can alter or vary the general responsibilities required by these rules, or create obligations of indemnity or contribution, by inserting appropriate clauses in the contract. Such variations, unless they violate public policy, will be given effect.

329   Assault and battery

Assault and battery are two separate intentional torts. Even though they are usually referred to as connected, one can exist without the other. Simply stated, an assault consists of placing a person in fear of bodily harm, and a battery is the infliction of bodily harm. In both cases, the intention to harm is an essential element.

In detail, an assault has been defined as:

An intentional, unlawful offer of corporal injury to another by force, or force unlawfully directed toward the person of another, under such circumstances as create well-founded fear of imminent peril, coupled with the apparent present ability to execute the attempt, if not prevented. [*State* v. *Shaw*, 116 Atl. 425 (New Jersey).]

A battery has been defined as

Any unlawful beating, or other wrongful physical violence or constraint inflicted on a human being without his consent. (*Goodrum* v. *State*, 60 Ga. 511.)

The wrongful physical violence, as noted in the definition, has been construed to mean the slightest touching of another, of his clothes, or anything else attached to his person—even a dog on a leash—if done in a rude, insolent, and angry manner.

An assault may be committed without a battery, as where a person is placed in fear and apprehension of bodily harm but his person is never touched, either because the directed force missed him or was never exerted. Damages, however, are recoverable for the mental disturbance caused by the apprehension.

A battery may be accomplished without an assault, as where a sleeping man is subjected to physical violence or where a surgical operation is performed upon an anesthetized person without his consent. Damages are recoverable for the physical injury thus inflicted.

Where an assault *and* a battery are committed, damages may be claimed for the mental apprehension caused by the assault and for the physical injury inflicted as a result of the battery.

330   Defamation: Libel and slander

Defamation, which may consist of either libel or slander, is the wrongful invasion of the legally protected right of security of reputation. Originally, libel consisted of anything of a defamatory nature which was written or published by a printing or other process which had some degree of permanence, whereas slander consisted of defamation of an oral nature, being conveyed and published only by speech. Libel has since been enlarged to include such an action as dishonoring a valid check presented to a bank. The distinction today seems to be that slander is defamation which is conveyed by speech and is heard, whereas libel is defamation conveyed by sight. Thus, in addition to actions, libel could consist of pictures, cartoons, moving pictures, signs, and statues. In any case, libel is regarded as the greater offense because the damage sustained is greater: printed material may be seen by many whereas slanderous speech can be heard by only a few.

The elements of defamation, whether libel or slander are:

1. A false and malicious statement tending to hold the plaintiff up to public disgrace.
2. Publication of the statement.
3. Damage.

1. *A false statement.* This is defined as an untrue statement which, if believed, would hold the plaintiff up to hatred, contempt, or ridicule, or cause him to be shunned and avoided. Malice, or evil intent, is inferred from its utterance. Thus it is defamatory to say that a man will not pay his just debts, is immoral, a coward, a crook, a bastard, or a eunuch, or that he has committed an act which is morally reprehensible or dishonorable. On the other hand, it is not defamatory to say that a man is tight with his money, does not go to church, is not a member of any church, or that he has taken advantage of his legal rights. None of these things, even if believed, would hold the man up to public disgrace or ridicule.

2. *Publication.* The statement must be published, intentionally or negligently, to someone other than the person defamed. Publication is the act of making the defamatory matter known publicly, or communicating it to one or more persons.

3. *Damages.* In most cases, damages must be alleged and proved by the person asserting the cause of action. Some states consider libel as defamatory per se, and actionable without proof of special damages, on the theory that the permanence of the writing and its potential widespread harm justifies the rule. Other states require proof of actual damages. As to slander, some aggravated forms are actionable without proof of actual damages, and in states requiring proof of damages in libel actions, the same rule applies. The following are actionable without proof of actual damages:

1. Imputation of serious crimes.
2. Imputation of a loathsome disease, such as leprosy or syphilis.
3. Imputation adversely affecting the plaintiff in his business, trade, or profession, such as calling an attorney a shyster or a crook.

(In some states there is an additional category, the imputation of unchastity to a person. Some states restrict this to women and others apply it to both sexes.)

The defenses to actions for libel or slander are *truth* and *privilege*.

1. *Truth.* It is clear that if the statement is true, there is no cause of action, since the cause is founded upon the falsity of the statement.

2. *Privilege.* Utterances or writings which are privileged fall into two classes, *absolute*, and *qualified* or *conditional.*

Absolute privilege refers to judicial proceedings, legislative proceedings, executive communications between the chief executive and his officials of the executive departments, and husband and wife. Statements made in the course of any of these proceedings or relationships, if untrue and damaging, are not actionable.

Qualified or conditional privilege exists with reference to publication "when fairly made by a person in the discharge of some public or private duty, whether legal or moral, or in the conduct of his own affairs, in matters where his interest is concerned." Even in those situations, the privilege is lost if the person making the statement goes beyond what is necessary to protect his interest or what meets his duty, or if he communicates the information to another person who has no connection with the business and is in no position to give any assistance with the problem.

331   Right of privacy

The right of privacy has been defined as the right of an individual to be let alone, to live a life of seclusion, or to be free from unwarranted publicity. A wrongful invasion of that right will give rise to an action in tort for damages.

The right of privacy consists of two separate rights: (1) the right of solitude and (2) freedom from unwarranted publicity. The second right is seldom the subject of insurance or insurance claims. It refers to a person's right to have his private affairs as well as his photograph free from publicity without his consent. For example, an unauthorized fictional biography of Warren Spahn, the major league pitcher was held to be an invasion of his privacy. [*Spahn* v. *Julian Messner, Inc.*, 250 N.Y.S. 2d 529.] In *Olan Mills, Inc.* v. *Dodd* [353 S.W. 2d 22 (Arkansas)], the plaintiff had her picture taken. Some years later, the photographer, without the knowledge or consent of the plaintiff, sent out advertising postcards with the plaintiff's picture, implying an offer to make a picture of like kind and quality. The court held that the unauthorized publication of a photograph of a person not in public life is an actionable invasion of the plaintiff's privacy.

The right of seclusion is more likely to be involved in casualty claims. When a person makes a claim for bodily injury or property damage, it is reasonable to expect that the defendant or his insurance carrier will make some inquiry to determine the truth or falsity of the claim. In some cases, it is not uncommon for insurance companies to employ the services of a private detective to make activity checks to determine the claimant's physical ability to perform some type of work. This could involve the taking of motion pictures or placing the claimant under surveillance. Where the investigation is unobtrusive and within reasonable limits, there is no invasion of the plaintiff's privacy. [*Forster* v. *Manchester*, 189 Atl. 2d 147 (Pennsylvania).] The right of privacy is invaded where the investigation exceeds reasonable bounds, such as subjecting the claimant to obtrusive surveillance for a long period of time, coming on the premises at night, eavesdropping on conversations in the claimant's home, telephoning the claimant under various pretexts at all hours of the day, and other activities amounting to harassment of the claimant. In *Pinkerton National Detective Agency, Inc.* v. *Stevens* [132 S.E. 2d 119 (Georgia)], the court said:

> The right of privacy may be implicitly waived, and is waived by one who files an action for injuries from a tort to the extent of the defendant's intervening right to investigate and ascertain for himself the true state of injury. However, this includes only a waiver of that reasonably unobstrusive type of investigation which would be to the best interests of the defendant in preparing its case. Activities consisting of overt and prolonged trailing of the plaintiff in a conspicuous manner sufficient to excite the speculation of neighbors, constant following in public places, pursuit tactics conducted late at night such as would ordinarily alarm an average person, together with other acts amounting to trespass and eavesdropping, cannot as a matter of law be said to be reasonable conduct in defense of the damage suit within the implied waiver of investigation resulting from the filing of such action.

Electronic eavesdropping and wiretapping have both been held to be an unreasonable invasion of privacy and actionable, even though the purpose of each was to obtain information in the defense of a lawsuit which had already been filed. For example, in *McDaniel* v. *Atlanta Coca-Cola Bottling Co.* [2 S.E. 2d 810 (Georgia)], the plaintiff claimed to have swallowed a piece of glass from the defendant's bottle. The defendant secretly placed a microphone in the plaintiff's hospital room and overheard conversations that went on. These facts constituted an invasion of the plaintiff's privacy and she was awarded damages.

Although the right of privacy has been recognized for a comparatively short time, some 28 states have accepted it as a part of their common law. Three states have considered and rejected it. These states are Rhode Island, Nebraska, and Wisconsin.

332 Conversion

Conversion applies only to personal property. It consists of the wrongful assumption of ownership over items of personal property. The owner is entitled to the possession and use of his property. Any wrongful interference with this right of ownership, possession, or use is a conversion, and the wrongdoer is subject to liability. Conversion may also be defined as an unauthorized assumption and exercise of the right of ownership over goods or personal chattels belonging to another, to the alteration of their condition or the exclusion of the owner's rights.

The possession by the other party may have been lawful in the first instance, but his use of the property for his own purposes may constitute a conversion. For example, an automobile owner leaves his car at a garage for repairs and without the owner's permission, the garageman uses the car to take his wife to a dance. This is a conversion, even though the car is not damaged, and the garageman is liable to the automobile owner for the value of the use of the car. On the other hand, if the car is damaged, the garageman is liable not only for the unlawful use, but also for the damage as well.

In another illustration, a man takes his tuxedo to a dry cleaner for cleaning and pressing. After it is cleaned and before the owner has repossessed, the dry cleaner, without the permission of the owner, wears the suit to a dinner. This is a conversion, even though the possession by the dry cleaner in the first instance is legal.

333 Trespass

At common law trespass consisted of any unlawful entry on the lands of another. Originally trespass was confined to unlawful entry on land, but as time went on, the courts applied the principle to any transgression or offense against the laws of nature, of society, or of the country in which we live. This is applied whether it relates to a man's person or his property. Therefore the subject of trespass will be considered under the following categories: (1) trespass on land; (2) trespass to goods; (3) trespass to the person; and (4) justifiable entries.

1. Trespass on land. The ownership of land includes the right of exclusive possession. Anyone, who, without the permission of the owner, express or implied, enters upon the land of another is making illegal use of the property. He is liable in damages to the owner for any loss or damage to the property including shrubbery, or perennial or annual crops. Any entry on the land to remove crops or any nature is a trespass. The owner may adopt reasonable means to exclude trespassers, such as the erection of fences and walls as well as the ownership of a watchdog. Likewise, the owner may use reasonable force to exclude a trespass where the intrusion occurs in the owner's presence. What is "reasonable force" will depend upon the facts and circumstances of the intrusion and in most cases will be a jury question.

The wrongful entry upon the land of another does not necessarily have to be made by the trespasser himself. For example, if he allows his cattle to roam and to intrude upon the land of another, he is quilty of trespass. It has been said that the cattle owner "trespasses with his cattle."

The same rule would apply in cases where the defendant in the course of blasting operations on his own land caused rocks, rubbish, and other debris to be thrown upon the plaintiff's land. Also where the defendant felled a tree on his own land which fell on the plaintiff's land, the defendant is strictly liable for the damage. Likewise, where the defendant dammed a stream, operated an automobile, bus, or streetcar on his own property or on the public way, and his act resulted in the stream, or the vehicles going directly on the land of the plaintiff, he was liable for the consequences.

The common-law view was that the owner of real property owned not only the surface property but also the airspace above to the heavens and below to the center of the earth. This rule has given way to the circumstances of modern living and the use of aircraft. Judicial modifications of the common-law view have established two zones above the owner's land, the first being that which he has reduced to possession by erecting a building thereon and also the space needed for the enjoyment of his property, with the space above that zone being considered as being in the public domain and, therefore, available for use by anyone. However, one may not string wires across the owner's land without permission, shoot across the land, even though the bullets do not fall on the land. Also, where an adjacent building encroaches upon the property, either at the foundation or by an extension above which extends over the other's land, this is a trespass.

As to the ownership of the area beneath the land, the common-law rule seems to be applied. It is a trespass to mine under another's land, construct a tunnel or to invade it by a projecting foundation.

2. Trespass to goods. The owner of personal property is entitled to the possession and use of the property. Any wrongful interference with the possession, use or physical condition of the property is a trespass for which the perpetrator is liable.

3. Trespass to the person. The individual has the right to safety of person. Any wrongful invasion of that right is tortious and makes the tortfeasor liable in damages. Originally, any invasion of the right of safety of person was considered as a trespass and the individual could enforce a claim for damages. While this form of action is probably still available, other forms of action may be and are utilized in order to effect a recovery, such as assault and battery.

4. Justifiable entries. The ownership or possession of land is an exclusive right and generally no one may enter the premises without the permission of the owner, express or implied. There are, however, certain classes of persons who may enter the land without the permission of the owner. These include a police officer, serving a warrant, a sheriff or marshal serving a court order, as well as a fire fighter entering for the purpose of extinguishing a fire.

A problem arises where the owner of personal property is on the land of another, and the right of the personal property owner to enter on the land in order to remove it. Generally, the rule is that where the personal property was placed in the land through no negligence or intention on the part of the owner of the personal property, he may enter to remove it and is not required to secure the permission of the landowner. This situation would arise where the personal property is brought to the land by the forces of nature, such as a windstorm or tornado. In addition, where the personal property was originally owned by the landowner and was sold to a buyer, the buyer upon the payment of the purchase price, has the right to enter the land and remove it.

334   False imprisonment

Everyone has the right of safety of person, which, as we have seen, includes liberty and freedom of movement. Any wrongful interference with this right is an actionable tort. *Imprisonment* does not necessarily refer to confinement within the walls of a state prison, although this could be included, but it does consist of the use of any force which completely restricts the person's right of movement. Imprisonment also consists of any confinement in a house, a store, or by forcibly detaining a person on the streets against his will.

A person may be confined by the retention of his property. For example, a store detective retains a woman's purse and refuses to return it. Under those circumstances, the woman is confined. The same thing would be true where a woman's luggage was dumped from a train not at her station. The fact that the person voluntarily left the train to reclaim her luggage does not change the situation. She has been confined, because her movements have been restricted by the action of the conductor or train crew.

False arrest is another form of imprisonment in that the person is deprived of freedom of movement. While a private citizen may arrest another where the crime is committed in his presence, he may not deprive another of liberty without probable cause. On the other hand, a police officer may arrest a person without a warrant if the crime is committed in his presence, or is a crime has been committed and the officer has reasonable cause for believing that the person arrested has committed the crime. The officer is protected from liability where he executes a warrant valid on its face, even though it might have been issued by an official who was without jurisdiction.

335   Malicious prosecution

As an element of the right of safety of person, the individual has a right to be protected from the institution of criminal charges which are brought without probable cause for believing that the individual has committed the crime. It is an action which is begun with the intention of injuring the defendant, and, as a result, the defendant has a cause of action against the person bringing the charges.

The elements of an action for malicious prosecution are as follows:
1. A criminal proceeding instituted by the defendant accusing the plaintiff of a specific crime.
2. Absence of probable cause for believing that the plaintiff had committed the crime.
3. Termination of the proceeding in favor of the plaintiff.
4. Malice, or evil intent, which may be defined as the intentional doing of a wrongful act without just cause or excuse, with the intent to inflict an injury, or under circumstances from which the law would imply evil intent.

1. Institution of criminal proceedings. The proceedings must be instituted. Merely because a complaint has been filed with the proper authorities, where no official action has been taken, is not sufficient. On the other hand, where a warrant has been issued for the arrest of the plaintiff and it has been served is sufficient evidence of the beginning of criminal proceedings.

2. *Absence of probable cause.* It is the duty of each citizen to bring to the attention of the authorities any person who is reasonably suspected of having committed a crime. Probable cause has been defined as "a reasonable ground of suspicion supported by circumstances sufficient to warrant an ordinarily prudent man in believing the party is guilty of the offense." In each case the facts and circumstances will determine whether or not this test is met.

3. *Termination in favor of the accused.* This means that the proceedings must be terminated in favor of the accused. It does not mean that the proceedings have been terminated by the accused, where he agrees to a compromise in which he entered voluntarily. It also might be noted that in criminal proceedings the person's guilt must be established beyond a reasonable doubt; whereas in the action for malicious prosecution the defendant may prevail if he can show by a preponderance of evidence that the plaintiff was in fact guilty.

4. *Malice.* In an action for malicious prosecution, the plaintiff has the burden of proving that the defendant acted with an evil purpose. The mere fact that the defendant was motivated by hatred, or spite, is not enough to establish malice. Malice is usually found where the defendant uses the prosecution to extort money from the plaintiff, to collect a debt, to recover property or to compel the performance of a contract. The existence of these facts will spell out a bad motive or an evil intent. It should be noted that prosecuting attorneys who merely conduct the proceedings on complaints sworn to by others are in a quasi-judicial position and, as such, they are protected by absolute privilege and are immune from suit for malicious prosecution. Also, the police officer who serves the warrant of arrest is likewise protected.

Damages. The damages recoverable cover a variety of losses, which may include libel and slander to a plaintiff's reputation, business, or credit standing. In addition, the plaintiff may recover for the expenses to which he has been put in defending himself, the securing of witnesses, the humiliation following arrest and incarceration, as well as those damages sustained by being deprived of the society of his or her family during this period.

336 Wrongful civil proceedings

When a defendant is sued, he necessarily must expend the money necessary for a successful defense. This includes fees paid attorneys, depositions, subpoenas, and for expert witnesses. In addition, where property has been attached and the property is needed for the continued operation of the defendant's business, the cost of the bond to release the attachment adds another cost to the defendant. Included as well are the expenses incurred in defending a garnishment, replevin, search of the premises under a warrant, injunctions, proceedings in bankruptcy, or for the dissolution of a partnership. These include suits which have produced an interference with the business of the individual.

The English common law limited the successful litigant to the recovery of costs and many of our states have adopted that rule. However, in the United States, the costs to the successful litigant are fixed by statute and in no case is the litigant entitled to the amount of his expenses, legal and otherwise, nor to damages which he has sustained as a result of the interruption of his business. The states which follow this rule are: Iowa, Ohio, Rhode Island, and New Mexico.

In other states, this rule has been abrogated and the general rules applicable to malicious prosecution have been adopted, and have, under the following circumstances, considered the bringing of wrongful legal proceedings as a tort. To establish this as a tort, the plaintiff must show that the action was begun without probable cause, that the action was terminated in favor of the plaintiff, that the defendant was actuated by malicious motives or evil intent, and that specific damages were sustained.

The damages could consist of the expenses incurred in defending the original suit, compensation for the arrest of a person, seizure or interference with property, the resulting financial loss to a business, as well as injury to credit or reputation. In any case, the plaintiff must establish the amount of his or her damages. Thus far, this remedy has been limited to situations where the original lawsuit affected the person, property, or reputation of the plaintiff.

337   Damages

Damages awarded by the courts in tort causes of action may be defined as pecuniary compensation or indemnity recoverable by any person who has suffered loss, detriment, or injury, whether to his person, property, or rights. The money damages so awarded may be *compensatory* or *punitive*.

1. Compensatory. These damages consist of an award of money which will reasonably compensate the injured person for the loss which he has suffered up to the time of trial and, if the injury is a continuing one, the amount awarded will also indemnify him against losses which he will incur in the future.

2. Punitive. In addition to compensatory damages, some states permit the jury to award additional amounts by way of punishment where the defendant's conduct has been intentional, malicious, or outrageous. The award is made to the plaintiff over and above the amount of the compensatory damages to solace the plaintiff for mental anguish, laceration of his feelings, shame, degradation, or other aggravations of the original wrong, or else to punish the defendant for his outrageous behavior and to prevent him from repeating the same offense. These are referred to as punitive or *exemplary damages* (in the vernacular as "smart money") in the sense that payment thereof will cause the defendant some discomfort.

Punitive damages may also be assessed against the employer or the principal for the acts of his servant or agent, even though the employer or principal did not participate in the occurrence and was unaware of it. Punitive damages are assessed when any of the following situations are found to exist:

1. Where the principal authorized the act and the manner of its accomplishment, or ratified or approved the act after it was done.
2. Where the agent was not selected with due care and where the exercise of due care would have revealed the unfitness of the agent for the task.
3. Where the agent was employed in a supervisory or managerial capacity and performed the act within the scope of his authority.

Situation 1 is merely enunciative of the fundamental rule of agency that where a person performs an act through another under his control, he does the act himself. Therefore, having control of the method and means of doing the act, the principal is answerable for the entire act. The same thing is true where the principal ratifies or adopts the act as his own, after the offense has been committed. If the agent committed an outrageous act, the failure of the principal to set up safeguards against its repetition is construed as a ratification of the act, and subjects the principal to liability for punitive damages.

For example, *A* employs *B* as a bouncer in his bar. In ejecting a customer, *B* commits a brutal assault and battery and administers punishment far beyond that necessary for the purpose of ejection. *A* approves the action and continues to employ *B* in the same capacity. Punitive damages may be assessed against *A* as punishment not only because he approved the act but also because of his failure to protect future customers from the same sort of abuse by either discharging *B* or transferring him to another position where no opportunity for a repetition of the act would be afforded.

Situation 2 refers to the duty of care in the selection of employees which the principal must exercise in cases where others are exposed to a risk of injury. For example, *A* employs *B* as a janitor in his apartment house, giving him a master key which will enable him to enter any of the apartments. If *A* had checked *B*'s employment record, he would have ascertained that *B* had been discharged from his previous position because he viciously assaulted a woman tenant. *B* thereafter attacks a woman tenant in *A*'s apartment house, gaining access to the apartment with the master key.

A is liable for punitive damages for the reason that his failure to exercise care in the selection of *B* exposed his tenants to an unreasonable risk of harm, and in employing *B*, under those circumstances, *A* made *B*'s acts his own.

Situation 3 may seem to overlap Situation 2, but this is not entirely the case. Situation 3 refers to corporations or large firms where there has been no fault on the part of the employer, either in the selection or the retention of the employee with knowledge of the employee's character. Punitive damages are awarded against the employer because they employed this particular agent in a managerial capacity. Because the agent was on a management level, his acts then became the acts of the employer.

CHAPTER IV

Tort doctrines

400 Tort doctrines defined

A doctrine is a rule, principle, theory or tenet of the law. Whereas a statute is a rule of law enacted by the legislature, a doctrine is a rule of law originated by the courts. It derives its validity from its repeated application to factual situations by the courts. There are a number of these doctrines applicable to the law of torts. Some enlarge the area within which the defendant may be held liable, and others diminish or eliminate his liability entirely.

401 Last clear chance

The law imposes a duty on the part of every person to exercise due care for the safety of others. This means that the individual is under a duty to avoid injury to another if it is possible to do so. This duty continues even though the contributory negligence of the other has placed him in a position of peril. Where a party has the *last clear chance* of avoiding injury to another, he is under the duty of avoiding the accident, and failure to do so will create a liability. This is true even though the negligence of the other party has placed him in a position of peril. The theory here is that the negligence of the party

81

having the last opportunity of avoiding the accident is the sole proximate cause of the injury. Manifestly, the defendant must have had actual knowledge of the plaintiff's perilous position or in the exercise of ordinary care, should have known of it. In addition, there must have been an opportunity available to the defendant to avoid the accident. Where these elements appear and an accident occurs, the plaintiff is absolved of his contributory negligence, and a recovery is allowed against the defendant.

If the defendant by the exercise of reasonable care could not have discovered the peril of the plaintiff, or if there was no opportunity afforded to the defendant of avoiding the accident, the doctrine does not apply. The doctrine contemplates a situation where the plaintiff by his own negligence has placed himself in a perilous position from which he cannot extricate himself. The defendant can avoid injury to the plaintiff, and the defendant is liable if he fails to avoid the injury. It is a situation which is created by the negligence of both plaintiff and defendant, but assumes that there was a time after such negligence occurred when the defendant could, and the plaintiff could not, by the means available avoid the accident.

The classic example of last clear chance involves a man who drives a negligently maintained vehicle onto the tracks of a railroad at a time when signals are flashing, warning of an approaching train. The vehicle stalls on the tracks, and the driver has no means of extricating himself from the vehicle. The engineer of the approaching train has an unobstructed view of the vehicle and could bring the train to a stop within the range of his vision and before striking the stalled vehicle. If he fails to do so, his negligence is the proximate cause of the accident, and the railroad is liable.

For the defendant to have had an opportunity of avoiding the accident, it is clear that the plaintiff's contributory negligence must have occurred some time prior to the happening of the accident. If the plaintiff's contributory negligent act occurred simultaneously with the occurrence of the accident, it is obvious that the defendant could not have had an opportunity of avoiding the accident. In other words, there would have to be some interval of time within which the defendant could take some action which would avoid the accident.

Thus the doctrine of last clear chance is an exception to the general rule that the contributory negligence of the plaintiff defeats his recovery.

402   Foreseeability

The prudent man will have a reasonable anticipation of the risks of harm or injury to which others will be exposed as a consequence of his action or lack of action in a given situation. He will therefore govern his conduct accordingly, and avoid injury to others, when the injury can be reasonably anticipated. The failure on the part of an actor to conform to this standard is negligence.

The doctrine of foreseeability is applied in order to provide a limitation on the application of the reasonably prudent man standard. The actor is answerable for any injuries which occur to others which should be reasonably antici-

pated. He is not answerable for injuries which could not be reasonably anticipated.

For example, *A*, driving his automobile, negligently collides with a plainly
marked truck containing explosives. The truck carries a red flag and signs
indicating the purpose for which it is being used. In the ensuing explosion, *C*,
the driver of the truck, is seriously injured. *D*, a pedestrian on the sidewalk
near the point of impact, is injured, and *E*, who is sitting at a desk in his office
one block away, is injured by falling glass which shattered as a result of the
explosion.

A is liable to *C*, *D*, and *E*. *A* should have reasonably anticipated the risk of
injury to which all persons would be exposed as a result of his collision with a
truck which he knew contained explosives.

Let us use the same facts but assume that the truck was not marked at all
and that there was no way that *A* could anticipate that the truck was carrying
explosives. Under these circumstances, *A* would still be liable to *C* and *D*, but
he would not be liable to *E*. Even if the unmarked truck did not contain
explosives, *A* would be bound to reasonably anticipate injury to *C*, the driver,
and also the possibility of injury to *D*, the pedestrian near the scene of the
collision. *A* did not know that the truck contained explosives, and therefore he
could not have reasonably anticipated any risk of injury to which *E* might be
exposed. For this reason, *A* is not liable to *E*; *E* was not within the "foreseeable orbit of danger."

In the famous *Palsgraf* case (*Palsgraf* v. *Long Island Railroad*, 248 N.Y.
339), a subway guard in the defendant's employ roughly shoved a passenger
onto the platform of a moving train in such a way as to knock out of the
passenger's hand a small package. The plain covered package, unknown to the
guard, contained fireworks. They set off an explosion which injured the plaintiff, approximately 25 feet away. The court held that the guard had no reason
to foresee from carelessly jostling the passenger's arm any substantial risk of
injury to Mrs. Palsgraf 25 feet away on the station platform.

But before there can be negligence, there must be a rational duty of care
owed by the defendant to the plaintiff. The risk reasonably to be perceived
defines the duty to be obeyed, and the duty runs only to those persons who are
within the foreseeable zone of danger. Here a recovery was denied for the
reason that the guard could not anticipate injury to a person at that distance
from the scene of the act. Some courts have criticized the Palsgraf decision, and
cases decided since that time are indicative of a growing trend toward permitting a recovery in all cases where the defendant's conduct is a substantial
factor in causing injury, whether the injured person could qualify as a foreseeable victim or not. The majority of the courts adhere to the application of
the doctrine of the foreseeability as laid down in the *Palsgraf* case, but in most
instances even these courts allow a recovery, finding some facts in the evidence
on which to base a conclusion that the injured person was within the orbit of
foreseeability.

A driver passes a large cardboard box which is lying in the left lane of the road. He can see that the box is empty. On his return trip the box is still there, but unknown to the driver, a small child is inside the box. The driver, thinking the box is still empty, and since it is in his line of travel, runs over the box, causing injury to the child.

On those facts, the question to be decided is whether or not the driver should have anticipated the presence of the child in the box, especially having in mind that a short time before he had actual knowledge that the box was empty. There is a difference of opinion as to the applicability of the doctrine of foreseeability to such a situation. However, we add just one additional fact: as the driver was passing the box, he noticed a large number of children playing in the immediate vicinity. Most students agree that with this additional fact, the driver should have anticipated the possibility of children playing inside the box, and therefore he would be answerable for injuries sustained as a consequence of an accident.

403   Foreseeability as applied to motor vehicles

A person who owns or operates a motor vehicle is bound to anticipate the risks of harm to which others will be exposed as a consequence of its operation. Persons within this foreseeable zone of danger would include others using the highway, operators and passengers of other vehicles, pedestrians, and the owners of property on the highway, such as traffic stanchions, road dividers, and traffic signals. He is also bound to anticipate the risks of harm to others who are near the highway, such as pedestrians on the sidewalk, people on private property abutting the highway, and owners of property along the highway, such as owners of telephone poles, street lights, fences, advertising signs, and buildings. If the owner or operator of the motor vehicle fails to exercise due care for the safety of these persons, he is guilty of negligence.

Due care will consist of the careful operation of the motor vehicle, including obedience to traffic signs, speed laws, the maintenance of a careful and proper lookout, and the maintenance of control of the vehicle. Due care would also include the proper maintenance of the operating parts of the vehicle, and the owner is bound to foresee the risks of harm to others should he operate his vehicle with improper brakes, improper lights, or improper tires.

The owner of a motor vehicle is also charged with the duty of reasonable anticipation with respect to the risk of harm to others which would be occasioned by the use of his vehicle by an incompetent operator. Therefore, if the owner entrusts his vehicle knowingly to an unlicensed driver, an intoxicated person, or a driver who has a reputation for recklessness, the owner will be responsible for damages sustained by others as a result thereof. The owner is bound to anticipate the risks of harm which will accrue to other persons as a result of his action in giving permission to such a driver to operate his vehicle.

404   Foreseeability as applied to premises

With respect to the ownership and maintenance of public premises, the owner or lessee is bound to maintain the premises in a reasonably safe condition, to make periodic inspections, and to remove dirt, debris, and other foreign substances which may accumulate as a result of the use to which the premises are put. The maintainer of the premises is bound to anticipate or foresee all possible risks of injury to persons invited to make use of the premises. This duty would consist of a warning to the public of any unsafe or hidden defect, unusual construction, or repairs.

The extent of the warning will differ with the circumstances; it might merely require a sign or a barricade, or the nature of the condition might require the posting of an employee at the site of the defective repairs for the purpose of orally warning all people passing that point. If the condition is of an extremely dangerous nature, it might consist of closing off that portion of the premises entirely.

The duty of inspection and removal of dirt and debris will differ with the type of premises involved. The inspection must be reasonable and at reasonable intervals of time, although these intervals will differ, depending on the circumstances. For example, in a vegetable store where vegetables fall to the floor with frequency—where lettuce leaves, beet tops, and other debris are likely to find their way to the floor used by the customers—the duty of inspection and cleaning would require that this be done at much more frequent intervals than would be the requirement in a dry goods store.

As to private premises, the owner is likewise required to maintain them in a reasonably safe condition and to warn persons entering the premises with respect to any hidden defects of which he has knowledge and which are not open and apparent. The owner is required to reasonably anticipate the risk of harm to which persons lawfully on the premises will be exposed.

405   Foreseeability as applied to products

In the area of food, the rule of strict liability is imposed upon the manufacturer, grower, processor, canner, or baker, if the product is not fit for human consumption. This liability is imposed irrespective of negligence. He must reasonably foresee that all food products are bought for eating purposes, and the manufacture and sale of products which are not fit for human consumption is negligence per se.

With respect to products other than articles of food, the manufacturer must foresee the risks of injury to which purchasers of the article will be exposed. This means that the manufacturer must design the product with reasonable care, give detailed and proper instructions as to its use, and further warn the purchaser as to any inherent dangers which are not open and apparent. This warning must be adequate. The manufacturer is held to a high degree of scientific knowledge with respect to the ingredients, design, and purity of the product.

In the application of this knowledge, the manufacturer is also required to anticipate the risks of harm which may arise, not only from the use to which the product is normally put but also any attendant hazards which may exist in connection with such use. For example, a man applied Baume-Bengay to his chest in the course of treatment for a cold. While the product was so applied, and while attempting to light a cigarette, the head of the match came off and fell on the man's chest. The product ignited, causing severe burns. The court, in upholding a verdict for the plaintiff, took the position that the manufacturer was charged with the knowledge of the flammable nature of its product, and its failure to warn the use of this hazard constituted negligence. [*Morton* v. *Bengay*, 130 Atl. 2d 863 (New Jersey).]

406   Foreseeability—Illustrative cases

It has been held that in the application of the doctrine of foreseeability, an intervening crime is not a superseding cause where such criminal forces were reasonably foreseeable and the defendant was under a duty to protect the plaintiff from them.

In *Liberty National Life Insurance Company* v. *Weldon* [107 So. 2d 696 (Alabama)], the life insurance company issued policies on the life of a 2½ year-old girl to an aunt who had no insurable interest in the child's life. The aunt murdered the child by feeding her arsenic. An action was brought by the child's father against the insurance company on the theory that the issuance of the policy to a person without an insurable interest constituted negligence, and, in addition, was an inducement on the part of the beneficiary to shorten the life of the insured.

The defendants contended that any negligence on their part in issuing the policies was not causal negligence; that the intervening criminal act of the aunt in murdering the child was an intervening, superseding cause, as a matter of law.

The court held that a life insurance company has the duty to use reasonable care and not to issue a life policy in favor of a beneficiary who has no interest in the continuation of the life insured; that policies issued in violation of the insurable interest rule are void, since they constitute a stimulus for murder; and that intervening criminal acts may be found to be foreseeable by the jury, and if so found, actionable negligence may be predicated thereon. In finding for the plaintiff, the court held that the defendant's negligence consisted of subjecting the plaintiff to the specific risk of criminal harm, and because of the enormity of the wrong done, the court also awarded punitive damages.

In *Brower* v. *R. R. Company* (103 Atl. 166), the owner had goods stolen from his wagon by unknown thieves while the driver was unconscious as a result of a grade crossing collision which demolished the wagon and killed the horse. The court ruled the owner could recover the value of the stolen goods from the railroad company, whose train had negligently struck the plaintiff's vehicle.

In *Austin Jones Co.* v. *Nine* (119 Atl. 577), the state was held liable where the head of a state insane asylum negligently released a dangerous lunatic who thereafter set fire to the plaintiff's building.

In an extreme case, *Southwestern Bell Telephone Company* v. *Adams* (133 S.W. 2d 867), the telephone company was held liable when an employee of the telephone company left the plaintiff's building open and trespassers set the building on fire.

The doctrine of foreseeability has also been applied to cases where the negligence of the defendant exposed the plaintiff to the risk of harm by others. For example, in *Hines* v. *Garrett* (108 S.E. 690), the railroad negligently carried the plaintiff past her station and forced her to leave the train in a notoriously dangerous and desolate neighborhood. The railroad was held liable for her injuries when she was criminally attacked and raped by several unknown assailants.

In *Neering* v. *Illinois Central Railway Co.* (50 N.E. 2d 497), the railroad was held liable for resulting injuries where it negligently exposed women passengers to expectable assault in a tough neighborhood.

In *Kendall* v. *Gore Properties* (236 Fed. 2d 673), the landlord failed to investigate the character and dangerous traits of an employee who was hired to paint apartments. Investigation would have disclosed that the painter had a record of conviction of assault and rape upon unprotected women. The landlord was held liable for the death of a young unprotected woman tenant who was strangled by this employee. If the landlord had investigated the character of the employee, he should have foreseen the risk of harm to his tenants by the employment of such a person. The court held him accountable as if he had made the investigation, and charged him with the knowledge that he would have gained if he had exercised reasonable care in the selection of his employee.

407 Rescue doctrine

This is an extension of the doctrine of foreseeability. It means that the defendant must foresee that if his negligent act places an injured person in a perilous position or imminent danger, it is reasonable to expect that others will come to the aid of the injured. It is likewise reasonable to expect that if any of the rescuers are injured in the process of giving such aid, the injury to the rescuers could be considered as consequential in the sense that the defendant's negligence was the proximate cause not only of the victim's injuries but also of the injuries to the rescuers.

Among the foreseeable consequences of negligently endangering one person is the likelihood of injury to an intervening rescuer. Therefore, the rescuer is also entitled to maintain an action for damages against the person whose negligence placed the victim in the dangerous position. In order to sustain such a cause of action, the rescuer, in addition to proving his damages and injuries, must prove the following elements:

1. The negligence of the defendant as the proximate cause of the victim's position.
2. The imminent danger to which the victim is exposed.
3. The justifiable exposure by the rescuer to danger in aiding the victim.

1. *The defendant must be negligent.*   The plaintiff and his cousin were passengers on the defendant's train. The cousin was thrown from a car by the railroad's negligence. When the train was stopped, the plaintiff went through the darkness to search for his cousin and was injured in falling off a trestle.

Recovery against the railroad was unanimously affirmed, and the court held that ordinary human experience and prevision teach us that by setting the stage and creating the dangerous situation, the defendant thereby foreseeably invited potential rescuers into the zone of danger. [*Wagner* v. *International Railway Co.*, 133 N.E. 437 (New York, 1921).]

It has been argued that the rescuer assumes the risk of injury in intervening in a situation and attempting a rescue, and it is the law that no one is obligated to come to the aid of another person in distress. Where a rescue has been attempted, the courts uniformly hold that many rescue attempts are created by a sudden impulse or a sudden response to a dangerous situation. To hold that the rescuer must take time for detached reflection and evaluation of the dangers before coming to the aid of another would not only place in an undue burden upon the rescuer but also be contrary to human behavior. The courts reason that where an attempt is being made to save a human life or property, a reasonably prudent person will take greater risks than ordinarily may be justified. The risk to which the rescuer exposes himself is one that a reasonably prudent man might take under the stress of an emergency situation.

Likewise, the voluntary exposure by the rescuer to a known danger does not constitute contributory negligence if the rescue attempt has a reasonable chance of success and, further, if the attempt is one that the reasonably prudent man would make under the circumstances.

For example, plaintiff's decedent was killed while attempting to rescue a child imperiled by the defendant's negligence. The court held that the decedent had not voluntarily exposed himself to peril and that the conduct of the defendant, constituting negligence towards the child, was also negligent toward the decedent.

In another case, a child fell through an unguarded opening on a state's negligently maintained bridge and the father was drowned in an effort to rescue the child. The court allowed a recovery for the father's death even though there was evidence that the father could not swim. The court held that the father's effort was the normal response of a parent to a situation where his child was in grave danger.

In each of these cases the rescuer chose to encounter a known risk. The extent to which he may expose himself to this risk is the same as the extent to which a reasonably prudent man would expose himself under the stimulus of the situation created by the defendant's negligence. If his intervention is rash, reckless, or foolhardy, then the intervention might be found to amount to contributory negligence or assumption of risk. However, except in the clearest cases, where reasonable minds could not disagree, the question of whether the rescuer's effort is reasonable is a question of fact for the jury.

The application of the rescue doctrine is not limited to volunteers alone. It has been applied to police and firemen injured in the course of rescue operations on the theory that although a rescue operation is one of the risks of such employment to which the individual assented at the time of his employment, he did not assume any risk incidental to a danger arising out of the defendant's negligence.

For example, in an English case, the defendant's servant had left his van and horses unattended in a crowded street. The horses bolted when a boy threw a stone at them. Plaintiff, a police constable on duty inside a police station, saw that if nothing were done, a woman and some children were in grave danger. At great risk to himself, he managed to stop both horses, one of which fell upon him as he was stopping it. In disposing of the defense of assumption of risk, the court held that the plaintiff had not freely chosen to assume the risk of the defendant's wrong but rather had been coerced into encountering the danger caused by the defendant's breach of duty.

Conceiving that the risk run by the policeman was incidental to his employment as a constable, this does not mean that he assented to the risk so far as the third person, the defendant, was concerned. He was suing the negligent third person, whose indisputable wrong had caused him an injury, and had not assented any risk in relation to the third person, however much he had assented to it as far as his employers were concerned. The court used as an analogy the policeman's duty to arrest the criminal. The court observed that no one would seriously suggest that because a city policeman is bound to arrest dangerous criminals (although admitting that risks encountered in so doing are part of the risks of employment), he therefore forfeits his right to sue for assault and battery some criminal who half murders him while he is making the arrest.

In a New Jersey case, the plaintiffs were two members of a fire department rescue squad who suffered gas asphyxiation while going to the rescue of two of the defendant's employees, who were fatally asphyxiated by carbon monoxide gas while attempting, by the use of a gasoline pump, to pump water out of a main. The court held that the employer's requirement of the use of a gasoline pump capable of producing carbon monoxide gas in a confined area (namely, a 30-inch diameter pipe with little ventilation) raised an issue of negligence as to the two employees. The wrong to the employees was also a wrong to the plaintiff rescuers and the basis for their claims. The fact that the dependents of the deceased employees were limited to a remedy under the Workmen's Compensation Act would not foreclose enforcement of the rescuers' common-law action. In finding for the plaintiffs the court described the rescue doctrine as follows:

The cry of distress is the summons to relief. The wrong that imperils life is a wrong to the imperiled victim; it is a wrong also to his rescuer. The risk of rescue, if only it not be wanton, is born of the occasion. The emergency begets the man. The wrongdoer may not have foreseen the coming of a deliverer. He is accountable as if he had.

For the rescue doctrine to apply, the negligence involved does not necessarily have to be that of a third person, but may be the negligence of the victim himself in creating an emergency which gave rise to the rescue attempt.

In such a situation, the victim will be liable to anyone who is injured in making a rescue attempt, and will also be liable to anyone whose property was damaged as a result of the rescue attempt.

For example, in a very old case, the defendant balloonist came down in the plaintiff's garden and was held liable for the damage done by a crowd which rushed in to rescue him. The theory here is that the crowd's action was foreseeable insofar as the balloonist was concerned, and by placing himself in a dangerous position he became liable for any damage arising as a consequence thereof. Also, if a person attempts suicide he obviously has a reckless disregard for his own safety. He is liable to his rescuer, even though the danger to his own safety was a risk to which he intentionally exposed himself.

In *Seaboard Airline* v. *Johnson* [115 So. 168 (Alabama)], a brakeman was injured when he attempted to stop a "kicked" car and save some men in a caboose some distance down the track. The court made the following observation:

Neither contributory negligence or assumption of risk is charged to him who comes to the rescue of others in peril without their fault, unless the act of the rescuer is manifestly rash or reckless to a man of ordinary prudence acting in an emergency. One cannot be said to act rashly or recklessly in such case if the element of danger to himself is less imminent than that of his fellow servants whom he is charged with the duty of protecting.

In *Cote* v. *Palmer* [16 Atl. 2d 595 (Connecticut)], a mother was trying to save her infant daughter from being run over by a train. In finding in favor of the mother for the injuries which she sustained the court said:

An outstanding factor is the instinctive reaction of human nature to the need of one in danger, and where he stands in a close relationship of blood or affection to the rescuer, as in a case like this, a young child to a mother, the reactions are a natural incident.

The extent to which the rescue doctrine has been applied is illustrated by an unusual case which came up in Louisiana. An accident occurred solely as a consequence of the defendant's negligence. The rescuer, who moved the injured persons from the car, also removed a revolver which was in the glove compartment of the car. The rescuer then handed the revolver to the defendant's husband, whom he had removed from the car, and the injured husband promptly shot the rescuer. The court held that the defendant was liable on the theory that the victim, the injured husband, had no motivation for shooting his rescuer and therefore must have been temporarily deranged as a result of the accident.

2. *There must be imminent peril.* The mere fact that a person comes to the aid of another is not in itself sufficient justification for the application of the rescue doctrine. Mere assistance to a person who is injured, but who is not in any further danger, does not require the application of the rule.

In *Roach* v. *Los Angeles Railroad* [280 Pac. 1053 (Utah)], an employee tried to stop a moving railroad car and was injured. There was no evidence that the moving car created a danger to anyone, and under those circumstances the court held that the employee assumed the risk and could not recover.

Similarly, in *Hawkins* v. *Palmer* [188 Pac. 2d 121 (Washington)], the plaintiff came upon injured persons by the side of the road. They had been injured as a consequence of the defendant's negligence. He volunteered to help the ambulance operator take care of them. Another car came along and sideswiped the ambulance. The court refused to apply the rescue doctrine for the reason that the element of imminent peril was absent and that the plaintiff had assumed the risk of injury voluntarily. The court defined the rescue doctrine as follows:

The rescue doctrine is applicable where one acts impulsively, oblivious of peril, to save or assist any injured person, or a person whose injury is imminent, or when, conscious of the peril, and weighing the consequences, he nonetheless goes to the aid of the injured person or the person whose injury is imminent.

The court observed that the defendant was not negligent insofar as creating a perilous situation relating to the persons to be rescued. There was no imminent peril as a result of the accident. In order to invoke the rescue doctrine, the defendant must be guilty of some negligence toward the rescuer after the rescuer has begun the rescue. Here, the accident was all over at the time that the volunteer attempted to assist the ambulance driver. The accident which occurred subsequently was too remote to involve the original defendant's negligence, and was in itself an intervening cause.

In *Eversole* v. *Wabash* [155 S.W. 419 (Missouri)], a volunteer tried to assist an engineer recouple cars. There was a possibility that if the cars were not recoupled that one might break away. The court held that there was no peril and that life was not endangered; therefore the volunteer could not recover for his injuries. The court said that it requires more than mere suspicion that an accident might follow to justify the invocation of the doctrine.

3. The risks to which the rescuer exposes himself must be justifiable under the circumstances. If the rescuer is rash and reckless in voluntarily exposing himself to a risk, he is guilty of contributory negligence, or at least the assumption of the risk. The general rule is that a voluntary exposure is not to be regarded as rash or reckless if it appears to have a fair chance of success, but the extent of the exposure will be governed by the circumstances in each case and the peril to which the victim is exposed. In all cases, this will pose a question of fact for the jury, and the jury will decide whether or not the rescuer's conduct conformed to the reasonably prudent man standard or whether it went beyond what would be considered necessary under the circumstances.

The rescue doctrine has been applied to cases involving property as well as human life. Obviously, the risks to which the volunteer can expose himself would be considerably less in the case of property than where human life is concerned. Also the kind, quality, and value of the property involved will dictate the extent of the exposure to danger that would be justified.

For example, a volunteer might be justified in entering a burning building in order to rescue the *Mona Lisa*. He would be encountering a known risk for the purpose of preserving a priceless, irreplaceable art treasure. His exposure to the risk, under those circumstances, might be justified. However, he would not be justified in exposing himself to such a risk in order to save his new hat.

408   Foreseeability as applied to public utilities

A public utility is defined as a business or service which is engaged in regularly supplying the public with some commodity or service which is of public consequence and need, such as electricity, gas, water, transportation, and telephone or telegraph service. Its right to render this service to the public exists as a result of a grant of authority, or franchise, given by the state. The state fixes the limitations within which the utility may operate and also sets up the standards of care the utility is required to observe for the protection of the general public. These rules may be fixed by the state legislature, or the legislature may delegate part of its lawmaking power to a public service commission or similar agency which will, from time to time, make regulations with respect to the operation of the public utilities.

In the case of electric companies, these regulations will determine the height at which certain types of wires must be maintained and certain precautions with regard to the use of high tension wires, as well as the location, operation, and maintenance of substations. As to gas companies, regulations may indicate where gas mains are to be located and specify the minimum depth they must be laid below the surface. The same regulations might likewise apply to a water company, as to location of mains, minimum depth at which they must be laid, and minimum safeguards which the water company must take in order to insure the purity of the water delivered. A failure to conform to these standards, which results in injury to any person, is negligence.

Compliance with the minimum regulations applied to the particular public utility will not entirely insulate the utility from liability in tort. The utility is bound to anticipate the risks of harm to which others will be exposed because of its operations, and it must adopt whatever measures are necessary to avoid or prevent the happening of a foreseeable incident which results in injury.

For example, with respect to companies supplying electricity, the regulations will provide the minimum height at which wires must be placed, but mere compliance with this rule is insufficient to entirely protect the power company. The company in the location of its wires is charged with the additional duty of either insulating its wires or placing them beyond the range of contact with persons who are rightfully present in the area. The company is bound to anticipate the activities of these persons and to take reasonable precautions against injury to them. This duty is elastic in the sense that changing conditions will either enlarge or diminish it.

The duty is greater in a populated area than in the open country, and where the open-country location changes its character (because of human activity in the form of home development), a higher duty of care is imposed. The power company is bound to foresee that at the present time people erect television antennas, and the company is bound to protect people from possible injury as a result of contact between these instrumentalities and its power lines. Before television was in general use the company was not required to anticipate these risks of harm to others. Now, however, with the widespread use of television receiving sets and the erection of such antennas, the duty of the company to anticipate the risk of injury is much greater than it was when no such activity was undertaken. Changes in living conditions, therefore, produce changes in the extent of the duty owed.

In a leading case, the facts indicated that a group of men and boys were attempting to erect a television antenna more than 50 feet in height. When the tower was raised, the men lost control and it fell, striking the company's high tension wire, which was uninsulated. One of the boys was killed, and one of the plaintiffs suffered severe shock.

The uninsulated high tension wire was mounted on poles located on a 3-foot easement running across the rear of lots belonging to the plaintiff's father and a neighbor. The wire was about 32 feet above the ground. There were no signs warning of the presence of the wire or of the fact that it was uninsulated. There were a number of houses in the vicinity, a fast-growing community, and there was evidence that the poles were leaning, the line sagging, and that a transformer had been installed on the wrong side of the pole (whose guy wires were improperly placed).

The court held that in locating its wires an electric company must either insulate them or place them beyond the range of persons present. When the likelihood of danger to human life must be balanced against the cost of insulation, the court felt that a defense as to the increased cost of more adequate insulation was not a very good argument. The court further pointed out that in an age marked by the common use of television sets, the duty of the power company to foresee the erection of television antennas was a reasonable one. [*Kingsport Utilities, Inc.* v. *Lamson,* 357 Fed. 2d 553.]

Brillhart v. *Edison Co.* (82 Atl. 2d 44) was a suit against the power company for the wrongful death of a workman. The decedent and a helper, while trying to install a metal pipe in a well pump, projected the pipe through a trapdoor in the roof of the pumphouse and it came in contact with the defendant's high-tension line, which passed to one side of the pumphouse at a distance of $10\frac{1}{2}$ feet from the roof of the pumphouse.

The court held that the evidence raised a submissible issue to the jury as to the power company's causative negligence in maintaining a wire in such close proximity to a building. The question for the jury was whether or not the power company should have foreseen the possible risk of harm to people making normal use of the pumphouse. The court further held that the evidence was insufficient to require, as a matter of law, a finding of contributory negligence on the part of the deceased. The court said that "The general public is not bound to the high degree of foresight in respect to danger from electric wires as is the company who maintains them."

With respect to unusual weather conditions, the power company is not bound to anticipate or guard against all of the hazards that the maintenance of its equipment might create in cases of unusual or unexpected weather. Where a hurricane has damaged the equipment, and electric power lines are down, the company must foresee the possible risk of injury to others and take whatever precautions are necessary to prevent injury to them. For example, in *Buccafusco* v. *Public Service Electric and Gas Co.* (410 Atl. 2d 79), the decedent was electrocuted when he came in contact with the defendant's uninsulated 2,400-volt line, which fell during Hurricane Carol. There was a verdict for the plaintiff.

The court held that the finding was not based upon the duty of the company to reasonably anticipate hurricanes, but that upon the occurrence of the damage, there was a duty on the part of the electric company to foresee the risk of injury to the public, to cut off power, and to make repairs within a reasonable time.

Other utility companies are subject to the same general rules of responsibility. The gas company and the water company are bound to anticipate the effect that ordinary weather will have upon their pipes and the commodity carried through them. They are not bound to anticipate unusual weather and are not bound to foresee the risk of injury which might come about as a consequence of unusual weather conditions. They are bound to anticipate the risk of injury or damage to property which may ensue following the exposure of their pipes to ordinary weather.

For example, in one case the water company maintained its pipes at a level which was not below the frost line. During the winter the pipes froze and the subsequent leakage into the plaintiff's basement inundated the entire basement. The water company was held liable for the damage on the theory that in maintaining their pipes at a place which was not normally below the frost line, they should have reasonably anticipated the risk of harm to the plaintiff's property.

409   Dangerous instrumentality doctrine

This doctrine contemplates the application of a rule of absolute or strict liability. Anyone who possesses, stores, maintains, or transports a dangerous instrumentality is absolutely liable for any injury or damage caused by the instrumentality, regardless of the presence or absence of due care. The reasoning behind this rule is that the person in possession of the dangerous instrumentality has exposed the community to an unreasonable risk of injury or damage and therefore he should be responsible for such injury or damage regardless of fault. The members of the community are required to guard against all ordinary, foreseeable risks of harm to their persons and property. They are not required to anticipate extraordinary risks of harm which the presence of a dangerous instrumentality will create. Consequently, where a dangerous instrumentality is involved, the defense of contributory negligence will not be available.

The dangerous instrumentality may consist of the possession, storage, or use of commodities such as dynamite, gasoline, explosives, and firearms. With respect to explosives, the possessor is absolutely liable to any member of the community for any injury or damage caused by the explosion thereof. The community is not required to take any precautions with respect to a possible explosion, such as boarding up windows, living in the basement while the explosive material is in the neighborhood, or the erection of a bomb shelter to avoid the risk of injury. There is, therefore, no defense on the grounds of contributory negligence if the community fails to take any of these precautions.

The rule of strict liability also applies with respect to the use of firearms. A person who entrusts firearms to another person, unfamiliar with their use, creates a dangerous instrumentality situation. The firearm in the hands of an incompetent person then becomes a dangerous instrumentality, and the owner is absolutely liable to anyone injured as a result. Likewise, a parent who carelessly leaves firearms in places where they are accessible to children becomes absolutely liable to anyone injured as a result of the use of the firearms by the children. Again, the firearm in the hands of a child becomes a dangerous instrumentality.

While it is true that a parent is not responsible for the torts of a child, liability is imposed not because of the act of the child but because of the neglect of the parent in creating an extraordinary risk to others. The parent is liable for his own tortious act of leaving a dangerous instrumentality in a place where it was easily accessible to others unfamiliar with its use or irresponsible with respect to the use thereof.

If the individual who took the firearm is injured, he will have assumed such a risk and, as to him, the other has no responsibility. Should others be injured as a result of the use of the firearm by the one in possession thereof, the owner would be responsible to them. The same situation is true with respect to explosives. If a trespasser, licensee, or invitee disturbs the explosive so as to cause an explosion, the owner will not be answerable for his injuries. The owner, however, would be answerable for the injury or property damage sustained by others. In both of these cases, the person actually taking the firearm, or interfering with the explosives, invited injury to himself and assumed all of the risks to which his action exposed him.

Absolute liability is imposed upon the owner of land who uses explosives for the purpose of blasting and excavation. This duty of care is nondelegable. Absolute liability is imposed upon the owner of the land even though he has delegated the blasting operation to an independent contractor and has used reasonable care in the selection of a competent contractor. The owner is still absolutely liable for any injury or property damage caused by the use of explosives on his land.

The rule of absolute liability does not apply to municipalities, counties, and other arms of government. The use of dynamite for blasting in the construction of roads, clearing of land, and other governmental activities, is quite common. The activity is one which is undertaken by the community at large, and therefore all of the members of the community have assented to the dangers which are occasioned thereby. Therefore, the municipality and the public officers engaged in this activity are not subject to the rule of absolute liability. They are, however, answerable where the injury or damage is caused by their own negligence or carelessness in the handling of the blasting operation.

410   Animals as dangerous instrumentalities

For the purposes of determining the duties and responsibilities of the owner or harborer of an animal, the law divides animals into two classes—domestic and wild. A domestic animal is defined as an animal which is in the service of mankind, such as dogs, cats, horses, sheep, pigs, cattle, chickens, turkeys, and even bees. On the other hand, wild animals are those which are hostile to man, and such would include bears, lions, tigers, snakes, elephants, etc.

Wild animals.   The rule is that wild animals are dangerous instrumentalities and the mere ownership thereof imposes liability upon the owner where damage or injury occurs. The theory is that the owner, in bringing the animal into the neighborhood, subjects his neighbors to an abnormal risk of harm, and regardless of whether the animal escapes as a result of the owner's negligence or not, the mere ownership or possession of such an animal imposes liability upon the owner for any injury or damage which the animal may do. A distinction must be made between animals which are indigenous to the locality in which they are kept and animals which are indigenous to a distant location. Where the wild animal is native to the location in which it is kept, and it escapes from the possession of the owner, the animal has then returned to the wild state, and since the owner can no longer exercise possession, he has neither ownership nor responsibility. Where the animal is not native to the community in which it is kept and it escapes, the owner or harborer is liable to anyone who is injured or whose property is damaged by the animal, and this liability would continue until the animal reached its native habitat, wherever that may be.

An exception to the imposition of the rule of absolute liability concerns persons who exercise possession of the wild animal in response to a public duty. Such persons are liable only for negligence in the exercise of possession in allowing the animal to escape or otherwise injure others. Possessors in this category would include a municipality maintaining a city zoo, its employees engaged in such operations, as well as common carriers, such as a railroad or an express company, both of which are required by law to transport wild animals. The rationale behind this rule is that where the owner of a wild animal brings it into the neighborhood, he voluntarily exposes his neighbors to an abnormal risk of harm, and for that reason strict or absolute liability is imposed upon him. The persons who respond to a public duty in possessing a wild animal do not have any discretion in the matter, but are required by law to bring the animal into the neighborhood.

The doctrine of strict liability with respect to the actions of wild animals has been applied to persons other than the owners or possessors of the animal, but who stood in some relationship of responsibility to the injured person. For example, in *Abrevaya* v. *Palace Theatre & Realty Co.* (197 N.Y.S. 2d 27), the plaintiff was attending a performance at the defendant's theater when a monkey, which was part of the performing act, came down into the audience and bit him. Strict liability was imposed on the theater owner, even though he did not own or possess the animal. Also, in *Smith* v. *Jalbert* (221 N.E. 2d 744), a licensor of premises upon which an exposition was conducted was held strictly liable for property damage inflicted by an escaped zebra owned by an exhibitor.

Certain wild animals may be so far domesticated and tamed as to bring them within the classification of a domestic animal. In such a case, the liability of the owner will depend upon the principles applicable to a domestic animal rather than the rule of strict liability which is applied to wild animals generally. Just what animals will come within this category usually will be a jury question. The jury will decide whether or not the animal is one which can be domesticated, having in mind the characteristic nature of the species to which the animal belongs, as well as the age of the animal and the length of time that it has been subjected to domestication.

Mere possession of land does not include ownership or possession of the indigenous wild animals which are found upon it. Therefore, the owner of land is not liable for injuries which may occur as the result of the actions of wild animals on his property but not under his control. Likewise, an owner who stocks his land with game indigenous to the locality and releases such animals loses his ownership and responsibility upon release. He owes no duty to his neighbors nor does he owe a duty to confine the game to the limitations of his property.

Domestic animals. These are generally regarded as harmless, and the owner is not liable for their actions unless the injury or damage is caused by animals which fall into one of the following three classes:

1. Livestock—animals which because of their size or habits are known to cause damage when they intrude on another's property.
2. Animals in which dangerous propensities are normal.
3. Abnormally dangerous animals.

1. *Livestock.* These are defined as those kinds of domestic animals and fowls which are normally susceptible of confinement within boundaries with-

out seriously impairing their utility and the intrusion of which upon the land of others normally causes harm to the land or the crops thereon. Thus, the term includes horses, cattle, pigs, and sheep as well as poultry, unless by custom in the area poultry are permitted to run at large.

The English common-law rule which has been adopted in the majority of American states is that the intrusion of livestock upon the land of another is a trespass and that the owner of the livestock is absolutely liable for the damage so caused. It has been said that "the owner trespasses with his cattle." Therefore, where trespassing cattle are concerned, the liability of the owner is exactly the same as if he himself had intentionally trespassed on the lands of another and caused the damage. The damages recoverable include not only the damage to the land itself but all consequential damages, such as personal injuries sustained by the owner of the land in attempting to exclude the animals, injuries to the property owner's cattle sustained as a result of fights with the intruding animals, the communication of a disease to the property owner's cattle, and any other damage in which a causal connection with the trespass can be established.

In a minority of states, especially those in the western part of the United States, they did not accept the English common-law rule, but promulgated one of their own which permitted cattle to roam on the open range at will and required the owner of land to fence in his property in order to keep the cattle out. The failure of the owner of land to fence out the livestock not only precludes him from recovering for the damage to his property but might in an appropriate case give rise to a cause of action by the owner of the cattle for injuries sustained by the cattle. This is particularly true in cases where a railroad is required to fence its right of way, and upon its failure to do so, cattle wander onto the tracks and are struck by locomotives.

2. *Animals in which dangerous propensities are normal.*   These are certain species of domestic animals in which dangerous or vicious propensities are normal and are known to exist. A bull, a stallion, and Burma cattle are all regarded as being mean and dangerous, and these characteristics are inherent in the nature of the animal. When such animals are possessed, the owner is not subject to the rule of strict or absolute liability as in the case of trespassing livestock, but he is liable to anyone who is injured as a result of his failure to exercise that degree of care which is commensurate with the nature of the animal, such care being exercised for the safety of others.

3. *Abnormally dangerous animals.*   This division refers to animals normally regarded as harmless, such as dogs and cats. The rule is that the owner of such an animal is not responsible for the property damage or injury sustained as a result of the animal's activities. The amount of property damage which a dog or cat could do to the premises of another is inconsequential, and the injury that they could cause would be considered as negligible when these things are balanced against the owner's right to possess such an animal. However, if the owner has knowledge (*scienter*) of a particular characteristic or vicious tendency on the part of the animal, the existence of which exposes

others to a risk of injury, the rule of strict liability will be applied. The liability is imposed on the owner of such a dog not because of his failure to exercise care in confining the dog, but in possessing the dog at all, having in mind that he has knowledge of dangerous characteristics which expose others to the risk of injury.

The dangerous characteristics referred to above include not only vicious traits which the animal may have exhibited but also habits which while not vicious in themselves are likely to cause injury. For example, where an owner of a large dog knows of the animal's habit of jumping at people in an overabundance of affection, the owner is liable regardless of the dog's intent. It should be emphasized that where liability is sought to be imposed to bring the case within this rule, the incident must have occurred as a result of the trait or characteristic of which the owner has knowledge. For example, the owner of a very large dog knows of the dog's habit of jumping at people. The dog bites a child. The owner had no knowledge of any characteristic of the dog which would put him on notice that the dog was likely to bite anyone. Therefore, knowledge of the habits which the dog did have will not spell out knowledge of other characteristics which have not been previously manifested.

Watchdogs. An owner has the right to maintain a watchdog for the purpose of excluding unwelcome strangers from his premises. He is subject to the same rules which govern his liability, if any, to trespassers. He is not required to maintain his premises in reasonably safe condition for the safety of a trespasser, but he is under a duty to refrain from maintaining any mechanical device or vicious dog on the premises, both of which are utilized solely for the purpose of injuring trespassers. In the case of a vicious watchdog, notice of the presence of the dog by signs or otherwise will subject the trespasser to the defense of either assumption of risk or contributory negligence, where it is established that such notice has been brought to the attention of the trespasser. As to others—licensees and business invitees—the right to possess a watchdog does not relieve the owner of his duty to maintain the premises in reasonably safe condition for the safety of those who are present on the premises by invitation or license. Similarly, the right to keep a watchdog on the premises does not relieve the owner of his duty to persons on adjacent land or on the public highway.

Mad dogs. At common law the owner of an otherwise normal dog who becomes afflicted with rabies is not liable for injury or damages sustained by a person or an animal bitten by such dog. Where the owner has reason to know that the dog is afflicted with rabies, then he is under a duty to use every precaution to prevent the animal from inflicting injury on others, this duty even being imposed to the extent of killing the dog, if necessary. On the other hand, if the dog is an abnormally dangerous animal and the owner has knowledge of the dog's vicious tendencies toward biting people, then if such a dog should bite another person, the owner is liable. If such dog becomes rabid, the owner's strict liability remains the same, but in addition he is liable for all damages sustained including the transmission of the disease. If the owner does not know of the vicious propensities of the dog, if any, before the appearance of rabies, and does not know and has no reason to believe that it is suffering from rabies, he is not liable for the injury or death of a person or an animal bitten by the dog and contracting the disease.

Dogs—statutory modifications.   Some states have enacted legislation modifying the common-law rule by making the owner or harborer of a dog strictly liable for bodily injury caused by the dog, regardless of whether the owner knew of any habits or vicious tendencies on the part of the dog. The statutes are in two classes. One type refers only to cases where the dog actually bites a person, applying the strict liability rule to that situation alone. Therefore, if a person were injured by the dog but not bitten, the statue would not apply. The other type of statute is much broader and applies the strict liability rule to all cases where injuries are sustained as a result of an attack by the dog. Under both statutes, as a prerequisite to the statutory application, the person injured or bitten as the case may be must establish that he was "peaceably conducting himself in any place where he may lawfully be." This would seem to exclude trespassers from the application of the statute.

It should be emphasized that the statute does not change the common-law rule, but it does add another cause of action in favor of the victim. The injured victim may bring his action at common law or under the statute, if such applies.

411   Ultrahazardous operations doctrine

This doctrine is related to the dangerous instrumentality doctrine and is based on the same duty of care which the owner of land owes to the community with respect to making reasonable use of his property. If he should conduct an operation which involves an abnormal risk of harm to the neighborhood, he will be held strictly liable for any damage which occurs as a result, irrespective of whether the ultrahazardous or inherently dangerous operation was conducted with due care. The general reasoning is that by conducting such operations and making abnormal use of his land, the owner has subjected the community to an unusual risk of harm and, having done so, the risk should be his and not that of the community. Nor is the community contributorily negligent if it fails to protect itself against the threatened harm. Thus, if a blasting operation were to be conducted, neighboring landowners are not required to live in the basement and board up their windows as protection against the effects of the operation.

The duty of the landowner making abnormal use of his property is to protect the rest of the community from all harm resulting from the abnormal use. This is a nondelegable duty, and he may not shift the responsibility to a contractor to whom he has assigned the task, even though the contractor was selected with due care and even though the owner has no control over the work of the contractor.

What usually happens when an independent contractor is employed is that the contract for the work contains a *hold harmless agreement*, whereby the contractor agrees to indemnify and hold the owner harmless from any liability imposed upon him as a result of the operation. The existence of this agreement does not affect the landowner's liability and duty to his neighbors, but merely provides a means of reimbursement to him should he be required to respond in damages to any member of the community.

Clearly, if the contractor does not conduct the operations with due care, he is responsible for his own negligent acts, and he may be held answerable in damages. In such a case, the injured person may sue either the contractor, or the owner, or both. The *quantum* of proof necessary to hold the owner responsible will be less than that required for the contractor. The elements of proof necessary, as against the owner, will be (1) proof of the abnormal use of the property, and (2) damages. Against the contractor, proof would have to show (1) the nature of the operation, (2) his negligent act or acts, and (3) damages as a result thereof.

412   Intrafamily immunity

The common-law rule, which has been adopted in the majority of the states, is that no lawsuits based on tort liablity are permissible between certain members of the family. Under this rule, a husband may not sue his wife, a wife may not sue her husband, a child may not sue his parent, and a parent may not sue his child. The reason behind this rule is that since the family unit is one of the cornerstones of our society, the preservation of the family is a matter in which the public interest is involved. The court will not lend its aid to litigation which can only have a disruptive influence on family life and could completely destroy the peace and harmony of the home. Regardless of the severity of the injury or the complete absence of care where reasonable care should have been exercised, a person standing within the relationships noted above may not maintain a cause of action against the negligent defendant.

From a practical standpoint, there would be no particular incentive for suits of this character where the family relationship is a continuing one. The payment of the judgment from one to the other would merely result in a realignment of the ownership of family assets. Attorneys' fees and court costs would be involved, and the actual result would be some impairment of the family resources with no particular advantage being gained by the successful litigant.

Husband and wife. The original common-law concept of the unity of marriage merged the legal personality of the wife into that of her husband. She could sue or be sued only in her husband's name, with him acting as her "guardian." With the coming of the Married Women's Acts, which in essence emancipated married women from the common-law disability and allowed them to sue or be sued in their own names without the involvement of their husbands, the courts reexamined the question of whether or not a married woman could sue her husband in tort. The majority felt that the family immunity doctrine constituted a bar to the maintenance of any action based on tort liability. Conversely, it was held that the family immunity doctrine likewise barred the husband from maintaining an action against his wife. A few courts, definitely in the minority, have taken the position that the Married Women's Act abrogated the family immunity doctrine insofar as it related to actions between husband and wife. They reasoned that if the legislature intended that suits between husband and wife were not included within the scope of the act, they could have said so.

As to torts committed by the husband or wife prior to marriage, and where the cause of action is asserted after the marriage has taken place, there are only a few cases reported.

In the following cases, recoveries have been allowed: *Brooks* v. *Robinson* [284 N.E. 2d 794 (Indiana)]; *O'Grady* v. *Potts* [396 Pac. 2d 285 (Kansas)]; and *Brown* v. *Gasser* [262 S.W. 2d 480 (Kentucky)]. The other jurisdictions which have considered the problem have concluded that such a suit would impair the peace and harmony of the marriage and even though the tort was committed prior to the inception of the relationship of husband and wife, as long as the relationship continued, the injured spouse would be prevented from asserting a tort cause of action against the other. The cases adopting this view are as follows: *Amendola* v. *Amendola* [121 So. 2d 805 (Florida)]; *Koenigs* v. *Travis* [75 N.W. 2d 478 (Minnesota)]; *Koplik* v. *C. P. Trucking Co.* [141 Atl. 2d 34 (New Jersey)]; and *Benevides* v. *Kelley* [157 Atl. 2d 821 (Rhode Island)]. Most of these cases are quite old, and, in view of the latest pronouncements of the same courts on the subject of interspousal immunity, it is doubtful whether the same cases would be decided the same way if the cases were presented now.

Effect of divorce or separation.   There are few cases on this subject, but it would seem that where there has been a divorce and the marital relationship has terminated that there would be no peace and harmony of the home which could be disrupted. Therefore, the injured spouse would not be precluded from bringing an action in tort for bodily injury, even though the injury occurred during the period of the marriage. *Sanchez* v. *Olivarez* [226 Atl. 2d 752 (New Jersey)] supports this view. See also *Purcell* v. *Kapelski* [444 Fed. 2d 380 (3d Cir.)] and *Juaire* v. *Juaire* [259 Atl. 2d 786 (Vermont)].

Although there are no cases directly on the point, it would seem that the same reasoning should apply where the parties are permanently separated and the immunity doctrine should not apply. However, in separation cases, there is always the possibility of reconciliation, and the court might be persuaded to invoke the doctrine so as to preserve whatever peace and harmony there may be left in the relationship. Therefore, we must regard the question as an open one at this time.

Wife versus husband's employer.   It sometimes happens that when the husband is acting in the course and scope of his employment he negligently injures his wife. Because of the family immunity doctrine, the wife is precluded from maintaining an action against her husband. However, there is no impediment in the way of her action against the employer based upon his vicarious liability for the negligent acts of his agents. Therefore, while the wife may not maintain an action against the negligent agent (her husband), she may maintain her cause of action against her husband's employer. See *Mulally* v. *Langenberg Bros.* [98 S.W. 2d 645 (Missouri)]; *Schubert* v. *Schubert Wagon Co.* [164 N.E. 42 (New York)]; *Fields* v. *Synthetic Ropes, Inc.* [215 Atl. 2d 427 (Delaware)]; and *Littleton* v. *Jordan* [428 S.W. 2d 472 (Texas)]; see also, 1 ALR (3) 677.

It has been urged that if the negligent agent is not liable to the injured person, whether due to the application of the family immunity doctrine or not, it would seem to follow that the principal likewise should be free from liability. This view has been adopted by very few of the courts, with the overwhelming majority holding the employer or principal liable. For a case enunciating the minority view, see *Riegger* v. *Bruton Brewing Co.* [16 Atl. 2d 99 (Maryland)].

Effect of death of either spouse. As between husband and wife, the death of either ends the family relationship, and since there is no possibility of the litigation having any effect upon the peace and tranquility of the home, the family immunity doctrine does not apply. Thus, if a husband or wife suffers bodily injuries in an accident due to the negligence of the other spouse, who is killed in the accident, there is no legal impediment to the bringing of suit against the legal representative of the deceased spouse. Likewise, where both husband and wife are killed in the accident which was due to the negligent driving of the husband, an action for the wrongful death of the wife may be maintained.

For example, in *Kaczorowski* v. *Kalkosinski* [183 Atl. 663 (Pennsylvania)], both husband and wife were killed in an automobile accident which occurred through the negligence of the husband. The court held that the wife's surviving father could maintain a wrongful death action against the administrator of the husband's estate. The family relationship no longer continued, and the court held that the parties to the action were "free from personal disabilities."

See also *Mosier* v. *Carney* [138 N.W. 2d 343 (Michigan)]—widow's recovery from the estate of her deceased husband allowed; *Poepping* v. *Linderman* [127 N.W. 2d 512 (Minnesota)]—surviving spouse may maintain a negligence action against the deceased spouse's estate for injuries caused during the marriage by the decedent's negligence.

Where an unemancipated child or children are the sole beneficiaries of the wrongful death action brought because of the death of a parent caused by the negligence of the other parent, who was also killed in the same accident, the action may be maintained without any involvement of the family immunity doctrine. Complications arise when the same action for wrongful death is brought against a surviving parent, whose negligence caused the death of the other. Clearly, the family relationship between the child or children and the surviving parent is a continuing one, and the maintenance of the action could have some disruptive influence on the relationship. This is true even though in most states the wrongful death action is brought by an administrator or other type of representative, since the real parties in interest are the ultimate beneficiaries, namely, the children. As to this phase of the problem, there are few cases, but those that have been decided indicate that there is a difference of opinion as to whether or not the family immunity doctrine is applicable.

For example, in *Russel* v. *Cox* [148 Pac. 2d 231 (Idaho)], the court held that a suit brought by the administrator of the wife's estate for the benefit of the minor children stated a cause of action for wrongful death against the surviving husband whose negligence caused the accident. In *Minkin* v. *Minkin* [7 Atl. 2d 461 (Pennsylvania)], the husband's death was caused by the negligent operation of a motor vehicle by his wife. The wife, as mother of the surviving child, qualified as guardian and next friend of the minor. She then brought suit in her representative capacity against herself as the negligent defendant. In other words, the mother was only a nominal plaintiff, and the suit actually was one by the minor child, using the vehicle of a representative because the minor was legally incapable of bringing the action himself. The representative so selected happened to be the same person against whom the suit was brought. The court approved the action and did not interpose the family immunity doctrine. Since the relationship of parent and child as to the mother and the child was a continuing one, it is difficult to see how the Pennsylvania court came to its conclusion. It may have been persuaded that the parent would not have brought the action unless she had access to some means of indemnification such as an insurance policy.

In *Heyman* v. *Gordon* [40 N.J. 52 (New Jersey)], the issue was whether a wrongful death action for the sole benefit of an unemancipated minor child could be maintained against the father, grounded on the latter's negligence which resulted in the death of the wife and mother. In holding that the cause of action could not be maintained, the court said:

Our law is settled that one spouse may not sue the other for injuries negligently inflicted, at law or in equity, for reasons of policy based primarily on the family relationship. Where the policy reason has disappeared, as for example, because of the death of the defendant spouse, the reason for the bar is gone and the action is permitted against the latter's estate. Here, the basic consideration still exists despite the death of the injured spouse, as the only beneficiary is still within the family relationship giving rise to the reason for the bar. The real party in interest is the child and there is no essential difference between these facts and where an unemancipated child sues his parent for his own injuries negligently caused. Such a cause of action may not be prosecuted in New Jersey even when the parent is insured.

Rejection of the interspousal immunity doctrine.   While the majority of the courts uphold the interspousal immunity doctrine, there are some decisions in which the courts have reexamined the doctrine and decided that it should be abolished. No doubt some consideration was given to the availability of insurance in our modern society as well as the changed status of the wife under present concepts. The following cases have rejected the interspousal immunity doctrine and have upheld the wife's right to maintain an action against her husband based on injuries caused by his negligence:

Alaska   *Cramer* v. *Cramer*, 379 Pac. 2d 95.
California   *Self* v. *Self*, 376 Pac. 2d 65.
Michigan   *Hoska* v. *Hoska*, 178 N.W. 2d 236.
Minnesota   *Beaudette* v. *Frana*, 173 N.W. 2d 416.
New Jersey   *Immer* v. *Risko*, 267 Atl. 2d 481 (abolished as to automobile liability cases only).
Vermont   *Richard* v. *Richard*, 300 Atl. 2d 637.
Virginia   *Surratt* v. *Thompson*, 183 S.E. 2d 200 (abolished as to automobile liability cases only).
Washington   *Freehe* v. *Freehe*, 500 Pac. 2d 771.

It might be added, parenthetically, that while suits between husband and wife are permitted in New York, the Insurance Law of that state provides that no policy of liability insurance shall be deemed to afford protection or indemnity in suits between husband and wife unless the policy is specifically endorsed to cover them. This means that any contract of liability insurance entered into in the state of New York is made in contemplation of this restriction irrespective of where the accident happens.

In *Bogen* v. *Bogen* [12 S.E. 649 (1941)], the Supreme Court of North Carolina refused to apply the interspousal immunity doctrine to an intentional tort. The court said:

Whether a man has laid open his wife's head with a bludgeon, put out her eye, broken her arm, or poisoned her body, he is no longer exempt from liability to her on the ground that he vowed at the altar to "love, cherish and protect" her. We have progressed that far in civilization and justice.

While the interspousal immunity doctrine may have originally been applied to all torts involving husband and wife, the later cases seem to apply the doctrine only to "nonwillful" torts and no others. Therefore, it can be concluded that even in states which recognize the doctrine that it will not be applied to intentional torts. For example, in *Flores* v. *Flores* [506 Pac. 2d 345], a New Mexico intermediate appellate court refused to apply the immunity doctrine in favor of a husband who had knifed his wife.

In *Korman* v. *Carpenter* [216 S.E. 2d 195 (Virginia)], the husband fatally shot his wife from whom he was separated and was convicted and sentenced to 20 years. Wrongful death action was brought by the administrator of the wife's estate for the benefit of the wife's parents and brothers. The court refused to apply the interspousal immunity doctrine, and allowed a recovery.

For some years legal text writers have urged the abolishment of the interspousal immunity doctrine. The argument is advanced that neither spouse should be able to injure the other and then be immune from liability. Even though the act complained of is later used as a grounds for divorce, the injured spouse is without a remedy for the reason that divorce settlements only contemplate the future losses which the spouse will bear and do not compensate for injuries already sustained. In *Freehe* v. *Freehe,* above, the court said:

A second major reason given for the disability is the notion that to allow a married person to sue his or her spouse for tort damages would be to destroy the peace and tranquility of the home. On reflection, we are convinced that this is a conclusion without basis. If a state of peace and tranquility exists between the spouses, then the situation is such that no action will be commenced or that the spouses—who are, after all, the best guardians of their own peace and tranquility—will allow the action to continue only so long as their personal harmony is not jeopardized. If peace or tranquility is nonexistent or tenuous to begin with, then the law's imposition of a technical disability seems more likely to be a bone of contention than a harmonizing factor.

While these cases may be some evidence of the court's willingness to reexamine the doctrine, the fact remains that the doctrine is still valid in the majority of states.

Parent and child.   The family immunity doctrine applies to actions in tort between parent and child on the theory that the barring of such suits is necessary for the preservation of family accord and parental authority. The rule applies to any family situation: natural father and mother, stepfather or stepmother, or any other person standing in place of a parent (*in loco parentis*) to the child. The doctrine applies to any relationship where there is an unemancipated minor child and a parent. The suit between these two parties is barred, whether brought by the child against the parent or by the parent against the child.

Where the child has attained the age of majority or has been emancipated (released from parental authority) prior to the occurrence of the accident, the reason for the rule no longer exists. Therefore, the doctrine is not applicable, and suits by such a child or suits by a parent against such a child are maintainable.

Where the child has not attained his majority or has not been emancipated at the time of the accident and suit is begun either by the child against the parent or by the parent against the child after the child has been emancipated or has attained his majority, the general rule is that such suits are not maintainable. The ruling is that the rights of the parties are determined as of the date of the accident. If the plaintiff—be it the child or the parent—could not maintain the action as of the date of the accident, the subsequent change in the child's legal status does not create a cause of action where none existed before.

A contrary view was expressed in *Logan* v. *Reaves* [354 S.W. 2d 789 (Tennessee)]. In that case, the child was a minor at the time of the accident but was emancipated by marriage prior to the time suit was filed. The court held that when the public policy of protecting the family relationship ceases, then the rule disallowing a parent's suit against the child no longer applies. Emancipation having terminated the family relationship, the rule did not apply, and the action against the emancipated child could be maintained.

The overwhelming majority of the cases sustain the view that cases of this type cannot be maintained. In *Brown* v. *Parker* [375 S.W. 2d 594 (Missouri)], the minor was unemancipated at the time of the accident but had reached majority before the issue was joined. The court stated that an unemancipated minor child could not sue his parent for an unintentional tort and held the same rule would apply to prevent a parent from suing an unemancipated child. In each situation the basis for the rule is a "public policy which refuses to allow the family relationship to be disturbed by such action." It was argued that the parent's disability to sue disappeared upon the defendant's reaching the age of 21 prior to trial. It was further argued that the rule prohibiting the parent's action against the child should not apply, since the basis for the rule had vanished. This is the same argument that was accepted in *Logan* v. *Reaves, supra,* but it was not accepted in Missouri. The court said:

However logical such an argument may be, the same considerations of public policy prevent our adopting it. In the first place the effect of such a ruling would be to allow a parent to sue an unemancipated minor child providing he could keep the case alive until after the child reaches legal age. Such a state of events would clearly violate the sound considerations upon which the rule is based. The family relationship would be disturbed during the time the parent waited for the child to become of age. . . .

The same policy considerations apply to prevent suits by an emancipated minor or a child who has attained his majority against a parent for negligent injury inflicted by the parent at a time when the child was unemancipated. [*Tucker* v. *Tucker,* 395 Pac. 2d 67 (Oklahoma); *Reingold* v. *Reingold,* 181 Atl. 153 (New Jersey); *Shea* v. *Pettee,* 110 Atl. 2d 492 (Connecticut)]. [*Nahas* v. *Noble,* 420 Pac. 2d 789 (New Mexico)].

A minor child might occupy two legal relationships with his parent, each independent of the other. For example, a minor son was employed by his father at the same wages as were paid to other employees and was required to do the same work during the same hours as other employees. He was injured in the course and scope of his employment and filed a claim for workmen's compensation against his father-employer. The court held that the accident arose out of the relationship of employer and employee and awarded compensation. Since the transaction did not involve the parent-child relationship, the family immunity doctrine had no application.

Child versus parent's employer. The same considerations and the same general rule which we found were applicable to cases involving a suit by the wife against the husband's employer are applicable here. The employer is vicariously liable to a minor child injured through the negligence of the father acting within the scope of his employment. Although the father-employee is immune to suits brought on behalf of his infant son, this immunity does not extend to his employer. See *Littleton* v. *Jordan* [428 S.W. 2d 472 (Texas)].

Child versus child. It is understandable why there are very few cases involving a suit between two unemancipated children in the same family, since there would seem to be little inducement for such litigation. The cases which have been decided point to a rule that the family immunity doctrine is not involved in such litigation. See *Emery* v. *Emery* [289 Pac. 2d 218 (California)].

To the same effect are the cases of *Overlook* v. *Ruedemann* [165 Atl. 2d 355 (Connecticut)] and *Rozell* v. *Rozell* [22 N.E. 2d 254 (New York)]. See also *Bush* v. *Bush* [231 Atl. 2d 245 (New Jersey)].

Effect of death. In cases where either the child or the parent has suffered death, the immunity doctrine does not apply to a suit between the survivor and the estate of the deceased. The family relationship has been terminated by death, and the nonapplication of the rule barring suits between family members would not in any way disturb the family relationship, since it has ceased to exist. For example, in *Oliveria* v. *Oliveria* [24 N.E. 2d 766 (Massachusetts)], it was held that a parent's administrator could maintain an action against an unemancipated child for negligence in causing the death of the parent, since the reason for the application of the immunity doctrine disappears with death.

A further reason advanced by some courts for not applying the immunity doctrine in death cases is that the legislature in passing the wrongful death statutes created a cause of action which could be asserted against the tortfeasor, or his estate as the case may be, by either a living plaintiff or the administrator of the estate of a deceased person. The following cases are illustrative of this principle and in each case a recovery was allowed:

Florida	*Shiver* v. *Sessions*, 80 So. 2d 905.
Illinois	*Calvert* v. *Morgan*, 190 N.E. 2d 1;
	Johnson v. *Meyers*, 277 N.E. 2d 778.
Kentucky	*Thurman* v. *Etherton*, 459 S.W. 2d 68.
Michigan	*Plumley* v. *Klein*, 199 N.W. 2d 169.
Minnesota	*Shumway* v. *Nelson*, 107 N.W. 2d 531.
Missouri	*Brennecke* v. *Kilpatrick*, 336 S.W. 2d 68.
South Carolina	*Fowler* v. *Fowler*, 130 S.E. 2d 568.
Wisconsin	*Lasecki* v. *Kabara*, 294 N.W. 33.

Emancipated children. The rule is that in the case of an emancipated child, either the child or the parent may sue the other in tort. A child may become emancipated (legally free from parental discipline) by attaining the age of 21, by being married, or by the consent of the parents who completely surrender of the right to the care, custody, and earnings of the minor child. The mere fact that the parent continues to support the child after one of these events has happened does not change the legal status of the child. For example, in *Fitzgerald* v. *Valdez* [427 Pac. 2d 655 (New Mexico)], the parent was allowed to bring an action against the child who was over the age of 21 at the time of the accident, even though the child continued to reside in the parent's home under the parent's care, custody and control, attending school, and was completely supported by the parent. Undoubtedly there was an insurance element in this case.

In *Carrieato* v. *Carrieato* [384 S.W. 2d 85 (Kentucky)], the daughter was 20 years and 10 months old at the time of the accident. At that age, the court held that she was emancipated even though she continued to live at home and take her meals there. Therefore her mother could bring suit against her. In intentional torts, the general rule is that the parent-child immunity doctrine will not be applied, the courts holding that an intentional injury by the parent constitutes an abandonment of the parental relation. This rule is applied only where the facts of the case go far beyond the mere exercise of parental discipline. For example, in *Mahnke* v. *Moore* [77 Atl. 2d 923 (Maryland)], a child approaching the age of five was forced by her father to witness the murder of her mother and was kept for a week with the corpse and finally was compelled to witness her father's suicide. The little girl was splattered with the suicide's blood. In an action against the father's estate the court held that there was a complete abandonment of the parental relation and the little girl could recover for the severe emotional disturbance and illness which she sustained. The court held that its interest in preserving domestic tranquility and strengthening parental authority against undermining should not be blindly enforced so as to shield a depraved or wantonly malicious parent.

Rejection of the parent-child immunity doctrine. A number of states have reexamined the application of the doctrine and have decided that in the light of modern-day conditions that the doctrine should be overruled. In most cases there was some recognition of the existence of insurance. The following cases have abrogated the parent-child immunity defense:

Alaska	*Hebel* v. *Hebel*, 435 Pac. 2d 8.
Arizona	*Streenz* v. *Streenz*, 471 Pac. 2d 282.
California	*Gibson* v. *Gibson*, 479 Pac. 2d 648.
Hawaii	*Tamashiro* v. *DeGama*, 450 Pac. 2d 998.
Illinois	*Schenk* v. *Schenk*, 241 N.W. 2d 12.
Kentucky	*Rigdon* v. *Rigdon*, 463 S.W. 2d 631.
Louisiana	*Rouley* v. *State Farm Mut. Auto. Ins. Co.*, 235 Fed. Supp. 786 (W.D. La.).
New Hampshire	*Briere* v. *Briere*, 224 Atl. 2d 588.
New York	*Gelbman* v. *Gelbman*, 245 N.E. 2d 192.
North Dakota	*Nuelle* v. *Wells*, 154 N.W. 2d 364.
Pennsylvania	*Falcon* v. *Pados*, 282 Atl. 2d 351.
Virginia	*Smith* v. *Kauffman*, 183 S.E. 2d 190.
Wisconsin	*Goller* v. *White*, 122 N.W. 2d 193.

These cases involve not only claims by an unemancipated child against the parent, but also actions by a parent against the unemancipated child. For example, in *Gelbman* v. *Gelbman,* supra, the plaintiff was a passenger in an automobile owned by her and driven by her unemancipated 16-year-old son. In affirming her right to recovery, the court said:

The parties recognize, as we must, that there is compulsory automobile insurance in New York. Such insurance effectively removes the argument favoring continued family harmony as a basis for prohibiting this suit. The present litigation is, in reality, between the parent passenger and her insurance carrier. Viewing the case in this light, we are unable to comprehend how the family harmony will be enhanced by prohibiting this suit.

Effect of insurance. With the increase in the writing of liability insurance, especially automobile, suits have been brought attacking the application of the family immunity doctrine where insurance was in existence at the time of the accident. It is usually urged that where there was insurance, there was no possible impairment of the peace and tranquility of the home. As a matter of fact, a recovery against the insured family member would provide a fund to take care of the medical and hospital expense as well as providing other funds to cover loss of wages and pain and suffering. Therefore, far from disturbing the tranquility of the home, the family purse would be increased rather than being depleted by having to assume the costs of the medical and other attention that the injured member would have to receive. Therefore the peace and tranquilty of the home would be undisturbed. In opposition it has been argued that to abrogate the immunity doctrine would open the door to fraud and collusion with the eventual result that the family integrity would be impaired. There are other types of available insurance, other than liability, which will provide payment for accidents and the medical expense incurred as a result. Some of the courts who have reexamined the rule, have decided to retain it in its present form, holding that the existence of insurance would not create a recoverable cause of action where none existed before. In *Clark* v. *Ruidoso-Honda Valley Hospital* [380 Pac. 2d 168 (New Mexico)], the court said:

The question is whether the parent's suit may be maintained against the child. So far as the plaintiff is concerned, liability insurance pertains to the collection of any judgment which might be obtained, and accordingly its presence or absence is not relevant in determining whether the action lies in the first instance.

In the same case, it was urged that the purchase of insurance should be construed as a waiver of immunity since if the defendant is immune from suit, there could be no other reason for carrying insurance. Obviously, liability policies cover a variety of risks including areas in which the defendant might be immune from suit. The court held that where the defendant is immune from suit, the mere purchase of liability insurance could not be regarded as evidence of a clear unequivocal intention to waive that immunity. Thus it was not construed as a waiver. One of the arguments offered in favor of the abolition of the family immunity doctrine is in reference to a factual situation in which a father took his son and some of the neighbor's children for a ride in his automobile. There was an accident due solely to the negligence of the father. All the children were injured. The neighbor's children were entitled to a recovery from the father. The son was not. Therefore the law should be overruled so that the son would participate on an equal basis with the neighbor's children. It is clear that the insurance policy on the automobile was purchased with an understanding of the law as it existed at the time of the purchase. If the father desired to obtain insurance protection for his son covering injuries received in an automobile accident, he could have done so. The argument is that except for an accident of birth, the son could have a recovery the same as the other children. The same thing might be true in a case where the automobile owner collides with another car. If the car is owned by someone other than the automobile driver, there is a possible recovery. If the car is owned by the automobile driver, there can be no recovery. Therefore, as far as the recovery for the damage is concerned, the mere accident of ownership will be determinative. As has been noted above, New York is one of the states in which tort suits between husband and wife may be maintained. In recognition of the possibility of fraud and collusion on the part of the parties, the New York Insurance Law provides that no policy of liability insurance shall be deemed to afford protection or indemnity in such suits unless the policy is specifically endorsed to cover them. Under a liability policy purchased in the state of New York, there is no coverage provided for husband-wife suits regardless of where the accident happens.

In the states which have overruled the intrafamily immunity doctrine, it seems clear that some recognition, tacit or otherwise, has been given to the existence of insurance. There would hardly be much incentive for such suits unless there was an insurance fund at the end of the litigation.

Application of the family immunity doctrine. The majority of the state courts apply the family immunity doctrine without any exceptions. For example, in *Hanna* v. *Hanna* [1968 Automobile Negligence Cases, (CCH) 19,675 (Indiana)], the court was called upon to determine whether or not the Married Women's Acts effected any change in the common law of the state so as to provide for a recovery by a husband against his wife for a nonwillful tort. In upholding the intrafamily immunity doctrine as part of the common law of the state, the court said:

> The rule of the common law proceeds upon the theory that in legal contemplation the HUSBAND AND WIFE ARE ONE PERSON AND NOT UPON THE THEORY THAT THE WIFE IS UNDER A LEGAL DISABILITY. This is unquestionably the common law, and that is part of the law of the State, so that it still prevails unless abrogated either by the express words of the statute or by necessary implication. (Emphasis by the Court.)
>
>   *   *   *   *   *
>
> Our General Assembly modified the common law legal relationship between husband and wife with the enactment of the Married Women's Acts. . . . which now provide certain independent rights and disabilities between spouses. The General Assembly, however, did not enact a statutory provision specifically stating that one spouse may sue another spouse for a negligent tort. The absence of any explicit statutory authority coupled with our long standing adherence to the common law precludes recovery in the case at bar. Indiana has, in fact, provided definite statutory exceptions which have abrogated various common law principles

of the husband-wife relationship, but in the absence of such statutory authority, this court is required to consider the husband and wife an entity in all remaining situations.

*   *   *   *   *

The General Assembly in its wisdom has enacted certain statutes bearing on the husband-wife relationship, and, had our General Assembly desired to provide a remedy to a spouse when injured by the tortious act of a negligent spouse, it would have expressly done so.

In *Nahas* v. *Noble* [420 Pac. 2d 127 (New Mexico)], the question was that where the unemancipated child negligently injures a parent, may the parent sue the child for those injuries after the child becomes emancipated? The court held that public policy demands that such suits be barred and that if there is to be any change in that policy it is a matter for proper consideration by the legislature and that it should not be overturned by the court. The court pointed out that what the plaintiff opposes is the application of the rule prohibiting her suit against her daughter, since it is claimed that any family disharmony created by the injury has already occurred. The court pointed out that what public policy forbids is litigation between parent and child based on the negligent acts of the defendant occurring at the time the child was a member of the family unit and subject to parental care and discipline. In 60 ALR 2d 1285, the annotation reads:

Although there is some authority to the contrary, the overwhelming majority of the cases sustain the view that a parent or his representative cannot maintain an action in tort against an unemancipated minor child, at least in the absence of a statute conferring that right, the reasons advanced for the rule being the necessity for the encouragement of family unity and the maintenance of family discipline, which are also the reasons advanced for the majority rule forbidding a minor child to maintain a tort action against its parent. . . .

In *Eule* v. *Eule Motor Sales* [162 Atl. 2d 601 (New Jersey)], the plaintiff suffered injuries when an automobile operated by her husband and owned by Eule Motor Sales, a partnership, was involved in an accident. Suit was brought against the Eule Motor Sales, and since her husband was a general partner in the firm holding a 50 percent interest, the defense of interspousal immunity was interposed. The court held that since the husband's interest in the partnership was involved, the suit could not be maintained. The court said:

The determination of whether Mr. Eule is in fact a real party in interest thus becomes focally significant and involves a survey of the rights and obligations of a general partner, and specifically his rights and obligations with respect to the net assets of the partnership. He was entitled to 50% of the net assets. Hence, if such assets should be diminished to satisfy a judgment by the wife against the partnership, his share therein would be reduced pro tanto. And, if the partnership assets proved to be insufficient to satisfy the judgment, his joint and several liability as a partner would require him to respond to his wife personally.

Since, in either event, maintenance of this action by the wife would in effect deprive the husband of the benefits of interspousal immunity granted by N.J.S.A.

37:2–5, it is held that for the purpose of conforming with the public policy implicit in the statute the husband must be regarded as a "litigant" and a real party in interest.

Other recent cases in which the courts have reexamined the intrafamily immunity doctrine and have decided that it still exists are the following: *Rickard* v. *Rickard* [203 So. 2d 7 (Florida Dist. Ct. Appeal)]; *Downs* v. *Paulin* [216 Atl. 2d 29 (Maine)]; *Watson* v. *Nichols* [155 S.E. 2d 154 (North Carolina)]; *Badigan* v. *Badigan* [174 N.E. 2d 718 (New York)]; *Termano* v. *Termano* [216 N.E. 2d 375 (Ohio)]; *Wooden* v. *Hale* [426 Pac. 2d 679 (Oklahoma)]; and *Chaffin* v. *Chaffin* [397 Pac. 2d 771 (Oregon)]. See also *Balts* v. *Balts* [142 N.W. 2d 66 (Minnesota)]; and *Hastings* v. *Hastings* [33 N.J. 274]. Suits by the parent against the child have been dismissed in *Schneider* v. *Schneider* [152 Atl. 498 (Maryland)], and in *Shaker* v. *Shaker* [29 Atl. 2d 765 (Connecticut)].

Other courts have held that in cases involving intrafamily immunity the question of liability insurance should not be considered. See *Tucker* v. *Tucker* [395 Pac. 2d 67 (Oklahoma)], and *Rambo* v. *Rambo* [114 S.W. 2d 468 (Arkansas)].

413　Immunity of charitable institutions

A charity is an institution, corporation, organization, or association which freely and voluntarily administers to the physical needs of those pecuniarily unable to help themselves. This would include schools, hospitals, churches, rescue missions, goodwill industries, and organizations of like kind and character, which are supported entirely by gifts in the form of actual donations from the public or bequests by will.

At common law all charitable organizations enjoyed complete immunity from liability in tort. There were two reasons given for the establishment of this doctrine: the *trust fund theory*, and the *quasi-governmental theory*.

Under the trust fund theory, the courts reasoned that where a gift or bequest by will was made to the charity, the donor or the testator affixed by implication that the gift was made on the condition that the money so donated would be devoted entirely to the charitable purpose. Therefore, the charity held all such money received in trust, and the money could be only expended for the charitable purpose and no other. Should the charity breach the condition and utilize this money for a purpose other than a charitable purpose, the donor or the estate of the testator could conceivably recover the amount of the gift. (A condition is an absolute requirement, and if there is a breach of the condition, there is no gift.)

The courts reasoned that since the charity had no funds other than those received as a consequence of gifts, it had no right to utilize the gifts for the purpose of paying claims. Should the money be used to pay claims, the charity would be guilty of a breach of trust and answerable to the donor of the gift. The courts reasoned that they could not, in the exercise of the administration of justice, compel the commission of an act, namely a breach of trust, which is legally reprehensible. Therefore, the charity could not be compelled to respond in damages for a liability based on a tort.

The quasi-governmental theory is that in supplying the needs of indigent or poor people, the charity is actually assuming some of the responsibilities of government. Having done so with the consent of the government, the same immunity which would be available to the government, if it undertook this duty, would likewise be available to the charity. In any case, the result is the same, and at common law a charitable organization, institution, or corporation was immune from tort liability.

As liability insurance became available, some courts reasoned that the payment of premiums for liability insurance would not be a breach of trust and that such an expenditure could reasonably be considered as being made in furtherance of charitable purpose. Therefore, these courts have specifically repudiated the *charitable immunity* doctrine.

The courts in other states have taken the position that the charitable immunity doctrine will be applied to all cases where a cause of action is asserted by a beneficiary of the charity, but hold the charitable organization responsible for tort liability arising from the injury or damage to the person or property of a stranger. A stranger would mean a person who is not an object of the charity and who was injured as a result of the operations of the charity, such as a pedestrian injured by being struck by an ambulance or automobile operated by the charity.

Still other courts make a distinction between nonpaying and paying beneficiaries of the charity. This is usually found in the cases of hospitals, where certain patients are treated through the social service division of the hospital as charity cases, in which no payment is demanded or received, as opposed to patients who pay for the accommodations received in the very same hospital. As to the charitable beneficiaries, the charitable immunity doctrine is applied, and as between the paying patient and the hospital, the courts hold that the relationship is not one of a charitable institution to its beneficiary but rather a business organization to its customer. In the latter case, the charitable immunity doctrine has no application.

From these observations it can be seen that there is a wide diversity of opinion among the courts of the various states. It is a changing situation and the trend is generally toward the elimination of charitable immunity rather than its extension. As of the present time, the rulings in the various states where the question has been considered are as follows.

Alabama.   A charity is liable for damages in tort to the same extent as a private person or a private corporation. *Supreme Lodge L.O.M.* v. *Kenny*, 198 Ala. 332; *Alabama Baptist Hospital Board* v. *Carter*, 226 Ala. 109; *Tucker* v. *Mobile Infirmary Assoc.*, 191 Ala. 572.

Arizona.   A charity is liable in damages for torts to the same extent as a private person or a private corporation; earlier cases to the contrary have been overruled. *Ray* v. *Tucson Medical Center*, 72 Ariz. 22.

Arkansas.   Charities have complete immunity from tort liability. *Arkansas*

Midland R.R. Co. v. *Peerson,* 98 Ark. 399. Moreover, the immunity of charities from tort liability has been recognized by an Arkansas statute (Sec. 66–517) which provides that an injured person shall have a direct cause of action against the liability insurance carrier of any nonprofit organization not subject to suit for tort. *Michael* v. *St. Paul Mercury Indemnity Co.,* 92 Fed. Supp. 140.

California. A private charity is liable in damages for torts in the same way as a private person or corporation. It makes no difference whether the injury is sustained by a paying or a nonpaying beneficiary. *Malloy* v. *Fong,* 37 Cal. 2d 356; *Muskopf* v. *Corning Hospital Dist.,* 359 Pac. 2d 457.

Colorado. The fact that the defendant is a charitable institution does not, of itself, prevent the plaintiff from maintaining an action in tort, irrespective of whether the injured person is a stranger or a beneficiary. *St. Luke's Hospital Assoc.* v. *Long,* 240 Pac. 2d 917; *St. Mary's Academy* v. *Solomon,* 77 Colo. 463.

Connecticut. Charitable immunity abolished by statute. Public Acts, 1967, p. 66.

Delaware. A charitable corporation is liable in damages for tort to the same extent as a private individual or corporation would be. *Durney* v. *St. Francis Hospital,* 83 Atl. 2d 753.

District of Columbia. Charitable corporations are responsible for the negligence of their servants causing injury to strangers, and it is believed that the same rule applies where a servant of a charity is the victim of its negligence. It is also indicated that the District would follow the rule that the charitable corporation is liable for its negligence in the selection and retention of servants. *President & Directors of Georgetown College* v. *Hughes,* 76 App. D.C. 123, 130 Fed. 2d 810; *White* v. *Providence Hospital,* 80 Fed. Supp. 76.

Florida. A charitable institution has no immunity for injuries sustained by a paying person. *Suwannee County Hospital* v. *Golden,* 56 So. 2d 911; *Nicholson* v. *Good Samaritan Hospital,* 145, Fla. 360.

There has been no ruling in this state as to the liability of the charitable corporation to a beneficiary of its service, but the indications are that Florida will follow the general trend toward imposing liability, rather than granting immunity.

Georgia. Aside from negligence in the selection or retention of personnel, a charity is generally immune from liability in tort. *Morton* v. *Savannah Hospital,* 148 Ga. 348; *Burgess* v. *James,* 73 Ga. 857; *Bailey* v. *YMCA,* 130 S.E. 2d 242.

Idaho. A charitable hospital is exempt from liability for injuries sustained by a paying patient. *Wilcox* v. *Idaho Falls Hospital,* 59 Idaho 350. (On the basis of this decision, it would appear that the charitable immunity doctrine would extend to cases involving servants, beneficiaries, or strangers.)

Illinois. A charity may be sued in tort. However, it has been held that the charity trust fund cannot be reached to satisfy the judgment, but its nontrust assets can be reached. *Marabia* v. *Mary Thompson Hospital,* 309 Ill. 147; *Fairall* v. *St. Mary's Hospital,* 187 N.E. 2d 15. Liability insurance has been held to be a nontrust asset. *Moore* v. *Moile,* 405 Ill. 555. See also, *Molitor* v. *Kaneland Community District No. 302;* 163 N.E. 2d 89.

Indiana. Grants no immunity. *Harris* v. *YWCA,* 237 N.E. 2d 242; *Ball Memorial Hospital* v. *Freeman,* 196 N.E. 2d 274. Prior decisions held that a charitable institution is liable for torts committed against a stranger. It has been held immune from liability for torts committeed against a beneficiary, including paying patients, unless it failed to exercise reasonable care in the selection of employees. *Winona Technical Institute* v. *Slolpe*, 173 Ind. 39; *Old Folks and Orphan Children's Home* v. *Roberts*, 83 Ind. App. 546; *St. Vincent's Hospital* v. *Stine*, 195 Ind. 350. The Harris and Ball decisions seem to overrule the cases granting immunity.

Iowa.   Charitable organizations are liable for damages in tort to the same extent as private persons and private corporations. *Haynes* v. *Presbyterian Hospital Assn.*, 241 Iowa 1269; *Sullivan* v. *First Presbyterian Church*, 152 N.E. 2d 628.

Kansas.   Charities have complete immunity from tort liability. *Davin* v. *Kansas Med. Assoc.*, 103 Kan. 48.

Kentucky.   A charitable institution is liable in tort, and the doctrine of *respondent superior* applies, regardless of whether the person negligently injured is a paying or nonpaying patient. *Mullikin* v. *Jewish Hospital Assn.*, 348 S.W. 2d 930.

Louisiana.   Grants no immunity as to strangers, but charities do have immunity as to beneficiaries. *Bougon* v. *Volunteers of America*, 151 So. 797; *Lusk* v. *U.S.F. & G. Co.*, 199 So. 666.

Maine.   The only case on this subject is not very recent. It follows the doctrine of complete immunity. *Jenson* v. *Maine Eye & Ear Infirmary*, 107 Me. 408. However, in 1965, Maine enacted a statute which in essence provides that a charitable organization shall be considered to have waived its immunity from liability for negligence or any other tort during the period a policy of insurance is effective covering the liability of the charitable organization for negligence or any other tort. Each policy issued to a charitable organization shall contain a provision to the effect that the insurer shall be estopped from asserting, as a defense to any claim covered by said policy, that such organization is immune from liability on the ground that it is a charitable organization. The amount of damages in any such case shall not exceed the limits of coverage specified in the policy, and the courts shall abate any verdict in any such action to the extent that it exceeds such policy limit. RS. Title 14, Sec. 156.

Maryland.   Immunity doctrine abolished by statute. Maryland Code Annotated, Sec. 566A.

Massachusetts.   Grants no charitable immunity. *Colby* v. *Carney Hospital*, 254 N.E. 2d 407.

Michigan.   A charitable corporation has no immunity with respect to torts committed against a stranger. *Bruce* v. *Central Methodist Episcopal Church*, 147 Mich. 230. A charitable institution has immunity against claims by those who are the recipients of its bounty. *DeGroot* v. *Edison Institute*, 306 Mich. 339; *Parker* v. *Port Huron Hospital*, 361 Mich. 28; *Greatrex* v. *Evangelical Hospital*, 246 N.W. 137.

Minnesota.   Grants no immunity to charitable institutions for the negligence of their officers or employees. *Mulliner* v. *Evangelischer Diakonniessenderein*, 144 Minn. 392; *Moeller* v. *Hauser*, 54 N.W. 2d 639.

Mississippi.   Grants no immunity to charitable organizations. *Mississippi Baptist Hospital* v. *Holmes*, 55 So. 2d 142; *Rhodes* v. *Millsaps College*, 176 So. 2d 253.

Missouri.   Charitable immunity doctrine abolished. *Abernathy* v. *Sisters of St. Mary's*, 446 S.W. 2d 599.

Nebraska. No immunity. *Meyers* v. *Drozda*, 141 N.W. 2d 852.

Nevada. Generally grants qualified immunity, with immunity applicable to claims of beneficiaries. *Springer* v. *Federated Church*, 283 Pac. 2d 1071. It has been held that a YMCA member who paid only nominal dues could recover because of injuries sustained as a result of a gymnasium defect. *Bruce* v. *YMCA*, 51 Nev. 372.

New Hampshire. Grants no immunity whatsoever. *Welch* v. *Frisbie Memorial Hospital*, 90 N.H. 337; *Hewett* v. *Workmen's Hospital*, 73 N.H. 556.

New Jersey. No immunity to charitable hospitals for injuries to a beneficiary. *Callopy* v. *Newark Eye & Ear Infirmary*, 141 Atl. 2d 276. See N.J. Immunity statute 2A:53A–7 *et seq.* As to other charities, grants immunity as to beneficiaries. *Peacock* v. *Burlington County Historical Soc.*, 230 Atl. 2d 513; *Makar* v. *St. Nicholas Greek Catholic Church*, 187 Atl. 2d 353. No immunity as to strangers. *Mayer* v. *Fairlawn Jewish Center*, 186 Atl. 2d 274.

New York. Grants no immunity against claims of strangers, servants, or beneficiaries. *Kellogg* v. *Church Charity Foundation*, 203 N.Y. 191; *Sheehan* v. *No. Community Hospital*, 273 N.Y. 163.

Also holds a charitable hospital liable for medical negligence. *Bing* v. *Thunig*, 143 N.E. 2d 3.

North Carolina. Charitable immunity abolished. *Rabon* v. *Rowan Memorial Hospital*, 152 S.E. 2d 852.

North Dakota. Grants no immunity for tort liability. *Rickbeil* v. *Grafton Hospital*, 74 N.D. 525.

Ohio. Grants no immunity from liability for torts committed against a stranger or a servant of the charity. *Sisters of Charity* v. *Duvelius*, 123 Ohio State 52.

No immunity as regards injuries sustained by a beneficiary as a result of the charity's negligence in selecting and retaining employees, but it is otherwise not liable for the negligence of its employees. *Taylor* v. *Flower Deaconess Home*, 105 Ohio State 61.

Institutions other than hospitals have immunity as to beneficiaries except where there is negligence in the selection and retention of employees. *Gibbon* v. *YWCA*, 170 Ohio State 280.

No immunity as to noncharitable activities. *Blankenship* v. *Alter*, 167 N.E. 2d 922; *Pearlstein* v. *A. M. McGregor Home*, 73 N.E. 2d 106. The fact that the charity carries liability insurance is in no way construed as affecting its liability. *Avellone* v. *St. John's Hospital*, 104 Ohio State 274.

Oklahoma. The question is unsettled, but the trend would seem to be toward a denial of immunity on account of the defendant's character as a charity. See *Gable* v. *Salvation Army*, 186 Okla. 587. Immunity of hospitals against claims by paying patients was denied in *Sisters of Sorrow* v. *Zeidler*, 183 Okla. 454.

Oregon. Grants no immunity. Immunity doctrine was abrogated in *Hungerford* v. *Portland Sanitarium & Benevolent Assn.*, 384 Pac. 2d 1009.

Pennsylvania. Grants no immunity. The doctrine to which Pennsylvania subscribed for many years was finally abrogated in *Flagiello* v. *Pennsylvania Hospital*, 208 Atl. 2d 193. See also, *Nolan* v. *Tifereth Synagogue*, 227 Atl. 2d 675.

Rhode Island. Grants no immunity. *Glavin* v. *R.I. Hospital*, 12 R.I. 411; *Basafo* v. *Salvation Army*, 35 R.I. 22. However, in 1938, Rhode Island enacted a statute which provided that no hospital incorporated in Rhode Island by the General Assembly, sustained in whole or in part by charitable contributions, shall be liable for neglect, carelessness, or want of skill, or for the malicious acts of any of its officers, agents, or employees in the management of, or in the care of treatment of any patients or inmates of such hospital.

South Carolina. Grants complete immunity irrespective of whether the victim is a stranger or a beneficiary. *Linder* v. *Columbia Hospital,* 98 S.C. 25; *Vermittion* v. *Women's College,* 104 S.C. 197.

Tennessee. The only immunity accorded to a charity is that such of its property as is used exclusively for charitable purposes is exempt from execution under a judgment rendered against it as a result of an action in tort. *McLeod* v. *St. Thomas Hospital,* 170 Tenn. 423.

The rule of immunity extends no further than the protection of the trust property of the charitable institution and the prevention of its being diverted from the purposes of the charity to the satisfaction of tort liability judgments. *O'Quinn* v. *Baptist Memorial Hospital,* 184 Tenn. 570.

Where a charity carries liability insurance, such insurance is not trust property of the institution and may be appropriated to the satisfaction of the tort judgment. *McLeod* v. *St. Thomas Hospital, supra.*

Texas. Charity is liable to employees, but is not liable to beneficiaries of the charity, providing it was not negligent in hiring or keeping an agent who proximately causes the injuries. *Southern Methodist Hospital* v. *Clayton,* 176 S.W. 2d 749. In *Watkins* v. *Southcrest Baptist Church,* 399 S.W. 2d 530, the court indicated that it would abolish the doctrine prospectively as to future cases if the legislature did not act in the meantime. See also *Villareal* v. *Santa Rosa Medical Center,* 443 S.W. 2d 622, wherein an appellate court abolished the immunity doctrine as being inapplicable to a paying patient.

Utah. Grants no immunity. The charity is liable in damages to the same extent and in the same manner as any private individual or corporation. *Sessions* v. *Thomas B. Dee Memorial Hospital,* 94 Utah 460.

Vermont. Grants no immunity. *Foster v. Roman Catholic Diocese,* 116 Vt. 124.

Virginia. A charitable institution has no immunity from liability for torts committed against a stranger. *Hospital of St. Vincent* v. *Thompson,* 166 Va. 101. A charitable hospital is liable to its patients for negligence in the selection and retention of its servants, but it is immune from liability for torts committed against the patient by its employees and by agents which were selected with due care. *Norfolk Protestant Hospital* v. *Plunkett,* 162 Va. 151; *Weston* v. *Hospital of St. Vincent,* 131 Va. 587; *Hill* v. *Leigh Memorial Hospital,* 132 S.E. 2d 411.

Washington. The charity has no immunity with regard to its liability to strangers, beneficiaries, or employees. *Pierce* v. *Yakima Valley Memorial Hospital Assn.,* 260 Pac. 2d 765. See also, *Friend* v. *Cove Methodist Church, Inc.,* 396 Pac. 2d 546.

West Virginia. Grants no immunity. *Adkins* v. *St. Francis Hospital of Charleston,* 143 S.E. 2d 154.

Wisconsin. No immunity. *Kojis* v. *Doctor's Hospital,* 107 N.W. 2d 131.

Wyoming. Grants no immunity. *Lutheran Hospital* v. *Yepsen,* 469 Pac. 2d 409.

In New Mexico and South Dakota, there are no reported cases on this subject. In Montana, there is a federal court decision in which the Federal District Court held that in absence of a controlling precedent by the state supreme court, it would follow the trend of modern authorities and permit a patient to maintain an action in tort against a hospital, notwithstanding the latter's claim of immunity as a charitable institution. [*Howard* v. *Sisters of Charity*, 33 Auto. Cas. 2d (CCH) 1111.]

414 Noncharitable activities

Even in states which subscribe to the charitable immunity doctrine, the cases generally hold that the charity is not entitled to immunity when engaged in any noncharitable function. The charity must respond in those cases in exactly the same manner as any other person or corporation conducting a business enterprise. The following are illustrative examples of cases wherein the activity engaged in was entirely disassociated from the charitable purpose.

Church conducting a public bingo game. Blankenship v. *Altar*, 167 N.E. 2d 922 (Ohio).

Plaintiff injured while leaving a church's premises after participating in an illegal bingo game. *Mannings* v. *Noa*, 76 N.W. 2d 75 (Michigan).

Customer in store maintained by the Salvation Army. *Berube* v. *Salvation Army*, 157 Atl. 2d 493 (Connecticut). Defendant, a charitable organization founded to maintain a living place for aged women, rented the entire office space in an office building it owned to tenants, using the entire profits to operate the home for the aged, located elsewhere. Plaintiff, an invitee of one of the tenants in the office building, was injured while using a common stairway negligently maintained in the building. It was held that use of the net profits from the operation of a commercial building in support of the charity's principal function did not entitle the charity to immunity from liability for injuries resulting from negligent maintenance. *Blatt* v. *George H. Nettleton Home for Aged Women*, 275 S.W. 2d 344 (Missouri).

Selling merchandise in a store to raise money did not entitle the charity to the defense of immunity. *McKay* v. *Morgan Corp.*, 272 Mass. 121.

Negligent operation of an elevator in an educational institution did not warrant the imposition of charitable immunity. *Roads* v. *Millsaps College*, 179 Mass. 596.

The charity operated an apartment house, the proceeds and profits thereof being devoted entirely to the charitable purpose. It was held that in the operation of the apartment house the charity must respond in damages for its tort liability the same as any private person or corporation, and that the immunity defense would not be available. *Pearlstein* v. *A. McGregor Home*, 73 N.E. 2d 106 (Ohio).

415 Governmental immunity

Sovereign immunity is a rule which we inherited from the English common law. It came into existence at a time when England was under the feudal system and when all of the powers of government were exercised only by the king. The king created, amended, or repealed the laws which he had made by his every act and deed. Therefore, all of the king's conduct was bound to be lawful, and hence the expression "The king can do no wrong."

It was possible, however, for the king to establish a law which would have retroactive effect and which, conceivably, could condemn as unlawful some prior act of the king himself. Where such a situation obtained, it would seem that a subject injured as a result of the king's prior unlawful act would have a cause of action against the king in damages. The king, however, as an absolute monarch, was not accountable to his subjects and could be sued even in this situation only if he gave his consent. The king was therefore immune from suit, even for damages caused by his own wrongful acts, unless he consented to be sued.

We adopted this rule, and substituted for the king the various sovereign states and the federal government. These political entities cannot be sued in tort without their consent, even where the act causing the injury is in violation of the law of the state itself. The state and the federal government occupy exactly the same position with relation to the citizens of this country that the king occupied with relation to his subjects. Like the king, the state and the federal government can consent to be sued. This can be done in a specific case or can be done on an overall basis. In most states there are court of claims acts wherein the sovereign has consented to be sued, and actions may be brought within the limitations of those statutes. The same thing is true with respect to the federal government in that it has enacted the Federal Tort Claims Act.

416   Proprietary functions of government

In the complexities of modern-day living, frequently the government, the state, or a political subdivision thereof will engage in what would normally be considered a business activity. A municipality may supply gas, water, and electricity to the residents, or it may maintain a swimming pool, skating rink, athletic stadium, or theater. When the government functions in a business area, it is not performing functions reserved exclusively to the government but is in an area which could be occupied by a private corporation. When this occurs, the function is referred to as a proprietary as opposed to a governmental function, which only the government can perform.

In the case of a governmental function, the sovereign, or a representative thereof, in the form of a political subdivision, can be sued in tort only with its consent. With respect to proprietary functions, the government is in the same status as a private individual or corporation and may be sued in exactly the same way as a private individual or corporation may be sued. There is no governmental immunity which shields the government from its liability while engaged in a proprietary function.

It is sometimes difficult to draw the line between what functions could be considered governmental, in which the immunity will attach, and those which would be considered proprietary, and in which no immunity defense is available. The general rule is that if the function undertaken by the government is one which could be performed by a private person or private corporation, then the function is proprietary. On the other hand, if the function is one which only the government may perform, and which cannot be performed by a private individual or corporation, then the function is governmental and the immunity defense will be available.

For example, the planning of a municipal sewer system is a governmental function. Only the government can plan and lay out the details of a sewer system which will utilize city property and provide for the disposal of waste. The actual construction of the sewer is a proprietary function if done by the city, since a private contractor could build it just as well. For that reason, the city then is in a business area when it builds a sewer, and in a governmental area when it plans the sewer.

As a further illustration: The regulation of traffic is a governmental function and no private corporation can exercise this function. The city can and does erect traffic controls in the form of traffic lights and other devices for the regulation of traffic. But the maintenance of the traffic light or the stop sign is a function which can be performed by a private individual or corporation. Therefore, if the municipality or the state undertakes this duty it is operating in a business area, and this is construed to be a proprietary function. The same rules would apply to streets and sidewalks. Only the governmental unit can plan the location of streets and sidewalks. Once planned, a private corporation can build and maintain them. Therefore, the building and maintenance of streets and sidewalks is a proprietary function when performed by a governmental entity.

The following activities have been held to be proprietary and not subject to the immunity doctrine.

Swimming pools. *Weeks* v. *City of Newark*, 162 Atl. 2d 341 (New Jersey).

Skating rinks. *Flowers* v. *Board of Commissioners*, 168 N.E. 2d 224 (Indiana).

Municipal garage. *Dallas* v. *City of St. Louis*, 338 S.W. 2d 39 (Missouri).

City hospitals. *Stolp* v. *City of Arkansas City*, 310 Pac. 2d 888 (Kansas). It should be noted, however, that this is not the universal rule. Most states hold that the operation of a city-owned hospital is a governmental function.

State-owned railroads. *People* v. *Superior Court*, 178 Pac. 2d 1 (California).

State fairs. *Guidi* v. *State*, 362 Pac. 2d 3 (California).

Summer recreational programs. School district conducting of summer recreational programs, which it was not required by statute to do and which were open to the public upon the payment of a fee, was held to be a proprietary function. *Morris* v. *School District*, 144 Atl. 2d 733 (Pennsylvania).

Turnpike commissions. These were held to be a separate instrumentality from the state, and hence are not clothed with immunity in the performance of any of its functions. It would seem that a turnpike authority would be exercising a governmental authority in planning and laying out the plans and specifications for the construction of a turnpike. The maintenance of the turnpike, if done by the state, would be a proprietary function, and therefore there would be no immunity. However, in the only two cases that have been decided, the courts have both held that the turnpike authority is a separate instrumentality which functions independently of the state even though created by it, and does not succeed to any of the rights of immunity which might be afforded to the state. *Gerr* v. *Ernick*, 283 Fed. 2d 293 (3d Cir. Pennsylvania), and *Hoffmeyer* v. *Ohio Turnpike Commission*, 166 N.E. 2d 543 (Ohio).

There are some cases in which the performance of one act will represent concurrently the exercise of a governmental function and a proprietary one. If such be the case, the courts generally require that the government respond in damages because of the proprietary aspect of the act. For example, in a Texas case, the client was injured when she slipped on fresh paint which the city had applied to the street in marking off parking meter stalls. It had failed to erect any signs warning the public of the wet paint. It was held that while the regulation of traffic was a governmental function whose negligent performance would not expose the city to liability, the maintenance of the streets in a reasonably safe condition was an element of the proprietary function of the city. Therefore, a recovery was allowed on the basis of the failure of the city to meet its duties with respect to the maintenance of the street. [*City of Austin v. Daniels,* 335 S.W. 2d 753.]

417   Limitations of the governmental immunity defense

The sovereign immunity defense has come in for some harsh criticism over the years mainly because there seemed to be no logic to a legal system which compensated innocent victims who had been injured as a result of the tortious conduct of others, but denied relief to the same victims if the tortious conduct was committed by the government or a political subdivision thereof. Consequently a number of states enacted statutes which either abolished the defense of immunity or severely limited its application. These states are Hawaii, Iowa, New York, Oklahoma, Oregon, Utah, and Washington. The application of the defense has been modified in Connecticut, South Carolina and Texas.

In addition to these statutes where there is statutory authority for the purchase of insurance by the governmental units, some courts hold that the purchase of insurance constitutes a waiver of governmental immunity to the extent of the insurance actually secured. The following states adhere to this theory:

Georgia	Missouri	North Carolina	Vermont
Kansas	Montana	North Dakota	West Virginia
Maine	New Hampshire	Ohio	Wyoming
Mississippi	New Mexico	Tennessee	

Since the doctrine of sovereign immunity is a creature of the courts, they are at liberty to reject the doctrine at any time. In the following cases the courts have reconsidered the doctrine and have expressly renounced it. While holding that the functions involved in each case were governmental in character, it was concluded that there was no further reason for the application of the doctrine in view of present-day conditions:

Alaska	*City of Fairbanks* v. *Schaible,* 375 Pac. 2d 201; *Scheele* v. *City of Anchorage,* 385 Pac. 2d 582.
Arkansas	*Parrish* v. *Pitts,* 429 S.W. 2d 45.
Arizona	*Stone* v. *Arizona Highway Comm.,* 381 Pac. 2d 107; *Veach* v. *City of Phoenix,* 427 Pac. 2d 335.
California	*Muskopf* v. *Corning Hosp. Dist.,* 359 Pac. 2d 457.

Colorado	*Evans* v. *Bd. of Commrs.*, 482 Pac. 2d 969; *Flourney* v. *School Dist. No 1*, 482 Pac. 2d 966.
District of Columbia	*Spencer* v. *General Hosp.*, 425 Fed. 2d 479; *Harbin* v. *Dist. of Col.*, 336 Fed. 2d 950.
Florida	*Hargrove* v. *Town of Cocoa Beach*, 96 So. 2d 130.
Idaho	*Smith* v. *State*, 473 Pac. 2d 937.
Illinois	*Molitor* v. *Kaneland Community District No. 302*, 163 N.E. 2d 89; *Harvey* v. *Clyde Park Dist.*, 203 N.E. 2d 573.
Indiana	*Klepinger* v. *Bd of Commrs.*, 239 N.E. 2d 160; *Brinkman* v. *City of Indianapolis*, 231 N.E. 2d 169.
Kentucky	*Haney* v. *City of Lexington*, 386 S.W. 2d 738.
Louisiana	*Board* v. *Splendor S. & E. Co.*, 273 So. 2d 19.
Michigan	*Williams* v. *City of Detroit*, 111 N.W. 2d 1.
Minnesota	*Spanel* v. *Mounds View School Dist.*, 118 N.W. 2d 795.
Nebraska	*Brown* v. *City of Omaha*, 160 N.W. 2d 805; *Johnson* v. *University*, 169 N.W. 2d 286.
Nevada	*Rice* v. *Clark County*, 382 Pac. 2d 605.
New Jersey	*Willis* v. *Dept. of Conservation*, 264 Atl. 2d 34.
Pennsylvania	*Ayala* v. *Phila Bd. of Ed.*, 305 Atl. 2d 877.
Rhode Island	*Becker* v. *Beaudoin*, 261 Atl. 2d 896.
Washington	*Kelso* v. *City of Tacoma*, 390 Pac. 2d 2; *Hosca* v. *City of Seattle*, 393 Pac. 2d 967.
Wisconsin	*Holytz* v. *City of Milwaukee*, 115 N.W. 2d 618.

It should be emphasized that the sovereign immunity doctrine, where applied, is available only to the governmental body against whom a claim is asserted; this immunity is not a defense to an action against a public officer based upon his own negligence. A public officer or governmental agent is responsible for any injury or damage caused by his negligence, whether in the scope of employment or not. The immunity which the government enjoys does not include its agents and employees. They are personally liable for the results of their own negligence just as any other private person, whether the acts complained of were committed within the scope of authority and in the course of employment or not.

Effect of insurance. It sometimes happens that a government unit will purchase liability insurance either voluntarily or under the authorization or compulsion of a statute. The problem in all cases is whether or not the government unit by the purchase of insurance has thereby waived its governmental immunity. There are five variations of circumstances under which the insurance may be purchased, and the answer to the question as to whether or not immunity has been waived will depend upon which of the five categories are involved. The classifications are: (1) voluntary purchase, (2) purchase authorized by legislative enactment, (3) purchase authorized by legislative enactment with no express waiver contained in the statute, (4) waiver to the extent of the insurance purchased, and (5) mandatory purchase of insurance.

1. *Voluntary purchase.* It is the general rule in the majority of states that voluntary procurement of liability insurance by a government subdivision

does not waive that unit's immunity from suit because, as it is generally stated, the power to waive such immunity lies with the legislature of each state, not with the department or the department head. Cases enunciating this rule are: *Holland* v. *Western Airlines, Inc.* [154 Fed. Supp. 457]; *Taylor* v. *State* [311 Pac. 2d 733 (Nevada)]; *Wallace* v. *Laurel County Bd. of Ed.* [153 S.W. 2d 915 (Kentucky)]; *Kesman* v. *School District of Fallowfield Tp.* [29 Atl. 2d 17, 68 ALR 2d 1445 (Pennsylvania)].

2. *Authorized purchase.* Where there is merely a statute which authorizes the purchase of insurance in the discretion of the governmental unit, the cases hold that there is a continuation of immunity notwithstanding the authorization and the actual purchase of insurance. The cases are:

Georgia	*Ware County* v. *Cason*, 5 S.E. 2d 597.
New Mexico	*Livingston* v. *Regents*, 328 Pac. 2d 78.
North Carolina	*Stephenson* v. *City of Raleigh*, 59 S.E. 2d 195.

3. *Authorized purchase with no express waiver.* This category might seem to overlap and be a part of number 2, but in all of the cases, the court made specific reference to the fact that the legislation did not contain an express waiver, and under those circumstances held that the procurement of insurance against tort liability as authorized by the statute did not require the conclusion that the unit's immunity from liability had been abrogated in whole or in part. The cases so holding are:

Idaho	*Pigg* v. *Brockman*, 314 Pac. 2d 609.
Indiana	*Hummer* v. *School of Hartford City*, 112 N.E. 2d 891.
Iowa	*McGrath* v. *City of Bettendorf*, 85 N.W. 2d 616.

4. *Waiver to the extent of insurance purchased.* Cases in this category hold that where the government unit is authorized to purchase insurance, the otherwise existing immunity of that unit is removed to the extent that the liability insurance protects the unit. This would seem to be the more logical view, and it is the conclusion reached by an expanding line of authority. In the other categories, as far as the performance of a governmental function is concerned, the government unit had no liability because of its immunity, and therefore the insurance so purchased would seem to be of doubtful value. Cases in this category are:

Illinois	*Molitor* v. *Kaneland Community District, No. 302,* 163 N.E. 2d 89.
Oregon	*Vendrell* v. *School Dist.*, 360 Pac. 2d 282.
Tennessee	*Wilson* v. *Maury County Bd. of Ed.*, 302 S.W. 2d 502; *City of Kingsport* v. *Lane*, 243 S.W. 2d 289.
Wyoming	*Maffai* v. *Town of Kemmerer*, 338 Pac. 2d 808.

5. *Mandatory purchase of insurance.* Some states have by statute required that certain government units carry liability insurance with certain stated limits. The units usually are school districts operating school buses, and other types of service where the risk of injury is high. The problem then posed is whether or not the requirement that insurance be carried is indicative of the

legislative intent to abrogate the governmental immunity as to that particular unit where there is no express waiver of immunity in the statute. The general rule is that where the statute requires that insurance be carried, the immunity has been waived at least to the extent of the limits of insurance. In *Longpre* v. *Joint School District No. 2,* 443 Pac. 2d 1 (Montana)], the court said:

Since it is clear that the liability insurance, which section 75–3406, R.C.M. 1947, requires school districts to carry, was meant to cover injuries arising from the operation of school buses, this court fails to see how it can be argued that the Legislature would require insurance to be carried and then deny any means of recovery to an individual injured in connection with the operation of a school bus. We do not think that the Legislature would, on the one side, require school districts to purchase liability insurance, and then on the other side, deny any means of recovery to one injured, otherwise the Legislature would simply have meant to enrich insurance companies. This cannot be.

In the present case, we hold that the . . . Assembly by requiring school districts to carry liability insurance, waived only to the extent of the insurance required or actually carried, the school district's immunity from suit.

Statutory immunity. There are situations in states where the courts have rejected the common-law doctrine of governmental immunity and where the legislature has reinstated the immunity defense by a specific statute. In such a case, regardless of whether insurance is carried, the statute will control, and the defense of immunity may be interposed as a complete bar to liability. See *Zapf* v. *Board of Chosen Freeholders* [209 Atl. 2d 660 (New Jersey)].

418 Governmental responsibility for riot and mob violence

In England, the community is answerable in damages for any injury or property damage caused by riot or mob violence, and this liability is imposed whether the local police are negligent in the performance of their duties or not. American courts have not adopted this rule. They have held that the maintenance of law and order is a governmental function, and, therefore, the immunity doctrine applies to the governmental unit charged with that responsibility. Because of this view, many municipalities, counties, and states have by legislation assumed the responsibility for damages arising out of riot and mob violence and have permitted recoveries under the statutory provisions where the state or political subdivision thereof has failed to provide the necessary police protection. In general, in the absence of specific legislation along these lines, claims for injury or damage as a result of mob violence and riot are not actionable.

419 Responsibility for streets and sidewalks

The state has the governmental authority to plan and lay out streets and sidewalks, and also the proprietary function of maintaining them. The state may delegate all of this authority to various political subdivisions of the state, such as counties, cities, and municipalities. Where such a delegation of authority takes place, the responsibility for the maintenance of the streets and sidewalks is that of the political subdivision alone. As to roads maintained by the state, the responsibility of the state remains. Since this is a proprietary function, the state or the governmental authority responsible for the maintenance of the streets and sidewalks may be sued in the regularly constituted courts, just as any other private individual or corporation.

The governmental authority responsible for the maintenance of streets and sidewalks is required to exercise due care for the safety of all persons privileged to use them. This duty of care consists of proper maintenance, the repair of any defects, and where the defect cannot be remedied immediately, the posting of adequate warning by means of signs, lights, barricades, and other protective devices. The governmental authority is only required to remedy such defects concerning which it has knowledge or which by the exercise of reasonable inspection it could discover. The mere presence of a defect is not enough. It must be shown that the authority had notice of the defect or that the defect had existed for such a period of time that reasonable inspection would have revealed its presence.

It would be virtually impossible for the governmental authority to maintain its streets and sidewalks in an absolutely level condition. There is bound to be some variation due to wear and the impact of extreme temperatures. Whether or not a condition is one which is defective and dangerous to the users of the highway or sidewalks is a question of fact for the jury, and they will be entitled to take into account its dimensions, the amount of depression, and also whether or not it is a condition that is open and obvious so as to be discoverable by the users of the facility.

In addition, the defense of contributory negligence is always available where the depression or defect is one which should be anticipated. If the depression is slight, the court could find the injured person guilty of contributory negligence as a matter of law. For example, in *Evans* v. *Batten* [138 S.E. 2d 213 (North Carolina)], there was an "indenture" in the defendant's walkway in a parking area which was the size and shape of a "shoe print" and was 9/16th of an inch deep. In sustaining the demurrer, the court said:

Slight depressions, unevenness and irregularities in outdoor walkways, sidewalks and streets are so common that their presence is to be anticipated by prudent persons.

As to whether or not a particular condition constitutes a defect, some courts have endeavored to establish an arbitrary rule taking a position, for example, as one court did, that a depression of 4 inches or more was a defect while any depression which was less than 4 inches was not. Arbitrary standards such as this have been considered by the highest courts of the state, and in each case the arbitrary standards have been rejected on the theory that whether or not a particular condition is a defect is a question of fact for the jury.

The duty of the governmental authority to maintain the streets will also extend to the proper maintenance of the shoulder of the highway and does require the authority to warn of any unsafe condition, such as a soft shoulder or other hazard which could make the use of the shoulder dangerous. In addition, where highway repairs are being undertaken, either by the governmental authority or by a private contractor, the duty of the governmental unit to maintain the highways in safe condition still remains, since the duty is nondelegable. For example, in *Beeman* v. *State of New York,* judgment was affirmed in favor of the plaintiff in his action for damage to his tractor and trailer when he was detoured on to a soft shoulder along the highway that was under repair, sank into the shoulder, turned, and went down an embankment. The court held that evidence of the state's failure to warn of the soft shoulder, and the state's failure to delineate the safe roadway to follow by the use of reflectorized stakes supported the plaintiff's claim of negligence on the part of the state.

It is customary where the state or the governmental unit having the responsibility for the maintenance of streets and sidewalks contracts with a private contractor for the reconstruction or repair of the street or sidewalk for the governmental unit to require a hold harmless agreement from the contractor by the terms of which the contractor agrees to protect the government unit from liability. The existence of this hold harmless agreement does not change the responsibility of the government unit, and claims may be brought against it. All the hold harmless agreement does is to provide the government unit with an indemnitor for its liability.

With respect to the private property owner, he is not responsible for the maintenance of the public street or sidewalk which abuts or adjoins his property, but he is responsible for any private walks, or driveway, or road on his own property. As to the public sidewalks and the public roads, these are responsibilities of the governmental authority, and even though the property owner is aware of an existing defect he has no responsibility to others who are injured as a result of its presence.

If the property owner himself should create an unsafe condition in the street or on the sidewalks, he is responsible for any injuries which occur as a result of its presence. He is required to remedy any defects or unsafe conditions which he himself created. If he fails to do so, and a pedestrian is injured because of the defect, he will be responsible to the pedestrian. If the defect is of such a nature that the government authority had notice of it or if it had existed for a sufficient period of time so as to spell out constructive notice on the part of the government authority, the injured person could sue both the landowner and the government authority as joint tort-feasors.

In some states, the abutting property owner owns the land to the center of the public street, subject to the public easement. An easement is a right of use. Therefore, the property owner can make any use of this land he sees fit, provided that he does not impair the right of the public to use it as a sidewalk or as a highway. For that reason, in many cities the landowner has excavated under the public sidewalk, extending his basement or other part of the building, and in addition has installed a sidewalk elevator or sidewalk doors for the purpose of access. In maintaining the sidewalk elevator or the sidewalk door, the property owner is required to exercise reasonable care for the safety of persons using the sidewalk, and he is responsible for any injuries which occur as a result of his failure to observe this duty. This same duty would apply to gratings, glass blocks, and other materials used to permit the access of light or air into the room under the sidewalk.

In some states and in some municipalities, there are laws or ordinances which require that a property owner keep any adjoining sidewalks in good repair. This does create a public duty and does make the property owner liable for the cost of the repair, but unless the statute specifically creates an obligation to respond in damages to a third person who may be injured as a result of the property owner's failure to repair a defect, there is no such obligation. The rule is stated in 63 CJS, Municipal Corporations, 861, p. 227, as follows:

Liability of an abutting owner or occupant for injuries to a traveler through failure to maintain a sidewalk in repair ordinarily will not grow out of statutes or ordinances requiring him to construct or repair sidewalks or merely declaring that a sidewalk in dangerous condition is a nuisance and unlawful; but such liability may be imposed by express statutory provision.

In a case where the abutting landowner or occupant is required to keep the sidewalk in repair and he fails to do so, with the result that the municipality is required to respond in damages to an injured person, such statute does not create a cause of action on the part of the municipality against the property owner to recover the amount that it has been compelled to pay to the injured person. In *Levendoski* v. *Geisenhaver* [134 N.W. 2d 228 (Michigan)], the court made this observation:

It is of some significance that in this case the ordinance permits immediate repair of the sidewalk by the city "to prevent the possibility of City liability for personal injury or property damage and does NOT provide that the city may sue the abutting property owner to recoup a claim it may have had to pay. Since the duty here imposed upon a property owner is to the city, which has the primary responsibility for the maintenance and control of its sidewalks as well as a liability to those injured by defective sidewalks, in the absence of an express (statutory) provision imposing liability on the property owner, there is none.

Therefore, when handling a case of this kind where there is a claim made against the abutting landowner by a traveler on the public sidewalk, the adjuster would be well advised to study the statute or ordinance (if there is one applicable) to ascertain whether or not it does specifically create a cause of action on behalf of the traveler against the abutting property owner. If it does not, then there is no liability.

420   Responsibility for snow and ice

The rules with respect to the proper maintenance and regard for the safety of those using the streets and sidewalks also apply to the hazards created by the presence of snow and ice. The governmental authority is required to use reasonable care to keep the streets and sidewalks in a safe condition. The matter of what would constitute reasonable care is dependent to a great extent upon the particular circumstances, the severity of the storm, say, as well as the question of whether or not the governmental authority had any notice of a particularly unsafe condition not of a general nature and failed to correct it. The authority cannot be required to keep all of the streets within its limits entirely free from snow and ice in cases where such snow and ice is present in the entire area. The authority is not required even to attempt to keep the streets and sidewalks free of snow during the progress of a storm, and it is generally held that there is no duty upon the authority to take any action until the storm has abated. The duty thereafter is only to remove the snow and ice at places where its presence constitutes a hazard or a dangerous condition, especially in those parts of the area where the streets and sidewalks receive the greatest public use.

Any recovery against the governmental authority would have to be based upon negligence. It is not an insurer of the safety of the traveling public privileged to use the streets or sidewalks. In order to make out a cause of action, the plaintiff would have to show that the failure of the authority to remove the ice amounted to actionable negligence. This would not mean that the authority has any particular duty to combat a general condition, but that it is under a duty to remedy unsafe conditions which, for example, might result from the overflow of sewers, or the accumulation of an unusual amount of water, or the failure of other drainage facilities to carry off the excess.

Even in these situations, it must be shown that ice, which accumulated as a result, actually constituted an unsafe condition in that there were substantial ridges and peaks in the ice which were of a sufficient size and were either rounded, jagged, or presented a distinct hazard which could not be anticipated by the person using the thoroughfare. In addition, the authority must have notice of the unsafe condition and a reasonable time within which to take corrective measures.

The question of whether or not the streets or sidewalks were in a defective or dangerous condition due to the accumulation of snow and ice is a question of fact for the jury, and even though the court can find as a matter of law that the claimant was contributorily negligent, when it comes to the question of the defective condition, this is a question entirely for the jury to decide.

As in the matter of the maintenance of the public sidewalk, we will find statutes or ordinances in some states which require that the abutting owner remove the snow and ice from the public sidewalk, and if he fails to do so that the municipality may do so at the expense of the owner. This does not create a cause of action on the part of an injured person against the property owner where the owner has failed to remove the snow. Just as in the case of the sidewalk defect, the statute or ordinance creates a public duty to the municipality on the part of the owner, but his failure to comply with such public duty does not make him liable to an injured pedestrian. The usual statute reads as follows:

No person shall permit any snow or ice to remain on the sidewalks in the front, rear or sides of any house owned by him longer than 24 hours after it has fallen or formed.

Where the property owner complies with the statute by attempting to remove the snow, but in so doing creates an unsafe condition or worsens the condition brought about by the snow, he is then liable to any person injured because of the unsafe condition which he created. For example, in *Foley* v. *Ulrich* [228 Atl. 2d 702 (New Jersey)], the plaintiff fell in front of the defendant's house. Plaintiff claimed that the defendant, in clearing the snow from the sidewalk, had shoveled the snow into mounds on either side of the walk. The sidewalk was a sloping walk, and it was contended that the creation of these mounds at a higher level was the cause of the icy condition due to which the claimant fell. In holding the landowner liable, the court stated the rule as follows:

The general common law rule applicable to this situation was that an owner had no duty to keep the sidewalk abutting his land free from the natural accumulations of snow and ice. The theory behind this rule was that a traveler should be expected to endure the ordinary hazards created by natural conditions, including ice formed by the natural accumulation of surface water. However, there was a necessary corollary to this rule, namely, a traveler should not be expected to assume responsibility for a peril which but for the conduct of the property owner would not have existed at all or not for the same length of time or degree. Thus, where the land owner, through his negligence, adds a new element of danger or hazard other than the one caused by the natural forces to the safe use of the sidewalk by the pedestrian, the land owner would be liable.

In these cases, the jury can find that there is no probability or certainty that had the snow remained unshoveled on the sidewalk the same condition would have been created, in which case there would be no liability on the part of the landowner. Therefore, the liability of the landowner will depend in a great measure upon the proof that the plaintiff is able to offer that the activity of the owner created a greater hazard than would have existed if he had done nothing. Clearly, there are obstacles in the way of the plaintiff's proof in that icy conditions seldom remain the same over an extended period of time, and as a result the plaintiff very often is confronted with an insurmountable problem in establishing the exact condition as it existed at the time of the accident.

In addition, if the abutting owner creates an unsafe condition himself, by depositing an unusual amount of water on the sidewalk by having a downspout drain on it, or by changing the level of his land so that an excessive amount of drainage water is deposited on the sidewalk, then the owner would be responsible for the dangerous condition thus created and would be answerable in damages for any injuries sustained as a result.

As to his own private sidewalk, driveway, or private road, the owner is responsible for their condition, and the degree of his responsibility will be governed by the status of the person lawfully using such facilities.

421 Nuisance as a basis of tort liability

A nuisance is defined as anything which is dangerous to health, is indecent or offensive to the senses, or an obstruction to the free use of property, so as to interfere with the comfortable enjoyment of life or property, or anything which unlawfully obstructs the free passage, or use in the customary manner, of any lake, river, square, street, or highway.

The question of whether or not a condition is a nuisance is determined by whether it will produce such a condition of things as, in the judgment of reasonable men, would naturally cause actual physical discomfort to persons of ordinary sensibilities, tastes, and habits. It arises from the unreasonable, uuwarranted, or, unlawful use by a person of his property, either real or personal, or from his own improper, indecent, or unlawful personal conduct, working an obstruction of or injury to the right of another, or of the public, and producing such material annoynance, inconvenience, discomfort, or injury that the law will presume resulting damages. The creator and maintainor of the nuisance is liable in tort to anyone injured as a result of its existence. It may consist of an unreasonable use of the public street or sidewalk so as to prevent others from using the street or sidewalk. Or it might consist of the production of noxious fumes which permeate the neighborhood and cause illness to persons or animals, destruction of growing crops, or otherwise interfere with the comfortable enjoyment of property.

The creator and the maintainor of the nuisance need not be the same person. The creator may be held liable after he has disposed of the premises, and the new owner may be held liable also for continuing to maintain the nuisance after he has acquired the premises. This liability will attach to both individuals, irrespective of when the accident or injury occurs.

The difference between the tort of negligence and that of nuisance is that, in nuisance, contributory negligence is not a defense. Proof that the nuisance exists, plus the injuries sustained as a result thereof, will make out a prima facie case. In a negligence action, it will be necessary to show that there was a duty on the part of the defendant, a breach of that duty, and damages as a proximate result thereof. To this the defendant can interpose the defense of contributory negligence. To an action for nuisance, there are only two general defenses: that the condition complained of is not a nuisance, or that the defendant did not create or maintain it.

422 Attractive nuisance doctrine

The rule is that a person who has an instrumentality, agency or condition upon his premises, or who creates such conditions on the premises of another, or in a public place, which may reasonably be apprehended to be a source of danger to children, is under the duty to take the precautions a reasonably prudent man would take to prevent injury to children of tender years whom he knows are accustomed to be there, or who may, by reason of something there which may be expected to attract them, come to play. It does not apply to natural conditions or common dangers existing in the order of nature; it applies in favor of children of tender years—too young to appreciate danger.

The doctrine had one of its origins in the famous *Turntable* case [*Sioux City R.R.* v. *Stout,* 17 Wall. (U.S.) 657], decided in 1873. The court upheld a recovery by a six-year-old trespassing boy, who lost his foot playing on the defendant's turntable. The rationale of the case was that the defendant knew or should have known that the turntable was dangerous to children and further that children played in the vicinity. The turntable was clearly visible from the place where the children normally played. The defendant was further charged with the knowledge that children, unable to appreciate the extent of the danger, would be attracted to the turntable. The defendant, therefore, was under a duty to protect the children from an unreasonable risk of harm created by the presence of the turntable. His failure to fence in the area, to erect warning signs, or, if necessary, to post a watchman to prevent access by children constituted negligence on his part and for which he was answerable in damages.

The original theory, as announced in *Keffe* v. *Milwaukee R.R. Co.* (21 Minn. 207), was that the defendant was liable because the child was enticed upon the premises by the condition created thereon by the defendant. Conversely, there was no liability if the child had not been attracted to the premises by the condition. (*United Zinc Co.* v. *Britt,* 258 U.S. 268.) From these decisions the rule of liability to children acquired the name of "attractive nuisance." This theory has now been generally rejected, and the more generally accepted rule is that the owner of premises has a duty of reasonable care not to maintain a dangerous condition on his land, the use of which could result in foreseeable harm to another; or where such a dangerous condition does exist, the owner has a special duty to trespassing children where he knows, or in the exercise of reasonable care should know, that they are likely to trespass on his premises. The fact that the child is a trespasser may be a fact to be considered, but the responsibility arises when the owner knows that children are likely to trespass. Therefore, he is under a duty to prevent the foreseeable harm to a child against which the child cannot be expected to protect himself.

The Restatement of the Law of Torts, Second, Section 339, states the rule as follows:

ARTIFICIAL CONDITIONS HIGHLY DANGEROUS TO TRESPASSING CHILDREN

A possessor of land is subject to liability for physical harm to children trespassing thereon caused by an artificial condition upon the land if

(a) the place where the condition exists is one upon which the possessor knows or has reason to know that children are likely to trespass, and

(b) the condition is one of which the possessor knows or has reason to know and which he realizes or should realize will involve an unreasonable risk of death or serious bodily harm to children, and (*c*) the children because of their youth do not discover the condition or realize the risk involved in intermeddling with it or coming within the area made dangerous by it, and

(*d*) the utility to the possessor of maintaining the condition and the burden of eliminating the danger are slight as compared with the risk to children involved, and

(*e*) the possessor fails to exercise reasonable care to eliminate the danger or otherwise protect the children.

It should be noted at the outset that this rule refers only to artificial conditions on the land and does not apply to natural conditions, regardless of how hazardous those natural conditions may be. The possessor of land (which would include within its terms not only the owner, but the occupier, such as a tenant) is not subject to liability if the injury is occasioned by a natural condition. Thus, where there is a swamp, pond, lake, stream, poisonous weeds, deceased trees, etc., on the land, the possessor is not liable for any injury sustained because of their presence.

The doctrine contemplates the existence of two basic elements: (1) a dangerous condition which involves an unreasonable risk of harm to trespassing children, and (2) the nature of children, who because of youth, are unable to recognize the existence of the peril.

1. Dangerous condition. Any structure or artificial condition on land could under certain circumstances present a danger to children, but the dangerous condition to which the rule refers is one which has a hidden peril which is not open and obvious to children. When a child is permitted to roam, it is contemplated that he is aware of certain hazards which are inherent in his activities, such as the danger presented by height, water, fire, etc. Comment (*j*) which followed the Restatement Rule makes the following observations:

There are many dangers, such as those of fire and water or falling from a height, which under ordinary conditions may reasonably be expected to be fully understood and appreciated by any child of an age to be allowed at large. To such conditions the rule stated in this Section ordinarily has no application, in absence of some other factor creating a special risk that the child will not avoid the danger, such as the fact that the condition is so hidden as not to be readily visible, or a distracting influence which makes it likely that the child will not discover and appreciate it.

Where, however, the possessor knows that children too young to appreciate such dangers are likely to trespass on his land, he may still be subject to liability to such children under the rule stated.

Thus, the decided cases turn on the question of whether or not the peril was one which the child could and should apprehend or one which children were likely to overlook. In *Senders* v. *Baird* [112 S.W. 2d 966 (Arkansas)], the court said:

If every instrumentality that is attractive to a venturesome boy and, also, has an element of danger about it constitutes an attractive nuisance then there is no limit to its application. Perils or dangers, such as exist from climbing, are obviously known to children who are old enough to be unattended and capable of venturesome conduct. Any child capable of climbing knows that if he falls from a fence, a tree or any elevated structure injury can result.

Water accidents. In *McCormick* v. *Williams* [397 Pac. 2d 393 (Kansas)], the case involved the drowning death of a six-year-old child in a backyard swimming pool. The court pointed out that the danger inherent in a swimming pool was patent rather than latent, and in denying a recovery, the court said:

Unfortunate as the accident to the child may be, a case must not be determined on sympathy rather than sound principles of law. A higher degree of care for the protection of the trespassing child should not be imposed on a property owner than is expected of a parent or custodian. Rules should not be adopted which, if carried to their logical conclusion, would make a property owner an insurer of a trespassing child against all injury. Such rules would make the ownership of property and modern conveniences well-nigh intolerable.

The majority of cases dealing with drowning in areas where there is an artificial accumulation of water, whether because of the construction of a swimming pool or otherwise, without any additional circumstances creating a greater duty, have been held not to involve the attractive nuisance doctrine. See *McGill* v. *City of Laurel* [173 So. 2d 892 (Mississippi)]; *Eades* v. *American Cast-Iron Pipe Co.* [94 So. 593 (Alabama)]; *Gilliland* v. *City of Topeka* [262 Pac. 2d 493 (Kansas)]; and *Newby* v. *West Palm Beach Water Co.* [47 So. 2d 527 (Florida)].

In the case of natural bodies of water on the land, the same rule of nonliability applies, except in cases where the landowner has created a greater hazard because of his activities thereon. If he does nothing more than to merely allow the condition to remain in its natural state, he is under no duty to anyone, including children, to take any precautions for their safety. For example, in *Ramundo* v. *Turi* [222 Atl. 2d 189 (New Jersey)], the action arose out of the drowning death of a 15-year-old boy in a pond located on the defendant's premises. The plaintiff contended that the defendant was required to fence in the pond or to keep children out because "there were numerous cold springs in the water which varied the temperature of the water so greatly that it adversely affected the swimming ability of anyone so using the pond." In dismissing the complaint, the court held that the defendant had no such duty, citing with approval the Restatement Rule.

Where in addition to the water hazard there is another condition created by the landowner which is dangerous to children, there may arise a special duty on the part of the landowner, which would compel the court to invoke the attractive nuisance doctrine. For example, in *Allen* v. *Wm. P. McDonald Corp.* [42 So. 2d 706 (Florida)], the defendant constructed spoil banks of white sand which sloped down to the water. A two-and-one-half-year-old child slid down the bank into the water and was drowned. The court held that the sand banks were not only an attractive nuisance but also were the proximate cause of the child's death, causing him to fall into the water. In *Everett* v. *White* [140 S.E. 2d 582 (South Carolina)], the defendant maintained a construction site where children were accustomed to play with his consent. A child sustained injuries when he fell into an excavation practically filled with mud, water, slime, and debris, which gave the appearance of a mud puddle but which was actually quite deep. Recovery was allowed on the theory that the existence of the excavation constituted a hidden peril, which created a duty on the part of the defendant to protect the children from the unreasonable risk of harm which this condition presented. See also, *Long* v. *Standard Oil Co.* [207 Pac. 2d 837 (California)]; *Hankins* v. *Southern Foundation* [216 Fed. Supp. 554 (District of Columbia)]; *Cicero State Bank* v. *Dolese* [18 N.E. 2d 574 (Illinois)]; *Cooper* v. *Reading* [140 Atl. 2d 792 (Pennsylvania)]; *Williams* v. *Morristown* [222 S.W. 2d 607 (Tennessee)].

Climbing accidents. The same rules and the same court decisions as are applicable to water accidents apply equally to climbing accidents where the child is injured because of fall from a height. Children who are allowed to roam are generally aware of the dangers which are posed by the possibility of a fall from a height. Therefore, the landowner, who merely maintains a structure, tower, pole, scaffold, or a construction activity on his premises is under no duty to prevent children from climbing them, even though he is aware that trespassing children are likely to intrude on his premises. For example, in *Pardue* v. *City of Sweetwater* [390 S.W. 2d 683 (Tennessee),] the court held that a city was not liable for the injuries sustained by an 11-year-old boy who fell while climbing on the city's water tank. The doctrine of attractive nuisance did not apply, since the only danger present was that of falling, which was a danger easily recognizable by the child. To the same effect is *Crawford* v. *Cox Planing Mill & Lumber Co.* [383 S.W. 2d 291 (Arkansas)], where the court also held that the doctrine of attractive nuisance did not apply to a scaffold from which a child fell, since the scaffold itself was not a dangerous instrumentality and it embodied no perils not readily apparent to children who respond to their instinct for climbing. The following cases are illustrative of the same principle and recovery was denied in each instance:

Railroad overpass or similar structure	*McHugh* v. *Reading*, 30 Atl. 2d 122 (Pennsylvania).
	Hocking v. *Duluth R.R.*, 117 N.W. 2d 304 (Minnesota).
	Davis v. *Goodrich*, 340 Pac. 2d 48 (California).
	Schroeder v. *Texas & Pac.*, 243 S.W. 2d 261 (Texas).
	Berwert v. *Atchison R.R.*, 289 S.W. 2d 112 (Missouri).
	Fourseam Coal Co. v. *Greer*, 282 S.W. 2d 129 (Kentucky).
Retaining walls	*Hageage* v. *District of Columbia*, 42 App. D.C. 109 (District of Columbia).
	Coon v. *Kentucky R.R.*, 173 S.W. 325 (Kentucky).
	Kayser v. *Lindell*, 75 N.W. 1038 (Michigan).
	Kansas City v. *Eillison*, 220 S.W. 498 (Missouri).

Playground swing	*Gleason* v. *Pittsburgh*, 47 Atl. 2d 129 (Pennsylvania). *Severance* v. *Rose*, 311 Pac. 2d 866 (California).
Playground slide	*Cooper* v. *Pittsburgh*, 136 Atl. 2d 463 (Pennsylvania).
Roofs	*Williams* v. *Overly Mfg. Co.*, 34 Atl. 2d 52 (Pennsylvania).
	Coughlin v. *U.S. Tool Co.*, 145 Atl. 2d 483 (New Jersey).
	Prickett v. *Pardridge*, 189 Ill. App. 307 (Illinois).
	Brennan v. *Kaw Const. Co.*, 271 Pac. 2d 253 (Kansas).
Construction sites	*Neal* v. *Home Builders*, 111 N.E. 2d 280 (Indiana).
	State v. *Bealmear*, 130 Atl. 66 (Maryland).
	Labore v. *Davison Const. Co.*, 135 Atl. 2d 591 (New Hampshire).
	Miller v. *Guernsey Const. Co.*, 112 So. 2d 55 (Fla.).
Fences	*Brown* v. *City of Scranton*, 169 Atl. 435 (Pennsylvania).
Lumber pile	*Hunter* v. *Turner Lbr. Co.*, 187 Fed. Supp. 646 (Florida).
Scaffolds	*Lopez* v. *Capitol Co.*, 296 Pac. 2d 637 (California).
Fire	*Arkansas Valley Trust Co.* v. *McIlroy*, 133 S.W. 816 (Arkansas).
	McCall v. *McCallie*, 171 S.E. 843 (Georgia).
	McKiddy v. *Des Moines Elec. Co.*, 206 N.W. 815 (Iowa).
	Krystopowicz v. *Reading Co.*, 40 Pa. D&C 304 (Pennsylvania).
	Tiller v. *Baisden*, 35 S.E. 2d 728 (West Virginia).
	Brannon v. *Harmon*, 355 Pac. 2d 792 (Washington).

Conversely, the child is not expected to appreciate a danger presented or exaggerated by a defect in the structure or other peculiar circumstance, which is hidden from the child or which the child would fail to appreciate because of his immaturity. For example, in *Diglio* v. *Jersey Central Power & Light Co.* [120 Atl. 2d 650 (New Jersey)], the defendant erected a high woven-wire fence around its premises. It was topped with sharp spikes projecting upward, and suspended above the spikes were three strands of barbed wire. Horizontal crossbars between sections of the fence were so placed as to resemble a ladder. In spite of this fence, the defendant permitted children to play on its premises without molesting, warning, or even chasing them away. The plaintiff, a nine-year-old girl, while climbing the fence on the ladderlike crossbars, slipped and impulsively grabbed the sharply barbed wire. The court held that the condition was an attractive nuisance and that the defendant was liable for the reason that it maintained a dangerous condition which exposed the child to an unreasonable risk of harm.

In *Klingensmith* v. *Scioto Valley Traction Co.* (18 Ohio App. 290), the court held the doctrine applicable to a $16\frac{1}{2}$-year-old boy, who had climbed the defendant's steel electric tower, and was killed by a disruptive discharge or "burst" of electricity. The court observed that if the dead boy knew of the possibility that disruptive discharges from high-voltage wires, such as those on the tower, might cause death without contact with the wires, then he knew more of the qualities of electricity than any member of the court prior to the information obtained in the case. See also *Schorr* v. *Minnesota Utilities Co.*

[281 N.W. 523 (Minnesota)], which involved a 16-year-old boy electrocuted while playing with an electric cable and in which a recovery was allowed.

2. *The nature of children.* The age and mentality of the child are among the determining factors in deciding whether or not a particular condition is one which exposes the child to an unreasonable risk of harm. A condition which is dangerous to a child of 6 years because he is unable to appreciate the danger, might not be a dangerous condition to a 14-year-old. Therefore, as the child grows older, the number of conditions which could be regarded as dangerous will decline. It is for this reason that courts seldom apply the rule to children over the age of 14 unless the hazard which is posed by the instrumentality is so hidden that even a 14-year-old could not be expected to realize the danger. In any case, the courts have been reluctant to establish any arbitrary age limits for the application of the doctrine, but rather have compared the age and mental attainments of the child against the particular condition to determine whether or not the rule has any application.

Creation of the dangerous condition by other than the property owner. It is possible in some instances for a dangerous condition to be created by one other than the property owner. If the owner maintains the condition, he will be liable to the child just as if he had created the condition himself. In other cases, where the condition is created and maintained by one other than the property owner, then he could be held liable together with the property owner as joint tort-feasors. This situation usually comes about in connection with the maintenance of streets and highways where a contractor is allowed to store supplies, etc., on the shoulder or some other part of the public land.

Pied Piper cases. In at least two instances, successful attempts have been made to apply some of the principles of the attractive nuisance doctrine to vendors or hucksters who attract children of the street. In *Mackey* v. *Spradlin* [397 W.S. 2d 33 (Kentucky)], a seven-year-old boy was killed by a dump truck after buying ice cream from a vendor whose truck was parked on the street. The accident happened at night. The court held that the jury could find the vendor equally liable with the dump truck operator in causing the accident, since the vendor "knowingly provoked into action with natural recklessness of irresponsible children."

In *Vought* v. *Jones* [139 S.E. 2d 810 (Virginia)], the court defines the duty of the ice cream vendor as follows:

Under elementary principles it was the duty of the defendant operator of the truck to exercise ordinary care to provide a reasonably safe place for this child who was his business invitee. To that end, he was required to exercise ordinary care to select a position on the road where he could stop his vehicle and dispense his merchandise to the plaintiff without exposing her to danger.

In a more recent case, *Bishop* v. *Hamad* (350 N.Y.S. 2d 270), the New York Supreme Court, Appellate Division, considered the duty of care owed by an ice cream vendor to a four-year-old child. The court said that

. . . the infant plaintiff was Hamad's business invitee to whom he owed a duty of providing a safe means of ingress to the vending truck and a safe exit from it . . . and of using reasonable care to protect her from harm . . . anticipating and taking into account her inability to understand or appreciate the danger and to protect her against it.

CHAPTER V

Statutory modifications of the law of torts

500 Statutory construction

A statute is a written enactment of the legislature and is reflective of the will of the people represented. There are some statutes which affect the law of torts. Where a need arises, whether due to a change in customs or usages because of the development of new machines or new conditions, or whether the need arises from the recognition of the necessity for a change from the old rules, the legislature, responsive to the will of the people, will enact laws which enlarge or diminish the liability imposed by the common law or laws, which will create new causes of action.

When a new statute is enacted, it will then be the task of the courts to construe it and to determine its legal effect. The courts proceed on the basic premise that a statute which is contrary to or "in derogation of" the common law will be strictly construed, and they will hold that the statute changes the common law only in the areas and to the extent that it specifically sets forth that it does. Should there be any doubt as to the meaning of the statute, it will be construed most strongly in favor of the commonlaw rule then in existence, the courts looking to the plain lanugage of the statute and not to the legislative intent which inspired it.

501 Abatement and survival

The common law is that a person's earthly activity ceases at death. Therefore, a dead person could neither sue nor be sued, and if he had begun the action in his lifetime, or an action had been begun against him, his death ended or abated the action. Thus an action could not be begun by a dead person, nor could an action be taken against him. If a lawsuit was pending at the time of his death, whether he was plaintiff or defendant, his death ended the action. Thus the common law gave recognition to the physical impossibility of earthly actions in the form of a lawsuit by or against a deceased person, and it gave no consideration to the possibility of having the personal representative of the deceased, such as an administrator or executor of his estate, appear for or in behalf of the deceased.

Under this system, if a claimant received serious injuries, suffered excruciating pain, suffered a loss of earning capacity, and incurred medical and hospital expense, and he died before the case proceeded to judgment, there were no legal means by which his estate could recover damages or even the out-of-pocket expenses from the wrongdoer. This was true even though the payment of heavy medical expenses and other losses would diminish his estate and leave that much less to be divided among his heirs.

As to the defendant, if he should die prior to judgment, his estate would not be liable to the injured person, no matter how serious the injuries were and no matter how culpable the defendant's conduct was in causing them, and his estate would be divided among his heirs without regard to any obligation, moral or otherwise, which he may have had toward the seriously injured person.

In order to correct this situation, some of the states have enacted legislation relating to abatement and survival, and in others the courts have given recognition to a right of survival of the cause of action in favor of the estate of the deceased. The statutes provide that the action shall not abate by the death of the plaintiff, whether his death was caused by the injury or not, but shall survive for the benefit of his heirs, and that the action may be brought by his personal representative. This refers only to the cause of action which the deceased had in his lifetime, and the damages recoverable are those which he himself could have recovered had he lived.

The recoverable items of damage include medical expense, loss of earnings, and other out-of-pocket expenses as well as an amount reasonably calculated to compensate for his physical and mental distress. They do not include his funeral expenses, for the reason that the deceased never owned a cause of action against the tort-feasor in his lifetime which would contemplate the payment of his funeral expenses. The claim that can now be asserted by the personal representative of the deceased is the claim that the deceased could have made had he lived. This means that the action will be based upon damages suffered from the date of the accident to the date of the deceased's death and not thereafter.

In the case of the death of the tort-feasor, the statutes provide that the action shall not abate but will survive against his estate. This means that the defendant is compelled by law to be honest and pay his earthly obligations before he is generous in the distribution of his estate among his heirs. The action may be brought or continued against the defendant's personal representative.

In either case, if the lawsuit were settled and releases given, there would be no cause of action to survive. If the deceased had settled his case with the defendant and extinguished the cause of action by the receipt of a payment in settlement, giving back a release in exchange even if the injured person died as a result of the injuries received, he had no cause of action against the defendant as of the date of his death, and therefore there was no cause of action to survive to his personal representative. The same thing would be true in a case that was settled and in which the defendant died. Since there was no cause of action in existence as of the date of the defendant's death, there was no cause of action that would survive against his estate.

502   Death by wrongful act

In the normal cause of events, when a man reaches the end of his natural life-span, his worldly assets are distributed to the natural objects of his bounty, either by will or by operation of law. Also, where a man has lived out his normal life-span, he will have contributed gifts, support, or other things of value to the natural objects of his bounty, usually the members of his family and close relatives.

Where, however, a man's life has been shortened by an accidental death which occurs through the negligence of another, it is clear that the natural objects of his bounty have sustained a loss. They lose the support, gifts, or other emoluments which they would have received during his lifetime had he lived, and the amount which would be distributed at the time of death is that much less than it would have been had he lived; if he had lived, he would have added to his possessions, and the amounts to be distributed at his death would have been that much more. Therefore, as a result of his premature demise, his beneficiaries have suffered a distinct loss.

The common law did not recognize that these beneficiaries had any legal rights against the tort-feasor, nor did the common law recognize that this class of persons had sustained damage as a result of the death of their possible benefactor. Where an injured person survives, the personal injury claim is his and his alone. He may bring the action, and the damages recoverable belong solely to him. This is true even though his dependents or close relatives may have suffered some deprivation because of his injury and may have been required to perform some services for him during his illness. The common law did not recognize damages sustained by relatives as actionable where the injured person survives (and does not do so today), and therefore, since they were strangers to the claimant's cause of action in his lifetime, there was no reason why the death of the claimant should change their status.

In England, social conditions dictated the necessity for legislative change. When the breadwinner of the family lost his life, the family more often than not was left destitute, and since they had no remedy when the death was caused by wrongful act, they joined other destitute persons on the public charity rolls. The cases became so numerous that public sentiment caused Parliament to pass the Fatal Accidents Act of 1846, which is more commonly known as Lord Campbell's Act.

The act created a new cause of action which could be brought for and in behalf of the dependents of the deceased against the tort-feasor where death was caused by the wrongful act, neglect, or default of the defendant. The underlying purpose of the act was to create a means whereby the persons who normally would be supported by the deceased could recover an amount which would be the same as they would have received had he lived, thereby preventing them from becoming objects of charity. Therefore, the measure of damages was the pecuniary loss suffered by these people as a result of the death. There was no recovery allowed for mental anguish and bereavement, since these were not pecuniary in nature.

The majority of the American states have enacted wrongful death statutes, similar to Lord Campbell's Act, limiting the recoverable damages to the value of the deceased's future contributions to the beneficiaries. The other states have enacted three general types of statutes to cover the situation: (1) punitive statutes, which base the measure of damages on the culpability of the defendant's conduct, (2) statutes which base damages on the loss to the estate, and (3) combined death and survival statutes, by means of which one action be brought for both the survival claim and the claim for wrongful death. (See Section 2029: Measure of Damages, Wrongful Death.)

A typical statute patterned after Lord Campbell's Act is the New Jersey Wrongful Death Statute, which reads as follows:

When the death of a person is caused by a wrongful act, neglect, or default, such as would, if death had not ensued, have entitled the person injured to maintain an action for damages resulting from the injury, the person who would have been liable in damages for the injury, if death had not ensued, shall be liable in an action for damages, notwithstanding the death of the person injured, and although the death was caused under circumstances amounting in law to a crime.

Every action commenced under this chapter shall be brought in the name of the administrator *ad prosequendum* of the decedent for whose death damages are sought, except where the decedent dies testate and his will is probated, in which event the executor named in the will and qualifying, or the administrator with will annexed, as the case may be, shall bring the action. Every action brought under this chapter shall be commenced within two years after the death of the decedent and not thereafter.

The amount recovered in proceedings under this chapter shall be for the exclusive benefit of the persons entitled to take any intestate personal property of the decedent in the proportions in which they are entitled to take the same. If any of the persons so entitled were not dependent on the decedent at his death, the remainder of the persons so entitled shall take the same as though they were the sole persons so entitled. If all or none of the persons so entitled were then dependent on him, they shall all take as aforesaid.

In every action brought on the provisions of this chapter, the jury shall give such damages as they deem fair and just with reference to the pecuniary injuries resulting from such death to the persons entitled to any intestate personal property of the decedent.

Beneficiaries. In some states the action for wrongful death is brought by the executor or administrator of the estate of the deceased for the benefit of a class of persons which includes the husband, wife, children, or if none of these, for the benefit of the mother and father of the deceased. In other states the action may be brought by the persons immediately concerned. It might be added parenthetically that the "husband" and "wife" refer to a legal relationship. Since most, if not all, states do not recognize a common-law relationship as legal, the so-called common-law wife and husband have not status under the wrongful death statutes and therefore cannot recover.

If any of the beneficiaries should die before the action is begun, or even if they should die after the commencement of the action, the claim dies with them and does not inure to the benefit of their estates. Of course, if there are other beneficiaries, the death of one of their number would not have any effect on their rights. Obviously, if all of the beneficiaries should die prior to judgment, the action will fail. As one of the elements of the cause of action, the plaintiff must establish that the claim was one which the deceased could have maintained had he lived.

Most states have a statute of limitations which requires that actions for personal injury must be brought within a certain period of time from the date that the cause of action accrued. For example, let us assume that the statute of limitation is two years from the date of the accident. If we assume that no action was brought, and at the time of the decedent's death more than two years had passed from the date of the accident, then it is clear that the injured person could not have maintained an action for his injuries if death had not ensued. His cause of action is already outlawed by the passage of time and by the expiration of the period of limitation. Under those circumstances there could be no qualification under the provisions of the statute. However, if the injured person died within the two years from the date of the accident, then an action for wrongful death under this statute could be brought at any time within two years from the date of the decedent's death.

If we assume that the decedent died one year, 11 months, and 29 days after the date of the accident, it is clear that he could have brought an action for personal injuries had he lived. He only had one more day within which to accomplish this, but the requirements of the statute are met if the injured person could have maintained the action had he lived. In such a case, he would have been able to maintain the action had he lived, and therefore the action for wrongful death could be brought at any time within two years after the decedent's death. This would mean that the interval of time would amount to 3 years, 11 months, and 29 days from the date of the accident.

On the other hand, if the deceased had settled the claim during his lifetime, or brought an action which proceeded to judgment, he could not have maintained a further action had he lived. Under those circumstances, the general rule is that this beneficiaries do not qualify under the statute so as to bring a wrongful death action. The majority of American courts follow this rule.

However, in *Alfone* v. *Sarno*, 87 N.J. 99 (1981), the New Jersey Supreme Court refused to follow this general rule and allowed a claim by a statutory beneficiary after the decedent had already recovered damages for her injuries. The facts showed that the deceased (daughter of the plaintiff) had recovered a judgment of $100,000 from the defendant physician alleging that his malpractice had caused her condition. The recovery was had in 1968. She subsequently died in 1974 as a result of the same injuries which were alleged in the previous malpractice suit. The court apparently took the position that in a wrongful death situation, the beneficiaries' cause of action arose at the time of the negligent act and was derived from the injuries to the deceased. Upon the death of the deceased, regardless of what action the deceased had taken during her lifetime, the beneficiaries' claim was enforceable after the decedent's death. The court was careful to point out that there could be no duplication of the damages recovered by the deceased since the same damages could not be recovered twice. This is a New Jersey decision and it is doubtful if other courts will be persuaded to follow this reasoning.

Damages. The original concept of Lord Campbell's Act was to provide a means by which the beneficiaries would recover as damages an amount which would reasonably compensate them for the monetary support they would have received from the deceased had he lived. The recovery was therefore limited to the pecuniary loss which these beneficiaries would have sustained due to the death and nothing more. The majority of American states which have enacted statutes similar to Lord Campbell's Act have the same restriction as to damages. Some states have a limitation on the amount of damages which may be recovered. These states are Colorado ($45,000 if there is no surviving spouse, minor children, or dependent parents): Kansas ($25,000); and Maine ($50,000). Some other states have added other and further elements of damages in addition to the pecuniary losses. These states are Ohio (damages include funeral and burial expenses, damages for injury or loss including loss of support, services, society, prospective inheritance and mental anguish); and Oklahoma (damages for spouse's loss of consortium; grief; children's parents' grief; loss of companionship; and, in a proper case, punitive damages). Wisconsin also provides for an award of up to $10,000 for loss of companionship. In addition, New Hampshire law provides for a limitation of $50,000 but there is no limitation if the deceased was survived by a widow, widower, child, father, mother, or dependent relative. Since these statutes are subject to change by the legislature, it is recommended, the claims representative is confronted by claims of this type, that reference be made to the current statute.

Death of a minor child. At one time a minor child was an economic asset in that he or she could be sent to work at a very early age and his wages were contributed to the family maintenance. With the coming of child labor laws, this is not possible today. Therefore, even today, a minor child's contribution to family maintenance would hardly balance the cost of raising and educating the child, so that in most cases the child is an economic liability rather than an asset. In states where the wrongful death statute is similar to the original Lord Campbell's Act, the only element of damages which are recoverable would be the child's funeral expenses. However, sometimes a jury will award much more than the funeral expenses, and such an award will not be set aside by the court. In such cases, the court is giving tacit recognition to mental anguish suffered by the parents. In states where the statute provides for a recovery for mental anguish and bereavement, such awards are customarily made. For a case discarding the "wage-profit" formula (the expected earnings of the child less the cost of raising him), see *Wycko* v. *Gnodtke*, 105 N.W. 2d 118 (Michigan). This case valued the life of the child in connection with his relationship with the family as part of the family unit. See also *Currie* v. *Fitting*, 134 N.W. 2d 611 (Michigan) and *Fussner* v. *Andert*, 113 N.W. 2d 355 (Minnesota).

Defenses. In order to recover, the beneficiaries must establish that the injuries to the deceased were caused by the "wrongful act, neglect, or default" on the part of the defendant and that the injuries were causally related to the death which ensued. The defendant may interpose any defense which he may have had against the deceased had he lived. This means that the defendant has available the defenses of contributory negligence, assumption of risk, or consent to the defendant's conduct. In addition, in most states, the defendant may interpose the defense that the defendant has available the defenses of contributory negligence, assumption of risk, or consent to the defendant's conduct. In addition, in most states, the defendant may interpose the defense that the claim has been released or has proceeded to verdict. In addition, the defense of the statute of limitations can be pleaded in an appropriate case.

503 Joint tort-feasors contribution law

At common law, there was no contribution among joint tort-feasors. Thus, where a cause of action was asserted against only one of several joint tort-feasors, and a judgment recovered, the defendant would be required to respond and pay all of the damages. The tort-feasor paying all of the damage would not have a cause of action, nor would he have a right to contribution from the other wrongdoers. The common-law concept was that all were wrongdoers, and therefore none had any status in court for the purpose of minimizing or in any way recouping any part of the loss which he sustained, partly as a consequence of his own wrongdoing. Since the injured party had elected to hold only one of several joint tort-feasors, the common-law courts felt no compulsion to change the situation.

Some states have felt that the common-law rule should be modified and, as a consequence, have enacted statutes creating a right of contribution from other joint tort-feasors in favor of the joint tort-feasor making the payment. The statutory language differs state by state, but the uniform law, which generally forms the basis of the statutes, reads as follows:

The right of contribution exists among joint tort feasors.

Where injury or damage is suffered by any person as a result of the wrongful act, neglect, or default of joint tort feasors, and a person so suffering injury or damage recovers a money judgment of judgments for such injuries or damage against one or more of the joint tort feasors, either in one action or in separate actions, and any one of the joint tort feasors pays such judgment in whole or in part, he shall be entitled to recover contribution from the other joint tort feasor or tort feasors for the excess so paid over his *pro rata* share; but no person shall be entitled to recover contribution under this act for any person entitled to be indemnified by him in respect to the liability for which the contribution is sought.

To be joint tort-feasors, parties must either act together in committing the wrong, or the acts, if independent of each other, must unite in causing a single injury. By this definition, the wrongful act or acts must be actively committed by the persons in order to constitute them joint tort-feasors. This will eliminate those whose liability is vicarious, such as a principal for the acts of his agent or an automobile owner for the negligence of his driver.

504   Lateral support of party walls

The common-law duty on the part of a landowner is to refrain from any abnormal use of his land which would cause damage to that of his neighbor. This would include any disturbance in the lateral or side support which he is required to give to the land of his neighbor. Therefore, a major excavation will deprive the neighbor of this lateral support, and constitutes a wrongful act.

Clearly, the necessity of providing lateral support for the land of his neighbor imposes a restriction upon the owner of land with respect to the use of his own property. If he does excavate, he does so at his peril and will be absolutely liable to his neighbor for any damage which occurs as a result. On the other hand, the owner of the property does not have the right to enter upon the land of his neighbor to erect any safeguards in order to prevent damage. These restrictions were especially onerous where there was in existence a party wall on the boundary, or the wall of the neighbor's building was so close to the boundary line that any excavation would be sure to cause damage to the existing structure. Therefore, many states have enacted statutes defining the rights of the parties and limiting the liability of the owner for the excavation where his entry into the land of the neighbor in order to erect safeguards is refused. This statute is in the public interest in the sense that it encourages the owner of property to erect buildings and make other improvements thereon.

A statute of the state of New Jersey (R.S. 46: 10–1) is typical of the form that the statute takes. It reads as follows:

> Whenever excavations for buildings or other purposes on any lot or piece of land shall be intended to be carried to a depth of more than 8 ft. below the curb or grade of the street, and there shall be any party or other wall wholly or partly on adjoining land, and standing upon or near the boundary lines of such lot or piece of land, the person causing such excavations to be made, if afforded the necessary license to enter on the adjoining land, but not otherwise, shall at all times, from the commencement until the completion of such excavations, preserve, at his own expense, such party or other wall from injury, and so support the same by proper foundation, that it shall remain as stable as before such excavations were commenced.

This statute modifies the common-law rule to the extent that the owner of property will be granted permission to erect safeguards on the land of a neighbor where excavations are being made, and in the absense of such permission, the owner is relieved of liability. Should the owner be granted permission to enter on the land of his neighbor, he will be required to erect adequate safeguards, and should any damage occur, his absolute liability at common law will be imposed.

505   Uniform aeronautics law

The common-law concept of ownership of land was that such ownership included not only the surface of the land itself but the airspace above the land to the heavens. Therefore, anyone making unauthorized use of the airspace above a person's land is a constructive trespasser. As such, he is responsible for any loss or damage caused by such intrusion upon the property of another. Obviously, this concept was formulated at a time when there were no aircraft in existence, and certainly not in contemplation of present-day conditions. If it were to be imposed with full vigor, it is clear that property owners could effectively prevent any aircraft from taking off from the ground.

The courts, hampered by the common-law concept of ownership, have wrestled with the problem for quite a few years. Some of the courts took the position that while the owner did have the property rights to airspace over his land, until he reduced the airspace by actually building a building or other structure into the airspace, the area above the land not required for the effective enjoyment of the property and the use of the building was held to remain in the public domain. Therefore, until such space was reduced to possession or was necessary for the enjoyment of the owner of the property beneath, the public could exercise a privilege of use without any liability to the owner.

In this sense, the courts created two zones above the owner's property. The first zone would consist of the area reduced to possession, plus whatever space above that point was needed in order to properly enjoy the land. The second zone was an area which was not reduced to possession and not used by the owner, not necessary for the peaceable enjoyment of his property. Therefore, the public had a privilege of use insofar as the second zone was concerned and could exercise such privilege without any interference by, or liability to, the owner.

The Restatement, Torts Second, Section 159 under the caption of Intrusions Upon, Beneath, and Above the Surface of the Earth, recommends the following rule:

(1) Except as stated in Subsection (2), a trespass may be committed on, beneath, or above the surface of the earth.
(2) Flight by aircraft in the air space above the land of another is a trespass, if, but only if
    (a) it enters into the immediate reaches of the air space next to the land, and
    (b) it interferes substantially with the other's use and enjoyment of his land.

No recommendation or opinion is expressed as to whether the rule in Subsection (2) is to be applied to the flight of space rockets, satellites, missiles, and similar objects. The phrase "surface of the earth" includes soil, water, trees and other growths, and any structures on the land or affixed to it.

In *United States* v. *Causby* [328 U.S. 256 (1946)], the U.S. Supreme

Court declared that federal statutes, together with administrative regulations adopted pursuant to them, had the effect of making the upper air, above the prescribed minimum altitudes of flight, a public highway. Later cases recognize that this decision had the effect of superseding any state law on the subject, so that liability for the entry into the air space generally is governed by federal law, and, as far as aviation is concerned, private rights in the upper air no longer exist.

As to the territory within the jurisdiction of the states, most states have enacted a recommended statute called the Uniform State Law for Aeronautics. The uniform law also recommends an additional provision providing for a rule of absolute liability on the part of the owner of any aircraft to persons or property on the land or water beneath the flight of the aircraft. The statute reads as follows:

> The owner of every aircraft which is operated over the land or waters of this state is absolutely liable for injuries to persons or property on the land or water beneath, caused by the ascent, descent, or flight of the aircraft, or the dropping or falling of any object therefrom, whether such owner was negligent or not, unless the injury is caused in whole or in part by the negligence of the person injured, or of the owner or bailee of the property injured. If the aircraft is leased at the time of the injury to person or property, both owner and lessee shall be liable, and they may be sued jointly, or either or both of them may be sued separately. An airman, who is not the owner or lessee, shall be liable only for the consequences of his own negligence. The injured person, or owner or bailee of the injured property, shall have a lien on the aircraft causing the injury to the extent of the damage caused by the aircraft or object falling from it. A chattel mortgagee, conditional vendor or trustee under an equipment trust, of any aircraft, not in possession of such aircraft, shall not be deemed an owner within the provisions of this section.

All states have not adopted this provision. Some have enacted it, and others have imposed it as a consequence of a judicial decision. The states in which absolute liability is imposed upon the owner of the aircraft for injury or damage to structures on the ground are Delaware, Hawaii, Minnesota, New Jersey, North Dakota, South Carolina, and Vermont.

(In Montana and Wyoming the statute provides for absolute liability in the case of forced landings only.)

Eight states apply the rule of ordinary negligence, requiring the plaintiff to show some negligence on the part of the owner or pilot of the aircraft before liability can be imposed. These states are Arizona, Arkansas, California, Idaho, Missouri, Pennsylvania, South Dakota and Tennessee.

Five states by statute create a rebuttable presumption of negligence in the case of injuries to persons or structures on the ground. This could be said to involve the application of the rule of *res ipsa loquitur* in those cases. These states are Georgia, Maryland, Nevada, Rhode Island, and Wisconsin.

It must be emphasized that the law with respect to aircraft is in a state of development. As each advance is made in the development of the aircraft itself, there will be corresponding legislation with respect thereto, as well as rulings of the courts with regard to specific factual situations. Therefore, an adjuster handling cases in this particular area must keep abreast of the new legislation as well as current decisions of the courts.

By the passage of the Federal Aviation Act of 1958, Congress provided for federal regulation of aviation, both commercial and private. It also created the Federal Aviation Administration whose duty it is to formulate and enforce air safety regulations. In very few areas is there any conflict between the federal regulations and the state laws, but where there is a conflict the federal rule will be controlling.

506   Statute of limitations

In the public interest, the legislatures of the various states have decided that there must be some point in time at which the threat of possible litigation must cease. Therefore, they have enacted statutes which prescribe the periods of time within which actions may be brought upon certain claims, and declare that no suit shall be maintained on such causes of action unless brought within the period of time specified. A statute setting forth the limitations of time within which certain causes of action must be brought is called a statute of limitations. Failure to bring suit within the period of time prescribed deprives the plaintiff of his right to enforce his claim.

There are different periods of time prescribed for different forms of action, the period of time referable to personal injury actions being different from property damage actions, and the limitation applicable to tort claims is generally a shorter period of time than that applicable to contract actions. Reference must be had to the specific state statute applicable to the cause of action to determine the limitation of time applicable.

Since the statute of limitations is a rule of substance, the law of the place where the cause of action arose is determinative of the period of limitation applicable, irrespective of where the action is tried. For example, if an accident causing personal injuries occurred in New Jersey, which has a two-year period of limitation within which the action must be brought, and suit was brought in New York, which has a three-year period applicable to personal injury claims, two years and three months after the accident, the cause of action would be barred by the New Jersey statute of limitations (which would be applicable to the claim) even though the action was brought in New York which grants a longer period of time.

The statutes usually provide that the limitation will not run against an infant during the period of his infancy and that the infant, upon attaining his majority, has an additional period of time within which the action must be brought before it is barred. There are other provisions, with regard to insane persons, which toll (nullify) the running of the statute during the period of insanity, or during the period in which the insane person is without a guardian to protect his interests.

Were it not for these statutes, the potential defendant would have to be prepared to defend the lawsuit at any time, no matter when it was brought.

This would place upon him the burden of perpetuating all his evidence, if it were possible to do so, and in cases where vital evidence could be destroyed by the passage of time, the defendant would be at a decided disadvantage. In addition, life is short and human memory faulty, so that the defendant may be deprived of his defense by the death of an important witness or the failure of other witnesses to recall the event with absolute clarity.

Technically, the statute of limitations does not destroy the claim; it merely makes it unenforceable. Therefore, the defendant may waive the statute or fail to interpose it as a defense, in which case the claim can be prosecuted to judgment even though the statute of limitations has run.

The time period of the statute of limitations begins to run from the date the cause of action accrues. In tort cases, this would mean that the statute begins to run from the date of the accident, or the date the tortious act was committed. In addition, most statutes provide that any period during which the defendant is absent from the state or secretes himself within the state is deducted from the period of limitation.

Medical malpractice cases and others of similar nature pose a special problem where the negligent act cannot be discovered until some time after it has occurred. For example, a surgeon leaves a surgical instrument or a sponge in the patient's body at the time of the operation. The patient is unaware of this, and after he has suffered some pain for a period of time, it is finally discovered. It is possible that by the time that the discovery is made, the statute of limitations has run against the claim. In other words, the statute could run against the patient's claim even before he knows that he has a claim. To correct this, some states have amended their statutes [cf. New York, CPLR 203 (f)] so as to provide that the period of limitation is to be computed from the date when the facts were discovered, or from the time when the facts could have been discovered by the exercise of due diligence. In other states, the courts have accomplished the same result without the aid of the legislature. In the following cases—all involving medical malpractice—the courts have adopted the "discovery" rule that where a foreign object is negligently left in a patient's body by a surgeon and the patient is ignorant of that fact, and consequently of his right of action for malpractice, the cause of action does not accrue until the patient learns of, or in the exercise of reasonable care and diligence should have learned of, the presence of such foreign object in his body.

Arizona	*Morrison* v. *Acton*, 198 Pac. 2d 590.
Arkansas	*Burton* v. *Tribble*, 70 S.W. 2d 503.
California	*Hemingway* v. *Waxler*, 274 Pac. 2d 699; *Stafford* v. *Schultz*, 270 Pac. 2d 1.
Colorado	*Davis* v. *Bonebrake*, 313 Pac. 2d 982; *Rosane* v. *Senger*, 149 Pac. 2d 372.
Florida	*City of Miami* v. *Brooks*, 70 So. 2d 306.
Idaho	*Billings* v. *Sisters of Mercy*, 389 Pac. 2d 224.
Louisiana	*Perrin* v. *Rodriquez*, 153 So. 555.

Michigan	*Johnson* v. *Caldwell*, 123 N.W. 2d 785.
Nebraska	*Spath* v. *Morrow*, 115 N.W. 2d 581.
New Jersey	*Fernandi* v. *Strully*, 173 Atl. 2d 277.
Oklahoma	*Seitz* v. *Jones*, 370 Pac. 2d 300.
Pennsylvania	*Ayers* v. *Morgan*, 154 Atl. 2d 788.
West Virginia	*Morgan* v. *Grace Hospital*, 17 Neg. Cas. 2d (CCH) 1469.

507   Comparative negligence

The theory of comparative negligence is not new to the law. It had its genesis in admiralty and is traditionally applied in all cases of admiralty and maritime jurisdiction. The common law never accepted it, adhering to the rule that the contributory negligence of the plaintiff, no matter how slight, will defeat his recovery. Comparative negligence applies the rule that the contributory negligence of the plaintiff will not defeat his recovery but will be taken into account by the jury in reducing the amount of his recovery.

The comparative negligence rule has been adopted in several federal statutes, such as the Federal Employers Liability Act, applying to injuries sustained by employees of an interstate carrier by railroad (see Section 1304, below), the Jones Act, applying to injury or death of seamen (see Section 1411, below), and Death on the High Seas by Wrongful Act, applying to death sustained on American vessels on the high seas (see Section 1412, below).

Some states have adopted the comparative negligence rule either by statute or judicial determination. Unfortunately, these states are not uniform in their approach to the rule and the result is that we have three distinctly different rules applicable. These statutes take the form of (1) pure, (2) modified, and (3) slight versus gross.

1. *Pure form.* Under this form, the plaintiff is entitled to recover, regardless of the amount of contributory negligence that is applicable to him, provided that the defendant was in some degree negligent. Theoretically, the plaintiff would recover if he was 99 percent negligent and the defendant 1 percent. The amount of the plaintiff's recovery would be reduced by the percentage of negligence of which he is guilty. Thus, if the plaintiff was 75 percent contributorily negligent, he would be entitled to recover only 25 percent of his damages. Likewise, the defendant could counterclaim for his damages and he would be entitled to a 75 percent recovery, since his contributory negligence amounted to only 25 percent. Obviously, where the defendant had sustained no damages, the only recovery involved would be by the plaintiff. The states subscribing to this rule are as follows:

State	*Statute or Judicial Decision*
Alaska	*Kaatz* v. *Alaska*, 540 Pac. 2d 1037
California	*Nga Li* v. *Yellow Cab*, 119 Cal Rptr 858
Florida	*Hoffman* v. *Jones*, 280 So. 2d 431
Illinois	*Alvis* v. *Ribar* (Ill. Supr. Ct)
Mississippi	3 M.C.A. 11-7-15

New York   Civil Practice Act, 1411-13
Rhode Island 2A G.L. of Rhode Island, Sec. 9-20-4
Washington   Laws of 1973, C. 138 Section 1

2. Modified form. This type of statute allows a recovery by the plaintiff
if his negligence did not exceed that of the defendant. There are, however,
two variations of this type of statute. The first requires that the plaintiff's
contributory negligence be less than the negligence of the defendant. Thus,
the plaintiff can be up to 49 percent negligent and still recover. However, if
the plaintiff's contributory negligence equals or exceeds that of the defendant,
there will be no recovery. States which currently have this type of statute
are as follows:

State	Statute
Arkansas	3A A.S.A. Section 27.17
Colorado	12 C.R.S. 1963 Ch. 41, Section 2-14
Connecticut	P.L. 73-622
Georgia	Ga. Code Anno. 105-603
Hawaii	Rev. Stat. Title 36 Ch. 663, Sec. 31
Kansas	St. Anno. 60-258A
Maine	7 M.R.S.A. Title 14, Sec. 156
Massachusetts	38 M.G.L.A. Ch. 231, Sec. 85
Minnesota	38 M.S.A. Sec. 604.01
Montana	Rev. Codes Anno. 60-258-A
Nevada	Rev. Stat. 41-141
Oregon	1 O.R.S. Sec. 18.470
Pennsylvania	Stat. Anno. Title 17, Sec. 2101
Puerto Rico	Title 31: Sec. 5141
Texas	Civ. Stat. 2212A
Vermont	12 V.S.A. Sec. 1036
Wyoming	2 W.S. Title 1, Sec. 7.2

The second variation of the modified form allows a recovery by the plaintiff
if his contributory negligence equals or is less than that of the defendant.
Under this type of statute, the plaintiff could be 50 percent negligent and
still recover. The states having this type of statute are as follows:

State	Statute
New Hampshire	4A N.H.R.S. Ch. 507, Sec. 7A
New Jersey	N.J.S.A. Ch. 507.7a
North Dakota	Code 9-10-07
Oklahoma	Stat. Anno. Title 23;P
Utah	Code. Anno. 78-27-37
Wisconsin	W.S.A. 331.045

3. Slight v. gross negligence. Some states by statute apply the rule of
comparative negligence only where the court finds that the plaintiff's contributory negligence as compared with defendant's negligence is gross. In
all other cases, the common-law rule of contributory negligence as a complete
defense applies. The states are:

State	Statute
Nebraska	N.R.S. 25-1151
South Dakota	7 S.D.C.L. Title 20, Section 9-2

As to states not included in the list above, there is always a possibility that there might be a legislative change or a judicial modification of the present law. Therefore, the claims representatives in such states should be alert for any changes which might occur.

508   Dram shop acts

At common law a third person who was injured as a result of the intoxication of one who had imbibed liquor at a tavern had no cause of action against the tavern keeper, regardless of the amount of liquor or the circumstances under which it was sold. To create such a cause of action, some states passed legislation known as "dram shop" or "civil damage" laws. While there is some variation in the language of each act, they are similar in form and generally cover the same area. For example, the Minnesota Civil Damage Act (MSA 340.95), reads as follows:

Every wife, husband, child, parent, guardian, employer, or other persons who are injured in person or property, or means of support, by an intoxicated person, or by the intoxication of any person, has a right of action in his own name against any person who, by illegally selling, bartering or giving intoxicating liquors, causes the intoxication of such person for all damages sustained.

Other states having similar legislation are:

Alabama	Code, Tit. 7, 121
Connecticut	Rev. Stat. 30–102
Illinois	Rev. Stat. Ch. 43, 135
Iowa	Code 129.2
Maine	Re. Sta. Ch. 61, 95
Michigan	Code Stat. Ann. 18.993
New York	Civil Rights Law, 16
North Dakota	Cent. Code 5–01
Ohio	Rev. Code 4399.01
Rhode Island	Gen. Laws 3–11–1
Vermont	Stat. Ann. Tit. 7, Ch. 17,501
Washington	Rev. Code 71.08.080
Wisconsin	Stat. 176.35

The laws of all states relating to the operation of establishments licensed to sell intoxicating beverages forbid the sale of intoxicating liquor to a minor (states differ as to the age requirement) or to an obviously intoxicated person. Therefore, any sale in violation of these regulations would be an "illegal" sale within the meaning of the Civil Damage Act. Likewise, the sale of an excessive amount of liquor consumed on the premises would be an illegal sale, since at some point it would be a sale to an intoxicated person.

In some states which do not have dram shop legislation, the courts have imposed what might be termed a common-law dram shop rule. For example, in *Rappaport* v. *Nichols* [156 Atl. 2d 1 (New Jersey)], three tavern owners sold and served alcoholic beverages to a minor (an illegal sale under the New Jersey statute and regulation). Thereafter, while in an intoxicated condition, the minor drove his car and collided with a car driven by the plaintiff's intestate. The court held all three tavern owners liable on the theory that when alcoholic beverages are sold by a tavern keeper to a minor or an intoxicated person, the unreasonable risk of harm not only to the minor or the intoxicated person but also to members of the traveling public may be readily recognized and foreseen. This is particularly evident in current times when traveling by car to and from the tavern is so commonplace and accidents resulting from drinking are so frequent. See also, *Nally* v. *Blandford* [291 S.W. 2d 832 (Kentucky)], where the deceased, while intoxicated, made a bet that he could drink an entire quart of whiskey without stopping. The defendant tavern owner sold the whiskey with the knowledge that the deceased intended to drink the entire quart on the premises, which he did. The deceased died the following day. The tavern owner was held liable for the death of the deceased, the court holding that the act of the defendant to be "an intentional wrongful act, and not a negligent one," and therefore the contributory negligence of the deceased in drinking the whiskey did not bar recovery.

The common-law dram shop liability has been applied in some states to individuals who supplied whiskey or other alcoholic beverages to a person who was involved in an accident while intoxicated. For example, in *Williams* v. *Klemesrud* [197 N.W. 2d 614 (Iowa)], there was a successful tort action brought against a college student who purchased vodka for a minor driver. The driver drank the vodka, became intoxicated and was involved in an accident which resulted in injuries to the plaintiff. Inasmuch as the Dram Shop Act imposed strict liability without negligence on the defendant, there was no reason why the same rule should not apply to an individual defendant. The court further held that the defense of contributory negligence is not available to the defendant under these circumstances.

In *Brockett* v. *Kitchen Boyd Motor Co.* (100 Cal. Rptr. 752), the employer was held liable to third persons who were injured as a result of the drunken driving of a minor employee following a Christmas party given by the employer. The employee was supplied with large amounts of liquor at the party. The employer knew or should have known that the employee would be driving on the highway to return home. The court held that those who illegally sell or furnish liquor to minors or to those visibly intoxicated in circumstances where it is foreseeable that the irresponsible imbiber will drive on the highway are responsible to third persons who may be injured as a consequence of the illegal supplying or selling. It is to be noted that in this case and the case which preceded it the intoxicated driver was a minor to whom it was illegal to furnish or sell liquor.

If, in the above case, the drunken driver had been an adult the question of the liability of the host-company would seem to be an open one at this time.

CHAPTER VI

Judicial modifications of the law of torts

600   Judicial authority

The common law consists of rules of law promulgated by the courts and based on the customs and usages of the people. It is clear that customs change with the passage of time and with the introduction of new inventions, as well as with advances made in science, sociology, and medicine. As customs change, the courts sometimes find that the reason for a common-law rule has ceased to exist, or that the application of an old rule would be unjust. Since the common law was originally the judicial reflection of general customs, the courts can be responsive to the changes as they occur, replacing old rules with new ones or abandoning some rules entirely. This the courts have the authority to do.

Under our political system, the states have retained certain rights of sovereignty, one of which is the right to maintain a judiciary independent of the federal government, and independent of all other states. The supreme court of each state therefore has the power and the authority to decide the common law and the rules thereunder applicable in the state. The common law, thus announced, may parallel the common law of another state or it may be diametrically opposed.

When a change in conditions is called to the attention of the supreme court of any state, and it is urged that the change requires a modification of the common law, the supreme court will determine whether or not there has in fact been a change, and if so, whether or not the change requires a modification of the common law, and, finally, the extent of the modification required. The views of each state supreme court will not always be the same, and the response to the change in conditions likewise may not be the same. Thus we do not have a uniform system of the common law in the United States, and to ascertain the applicable common law in a given state, recourse must be had to the latest pronouncements of the supreme court of that state on the particular subject.

This is a confusing problem for the claimsman, but it is one which he will have to face. He can accomplish this only by keeping abreast of the decisions of the supreme court of the state, or states, within the territory assigned to him.

We will consider in the following paragraphs some of the judicial modifications of the common law as they relate to the law of torts, reflecting as far as possible the common law on each subject as applied in the states which have considered the problem.

601   Fright without impact

The original common-law rule was that without physical impact there can be no recovery for injuries, physical or mental, incurred by fright negligently induced. This is contrary to the fundamental principle of the common law that a wrongdoer is responsible for the natural and proximate consequences of his conduct. The courts felt that it was necessary to establish this rule of nonliability on the grounds of public policy. The leading case on the subject was decided in New York state in 1896, and is titled *Mitchell* v. *Rochester Ry. Co.* (151 N.Y. 107, 45 N.E. 354).

In that case, Mrs. Mitchell suffered a miscarriage as a result of her apprehension that the horses driven by the defendant's agent were about to trample her. There was no actual physical contact between the horses and Mrs. Mitchell, and it developed, that while the horses were negligently driven, Mrs. Mitchell suffered no injuries as a result of any physical contact with them. In placing its decision on the basis of public policy, the court said:

> If the right of recovery in this class of cases should once be established, it would result in a flood of litigation in cases where the injury complained of may be easily feigned without detection, and where the damages must rest upon mere conjecture or speculation . . . to establish such a doctrine would be contrary to principles of public policy.

Most states follow this rule and do not permit recoveries for fright unless there is some impact upon the claimant's person. This impact may be very slight and, in the nature of things, would not in and of itself be the entire cause of the claimant's mental apprehension. The reasoning seems to be that there is a recovery for fright if such is the natural and probable consequence of a wrongful act, but that public policy demands that there be some impact before a recovery will be allowed.

In 1961, New York specifically reversed the rule in the *Mitchell* case in sustaining a complaint which alleged that the claimant was negligently caused to suffer "severe emotional and neurological disturbances with residual physical manifestations." The complaint alleged that the infant plaintiff was placed in a chair lift at a state-operated ski center by a state employee who failed to secure and properly lock the belt intended to protect the occupant; that as a result of this negligent act the infant plaintiff became frightened and hysterical upon descent, with consequential injuries. The court said:

> It is our opinion that Mitchell should be overruled. It is undisputed that a rigorous application of its rule would be unjust, as well as opposed to experience

and logic. On the other hand, resort to the somewhat inconsistent exceptions would merely add further confusion to a legal situation which presently lacks that coherence which precedent should possess.

In disposing of the public policy theory of the *Mitchell* case, the court remarked that the possibility of fraud, extra litigation, and speculative damages "is no reason for a court to eschew a measure of its jurisdiction"; that even if "a flood of litigation were realized by abolition of the exception, it is the duty of the courts to willingly accept the opportunity to settle these disputes." In referring to the speculative nature of the damages in such cases, the court said:

In the difficult cases, we must look to the quality and genuineness of the proof, and rely to an extent on the contemporary sophistication of the medical profession and the ability of the court and jury to weed out the dishonest claims. Claimant should, therefore, be given an opportunity to prove that her injuries were proximately caused by the defendant's negligence.

The case above cited is *Battalla* v. *State of New York* (10 N.Y. 2d 237). It will be noted that the court placed its decision on two grounds, namely (1) that the reason for the rule no longer existed, and (2) the advances in medical technology were such that fraudulent claims can now be easily detected.

The courts in some states have specifically reversed the impact rule by clear-cut decisions. The majority of states adhere to the impact requirement and deny recovery where it is not met. The following is a list of other states, which, like New York, have expressly repudiated the impact requirement where the plaintiff was within the zone of danger, together with the cases involved and the facts of each:

Connecticut. [*Orlo* v. *Connecticut Co.*, 21 Atl. 2d 402.] Plaintiff, a passenger in an automobile following the defendant's streetcar, suffered a reactivation of a diabetic condition as a result of fright and shock negligently caused by the breaking of a trolley pole and wires, which fell and struck the top of the car in which the plaintiff was riding.

Delaware. [*Robb* v. *Pennsylvania Railroad Co.*, 210 Atl. 2d 709.] A driver whose car became stuck in a rut on a grade crossing negligently maintained by the railroad, jumped out of her car immediately prior to the time the car was struck and demolished by an oncoming train. She was allowed a recovery for her physical injuries induced by fright and fear for her own safety, even though there was no physical impact.

Maryland. [*Bowman* v. *Williams*, 165 Atl. 182.] The plaintiff, a father looking out of his dining room window, saw a large truck crash through the basement of his house. Recovery was allowed for his physical illness occasioned by nervous shock resulting from fear for the safety of the house, himself, and his two little boys in the basement.

Minnesota. [*Okrina* v. *Midwestern Corp.*, 165 N.W. 2d 259.] Due to the negligent construction work, a wall collapsed next to the store in which the plaintiff was trying on clothing. She was not struck by any flying debris, but she did sustain a physical illness due to the noise and the proximity of the crash. Recovery allowed.

Nebraska. [*Rasmussen* v. *Benson,* 280 N.W. 890.] The defendant negligently sold to the plaintiff's intestate, a dairyman, a sack of bran infected with arsenic. He innocently fed this bran to his cows. After he had milked the cows and delivered milk all around the community, he returned to discover his stock dead, dying, or ailing. He was erroneously told that the arsenic would have poisoned the milk which he sold to his customers. Fearing the result, he made frantic efforts to contact all of his customers, and as a result of these exertions, he collapsed from shock, fear for the safety of his customers, and overexertion. He died nine months later of a decompensated heart. Although there was no physical impact, a recovery was allowed.

New Jersey. [*Falzone* v. *Busch,* 214 Atl. 2d 12.] The claimant's husband, standing in a field adjacent to the roadway, was struck and injured by a negligently operated automobile, which then veered and headed toward the parked automobile occupied by the claimant, coming so close to the claimant to put her in fear of her safety. Recovery for the physical injuries thus induced were allowed even though there was no physical impact.

Pennsylvania. [*Neiderman* v. *Brodsky,* 261 Atl. 2d 84.] The plaintiff was walking with his son and was narrowly missed by the defendant's automobile which skidded onto the sidewalk and struck the plaintiff's son. The plaintiff was not touched. Recovery was allowed for the heart trouble which he experienced as a result.

Texas. [*Houston Electric Co.* v. *Dorsett,* 194 S.W. 2d 546.] Petition, alleging that as plaintiff was carefully crossing the street the defendant's bus, negligently driven, nearly missed striking her, causing her to suffer great emotional shock resulting in such derangement of her nervous system that she was compelled to remain away from her work for a year, stated a cause of action against the bus company.

Vermont. [*Savard* v. *Cody Chevrolet, Inc.,* 234 Atl. 2d 656.] Defendant's agent was driving a truck which was known by both the defendant and his agent to have defective brakes. He thought he could control the truck by using various shifting of the gears. These attempts failed when the drive shaft flew out of the truck and it crashed into a house. The plaintiff and her parents were inside the house when it was struck by the truck. The impact of the collision caused severe damage to the house with consequent loud noise, loss of light and with a showering of light debris on the person of the plaintiff. There was no impact between the truck of the defendant and the plaintiff nor did she sustain any physical injury at the time. As a result of the accident the plaintiff claimed that she suffered severe nervous shock, emotional distress, sleeplessness, and loss of appetite which caused a loss of weight. The Supreme Court of Vermont sustained a recovery, adopting the following rule:

. . . where negligence causes fright from reasonable fear of immediate personal injury, and such fright is adequately demonstrated to have resulted in substantial bodily injury or sickness, the injured person may recover if such injury or sickness would be proper elements of damage if they had resulted as a consequence of direct physical injury rather than fright. This is the more modern rule followed in most jurisdictions, and we adopt it here.

Wisconsin. [*Colla* v. *Mandella,* 72 N.W. 2d 755.] At the time of the accident the plaintiff was 53 years of age, suffering from high blood pressure and a mild heart condition. He was taking a nap in the bedroom beside an adjoining alley. A driverless truck crashed into the side of his house near the bedroom windows, making a loud noise. The evidence showed that he was frightened and upset by the accident, that his heart condition became progressively worse, and he died of heart failure ten days after the accident. Recovery was allowed even though there was no contact between the truck and the deceased, and even though there was no possibility of any injury to his person.

It is to be noted that in all of the foregoing cases, the emotional shock or fright was produced by an apprehension of injury by the person who suffered the mental shock brought on by fear for his own safety, and in each case, he was in a position where injury could have resulted. There is another class of case involving emotional shock brought on not by fear for the person's own safety but from fear of harm or peril to another, such as the shock sustained by a mother who witnessed the death of her child under the wheels of a truck. The general rule is that there is no recovery allowed in such cases, even though it cannot be denied that the mother under those circumstances has suffered a mental lesion from which she might never recover. The rationale of the decision denying recovery is that while the driver of a vehicle has a duty of care which extends to others on the highway who may be injured by his negligent operation of the automobile, he owes no duty to others who are not themselves endangered by his use of the vehicle. Other reasons given for the decision are lack of foreseeability, proximate cause, and the lack of fear by the mother for her own safety. For example, in *Waube* v. *Warrington* (216 Wis. 603), the court said:

> The answer cannot be reached by logic . . . it must be reached by balancing the social interests involved in order to ascertain how far the defendant's duty and the plaintiff's right may justly and expediently be extended.

Another reason given for denying recovery, which has been discussed in several cases, is the matter of public policy in the sense that if a recovery were allowed it would place an unreasonable burden on the users of the highway, and furthermore, if a recovery were allowed in the case of a mother, could not the same right of recovery be extended to the father, sister, brother, the grandparents, a baby-sitter, who had charge of the deceased infant, the next-door neighbor, or even a stranger? As one court put it, allowing a recovery would "enter a field that has no sensible or just stopping point." Some text writers have suggested that the recovery be limited to only the mother or to some other close relative, but this limitation would have no reason in itself and would be arbitrary, being imposed solely for the purpose of defining the limits beyond which recovery would not be allowed.

A further phase of this problem is posed by the situation where the mother did not actually see the accident but suffered an emotional shock when told about the details of the accident and later viewed the body of her deceased child. Recoveries have also been denied in such cases.

In the following cases, the emotional shock was sustained by a person who was outside the zone of danger, and recovery was denied.

California	*Amaya* v. *Home Ice Co.*, 59 Cal. 2d 295.
Maryland	*Resavage* v. *Davies*, 199 Md. 479.
New Hampshire	*Cote* v. *Litawa*, 71 Atl. 2d 792.
	Barber v. *Pollock*, 104 N.H. 379.
	Jelley v. *LaFlame*, 238 Atl. 2d 728.
New Mexico	*Curry* v. *Journal Pub. Co.*, 68 Pac. 2d 168.
New York	*Tobin* v. *Grossman*, 249 N.E. 2d 419.
Wisconsin	*Waube* v. *Warrington*, 258 N.W. 497;
	Colla v. *Mandella*, 1 Wis. 2d 594;
	Klassa v. *Milwaukee Gas Light Co.*, 273 Wis. 176.

In *Dillon* v. *Legg* [69 Cal. Rptr. 72 (1968)], the California Supreme Court by a split decision (4–3) reversed the decision in the *Amaya* case noted above and held that a mother who witnessed the negligently caused death of her daughter and as a consequence suffered emotional shock and physical injury could recover from the tort-feasor even though at the time of the accident she was in a place of safety and not within the zone of danger.

In *Archibald* v. *Braverman* [79 Cal. Rptr. 723 (1969)], the California Court of Appeals reversed a summary judgment for the defendant in the case of a mother who was not an eyewitness to the accident involving her child, but who had come upon the scene almost immediately and had seen the child's injured condition. The California Supreme Court denied a rehearing so that this will represent the California law on the subject. In these two cases, California has gone the whole route and allowed recoveries not only where the mother was an eyewitness to the accident, but also to a mother who was not. So far no other courts have been so persuaded.

602   Mental anguish and emotional disturbance

At common law no recovery was allowed for mental anguish or emotional disturbance except in cases of intentional torts, such as assault, slander, and libel. In the tort of negligence, no recovery was allowed in the absence of some actual impact or physical injury.

There is evidence that some courts are departing from this common-law rule. This is especially true in the area of food cases. Recoveries have been allowed for emotional disturbance caused by the sight of particularly revolting substances in food, such as cockroaches, dead mice, and the like. Obviously, if the plaintiff had eaten any of the food, there would have been physical contact and a recovery would be allowed. The cases in which the courts have departed from the rule are those in which a particularly offensive sight is the cause of the disturbance—and nothing more. This appears to be a growing trend, and at the present time the rule followed in the majority of states seems to be that where a causal connection can be established between the particularly offensive sight in food and the emotional disturbance, a recovery will be allowed.

In areas other than food cases, emotional disturbance resulting from the sight of a particularly gruesome object or the happening of an accident to another person—even a member of the beholder's immediate family—is usually not recoverable. But in some isolated cases, recoveries have been allowed for emotional disturbance caused by an unauthorized autopsy on the body of a close relative, mishandling of dead bodies of deceased relatives, and the burial of the wrong body in a grave.

The intentional infliction of mental anguish and mental suffering is actionable only where the conduct of the defendant was extreme and outrageous. In other cases, more insulting words and conduct which does not amount to such extreme action, even though it does cause some mental distress, is not actionable. In *Alsteen* v. *Gehl* [124 N.W. 2d 312 (Wisconsin)], the court held that the following elements must be established to effect a recovery for intentional mental distress. There must be:

1. Intentional misconduct by the defendant.
2. Defendant's conduct must be extreme and outrageous, exceeding the bounds of decency.
3. Defendant's misconduct was a cause-in-fact of the plaintiff's emotional distress.
4. The plaintiff must have suffered "an extreme emotional response" to the defendant's conduct.

For example, in *Zayre of Atlanta, Inc.* v. *Sharpton* [139 S.E. 2d 339 (Georgia)], a floorwalker in a department store loudly accused the plaintiff of larceny and shoplifting. Plaintiff recovered a judgment based upon her humiliation and emotional distress against the corporate defendant. See also the following cases: *Solazar* v. *Bond Finance Co.* [410 S.W. 2d 839 (Texas)], relating to the outrageous conduct of debt collection agencies; *Kaufman* v. *Abramson* (363 Fed. 2d 865), describing the outrageous conduct of evicting landlords; and *Frishett* v. *State Farm Mutual Automobile Insurance Co.* [143 N.W. 2d 612 (Michigan)], involving the deliberate infliction of mental suffering upon a claimant by the agents of the liability insurance carrier.

In *Crisci* v. *Security Insurance Co. of New Haven* [426 Pac. 2d 173 (California)], it was claimed that the insurance carrier's wrongful refusal to settle a case within the policy limits where there was an opportunity to do so, was the proximate cause of the plaintiff's mental suffering and suicide attempts. An excess award had stripped the plaintiff of all of her property and caused her to be dependent upon the charity of her grandchildren. The court held that the insurance carrier was guilty of tortious conduct under the circumstances and awarded damages not only as to the excess verdict but also an award for mental distress. This case is reviewed in detail in Section 1605, infra. Section 46, Restatement, Torts, Second, states the rule as follows:

Outrageous Conduct Causing Severe Emotional Distress

(1) One who by extreme and outrageous conduct intentionally or recklessly causes severe emotional distress to another is subject to liability for such emotional distress, and if bodily harm to the other results from it, for such bodily harm.
(2) Where such conduct is directed at a third person, the actor is subject to liability if he intentionally or recklessly causes severe emotional distress

> (a) to a member of such person's immediate family who is present at the time, whether or not such distress results in bodily harm, or
> (b) to any other person who is present at the time if such distress results in bodily harm.

The comments following this section point out that the rule is intended to apply only to conduct which is of such outrageous character that it exceeds the bounds of decency. It will not be enough that the defendant acted with a malicious intent or that he intended to inflict emotional distress. Likewise the rule does not extend to mere insults, threats, indignities, or other annoyances since the law is not required to intervene in every case where the plaintiff's feelings are hurt.

In some cases the circumstances under which the defendant's action is taken will have some bearing on the question of whether the conduct is outrageous or not. For example, *A* is in the hospital suffering from heart disease. *B*, an insurance adjuster calls on *A* in an effort to settle a claim which *A* has. Due to the adjuster's harassment and boisterous attitude, *A* suffers from emotional distress and has a heart attack. If *B* was aware of *A*'s heart condition, his conduct could be deemed "outrageous." On the other hand, if *B* did not know of *A*'s condition, his conduct will not be so classified. This example follows the comment in the Restatement.

603   Consortium

At common law a husband was entitled to the services of his wife. He was required to pay her medical bills in the case of illness or injury. Where the wife was injured, the husband only could bring the action, which consisted of two counts: one for the personal injury to his wife, including her physical and mental distress, and the other for his own loss of services, for his medical expenses, and related damages. A married woman was under a disability and could not sue in her own name. Suit could be brought only by her husband for and in her behalf.

At common law the wife was considered as a sort of superior servant, who as a consequence of the marriage contract owed certain duties to her husband. These duties collectively are called *consortium*. They consist of the three S's, namely, sex, society, and services. "Sex" means the right of the husband to have sexual relations with his wife. "Society" means that the husband is entitled to the companionship of his wife. "Services" consist of the usual household chores, such as keeping the home in proper condition, cooking his meals, and other duties made necessary for the maintenance of the home. Any injury to the wife which impaired her ability to perform these duties and deprived the husband of his right to have them performed gave rise to a cause of action by the husband against the wrongdoer who caused the wife's injuries. Also as part of the marriage contract, the husband is obligated to provide for the care and comfort of his wife where such becomes necessary as a result of sickness, illness, or injury sustained by her.

With the emancipation of married women from this common-law disability, the same two causes of action remained, but now the injured wife may sue in her own name for the injuries she has sustained, including her physical distress. The husband still has his cause of action for loss of services and medical expenses which he can assert in his own name. Thus, where a married woman is injured at the present time, both the husband and the wife have causes of action arising out of the same event, which can be prosecuted jointly or separately. A release by the wife alone will not extinguish the husband's cause of action and, conversely, a release by the husband alone would not extinguish his wife's cause of action.

At common law, when the husband himself was injured, only he had a right of action against the wrongdoer, and the release by him of his cause of action would extinguish the entire claim. Whether or not any right on the part of the wife to the services of her husband existed is obscure. Possibly one reason, at least, why such a right was never recognized was due to the fact that the wife could not assert such a right even if she had one, since she was under a legal disability and could not enforce such a cause of action.

In *Hitaffer* v. *Argonne Products* [183 Fed. 2d 811; certiorari denied in 340 U.S. 852], the Circuit Court of Appeals for the District of Columbia, recognizing the irrationality of denying the wife a remedy available to her husband, modified the common law of the District of Columbia and held that the wife had an assertable cause of action for the loss of consortium where her husband had been injured by the tortious act of the defendant. The court reasoned that since the husband had a cause of action for loss of his wife's services where she was injured, the wife, likewise, in the case of injury to her husband had sustained similar damage.

The wife, being under a legal disability at common law could not assert this cause of action. Since married women now by statute have been emancipated from the legal disability imposed by the common law, the court said that the wife now could assert such a cause of action and recover. Therefore, under the ruling of the case, where a husband is injured, a cause of action arises on the part of the wife for damages for the loss of her husband's services.

At first the Hitaffer decision was generally rejected, but at the present time there seems to be a trend toward a reexamination of the question, with the result that the following courts have now adopted the Hitaffer rule:

Alaska	*Schreiner* v. *Clay Fruit et al.*, 519 Pac. 2d 462.
Arizona	*City of Glendale* v. *Bradshaw*, 503 Pac. 2d 803.
Arkansas	*Missouri Pacific Trans. Co.* v. *Miller*, 299 S.W. 2d 41.
Delaware	*Stenta* v. *Leblang*, 185 Atl. 2d 759.
Florida	*Gates* v. *Foley*, 247 So. 2d 40.
Georgia	*Brown* v. *Georgia-Tennessee Coaches, Inc.*, 77 S.E. 2d 41.
	Bailey v. *Wilson*, 111 S.E. 2d 106.
Illinois	*Dini* v. *Naidich*, 170 N.E. 2d 881.
Indiana	*Troue* v. *Marker*, 252 N.E. 2d 800.
Iowa	*Acuff* v. *Schmidt*, 78 N.W. 2d 480.
Kentucky	*Kotsiris* v. *Ling*, 451 S.W. 2d 411.

Maryland	Deems v. Western Maryland Ry. Co., 231 Atl. 2d 514.
Massachusetts	Diaz v. Eli Lilly & Co., 302 N.E. 2d 555.
Michigan	Montgomery v. Stephan, 101 N.W. 2d 227.
Minnesota	Thill v. Modern Erecting Co., 170 N.W. 2d 865.
Mississippi	Chevrolet v. Ward, 51 So. 2d 443.
Missouri	Novak v. Kansas City Transit, Inc., 365 S.W. 2d 539.
New Hampshire	LaBonte v. National Gypsum, 269 Atl. 2d 634.
New Jersey	Elko v. Constr. Serv. Corp., 215 Atl. 2d 1.
New York	Millington v. Southeastern Elevator Co., Inc., 239 N.E. 2d 897.
Ohio	Clouston v. Remlinger, 258 N.E. 2d 230.
Oregon	Ross v. Cuthbert, 397 Pac 2d 529.
Pennsylvania	Hopkins v. Blanco, 302 Atl. 2d 855.
Rhode Island	Mariani v. Nanni, 185 Atl. 2d 119.
South Dakota	Hoekstra v. Helgeland, 98 N.W. 2d 669.
Wisconsin	Moran v. Quality Aluminum Casting Co., 150 N.W. 2d 137.

In addition, there are federal court decisions interpreting the law of the following states, which allow a recovery by the wife for loss of consortium:

Montana	Duffy v. Lipsman-Fulker Son & Co., 200 Fed. Supp. 71.
Nebraska	Cooney v. Moomaw, 109 Fed. Supp. 448;
	Luther v. Mample, 250 Fed. 2d 922.

The following states have considered and have rejected the Hitaffer rule:

Alabama	Smith v. United Constr. Workers, 122 So. 2d 153.
California	Deshotel v. Atchison, T. & S. F. Ry., 328 Pac. 2d 449.
Colorado	Weng v. Schleiger, 273 Pac. 2d 356.
Connecticut	Lockwood v. Lee, 128 Atl. 2d 330.
Maine	Potter v. Schafter, 211 Atl. 2d 891.
Oklahoma	Nelson v. Lockett, 243 Pac. 2d 719.
South Carolina	Page v. Winter, 126 S.E. 2d 570.
Tennessee	Rush v. Great American, 376 S.W. 2d 454.
Texas	Krohn v. Richardson-Merrell, 406 S.W. 2d 166.
Vermont	Baldwin v. State, 215 Atl. 2d 492.
West Virginia	Seagraves v. Legg, 127 S.E. 2d 605.

Some of the above cited cases are quite old, and even though the courts have rejected the rule, there is no guarantee that they will not reconsider the adoption of the rule in an appropriate case. It undoubtedly will be argued that in view of the opinion in the majority of states which have adopted the Hitaffer rule that the continued rejection of the rule denies to women equal protection of the laws. Therefore no reliance should be placed on these decisions.

In states where the Hitaffer rule has been adopted, two causes of action arise in cases where the husband in injured—one by the husband for his own injuries, pain and suffering, and medical expense and one by the wife for her loss of consortium. A release of one cause of action will not extinguish the other. Therefore, it is recommended in all cases where the injured person (man or woman) is married that releases be taken from both husband and wife. This procedure is recommended even in those states which have specifically rejected the Hitaffer rule.

604 Prenatal injuries

The common-law rule is that an injury to an unborn child is solely an injury to the mother. The reasoning is that an unborn child is not a person endowed with legal rights until actually born. A fetus *en ventre sa mere* is considered to be part of the mother's anatomy until birth. Therefore, any injury to the fetus prior to birth is considered to be an injury to the mother only. This rule is applied even though the infant is born later with some physical or mental defect which can be directly traced to the injury sustained by the mother. Under those circumstances, settlement by the mother of her claim for personal injuries will extinguish the entire cause of action.

Some courts felt that the application of this common-law rule was entirely unjust, especially in cases where the child was forced to go through life with a physical or mental impairment which was visited upon it as a result of the wrongdoing of another. Therefore, these courts changed the rule and permitted recoveries in actions brought by such children whose injuries could be traced to the injury to the mother. This sounds like a fairly simple rule to apply, but the decisions of the courts are in hopeless confusion as to the situations in which they will apply the rule and the situations in which they will not.

The first distinction introduced was the application of the rule of viability. A viable child is a child which has proceeded to such a point in its development that, although not born, it still is capable of life outside of the mother. A nonviable unborn child is one that has not proceeded to such a state of development and cannot exist outside of the mother. In determining this question, reliance must be placed upon medical testimony, and the presence or absence of a fetal heartbeat will have some bearing on the question. A number of courts have allowed recoveries where the injury was sustained by a viable child, and denied recovery in cases where personal injuries were sustained by a nonviable fetus. Still other states made no distinction between the two and have allowed recoveries in all cases where the child was born with an injury or mental disability traceable to the injury to the mother, whether the child was viable or nonviable at the time of the injury to the mother.

The question has not been presented to all of the states, and therefore it is impossible at this time to make too many distinctions as to those states which will apply the viability rule and those which will not. The cases in which recoveries have been allowed for personal injury sustained by a viable child prior to birth are as follows:

Connecticut   *Tursi* v. *New England*, 111 Atl. 2d 14.
District of Columbia *Bonbrest* v. *Katz*, 65 Fed. Supp. 138.

Delaware	*Worgan* v. *Greggo*, 128 Atl. 2d 555.
Georgia	*Tucker* v. *Carmichael*, 65 S.E. 2d 909.
Illinois	*Amann* v. *Faidy*, 114 N.E. 2d 412.
Kentucky	*Mitchell* v. *Couch*, 285 S.W. 2d 901.
Minnesota	*Verkennes* v. *Corniea*, 38 N.W. 2d 838.
Mississippi	*Rainey* v. *Horn*, 72 So. 2d 434.
Missouri	*Steggal* v. *Morris*, 258 S.W. 2d 577.
New Hampshire	*Proliquire* v. *MacDonald*, 135 Atl. 2d 249.
New Jersey	*Smith* v. *Brennan*, 157 Atl. 2d 497.
New York	*Woods* v. *Lancet*, 102 N.E. 2d 691.
Oregon	*Mallison* v. *Pomeroy*, 291 Pac. 2d 225.
Washington	*Seattle First National Bank* v. *Rankin*, 367 Pac. 2d 835.

The states in which the question has been presented, and where the viability rule has been rejected, make no distinction in cases of personal injury as to whether the injury was sustained by a viable or nonviable fetus. The states allowing recoveries for personal injuries in such cases are as follows:

Georgia	*Hornbuckle* v. *Plantation Pipe Line*, 93 S.E. 2d 727.
Maryland	*Damasiewicz* v. *Gorsuch*, 79 Atl. 2d 55.
Massachusetts	*Torigan* v. *Watertown News*, 225 N.E. 2d 926.
New Hampshire	*Bennett* v. *Hymers*, 147 Atl. 2d 108.
New Jersey	*Smith* v. *Brennan*, 157 Atl. 2d 497.
New York	*Kelly* v. *Gregory*, 125 N.Y.S. 2d 696.
Pennsylvania	*Von Elbe* v. *Studebaker-Packard*, 15 Pa. Dist. & Co. R. 2d 635.
Rhode Island	*Sylvia* v. *Gobielle*, 220 Atl. 2d 222.
Texas	*Leal* v. *C. C. Pitts*, 419 S.W. 2d 820.
Wisconsin	*Puhl* v. *Milwaukee*, 99 N.W. 2d 163.

In cases involving the death of the unborn child, either prior to birth or immediately thereafter, we find still more diversity of opinion among the courts. We will consider death cases below under three categories of infants born alive, stillborn infants, and nonviable fetuses.

Death of viable infant born alive.   In the following states recoveries have been allowed in cases where the viable infant sustained injuries and survived birth, but died soon thereafter as a result of the injuries.

Connecticut	*Gorke* v. *LeClerc*, 181 Atl. 2d 488;
	Prates v. *Sears*, 118 Atl. 2d 633.
Illinois	*Amann* v. *Faidy*, 114 N.E. 2d 412.
Iowa	*Wendt* v. *Lillo*, 182 Fed. Supp. 56.
Missouri	*Steggall* v. *Morris*, 258 S.W. 2d 577.
Massachusetts	*Keyes* v. *Construction Services*, 165 N.E. 2d 612.
New York	*Woods* v. *Lancet*, 102 N.E. 2d 691.
South Carolina	*Hall* v. *Murphy*, 113 S.E. 2d 790.

Death of viable infant prior to birth or stillborn.   In the following states recoveries have been allowed in these cases. :

Connecticut	*Gorke* v. *LeClerc*, 181 Atl. 2d 448.
Delaware	*Worgan* v. *Greggo et al.*, 128 Atl. 2d 557.
Georgia	*Porter* v. *Lassiter*, 87 S.E. 2d 100; action brought under a statute permitting a recovery for the "homicide" of a child.
Illinois	*Chrisafogeorgis* v. *Brandenberg*, 304 N.E. 2d 88.
Iowa	*Wendt* v. *Lillo*, 182 Fed. Supp. 56; federal court decision interpreting the law of Iowa.
Kansas	*Hale* v. *Manion*, 368 Pac. 2d 1.
Kentucky	*Mitchell* v. *Couch*, 285 S.W. 2d 901.
Maryland	*Odham* v. *Sherman*, 198 Atl. 2d 71.
Minnesota	*Verkennes* v. *Corniea*, 38 N.W. 2d 838.
Mississippi	*Rainey* v. *Horn*, 70 So. 2d 434.
New Hampshire	*Proliquire* v. *MacDonald*, 135 Atl. 2d 249.
Ohio	*Stidam* v. *Ashmore*, 167 N.E. 2d 106.
Pennsylvania	*Gullborg* v. *Rizzo*, 331 Fed. 2d 557; construing Pennsylvania law.
	However, in *Carroll* v. *Skloff*, 202 Atl. 2d 9, the Pennsylvania Supreme Court denied recovery for stillbirth.
South Carolina	*Fowler* v. *Woodward*, 138 S.E. 2d 42.
Wisconsin	*Kwaterski* v. *State Farm Mutual*, 148 N.W. 2d 107.

The following states have denied recoveries in cases brought by the personal representatives of a viable child who died prior to birth or was stillborn.

California	*Scott* v. *McPheeters*, 92 Pac. 2d 678; (construing a statute).
Louisiana	*Cooper* v. *Blanck*, 397 So. 2d 352; (construing civil code).
Michigan	*Powers* v. *City of Troy*, 4 Mich. App. 572.
Nebraska	*Drabbels* v. *Skelly Oil Co.*, 50 N.W. 2d 229.
New York	*Muschetti* v. *Pfizer*, 144 N.Y.S. 2d 235.
Oklahoma	*Howell* v. *Rushing*, 261 Pac. 2d 217.
Tennessee	*Hogan* v. *McDaniel*, 319 S.W. 2d 221.

Death or destruction of nonviable fetus. In this classification, recoveries have been allowed for and in behalf of the unborn child in the following cases:

Georgia	*Porter* v. *Lassiter*, 87 S.E. 2d 100.
Illinois	*Daly* v. *Meier*, 178 N.E. 2d 691;
	Sana v. *Brown*, 183 N.E. 2d 187.
New Hampshire	*Bennett* v. *Hymers*, 147 Atl. 2d 108.
Pennsylvania	*Sinkler* v. *Kneal*, 164 Atl. 2d 93.

Most of the other states which have considered the problem of the death or destruction of a nonviable fetus have regarded this as part of the injury to the mother and have denied recoveries for and in behalf of the unborn child.

These differences of opinion among the courts pose a real problem for the adjuster who is faced with a claim for personal injuries by a pregnant woman. In cases where there is a possibility of an injury to the unborn child, settlement with the injured mother will not extinguish a possible claim for and in behalf of the infant who is later born with a physical or mental disability due to the accident.

605   Center-of-gravity rule

This rule relating to the exercise of jurisdiction by a court over a transaction, event, or accident which occurred outside the borders of the state is sometimes referred to as the Grouping of Significant Contacts Rule.

In tort cases, the general rule is that the place of the tort is determinative of the applicable law. This rule includes torts arising out of contract. Actions in tort are transitory in the sense that the action may be brought in any court having jurisdiction of the parties, regardless of the situs of the accident. The law of the forum (*lex fori*) is applied only to procedural matters, but the law governing the rights of the parties (substantive law) as between themselves will be governed by the law applicable at the place of injury, or the *lex loci delicti*. An exception to this rule has developed where there are special circumstances, usually where the parties to the action are citizens and residents of the forum state and where the accident has occurred elsewhere. In such a case, since the forum state has a greater interest in the outcome (greater significant contacts) because it involves only its own citizens, the local law of the forum state may be applied.

The practical result of this rule is that at the outset, the plaintiff has a choice of the law under which he will bring his action. He may proceed in the state where the accident occurred, in which case the law of that state will be applied. He may proceed in his own state of residence, in which case the law of the forum state will be applied. As a result, the plaintiff will select the jurisdiction which is more favorable to his recovery, whether it refers to the required quantum of proof, as in ordinary negligence states as opposed to guest statute states; or nonprivity states, as against privity states in products cases; or the amount of recovery, as in states which have a monetary limitation on recoveries for wrongful death as against those having no limitation whatsoever on such recoveries. However, it must be emphasized that the rule is applicable only when those special circumstances exist and there are greater significant contacts with the parties to the litigation on the part of the forum state than those of the state of the accident. The Restatement (Second) on Conflict of Laws reads as follows:

In an action for a personal injury, the local law of the state where the injury occurred determines the rights and liabilities of the parties, unless some other state has a more significant relationship with the occurrence and the parties as to the particular issue involved, in which event the local law of the latter state will govern.

Not all states have accepted this rule. Some have approved it, some have rejected it, and still others have not had occasion to examine it at all. Therefore, the best that can be accomplished at the present time is to make reference to the decided cases and the specific states of fact to which the rule has been either applied or rejected.

Aircraft. In *Kilberg* v. *Northeast Airlines, Inc.* (9 N.Y. 2d 34; 172 N.E. 2d 526), the decedent, a New York resident, purchased a plane ticket to Nantucket, Massachusetts, in New York as a paying passenger on the defendant's flight originating in New York and was killed when the plane crashed in Massachusetts. The Massachusetts wrongful death statute then limited recovery to $15,000. The deceased's administrator brought action in New York for wrongful death and for breach of an implied contract of safe carriage arising from the purchase of the plane ticket in New York. The plaintiff contended that the death limit of $15,000 as set forth in the Massachusetts wrongful death statute was merely a procedural rule and as such was not binding on the New York court. It was also argued that since the deceased was a citizen and resident of New York, since the ticket was purchased in New York and since the flight originated in New York, and, in addition, the defendant corporation conducted some of its business in New York that New York State had greater significant contacts with the tort than did Massachusetts, which was merely the site of the accident; and therefore the Massachusetts limitation of $15,000 was not applicable, and the New York court could apply its own law to the recovery. Since New York has no limitation in its wrongful death statute, an award of $150,000 was made, which was subsequently affirmed by the New York Court of Appeals.

In *Pearson* v. *Northeast Airlines, Inc.* (309 Fed. 2d 553), the plaintiff's decedent was killed in the same air crash which took the life of Kilberg. Action was begun, however, in the federal court and the constitutionality of the Kilberg decision was attacked on the theory that New York had failed to give full faith and credit to the statutes of the state of Massachusetts and, in so doing, had violated the federal Constitution in that regard. The court held there was no constitutional violation and gave judgment in the sum of $160,000 applying the New York unlimited damage rule, which judgment was upheld by the Circuit Court of Appeals. The U.S. Supreme Court denied certiorari in 372 U.S. 912.

Where the forum state has no significant contacts with the occurrence or the parties, the center-of-gravity rule does not apply. For example, in *Cherokee Laboratories* v. *Rogers* (398 Pac. 2d 520), the Oklahoma Supreme Court held that in an action brought in Oklahoma for the wrongful death of a person killed in a crash of an airplane in Missouri, the substantive law of Missouri was controlling and that the statutory wrongful death limit of Missouri should be applied. The court refused to follow Kilberg and Pearson (*supra*), since there was a failure of proof that Oklahoma had any significant contact with the event.

The same result obtained in *Skahill* v. *Capital Airlines* (234 Fed. Supp. 906), where the Federal District Court for the Southern District of New York held that in an action for wrongful death arising from an airplane crash in Virginia, the Virginia limitation on wrongful death recovery was applicable even though such limitations are against public policy in New York, where the action was brought, since a New York Court can refuse to apply the law of the state where the accident occurred only if New York has some interest or contact with the transaction. Here neither the deceased nor his dependents were residents of New York nor was the flight scheduled to pass through New York. See also, *Griffith* v. *United Airlines* [203 A 2d 796 (Supreme Court of Pennsylvania)].

There is still a third class of cases involved in the consideration of the rule, that is, where the law of the state where the accident occurred does not create a cause of action and the law of the forum state does. For example, in *Long* v. *Pan American Airways*, decided by the New York Supreme Court, Appellate Division on June 22, 1965, the facts indicated that suit was brought in New York against the defendant, which maintained its main office in New York State. The action arose as a result of the wrongful death of several passengers on a flight from Philadelphia to San Juan, P.R. The tickets were purchased in Philadelphia, and all of the deceased persons were residents of Pennsylvania as were the next of kin who brought the action. The accident occurred in Maryland, where the wrongful death statute creates a cause of action for wrongful death only in favor of persons dependent on the deceased. Pennsylvania, on the other hand, under its wrongful death statute, creates a cause of action by the next of kin, regardless of dependency. The plaintiffs urged that the Pennsylvania law should apply, since, under the ruling in the *Kilberg* case, Pennsylvania had the greater significant contacts with the persons involved in the event than did Maryland. The court held that there was no choice of law situation here for the reason that the Maryland wrongful death statute did not give the plaintiffs the right to sue, and since no cause of action was created in their behalf by the Maryland law, the procedural aspects of the Pennsylvania law could not be applied. The court distinguished the case from the *Kilberg* case in pointing out that in Kilberg the Massachusetts law created a cause of action on behalf of the plaintiffs and the question of whether or not there is a cause of action for wrongful death is a matter of substantive law governed only by the place of accident. The question of limitations on recovery is a procedural matter, and in the *Kilberg* case, the New York court disregarded the procedural limitations of the Massachusetts statute. In this case, the Maryland law created no substantive right in favor of the plaintiffs, and therefore there was no cause of action. There was a strong dissenting opinion, and it is possible that this case will be the subject matter of further appeal.

Automobiles.   In *Babcock* v. *Jackson* (12 N.Y. 2d 473; 191 N.E. 2d 379). the facts indicated that the plaintiff and her husband were both residents of Rochester, New York, as was the defendant. They drove from that city on a trip which took them into the Canadian Province of Ontario, where the accident occurred when the car went out of control and collided with a stone wall. When the plaintiff sued in New York State to recover for serious resulting injuries, the defendant pleaded as a defense the Ontario guest statute which denied a gratuitous guest any and all remedies against the host-driver or owner. This defense was upheld by the trial court, and the complaint was dismissed. The Court of Appeals reversed the decision, holding that the New

York law, which contained no guest statute, controlled the substantive law questions in the case, since New York was the "center of gravity" of the case and had a more relevant interest in the issues than did Ontario, which was merely the place of the accident. This case is significant since it applies the substantive law of the forum state to the accident and the rights of the parties, whereas all other cases make a distinction between rules of substance and rules of procedure.

In *Grant* v. *McAuliffe* (41 Cal. 2d 859), the case involved a collision in Arizona between two California automobiles containing California residents. Arizona law would not permit an action to be commenced after the death of the tort-feasor. California imposed no such limitation. In order to avoid the application of the law of the place of accident, the California court characterized the survival question as a matter of the administration of decedents' estates, governed by the law of the forum since it was procedural and not a matter of substantive law.

In *McDaniel* v. *Sinn* (400 Pac. 2d 1018), the Kansas Supreme Court refused to apply the substantive law of Kansas to an automobile accident occurring in Missouri and involving Kansas citizens. The court noted that some states have decided that where all the parties are residents of one state, the substantive law of that state could be applied to accidents occurring in another jurisdiction. The court cited *Richards* v. *United States* (369 U.S. 1) in which the headnote reads as follows:

The general conflict of laws rule followed by a vast majority of the states is to apply the law of the place of injury to the substantive rights of the parties, but the recent tendency of some states has been to depart from his rule in order to take into account the interests of the state having significant contact with the parties to the litigation.

The court also noted the Annotation in 15 ALR 2d 762 as follows:

The great weight of judicial authority is inclined to view that question as to the measure and amount of damages recoverable or a limitation on that amount are just as much questions of substantive law and therefore governed by the law of the place where the fatal injury was inflicted as the right generally to recover for the wrongful death.

The court also referred to a later Annotation in 92 ALR 2d 1180 and cited the following:

It is the general rule, subject to some exceptions . . . that questions as to the measure, extent of amount of damages recoverable in wrongful death actions are to be determined by the law of the place where the wrong causing the death occurred, this rule being founded upon the view that the measure, extent or amount of damages for wrongful death pertains to a matter of substance of the right to recovery, which should be governed by the law of the place wherein the cause of action arose.

The court decided to follow the rule applying the substantive law of the place of the accident to tort cases irrespective of any contacts with the parties to the litigation which Kansas might have.

Contracts.   In tort cases arising out of the negligent performance of contracts, the same questions are presented. In *Dyke* v. *Erie Railroad* [45 N.Y. 113 (1871)], the contract referred to a contract of carriage by rail between New York points but through Pennsylvania. Damage was sustained in Pennsylvania by whose law the recovery would be limited to $3,000. However, the New York court held that the Pennsylvania limitation did not apply, since this was a contract for safe carriage, executed in New York by residents of the State of New York, and therefore the substantive law of New York, which had no limitation, applied. A judgment of $35,000 was sustained. See also, *Bowles* v. *Zimmer Mfg. Co.* (277 Fed. 2d 868; 76 ALR 2d 120), involving a breach of warranty in the sale of a defective surgical nail; and also *Lowe's Hardware, Inc.* v. *Fidelity Mutual Insurance Co.* (319 Fed. 2d 469), which involved a life insurance contract.

As contracts of release executed in a state other than the state in which the tort occurred, see *Daily* v. *Somberg* (146 Atl. 2d 676; 69 ALR 2d 1024). In that case, a release executed in New Jersey for a malpractice cause of action against doctors who aggravated a previously existing injury sustained as a result of an Ohio tort was held to be governed by the law of New Jersey as to its effect. As to contracts made in one state to be performed in another, see *Clay* v. *Sun Insurance Office, Ltd.* [84 Sup. Ct. 1197; 12 Fire & Cas. (CCH) 30]. In that case the Supreme Court of the United States held that the five-year statute of limitations of the Florida law was applicable to a Florida suit brought against the insurer by a Florida resident who had formerly lived in Illinois, where the contract of insurance was executed. The Illinois cases uphold the 12-month-suit clause in the insurance contract as valid, whereas the Florida law by statute has nullified such limitations if they require that suit be brought in less than five years. The Court said that Florida had ample contacts with the transaction and the parties so as to satisfy any conceivable requirement of full faith and credit or of due process.

Defamation.   The following cases are involved in multistate defamation and invasion of privacy: *Dale System, Inc.* v. *Time, Inc.* (116 Fed Supp. 527), in which the law of the plaintiff's domicile applied to a multistate libel; and *Mattox* v. *News Syndicate Co.* (176 Fed 2d 897), in which the Virginia law was applied to a libel suit brought by a Virginia resident against a New York newspaper. See also, 60 *Harvard Law Review* 941–52.

Dram shop acts.   In *Schmidt* v. *Driscoll Hotel* (82 N.W. 2d 635), Minnesota applied its Civil Damage Act so as to provide a remedy against a liquor seller for the illegal sale within the state which resulted in an out-of-state automobile accident in Wisconsin.

In *Zucker* v. *Vogt* (200 Fed. Supp. 340), the Federal Court in Connecticut applied that state's dram shop act to allow a recovery for the death of a New York motorist in a New York automobile accident caused by the defendant's sale of liquor in Connecticut to an intoxicated motorist whose domicile was unknown. The court reasoned that the purpose of the Connecticut statute was not limited to local injuries but extended to out-of-state injuries when caused by local illegal sales of liquor.

Interfamilial immunity. The general rule seems to be that the law of the matrimonial domicile will determine whether or not one spouse has a cause of action against the other regardless of where the injuries were inflicted. For example, in *Haumschild* v. *Continental Casualty Co.* [95 N.W. 2d 814 (Wisconsin)], the capacity of one spouse to sue the other for a personal tort was held to be governed by the law of the matrimonial domicile and not by the place of the accident. The accident occurred in California, but the suit was filed in Wisconsin. Wisconsin law was held to be applicable.

In *Thompson* v. *Thompson* [193 Atl. 2d 439 (New Hampshire)], it was held that the law of the family domicile applied to determine the capacity of one spouse to sue the other even for an out-of-state automobile tort. In *Koplik* v. *C. P. Trucking Corp.* [141 Atl. 2d 34 (New Jersey)], the court held that the New Jersey law which was the law of the forum as well as the family domicile controlled rather than the law of New York in which state the injury was sustained. To the same effect is *Emery* v. *Emery* [289 Pac. 2d 218 (California)].

Interstate bailments. In *Levy* v. *Daniel's U-Drive Auto Renting Co.* [143 Atl. 163 (Connecticut)], there was a Connecticut commercial bailment of an automobile which was involved in an accident in Massachusetts resulting in an injury to a passenger. The Connecticut statute provided that anyone renting a car to another is liable for any damage caused to any person by the operator of such vehicle while rented. The plaintiff-passenger sued the defendant in Connecticut, seeking to impose the liability created by the Connecticut statute. The claim was resisted on the ground that since the action sounded in tort, its validity must be determined only by the law of Massachusetts, which imposed no liability on commercial bailors. The Connecticut court held that since the statute was part of the bailment contract entered into with the driver, and since the plaintiff was a beneficiary of that contract, the plaintiff's claim against the defendant was one in contract and the Connecticut law applied.

CASE TABLE

Rule Applied	Aircraft
New York	*Kilberg* v. *Northeast Airlines, Inc.,* 9 N.Y. 2d 34; 172 N.E. 2d 526.
New York	*Pearson* v. *Northeast Airlines, Inc.,* 309 Fed. 2d 553, certiorari denied in 372 U.S. 912.
Pennsylvania	*Kuchinic* v. *McCrory,* 22 Atl. 2d 897.

Rule Denied	
Florida	*Hopkins* v. *Lockheed Aircraft Corp.* 201 So. 2d 743.
New York	*Skahill* v. *Capital Airlines,* 234 Fed. Supp. 906.
Oklahoma	*Cherokee Laboratories* v. *Rogers,* 398 Pac. 2d 520.
Pennsylvania	*Griffith* v. *United Airlines,* 203 Atl. 2d 796.
Ohio	*Goranson* v. *Capital Airlines,* 345 Fed. 2d 750.

Rule Applied	*Automobiles*
California	*Grant* v. *McAuliffe*, 41 Cal. 2d 859.
Kentucky	*Wessling* v. *Paris*, 1967–1 Auto Neg. (CCH) 15, 766.
New York	*Babcock* v. *Jackson*, 12 N.Y. 2d 473, 191 N.E. 2d 379.
New York	*Keller* v. *Greyhound Corp.*, 244 N.Y.S. 2d 882.
Wisconsin	*Wilcox* v. *Wilcox*, 133 N.W. 2d 408.

Rule Denied	
Delaware	*Friday* v. *Smoot*, 211 Atl. 2d 594.
Kansas	*McDaniel* v. *Sinn*, 400 Pac. 2d 1018.
Maryland	*White* v. *King*, 223 Atl. 2d 763.
New York	*Dym* v. *Gordon*, 16 N.Y. 2d 120.
New York	*Kell* v. *Henderson*, 47 Misc. 2d 992.
Wisconsin	*Brunke* v. *Popp*, 124 N.W. 2d 642.

CHAPTER VII

Law of contracts

700 Elements of contracts

For the most part, the claimsman will be concerned with contracts which are already in existence. These include, among others, insurance contracts, leases, hold harmless agreements, and arbitration agreements. He will be involved in the formulation of only a few. These are contracts of release, covenants not to sue, nonwaiver agreements, and instruments of similar character.

A contract may be defined as an agreement relating to a legal subject matter between two or more persons, having the capacity to contract, whereby for a valuable consideration one or more become entitled to acts or forebearance to act on the part of the other or others. The element which distinguishes a contract from a mere unenforceable agreement is the consideration. Consideration, called *quid pro quo*, means "something for something." For example, *A* has the right to bring a personal injury action in tort against *B*. *B* agrees to pay, and *A* agrees to accept $100 to settle his case. The consideration running from *B* to *A* is $100, and the consideration running from *A* to *B* is *A*'s forebearance of his right to sue. Therefore, this is a contract and, as such, enforceable at law.

175

A contract comes into existence as a result of two preliminary steps: (1) an offer by one and (2) an acceptance by the other. When both of these preliminary steps have been taken, and where both are supported by a valuable consideration, there is a contract.

701   Offer

An offer is a proposal to make a contract. It must be made by the person who is to make the promise, and it must be made to the person to whom the promise is made. It may be made either by words or signs, either orally or in writing, either personally or by messenger, but in whatever way it is made, it is not in law an offer until it comes to the knowledge of the person to whom it is made.

The insurance industry uses two terms to differentiate between an offer of settlement made by the company and an offer of settlement made by the claimant. These terms are *offer* and *demand*. An offer refers to the amount which the company has already transmitted to the claimant as the amount that it will pay in full settlement of the claim. A demand is the amount that the claimant has submitted to the company for which he will settle his claim. Both are offers or proposals to enter into a settlement contract. In both instances, no contract will result until the amount so offered or demanded, as the case may be, is accepted by the opposite party.

The person making the offer, the offeror, has the right to decrease, increase, vary, or withdraw the offer at any time before it is accepted. Any such change in the offer is not legally effective until it is brought to the attention of the person to whom the original offer was made, the offeree. If the original offer is accepted prior to the time that the offeror's intention to change the offer has been received by the offeree, then there is a contract based on the original offer.

Once an offer has been made, the offeror is in a less favorable position than the offeree. Unless the offer is altered or withdrawn, the offeree can bring a legal contract into existence by an act of acceptance. There is no further step which the offeror can take, once the offer is made, in order to bring a contract into existence. The initiative is with the offeree. He can, at his option, bring a contract into existence or refuse to enter into a contract.

702   Duration of offer

The period of time within which the offer will remain open, and during which the offeree may accept, can be specifically stated by the offeror at the time of making the offer. Then, if the offer is not accepted within the time so limited, the offer will terminate by its own terms. If no time is stated at the time the offer is made, in the absence of any withdrawal of the offer by the offeror, the offer is considered to remain open for a reasonable time. What would constitute a reasonable time would depend upon the facts and circumstances of the situation. In the case of litigation, what would constitute a reasonable time under the circumstances is a question of fact for the jury.

What would be a reasonable time in one case might be an unreasonable time in another. For example, if an offer were made to a claimant who was still under medical treatment, and the facts indicated that he expected to be discharged by his doctor within the next two weeks, under such circumstances it would be reasonable to expect that the claimant would not be in a position to accept the offer or reject it until such time as his medical treatment had terminated. Therefore, in that case, the claimant would be at least the two-week period of time contemplated within which to accept the offer. In the absence of any change or withdrawal of the offer during that period of time, the acceptance of the offer at any time within the two-week period or perhaps even one week beyond the termination of treatment might not be an unreasonable length of time. Therefore, it would be considered that the offer remained open at least until the termination of the claimant's treatment, and then perhaps for a short time thereafter.

If the claimant waited six months after the termination of his treatment before deciding to accept the offer, the offeror could treat the offer as having expired by the passage of time and regard the claimant's acceptance as an offer itself. It is not required that an offer remain open indefinitely, and where a reasonable time has expired between the time of the offer and the time of the attempted acceptance, the offeror can treat the offer as no longer in existence.

To take another example, let us assume that during the course of the trial of a personal injury action, the defendant's attorney offered to settle the case for a stated amount. Even if no other words were spoken, it would be contemplated under the circumstances of the offer that an immediate acceptance was required and that the offer would terminate if not immediately accepted. Clearly, the plaintiff could not regard the offer as continuing until after verdict. The circumstances under which the offer was made indicate that the offer was made in order to avoid submitting the matter to the jury and that a reasonable time within which the offer must be accepted would be a matter of minutes rather than a longer period of time.

703   Offer to an attorney or agent

An attorney is a special or limited agent of his client. He has no authority to release his client's claim unless and until the client authorizes him to do so. Anyone dealing with an attorney is on notice of the fact that he is dealing with a limited agent who cannot bind his client to a settlement without his client's consent. An offer to an attorney is then an offer to an agent or messenger of the offeree, and unless there is a time limit expressed in the offer, or it is revoked before acceptance, the offer will be considered to remain open for a reasonable period of time. Since the offeror knows that the offer must be communicated to the client, a reasonable period of time would be of at least sufficient duration to give the attorney an opportunity to communicate with his client and receive a reply. If the client is located in the same city as the attorney, the period of time would be of short duration, whereas if the client is located in a distant city, or in a foreign country, the period of time constituting a reasonable time would be that much longer.

When an offer is made to an attorney he will sometimes venture his own opinion as to whether or not the offer will be acceptable to his client. This expression of opinion is in no way binding on his client. He may say that the amount offered is too small and that he doubts that his client will accept it, but if he is successful in securing the client's consent to a slightly higher figure, he inquires as to whether the company will pay it. The objective is to obtain an increase in the offer before making any sort of a demand.

For example, if an offer of $500 were made, the attorney might say that he knows that his client will not accept it, but he will communicate it anyway. He will venture the opinion that he is sure that his client would be interested in a settlement of $750, and he then inquires as to whether or not the company would be willing to pay $750, provided that he can induce his client to accept that amount. If the company agrees that it will pay $750 under those circumstances, it has actually increased its offer to $750. The mere fact that this increased offer is made on the condition that the client accepts it doesn't change its character from an offer into something else; it is still an offer of $750. If the company intended to stand on its original offer of $500 it should have said so, and it should have advised the attorney that if his client wishes to submit a counteroffer of $750, or any other figure, the client may do so, and the company will give due consideration to any such counteroffer.

While the attorney is a limited agent of his client, it is possible for the client to give him the authority to settle the claim. This happens most frequently where the client is absent from the state or from the country. Under those circumstances, an agreement by the attorney to settle at a certain figure is binding on his client, and where the attorney warrants that he has such authority, the claimsman may deal with him on that basis. Whether or not the attorney has actually warranted his authority to so act will be determined by the words which were said and the conditions under which they were spoken. If the attorney were to say, "You can deal with me because my client will take whatever I tell him is reasonable," the attorney has not warranted his authority to settle the claim for his client. He has merely expressed an opinion as to how his client will react to his recommendations and nothing more. To be a warranty of authority, the words spoken must clearly communicate the fact that the authority has already been delegated to the attorney and that he can bind his client to a contract of release. Anything less than this will not be construed as a warranty of authority. For these reasons, the claimsman should exercise extreme care in deciding whether or not a warranty has been given. Nothing is more frustrating than a situation where the claimsman has mistakenly construed some words spoken to be a warranty and, in proceeding on that basis, has offered the limit of his authorization, not only to find that there was no warranty but also to be confronted with a demand for more money. Therefore, if there is any doubt as to whether or not the attorney is giving a warranty as to his authority to settle, a letter or other writing from the attorney spelling out his authority should be secured. This writing can be relied upon, since no attorney will put himself on record as having authority unless he actually has it.

In addition to the authority to settle the claim for the client, the attorney may be given the power to execute a release or other document extinguishing the claim. Where such is the case, the claimsman may accept such a document, executed by the attorney only, but for the protection of the file he should obtain a verified copy of the document granting such authority (usually a power of attorney).

When dealing with an agent of the claimant, other than an attorney, the claimsman is likewise on notice that the agent has no greater authority than that granted to him by the claimant. Inquiry should be directed to the authority and to the basis on which the agent is purporting to act, and copies of the documents granting the authority should be secured. Dealings with the agent can be had but only to the extent of the authority set forth in the documents submitted.

The situation comes up most frequently where the husband is in the service and has executed a power of attorney to his wife whereby she can act in his place and stead during this time. Where the wife has been injured through the negligence of another, she can, by means of this power, execute a release extinguishing the husband's cause of action for loss of consortium and medical expense. She could also release any other claim which the husband may have for his own personal injuries. A verified or photostatic copy of the power of attorney should be obtained and filed in support of the release executed.

704   Offer through an authorized agent

The offer does not have to be made directly by the person, firm, or corporation making the offer, but can be made through an agent selected and authorized for that purpose. The agent selected for the purpose of communicating the offer may be a telegraph company, a telephone operator, an attorney, an employee, or an adjuster. When an offer is made through an agent, the offeror is bound by the mistakes of the agent in transmitting or communicating the offer. If this were not so, business of any kind could not be conducted with any degree of certainty or dispatch. The offeree therefore can rely on the offer as it is received, and when accepted in good faith as received, a contract will result. For example, a claimant makes a demand of $500 for the settlement of his claim. The insurance company sends a telegram offering to settle for $250. Through an error in transmission, the telegram actually received offers $350, which the claimant accepts. The company is bound to a settlement for $350.

Now let us assume that the error in transmission had to do with an additional cipher, and the telegram received by the claimant read $2,500, rather than the $250 intended, and the claimant accepted the $2,500. The company is not bound to a $2,500 settlement. The acceptance was not in good faith. The claimant knew or should have known, in the face of his demand of $500, that the telegram was an obvious error, and he was therefore put on inquiry as to the exact terms of the offer.

The same principles apply where the offeror has selected other agents for the purpose of transmitting an offer. Suppose that an adjuster was authorized to settle for $250 a case in which there was a $500 demand. By mistake the adjuster offers $350, which the claimant accepts. The company is bound to the

$350 settlement. On the other hand, let us assume that the claimant authorized his attorney to make a demand of $500 and by mistake the attorney makes a demand of $350, which the company accepts. The claimant is bound to a settlement of $350. It should be noted that the attorney's authority to make the offer of settlement came directly from his client and that a demand or offer of settlement was actually made on the strength of that authority. If the attorney merely gives his opinion as to the amount that his client should receive for the injury, he has not made a demand nor has he transmitted an offer of settlement from his client to the company. In such a case, the client would not be bound by the attorney's own opinion as to value.

The same principles of good faith in the acceptance of the offer are applicable in the foregoing cases. If the claimant demanded $500 and the adjuster offered $2,500, the claimant would be put on inquiry as to the *bona fide* of the offer. Or where the offer of settlement to the claimant's attorney was $2,500 and the attorney offered to settle for $500, the company likewise would be put on inquiry as to the possibility of a mistake.

Where an offer is made by an agent outside the scope of his agency, or without authorization so to do by the principal, the law of agency will be applied in determining whether the principal is or is not bound to a contract created by the acceptance of such an offer. Where the agent has made a mistake in transmitting the offer, or where the agent exceeds his authority in making the offer, the rights and liabilities of the parties as between themselves are governed by the principles of the law of agency. (See Chapter VIII.)

705   Termination of offer

An offer of settlement may be terminated by any one of the following:

1. Rejection by the offeree.
2. Lapse of time.
3. Death of the offeree.
4. Revocation by the offeror.

Rejection.   A rejection by the offeree immediately terminates the offer. This is true even though the offeror indicated by the terms of the offer that it would remain open for a certain period of time. For example, if *A* makes an offer of settlement to *B* with the understanding that the offer would remain open for the next 14 days, and if *B* rejects the offer the very next day, the offer is terminated as of the time of rejection.

A counteroffer by the offeree is a rejection of the original offer. While the original offer does not necessarily have to be rejected specifically, the making of a counteroffer by the offeree indicates his unwillingness to accept the original offer as made and, as such, terminates it.

Lapse of time.   An offer not accepted within a reasonable time will terminate. An acceptance after a reasonable time has passed is regarded as an offer itself, since there is no outstanding offer which can be accepted.

Death of offeree.   The death of the offeree prior to his acceptance of the offer terminates it. The offeree is an essential person in the making of a contract, and his death terminates the offer and likewise terminates any unfinished negotiations.

Revocation by offeror. Prior to acceptance, the offeror may withdraw or revoke the offer he has given. This termination of the offer is effective only when brought to the attention of the offeree. If the information is communicated to the offeree prior to acceptance, the offer terminates, and an acceptance after receipt of this information will not result in a contract.

706   Acceptance

The acceptance of an offer is an expression of assent to the terms thereof made by the offeree to the offeror. This assent must comply exactly with the terms and conditions of the offer. If there are any variations in the terms of the acceptance, as compared with the terms of the offer, it is not an acceptance but a counteroffer.

The acceptance may be made by the offeree or by someone in his behalf authorized by him to do so. Therefore, the offeree may authorize his attorney to accept the offer for him or authorize an agent to perform the same function. However, where an offer is made to an offeree, and before acceptance the offeree dies, acceptance by the offeree's personal representative or executor within a reasonable time will not constitute a contract. The offer expires as of the time of the offeree's death, and therefore the act of the executor cannot bring a contract into existence.

707   Acceptance by silence

The silence of the offeree, or his lack of response to an offer, does not constitute an acceptance. This is true even though the offer stipulated that a failure to reply would be construed as an acceptance. For example, if an adjuster wrote to the claimant, offering him $100 in full settlement of his claim, further advising that if he, the adjuster, did not hear from the claimant by a certain date, he would assume that the $100 is acceptable, the lack of response by the claimant under those circumstances would not constitute an acceptance and there would be no contract.

708   Acceptance by conduct

If a person accepts and uses goods or merchandise which are forwarded to him on an unsolicited basis, his use of the goods implies an acceptance of an offer to sell, and also implies an obligation to pay for the goods. The same principle would apply to a situation where the adjuster sends the claimant a release form draft with a letter stating that the payment therein constitutes a full and complete settlement of any cause of action which the claimant may have against the insured. The acceptance and deposit of such a draft under those circumstances would constitute an acceptance of the offer. The claimant is precluded from claiming that he did not accept an offer of settlement. He could not claim that he accepted the check as part payment, since the terms of the tender of the draft contemplated a settlement in full.

709   Consideration

Even though there is an offer and an acceptance, one additional element is necessary to give the resulting agreement the binding force of a contract. The agreement must be supported by adequate consideration. Consideration for a promise is either an act or a forebearance. It is the price bargained for and paid for a promise.

For example, in the giving of a release of a personal injury claim, the consideration for the claimant's promise to forego his right to bring suit is the amount of money paid to him. The agreement by the insurance carrier to pay an amount of money which it is not legally required to do until the claimant has secured a judgment, represents a legal detriment to the insurance carrier. The forebearance by the claimant from asserting his legal rights is a legal detriment to him. Neither of the parties is obligated to do either act. Therefore, there is some benefit moving from each party to the other. This benefit to one, and legal detriment to the other, is called consideration.

Consideration has also been defined as any benefit conferred or agreed to be conferred upon the promisor by any other person to which the promisor is not lawfully entitled, or any prejudice suffered, or agreed to be suffered by such person, other than such as he is at the time of consent lawfully bound to suffer, as an inducement to the promisor. This means that consideration consists of the doing of something which a person is not legally obligated to do, such as the payment of money or the waiver of some legal right.

The courts generally will not inquire into the relative value of the consideration moving from one party to the other, taking the position that the parties may enter into any type of agreement they please and that it is no part of the court's function to determine whether the value of the consideration moving from one party to the other is commensurate with the value of the consideration moving from the other. Under this theory, where only a nominal consideration is expressed, $1, the courts generally will not inquire as to whether or not the action required of the other party has the value of $1 or something in excess of that amount. The only time that the courts will consider the question of the adequacy or value of the consideration is where there is a promise of goods for goods or money for money, or where the consideration is so inadequate so as to be unconscionable. For example, it has been held that a consideration of $1 would be insufficient to support the payment of $5,000 by the other party. The delivery of 100 bales of cotton would hardly support the promise as a return of the delivery of 1,000 bales of the same kind of cotton.

While the courts will not inquire into the adequacy of the consideration, where there is a claim of misrepresentation, fraud, or mutual mistake of fact, and an attempt is made to set aside and vacate the release, the amount paid as the consideration will have some bearing on the issues. For example, a small payment might support a claim that it was accepted as part payment and that the release was signed on the representation that it was a receipt for such payment. On the other hand, a large payment, or one which, when viewed in comparison with the injuries suffered, was entirely adequate, would not be evidence in support of a claim that it was accepted as a partial payment.

710 Void and voidable contracts

An agreement may have all of the incidents of a contract, such as offer, acceptance, and a valuable consideration. The parties may have intended to enter into a legal contract, but the contract may not be recognized by the courts either because it contemplated the doing of an illegal act, is against public policy, because there was fraud in the execution of the instrument, or because of a mutual mistake as to the subject matter. These contracts, if they are contracts at all, are void *ab initio* (from the beginning), and no rights, duties, or obligations arise because of their existence. No action is required on the part of either party to declare it to be a void contract, since it is void and unenforceable from the very beginning.

There are some contracts which may be disaffirmed by one of the parties, either because he was an infant, or under some other legal disability when he entered into it, or because there was fraud in the inducement, or because of a mistake on his part caused or induced by the other party. Such a contract is treated as valid until the party who has the right to disaffirm it has manifested his election to do so. If he does not do so, it is a valid and enforceable contract. During the time he still has the right of disaffirmance, it is called a voidable contract.

711 Mistake of fact

A mistake of fact may be *mutual* (by both parties) or *unilateral* (by only one party). A mutual mistake of fact as to the existence of the subject matter, its quantity, quality, nature, and the law relating to the situation will usually prevent the formation of a contract.

For example, *A* has what he believes to be a diamond ring. He agrees to sell the ring to *B*, who also believes the ring to be a diamond, for $1,000; but the stone is glass and not a diamond. There is no contract for the reason that there was a mutual mistake of fact. *A* thought he was selling a diamond ring and *B* thought he was buying a diamond ring. The nature of the subject matter was such that they were both mistaken as to its nature and quality.

In another example, *A* sustained injuries to his leg which were described by his doctor as lacerations and contusions. Both *A*, and *B*, the insurance adjuster, relied on these statements as being an accurate description of the injury. Under those circumstances, a release of the claim by *A* for $250 and the payment of that amount by the adjuster would constitute a full and complete release of the claim. However, suppose, unknown to both *A* and *B*, that *A* was suffering from a thrombosis which ultimately set up an occlusion, as a result of which the leg was subsequently amputated. At the time that the contract of release was made, neither *A* nor *B* was aware of the existence of this other condition.

Therefore, there was a mistake on the part of both parties as to the nature and extent of *A*'s injuries. *A* thought he was settling a case which involved only lacerations and contusions of his leg, and *B* thought he was settling a case involving those same injuries. Both parties were mistaken as to a material fact, and both were mistaken as to the same fact: the extent of *A*'s injuries. The contract did not comtemplate the release of any claim except one involving lacerations and contusions of the leg. The case involved a much more serious injury, and therefore a contract entered into under a mutual mistake as to a material fact is no contract at all. Both parties may proceed as if there were no contract in existence.

To take another example, let us assume that *A* thought he had sustained some internal injuries, the nature of which he did not know. *B*, the insurance adjuster, believed that *A* had suffered some injuries. *A* and *B* agreed to settle the case for $500, but prior to giving *A* a draft, *B* insisted that *A* be examined by the company doctor. The company doctor found no injuries whatsoever. There is no enforceable contract. *A* thought he was injured, *B* thought he was injured, and they were both mistaken as to a material fact, namely the extent of *A*'s injuries. Under those circumstances, even though an offer and acceptance had been made, and a consideration agreed upon, there is no contract for the reason that the mutual mistake of fact prevented the formation of a valid contract.

With respect to a unilateral mistake of fact the general rule is that there is a binding contract provided that the mistake on the part of the one party was not caused or induced by the opposite party. Therefore, if the case were settled by the adjuster with the claimant, where no reliance was placed upon any medical reports and where there was no assumption as to the extent of the injuries, the release is binding and enforceable even though the injuries prove to be more serious than the claimant anticipated at the time the release was given.

The distinction between this situation and the mutual mistake of material fact is that in the first instance both parties relied upon certain information and assumed that the injuries were limited to that diagnosis. In the second case, neither had any information as to the extent of the injuries and neither relied on any medical expressions as to the extent thereof. The intent was to settle the case, and the mere fact that the claimant underestimated the extent of his injuries will not enable him to avoid the contract.

These are, however, close questions of fact which will be decided by the jury under appropriate instructions from the court. If the evidence indicates a mutual mistake of fact, there is no contract. If the mistake was merely unilateral, the release will be sustained.

In *Harvey* v. *Georgia* (266 N.Y. Supp. 168) the court stated the rule as follows:

Where the release is executed under a mistake as to the future developments or effect of the injury or injuries then known to exist, the release bars suit in spite of the mistake, if the injuries prove more serious than supposed; but where at the time the release is executed, unknown injuries exist which were not taken into consideration by the parties, the release can be set aside and is no bar to the suit.

A unilateral mistake which is caused or induced by the opposite party will prevent the formation of a contract. For example, in a case where the claimant had been examined by the insurance company's physician and the report indicated that the claimant had sustained a very serious injury, the adjuster represented to the claimant that the doctor's report indicated the injuries to be of trivial nature. On the basis of the adjuster's statement, the claimant was induced to settle his case by giving a release for a nominal amount. The claimant was mistaken as to the extent of his injuries. This mistake was caused by, or induced by the adjuster's assurance to him of the insurance company doctor's findings. Therefore, the mistake was caused by the opposite party, and therefore there is no contract.

712   Fraud

A contract may be avoided or may never come into existence at all because of the fraud of one of the parties thereto. The fraud may be in the *factum* (the making) or in the *inducement*. In the first instance, there is no contract at all, and in the second instance, the contract may be avoided by the party defrauded.

Let us assume that the claimant is unable to read and write and that he signs a contract of release under those circumstances, using a mark which is properly witnessed. He is told that the paper he is signing is merely a receipt for the draft being delivered to him, or is an acknowledgement of the fact that the adjuster called on him. This is an example of fraud in the factum (in the making). The claimant never intended to give a general release and was misled into believing that he was signing some other type of instrument. There is no contract.

If the adjuster should represent to the claimant that even though the language of the instrument that he is signing does take on the appearance of a general release, but in spite of this the instrument will be regarded by the company as merely a partial release, this is fraud in the inducement. There is a contract, but it may be disaffirmed or avoided by the claimant if he so elects. On the other hand, if the claimant is satisfied with the contract, he may accept it, and it is a perfectly legal instrument. It should be emphasized that the claimant alone has the option and can bind or discharge the company as he sees fit.

The courts have never defined fraud. They have concluded in specific cases that the action complained of was fraudulent, but they have never felt that they should be bound by any definition of the term. For our purposes, fraud normally will consist of the following elements: (1) He lied. (2) He knew he lied. (3) He lied with the intent that the other party should rely on his statement. (4) The other party did rely. (5) The other party sustained damage as a result thereof.

All five of these elements must be present in order to constitute fraud. For example, if a claimant made false statements to us, known by him to be false, but we did not rely on them, nor did we take any action as a result of such reliance, then there is no fraud. On the other hand, if the adjuster makes false representations to the claimant with the intent that the claimant rely on such false representation, and also if these false representations were known to the adjuster to be untrue, there is no fraud unless the claimant actually did rely on the statements and actually did sustain damages as a consequence of such reliance.

713   Parol evidence rule

Where a written instrument is complete on its face, the general rule is that oral testimony may not be received to alter or vary any of the terms thereof. This is called the parol evidence rule. Like any other rule of law, this rule is subject to certain exceptions. Oral testimony in such cases is admissible for the following purposes:

1. To explain the meaning of ambiguous words in the instrument.
2. To prove facts rendering the agreement void or voidable for illegality, fraud, mistake, or insufficiency of consideration.
3. To prove facts in a suit for rescision of the written agreement, showing such mistake as affords grounds for such a remedy.
4. To prove facts in a suit for specific performance, showing such mistake, oppression, or unfairness as affords ground for denying that remedy.

These exceptions give a party to the contract the means of showing outside facts which will establish fraud in the factum, fraud in the inducement, and mistake of fact, be it mutual or unilateral, or will explain any words in the contract which are not subject to interpretation by the average person.

714   Representations

Any statement made by either party to the contract, prior to its making or concurrently with its making, is either a *representation* or a *warranty*. A representation, if untrue, will not entitle the opposite party to rescind or avoid the contract unless the representation is material to the contract itself. A warranty, if untrue, goes to the heart of the contract and prevents the formation of a contract. A representation, in order to have any influence on the contract, must be in relation to a material fact and be untrue. If the representation be material and untrue, it will enable the party to whom the representation is made to avoid the contract at his option.

In relation to an insurance contract, the same distinction is made between a representation and a warranty. The former, which precedes the contract of insurance and is no part of it, need only be materially true, and the latter is part of the contract and must be exactly and literally fulfilled, or else the contract is broken and inoperative.

In most insurance contracts, statements are required from the proposed insured with respect to some of the conditions of the risks to be assumed by the insurance company. These are representations and not warranties. They are statements which are made by the proposed insured to the insurance carrier before or at the time of the making of the contract in regard to some past or existing fact, circumstance, or state of facts pertinent to the contract, which is influential in bringing about the agreement. To avoid the contract once it is made, the insurance company will have to show not only that the representations were untrue but that they were material to the risk in that if the insurance carrier had known of the existence of the fact misrepresented, it would not have entered into the contract. The question of whether a misrepresentation is material or not is a question of fact for the jury.

The same fact may be material in one case and immaterial in another. For example, if a prospective insured represented that his name was John Smith, and in truth and in fact his name was originally John Brown, and he decided to change it for no reason at all, this might be considered a misrepresentation, but it certainly would not be material to the risk, since the insurance carrier intended to contract with this particular person, irrespective of his name. However, if we assume the same set of facts, but add to them the fact that under the name of John Brown the prospective insured had been convicted of automobile homicide and had a long record of convictions for traffic violations and accidents occurring as a result thereof, then the prospective insured's representation to the company that his name was John Smith and not John Brown would be material to the risk. This is for the reason that if the insurance carrier had known that the person requesting insurance had the driving record of John Brown, they would not have entered into the contract in the first place. The insurance carrier can avoid this contract. There was a misrepresentation, and such misrepresentation was material to the risk.

715   Warranties

All statements made in the formation of a contract are either representations or warranties. The factor which determines into which of these two categories a statement will fall is the *intention* of the parties. If no intention is expressed, then the statement is considered to be a representation. To be a warranty, there must be some evidence that the parties to the contract intended that the statement be a warranty. This intention may be evidenced by the fact that the warranty is contained in the contract itself, or the warranty may be implied by law from the nature of the transaction.

For example, where an agent contracts with another for his principal, the agent by that act impliedly warrants to the third person that he has the authority to bind his principal by making a contract for him. In a contract of sale, the seller impliedly warrants that the product sold is reasonably fit for the purpose and also that it is of merchantable quality. These warranties arise from the nature of the transaction and are not expressed. They are regarded as implied warranties.

Where the warranty is untrue, this is referred to in law as a breach of warranty. Where that happens, the aggrieved party has a choice of remedies. He may regard the contract as void, or no contract at all, and he may refuse to perform his part of the bargain. He may sue the other party for any damages which may arise as a result of the breach of warranty.

For example, in a sales transaction where the product is not of merchantable quality, the buyer may return the article to the seller and rescind the contract. If the buyer had used the product and was injured because of some defect in the product, the buyer can maintain a cause of action against the seller for any damages which he incurred as a result of the defect in the product.

Therefore, a representation, if untrue, will not affect the contractual relationship between the parties unless it is material to the agreement. A warranty, if untrue, will void the contract whether it is material to the contract or not. In addition, where the warranty is untrue, the aggrieved party has a remedy in the form of an action to recover damages for any injury suffered as a result of the breach of warranty.

716   Conditions

A condition is a qualifying agreement in the contract which describes the circumstances under which the contract is to operate. Its object is to modify, suspend, or rescind the principal obligation. For example, in a contract of sale, the buyer agrees to pay the purchase price prior to delivery, and the seller agrees to deliver upon receipt of the purchase price. The principal obligation of the seller is to deliver, but this obligation is conditioned upon the prior payment of the purchase price. The failure of the buyer to make the payment relieves the seller of his principal obligation.

All liability insurance policies require as a circumstance of the performance of the principal obligation by the insurance carrier that the insured report all accidents as soon as practicable. This is a condition, since it describes the circumstances under which the contract of insurance is to operate. The failure of the insured to meet this condition will relieve the insurance carrier of its principal obligation, which is to defend and to indemnify the insured.

There is a difference in the two examples given. In the first, the failure of the buyer to tend the purchase price within a reasonable time will not only relieve the seller of his obligation to deliver but will nullify or rescind the contract entirely. In the second, the failure of the insured to meet the condition merely suspends the carrier's principal obligation as to that particular event; namely, the accident which was not reported as soon as practicable. As to future events or as to past events, if the condition is met, the policy of insurance is still operable. Therefore, should the insured fail to report a particular accident "as soon as practicable" the principal obligation of the insurance carrier is rescinded only as to that particular event. The breach of condition does not, as in the first example, bring the contract to an end, or nullify the entire contract, but the contract continues as to other events with the same obligations and subject to the same conditions.

Conditions are classified by the times at which they are to be performed, such as conditions precedent (before the contract), conditions subsequent (after the contract), and conditions concurrent (simultaneously with the formation of the contract).

717   Waiver and estoppel

A waiver is the intentional or voluntary relinquishment of a known legal right. Estoppel is the legal result of a waiver, or of conduct from which a waiver can be implied. It prevents the party from asserting his original right. We meet this most frequently in insurance practice when there had been a breach of a condition of the policy contract. Where such a breach occurs, the aggrieved party may consider the breach as having the effect of relieving him of his obligation to perform, or he may forgive the breach and treat the contract as being in full force and effect. In the latter case, he will have voluntarily relinquished any rights which he may have acquired as a result of the breach. This constitutes a waiver.

A waiver may be express or implied. An express waiver, as the term suggests, is an oral or written statement specifically relinquishing the rights which accrued as a result of the breach. A waiver is implied where one party has pursued such a course of conduct with reference to the other party as to evidence an intention to waive his rights. To make out a case of implied waiver of a legal right, there must be a clear, unequivocal, and decisive act of the party showing such a purpose, or an act amounting to an estoppel on his part.

For example, in a liability insurance contract situation where the insured has failed to make a report of an accident to the insurer as soon as practicable after it has occurred, the insurer has the choice of either waiving the breach of condition and accepting the claim, or of considering the breach as relieving it of its obligation and rejecting the claim. If it decides to waive the breach, then it has relinquished its right to disclaim responsibility, and it must perform all the obligations of the contract as if there had been no breach. If it decides to consider the breach of condition as relieving it of the responsibility to perform, it must give notice to the insured of its position, and may not thereafter take any action or pursue any conduct which is inconsistent with that position.

For example, the insurance contract gives the insurer the right to investigate, settle, or defend any claims made against its insured within the coverage afforded by the policy. If a claim is made that is not within the coverage of the policy, either because it does not arise out of the hazards insured against, or because of a breach of a condition of the contract by the insured, the insurer has no right to investigate, settle, or defend. Where there has been a breach of a condition of the policy, and the insurer has given notice of the fact that it considers the breach as relieving it of its obligations thereunder, it may not thereafter exercise rights granted to it only with respect to claims within its coverage. If it should investigate, settle, or defend the claim, such action would constitute an implied waiver of the breach of condition.

The aggrieved party must have knowledge of the breach of condition before its actions can be construed as a waiver. However, immediately upon the acquisition of knowledge of the breach of condition, the aggrieved party must make its decision. If it continued with a course of conduct which would be inconsistent with a denial of liability under the contract, such action would constitute a waiver.

For example, let us assume that the insured has made an untruthful statement with regard to the facts of the accident to the insurance carrier. This is in violation of the cooperation clause of the insurance contract. The insurance carrier is not aware of the untruthful statement and does not acquire this knowledge until the insured admits under oath in the trial of the case that the statement is untrue, or, in the alternative, testifies to an entirely different version of the accident. At that moment the insurance carrier acquires knowledge of the fact that there has been a breach of condition and that the insured has not cooperated. It is at that time that the insurance carrier must give notice of its election to treat its obligations under the policy as nonexistent.

It is quite true that up until that point, in the history of the case, the insurance carrier did exercise its rights under the contract, but it did so under the mistaken apprehension that the insured had made a truthful statement to it concerning the accident. As soon as the aggrieved party acquires knowledge of the breach of a condition, it must retire from the case and take no further action that would be inconsistent with a denial of liability under the contract.

In many instances it is the duty of the aggrieved party to give notice to the other party that he has decided to disclaim any responsibility under the contract because of the breach of condition. Failure to give notice in some cases might amount to a waiver. For example, if an insured gave a delayed notice to his insurance carrier, the insurance carrier could treat the condition as breached and refuse to carry out its obligations under the contract. However, the insurance carrier must notify the insured of its position. If it does not, the insured would be perfectly within his rights in assuming that the insurance company was performing in accordance with its contract. For that reason, the insured would take no steps toward protecting himself by making his own investigation and arranging for either settlement or defense, as the case might be. Therefore, the failure of the insurance carrier to notify the insured so that he could take steps to protect himself could constitute a waiver in and of itself.

The courts of the various states have not been consistent in the use of the terms waiver and estoppel. Some do not refer to an implied waiver, as defined above, but consider such a situation merely as an estoppel by conduct or an equitable estoppel, and not a waiver at all. They consider only an affirmative, overt act as a waiver. Still others do not refer to estoppel at all. When they decide that there is a waiver, it abrogates any defense which may be interposed on the theory of a breach of condition. Whatever terms are used, the result is usually the same.

718   Nonwaiver and reservation of rights

In insurance contract situations where there has been a breach of a condition by the insured, the insurance carrier, for a variety of reasons, sometimes desires to investigate the case and defend the insured without waiving its rights under the contract. It may accomplish this by a notice of reservation of rights, a nonwaiver agreement, or a reservation-of-rights agreement. (The procedure and the legal implications of such actions are discussed in Chapter XVI, which deals with liability insurance contracts.)

719   Ambiguities

In a written instrument, an ambiguity is defined as duplicity, indistinctness, or uncertainty of meaning. In the law of contracts the rule is that where there is any doubt as to the meaning of any particular clause in the contract, or where the clause is amendable to more than one interpretation, the language will be construed against the maker of the contract and most strongly in favor of the other party. The person who wrote the contract had the opportunity to make his meaning clear. If he did not do so, and his language is subject to more than one interpretation, the court will adopt the interpretation most favorable to the party who did not write the contract.

The insurance policy contract is constructed by and offered by the insurance carrier. If any of the terms or conditions of the policy contain any ambiguities, in the sense that they are susceptible to more than one meaning, the meaning most favorable to the insured will be adopted. In construing insurance contracts we can expect that the courts will, if possible, find there is insurance coverage unless there is clearly an intent, expressed in the language of the policy, to exclude or limit the amount of coverage afforded.

720   Assignments

All contracts, with the exception of contracts for personal services, are assignable unless there is an express provision in the contract preventing assignment. In all casualty insurance policies, the contract by its terms provides for an assignment on the condition that the assignment be approved by the company and evidence thereof be attached to the policy in the form of an approval from an officer of the company authorized to do so. The policy can be assigned only with the consent of the insurance carrier.

721   Capacity to contract

There are some classes of persons who are either totally or partially incapacitated when it comes to making a binding contract. These are infants, married women, idiots and insane persons, and drunkards. We will consider each in their relationship to the making of a contract.

1. *Infants.* An infant or minor is a person who has not attained the age of full maturity of mind and judgment and for that reason receives special protection from the law. The age at which a person attains full maturity and the right to exercise full legal capacity to contract is fixed by the state law. Most states fix the age of majority at 21 for both sexes. Some have a lesser age, and in others the age differs between male and female. Some states grant full capacity to contract to infants who are married. In any case where age is the criterion, the person attains his full maturity on the day before his 18th or

21st birthday, as the case may be, since the law does not take cognizance of a fraction of a day. An infant may be emancipated prior to attaining majority. This merely means that he is no longer subject to parental control and, as a result thereof, he may retain his own earnings. This does not affect his legal capacity to contract.

A contract entered into by an infant is voidable, not void. At any time prior to attaining his legal age, and for a period of time thereafter as fixed by law (usually one year), an infant may disaffirm a contract which he has made, and there is no further liability on his part under the contract. He is required to return to the other party any advantage that he may have gained under the contract.

A guardian may act for an infant and may enter into a binding contract for and in behalf of the infant within the statutory limitations provided for in the state of his appointment. In most states, a contract releasing a claim arising out of bodily injuries sustained by the infant must be submitted to a court of competent jurisdiction for review and approval before the contract will be binding on the infant and effectively extinguish the claim. The rules of court in the particular jurisdiction involved will determine the type of proceeding necessary to bring the matter to the attention of the court.

2. Married women.   At common law a married woman had no legal capacity to enter into a contract while her husband was alive. This disability has been removed in most states by emancipation statutes, and while the statutes differ somewhat as to whether or not she can engage in business on her own account, the general rule is that she can contract as freely as if she were a single woman. In some states, she cannot make a contract with her husband. In others, she can contract with her husband only in limited areas. In all states, the common-law rule is that she cannot make a contract with her husband to perform services which she is bound to perform as a result of the marriage contract. These are household duties, such as the care of their children, washing, cooking, and caring for her husband when he is ill. In some states, she cannot enter into a contract of employment with her husband with respect to services which she will render in connection with her husband's business, and, consequently, she cannot become his employee, even if she does render services, so as to qualify under the Workmen's Compensation Act as an employee.

3. Idiots and insane persons.   An idiot is defined in law as a person with no mind at all. Therefore, he cannot form an intent to enter an contract, and consequently any contract entered into by an idiot is a nullity and is void.

The contract of a person of unsound mind, who has not been judicially declared insane, is voidable and not void. He occupies the same position as an infant, and may disaffirm his contract through a guardian after he has been declared to be incompetent, or may himself disaffirm should he regain his sanity. The burden of proving that he was of unsound mind at the time the contract was made is on the party seeking to disaffirm. In the case of persons who are mentally incompetent due to senility, the burden of proof is less onerous than in other cases, since the opposite party is charged with the knowledge of his age and apparent mental capacity as of the time of the contract.

An offer made to a person who becomes insane to such a degree that he himself cannot manifest an assent to the terms is terminated by such insanity. It may not be accepted by the insane person's guardian in order to create a contract.

Where a person has been judicially declared to be insane, and has been committed as an insane person, he no longer has the capacity to enter into a contract. A contract with him is void. In dealing with cases involving bodily injuries sustained by such a person, the settlement may be concluded with the guardian of his property, who is also called the committee of the property, or the conservator of the insane person's assets. The settlement and the release of the claim must be submitted to and have the approval of the court having jurisdiction of the incompetent.

4. Drunkards.   If it can be established that at the time he entered into the contract, a person was so intoxicated that he was unable to understand the nature of the transaction, the contract is voidable. He may disaffirm it when he becomes sober. His failure to disaffirm the contract upon regaining his sobriety (with knowledge of its existence) will extinguish his right to avoid it. If a case were settled with a person under those conditions, and upon regaining his sobriety, he spent the money paid to him under the contract of release with knowledge of its source, such action would be construed as a ratification of the contract and will likewise extinguish his right of avoidance.

722   Contracts to compound a crime

Any contract whose purpose is to conceal a crime or to hamper the prosecution thereof, or to refrain from making a criminal complaint, is void as against public policy. In some states, the mere entering into such a contract will constitute a crime in itself as to both parties. The theory behind this reasoning is that where such contracts are made, the criminal is free to continue his nefarious conduct with the result that other members of the public may become victims of the same criminal. The public good, or public policy, demands that where a crime has been committed, the perpetrator thereof be tried and convicted if the evidence so warrants.

This type of contract should not be confused with an agreement between the wrongdoer and the person injured for the return of his property or the payment of damages therefore. Where a criminal prosecution is pending, it would be to the defendant's advantage in mitigation of sentence to be able to show that full restitution had been made to the injured party. Therefore, any agreement made with respect to the returning of property or payment therefor, following the initiation of criminal proceedings, is a valid and binding agreement.

In *Board of Education* v. *Angel* [84 S.E. 747 (West Virginia)] the court said:

It is well settled law, that, where no criminal proceedings have been begun and pending against the wrongdoer for the crime, one whose money or property has been embezzled, or fraudulently procured may contract with such wrongdoer for repayment or satisfaction of the loss and take security therefor without invalidating such a contract, unless there be included therein and as part consideration therefor, some promise or agreement, express or implied that such prosecution shall be suppressed, stifled or stayed.

723   Contracts to procure evidence

It is perfectly legal to employ an investigator or an adjuster to procure evidence in connection with any claim or lawsuit, provided that the agreement for payment has reference to the actual work performed and is not conditioned upon the outcome or the amount of recovery obtained. Such latter contracts are illegal and void. The defense to such a contract action would be interposed by the person sought to be charged, and the existence of such an agreement would not be a complete defense to the cause of action against the tort-feasor. The reason that such contracts are void and are against public policy is due to the fact that it places a premium upon the manufacture of evidence and subornation of perjury. In any case, the existence of the contract could be brought out in the trial of a main case in order to reflect upon the credibility and reliability of the evidence so procured.

A contract with an expert conditioned upon the amount of recovery is also void. For example, in *Laffin* v. *Billington* (86 N.Y. Supp. 267), it was held that a contract with a physician for expert testimony in a personal injury action, in which his fee was contingent upon the amount of the verdict, was contrary to public policy and therefore void. Also, in *Beigoff Detective Service, Inc.* v. *Walters* (267 N.Y. Supp. 464), a husband contracted to pay a detective agency a sum of money if it was successful in securing evidence to prove that his wife had been guilty of adultery. The contract required that the husband pay for the disbursements necessarily made in the course of investigation, but that no payment was to be made for the actual services rendered unless the evidence was discovered which would enable him to successfully maintain his action for divorce. The contract was held to be void as against public policy and unenforceable.

724   Attorney's contingent fee contracts

A contract of retainer between an attorney and his client whereby the attorney's fee is conditioned upon a recovery and is based on a percentage of the amount so recovered is a valid contract provided that the amount of compensation agreed upon is fair and reasonable. These contracts are recognized on the theory that they are a social necessity. To require a retainer fee be paid in advance, and the full fee be paid irrespective of the outcome of the lawsuit, would work a serious injustice to poor people who could not afford counsel under those circumstances.

As between the attorney and client, the percentage of the recovery to be paid must be fair and reasonable and not extortionate. This is a matter which is solely between the attorney and the client, and even though the amount of compensation paid to the attorney will have a considerable influence upon the amount demanded in settlement, the defendant cannot complain. Also, the defendant cannot complain even though this type of arrangement makes the attorney a coproprietor of the personal injury cause of action.

In some states, the rules of court require that all such contingent fee contracts be filed with the clerk of the court having jurisdiction in the area in which the attorney maintains his office. The retainers thus filed become public records and in most instances are available to the public for inspection.

725 Exculpatory contracts

The public has an interest in the maintenance of conditions which are conducive to the preservation of wealth, property, and human life. Therefore, contracts which exculpate or relieve a tort-feasor from the consequences of his own negligence are void if the public interest is involved. On the other hand, if the only persons who are affected by the contract are the immediate parties and there is no danger or involvement of the public interest, then such contracts have been upheld.

Let us assume that an employer inserted a clause in the contract of employment whereby the employer was exonerated in advance from any liability arising out of the injuries to the employee, be they due to the negligence of the employer, or occurring under such circumstances as to permit a recovery under the compensation law. The public policy of the state, as expressed by the workmen's compensation law, would be defeated if such a clause were upheld. Therefore, the public interest would demand that the clause be considered void as against public policy. Another reason for rejecting the contract would be that if such a contract were allowed to stand, the employer would be under no duty to maintain his premises in a safe and satisfactory condition, or to provide the proper tools, machinery, and safeguards.

In another case, let us assume that a public utility, such as an electric power company, refused to supply electricity to a householder unless the householder would agree in advance that the electric company be exonerated from any liability arising from the negligent acts of its employees, servants, or agents. This contract would be void as against public policy. Public policy would demand that a utility make its services available to all members of the community and that it bargain fairly. Here, the utility was taking advantage of its superior bargaining power so as to deprive the householder of its services unless the householder agreed to unacceptable terms. Such a contract is unenforceable and void for the reason that the parties did not bargain on equal terms and that advantage had been taken of the weaker party.

Generally, the burden of proof as to the public interest involved in a contract of this sort is on the party asserting such a defense. The contracts are upheld unless there is evidence that the public interest is involved. For example, a clause in a lease of a private dwelling providing that the landlord shall not be responsible for damage from leakage, whether due to the negligence of the landlord or not, is a valid condition of the lease, and since there is no public interest involved, the clause will be given legal effect. Here, both the landlord and the tenant bargained on equal terms in the sense that neither had to enter into contractual relations with the other, and therefore it is a matter in which the parties were free either to accept or reject the clause as they saw fit.

In an action for damages for injuries sustained in a fall at the edge of a swimming pool, arising out of the alleged negligence of the defendant Gymnasium Corporation, it appeared that in becoming a "member" or patron of the gymnasium, the plaintiff signed a membership contract containing an agreement to assume full responsibility for any injuries which occur in and about the gymnasium premises "including, but without limitation, any claims for personal injuries resulting from or arising out of the negligence of" the defendant. The court held that the clause was valid, and in considering the legal relationship between the contracting parties and the possible public interest involved, the court said:

Here there is no special legal relationship and no overriding public interest which demand of this contract provision, voluntarily entered into by competent parties, should be rendered ineffectual. Defendant, a private corporation, was under no obligation or legal duty to accept the plaintiff as a member or patron. Having consented to do so, it had the right to insist upon such terms as it deemed appropriate. Plaintiff, on the other hand, was not required to assent to unacceptable terms, or to give up a valuable legal right, as a condition precedent to obtaining employment or being able to make use of the services rendered by a public carrier or utility. She voluntarily applied for membership in a private corporation, and agreed to the terms upon which this membership was bestowed. She may not repudiate them now. [*Ciafalo* v. *Vic Tanny Gyms, Inc.*, 214 N.Y.S. 2d 99.]

In *Johnson* v. *Star Permanent Wave Corporation* (261 N.Y.S. 209), the plaintiff went into the defendant's beauty parlor to receive a permanent wave. In consideration of a reduced rate charged for the work, she was asked to sign and did sign a document agreeing to release and save harmless the defendant from any and all liability which might arise as a result of any injury sustained for any reason while receiving a permanent wave. It was held that she could not recover for injuries received because the document signed was a complete bar to her cause of action. Here again, there was a private agreement between two contracting parties, and one in which the public had no interest whatsoever.

In the two preceding cases, the contract set forth an intent to absolve the defendants from all liability arising out of the particular transaction. Since the intention of the parties was clear, the court gave effect to the agreement. On the other hand, if the intention to absolve the defendant from his liability for his negligence is not clear, the courts will not construe the agreement as exculpating him from liability. For example, in *Bernstein* v. *Seacliff Beach Club, Inc.* (228 NYS 2d 567), the court held that a clause in the plaintiff's membership application to the effect that all claims for injury to person or property were waived did not clearly exhibit an intention to absolve the defendant from liability for its negligence. Therefore, it was ineffectual to relieve the beach club of its liability. Also, in *Hertzog* v. *Harrison Island Shores, Inc.* (251 N.Y.S. 2d 164), the plaintiff's membership application stated that the member agreed to "waive claim for any loss to personal property, or for any other personal injury while a member of the said club." The court held that the language did not possess the clarity or explicitness necessary in an exculpatory agreement to express the intention of the parties to absolve one of them from liability for negligence. Both of these cases enunciate the general rule that an exculpatory clause or agreement will be strictly construed against the party it favors.

Exculpatory agreements are frequently encountered in the recreation area where the operators of the facility seek to avoid liability for their own negligence by this means. The cases can be divided into two groups: (1) those involving signed agreements and (2) those involving unsigned agreements where the agreement is contained on the back of a ticket or there is a notice posted to that effect.

1. Signed agreements.   When an exculpatory agreement with an amusement operator is signed by an adult, whether he read it or not, the courts hold that the adult is bound by the agreement. For example, in *Moss* v. *Fortune* [340 S.W. 2d 902 (Tennessee)], the court held that the plaintiff, by signing a written agreement that he exonerated the defendant from liability and that he assumed the risk of injury to which he would be exposed in hiring and riding a horse from the defendant's riding academy, could not recover for bodily injuries sustained as a result of the defendant's negligence. The court specifically stated that the parties could agree between themselves that one would not be liable to the other.

In *Broderson* v. *Rainier National Park Co.* [60 Pac. 2d 234 (Washington)], the plaintiff signed a printed slip which contained an assumption-of-risk clause on the part of patrons using the defendant's toboggan course. The court held that the signing of the agreement absolved the defendant from liability, even though the plaintiff claimed that he had not read it and he was unaware of its terms.

In *Lee* v. *Allied Sports Associates* [209 N.E. 2d 329 (Massachusetts)], the plaintiff signed a release prior to entering the pits on a speedway operated by the defendant. The court held that the plaintiff could not recover for injuries sustained as a result of being hit by a wheel which had become detached from a racing car. The plaintiff claimed that he had not read the release prior to signing it, but the court held that his failure to read the release did not affect its validity. In the absence of fraud or duress, the agreement was enforceable as a complete exoneration of the defendant from liability.

2. Unsigned agreements.   Attempts have been made by the operators of amusement devices and other recreational areas to create an exculpatory contract by printing an agreement on the reverse side of the ticket, which stated that the use of the device would constitute an acceptance of the exculpatory clause. If it can be shown that the customer was aware of the agreement and consented to its terms, then the customer is bound by it, and the defendant is exculpated from liability for his own negligence. The difficulty is that the operator seldom is able to establish that the customer actually read the agreement or used the device with any awareness of the existence of operator's lack of liability. In the absence of being able to establish notice to the customer and the customer's assent to the agreement, the courts will not release the operator. In many of the cases, the agreement is printed in fine print on a small ticket, which the customer holds only momentarily until it is collected, or torn in half with the customer retaining only the stub. In *Kushner* v. *McGinnis* [194 N.E. 106 (Massachusetts)], the ticket contained a disclaimer of liability, and the defendant sought to utilize it as a defense to a claim for bodily injuries sustained by the plaintiff. The evidence showed that the plaintiff was a Russian, who could not read English, and furthermore the ticket was taken and torn up within four or five steps from where it was purchased. Since the defendant could not prove that the plaintiff had notice of the agreement, the court held that the defense could not be interposed. See also, *Brennan* v. *Ocean View Amusement Co.* [194 N.E. 911 (Massachusetts)]; *O'Brien* v. *Freeman* [11 N.E. 2d 582 (Massachusetts)].

Many amusement operators post signs on the premises which read "Use at your own risk." While these signs might have the effect of discouraging small claims, they are not exculpatory in nature and do not absolve the operator from liability for his own negligence.

Effect of infancy.   An infant who signs an exculpatory contract has the same right of disaffirmance as he has in respect to any other contract. In *Cunningham* v. *State* [32 N.Y.S. 2d 275 (New York)], the court held that a minor was not bound by a waiver of liability which she had signed, since she had disaffirmed the contract. Because of the minor's right of disaffirmance, some operators of summer camps and other similar facilities require that the parent or guardian of the child sign a release-of-liability form of contract, exculpating the operators from liability for their own negligence. There are few cases on the subject, and it may well be that the contract may have the effect of discouraging litigation. In *Fedor* v. *Mauwehu Council, Boy Scouts of America, Inc.* [143 Atl. 2d 466 (Connecticut)], the infant-plaintiff's father signed a contract, which included a clause containing a waiver of all claims for damages in the event of injury. The court placed its decision on the matter of public policy, holding that they would not confer immunity because of the unequal bargaining positions of the parties, but the court also stated that it was doubtful whether a parent had the authority to waive the rights of his child against the defendant, for the defendant's negligent acts.

726   Hold harmless agreements

It frequently happens that, as a condition of a business contract, one party agrees to hold harmless or to indemnify the other party from certain liabilities, which may be imposed upon him by law, that arise out of the subject matter of the contract. The terms and the responsibility assumed differ with the agreement, and it may run from the assumption of all liability arising out of the premises or the operation, irrespective of whether the liability arises because of the negligence of his own employees or the negligence of the other contracting party and his employees, to merely the assumption of liability for the negligence of his own employees.

For example, under the ultrahazardous operations doctrine, the owner of land is held to a strict liability for any accidents or injuries which are sustained as a result of the operations, whether they are under the control of the owner or an independent contractor. Let us assume that the owner hires an independent contractor to do the work, but insists that he, the owner, be held harmless from any liability which may be imposed upon him by law arising out of the ultrahazardous operations. The contractor may execute a hold harmless agreement which will so indemnify the owner in respect to all liability which may be imposed, irrespective of whether the accident occurred as a result of the negligence of the contractor's employees, the employees of the owner, or the owner himself. *The hold harmless agreement may be restricted to the liability imposed on the owner which arises out of the negligence of the contractor's employees only.*

Hold harmless agreements must be distinguished from an exculpatory contract, under which the agreement exonerates the tort-feasor from liability arising from his own negligence. Under a hold harmless agreement the tort-feasor is not absolved from liability. He still remains liable to the injured person for his negligence, but when his liability is established, the hold harmless agreement may require someone else to respond for him or to reimburse him for the damages which he has paid.

There are two general forms of hold harmless agreements: (1) an agreement to hold the indemnitee harmless which may be imposed by law because of the negligence of the indemnitor, and his servants, agents, or employees, and (2) an agreement which not only indemnifies the indemnitee for the acts of the indemnitor's servants, agents, and employees, but also agrees to hold the indemnitee harmless from any liability imposed upon him because of the negligence of his own employees, servants or agents.

1. *Liability for the acts of the indemnitor.* In most cases an agreement of this type is not against public policy and is valid. An exception arises where there is a disparity in the bargaining power of the parties and the stronger party has taken advantage of the weaker party, in which case the agreement is void. For example, an electric utility refuses to supply electricity to a homeowner unless the homeowner will execute a hold harmless agreement under which the utility is indemnified against liability for the acts of its agents or employees. Obviously, the homeowner has no choice if he is to receive the necessary service. Such a hold harmless agreement is void as against public policy.

2. *Liability for the acts of the indemnitee.* Ordinarily a contract whereby one party assumes the liability of the other for the negligent acts of the other and his employees is not invalid as being against public policy. However, in a number of states, legislation has been enacted which prohibits, voids or modifies the use of such hold harmless agreements on construction contracts.

Typical of the statutes is the Tennessee enactment, which reads as follows:

A covenant, promise, agreement or understanding in, or in connection with or collateral to a contract or agreement relative to the construction, alteration, repair or maintenance of a building, structure, appurtenance and appliance, including moving, demolition and excavating in connection therewith, purporting to indemnify or hold harmless the promisee against liability for damages arising out of bodily injury to persons or damage to property caused by or resulting from the sole negligence of the promisee, his agents or employees, or indemnitee, is against public policy and is void and unenforceable.

Although most states having similar provisions exclude insurance contracts of indemnity by court decision, the California statute specifically exempts insurance contracts from the effect of the legislation. This statute reads as follows:

All provisions, clauses, covenants or agreements contained in, collateral to, or affecting any construction contract and which purport to indemnify the promisee against liability for damages for (a) death or bodily injury to persons, (b) injury to property, (c) design defects or (d) any other loss, damage or expense arising under (a), (b), or (c) from the sole negligence or willful misconduct of the promisee or the promisee's agents, servants or independent contractors, who are directly responsible to such promisee, are against public policy and are void and unenforceable; provided, however, that this provision shall not affect the validity of any insurance contract, workmen's compensation, or agreement issued by an admitted insurer as defined in the insurance code.

Nothing contained in Section 2782 (above) shall prevent a party to a construction contract and the owner or other party for whose account the construction contract is being performed, from agreeing with respect to the allocation or limitation as between the parties of any liability for design defects.

Other states which have similar legislation relating to construction contracts include the following:

Delaware	Illinois	New Mexico	South Dakota
Florida	Michigan	New York	Texas
Georgia	Mississippi	North Dakota	Utah
Hawaii	New Hampshire	Pennsylvania	Washington
Idaho			

It should be emphasized that these statutes all refer to construction contracts only. Other hold harmless agreements which assume the liability of the promisee are not affected. This latter would include the standard sidetrack agreements executed in favor of the railroad, whereby the person for whose benefit the sidetrack is built assumes all the liability of the railroad, including liability for the negligent acts of the servants, agents and employees of the railroad.

These agreements are of importance to the claimsman for the reason that if the person indemnified is the insured, he can call on the other party to perform under the contract. Should the insurance carrier be compelled to pay the claim, it will succeed to the insured's rights and can subrogate against the indemnitor.

Liability assumed under a contract or hold harmless agreement can be the subject of insurance, so that the claimsman may be called upon to represent the indemnitor in such cases.

727 Arbitration agreements

There are many insurance policies containing an agreement to arbitrate differences in evaluation, or liability, which may arise between the parties to the contract, namely, the insurance carrier and the insured. These are contracts to arbitrate future disputes. The common-law rule is that such contracts are unenforceable and are voidable at the will of either party. The reasoning behind the rule is that private persons cannot by a contract to arbitrate oust the jurisdiction of the courts. As to disputes which are in existence, the parties then may waive their rights to a trial by jury, and dispose of the dispute in any manner they see fit, be it by negotiation, arbitration, or recourse to the courts. The prohibition is not against arbitration as such, but is against an agreement which obligates the parties to submit disputes which have not now arisen but which may arise in the future to arbitration. Therefore, in those states which adhere to the common-law rule, the policy provisions with regard to arbitration are not enforceable, and neither the insured nor the insurance carrier can compel the other to submit the dispute to arbitration, notwithstanding the policy provisions.   See *Hill* v. *Seaboard Fire & Marine Ins. Co.* [374 S.W. 2d 606 (Missouri)]; *Boughton* v. *Farmers Insurance Exchange* [354 Pac. 2d 1085 (Oklahoma)]; *State Farm Ins. Co.* v. *Spears* [32 Auto. Cas. (CCH) 2d 484]; *Barnhart* v. *Civil Service Employees Ins. Co.* [308 Pac. 2d 873 (Utah)]. The following states follow the common-law rule, either by statute or by court decisions:

Alabama	Georgia	New Mexico	Texas
Alaska	Missouri	North Dakota	Vermont
Arkansas	Montana	Oklahoma	Virginia
Delaware	Nebraska	South Dakota	West Virginia

All other states and the District of Columbia have passed statutes modifying the common-law rule by making contracts to arbitrate future disputes valid, enforceable, and irrevocable.

728 Beneficiary contracts

It is possible for two parties to enter into a contract which is for the benefit of a third person who is not a party to the contract. Upon the happening of the event, or the payment, or performance which is provided by the contract, the third-party beneficiary acquires legal rights under the contract which are enforceable at law. The most common form of a beneficiary contract is a life insurance policy wherein the insured pays the premium to an insurance company, which company agrees to pay a stated sum to the beneficiary upon the happening of the death of the insured. When the event takes place, the beneficiary, although not a party to the contract, may bring legal action against the life insurance company if it does not perform within the terms of its contract.

The medical payments provision of various liability insurance policies is also a beneficiary contract. It does not name a specific beneficiary by name but does designate the beneficiaries by class. When any member of this class or group of persons qualifies as a beneficiary by sustaining injury in the automobile or on the insured premises, the right of such a beneficiary comes into existence. Should the company fail to make the payments required under its contract, the beneficiary may enforce his claim by bringing suit for damages for breach of contract directly against the company.

729   Leases

A lease is a contract whereby for a consideration called the rent, the owner of real property transfers possession for a period of time to the other party, called the tenant. A lease merely transfers temporary possession of real property and nothing more. The tenant is obligated to return the premises to the owner in the same condition as he received them, subject only to ordinary wear and tear. In the case of any deterioration or damage to the premises, the tenant has the obligation of making repairs, since he has a responsibility to return the premises to the owner in reasonably the same condition as he received them.

As in any other agreement, the parties may insert any legal terms and conditions, either imposing greater liability upon one party or the other, or relieving one party or the other from the normal lease obligations. Therefore, one of the most important steps in the investigation of accidents due to defects in the premises, where such premises are occupied by a tenant, is the securing of a copy of the lease to determine exactly what obligations were assumed by each party.

Under the terms of a lease, the landlord may transfer possession of an entire building and the grounds around it, or part of a structure, retaining some parts of it for his own use; or he may lease a number of parts or apartments to various tenants, reserving to himself the grounds, access ways, and other parts of the building, some of which he makes available to the tenants for their own use. As to the parts of the property which the landlord reserved to himself for the use of the tenants, the landlord is ordinarily responsible for their condition and will be answerable in damages should he fail to exercise reasonable care in maintaining them. This would refer to the elevators, stairways, lobby, the laundry room, and private sidewalk to the building, as well as those portions of the grounds which are made available to the tenants for their use. In addition, the landlord retains to himself the electric conduits in the walls, water pipes, sewer pipes, the roof, the heating facility, etc. He is liable to the tenant if he fails to maintain these in safe condition and the tenant is injured thereby. The parties to the contract of lease can vary, diminish, or enlarge these responsibilities. Likewise, the tenant could exculpate the landlord from all liability for his own negligence. In addition, some leases contain hold harmless agreements whereby the tenant agrees to indemnify the landlord for any liability imposed upon him as a result of an injury to a social guest of the tenant.

Unless the lease so stipulates, the landlord may not enter the leased premises during the term of the lease. Some leases permit the landlord to enter at certain reasonable times for the purposes of inspection or repair. Some leases obligate the landlord to make necessary repairs to the leasehold and contain a clause allowing him to reenter the premises for that purpose. Should the tenant notify the landlord of the need for repairs, and the landlord makes an inspection which confirms the tenant's opinion, and the landlord promises to make the necessary repairs, the failure of the landlord to make those repairs does not subject him to liability to someone who is injured as a result of the condition. If the landlord is obligated to make repairs under the lease, and he fails to do so within a reasonable time after he has notice of the necessity of repairs, the tenant's only remedy is to have the repairs made himself at the expense of the landlord. This is contrary to the popular motion that where this condition exists, the tenant may expose himself to the unsafe condition, and in the case of injury the landlord will be strictly liable. The defense on contributory negligence would always be available to the landlord.

Where the landlord does make the repairs, whether the lease obligates him to do so or not, he is liable if the repairs are made in an unsafe or negligent manner with the result that the tenant, his family, or social guests are injured.

730   Accord and satisfaction

A disputed claim of any kind may be settled by the agreement of the parties. This agreement may involve the extinguishment of the claim by one party in return for a payment of money by the other. The agreement by the parties to settle the disputed claim, and the terms thereof, is called an *accord*. This is merely an agreement to settle and is executory, since it contemplates that something more must be done to complete the transaction. *Satisfaction* is the payment required by the accord. When the payment is made and received, the contract is executed and complete. Both sides are bound by the transaction and the disputed claim is extinguished. Therefore, to have a completed transaction, the two necessary steps are (1) the agreement to settle (accord), and (2) performance by payment under the agreement (satisfaction).

An accord is a contract in and of itself. It comes into existence as a result of an offer from one party and the acceptance by the other, both supported by adequate consideration. The consideration moving from the party offering the satisfaction is the payment of a sum of money for a disputed claim which the party has a legal right to resist. The consideration moving from the opposite party is the agreement to forego pressing a claim for a larger amount. When either party fails to perform his promise under the agreement, the contract is breached. If the party who is to make the payment fails to do so, the opposite party has the option of considering the contract rescinded by the nonperformance of the other, thereby releasing his obligations under the contract, or he may stand on the contract and sue the party for the payment which the contract demands. Therefore, where an agreement was made with a claimant to settle his case for a certain amount, for which he signed a release, and the company thereafter declined to make the payment, the claimant has the option of regarding the contract of release as rescinded, releasing him from his obligations and permitting him to sue on the original claim, or he may sue the company for damages for breach of contract, the damages being the amount that he should have received under the accord (the release), together with the cost of the action.

Conversely, where the claimant has a change of mind after he has signed the release, thereby evidencing an intention to settle the claim, and he returns the draft uncashed, or if there is a period of time between the execution of the release and the delivery of the draft and he refuses the draft when tendered, the majority rule, in the absence of fraud and deceit, and in the absence of a statute modifying the rule, is that the accord is a contract and the claimant is bound. In *Reynard* v. *Bradshaw* (196 Kansas 97), the claimant signed a release for $2,500 which was delivered to the adjuster representing the insurance company. The adjuster was employed by an independent firm and did not have draft authority, so that no payment of money was made to the claimant at the time of the execution of the release. The day after the release was signed, an attorney representing the claimant notified the adjuster that the sum of $2,500 would not be acceptable in settlement, and demanded the return of the release. The insurance company in the meantime mailed its check in the sum of $2,500 to the claimant some four days after the date of the release. The claimant thereafter brought suit against the tort-feasor, and an affirmative defense that the claim had been released was interposed. The plaintiff admitted the release, but claimed that since the consideration was not accepted by her, the release was nothing more than an offer to settle as opposed to a binding contract. In upholding the defense, the court said:

. . . To accept plaintiff's contention would be in effect to say that plaintiff's acceptance of the defendant's proposition to pay amounted to an agreement to accept money when and if offered, and not to accept an agreement to pay, and that the plaintiff had the right to refuse acceptance even though she had previously agreed to accept. In short that plaintiff's acceptance without further performance amounted to nothing at all. We think the parties intended more than just a hollow ceremony. As a matter of law it would make no difference who made the offer and who made the acceptance. What is essential is that there was a definite proposition accepted by both parties. In other words, the release shows a mutual meeting of the minds of the parties resulting in mutual promises and we think the release on its face shows it was so intended by them. The compromise of a disputed claim furnishes good consideration for a contract. . . . Here there are all the elements of a valid contract and we have no doubt either of the parties could have enforced it. The law favors contracts in settlement of disputed matters and the avoidance of litigation and it ought not to circumscribe the means of carrying such settlements into effect.

The plaintiff also contended that the consideration was not paid at the time the release was executed, even though the release recited that the consideration was paid. On this point, the court said:

The fact that the $2,500.00 was not tendered until a few days after the execution of the instrument would not constitute such a material failure of consideration as would entitle the plaintiff to rescind the contract. Mere delay in performing a contract is not such substantial breach, justifying rescission, unless the delay is such as to warrant the conclusion that performance is not intended. Performance within a reasonable time would be sufficient.

Similarly, in *Johnson* v. *Norfolk* [82 N.W. 2d 656 (South Dakota)], the plaintiff, a passenger in an automobile involved in a collision, signed a release of all claims, and although the instrument acknowledged receipt of the sum agreed upon, nothing was paid at the time. The following day plaintiff employed counsel, who, five days thereafter, wrote the adjustment firm handling the claim asking for a return of the release and advising that the plaintiff would return any payment tendered for the purported settlement. The defense of accord was interposed, and the court held that the release constituted a binding contract of compromise and settlement of the claim.

For other cases reaching the same conclusion on a similar state of facts, see *Hofland* v. *Gustafson* [282 Pac. 2d 1039 (California)]; *Ulrich* v. *McDonough* [101 N.E. 2d 163 (Ohio)]; *Segal* v. *Allied Mutual Ins. Co.* [188 N.E. 504 (Massachusetts)]; *Tooke* v. *Houston Fire & Casualty Insurance Co.* [122 So. 2d 109 (Louisiana)].

In some states there are statutes which provide for a written accord to be set up as a defense or as a counterclaim to an action based on the original claim. [New York, Personal Property Law, Sec. 33a & 33b. Also see *Trenton St. Ry. Co.* v. *Lawlor* (N.J.) 71 Atl. 234.]

Where an accord and satisfaction has been afforded to the creditor by a third party other than the debtor, and it is accepted by the creditor as the full satisfaction of the claim, the debt is discharged. This would have reference to the settlement of a claim against the insured by a third party, the insurance company. The settlement, by means of an accord and satisfaction by the insurance company, will operate as a discharge of any debt which the insured may have to the claimant.

Where the debtor and the creditor have mutual claims against each other arising out of the same event, an accord and satisfaction between them will merge the conflicting claims and operate as a discharge of all claims between them unless there are specific reservations in the agreement of accord. In such a situation, most lawyers would insist on an exchange of releases so that there could never be any question of the intentions of the parties.

Thus, in a case where *A* and *B* are driving their own cars and collide at an intersection, and each claims that the other was to blame, an agreement of settlement (an accord) whereby *A* agrees to pay, and does pay (satisfaction) *B* a certain sum, will usually extinguish any claim which *A* may have had against *B*. In the agreement of accord, *A* could specifically reserve any rights which he may have to make a claim against *B*, and set up that the payment made was in satisfaction of a doubtful and disputed claim in which liability was specifically denied. It could be further agreed that the fact of settlement may not be pleaded as a defense to any action *A* might have, or that the settlement may not be introduced in evidence and used in any way, either as a defense or in mitigation of *A*'s action against *B*. Thus the parties may agree on any terms which are mutually acceptable.

Where an accord and satisfaction is entered into between the creditor and a third party acting as agent for the debtor, the acts of the third party are the acts of the debtor, and the rights of the parties are determined as if the debtor himself had participated in the agreement. Where the third party is not the agent of the debtor nor under his control (such as an insurance company carrying out its obligations of indemnity under the policy), an entirely different question is presented. If, in the preceding example, *A*'s insurance carrier had made the settlement with *B*, either without *A*'s knowledge, or with his knowledge but over his protest, the question is whether or not the insurance company's action, independent of *A* as it was, had any effect on *A*'s cause of action against *B*.

The earlier cases took the view that whatever the insurance company did with respect to the settlement was not binding on its insured, whether he agreed to the settlement or not, since the insurance company was not the agent of the insured and could act independently of its insured, and further that no subsequent action on the part of the insured would change the situation, nor was there any action required of him when he acquired knowledge of the settlement.

While the above is still the law in most states, there is some evidence of a contrary view. The Restatement (Law of Contracts, Sec. 421) suggests the following rule:

A payment or other performance by a third person, accepted by the creditor as full or partial satisfaction of his claim, discharges the debtor's duty in accordance with the terms on which the third person offered it. But the debtor on learning of the payment or other performance has power by disclaimer within a reasonable time to make the payment or other performance inoperative as a discharge.

This rule suggests that upon learning of the settlement by the third party, the debtor is bound by it and ratifies it unless he disclaims within a reasonable time.

Only a few courts have had occasion to consider the problem, and those that have have placed their decision on the basis of agency, or ratification and adoption of the settlement by the insured, rather than on the rule itself. In most states, the question of whether or not the action of an insurance carrier in settling a claim has any influence on the insured's cause of action against the person with whom the settlement has been made is an open one. The majority of the cases decided tend toward the view that the settlement has no influence on the insured's cause of action unless he participated in the settlement, or adopted, or ratified the act of the insurance carrier as his own act.

731   Releases

A release is a formal document providing for the relinguishment, concession, or giving up of a right or claim by the person in whom it exists, or to whom it accrues, to the person against whom it may be demanded or enforced. It is a contract, which is supported by a good and valuable consideration. A release may be (1) general, or (2) partial or *restrictive*.

1. *General*.   As its designation implies, a general release extinguishes all claims which the releasor may have against the releasee. The releasor clearly cannot release a claim which he does not own, either because he never had it or because he has assigned it to another. Thus an injured wife in most jurisdictions can release her claim for her injuries, but a release from her will not be a bar to others who may have a claim arising out of her injuries or the same accident. Her release will not affect her husband's claim for loss of consortium, since this claim is owned by the husband and the husband alone. Conversely, a release from the husband will not release the wife's claim for her injuries. His release will effectively release any claims which he might have, such as a claim for loss of consortium, and his own injuries if he were involved in the same accident.

Since the releasor cannot release a claim which he does not own, it follows that if he has assigned any part of the claim, he can release only that part which he retains. Where he has assigned part of the claim, and he executes a general release, the question of whether or not the release so given affects the rights of the assignee will depend upon the circumstances. If the releasee settles the case and takes back the release with knowledge or notice of the assignment, then the rights of the assignee are not affected by the release, but where the releasee has no knowledge, or is not chargeable with knowledge of the assignment nor any notice of it, settles the case believing that he was extinguishing the entire claim, the assignee may be estopped from enforcing his claim.

This situation usually arises where there is collision coverage on the claimant's car, and payment less the deductible has been made by the collision carrier. If the releasee has knowledge of the collision carrier's rights, he cannot obtain a full release from the claimant, since the claimant no longer owns part of the property damage claim. He does own that part of it which is represented by the deductible, and a general release from him will include the deductible but will not extinguish the collision carrier's claim for the balance. Some companies will add language to the release indicating that it covers only the property damage represented by the deductible, stating the exact amount of the deductible.

In all cases the release will effectively extinguish any claim which the releasor has against the releasee. Whether or not it also releases the claims which the releasor may have against others who stand in the relationship of tort-feasors depends upon the applicable law.

In cases where the insured has a possible cause of action against the releasor and the insurance carrier seeks to avoid the possibility of the release being pleaded in bar to the insured's cause of action, some companies have inserted a condition in the release, which reads substantially as follows:

It is understood and agreed between the releasor and the releasee that this release and settlement is not construed as an admission of liability on the part of the releasee, by whom liability is expressly denied. It is further understood and agreed that this release and settlement shall not be available as a defense by the releasor or anyone on his behalf, or as an estoppel, in any action which is now pending, or which hereafter may be brought by the releasee, or anyone in his behalf against the releasor.

2. *Partial or restrictive.* It is possible for a releasor to release part of his claim and retain the balance. This can be done by appropriate language in the instrument itself. It is seldom used in insurance matters where the part retained can be asserted against the insured. While most of the states, in the absence of statutes on the subject, still adhere to the common-law rule that the release of one of the tort-feasors releases all, there are some states which give effect to restrictive words in the release, which limit the surrender of the releasor's legal right to merely a release to the releasee and no one else. Some of these even give effect to an oral agreement which accompanies the release.

732   Covenant not to sue

A solution was sought to the problem presented where a plaintiff desired to release one of the tort-feasors, and not all, without extinguishing his entire claim. In states where the common-law rule is rigidly imposed, a release would not accomplish the desired result. A covenant not to sue was the device adopted for the purpose of avoiding the consequences of a release and also of accomplishing the result. A covenant not to sue is an agreement by one who has a right of action at the time of making it against another person by which he agrees not to sue to enforce such right of action forever in return for the payment of a consideration. Technically, the person giving such a covenant does not extinguish his claim. The claim is still in existence, but he has given up his right to bring legal action in order to enforce it. Since no other means of enforcement are available, the practical result is that the person giving the covenant is prevented from recovering on his claim against the coventee. Should the person giving the covenant attempt to bring action on his claim, the defendant could counterclaim for damages arising out of the breach of the covenant. The damage recoverable for the breach would be exactly the same amount which the plaintiff was claiming to be due to him. The result would be that any judgment obtained by the plaintiff would be offset by a judgment on the counterclaim for exactly the same amount. In order to avoid such a circuitry of action, most courts regard the covenant as a bar to the action, and will render judgment for the defendant accordingly.

733 Law governing contracts

The general rule is that unless there is a contrary intent expressed in the contract itself, the place where the contract is made is determinative of the law governing the contract. The theory is that in making the contract at that particular place, both parties entered into the agreement in contemplation of the law of the state which was applicable at the place of contract. This has no reference whatsoever to the place where the contract is to be performed.

Contracts come into existence as a result of an offer and an acceptance. If we assume that the offeror is located in one state, and he sends his offer to the other party in a second state, the contract will come into existence as soon as the second party accepts the offer. Therefore, the contract is made in the state where the offer is accepted. If the offeror had intended that the laws of the state in which he was located should govern the rights of the parties, he could easily have included that stipulation in his offer; then acceptance of the offer with that stipulation attached would establish that the parties intended that the law of a place other than the place where the contract was made should govern the rights of the parties.

This same rule will apply to contracts of insurance. The law of the place where the contract is made will govern the rights of the parties to the insurance contract, namely, the insured and the insurance company. In automobile liability contracts it is quite possible that the performance of the contract by the insurance company might take place in a state other than the state in which the contract was made. The fact that performance is required in another state will not in any way alter the rights of the parties insofar as the contract of insurance is concerned. The place where the contract is made will still govern the rights of the parties.

In the law of torts, the place of the happening of the event will determine the substantive law governing the rights of the parties involved. Under those circumstances, where insurance is involved, it is possible to have two different jurisdictions concerned with the handling of the claim. In the first place, if the place of contract is a state different from the one where the tort was committed, the laws of that state will govern the rights of the parties to the insurance contract and will measure the responsibility of the insurance company to its insured. The tort law of the place of accident will govern the rights of the parties involved in the accident and will be determinative of whether or not there is any liability imposed upon the insured by law.

For example, if an automobile liability insurance policy were entered into in the state of Louisiana, the rights of the parties under the contract of insurance would be determined by the state law of Louisiana. If an accident occurred in the state of Texas, the law which would be applicable to the rights and liabilities of the parties to the accident would be the law of Texas.

The insurance law of the state of New York provides that no policy of automobile liability insurance shall be deemed to indemnify the insured against any tort liability he may have, brought by his spouse, unless such coverage is afforded by a specific endorsement on the policy. If an accident should occur in New York State, the wife does have a cause of action against her husband in tort, but because of this provision of the insurance law, no policy of insurance would indemnify the husband in such a case, unless the policy were specifically endorsed to afford such coverage.

In a specific case, a man purchased a policy of automobile liability insurance in the state of New York. He thereafter moved his home from the state of New York to the state of Connecticut, still within the policy period. The policy was endorsed to show the change of address, but no endorsement was attached to the policy covering the insured's liability to his wife. An accident occurred in the state of Connecticut, which has no similar provision in its insurance law, which accident resulted in serious injuries to the insured's wife. The insurance carrier refused to defend, and, after judgment was obtained, an action was brought against the insurance carrier on the policy. The court upheld the insurance carrier in its disclaimer, taking the position that when the contract was entered into, the parties contemplated that the insurance law of the state of New York was part and parcel of the agreement, even though not written therein. The subsequent change of address on the part of the insured did not in any way change the agreement. Therefore, the law of the state of New York governed the rights and liabilities of the parties to the contract. The mere fact that there was an endorsement attached to the policy changing the place of residence of the insured did not amount to the making of a new contract, but merely an amendment to the old one.

CHAPTER VIII

Law of agency and contractors

800 Agency defined

The fundamental principle of the law of agency is that when a person does an act through an agent under his control, he does the act himself. Since he is answerable for the legal consequences of his own acts, he is likewise answerable for the acts of his agent. The person for whom the act is done is called the *principal.*

The word *agent* has various connotations in our everyday language and may mean different things under numerous circumstances. We have real estate agents, book agents, insurance agents, and theatrical agents. We are concerned with agents in the legal sense, and whether or not any of the persons described will qualify as legal agents depends on their relationship with an employer or principal. An agent is defined as one who is authorized to do certain acts for or in relation to the rights and property of another at his request, instruction, or command. The two elements which distinguish an agency relationship from other types of relationships are (1) authority to act for the principal, and (2) control by the principal.

1. *Authority to act.* For the agency relationship to exist, the principal must delegate some authority to the agent to do some act, ministerial or commercial, for and in behalf of the principal. If a person has no authority to act for the principal, he is not an agent, and his acts are not the acts of the principal. For example, an individual is in the real estate business, and he fraudulently represents to another that he is my agent for the purpose of selling my house. He has never received any authority from me. He executes a

211

contract of sale with the other, and when the purchase price is tendered, it is refused. The principal is not bound to the contract for the reason that the purported agent had no authority.

To take another situation, let us assume that *A* employs *B*, a real estate agent, to sell his house. *B* sells *A*'s car instead. *A* is not bound to the contract for the sale of his car, since *B* had no authority to sell the car. *B* was *A*'s agent for the purpose of selling *A*'s house, but not for any other purpose. If *B* had sold *A*'s house, *A* would be bound to the contract for the reason that *B* had the authority to so act for and in behalf of *A*.

2. *Control by the principal.* Merely because an act is done for and in behalf of a person does not make the person doing the act the agent of the beneficiary of the act unless the act was done under the control of the beneficiary as to the methods and means of accomplishment. For example, *A* takes a suit of clothes to the dry cleaner for the purpose of having it cleaned and pressed. *A* gives the dry cleaner the authority to clean the suit, but *A* does not exercise control and supervision over the methods and means employed by the dry cleaner to accomplish the result. Since there is no control by *A*, the dry cleaner is not his agent.

To take a converse situation, *A* employs *B* as a handyman. *A* fixes the hours of employment, furnishes the tools, and directs *B*'s work. While so engaged, *B* sells *A*'s house to a purchaser. *A* is not bound by the contract of sale. *B* was under *A*'s control, but *B* had no authority to sell the house, and hence was not *A*'s agent for the purpose of selling the house. If, however, *B* had been instructed to buy some fertilizer, and did so, *A* would be liable to the supplier for the cost of the fertilizer, since *B* had the authority and acted under *A*'s control and direction in making the purchase.

An agent may devote his full time to the business of the principal, as in the relationship of employer and employee, or he may merely represent the principal in one or more isolated transactions. The acts done for the principal may be of both a business and a social nature, and they may also be done either for a fee, or salary, or gratuitously. For example, the principal asks his neighbor to drive the principal's car to a garage, or to take the principal's car and drive his wife to the store. The neighbor is the agent of the principal while engaged in driving the principal's car for these purposes.

An independent contractor is not an agent, and the acts of an independent contractor are not the responsibility of the principal who employs him. An independent contractor is defined as one who represents another as the result to be accomplished and not as to the methods and means of doing the work. Thus, if the principal employs a painter to paint his house for an agreed price, even though the principal chooses the color of the paint and directs the painter as to where the paint is to be applied, under those circumstances the painter is an independent contractor. On the other hand, if the principal furnished the paint, the ladders, brushes, etc., and fixed the hours of employment and directed the means of doing the work, paying for the job on a fixed daily rate, then the painter would be an employee and the agent of the principal. The question of whether or not an individual is an independent contractor always turns on the question of control. If there is no control exercised, there is no agency.

The agency relationship is created by the mutual agreement of the parties. The principal must offer to delegate some authority to the agent to be exercised under the control of the principal. The agent must accept the delegation of authority and the terms on which it is offered. Both elements must be present for the relationship of principal and agent to arise. If either element is lacking, there is no agency.

801   *Respondeat superior*

Where a principal does an act through an agent, and the agent is negligent in the performance thereof to the extent that some third person sustains injury, the negligence of the agent is imputed to the principal. The principal is answerable in damages to the injured person, even though the principal himself did not participate in the event. This response for the actions of another which the law imposes on the principal is called vicarious liability. The doctrine under which it is imposed is called the doctrine of *respondeat superior* (let the master answer). The doctrine applies only where there was a relationship of principal and agent in existence at the time the event occurred and in respect to the very transaction from which it arose. The doctrine is inapplicable when the agent is acting outside the legitimate scope of his authority.

802   Types of agents

Agents are generally classified by the nature and extent of the authority given to them by the principal. These classifications include *universal, general, limited, implied,* or *apparent agents.*

A *universal agent* is one who is appointed to do all the acts which the principal can personally do, and which he may lawfully delegate the power to another to do. Agents of this type are extremely rare. Since the occasion for the delegation of such complete authority comes about only in extreme cases of necessity, the law presumes that the agent is not a universal agent unless there is clear and convincing evidence of the principal's intent to create that type of agent.

A *general agent* is one to whom the principal confides his whole business, or all transactions or functions of a designated class. In the insurance business, a general agent is one who exercises complete underwriting authority in the territory to which the principal assigns him. The acts of a general agent of an insurance company are the acts of the company. This is true even though the company may have placed some limitations upon his authority. Unless the limitations of the authority of the general agent are actually brought to the attention of the third person dealing with the general agent, the third person has a right to assume that since this man is held out to the public as a general agent, that he has all of the powers normally delegated to a general agent.

A *limited agent* is one who is an agent for the principal within a certain area, limited either by contract or by the usage in the particular trade or occupation in which he is engaged. For example, a grocery clerk is an agent of the owner of the grocery store. He has authority to sell groceries at retail to customers and to collect the purchase price. His authority is limited to this particular function. He could not, without additional specific authority, undertake to sell the entire grocery store, including the stock, fixtures, the building, and the goodwill. A person dealing with the grocery clerk would be bound to recognize that grocery clerks by the usage of the business are not clothed with the authority to sell the business. Likewise, a truck driver employed to drive a truck from one place to another would not have authority to sell the truck, or to pledge it as security for a loan on behalf of his principal without actual authority so to do. He would have authority, however, to have the truck repaired should it break down and the principal would be liable for the repair bill.

An *implied* or *apparent agent* is one whom the principal, either intentionally or by want of ordinary care, constitutes his agent, though he is not either expressly or by implication, clothed with any specific authority by the principal. This situation is also classified as one involving an ostensible agent or an agent by estoppel.

For example, if a grocer leaves a person in charge of his store, with directions merely to watch the store and do nothing further, the limitation of this person's authority would be known only to the grocer and the person he placed in charge of the premises. If this person undertook to sell some of the groceries to retail customers, the grocer as principal would be bound by the transaction. This is true, even though the grocer may have expressly instructed the person in charge that this was not to be done.

As to the third persons dealing with the agent in charge of the store, since they had no knowledge of the limitation of the authority of the agent, and since the principal had created a situation wherein third persons would assume that the person in charge had authority to act, the grocer is estopped from denying the authority of his agent. He is bound by the unauthorized transactions which the agent undertook on his behalf.

An *insurance broker* is a limited agent. He is the agent for the insured, and his agency is limited to the procuring of insurance coverage for his principal. Therefore, his acts within the scope of his agency are the acts of his principal, or the person for whom the insurance is being procured, and not the acts of the insurance companies with whom he deals. He differs from an insurance agent who is employed by an insurance company for the purpose of selling insurance, or a subagent employed by the general agent for the purpose of selling insurance, in that the broker is the representative of the insured. The other two types of agents are agents of the insurance company.

803   Specific agency relationships

The most common form of agency relationship is that of employer and employee. It is also referred to as a relationship of master and servant. An employee is defined as anyone who, for a lawful consideration, undertakes to perform a lawful pursuit at his employer's direction. This contemplates a contract of hire between employer and employee, control by the employer, not only of the result to be accomplished, but the methods and means of performing the work. It also contemplates that the employer or employee shall have the right to terminate the agreement at any time.

An employee is a limited agent and may act for the employer in all matters within the scope of his employment. The tests as to whether or not an employer-employee relationship exists include the following:

1. Does the employer fix the hours of work?
2. Does the employer supply the tools, equipment, and protective industrial clothing for the person hired?
3. Does the person hired receive pay in accordance with stated periods of time, stated units of work, or is he paid an agreed price for the entire job?
4. Does the employer withhold income taxes from the person's salary, provide unemployment insurance, provide compensation benefits, and pay social security tax?

If the answers to all of these questions are in the affirmative, and the answer to 3 is that the pay is in accordance with stated periods of time or stated units of work, then the employer-employee relationship exists. If it does, the negligence of the employee acting in the scope of his employment will be imputed to the employer, and, in addition, any acts performed by the employee within the scope of his employment are binding upon the employer under the doctrine of *respondeat superior.*

A corporation is loosely defined as an artificial person created by statute. It can function only through agents. An individual operating a business as such can exercise all the powers incidental to the management of the business. In the case of a corporation, the management of the business is placed in the hands of a board of directors. These directors exercise all of the powers of management and may specifically delegate powers to officers of the corporation or other employees. Therefore, in those cases of administrative management where the authority has been specifically delegated in advance, the corporation is bound by and responsible for the acts of such designated employees within the scope of the authority thus given.

For example, the secretary of a corporation is normally given the authority to sign legal documents in behalf of the corporation. This authority may be on a blanket basis or it may be specifically limited to a certain kind or class of legal documents. If the secretary of the corporation is authorized to compromise claims which the corporation may have and is further authorized to execute a release for and in behalf of the corporation, then the adjuster may deal with him. On the other hand, such authority may have been delegated by the board of directors to some other officer. In either case, the adjuster would have no way of knowing the exact authority of the officer executing the release, and in the absence of an actual examination of the minutes of the board of directors meeting, the adjuster may rely upon a sworn statement attached to the release signed by an appropriate officer who has knowledge of the director's action, indicating that the officer executing the release has been specifically authorized to do so by action of the board of directors.

As to purely ministerial functions, all executive officers, and all employees, are authorized to act for the corporation within the scope of their authority or employment. Torts committed or contracts executed within this area of employment then become the responsibility of the corporation.

Government agents present a problem all their own. Agents of the government, be they local, state, or federal, and be they elective or appointed, have only such authority as is given to them by the statutes creating their positions. Certain officers are authorized by law to delegate some part of their responsibilities to others by means of a directive or executive order. The general public passed the laws which created all of these government agents. It did this either directly or through representation. Therefore, the general public is on notice of the limitation of authority of government agents. Any action taken by a government agent in excess of his authority, even though he has apparent authority to so act, is not binding on the government. The government is not subject to liability on the theory of implied agency, ostensible agency, or agency by estoppel.

A partnership is a form of business enterprise which is created by a voluntary contract between two or more competent persons wherein they agree to place their money, efforts, labor, and skill in lawful business or lawful commerce, with the understanding that there shall be a proportional sharing of the profits and losses between them. Each partner is an agent of the partnership, and because of the nature of the business, he represents all of the individuals who make up the partnership, including himself.

Partners are jointly and severally liable for the obligations incurred by the partnership in the course of the partnership enterprise. This means that a person having a cause of action against the partnership could sue one partner, some of the partners, or all of the partners. Partnerships, like any other business enterprise, can have employees who are not partners. The liability of the partnership for the imputed negligence of its employees would be the same as that of any other employer.

A joint enterprise is an undertaking somewhat similar to that of the partnership. It does not connote a permanent arrangement, but refers to an association formulated to accomplish some specific purpose. To be a joint enterprise, all of the persons engaged in the common purpose must have an equal right to control, or at least have a voice in the management. A joint enterprise therefore can be defined as the joint prosecution of a common purpose under such circumstances that each has authority, express or implied, to act for all in respect to control, means, or agencies employed to execute such a common purpose. The existence of a joint enterprise, which is sometimes otherwise referred to as a joint adventure or common purpose, depends entirely upon the right of joint control. Even though people having the same objective are involved, there is no joint enterprise unless each of the people so engaged have a voice in the control of the methods and means utilized in order to accomplish the common purpose.

We will find joint enterprise most frequently involved in automobile cases. For example, *A* and *B* decide to go on a vacation in *A*'s car. The understanding is that both will equally share the expenses incurred for gasoline and oil, as well as any repairs that might be necessary to the vehicle during the vacation trip. On those facts alone, there is no joint enterprise. There is no understanding that the right to control the vehicle will be joint, and under the circumstances, it would appear that *A* would control the movement of his vehicle, would decide whether or not he would allow *B* to drive, and also decide what route would be taken in order to reach their vacation spot. Since *B* had no right to control the movement of the vehicle, there is no joint enterprise.

Suppose *A* and *B* decide to go on a vacation and they jointly rent an automobile for that purpose. It is understood that both will drive the car on occasions, both will be responsible to the renting agency for the return of the vehicle, and both will be responsible for the charges incurred in connection with the use of the vehicle. Here there is a joint right of control, and there is a joint enterprise.

Joint enterprise has importance only on the issue of liability. Where there is a joint enterprise, all joint adventurers are liable to third persons, and the negligence of one member of the joint enterprise is imputable to the others. Just as in a partnership, the injured third person may sue one of the joint adventurers, some, or all. He is not required to join all joint venturers.

With regard to the liability among themselves, the same rules are applicable to joint adventurers as are applicable to members of a partnership. Where a joint venturer or a partner is injured through the negligence of another joint venturer or partner, the negligence of the person causing the injury is not imputed to their partner or joint venturer who is injured so as to prevent a recovery by him against the negligent partner. Imputed negligence occurs only where a third person, or a stranger to the joint enterprise or partnership is injured. It does not apply as between partners or joint venturers.

804   Appointment of subagents

An agent normally does not have the authority to delegate any part of his duty to someone else unless he is specifically authorized to do so by the principal, or where custom or usage in the particular trade in which they are engaged normally gives the agent that authority. If an agent does employ the services of another where he has no authority to do so, and where the custom or usage in the trade or business does not authorize such employment, the person so employed is not a subagent of the principal and cannot bind the principal in contract, nor can this person's negligent act be imputable to the principal.

Illustrations. *A* employs *B* to deliver milk at retail to private homes. It is not customary for such drivers to employ helpers. Unknown to *A*, *B* employs a boy to assist him in making the deliveries. The boy is not the agent of *A*.

A employs *B*, an attorney, for the purpose of collecting a debt from a debtor located in a distant state. Litigation is anticipated. *B* may employ an attorney in the distant state and this attorney is the subagent of *A*.

The *X* Insurance Company appoints *A* as its general agent for the state of *Y* with the understanding that *A* will maintain offices in several parts of the state. *A* is authorized to employ subagents who will have authority to bind the *X* Insurance Company, even though there is no specific agreement between *A* and the *X* Insurance Company that *A* was authorized to appoint subagents. The custom and usage of the business, together with the area to be covered, impliedly contemplates the employment of subagents.

805   Agency by emergency

Normally an agent performing a purely ministerial function does not have the authority to delegate any part of his work to another. However, there are situations where an emergency arises and where efforts to communicate with the principal or employer have failed. In such a case, the agent or employee would have the implied authority to make whatever arrangements the facts of the situation demanded.

For example, if a truck driver suffered an illness while on his route, unsuccessfully attempted to communicate with his employer, and was unable to continue with the truck, and where his load consisted of a perishable commodity, the driver would have the implied authority under those circumstances to employ another driver to complete the trip at the expense of his employer. In such a case, even though the employer had no knowledge of the employment of the other driver, should an accident occur, the other driver's negligence would be imputed to the principal, or employer.

On the other hand, if the driver were taken ill and the load did not consist of a perishable commodity and there was no requirement that the load be delivered promptly, then no emergency would be present and the truck driver would have no authority, implied or otherwise, to engage the services of another to complete the trip.

Therefore, in all cases involving an agency by emergency, a meticulous investigation is required to determine whether or not an emergency was in existence, whether or not the truck driver had actual authority to employ the services of others, or whether or not such authority could be implied from the facts of the particular situation.

In another case, the truck may be on a public highway and the driver injured as a consequence of an accident. The driver would have the implied authority to hire someone else to drive the truck off the highway. This could be done by hiring an individual who would then act as agent for the owner of the truck, or, in the alternative, he could secure the services of a towing concern for the same purpose. In the latter case, the towing concern would be an independent contractor and there would be no agency relationship between the owner of the truck and the towing concern. However, as agent for his employer, the truck driver would have the implied authority to obligate his employer to pay for the services rendered by the towing concern.

To constitute an agency by emergency, three elements must be present: (1) There must be an emergency requiring immediate action. (2) Efforts to contact the principal for instructions must have failed. (3) There must be an actual contract of hire made with the subagent.

To illustrate the extent to which this concept has been applied, a private carrier made a contract to transport a U.S.O. troupe from an army camp to a major city. On an extremely cold day, the carrier's driver picked up the troupe and proceeded on his way. En route, the bus broke down, and in addition, the heating apparatus ceased to function. The driver attempted to contact his employer without success, and finally made a contact with the army camp. He arranged for the Army to provide a bus and driver for the purpose of completing the trip. Before the army bus reached its destination, an accident occurred through the negligence of the driver of the army bus.

In actions brought against the bus company, the court held that the driver of the army bus at the time of the accident was acting as the agent of the bus company, and therefore his negligence was imputed to the bus company. In this case, it will be seen that all three elements of the principal of agency by emergency were present. There was an emergency, there was an attempt to contact the principal, and there was an actual contract of hire made by the employment of the army bus and its driver.

806   Special and general employers

This concept of agency is sometimes referred to as the *borrowed servant rule,* or the *rule of the loaned employee.* It comes about where the employee's regular or general employer, with the consent of the employee, temporarily loans the services of the employee to another, called a *special employer,* for the purpose of doing some specific task. The employee still remains in the employ of the general employer, and there usually is some arrangement by which the special employer will reimburse the general employer for the salary earned by the employee while absent from his regular job. The question is whether or not by such an arrangement the employee becomes at least temporarily an employee and/or agent of the special employer. The answer to the question will turn on the matter of control. If the general employer retains his entire control over the employee, then the employee is an agent of the general employer and not of the person for whom he is working. On the other hand, if the general employer relinquishes the entire control of the employee's actions to the special employer, then the employee becomes an employee or agent of the special employer while under such control and direction, even though the employee still remains on the payroll of the general employer.

Therefore, the question of whether or not the employee becomes a temporary employee of the special employer, or remains a regular employee of his general employer, will almost always be determined by which employer has the right to control and direct his activities in the performance of the act and whose work is being performed. The negligence of the loaned employee will be imputed to the employer who has the right of control and direction at the time of the accident.

807   Attorneys as limited agents

An attorney engaged for the purpose of bringing an action at law against a defendant is a limited or special agent of the client who employs him. His agency is limited to the cause of action for which he is engaged, and he may act for the client only in connection with legal representation in that case and no other. Within the scope of his authority, he may do the following acts without consultation with his client, and the action so taken will be binding upon the client. He may:

1. Admit facts.
2. Waive a jury.
3. Consolidate actions.
4. Waive rights of appeal.
5. Dismiss an action.
6. Submit a matter to arbitration or reference.
7. Engage experts at the client's expense if the fee is reasonable.

He may *not* release the cause of action without his client's consent. He is bound to transmit to his client all offers of settlement so that the client may accept or reject them. This is a duty that he has only to his client. His failure to do so, which results in damage to the client, will subject him to liability to the client alone. He does not owe this duty to any other party to the action.

Unless the attorney warrants that he has specific authority to do so, an agreement on the part of the attorney to settle a certain case at a specific figure will not be binding on his client. If the attorney warrants that he has such authority and he does not, the client still is not bound by the agreement, but the attorney does expose himself to liability for damages arising from the breach of this warranty of authority.

808   Fiduciary agents

An agent is said to act in a fiduciary capacity, or to receive money or contract a debt in such capacity, when the business which he transacts, or the money or property which he handles, is not his own or for his own benefit, but for the benefit of another person as to whom he stands in a relation implying and necessitating great confidence and trust on one part and a high degree of good faith on the other. A fiduciary agent, therefore, is one who not merely performs ministerial functions but is entrusted with the title to or custody of the property of another, concerning which he has undertaken the responsibility of performing some function. Examples of this type of relationship include trustees, under a technical or express trust; executors, under a last will and testament; attorney-at-law, guardian, broker, director of a corporation, public officer.

All of these are held to a high degree of care in the faithful performance of the duties that they have undertaken. All of these agents receive money or contract a debt in a fiduciary capacity. The business which he transacts or the money or property which he handles is not his own, nor are the transactions which he makes for his own benefit, but for the benefit of another person or persons as to whom he stands in a relationship implying and necessitating great confidence and trust.

Basically, the relationship arises when one party has entrusted his property, his money, all the power to contract debts to the agent, with the understanding that the agent will exercise judgment as to the management, sale, purchase, or settlement of obligations. The principal has divested himself of most of the control of the property and relies entirely upon the exercise of good judgment and faithfulness on the part of the agent.

Out of such a relationship the law raises the rule that neither party may exert influence or pressure upon the other, take selfish advantage of the trust, or deal with the subject matter of the trust in such a way as to procure it for himself or to prejudice the other, except in the exercise of the utmost good faith and with the full knowledge and consent of the other. Business shrewdness, hard bargaining, and astuteness to take advantage of the forgetfulness or the negligence of another being is totally prohibited between persons standing in such a relation to each other.

A fiduciary agent may not deal with the principal's property in his hands in any other way except for the advantage of the principal. The agent may not exercise any self-interest in dealing with the property in his hands. This is for the reason that the law presumes that a man cannot serve two masters. The agent cannot sell the property to himself, sell his own property to the principal, or exercise such a use of the property so as to produce an income for himself, independent of the fees arising out of the fiduciary relationship.

Where an agent does deal with the property in his possession and buys the property for his own account, or sells property of his own to the principal, on the principal's account, then the law *conclusively* presumes the transaction to be fraudulent. This means that even though the agent dealt with the property fairly, and paid more than the market price, the agent is precluded from presenting this evidence. A conclusive presumption is one which cannot be overcome by any evidence, and the court will not receive any evidence with respect to it. In other words, a fiduciary agent must act solely for his principal and cannot, in the exercise of this agency, deal with himself personally in any way.

In many of these relationships, which are created by operation of law, an additional guarantee is required which may take the form of a bond with a good and sufficient surety as to the faithful performance of the duties undertaken by the agent. This guarantee may take the form of a surety bond written by an insurance company or an undertaking from a private individual, both of which bind themselves to the agent for the benefit of the person or persons for whom the agent is obligated to act.

Public officers in some cases occupy a fiduciary relationship with respect to the people of the state, city, or municipality by whom they are employed. They are required to deal in all matters for and in behalf of the political subdivision which they represent and may not deal with the property or money or power entrusted to them with any considerations of self interest. In most instances the law requires that such public officers be covered by a bond to guarantee the faithful performance of these duties.

An adjuster is a fiduciary agent of the company which he represents, at least in certain phases of his activities. He is an agent who is given the authority to contract a debt, to receive property for and in behalf of his principal, and is required in the performance of his duties in connection therewith to inform his principal of any facts coming to his knowledge which will have any influence upon the contracting of the debt or the disposition of the property.

809   Trustees

There are fiduciaries who are in possession and control of property for the benefit of others, whose relationship comes about as a result of an appointment by the court. They are responsible to the court for the faithful performance of their duties and are not under the control of the parties for whose benefit they act. Therefore, they are not agents, although acting in a fiduciary capacity. In this classification we find *receivers, executors,* or *administrators* of the last will and testament of a deceased, and *guardians* of infants or incompetents.

A *receiver* is a fiduciary and has the power to bind the organization of which he is the receiver to contract and tort liability. He is not appointed by the organization or, necessarily, with its consent. He is a representative of the court, and he acts only under the court's direction. The persons for whose benefit he is appointed, be they stockholders or creditors, have no right of control over his actions. His actions are his own.

Executors and *administrators* under a last will and testament are fiduciaries, but they are not the agents of the beneficiaries under the will. Like the receiver, they are responsible to and under the direction of the court which appointed them. They may bind the estate in contract or expose the estate to liability in tort. However, the negligence of the executor or administrator is not imputed to the ultimate beneficiaries of the estate.

Guardians of infants and incompetents are the same type of fiduciaries. They are appointed by the court, subject to its control and direction, and are personally responsible for their acts in connection with the administration of the trust. They are not the agents of the infant or the incompetent.

The same rule applies to fiduciaries of this character as to fiduciary agents. The trustee may not deal with the property in his hands for his own benefit nor may he sell property of his own to the estate or organization that he represents. Such acts are conclusively presumed to be fraudulent, irrespective of the nature or character of the act.

810   Independent contractors

An independent contractor is defined as one who exercises an independent employment and contracts to do a piece of work according to his own judgment and methods, and without being subject to his employer except as to the results of the work. He has the right to employ and direct the action of the workmen, independently of such employer, and is free from any superior authority in him to say how the specified work shall be done or what the laborers shall do as it progresses. It is very generally held that the right of control as to the mode and method of doing the work is the principal consideration in determining whether one employed is an independent contractor or a servant. Therefore, one who represents another as to the result to be obtained and not as to the methods and means of accomplishing that result is an independent contractor.

In the case of an independent contractor, the principal does not fix the hours of employment, furnish the tools to be used in accomplishing the purpose, or furnish the industrial clothing to be worn by the workmen so engaged; nor does he interfere with the methods or mode of operation conducted by the contractor. On the other hand, if the principal has the right to fix the hours of employment and to control the methods and means of doing the work, then the person with whom he contracts in this relationship is not an independent contractor.

An independent contractor is not the agent of the principal. He is liable for his own tortious acts, and his negligence in the performance of his work is not imputed to the principal.

The employment of an independent contractor does not always insulate the principal from liability for the negligent acts of the contractor. There are certain duties which the principal, as an owner of land or as an operator of a business, is bound to perform with respect to the risk of harm to third persons. The duty of care in certain areas cannot be delegated to an independent contractor. The principal is liable for any failure to meet the duties imposed upon him by law in the following situations:

1. Where the principal has failed to exercise due care in the selection of a reasonably competent contractor.
2. Where the work to be done by the independent contractor is by its nature inherently dangerous.
3. Where the negligent act or omission involves a violation of a duty imposed upon the principal either by the common law or by statute.
4. Where the work to be done by the independent contractor is forbidden by law.

Where any one of these conditions prevails, the negligence of the contractor is the negligence of the principal. For example, if the owner of a piece of property required the removal of some stone or tree stumps on his property, and engaged a contractor for the purpose of blasting out these things, the mere employment of an independent contractor to do this work will not absolve the owner from his common-law duty to his neighbor. If the project resulted in damage to the neighbor's property, both the contractor and the owner of the property would be liable to the neighbor. The work is inherently dangerous. Also, in the same case, if damage ensued, the neighbor could allege that the owner had failed to exercise due care in the selection of a competent contractor to do the work.

The owner of property is under a statutory duty to refrain from any acts which impair the proper use of the street in front of the premises or the adjacent sidewalk. If construction or repairs are being made to the premises which in any way affect the street or sidewalk, the owner has a duty of care to the general public and must provide for a means of passage and also must maintain safety devices in the form of barricades, fences, and warning signs, to protect the public from injury. This is a duty which is imposed upon the owner of the land, and he cannot contract away his responsibility by means of the employment of an independent contractor.

The owner's liability to the members of the public who may be injured as a consequence of this operation remains, irrespective of any of the terms of the contract which may be made between the owner and the contractor. It is customary in such situations for the contractor to agree to indemnify the owner from any liability arising out of the operations of the contract. This is referred to as a "hold harmless agreement." (This agreement is discussed in detail in the chapter on the Law of Contracts.) For the purpose of this illustration, the owner's liability to the public remains, and all that a hold harmless agreement does is to provide for a means of protection or reimbursement to the owner after the liability has been imposed upon him. As between the owner and the injured member of the public, the duties and responsibilities remain exactly the same, and the existence of the hold harmless agreement does not in any way alter the responsibilities of the rights of the parties.

As to the duties and responsibilities which can be delegated to the independent contractor, he is liable for his own negligent acts committed by him, his agents, servants, or employees. As to nondelegable duties which are imposed upon the owner, both the owner and the independent contractor are liable in damages to a person injured. In the delegable duty area, only the independent contractor is liable for his own negligence. If the subject matter of the contract is one where it is within the contemplation of the parties that some part of the work be subcontracted to others, such subcontractor is liable for his own negligence and the negligence of his agents, servants, or employees.

The contractor who has the contract with the owner of the property, and who subcontracts some portion of the work, is referred to as the *general* or *prime contractor*. As such, he has the responsibility to the owner for the completion of the job as well as responsibility for the direction of the work. He is responsible for the general housekeeping on the job, the maintenance of fences, barricades, lights, and other warning devices. These latter duties are owned not only to the members of the public but to the employees of subcontractors injured as a consequence of the failure to meet such responsibilities. The general contractor has the duty of maintaining the premises on which the work is in progress in a reasonably safe condition, and he is liable to employees of the subcontractor or other persons legally on the premises, if they are injured as a result of the failure to meet this duty.

The subcontractor is liable for any injuries occasioned by his negligence or the negligence of his servants, employees, or agents. This responsibility not only extends to the general public and persons legally on the premises, but also to employees of the general contractor and employees of other subcontractors as well.

The existence of these various responsibilities on the part of the general contractor and the subcontractor sometimes poses a very difficult problem of investigation, especially on a large construction project where a number of subcontractors are involved. For example, if a brick falls from the building during the course of construction and injures a member of the public, how can the offending subcontractor be identified? The mere fact that the commodity which fell was a brick would not necessarily point to the bricklayer, unless the bricklayer was the only subcontractor working on the job at that particular time. A subcontractor or his employees will seldom admit that they dislodged the brick, and therefore the plaintiff has the problem of proof. The contractors against whom claims are asserted likewise have a problem of defense.

Some insurance companies have met this problem by refusing to insure any large construction project unless the general contractor and all of the subcontractors take out liability insurance coverage with them, either on a general or specific job basis. This avoids any controversy between insurance carriers and leaves the management and control of the defense of any action arising on the job to the one insurance carrier. Where this situation obtains, it is extremely important that the adjuster check the insurance coverage.

Sometimes, a subcontractor will have insurance in one company and will take out a specific short-term policy with a second company in order to conform with the general contractor's obligation or the contract which the subcontractor made to insure in a specific company. This is usually on a specific job basis, and the policy issued to the subcontractor covering all of his other obligations should be endorsed so as to eliminate any coverage for the specific job in which specific insurance coverage has been obtained. If this is not done, there may be dual insurance, in that the subcontractor will have insurance with his usual insurance carrier which covers all of his operations, plus the specific short-term policy which he has purchased for the particular job.

811   Scope of agency

In the performance of the principal's business, all of the acts of the agent are within the scope of his agency. When the agent is performing acts solely for his own purposes, he is not within the scope of his agency. In applying these rules, we should make a division between agents who are regularly employed by the principal and those agents who are employed for some specific purpose. As to employees, all acts performed in the course of employment designed to further the interests of the principal are within the scope of the agency. This is for the reason that during the hours of employment and with respect to the work itself, the agent-employee is under the control of the principal-employer. Acts done by employees for their personal convenience, or for some private purpose entirely disassociated from the business of the employer, are outside the scope of the agency.

Agents who are employed for a specific purpose are within the scope of the agency only when they are acting for the principal within the area of their particular employment. All other acts, preliminary to or subsequent to action within the specific purpose, are outside the scope of the agency. For example, P employs A, a real estate agent, for the purpose of selling a piece of real property which P owns. A drives T, a prospective purchaser, to the real property. In the course of so doing, an automobile accident occurs which is due entirely to A's negligence. T is injured. P is not liable to T because A was not within the scope of his agency at the time of the accident.

Using the same example, let us assume that A opened the house for T's inspection. A knew of a dangerous condition on the premises and failed to warn T. T is injured as a result of this dangerous condition. P is liable to T. In this situation, A was within the scope of his agency. P knew of the dangerous condition and A, his agent, also knew of the danger. As to P, T is a business invitee. Therefore, P owed T the duty of warning him of any dangerous condition on the premises which was not open and obvious. P delegated this duty to A, who did not perform it. Hence P is liable for the nonfeasance of his agent, A.

812   Deviation from the scope of agency

The fundamental rule under which the negligence of an agent is imputed to the principal is that where a person does an act through another under his control, he does it himself and is responsible for the result. As long as the agent is performing his duties under the control of the principal, the agent is within the scope of his agency. When the agent performs an act for his own purposes, the element of the principal's control is lacking and therefore, until the agent returns to the control of the principal, his acts in the interim are his own. Clearly, an agent does not represent his principal 24 hours a day, and the agent does perform acts which are strictly personal and have no relation to the business of the principal. The negligence of an agent in the performance of personal acts is not attributable to the principal.

These seem fairly simple rules to apply when the personal act of the agent is entirely disassociated from the business of the principal. A difficulty arises where there is the combination of both. Let us assume that a truck driver is instructed to take a load from New York City to Albany, New York. There is no question that if the truck driver takes a reasonably direct route to Albany, all of his acts in connection therewith would be solely for the benefit of his principal, under the control of the principal, and therefore within the scope of his agency. Should an accident occur under these circumstances, the negligence of the agent would be imputed to his principal. However, let us assume that for some reason personal to himself, the truck driver decides that instead of going directly to Albany he will stop off at Stamford, in Connecticut, to attend to some of his own business and then proceed from that point to Albany. If the truck driver commits a wrongful act while en route from New York to Stamford, the cases uniformly hold that while on this leg of the journey, the employee had abandoned his employment and was not under the control of the principal. Therefore, the risks of the highway are his own and not those of the principal.

If a negligent act is committed between Stamford and Albany, the courts are divided as to whether or not the principal's liability is involved. The most liberal view is that once the truck driver's personal business has been completed that at that moment, in proceeding toward Albany, he has resumed his employment. Therefore, as to any negligent act occurring between Stamford and Albany, the negligence of the agent would be imputed to the principal.

Other states have held that until such time as the truck driver is actually back on what could be considered a direct route to Albany from New York, his deviation from the employment was still in progress. To illustrate, if a truck driver took Route 1 from New York to Stamford and then took Route 5 from Stamford to Route 9, and the most direct route between New York and Albany was Route 9, under the second theory, the liability of the principal would not be involved until the truck driver was actually back on Route 9. The theory here is that during the entire deviation from the normal route, the truck driver was not engaged in his employer's business.

In the previous illustrations, the main purpose of the trip involved the interest of the principal in moving the truck from New York to Albany. It is on this basis that at least part of the trip is chargeable to the principal. A more perplexing question arises when the agent is making a trip solely for a purpose of his own and is asked by his employer to perform some trifling service while en route. The entire purpose of the trip is personal to the agent. The trifling service required by the principal would not have justified a special trip for that purpose. Therefore, if the agent's personal purpose was not involved, the trip would have been abandoned. In such situations, the imputed negligence of the employer would be involved only with respect to acts performed while actually doing the act required by the principal. As to the trip itself, the risks of the highway were entirely those of the employee and not those of the employer.

813   Vicarious liability of the principal

The theory of vicarious liability on the part of the principal is a theory that was developed by the English common law. It came into existence at a time when the master of the household had serfs, bounden servants, and others who were members of his household, and over whom the master exercised absolute authority. All of their actions, therefore, were within the master's control, and under those circumstances, since none of these people had any property of their own, the English common-law courts developed the theory of the master's liability for the acts of the servants. This means that the master must respond for the acts of an agent or servant under his control. This type of responsibility has been variously called *vicarious liability, imputed liability,* and *respondeat superior.*

Today we do not have bounden servants and serfs, but we do have other types of agents. These may be employees or agents employed for a specific purpose. The responsibility of the principal, however, is the same. The principal must respond in damages for the acts of his agents performed while acting within the scope of his agency. This is true even though the acts of the agent in furtherance of the principal's business are done improperly, carelessly, or negligently.

Where the principal requires his agent to drive an automobile, and where the master especially instructs the agent that the automobile is to be driven carefully, it could be argued that if the agent operates the automobile in a careless manner, such agent is outside the scope of his authority.

The courts, no doubt influenced by the development of the law from the bounden servant days, have not accepted this theory. They hold the principal responsible for all of the acts of the agent within the scope of his agency or while furthering the interests of the principal, whether carelessly done or not. For example, let us assume that the principal instructs his agent to go to a certain parking lot and drive the principal's black Chevrolet sedan to the principal's home. The agent goes to the parking lot but mistakenly takes a black Chevrolet sedan owned by X. On the return trip, the agent is involved in an accident and the Chevrolet is damaged. Under those circumstances the principal is liable to X, even though his instructions to his agent were to bring only the principal's car to his home and no other.

As to intentional torts committed while acting for the principal, the general rule is that if the intentional act is committed while serving the interest of the principal, however much of a mistake in judgment it might be, the doctrine of *respondeat superior* applies, and the principal is answerable. On the other hand, if the intentional act was neither intended to serve nor did serve the master's interest, then it is a deviation from the scope of the agency, and the principal is not answerable. Two District of Columbia cases illustrate the distinction between the two situations. In *Dilli* v. *Johnson* (107 Fed. 2d 669), an assault occurred when the plaintiff told the defendant's employee in charge that his hamburger contained unground meat. It was the employee's duty to adjust any disputes or differences with the customers, and the court held that he was acting within the scope of his employment when he resented the complaint by violently attacking the plaintiff. Conversely, in *District Certified TV Service, Inc.* v. *Neary* (350 Fed. 2d 998), the facts indicate that one Singleton, while driving his employer's truck collided with the plaintiff's parked car. Hearing the noise, the plaintiff emerged from a nearby house and gave chase in his damaged automobile. Singleton was without question leaving the scene without stopping to identify himself or for any other purpose. The plaintiff caught up with him at a traffic light, but he refused to stop and the chase continued, during which time Singleton ran through red lights and stop signs and finally brushed a traffic officer, who joined the chase. Finally, the chase ended when Singleton smashed into the plaintiff's automobile, attempted to assault the officer with a metal stanchion, and the event was finally ended when the police officer shot and wounded Singleton.

In noting that there are instances of intentional torts which would involve the liability of the master, the court held that on these facts, the doctrine of *respondeat superior* did not apply, and the principal was not liable. The court said:

> Singleton's extended flight following the first collision, involving reckless disregard of traffic regulations and human life, must be denominated his own "frolic" and none of the Appellant's (employer's) affair. Singleton's actions after his collision with the police officer and perhaps at all times after his contact with the parked car were essentially unlawful. His attempt to use a weapon on the officer was in the same pattern; . . . It cannot by any stretch of the imagination be thought to have served his master's interests in any way.

814   Direct liability of the principal

The principal has been held liable for the acts of his agents to persons to whom the principal owes a duty of protection. For example, a conductor on a railroad assaults a female passenger. The railroad is required to respond in damages for the injuries to the passenger. It is clear that the act of the conductor in assaulting the passenger is outside the scope of his agency. Certainly, the railroad did not authorize or approve of the action of the conductor. The conductor was employed for a certain specific act, and conduct of this character is clearly outside of the scope of his authorization. However, the railroad owes a high degree of care to its passengers. It is for that reason that the railroad is responsible for the injuries where its failure to perform the duty results in damage. In cases where there is a special duty of protection, this liability is imposed upon the principal whether the principal knew, or by the exercise of reasonable care should have known, that such conduct on the part of its agents was likely to occur.

In other cases, where the principal is under no specific duty of protection to the person injured, the principal will be liable only when he is negligent in the selection or retention of his agents. For example, a landlord employs a janitor for his apartment house. The janitor is given master keys and has the means of access to all portions of the building. The janitor has a clear employment record and has never been accused of or convicted of a criminal act of any sort. The janitor enters the apartment of a tenant and assaults a woman tenant. The landlord is not liable for the injuries to the tenant.

On the other hand, let us add to the same factual situation one additional

item. Assume that the janitor had been discharged from his previous employment because of complaints by tenants that his conduct consisted of entering
their apartments without authorization and attempting to molest female tenants. This fact was not known to the landlord at the time that he hired the
janitor, but could have been ascertained by making reasonable inquiries.
Under those circumstances, the landlord would be liable to the female tenant
assaulted by the janitor. The liability is based upon the landlord's negligence
in employing a janitor of this character and his failure to exercise reasonable
care in the selection of such an employee. The landlord is chargeable with the
knowledge which he has of the character of the employee or knowledge which
he would have gained by the exercise of reasonable care in making the selection.

815   Liability of agent to principal

The agent is liable to the principal for any damages sustained by the
principal as a result of the acts of the agent amounting to (1) negligence, or
(2) misrepresentation, concealment, and nondisclosure.

1. Negligence. It is fundamental in the law of torts that the tort-feasor is
answerable for the legal consequences of his own acts. The fact that another
may be vicariously liable for the acts will not absolve the tort-feasor from
responsibility. Therefore, where the principal is required to respond in damages because of the negligent act of the agent, the principal is entitled to a
recovery from the agent for the damages so sustained.

As between the agent and the principal, the negligence of the agent is not
imputed to the principal, and the principal may recover damages from the
agent for any injuries sustained by the principal himself as a result of the
agent's negligence. The damages sustained by the principal might be bodily
injury or property damage, or they might consist of business losses sustained
by reason of the agent's negligent performance of his duty.

The typical bodily injury or property damage situation in which the duty
of the agent to the principal is involved is where the principal is riding as a
passenger in his own car, driven by the agent. An accident occurs due solely
to the negligent driving of the agent. The principal sustains bodily injuries as
well as property damage to his vehicle. The principal is entitled to recover
from the agent for the damages so sustained. The relationship of principal and
agent does not absolve or insulate the agent from the responsibility of responding in damages for his own negligence. As between the principal and the
agent, the agent's negligence is not imputed to the principal.

Where the principal has sustained a business loss due to the agent's negligent performance of his duties, the principal is likewise entitled to recover
damages from the agent. The agent's negligence might consist of an act which
is incompetently done, or it might consist of the failure to act at all when there
was a duty to act. This latter situation frequently arises where the agent is
under a duty to supply information to the principal. If the agent fails to
exercise care and competence in obtaining and communicating information

which the principal is justified in expecting, and the information so supplied is erroneous, and the principal relies upon it, the agent is answerable to the principal for the damage so sustained.

In all actions against the agent based on negligence, the usual defenses to negligence actions are available to the agent, such as contributory negligence of the principal, assumption of risk, etc.

2. *Misrepresentation, concealment, and nondisclosure.* Where the agent supplies information to the principal which he either knows is false or has reason to believe is false, and the principal acts in reliance thereon, the agent is absolutely liable to the principal for any losses sustained as a result. This is an intentional tort, and the rule of absolute or strict liability is imposed. The defense of contributory negligence or assumption of risk is not available. The same result will obtain where the agent is under a duty to report, and he conceals or fails to disclose information which he obtained in the course of his employment as agent.

The distinction between the intentional tort, deceit, or misrepresentation, and negligence, lies in the knowledge and intent of the agent. If the agent is under a duty to secure information, and he fails to do so, he is negligent. If he obtains the information and either fails to disclose it or intentionally makes a report which is false and contrary to the information he has, he is chargeable with an intentional tort and is subject to absolute liability.

816 Liability of the agent to third persons

An agent is answerable for his own acts to third persons just as if there were no relationship of principal and agent in existence. Merely because the injured person has a cause of action against the principal, based on his vicarious liability, it does not protect or insulate the agent from his responsibility to answer for the legal consequences of his acts to third persons who may be injured thereby. The injured person may elect to hold the agent responsible and waive any rights which he may have against the principal. He may elect to hold the principal and waive his rights against the agent, and, finally, he may (and he usually does) proceed against both the agent and the principal.

An agent in acting for the principal in dealings with third persons impliedly warrants that he has the authority to act for the principal. If it should occur that the agent did not have the authority, the agent is liable to the third person for any loss sustained as a result of the reliance by the third person on the agent's warranty of authority.

817 Liability of principal to agent

The principal is answerable in damages for the consequence of all his tortious acts. The fact that the injured person is an agent of the principal will have no influence upon the principal's responsibility. The extent of the response by the principal for his own acts might be altered in the case of agents who are employees by the state workmen's compensation act, but in any case, the legal requirement that the principal be answerable for his own tortious acts is not in any way altered or changed because of the existence of the relationship of principal and agent.

818   Ratification or adoption of unauthorized acts

Sometimes agents act outside the scope of their authority. Where this happens, the principal may repudiate the transaction, or ratify or adopt the agent's action. In the first case, the principal is not bound by the acts of the agent. Where the principal has adopted or ratified the act of the agent, the principal in effect has waived any defect in the agent's authority and is therefore bound by the act of the agent just as if the agent had actual authority to so act.

For example, an insurance company and an insurance agency terminate their contract of agency by mutual consent. Therefore, the insurance agent has no further authority to represent this particular insurance company. However, the agent does issue an insurance policy for the company, collects the premium, and remits the premium to the company. The acceptance and retention of the premium payment by the company will amount to a ratification or adoption of the agent's act in issuing the policy. Therefore, the company is estopped from denying the agent's authority to issue the policy, even though the agent has no actual authority to do so. On the other hand, if the company had immediately returned the premium and notified both the agent and prospective insured of the lack of authority on the part of the agent, then no contract of insurance would result, and there would be no ratification.

819   Termination of the agency relationship

The agency relationship may be terminated by (1) *mutual consent,* (2) *termination of authority,* or (3) *loss of capacity.*

1. *Mutual consent.* The agency relationship comes into existence as a result of the mutual consent of the principal and the agent. It may be terminated in exactly the same manner. When such an agreement is reached, the authority of the agent ceases and the responsibility of the principal for the acts of the agent likewise ceases as of that moment.

2. *Termination of authority.* The agency relationship can be ended by either party unilaterally. The principal may do so by specifically informing the agent of the termination of his authority to act and also by giving notice to all third persons who may deal with the agent of the termination of the agent's authority. The agent likewise may terminate his authority to act by notifying the principal, as well as all third persons who may be affected thereby, of the fact that he is no longer acting as agent for the principal and has terminated his relationship with the principal. As of the moment that this renunciation of authority takes place, all of the incidents of the principal and agent relationship, and the liability thereunder, cease as to both parties.

3. *Loss of capacity.* When either party to the contract of agency suffers a loss of the capacity to further continue with the contract, the relationship of principal and agent ceases as of that moment. This could come about as the result of the death of either principal or agent. Death will terminate the relationship whether the other party to the contract has notice of such death or not. In the case of a corporation, the dissolution of the corporation will terminate the agency relationship. The bankruptcy of either principal or agent will also act as a terminating factor.

Where the agency relationship is based upon the fact that the agent has a license to perform, the loss of such license will immediately terminate the relationship. For example, where a client has engaged the services of an attorney, and the attorney is disbarred, the disbarment of the attorney terminates his capacity to act as an attorney for the client and therefore terminates the agency relationship.

CHAPTER IX

Law of bailments, innkeepers, and carriers

---

900 Bailments defined

A bailment is the delivery of personal property by the owner to another for some specific purpose, on a contract, express or implied, with the understanding that after the purpose has been fulfilled, the property will be returned to the owner, or otherwise dealt with according to the specific purpose to be accomplished. It contemplates situations where personal property is voluntarily placed by the owner in the possession of another person with the intent that title and ownership will be retained by the owner. The owner who transfers possession is called the bailor, and the person to whom the possession is transferred is called the bailee. While the subject matter of a bailment can be any species of personal property, the claimsman will be concerned for the most part with automobiles and instrumentalities of like nature, which are involved in accidents while in the hands of a bailee.

To constitute a bailment, there must be (1) a voluntary transfer of possession by the owner to another person, and (2) an acceptance of possession by the other person. For example, if a man entered a restaurant and hung his overcoat on a hook provided for that purpose, and while he was eating the overcoat disappeared, the action would not constitute a bailment. The owner had not transferred possession of his overcoat to the restaurant keeper, and the restaurant keeper did not accept possession.

Let us use the same facts again but add that when the man entered the restaurant, he handed his overcoat to a waiter, asking him to check it for him. Upon finishing his meal, and requesting his coat, he was informed by the waiter that it was missing from the hook where the waiter had hung it. The delivery of the coat to the waiter constituted a bailment, since it involved a transfer of possession of the coat. The difference between the first situation and this one is that in the first case, irrespective of the intention of the owner of the coat, there was no actual transfer of possession from the owner to the restaurant keeper. Furthermore, there was no acceptance of possession by the restaurant keeper. Thus, the two necessary elements of a bailment were lacking, namely, a transfer of possession and the acceptance of possession by another. In the second case, there was an actual transfer of possession as well as an acceptance of possession by the waiter, and therefore the requirements of a bailment were fulfilled.

Where there is a bailment, the bailee is required to return the property to the bailor, and he is liable in damages if he fails to do so. Where there is no bailment, clearly no liability to respond in damages can arise.

901   Bailment as distinguished from a sale or exchange

One of the essential elements of a bailment contract is that it contemplates that the identical property in the same or in an altered state be returned to the owner. Fungible goods[1] are the exceptions to this situation. In all other cases, to constitute a bailment, the contract must contemplate the return of the identical property. In a sale, there is not only a transfer of possession of the goods but also a transfer of title and ownership. This is true even though the sale is made on a credit basis under a conditional sales contract, or where the seller retains a chattel mortgage. The fact that the seller retains some documents of title or the right to repossess the goods in the event of the buyer's failure to make the agreed payments would not in any way alter the character of the transaction. It is still a sale.

There are situations where there is a bailment which may or may not lead to an ultimate sale. This happens most frequently in cases involving the sale of automobiles, where the seller or vendor permits the prospective purchaser to try the car out in order to decide whether or not he wishes to purchase it. Under these facts, this is a bailment. However, once the customer evidences his intent to purchase the vehicle, there is a sale, rather than a bailment.

With the exception of fungible goods, as has been previously noted, the agreement of bailment contemplates the return of the identical property. If the agreement contemplates the return of property of like kind and quality, or

---

[1] Such as grain, which is delivered to a warehouse or grain elevator. When the grain is so deposited, it is not contemplated by the contract or custom that the bailee shall return the identical grain stored, but only an equal amount of grain of the same kind and grade from the comixed mass. The contract is still a bailment.

other property of any description, the transaction is a sale or exchange. In a sale or exchange, title to the goods immediately passes with the transfer of possession, whereas in a bailment the title or ownership of the goods never leaves the original owner.

Let us assume that a farmer delivered a quantity of apples to a cider processor with the agreement that the farmer would receive one gallon of cider for each two bushels of apples. This is not a bailment, but an exchange. In a bailment, the bailee receives only the possession; the title remains in the bailor. Hence, the bailee is obligated to return the identical article given to the bailor, even though in altered form. In this case, the title of the apples passed to the processor for the reason that the processor was not obligated to return cider made from the identical apples. If he were so obligated, then and only then would the transaction constitute a bailment.

902   Bailment as distinguished from custody

The employer provides tools to be used by his employee in the course of the employment. As to these tools, the employee is not a bailee. He has mere custody of his employer's property while acting as the agent of the employer in the course and scope of his employment. Possession by an agent within the scope of his agency is the possession of the principal. Therefore, the possession of the tools never was transferred by the owner or employer, and for that reason the transaction is not a bailment.

Should the employer, however, permit the employee to use the tools for his own personal purposes, either in the plant or at the employee's home, the goods, which in this case would be the tools, while being so used constitute a bailed property. The same reasoning would apply to other property owned by the employer, the custody of which was given to the employee. The most common form of such property would be an employer-owned automobile. While this automobile is being used on the employer's business, the employee has mere custody of the property. He is acting as an agent for the owner of the property. The relationship of bailor and bailee, therefore, does not exist. However, many employers do permit their employees to use company-owned vehicles for personal use. While the employer's property is being used for the personal convenience of the employee, and not on the employer's business, the relationship under those circumstances is that of bailee and bailor, and all of the incidents of a bailment attach. Therefore, whether there is a bailment or mere custody at a given time will depend upon the use to which the article is being put at the time.

903   Bailment as distinguished from a rental of space

This subject will come up most frequently with respect to automobile parking lots. If the owner of an automobile transfers possession of his vehicle to the operator of an automobile parking lot, by giving him the keys to the vehicle, or permitting him to move the vehicle from place to place while it is on the parking lot, the transaction is a bailment.

On the other hand, some parking lot operators seek to escape the liability of a bailee with respect to parked automobiles by merely renting the parking space to the automobile owner. In these cases, the automobile owner parks and locks his car himself, and retains the keys. The parking lot operator does not have any control over the vehicle while it is in the rental space, and under those circumstances there is no bailment. If the owner transfers possession of the vehicle to the parking lot operator by delivering the keys of the vehicle to him, and these keys are accepted by the parking lot owner, then in spite of posted notices to the contrary, the transaction is a bailment. This is for the reason that possession and control of the vehicle has been transferred from the owner to the parking lot operator, and such transfer has been accepted.

904   Bailment as distinguished from theft or conversion

The relationship of bailor and bailee can never exist between the owner of the property and a thief. The essential element that is missing from such a transaction is the voluntary relinquishment of possession of the property by the owner. The owner is entitled to the return of his property irrespective of the person who has possession thereof and irrespective of the circumstances under which that person received the property. Let us assume that a thief stole a valuable diamond ring from the owner. The thief pledged it to a pawnbroker. The owner of the ring is entitled to possession of the ring and is not required to reimburse the pawnbroker for the amount of money which he had advanced to the thief on the security of the ring. The relationship between the thief and the pawnbroker was that of bailor and bailee. The pawnbroker-bailee acquired no greater right to the possession of the goods than his bailor had. His bailor had no legal right to the possession of the diamond ring and therefore could transfer no rights whatever to the pawnbroker. The pawnbroker's action in retaining the diamond ring, however innocently possession thereof was acquired, is a tortious act and subjects him to liability for damages if the possession of the ring continues after proper demand for the return thereof is made by the owner. The guilt or innocence of the pawnbroker would have no bearing whatsoever upon the true owner's right to possession of his property.

The taking of a chattel from the owner without legal justification, and with the intention of exercising dominion or ownership over it, is a *conversion*. The wrongful taking or wrongful use of a chattel, without the consent of the owner, amounts to a tort and will subject the tort-feasor to liability for damages. To constitute a conversion, the chattel does not have to be taken from the owner's actual possession.

For example, an employee is given a company-owned car to be used solely on company business. If the employee should use the car for personal errands, such an act would constitute a conversion. It is the wrongful exercise of dominion or ownership over the automobile and the conversion of the use of the chattel. The mere fact that the employee returns the automobile to his employer, or that he uses the automobile in an authorized manner after his personal errand has been accomplished, will not in any way change the nature of the transaction.

In another example, the owner of a suit of clothes takes the suit to a dry cleaner for the purpose of having it cleaned. While the suit is in the possession of the dry cleaner, the dry cleaner decides to wear the suit to a wedding. The dry cleaner is guilty of conversion, since the agreement of bailment did not in any way authorize the dry cleaner to use the clothing for his own personal purposes.

In both examples, the person converting the property to his own use is liable to the true owner for the full value of the use thereof, for any damage which may have occurred to the chattel, and for any diminution in value which might have occurred as a result of such use. To recover, the owner would not have to show a negligent act or lack of due care. His case would be established merely by showing that the chattel was used in an unauthorized manner and that he had sustained damage as a consequence thereof. In a bailment situation, the bailee is liable to the bailor only when damage occurs to the bailed property through his negligence and not otherwise. In both of these cases, there was a breach of the bailment agreement and it was suspended during the period of conversion. During that time the relationship of the parties was not that of bailor and bailee.

905   Subject matter of bailments

Any species of personal property can be the subject matter of a bailment. This definition would include all chattels, including animals, both domestic and wild. It likewise would include evidences of ownership, such as stock certificates, shares of stock, bills or notes, or other evidences of debt. Real property can never be the subject matter of a bailment, and the use or possession of real property can be acquired by lease, tenancy at will, or by mortgage foreclosure, but never by means of a bailment contract.

906   Kinds of bailments

Bailments are classified according to the purpose for which they arise, and the obligations between the parties are governed by the class in which the bailment falls. The classifications are as follows:

1. Bailments for the sole benefit of the bailor.
2. Bailments for the sole benefit of the bailee.
3. Bailments for the benefit of both bailor and bailee.

The average man in the course of his lifetime is involved in many contracts of bailment. If he permits a friend to park his automobile in his driveway or in his backyard, or leave some property in his possession for storage, and no charge was made for this service, this would be an example of a bailment for the sole benefit of the bailor. On the other hand, if the man borrows his neighbor's lawn mower, tools, or other appliances for temporary use for his

own benefit, a bailment would be implied while such articles are in his possession. This is an example of a bailment for the sole benefit of the bailee or
borrower. It is contemplated that the same article will be returned in the same
condition as it is received.

If the man took his clothing to a dry cleaner for the purpose of having it
cleaned and pressed, this would be a bailment. It is contemplated that the
property will be returned in an altered state but that the same property will be
returned. For a price, the bailee agrees to exercise his skill in accomplishing
the objective of cleaning. This is an example of a bailment for the benefit of
both bailee and bailor. It is also referred to as a mutual benefit bailment for
the reason that both parties profit from the arrangement. The man receives his
clothing in a more wearable state, and the bailee receives a fee for his work.

907   Degrees of care required

The classification into which the bailment falls will determine the degree of
care which is required of the bailee. These classifications are as follows:

1. *For the sole benefit of the bailor.* In this class the bailee receives
no compensation for the deposit of the goods on his property, and therefore he
owes to the bailor a slight degree of care. This has been defined as the duty of
refraining from the commission of any act which would damage the property.
The bailee is responsible only for his own wrongdoing, and if he commits any
act which act does damage to the property while it is on his premises, this will
impose a liability. The bailee, however, is not liable for his failure to act. He
is under no duty to protect the property from the weather or to perform any
other act for its preservation. He is liable only if his own active wrongdoing
results in damage to the bailed property.

2. *For the sole benefit of the bailee.* In this class of bailments, the
bailee owes a high degree of care to the bailor and is liable for any loss caused
by slight negligence on his part. He is bound to exercise all the care and
diligence that the most careful persons are accustomed to apply to their own
affairs, and the want of the most exact and scrupulous caution is regarded by
the law as culpable neglect. If the neglect or imprudence of the bailee contributes to the damage to the property, the bailee is liable, even though the
loss is caused by inevitable accident or irresistible force.

This, however, does not mean that the bailee is responsible under all circumstances where the property is damaged or lost. He is liable only if his lack
of care played some part in the loss or damage to the property. He is required
to exercise a high degree of care. If he meets this obligation, and in spite of
the exercise of a high degree of care, the property is damaged or lost, the
bailee is not responsible. Should the property be stolen or taken away without
any negligence or lack of the high degree of care imposed, the bailee will not
be liable for the loss or damage. A borrower of property is not an insurer of
it, even when it is gratuitously loaned.

3. *Those for the benefit of both bailor and bailee.* The bailee is
required to exercise ordinary care, which means such care as the ordinary,

prudent man would exercise in caring for his own property under like circumstances. Obviously, the quantum of care which is required, would have some relationship to the kind and value of the article bailed. One would not expect the bailee to exercise the same degree of protective security over a pound of steel that would be required if the article were a pound of gold. Thus, what would constitute ordinary care in the case of a pound of steel might amount to even gross negligence in the care required to preserve and protect a pound of gold.

908   Presumptions in bailment cases

When the bailee returns the property in a damaged condition, or fails to return the property at all, upon the termination of the bailment, there arises a presumption of negligence on the part of the bailee. The bailor will make out a prima facie case when he establishes the contract of bailment, the delivery of the property to the bailee, and either the return of the property in the damaged condition or a failure to return the property at all.

The duty then is on the bailee to go forward with the evidence and to show affirmatively that the loss or damage to the property was occasioned by circumstances which did not involve any negligence on his part. If the bailee cannot sustain this burden, then the verdict must be in favor of the bailor. On the other hand, if the bailee is successful in showing that he exercised the degree of care required under the conditions of the bailment and that the loss or damage was occasioned by circumstances which did not involve any lack of care on his part, the bailee would be entitled to a verdict. Of course, where the bailee has introduced evidence to show lack of negligence on his part, the bailor may rebut this evidence by introducing evidence of his own to support a theory of liability on the grounds of negligence. In most states, the presumption in favor of the bailor disappears when specific evidence is introduced by the bailee showing that he was not guilty of any negligence.

909   Liability, bailor to bailee

In bailments for the sole benefit of the bailee or the sole benefit of the bailor, there is no duty of care owing from the bailor to the bailee with respect to the bailed property. In the case of a bailor for hire, he owes to the bailee a duty to inform him of any known defects in the bailed item which would constitute an unreasonable risk of harm. The bailor is under a duty to inspect and to ascertain whether or not there are any defects. The bailor is charged with knowledge of the defects which he actually knew about as well as defects which would have come to his attention had a reasonable inspection been performed.

Let us suppose that *A* rents an automobile to *B*. The automobile has defective brakes, and this fact is known to *A*, but he fails to disclose this condition to *B*. *B* is injured as a result of a sudden brake failure while driving the automobile. *A* is liable to *B*.

Let us consider a second situation. *A* rents his automobile to *B*. Unknown to *A* the automobile had a defective fuel pump, the existence of which could not have been ascertained by reasonable inspection by *A*. *B* is injured as a consequence of an explosion caused by the defective fuel pump. *A* is not liable to *B*.

It therefore should be emphasized that the bailor is not an insurer or guarantor of the safety of the bailed appliance. He likewise is not liable for injuries from known risks assumed by the bailee. The bailor is answerable in damages only where he has knowledge of a defect which constitutes an unreasonable risk of harm and fails to disclose the existence of such defect to the bailee, or where by the exercise of reasonable care, in the form of inspection, he would and should have discovered a harmful defect but did not ascertain its existence.

910   Liability, bailee to third persons

The liability of the bailee arising out of the maintenance or use of a bailed article, be it an automobile, a horse, or machinery, is the same as if the bailee were the actual owner of the property. His liability to third persons would rest in tort, and he would be responsible for his own negligence in operating or using the particular article. It would make no difference as to the circumstances under which the bailee acquired possession of the bailed article, and his liability would be the same whether it was a gratuitous bailment or one for hire. While it is true that the bailee may have an action over against his bailor for the bailor's failure to supply an article without defects, or for the failure of the bailor to warn the bailee of defects of which the bailor had knowledge, this would not in any way affect the bailee's responsibility to third persons.

911   Liability, bailor to third persons

In the case of gratuitous bailments, the few cases that are available hold that there is no greater obligation on the part of the bailor toward a third person than there would be to his immediate bailee. Therefore, when there is a borrowed or loaned article, and no compensation is paid for the use thereof, the bailor has no duty to the bailee with respect to warning of known defects or to inspection of the appliance.

This duty is no greater when a third person, other than the bailee, is injured. Therefore, in cases involving gratuitous bailments it can be said that the bailor has no liability to a third person who is injured as a consequence of the use of the article by the gratuitous bailee. In torts we learned that where one person places a dangerous instrumentality in the hands of another who is unfamiliar with its use or incapable of exercising care in its use, he is liable to anyone injured as a result of the use of the dangerous article. For example, if a person gave a gun to a child, who is obviously incompetent in the use of firearms, the person supplying the gun would be liable to anyone suffering injury as a consequence of its use. This responsibility, however, does not arise out of the contract of bailment. It arises because of the duty on the part of the owner of the gun to use reasonable care in its use, and this duty runs to anyone injured as a result of the use of the firearm.

Along the same lines, a gratuitous bailor of an automobile has been held liable where he knowingly entrusted the use of the vehicle to an inexperienced, intoxicated, or habitually careless driver and the accident, involving an injury to a third person, was proximately caused by the negligence of such a driver. Also, a gratuitous bailor will be liable if he knowingly transfers the possession and use of a vehicle which is unfit to drive, due to the fact that it had no brakes or is otherwise seriously defective. This liability will extend to third persons injured as a result of the use of such a vehicle.

In the case of a bailor for hire, he is not only subject to the same responsibilities as noted above but he also has a duty of making reasonable inspection of the vehicle, not only for the safety of third persons but also for the safety of the bailee as well.

912   Liability, third person to bailee

One of the quirks of the common law, which goes back to a decision made in 1902, is that where the chattel is wrongfully damaged while in the possession of a bailee, only the bailee may sue and recover from the wrongdoer, not only for the value of his interest but also for the entire loss. In the *Winkfield* case the court said:

> . . . I have now shown by authority, the root principles of the whole discussion is that, as against a wrongdoer, possession is title. The chattel that has been converted or damaged, is deemed to be the chattel of the possessor and of no other, and, therefore, its loss or deterioration is his loss, and to him, if he demands it, it must be recouped. His obligation to account to the bailor is really not *ad rem* in the discussion. . . . As between bailee and stranger possession gives title—that is, not a limited interest, but absolute and complete ownership, and he is entitled to receive back a complete equivalent for the whole loss or deterioration of the thing itself.

Unfortunately, an overwhelming majority of the courts favor the "possession theory" set forth in this case. The case further emphasizes the rights of the bailor in the amount of the recovery by the following:

> . . . the bailee has to account for the thing bailed, so he must account for that which has become its equivalent and now represents it. What he has received above his own interest, he has received to the use of his bailor.

Nevertheless, the import of the decision and cases which have followed it is that the bailee, whose interest is usually very small in contrast to that of the bailor, may sue without the knowledge or consent of the bailor for the full value of the damages to the bailed property caused by the tort-feasor. [See *Berger* v. *34th St. Garage*, 84 N.Y.S. 2d 348 (1948).]

A recovery by the bailee for the full value of the damage will preclude another and further suit by the bailor for any damages whatsoever, since, from the standpoint of the tort-feasor, he "cannot be vexed twice for the same wrong."

In recognition of this common-law rule, many of the drive-it-yourself companies have taken care of the situation by clauses in the contract transferring possession. In any case where the claimsman is faced with a claim by the bailee, he should first ascertain whether or not the bailee has a right to the possession of the chattel, and also check whatever contractual limitations there may be on his right to recovery.

913   Liability, third person to bailor

The common-law rule, as noted above, applies to the person who has the immediate right of possession. If the bailor has a right to demand possession at once, then he, and not the bailee, may maintain an action for damages against the tort-feasor.

In an action brought by the bailee against the tort-feasor, the defense of contributory negligence of the bailee may be interposed, and if it is sustained, it is a complete defense to the action by the bailee. However, in an action by the bailor against the tort-feasor, the contributory negligence of the bailee is not imputed to the bailor, and the defense of the bailee's contributory negligence may not be interposed against him. (*New York L.E. Co.* v. *New Jersey Electric Railway Co.*, 38 Atl. 828.) This rule has been adopted in the majority of states.

Some states have modified the common-law rule by statute, permitting the contributory negligence of the bailee to be interposed as a proper and valid defense to an action brought by the bailor.

The recovery by the bailee of the full value of the damage will, as has been noted, preclude another and further action by the bailor against the tort-feasor (*Knight* v. *Davis*, 71 Fed. 662), but where the bailee sues the tort-feasor, and there is a verdict for the defendant based on the bailee's contributory negligence, the judgment is not binding on the bailor, and he may thereafter bring an action against the tort-feasor. [*Peck* v. *Merchants*, 116 Pac. 365 (Kansas); *Standard* v. *Schloss*, 43 Mo. App. 304.]

Some states have statutes which impose vicarious liability on the owner of a motor vehicle where the vehicle is being used by another with the owner's consent, express or implied. These statutes impute the negligence of the driver to the owner. One state has taken the view that the statute also authorizes the court to impute the contributory negligence of the driver to the owner, or bailor, thus overcoming the common-law rule. [*Milgate* v. *Wraith* (California), 121 Pac. 2d 10.]

Two other states have refused to so interpret their statutes, holding that the common-law rule is that the contributory negligence of the driver is not imputable to the owner when the car is being driven with his consent but not on his business, and, further, that unless the statute changes this rule by specific language, the common-law rule remains. They held that the statute merely created a liability on the part of the owner for the negligence of the driver but did not impute the contributory negligence of the driver to the owner so as to defeat his right to recovery for the damage to his vehicle. [*Mills* v. *Gabriel* (New York), 18 N.Y.S. 2d 78, aff'd in 31 N.E. 2d 512; and *Christenson* v. *Hennepin Transportation Co.* (Minnesota), 10 N.W. 2d 406.]

914   Limitation of liability

In the absence of an agreement to the contrary, with respect to the liability of the bailee for damage to the goods while in his possession, he is liable to the bailor for any loss or damage caused by his negligence. The parties may enter into any contract which they desire, and such a contract can provide for a maximum amount for which the bailee would be responsible in the event of damage or loss. This must be the subject matter of a contract, and both parties must have knowledge of and agree to such terms.

It frequently happens that a bailee, operating an automobile parking lot, a checkroom, or a dry cleaning establishment will attempt to limit his liability by the posting of notices on the premises to the effect that he is not responsible for goods left over 30 days, or that in the event of loss the maximum liability shall be $25, or similar types of limitation.

It is fundamental in the law of contracts that for the limitation to be an effective element of the contract both parties must mutually assent to the terms. Where notices are posted, the limitation of liability will not be effective unless it is shown that the bailor had actual knowledge of the limitation and delivered his property to the bailee upon the terms of limitation. In the absence of knowledge on the part of the bailor and his agreement to the terms, the notices, however conspicuously posted, will not effectively limit the liability of the bailee. The following cases are examples of this principle.

A delivered a parcel to an agent in charge of a parcel room and received from the agent a parcel check, paying the requisite fee of 10 cents therefor. The agent, upon presentation of the check, stated that the parcel had been delivered to another. At the parcel room, notices limiting the liability of the agent's employer to $25 in the event of loss were posted. *A* did not know of such notices or their content. Under those circumstances, *A* would not be limited to the amount stated in the notices. In order to limit *A*, the notice must be made part of his contract, and this can be done only by specifically calling to his attention and securing his agreement to those terms.

In another case, a manufacturer delivered goods to a dyer to be dyed. Attached to the goods when returned from the dyer was a printed notice that claims for damages must be made within three days after delivery of the dyed goods or such claims would not be recognized. On the bill rendered for dyeing, the same notice was printed. Some months afterward the manufacturer first brought suit against the dyer for damage to the goods, and the dyer attempted to interpose the defense that no notice of the defect nor claim for damages was made within three days after the delivery of the goods.

This defense was not a valid one for the reason that limitation was not a part of the contract of bailment. The bailee could not thereafter, without the express assent of the bailor, alter the contract, even though the limitation was actually brought to the attention of the bailor. This was a contract of bailment in which no limitation was expressed. After the contract of bailment had been completed, the bailee attempted to alter the terms of the contract and to impose a limitation which was not one of the terms of the original agreement.

In still another case *A* parked his automobile in a public parking lot, owned by *B*, which lot was enclosed by a wire fence, except for the entrances and exits. The agent instructed *A* that the keys be left in the ignition switch. After receiving the fee of 75 cents, which was demanded, *B* fastened a stub with a large number thereon on the windshield of the car. He gave a similar stub to *A* which, without examining, *A* placed in his pocket. On the reverse side of the stub given to *A*, in fine print, appeared the following: "We are not responsible for this car, its accessories, or contents while parked in our lot."

There was a relationship of bailor and bailee between *A* and *B*. Unless altered by an agreement of the parties, all of the incidents of a bailment contract would arise, including the liability for loss or damage which the law imposes upon the bailee. The limitation of liability, as expressed on the stub, was not brought to *A*'s attention, and therefore *A* would not be charged with the knowledge of a limitation, and since he had no knowledge of the limitation, there is no evidence that he assented to any such terms. Therefore, the bailee has not limited his liability by this means and must respond in the event of loss to the full amount of the loss or damage.

915 Conversion or unauthorized use by the bailee

The contract of bailment requires that the bailee perform in accordance with its terms. If the contract contemplates storage of the goods at a certain place, the bailee is bound to store the goods at that place and no other. If the contract contemplates that the bailee will exercise some process in connection with the goods, he may exercise that process and no other. He may not use the goods for his own purposes, nor may he use any different process than that which was agreed upon. If he performs any of these unauthorized acts, it is a conversion, and he is responsible to the bailor for any loss or damage occasioned thereby.

In one case, *A* delivered an expensive fur coat to a fur storage company in Trenton, New Jersey, for storage in its vault at that place. *A* paid the charges demanded. After *A* left the store, the manager discovered that the company's vaults at Trenton were filled, and for that reason he arranged with the *X* Trucking Company to transport *A*'s coat from Trenton to New York City, where the company had a similar vault. While en route to New York, the truck carrying the coat, and its contents, were completely destroyed by fire.

Under these circumstances the fur storage company is liable to *A* for the value of the coat. If a bailee deviates from his contract as to the place of storage or keeping of the bailed property, and a loss occurs, which would not have occurred if the property had been stored or kept in the place agreed upon, the bailee is liable even though he is not negligent. It is a conversion by the bailee to store goods at a place other than the specific place where he agreed to keep the goods, and therefore the bailee is subject to liability for the loss, independent of any negligence.

Unauthorized use would also create a liability on the part of the bailee to the bailor. For example, *A* hired an automobile from *B* for use in his business and put it in charge of his employee, who, at the close of the day's work, was to put the automobile in *A*'s garage. In violation of *A*'s instructions, the employee used the car to attend to some personal business of his own and left the car on the street. The car was stolen.

Under these circumstances, *A* is liable to *B* under the doctrine of *respondeat superior* for the act of his servant, and also for the breach of the contract of bailment. The employee was in the employment of *A* until he returned the automobile. The automobile was hired only for business use, and neither *A* nor his employee was authorized to use it in connection with the employee's private affairs. *A* thus became answerable upon the contract of bailment, since he made it possible for the employee to make an unauthorized use of the automobile.

916   Exculpatory contracts as applied to bailments

The general rule in contract is that the parties to the contract may include within its terms any agreements to which they are mutually agreed. Therefore, while the parties may make any contract that they desire, any provisions which violate public policy will have no legal effect. Therefore, it would seem that a bailor and bailee could agree in the contract of bailment that in the event of loss due to the bailee's negligence, the bailor waives in advance any cause of action that he may have to recover for such damage.

Unfortunately, the courts are not in agreement with respect to this legal proposition, some taking the position that it is against public policy for one party to contract away liability for his own negligence, and others the position that if the parties involved are private parties, and the general public is not involved, they may make any contract they wish, providing that both parties to the contract bargain on equal terms.

For example, if a public utility, having the exclusive franchise in a given locality to supply gas for heating, rented heating appliances to its customers and had a provision in the rental contract absolving the public utility from liability arising out of the negligent acts of its agents or servants, all courts would agree that such a provision is void as being against public policy. The public utility is a business which is affected with the public interest. The customer could deal with the public utility only in order to obtain the required service, and could not obtain the same service from any other source. The parties did not bargain on equal terms, and the public utility, because of the nature of its public duty, is precluded from contracting away its liability for negligence.

On the other hand, if two private parties agreed that the bailment contract was merely one of storage, and that the bailee was relieved of any liability arising out of the loss or damage to the goods due to freezing, water damage, or any other specific peril, whether the bailee was negligent or not, it would seem to be a proper provision of the contract, and the public interest would not be involved in any way. In this case, the bailee will be absolved of liability because of the terms of the contract.

917   Innkeepers: Common-law liability

In feudal times there was little or no police protection afforded to travelers on the highway. Outlaws were numerous, and as a result the traveler and his property were in jeopardy when on the open highway. They therefore traveled in groups or caravans in order to afford mutual self-protection. At nightfall, the travelers sought protection and lodging at an inn. The inn was required not only to furnish accommodations for the traveler himself, but also stable room and provender for the traveler's horses or cattle or whatever animals he had with him.

The primary purpose of travel in those days was to bring products to market. These might consist of grain or animals. Therefore, the traveler was carrying with him a certain amount of valuable personal property. It would be easy for the innkeeper to enter into a conspiracy with outlaws in the vicinity whereby the guest would be relieved of his property during the nighttime hours.

To meet this contingency, the courts imposed the rule of strict liability upon the innkeeper with respect to the guest's property. This rule made the innkeeper an insurer of the guest's property while the relationship of innkeeper and guest continued. This means that if the guest's property was lost or damaged, from any cause whatsoever, the innkeeper was absolutely liable. This has no reference to the negligence of the innkeeper, and his liability attached whether he had anything to do with the loss or damage to the property or not.

There are three situations in which the innkeeper is relieved of this responsibility: (1) an act of God, (2) an act of the public enemy, and (3) negligence of the guest, his servant, or companion.

It is clear that the innkeeper could not provide protection against an act of God, such as a hurricane, storm, flood, or lightning. Likewise, he could not provide protection for the guest from the actions of another nation with whom his nation is at war. It is also clear that the innkeeper should not be responsible for any loss or damage occasioned by the guest's own neglect of his property or the act of the guest's servants or companions.

918   Innkeepers: Liability for personal injury to guests

While the common law exercised great concern with respect to the property of the guest, the safety of the person of the guest was not similarly protected. As to the innkeeper, the guest has the status of a business invitee. The innkeeper owes him the duty of keeping the premises in reasonably safe condition for his safety, making reasonable inspections, and warning the guest of any unsafe conditions which are not open and obvious. The innkeeper owes the same duties to persons who visit the guest, since these persons are also classified as business invitees. In order to maintain the premises in reasonably safe condition for the safety of the guest, the innkeeper has the additional duty to maintain a security staff whose duty it is to protect the guest against misconduct of any kind on the part of other guests, employees, or strangers at any place on the premises, including the room occupied by the guest. In order to meet this duty, the security personnel must make tours or inspections at reasonable intervals of all parts of the inn, including the corridors, stairways, and the public rooms. What would constitute reasonable intervals will depend upon the nature of the premises and its their accessibility to strangers and others on the outside. In addition, the innkeeper must exercise reasonable care in the selection of employees and must make inquiries as to the employee's previous work record and the reasons why he left his last employment. Failure on the part of the innkeeper to meet these duties, where such failure results in injury to the guest, will create a liability for damages on the part of the innkeeper.

919   Statutory modifications of innkeepers' liability

The innkeeper's liability as an insurer of the property of his guests has been modified in some states by statute. The statutes usually provide that where the inn maintains a safe on the premises for the deposit of certain valuables, such as jewelry, precious stones, negotiable instruments, money, and certificates, and the availability of such safe is brought to the attention of the guest either by a printed notice in each room or a printed notice placed in a conspicuous place in the public rooms of the inn, the limit of liability of the innkeeper for the loss of articles of this type, not deposited in the safe, is limited to a certain sum of money, usually $500. This means merely that where the articles mentioned in the statute are actually deposited in the safe, the innkeeper's liability as an insurer remains.

The innkeeper would be liable for the value of any articles lost from the safe, and this liability would be subject to no limitation whatsoever. However, as to articles of the kind and class noted in the statute and not deposited in the safe, where notice of the existence of the safe has been brought to the attention of the guest, the innkeeper's liability for the loss of these articles is limited to the amount stated in the statute. As to all other property not covered by the statutory modification, the innkeeper is still an insurer.

920   Inn defined

An inn has been defined as a house where a traveler is furnished with everything which he has need for while on his way. It is a house where all who conduct themselves properly and who are able and ready to pay for their entertainment are received if there are accommodations for them, and who, without any stipulated engagements as to the duration of their stay, or as to the rate of compensation, are, while there, supplied at a reasonable charge with their meals, their lodging, and such services and attention as are necessarily incident to the use of the house as a temporary home.

An inn is synonymous with hotel, motel, or a place for the entertainment of travelers, where all their wants as travelers can be supplied. A restaurant where meals only are furnished is not an inn. An inn likewise is distinguished from a private boardinghouse in that the keeper of a boardinghouse is at liberty to choose his guests, while the innkeeper is obligated to entertain and furnish all travelers of good conduct and means of payment with what they may have occasion for while traveling on their way. Another distinction is that in a boardinghouse the guest is under an express contract for a certain time at a certain rate, whereas in an inn the guest is entertained from day to day upon an implied contract.

The liabilities of an innkeeper are imposed upon a hotel or a motel. Boardinghouses and rooming houses, since they do not come within the definition of an inn, are not subject to innkeeper's liability as an insurer of the property of its guests.

It is possible for a hotel owner to occupy the position of innkeeper as to some of his guests, and to occupy the position of a boardinghouse or rooming house keeper as to all others. If a guest engages accommodations at the hotel on a daily basis, without any engagement as to the length of his stay, the relationship is one of innkeeper and guest. One the other hand, if a guest makes an agreement with the hotel to engage accommodations on a monthly basis under a contract wherein it is stipulated that the guest will pay a certain amount each month as rental for the accommodations, and where there is some agreement as to the method of termination, then the relationship consists of boardinghouse or rooming house keeper and guest, and the liabilities of an innkeeper are not imposed upon the hotel owner. Therefore, even though the accommodations are the same, the liability of the hotel owner will turn on the method under which the premises are rented.

921 Guests defined

A guest has been defined as one who partakes of the accommodations offered by an inn, without any bargain for time, and remains without such an agreement. He may go when he pleases, paying only for the actual entertainment which he receives. To be a guest, the person must actually register and use the room accommodations of the hotel. Persons attending balls, banquets, and other functions at an inn or hotel are not guests. Likewise, one who merely goes to an inn to pass the time or to write letters, without registering or purchasing accommodations, is not a guest.

Therefore, as to these classes of persons, the relationship of innkeeper and guest is not in existence, and the liability of the innkeeper as an insurer of the property of these classes of persons does not accrue. As to the innkeeper's liability for personal injury, persons attending functions in the hotel would come within the classification of business invitees. As to all others, they would be considered licensees or trespassers, depending upon the circumstances of their use of the hotel premises.

922   Common carriers

A common carrier is defined as one who holds himself out or undertakes to carry persons or goods of all persons indifferently, or of all who choose to employ him.

Common carriers of passengers are those that undertake to carry all persons indifferently who may apply for passage, so long as there is room, and there is no legal excuse for a refusal. In this classification we would include airlines, railroads, public buses, taxicabs, subways, and trolley cars. Also included within the classification of common carriers of passengers would be elevators in buildings open to the public, escalators, and even a roller coaster in an amusement park.

Common carriers of property include airfreight lines, railroads, trucking companies, elevators, and express companies.

923   Liability of a common carrier

A common carrier of property is an insurer of the property it carries. It is liable if the property is damaged in any way while in transit or is delivered in a damaged condition at the point of destination. This liability as an insurer is subject to only three exceptions: (1) an act of God, (2) an act of the public enemy, or (3) the inherent vice of the goods.

An act of God would include a tornado, hurricane, earthquake, lightning, and the like. To absolve the common carrier from liability, the loss of the goods or the damage to the goods must be occasioned entirely by an act of God, and without any concurrent act on the part of the common carrier. The act of a public enemy would refer to belligerent action by a nation with whom we are at war. The last exception refers to the nature of the goods carried, in the sense that they are perishable or explosive, and such fact was not made known to the carrier by the shipper.

The common carrier may limit the amount for which he may be held liable in the event of loss or damage. This can be accomplished by a specific agreement made prior to acceptance of the shipment. However, the carrier cannot by agreement escape his liability as an insurer of the goods while in his possession.

With respect to common carriers of passengers, the carrier owes a high degree of care for the safety of its passengers. A high degree of care is not the legal equivalent of ordinary care. It means something involving care and caution in excess of what would be exercised by the ordinary prudent person under the same or similar circumstances. It has been defined as that degree of care which a very cautious, careful, and prudent person would exercise. It is for the jury to decide, in a proper case, as to whether or not the carrier has exercised that degree of care which the law imposes upon him in the exercise of his business.

924   Private carriers

A private carrier is one who does not hold himself out to the general public as a carrier for all who may employ him. He does transportation work only for such private individuals, firms, or corporations with whom he has made a contract. He is not bound to accept all contracts of carriage that are offered to him, and he may refuse employment if he does not regard the contract as being desirable. The liability of the private carrier is governed by the rules of ordinary negligence, both as to persons and property. He may, however, assume greater liability by means of a contract, but in the absence of any contractual assumption of liability, he is responsible only for personal injuries or property damage caused by ordinary negligence on his part.

It is possible for a common carrier to become a private carrier in certain specific instances, as a consequence of a private carrier contract made with a specific person, firm, or corporation. For example, a bus normally used for public transportation can be chartered by a private individual, firm, corporation, club, or other group for one specific purpose. Likewise, a specific contract can be made by a taxicab company wherein a certain taxicab is devoted to a specific contract as one to transport a large number of employees from one place to another, a church group, a club, or even smaller groups of people. In these instances, the particular instrumentality, be it a bus or a taxicab, has been withdrawn from public use and is devoted entirely to a private purpose. In such cases, the liability of the owner of the bus or taxicab is the same as that of a private carrier.

925   Common carrier as a joint tort-feasor

It should be emphasized that the responsibility of exercising a high degree of care on the part of the common carrier is only for the benefit of its passengers. Where personal injuries occur, and there is no relationship of passenger and common carrier, then the responsibility of the common carrier to respond for its negligence will be based upon its duty to exercise only ordinary care. It is only when the relationship of passenger and common carrier exists that the extended responsibility of the common carrier comes into existence, and then only in favor of the passenger.

It frequently happens that there is a collision between a private passenger automobile and a taxicab which is occupied by a passenger. The taxicab company, as a common carrier, owes a high degree of care for the safety of its passenger. The driver of the other car has no such relationship to the taxicab passenger and is liable only if his conduct constitutes ordinary negligence. To put it another way, the duty owed by the driver of the passenger car to the taxicab passenger is a duty of ordinary care, as opposed to the duty on the part of the taxicab to its passenger, which requires the exercise of a high degree of care. Therefore, since the duty of care required of the taxicab is much greater than that of the other driver, the possibilities of the taxicab escaping liability are more remote. The taxicab company, then, would have a more compelling reason for undertaking a settlement of the passenger's personal injury claim than would the owner of the other vehicle. These facts should be taken into consideration at any time that settlement discussions are undertaken in connection with this type of case.

If the passenger was occupying the passenger vehicle, and there was a collision between the taxicab and the private passenger vehicle, the duty of care owed by the taxicab to the passenger in the other car would be merely that of ordinary care. There would be no relationship of common carrier and passenger between the offending taxicab operator and the passenger of the private vehicle.

926   Exculpatory contracts, common carriers

It frequently happens that a common carrier, usually a railroad, will issue a gratuitous pass to employees and/or their families, clergymen, and others upon the express agreement that the carrier will have no responsibility to the passenger in accidents caused by its negligence. The courts, generally, will uphold agreements of this sort, some on the theory that where a gratuitous passage is given, the relationship of the common carrier and passenger does not exist, and others on the theory that since there was a gift or a reduced rate allowed, the donor could affix to the gift any conditions that he chose. Normally, courts will not uphold exculpatory contracts where one of the parties is at a bargaining disadvantage. But here the parties bargained on equal terms. The passenger could pay full fare for this transportation and the relationship of common carrier, with its attendant liabilities, would ensure. Taking advantage of the gift, the passenger must accept the terms on which it is offered.

CHAPTER X

Law of products

1000 Products liability generally

Caveat emptor, "Let the buyer take care," was the original rule of the marketplace. In the distant past, the merchandise offered for sale consisted primarily of the natural products of the soil or simple manufactured products. The buyer could and did inspect the articles, and in that way he could gain as much knowledge of the products as the seller himself had. The buyer did not rely on the expertise of the seller, but entirely upon what his own inspection of the article revealed. He saw what he bought and he bought what he saw. If he bought a defective product, he had only himself to blame. Should he seek to hold the seller responsible for selling the defective article, he could be confronted with the defense of contributory negligence since he had as much opportunity to ascertain the defective condition as did the seller. Thus, in the beginning, the common-law courts applied the rule of *caveat emptor* to all sales, and in so doing merely applied a rule in response to the customs and usages of the times.

In addition, because of the simplicity of the products involved, the possibility of someone other than the buyer sustaining injuries as a result of the use of the product was remote. As products became more complicated, it was possible for the seller, by packaging or coloring, to deceive the buyer by offering an inferior and defective product in place of one of merchantable quality. In such situations, the courts permitted the buyer to bring a tort action based on the seller's deceit, taking the position that the seller was under a duty to offer a product which would compare favorably with other products of like kind found on the market. While most of the early actions were based on tort liability, some courts referred to this duty of the seller as a "warranty" of merchantability, using a term which is usually referable to contracts in describing a tort action.

Products liability refers to the responsibility arising out of the manufacture, distribution, and sale of defective or dangerous products and the failure of the manufacturer, distributor, or retailer to meet the duties which the law imposes upon him with respect to the particular product. It also deals with the problem of the persons to whom these duties are owed, or, to put it another way, it deals with the persons who have a legally protected right as to the use of the product and the wrongful invasion of that right. It also deals with the statutory modifications of the contract of sale as well as the judicial modifications of the applicable common law.

1001   Early concepts

The early cases all turned on the relationship of the parties as being determinative of whether or not any duty existed. Unless the parties had some relationship to the transaction, or were in privity with each other, the courts could not see where there was an existing duty. One of the earliest cases, *Winterbottom* v. *Wright* (10 Meeson & Welsby 109), decided in 1842 is illustrative of this concept. In that case an action was brought by a mail-coach driver against a contractor who had contracted with the postmaster-general to provide and keep in repair the mail coach. It was claimed that the contractor so disregarded his duties so as to place an unsafe coach on the road, which coach overturned and injured the plaintiff. In holding that the plaintiff's complaint did not state a maintainable cause of action, the court said:

> There is no privity of contract between these parties; and if the plaintiff can sue, every passenger, or even any person passing along the road, who was injured by the upsetting of the coach, might bring a similar action. Unless we confine the operation of such contracts as this to the parties who entered into them, the most absurd and outrageous consequences, to which I can see no limit, would ensue.

. . . The plaintiff in this case could not have brought an action on the contract; if he could have done so, what would have been his situation, supposing the Postmaster-General had released the defendant? That would, at all events, have defeated his claim altogether. By permitting this action, we should be working this injustice, that after the defendant had done everything to the satisfaction of his employer, and after all matters between them had been adjusted, and all accounts settled on the footing of their contract, we should subject them to be ripped open by this action of tort being brought against him.

Thus, the court established the rule that the contractor was not liable to one who was not in privity of contract with him. However, some ten years later in 1852, the Court of Appeals of New York announced an exception of the privity requirement in *Thomas* v. *Winchester* (6 New York 397), by holding that where the negligence of the manufacturer produced an article which was "imminently dangerous to the lives of others," the manufacturer was liable to the person injured whether there was a contract between them or not. In this case, the plaintiff's husband purchased a jar of what was supposed to be extract of dandelion, a simple and harmless medicine, but which, because of the mislabeling by the manufacturer, actually contained extract of belladonna, a deadly poison. The court held the manufacturer liable even though the drug had passed through numerous hands before it found its way to the plaintiff.

The imminently dangerous, or inherently dangerous, exception to the rule requiring privity of contract in negligence actions was further defined and enlarged by the same court in *MacPherson* v. *Buick Motor Co.* [217 N.Y. 382; 111 N.E. 105 (New York Court of Appeals)]. In that case, the plaintiff was injured when a spoke wheel on the automobile crumbled while the automobile was being operated. The automobile was bought from a dealer and there was no privity of contract between the plaintiff and the manufacturer. The court held that an automobile defectively made was an inherently dangerous instrumentality and this fact brought it within the exception to the privity requirement. The court reiterated the rule of *Thomas* v. *Winchester,* and stated that it could see no difference between a dangerous drug and an automobile which is dangerous because it was defectively manufactured. The court said:

We hold, then, that the principle of *Thomas* v. *Winchester* is not limited to poisons, explosives, and things of like nature, to things which in their normal operation are implements of destruction. If the nature of a thing is such that it is reasonably certain to place life and limb in peril when negligently made, it is then a thing of danger. Its nature gives warning of the consequences to be expected. If to the element of danger there is added knowledge that the thing will be used by persons other than the purchaser, and used without new tests, then, irrespective of contract, the manufacturer of this thing of danger is under a duty to make it carefully.

It might be noted that one of the defenses urged by the defendant was that they themselves had not manufactured the wheel, but that they had purchased it from a reputable and competent manufacturer. The court held that the manufacturer of the finished product was under a duty of inspection, and if he put a finished product on the market which is defective, he is liable even though some component part not manufactured by him is negligently made.

A second exception to the privity requirement was announced in the case of *Huset* v. *J. I. Case Threshing Machine Co.* [120 Fed. Rep. 865 (1903)]. There it was held that a manufacturer or vendor, who, without giving notice of its character or qualities, supplies or delivers to another a machine or article which, at the time of delivery, he knows to be imminently dangerous to the life or limbs of anyone who may use it for the purpose for which it is intended, is liable to anyone who sustains injury from its dangerous condition, whether he has any contractual relations with him or not.

In summary, the early cases established the rule that if there was privity of contract between the parties, the injured plaintiff could bring an action in tort based upon negligence or deceit, or bring an action for breach of contract based upon the failure of the seller to meet the contract specifications. If there was no privity of contract between the parties, the injured party could not maintain a cause of action unless the facts of the case brought it within either of the following two exceptions:

1. The product involved imminent danger to the lives of others if it were negligently labeled (poison or explosives), or became a thing of danger if defectively made (automobiles).
2. The product was dangerous to the life and limbs of anyone who may use it, and the manufacturer or supplier, having knowledge of this danger, failed to give notice of the danger.

1002   Liability of the retailer for negligence

Since the retailer is in privity of contract with the buyer, there is no impediment in the way of the buyer maintaining an action against the retailer for damages sustained as a result of the retailer's negligence. If the retailer is to be charged with negligence it must be because of his failure to meet some duty which he owed to the buyer. The duties are few since the retailer is merely the conduit through which the product finds its way from the manufacturer to the consumer and unless the nature of the product, or the duties assumed by the retailer require that the retailer exercise care, he is under no duty to do so. Retailers have been held liable for negligence in the following categories:

1. Failure to inspect or test the product.
2. Failure to warn of the dangers of the product.
3. Failure to properly assemble the product.
4. Negligent sales.
5. Sales in violation of a statute.

1. *Failure to inspect or test the product.* Ordinarily the retailer is under no duty to inspect or test the product. This is especially true in the cases of products sold in a sealed container, such as tin cans, bottles, and other types of containers. It is clear that it would be unreasonable to expect the retailer to open and test each sealed container and it is obvious that because of the buying habits of the public that the retailer would have difficulty in selling any product which had been subjected to such testing. There is one exception referable to the automobile business, which includes automobile agencies as well as used car dealers. Such retailers have been held liable for their failure to test and inspect their products before sale when subsequent facts revealed that defects were present which a reasonable inspection would have uncovered. Thus in *Gaidy Motors, Inc.* v. *Brannon* [268 S.W. 2d 627 (Kentucky)], a used car dealer was held liable where the purchaser after driving several blocks ran into a pedestrian because the brakes failed. The court held that the dealer was under a duty to exercise reasonable care to discover such defects and to either repair them or to warn the buyer of the existence of the defect.

With respect to other products, the cases generally hold that the retailer who purchases the article from a reputable manufacturer is under no duty to inspect it, and is not liable even in cases where an inspection might have revealed a defect. For example, in *Bravo* v. *C. H. Tiebout & Sons, Inc.* (243 N.Y.S. 2d 335), the retail seller of a grinding wheel was held to be not liable to the buyer because of his failure to inspect the wheel and discover the defect. The retailer had purchased the wheel from a reputable manufacturer and had reasonable grounds for believing that the wheel was free from defects. To the same effect is *Alfieri* v. *Cabot Corp.* (235 N.Y.S. 2d 753), where the retailer sold a package of charcoal briquettes, which he had obtained from a reputable manufacturer. It was held that the retailer was not liable for wrongful death and injuries caused by carbon monoxide poisoning resulting from the use of the briquettes for heating. There was no evidence in the case that the plaintiffs relied on the retailer's expertise or that the seller had actual knowledge of the dangerous properties of the briquettes. Even though the seller might have discovered the danger by testing the briquettes for heating under controlled conditions, the court held that he was under no duty to do so. See also, *Continental Casualty Co.* v. *Belknap Hardware Co.* [281 S.W. 2d 914 (Kentucky)] (cant hook); *Dipangrazio* v. *Salamonsen* [393 Pac. 2d 936 (Washington)] (glass door); *Kratz* v. *American Stores* [59 Atl. 2d 138] (stove polish); *Sears, Roebuck & Co.* v. *Marhenke* [121 Fed. 2d 598 (9th Cir.)] (hot-water bag); *Ringstad* v. *I. Magnin & Co.* [239 Pac. 2d 848 (Washington)] (flammable cocktail robe); *R. H. Macy & Co.* v. *Vest* [140 S.E. 2d 491 (Georgia)] (flammable dress); *Guyton* v. *S. H. Kress & Co.* [5 S.E. 2d 295 (South Carolina)] (exploding bottle of nail polish).

There is also a line of cases holding that the retailer is under no duty to inspect and test for the purpose of discovering latent defects. See *Long* v. *Flanigan Warehouse Co.* [382 Pac. 2d 399 (Nevada)] (ladder); *Hector Supply Co.* v. *Carter* [122 So. 2d 22 (Florida)] (lawn mower); *Mississippi Butane Gas Systems* v. *Welch* [45 So. 2d 262 (Mississippi)] (tank); *Levis* v. *Zapolitz, Inc.*, 178 Atl. 2d 44 (New Jersey)] (slingshot).

Where the retailer sells a reconditioned product and guarantees that it "is as good as new" or that it is "safe to use," the cases hold that such a retailer is under a duty to inspect, and, if he fails to do so, and a defective condition causes an accident, he is negligent and consequently liable to the purchaser. See *Ward* v. *Nance* [115 S.E. 2d 781 (Georgia)] (rebuilt refrigerator); *Witt Ice & Gas Co.* v. *Bedway* [231 Pac. 2d 952 (Arizona)] (refurbished valve); *Veach* v. *Bacon American Corp.* [146 S.E. 2d 793 (North Carolina)] (buffing machine).

2. *Failure to warn of the dangers of the product.* Whether or not there is a duty to warn on the part of the retailer depends upon the nature of the product, and the retailer's knowledge of the danger. If the product is one which as a matter of common knowledge is dangerous, then the retailer has no more information than does the buyer, and consequently the retailer is under no duty to warn him. It is only where the retailer has knowledge of the danger and where he has reason to believe that the purchaser will not discover the danger that the retailer has a duty to warn. This duty can normally be met by adequate labeling. For example, in *Gall* v. *Union Ice Co.* [239 Pac. 2d 48 (California)], a distributor of sulfuric acid was held liable for his negligence in failing to warn the buyer of the dangers of not keeping a drum of acid cool and vented, when the buyer was ignorant of the dangers involved. Also, in *Harp* v. *Montgomery Ward & Co.* [336 Fed. 2d 255 (Oregon)], the defendant contracted to sell and install an electric clothes drier. It failed to ground the machine and failed to warn the purchaser of the danger of death by electrocution as a result. The court held the defendant liable for its negligence in failing to give the necessary warning.

The age and intelligence of the buyer will have some influence upon whether or not there is a duty to warn. If the retailer knows or has reason to know that because of his age or intelligence the buyer is not aware of the dangers of the product and the retailer had such knowledge, the retailer must warn of the danger. For example, in *Krueger* v. *Knutson* [111 N.W. 2d 526 (Minnesota)], a druggist sold potassium chlorate as rocket fuel to a teen-age member of a rocket club without warning the purchaser of the explosive properties of the product. Liability was imposed on the druggist. In *Walker* v. *Gun Traders, Inc.* [116 So. 2d 792 (Florida)], the retailer sold a secondhand revolver with a defective safety notch to a minor purchaser without warning him of the dangerous potentiality of the weapon. The retailer was held liable for the injury which resulted from the use of the dangerous product.

Where the properties of the product and the dangers attendant to its use are matters of common knowledge or where the danger of the product is open and obvious, the retailer is under no duty to warn. Thus, a supplier of redimix concrete was under no duty to warn the buyer that prolonged contact of the cement with the skin would produce chemical burns. *Katz* v. *Arundel-Brooks Concrete Corp.* [151 Atl. 2d 731 (Maryland)]. To the same effect is *Baker* v. *Stewart Sand & Material Co., Inc.* [353 S.W. 2d 108 (Missouri)]. Likewise, in *Strahlendorf* v. *Walgren Co.* [114 N.W. 2d 823 (Wisconsin)], the seller of plastic airplanes propelled by rubber bands was held not liable for his failure to warn the purchaser of the danger of injury to a person who might be struck in the eye by the toy. Other cases holding the retailer not liable for his failure to warn with respect to open and obvious danger are *Bradshaw* v. *Blystone Equipment Co.* [386 Pac. 2d 396 (Nevada)]; *Villanueva* v. *Nowlin* [420 Pac. 2d 764 (New Mexico)]; *Verdiglione* v. *Rosignolo* [258 N.Y.S. 2d 471].

Where it is established that there is a duty to warn, the question of the retailer's liability will turn on the question of whether or not the warning was adequate or not. If no warning was given, then the retailer is liable for any injuries sustained as a consequence of his failure to do so. If the warning was given but it was inadequate in the sense that it was not conspicuously placed on the package, was not large enough, or was not readable, the retailer is likewise liable. For example, in *Tampa Drug Co.* v. *Wait* [103 So. 2d 603 (Florida)], the label warned that the vapor of the carbon tetrachloride purchased was harmful and that prolonged breathing of it or repeated contact with the skin should be avoided and that the product should be used with adequate ventilation. The purchaser used the product to clean the floors of his home. Several days later he died of carbon tetrachloride poisoning. The court held the defendant liable on the theory that since the warning did not call attention to the deadly effects or the potentially fatal consequences which might follow the use of the product, which rendered the warning inadequate. On the other hand, a warning "Caution: do not use near fire or flame" and a further warning, "Use in a well-ventilated area. Do not smoke, extinguish all pilot lights" was held to be adequate for the purpose of warning the purchaser of the danger of using an adhesive product. *Moschkau* v. *Sears, Roebuck & Co.* [282 Fed. 2d 878 (7th Cir.)].

3. Failure to properly assemble the product. Where the retailer assembles, or assembles and installs the product, he is under a duty to the purchaser to exercise care in so doing. This would mean that he would have to follow the manufacturer's assembly instructions or installation instructions, but, more importantly, he would have to test and inspect the completed article. For example, in *Parisi* v. *Carl W. Bush Co.* (New Jersey), the defendant-vendor negligently assembled a bicycle so that it could not be controlled, and as a result he was held liable for the injuries sustained by the purchaser's daughter. Similarly, in *Cornett* v. *William Lang & Sons Co.* [175 N.E. 2d 105 (Ohio)], the installer of a fire escape was held liable where the jury found that he was negligent in installing a cable of insufficient size and strength. Also, in *Phillips* v. *Ogle Aluminum Furniture, Inc.* [235 Pac. 2d 857 (California)], the vendor in assembling an aluminum chair used screws which were too short, and therefore he was held liable to the purchaser for injuries sustained as a result of the back coming off the chair.

4. Negligent sales. Where the retailer delivers a dangerous product in place of a comparatively safe product, which was ordered, and the substitution cannot be detected upon reasonable inspection, the retailer will be liable for the resulting damage. Most of the cases in this category involve druggists where the retailer failed to deliver the product called for in a prescription and substituted some other ingredient, which he knew or should have known was dangerous to the purchaser. In *Thomsen* v. *Rexall Drug & Chemical Corp.* (45 Cal. Rptr. 642), the druggist negligently filled a prescription calling for cortisone pills with penicillin or sulfa pills. He was held liable to the purchaser who developed vasculitis as a result of taking the substituted drugs. See also, *Burke* v. *Bean* [363 S.W. 2d 366 (Texas)], where the druggist improperly dispensed capsules to effect a suntan when the prescription called for gall bladder tablets, and was held liable for the resulting injury suffered by the purchaser. Similarly, in *Acherman* v. *Robertson* [3 N.W. 2d 723 (Wisconsin)], a veterinarian through his agent delivered Lysol to the purchaser instead of mange oil which was ordered. The purchaser sprayed his hogs with the Lysol, thinking that it was mange oil and as a consequence many of them died. The veterinarian was held liable to the purchaser.

Also in this category, we can include sales made to persons who, because of their age or condition, are not in a position to appreciate the dangers of the product sold. Thus, where the retailer sold gasoline to a child [*Clark* v. *Ticehurst,* 271 Pac. 2d 295 (Kansas)] and where a retailer-druggist sold carbolic acid to a man in such a state of intoxication that he could not appreciate the danger, and died as a result of drinking it [*Bennet Drug Stores, Inc.,* 20 S.E. 2d 208 (Georgia)], the retailers were held liable for the resulting injuries.

5. *Sales in violation of a statute.* Generally, a sale made in violation of a statute or ordinance is negligent per se, and the retailer is liable if the person injured is within the class of persons the statute or ordinance was designed to protect. The majority of the cases in this category arise under pure food laws where the vendor has sold contaminated food which was unfit for human consumption and thus was in violation of the statute. Other areas include the sale of firearms to a minor in violation of a local ordinance [*Zamora* v. *J. Korber & Co.,* 278 Pac. 2d 569 (New Mexico)], the sale of penicillin ointment without a prescription in violation of the Federal Food, Drug and Cosmetic Act [*Cox* v. *Laws,* 145 So. 2d 703 (Mississippi)], the sale of cartridges to a boy under the age of 16 in violation of a state statute [*Mautino* v. *Piercedale Supply Co.,* 13 Atl. 2d 51 (Pennsylvania)], the sale of gasoline in an unlabeled jug in violation of a statute [*Reynolds* v. *Murphy,* 84 S.E. 2d 273 (North Carolina)].

Most states have either statutes or regulations of the Alcohol Beverage Control Commission, which have the force of law, making the sale of intoxicants to a minor or a visibly intoxicated person unlawful. Such a sale is negligence per se and the purchaser may recover for injuries he received as a consequence of the unlawful sale. See *Soronen* v. *Olde Milford Inn, Inc.* [218 Atl. 2d 630 (New Jersey)] (reversed on other grounds); *Majors* v. *Brodhead Hotel* [205 Atl. 2d 873 (Pennsylvania)]; *Galvin* v. *Jennings* [289 Fed. 2d 15 (3d Cir.)]; *Ramsey* v. *Anctil* [211 Atl. 2d 900 (New Hampshire)]. As to the retailer's liability to persons not purchasers, see Section 508, Dram Shop Acts, above.

1003   Liability of the retailer for breach of contract

The parties to a contract of sale like the parties to any other type of contracts may mutually agree to any terms and conditions they desire. The party who breaches the contract may have to respond in damages to the other. In the early cases involving sales where there was no express warranty or guarantee in the contract itself, the rule of *caveat emptor* was applied with no warranty or guarantee implied from the nature of the transaction. Later, as commercial transactions multiplied, the courts recognized that the seller had superior knowledge of the ingredients of the article, and the quality of the article with respect to its salability and its fitness for the particular purpose for which it was bought. Therefore, where there was a contract of sale, the courts imposed the obligation on the seller to warrant or guarantee certain things about the article sold which were implied from the nature of the transaction and without any specific agreement between the parties with reference to it. The implied warranties are (1) warranty of title, (2) warranty of merchantability, and (3) warranty of fitness for a particular purpose. These are described as follows:

1. *Warranty of title.* When an article is offered for sale, the seller guarantees that he has title and ownership, or that he has been authorized by the owner to pass good and sufficient title. The purchaser is not required to trace the chain of ownership from the manufacturer to the seller, but may rely on this implied warranty.

2. *Warranty of merchantability.* This has come to mean a guarantee that the goods are of such quality to pass under the same kind of description specified in the agreement and must be reasonably fit for the ordinary uses to which such goods are put.

One of the earlier cases to announce this rule was *Gardiner* v. *Gray* [(1815), 171 Eng. Rep. 46], which involved the sale of "waste silk" by sample and in which neither the buyer nor the seller was able to inspect the goods before delivery. The goods delivered did not meet the sample or the requirements as "waste silk." In finding for the plaintiff, the court said:

I am of the opinion, however, that under such circumstances, the purchaser has a right to expect a saleable article answering the description in the contract. Without any particular warranty, this is an implied term in every such contract. Where there is no opportunity to inspect the commodity, the maxim of caveat emptor does not apply. He cannot without a warranty insist that it shall be of any particular quality or fineness, but the intention of both parties must be taken to be, that it shall be saleable in the market under the denomination mentioned in the contract between them. The purchaser cannot be supposed to buy goods to lay them on a dunghill.

Thus the court equated merchantability with "salability" and if the goods did not meet the ordinary tests of the marketplace for goods of similar kind, they would be unmarketable and not within the scope of the unexpressed intention of both parties. Certainly, no purchaser would buy goods which were unsalable only to be forced to throw them away.

3. Warranty of fitness for a particular purpose. This implied warranty came as a sequence to the preceding warranty, and means generally that "if a person sold a commodity for a particular purpose, he must be understood to warrant it reasonably fit for such purpose." [*Gray* v. *Cox* (1825), 107 Eng. Rep. 999]. To obtain the benefit of this warranty, the purchaser must show that the seller was aware of the purpose for which the commodity was bought.

1004   Liability of the manufacturer or distributor for breach of contract

Generally, the manufacturer and distributor are not in privity of contract with the ultimate consumer and therefore, in the absence of statute, there are no implied warranties arising out of the relationship of the manufacturer and distributor and the product. However, the manufacturer or distributor or both may make express warranties to the ultimate consumer as an inducement to the purchaser to buy the product, in which case the manufacturer or distributor will have to respond in damages if the express warranty is untrue and results in injury to the purchaser.

As between the retailer and the distributor, they are in privity of contract, with the retailer being the purchaser and the distributor the seller. Should the retailer be required to respond in damages to the ultimate consumer because of a breach of warranty, the retailer could then sue the distributor on the same warranty theory. Clearly, there were implied warranties in the contract of sale between the distributor and the retailer, and if the retailer sustained damages as a result of the breach, he is entitled to damages from the distributor. The same situation obtains as between the manufacturer and the distributor, with the manufacturer in the position of the seller and the distributor in the role of the purchaser. Therefore, the manufacturer would be liable to the distributor on the same theory as the recovery was first obtained against him for the retailer. Thus, by means of these circuitous actions, the manufacturer would be the one ultimately to pay the claim originally asserted by the ultimate consumer, but where there is a privity requirement, the ultimate consumer has no cause of action directly against the manufacturer or distributor.

1005   Elimination of the privity requirement

In recent years many of our courts have had occasion to reexamine the privity requirement set down in the *Winterbottom* case as well as the exceptions to that requirement in cases where the product was "inherently dangerous" to life and limb. The majority of the states which have considered the problem have either by legislation or court decisions eliminated the privity requirement as an element to be established in order to maintain a cause of action against the manufacturer, distributor, or retailer arising out of the sale of a defective product made so by the defendant. In historical sequence, the courts considered such cases in three categories: (1) food products, (2) products for intimate body use, and (3) all other products.

1. Food products. It is probably safe to say that where food or beverages are sold which are unfit for human consumption, all states will impose a rule of strict liability upon the manufacturer, processor, distributor, or retailer. The reasoning behind the decisions may differ but the result is the same. Some take the position that the sale of food and drink comes within the exception applicable to inherently dangerous products, and others utilize the warranty theory that the defendant in offering food products for sale impliedly warrants that they are fit for human consumption. Two exceptions to the rule of strict liability are (a) the sealed container doctrine, and (b) the raw pork exception.

(a) *Sealed container doctrine.* In a few states, the courts have relieved the retailer from liability where the food or beverage was sold in a sealed container, purchased from a reputable manufacturer or processor, and where the retailer had exercised reasonable care of the product while it was in his possession. The states allowing this exception are:

Alabama, *Kirkland* v. *A.&P.*, 171 So. 735; Louisiana, *Lescher* v. *A.&P.*, 129 So. 2d 96; Mississippi, *Kroger Grocery Co.* v. *Lewelling*, 145 So. 726; Tennessee, *Calhoun* v. *Coca-Cola Bottling Co.*, 14 Neg. Cas. 2d (CCH) 929; Texas, *Bowman Biscuit Co.* v. *Hines*, 251 S.W. 2d 153; and West Virginia, *Pennington* v. *Cranberry Fuel Co.*, 186 S.E. 610.

All of the above states with the exception of Louisiana have now adopted the Uniform Commercial Code, under which the retail seller is required to affirm that anything he sells is reasonably fit for the purpose for which it is sold. There is therefore some question as to whether or not this exception will be applied in cases arising in the future.

(b) *Raw pork exception.* It is a well-known fact that most raw pork contains trichina, a parasite, which when introduced into the human body will cause a disease called trichinosis. It is also well known that the parasites are destroyed if the pork is properly cooked. Trichinae will not survive heat of 137° F. and for that reason the plaintiff is faced with difficulties in the way of proof that he did properly cook the pork before eating it. Cases supporting this exception are:

Connecticut, *Silverman* v. *Swift & Co.*, 107 Atl. 2d 277; Illinois, *Golaris* v. *Jewel Tea Co., Inc.*, 22 FRD 16, *Nicketta* v. *National Tea Co.*, 87 N.E. 2d 30; Maine, *Kobecis* v. *Budzko*, 225 Atl. 2d 418; Michigan, *Cheli* v. *Cudahy Bros. Co.*, 255 N.W. 414; Pennsylvania, *Adams* v. *Scheib*, 184 Atl. 2d 700.

It should be emphasized that all of these cases refer to the sale of raw pork. The rule is to the contrary where the processor or seller cooked the pork himself, such as the sale of a smoked ham, or a picnic smoked pork shoulder. [See *Swift & Co.* v. *Wells*, 110 S.E. 2d 203 (Virginia).]

In all of these cases, the burden will be upon the plaintiff to establish that the food involved was in fact unwholesome and not fit for human consumption. There are a number of foods which contain substances which are not fit for human consumption, but which are natural to the food. One would expect to find bones in fish, chicken bones in chicken, a T-bone in a T-bone steak, pits in peaches or seeds in grapes. The majority view is that these are not foreign substances so as to make the food unfit for human consumption. Cases upholding the "naturalness" test and denying recoveries are:

California, *Lamb* v. *Hill*, 245 Pac. 2d 316; Iowa, *Brown* v. *Nebiker*, 296 N.W. 366; Louisiana, *Musso* v. *Picadilly Cafeterias, Inc.*, 178 So. 2d 421; Massachusetts, *Webster* v. *Blue Ship Tea Room, Inc.*, 198 N.E. 2d 309; New York, *Courter* v. *Dilbert Bros.*, 186 N.Y.S. 2d 334; North Carolina, *Adams* v. *A.&P.*, 112 S.E. 2d 92; Ohio, *Allen* v. *Grafton*, 164 N.E. 2d 167; Oregon, *Hunt* v. *Ferguson-Paulus Enterprises*, 415 Pac. 2d 13.

A minority of the courts have rejected the naturalness test, and substituted therefore the reasonable expectation test. This means that the test is not whether or not the substance is natural to the food, but whether or not the consumer could reasonably expect to find it in the food. In each of the cases, however, there was either an assurance from the processor that the food did not contain anything not fit for human consumption, or that there was some duty on the part of the retailer (usually a restaurant operator) to remove even natural substances from the food. For example, in *Bryer* v. *Rath Packing Co.* [156 Atl. 2d 442 (Maryland)], the defendant advertised its product as "Ready to Serve Boned Chicken." The court held that under the circumstances even though a chicken bone would be natural to the food, a consumer could reasonably expect, because of the advertising, that the food did not contain chicken bones. In *Wood* v. *Waldorf System, Inc.* [83 Atl. 2d 90 (Rhode Island)], a patron in a restaurant who swallowed a chicken bone while eating a bowl of chicken soup containing rice and diced carrots was allowed a recovery. [See also *Zabner* v. *Howard Johnson's, Inc.*, 201 So. 2d 824.]

2. Products for intimate body use. The courts, in turning their attention to drugs, cosmetics, cigarettes, and articles of like nature which were applied to the body in some form or another, could see no particular distinction between such products and food or beverage items, and therefore extended the special rule heretofore applicable only to food cases to include these items. Thus the plaintiff could bring action directly against the manufacturer without any showing of privity. The leading case on this subject is *Gottsdanker* v. *Cutter Laboratories* (6 Cal. Rptr. 320), wherein the California District Court of Appeal allowed an action for breach of warranty to be maintained against the manufacturer of Salk vaccine without any evidence of privity being required. See also, *Esborg* v. *Bailey Drug Co.* [378 Pac. 2d 298 (Washington)] (hair tint preparation); *Gober* v. *Revlon, Inc.* [317 Fed. 2d 47 (4th Cir.)] (fingernail base coat); *Bowles* v. *Zimmer Mfg. Co.* [277 Fed. 2d 868 (7th Cir.)] (defective surgical nail) applying Michigan law; and *Chapman* v. *Brown* [304 Fed. 2d 149 (Hawaii, 9th Cir.)] (flammable hula skirt).

The cases alleging lung cancer from smoking cigarettes usually allege an express or implied warranty, and the following cases have held that privity of contract is not a necessary element in establishing the cause of action:

Florida   *Green* v. *American Tobacco Co.*, 304 Fed. 2d 70; on remand 325 Fed. 2d 673.

Louisiana	*Lartigue* v. *R. J. Reynolds Tobacco Co.*, 317 Fed. 2d 19.
Missouri	*Ross* v. *Philip Morris & Co., Ltd.*, 328 Fed. 2d 3.
Pennsylvania	*Pritchard* v. *Liggett & Myers Tobacco Co.*, 295 Fed. 2d. 292.

3. All other products. After making partial inroads on the requirement of privity, a majority of the legislatures and the courts reexamined the question of the privity requirement on an overall basis, and by either legislation or court decision have eliminated the privity requirement. A minority of states still require privity and a small number have not reexamined the question at all. The present status is reflected in the following divisions: (1) Legislation eliminating privity; (2) Nonprivity states where by court decision the privity requirement has been eliminated; (3) Privity states where the privity requirement has been retained; and (4) States in which there has been no determination and the question is still open.

1. *Legislation.* The following states have eliminated the privity requirement in actions brought against the manufacturer, distributor or retailer, by specific statutes:

Alabama	Laws 1965, Act 549, Section 2-318, effective January 1, 1967 and amending the Uniform Commercial Code.
Arkansas	Ark. Stat. Ann. Section 85-2-318.1.
Colorado	Colo. Rev. Stat. Ann. 155-2-318.
Georgia	Ga. Code Ann. 96-307 (1958). This statute was repealed and is superseded by Ga. Code Ann. 109A-2-318, which is the Uniform Commercial Code.
Virginia	Va. Code Ann. 8.2-318.
Wyoming	Wyo. Stat. Ann. 34-2-318.

2. *Nonprivity states.* In the following states, the courts have by decision eliminated the privity requirement:

Arizona	*Crystal Coca-Cola Bottling Co.* v. *Cathey*, 317 Pac. 2d 1094; *Nalbandian* v. *Byron Jackson*, 399 Pac. 2d 681.
California	*Vandermark* v. *Ford Motor Co.*, 391 Pac. 2d 168; *Greenman* v. *Yuba Power Prods.*, 377 Pac. 2d 897.
Connecticut	*Mitchell* v. *Miller*, 214 Atl. 2d 694; *Simpson* v. *Powered Products, Inc.*, 192 Atl. 2d 555.
District of Columbia	*Picker X-ray Corp.* v. *General Motors Corp.*, 185 Atl. 2d 919; *Simpson* v. *Logan Motor Co.*, 192 Atl. 2d 122.
Florida	*Bernstein* v. *Lily-Tulip Cup Corp.*, 177 So. 2d 362.
Illinois	*Suvada* v. *White Motor Co.*, 210 N.E. 2d 182.
Iowa	*State Farm Mutual Ins. Co.* v. *Anderson-Weber*, 110 N.W. 2d 449.
Kentucky	*Dealer Transp. Co.* v. *Battery Distrib. Co.*, 402 S.W. 2d 441.
Michigan	*Spence* v. *Three Rivers Builders & Masonry Supply*, 90 N.W. 2d 873; *Hill* v. *Harbor Steel & Supply Corp.*, 132 N.Y. 2d 54.
Minnesota	*Beck* v. *Spindler*, 99 N.W. 2d 670.
Mississippi	*State Stove Mfg. Co.* v. *Hodges*, 189 So. 2d 113.

Missouri	*Morrow* v. *Caloric Appliance Corp.*, 372 S.W. 2d 41.
New Jersey	*Santor* v. *A. & M. Karagheusian, Inc.*, 207 Atl. 2d 305; *Henningsen* v. *Bloomfield Motors*, 161 Atl. 2d 69.
New York	*Goldberg* v. *Kollsman Instr. Corp.*, 191 N.E. 2d 81.
North Dakota	*Lang* v. *General Motors Corp.*, 136 N.W. 2d 805.
Ohio	*Lonzrick* v. *Republic Steel Corp.*, 205 N.E. 2d 92.
Oklahoma	*Marathon Battery Co.* v. *Kilpatrick*, 418 Pac. 2d 900.
Oregon	*Wights* v. *Staff Jennings, Inc.*, 405 Pac. 2d 624.
Tennessee	*General Motors Corp.* v. *Dodson*, 338 S.W. 2d 655.
Washington	*Brewer* v. *Oriard Powder Co.*, 401 Pac. 2d 844.

3. *Privity states.* The following states have retained the requirement of privity, and in the absence of privity of contract between the parties, there is no maintainable cause of action which can be asserted. The states are as follows:

Delaware	*Barni* v. *Kutner*, 76 Atl. 2d 801 (1950). See also Laws of 1966, Ch. 349 Sec. 2-318 which provides for an action on an implied warranty without privity.
Idaho	*Abercrombie* v. *Union Portland Cement Co.*, 205 Pac. 1118 (1922).
Maine	*Pelletier* v. *Dupont*, 128 Atl. 186 (1925).
Maryland	*Vaccarino* v. *Cozzubo*, 31 Atl. 2d 316 (1943).
Massachusetts	*Kennedy* v. *Brockelman Bros.*, 134 N.E. 2d 747 (1956).
New Hampshire	*Smith* v. *Coca-Cola Bottling Co.*, 25 Atl. 2d 125 (1942).
North Carolina	*Terry* v. *Double Cola Bottling Co.*, 138 S.E. 2d 753 (1964).
Rhode Island	*Minutilla* v. *Providence Ice Cream Co.*, 144 Atl. 884 (1929).
South Dakota	*Whitehorn* v. *Nash-Finch Co.*, 293 N.W. 859 (1940). Changed by statute—see Laws of 1966, Ch. 150, Sec. 2-318.
West Virginia	*Burgess* v. *Sanitary Meat Market*, 5 S.E. 2d 254 (1939).

It is to be noted that some of the cited cases are quite old, and there is some question as to whether or not the courts would reach the same conclusion if the matter were again presented to them. No doubt they will be influenced by the trend which is evident in the other states.

In the following states and one territory, the courts have eliminated the privity requirement only in the areas of food and beverages, while apparently retaining the requirement as to all other cases. These are:

Montana	Privity requirement eliminated in food cases by the pure food laws. Privity is a requirement in all other cases. *Larson* v. *U.S. Rubber Co.*, 163 Fed. Supp. 327.
Nebraska	*Asher* v. *Coca-Cola Bottling Co.*, 112 N.W. 2d 252.
Puerto Rico	*Coca-Cola Bottling Co.* v. *Torres*, 255 Fed. 2d 149.
South Carolina	*Springfield* v. *Williams Plumbing Supply Co.*, 153 S.E. 2d 184. In this case the court noted the adoption of the Uniform Commercial Code since the date this cause of action arose and indicated the possibility that the privity requirement would be eliminated in future cases.

In the following two states, the privity requirement has been eliminated as to food and products intended for intimate bodily use:

Hawaii   *Brown* v. *Chapman*, 304 Fed. 2d 149.
Louisiana   *Miller* v. *Louisiana Coca-Cola Bottling Co.*, 70 So. 2d 409;
            Gilbert v. *John Gendusa Bakery, Inc.*, 144 So. 2d 760;
            Lartigue v. *R. J. Reynolds Tobacco Co.*, 317 Fed. 2d 19.

4. *Question still open.*   In the following states the question of privity or nonprivity as a prerequisite to a cause of action against the manufacturer for breach of warranty is an open one, although each has adopted the Uniform Commercial Code since the date of the last court decision on the subject. These states are:

Alaska   No decision. Uniform Commercial Code adopted 1962.
New Mexico *Phares* v. *Scandia Lumber Co.*, 305 Pac. 2d 367 (1956). Uniform
            Commercial Code adopted 1961.
Utah   *Schneider* v. *Suhrman*, 327 Pac. 2d 822. This case eliminates the
            privity requirement as to food. No decision as to other products.
            Uniform Commercial Code adopted in 1965, but Utah struck out
            the provision relating to actions for breach of implied warranties.

1006   Effect of the elimination of privity

Tracing the privity requirement as one of the prerequisites of the cause of action, from the time of the *Winterbottom* v. *Wright* case where in the absence of privity there was no assertible cause of action, through the various exceptions to the requirement of privity up to the present time, it can be seen that the cases in which the privity requirement is an element of the cause of action are diminishing, and in some jurisdictions it has disappeared entirely. With the elimination of the privity requirement, more and more cases are added to the list of assertible causes of action. Therefore, the effect of the elimination of the privity requirement is to create causes of action where none existed before.

It should be emphasized, however, that the elimination of the privity requirement merely gives this class of plaintiff the legal capacity to sue the manufacturer, but in order to recover, the plaintiff must make out a prima facie case either of negligence or breach of warranty which the manufacturer owes to him, either at common law or under the Uniform Commercial Code.

In a number of products the package contains an approved stamp or a certification from a testing laboratory or a testing company that the product has been tested and is safe for us. Where the product is defective and the buyer is injured because of the use of it, under the old rule of privity, the buyer would have no cause of action against the tester. See *National Iron & Steel Co.* v. *Hunt* [143 N.E. 833 (Illinois 1924)]. However, with the eclipse of the privity requirement in the products liability field, we can expect that claims will be asserted in this area. For example, in *Hempstead* v. *General Fire Extinguisher Corp.* [269 Fed. Supp. 109 (Delaware)], a testing company was held liable to the consumer for negligently approving the design of a fire extinguisher. In *Hardy* v. *Carmichael* [24 Cal. Rptr. 475], a termite inspector, employed by the seller through a real estate agent, was held liable to the purchaser for negligent misrepresentation in his report concerning the house, which was the object of sale.

1007   Duties of the manufacturer

Generally, the manufacturer is required to exercise reasonable care in the design, production, and assembly of the product, the degree of care being governed by the risk of harm to which the consumer is exposed. The Restatement, Second, Law of Torts, states the following rule:

395   Negligent Manufacture of Chattel Dangerous Unless Carefully Made
A manufacturer who fails to exercise reasonable care in the manufacture of a chattel which, unless carefully made, he should recognize as involving an unreasonable risk of causing physical harm to those who use it for a purpose for which the manufacturer should expect it to be used and to those whom he should expect to be endangered by its probable use, is subject to liability for physical harm caused to them by its lawful use in a manner and for a purpose for which it is supplied.

This Restatement rule states the law as it has been generally adopted, and it contemplates the duty of the manufacturer to the general public, arising out of the purchase of the product by the ultimate consumer. Since the manufacturer made the product, he supposedly knows more about it than the consumer. He knows what raw materials or ingredients were used. He knows the properties of those materials and he is charged with the knowledge of the possible harm to others which may come about if proper care is not exercised. Finally, by placing the article on the market there is a representation that it can be safely used. Since the manufacturer derives an economic benefit from placing the article in the stream of commerce, liability is imposed if he fails to exercise reasonable care in its manufacture.

It should be noted that the rule creates a liability to "those who use" the article, which means that the rule is not only for the benefit of the buyer, but also all others who may be reasonably anticipated to use it. In addition, liability also is imposed upon the manufacturer for injuries suffered by "those whom he should expect to be endangered by its probable use." This could encompass a large number of people who are not directly or indirectly involved in the sale. For example, let us assume that an automobile manufacturer placed a defective automobile on the market, the defect consisting of ineffective braking power when the brakes are suddenly applied. The buyer takes a few friends for a drive, and the brakes fail as a result of the defect. The passengers in the car are injured, including the driver-buyer. Under this rule all would be "using" the vehicle and therefore entitled to hold the manufacturer responsible for their injuries. Let us further assume that because of the brake failure, the car mounted the curb and injured a group of pedestrians. Under this rule, the pedestrians would come within the definition of those whom the manufacturer "should expect to be endangered by" the probable use of the automobile.

The "manufacturer" of the article is the one who makes or assembles the article and places it on the market under his name. The mere fact that he purchased raw material or a component part from another supplier will not insulate him from liability, even if the material or the component part is the cause of the defect. Since he is the one who had the duty to inspect the article for defects prior to its release to the market, the person injured does not have to go any further back in the chain than such manufacturer.

What will constitute reasonable care in the manufacture of an article will be commensurate with the foreseeable danger in its use if defective. This is a relative term and the greater the danger imposed by the article the greater the duty of care. Conversely, if the article is one which poses little or no danger of anything more than trivial risk, then the duty of care is that much less. Also, in the exercise of care, the manufacturer is not bound to anticipate an abnormal use of the product, and is not liable for injuries sustained as a result of such use. For example, the manufacturer of a dining room table would not be liable for injuries sustained when six people decide to stand on it and dance and the table gives way under their weight. This type of abnormal use, the manufacturer is not bound to anticipate.

1008   Duty of safe design

The manufacturer is bound to exercise reasonable care in designing his product, and is also bound to foresee the possible risks of harm to which others will be exposed because of unsafe design. If a person suffers injury as a result of the unsafe design of the product, the manufacturer is liable. For example, in *Greenman* v. *Yuba Power Products, Inc.* [377 Pac. 2d 897 (California)], the defendant designed and marketed a power tool, called a Shopsmith, which contained an inadequate set of screws which would sometimes allow the tailstock of the lathe to move away from the piece of wood and thus cause the piece to fly out of the machine. The court held that strict liability might be imposed because there was a defect in design which made the Shopsmith unsafe for its intended use. The court pointed out that the duty of the manufacturer was not to design a product which was perfectly safe or foolproof, but that the product in this case was not reasonably safe, and furthermore, it was not safe for its intended purpose.

1. *Automobiles.*   The design of automobiles has generated more controversy and more court attention perhaps than any other product. There is no question but that if the design of the automobile was such that it was the cause of the accident, the manufacturer is liable. For example, in *Carpini* v. *Pittsburgh & Weirton Bus Company* [216 Fed. 2d 404 (West Virginia)], the court permitted a recovery against the manufacturer because of a defectively designed petcock in the undercarriage of a bus which became dislodged by an obstruction in the road, causing the brakes to fail. Likewise, if the design causes an injury, or exposes the person to a greater injury, the manufacturer is liable. For example, in *Ford Motor Co.* v. *Zahn* (265 Fed. 2d 729), the plaintiff sued to recover damages for the loss of an eye, caused by a defective ashtray in a Ford car manufactured by the defendant. The plaintiff was riding as a guest in the front seat of the Ford. The ashtray which had a "jagged edge" was located on the top of the right-hand front corner. The plaintiff was bending forward to deposit ashes in the tray when the owner-driver suddenly applied his brakes to avoid a collision with an unidentified car. The plaintiff was thrown against the ashtray and the injury he sustained resulted in the loss of his right eye. The court held that since the defendant admittedly realized the importance of assembling the dash portion of the car so that there would be nothing there that would endanger passengers suddenly catapulted forward, the defendant should have foreseen that the defective ashtray was apt to result in injury to passengers. Under those circumstances, the court sustained a recovery by the plaintiff.

On the other hand, the manufacturer is not bound to anticipate the actions of others when the car is not in use. In *Kahn* v. *Chrysler Corp.* (221 Fed. Supp. 677), a minor drove his bicycle into the rear end of a Dodge automobile. The court held that the manufacturer had no duty to design a vehicle which would be safe for a child to ride his bicycle into while the vehicle was parked. To the same effect is *Hatch* v. *Ford Motor Co.* [329 Pac. 2d 695 (California)], in which a six-year-old boy walked into a radiator ornament which, in violation of the statute, protruded beyond the front of the radiator grill of a parked car. He sustained a severe injury which destroyed the sight of his left eye.

The court held that the manufacturer was not liable for the unsafe design of the ornament, and that there was no duty on the part of the manufacturer to design a car with which it was safe to collide, and further, that even if the ornament was so placed upon the car as to violate the statute, "the statute here was designed to decrease the hazard created by driving of such automobiles on the highway. It was not designed to protect those, who solely by reason of their own act or omission, might come in contact with it as an inert object lawfully standing unattended upon a highway."

In *Evans* v. *General Motors Corporation* (359 Fed. 2d 825), the deceased was driving a Chevrolet station wagon, designed with an X-frame chassis, when it was struck on the left side by another automobile at an intersection. The plaintiff contended that the manufacturer was negligent in designing a vehicle with an X-frame rather than a perimeter frame, because the X-frame provided insufficient protection to an occupant in the event of a collision. In holding that the manufacturer was under no duty to design an automobile which would be safe in the event of a collision, the court said:

The intended purpose of an automobile does not include its participation in collisions with other objects, despite the manufacturer's ability to foresee the possibility that such collisions may occur. As defendant argues, the defendant also knows that its automobiles may be driven into bodies of water, but it is not suggesting that defendant has a duty to equip them with pontoons.

In *Schemel* v. *General Motors Corporation* (384 Fed. 2d 802), the plaintiff was injured when his car was struck by a Chevrolet Impala which was operated at a speed of 115 miles per hour. The court held that the manufacturer was under no duty to produce a vehicle which would be restricted to a certain speed and that the manufacturer was not an insurer of the use of its products. The misuse of the automobile by the driver created no liability on the part of the defendant. Likewise, in *Willis* v. *Chrysler Corporation* (264 Fed. Supp. 1010), the plaintiff claimed that the defendant had breached the warranty of fitness for its intended use when the automobile broke in two when involved in a collision with another vehicle. In finding for the defendant, the court said:

> The court is of the opinion that the defendant had no duty to design an automobile that could withstand a high speed collision and maintain its structural integrity. It would require tenuous reasoning to broaden the implied warranty of "fitness for intended use" to an implied warranty of "fitness to survive a collision."

Claims have been made that the automobile was unsafely designed where the car was set on fire following a collision. The courts have uniformly held that the manufacturer was not obligated to design an automobile which was fireproof. See *Shumard* v. *General Motors Corp.*, (270 Fed. Supp. 311).

2. Roadworthiness versus crashworthiness. In spite of *Evans* v. *General Motors, supra,* there is a continuing dispute between consumer advocates and the automobile manufacturers as to the extent of the duty of safe design on the part of the manufacturers. Consumer advocates feel that since the automobile manufacturers can reasonably foresee the risk of injury to passengers arising from a collision with another vehicle or another object, the duty of safe design should include such design that would reasonably protect the users of the automobile from the consequences of a collision. The manufacturers, on the other hand, contend that their design duty consists merely of a product that will provide reasonably safe transportation and nothing more. The manufacturers claim that they are not under any obligation to design a vehicle that would be safe under all circumstances, whether the vehicle was misused or not. Thus, it is the position of the manufacturers that they have only the obligation of designing a vehicle which is roadworthy, but not crashworthy or crashproof.

The Mississippi Supreme Court considered this question in *Walton* v. *Chrysler Motor Corporation* (229 So. 2d 568). In that case the vehicle which the plaintiff was operating struck another car. The impact caused the plaintiff's seat to break and caused him to be thrown about in the interior of the car. In finding for the defendant on the theory that the manufacturer had no duty to design a car which would be safe for collisions, the court said:

> We are of the opinion that the automobile manufacturer is not an insurer against the possibility of accidental injury arising out of the intended use of its products. Although it is true that the manufacturer is liable for defects in its products which cause injury arising out of the intended use for which the product is manufactured, we are, nevertheless, of the opinion, and so hold, that an automobile manufacturer is not liable for injury arising from defects in the auto which did not cause or contribute to the cause of the accident, such as rear-end collision.

This is true although such accidents may have been foreseeable as a misuse of this manufactured product.

3. *Second accident or enhanced injury.* Where the design of the automobile is such that in the event of a collision the driver and passengers are exposed to an unreasonable risk of harm, generally the cases hold that the manufacturer is liable. For example, in *Mickle* v. *Blackmon* [166 S.E. 2d 173 (South Carolina)], a passenger was thrown against a gear shift lever knob which shattered and impaled her following a collision with another vehicle. In finding for the plaintiff, the court said:

The duty of care applicable to this case was to take reasonable precautions in light of the known risks, balancing the likelihood of harm, and gravity of harm if it should happen against the burden of feasible precautions which would tend to, avoid or minimize the harm.

To the same effect is *Dyson* v. *General Motors Corp.* (298 Fed. Supp. 1064). There, the plaintiff, a passenger in a 1965 Buick Electra hardtop was injured when the car overturned following a collision and the roof collapsed. In finding for the plaintiff, the court said:

. . . the correct rule, in my opinion, can be stated either of two ways: (1) vehicular accidents are so commonplace as to constitute a readily foreseeable misuse of motor vehicles; or (2) vehicular accidents are incidental to the normal and intended use of motor vehicles on today's highways. Under this approach to the concept of intended purpose and normal use, the manufacturer would not be held liable for the vicissitudes of using a passenger automobile on a race track or a plowed field, for example, but might be held liable for the foreseeable, though accidental, traumatic consequences of the use of passenger cars on highways by occupants.

The court has used rather broad language, and, if taken literally, then the manufacturer would be liable in every case where there was a collision and an injury to passengers. All the court was called upon to decide here was whether or not a roof which collapsed in a rollover accident was defective in design. The court held that it was.

From this case and the cases which followed, it seems clear that there must be some causal connection between the injuries and the alleged defective design. For example, in *Larsen* v. *General Motors Corporation* [391 Fed. 2d 495 (8th Cir.)], the plaintiff was involved in a head-on collision with another vehicle while driving a Corvair automobile. The plaintiff alleged that the automobile was defectively designed in that the steering shaft was so constructed so as to produce a rearward displacement in a head-on collision. In finding for the plaintiff, the court said:

While automobiles are not made for the purpose of colliding with each other, a frequent and inevitable contingency of normal automobile use will result in collisions and injury producing impacts. . . . Where the injuries or enhanced injuries are due to the manufacturer's failure to use reasonable care to avoid subjecting the user of its products to an unreasonable risk of injury, general negligence principles should be applicable. The sole function of an automobile is not just to provide a means of transportation, it is to provide a means of safe transportation or as safe as is reasonably possible under the present state of the art.

See also *Badorek* v. *General Motors Corporation* (90 Cal. Rptr. 305).

No doubt influenced by the opinion of the *Larsen* case, the Supreme Court of Tennessee decided *Ellithorpe* v. *Ford Motor Company* (503 S.W. 2d 516). There the plaintiff was injured in a rear-end collision in which she struck another vehicle. She was injured when her face struck the hub of her steering wheel on which the manufacturer placed its emblem which consisted of three plastic prongs. The court held that the intervening accident will not relieve the manufacturer of design defects, even if the accident was due to the fault of the plaintiff. The court said:

. . . that collisions are clearly foreseeable by the manufacturer and that he therefore has the duty to minimize the harm of inevitable accidents by utilizing reasonably safe design. This does not require construction and design of an automobile which will be absolutely safe in a collision. It does require the manufacturer to design an automobile which, in the event of an accident, is "as safe as is reasonably possible under the present state of the art." . . . We agree with the defendant that abnormal use of a product is generally a defense in strict liability cases. . . . However, the use of the product will not bar recovery if it is reasonably foreseeable by the manufacturer.

The court held that the damages for which the defendant was liable was limited to pay only such damages for the injuries which were caused by the defect and not those sustained in the collision. In other words, the defendant was liable only for the injuries caused by the defect and not for other injuries which were not causally connected with the defect.

4. National Traffic and Motor Vehicle Safety Act. In 1966, Congress passed the National Traffic and Motor Vehicle Safety Act (15 USCA 1381). The act created a National Traffic Safety Agency, to create standards of motor vehicle design under the following four categories:

1. Engineering design which reduces the risk of accidents.
2. Engineering design which reduces the risk of injury when accidents occur.
3. Engineering design which provides greater tolerance for pedestrians on impact.
4. Engineering design which protects persons from injury while the vehicle is not in operation.

Obviously whether or not the manufacturer complied with the standards will not determine his common-law liability for unsafe design. It will, however, be evidence of his lack of due care where he did not comply.

In addition mere compliance with the standards created will not insulate the manufacturer from liability for unsafe design if there are other areas in which the manufacturer has failed to exercise due care in creating the design.

The statute (15 USCA 1397) provides that "compliance with any Federal motor vehicle safety standard issued under this Title does not exempt any person from any liability under common law."

5. *Consumer Product Safety Act.* This act was passed by Congress in 1972 and is found in 15 USCA 205 et seq. The primary purpose of the act is to reduce the unreasonable risk of injuries to consumers caused by consumer products. It creates a commission known as the Consumer Product Safety Commission, whose duty it is to determine the products which contain a defect which would create a "substantial products hazard." When this was determined, the Commission could take certain actions for the protection of the consumer:

1. Under Section 8 of the act (15 USCA 2057) the Commission may under certain circumstances ban an allegedly hazardous product; and
2. Under Section 7 of the act (15 USCA 2056), the Commission has the power to promulgate standards for consumer products; and
3. Under Section 10 of the act (15 USCA 2059), the Commission has the power to issue consumer products safety rules.

An important tool which is used by the Commission in determining the kind and type of products which are hazardous is the National Electronic Injury Surveillance System (NEISS) which is operated by the Injury Data Control Center of the Federal Drug Administration, Bureau of Product Safety. This system is designed to gather injury data from hospital emergency rooms situated throughout the country. The NEISS system automatically polls each of the hospitals tied in with the system recording the injury data and stores this information for a daily summary register and a detailed case printout for review. Products which produce a high frequency of injury or severity of injuries are referred to the Commission for field investigation by the local Consumer Products Safety Commission offices. The investigation will thus determine what remedial action, if any, the Commission will ultimately take.

The Commission's actions are matters of public record and are available to the public. This act is of importance to the claims industry for that reason. The products investigated by the Commission and the action taken will have some influence on the possible liability of the manufacturer.

Where the Commission has made findings that a certain product is hazardous, generally there has been voluntary compliance with the recommendations, in that either the product is improved or is taken off the market. While there is an appeal procedure, it would be foolhardy for a manufacturer to continue to put such a product in the stream of commerce in the face of the Commission's findings. In addition, the Commission has the power to impose civil penalties (Section 2069) and Section 2071 gives the federal district courts injunctive and seizure powers with respect to the products banned by the Commission.

Under Section 15 of the act (which the Commission calls the "tattle-tail" provision) the consumer may give notification of any products which contain defects. In almost every instance, the manufacturer, distributor, or retailer has taken voluntary action, which means that one of the three options open has been taken, namely to repair the product, to replace the product, or to return the money to the consumer. These consumer notifications are on the increase. Where an accident has happened as a result of the use of an alleged defective product, it is possible for the claimant to file a notification with the Commission and get some sort of a ruling as to the hazardous nature of the product. An adverse ruling in favor of the claimant might have some influence on the settlement of the claim.

In addition, where the Commission has set some safety standards, the fact that the product which is the cause of the accident did not meet these safety standards would be evidence of negligence on the part of the manufacturer.

In any case, the Consumer Product Safety Act is an important piece of legislation and will have its impact on the handling of products liability claims.

1009 Duty to warn

The manufacturer who places his product in the stream of commerce is held to possess a high degree of scientific knowledge with respect to his product. He is bound to anticipate all of the uses to which the product will be put, and, if there are any dangers in connection with such use, the manufacturer is under a duty to warn the ultimate user of any dangerous propensities inherent in the product.

Where there is a duty to warn, the warning must be adequate. If the warning is placed on the package, but in such an inconspicuous place as normally not to come to the attention of the user, the courts generally hold that the manufacturer has failed in performing the duty. For example, in *Haberly* v. *Reardon Co.* (319 S.W. 2d 859), the manufacturer of a cement-base paint printed the ingredients of the paint in very small type on the package. The ingredients indicated that the paint contained lime, but there was no warning that the paint would cause blindness if it got into one's eyes, and a 12-year-old boy lost his eye through contact with a paint brush in his father's hand. Recovery was upheld on the theory that the manufacturer had failed to give adequate warning of the propensities of its product, and that the mere mention of lime as one of the ingredients was not a sufficient warning of the inherent dangers.

The duty to warn exists not only as of the time of the sale of the product, but also where the manufacturer subsequently acquires knowledge that the product sold is dangerous. For example, a laboratory sold a certain batch of vaccine. At the time of the sale, the laboratory believed that the vaccine was safe for use, and that tests that had been conducted up to that time verified such a belief.

Subsequent events proved that the vaccine, if used in a certain way, was dangerous to human life. The laboratory was then under a duty to warn all who may have purchased the product of its dangerous propensities, and failure to do so would constitute negligence, even though at the time of the sale the laboratory had no knowledge that the vaccine was dangerous.

The extent of the warning thus required to be given, and the adequacy thereof, are questions of fact for the jury. It would appear that the minimum requirement would consist of publicity and advertising calling attention to the danger at least comparable to the advertising and publicity that was originally given in order to sell the product.

In *Comstock* v. *General Motors Corp.* (99 N.W. 2d 627), the facts indicated that immediately following the introduction of the 1953 Buick, General Motors and its dealers discovered that the braking system on the 1953 Buick Roadmaster was defective. It was learned that failure of a ring sealer in the hydraulic brake master cylinder allowed brake fluid to escape. The manufacturer then issued written notices to dealers to replace the defective part in the braking system at General Motors' expense whenever 1953 Buicks came in for service. These repairs were made without notice to the owners and even if the owners made no complaint about the brakes. No warning was ever given to owners of 1953 Buicks by General Motors or by the dealer who sold the cars. Testimony also indicated that General Motors did not want the public to know that the brakes were bad, and for that reason did not contact the car owners, did not advertise about the defective braking system, and did nothing to find out who the owners were.

Under those circumstances, the plaintiff who was injured as a result of the brake failure of a 1953 Buick was allowed to recover for the reason that General Motors failed in its duty to take all reasonable means to convey an effective warning to those who had purchased 1953 Buicks when the latent defect was discovered.

In defining the duty to warn on the part of General Motors, the court said:

If such a duty to warn of a known danger exists at the point of sale, we believe a like duty to give prompt warning exists when a latent defect which makes the product hazardous to life becomes known to the manufacturer shortly after the product has been put on the market. . . .

This duty has now been the subject of legislation by the federal government. The National Traffic and Motor Vehicle Safety Act of 1966 (15 USCA 1381 et seq) reads as follows:

1402. Discovery of defects by manufacturer—Notice to purchaser (a) Every manufacturer of motor vehicles or tires shall furnish notification of any defect in any motor vehicle or motor vehicle equipment produced by such manufacturer which he determines, in good faith, relates to motor vehicle safety to the purchaser (where known to the manufacturer) of such motor vehicle or motor vehicle equipment, within a reasonable time after such manufacturer has discovered such defect.

Paragraph (b) of this section sets forth the means of notification to be by certified mail to the first purchaser of the motor vehicle or motor vehicle equipment containing the defect.

In all cases, the "recall" letter sets forth the defect and also directs the purchaser to return the motor vehicle to the dealer who will make repairs at no charge.

Where the purchaser has received the recall letter and thus has knowledge of the defect and continues to drive the car thereafter, the cases hold that he is guilty of contributory negligence or at least he has assumed the risk of injury. In *Buttrick* v. *Arthur Lessard & Sons, Inc.* (260 Atl. 2d 111), the New Hampshire Supreme Court held that the plaintiff's action in operating his car with the knowledge of a defect in the lighting system constituted contributory negligence, and was a bar to his recovery. See also *DeFelice* v. *Ford Motor Co.* (255 Atl. 2d 636); *Hunt* v. *Firestone Tire & Rubber Co.* [448 Pac. 2d 1018 (Oklahoma)].

In *Barth* v. *B. F. Goodrich Tire Co.* (71 Cal. Rptr. 306), the defendant sold a set of tires to the plaintiff for use on his station wagon. The defendant knew that the use of these particular tires on a station wagon such as the plaintiff's, fully loaded, would cause the tires to rupture. For the purposes of making the sale, the defendant did not warn the plaintiff of this dangerous condition. The court in finding in favor of the plaintiff held that the failure to warn is in itself a defect in the product.

There are products which are unavoidably unsafe, especially in the field of drugs, but the manufacturer is absolved of liability, provided that adequate warnings are given. The question of whether or not the warning given (usually to the physician) is adequate is a question for the jury. For example, in *Yarrow* v. *Sterling Drug Co.* [263 Fed. Supp. 159, affirmed in 408 Fed. 2d 987 (South Dakota)], the plaintiff was given Aralen as treatment for an arthritic condition. The drug was known to the manufacturer to have some ocular complications and the plaintiff's doctor received instructions to that effect. As a result of the daily administration of the drug, the plaintiff became 80 percent blind. The court found that, although the drug was not defective, liability was imposed because of the defendant's failure to adequately warn the plaintiff's doctor of the possible side effects from the use of the drug. The court further held that the treatment by the doctor did not insulate the manufacturer from liability. On the other hand, where the dangers attendant with the use of the product are open and obvious, there is no duty on the part of the manufacturer to warn. He can assume that most individuals are aware of the dangers of gasoline, kerosene, acids, natural gas, electricity and other commodities and there is no duty to warn involved. Also, there is no duty to warn in the case of knives, hammers, hatchets, and other implements of like kind.

Likewise the duty to warn will be conditioned by the type of individual using the product. For example, in *Lockett* v. *General Electric Company* (375 Fed. Supp. 1201), the plaintiff was employed by the Sun Shipbuilding and Dry Dock Company. He was seriously injured when caught in the gears of a drive shaft of a vessel being constructed by his employer. He sued the manufacturer of the gears, General Electric, alleging that it should have warned of the need to guard the gears and that it should have supplied the needed guards. The court held that

. . . even assuming that the condition was not readily observable to a person without special experience, it certainly can be assumed that Sun Ship has special experience in the assembly and construction of vessels, and G.E. had reason to believe that those in Sun Ship's employ, working in the vicinity of the gears, would be able to perceive the danger. . . . there is ordinarily no duty to give a warning to members of a profession against dangers generally known to that profession. . . . Where a dangerous condition is equally within the technical knowledge of the supplier and the employer, there is no duty on the part of the supplier to warn the employer of the danger.

1010   Identification of the manufacturer

The person who has suffered bodily injury or property damages as a result of the use of a product, and brings action against the alleged manufacturer, has the burden of proving that the product which caused the injury or property damage was in fact a product made by the manufacturer sought to be charged. The liability may be imposed upon the manufacturer by anyone who was injured as a result of the use of the product, and the liability is not confined to injuries or damage suffered by the actual buyer. The person injured could be in the buyer's family, a neighbor, or even a stranger, but in order for a recovery to be had it must be established that the particular product, which it is claimed was defective or harmful, was actually produced by the manufacturer who is to be charged with liability.

For example, let us assume that a farmer bought a certain fungicide, produced under a trade name, and used this product for dusting his own crops. If the product is defective, and causes damage not only to his own crops but also to the crops of his neighbor, both the farmer and his neighbor would have a cause of action in tort against the manufacturer for the damage caused by the product to both crops. In order to recover, however, both the farmer and his neighbor would have to show that the damage was caused by the use of the particular product, that it was used in accordance with the instructions, and that no other product was used to mixed with it.

It frequently happens that because of the usages of the trade, a distributor or retailer will market a product under his own brand name or label, which product is made by someone else. This is especially true in the canning industry, and it is not unusual to find one cannery labeling the same product for three or four different distributors under three or four different brand names. Under those circumstances, the distributor by the use of his own trade name has adopted the product as his own and will be charged with liability in the case of a defective product just as if he had made it himself. Having used his own trade name, or brand, or label on the product, the distributor may not interpose the defense that the product was processed or manufactured by someone else. It is true that as between the canner and the distributor there may be a hold harmless agreement, or the distributor may have a cause of action against the canner for breach of warranty, but the existence of either the agreement or the cause of action will not in any way affect the action brought by the injured person against the distributor.

1011   *Res ipsa loquitur* as applied to products

In actions against the manufacturer based on his negligence in placing a defective product in the stream of commerce, the consumer has the burden of proving that (1) the product was defective when it left the manufacturer's hands, and (2) the defect was the result of the failure of the manufacturer to exercise reasonable care in its production or inspection. Since both of these processes are within the control of the manufacturer, the plaintiff-consumer was faced with a problem of proof, a problem which in some instances was difficult to sustain and in others impossible.

The courts, however, in some instances have applied the rule of *res ipsa loquitur* and allowed a recovery. Literally translated, *res ipsa loquitur* means "the thing speaks for itself." It is a rule of evidence which creates an inference or a presumption of negligence when certain basic elements are established. These elements are: (1) the accident must be one which normally will not occur unless the defendant was negligent; (2) the instrumentality which caused the accident was within the control of the defendant; and (3) the injured person did not contribute in any way to the causation of the accident. In products cases, the instrumentality which causes the injury is not in the physical control of the defendant-manufacturer at the time of the injury, but the courts applying the rule have held that if the negligent act was committed while the instrumentality was in the control of the defendant, such as the failure to inspect or the production of a defective product, this fact is sufficient to meet the requirement. For example, a bottler overfills a bottle, which subjects the bottle to pressure beyond its capacity to withstand, and when the consumer picks it up, the bottle explodes. If it can be established that the bottle as used by the consumer was in the same condition as it was when it left the bottler, the courts will apply the rule of *res ipsa loquitur*. This means that the plaintiff can establish the basic elements by mere proof of the facts of the accident without any showing of the specific act of negligence claimed to have been committed by the defendant, and this proof will raise an inference of negligence on the part of the manufacturer. Thus, the plaintiff has made out a prima facie, or basic case and is entitled to go to the jury. The defendant-manufacturer then may go forward with the evidence and establish either (1) that there was no defect, or (2) if there was a defect, it did not occur through the negligence of the manufacturer. If the defendant-manufacturer should fail in his proof of either of these defenses, the plaintiff should prevail.

It should be emphasized that in order for the plaintiff-consumer to gain the advantage of the rule he must show that the product which caused the accident was in the same condition at the time of the accident as it was when it left the manufacturer. In a word, the plaintiff must by proof negative any possibility of mishandling of the product from the manufacturer to the consumer. Clearly, the manufacturer would not be liable in a case where the product was mishandled, or interfered with while en route or while it was in the hands of the consumer. The failure of the plaintiff to establish this will deny him the advantage of the rule.

The courts are not in total agreement as to the application of the rule to products cases, some taking the position that it is inapplicable to all cases, but the majority apply the rule sparingly and only when the basic requirements are met. The areas in which the rule is most frequently applied are (1) exploding bottles, (2) foreign substances in bottled goods or goods in sealed containers, and (3) foreign substances in drugs and cosmetics.

1012   Strict liability in tort

As an extension of the doctrine of strict liability applicable in food cases, some courts have applied the same doctrine to all other products which, if defectively made, are dangerous to the consumer. There are two theories in support of this conclusion. The first to be enunciated was the *warranty* theory and the second was the *tort* theory. The warranty theory was first originated in Mississippi in *Coca-Cola Bottling Works* v. *Lyons* [111 So. 305 (1927)]. The court held that the manufacturer's warranty or guarantee that the goods were not defective and fit for the purpose for which they were sold ran with the product for the benefit of the ultimate consumer, thus eliminating the necessity for privity of contract. Thus, if the warranty were breached, the consumer could recover of the manufacturer without any evidence of negligence on his part. This created the imposition of liability without fault on the sellers of defective products.

Later, some courts felt that the warranty theory was too confusing, especially since the word "warranty" was closely associated with the law of contracts. The later cases seem to have discarded the warranty theory and adopted the strict liability in tort doctrine, which more accurately describes the applicable rule of law. The American Law Institute in the Restatement of the Law of Torts, Second, recommends the following rule as being enunciative of the strict liability in tort doctrine:

402A. Special Liability of Seller of Product for Physical Harm to User or Consumer.

(1) One who sells any product in a defective condition unreasonably dangerous to the user or consumer or to his property is subject to liability for physical harm thereby caused to the ultimate user or consumer, or to his property, if

(a) The seller is engaged in the business of selling such a product, and

(b) It is expected to and does reach the user or consumer without substantial change in the condition in which it is sold.

(2) The rule stated in Subsection (1) applies although

(a) The seller has exercised all possible care in the preparation and sale of his product, and

(b) The user or consumer has not bought the product from or entered into any contractural relation with the seller.

The Comment which followed the rule makes it clear that this special liability of the seller is an imposition of liability without fault where a defective product is involved, and regardless of whether the court follows the warranty theory or the tort theory, the result is the same. The following states who have accepted the rule under one theory or the other are as follows:

Tort Theory	*Warranty Theory*
Alaska	Arkansas
Arizona	District of Columbia
California	Florida
Colorado (Fed. Ct. interpreting	Hawaii
Colorado law.)	Iowa
Connecticut	North Dakota
Illinois	Washington
Indiana (Fed. Ct. decision.)	
Kansas	
Kentucky	
Michigan	
Minnesota	
Mississippi	
Missouri	
Nevada	
New Jersey	
New York	
Ohio	
Oklahoma	
Oregon	
Pennsylvania	
Rhode Island (Fed. Ct. decision.)	
Tennessee	
Texas	
Vermont (Fed. Ct. decision.)	
Wisconsin	

In ten states there are decisions which have rejected the application of strict liability without privity of contract. These states are:

Delaware	Rhode Island (But see
Idaho	*Klimas* v. *I.T.&T. Corp.*,
Maine	297 Fed. Supp. 937.)
Massachusetts	South Dakota
New Hampshire	West Virginia
North Carolina	

With the exception of Idaho, all of these states have enacted legislation which would seem to overcome the impact of these decisions. The application of the rule contemplates the existence of a number of elements, which must be considered. These are (1) the seller of the product, (2) a defective product, (3) a dangerous product, (4) a user or consumer, and (5) physical harm to the user or consumer of his property.

1. Seller. The comment which follows the rule defines the seller as the one who markets the product for the use and consumption of the general public. The seller then is the one who places the product in the stream of commerce, or the one who manufactures it or assembles it into one complete unit. The doctrine has been interpreted to include manufacturers, component suppliers, distributors, retailers, bailors, and in two cases builders of housing developments.

Manufacturers. Most of the cases involve suits between the consumer and the manufacturer, and where the manufacturer has placed a defective product in the stream of commerce and it has not been subjected to mishandling from the time it left the manufacturer until it reached the consumer, the rule has been applied.

Component suppliers. There is some doubt as to the application of the rule to a supplier of component parts who supplies them to the manufacturer to be made into the finished product. It would appear that the supplier had delegated the duty of inspection to the manufacturer and that the primary responsibility for placing the finished product on the market rests with the manufacturer. In *MacPherson* v. *Buick Motor Co., supra,* it will be recalled that the court struck down the defense by Buick that the defective wheel which was the cause of the accident was made and supplied by a subcontractor, the court holding that the plaintiff was not required to go beyond the manufacturer of the finished product in order to recover. This may account for the scarcity of cases wherein the ultimate consumer seeks to hold the supplier of a component part liable for the accident. In the following cases, a supplier of component parts was held to be liable to the ultimate consumer, even though the components were incorporated into the finished product by a manufacturer:

Admiralty:	*Sevits* v. *McKiernan-Terry Corp.*, 264 Fed. Supp. 810.
Florida	*Power Ski* v. *Allied Chemical Corp.*, 188 So. 2d 13.
Illinois	*Suvada* v. *White Motor Co.*, 210 N.E. 2d 182.
Michigan	*Hill* v. *Harbor Steel & Supply Corp.*, 132 N.W. 2d 54[1].

In the following New York cases, the court in each instance found that the rule of strict liability was not applicable to the supplier of a component part of the finished product:

Goldberg v. *Kollsman Instrument Corp.*, 191 N.E. 2d 81.
Montgomery v. *Goodyear Tire & Rubber Co.*, 231 Fed. Supp. 447.
Halpern v. *Jad Constr. Corp.*, 244 N.Y.S. 2d 147.

Distributors. There are few cases involving the application of the strict liability rule to distributors, although the distributors would come within the Restatement definition of sellers of products. One of the reasons for the lack of cases may be that the same rule of liability would be applicable to the manu-

---

[1] In this case the jury found that the component part (a valve) was not defective and the submanufacturer was relieved of liability. The court indicated, however, that the supplier of this component part would be liable if the valve had been found to be defective.

facturer so that it would be just as easy to sue the manufacturer as it would be to sue the distributor. Also the relative size and wealth of the defendant-manufacturer is greater than that of the distributor, so that it would be to the plaintiff's advantage to sue the more prosperous defendant, who would also be known to the jury because of his advertising than would be the distributor. In the following cases, actions against the distributor were sustained and the rule applied:

California	*Canifax* v. *Hercules Powder Co.*, 46 Cal. Rptr. 552.
Michigan	*Piercefield* v. *Remington Arms Co.*, 133 N.W. 2d 129.
New York	*Pimm* v. *Graybar Elec. Co.*, 278 N.Y.S. 2d 913;
	Schwartz v. *Macrose Lbr. Co.*, 272 N.Y.S. 2d 227.

For a case refusing to apply the rule to a nonnegligent wholesaler, see *Price* v. *Gatlin* [405 Pac. 2d 502 (Oregon)].

Retailers. The rule has been applied to retailers although at least four states have retained the sealed container exception, holding that where the retailer sold the product in a sealed container, liability would not be imposed upon him if the product proved to be defective and dangerous. The states are as follows:

Florida	*McLeod* v. *W. S. Merrell Co.*, 174 So. 2d 736.
Louisiana	*Lescher* v. *A.&P.*, 129 So. 2d 96.
Mississippi[2]	*Kroger Grocery Co.* v. *Lewelling*, 145 So. 726 (1933).
Texas[2]	*Bowman Biscuit Co.* v. *Hines*, 351 S.W. 2d 153 (1952).

Bailors. While the rule would seem to apply to a sale wherein there is a transfer of title to the product, the rule has been applied to bailors for hire where there was a sale of the use of the product with no transfer of title or ownership contemplated. Some courts have applied the strict liability in tort rule to bailors who lease defective products, which endanger the person or property of those who may foreseeably use the product even though there was no privity between the injured person (usually an employee of the bailee) and the bailor. The following cases have applied the rule:

Florida	*Brookshire* v. *Florida Bendix Co.*, 163 So. 2d 881.
New Jersey	*Cintrone* v. *Hertz Co.*, 212 Atl. 2d 769.
New York	*Delaney* v. *Townmotor Corp.*, 339 Fed. 2d 4;
	Bengait v. *State of New York*, 256 N.Y.S. 2d 876.
Oregon	*Gray Line Co.* v. *Goodyear*, 280 Fed. 2d 294.

Builders. The rule of strict liability has been applied in two cases involving building developers who sold houses which were defective and which caused physical harm to the owner or occupants. The cases are:

Mississippi	*State Stove Mfg. Co.* v. *Hodges*, 189 So. 2d 113.
New Jersey	*Schipper* v. *Levitt & Sons, Inc.*, 207 Atl. 2d 314.

---

[2] Both of these cases were decided prior to the promulgation of the Restatement Rule.

2. Defective product.   Even though the rule imposes strict liability, it is still necessary that the plaintiff meet the burden of proving that the product was defective. He may do this by invoking the rule of *res ipsa loquitur* in appropriate cases, but in every case the plaintiff must establish that the product was defective when it left the hands of the manufacturer and that the product was in the same defective condition when the accident happened. Failure on the part of the plaintiff to establish these elements will deny him the application of the rule.

3. A dangerous product.   Not only must the plaintiff establish that there was a defect in the product, but also that the defect was unreasonably dangerous to the user or consumer. For example, a manufacturer produces a needle that has neither an eye nor a point. The product is defective, but the defect is not of such a nature that it is dangerous to the user. In *Montgomery* v. *Goodyear Tire & Rubber Co.* (231 Fed. Supp. 447), 11 servicemen were killed in the crash of a dirigible. Action was brought against the manufacturer of the envelope fabric or skin of the aircraft. Since there was a competent eyewitness, evidence of the fact that there was no tear in the fabric prior to impact, the court held that the plaintiffs had failed to prove any manufacturing defect in the airship. Also in *Rossignol* v. *Danbury School of Aeronautics, Inc.* [227 Atl. 2d 94 (Connecticut)], the plaintiff, the purchaser of a used airplane failed to allege and establish that the airplane was in the same condition when it reached him as it was when it left the manufacturer, was denied the application of the strict liability rule. The longer the plaintiff has owned and used the product, the more difficult will be his burden of proof. For example, in *Paton* v. *General Motors Corp.* [401 S.W. 2d 446 (Missouri)], the plaintiff drove the car 73,000 miles before the accident happened. It was claimed that there were defects in the car which were never remedied. The court discounted the plaintiff's testimony because of its obvious exaggeration and affirmed a judgment in favor of the defendant. See also *Brown* v. *General Motors Corp.* [407 Pac. 2d 461 (Washington)], which involved a two-year-old car which had been driven 33,000 miles and in which the court reached the same conclusion that the claimed defect did not exist.

4. User or consumer.   Within this definition would come the purchaser, but the terms have been held to include the following:

Members of the purchaser's family	*Klein* v. *Duchess Sandwich Co.*, 93 Pac. 2d 799 (California);
	Blanton v. *Cudahy Packing Co.*, 19 So. 2d 313 (Florida);
	Knab v. *Alden's Irving Park, Inc.*, 199 N.E. 2d 815 (Illinois);
	Hardman v. *Helene Curtis Indus.*, 198 N.E. 2d 681 (Illinois);
	Davis v. *Van Camp Packing Co.*, 176 N.W. 382 (Iowa);
	Nichols v. *Nold*, 258 Pac. 2d 317 (Kansas);

	Manzoni v. *Detroit Coca-Cola Bottling Co.*, 109 N.W. 2d 918 (Michigan) ; *Henningsen* v. *Bloomfield Motors*, 161 Atl. 2d 69 (New Jersey) ; *Greenberg* v. *Lorenz*, 173 N.E. 2d 773 (New Jersey) ; *Griggs Canning Co.* v. *Josey*, 164 S.W. 2d 835 (Texas) ; *Swift & Co.* v. *Wells*, 110 S.E. 2d 203 (Virginia).
Guests of the purchaser	*Tomczuk* v. *Town of Cheshire*, 217 Atl. 2d 71 (Connecticut) ; *Miller* v. *Louisiana Coca-Cola Bottling Co.*, 70 So. 2d 409 (Louisiana) ; *Welch* v. *Schiebelhuth*, 169 N.Y.S. 2d 309 (New York) ; *Thompson* v. *Reedman*, 199 Fed. Supp. 120 (Pennsylvania) ; *Deveny* v. *Rheem Mfg. Co.*, 319 Fed. 2d 124 (Vermont) ; *Dipangrazio* v. *Salamonsen*, 393 Pac. 2d 936 (Washington).
Employees of the purchaser	*Delta Oxygen Co.* v. *Scott*, 383 S.W. 2d 885 (Arkansas) ; *Jones* v. *Burgermeister Brewing Corp.*, 18 Cal. Rptr. 311 (California) ; *Dagley* v. *Armstrong Rubber Co.*, 344 Fed. 2d 245 (Indiana) ; *Hill* v. *Harbor Steel & Supply Corp.*, 132 N.W. 2d 54 (Michigan) ; *Cintrone* v. *Hertz Truck Leasing & Rental Service*, 212 Atl. 2d 769 (New Jersey) ; *Thomas* v. *Leary*, 225 N.Y.S. 2d 137 (New York) ; *Lonzrick* v. *Republic Steel Corp.*, 205 N.E. 2d 92 (Ohio) ; *Brewer* v. *Oriard Powder Co.*, 401 Pac. 2d 884 (Washington).
Lessee of the purchaser Donee of the purchaser	*Simpson* v. *Powered Products, Inc.*, 192 Atl. 2d 555 (Connecticut). *Brown* v. *Chapman*, 304 Fed. 2d 149 (Hawaii) ; *Blarjeske* v. *Thompson's Restaurant Co.*, 59 N.E. 2d 320 (Illinois) ; *Coca-Cola Bottling Works* v. *Lyons*, 111 So. 305 (Mississippi) ; *Nemela* v. *Coca-Cola Bottling Co.*, 104 S.W. 2d 773 (Missouri).
Passengers in automobiles	*Thompson* v. *Reedman*, 199 Fed. Supp. 120 (Pennsylvania).
Passengers in airplanes	*King* v. *Douglas Aircraft Co.*, 159 So. 2d 108 (Florida) ;

Ewing v. *Lockheed Aircraft Corp.*, 202 Fed. Supp. 216 (Minnesota) ;

Goldberg v. *Kollsman Instrument Corp.*, 191 N.E. 2d 81 (New York).

Customer treated with the product in a beauty shop

Garthwait v. *Burgio*, 216 Atl. 2d 189 (Connecticut) ;

Graham v. *Bottenfield's*, 269 Pac. 2d 413 (Kansas).

Child injected with vaccine

Gottsdanker v. *Cutter Labs.*, 6 Cal. Rptr. 320.

Bernstein v. *Lily-Tulip Cup Corp.*, 181 So. 2d 641 (Florida).

Hospital patient supplied with paper cup

Matthews v. *Lawnlite Co.*, 88 So. 2d 299 (Florida) ;

Delaney v. *Townmotor Corp.*, 339 Fed. 2d 4 (New York).

Prospective purchasers testing product

Bystanders.   The American Law Institute in promulgating Rule 402A refused to express any opinion as to whether or not a bystander per se would come within the rule. As to whether or not bystanders, pedestrians, and others in the vicinity who are injured because of the use of the product come within the terms of a "user or consumer" seems to be an open question at this time. In one case (*Piercefield* v. *Remington Arms Co.*, 133 N.W. 2d 129), a Michigan court applied the rule of strict liability against the manufacturer in favor of a bystander injured by the explosion of a defective shotgun. In a Connecticut case (*Mitchell* v. *Miller*, 214 Atl. 2d 694), the plaintiff while playing golf was killed when a car which had been left parked rolled down an incline and struck him. Suit was brought against the owner of the car and the manufacturer. As to the manufacturer it was alleged that the defendant "through extensive advertising" warranted to the owner and to the plaintiff and "to the public generally" that the automobile was reasonably fit for the purposes of proper use, including parking. The court sustained the complaint.

Conversely, in *Hahn* v. *Ford Motor Co.* [126 N.W. 2d 350 (Iowa)], action was brought by a motorist who was injured when his automobile was struck in the rear by a truck with defective brakes. The court held that the motorist had no cause of action against the manufacturer or the seller of the truck. The same facts were involved in *Berzon* v. *Don Allen Motors, Inc.* [256 N.Y.S. 2d 643 (New York)]. The court held that the strict liability doctrine protects only contemplated users of a defective product and that strangers and bystanders are not afforded the protection of the doctrine.

In *Rodriguez* v. *Shells City, Inc.* [141 So. 2d 590 (Florida)], the plaintiff who was watching his brother use a sand kit was injured when a rubber disk disintegrated and a part flew into his eye. Suit was brought against the retailer. In finding in favor of the defendant, the court said:

. . . we find that the plaintiff, Rene Rodriguez was not an injured user of the product but was merely a bystander at the time the accident took place. Whatever inroads have been made in recent years toward liberalizing the availability of the implied warranty action against one not in privity with the injured, the courts of this state have never relaxed the requirement that the injured be a user of the product.

This decision should be compared with another Florida case, *Toombs* v. *Fort Pierce Gas Co.* (208 So. 2d 615), in which a propane gas tank exploded injuring the purchaser and members of a neighbor's family. The trial court held that the bystanders could not recover, citing *Rodriguez* v. *Shells City.* The Supreme Court reversed the decision, holding under the Florida doctrine of implied warranty "dangerous instrumentalities" constituted an exception to the requirement of privity. However, the court did not overrule the Rodriguez decision. Therefore, it would seem that in the absence of a dangerous instrumentality coming within the Florida special doctrine, the *Rodriguez* case still represents the law of Florida with respect to claims by a bystander.

There are several cases which do apply the doctrine of strict liability in favor of a bystander. These are in Arizona, California, Indiana, and Texas. The Arizona case is *Caruth* v. *Mariana* (463 Pac. 2d 83), in which there was a rear-end collision and there was a claim by the plaintiff-motorist that the purchaser's car had defective brakes. In a suit against the manufacturer and the retailer, the court held that both could be held strictly liable to the bystander. The bystander here is the operator of the other car who was a stranger to the transaction between the offending motorist and the retailer and the manufacturer.

In the California case of *Elmore* v. *American Motors* (451 Pac. 2d 84), the facts indicated that Mrs. Elmore due to an alleged defect in the automobile manufactured by the defendant swerved to the wrong side of the road and collided with the car of plaintiff Waters. Both she and Waters sued the retailer and the manufacturer. The court held that Waters, the bystander, was entitled to the benefit of the strict liability doctrine if there was a defect. The question of the existence of the defect was for the jury. The court stated that the purpose of strict liability upon the manufacturer is to shift the costs from the injured persons who are "powerless to protect themselves" to the maker of the offending instrumentality. The court also pointed out that the bystander was in an inferior position as opposed to the consumer, since the purchaser had an opportunity to inspect the product whereas the bystander did not. In spite of this opinion, the court did not relieve the retailer from liability. The court held that to hold the retailer also liable in such cases it would be expected that he would be able to exert pressure on the manufacturer to produce a safe product and the retailer's strict liability "thus serves as an added incentive to safety." [See also *Codling* v. *Paglia*, 327 N.Y.S. 2d 978.]

The Indiana case of *Sills* v. *Massey-Ferguson* (296 Fed. Supp 776), is a federal court decision in which the court was called upon to determine the Indiana law on the subject of the recovery by a bystander. Unfortunately there were no Indiana cases on the subject, but the court decided that the "direction of the law in Indiana was clear." It then decided to adopt a rule protecting the bystander. The facts indicated that the defendant had manufactured a rotary lawn mower and sold it to a car dealer. The plaintiff was on the dealer's premises for the purpose of purchasing a car, while an employee a short distance away was using the lawn mower on the grounds. It passed over a bolt lying on the ground and hurled it 150 feet through the air, striking the plaintiff in the jaw. In deciding that the manufacturer was subject to strict liability to the plaintiff, the court noted the Restatement limitation to "users and consumers," but placed its decision on the emerging weight of authority, citing the *Piercefield* and *Mitchell* cases noted above. This, of course, is a Federal court decision in which the court was "guessing" what the Indiana law is. The Texas case is a state court decision. In *Darryl* v. *Ford Motor Co.* (440 S.W. 2d 630), the plaintiff's car was struck by a truck which allegedly had defective brakes. In an action against the manufacturer, the court cited the *Piercefield* and *Mitchell* cases, holding that "there is no adequate rationale or theoretical explanation why non-users and non-consumers should be denied recovery against the manufacturer of a defective product."

In another federal court case, the court was called upon to apply the law of Vermont to an action involving a bystander in *Wasik* v. *Borg* (423 Fed. 2d 44), which again involved a rear-end collision. It was claimed by the defendant that a sudden uncontrollable acceleration caused the accident. The plaintiff brought action against the purchaser of the car, and the purchaser in turn joined the manufacturer as an additional defendant by means of a third-party complaint. Since there were no cases in Vermont on the subject, the court had to make a "guess" as to the law of Vermont. The trial court estimated that since Vermont had adopted the doctrine stated in the Restatement, Section 402A, there was ample reason to find that the Vermont court would apply the rule of strict liability of the manufacturer to a claim involving a bystander. The Court of Appeals agreed and stated that "this is an advanced doctrine for any court to adopt, particularly for a federal court applying state law which has not yet fully crystalized." The court reasoned that since Vermont had adopted Alternative B of Section 2–318 of the Uniform Commercial Code which extends coverage to "any person who may reasonably be expected" to be affected by the goods, there was every reason to believe that the Vermont courts would extend the right of recovery under strict liability to a bystander.

In a lower court decision (Court of Claims), *Forgione* v. *State of New York,* the court held that where the state had rented a pair of defective roller skates, it was liable not only to the bailee for his injuries sustained as a result of the use of the product, but also to the bailee's companion who was knocked down when the bailee fell. The case was not appealed.

Therefore, while the question of the application of the doctrine of strict liability in tort to injuries sustained by bystanders is still an open one in most states, there appears to be a general trend toward utilizing the doctrine for the protection of an injured bystander, thus including him within the definition of a "user or consumer."

5. *Physical harm.* The plaintiff must establish that as a user or consumer he or his property have suffered physical harm proximately caused by the defect. Merely to establish that physical harm has occurred is not enough. The causal relationship between the defect claimed and the physical harm is an essential element of the plaintiff's proof. For example, in *State Stove Mfg. Co. v. Hodges* [189 So. 2d 113 (Mississippi)], a water heater which was equipped with defective thermostats exploded and completely demolished a new home. In the suit against the manufacturer of the heater, the evidence indicated that the building contractors had failed to install a temperature relief valve on the heater in accordance with the manufacturer's instructions. The jury found that the negligence of the building contractor in failing to follow instructions was the proximate cause of the explosion and exonerated the manufacturer from liability.

1013 Misrepresentation by the seller

Where a seller makes untrue statements either through the general advertising media such as newspapers, television commercials, radio, billboards and sales brochures, he is liable to the consumer or user if the products do not meet the standards of quality as set forth in the advertising. The Restatement rule is as follows:

402B. Misrepresentation by Seller of Chattels to Consumer

One engaged in the business of selling chattels who, by advertising, labels or otherwise, makes to the public a misrepresentation of a material fact concerning the character or quality of a chattel sold by him is subject to liability for physical harm to a consumer of the chattel caused by justifiable reliance upon the misrepresentation, even though

(a) it is not made fraudulently or negligently, and

(b) the consumer has not bought the chattel from or entered into any contractual relation with the seller.

The application of this rule requires the existence of two elements, namely, (1) a misrepresentation of a material fact concerning the chattel made to the public, and (2) justifiable reliance on the misrepresentation by the consumer.

1. *Misrepresentation.* The misrepresentation consists of an untrue statement of the character, ingredients, and the quality of the product as distinguished from mere "puffing" which consists of an opinion by the seller. Therefore, where the seller says that a suit will "wear like iron" this is mere opinion and is not a representation as to the character or ingredients of the product. Also, where the seller's advertising asserts that the product contains some ingredient, such as GL-70, solium or TCP, the nature of which is unknown to the buying public, and which in most instances exists merely in the fertile imagination of the advertising manager, there is no misrepresentation involved. Also where the advertising insists that the product is the "best of its kind" or the "best in its price class," these are matters of opinion and are not misrepresentations even though evidence can be offered that they were untrue and the falsity was known to the seller when he made the statement. Thus, where the seller of a nine-year-old yacht represented that the vessel was in perfect shape, the court held that this was merely an expression of belief or judgment and not a misrepresentation. [*Keating* v. *DeArment*, 193 So. 2d 694 (Florida).] The representation made must be accepted in accordance with its terms and the determination of its truth or falsity will be made on the basis of the actual representation when applied to the facts. For example, in *Jackson* v. *Muhlenberg Hospital* [232 Atl. 2d 879 (New Jersey)], a statement on a bottle of blood that, although the utmost care is used in the selection of donors, the blood may contain hepatitis virus, was construed to mean that the utmost care had been exercised and not a warranty that the blood did not contain hepatitis virus. The court observed that a patient who had contracted hepatitis after an infusion of the blood could recover of the manufacturer or processor if the utmost care had not been exercised in the selection of donors, otherwise not. To the same effect is *Denna* v. *Chrysler Corp.* [206 N.E. 2d 221 (Ohio)], where the manufacturer advertised that the automobile was equipped with "full-time constant control power steering." The court held that this was a mere description of the type of steering mechanism and not a promise with regard to the performance of the particular automobile sold and made to induce the purchase.

The cases are many in which there were misrepresentations of material facts and in which recoveries have been allowed. The earlier cases required that the seller have knowledge of the falsity of his representation and liability was imposed because of the deceit practiced by the seller. This requirement has now all but disappeared and under this rule liability is imposed upon the seller where a misrepresentation is made by him regardless of whether he was aware of its falsity or not. For example, in the cigarette lung cancer cases it was held that where the cigarette manufacturer advertised that smoking its cigarettes would not be harmful to the nose, throat, and lungs such evidence would make out a submissible case to the jury on the issue of whether or not the representation was true. [*Pritchard* v. *Liggett & Meyers Tobacco Co.*, 295 Fed. 2d 292 (Pennsylvania); *Green* v. *American Tobacco Co.*, 325 Fed. 2d 673 (Florida).] Other products which come in contact with the human body or are ingested have also been advertised as being "harmless" or "safe" and in each instance where it could be established that the representation was untrue liability followed. See *Hamon* v. *Digliani* [174 Atl. 2d 294 (Connecticut)] (detergent advertised as being safe for household cleaning tasks); *Toole* v. *Richardson Merrell* [60 Cal. Rptr. 398 (California)] (MER29 advertised as being nontoxic, free from side effects and completely safe); *Schilling* v. *Roux Distributing Co.* [59 N.W. 2d 907 (Minnesota)] (hair dye warranted safe if used according to directions); *Spiegel* v. *Saks 34th St.* (252 N.Y.S. 2d 852) (hand cream advertised to be hospital tested and safe); and *Rogers* v. *Toni Home Permanent Co.* [147 N.E. 2d 612 (Ohio)] (home permanent advertised as safe and "gentle").

Cases involving other products purchased as a result of misleading advertising and in which recoveries were allowed because of injuries sustained are: *Randy Knitwear, Inc.* v. *American Cyanamid Co.* [181 N.E. 2d 399 (New York)] (labels and advertising which accompanied the fabric represented it to be shrink-proof); *Hansen* v. *Firestone Tire & Rubber Co.* [276 Fed. 2d 254 (6th Cir.)] (advertising extolling the safety features of the tire); *McCormack* v. *Hankscraft Co., Inc.* [154 N.W. 2d 488 (Minnesota)] (advertising vaporizer as "safe" and "practically fool-proof"); *Maecherlein* v. *Sealy Mattress Co.* [302 Pac. 2d 331 (California)] (purchase induced by billboard and radio advertising as well as the label on the mattress giving a ten-year warranty).

2. Reliance. The second element is the justifiable reliance by the consumer on the advertising. This assumes that the advertising came to the attention of the consumer and that he was induced either to purchase or to use the product in response to the guarantee or warranty expressed in the advertising.

1014 Market share liability

In the ordinary case where a drug is prescribed for a patient, most adverse effects will manifest themselves within a short time after taking the drug. In most cases, the patient will have no difficulty in identifying the manufacturer, and, if he has a cause of action against him, it can be instituted. In other cases, the effects of the drug may not be apparent for long periods of time —and in some cases, for years. For example, DES (diethylstilbestrol) has been prescribed for expectant mothers during pregnancy in order to prevent miscarriages. This drug had been prescribed since the early 1940s and 1950s. In 1971, it was discovered that a number of the daughters of women who had received DES during pregnancy were developing vaginal and cervical cancer. Because of the passage of time, none of the mothers could establish which pharmaceutical manufacturer made the drug they had taken.

In *Sindell* v. *Abbott Laboratories*, 426 Cal. 3d 588 (California Supreme Court, 1980), the plaintiff was the daughter of a mother who had taken DES during pregnancy to prevent miscarriage. It was claimed that taking the drug caused cancer in the daughter. Since the plaintiff could not identify the manufacturer of the particular product her mother took, she sued a number of manufacturers who produced drugs under the same formula. In making its decision, the court created the market share theory of liability, holding that the defendants were liable to the plaintiff in proportion to their share of the product market unless they could show that they could not have marketed the product taken by the mother. In addition, where all manufacturers were not joined by the plaintiff, they could cross-complain against the others and join them in the lawsuit. Inferentially, the court pointed out that the manufacturers were better able to bear the cost of injury resulting from the manufacture of a defective product, the rationale being that the manufacturers could recover their losses by increasing the price of the product, whereas the plaintiff had no other source of recovery.

Several states are considering legislation with respect to products liability, and the United States Department of Commerce sponsored a study which resulted in the publication of a Model Uniform Products Liability Act. Just how far these acts will be toward restricting the courts in applying the strict liability theory to the market share liability is an open question.

1015   Blood transfusions as a sale

Hospitals and other medical institutions have for years taken the position that the supplying of blood for transfusions constituted a service rather than the sale of the blood as a product, and therefore the rule of strict liability was not applicable. However, in *MacNeal Memorial Hospital* v. *Cunningham*, 266 N.E. 2d 785, the Illinois Supreme Court held that the furnishing of blood for transfusions constituted a sale, and therefore the rule of strict liability would apply. In that case, the blood which was furnished was infected with serum hepatitis, and even though the hospital had no means of testing the blood to determine its purity, the transaction amounted to a sale of impure blood and thus was subject to the rule of strict liability.

As a result of this case, hospitals were reluctant to give transfusions unless the patient released them from liability in advance. This was unfortunate since in many cases the patient was in no physical condition either to give the release or to understand its terms.

The Illinois legislature responded to this situation by passing a declaration of public policy, followed by a statute limiting the liability of any person, firm, or corporation furnishing human blood. The declaration follows:

Declaration of Public Policy.   The availability of scientific knowledge, skills, and materials for the purpose of injecting, transfusing or transplanting human whole blood, plasma, blood products, blood derivatives and products, corneas, bones or organs or other human tissue is important to the health and welfare of the people of this state. The imposition of legal liability without fault upon the persons and organizations engaged in such scientific procedures inhibits the exercise of sound medical judgment and restricts the availability of important scientific knowledge, skills and materials. It is therefore the public policy of this State to promote the health and welfare of the people by limiting the legal liability arising out of such scientific procedures to instances of negligence or willful misconduct. (Ill. Rev. Stat. Ch. 91, Sec. 181.)

The statute enacted in furtherance of this declaration reads as follows:

Limitation of Liability.   The procuring, furnishing, donating, processing, distributing, or using human whole blood, plasma, blood products, blood derivatives and products, corneas, bones or organs or other human tissue for the purpose of injecting, transfusing or transplanting any of them in the human body is declared for the purposes of liability in tort or contract to be the rendition of a service by every person, firm or corporation participating therein, whether or not any remuneration is paid therefor, and is declared not to be a sale of any such items and no warranties of any kind of description nor strict tort liability shall be applicable thereto. . . . (Ill. Rev. Stat. Ch. 91, Sec. 182.)

It is to be noted that under this statute not only hospitals are relieved of the application of the principle of strict liability in tort, but also donors, blood banks, blood processors as well as eye banks and other persons engaged in processing human tissue.

In addition to the state of Illinois, the following states have enacted similar legislation:

State	Statute
Alabama	Code, Title 7A, Sec. 2-314 (4)
Alaska	Section I, AS 45.05-100
Arizona	Revised Statutes, 36-1151
Arkansas	Statutes, Sec. 85-2-316, Subsection (3) (d)
California	Health & Safety Code, Sec. 1623
Colorado	Laws of 1971, S.B. 83 Sec. 41-2-11
Connecticut	Laws of 1971, S.B. 885
Delaware	Del. Code—Sec. 2-316 of Title 5A
Florida	Laws of 1969, Ch. 69-157, Subsections 672-316
Georgia	Laws of 1971, H.B. 582, Sec. 105-1105
Hawaii	Laws of 1971, H.B. 666
Idaho	Code, Sec. 39-3702
Iowa	Code, Sec. 142 A 8
Kansas	Laws of 1971, S.B. 209
Kentucky	Revised Statutes, 139.125
Louisiana	Civil Code, Art. 1764
Maine	Revised Statutes, Title 11, Sec. 2-108
Maryland	Article 43, Sec. 136B
Massachusetts	Genl. Laws, Sec. 691.1511
Michigan	Complied Laws of 1948, Sec. 691.1511
Mississippi	Code, Ch. 6, Sec. 7126-71
Missouri	Laws of 1971, S.B. 7
Montana	Laws of 1971, Ch. 284
Nebraska	Revised Statutes, Ch. 284
Nevada	Revised Statutes, 460.010
New Mexico	Statutes, Sec. 12-12-5
New Hampshire	Laws of 1971, Ch. 471, Sec. 507:8H
New York	Public Health Law, Sec. 580.4
North Carolina	G.S., Sec. 90-220.10, Laws of 1971, Ch. 836
North Dakota	Code, Sec. 41-02-33, Subs. 3
Ohio	Code, Sec. 2108.11
Oklahoma	Statutes, Ch. 34, Sec. 2151
Pennsylvania	Pa., Act of Jan. 28, 1972
South Carolina	S.B. 754, Law 1968
South Dakota	Section 2-315
Tennessee	T.C.A. Sec. 47-2-316 (5)
Texas	Bus. & Com. Code, Sec. 2-316 (e)
Virginia	Code, Sec. 32-304.2
Washington	Laws of 1971, S.B. 157, Ch. 56
Wisconsin	Statutes, Sec. 146-31
Wyoming	Statutes, Sec. 34-2-316 (3) (d)

As to the states which are not listed above, it is possible that the courts or the legislatures have not addressed the problem so that in those areas, the question must be regarded as still open. However, in Utah, the court decided that the furnishing of blood for a transfusion amounts to a service and not a sale, so that no warranty attaches as to the quality of the blood furnished. See *Dibblee* v. *Dr. R. W. Groves Latter Day Saints Hospital,* 304 Pac. 2d 1085.

It should be emphasized that these statutes merely insulate the hospital from liability with respect to the quality of the blood furnished. The hospital still is under a duty to provide sanitary conditions for the transfusion as well as proper equipment and a competent staff. In addition, the hospital or supplier would be liable if the blood were incorrectly typed or mislabeled.

1016   Defenses: Abnormal use

The seller is not bound to foresee that the consumer or user will make abnormal use of the product and will use it for a purpose not intended. The general rule is that the manufacturer has assumed the responsibility only for normal uses and no others. Thus the manufacturer is not bound to anticipate that an automobile will be negligently driven, or an airplane negligently flown. He is not required to produce an accident-free automobile or plane. Likewise where a tire manufacturer produces a tire which is safe for ordinary driving, he is not liable to a consumer who uses the tire on a racing car and sustains injury when the tire blows out in the course of a race. Other cases involving abnormal use in which recoveries were denied are: *Moore* v. *Jefferson Distilling & Denaturing Co.* [126 So. 691 (Louisiana)] (examining oil drum with a lighted match); *Cohagen* v. *Laclede Steel Co.* [317 S.W. 2d 452 (Missouri)] (wire binder for wrapping steel used as a sling to lift bundle of steel with a crane); *Dubbs* v. *Zak Bros. Co.* [175 N.E. 626 (Ohio)] (wearing shoes that did not fit); *Schfranek* v. *Benjamin Moore & Co.* [54 Fed. 2d 76 (New York)] (wall-decorating compound stirred by hand); *McCready* v. *United Iron & Steel Co.* [272 Fed. 2d 700 (10th Cir.)] (casements for use as window frames used by workman as a ladder).

The failure to use the product in accordance with the directions which accompany it is also regarded as an abnormal use for which the manufacturer is not liable. For example, almost without exception all hair dye preparations warn of the danger of using the product without first conducting a "patch" test to determine whether or not the user is allergic to the product. This patch test is made by placing a portion of the dye on the skin and allowing it to remain for a period of time (usually 24 hours) and if there is a reaction the product is not to be used. If no reaction the product can then be used. The failure of the user—be it a beauty parlor or the actual consumer—to conduct the patch test amounts to an abnormal use of the product and which will provide a complete defense to the cause of action. [See *Quist* v. *Bressard Distributors, Inc.,* 260 N.Y.S. 2d 394 (New York); *Romero* v. *And'ra,* 30 Cal Rptr. 645; *Pinto* v. *Clairol, Inc.,* 324 Fed 2d 608 (Kentucky); *Arata* v. *Tonegato,* 314 Pac. 2d 130 (California).]

The failure of a physician to follow the manufacturer's directions in administering a drug exonerates the manufacturer from liability. (*Magee* v. *Wyeth Labs., Inc.*, 29 Cal. Rptr. 322). Other cases involving the failure to follow the manufacturers' instructions include: *Vincent* v. *Tsiknas Co.* [151 N.E. 2d 163 (Massachusetts)] (glass jar pried open with beer can opener contrary to instructions as to opening jar); *Wood Motor Co.* v. *Tobin* [1 Atl. 2d 199 (New Jersey)] (antifreeze used contrary to instructions); *Kaspirowitz* v. *Schering Corp.* [175 Atl. 2d 658 (New Jersey)] (sale and use of product without a prescription as required by the manufacturer's instructions); *Landers* v. *Safeway Stores, Inc.* [139 Pac. 2d 788 (Oregon)] (bleaching solution not diluted as required by instructions); *Bender* v. *William Cooper & Nephews, Inc.* [55 N.E. 2d 94 (Illinois)] (disinfectant not diluted); *Schipper* v. *Levitt & Sons, Inc.* [207 Atl. 2d 314 (New Jersey)] (heating unit installed without recommended safety valve).

On the other hand, there are unusual uses to which the product may be put and which the manufacturer is bound to anticipate. His failure to warn of these possibilities may subject him to liability. Strict liability has been imposed upon the manufacturer of a chair which collapsed while the user was standing on it [*Phillips* v. *Ogle Aluminum Furniture Co.*, 235 Pac. 2d 857 (California)]; the manufacturer of a cocktail robe which caught fire when worn in close proximity to the flame of a kitchen stove [*Ringstad* v. *I. Magnin & Co.*, 239 Pac. 2d 848 (Washington)]; flammable hair spray used without warning of its properties near a candle [*Hardman* v. *Helene Curtis Indus., Inc.*, 198 N.E. 2d 681 (Illinios)].

Where the manufacturer may reasonably anticipate that the product can come into the hands of children, he is held to strict liability if he fails to take all means at his command to label and otherwise warn of the dangers to children which might come about from its use. See *Spruill* v. *Boyle-Midway, Inc.*, 308 Fed. 2d 79 (furniture polish drunk by child); *Haberly* v. *Reardon Co.* [319 S.W. 2d 859 (Missouri)] (child getting lime-based paint in his eye.).

1017 Defenses: Contributory negligence

The defense of contributory negligence as well as the defense of assumption of risk may be interposed to an action based upon the rule imposing strict liability. In products cases there does not appear to be any appreciable distinction between the two defenses, the main difference being in the nomenclature employed.

Generally, the cases hold that the plaintiff is under no duty to discover the existence of a defect in the product and the defense of contributory negligence under those circumstances has not been sustained. Therefore, if he drives on a defective tire without any knowledge of the defect even though he could have discovered it, he is not charged with contributory negligence. On the other hand, if he is aware of the defect and he continues to use the product with knowledge of the defect, he is chargeable with contributory negligence. For example, in *Saeter* v. *Harley Davidson Motor Co.* [21 Auto Cas. (CCH) 2d 643 (California)], the plaintiff continued to operate a motorcycle after he had discovered a defective damper that caused the front wheel to wobble. He was denied recovery since he was guilty of contributory negligence in so doing. Also in *Stevens* v. *Allis-Chalmers Mfg. Co.* [100 Pac. 2d 723 (Kansas)], the manufacturer failed to provide a cover for the takeoff shaft, and since the farmer who used it was well aware of the defect and the danger, he was denied recovery since his continued use of the harvester constituted contributory negligence.

Where the plaintiff's conduct is such that it violated a statute or safety regulation, he is guilty of contributory negligence even in cases where it can be established that there was a defect in the product. For example, in *Walsh* v. *Miehle-Gass-Dexter, Inc.* [378 Fed. 2d 409 (Pennsylvania)], the plaintiff sought damages on the theory that the printing press on which he was injured was negligently designed. The facts indicated that he had attempted to clean a foreign substance from a cylinder while the machine was in operation. A safety regulation promulgated by the Department of Labor and Industry prohibited the oiling or cleaning of machinery while in motion in all places where exposure to hazardous contact is involved. The plaintiff's violation of the safety regulation amounted to contributory negligence per se.

The failure of the user or consumer to follow the manufacturer's instructions as to the installation or use of the product in most cases amounts to contributory negligence. Therefore, in *Oettinger* v. *Norton Co.* [160 Fed. Supp. 399 (Pennsylvania)], the failure of the operator of a grinding wheel to consult the available information concerning the safe operating speed of the grinding wheel constituted contributory negligence when he operated the wheel in excess of its safe maximum speed.

1018   Defenses: Allergy and susceptibility

This defense is involved in the use of cosmetics and other products for intimate body use. The general rule is that the manufacturer is not an insurer against rare and unforeseeable allergies and susceptibility which might exist in a particular person. The manufacturer has a right to assume that the product will be used in a normal manner by persons who have normal reactions. However, where the manufacturer knows, or in the exercise of care should know, that a large number of persons would be likely to be affected by the use of the product, he is liable if he should fail to warn them. Thus in *Sterling Drug, Inc.* v. *Cornish* [370 Fed. 2d 82 (Kansas)], the court held that if the manufacturer knew or should have known that a group of users of its drug would suffer side effects, particularly retinal damage, he had the duty to warn the medical profession of the susceptibility of such a group even though their numbers might be small. Other cases hold that there is no liability on the part of the manufacturer in absence of proof that the use of the product will affect a "substantial" number of persons. [See *Magee* v. *Wyeth Laboratories, Inc.*, 29 Cal. Rptr. 466.] It would appear that if the manufacturer knows or should know that a number of persons will develop an allergy or sensitivity to his product, he is under a duty to warn.

1019 Defenses: Intervening negligence

If the manufacturer puts a defective product in the stream of commerce, he will be held strictly liable even though some intermediate party should have discovered the defect and remedied it. In such a case, the intermediate party who should have discovered the defect can be brought in as a joint tort-feasor, and if there was a duty owing from the intermediate party to the manufacturer, there is always the possibility of a claim for contribution. For example, in *Duckworth* v. *Ford Motor Co.* [320 Fed. 2d 130 (Pennsylvania)], the injuries were sustained when the steering mechanism on a new car failed. The manufacturer brought in the dealer as a joint tort-feasor. The court found that the manufacturer and the dealer were joint tort-feasors, even though their negligent acts were not simultaneous. The manufacturer was negligent in failing to properly assemble the steering mechanism at the factory and the dealer was negligent in failing to repair the steering mechanism properly after the defect had been called to his attention by the buyer. Under the circumstances the manufacturer was entitled to contribution from the dealer.

In *Vandermark* v. *Ford Motor Co.* [391 Pac. 2d 168 (California)], the defendant sought to escape liability for injuries sustained as a result of defective brakes on a new car on the theory that it was the duty of its dealer to service the car before delivery. Therefore the defect in the brakes was caused by something the dealer "did or failed to do" in connection with its servicing duty. In reviewing the applicable law and holding that the manufacturer cannot delegate its duty to place a nondefective product in the stream of commerce, the court said:

In *Greenman* v. *Yuba Power Products*, 59 Cal. 2d 57, we held that "A manufacturer is strictly liable in tort when an article he places on the market, knowing that it is to be used without inspection for defects, proves to have a defect that causes injury to a human being." Since the liability is strict it encompasses defects regardless of their source, and therefore a manufacturer of a completed product cannot escape liability by tracing the defect to a component part supplied by another. . . . Moreover, even before such strict liability was recognized, the manufacturer of a completed product was subject to vicarious liability for the negligence of his suppliers or subcontractors that resulted in defects in the completed product. . . . These rules focus responsibility for defects, whether negligently or nonnegligently caused, on the manufacturer of the completed product, and they apply regardless of what part of the manufacturing process the manufacturer chooses to delegate to third parties. It appears in the present case that Ford delegates the final steps in that process to its authorized dealers. It does not deliver cars to its dealers that are ready to be driven away by the ultimate purchasers but relies on its dealers to make the final inspections, corrections and adjustments necessary to make the cars ready for use. Since Ford, as the manufacturer of the completed product, cannot delegate its duty to have its cars delivered to the ultimate purchaser free from dangerous defects, it cannot escape liability on the ground that the defect in Vandermark's car may have been caused by something one of its authorized dealers did or failed to do.

On the other hand where the product leaves the manufacturer free from defects, or where the user or consumer cannot sustain the burden of proving that the product causing the injury was in the same condition at the time of accident as it was when it left the manufacturer, the manufacturer cannot be held liable. Such a situation might come about where the intermediate parties failed to exercise care in its preservation, as for example in the case of frozen foods which the intermediate parties failed to keep under refrigeration.

1020   Defenses: Disclaimers

In a contract of sale, just as any other contract in which the parties bargain on equal terms, the parties can agree upon any terms or conditions that they see fit. Thus, where the goods are sold "as is" without any warranty or guarantee as to the quality thereof, and the buyer is willing to make the purchase under those circumstances, the seller or manufacturer assumes no responsibility to the user or consumer for any defects which cause injury. This situation is most frequently found in the sale of second-hand or used goods, or goods sold as "factory seconds." Thus, the manufacturer or seller can disclaim liability for defects in any product and escape legal responsibility for injury.

The courts have been quick to recognize that the application of this contractual principle would in some cases result in injustice to the user or consumer. Therefore, they have insisted that the facts must show that the buyer was aware of the disclaimer and took the goods with a full realization of the consequences. Thus, they have not upheld disclaimers where the buyer was unaware of them, or where he bought the product and later discovered notice of the manufacturer's disclaimer in the package. The rationale behind this reasoning is that since the buyer never assented to such terms, he is not bound by them. Also, where there is a disproportion in the bargaining power of the parties, the courts have been quick to come to the aid of the weaker party. In *Henningsen* v. *Bloomfield Motors* (161 Atl. 2d 69), the court struck down the standard automobile warranty which limited the manufacturer's liability to the replacement of defective parts and absolved the manufacturer of any responsibility for bodily injuries for the reason that the parties did not bargain on equal terms, the court noting that the same disclaimer was used by all American automobile manufacturers and a buyer would be forced to assent to these terms if he wanted to buy an American-made automobile. In addition, the Michigan court in *Browne* v. *Fenestra, Inc.* (123 N.W. 2d 730), struck down a disclaimer as contrary to public policy where the product involved was one dangerous to human safety.

In any case, the defense of disclaimer is subject to limitation, and while each case will have to stand on its own facts, the likelihood is that unless the agreement of the parties is clear and there is no difference in the bargaining power of each, the courts will not give effect to a disclaimer.

1021 Uniform Commercial Code

In view of all the various decisions dealing with the matter of products and their sales, it was deemed desirable that the existing law be codified in one statute and that each state enact the same statute. In this way, commercial transactions would be treated on a uniform basis for the benefit of business and the general public. For that reason the National Conference of Commissioners on Uniform State Laws were formed for the purpose of promulgating proposed laws in certain general areas which would be submitted to the various state legislatures with a recommendation that they be accepted and passed. Since the same law would be submitted to each state they were called uniform laws. In the area of products, the first such law was the Uniform Sales Act. This was a codification of the common law and in some ways patterned after the English Sale of Goods Act. From the time of its first submission in 1906, 36 states accepted it as part of their law. In 1958, it was deemed desirable to recodify the law and to combine into one statute the Uniform Sales Act and other uniform laws covering somewhat the same area. The recodification is called the Uniform Commercial Code and at the present writing it has been accepted and enacted into law in 49 of the 50 states, Louisiana being the sole exception. It has also been enacted in the District of Columbia.

1022 Express warranties

An express warranty both at common law and under the Uniform Commercial Code consists of any affirmation of fact or any promise relating to the quality or safety of the product offered for sale. An expression of opinion is not a warranty. If a warranty is breached or is untrue and the buyer sustains injury to his person or property as a result of his reliance thereon, the seller is liable in an action for damages. If there is a mere expression of opinion and the buyer is damaged because of his reliance thereon, there is no liability on the part of the seller. It is sometimes difficult to distinguish between an express warranty and an expression of opinion, but the courts have uniformly held that where there is any doubt, they will find a warranty, thus construing the statements made most strongly in favor of the buyer.

Under the Uniform Commercial Code, the element of reliance by the buyer on the express warranty which was a common-law requirement is no longer necessary in order to maintain an action for breach of warranty. The Commercial Code, Section 2–313 reads as follows:

(1) Express warranties by the seller are created as follows:
    (a) Any affirmation of fact or promise made by the seller to the buyer which relates to the goods and becomes the basis of the bargain creates an express warranty that the goods shall conform to the affirmation or promise.
    (b) Any description of the goods which is made part of the basis of the bargain creates an express warranty that the goods shall conform to the description.

(c) Any sample or model which is made part of the basis of the bargain creates an express warranty that the whole of the goods shall conform to the sample or model.

(2) It is not necessary to the creation of an express warranty that the seller use formal words such as "warrant" or "guarantee" or that he have a specific intention to make a warranty, but an affirmation merely of value of the goods or a statement purporting to be merely the seller's opinion or commendation of the goods does not create a warranty.

The seller mentioned in the statute is not limited to the immediate retailer but with the elimination of the privity requirement includes the manufacturer as well. Either or both may make an express warranty and will be held responsible for any damages caused by the breach. Where one makes an express warranty and the other does not, the one making the warranty will be responsible and the other will not be liable. For example, in *Cochran* v. *McDonald* [161 Pac. 2d 305 (Washington)], the manufacturer affixed a label to each can of antifreeze attesting to its quality and safety and the purchase was made in reliance upon the truth of the label. In an action against the distributor for breach of warranty, the court held that the distributor had made no warranty nor had he adopted the manufacturer's warranty as his own, and therefore, he was not liable to the purchaser. In *Pemberton* v. *Dean* [92 N.W. 478 (Minnesota)], a card attached to a grinding wheel by the manufacturer warranted that the wheel would operate satisfactorily and safely at 1,800 revolutions per minute. In an action against the retailer for breach of warranty, the court held that the dealer by the sale did not adopt as his own the manufacturer's warranty and therefore was not liable to the purchaser for the breach of an express warranty.

1023   Implied warranties of quality

As opposed to an express warranty, an implied warranty arises from the nature of the transaction and by operation of law rather than by agreement of the parties. The two types of implied warranty arising from sales transactions are: (1) warranty of merchantability and (2) warranty of fitness for a particular purpose. One may seem to overlap the other and in many cases recovery may be had based on the breach of either.

1024   Implied warranty of merchantability

The term "merchantable" as used in the Sales Act and the Commercial Code has a broader meaning than salable. It has been construed to mean that at least the article is of medium quality or goodness, and that such goods are reasonably fit for the purposes for which such goods are ordinarily used. It also must compare favorably with other goods of like kind and description that are on the market. The Uniform Commercial Code provides under Section 2–314 as follows:

(1) Unless excluded or modified (Section 2–316), a warranty that the goods shall be merchantable is implied in a contract for their sale if the seller is a

merchant with respect to goods of that kind. Under this section the serving for value of food or drink to be consumed either on the premises or elsewhere is a sale.

(2) Goods to be merchantable must be at least such as

    (a) pass without objection in the trade under the contract description; and

    (b) in the case of fungible goods, are of fair average quality within the description; and

    (c) are fit for the ordinary purpose for which such goods are used; and

    (d) run, within the variations permitted by the agreement, of even kind, quality and quantity within each unit and among all units involved; and

    (e) are adequately contained, packaged, and labeled as the agreement may require; and

    (f) conform to the promises or affirmations of fact made on the container or label if any.

(3) Unless excluded or modified (Section 2–316) other implied warranties may arise from course of dealing or usage of trade.

Section 2–316 (3) (b) of the Commercial Code reads as follows:

When the buyer before entering into the contract has examined the goods or the sample or model as fully as he desired, or has refused to examine the goods there is no implied warranty with regard to defects which an examination ought in the circumstances to have revealed to him. . . .

1025 Implied warranty of fitness

The implied warranty of fitness for a particular purpose arises from the nature of the transaction and the operation of law. The transaction must be one in which the buyer can establish that the seller knew the purpose for which the product was bought and that he, the buyer, relied on the judgment of the seller in selecting the particular product. This rule is subject to two exceptions (1) there is no warranty when an examination by the buyer would have revealed the defect (Section 2–316 (3) (b), *supra*) and (2) there is no warranty of fitness by the retailer where the product is sold under its patent or other trade name.

The Commercial Code provision, Section 2–315 reads as follows:

Where the seller at the time of contracting has reason to know any particular purpose for which the goods are required and that the buyer is relying on the seller's skill or judgment to select or furnish suitable goods, there is, unless excluded or modified under the next section an implied warranty that the goods shall be fit for such purpose.

In most instances the seller's knowledge of the purpose for which the goods are bought can be implied from the nature of the goods. Thus it is not necessary that the buyer actually tell the seller that food is bought to be eaten and other products of like kind which are normally bought for only one purpose. In other cases where the buyer's purpose is unknown to the seller and the purported use is not one for which the article is usually sold, there is no implied warranty.

1026   Sales requirement: Service contracts

In some instances there is a question as to whether or not the contract involved the sale of property or the rendition of services. Clearly, if there is no sale, the provisions of the Uniform Commercial Code have no application and also the strict liability in tort doctrine cannot be applied. The general rule requires a determination of whether or not the predominate basis of the contract contemplates a sale of property or the rendition of services with the transfer of property a mere incident of the services rendered. If the predominating feature of the transaction is the rendition of services, even though there may be a transfer of property involved, it is not a sale. For example, in *Magrine* v. *Krasnica* [227 Atl. 2d 539 (New Jersey)], a patient sustained injury when a latently defective hypodermic needle broke off in her gum. In an action against the dentist the court refused to apply the strict liability doctrine on the theory that the essence of the contract was the rendition of professional services and did not involve a sale. To the same effect, is *Texas State Optical, Inc.* v. *Barbee* [417 S.W. 2d 750 (Texas)], where it was held that the making and fitting of contact lenses by an optometrist for his patient involved a contract for professional services to which no implied warranty attached even though as an incident thereto there was a transfer of property (contact lenses). Also, in *Shaw* v. *Fairyland at Harvey's, Inc.* [271 N.Y.S. 2d 70 (New York)], the court held that the overturning of the gondola on a ferris wheel did not create a cause of action on the part of the occupants for breach of implied warranty of fitness. The court said that the warranty was confined to the sale of goods and, the tranfer of objects as distinguished from an abstract right to occupy an amusement device. Here again the rationale was that the contract involved merely service and not a sale.

1027   Effect of rescission of contract of sale

The general rule is that where two parties to a contract rescind the contract by agreement, such agreement cancels the contract. It is as if there never had been any contract, and the parties to the rescinded contract have neither rights nor obligations under it.

In a contract of sale, the problem has arisen as to whether or not, after the contract has been rescinded by the buyer, he has any cause of action against the seller for breach of warranty which may have occurred prior to the time that the contract was rescinded. Before the contract was rescinded, there would be no question but that if the buyer suffered injury, which injury was traceable directly to a breach of warranty, express or implied, he would have a cause of action against the seller for damages for breach of warranty. The question then to be decided would be whether or not, by a later agreement to rescind the contract, the buyer has by that act extinguished his cause or action for damages for breach of warranty.

There is no clear-cut answer to this question since the problem has been considered in only five states and the decisions are not in agreement. For example, in *Marko* v. *Sears, Roebuck & Co.* [94 Atl. 2d 348 (New Jersey)]] the facts indicated that the plaintiff purchased a rotary power mower from the defendant. At the time of the sale, the plaintiff made known to the seller that he intended to cut grass and weeds on a slope which was very rough and which contained some small stones. The seller pointed out the advantages of this particular mower and expressly warranted that in case the blade came in contact with any rock or other like substance, the motor would automatically shut itself off.

The plaintiff, in the course of using the mower, was injured when the blade struck a rock and the motor did not turn itself off. While the plaintiff was in the hospital recovering from his injuries, he asked a friend to return the lawn mower to the defendant and get his money back. This was done. Thereafter, the plaintiff brought an action against the seller for damages arising out of the breach of the express warranty which the seller had given. The seller defended on the theory that there was not now in existence any contract of sale because of the rescission of the contract at the request of the plaintiff. Therefore, since there was no contract of sale, there could not possibly be any incident of a contract of sale, such as an express warranty on the basis of which the plaintiff could recover.

The court, in disposing of this defense and finding in favor of the plaintiff, called attention to the following provision in the Sales Act: "Nothing in this Act shall affect the right of the buyer or seller to recover interest or special damages in any case where by law interest or special damages may be recoverable." The court held that this provision included personal injuries which had already been sustained as a result of a breach of warranty despite the fact that thereafter there had been a rescission and repayment of the purchase price.

Therefore the court allowed a recovery by the buyer and specifically held that the provision of the Sales Act, which required the buyer to elect between several remedies for breach of warranty, did not deprive him of his cause of action for personal injuries which had already accrued prior to the time of rescission. A similar result was reached in *Garback* v. *Newman* [51 N.W. 2d 315 (Nebraska)] and in *Hochshild* v. *Kohn & Co.* [41 Atl. 2d 600 (Maryland)].

The contrary view has been adopted in Arizona [*Authorized Supply Co.* v. *Swift & Co.*, 271 Fed. 2d 242] and Washington [*Clyde Eq. Co.* v. *Fiorito*, 16 Fed. 2d 106; and *Houser* v. *McKay*, 101 Pac. 894]. In these cases the courts held that the rescission of the contract extinguished all of the rights and obligations of the parties under the contract, even though some rights and obligations were in existence as a result of a breach of warranty. The holding here is that when a contract is rescinded, it is cancelled as of the date it was entered into and it is as if there never was any contract at all.

It should be emphasized that in both of these situations we are dealing with the problem of a claim for breach of warranty which came into existence prior to the date on which the contract was rescinded. It is clear that all states are in agreement that when the contract is rescinded, at least from that point forward, there are no contractual obligations whatsoever. Therefore, if after rescission of the contract, an event took place, such as a personal injury as a result of the use of the product, or property damage resulting therefrom, there would be no liability under the contract, which had already been cancelled and rescinded.

1028   Beneficiaries of the contract of sale

As we have seen, the original concept of liability under a contract of sale was limited to the parties to the contract and unless there was privity of contract between the injured person and the seller, there was no actionable claim. Recognizing the injustice of this harsh rule, the courts sought to make exceptions on the theory that the housewife was the agent of the family for the purpose of purchasing food and in the case of guests she was likewise their agent for the same purpose. Ultimately the courts abandoned the privity requirement and all the artificial rationales that were used to circumvent the rule. The Uniform Commercial Code as being enunciative of the existing law contains the following provision under Section 2–318:

A seller's warranty whether express or implied extends to any natural person who is in the family or household of the buyer or who is a guest in his home if it is reasonable to expect that such person may use, consume or be affected by the goods and who is injured in person by breach of the warranty. A seller may not exclude or limit operation of this section.

In adopting the Uniform Commercial Code, seven states extended the scope of this provision to include "any injured person who may reasonably be expected to use, consume or be affected by the goods." These states are: Alabama, Colorado, Delaware, South Carolina, South Dakota, Vermont, and Wyoming. Arkansas and Virginia have by statute abolished the defense of privity entirely as to the manufacturer and the seller with respect to any injured person who the manufacturer or seller might reasonably have expected to use, consume, or to be affected by the product.

1029   Disclaimer or limitation of warranty

It is possible for a sale to be made in which both parties agree that there will be no warranties, express or implied, or that the liability of the seller will be limited to replacement of certain parts or limited to the liability incurred because of the failure of certain parts of the product to conform to the contract. Any such deviations from the normal contract of sale will be carefully scrutinized by the courts and unless the disclaimer or limitation is clear and understandable no effect will be given to it. Also where the court finds that there was a disproportion in the bargaining power of the parties, it might find the disclaimer to be against public policy. Recognition has been given to the rights of the parties to enter into such agreements by the Uniform Commercial Code under Section 2–316 which reads as follows:

(1) Words or conduct relevant to the creation of an express warranty and words or conduct tending to negate or limit warranty shall be construed wherever reasonable as consistent with each other; but subject to the provisions of this Article on parol or extrinsic evidence (Section 2–202) negation or limitation is inoperative to the extent that such construction is unreasonable.

(2) Subject to subsection (3), to exclude or modify the implied warranty of merchantability or any part of it the language must mention merchantability and in case of a writing must be conspicuous, and to exclude or modify any implied warranty of fitness the exclusion must be in writing and conspicuous. Language to exclude all implied warranties of fitness is sufficient if it states, for example, that "There are no warranties which extend beyond the description on the face hereof."

(3) Notwithstanding subsection (2)

    (a) unless the circumstances indicate otherwise, all implied warranties are excluded by expressions like "as is," "with all faults" or other language which in common understanding calls the buyer's attention to the exclusion of warranties and makes plain that there is no implied warranty; and

    (b) when the buyer before entering into the contract has examined the goods or the sample or model as fully as he desired or has refused to examine the goods there is no implied warranty with regard to defects which an examination ought in the circumstances to have revealed to him; and

    (c) an implied warranty can also be excluded or modified by course of dealing or course of performance or usage of trade.

With respect to the limitation of liability as well as additional remedies in the case of a breach of warranty, the Code under Section 2–719 provides as follows:

(1) Subject to the provisions of subsections (2) and (3) of this section and of the preceding section on liquidation and limitation of damages,

    (a) the agreement may provide for remedies in addition to or in substitution for those provided in this Article and may limit or alter the measure of damages recoverable under this Article, as by limiting the buyer's remedies to return of the goods and repayment of the price or to repair and replacement of non-conforming goods or parts; and

    (b) restort to a remedy as provided is optional unless the remedy is expressly agreed to be exclusive, in which case it is the sole remedy.

(2) Where circumstances cause an exclusive or limited remedy to fail of its essential purpose, remedy may be had as provided in this Act.

(3) Consequential damages may be limited or excluded unless the limitation or exclusion is unconscionable. Limitation of consequential damages for injury to the person in the case of consumer goods is prima facie unconscionable but limitation of damages where the loss is commercial is not.

Just as in the common law, rules with respect to disclaimers and limitation of liability, there must be an agreement or meeting of the minds of the parties as to the details of the disclaimer. Where the manufacturer merely places a notice of disclaimer on the product in an inconspicuous place after the contract of sale is made, he does not have the advantage of the disclaimer, the courts holding that a unilateral attempt at disclaimer is not binding on the other party. [See *Admiral Oasis Hotel* v. *Home Gas Industries,* 216 N.E. 2d 282 (Illinois).]

1030   Damages for breach of warranty

In actions for breach of warranty, the measure of damages in the loss directly and naturally resulting in the ordinary course of events from the breach of warranty. This might mean the difference between the value of the goods as delivered and the purchase price agreed upon. It might mean damages far in excess of the purchase price in cases of personal injuries or of damage to property as a result of the use of the goods.

In personal injury cases, the same elements of damages as would be alleged in any tort cause of action for personal injuries are allowable. These are considered as consequential damages. As to damage to property caused by the use of a defective product, recoveries have been allowed in the following instances:

Value of goods destroyed by using warranted coloring matter which was damaging (*Swain* v. *Schieffelin,* N.Y., 31 N.E. 1025).

Inferior oil for use in making carpets, sold under an express warranty, the buyer being allowed the difference between the value of the carpet as made with defective oil and the value of the carpet if the oil had been of merchantable quality (*Wait* v. *Borne,* N.Y., 25 N.E. 1053).

Damage to flowers due to defective condition of engine in order to pump water into a greenhouse (*Carter* v. *Fisher,* 12 1 N.Y. Supp. 614).

Breach of warranty as to seeds, the damage recoverable being the difference in value between the crop actually raised and the crop which ordinarily would have been raised, less the cost of raising the crop (*White* v. *Miller,* 71 N.Y. 118).

The applicable sections of the Uniform Commercial Code with respect to damages are Sections 2–714 and 2–715. Section 2–714 reads as follows:

(1) Where the buyer has accepted the goods and given notification (Subsection (3) of Section 2–607) he may recover as damages for any nonconformity of tender the loss resulting in the ordinary course of events from the seller's breach as determined in any manner which is reasonable.

(2) The measure of damages for breach of warranty is the difference at the time and place of acceptance between the value of the goods accepted and the value they would have had if they had been as warranted, unless special circumstances show proximate damages of a different amount.

(3) In a proper case any incidental and consequential damages under the next section may also be recovered.

Section 2–715 reads as follows:

(1) Incidental damages resulting from the seller's breach include expenses reasonably incurred in inspection, receipt, transportation and care and custody of goods rightfully rejected, any commercially reasonable charges, expenses or com-

missions in connection with affecting cover and any other reasonable expense incident to the delay or other breach.

(2) Consequential damages resulting from the seller's breach include
  (a) any loss resulting from general or particular requirements and needs of which the seller at the time of contracting had reason to know and which could not reasonably be prevented by cover or otherwise; and
  (b) injury to person or property proximately resulting from any breach of warranty.

The notice provision referred to in Section 2–714 subsection (1) and designated as Section 2–607 reads as follows:

(3) Where a tender has been accepted
  (a) the buyer must within a reasonable time after he discovers or should have discovered any breach notify the seller of breach or be barred from any remedy. . . .

1031 Breach of warranty and wrongful death

An action for wrongful death may be maintained under the statues of each state where the death was caused by the wrongful act, neglect, or default of another. Where death has ensued as a consequence of a breach of warranty express or implied, the question is whether or not a breach of warranty is a "wrongful act, neglect or default" so as to meet the requirements of the wrongful death statute for the maintenance of the action. Some states construe these words to mean that no recovery will be allowed unless the death was negligently or culpably caused. Since a breach of warranty is neither negligent nor culpable, some states hold that it cannot be the basis of a wrongful death action. States denying a recovery in actions for wrongful death based on a breach of warranty are:

California	*Hinds* v. *Wheadon*, 115 Pac. 2d 35.
Connecticut	*Burkhardt* v. *Armour & Co.*, 161 Atl. 385.
Florida	*Whiteley* v. *Webb's City, Inc.*, 55 So. 2d 730.
Mississippi	*Goodwin* v. *Misticos*, 42 So. 2d 397; *Hasson Grocery Co.* v. *Cook*, 17 So. 2d 791.
Missouri	*Sterling Aluminum Products* v. *Shell Oil Co.*, 140 Fed. 2d 801.
New Hampshire	*Wadleigh* v. *Howson*, 189 Atl. 865.
Pennsylvania	*Miller* v. *Preitz*, 221 Atl. 2d 320. *DiBelardino* v. *Lemmon Pharmacal Co.*, 208 Atl. 2d 283.

Actions for wrongful death based on a breach of warranty have been held to be maintainable in the following states:

Arkansas	*Heinemann* v. *Barfield*, 207 S.W. 62.
Illinois	*Greenwood* v. *Thompson*, 213 Ill. App. 371.
Indiana	*Dagley* v. *Armstrong Rubber Co.*, 334 Fed. 2d 245.
Massachusetts	*Schuler* v. *Union News Co.*, 4 N.E. 2d 465.
Minnesota	*Keiper* v. *Anderson*, 165 N.W. 237.
New York	*Greco* v. *S. S. Kresge Co.*, 12 N.E. 2d 557.

It should be emphasized that these cases involve only the question of whether or not an action for wrongful death can be maintained for breach of warranty. It is possible that the same set of facts could form the basis for a negligence action in which case the action conceivably could be maintained in every state.

1032   Indemnity and contribution

The terminology of buyer and seller is not necessarily restricted to a retailer and his customer, but in the chain of distribution from the manufacturer to the retailer the product may pass through several hands and each of these including the manufacturer could occupy the position of buyer or seller with relation to the other. As between the retailer and the manufacturer, the retailer is the buyer and the manufacturer is the seller. The retailer in that case would be entitled to all the rights of a buyer as against the manufacturer. Consequently, when a retailer, acting as a seller, has been forced to settle a claim brought against him by his buyer, he has suffered damage as a result of the sale made by the manufacturer to him. Therefore in that case, the retailer as the buyer from the manufacturer can assert a cause of action against the manufacturer either for breach of warranty or for negligence in the production of a defective product. The retailer then is entitled to indemnity from the manufacturer and the measure of such indemnity will be the damages which he, the retailer has suffered. This will include the settlement made and any other expenses which may have been imposed upon him, such as legal fees, court costs, and the like. Also, if he can show that he has suffered a deprivation of business, loss of goodwill or damage to his reputation, he would be entitled to a recovery for these items as well. Where the retailer or other person in the chain of distribution is sued, the Uniform Commercial Code provides for the vouching in of the responsible party as an additional defendant. Section 2–607 provides as follows:

(5) Where the buyer is sued for breach of warranty or other obligation for which his seller is answerable over

(a) he may give his seller written notice of the litigation. If the notice states that the seller may come in and defend and that if the seller does not do so he will be bound in any action against him by his buyer by any determination of fact common to the two litigations, then unless the seller after seasonable receipt of the notice does come in and defend, he is so bound.

Under this section, if the retailer were sued for breach of warranty of merchantability in that the product was defective, notice to the seller or manufacturer to come in and defend will require the manufacturer to do so, otherwise the manufacturer would be bound by any determination of fact reached in the litigation, such as the existence of the defect, and in a subsequent suit against the manufacturer he could not relitigate the issue of whether or not there was a defect.

As to contribution, at common law there was not contribution between joint tort-feasors. Some states have passed Joint Tortfeasors Contribution Laws which enable one joint tort-feasor who has paid more than his proportionate share of the judgment to recover the excess from the other. In products cases this might come about where the manufacturer produced a defective article which in turn was improperly assembled by the retailer and who failed to discover the defect, in which case both the retailer and the manufacturer are joint tort-feasors.

1033   Statutes of limitations

The general rule is that the statute of limitations in sales contracts begins to run from the time of sale or from the time of the delivery of the product. There are a limited number of cases where the courts have held that the time period begins to run when the defect is discovered, which defect could not have been discovered at the time of sale. For example, where a manufacturer warranted that his carpet would last for a period of six to eight years following its installation, the court held that the right of action on the warranty did not accrue until it became apparent that the carpet would not last for the guaranteed period, and not the date of the sale since the truth of the warranty could not be determined at the time it was made but was ascertainable only by the passage of time. [See *Southern California Enterprises* v. *D. N. E. Walter & Co.*, 178 Pac. 2d 785 (California).]

The Uniform Commercial Code under Section 2–725 provides as follows:

(1) An action for breach of any contract for sale must be commenced within four years after the cause of action has accrued. By the original agreement the parties may reduce the period of limitation to not less than one year but may not extend it.

(2) A cause of action accrues when the breach occurs, regardless of the aggrieved party's lack of knowledge of the breach. A breach of warranty occurs when tender of delivery is made, except where a warranty explicitly extends to future performance of the goods and discovery of the breach must await the time of such performance the cause of action accrues when the breach is or should have been discovered.

(3) When an action commenced within the time limited by subsection (1) is so terminated as to leave available a remedy by another action for the same breach such other action may be commenced after the expiration of the time limited and within six months after the termination of the first action unless the termination resulted from voluntary discontinuance or from dismissal for failure or neglect to prosecute.

(4) The section does not alter the law on tolling of the statute of limitations nor does it apply to causes of action which have accrued before this Act becomes effective.

The first problem posed by this legislation refers to the matter of personal injury claims, since most states have statutes of limitations applicable to such claims which require that the action be begun within a shorter period of time than the four years set forth in this statute. In *Gardiner* v. *Philadelphia Gas Works* (197 Atl. 2d 172), the Pennsylvania Supreme Court held that an action for personal injuries brought for breach of warranty was governed by the four-year limitation of the Commercial Code rather than the general statute which required that personal injury actions be commenced within two years after the cause of action accrues.

1034   Long-arm statutes

Where the manufacturer is located outside of the state of the plaintiff's domicile and is not subject to the service of process within the state, some states, for the protection of their citizens, have enacted so-called long-arm statutes. These are designed to enable the plaintiff to obtain personal jurisdiction over nonresidents who otherwise would not be subject to the service of process within the confines of the state.

There is no uniformity among these state statutes. Some "borrow" from their nonresident motorist acts, and require that in addition to notice to the defendant that the service of process be made upon some state official. Others merely require that service to be made upon the nonresident defendant. (See Ill. Rev. Stat. c. 110, Sections 16, 17.) Usually these statutes base their jurisdiction, as in the nonresident motorist acts, upon the doing of some act within the state. For example, North Carolina (Gen. Stat. Sec. 55–145) confers jurisdiction on the North Carolina courts with respect to any cause of action arising "out of the production, manufacture or distribution of goods by such corporation with the reasonable expectation that such goods are to be used or consumed in the state and are so used or consumed, regardless of how or where the goods were produced, manufactured, marketed or sold or whether or not through the medium of independent contractors or dealers."

Virginia by the Va. Code Ann. Section 8–81.2, confers jurisdiction on its courts to a cause of action by a Virginia resident arising from a person's "causing in this state to any person by breach of warranty expressly or impliedly made in the sale of goods outside the state when he might reasonably have expected such person to use, consume, or be affected by the goods in this state, provided that he also regularly does or solicits business, or engages in any persistent course of conduct, or derives substantial revenue from goods used or consumed or services rendered in the state."

Illustrative of the problems in this type of jurisdictional proceeding is the case of *Gray* v. *American Radiator and Standard Sanitary Corp.* [176 N.E. 2d 761 (Illinois)], wherein the defendant manufactured a safety valve in Ohio and sold it to an independent dealer outside of Illinois. The valve was later attached to a water heater in Pennsylvania and later sold to an Illinois consumer. While being used in Illinois, the valve exploded, injuring the plaintiff. The defendant was served with process in Ohio. The Supreme Court of Illinois held that a "tortious act" within the meaning of the Illinois long-arm statute, had been committed in Illinois and upheld the recovery.

The Nevada long-arm statute (N.R.S. 14.080) provides as follows:

Any company . . . which manufactures, produces, makes, markets or otherwise supplies directly or indirectly any product for distribution, sale or use in this state may be lawfully served with any legal process in any action to recover damages for injury to person or property resulting from such distribution, sale or use in this state.

In *Metal-Matic, Inc.* v. *The Eighth Judicial District* (415 Pac. 2d 617), the injuries were allegedly caused by a defective boat railing, manufactured by *D* Corporation, a Minnesota corporation. *D* Corporation contended that it never directly or indirectly solicited or conducted any business in Nevada. *D* Corporation was the manufacturer of a component part of the boat, the railing, and the final product was assembled by a different manufacturer who then shipped it to a distributor in Nevada. The boat was purchased from a retail dealer. While the boat was being used by the purchaser, a passenger leaned against the railing, which gave way and he fell into the water and was drowned. In sustaining Nevada jurisdiction, the court said:

In our case, a manufacturer of a component part of a boat can presume or reasonably foresee that its potential market would be Lake Mead or Lake Tahoe, in Nevada, as well as the lake areas of Minnesota, Wisconsin, Michigan or any other part of the United States where navigable lakes or waters are located. It should not matter that the purchase was made from an independent middleman or that someone other than the defendant shipped the product into this state. . . . Our statute says directly what the Illinois and New York courts had to interpret. . . . Where it is reasonably foreseeable that a product will enter the flow of commence, the manufacturer of that product can expect to be sued in any state where the product is alleged to have caused an injury. This is without regard to how many hands have touched the product from it production to the time of injury.

Therefore, whether or not jurisdiction will be assumed will depend upon the type of statute and the extent to which it will apply to a given situation. In addition, the Supreme Court of the United States has not as yet directly ruled on the constitutionality of these statutes. They have been attacked as being violative of the due process clause. However, *International Shoe Co.* v. *Washington* [326 U.S. 310 (1945)], laid down the test for determining the validity of service of process on nonresidents under the due process clause. The court said:

[The due process clause] requires only that in order to subject a defendant to judgment in personam, if he be not present within the territory of the forum, he have certain minimum contacts with it such that the maintenance of the suit does not offend traditional notions of fair play and substantial justice.

In *McGee* v. *International Life Insurance Co.* [355 U.S. 220 (1957)], the Supreme Court upheld the jurisdiction of the California court to hear and determine a case involving a nonresident defendant based on a single act within the state. Thus, these cases may give some insight as to the position that the Supreme Court is likely to take with respect to long-arm statutes.

1035 Completed operations as a product

Frequently an owner or an employer will engage the services of an independent contractor to do some construction or alteration work. The work could consist of the erection of an entire building, alterations to an existing building, the installation of furnaces, plumbing, roofing, or electrical wiring as well as the building of a road. The employer or owner could be a person, firm or corporation, which would include the state, county, or municipal corporation.

The "product" is the completed work after the independent contractor has removed his men and materials from the job and after the work has been accepted by the owner or employer. A problem arises where the work has been completed and accepted, but the work was defectively or negligently done so much so that an accident occurred which resulted in bodily injury or property damage to third parties. The courts have been called upon to consider the liability, if any, of the independent contractor and the liability of the owner who accepted the work and continued to maintain the premises. There are two schools of thought among the courts. Some have adopted the accepted work doctrine with its exceptions. Others apply the rule of strict liability on the part of the contractor, thus utilizing the general products liability rule. We will consider each view as follows:

1. *Accepted work doctrine.*   This view establishes the rule that the independent contractor is not liable for negligently causing injury to third persons after the completion of his work and the acceptance of it by the owner, the courts holding that there is no privity of contract between the contractor and the third persons and that the only duty owed by the contractor is to the owner arising out of their contractual relationship. For example, in *Southwestern Bell Telephone Co.* v. *Travelers Indemnity Co.* [479 S.W. 2d 232 (Arkansas)], an independent contractor was employed to perform certain plowing and trenching work and to lay the telephone company's ground cables and wires. The work was completed and accepted by the telephone company. About two months after the acceptance and payment to the independent contractor, a third party was injured when he tripped and fell because of a depression in the trench which had resulted from the settling of the backfill due to rainfall. Even though evidence was offered to the effect that after acceptance of the work by the telephone company, it was agreed that upon notice the contractor would return to the job and refill any sunken trenches, the court found that the telephone company was solely liable and exonerated the contractor from liability. The court said:

. . . we recognize the general rule that where there is a practical acceptance of the contractor's work thereupon the liability of the contractor as to third persons ceases and the responsibility for maintaining or using the property in its defective state is shifted to the proprietor.

In *Black* v. *Peter Kiewit Sons Co.* [497 Pac. 2d 1056 (Idaho)], the plaintiffs brought a negligence action against the independent contractor and the Idaho Department of Highways when an oil slick on the highway caused their automobile to go out of control. It was stipulated that the contractor had constructed the highway in accordance with the plans and specifications published by the state and that the State Highway Engineer had accepted the work as completed prior to the time of the accident. Summary judgment in favor of the contractor was granted. The court said:

A contractor is required to follow the plans and specifications and when he does so, he cannot be held to guarantee that the work performed as required by his contract will be free from defects, or withstand the action of the elements, or that the completed job will accomplish the purpose intended. He is only responsible for improper workmanship or other faults, or defects resulting from his failure to perform.

The rationale behind both of these cases is that the employer or owner having accepted the work as completed and having maintained the premises from that point on is liable to third persons who may be injured as a result of a defect on the premises. The owner, having accepted the work, adopted the finished product as his own. In the second case, there is another reason to hold the Highway Department responsible. They designed the work and set the specifications. The contractor was merely the medium through which their design was put into existence.

2. *Exceptions to the accepted work doctrine.* Where the completed work has an inherently dangerous defect imminently dangerous to third persons, the immunity doctrine does not apply, even though the employer or owner accepted the work with the knowledge of the dangerous nature of the work. In *Paul Harris Furniture Co.* v. *Morse* [139 N.E. 2d 275 (Illinois)], the court pointed out the exceptions to the general rule insulating the contractor from liability after the work was completed and accepted. The court said:

Plaintiffs, on the other hand, maintain that this case falls within the exceptions to the general rule. The general rule is that where an independent contractor is employed to construct or install any given work or instrumentality, and has done the same and it has been accepted by the employer and the contractor discharged, he is no longer liable to third persons for injuries received as the result of defective construction or installation. This rule, however, is subject to certain well recognized exceptions whereby a contractor may be held liable even after acceptance of his work by the contractee (1) where the thing dealt with is imminently dangerous in kind, such as explosives, poisonous drugs and the like, (2) where the subject matter of the contract is to be used for a particular purpose, requiring security for the protection of life, such as a scaffold, and (3) where the thing is rendered dangerous by a defect of which the constructor knows but deceitfully conceals, and which causes an accident when the thing is used for the particular purpose for which it was constructed. . . .

In this case, the contractor was employed to excavate a hole and to install a propane gas tank therein. In the course of the operation, he negligently cut the tile leading to the sewer, and after putting the tank in place, he sealed off the tank but did nothing to seal up the hole leading to the sewer. He was held liable for the ensuing explosions which damaged several stores. [See also *Welding Products of Georgia* v. *S. D. Mullins Co.*, 193 S.E. 2d 881 (Georgia).]

3. *Abrogation of the accepted work doctrine.* A number of courts which have had occasion to reexamine the accepted work doctrine have concluded that the contractor should be held liable for his negligent work, regardless of whether the injury is sustained by the owner or employer or by a third person, and further that the failure of the owner to inspect the work or to act to prevent harm after discovering that the work has not been done properly is not necessarily a superseding cause. Such a failure of the owner would subject him to a liability which is concurrent with that of the contractor, but does not, as a matter of law, absolve the contractor of his negligence.

In *Hilla* v. *Gross* [204 N.W. 2d 712 (Michigan)], a sun deck constructed by an independent contractor collapsed and injured the plaintiff who was a social guest on the owner's premises. The work had been completed by the independent contractor and the work was accepted by the owner. The independent contractor interposed the defense of the accepted work doctrine under which the contractor would be absolved from all liability for his own negligence once the work had been completed and accepted by the owner. The court held that the accepted work doctrine was no longer the law in Michigan and specifically overruled the defense. The court further stated that the consequence of this holding is that the contractor continues to be liable for his negligent work subject to the usual proof in tort litigation as to negligence and proximate cause. In *Talley* v. *Skelly Oil Co.* [433 Pac. 2d 425 (Kansas)], the court specifically overruled the accepted work doctrine, noting that an increasing number of jurisdictions have discarded the old and somewhat discredited rule of nonliability on the part of the independent contractor where the work had been completed and accepted by the owner. The court said that the more modern view, which simply stated, imposes liability upon a contractor for injuries to a third person occurring after the completion of his work and its acceptance by the contractee, where the work is reasonably certain to endanger third persons if the work has been negligently performed. [See also *Atkinson* v. *St. Paul Ins. Co.*, 263 So. 2d 85 (Louisiana).]

4. *Strict liability.* Where the negligence of the contractor is the cause of an injury to a third party, some courts have held the contractor liable under the strict liability in tort doctrine in much the same way as a manufacturer is liable to the ultimate user or consumer for a dangerous and defective product. For example, in *Schipper* v. *Levitt & Sons, Inc.* [207 Atl. 2d 314 (New Jersey)], the defendant was held liable to a tenant who was injured by a defectively designed hot-water system. The house was built for the owner and accepted by him. It was subsequently leased to the plaintiff's family. There was, of course, no privity of contract between the tenant and the builder. However, the court could see no difference between the sale of a house and the sale of a chattel, such as an automobile and that strict liability would be imposed on the builder. The court further pointed out that the plaintiff's burden still remains of establishing to the jury's satisfaction from all the circumstances that the design of the hot-water system was unreasonably dangerous and proximately caused the injury.

New Jersey finally overruled the "completed and accepted" rule in *Totten*

v. *Gruzen* (245 Atl. 2d 1). In this case there was a claim by a tenant against the architects and the general contractor as well as the heating contractor. The work had been completed and accepted by the owner, Housing Authority of the City of Hackensack as a project for low-income families. The premises were rented by the housing authority to the plaintiff. In overruling the accepted work doctrine, the court could see no good reason why the negligence principles adopted in the *Schipper* case with respect to mass housing developers should not be applied to all builders and contractors. Such liability may rest on architects and engineers on the basis of improper design as well as contractors for defective materials, equipment, and workmanship.

5. *Effect of the passage of time.* It is sometimes urged that where there has been a period of time elapsing between the time the work was done by the independent contractor and the time of the accident, the failure of the owner to correct the condition or to require the contractor to remedy the defect becomes a superseding cause of the accident, thus relieving the contractor from liability. It is urged that where the defective condition existed for a long period of time, the owner knew or should have known of the condition. It is further urged that the contractor has no right to reenter the premises to do any further work after his operation has been completed and the work accepted by the owner. In all the cases in which this contention has been advanced the courts have held that the mere passage of time presents a fact question and is not a question of law for the court. For example, in *Hanna* v. *Fletcher* (231. Fed. 2d 469), the U.S. Court of Appeals for the District of Columbia stated: "If a porch stands for seven years and then collapses the fact that it stood for seven years would not eliminate negligence as a cause of its collapse." In *Hale* v. *Depaoli* [201 Pac. 2d 1 (California)], it was contended that the passage of 18 years from the date of construction of the structure causing the accident relieved the contractor from liability to a third person. In rejecting the contention the court stated that "the mere passage of time presents questions of fact and not of law." Therefore, in each case, the question of the effect of the passage of time in a given situation will be determined by the jury and not by the court. In other words, there is no standard by which a measurement can be made as to when the independent contractor can be free from possible liability.

On the other hand, if the owner has maintained the structure in an unsafe condition and this fact is known to him or because of the length of time involved he should have known of it, the owner is liable to the injured third party as a tort-feasor.

The Restatement, Second, Torts, Section 452 recommends the rule, as follows:

Third Person's Failure to Prevent Harm

(1) Except as stated in Subsection (2), the failure of a third person to act to prevent harm to another threatened by the actor's negligent conduct is not a superseding cause of such harm.

(2) Where, because of the lapse of time or otherwise, the duty to prevent harm to another threatened by the actor's negligent conduct is found to have shifted

from the actor to a third person, the failure of the third person to prevent such harm is a superseding cause.

The Restatement gives the following example of the application of the rule:

The *A* Electric Company, under contract with *B* Village, constructs an electric transformer pole, and turns it over to the Village. The contract expressly provides that the Village assumes all responsibility for inspection, care, and maintenance of the pole and for its condition after it is turned over. Through the negligence of *A* Electric Company, two wires on the pole are set too close together, so that high winds, which are not uncommon in the vicinity, rub the wires together and wear off the insulation. *B* Village does nothing to inspect or maintain the pole. At the end of a year and a half, the insulation on the wires is worked through, and as a result a current of 2,300 volts comes over the wire of a telephone while *C* is using it. *C* is injured. *A* Electric Company is not liable to *C*.

Thus, in this illustration, the duty of inspection fell to *B* Village and although there was no inspection, the Village is charged with the knowledge that it would have received had an inspection been made. Therefore, its failure to act for the protection of *C*, and its failure to correct the dangerous condition absolved the *A* Electric Company from liability, even though it was guilty of the initial negligent act. Actually, the duty of maintaining the pole in reasonably safe condition passed to *B* Village and there was no further duty on the part of *A* Electric Company. Comment (f) of the Restatement which follows this example further explains the application of the Rule. It reads as follows:

Even in the absence of any contract or agreement, the circumstances may be such that the court will find that all duty and responsibility for the prevention of harm has passed to the third person. It is apparently impossible to state any comprehensive rule as to when such a decision will be made. Various factors will enter into it. Among them are the degree of danger and the magnitude of the risk of harm, the character and position of the third person who is to take the responsibility, his knowledge of the danger and the likelihood that he will or will not exercise proper care, his relation to the plaintiff or to the defendant, the lapse of time, and perhaps other considerations. The most that can be stated here is that when, by reason of the interplay of such factors, the court finds that full responsibility for control of the situation and prevention of the threatened harm has passed to the third person, his failure to act is then a superseding cause, which will relieve the original actor of liability.

Therefore, it would seem that in the case of completed operations, where the construction or alteration was negligently performed, the duty of care would not pass to the owner or employer unless the defect was open and obvious or that there were other factors that would put the owner on notice of the fact that there was a defect. With this knowledge, a failure on the part of the owner to repair the condition would then become a superseding cause of the accident insulating the contractor from liability. On the other hand, if the defective condition were so concealed that the owner would have no reason to suspect the existence of a defect until an accident occurred, then the contractor's liability and responsibility would continue, regardless of the amount of time which had passed from the time of the work and the happening of the accident. For example, in *Hilla* v. *Gross, supra,* the contractor substituted aluminum support columns for the steel columns specified in the original plans in the construction of a sun deck. Approximately two-and-one-half years after completion, the accident occurred. There was no way that the owner could have been aware of the substitution since the columns were completely covered. Under those circumstances there was no duty of care transferred to the owner and the contractor's liability remained. There is another example given in the Restatement, which, while it does not refer to completed operations, is illustrative of the point that where the owner is aware of the defect, even though it is caused by the negligence of the contractor, he is under a duty to correct it and his continued use of the defective article or premises shifts the burden of responsibility from the contractor to the owner. The example is as follows:

A manufactures and sells an automobile with a defective hood catch, creating the danger that on a rough highway the hood will fly up and obscure the vision of the driver. The car is sold by the dealer to *B*. *A* is notified of the defect in the car and the danger, and sends out to its dealers a new safety catch for installation in all such cars, in order to remedy the defect. The dealer calls *B*, and offers him the new safety catch, warning him of the danger and urging him to install it. *B* refuses to do so. After driving the car for a year, *B* sells it to *C*, who is ignorant of the danger. While *C* is driving the car, the hood flies up, and *C* is injured. *A* is not liable to *C*.

Therefore, even though the work (the manufacture of the car) was negligently performed, the failure on the part of the owner to remedy the defect when its existence came to his knowledge shifted the responsibility for the accident from the manufacturer to the owner.

1036 Products liability insurance

Coverage for the "products hazard" is usually added to a public liability policy covering premises and operations. The main policy will exclude property damage or bodily injury arising out of the products hazard, but the addition of the products endorsement will eliminate the exclusion. If there is no products hazard insurance, the exclusion will be applied.

The products hazard is defined as follows:

. . . "products hazard" includes bodily injury or property damage arising out of the named insured's products or reliance upon a representation or warranty made at any time with respect thereto, but only if the bodily injury or property damage occurs away from premises owned by or rented to the named insured and after physical possession of such products has been relinquished to others.

The products of the named insured are defined as follows:

. . . "named insured's products" means goods or products manufactured, sold, handled or distributed by the named insured or by others trading under his name, including any container thereof (other than a vehicle), but named insured's products shall not include a vending machine or any property other than such container, rented to or located for use of others but not sold.

Premises and operations coverage alone does not cover the normal products liability claim. Premises and operations coverage applies only to injuries occurring on, or adjacent to, the insured's premises. The coverage applies as well to injuries occurring during the progress of the insured's operations away from the premises. It does not apply where the injury occurred away from the insured's premises and after the insured's operations were completed. The insured may purchase products liability insurance as well as completed operations coverage. (See Section 1035, *infra*.) However, problems of coverage do arise where the insured has only premises and operations coverage and the accident occurs from a cause closely related with the operations of the premises. For example, in *St. Paul Fire & Marine Ins. Co. v. Coleman* (316 Fed. 2d 77), the court found that the products and completed operations exclusion was not broad enough to avoid coverage. The insured boatyard negligently refueled a boat at the boatyard's pier. The boat left the pier and caught fire some 73 feet away. The court held that the premises and operations coverage applied to these particular facts. The rationale of the court's decision was that it was not altogether clear that the coverage actually purchased, which included occurrences arising out of the "ownership, maintenance and use of premises and all operations" would not apply to a fire on a boat where the negligent act complained of actually occurred on the premises even though the fire as a result thereof occurred away from the insured's premises. It is to be expected that in close situations, such as this, the court will find coverage, in spite of the exclusion to the contrary.

Damage to the product itself.   Damage to the insured's products themselves out of which the accident arises is specifically excluded from the policy coverage. Obviously, this would not seem to be an insurable item for the reason that the insurer would in effect be guaranteeing the quality of the insured's products. If such insurance were to be made available, the insured could produce an inferior product and make claims against the insurer for all such loss. The exclusion was applied in *Advanced Refrigeration & Appliance Co. v. Insurance Company of North America* (349 N.Y.S. 2d 195), where a refrigerator sold by the insured was defective. The purchaser's claim was for breach of warranty. The court held that the insured's products liability coverage did not provide coverage for the reason that the only damage was to the refrigerator itself. The court said:

"Products liability" as contemplated under the only reasonable interpretation which can be placed upon the policy issued to plaintiff, must be held to mean the liability arising when, as a result of a defect in the product, there is bodily injury, or damage to *some* property other than the product.

In *Hauenstein* v. *Saint Paul-Mercury Indemnity Co.* [65 N.W. 2d 122 (Minnesota)], the insured sold plaster to a contractor who applied the plaster to a wall of a hospital that he was building. The plaster was defective and had to be replaced.

The insurer disclaimed coverage because of the policy exclusion. The court rejected the insured's argument that the plaster lost its identity when it was mixed with water and applied to a wall. However, the court held that the defective plaster did cause damage to the wall of the building, and the damage to the building as a whole consisted either the diminution in the market value of the building or the cost of removing and replacing the plaster, whichever was less.

Along the same lines is *St. Paul Fire & Marine Ins. Co.* v. *Northern Grain Co.* [365 Fed. 2d 361 (8th Cir.)], in which seed sold by the insured was defective and resulted in a stunted crop. The purchaser sued the insured for damages. The court held that the insured's products liability coverage was involved, in spite of the specific exclusion with respect to damage to the product itself. The court held that liability under the policy could be sustained on either of two theories. First, the stunted crop into which the seeds grew was property distinct from the seed itself, or second, that damage has been incurred from the loss of use of the land in which the defective seed was planted.

To meet these and other cases of similar import, the 1973 revision of the standard policy contained exclusion (m) which revised the policy so as to exclude the following:

. . . loss of use of tangible property which has not been physically injured or destroyed resulting from . . . the failure of the named insured's products . . . to meet the level of performance, quality, fitness or durability warranted or represented by the name insured.

This further supports the original intention that insurance should not in any way be construed as a guarantee of the quality of the insured's products or of the representations made by the insured with regard to the product itself.

Withdrawal of a defective product. Under present business conditions and under some statutes, it is necessary for the insured to withdraw a defective product from the market and to refund the purchase price to persons who have bought the product. In some cases the cost of such procedure will be astronomical. Since it is not the intention of the insurance industry to guarantee the quality of the product, it follows that they would be unwilling to assume the cost of product withdrawal even though such procedure might possibly avoid some claims. Therefore the policy excludes from its coverage such damages. The exclusion reads as follows:

This insurance does not apply: . . . (n) to damages claimed for the withdrawal, inspection, repair, replacement, or loss of use of the named insured's products or work completed by or for the named insured or of any property of which such products or work forms a part, if such products, work or property are withdrawn from the market or from use because of any known or suspected defect or deficiency therein.

This exclusion was tested in *Lipton, Inc.* v. *Liberty Mutual Insurance Co.* (34 N.Y. 2d 356). In that case the insured's products were contaminated and had been sold to Lipton and incorporated in their dried soup mixes. Lipton launched a major effort to recall from the market and to destroy all of

Lipton's products which had been thus contaminated. Lipton had purchased macaroni and noodle products from Gioia who carried products liability insurance with Liberty Mutual. In disclaiming coverage for the costs of Lipton's recall of its products from the market, Liberty Mutual argued that the claim came within the scope of the exclusion. The court found that there was an ambiguity in the language of the exclusionary clause in that it could be read as referring only to the withdrawal of the insured's products from the market by the insured itself and not a withdrawal by a third party like Lipton. It seems clear that the drafters of the exclusion intended to exclude all claims for damages for the withdrawal of a product and that the current language must be revised.

1037   Completed operations insurance

Originally, the products hazard and the completed operations insuring agreements were combined in one paragraph. In the 1966 and 1973 revisions they were divided into separate coverages with separate insuring agreements, even though some of the exclusions were applicable to both. Completed operations is defined as follows in the 1966 revision:

"Completed operations hazard" includes bodily injury and property damage arising out of operations or reliance upon a representation or warranty made at any time with respect thereto, but only if the bodily injury or property damage occurs after such operations have been completed or abandoned and occurs away from premises owned or rented by the named insured. "Operations" include materials, parts or equipment furnished in connection therewith. Operations shall be deemed completed at the earliest of the following times:
(1) when all operations to be performed by or on behalf of the named insured under the contract have been completed,
(2) when all operations to be performed by or on behalf of the named insured at the site of the operations have been completed, or
(3) when the portion of the work out of which the injury or damage arises has been put to its intended use by any person or organization other than another contractor or subcontractor engaged in performing operations for a principal as part of the same project.
Operations which may require further service or maintenance work, or correction, repair or replacement because of any defect or deficiency, but which are otherwise complete, shall be deemed completed.

Item 3 of the Declarations sets forth the following:

The insurance afforded is only with respect to the Coverage Part(s) indicated below by specific premium charge(s) and attached to and forming a part of this policy.

Therefore, if there is no premium charges and no coverage parts attached to the policy referring to completed operations and products liability insurance, then there is no coverage for these items. If there is no coverage, then none of the coverages defined under the completed operations hazard and the products hazard are covered.

The completed operations hazard is further modified by the policy definition, as follows:

The completed operations hazard does not include bodily injury or property damage arising out of
(a) operations in connection with the transportation of property, unless the bodily injury or property damage arises out of a condition in or on a vehicle created by the loading or unloading thereof,
(b) the existence of tools, uninstalled equipment or abandoned or unused materials, or
(c) operations for which the classification stated in the policy or in the company's manual specifies "including completed operations."

The premises and operations coverage will indemnify the insured for any liability imposed because of operations away from the premises, which arises out of and during the progress of the work. Completed operations coverage takes over after the work has been completed and covers any liability which the insured may have as a consequence of accidents or occurrences which happen after the insured is no longer actively engaged in doing the work.

1038 Products liability investigation

The investigation of a products liability claim requires a certain amount of resourcefulness and imagination. The factual situations are so varied that it is impossible to forecast exactly what will confront the claims representative. It is best to start out with the initial premise that for the claimant to recover it must be esablished that the product was defective. If the claimant cannot establish a defect, either in the product itself or from the lack of warning or the lack of adequate instructions for its use, the claimant cannot recover.

Therefore, the first inquiry made in the products liability investigation will be directed toward ascertaining the defect, if any, that is the basis of the claim. In serious cases involving bodily injury, the claim should be reduced to a signed statement from the person making the claim. The statement should establish that there was a sale of the product, what instructions, if any, accompanied the product, what warnings, if any, were attached to the label and exactly how the product was used.

Among the defenses to products claims are the following: (1) unforeseeable use; (2) use with knowledge of the danger or of the defect; (3) disregard of the warning; (4) use contrary to instructions; and (5) misuse of the product.

1. *Unforeseeable use.* The manufacturer has a duty to make a product that will be safe for a purpose for which the manufacturer should expect it to be used. There is no duty to design or make a product which would be safe for every possible use to which it may be put. For example, in *Speyer, Inc.* v. *Humble Oil & Refining Co.* (275 Fed. Supp 861, affirmed in 403 Fed. 2d 766), the plaintiff leased some gasoline pumping equipment from the defendant. A customer, a cab driver, who was refueling his car failed to remove the nozzle from the tank of his car before he pulled away from the pump. The strain on the hose caused a meter casting in the pump to break and a quantity of gasoline escaped. A fire occurred before the condition could be remedied. The action was brought to recover damages for the fire and the allegation was that the manufacturer or lessor was guilty of negligent design. The court held that this type of misuse was unforeseeable and therefore rendered a verdict for the defendant.

2. Use with knowledge of the defect.   Where the purchaser or user is aware of a defect in the product and uses it even with that knowledge, the seller or manufacturer is not liable. The defense would be either contributory negligence since the user did not exercise care for his own safety, or assumption of risk in that the user was aware of the risk and voluntarily exposed himself to it. In every case, the purchaser has the opportunity of examining the product, and whether he does or not, he is charged with the knowledge that he would have gained if he had examined it. For example, in *Hunt* v. *Firestone Tire & Rubber Co.* [448 Pac. 2d 1018 (Oklahoma)], the plaintiff was injured when a tire on his two-and-one-half-month-old car blew out. The evidence showed that when the car was delivered, the purchaser noted that the tire was defective since there were cuts in the sidewall. Although the plaintiff was employed for many years as a truck driver, nevertheless he did not change the tire but drove on the tire for over 8,000 miles when the blowout occurred. Under the circumstances, the court held that he assumed the risk of injury and that the seller was not liable. Therefore in investigating such cases, the facts must be developed as to when for the first time the plaintiff noticed the defect, whether or not he complained to the seller and whether or not he used the product, knowing of the defect.

3. Disregard of the warning.   The manufacturer or seller has the duty of adequately warning the purchaser of any dangers in the use of the product which is not open and apparent to the average person. Where the warning has been given and the warning is so placed on the package or the product so as to come to the attention of all users, the failure of the user to heed the warning which causes the injury will provide the seller or manufacturer with a complete defense. For example, in *Shanklin* v. *Allis-Chalmers Mfg. Corp.* [254 Fed Supp. 223 (West Virginia)], the plaintiff lost his arm in a harvester machine. While the machine was running, he opened the door to remove cornstalks which had clogged the rollers. His glove was caught in the rollers and his arm was drawn into the machine. The door which he opened had a warning on it which stated: WARNING—KEEP AWAY FROM ROLLERS UNLESS POWER IS OFF. The court held that the warning was adequate and easily understood, but that the plaintiff assumed the risk of injury by proceeding in a course of conduct in spite of the knowledge of the obvious danger.

4. Use contrary to instructions.   Comparable to the factual situation with respect to warnings, the instructions supplied with the product must be followed, or the seller may have another defense. The adequacy of the instructions and the plaintiff's actions with regard to them will be the primary questions to be decided. For example, in *Pinto* v. *Clairol, Inc.* (324 Fed. 2d

608). the instructions which accompanied the defendant's hair dye solution required that the user make a "patch" test by applying the solution to a small amount of hair to determine whether or not the user had an allergy and to determine whether or not the user would have an adverse reaction. The plaintiff failed to make the patch test. The court held that even though the plaintiff had been using this particular type of dye for years without any adverse reaction did not absolve her from the responsibility of making the patch test. Therefore, in each case where instructions accompany the product, the investigation should determine whether or not the instructions were followed.

5. *Misuse of the product.* Where the plaintiff uses the product for a purpose other than its intended use, there will be a question of fact as to whether or not this action caused the accident. For example, in *McKay* v. *Upson-Walton Co.* (317 Fed. 2d 826) the defendant sold a block and tackle which had a $2\frac{1}{2}$ ton load capacity. This limitation was plainly set forth in the instructions. Where the plaintiff used the product to lift a load of about 5 tons, he was denied recovery. In this case the product was used for its intended purpose, but was exposed to conditions beyond its capacity. The investigation should show exactly the use to which the product was put—whether or not it was used for a purpose not intended or used beyond its capacity to function. It sometimes happens that the injured person will tamper with the safety devices on the product making such device inoperable. When this happens and the injury is caused by the lack of the safety device, obviously there is no liability on the part of the manufacturer.

The same result would obtain if a person other than the injured either removed the safety device or the machine is altered so as to operate when the safety device is off.

Conduct of a third party. The classic example of the conduct of a third party occurs where a physician administers a drug without following the manufacturer's instructions. If the failure to follow the instructions was the proximate cause of the injury or death, the manufacturer is insulated from liability. For example, in *Magee* v. *Wyeth Laboratories, Inc.* (26 Cal. Rptr. 322), the evidence indicated that the physician's failure to follow the instructions which accompanied the drug and not the drug itself was the cause of the patient's death.

Contact with the insured. It is important to have all of the insured's records available. This would include descriptive material pertaining to the product involved and how it was manufactured and what purpose it was intended to serve. Also all instructions, warnings and other material which accompanied the product. Most companies have detailed records, keyed to serial numbers and descriptive model numbers which will identify the time of production and sale and the procedures used in manufacturing the particular product. Quality control records may also be utilized. Such evidence may be used to nullify the claim that there was a defect in the product.

Safety standards. There are a number of industry organizations which have promulgated safety standards for a number of products. Thees include the American Standards Association and the Underwriters Laboratories. Certain products are certified. The National Safety Council is also active in this area. In addition, there are governmental agencies at both the federal and state level which establish either by statute or regulation the standards of certain products which must be met. If the product meets the average safety standard and has been certified by one of thees organizations, it is some evidence that the product is not defectively designed. Inquiry should be made through the insured, and in appropriate cases through the organization having the duty of setting such standards.

Plaintiff's burden of proof. It must be emphasized that regardless of whether the action is brought under the Uniform Commercial Code or strict liability in tort, the plaintiff in order to recover must establish that the offending product was defective. The purpose of the investigation is to ascertain the facts and to determine whether or not the plaintiff can in fact meet the burden which is thus placed upon him.

1039   Comparative negligence and products liability

In the case of a defective product causing injury, many states have adopted the rule of strict liability in tort in actions against the manufacturer. (See Section 1012, supra.) Under this rule, the courts have uniformly held that contributory negligence of the user was not a defense to this type of action. The only cases where there was a defense were limited to assumption of risk (where the user knowingly drove an automobile with defective brakes) or abnormal misuse (where the user attempted to hammer a nail with a glass bottle).

Subsequently, the legislatures by statute and the courts by judicial modification have approved the rule of comparative negligence. This immediately raised the question as to whether or not comparative negligence should be applied to cases involving strict liability in tort. Some courts took the position that strict liability in tort was a form of negligence per se and under such circumstances the rule of comparative negligence could be applied. See *Hagenbuch* v. *Snap-on Tools Corp.*, 359 Fed. Supp. 676, applying New Hampshire law; and *Stephen* v. *Sears, Roebuck & Co.*, 266 Atl. 2d 585 (New Hampshire) and *Franklin* v. *Badger Ford*, 201 N.W. 2d 866 (Wisconsin).

In *West* v. *Caterpillar Tractor*, 330 So. 2d 80, the Florida Supreme Court was confronted with the same problem. It held that under Florida law, the lack of care on the part of the plaintiff's intestate constituted a defense to strict tort liability. The facts in this case indicated that Mrs. West, in order to board a bus, walked in the path of a grader that was backing up, and she received injuries from which she subsequently died. The jury found that she was 35 percent contributorily negligent, and the verdict was reduced accordingly. The plaintiff contended that the grader was defectively designed in that it was not provided with an audible warning system for use while backing the grader, by failing to provide adequate rear view mirrors, and by designing the grader with a blind spot created by obstructions while looking to the rear while driving in reverse.

In *Butaud* v. *Suburban Marine and Sporting Goods, Inc.,* 555 Pac. 2d 42 (Alaska), the plaintiff was injured while racing a snowmobile which was not designed for that purpose. A drive belt broke which caused a guard to shatter, injuring the plaintiff's eye. The defendant contended that the plaintiff had failed to maintain the snowmobile properly and further that racing such a vehicle constituted contributory negligence. The court held that a product liability defendant was entitled to offer evidence on the general misuse of its product. Once misuse is established, the principles of comparative negligence will apply.

A contrary view was taken by the Colorado Court of Appeals in *Kinard* v. *Coates,* 553 Pac. 2d 835, holding that comparative negligence does not apply to product liability actions brought on the theory of strict liability in tort.

Doubtless there will be many more appeals undertaken in this particular area, and therefore the claims representative should keep abreast of developments in his state.

CHAPTER XI

Professional liability

1100 Profession defined

A profession is a vocation, calling, or occupation involving labor, skill, education, and special knowledge. The labor and skill involved is predominately mental or intellectual, rather than physical or manual. The term was originally used in reference to theology, law, and medicine, but as the applications of learning and science have expanded, other vocations have come within the meaning of the term. In any case, the practice of a profession requires a license, which is granted by the state or federal authority after the applicant has passed a detailed examination. Such license will remain in effect only so long as the person observes the ethics of the profession and complies with the rules of conduct prescribed by the granting authority. Thus, the license can be revoked or suspended by the granting authority when it receives evidence that the person has been guilty of unethical conduct or has failed to comply with the rules and regulations under which the license was issued.

1101 Professional liability defined

When a person holds himself out as a practitioner in any profession, he impliedly warrants that he possesses the average skill of others practicing the same profession in the same community. He also warrants that he will exert his best efforts in behalf of any client or patient who employs him.

Where he fails to use his best efforts in behalf of the client or patient, either through neglect, inattention, or indifference, and the client or patient suffers a physical or pecuniary injury, he is answerable in damages to the client or patient to the extent of his loss. His failure to exert his best efforts will be construed as a lack of due care. The Restatement, Second, Torts, Section 299A suggests the following rule:

Unless he represents that he has greater or less skill or knowledge, one who undertakes to render services in the practice of a profession . . . is required to exercise the skill and knowledge normally possessed by members of that profession . . . in good standing in similar communities.

Under this rule, when a person who engages another who is engaged in the practice of a profession, he has a right to assume that the professional person has the skill and knowledge possessed by other members of the profession, practicing in similar communities. If he represents that he has greater skill than others in his profession, he will be held to a higher degree of care and performance. On the other hand, if he admits that he has less knowledge and skill than others in the particular transaction in which he has been engaged, and the client engages him with that knowledge, he will not be held to the degree of care and performance that would ordinarily be required.

MEDICAL MALPRACTICE

1102 Scope

Physicians, surgeons, dentists, nurses, and hospitals have not escaped attention as possible personal injury defendants in cases where an unexpected result occurs, or where an allegation can be made that the person or institution rendering the medical service was lacking in experience, application, attention, or skill. Claims in the malpractice category are on the increase. This may be due partly to the claim consciousness of the times and, more particularly, to the miraculous advances that medical science has made in the past few years. The public has come to expect miracles from medical science and when the miracles do not occur, suit is inevitably brought against the physician or surgeon responsible for the result.

In these cases there is more involved than a mere suit for damages. Where a plaintiff's verdict is obtained or where a large settlement has been made, the physician stands condemned in the eyes of the public as an incompetent practitioner. This is an unfortunate by-product of malpractice litigation.

In recent years, malpractice claims have increased so rapidly and the verdicts have increased so markedly that insurers are reluctant to carry these risks unless there is a substantial increase in premium, which the medical profession finds it almost impossible to meet. Several solutions have been advanced to meet the problem and most require legislative implementation. Just what form the legislation will take is unknown at this time, but it is known that this is a problem to be solved by each individual state and thus we can expect that the legislation, when it comes, will differ on a state-by-state basis. Therefore, the claims representative should be alert to any legislative changes which may occur in his territory.

The following discussion will represent the common-law approach to the medical malpractice problem and when new legislation is enacted, the claims representative should compare the new statute with the common law as set forth here.

1103   Creation of physician-patient relationship

The relationship of physician and patient comes into existence as a result of the mutual agreement of the parties; neither is under any legal obligation to enter into this relationship. The patient may refuse the services of the physician or surgeon, however great the patient's need for such services may be. The patient may select one doctor in preference to another, or he may decide not to accept any medical attention at all. On the other hand, the doctor is under no legal obligation to accept all who seek his services as patients, nor is he under any duty to enter into the relationship of physician and patient even in cases of emergency. With respect to the latter, the physician is in the same legal position as any other person who is at the scene of an accident or other emergency. If he voluntarily undertakes to treat an injured victim, he assumes the same liabilities and obligations which would be assumed by a volunteer under similar circumstances. On the other hand, if a physician does not offer his services or does not render service when it is requested, his refusal to treat an injured victim will not subject him to any legal liability. This is true even though the victim dies or suffers permanent injury as a result of the lack of immediate medical attention.

1104   Termination of physician-patient relationship

Since the relationship is created by mutual agreement, either party may terminate the relationship by giving notice to the other. The patient may refuse further treatment or neglect to call at the doctor's office for the necessary treatment. Where this happens, the physician is under no further obligation to the patient.

The physician may terminate the relationship by giving notice to the patient. This must be by actual notice, and it is the doctor's duty to see that the fact of his termination comes to the knowledge of the patient. While the relationship continues the doctor may not abandon the patient or fail or neglect to render whatever treatment the condition of the patient requires. He can terminate his obligations to the patient only by giving actual notice of such termination, and the relationship terminates as of the time that notice is received by the patient. Therefore, if any act of abandonment or neglect occurred prior to the time that the notice of termination by the physician was received, the physician's liability will attach.

1105   Physician's duty to his patient

The physician in undertaking treatment of the patient's illness or injury does not guarantee either a cure or a successful result. But does warrant that he possesses the average medical skill available in the community; that he will employ his skill for the best interests of the patient; that the treatment which he prescribes will conform to the standard medical practice in cases of that kind, and that, where necessary, he will recommend competent nurses, sanitarium, nursing home, or hospital. He also warrants to see that the nurses or hospital receive proper instructions as to the management of the case and the treatment and medications to be given. These are the only duties undertaken by the physician, and unless there has been a failure to meet these obligations he is not answerable in damages for the result, unfortunate as it might be.

In *Ewing* v. *Goode* (78 Fed. 442) the court said:

Before the plaintiff can recover, she must show by affirmative evidence—first, that the defendant was unskillful or negligent; and second, that his want of skill or care caused injury to the plaintiff. If either element is lacking in her proof, she has presented no case for the consideration of the jury. The naked facts that the defendant performed operations upon her eye, and that pain followed, and that subsequently the eye was in such a bad condition that it had to be extracted, establishes neither the neglect and unskillfulness of the treatment, nor the causal connection between it and the unfortunate event. A physician is not a warrantor of cures. If the maxim Res Ipsa Loquitur were applied to a case like this, and a failure to cure was held to be evidence, however slight, of negligence on the part of the physician or surgeon causing the bad result, few would be courageous enough to practice the healing art, for they would have to assume financial liability for nearly all the ills that flesh is heir to.

1106   Vicarious liability: *Respondeat superior*

The physician is responsible for the acts of others done under his direction in connection with the treatment of the patient. These acts may consist of treatment rendered by the physician's own office personnel, treatment rendered by a nurse, physiotherapist, or other technicians. The physician has the obligation of selecting competent personnel for this purpose and the additional obligation of properly instructing them as to the treatment to be rendered, the duration of the treatment, and the methods and means to be employed in connection with the particular case. Should any of these individuals fail in their duties as a consequence of the physician's failure to properly instruct them, there is a liability on the part of the physician.

In the case of hospital personnel, the physician has the duty of properly instructing them as to medical acts to be done by them in connection with the treatment of his case. He is responsible for the results of their actions taken under his instructions. As to acts of hospital personnel in the course of their employment, and in the course of administrative acts of the hospital, the physician has no responsibility. Hospital medical personnel are the agents of the physician only when they are performing medical acts as instructed by him. Otherwise they are the agents of the hospital.

1107   Physician's duty to others

The physician is under a duty to instruct and to supervise the work of others in connection with the treatment of his case. He likewise is under a duty to disclose to such others any unusual condition which would affect the handling of the patient as well as any dangers to which these others would be exposed in connection with the treatment. For example, a nurse was employed for the purpose of attending a paranoic patient. The doctor was aware that this patient was subject to periods of violence but failed to inform the nurse, who was injured as a result of a violent episode on the part of the patient. She was allowed to recover damages from the physician, arising out of the personal injuries she sustained, on the theory that the physician had failed in his duty to warn her and, as a consequence, she did not have the opportunity of creating safeguards.

In another situation, let us assume that the physician is treating a patient with a virulent communicable disease. He enters the patient in a hospital but fails to disclose to the hospital the communicable nature of the patient's illness. The patient is then admitted to the hospital on general service and is not isolated. As a result of the failure to isolate the patient, many other patients in the same ward are infected with the disease. Under those circumstances, the physician, because of his failure to disclose the dangerous condition of his patient, would be liable to the hospital as well as to any patients in the hospital who suffered damage as a result thereof.

In *Freese* v. *Lemmon* [210 N.W. 2d 576 (Iowa)], the defendant Lemmon's car collided with that of the plaintiff. It was claimed that Lemmon suffered a seizure and therefore lost control of the car, causing the accident. Lemmon's physician was also joined as a defendant. He had consulted the physician for a seizure which he had suffered three months earlier. The complaint alleged that the negligence of the physician consisted of the following: (1) failing to diagnose and ascertain the cause of the first seizure of the defendant Norman Lemmon and to learn of its reoccurrence; (2) negligently failing to advise defendant Lemmon not to drive an automobile; (3) negligently failing to warn the defendant Lemmon of the dangers involved in driving an automobile in view of all the facts and circumstances; (4) negligently failing to employ recognized and appropriate tests for the diagnosis of the cause of defendant Lemmon's first seizure; (5) negligently failing to take a spinal tap of the defendant Lemmon; (6) negligently advising defendant Lemmon that he could drive an automobile; and (7) negligently failing to consult a specialist to whom the patient had been referred prior to advising the defendant Lemmon that he could drive an automobile. The court held that the complaint stated a cause of action against the physician.

1108 Standards of care

The law requires that the physician exercise reasonable care in the treatment of his patient. This means that the treatment which he gives must conform to the standard medical practice in the community where treatment is rendered. This is another way of saying that the physician is judged by the reasonably prudent man standard. A reasonable prudent physician in acting under the circumstances of treatment will conform to the general medical practice followed in connection with the particular type of case under his care. The physician is required to know just what the standards of medical practice are and to render his treatment in accordance therewith.

Whether or not treatment conformed to the standard medical practice is a question of fact for the jury. The jury is not experienced in medical matters and therefore must have some guidance in the medical area. Therefore, the plaintiff must establish the standard medical practice by the testimony of a physician. With this guidance the jury can perform its duty and decide whether or not the defendant's conduct of the case conformed to the standard medical practice. This is a departure from the general rule that no expert testimony is admissible in order to show the standards of conduct that would be pursued by the reasonably prudent man. In all other matters, the jury is competent to judge the presence or absence of due reasonable care on the basis of their own experience. However, since the jury is not expected to have any medical knowledge, the guidance of an expert becomes a necessity.

Conformity with the standard medical practice will include the type of treatment rendered, the extent of the attention that the physician must give the case (as well as the normal safeguards which should be undertaken in the form of the employment of nurses), the use of diagnostic aids, and the frequency of the physician's visits. Failure to utilize all of the means available to the physician, if standard medical practice demands it, will constitute negligence.

1109 Substitute physician

It happens frequently that during the course of treatment the attending physician is absent due to illness, vacations, or medical conventions. Usually he arranges for another physician to maintain his practice in his absence. If the attending physician selects as a substitute a competent practicing physician, who is licensed in the state in which the medical treatment is rendered, then the first physician has no liability in tort to the patient as a result of any negligent act of the substitute physician. The substitute physician is in the position of an independent contractor who is not under the control of the attending physician and therefore is not the agent of the attending physician. However, the failure of the attending physician to select a competent substitute, or his failure to fully inform him as to the nature of the case, the treatment regimen, the allergies of the patient, and other peculiarities which could not be detected by examination, could constitute negligence on the part of the first physician and subject him to liability. Otherwise, there is no liability on the part of the first physician for the tortious conduct of his substitute.

1110   Multiple physicians

It sometimes happens that, because of the various specialties in which physicians are engaged, more than one physician will treat the various conditions from which the patient is suffering. For example, in a case where the patient has sustained a fractured skull, there may be an eye complication, and, while the attending physician is treating the skull fracture, the case is referred to an ophthalmologist. With respect to liability, the general rule is that if complications develop, and are observed by either of these two physicians, and there is a failure to adequately treat the complications, both physicians are responsible. If the eye doctor observes symptoms which indicate serious brain damage or pressure which would require an immediate operation, the eye physician, even though his treatment of the case is limited to the eyes alone, is under a duty to communicate this information to the other physician or make whatever arrangements are necessary to preserve the patient's life. The failure of the eye doctor to do so would subject him to liability and the failure of the attending physician to recognize and correct the condition would likewise subject him to liability. Neither the eye doctor nor the attending physician may ignore symptoms relating to the condition treated by the other without incurring personal liability.

1111   Assault and battery

The rule, as expressed in *Schloendorff* v. *New York Hospital* (105 N.E. 92), is as follows:

> Every human being of adult years and sound mind has a right to determine what shall be done with his own body; and a surgeon who performs an operation without his patient's consent, commits an assault, for which he is liable in damages. This is true, except in cases of emergency where the patient is unconscious and where it is necessary to operate before consent can be obtained.

This means that the surgeon may not surgically invade any part of the patient's body without his consent. Should the surgeon do so, he is guilty of an assault and battery which will subject him not only to civil liability but to criminal responsibility as well. For this reason, most surgeons and hospitals require that the patient sign a written consent to an operation before one will be performed. This will establish the surgeon's right to operate and insulate him from liability for so doing.

With respect to infants and insane persons, both of whom are incapable of giving consent, consent is given by the parents or guardian, as the case may be. In the case of infants, it sometimes occurs that the parents, because of religious scruples, refuse to consent to an operation which, in the opinion of the surgeon, is necessary to prolong the infant's life. In such cases a proceeding may be instituted in a court of competent jurisdiction, by the surgeon or hospital, asking for a court order permitting the operation. This is in the nature of a quasi-criminal proceeding directed against the parents of the infant. The basis of the complaint is that the parents are lacking in their duty of protection to the infant, and the prayer for relief asks for a finding by the court that the parents are neglecting their duty—and an assumption by the court of guardianship of the infant for the infant's benefit. These cases are rare, but do occur and do receive considerable publicity.

Should the guardian or committee of the lunatic refuse an operation where such is necessary, a similar action may be instituted in order to obtain the court's consent to an operation if such is necessary to save the lunatic's life.

In the case of an unconscious person, where an immediate operation is necessary, the court, by means of a legal fiction, will regard the surgeon as the patient's agent by necessity, and therefore regard him as having the power to consent to the operation for and in behalf of the unconscious patient. This is for the reason that the necessity of the situation demands it.

Where the doctor has obtained the consent of the patient to an operation, he is authorized to do only the operation set forth in the consent signed by the patient. The physician or surgeon is liable if he performs an unauthorized operation, even though the surgical procedure undertaken did, in the final analysis, benefit the patient's health. The surgeon is bound to anticipate the ordinary complications which will arise at the time of the operation. The patient should be consulted and his consent obtained in advance to any possible surgical procedures (in addition to the one contemplated) prior to the operation. Merely because the surgeon has obtained the patient's consent to an operation of a specific type does not in any way authorize the surgeon to invade any other portion of the patient's body or to perform any other surgical procedure without first having the patient's consent. Where an exploratory operation is contemplated, it is customary to explain the necessity of such an operation to the patient and to obtain a general consent in advance.

This brings us to a consideration of situations where the operation is performed as covered by the consent, but is done on the opposite side. For example, when the surgeon obtains consent to an operation on the right ear, and, when the patient is prepared for the operation and under total anaesthesia, it is discovered that there is a much more acute condition in the left ear. An operation therefore is performed on the left ear and no surgical procedure is directed toward the right ear.

There are two schools of thought among the states as to the liability of the surgeon under those circumstances. The majority view is that the physician has performed an unauthorized operation and is therefore guilty of assault with the resultant liability for damages. In that view, it makes no difference if the operation performed on the opposite side is of exactly the same nature and scope as the contemplated operation. The patient consented only to the invasion of his body on one side, and an invasion on the opposite side is beyond the scope of the authorization given by the patient. But in a minority of states the position is taken that, since the operation is of the same type and directed toward the same type of recovery, the physician or surgeon was the agent of the patient by necessity, and consent is amended.

1112   Doctrine of informed consent

The relationship of physician and patient is one of trust and confidence. The patient relies on the doctor's knowledge of the medicine, which is superior to his own. Therefore, when the patient's consent to surgical operation or any type of treatment is necessary, the doctor is under a duty to disclose to the patient all of the possibilities and the dangers inherent in the recommended treatment. The courts generally hold that a consent obtained without a full and frank disclosure to the patient of all the facts and the dangers to which the treatment will expose him is no consent at all. The courts have not gone so far as to regard a consent so obtained as fraudulent, but they hold that for consent to be valid it must be given under circumstances where the patient is fully cognizant of the possible consequences. Failure to acquaint the patient with all the facts which are necessary to form the basis of an intelligent consent will subject the doctor to liability.

An exception to this rule requiring a disclosure of dangers is, of course, an actual emergency where the patient is in no condition to determine the question himself. Some courts have said that another exception is where an explanation of every risk attendant upon a treatment procedure may alarm a patient who is already apprehensive and who may refuse surgery or treatment in which there is minimal risk, or where such disclosure may result in actually increasing the risk by reason of the psychological results of the apprehension itself. Some courts recognize a further exception that each patient is to be treated as a separate problem on the theory that the patient's mental and emotional condition is important and that a certain amount of discussion, consistent with full disclosure of facts necessary to an informed consent, should be employed.

A physician who misleads a patient by not only failing to give a warning of reasonable and recognized risks inherent in a treatment (after which the patient may have refused the treatment) but also by affirmatively assuring him that there are no risks (knowing such statement could be untrue), is liable for the harmful consequences of the treatment. Such failure to disclose, or giving of an untrue answer as to the probable consequences of a treatment, constitutes malpractice unless such action comes within exceptions to the rule requiring candor and disclosure. In all cases where an exception to the full disclosure duty of the physician is urged, a question of fact will be raised for the determination of the jury. It will be its duty to decide whether or not the circumstances of the case are such as to relieve the physician of his duty of disclosure.

It must be emphasized that in order for the plaintiff to recover damages, it must be established that the lack of informed consent was the proximate cause of the plaintiff's injuries. For example, in *Downer* v. *Veilleux* [322 Atl. 2d 82 (Maine)], the plaintiff suffered multiple injuries including a fracture of the right femoral neck. The doctor decided to treat this fracture by traction and did not perform an open reduction. In the plaintiff's suit against the doctor, the plaintiff contended that if she had been informed of the condition that she would have insisted on surgery or other treatment, and she would not have sustained the ununited fracture which occurred as a result. She also contended that if she had been informed, she would have insisted upon a consultation with an orthopedic specialist. On the latter point, the court stated that:

if we were to hold that the evidence in the present case established a duty on the defendant's part to consult an orthopedic specialist, the effect of our decision would be to say that a physician, even though shown to be competent to treat the illness or injury at hand, subjects himself to liability whenever he relies on his own skills and applies them diligently, but fails to effect a cure. Since there is no evidence in this case that the defendant's failure to consult a specialist proximately caused or aggravated the plaintiff's injuries, such a holding would not only inhibit the practice of medicine to the point where even the simplest procedure would have to be performed in tandem, but also it would render the self-reliant physician an insurer contrary to what this Court has held the law of Maine to be.

The plaintiff also contended that the physician failed to inform her of the risks of the treatment undertaken and the alternatives available, thus transforming the type of treatment rendered into an unconsented contract and thus a technical battery. The court rejected this approach based on the lack of informed consent. The court held that in order for the plaintiff to recover under the lack of consent theory, she must establish (1) that the lack of consent was a proximate cause of the injury suffered; and (2) that had the patient been informed of the risk, she would have submitted to surgery or other type of treatment. The plaintiff must also prove by expert testimony what the risks were and that alternative treatment was feasible. The court held that a physician need not advise a patient of alternatives which if applied would be futile. A judgment for the physician was affirmed.

Some states have legislated with respect to the obligation of the physician to inform the patient of the risks involved in the treatment recommended and in some cases have limited his liability. For example, the New York Statute (Chapter 109, Laws of 1975, effective September 1, 1975) reads as follows:

2805–d. Limitation of medical malpractice action based on lack of informed consent.

1. Lack of informed consent means the failure of the person providing pro-

fessional treatment or diagnosis to disclose to the patient such alternatives thereto and the reasonably foreseeable risks and benefits involved as a reasonable medical practitioner under similar circumstances would have disclosed, in a manner permitting the patient to make a knowledgeable evaluation.

2. The right of action to recover for medical malpractice based on a lack of informed consent is limited to those cases involving either (*a*) non-emergency treatment, procedure or surgery, or (*b*) a diagnostic procedure which involved invasion or disruption of the integrity of the body.

3. For a cause of action therefor it must also be established that a reasonably prudent person in the patient's position would not have undergone the treatment or diagnosis if he had been fully informed and that the lack of informed consent is a proximate cause of the injury or condition for which recovery is sought.

4. It shall be a defense to any action for medical malpractice based upon an alleged failure to obtain such an informed consent that:

(*a*) the risk not disclosed is too commonly known to warrant disclosure; or

(*b*) the patient assured the medical practitioner he would undergo the treatment, procedure or diagnosis regardless of the risk involved, or the patient indicated to the medical practitioner that he did not want to be informed of the matters to which he would be entitled to be informed; or

(*c*) consent by or on behalf of the patient was not reasonably possible; or

(*d*) the medical practitioner, after considering all of the attendant facts and circumstances, used reasonable discretion as to the manner and extent to which such alternatives or risks were disclosed to the patient because he reasonably believed that the manner and extent of such disclosure could reasonably be expected to adversely and substantially affect the patient's condition.

4401–a. Motion for judgment. A motion for judgment at the end of the plaintiff's case must be granted as to any cause of action for medical malpractice based solely on lack of informed consent if the plaintiff has failed to adduce expert medical testimony in support of the alleged qualitative insufficiency of the consent.

Only a few states have considered changes in the doctrine of informed consent. These are:

State	Statute
Florida	Cause of action to be based on local standards. If consent is in writing the presumption that it was obtained is conclusive.
Idaho	Persons who may consent are defined. Sufficiency of consent based on local practice. Written consent is presumed to be valid and sufficient.
Iowa	A presumption of consent is created if in writing, signed and in general terms sets forth purpose, risks probability and all questions answered satisfactorily.
Indiana	No liability for breach of contract guaranteeing results unless in writing and signed.
Louisiana	Guaranteed results—no liability unless in writing. Written, signed consent is valid and cannot be limited or modified if risks and procedures are explained in general terms and questions satisfactorily answered.

Ohio	Guaranteed results—statute of frauds applies and must be in writing and signed. If written in general terms the consent can be overcome by a preponderance of evidence.
Nevada	Conclusive presumption of consent if in writing and signed and procedure, alternatives and risks explained in general terms. Implied presumption where delay would cause serious harm.
Tennessee	Applies local standards to informed consent or standards of surrounding states where relevant.

In many of the states there is legislation under consideration. Therefore, the claims representative should remain abreast of the situation and make such changes in his approach to cases of this type as is dictated by the provisions of the statute, if any.

1113   Liability in contract

When a physician accepts a case for treatment he impliedly warrants that he will use his best skill and care in the management and treatment of the case. This is an instance of the contract of employment. Failure to exercise skill and care in treatment will subject a physician to liability for breach of contract.

Some physicians and surgeons go beyound this implied warranty and make express guarantees with regard to the outcome of the treatment or operation. This usually comes about when the physician is anxious to operate and gives the guarantee in order to induce the patient to submit himself to the operation. Usually, when a major operation is contemplated, the physician will discuss the matter with the patient and his wife, at which time the physician will guarantee that the surgical shock will be minimal and, further, that the patient will be able to resume his normal occupation within a certain period of time after the operation. If the patient should die, or get a poor result, a cause of action in contract could arise which the patient or his wife (as his personal representative in case of his death) could bring against the physician for breach of contract. The basis of action would be the surgeon's guarantee of a successful result, the patient's submission to the operation as a result of such inducement, the doctor's failure to produce the result required by his guarantee, plus the damages that came about as a proximate result.

This type of guarantee is most often given by a plastic surgeon in connection with facial surgery. In these cases there is no medical requirement that an operation be performed; the sole purpose of the operation is to improve the patient's facial appearance. Therefore, the doctor not only guarantees the surgical result but also that the cosmetic result will be an improvement in the patient's appearance. The plastic surgeon must not only perform a successful medical operation but must produce an improvement in the patient's facial characteristics. Many plastic surgeons are extremely careful in their negotiations with the patient so that there is no misunderstanding as to the exact result to be accomplished. Some surgeons make an artistic sketch of the result which they will accomplish and then secure the patient's agreement to the operation with that particular result in mind. Then, if an allegation is made that the doctor did not perform in accordance with his guarantee, the doctor has evidence of his agreement with the patient and of the result he guaranteed to accomplish.

1114   Burden of proof

In order to establish the tort of malpractice, the plaintiff has the burden of showing (1) the existence of the legally protected right; (2) the wrongful invasion of that right by an act of commission or omission; (3) damages as a proximate result thereof. In malpractice cases the legally protected right will consist of the patient's right to receive medical attention in accordance with standard medical practice. He will have to establish what the standard medical practice is, and, in addition, show wherein the defendant's treatment did not conform thereto. The plaintiff must also show that he sustained an injury or damages as a result of the failure of the physician to conform to standard medical practice. The jury is not informed with respect to standard medical practice. Therefore, the plaintiff will be obligated to establish such practice by the testimony of an expert witness. This expert witness can only be another physician, and few physicians are willing to testify against a fellow practitioner. There are many reasons for this.

First of all, the expert witness may find himself a defendant in a malpractice suit at some time in the future, and the present defendant may "return the compliment" by testifying against him. In addition, medical societies are extremely sensitive about malpractice suits and discourage their members from testifying against other practitioners. Some courts have referred to this reluctance as a "conspiracy of silence." Therefore, in tort actions the plaintiff is always confronted with the difficulty of securing an expert witness.

In order to overcome the disadvantages posed by the difficulties in obtaining medical testimony to support the claimant's claim, plaintiff's counsel have utilized two methods to overcome this problem. They are (1) *res ipsa loquitur* in appropriate cases and (2) the testimony of the defendant doctor to establish the standard of medical practice.

1. *Res ipsa loquitur.* This doctrine contemplates a state of facts wherein the jury can conclude that (1) the character of the occurrence and the circumstances attending it lead reasonably to the belief that, in the absence of negligence, it would not have occurred, and (2) the thing which caused the injury is shown to have been under the management and control of the alleged wrongdoer. For example, in *Ybarra* v. *Spangard* [154 Pac. 2d 687 (California)], following an appendix operation, the patient found that he had a traumatic injury to his shoulder, which apparently was acquired while he was unconscious during the operation. The court held that the patient was entitled to rely on the doctrine of *res ipsa loquitur*, and that the failure of the surgeon to explain the injury as having occurred without negligence on his part, compelled a finding of negligence. Other cases involving the same doctrine are: *Daiker* v. *Martin* [91 N.W. 2d 747 (Iowa)] (subsequent infection and amputation of fractured leg as a result of the application of a tight cast);

Leonard v. *Watsonville Community Hospital* [305 Pac. 2d 36 (California)] (Kelly clamp left in abdominal cavity); *Tiller* v. *Von Pohle* [230 Pac. 2d 213 (Arizona)] (cloth sack left in patient's body following an operation); *Terhune* v. *Margaret Hague Maternity Hospital* [164 Atl. 2d 75 (New Jersey)] (woman in childbirth awoke to find face burned from anesthesia); and *Sawyer* v. *Jewish Chronic Disease Hospital* [234 N.Y.S. 2d 372 (New York)] (anesthesia death of a two-year-old child).

A doctor or hospital is not a guarantor of the success of the treatment, and the mere fact that the treatment did not result in a complete cure is not enough to compel the application of *res ipsa loquitur.* The result must be such that a reasonable man could conclude that it would not have happened unless the doctor or hospital was negligent. In *Silverson* v. *Weber* [372 Pac. 2d 97 (California)], the court said:

> To permit an inference under the doctrine of res ipsa loquitur solely because an uncommon complication develops would place too great a burden upon the medical profession and might result in an undesirable limitation on the use of operations or new procedures involving an inherent risk of injury even when due care is used. Where risks are inherent in an operation and an injury which is rare does occur, the doctrine should not be applicable unless it can be said in the light of past experience, such an occurrence is more likely the result of negligence than some other cause for which the defendant is not responsible.

In addition, the defendant can overcome the effect of *res ipsa loquitur* by showing that the standards of medical practice were followed and the medical procedures utilized in the treatment of the case were the same as those used in the locality for the treatment of similar cases.

2. Defendant's testimony. Since the plaintiff has the burden of establishing the standard medical practice applicable to his case, some have sought to accomplish this by taking the testimony of the defendant-doctor, either by deposition in discovery proceedings or by calling him as an adverse witness. For example, in *Rogotzki* v. *Schept* [209 Atl. 2d 426 (New Jersey)], the court upheld the use of discovery procedures for the purpose of compelling the defendant-doctor to answer questions on deposition calling for his expert opinion relative to the treatment he rendered. The court said:

> Where the expert testimony of a defendant-doctor is brought into issue as a result of his exercise of expert judgment, pre-trial discovery relating to his opinion and exercise of judgment in the course of treating his patient is no different from any case in which an adverse party has knowledge of relevant matters; to hold otherwise would, particularly in a medical malpractice case, put a plaintiff to a disadvantage. The critical information necessary to a proper understanding and presentation of the case is almost exclusively within the knowledge of the defendant-expert. Further, courts have generally recognized how difficult it is for a plaintiff to obtain competent expert testimony in a medical malpractice case.

In *McDermott* v. *Manhattan Eye, Ear and Throat Hospital* [203 N.E. 2d 469 (New York)], the plaintiff did not call a medical expert of her own, but called the defendant-doctor for the purpose of showing the standard medical practice in cases such as hers and also his nonconformity therewith. The court held that she was entitled to do so. [See also *State of Maryland* v. *Brainan,* 167 Atl. 2d 117; *Walker* v. *Distler,* 296 Pac. 2d 452 (Idaho) ; *Harnden* v. *Mischel,* 246 N.W. 646 (North Dakota); *Dark* v. *Fitzer,* 149 N.W. 2d 222 (Michigan) ; and *Shurpit* v. *Brah,* 141 N.W. 2d 266 (Wisconsin).]

While all of the courts have not been called upon to decide the question, the trend seems to be that the plaintiff may call the defendant-doctor and elicit testimony from him as to the standard medical practice and his activity in connection with the case. This does not mean necessarily that the doctor's testimony will be adverse to himself and much will depend upon his competence as a witness and the facts of the case. Therefore, in investigating cases of this nature, the investigator should bear in mind the possibility of the doctor as a witness and should evaluate his ability in that direction, bearing in mind that this contingency might arise.

The plaintiff can establish his claim much more easily in contract actions. For example, if the surgeon guaranteed that an operation would be performed and the patient would be back at work within one month, mere proof that the patient died on the operating table would be sufficient to establish that the surgeon did not perform in accordance with his guarantee. No expert testimony is necessary to establish the fact of death. Also, the plaintiff must merely establish the existence of the guarantee and the failure of the doctor.

It may well be asked then why plaintiffs persist in bringing malpractice actions based on the physician's tort liability rather than on contract. The reason for it is that most malpractice insurance policies exclude from their coverage any claims based upon a contractual guarantee made by the insured physician. Therefore, unless the physician involved is one who can financially respond in damages, to the extent of the plaintiff's claim, a tort action in malpractice is usually brought in order to reach the doctor's insurance protection.

1115   Liability of consulting physician or surgeon

It frequently happens that the attending physician will require some advice or guidance from a physician of greater experience or one who specializes in the particular illness. In such cases the attending physician will arrange for a consultation and be guided as to the future course of treatent by the result of that consultation. Where the consulting physician makes his own diagnosis and recommends a course of treatment which is in accordance with standard medical practice, he has no further responsibility. Whether or not his recommendations are carried out is the responsibility of the attending physician.

However, where the attending physician calls in a surgeon for the purpose of doing an operation which the attending physician does not feel competent to perform, the usual arrangement is that the surgeon will do the operation and the attending physician will assume the responsibility for aftercare following the operation. Under those circumstances, the surgeon is responsible for the application of standard medical practice and the successful completion of the operation. Unless he is further consulted, the responsibility of the case then rests with the attending physician.

What very frequently happens, however, is that complications develop and the attending physician again consults the operating surgeon as to further treatment. The question then will arise whether the operating surgeon, under those circumstances, is free to rely upon the information given to him, usually by telephone, by the attending physician, or whether the surgeon is under a further duty and obligation to actually examine the case and to undertake some portion of the future treatment. If the operating surgeon knows the limitations of the attending physician and fails to take action, he may be liable to the patient for any unfortunate result that may follow. Therefore, it is possible to spell out negligence on the part of the operating surgeon when he knows that complications have developed which require his attention but nevertheless places the responsibility for these procedures in the hands of a physician who is incompetent to perform them.

1116 Liability of hospitals

A hospital, generally, is an institution wherein medical service is rendered by others. It provides certain services, such as beds, meals, operating room facilities, and medicines, as well as instruments to be used in connection with treatment. The hospital, as such, does not practice medicine and does not offer medical service. The responsibility for rendering medical service is placed squarely on the shoulders of those who are licensed to perform such service. These could include doctors, nurses, anesthetists, and laboratory technicians of various kinds. The common-law rule is that a hospital is responsible for negligent performance of administrative acts, and not responsible for any medical acts done by the hospital. The latter are considered to be the responsibility of licensed medical practitioners.

It is sometimes difficult to distinguish between a medical and an administrative act. For example, if a hospital furnishes a defective injection needle this is considered to be an administrative act, and if any liability results from such negligence, the hospital is responsible. However, if the injection is administered improperly, and as a result thereof damage is caused, this is considered a medical act and as such is not within the responsibility of the hospital.

The furnishing of blood properly typed and preserved is an administrative act of the hospital. Likewise, any errors made in mislabeling blood samples taken from the patient, or mislabeling blood in the hospital's blood bank, are in the area of administrative rather than medical functions.

The hospital can function only through its agents, and it is responsible administratively for any negligence in the selection and retention of hospital personnel: it has the administrative function of selecting properly qualified personnel and of discharging incompetent personnel. Should an employee fail to follow the orders of the attending physician, or follow them negligently, the hospital could be liable for its administrative failure to provide competent employees but not for the negligent medical act of such an employee.

As can be seen, medical employees of the hospital occupy a dual relationship with respect to their employer. Interns, resident physicians, and registered nurses are all licensed to practice their professions. In the course of so doing they will perform administrative acts for the hospital, and likewise will perform some medical acts. The rule is that while performing administrative acts they are employees of the hospital, and as such, their negligence is imputed to the hospital under the doctrine of *respondeat superior*. As to medical acts, they are considered to be independent contractors, and any negligence in the performance of such acts is not imputed to the hospital. The theory is that the hospital has control over all administrative acts of such personnel, but that such personnel are obligated by their licenses to practice to exercise their own independent judgments with respect to the accomplishment of medical acts. They are, therefore, personally liable for their own negligence in the performance of medical acts.

There are some instances where hospital authorities interfere with and control the medical acts of some of their employees. If the hospital undertakes to do this, the hospital will be assuming other and further liability beyond that imposed by the general rule.

The majority of cases involving the liability of hospitals are those dealing with the failure of the hospital attendants to properly care for the patients, failure to provide bed rails, and the failure to prevent falls from beds as well as the failure to properly confine mentally disturbed patients. Also, hospitals have been held liable for their failure to foresee the risk involved in allowing a dentist to use the operating room for dental procedures under total anesthetic without having a medical doctor present, and under the doctrine of *respondeat superior*, one hospital was held liable for a resident's referral of a patient to an incompetent employee for treatment, although the hospital would not have been liable for an error of professional judgment by the same resident physician.

1117   Operating room responsibility

A surgical operation is a medical act. It is done by a surgeon whose relationship to the hospital is that of an independent contractor. The hospital furnishes the operating room, the equipment, and some personnel. It is responsible administratively for its failure to provide proper equipment, proper surgical instruments, and competent operating room personnel.

The general rule is that the surgeon has the sole responsibility for the success of the operation. All operating room personnel are under his direction and control while the operation is in progress. Thus the courts have referred to the operating surgeon as the "captain of the ship." He is responsible not only for his own surgical acts but also for the medical acts of all others on the surgical team.

This rule was easy to follow in the past where operating room procedures were fairly simple. Today, many of these procedures are prolonged and extremely complicated. The courts are recognizing more and more the fact that the operating surgeon must devote his entire attention to the surgical operation and cannot, in addition thereto, supervise the work of others. Therefore, there are cases where the operating surgeon has been absolved from liability where the negligent act was done by another physician acting as anesthetist or by a registered nurse who acted as an instrument nurse, sponge nurse, or in another operating room capacity. However, the common-law rule still remains that the operating surgeon has absolute authority in the operating room and therefore, in the absence of mitigating circumstances, he is responsible for all actions performed in connection with the operation.

1118   Defenses: Statute of limitations

The general rule in tort causes of action is that the statute of limitations begins to run from the time of the commission of the wrongful act. This same rule is applied to malpractice cases, regardless of whether the patient is aware of the wrongful act or not. Thus, if a surgeon left a sponge or a surgical instrument in the patient's body at the time of the operation, the tortious act was committed at the time of the operation and the statute begins to run at that time. Should the patient discover the condition before the statute has run, he may sustain his cause of action, but if the discovery is after the statute has run, the patient cannot assert his claim. In view of this latter situation, some courts, recognizing the injustice and the harshness of the rule, began to develop exceptions. These exceptions are (1) the continuous treatment rule, (2) constructive fraud exception, and (3) the date of discovery rule. Not all courts have been confronted with the problem so that the present situation is that some courts apply the strict common-law rule that the statute of limitations begins to run from the date of the commission of the wrongful act, some have adopted one or more of the exceptions as noted, and still others have not spoken on the subject at all.

Therefore, unless the supreme court of a given state has adopted one or more of the exceptions, it should be assumed that the common-law rule will be applied, until the court rules otherwise.

1. *Continuous treatment.* Under this exception, the courts hold that the statute of limitations does not begin to run until the doctor discharges the patient from treatment for the same or related illness out of which the cause of action for malpractice arose. It should be emphasized that this does not mean that there is a continuity of the physician-patient relationship, but the treatment must involve the same or related injuries. This exception is sometimes referred to as the "continuing negligence" rule on the theory that in continuing the treatment the physician's original negligence continued throughout all of the remaining treatment. The following states have adopted this exception:

California	*Hundley* v. *Francis Hospital*, 327 Pac. 2d 131 (1958).
Minnesota	*Schmitt* v. *Esser*, 226 N.W. 196 (1929).

New York	*Hammer* v. *Rosen*, 165 N.E. 2d 756 (1960) ;
	Nervick v. *Fine*, 87 N.Y.S. 2d 534 (1949).
Ohio	*Gillette* v. *Tucker*, 65 N.E. 865 (1902).
Oregon	*Hotelling* v. *Walther*, 130 Pac. 2d 944.
Pennsylvania	*Ayers* v. *Morgan*, 154 Atl. 2d 788 (1959).

The following courts have refused to follow the continuous treatment rule, but in view of the dates of the decisions, there is some doubt as to whether or not the same cases would be decided the same way if the question were again presented in an appropriate case:

| Fed. Ct. (4th Cir.) | *Pickett* v. *Aglinsky*, 110 Fed. 2d 628 (1940). |
| Massachusetts | *Cappuci* v. *Barone*, 165 N.E. 653 (1919). |

2. Constructive fraud.   This exception is sometimes referred to as "fraudulent concealment" and is based on the theory that the relationship of physician and patient is one involving trust and confidence. Therefore, the physician is under a duty to disclose to the patient any facts which he knows or should have known by the exercise of reasonable care relating to the patient's condition, even though such disclosure would include evidence of the physician's wrongful act. The knowledge of the wrongful act is peculiarly within the control of the doctor and in many cases, the patient has no means of ascertaining the occurrence until some manifestation of the malpractice becomes evident. The courts, therefore, hold that the statute of limitations does not begin to run during the period of concealment or until the patient became aware of the malpractice, whichever came first. The states subscribing to this exception are:

Alabama	*Hudson* v. *Moore*, 194 So. 147.
Arizona	*Morrison* v. *Acton*, 198 Pac. 2d 590.
Arkansas	*Burton* v. *Tribble*, 70 S.W. 2d 503.
Georgia	*Saffold* v. *Scarborough*, 86 S.E. 2d 649.
Indiana	*Guy* v. *Schuldt*, 138 N.E. 2d 891.
Kentucky	*Adams* v. *Ison*, 249 S.W. 2d 791.
Minnesota	*Schmucking* v. *Mayo*, 235 N.W. 633.
North Dakota	*Milde* v. *Leigh*, 28 N.W. 2d 530.
New Hampshire	*Lakeman* v. *LaFrance*, 156 Atl. 2d 123.
South Dakota	*Hinkle* v. *Hargens*, 81 N.W. 2d 888.
Tennessee	*Hall* v. *DeSaussure*, 297 S.W. 2d 90.

For a case holding that for this exception to apply there must be some active misconduct, such as misstatements or misrepresentations to the patient, see *DeHann* v. *Winter* [241 N.W. 923 (Michigan)], decided in 1932.

3. Date of discovery.   This exception may seem to overlap the constructive fraud or fraudulent concealment exception, but the cases hold merely that the statute of limitations does not begin to run until the patient discovers the malpractice, whether this comes to him as a result of the physician's disclosure of the wrongful act or as a result of some physical manifestation of the wrongful act. Many of the cases in this category involve foreign objects which are left in the patient's body after an operation, such as sponges, hemostats, and things of like nature. In most of these cases the patient is entirely unaware of the condition, and it is only when complications arise as a result of the presence of the foreign object in the patient's body that he gains the knowledge of what had occurred. It is for that reason that some courts have adopted the date of discovery as being the date from which the statute of limitations will run. One of the elements of investigation in cases of this type will be to ascertain when the patient knew or by the exercise of reasonable care should have known of the malpractice. Then the time period of the statute of limitations will be measured from that date rather than the date of the wrongful act. Clearly, if the statute has run when measured by these criteria, it can be interposed as an affirmative defense. The states subscribing to the date of discovery rule are as follows:

Idaho	*Billings* v. *Sisters of Mercy*, 389 Pac. 2d 224.
Montana	*Grey* v. *Silver Bow County*, 425 Pac. 2d 819;
	Johnson v. *St. Patrick's Hospital*, 417 Pac. 2d 469.
New Jersey	*Fernandi* v. *Strully*, 173 Atl. 2d 277.
Oregon	*Berry* v. *Branner*, 421 Pac. 2d 996.
Pennsylvania	*Ayers* v. *Morgan*, 154 Atl. 2d 788.
Texas	*Gaddis* v. *Smith*, 417 S.W. 2d 577.
West Virginia	*Morgan* v. *Grace Hospital*, 144 S.E. 2d 156;
	Bishop v. *Byrne*, 265 Fed. Supp. 460.
United States	*United States* v. *Reid*, 251 Fed. 2d 691.

Other cases in which the statute of limitations was tolled and which do not fall within the categories noted above are as follows:

Georgia [*Lacy* v. *Ferrento*, 151 S.E. 2d 763]. Brain injury caused by doctor's employee caused insanity which prevented the plaintiff from filing action within the period of limitation. Held statute tolled during period of insanity.

Louisiana [*Hill* v. *Eye, Ear, Nose & Throat Hospital*, 200 So. 2d 34]. Timely institution of suit against one joint tort-feasor tolls the statute as to the other.

Massachusetts [*Pasquale* v. *Chandler*, 215 N.E. 2d 319]. Surgical instrument left in abdominal cavity at the time of operation. Court held that cause of action accrued at the time of the operation and that the statute of limitations was measured from that date, and the cause of action against the surgeon was barred. The failure of the attending physician to discover the presence of the surgical instrument where he had treated the patient within the period of the statute of limitations amounted to actionable negligence and this action was not barred since it was brought within the period of limitation. The failure of the attending physician was a continuing act of negligence which was repeated during the entire period of treatment.

Tennessee [*Frazer* v. *Osborne*, 414 S.W. 2d 118]. Sponge left in incision not discovered until ten years after the operation. Court held that statute of limitations did not run until the termination of the physician-patient relationship.

In some cases, the exceptions noted have been applied to claims against the state, a county, or municipality which in most instances are subject to a shorter period of limitation (usually 90 days). The limitation begins to run in the same manner as in other cases not involving a governmental agency.

1119   Defenses: Assumption of risk

It is clear that any patient that submits to treatment or to an operation assumes some risk. The patient must assume the risks of an allergic reaction to certain types of medication where there is no history or any evidence of any such possible allergy. In some cases, the patient will be treated by the use of narcotics if the condition so demands. The patient runs the risk of the results of such use. In cases of operative procedures, the patient assumes the normal risks of the operation, such as surgical shock and reaction to anesthesia.

If a person consults a doctor who is obviously intoxicated at the time of treatment, and the patient insists that the doctor treat him under those circumstances, the patient will be held to have assumed all of the risks of injury occasioned by the treatment. Also, where the patient insists that a doctor of limited professional skill undertake an extensive surgical procedure or procedures which are beyond his capacity, the patient will have assumed the risk for any unfortunate result.

1120   Defenses: Release of joint tort-feasor

On some occasions it will be found that the patient's injuries were caused by the negligent act of another. The person causing the injury is liable to the patient for any damages which accrue as a proximate result thereof. If the patient selects his doctor with reasonable care, and and the doctor's malpractice causes a greater injury than normally would ensue, the malpractice of the physician will not in any way reduce or mitigate the damages for which the wrongdoer is responsible. The question which is then posed in such cases is whether or not a general release given to the original wrongdoer automatically releases the physician from liability for malpractice in rendering the treatment. The general rule applying to joint tort-feasors is normally applied. Both the doctor and the original wrongdoer acted in concert, although not concurrently, in causing the patient's ultimate damage. Therefore, a release given to the original wrongdoer will automatically operate so as to release the physician. This follows the general rule of law that the release of one joint tort-feasor releases all, and is applied unless the claimant, in settling his case with the original wrongdoer, expressly reserves his right to proceed against the other tort-feasor, namely, the physician. This can easily be accomplished by the use of a covenant not to sue.

As to malpractice which occurs after the patient has settled with the original wrongdoer, the rule seems to be to the contrary. Clearly, the patient is not required to anticipate malpractice on the part of the physician. Therefore, the patient could not know at the time of settlement that malpractice would occur, and, as a result, the settlement would contemplate only the injuries sustained by the patient which were known at the time the settlement was made. It could not release future tortious acts unless the release so given was intended to cover them.

In a recent New York case the plaintiff's leg, having been broken when she was struck by a taxicab, required hospitalization and operation by the defendant's doctor. Believing herself on the road to recovery, she settled the case against the taxi driver who caused the injury, giving him a general release. Thereafter, discovering a permanent shortening of the leg, caused by the alleged malpractice of the doctor both before and after the execution of the release, she brought an action against the doctor. The court found no basis for the application of either the joint tort-feasor rule, or the reasons for that rule, where the parites were not true tort-feasors and where they did not combine to produce the wrong, but only shared a common element of liability. The court said:

We may not say, as a matter of law, that the release executed by the plaintiff bars the present action. The basic question, in the light of our analysis, is whether the plaintiff's settlement with the taxicab driver did, in fact, constitute satisfaction of all damages caused by his wrong, or was intended as such. If it did, or was so intended, no claim remained against the doctor. But, if it did not reflect full satisfaction, and was not so regarded, and the burden of proving such facts rests upon the plaintiff, the release will not prevent recovery against the doctor. However, as indicated, these are questions of fact to be decided upon trial; and, indeed, this is the conclusion which has been announced in well considered cases in other jurisdictions.

1121   Insurance coverage

There is no standard medical malpractice policy. The companies generally tailor existing liability policies or other types of agreements to meet the specifications of the physicians or medical society under whose sponsorship the policies are sold. There are some exclusions which are generally contained in all such policies. The following are usually excluded from the malpractice policy:

1. Acts involving the criminal liability of the physician.
2. Acts performed when the physician is intoxicated or under the influence of drugs.
3. Guarantees as to a specified result of the treatment.
4. Certain types of prescribed treatment, such as X-ray therapy, spinal anesthesia, plastic surgery, and the prescription of contact lenses.
5. Vicarious liability unless there is a specific agreement to cover such liability and a specific premium charged therefor.

The policies cover the tort liability of the physician together with his contractual liability arising under the implied agreement to use skill and care. As noted above, guarantees of a specific result are excluded. With respect to assault and battery, the policy generally excludes intentional acts which constitute assault and battery, but includes any liability arising out of the mere failure on the part of the doctor to obtain consent of the patient to the operation.

One departure from the usual liability coverage is found in malpractice policies. Since the reputation of the physician is a thing of value to him, there is an agreement contained within the policy itself that no case will be settled by the insurance carrier without receiving the prior approval of the insured physician. This means that where there is an offer of settlement the matter must be submitted to the insured physician before any commitments can be made with respect to the settlement. Therefore, the physician reserves to himself the right to decide whether or not a case against him will be settled.

Since this provision places the insurance carrier in a disadvantageous position, since it may not decide the question of settlement, many policies provide that where a proposition of settlement is submitted to the doctor and he does not approve it, the amount of the proposed settlement will represent the maximum liability of the insurance carrier in the case of any future judgment. This agreement will modify the limits of liability as expressed in the main contract, and will serve to reduce them if the physician refuses the proposed settlement.

The insurance industry has found it to be increasingly difficult to write medical malpractice insurance at a profit at existing rates. Some companies have increased their premium rates and others have retired entirely from the medical malpractice field. In order to provide such insurance as is needed, some states have by statute created a Joint Underwriting Association (JUA). Usually this is an unincorporated association, the members of which consist of all the insurance companies writing liability insurance within the state. The member companies are required to assume the expenses and the costs of claims made against the association under policies of insurance written by the association for physicians and hospitals. These measures are limited in duration and the projection is that other and further legislation will be enacted to replace them as experience develops. The following states have JUA legislation:

California	Iowa	New York	South Carolina
Florida	Maine	Ohio	Tennessee
Hawaii	Maryland	Rhode Island	Texas
Idaho	Massachusetts		

Other types of legislation calculated to provide medical malpractice insurance have been passed in the following states:

Arkansas	Michigan	North Carolina
Georgia	Nevada	North Dakota
Indiana	New Hampshire	Wisconsin
Louisiana		

The problem is under further study in these states and others so that it can be expected that other states will join the list as legislation is enacted.

1122   Investigation

Malpractice insurance involves a particularly hazardous exposure as far as the insurance carrier is concerned. For that reason, not all companies are interested in writing the coverage, and those who are insist upon a certain volume before undertaking to provide it. What usually happens is that negotiations for the coverage are conducted by the state or county medical society on behalf of the membership. The commitment usually is made that the writing of the insurance is conditioned upon the acceptance or purchase of the insurance by a certain percentage of the membership. Thus, while the policies are issued to the individual physicians, the medical society has an interest in the manner in which claims are handled. The society is likewise interested in the esteem in which the profession is held and, as a result, actively participates in the investigation and disposition of malpractice claims.

Most societies have a malpractice committee to whom copies of all claims are referred by the physicians involved. The commitee then makes its own investigation together with recommendations to the company, as well as to the society, with reference to further investigation which is necessary for settlement or a denial of liability, whichever seems to be appropriate under the circumstances. Usually, as each case is reported, the committee appoints one of its members as a "case manager" who will undertake personally to assist and guide the physician involved as well as to make recommendations to the insurance adjuster. The existence of such an arrangement can be of considerable assistance to the adjuster in that the committee or the case manager will aid the adjuster in developing information as to the standard medical practice as well as giving assistance with respect to the technical details of the treatment which was undertaken.

There no doubt will be situations where there will be a difference of opinion between the adjuster and the malpractice committee. This may have a definite influence upon the future relationship between the medical society and the company. Therefore, where points of difference arise, it is suggested that the underwriting department of the company be kept fully informed as to the details thereof, the requests made by the medical society, and the position taken by the adjuster with respect to them.[1]

It is difficult to pinpoint the motivation which impels a patient to bring an action against his physician in malpractice. The most common cause of the person's dissatisfaction arises with respect to the physician's bill for services. Where the physician's bill is much higher than the patient expected, the patient may resort to the threat of a malpractice action in order to compel the physician to reduce it. In other cases, the patient may object to the means adopted by the physician in attempting to collect his bill: making demands which the patient regards as unreasonable, referring the case to a particularly irritating collection agency, or even beginning suit against the patient for the collection of the bill. A great many malpractice claims therefore are interposed as counterclaims to an action on the part of the physician demanding

---

[1] More information is needed in situations of this type than normally is gathered in the ordinary liability investigation. For that reason, an outline of a malpractice investigation follows this section.

payment for his medical services. These matters introduce an additional element into the handling of malpractice claims, since, while it is no part of the adjuster's duty to inquire into the amount of the bill and how the medical charges will be paid, settlement of many of these cases will be accomplished merely by making arrangements satisfactory to both the physician and the patient with respect to the payment of his bill and will not necessarily require any payment whatsoever on the part of the company.

With respect to patients, most hospitals require that the doctor enter his orders on the patient's chart in writing and require that the doctor sign each order as given. This is done for the protection of the hospital so that there will be a record of exactly what the doctor ordered and the record will indicate that his directions were followed by such hospital personnel as were charged with the responsibility. In those cases it will be necessary for the adjuster to review the hospital records and, more particularly, the orders given by the doctor which are alleged to be carelessly or improperly given. The adjuster should be familiar with some of the abbreviations which are used in the directions for medications. (See Section 1833.)

The adjuster must recognize, in handling these cases, that there is more involved than a mere claim for damages for personal injuries. The doctor's reputation and future standing in medical circles may well depend upon the outcome of the malpractice claim. Therefore, the adjuster's responsibility is greater in this class of cases than in matters where the future status of the insured is not involved.

1123 Good Samaritan legislation

Where there is a relationship of physician and patient the duty of the physician to render treatment in accordance with the standard medical practice is imposed upon him, whether the relationship arose as a consequence of an emergency or not. Standard medical practice in all instances will consist of treatment under antiseptic conditions, with the proper equipment and tools of the trade, proper medication, and, where needed, a sufficient number of trained medical assistants. Any care which falls below this standard is negligence.

The doctor is not under any duty to accept all who apply for treatment as patients, and he may refuse to enter the relationship without incurring any liability, no matter how great the patient's need of immediate treatment may be. Thus, the doctor may legally walk by the victim of an automobile accident, who is bleeding to death, without making any offer of assistance and he will incur no legal liability whatsoever. If he should offer assistance and it is accepted, or if he assists an unconscious patient, the relationship of physician and patient arises and the doctor assumes the duty of care which the law imposes upon him. The circumstances under which an emergency arose do not in any way alter the duty of the physician in the rendering of the treatment.

It has frequently happened that the physician was on vacation, was on a hunting trip, or in any case way from his practice when an emergency arose with respect to an injured or sick person.   The doctor, being on vacation, did not have his kit with him, but recognized that if something wasn't done immediately the patient might die. Therefore, he undertook to treat the patient—or operate on him with whatever surgical instruments or knives were available—with the result that the patient recovered. Clearly, an operation performed or medical treatment rendered under these circumstances would not and could not meet the standards of accepted medical practice. Therefore, the physician is chargeable with negligence even though he was acting as a "good Samaritan" in relieving a person in extreme or dire need of the medical treatment, such as he could give. In some cases physicians who rendered treatment under these conditions were astonished to find that the gratitude of the patient was short-lived, and that the patient brought an action for malpractice where the results were not as could be expected under the best conditions. Because some large verdicts were returned in cases of this type, the various medical groups have been concerned to the extent that they have issued instructions to their membership as to the action each should take under emergency conditions. In addition, they have sponsored legislation which would relieve the "good Samaritan" doctor, who responded to an emergency, of the duty of conforming to the standards of medical practice, and which would allow a recovery only where an injury was caused by the gross negligence of the physician, abrogating any right of recovery based on ordinary negligence. These laws are receiving the consideration of the various state legislatures.

OUTLINE FOR MEDICAL MALPRACTICE CASES

It is suggested that the following or a similar outline be used in malpractice investigations.

Insured

1. Name
2. Age
3. Home Address   How long?
4. Business address   How long?
5. Occupation
6. Educational background
7. Professional qualifications
8. Medical societies
9. Special societies
10. Hospital connections
    Interned
11. Year licensed to practice in state
12. Concurrent insurance
    Date of policy
    With whom?
    Limits

Claimant

13. Date of first professional visit
    Last visit
14. Claimant's name
    Address
    Age
    Occupation
15. What is the malpractice, error, or mistake alleged to have been?
16. When did insured first become aware of any allegation or claim of malpractice, error, or mistake?
    How?
    By whom?
17. When did insured first notify company?
    Delayed notice
    Insured's explanation
    Reserve rights orally
18. Was patient referred to insured?
    By whom?
    Why?
19. Nature of patient's complaints
20. Dates of all visits
21. Past history
22. Findings on examination
23. Lab (including X ray)
    Diagnosis
    Prognosis
24. Treatment (full detail)
25. If surgical operation
    (1) Preoperative diagnosis
    (2) Postoperative diagnosis
26. Insured's witnesses
    Who are they?
    What do they say?
27. Unfavorable witnesses
28. Accepted practice
29. Names of all persons present at the time of treatments
30. Amount of patient's bill
    Amount paid
    Amount outstanding
    Is insured pressing to get bill paid?
    Has he turned unpaid balance over to a collection agency?
    Has agency filed suit to force collection?
31. Arrange with insured not to talk about the case except to those protecting his interests. Do not write letters to anyone without our approval. Forward summons or any other papers to us.
32. Any admissions against interest by insured? If so, obtain a copy.
33. Has insured voluntarily made any payment, assumed any obligation, or incurred any expense in connection with this case?

34. Will insured give written consent to settle the case?
35. Copies of all insured's records
    Can he obtain copy of hospital records?
    Can insured obtain any records on claimant prior to his treating him?

ACCOUNTANTS

1124   Profession of public accounting defined

With the rise of various tax and governmental regulations of business, the services of a professional accountant is almost indispensable, and because of this need, many have entered the profession.

Section 7401 of the New York Education Law defines the profession as follows:

> The practice of the profession of public accountancy is defined as holding oneself out to the public, in consideration of compensation received or to be received, offering to perform or performing for other persons, services which involve signing, delivering or issuing, or causing to be signed, delivered or issued any financial, accounting or related statement or any opinion on, report on, or certificate to such statement if, by reason of the signature, or the stationery or wording employed, or otherwise, it is indicated or implied that the practitioner has acted, or is acting, in relation to said financial accounting or related statement, or reporting as an independent accountant or auditor or as an individual having or purporting to have expert knowledge in accounting or auditing.

Other states have similar laws which define the profession of public accounting, and, in addition, require that the person submit to an examination as to his knowledge and capability in order to receive a certificate from the state authorizing him to practice the profession. Thus, persons who practice the profession as certified by the state are called certified public accountants. The granting of this certificate by the state subjects the accountant to regulation by the state.

1125   Liability to employer-client

The certified public accountant warrants that he possesses that degree of skill commonly possessed by others in the same employment, and he warrants that he will employ his skill for the best interests of his client. If he does not have the skill, then his application for employment is fraudulent, in which case his employer is not obligated to accept his work or pay his fee.

On the other hand, if he does have the skill, and he undertakes the task, he will be liable to his employer for any losses which might be incurred as a result of his negligently performing the audit, bad faith or dishonesty. He is not, however, liable for mere errors in judgment.

For example, in *1136 Tenants' Corporation* v. *Rothenberg*, (319 N.Y.S. 2d 1007, affirmed in 30 New York 2d 585), the accountants were retained by a manager of the corporation who had been embezzling funds from his employer to perform auditing services for a fee of $600 per year. The accountants became aware of the absence of bills and invoices from the books and accounts, but certified the audit as being true and correct. Upon discovery of the defalcations, the corporation sued the accountants for the losses sustained as a result of their reliance on the false audit, and recovered a judgment in the sum of $250,000. The accountants claimed that they were employed only to make "write-ups" of the company's books and that if their work was unsatisfactory, their maximum liability would consist of the amount of the fees which they had been paid. In affirming the judgment the court found that the accountants were paid to audit the books and that the procedures performed by the accountants were "incomplete, inadequate and improperly performed." The measure of damages was held to be the amount of the loss sustained by the client and not the amount of the fee paid, or the cost of a satisfactory audit.

The defense of contributory negligence is available to the accountant, where the client-employer fails to make adequate records available or where there has been a course of dealing over the years which entailed a loss caused by the lack of due care on the part of the client and which could have been prevented by the exercise of ordinary prudence. For example, in *Craig* v. *Anyon* (208 N.Y.S. 259), the accountant was paid the sum of $2,000 to make an audit. He failed to discover that an employee had been guilty of embezzlement over the period of years and that the amount of the client's loss was $1,177,085.26. When the defalcation was discovered, the client sued the accountant seeking to recover his entire loss. The court held that while the accountant was negligent, such negligence was not the proximate cause of the plaintiff's loss, and therefore limited the recovery to $2,000, representing the amount of the fee paid. The court further held that as a matter of law, the only loss which resulted directly and proximately from the negligence of the accountant was the sum of $2,000, the fee paid for an unsatisfactory audit. The court said that "plaintiff's should not be allowed to recover for losses which *they* could have avoided by the exercise of reasonable care." It would appear that in this case, the loss had already been sustained and that the accountant's failure to discover it was the basis for the suit.

1126   Liability to third persons

Where an accountant prepares a financial statement which he knows is for the benefit of a particular person, the accountant is liable to that third person if the financial statement is inaccurate or fraudulent, or does not truthfully reflect the condition of the person or corporation covered by the report. For example, in *Glanzer* v. *Shepard* [135 N.E. 275 (New York)], a public weigher was employed by the owner of some beans to certify the correct weight to a prospective purchaser. The weight certified was incorrect, and the weigher was found liable to the purchaser for the damages which he had sustained in buying the short weight. The weigher was employed solely by the owner, but since he knew the purpose of the certification and since the purchaser was the beneficiary of the contract with the owner, the court held the weigher liable. While this case does not deal specifically with the relationship of an accountant with his client, it is frequently cited as representing the principle that the accountant is liable to a third party for an incorrect audit where the accountant knows that the third party will rely on the audit. On the other hand, where the accountant prepares a financial statement for his employer and he has no knowledge or relationship with the third party, there are two schools of thought among the courts. The New York rule as illustrated in *Ultramares* v. *Touche* (174 N.E. 441), holds that the accountant is not liable to unknown third parties who may rely on the financial statement negligently prepared for the client. Since there was no contract of employment with the unknown third party and since the unknown third party could not qualify as a beneficiary of the accounting contract, there was no liability on the part of the accountant. The court said:

> If liability for negligence exists, a thoughtless slip or blunder, the failure to detect a theft or forgery beneath the cover of deceptive entries may expose accountants to a liability in an indeterminate amount to an indeterminate class. The hazards of a business conducted on these terms are so extreme as to enkindle doubt whether a flaw may not exist in the implication of a duty that exposes to these consequences.

Thus, the rule is stated that where the accountant has no relationship with the third party, sometimes referred to as "privity," or no knowledge of the existence of a third party or of the reliance that such third party may place on the statement, there is no liability on the part of the accountant to the third party for negligence in preparing the statement. This rule has been cited with approval in *Investment Corporation of Florida* v. *Buchman* [298 So. 2d 291 (Florida District Court of Appeal)]; *Canaveral Capital Corporation* v. *Bruce* [214 So. 2d 505 (Florida District Court of Appeal)]; *Stephens Industries, Inc.* v. *Haskins & Sells* [438 Fed. 2d 357 S.E. (Colorado)]; *MacNederland* v. *Barnes* [199 S.E. 2d 564 (Georgia)]; and *Bunge Corp.* v. *Eide* [372 Fed. Supp. 1058 (North Dakota)]. Conversely, there are a number of courts which have rejected the Ultramares rule as well as the Restatement. The Restatement, Torts, Second, under Section 552, the following rule is suggested:

> (1) One who, in the course of his business, profession or employment, or in a transaction in which he has pecuniary interest, supplies false information for the guidance of others in their business tranactions, is subject to liability for pecuniary loss caused to them by their justifiable reliance upon the information, if he fails to exercise reasonable care or competence in obtaining or communicating the information.
> (2) Except as stated in subsection (3), the liability stated in subsection (1) is limited to loss suffered (a) by the person or one of the persons for whose benefit and guidance he intends to supply the information, or knows that the recipient intends to supply it; and (b) through reliance upon it in a transaction which he intends the information to influence, or knows that the recipient so intends, or in a substantially similar transaction.

(3) The liability of one who is under a public duty to give the information extends to loss suffered by any of the class of persons for whose benefit the duty is created, in any of the transactions in which it is intended to protect them.

In *Ryan* v. *Kanne* [170 N.W. 2d 395 (Iowa)], the court rejected the accountant's defense of the lack of privity between them and the plaintiff, holding the accountants liable to third parties who rely on the financial statement. The court said:

When the accountant is aware that the balance sheet to be prepared is to be used by a certain party or parties who will rely thereon in extending credit or in assuming liability for the obligations of the party audited, the lack of privity should be no valid defense to a claim for damages due to the accountant's negligence. We know of no good reason why accountants should not accept the legal responsibility to known third parties who reasonably rely upon the financial statement prepared and submitted to them.

Other cases reaching this same conclusion are *Shatterproof Glass Corporation* v. *James* [466 S.W. 2d 873 (Texas)]; *Fischer* v. *Kletz* [266 Fed. Supp. 180 (New York)]; and *R. I. Hospital* v. *Schwartz* (455 Fed. Supp 847).

1127   SEC liability

The accountant is responsible for the financial statements filed with and required by the Securities and Exchange Commission. When such filing is made and the registration statement contains an untrue statement of a material fact or fails to include and state a material fact required to be stated or necessary to make the statement clear and not misleading, the investor can sue the accountant for damages. For a complete discussion of the accountant's liability, see *Escott* v. *BarChris Construction Corporation* [283 Fed. Supp. 643 (Federal District Court, Southern District, New York)].

1128   Statute of limitations

The general rule is that the statute of limitations begins to run from the time the cause of action accrues. This usually is from the time that the negligent act occurs. In the case of accountants, however, the negligent act may have occurred at the time of the audit, but the infliction of damages may not occur until a later time. Obviously, the plaintiff would have no assertable cause of action until some damages were sustained, and therefore the rule is that the statute of limitations will not begin to run until the cause of action has accrued. For example, in *Atkins* v. *Crosland* [417 S.W. 2d 150 (Texas)], the defendant-accountant prepared the plaintiff's income tax returns for the year 1960, said work being completed on December 31, 1960. The return was improperly prepared and the plaintiff was deprived of a tax savings in a substantial amount. As a result, on October 20, 1961 the Commissioner of Internal Revenue assessed the plaintiff with a tax deficiency. On September 3, 1963, the action was begun. The defendant-accountant moved to dismiss the complaint since the action was brought more than two years after December

31, 1960. In denying the motion, the court held that the cause of action arose at the time the deficiency was assessed, and therefore was brought within the two-year period. The court said:

The test to determine when the statute of limitations begins to run against an action sounding in tort is whether the act causing the damage does or does not of itself constitute a legal injury, that is, an injury giving rise to a cause of action because it is an invasion of some right of plaintiff. If the act is of itself not unlawful in this sense, and the plaintiff sues to recover damages subsequently accruing from, and consequent on, the act, the cause of action accrues, and the statute begins to run, when, and only when, the damages are sustained; and this is true although at the time the act is done it is apparent that injury will inevitably result.

The court held that the plaintiff's cause of action did not arise until the tax deficiency was assessed. Until that time, the plaintiff had not been injured and could not assert a cause of action.

If, however, the act of which the injury is the natural sequence is of itself a legal injury to the plaintiff, a completed wrong, the cause of action accrues and the statute begins to run from the time the act is committed, even where little of any actual damage occurs immediately on the commission of the tort. [See *Tennessee Gas Transmission Co.* v. *Fromme.* 269 S.W. 2d 336 (Texas).]

ARCHITECTS

1129   Architect defined

An architect may be defined as a person whose profession it is to devise plans and specifications, ornamentation, and alterations of buildings or other structures, and, in some cases where the contract so requires, to supervise each step of the construction. An architect or engineer has also been identified as one whose special occupation is to design buildings, both residential and commercial, to fix the thickness of the walls and the supports necessary to hold them in proper position. He also determines the kind and quality of the material which is to be used, as well as giving guidance and supervision to the builders in the course of the construction.

The practice of architecture requires learning, skill, and integrity. It is an occupation that is affected with the public interest in the sense that the protection and welfare of the public requires that buildings and other structures to be properly designed and safely constructed, not only as to the end result but also during the course of construction. The state therefore has the power to regulate the profession and to determine who is qualified to engage in it. The state may issue a license to those who qualify and may deny the use of the title of "architect" and forbid the practice of architecture to anyone not properly licensed. A typical statute (Ala. Code Tit. 46. Section 8) reads as follows:

In order to safeguard life, health and property, no person shall practice architecture in this state or use the title "architect" or any title, sign, card or device to indicate that such person is practicing architecture or is an architect unless such person shall be registered as an architect as hereinafter, provided and shall thereafter comply with the provisions of this chapter.

In most states, persons desiring to enter the business of drawing plans and specifications of buildings and residences, as well as other structures, are required to demonstrate the past education which they have received, and also to demonstrate their ability to perform by passing an examination before they are licensed and permitted to offer their services to the public.

1130   Responsibilities to the employer

The duties and responsibilities of the architect are spelled out in his contract of employment. Some contracts merely require the architect to draw the plans and specifications and nothing more. Others require in addition that the architect supervise the work, and in most cases he is given the authority to stop the work at any time when the contract with the builder is not being properly performed. There are a number of contract forms recommended by the American Institute of Architects, which are used generally by the profession. These contracts are subject to change and are amended frequently. The claims representative who is involved with claims for or against architects should in each instance review the particular contract that is involved.

Regardless of the form of contract that is being used, the architect impliedly warrants that he possesses that degree of skill and learning ordinarily possessed by architects in good standing, practicing in the same locality and under the same circumstances. He must exert his best efforts on behalf of his client in the exercise of due diligence and his best judgment in an effort to accomplish the purpose for which he is employed. He will be subject to liability to his employer if he does not possess the skill he impliedly warranted that he had or if he does not expend his best efforts in behalf of his client.

1131   Duties and responsibilities to third persons

Until recent years, architects had a peculiar type of immunity from suit by third persons. The courts felt that the architect in most cases was an adviser to the builder or owner and that the responsibility, if any, for accidents occurring at the construction site was the responsibility of either the owner or the contractor. At the present time, there is a trend toward placing responsibility upon the architect for defective plans, inadequate improper specifications of materials and for failure to properly supervise the job where an accident has occurred. The injured person would be an employee of the builder or his subcontractors or a member of the public.

Frequently, the architect is brought in as an additional defendant by the service of a third-party complaint by the defendant-builder or defendant-owner. If the circumstances are such that the accident was caused by lack of proper supervision by the architect, lack of care in determining the specifications for the material to be used or a defective design of the building, the architect may be liable for the entire judgment, even though the work was actually performed by others.

There is a growing tendency on the part of the courts to apply products liability principles to the completed work product of the architect. In *Inman* v. *Binghampton Housing Authority* [143 N.E. 2d 895 (New York)], the court could see no difference in principle between real property and chattels, or personal property. Calling attention to *MacPherson* v. *Buick Motor Co.* (111 N.E. 1050), which held a manufacturer of an inherently dangerous chattel (an automobile) which was defectively made, liable for injuries to remote users, the court could see no difference between the liability of the manufacturer in that case than the liability of those who plan and put up structures on land. To the same effect is *Foley* v. *Pittsburgh-Des Moines Co.* [68 Atl. 2d 517 (Pa)].

1132   Statute of limitations

There are only a few cases on this subject, but the general rule seems to be that the statute of limitations begins to run from the date of the accident and not from the date that the work was defectively done. This would seem to parallel the conclusions drawn in the case of accountants on the same subject.

ATTORNEYS

1133   Attorney defined

Strictly speaking, an attorney is a term which denotes an agent or substitute, or one who is appointed and authorized in the place or stead of another. A person who is so authorized is called an attorney-in-fact, and his authority is usually derived from an instrument called a "power of attorney." He may or not be an attorney-at-law.

An attorney-at-law is an advocate, counsel, or official agent employed in preparing, managing, and trying cases in the courts. He is an officer of the court. To so act, he must be licensed by the state, which license is issued only after the successful completion of a law school course of study and the passing of a bar examination. Some states require that he also serve a period of clerkship with an admitted attorney before a plenary license is issued.

The bar, being a footrail in front of the judge's bench beside which attorneys plead their partys' causes became a symbol of law practice in this country. Since only attorneys-at-law may so appear and plead before this bar, the term "admission to the bar" arose and associations of lawyers are usually referred to as Bar Associations.

1134   Practice of law defined

There is no general definition of the practice of law laid down by the courts. They have preferred to decide each case coming before them on its particular merits and then to decide whether or not the particular facts brought the case within the compass of the practice of law. 7 CJS Attorney & Client, Section 3g sets forth the following definition:

The general meaning of the term "practice of law" is of common knowledge, although the boundaries of its definition may be indefinite as to some transactions. As generally understood, it is the doing or performing of services in a court of justice, in any matter pending therein, throughout the various states, and in conformity with the adopted rules of procedure; but it is not confined to performing services in an action or proceeding pending in courts of justice, and, in a larger sense, it includes legal advice and counsel, and the preparation of legal instruments and contracts by which legal rights are secured, although such matter may or may not be pending in a court.

In spite of the lack of a definitive statement from the courts, persons who are not authorized to practice law are subject to injunction and criminal liability if they should engage in a practice which the court might define as the practice of law. The reason for this is the protection of the public. An attorney is subject to a Code of Professional Responsibility and the Canons of Legal Ethics. He is subject to discipline by the Grievance Committee of the Bar Association with the result that an injured client always has recourse to such committee by filing a complaint. A person, not a member of the bar is not subject to any discipline.

1135   Duties and responsibilities of the attorney

In discussing the duty owed by an attorney to his client, the court in *Olsen* v. *North* (276 Ill. App. 457) made the following pronouncement:

When a person adopts the profession of law, if he assumes to exercise the duties in behalf of another for hire and reward, he must be held to employ in his undertakings a reasonable degree of care and skill. If injury results to the client, from want of such reasonable care and skill, he must respond in damages to the extent of the injuries sustained. It is the duty of an attorney to bring to the conduct of his client's business the ordinary legal knowledge and skill common to the members of the legal profession, to act toward his client with the most scrupulous good faith and fidelity, and to exercise in the course of his employment that reasonable care and diligence which is usually exercised by lawyers.

The failure of the attorney to exercise his best efforts in behalf of his client is malpractice and is actionable as such.

The majority of claims involving legal malpractice stem from the failure of the attorney to exercise care in the handling of litigation. Damages have been allowed where the attorney has allowed the statute of limitations to run (*Parker-Smith* v. *Prince*, 158 N.Y.S. 346); failed to file an appearance with the result that the complaint was dismissed (*Grayson* v. *Wilkinson*, 13 Miss. 268); and failed to prosecute an action once begun (*Kash N'Kary Supermarkets* v. *Garcia*, 221 So. 2d 786). Other cases outside the litigation area in which the attorney has been held guilty of malpractice include the following: failure to observe a title defect (*Owen* v. *Neely*, 471 S.W. 2d 705, Florida); drafting an unenforceable contract (*Stein* v. *Kremer*, 112 N.Y.S. 1087);

failure to attach a lien on the debtor's property (*Orr* v. *Waldorf*, 291 Fed. 343).

INSURANCE ADJUSTERS

1136 Adjuster defined

Strictly speaking, the business of adjusting and investigating insurance claims is not a profession in the same sense as is the practice of law or medicine. The business does require a certain amount of education and experience. Therefore, the insurance adjuster may be defined as one who is a layman with expertise. As an educational background, he does require a certain amount of knowledge of law, medicine, and above all the psychology of dealing with others.

In some states adjusters are required to be licensed before they can engage in the business. Some states also require the successful passing of an examination and require that the license be renewed at periodic intervals. In some states independent adjusters are required not only to have a license but to be bonded as well. The license requirement arose during the Great Depression of the 1930s when attorneys took the position that adjusters were encroaching on the practice of law and furthermore they were not subject to the same discipline as are members of the bar. To meet this latter argument, the states supplied the disciplinary function by requiring a license, which could be revoked for cause by the state authority. To further meet this objection, an agreement was reached with the American Bar Association in January 1939 wherein it was agreed that laymen have a proper place in the adjustment of claims and that such occupation did not constitute the unauthorized practice of law. A Statement of Principles on Respective Rights and Duties of Lawyers and Laymen in the Business of Adjusting Insurance Claims was agreed upon, and these Principles are used as a guide for the adjuster in the handling of his claims.

1137 Principles on Respective Rights

The Statement of Principles on Respective Rights and Duties of Lawyers and Laymen in the Business of Adjusting Insurance Claims reads as follows:

1. Claims under insurance policies, for the purpose of this statement, are divided into two classes:

First—A claim in contract by a policy holder or beneficiary directly against the insurance company which issued the contract.

Second—A claim of a third person in tort against the holder of a policy of liability insurance.

2. In the first class the claimant and the insurance company each has the right to discuss the merit of the claim with the other and settle it.

3. In the second class, under a policy by which the company insures the liability of the policyholder, it is recognized that the company has a direct financial interest in the claim presented against the policyholder, and in a suit in which the name

of the company may not appear as a party litigant, but which the company is obliged to defend in the name of the policyholder. Therefore, the company has a right:

(*a*) To discuss with the policyholder or the claimant the merit of the claim, and to settle it.

(*b*) To investigate the facts, interview witnesses, appraise damages, consider and determine the liability of the company and its policyholder in the factual circumstances.

4. In handling claims under the second class—

(*a*) The companies or their representatives will not advise the claimant as to his legal rights.

(*b*) The companies and their representatives, including attorneys, will inform the policyholder of the progress of any suit against the policyholder and its probable results. If any diversity of interest shall appear between the policyholder and the company, the policyholder shall be fully advised of the situation and invited to retain his own counsel. Without limiting the general application of the foregoing, it is contemplated that this will be done in any case in which it appears probable that an amount in excess of the limit of the policy is involved, or in any case in which the company is defending under a reservation of rights, or in any case in which the prosecution of a counterclaim appears advantageous to the policyholder.

5. Under both classes of claims—

(*a*–1) The companies or their representatives will not deal directly with any claimant represented by an attorney without the consent of the attorney. (The word "deal" means to negotiate, settle, do business with and negotiate for a settlement or payment. Any definition of the word "deal" would not prevent a direct approach to the claimant for the purpose of checking his identification, or the bona fides of his representation by an attorney.)

(*a*–2) No lay person, lay firm, lay partnership or corporation serving as a representative of an insurance company, in the handling of a claim, shall engage in the practice of law.

(*b*) The companies may properly interview any witnesses, or prospective witnesses without the consent of opposing counsel or party. In doing so, however, the company representative will scrupulously avoid any suggestion calculated to induce the witnesses to suppress or deviate from the truth, or in any degree affect their free or untrammeled conduct when appearing at the trial or on the witness stand. If any witness making a signed statement so requests, he shall be given a copy thereof.

[Note: At a meeting of March 7, 1954, it was agreed: (1) that this language applies to all witnesses—plaintiff's, defendant's and neutral witnesses; (2) that no time limit is placed upon the witness requesting a copy of the statement; and (3) that the obligation to furnish a copy of the statement runs only to the witness himself or herself.

(*c*) The companies or their representatives will not advise the claimant to refrain from seeking legal advice, or against the retention of counsel to protect his interest.

(*d*)   The companies will respect the disabilities of minors and incompetents, and agrees that no settlement of a cause of action of an infant or incompetent shall be presented to the court for approval, except under provision for an investigation of the propriety of the settlement either by the court or by counsel independent of the defendant.

(*e*)   The companies will not permit their employees—whether laymen or lawyers—to collect for agents or policyholders claims or accounts in which the company has no interest.

(*f*)   The companies recognize that the Canons of Ethics of the American Bar Association apply to all branches of the legal profession, and that specialists in particular branches are not to be considered as exempt from the application of those Canons.

(*g*)   Lay adjusters will only be permitted to fill in blanks of release forms previously drafted by counsel, and they will be forbidden to draft special releases called for by the unusual circumstances of any settlement. All such special releases shall be prepared by counsel.

(*h*)   The companies will undertake to be responsible for the conduct of their employees in observing and executing the foregoing principles, and will endeavor to see that their representatives, other than employees, do likewise.

The Statement of Principles also created a Conference Committee on Adjusters, consisting of ten members, five of whom shall represent the American Bar Association and five who shall be representatives of the insurance companies. The Committee will continue to meet frequently and it is hoped that all complaints of the conduct of lawyers or insurance companies will be referred for consideration.

Since all of the companies have subscribed to this Statement of Principles, the adjuster is obligated to undertake his work within the framework of the rules. Most of the principles reflect the usual procedure in the adjustment of claims. The one section, namely 5 (a–1), has been the source of some difficulty. It is agreed that the adjuster will not deal with a claimant who is represented by an attorney. This would seem to mean that the adjuster must have some knowledge or notice that the claimant has employed an attorney. Otherwise, the adjuster is free to follow his normal procedure in contracting the claimant, securing a statement, or negotiating a settlement. If the attorney has put the company on notice of his employment by letter or other communication, then the adjuster may not deal with the claimant without the consent of the attorney. If the attorney has not given such notice, but the claimant tells the adjuster that he has employed an attorney, the adjuster cannot deal further with the claimant. In the absence of notice or knowledge on the part of the adjuster that an attorney has been employed, it would seem that the adjuster could deal with the claimant, unless the employment of an attorney is brought to his attention.

The section also recognizes the fact that in some cases attorneys have been known to send out representation letters when in truth and in fact, they have not been retained. The letter may have been sent under a misunderstanding or a misapprehension of the claimant's desires. In any case, the rule is that the adjuster may contact the claimant in such a case to determine whether or not in fact an attorney has been employed.

In the case of witnesses' statements, it should be noted that the obligation of the company to supply copies of the witness's statement is to the witness himself and no one else. Frequently, an attorney will request a copy of his client's statement. Technically, the company is under no obligation to comply, but it may waive the technicality and supply the copy. Otherwise, the copy of the statement will be given at the witness's request only.

1138   Unfair claim settlement practices acts

The adjuster's conduct of his business has been further circumscribed by the enactment of unfair claim settlement practices acts in a number of states. These statutes prohibit unfair settlement practices and in each case provide for a fine or other forfeiture to be imposed upon the insurance carrier whose employees are guilty of any violation. A typical act is Section 40-d of the New York Insurance Law, which is titled "Unfair Claim Settlement Practices by Insurers" and which reads as follows:

No insurer doing business in this state shall engage in unfair claim settlement practices. Any of the following acts by an insurer, if committed without just cause and performed with such frequency as to indicate a general business practice, shall constitute unfair claim settlement practices:

(*a*) knowing misrepresenting to claimants pertinent facts or policy provisions relating to the coverages at issue;

(*b*) failing to acknowledge with reasonable promptness pertinent communications with respect to claims arising under its policies;

(*c*) failing to adopt and implement reasonable standards for the prompt investigation of claims arising under its policies;

(*d*) not attempting in good faith to effectuate prompt, fair and equitable settlements of claims submitted in which liability has become reasonably clear; or

(*e*) compelling policyholders to institute suits to recover amounts due under its policies by offering less than the amounts ultimately recovered in suits brought by them.

Section 5 of the Insurance Law provides that each instance shall be treated as a separate violation and subject to penalties. A $500 fine shall be levied against the insurance company for each violation.

Under the act, the Insurance Commissioner is empowered to formulate rules and regulations to implement the enforcement of the provisions of the statute. The rules and regulations so promulgated are as follows:

Preamble

Section 40-d of the Insurance Law was added by Chapter 296 of the Laws of 1970, effective September 1, 1970. Section 40-d prohibits insurers doing business in this state from engaging in unfair claims settlement practices and provides that if any insurer performs any of the acts or practices proscribed by that section without just cause and with such frequency as to indicate a general business practice, then those acts shall constitute unfair claims settlement practices.

This regulation is issued for the purpose of defining certain minimum standards which, if violated without just cause and with such frequency as to indicate a general business practice, would constitute unfair claims settlement practices. This regulation is not exclusive, and other acts, not herein specified, may also be found to constitute such practices.

Section 216.1 Definitions

The definitions set forth in this section shall govern the construction of the terms used in this regulation.

a. "Agent" shall mean any person, firm, association, or corporation authorized to act as the representative of an insurer and licensed pursuant to the provisions of Sections 113, 115 or 119 of the Insurance Law. With respect to group life and group accident and health policies, an employer-policyholder shall be the agent of the insurer to the extent such employer has been authorized to act on behalf of such insurer.

b. "Claimant" shall mean any person, firm, association or corporation asserting, directly or indirectly, a right to payment under a policy of insurance.

c. "Investigation" shall mean any procedure adopted by an insurer to determine whether to accept or reject a claim.

d. "Notice of Claim" shall mean any notification, whether in writing or otherwise, to an insurer or its agent, by any person, firm, association, or corporation asserting, directly, or indirectly, a right to payment under a policy of insurance, which reasonably apprises the insurer of the facts pertinent to a claim.

Section 216.2 Applicability

This regulation shall apply to all insurers licensed to do business in this state, except:

a. It shall not be applicable to policies of workmen's compensation insurance issued pursuant to the provisions of Section 46(15); credit insurance issued pursuant to the provisions of Section 46(17); title insurance issued pursuant to the provisions of Section 46(18); inland marine insurance issued pursuant to the provisions 46(20)(a), 46(20)(b) and 46(20)(d) unless such policy is subject to the provisions of Sections 167–a or 167–b; and ocean marine insurance issued pursuant to the provisions of Section 46(21).

b. Sections 216.6(a) and 216.6(b) of this regulation shall not be applicable to policies of life insurance written pursuant to the provisions of Section 46(1) and to accident and health policies written pursuant to the provisions of Section 46(2).

c. Sections 216.4, 216.5 and 216.6(c) of this regulation shall not be applicable to policies of accident and health insurance written pursuant to the provisions of Section 46(2) where the claimant is neither a policyholder, nor a certificate holder under a policy of group insurance.

Section 216.3 Misrepresentation of Policy Provisions

a. No insurer shall knowingly misrepresent to a claimant the term, benefits, or advantages of the insurance policy pertinent to the claim.

b. No insurer shall deny any element of a claim on the grounds of a specific policy provision, condition, or exclusion unless reference to such provision, condition or exclusion is made in writing.

c. Any payment, settlement, or offer of settlement which, without explanation, does not include all elements of the claim which should be included according to the claim filed by the claimant and investigated by the insurer shall, provided it is within the policy limits, be deemed to be a communication which misrepresents a pertinent policy provision.

Section 216.4 Failure to Acknowledge Pertinent Communications

a. Every insurer, upon notification of a claim, shall, within fifteen working days, acknowledge the receipt of such notice. Such acknowledgement may be in writing if the notice is in writing. If an acknowledgement is made by any other means, an appropriate notation shall be made in the claimant's file. Notification given to an agent of an insurer shall be notification to the insurer. If notification is given to an agent of an insurer, such agent may acknowledge receipt of such notice. Notice to an agent of an insurer shall not be notice to the insurer if such agent notifies the claimant that the agent is not authorized to receive notices of claims. An appropriate reply shall be made within fifteen working days on all other pertinent communications.

b. Every insurer, upon receipt of any inquiry from the Insurance Department respecting a claim, shall within fifteen working days, furnish the Department with the available information requested respecting the claim.

Section 216.5 Standards for the Prompt Investigation of Claims

Every insurer shall establish procedures to commence an investigation of any claim filed by a claimant or by a claimant's authorized representative within fifteen working days of receipt of notice of claim. Every insurer shall mail to every claimant or the claimant's authorized representative a notification of all items, statements and forms, if any, which the insurer reasonably believes will be required of the claimant, within fifteen working days of receiving notice of the claim. If further items, statements, or forms may be required of the claimant, the insurer shall so notify the claimant or the claimant's authorized representative in the first notification, or, if no such notification is sent, then, within fifteen working days of receipt of notice of claim. A claim filed with an agent of an insurer shall be deemed to have been filed with the insurer unless such agent notifies the person filing the claim that the agent is not authorized to receive notices of claim.

Section 216.6 Standards for Prompt, Fair and Equitable Settlements

a. In any case where there is no dispute as to the insurer's liability for, and the extent of, coverage, it shall be the duty of every insurer to offer claimants or their authorized representatives amounts which are fair and reasonable as shown by its investigation of the claim, providing the amounts so offered are within policy limits and in accordance with the policy provisions.

b. "Actual cash value," unless otherwise specifically defined in the policy, means the lesser of the amounts for which the claimant can reasonably be expected to repair the property to its condition immediately prior to the loss, or to replace it with an item substantially identical to the item damaged. This shall not be construed to prevent an insurer from issuing a policy insuring against physical damage to property, where the amount of damages to be paid in the event of a total loss to the property is a specified dollar amount.

c. Within 30 days after receipt of notice by the insurer of a claim, the claimant or the claimant's authorized representative shall be advised in writing of the acceptance or rejection of the claim by the insurer. If the insurer needs more time to determine whether the claim should be accepted or rejected, he shall so notify the claimant, or the claimant's authorized representative within 30 days after receipt of notice of the claim. If the claim remains unsettled, the insurer shall, 90 days from the date of the initial letter setting forth the need for further time to investigate, and every 90 days thereafter, send to the claimant or the claimant's authorized representative a letter setting forth the reasons additional time is needed for investigation. If the claim is accepted, in whole or in part, the claimant or the claimant's authorized representative shall be advised of the amount offered. In any case where coverage is denied, the insurer shall notify the claimant or the claimant's authorized representative of any applicable policy provision limiting the claimant's right to sue the insurer.

d. In any case where there is no dispute as to one or more elements of a claim, payment for such element(s) shall be made notwithstanding the existence of disputes as to other elements of the claim.

e. Every insurer shall pay any amount finally agreed upon in settlement of all or part of any claim not later than five working days from the date of such agreement or from the date of the performance by the claimant of any condition set by such agreement, whichever is later.

Any notice rejecting any element of a claim shall contain the following statement:

"We will, of course, be available to you to discuss the position we have taken. Should you, however, wish to take this matter up with the New York State Insurance Department, it maintains a Complaint Bureau at _____."

(address)

It can be expected that other states will enact similar legislation. Also rules and regulations will be formulated which will govern the claim activities of the insurance carrier's representatives. The claims representative must therefore keep abreast of the situation in the state and regulate claims conduct in accordance with the statute.

CHAPTER XII

Law of automobiles

INTRODUCTORY NOTE

The Law of Automobiles is undergoing some drastic changes. About half of the states have already legislated and have abandoned the tort system of compensating automobile injuries and property damage in favor of a statutory automobile reparations system (no-fault), in which recoveries are allowed regardless of common-law liability. We will therefore consider the Law of Automobiles from two aspects: (1) the tort system and (2) the automobile reparations system.

THE TORT SYSTEM

1200   Rights and duties of the motorist

The operator of a motor vehicle is required to exercise reasonable care for the safety of others who may be endangered by its use. The operator owes this duty of care to the operators and occupants of other vehicles on the highway, occupants of the operator's own car, and pedestrians, as well as to owners of property, either on the highway or adjacent to it. Reasonable care is a relative term in that the extent of the care required is entirely dependent on the circumstances. It is measured by the reasonably prudent man standard. The question of whether the operator's conduct conformed to the standard, or fell below it, is usually a question of fact to be determined by the jury, unless the facts of the occurrence are so clear that reasonable minds could not differ as to the application of the standard.

The reasonably prudent man will maintain his vehicle in a reasonably safe condition, will obey the rules of the road, will conform to the highway regulations, will observe and obey traffic control signs and signals, will keep his car under control, and will do everything possible to avoid an accident. Clearly, the duty of care is a varying one which will be measured in each case by the circumstances and the degree of danger involved. As one court put it: "The danger to be perceived determines the duty to be obeyed."

Thus, if a motorist sees a pedestrian with a white cane crossing at an intersection, he is charged with the knowledge that the pedestrian is blind, and therefore the duty of care is greater than would be the situation if the pedestrian had no infirmity. In this case, the duty of care would require that the motorist yield the right-of-way to the blind man. Where a predestrian has normal faculties, and is crossing in the path of the motorist, the duty of care would consist of giving the pedestrian adequate warning of the motorist's approach by sounding the horn. When the motorist is on the highway, he must operate his vehicle with a degree of care which is commensurate with existing conditions. If it is a clear day, vision unimpaired, and the roads dry, the motorist will be expected to exercise a certain degree of care. Where the weather is bad, raining, snowing, or sleeting, with vision impaired and the roads wet or covered with snow and ice, a much greater degree of care is required.

The area in which the vehicle is being operated will also have some influence on the amount of care which is needed. A greater degree must be exercised in a congested city area as opposed to the open highway, and in dense as opposed to light traffic. A motorist passing a school, old folks' home, or an orphanage would be required to exercise more than the normal amount of care if he has notice of the existence of these institutions by means of warning signs. Likewise, if he is traveling through an area in which a number of children are playing, he would be required to exercise more care for their safety than if he was traveling through a business area where there are no children.

The motorist has the right to assume that others using the highway will exercise care for his safety as well as for their own, will obey the rules of the road, the highway regulations, traffic controls, etc. He may rely upon this assumption until it becomes clear that the other person will not act with reasonable care. Thus, if a motorist sees a vehicle approaching him on the wrong side of the road, he has a right to assume that the other motorist will return to the proper side before they meet. Just how long he can rely on this assumption is a question of fact for the jury. When it becomes clear that the other car will not return to its proper side of the road, the motorist must take some defensive action in order to avoid an accident if it is then possible to do so.

In a number of states, infants are licensed to operate a motor vehicle after they have attained a certain age. An infant, operating a vehicle under those circumstances, is required to exercise the same degree of care as is required of an adult. His conduct will be judged by the reasonably prudent man standard, and if his actions fall below that standard he can be charged with negligence. The fact that an infant is incapable of mature judgment is not a defense. His conduct in operating the vehicle will be judged as if he were an adult.

1201   Lack of operator's license not negligence per se

The fact that the driver of a vehicle involved in an accident did not have a driver's license is not evidence of negligence as a matter of law or in itself. It is evidence of the fact that the operator has failed to comply with the statute, and, in operating a motor vehicle, has committed a crime. The criminal act will subject him to criminal liability and the penalties imposed for such an offense. But the true test of whether or not the operator is chargeable with negligence is how he operated the car under the circumstances of the accident; the fact that he did nor did not have a valid driver's license at the time of the accident has no bearing whatsoever on the issue of negligence.

Evidence of his lack of a driver's license is admissible on the issue of credibility, and, since the jury is required to determine which witnesses it will believe and which it will not, any evidence that will assist in this determination is admissible. The jury is entitled to know that the driver operated his motor vehicle in violation of the law so that they can determine whether they will believe his version of the accident. The theory is that the jury would be less likely to believe the version of a person who was guilty of a crime than the testimony of someone who had never committed one. Therefore, the evidence is admissible only for a limited purpose, and not for establishing the negligence of the operator.

1202 Unregistered vehicles

The fact that the driver of a vehicle involved in an accident did not display license plates as required by law is not evidence of negligence on the part of the owner or operator. The ordinary rules of negligence will apply and the facts of the accident will be determinative of the liability of the driver or owner.

Obviously, the owner or driver of such a vehicle is making illegal use of the highway and will be answerable to the public authority for the infraction. The fact that the vehicle was being used in violation of the state law is a fact which is admissible in evidence, not as evidence of negligence, but as a fact to be taken into consideration by the jury in deciding upon the credibility of the driver. A person who will knowingly violate the law in making such use of the highway is ordinarily a person whose testimony as to the facts of the accident is subject to question, and the jury is entitled to take this into account in determining what weight they will give to his version of the accident.

1203 Assured clear distance rule

The application of this rule requires that the driver keep his car under such control that he can stop within the distance which he can clearly see, should such a stop be necessary in order to avoid an accident. The distance will vary according to the circumstances. At night the distance would be measured by the range of his headlights, whereas in the daylight hours his visibility will depend upon weather conditions. In any case, if he fails to maintain such control as would enable him to stop within the range of his vision, he is guilty of negligence. To be applied, the rule contemplates the existence of two elements: *visibility* and *opportunity*.

Visibility. The dangerous condition or object must be large enough or of such a nature as to be visible to an individual with average eyesight, or there must be adequate warning of its existence. Thus, if there is a slowly moving truck on the highway, a clearly marked barricade with warning signs, blinkers, lanterns, or flares, construction in progress with a signalman some distance in advance of it, or signs warning of a cattle crossing, the motorist is guilty of negligence if he is unable to avoid the objects by reducing his speed or stopping his vehicle. In each of these cases he saw, or should have seen, the object, or he received adequate warning of their existence.

Opportunity. The driver must have had an opportunity to slow down or stop. Where the dangerous condition or object is not visible, and he has had no warning of its existence, he is not negligent if he does everything possible to avoid the accident when the dangerous condition is apprehended. For example, if an excavation or hole in the highway is not visible at a greater distance than five feet, and there are no warning signs, the motorist cannot be deemed to be negligent if he cannot stop or avoid it since he had no opportunity to do so.

1204   Rules of the road

The highway and traffic regulations of a state constitute the rules of the road for that particular state. They determine how travelers may use the highway, which vehicle has the right-of-way, and the conditions under which the right-of-way is acquired, as well as the rights and duties of the vehicles which do not have the superior right-of-way. They also fix the maximum speed and the conditions under which motor vehicles may be driven on the public roads. Since they are designed to promote safety and do restrict extreme action by any individual, there is a general uniformity among the laws of the various states.

The rights granted by the rules of the road are not absolute in that they may be exercised under all circumstances; they are subject to the qualification that the motorist exercise care for the safety of others. For example, if a motorist is stopped at a controlled intersection, and the light changes to green in his favor, he must allow the traffic and the pedestrians already in the intersection to clear before he proceeds.

1205   Compliance with traffic signs

The state highway law in most jurisdictions contains the requirement that "No person shall fail, neglect or refuse to comply with any lawful traffic regulations displayed on any highway." This means that the motorist must observe and obey all regulatory signs posted along the highway, provided they are *lawful* and *displayed*.

Lawful.   The authority for the erection of any traffic control sign is granted either by a state law or by an ordinance passed by a political subdivision of the state to which lawmaking power of this kind has been delegated. If the sign is erected without the authority of a state law or ordinance, it is an unlawful sign and the motorist is not bound to obey it. The same result will follow where the ordinance is illegal because it was not enacted according to law, or covers a portion of the highway outside of the jurisdiction of the body enacting it.

Displayed.   This means that it must be possible for the motorist to observe the sign; it must be clearly readable and visible. If the sign has been damaged by exposure to weather so that it is not readable, or if the motorist's view of the sign is obstructed because of an overgrowth of shrubbery, weeds, bushes, or debris piled in front of it, the sign is not "displayed" and the motorist is not charged with the knowledge of the presence of the sign. And, where the sign has been damaged because of a prior accident or the action of vandals, or has been stolen, it is not being "displayed."

1206 Failure to see traffic warning signs

A motorist traveling on the highways has the duty of making reasonable use of his vision in order to determine whether or not there are any traffic control signs (erected for the protection and the protection of others). He cannot escape the duty imposed by the statute by stating that he did not see plainly visible signs, because he has the duty to see what, in the exercise of reasonable care, he should have seen. The motorist is charged with the knowledge that he would have acquired had he observed the sign, and his conduct is judged on that basis. Therefore, the failure to see and comply with plainly visible traffic control signs is negligence.

1207 Vehicles traveling in the same direction

Where two cars are traveling in the same direction on the same road, the general rule is that the car ahead has the superior right and may maintain its position. Further rights and duties arise in situations involving (1) passing, (2) reduction in speed or stopping, (3) turns at intersections, and (4) turns between intersections.

1. *Passing.* The leading vehicle is under the duty to keep to the right side of the road. There is no absolute legal duty on the part of the motorist to stop his car in order to permit a faster vehicle to pass, even though, when the passing is being attempted, there might be a duty to reduce speed or come to a full stop under special circumstances where such action might prevent an accident.

In some parts of the country, especially where there are long, winding, uphill roads, it is customary for the driver of a slow-moving truck to signal those behind that it is safe to pass. The signal is usually a hand signal or the blinking of marker lights. The truck driver is under no duty to give such a signal, and does so only as a matter of courtesy. Having voluntarily assumed the duty, however, the truck driver must exercise reasonable care in the execution of it. Should the truck driver give the signal, and the following motorist rely on it with the result that an accident occurs, the truck driver may be held partially responsible as a joint tort-feasor. In any case, reliance on the signals given by the truck driver will not relieve the passing driver of his duty to exercise care.

The overtaking driver may pass only when it is safe to do so. He must exercise care and judgment as to when and where the passing maneuver may be accomplished. Where there is insufficient room for safe passage, it is the duty of the following driver to maintain his position and wait until a place is reached where it can be done in safety. The driver of the overtaking vehicle is required to signal his intention to pass the forward vehicle by a blast or stroke of his horn. As to vehicles following him, he is required to signal his intention to pass by means of a hand signal or other signaling device. In both cases, the signal must be timely and must provide an adequate warning to all other vehicles of his intention.

Whether the passing motorist exercised care and judgment, and gave adequate warning of his intention to all vehicles concerned, are questions of fact to be determined by the jury in the light of all the circumstances. In *Simpson* v. *Snellenberg* [115 Atl. 403 (New Jersey)] the court said:

Important considerations . . . are the width of the road, at the place where the accident occurred, conditions of visibility, density of traffic, and the general condition of the road, whether icy, slippery, paved, muddy, etc.; all of which bear upon the degree of care and caution properly exercisable by a driver who seeks to pass another upon the road, as well as the duties of the driver in the front who becomes aware of a motorist in the rear who desires to pass him.

Most statutes require that the passing vehicle must be to the left of the overtaken vehicle. Where the statute requires that all vehicles pass on the left, violation of the statute has been held to be negligence per se. Most states, however, hold that passing other than on the left does not in and of itself establish negligence unless such movement was the efficient cause of the accident which ensured.

In some jurisdictions, ordinances prohibit the overtaking and passing of another vehicle at intersections. Violations of such statutes, where they exist, constitute negligence. In the absence of such a statute, the passing of an overtaken vehicle in an intersection in and of itself is not negligence.

2. Reduction in speed or stopping. Most highway statutes require that the motorist give warning by means of a hand signal or adequate signal device of any marked reduction in speed, or stopping on the highways, to the vehicles behind him, if he has an opportunity to do so. But where the forward driver is suddenly confronted by an object on the highway, such as an animal, a person, an unmarked barricade, or a defect in the roadway, and he has no opportunity of signaling his intention, he is relieved of the obligation to do so.

Where a motorist driving at night is suddenly confronted with glaring headlights which prevent him from seeing the road ahead, he is under a duty to slacken his speed or stop, as the occasion demands. He is not entitled to operate his vehicle on a public street when he cannot see. In addition, the fact that the oncoming motorist was negligent in keeping his headlights on a high beam will not relieve the blinded motorist from his duty to exercise care. In *Mathers* v. *Botsford* [97 So. 282 (Florida)], the court said:

While it may be negligence for a driver of an automobile to permit the bright lights on his car to obscure or obstruct the vision of a driver of another car on a public highway, yet this does not relieve the driver of the other car of the duty to exercise due care required by the circumstances, and even to stop if that is reasonably required to avoid injury to persons who may be lawfully on the road, but whose presence is not known to the driver because of the blinding light on another vehicle then approaching.

Thus the blinded motorist may have two duties: to exercise care as to persons on the highway whom he cannot see, and to signal his intention of markedly reducing his speed or stopping to the vehicle following him. If he has an opportunity to signal the following vehicle, he must do so.

Where the following vehicle runs into the forward vehicle because of a sudden stop or slackening speed, the defense is usually interposed that the vehicle was following the forward car too closely and was therefore contributorily negligent. What constitutes a safe following distance will depend upon the facts and circumstances of each case, with due regard being given to the density of traffic at the point of accident, the speed of the cars, and the condition of the road. The highway laws do not provide an answer as to what would constitute a safe following distance for the reason that what might be a safe distance in one case would be entirely unsafe in another.

For example, in a congested traffic condition where vehicles are moving at 3–5 miles per hour, a safe following distance might be 3 feet, whereas on the open highway where traffic is moving at 25 miles per hour, 3 feet would be unsafe. On the open highway, police officers calculate the safe following distance under the best driving conditions to be at least one car length for each 10 miles per hour of speed. Thus at 40 miles per hour, the following vehicle should be at least four car lengths behind the forward vehicle.

In approaching an intersection where a traffic officer is in control or where the intersection is controlled by traffic lights, drivers are under a duty to anticipate that vehicles ahead may have to stop on short notice and with less warning than would otherwise be given.

3. *Turns at intersections.* If a right or left turn is to be made at an intersection, the driver is required, in addition to checking traffic and signaling, to place the vehicle in the proper position and make the turn from one proper lane to the other proper lane when safe to do so. When a driver intends to turn right at an intersection, both the approach and the turn must be made as close as practicable to the right-hand curb or edge of the roadway. A driver intending to make a left turn at an intersection should approach in the lane nearest the center line of the roadway, pass to the right of such center line where it enters the intersection, turn wherever practicable to the left of the intersection, and leave the intersection to the right of the center line of the roadway being entered.

Signals for a right or left turn may be given by hand and arm, or by an approved mechanical or electrical device, and they must be given for a distance of not less than 100 feet before turning.

4. *Turns between intersections.* As to right turns into a private driveway, alley, or parking lot, the same rules referable to turns at an intersection are applicable. As to left turns, the general rule is that where the driver intends to make such a turn between intersections, he is under a duty to give a timely signal to motorists following him, under the same duty as in turns at intersections in that he must exercise care and caution to be certain that the turn can be made in safety. Where he is on notice that the car following him intends to pass, he must allow it to pass, and then make his turn in safety.

Some cases hold that the turning motorist is not bound to anticipate that the vehicles following him will attempt to pass and, in the absence of any knowledge or notice that they intend to pass, has the right to make the turn. However, it should be noted that at an intersection the following motorist is required to have his car under such control so as to be able to stop on short notice. But the same caution and vigilance is not required when the following motorist is driving between intersections. Therefore it would seem that the left-turning motorist should be required to exercise a greater degree of care and caution as to following motorists when making a left turn between intersections than would be necessary at an intersection.

1208   Vehicles traveling in opposite directions

The rules of the road require that all vehicles be driven on the right-hand side of the road. This means that vehicles must be driven on the extreme right side of the road, or to the right of the center line, except when overtaking and passing a vehicle ahead, or when a highway having more than one lane in each direction becomes congested with traffic to the extent that vehicles must be driven in all lanes so provided. Some statutes do not require that the vehicles be driven on the right-hand side at all times, but do require that, upon meeting another vehicle, the first vehicle must be on the right-hand side of the road. Thus, when the road is clear the vehicle can use any part of the road, but when another vehicle approaches the vehicle must then take to the right side of the road.

Specific situations involving vehicles traveling in opposite directions will arise in the following situations: (1) passing, (2) left turns at intersections, and (3) left turns between intersections.

1. *Passing.* When two vehicles traveling in opposite directions meet, each is required to keep to the right of the center line. When a collision occurs on the wrong side of the road, a presumption of negligence ordinarily arises against the driver of the vehicle who is on the wrong side. The presumption can be overcome by an explanation of the facts and circumstances of the accident which may absolve the driver of negligence or the lack of due care. For example, if it could be shown that the driver operating a vehicle with due care was hit by a negligent motorist, and his vehicle was forced onto the wrong side of the road, with another accident ensuing, the explanation, if believed, will overcome the presumption.

The problem arises as to what constitutes the right-hand side of the road. Does it include the shoulder, or the sidewalk, or is it restricted to the traveled portion of the highway? In an old case, which still represents the law today, the court was confronted with this very problem. In *Lavenstein* v. *Maile* [132 S.E. 844 (Virginia)], the court said:

It is argued that if it be contended that Lavenstein was driving too near the left side of the concrete, the truck had ample room to pass on the dirt section of the road. This appears to be true; but it must be kept in mind that the concrete was placed there for the use of the public travelling on the highway in both directions, was wide enough to allow automobiles to pass each other in safety, and one driver had no greater rights on the concrete than the other. It was Lavenstein's duty, therefore, to keep to the right-hand side of the concrete when the truck was passing his car.

2. *Left turns at intersections.* Where a left turn is being attempted at an uncontrolled intersection, or a controlled intersection not having left turn directional signals, the general rule is that the oncoming vehicle has the superior right-of-way and that the left-turning vehicle shall yield the right-of-way to the oncoming vehicle. In making a left turn or a curve across the line of traffic, the person must exercise due caution to see that the way is clear so that it is safe for him to cross traffic which is coming in the opposite direction. The motorist approaching an intersection is required to exercise care in having his car under control, maintaining a careful lookout, and he must avoid an accident if it is possible to do so. The left-turning motorist does not have to get out of his car and make a measurement to determine whether or not it is safe to cross. He will exercise his best judgment under the facts and circumstances and he will assume that the approaching motorist will have his car under control so as to be able to slow down, if such is necessary, to permit the left turn to be made safely.

When the left-turning motorist is entirely within the intersection, some cases hold that he has acquired the right-of-way and that the approaching motorist must yield. In any case, the left-turning and the approaching motorist must exercise due care for the safety of each other.

The mere fact that a collision occurs while a motorist is making a left turn does not in and of itself establish that he was responsible for the accident. The facts of the occurrence will be determinative of his responsibility. These facts will include, among others, the physical dimensions of the intersection, the density of traffic, the speed of the two cars, the presence of traffic signals, the positions of the cars at impact, and where they both came to rest.

3. *Left turns between intersections.* When he is coming to an intersection, the approaching driver must exercise care and must anticipate that other vehicles will cross, attempt left turns, or make right turns. Therefore, the duty of maintaining a proper lookout and of having the vehicle under control in anticipation of the movement of other cars is greater than at other times. When driving between intersections, the driver has a right to assume that approaching vehicles will keep to the right, and he has no reason to anticipate that a left turn will be made by a vehicle approaching him. Therefore, when a left turn is to be made between intersections, there is a greater duty of care on the left-turning driver than would be the case of a left turn at an intersection. Some statutes prohibit left turns between intersections and require that the vehicle proceed to the intersection and make the turn at that point. Clearly, if there is such a statute, a driver who violates it by making a left turn between intersections is ordinarily negligent.

1209 Vehicles traveling at right angles

This will involve the rights and duties of motorists approaching and driving through intersections. It is clear that a motorist approaching an intersection is on notice that others will use the intersection by crossing his lane of travel, either motorists or pedestrians. Therefore, he is charged with a greater duty of care and vigilance than would be the situation while driving on the open road. The duty of care would include maintaining a proper lookout for others, reducing speed, or sounding his horn to warn others of his approach, if the circumstances so required. Likewise, he is on notice of and must anticipate that other vehicles may stop short, turn, or reduce their speeds. This will involve controlled and uncontrolled intersections.

1. *Controlled intersections.*   The motorist is under a duty to obey the traffic directional signals at a controlled intersection and to yield the right-of-way to other vehicles where required, and to pedestrians on a crosswalk with a green light. The mere fact that the motorists has the right-of-way because the traffic signal is in his favor does not give him the right to proceed without the exercise of due care, and this duty continues even though another driver may negligently operate his vehicle in the intersection.

2. *Uncontrolled intersections.*   The general rule is that the motorist who first enters an uncontrolled intersection has the right-of-way over vehicles approaching the intersection. As in the controlled intersection, the fact that the driver has the right-of-way does not give him the right to proceed without the exercise of due care, nor would the fact that another driver is operating his vehicle negligently in the intersection excuse all other drivers from their duty of exercising due care.

Most highway rules further provide that where two cars approach the intersection simultaneously, the car on the right has the right-of-way and the other must yield, but there is some variation in the application of these rules by different states. Some follow the rule that where there is a collision in the intersection the driver in the inferior position (on the left) is presumptively to blame. Others hold that the reasonably prudent man standard should be applied to the conduct of the driver on the left. The test in evaluating the conduct of motorists who approach the intersection at about the same time is that if

. . . A man of ordinary prudence in such a situation in the exercise of due care would reasonably believe that, if the two automobiles continued to run at the rate of speed at which they were running, such continuance would not involve the risk of a collision, but would carry his automobile across the intersection of the highways in safety in front of the automobile approaching from his right, then the automobile from the left would not be negligent in crossing the intersection in front of the automobile approaching from the right.

In approaching an intersection where a traffic officer is stationed or traffic lights are in operation, motorists are under a duty to anticipate that the vehicles ahead may have to stop on short notice and with less warning than would be the case on the open highway.

1210   Violating rules of the road in an emergency

The application of the foregoing rules may be affected by an emergency. When a motorist is confronted with an emergency, he is not required to give detached reflection as to what course of action is the most desirable, but is required to take such action as a reasonably prudent man would take in order to avoid injury to himself and others, even though this action may involve a violation of the rules of the road. He may drive his vehicle to the right or to the left, onto the center island, or onto the shoulder. Each such act will be judged by the circumstances confronting the motorist, and the amount of time which he had within which to decide what to do. A violation of the rules of the road will not constitute negligence if the following evidence is available:

1. The violation of the rules was justifiable under the circumstances.
2. The motorist's own failure to exercise due care did not create the emergency.
3. He exercised reasonable care in facing the emergency.

It should be emphasized that the emergency rule applies only in favor of the innocent motorist whose conduct did not create the emergency. If the motorist was negligent and created the emergency, he is responsible for the consequences of his own acts, and the emergency rule is inapplicable. Thus a motorist is not exonerated from liability for a collision resulting from his sudden swerving from behind a car, in order to avoid smashing into it because it suddenly slowed up, where it appears that had the driver in the rear maintained a proper lookout and regulated his speed in accordance with what would constitute due care, he could have stopped in time to avoid a collision, thus avoiding the necessity of pulling to the left side of the road in the path of the oncoming vehicle. Therefore, the emergency was created by the motorist's own negligence, and for that reason the emergency defense cannot be invoked in his favor.

1211   Excusable violations of statutes

There are situations where a statute has been violated but where the defendant had no intention of so doing and where the violation occurred through circumstances over which the defendant had no control. The law does not require that the impossible be accomplished. Therefore, where the defendant has no knowledge of the possible violation of the statute, and has no means at his command whereby the violation can be avoided, the jury can find that the violation is excusable, thereby discharging the defendant from liability.

For example, state highway statutes provide that all motor vehicles using the highway be equipped with adequate and properly functioning brakes. If a motorist knowingly operates a vehicle on the highways with defective brakes, he has violated the statute and he is answerable for any damage which is proximately caused by his failure to comply with the statutory requirements. On the other hand, if there was a sudden brake failure which the defendant could not have anticipated, and which he could not have discovered upon reasonable inspection, the jury could find that the violation is excusable.

If there was an interval of time, however short it might be, between the time that the defect was discovered and the impact, it is the duty of the defendant to adopt such means and take such measures as are available to him to avoid the accident. If he fails to do so when he has the opportunity, he is lacking in due care and is negligent. Similarly, if the defect is of such a nature as to have been discoverable upon reasonable inspection, the defendant is chargeable with the knowledge that a reasonable inspection would have revealed.

1212   Stop signs

A motorist coming to a stop sign is required to come to a full stop. After stopping, he may proceed with caution, and at that point has the same right of use of the highway as any other car. The same duties and the same rights applicable to uncontrolled intersections apply equally here. The stop sign merely obligates the motorist to come to a full stop and make his observation. When he has done that, he has done all that the law requires of him, as far as the stop sign is concerned.

The fact that a motorist did not stop at a stop sign is not in and of itself evidence of negligence unless it can be shown that the failure to stop was the proximate cause of the accident. If it had no influence on the causation of the accident, it is regarded as an excusable violation.

1213   Vehicles entering the highway from private way

A motorist entering the highway from a private driveway, alley, or garage is required to exercise that degree of care and caution which the hazards of the situation demand. If the entrance to the driveway is obscured from the vision of motorists already on the highway because of the presence of foliage or other obstructions to vision, the care to be exercised is that much greater. As to the motorist already on the highway, he is not bound to anticipate that vehicles will enter the highway between intersections. He is required to exercise the usual care in having his vehicle under control as to speed and stopping ability. He is not held to the same degree of care as would be the case when he is approaching an intersection. As to the entering motorist, his conduct will be judged by the facts and circumstances of the occurrence, the weather conditions, the density of traffic, and the kind and type of driveway involved.

The vehicle already on the highway has the right-of-way, and equal rights to the use of the highway do not come into existence until the entering vehicle has fully entered upon the highway. The duty on the part of the entering motorist is to yield the right-of-way to the motorists already on the highway by slowing up or stopping, if necessary, before entering. Some state statutes require that a full stop be made by the entering motorist.

Where the driveway crosses the public sidewalk, some, if not all, statutes require that the motorist stop before driving on the sidewalk. Pedestrians on the sidewalk have an absolute right-of-way and the motorist must yield to that superior right. Failure to do so is negligence.

When the motorist enters the highway from a semipublic parking lot, such as a shopping center parking lot, state fairgrounds, or a drive-in movie, all of which are lighted and designated by signs, the motorist already on the highway is on notice of the possibility of other vehicles entering from the area, and therefore has a duty of care commensurate with the hazards which he must anticipate.

It should be emphasized that, in any case, private ways do not have the same status as public highways, and the rules of the road applicable to travel on such roads do not apply to private ways.

1214 Railroad crossings

In spite of the fact that at many grade crossings, the railroads still maintain signs directing people using the crossing to "stop, look and listen," it does not define the duty of the motorist. The rule is that motorists approaching a railroad crossing must reduce their speed to a safe limit after passing the warning sign, usually required to be erected 300 feet from the crossing. The motorist then is required to proceed cautiously and carefully, with his vehicle under complete control. He is not required to come to a full stop, look, and listen under all circumstances, as the signs indicate. However, most highway statutes require that he come to a full stop, usually not less than 15 feet from the nearest rail, under any one of the following circumstances:

1. When a clearly visible electrical or mechanical signal warns of the immediate approach of a train.
2. When a crossing gate is lowered or a flagman signals the approach or passing of a train.
3. When an approaching train, within 1,500 feet of the highway, gives an audible signal, or when it is plainly visible and dangerously close as it approaches the highway.

Most statutes require that certain vehicles make a full stop at railroad crossings at all times. These vehicles include buses with a capacity of more than six passengers, school buses, vehicles transporting explosives, and certain types of construction vehicles. Drivers in following vehicles, in the exercise of due care, are bound to anticipate such stops and to govern the conduct and driving accordingly.

1215 School buses

Under most statutes, the driver of a vehicle approaching or overtaking a school bus, displaying proper school bus signs at front and rear and stopped to pick up or discharge a school child, is required to stop his vehicle not less than 10 feet from the bus and remain stationary until the child has entered the bus or has alighted and reached the side of the highway. Two exceptions are usually provided to prevent unnecessary traffic delays when the safety of school children is not affected. A driver may pass a school bus, discharging or picking up children, at a speed of not more than 10 miles per hour only under the following conditions:

1. When a school bus is parked at the curb on the same side of the street as the school and is receiving children directly from the school or discharging them to enter.
2. On highways having dual or multiple roadways separated by safety islands or other physical separations, the driver of a vehicle approaching a stopped school bus on another roadway may pass at the reduced speed noted above. This does not apply to a vehicle overtaking the stopped bus on the same roadway.

The identification and equipment of the school bus will differ state by state, although most require the bus to be of yellow color and carry plain markings. Certain flashing stoplights, front and rear, are required, and in some states a gate is required to be extended from the left side of the bus when it is in a stopped position.

1216   Emergency vehicles

The emergency vehicles with which we will be concerned for the most part are ambulances, fire apparatus, and police cars.

Ambulances.   In the absence of a statute granting a preferential use of the highways, ambulances are subject to the same traffic rules as any other vehicle. They must obey the speed laws, traffic signals, and traffic control signs. Where statutes confer preferential rights and privileges to ambulances, these rights may be exercised only when the ambulance complies with the statute as to the use of a siren, flashing lights, and other signals as may be prescribed, and only when the ambulance is responding to an emergency. When used for any other purpose or driven at any other time, the ambulance has no rights superior to those of any other motor vehicle. However, even when responding to an emergency, the driver of the ambulance is charged with the duty of exercising that degree of care which is commensurate with the hazards involved. Where the statute requires that the motorist turn out of the way of an ambulance, the motorist who fails to do so, after receiving warning of the approach of the ambulance, is chargeable with contributory negligence if an accident should ensue.

Where it is claimed that the ambulance was responding to an emergency, it should be established that an emergency existed and its character was such as to justify the speed at which the ambulance was being driven. If there was no emergency or the call for assistance was such that speed was not essential, the duty of exercising due care would be the same as that imposed on other drivers. Where there is an emergency, and the ambulance has given the warning required, the ambulance driver has a right to rely on the assumption that all vehicles in the vicinity will yield the right-of-way and turn aside as required.

Fire apparatus.   The same rules as apply to ambulances govern the operation of fire apparatus on the highways. When responding to an alarm, the driver of the fire apparatus must exercise the care required under the circumstances by sounding the proper warning and affording other vehicles on the highway an opportunity to move out of the way.

Police cars. Police cars are privileged to exceed the speed limit and otherwise disregard traffic controls when engaged in pursuing a fleeing criminal. This privilege is granted only for the limited purpose of police duty and, even while it is being utilized, the driver must exercise whatever due care the hazards of the situation require. Should the privilege be abused, the officer is answerable.

1217 Motorcycles and bicycles

The riders of motorcycles and bicycles using the highway are subject to the same rights and the same duties as motor vehicles. Because of the slow speed of bicycles, there are several additional rules which are applicable. The statutes usually provide that every person operating a bicycle upon a roadway shall ride as near to the right side of the roadway as practicable and exercise due care when passing a standing vehicle or one proceeding in the same direction. Bicycles shall ride in single file except on paths or parts of the roadway set aside for their exclusive use. A person propelling or riding a bicycle shall not ride other than upon or astride a permanent and regular seat attached thereto, nor shall he ride with his feet removed from the pedals, or with both hands removed from the handlebars. No bicycle shall be used to carry more persons at one time than the number for which it is designed and equipped.

The statutes prohibit "hitching" rides when using a bicycle, coaster, skates, sled, or toy vehicle. This means that no person using these devices may attach same or himself to any streetcar or vehicle on the roadway.

The equipment required of a motorcycle is practically the same as any other motor vehicle as to lights, brakes, and horn. Mechanical or electrical directional signals are usually not required.

As to bicycles, they are required to have brakes which will enable the operator to make the braked wheels skid on dry, level, clean pavement. When in use in the nighttime, the bicycle shall be equipped with a lamp on the front which shall emit a white light visible from a distance of at least 500 feet to the front, and a lamp on the rear which shall emit a red light visible from a distance of at least 500 feet to the rear. In addition to the red lamp, a red reflector may be mounted on the rear. The bicycle must be equipped with a bell or other device capable of a signal audible for a distance of at least 100 feet. Local statutes and ordinances may increase or diminish these duties, and these should be consulted in each case.

As to motorists, the driver of a motor vehicle owes the same degree of care to the rider of a motorcycle or bicycle as he is required to exercise toward operators of other motor vehicles.

1218 Parked vehicles

A vehicle is parked when it is stopped, whether the driver is behind the wheel or not, except when it is stopped in obedience to a traffic officer, sign or signal, or taking on or letting off passengers or merchandise. The highway statutes and local ordinances specify how and where a vehicle may be legally parked. In cities and populated areas, the usual rule is that a vehicle may be parked on the right-hand side of the road, parallel to and within 6 inches of the curb and headed in the direction of traffic. Exceptions are parking on the left side of one-way streets or angle parking.

Outside of business and residential areas, the vehicle may be parked only on the shoulder of the road, off the improved portion of the highway. Buses, trucks, weighing over 5,000 pounds, and vehicles carrying flammables or explosives are required to carry flares and other emergency warning devices. When such vehicles are parked outside of a business or residential area during a period when lighted lamps are required, the driver must set out such warning devices, usually one a certain distance in front of the vehicle, one alongside the vehicle, and one a certain distance to the rear.

Generally, parking is prohibited in the following places:

1. Within an intersection, including the T-end type.
2. On a crosswalk.
3. Within 25 feet of an intersection.
4. Between or within 20 feet of a curb and an opposite safety zone.
5. Alongside or opposite any street excavation or obstruction where parking would obstruct traffic.
6. Alongside another vehicle parked at the curb (double parking).
7. Upon a bridge or elevated highway or within a highway tunnel or underpass.
8. Any officially marked "No Parking" space.

A motorist is negligent if he parks in violation of the parking rules, and liable in damages if such parking is the proximate cause of an accident. He is likewise negligent if he parks his vehicle in such a way that a part of it projects onto the traveled portion of the highway, rendering travel thereon unsafe for passing motorists. In determining whether or not the negligent parking was the proximate cause of the accident, the jury will take into account the width of the road, the density of traffic, visibility, and if at night whether or not lights were displayed on the parked vehicle, and whether or not the approaching motorist was afforded an opportunity of avoiding the accident—all these in addition to the other facts and circumstances of the accident.

As an example, let us assume that a vehicle was parked at night on the left side of the highway with its lights on. The approaching motorist would have every reason to assume that the vehicle was in motion, and would return to its right side of the road to permit safe passing. Just how long the approaching motorist should rely on his assumption, and at what point he should have seen that the other vehicle was not in motion, are questions of fact to be decided by the jury.

A motorist who parks his vehicle in a prohibited area may also become liable to others where the accident caused an obstruction to vision as a result of the improperly parked vehicle. The mere fact that the vehicle was illegally parked will not in and of itself impose liability. It must be shown that the fact of illegal parking was the cause or a contributing cause of the accident.

The statute requires that when the vehicle is parked the brakes be set and the motor turned off, and, where the vehicle is parked on an incline, that the front wheels be cramped against the curb. Any failure to so park the vehicle, which results in the unattended vehicle being set in motion, will impose liability on the driver for any damage caused thereby.

1219   Disabled vehicles

Where a vehicle is improperly parked on the highway, the law raises a presumption of negligence from this fact against the operator of the vehicle. The burden of overcoming the presumption by explanation is placed upon the defendant. If it can be shown that the parking was the result of an emergency, such as a mechanical failure or collision with another object or another motor vehicle, and that the driver of the vehicle exercised due care under the circumstances for the safety of others, the jury can find that the illegal parking was an excusable violation of the statute. We will consider, therefore, the emergency and due care.

Emergency.   The condition of the vehicle must be such that it cannot be removed from the traveled portion of the highway. If it can be so moved, the driver is under an obligation to move it to the shoulder. The burden of establishing the impossibility of moving the vehicle is imposed upon the driver of the vehicle.

Due care.   The statute usually provides that when in case of accident or emergency it becomes necessary to leave a vehicle on the highway at night, a red light be conspicuously displayed thereon and that the owner or operator of the disabled vehicle must notify, by the quickest means of communication, the nearest police authority. Where there is an opportunity to do so, it would appear that the minimum requirement of due care would be compliance with the statute. Where the owner or operator has been injured in the accident, or where the interval of time between the disablement and the subsequent accident is of short duration, the fact question to be decided by the jury will be the duty of such a person, under the circumstances, to exercise care, and the extent of it. The question of due care will turn on the application of the reasonably prudent man standard and the opportunity which the operator of the vehicle had to exercise the care which the standard requires.

Where a vehicle is stopped on the traveled portion of the highway for the purpose of emergency repairs, and an accident occurs, a number of fact questions re involved. The statutes usually provide that the vehicle must be removed from the highway unless it is impossible to do so. If it cannot be moved, the cases generally hold that the operator is not necessarily contributorily negligent because he attempts repairs in that situation. He has a right to assume that passing motorists will exercise care for his safety. In addition, he is charged with the duty of exercising care and vigilance for his own safety, but he cannot maintain constant vigilance and still make the repairs. Again, in this situation, whether or not he exercised the degree of care commensurate with the danger is a question for the jury.

1220   Commercial vehicles

The highway statutes prescribe the size, permissible weight per axle, equipment, lighting, markers, reflectors, and the speed at which commercial vehicles may be driven. The state statutes differ widely and recourse must be had to the law itself to determine its requirements. The average statute provides that the dimensions not exceed the following:

Width (outside)	96 inches
Height	$13\frac{1}{2}$ feet
Length (single vehicle)	35 feet
Length (tractor and semitrailer)	50 feet
Length (tractor and trailer)	50 feet

The average maximum weight limitations differ by the number of axles and their spacing. The maximum for one axle is 22,400 pounds. If the wheels of all axles are spaced more than 40 but less than 96 inches apart (tandem axle), the maximum is 32,000 pounds, with the maximum overall weight in any case being 73,280 pounds. Private house trailers and semitrailers are usually subject to the same limitations. Operating a vehicle of this type in violation of the law as to size and load is negligence, and if either is the proximate cause of an accident, the operator or owner will be liable.

The statutes prohibit loading or operating a loaded vehicle in such a way that the contents may be scattered or dropped on the highway. Thus, where part of the load falls to the pavement in the path of a following vehicle, and is the proximate cause of an accident, the persons injured thereby have a cause of action against the operator, or the person responsible for the loading, or both. In addition, where vehicles are carrying a projecting load, the statutes require that a red flag in the daytime and a red light at night be attached to the end of the projecting material.

1221   Rights and duties of passengers

The driver of a motor vehicle is required to exercise reasonable care for the safety of his passengers. This duty of reasonable care extends not only to the operation of the vehicle but to its maintenance as well. For example, if a driver knowingly operates a vehicle with faulty brakes, lights, or tires, he is liable to a passenger who may be injured as a result of an accident occurring because of the defect. Where there is a defect in the vehicle and the defect is unknown to the driver but could have been discovered upon reasonable inspection, some cases make a distinction between a gratuitous passenger or guest and one who is riding in the car for the business advantage of the driver. They use the analogy of licensee and business invitee in holding that the duty of reasonable inspection is imposed only in the case of the business passenger and not in the case of the gratuitous passenger or guest.

The passenger is required to exercise reasonable care for his own safety, and his failure to do so will bar his recovery in the case of an accident. The defenses interposed are assumption of risk and contributory negligence.

Assumption of risk.   Where a passenger knowingly entrusts his safety to an incompetent driver, whether such incompetence be due to illness, intoxication, or the lack of driving experience, he will have assumed all the risks which arise out of the driver's incompetence. The defense is based on the existence of two elements: (1) knowledge of the risk and (2) voluntary exposure to it.

Thus, if the passenger enters a car driven by a person with only a learner's permit, and the passenger has knowledge of the driver's lack of experience, he will have assumed all the risks arising out of the driver's lack of driving experience. But if the vehicle has faulty brakes, which fact is unknown to the passenger, and the accident occurs due to this condition, the passenger has not assumed this risk. If the driver has only a learner's permit, or is intoxicated, or ill, and these facts are unknown and could not be ascertained by the passenger by the exercise of reasonable care, he likewise will not be held to have assumed any risk on injury arising out of these conditions.

The courts sometimes combine assumption of risk and contributory negligence, holding that where a passenger enters the vehicle with the knowledge that the driver is intoxicated, the passenger has not only assumed the risk of injury but is also contributorily negligent in failing to exercise care for his own safety. For example, in *United* v. *Salter* (167 Pac. 2d 954) the court said:

> The effect of intoxicating liquor in depriving the driver of a car of care and caution and inducing physical incapacity in the operation of the car is universally known and illustrated tragically almost daily. When one becomes a guest and imprudently enters the car with the knowledge that the driver is so under the influence of intoxicants as to tend to prevent him from exercising the care and caution which a sober and prudent man would employ in the operation and control of the car, the guest is barred from recovery by reason of contributory negligence and as having assumed the risk involved. Where the evidence of such fact is without conflict, the plaintiff is barred from recovery as a matter of law. Where the evidence is sufficient to raise a question as to the plaintiff's knowledge and prudence, the determination of the issue must be submitted to the jury or other trier of the facts.

Contributory negligence.   The passenger is required to exercise reasonable care for his own safety. He may not interfere with the operation of the vehicle, distract the driver's attention, attempt to get out of the car while it is in motion, or do any other act which will involve a risk of injury to himself. He is entitled to rely on the driver when it comes to the operation of the vehicle and is not required to watch the road and warn the driver of impending dangers. As a matter of fact, he may even go to sleep, provided that in so doing he does not place himself in a position that interferes with the safe operation of the vehicle.

1222   Automobile guest statutes

In a number of states, it was felt that as a matter of legislative policy some modification should be made in the common-law rule imposing liability upon the host-driver for ordinary negligence where the injured person was given transportation without payment of any kind. Some states felt that the host, acting as a Good Samaritan, should be exposed to liability only where his conduct exceeded certain limitations which were set forth in the statute. Others decided that the statutes were necessary where insurance was involved to discourage collusive actions of both host and guest.

These actions would have an adverse effect upon insurance rates, and it was felt that automobile guest statutes were necessary in order to protect the insurance buying public. In any case, whatever the motivation, these states enacted statutes which limited the liability of the host insofar as it related to his gratuitous guest. Each state has fixed its own standards of responsibility to which the host is subject, but in each instance something more than ordinary negligence must be established. The following is a list of the states having guest statutes, together with the standards of responsibility for which the host is answerable. The references in each case are to the particular state statute.

ALABAMA

Owner, operator, or person responsible for operation of motor vehicle shall not be liable for loss or damage arising from injuries to or death of a guest while being "transported without payment therefor in or upon said motor vehicle, resulting from the operation thereof, unless such injuries or death are caused by the *willful or wanton misconduct*"[1] of such operator, owner, or person responsible for the operation of the motor vehicle. (Title 36, sec. 95)

DELAWARE

No person transported by the owner or operator of a motor vehicle as a guest without payment shall have a cause of action for damages against such owner or operator for injury, death, or loss in case of accident unless such accident was *intentional* on the part of such owner or operator, or was caused by his *willful or wanton disregard of the rights of others.* (Title 21, sec. 6101)

GEORGIA

No statutory provisions. Liability to guests, by the decisions of the courts, occurs only in cases where the owner or operator is guilty of gross negligence.

ILLINOIS

No person riding in a motor vehicle as a guest without payment or while engaged in a joint enterprise with the owner or driver, nor his personal representative, shall have a cause of action for damages against the driver or operator thereof or its owner, his employee or agent, for injury, death, or loss in case of accident unless such accident shall have been caused by the *willful and wanton misconduct* of the driver or operator of such motor vehicle or its owner or his

---

[1] Author's italics throughout.

employee or agent and unless such willful and wanton misconduct contributed to the injury, death, or loss for which the action is brought. This section shall not relieve a motor carrier of passengers for hire of responsibility for injury or death sustained by such passenger. (Chap. 95, 9–201)

INDIANA

The owner, operator, or person responsible for the operation of a motor vehicle shall not be liable for loss or damages arising from injuries to or death of a guest without payment, resulting from the operation thereof, unless such injuries or death are caused by the *wanton or willful misconduct* of such operator, owner, or person responsible for the operation of such motor vehicle.

This provision shall not relieve a common carrier or sales demonstrator of the responsibility for injuries sustained by a passenger or prospective purchaser. (47–1021, 1022)

MASSACHUSETTS

No guest statute; but court decisions hold that the host is not responsible to a gratuitous guest unless he is guilty of gross negligence.

NEBRASKA

The owner or operator of a motor vehicle shall not be liable for any damages to any passenger or person or within the second degree of consanguinity or affinity who is riding in such motor vehicle as a guest or by invitation and not for hire, unless such damage is caused by (1) the driver of such motor vehicle being under the influence of intoxicating liquor, or (2) the gross negligence of the owner or operator in the operation of such motor vehicle. For the purpose of this section, the term guest is hereby defined as being a person who accepts a ride in any motor vehicle without giving compensation therefor, but shall not be construed to apply to such passenger in any motor vehicle being demonstrated to such passenger as a prospective purchase. Relationship by consanguinity or affinity within the second degree shall include parents, grandparents, children, grandchildren, and brothers and sisters. Should the marriage of the driver or owner be terminated by death or dissolution, the affinal relationship with the blood kindred of his or her spouse shall be deemed to continue. (39-6, sec. 191.)

OHIO

The owner, operator, or person responsible for the operation of a motor vehicle is not liable for loss or damage arising from injuries to or death of a guest transported without payment, resulting from the operation thereof, unless the injuries or death are caused by the *willful and wanton misconduct* of such operator, owner, or person responsible for the operation of said motor vehicle. (4515.02)

TEXAS

(a) No person who is related within the second degree of consanguinity or affinity to the owner or operator of a motor vehicle and who is being transported over the public highways of this State by the owner or operator of a motor vehicle as his guest without payment for such transportation shall have a cause of action for damages against such owner or operator for injuries, death or loss, in the case of accident, unless such accident shall have been intentional on the part of said owner or operator or caused by his heedlessness or his reckless disregard of the rights of others. There shall be no such immunity for the owner or operator who is not related to the guest. (b) Nothing in this Act affects any judicially developed and developing rules under which a person is or is not totally or partially immune from tort liability to another by virtue of the family relationship. (c) When any liability claim is made by a guest against the owner or operator or his liability insurance carrier, the owner or operator or his liability insurance carrier shall be entitled to offset, credit or deduction against any reward made to such guest in the amount of money equal to the amounts paid by the owner, operator or his automobile liability insurance carrier for medical expenses of such guest, provided, however, that nothing herein shall be construed to authorize a direct action against a liability insurance company if such right does not presently exist at law. (Sec. 1)

This Act shall not relieve a public carrier or any owner or operator of a motor vehicle while the same is being demonstrated to a prospective purchaser, of responsibility for any injuries sustained by a passenger while being transported by such public carrier, or such owner or operator. (Sec. 2)

UTAH

Responsibility of owner or driver of a vehicle to guest.—Any person who as a guest accepts a ride in any vehicle, moving upon any of the public highways of the state of Utah, and while so riding as such guest receives or sustains an injury, shall have no right of recovery against the owner or driver or person responsible for the operation of such vehicle. In the event that such person while so riding as such guest, is killed, or dies as a result of injury sustained while so riding as such guest, then neither the estate nor the legal representatives or heirs of such guest shall have any right of recovery against the driver or owner of said vehicle by reason of the death of said guest. If such person so riding as a guest be a minor and sustain an injury or be killed or die as a result of injury sustained while so riding as such guest, then neither the parents nor guardians nor the state nor legal representatives or heirs of such minor shall have any right of recovery against the driver or owner or person responsible for the operation of said vehicle for injury sustained or as a result of the death of such minor. Nothing in this section shall be construed as relieving the owner or driver or person responsible for the operation of a vehicle from liability for injury to or death of such guest proximately resulting from the intoxication or willfull misconduct of such owner, driver or person responsible for the operation of such vehicle; provided, that in any action for death or for injury or damage to person or property by or on behalf of a guest of the estate, heirs or legal representatives of such guest, the burden shall be upon plaintiff to establish that such intoxication or willful misconduct was the proximate cause of such death or injury or damage. (Sec. 41-9-1)

"Guest" defined.—For the purpose of this section the term "guest" is hereby defined as being a person who accepts a ride in any vehicle without giving compensation therefor. (Sec. 41-9-2)

VIRGINIA

Liability for death or injury to guest in motor vehicle.—Any person transported by the owner or operator of any motor vehicle as a guest without payment for such transportation and any personal representative of any such guest so transported shall be entitled to recover damages against such owner or operator for death or injuries to the person or property of such guest resulting from the negligent operation of such motor vehicle. However, this statute does not limit any defense otherwise available to the owner or operator. (Sec. 8-646.1)

Some states have repealed their guest statutes. This means that the guest statute will be applicable only to accidents which occurred prior to the effective date of the repeal and not thereafter. These states are:

State	*Repeal Effective*
Arkansas	2/2/83
Colorado	4/9/75
Florida	2/14/72
Kansas	7/1/74
Montana	7/1/75
Oregon	10/3/79

The provision regarding motor vehicle passengers was removed from the guest statute. Provisions regarding aircraft and watercraft passengers remain.

South Dakota	7/1/78
Vermont	3/1/70
Washington	3/1/74

States which are not listed (including the District of Columbia) do not have guest statutes. Therefore the rule of ordinary negligence will be applied to the conduct of the host, and the guest may recover if the host is chargeable with ordinary negligence.

The constitutionality of guest statutes has been under continuous attack, The Supreme Court of the United States upheld the statutes on the theory that they were not violative of the Constitution of the United States [*Silver* v. *Silver*, 280 U.S. 117 (1929)]. Since that time guest statutes have been considered by the state courts and a determination made as to whether they were violative of the state constitutions. The courts of California, Idaho, Iowa, Michigan, Nevada, New Mexico, North Dakota, South Carolina, and Wyoming have invalidated their guest statutes by declaring them to be violative of the state constitution.

In *Thompson* v. *Hagan* (523 Pac. 2d 1370), the Supreme Court of Idaho while recognizing that the law was intended to prevent collusive lawsuits, took the position that by denying recovery to all guests the guest statute is all-inclusive in its sweep and bars all actions. In that respect the law is invalid and denies to the guest equal protection of the laws.

Conversely, the Delaware Supreme Court upheld the state's guest statute in *Justice* v. *Gatchell* (325 Atl. 2d 97). The court said:

... on the basis of the record before us, even on the basis of information of which we might take judicial notice, we are unable to say that there are no longer any evils to be corrected, or permissible objectives to be accomplished by the Guest Statute. Whether the concept of hospitality-protection or collusion-prevention has

been so eroded by changing conditions, as to have disappeared as acceptable justification for the Guest Statutes is a problem more appropriate for legislative solution than for judicial determination. The General Assembly has access to relevant
information bearing upon these matters more significant than any afforded this
Court, bound as it is by the limitations of this judicial proceeding.

1223   Guest defined

A guest in an automobile has been defined as a person who takes a ride in
an automobile driven by another person merely for his own pleasure or on his
own business, and without making any return or conferring any benefit on the
automobile driver. He is one who has received a gift from the host-driver in
the form of transportation with no return being given or expected. On the
other hand, for the purposes of the application of the guest statutes, one who
pays for his transportation, whether the amount approximates the cost or not,
or confers a benefit on the automobile driver, may or may not be considered a
guest, depending upon the circumstances. We will therefore consider the payment theory and the mutual benefit theory.

The payment theory.   Where the passenger pays for his transportation
in an amount which approximates its cost, there is no question but that he is
not a guest. Where a passenger is given transportation gratuitously and during
the course of the trip pays for a meal, or for some gasoline, which payments
are not intended to be payment for transportation and not received as such, the
mere payment of such small amounts will not change his status as a guest.
Between these two extremes will fall a certain group of cases where there is a
doubt as to whether the payment was intended and received as payment for
transportation and which are decided on the basis of their own particular
facts and circumstances.

For example, in *Wagnon* v. *Patterson* [70 S.E. 2d 244 (Alabama)], the
facts indicated that the defendant drove the plaintiff to and from work every
day. Each payday, the plaintiff gave the defendant 50 cents a week to "help
share the expense of the gasoline." The court held that the question of whether
or not the plaintiff was a passenger or a guest was properly submitted to the
jury, who found that the plaintiff was a passenger.

In *Vogreg* v. *Shepard Ambulance Service* [268 Pac. 2d 642 (Washington)], the plaintiff's husband, who was a paralytic, was being transported
home by ambulance. After he was placed in the vehicle, the plaintiff got in and
gave directions to the driver. No separate charge was made for the plaintiff's
transportation. The trial court held as a matter of law that she was guest on
the theory that the ambulance charge was made solely for the purpose of
transporting her husband. On appeal the Supreme Court, reversing the trial
court's decision, held that the host-guest relationship is a question of fact for
the jury unless reasonable minds can reach but one conclusion under the facts
of the particular case. In this case the jury might well conclude that carrying
the wife was as much part of the contract as carrying the husband.

In *Koriss* v. *Butler* [277 Pac. 2d 873 (California)], the district court of
appeal held that if nothing more is involved than the exchange of social

amenities and hospitalities, or extending ordinary courtesies of the road, such as paying bridge or ferry tolls, the host-guest relationship is not destroyed. Since the burden of establishing that he was a passenger and not a guest is on the plaintiff, the court held that the evidence was clearly insufficient to establish this fact. Therefore, as far as payment is concerned, it is usually a question of fact as to whether the payment was or was not made in return for the transportation.

Where payment is made for the transportation, it does not necessarily have to be made by the passenger in order to avoid the guest status. To illustrate, in *Thompson* v. *Lacey* (207 Pac. 2d 1), the facts indicated that the plaintiff's deceased husband and the driver were employees of the same company, the driver being branch manager and the deceased the sales supervisor of the area. They were going to a sales meeting in the manager's car. The company reimbursed employees for expenses incurred in going to meetings, including an allowance of 7 cents per mile when a private car was used. The employee driving the car would receive the mileage allowance and the others riding with him would not.

In holding that the deceased was a passenger rather than a guest, the Supreme Court of California observed that it is not necessary that the compensation for transportation be paid by the one transported, but may be paid by someone other than the rider. The company received an economic benefit because it would pay less traveling expenses to its employees attending the meeting by reason of their arrangement whereby only the owner of the car would receive the mileage allowance. Therefore the company was in effect paying one employee to bring others to the meeting.

Mutual benefit theory.   The general rule is that the occupant of a motor vehicle is not a guest where the ride is intended to further the business interests of the driver or owner, or where it is to promote the mutual business interests of both the host and the occupant. For example, in *Thomas* v. *Hughes* [279 P. 2d 286 (Kansas)], the plaintiff, as manager of a corporation, purchased an automobile for the corporation from a dealer, who agreed to make the customary mechanical checkups. During one such checkup, the dealer's mechanic requested that the plaintiff accompany him on a road test to be certain that the automobile was in perfect running order. As a result of the mechanic's negligence there was an accident in which the plaintiff was injured.

In holding that the plaintiff was a passenger and not a guest, the court observed that payment, required by the local guest statute to raise an occupant of a vehicle to the status of one who can recover for ordinary negligence, need not be a payment in money. It is sufficient to escape the restrictions of the guest statute that the plaintiff's presence conferred a business advantage on the owner or operator of the vehicle. Here, the mutual benefits arising from the contractual relationship, and the goodwill passing to the dealer's business because of the practice of service checkups, prevented the case from being governed by the guest statute.

In *Woodland* v. *Smith* [354 Pac 2d 391 (Washington)], the defendant transported the plaintiff to a business meeting in which both had an interest, and where the plaintiff, who was acquainted with others at the meeting, was to introduce the defendant to them. Plaintiff was held to be a passenger and not a guest. The following cases illustrate the same principle:

Robb v. *Ramey Associates* [14 Atl. 2d 394 (Delaware)]; purpose of the trip was to sell the plaintiff a cemetery lot; held not a guest.

Zaso v. *DeCola* [51 N.E. 2d 654 (Ohio)]; plaintiff was not a guest where he had gone with the defendant to his home in order to attempt to bring about a reconciliation between the defendant and his wife.

George v. *Stanfield* [33 Fed. Supp. 486 (Idaho)]; purpose of occupant's presence was to aid the defendant in locating a certain place; held not a guest.

Infants as guests.   The courts are divided on the question of whether or not an infant can attain the status of a guest in a vehicle so as to come within the provisions of the guest statute. To achieve the status of a guest, the decisions all agree that there must be an invitation, expressed or implied, and an acceptance, formal or informal. The courts further agree that an infant of tender years is incapable legally of accepting the invitation. The courts, however, part company on the question of whether or not the parent or guardian can accept the invitation for the infant so as to make such acceptance binding on the infant to the extent of making it subject to the guest statute. The cases holding that the parent or guardian can accept the invitation for the infant, thereby making the infant a guest, are as follows:

In re Wright's Estate [228 Pac. 2d 911], a four-year-old child, placed by his parents in the care of the driver, was held to be the driver's guest. (Kansas)

Welker v. *Sorenson* [306 Pac. 2d 737], a mother and her 29-month-old child were riding as guests of the defendant driver at the time of the accident. The court held that since the parent impliedly accepted a ride for her child, the infant thereby assumed the guest status of the mother, foreclosing a recovery under the guest statute in the absence of gross negligence. (Oregon)

Horst v. *Holtzen* [90 N.W. 2d 41], a 13-day-old infant was carried by her mother into the defendant's car for a gratuitous ride to a meeting of a church society. The Iowa Supreme Court held that while an infant of tender years is incapable of accepting the invitation, the parent may act for the child, and mere permission of the parent would classify the free-riding infant as a guest. (Iowa)

The contrary view emphasizes the infant's lack of capacity to accept the invitation, as well as the fact that in some cases the infant is an unwilling passenger in that he is forced to take the ride because of the dominant authority of the parent or guardian. The cases supporting this view are as follows:

Green v. *Jones* [319 Pac. 2d 1083 (Colorado)]: Plaintiff, aged 2, was injured while riding as a gratuitous guest in the defendant's car. The Supreme Court of Colorado found that a two-year-old child is incompetent to accept or reject an invitation. Since the status of "guest" under the statute can be acquired only by knowingly and voluntarily accepting the invitation to become one, there was no legal acceptance in this case, and therefore the infant was not a guest.

Fuller v. *Thrum* [31 N.E. 2d 670 (Indiana)]: A six-year-old child, incapable of accepting an invitation to ride in the car, could not be legally classified as a guest.

Rocha v. *Hulen* [44 Pac. 2d 478 (California)]: The driver of an automobile found a five-year-old child injured and unattended. He was involved in an accident while taking the child to a hospital. The court held that the child had not "accepted" the ride and consequently could not be a guest.

Hart v. *Hogan* [24 Pac. 2d 478 (Washington)]: A 12-year-old child in the custody of her mother was held not to be a guest of the car owner. The court pointed out that she was an involuntary occupant of the automobile and that she had no option other than to accompany her mother.

Owner as guest of driver.   The majority rule is that the owner of the car driven by another is not a guest and, not being subject to the guest statute, may recover from the driver upon a showing of ordinary negligence. While not all states having guest statutes have passed on the question, the following cases support the majority view: California: *Ahlgren* v. *Ahlgren* (313 Pac. 2d 88); Connecticut: *Gledhill* v. *Connecticut Co.* (183 Atl. 379); Delaware: *Wilson* v. *Workman* (192 Fed. Supp. 852); Ohio: *Henline* v. *Wilson* (174 N.E. 2d 122); Pennsylvania: *Lorch* v. *Englin* (85 Atl. 2d 841); and Virginia: *Helms* v. *Leonard* (170 Fed. Supp. 143).

In *Naphtali* v. *Lafazen* [165 N.Y.S. 2d 395, affirmed in 171 N.E. (2) 462], the New York court was called upon to construe the Ohio guest statute as it applied to a situation where the owner-husband and his wife brought personal injury actions, plus the husband's action for loss of consortium, against the driver. The car was being used on a pleasure trip with the owner-husband assuming all the expenses. As a defense, the Ohio guest statute was interposed. The court held that the husband-owner was not a guest and that he could recover not only for his own personal injuries but also for the loss of his wife's services and medical expenses. The wife was held to be a guest and therefore precluded from recovery in the absence of a showing of gross negligence. As to the recovery by the husband in his loss of services action, this would seem to be an inconsistent result, but the court held that the action for loss of services was one owned by the husband and was therefore subject to the law applicable to the husband's claim alone.

As opposed to the majority view, in *Phelps* v. *Benson* (90 N.W. 2d 533), the Minnesota court, in construing the South Dakota guest statute, held that the owner was a guest when suing the driver of his car. This case has been criticized in later decisions.

Bailee as guest of the driver.   In *Collie* v. *Aust* (342 Pac. 2d 998), the California court held that the bailee of the owner, like the owner, is not a guest of the person he allows to drive the car.

1224   Duration of guest status

Where there has been an invitation and an acceptance of gratuitous transportation, and while the transportation is being given, in the absence of special circumstances the occupant is a guest within the contemplation of the guest statutes. Questions as to the status of the occupant while the transportation is being given arise when (1) the guest gets out of the car intending to return and continue the trip; (2) when the driver is out of the car temporarily; and (3) when there has been a revocation of either the invitation or the acceptance.

Guest out of the car.   When the guest is entirely outside the automobile, the general rule is that the guest status has either terminated or is suspended during the time. Each case presents questions of fact for the jury as to exactly if and when the guest relationship was suspended or terminated. In some cases the guest will be entirely outside the automobile with both feet on the ground and not touching the car. In others, the guest will be partly in the car and partly on the ground, and in still others, the guest will be in the act of alighting without having reached the ground at all. The courts generally hold that it is the function of the jury to find whether the individual is or is not in a guest status when he is outside of, leaving, or entering the standing vehicle.

In *Rogers* v. *Lawrence* (296 S.W. 2d 809), the Supreme Court of Arkansas held that when a guest has left the vehicle, intending to later reenter after transacting other matters, the court cannot say, as a matter of law, that the intention to resume the journey makes the guest relationship continue while the guest is entirely away from the car. It was for the jury to say, whether the guest relationship was terminated when the guest had both feet on the ground and was not touching the car. In that case, the guest was injured when the driver moved the car and struck the guest with either the door or the fender. The jury found that the guest relationship had been suspended while the guest was outside of the vehicle, and this finding was not disturbed on appeal.

Questions of this type frequently arise when the guest gets out of the car to assist either in repairs or getting the car started by cranking or pushing. The general rule is that it is a question for the jury to decide as to whether or not the guest status is suspended. In most of the cases, the jury has found that the guest relationship was suspended.

Driver out of the car.   Where the guest remains in the automobile while the driver is outside of it and the guest is injured because of the driver's negligence in failing to set the brake properly, or leaving the motor running, the cases hold that the host-guest relationship is suspended during the period of the driver's absence. [See *Panopulos* v. *Maderis*, 293 Pac. 2d 121 (California) ; *Clinger* v. *Duncan*, 141 N.E. 2d 156 (Ohio) ; and *Waltzinger* v. *Birsner*, 128 Alt. 2d 617 (Maryland).]

Revocation of invitation or acceptance.   The status of host-guest comes into existence as a result of an invitation and the acceptance thereof. The driver may withdraw or revoke the invitation, and at that point the passenger ceases to be a guest. He must leave the vehicle at the first opportunity. If he remains, he is a trespasser. Should he be injured while leaving the vehicle after the invitation had been revoked (a rare situation) it would appear that the rule of ordinary negligence would apply.

A more common situation is where the guest withdraws his acceptance of the invitation and demands to be let out of the car. If the driver fails to accede to the demand, the host-guest relationship is at an end and the passenger is being transported against his will. A mere protest at the way the automobile is being driven will not destroy the host-guest relationship if it is not accompanied by a demand to be let out of the car. The demand is evidence of the withdrawal of the acceptance of the invitation, and with that withdrawal the host-guest relationship terminates.

Where the acceptance of the invitation is obtained by fraud, the cases generally hold that the host-guest relationship never came into existence, and that the guest statute has no application. For example, in *Coffman* v. *Godsoe* [351 Pac. 2d 808 (Colorado)], the driver represented to the guest that he had a driver's license and was fully capable of operating the vehicle. Both of these statements were untrue. The court held that since the passenger's consent was obtained by fraud, the acceptance of the invitation was a nullity and not binding on the passenger. The status of host and guest, therefore, could not come into existence, with the result that the guest statute was inapplicable to the case.

1225   Vicarious liability of the owner

Ordinarily, the owner of a motor vehicle who entrusts the use thereof to another person possessing competence to drive is not answerable for the driver's negligence unless, at the time of the accident, the driver was acting as agent for the owner. In the latter case, the basic principles of agency apply and the principal is liable for the acts of his agent within the scope of his agency under the doctrine of *respondeat superior*. In the absence of agency, the owner is not vicariously liable for the negligent acts of the driver.

Where the owner of an automobile is riding in the car driven by another, a presumption arises that the driver is the agent of the owner and is under his control. This presumption was once regarded as irrebuttable, but the present tendency of the courts is to allow evidence to be submitted for the purpose of showing that no agency did in fact exist. For example, in *Greyhound Lines* v. *Caster* [216 Atl. 2d 689 (Delaware)], the evidence indicated that the owner-passenger was asleep at the time of the accident. The court held that he had relinquished control and that the driver's negligence was not imputable to him. Other cases involving the same set of facts in which the same result was obtained are: *McMartin* v. *Saemish* [116 N.W. 2d 491 (Iowa)]; *Johnson* v. *Los Angeles Motor Freight* [352 Pac. 2d 1091 (Oregon)]. Cases in which the driver's negligence was imputed to the owner-passenger are: *Baber* v. *Akers Motor lines* [215 Fed. 2d 843 (District of Columbia)]; *Simaitis* v. *Thrash* [166 N.E. 2d 306 (Illinois)]; *Siler* v. *Williford* [350 S.W. 2d 697 (Kentucky)]; *Dowden* v. *Hartford Accident* [151 So. 2d 697 (Louisiana)]; *MacArthur* v. *Gendron* [312 S.W. 2d 146 (Missouri)]; *Merritt* v. *Darden* [176 Atl. 2d 205 (Maryland)]; *Shoe* v. *Hood* [112 S.E. 2d 543 (North Carolina)]; *Allstate Insurance Co.* v. *Combs* [206 N.E. 24 (Ohio)]; *Strupp* v. *Farmers' Mutual* [109 N.W. 2d 660 (Wisconsin)]. Thus it is to be noted that the majority of the states still adhere to the presumption of agency where an owner-passenger is involved, but there is evidence that the rule is being reexamined, and it is possible that some of these cases will be reversed.

Imputed contributory negligence. In many cases, it was urged that since the negligence of the agent is the negligence of the principal where a third party is seeking damages, it would seem to follow that the same rule of responsibility should apply where the principal is seeking damages from a third party for injuries to person or property which he has sustained. The courts universally adopted this rule and it came to be known as the "both ways" rule. Under it, the principal is charged with the negligence of his agent regardless of whether a third party is seeking damages from him or he is seeking to recover damages from the third party. The original Restatement of the Law of Torts adopted the both ways test as follows:

Sec. 485: Except as stated in 493 and 499, a plaintiff is barred from recovery by the negligent act or omission of a third person if, but only if, the relation between them is such that the plaintiff would be liable as defendant for harm caused to others by such negligent conduct of the third person.

Sec. 486: A master is barred from recovery against a negligent defendant by the contributory negligence of his servant acting within the scope of his employment.

Thus, if the master is riding in his own car driven by his servant, and is injured through the joint negligence of the servant and a third party, he is charged with the contributory negligence of his servant in his action against the third party, even though the master personally is entirely blameless and had no means at his command whereby he could have avoided the accident. It is true, that the master has a cause of action against his servant to recover any damages which he may have sustained as a result of the negligence of the servant, and the master in that situation would not be charged with a contributory negligence or the negligence of the servant. The contributory negligence of the servant is imputed to the master only for the benefit of other parties. The practical result here is that the servant could be held entirely responsible for the damage and the third party, although a joint tort-feasor, would escape liability.

The rule has been under attack for many years by legal scholars, who question its logic as well as its justice. It is pointed out that the application of the rule deprives a faultless plaintiff of his right to recovery solely because he stood in some relationship to one of the parties. As a consequence, there are some indications at the present time that the courts will reexamine the rule. Among the first cases to manifest this change in the attitude of the courts is *Jenks* v. *Veeder Contracting Co., Inc.* (30 N.Y.S. 2d 279, affirmed in 37 N.Y.S. 2d 230, appeal dismissed in 289 N.Y. 787, 46 N.E. 2d 848). The case involved the imputing of contributory negligence to a joint owner. The court said:

Parties having equal title to a motor vehicle cannot be permitted to contend for the wheel in moving traffic and hence the imputation of negligence to the joint owner present upon the theory of equal right to domination or control is untenable when applied to the facts of this case.

The realities of the actual operation of vehicles on highways cannot be entirely overlooked in dealing with the rights and obligations of those present with the driver.

There are other evidences of the intention of the courts to limit the application of the rule, especially in cases where there is evidence that the owner has relinquished control. For example, in *Greyhound Lines, Inc.* v. *Caster* [216 Atl. 2d 289 (Delaware)], the court approved a jury instruction that if they found that the owner-passenger was asleep at the time of the accident, they must find the driver's contributory negligence was not imputed to the owner, since the owner had relinquished control by going to sleep and there had been no claim that the owner was personally guilty of negligence in allowing the driver to operate the car. See also *Johnson* v. *Los Angeles Motor Freight* [352 Pac. 2d 1091 (Oregon)], where it was held that the contributory negligence of the driver was not attributed to the owner, because they were driving on a long trip and he was sleeping in the back seat of the car at the time of the collision with a bus, where the driver was competent and at the time of the accident the owner was not exercising control over her.

In the adoption of the new Restatement, Torts, Second, imputed contributory negligence was abandoned as to many of the relationships to which it originally applied. It now reads:

Sec. 485: Except as stated in 486, 491, and 494, a plaintiff is not barred from recovery by the negligent act or omission of a third person.

In the Comment, which accompanied this change in the rule, we find the following:

The rule stated in this Section rejects except as indicated by the reference to other Sections, the doctrine of "imputed contributory negligence" under which the plaintiff is barred from recovery against the defendant because the negligence of a third person, with whom the plaintiff stands in some relation, has contributed to his harm.

The Comment further notes that in many of the cases involving imputed contributory negligence, the decision was based on a fictitious agency relationship and should no longer be recognized as valid. Therefore, a passenger in a vehicle is held to be barred by the negligence of his own driver from recovery from a defendant who collided with the vehicle, on the basis that the driver was necessarily the agent of the plaintiff, even though the vehicle was that of a common carrier. Likewise, a child was held to be barred from recovery against a defendant who injured him, by the negligence of a parent who had the child in custody, on the theory that the parent was the child's agent to look after him and, therefore, the negligence of the parent was imputed to the child. There were similar imputations of the negligence of one spouse to the other, and of the negligence of a bailee to his bailor. It is now generally recognized that such theories of agency are entirely fictitious, and the doctrine of imputed negligence has been largely discredited. It is now applied only in the limited number of respects. These are as follows:

1. The negligence of a servant acting within the scope of his employment is imputed to bar the recovery of his master. (See Sec. 486.)
2. In a small number of jurisdictions which have the law of community property, the negligence of one spouse is still imputed to bar recovery by the other. (See Sec. 487, Comment c.)
3. The negligence of one member of a joint enterprise is imputed to bar recovery by the others. (See Sec. 491.)
4. In action for death or loss of services, the negligence of the person who is injured bars recovery by the person who has been deprived of the relation. (See Sec. 494.)

Unfortunately, the Restatement retains imputed contributory negligence where it applies to actual agency relationships and the purpose of the change in rule is to merely reject it with respect to fictional agency relationships such as are found in the Family Doctrine, etc.

In *Weber* v. *Stokely-Van Camp, Inc.* (144 N.W. 2d 540), the Supreme Court of Minnesota specifically reversed earlier cases embracing the Rule and abolished the "both ways" test as a rule of decision in that state. The court said:

We can think of nothing more dangerous in these days of congested travel on high-speed highways than to permit a master riding as a passenger in a car driven by his servant constantly to interfere with the servant's driving or his attempt to exercise a theoretic right of control. To do so would be the clearest evidence of active negligence on the part of the master, for which he would be chargeable without imputing to him the negligence of his servant. Imputed negligence, on the other hand, presupposes that the master is innocent of any fault. How, then, can we reconcile the theory of right to control, the exercise of which would charge the master with negligence and imputed negligence based on the theory that he is free from any fault? The two just do not hang together.

We are convinced the time has come to discard this rule, which is defensible only on the grounds of its antiquity. In doing so we realize we may stand alone, but a doctrine so untenable should not be followed so as to bar recovery of one entitled to damages.

This decision represents a total rejection of the "both ways" test whereas the new Restatement merely accomplishes a partial rejection by retaining the Rule and applying it only to a limited number of cases. It is possible that other courts will follow the lead of Minnesota.

In bailments, the element of control by the owner is lacking. The applicable common-law rule is that the contributory negligence of the bailee is not imputed to the bailor and, therefore, it cannot be interposed as a defense to the bailor's action against the negligent third party to recover his damages. This common-law rule has been modified by statute in some states. (See Sec. 913.)

Negligent entrustment. It is possible for the owner to be held liable for his own act of negligence if he knowingly entrusts the use of his vehicle to a person who is intoxicated, incompetent, reckless, or irresponsible with respect to the use of an automobile, and an accident occurs as a result. The liability thus imposed is not based on the negligence of the driver in causing the accident; it is based on the owner's own negligent act in making the vehicle available to such a person. In order to hold the owner responsible, it must be established that he knew, or by the exercise of reasonable care should have known, of the incompetence of the driver, and that he consented to the use of his vehicle by such a person. Both elements must be established or the action against the owner must fail.

1226   Family purpose doctrine

This doctrine creates a fictional relationship of principal and agent with regard to the use of a family automobile, whereby the member of the family driving the car is considered to be the agent of the father-owner whether there is any agency in fact or not. It is based on the theory that the father of the family has an obligation to provide recreation and entertainment for the members of his family. If he purchases an automobile, which is devoted to family purposes, then any member of the family driving the automobile with the owner's consent is acting as the agent of the father-owner in discharging the father-owner's responsibility to provide recreation and entertainment.

This doctrine is applied even where the member of the family is driving the car solely for his own purposes. The doctrine is a rule of expediency since it is applied solely for the purpose of permitting an action against a financially responsible person (the father) rather than limiting the plaintiff to a recourse against another member of the family who may not be able to respond in damages.

In *Turner* v. *Hall's Adm.* [252 S.W. 2d 30 (Kentucky)], the court said:

The Family Purpose Doctrine is a humanitarian one designed for the protection of the public generally, and resulted from recognition of the fact that in the vast majority of instances an infant has not sufficient property in his own right to indemnify one who may suffer from his negligent act.

Only about half of the states which have considered the doctrine have adopted it, either by specific statute or by judicial determination. The others have specifically rejected the doctrine and refuse to apply it.

1227   Statutory liability of the owner

Several states have by statute imposed liability upon the owner of a motor vehicle where the vehicle is being driven by another with his consent, express or implied. Some create an irrebuttable presumption of agency and others merely impose the liability from the fact of ownership with no attempt being made to create an agency relationship. Some have limitations as to the amount for which the owner is responsible under the statute, while others have no limitation whatsoever. Recourse must be had to the specific statute to determine the exact liability imposed and the limitations, if any.

Among the states having statutes imposing liability on the owner are: Florida (statute 51.12), California (Vehicle Code sec. 17150), District of Columbia (D.C. Code 40–424). Idaho (49:1404), Iowa (321.493), Michigan (1257.401), Minnesota (170.54), Nevada (41.440–460), New York (V. & T. law, sec. 388), and Rhode Island (31.33, 6.7).

In states where an operator's license is granted to an infant of the age of 16 and upwards, some statutes require that the infant be sponsored by an adult, who will assume responsibility for all damages arising out of the operation of a motor vehicle by the infant.

1228   Vicarious liability of person other than owner

In order to become vicariously liable for damages arising out of the operation of a motor vehicle, a person does not necessarily have to be the owner of the vehicle. Under the basic principles of agency, the person, firm, or corporation, on whose business and for whose benefit the vehicle is being operated by a driver under their control, is liable under the doctrine of *respondeat superior*. It makes no difference whether the vehicle is owned by the driver or by someone else. If the vehicle is being operated by an agent, servant, employee, or someone under the control of the principal, and on the principal's business, the principal is liable for the acts of such driver. Thus, if an employee is driving his own personal car, or one owned by someone else, on the business of his employer, the employer is vicariously liable for damages arising out of the employee's negligence in operating the vehicle.

1229   Driver's negligence not imputed to passengers

In absence of an agency relationship between the passenger and the driver, the negligence of the driver is not imputed to the passenger. The passenger or guest has no control over the operation of the vehicle or the actions of the driver, and therefore is not chargeable with or responsible for the lack of care on the part of the driver. This same rule applies even where there is some family relationship between the passenger and the driver, such as husband and wife, parent and child, niece and nephew, and the like.

Where there is an agency relationship between the driver and the passenger, as where the owner is riding in his own car driven by his chauffeur, the general rule of agency is usually applied in that the negligence of the agent is imputed to the principal. Under this rule, however, the passenger may recover for his injuries even though his own driver is at fault, and where two cars are involved and both drivers at fault, he may elect to hold either or both responsible for his injuries as joint tort-feasors. It must be pointed out that the duties of both drivers to the passenger may not always be the same, and the driver of the car in which the passenger is riding may have a greater or lesser duty than that of the other driver.

For example, in a guest statute state, the driver of the vehicle in which the guest is riding is liable, as a rule, only for gross negligence, but the other driver is responsible to the passenger if he fails to exercise ordinary care. If the passenger is riding in a common carrier, taxicab, or bus, the driver owes a high degree of care for the safety of his passengers, whereas the other driver still only owes a duty of ordinary care.

1230   Rights and duties of pedestrians

The pedestrian has certain rights and duties when he is (1) on the sidewalk, (2) crossing the street at a controlled intersection, (3) crossing at an uncontrolled intersection, (4) crossing between intersections, and (5) walking on the highway.

1. Sidewalks.   The pedestrian has a clear statutory right-of-way on the sidewalk and the motorist must yield to this superior right. When a pedestrian on the sidewalk is injured as a result of being struck by any part of a motor vehicle, a presumption of negligence on the part of the operator of the motor vehicle arises. It makes no difference whether the wheels of the vehicle are on the road. If the pedestrian is on the sidewalk and he is injured by any part of the vehicle, such as an overhang, or a projecting load, the same presumption of negligence arises. The driver may overcome the presumption by a showing that he was operating his vehicle with reasonable care, but that he was forced onto the sidewalk by the negligent act of another motorist.

2. Controlled intersections.   The pedestrian has a clear substantial right-of-way over any motorist when crossing on a crosswalk with a green light in his favor. Should the light change while he is in the intersection, the motorist has the duty of permitting him to clear the intersection before the motorist proceeds. The turning motorist is required to yield the right-of-way to pedestrians at a controlled intersection. The pedestrian has a right to assume that the motorist will obey the law and meet the duties thus imposed. On the other hand, the pedestrian must exercise reasonable care for his own safety, and, failing in this, he can be charged with contributory negligence.

3. Uncontrolled intersections.   The extent of the vigilance and care which the pedestrian must exercise for his own safety is greater at uncontrolled intersections than at an intersection controlled by a traffic officer or traffic lights. He has a right to rely on the direction of the traffic officer or the lights in crossing. When crossing at an uncontrolled intersection, he is on notice of the possible danger, and must meet the duty of observation which requires him to look before crossing. His failure to do so usually contributory negligence as a matter of law.

The motorist approaching the intersection must have his car under control, and if he sees a pedestrian, or his vision of the intersection is obscured by foliage, parked cars, or other objects, he is under a duty to warn of his approach by sounding his horn or other means. Under most statutes, the pedestrian has the right-of-way at unguarded and unlighted crosswalk intersections, as well as at those which are well lighted and guarded by stop signs or other warning signs.

The pedestrian has a right to rely on the assumption that the motorist using the intersection will exercise the duty of care as imposed on him by law. Having made an initial observation before crossing, the pedestrian is not bound to anticipate that a motorist will approach the intersection at a high rate of speed or that warning of his approach will not be given. He therefore is not normally under a duty to make constant observations, but only to maintain the same lookout as would be undertaken by the reasonably prudent man in the same or similar circumstances.

4. *Between intersections.* In the absence of a statute or ordinance which prohibits jaywalking, the pedestrian is not negligent merely because he crosses the street between intersections and not at a place set aside for a pedestrian crossing, but he is required to exercise a greater degree of care and caution. This under some circumstances would include a duty of constant observation and vigilance. When the pedestrian knows that the motorist's view is obscured, as when the pedestrian steps from between two parked cars, the duty of vigilance is greater than would be the case if the motorist's view was unobstructed. Whether the conduct of the pedestrian was or was not negligent is generally a question of fact for the jury applying the reasonably prudent man standard. If there is a statute or ordinance which forbids crossing between intersections, he is contributorily negligent as a matter of law if he does so.

5. *Walking on the highway.* In the absence of statute or ordinance, the basic rule is that both the pedestrian and the motorist have an equal right to use the highway for the purpose of travel. Upon approaching a pedestrian on the highway, the motorist has a duty to slow down and give proper warning of his approach. The generally accepted warning signal, and one which is required by most statutes, is the sounding of the horn.

It has been argued that the noisy operation of a truck, or the glaring headlights of an oncoming vehicle furnish sufficient warning. The cases hold, however, that while these conditions do convey the fact that the vehicle is approaching, they do not convey the fact that the pedestrian is in a position of danger. Where the statutes require that an audible signal be given, this is usually construed to mean the sounding of the horn, or other device calculated to perform the same function.

The pedestrian is under a duty of exercising reasonable care for his own safety. The extent of the care which he must exercise is determined by the facts and circumstances of each case, such as the density of traffic, width of the road, obstructions to the motorist's vision, and the extent of the warning signals given by the motorist. Thus a pedestrian, walking along a narrow road at night, dressed in dark clothing, would be required to exercise greater vigilance than the pedestrian walking along a wide road in the daytime, dressed in white clothing.

The pedestrian is not required to constantly look to the rear to ascertain the presence of approaching vehicles, but the circumstances of the case may demand that he maintain a close and observant watch for vehicles approaching from the rear. Nor is the pedestrian necessarily contributorily negligent if he walks on the highway at a place where there is a sidewalk or footpath available for his use. Since the pedestrian's and the motorist's right to use the highway is coextensive, the fact that the pedestrian is on the paved portion of the highway will not in and of itself be evidence of negligence. This is true even where there is a sidewalk or footpath, but the jury is entitled to take these facts into consideration in determining the question as to whether or not the pedestrian has exercised reasonable care for his own safety.

If the traffic is heavy and moving at a fast pace, the jury might reasonably find that the pedestrian, in walking on the highway where there was a footpath or sidewalk available, exposed himself to an unreasonable risk of harm and was therefore contributorily negligent. On the other hand, they might find that the pedestrian exercised the required amount of care if it is shown that the accident happened at night, the footpath or sidewalk was unlighted, and walking on it would expose the pedestrian to a greater risk than on the highway, or if the facts showed the sidewalk was covered with snow and the only plowed area on which the pedestrian could walk was the highway.

Statutes and ordinances have altered the rights and duties of pedestrians. In most cases, they have increased the duties and decreased the rights. For example, the statutes of most states provide that the pedestrian must walk on the sidewalk where one is provided and may only cross the streets at intersections. On the open highway pedestrians are required to walk on the left side of the roadway and face oncoming traffic. If the failure on the part of the pedestrian to obey the statute is the proximate or a contributing cause of the accident, he will be charged with contributory negligence.

1231 Traffic officers and workmen on the highway

A traffic officer must exercise reasonable care for his own safety and avoid being struck by a vehicle if it is possible to do so. Because of the nature of his work, however, he is not held to the same degree of care which is required of a pedestrian crossing the street, and, of necessity, he must rely to a greater degree upon the care and caution of motorists. He must exercise care in going to and from his post, and he must avoid placing himself in a place of known danger, such as stepping into the line of traffic. When the officer is directing traffic at an intersection, he may rely on the assumption that all motorists approaching the intersection will exercise the care and caution which the law requires at that place. Where the officer is directing traffic on the open road, the motorist normally has no reason to anticipate his presence unless he receives some advance notice. Usually this is done by warning signs, or by flashing lights at night. Where an accident occurs at such a place, there is almost always a question of fact for the jury as to whether there was sufficient notice given of the presence of the officer, or whether the motorist should have reasonably anticipated that an officer would be there.

The same rules are applicable to a workman on the road. He is not held to the same degree of care and caution as is imposed upon the pedestrian, and this also for reasons of necessity: he would never get his work done if he spent all his time watching for traffic. On the other hand, he must exercise some care. He must confine himself to the work area, and he may not carelessly step out into a lane of traffic without making a reasonable observation as to whether or not it is safe to do so. He is required to avoid any known danger.

The motorist, when he observes a workman in the road, or where he has notice of the existence of road repairs by means of warning signs or devices, is required to slow down, and to stop if necessary. In any case, he must guide his vehicle in such a way as to avoid any possibility of accident. He knows that the workmen cannot exercise the same degree of care and caution as a pedestrian would, and therefore he has a duty to exercise a higher degree of care for the safety of the workmen than would be required in the case of a pedestrian.

1232   No contact cases

It is fundamental that where negligence of the motorist is the proximate cause of an accident, the motorist is answerable. This is true whether there is any contact between the offending vehicle and the injured pedestrian or not. For example, if a motorist drives his car on the sidewalk, and, to avoid being struck, a pedestrian jumps out of the way and is injured in so doing, the proximate cause of the injury is the negligence of the motorist in driving on the sidewalk. While there was no actual contact between the offending vehicle and the pedestrian, nevertheless the motorist is answerable in damages.

In another case, let us assume that the offending motorist ran through a red traffic light into the path of another vehicle proceeding on the green. The vehicle stops short and there is no contact with the offending vehicle. Because of the sudden stop, vehicles behind are unable to stop and crash into the stopped vehicle. The proximate cause of the accident is the negligence of the motorist who ran through the red light, and he is liable for all the damage caused thereby, whether to the vehicle into whose path he drove or to the other vehicles which were following. The motorist who stopped suddenly in order to avoid an accident is not to blame for the accident which followed; the responsibility is entirely that of the motorist who ran the red light.

The difficulties attending these no-contact cases does not lie in the direction of the law governing the situation, but in the matter of proof. What usually happens is that the motorist who caused the accident escapes and is unidentified. When it is alleged that the motorist who stopped suddenly was negligent, he can absolve himself of negligence only by showing the necessity for his action. If there was no other vehicle involved, then a sudden stop without warning could be considered as a negligent act. Therefore the plaintiff is interested in establishing that there was no other car involved since, in that way, he can recover from the defendant. Otherwise, if the defendant was not negligent, and the accident was caused by the other car, which is unidentified, the plaintiff will have to find and identify him before a recovery can be had. Where a defense such as this is interposed, plaintiffs like to refer to the unidentified vehicle as the "phantom car," which tends to raise some question as to its existence.

1233   State licensing regulations

The license to drive a motor vehicle on the public highways of the state is a privilege and not a right. The distinction between the two is that a right is an element of citizenship which belongs to each individual citizen. A privilege is a license granted by the state permitting the performance of certain acts. In this category would fall the privilege of practicing certain professions, such as medicine, law, and dentistry. In granting a license to exercise these privileges, the state sets certain minimum requirements which must be met before the privilege will be granted. In the case of the professions, this takes the form of the successful passing of an examination following a prescribed period of study.

With respect to motor vehicles, the regulations usually require that the operator pass a driving test as well as meet certain physical standards. Thus, the state may grant the privilege to those who qualify and deny it to those who do not. The state may also attach to the granting of the privilege certain conditions with respect to its exercise and its duration. It may provide for a renewal of the privilege at certain intervals, and it may revoke the privilege at any time.

1234 Financial responsibility acts

As one of the conditions of the granting of the privilege to operate a motor vehicle, most states have imposed the provisions of a financial responsibility law. These acts generally provide that where the motorist has been involved in an accident for which he is responsible, and for which he is unable to respond in damages, his license to operate a motor vehicle is revoked unless he can furnish proof of future financial responsibility. This proof can take the form of an insurance policy covering the limits required by law, or he can qualify as a self-insurer by a deposit of security with the state. When an insurance policy is certified as proof of financial security, the insurance carrier must agree to abide by the conditions of the act as to cancellation and disclaimer (see Section 1615 below). Some acts provide that if the motorist presents to the state proof that the claim against him has been settled by him, the provisions of the act are not applicable, and he is not required to file proof of future financial responsibility.

As a means of enforcement, some states require that all drivers submit proof of insurance either concurrently with or within a short time after filing the state motor vehicle report of accident. Forms for this purpose are supplied (usually called SR 21's), and the insurance carried certifies that insurance is carried by submission of this form to the state. This system is the means by which the state can ascertain who is subject to financial responsibility and who is not. If the insurance form is not submitted within the time required by the act, the state assumes that no insurance is carried and that the operator is therefore subject to financial responsibility. The fact that insurance is carried is an indication that the operator can respond in damages if they are awarded against him, and thus he is not subject to the act.

1235 Unsatisfied judgment laws

The enactment of financial responsibility laws did not entirely solve the problem of the financially irresponsible motorist in the sense that there was no provision for compensating the victim of the first accident. The acts had only a prospective effect in that they required proof of future financial responsibility, responsibility that was not applied retroactively for the benefit of the first victim. Therefore, some states have enacted unsatisfied judgment laws. Under these laws a fund is created, usually by a tax on uninsured motorists and on automobile liability premiums earned in the state.

Where a judgment is obtained against an uninsured motorist and no recovery is possible, the plaintiff, if a qualified person, may have recourse against the fund for payment within the limitations prescribed in the law. A qualified person is defined as a citizen and resident of the state, or of another state which provides for a similar remedy. Some provide for a recovery for both personal injury and property damage (for example, Maryland and New Jersey) and others for personal injury only (for example, New York's Motor Vehicle Accident Indemnification Corporation Act). Where a qualified person is injured or killed in a hit-and-run accident and the offending motorist cannot be identified, these acts provide for an action against and payment by the fund in cases where the liability of the unidentified motorist can be established.

1236   Compulsory automobile insurance

Some states felt that the problem of the financially irresponsible motorist could be solved by compelling all motorists to carry automobile liability insurance with certain minimum limits. Therefore, compulsory insurance laws were passed requiring as a condition precedent to the renewal of a license, that the motorist present proof of insurance in the form of a policy or certificate from his insurance carrier. Clearly, this type of legislation would require insurance on all cars licensed within the state, but it falls short of the objective of having insurance available in every case involving an automobile accident. No insurance would be available in the case of a stolen car, an out-of-state vehicle, or an unregistered vehicle.

1237   Statutory policies of automobile liability insurance

Most state laws require, as a condition precedent to the license to operate on the streets and highways, that common carriers (passenger buses, freight carriers, and taxicabs) must file with the state a certified copy of a liability insurance policy, with minimum limits as prescribed in the law and subject to the conditions of the law. Interstate carriers, licensed by the Interstate Commerce Commission, are required to carry the amount of insurance prescribed by the commission. The policies must be filed with the Commission and conform to its rules and regulations as to cancellation and disclaimer.

1238   Service of process on nonresident motorists

A state may grant the privilege of operating a motor vehicle on its highways to drivers licensed in other states. This is done as a matter of reciprocity since the foreign state grants the same privilege. As with its own citizens, the state may affix conditions to the granting of this privilege. The condition attached to the grant of the use of the highways is that the foreign motorist constitutes some state official (usually the Secretary of State or Director of Motor Vehicles) as his agent upon whom service of process may be made in an action arising out of any accident which occurs within the state while the foreign motorist is using the highways.

This is sometimes referred to as "substituted service," and is a statute which is enacted for the protection of the citizens of the state whose highways are being used by the foreign motorist. Were it not for legislation of this type, the offending motorist could return to his home state and escape a lawsuit in the state where the accident happened. The injured person would then have to bear the financial burden of bringing his action in the defendant's home state. It should be emphasized, however, that service of process in this fashion is authorized only in the case of automobile accidents occurring in the state whose highways are being used. It does not apply to other litigation arising out of other matters which could be brought against the motorist.

1239 Seat belt defense

With the national publicity being given to the matter of safety which is afforded by the use of automobile seat belts, and the affirmative proof that has been offered that the use of seat belts will minimize or prevent injury, a number of states have passed statutes requiring that seat belts be made standard equipment on all new cars sold in the state after a given date. Most require seat belts only in the front seat, but the automobile manufacturers have voluntarily supplied seat belts for the front and rear seats beginning in 1965.

The legal problem presented by the use of seat belts involves the question of whether or not the driver or passenger of an automobile which is equipped with seat belts is contributorily negligent because of his failure to use them, and consequently may not recover. In addition, it has been urged that the failure of the injured person to use an available seat belt constitutes the failure to mitigate damages, and therefore the defendant is not responsible on the theory that the defendant is not liable for the avoidable consequences of the accident. In opposition, it has been argued that the failure to use seat belts has nothing to do with the causation of most accidents and further that the plaintiff's duty to mitigate damages or to take such steps as to eliminate the avoidable consequences of the accident is a duty which arises not before but after the accident has occurred. We will consider this problem under two headings: (1) contributory negligence and (2) avoidable consequences.

1. *Contributory negligence.* An automobile driver or passenger is required to exercise reasonable care for his own safety. If he fails to do so and such failure contributes to the causation of the accident, then in states applying the common-law rule he cannot recover. For example, if the claimant is riding as a passenger in the front seat of an automobile with available seat belts which he fails to use and the driver is confronted with a sudden emergency and suddenly applies his brakes, causing the passenger to move forward striking either the windshield or the dashboard, it could be argued that the

failure of the passenger to use the seat belt contributed to the causation of the accident. To support such an argument it must be shown by measurements of the claimant's body and the measurements of the car that the restraint exercised by the use of the seat belt would have avoided any contact by the claimant's body with any part of the windshield or dashboard. Therefore, in this case there is a definite chain of causation from the failure to use the seat belt and the occurrence of the injury. In cases where there are other factors and such a chain of causation cannot be established, it is doubtful that the defense of contributory negligence will be sustained. In a case where the driver negligently drives the car off the road and it hits a tree or overturns, it could hardly be said that the failure of his passenger to use the seat belt had anything to do with the causation of the accident. In *Lipscomb* v. *Diamiani* [226 Atl. 2d 914 (Delaware)], the court held that evidence of the failure to use seat belts was inadmissible in order to establish contributory negligence. [See also *Kavanagh* v. *Butoric*, 221 N.E. 2d 824 (Indiana).]

It should be pointed out that the legislation with respect to seat belts merely makes it mandatory that all new cars sold be equipped with them, but there is nothing in the legislation which requires that the passengers or the drivers of such cars use them. Also, there is nothing in the legislation which provides for any penalty by way of the deprivation of any rights of action where the seat belts are not used. The court in *Brown* v. *Kendrick* [192 So. 2d 49 (Florida)], summed up the present situation as follows:

> The problem of seat belts is coming to be more in the public eye today and there has been some legislative action with regard thereto. There has been and still exists controversy over the safety feature of the seat belts. The Florida Legislature has touched upon the subject only to the extent of requiring approval of the type to be used, if used.
>
> The Congress of the United States has considered several bills pertaining to motor vehicle and highway safety but in neither bill, as approved, has there been a mandatory use of seat belts. Further research is requested and required and a committee was established therefor with directions to report back to the Secretary of Commerce. So, in this state of quandary, the plaintiff and defendant could each have argued on the merits of the use of seat belts, but each argument would necessarily have been conjectural and of doubtful propriety. . . . Certainly, as pointed out by the appellee, the plaintiff's failure to fasten her seat belt was not such negligence as to contribute to the occurrence of the accident, nor to be the proximate contributing cause of the injury in absence of a showing that the accident could have been avoided in the absence of such negligent act.

2. Avoidable consequences.   There are no cases squarely on this point and as suggested above, the problem would be whether or not the law requires that the plaintiff mitigate damages before the damages have actually been sustained. If it could be shown that the plaintiff would not have suffered any injuries if he had fastened the seat belt, it could be urged that his failure so to do amounted to contributory negligence, but it is doubtful, in the absence of legislation so providing, that the avoidable consequences defense will go anywhere.

Closely related to the seat belt defense is the safety helmet defense which can be urged against motorcycle riders. Most states have statutes which require that operators and passengers of motorcycles wear safety helmets. The failure of the plaintiff to obey the safety statute has been held to be contributory negligence as a matter of law in some states or at least evidence of contributory negligence in others.

In *Spier* v. *Barker* [323 N.E. 2d 164 (1974)], the New York Court of Appeals considered for the first time the seat belt defense and the effect of the failure of the plaintiff to use them even though the automobile in which she was riding was so equipped. The facts indicated that she was involved in an intersection accident with a tractor-trailer, and as a result of the impact she was ejected from her automobile, which then ran over her legs. She was not wearing the seat belt. The jury found that she was guilty of contributory negligence and brought in a verdict for the defendant. The Appellate Division affirmed the verdict on appeal. Upon further appeal to the Court of Appeals, the court considered three theories in support of the seat belt defense: (1) Nonuse of a seat belt constitutes negligence per se, precluding the plaintiff's recovery; (2) nonuse is the failure of the plaintiff to act as a reasonable man and the plaintiff may be found to be contributorily negligent; and (3) nonuse may, in particular circumstances, mean that the plaintiff acted unreasonably and should not be permitted to recover damages for injuries which a seat belt would have prevented. The court adopted the third proposition, holding that the seat belt offers an automobile occupant the opportunity, prior to the accident to minimize damages. The court said that there is no doubt of seat belt effectiveness in preventing injuries and juries should be able to separate injuries caused by the initial impact from those caused by the plaintiff's nonuse of a seat belt. Thus, injuries which can be directly traceable to the nonuse of the seat belt will be classified as avoidable consequences for which injuries no recovery can be had.

It should be emphasized that the mere nonuse of an available seat belt will not in all cases constitute a defense unless it can be shown that the injuries or the aggravation thereof were directly caused by such nonuse, or, to put it another way, any injuries sustained which the use of the available seat belt would have prevented are not recoverable.

2. THE AUTOMOBILE REPARATIONS SYSTEM

1240 Purpose and scope

When the automobile first appeared on the American scene, the courts had no difficulty in applying common-law principles which were formerly utilized in determining liability in cases involving horse-drawn vehicles. Statutes, implementing the common-law rules were enacted, and the courts adopted certain doctrines which were especially applicable to automobiles.

Almost from the beginning some legal scholars and others felt that the application of horse-and-buggy rules to the operation of automobiles was unfair. They pointed to the potential for personal injury which the automobile brought with it and recommended that some other legal system should be created which would provide for compensation for each person injured as a result of an automobile accident, regardless of who was at fault. They pointed to the automobile as the offending instrumentality and that if automobiles were to be used that some method of redress should be available to all injured persons. One of the first published documents on the subject was a Columbia University study in 1932. This recommended a compensation scheme for automobile accidents, which would be patterned after the workmen's compensation law, and which would compensate all persons who suffered personal injuries as a result of automobile accidents. The idea lay dormant until 1954, when other no-fault compensation plans were recommended. The first to have some impact was Ehrensweig, "Full Aid Insurance for the Traffic Victim." In 1958, there was another suggestion in Green, "Traffic Victims: Tort Law and Insurance." Finally, in 1965, the plan which had the greatest impact on the problem was Keeton and O'Connell, "Basic Protection for the Accident Victim." This latter plan came to the attention of many of the state legislatures, and was seriously considered. In view of this, other plans were suggested by the American Insurance Association (see Report of Special Committee to Study and evaluate the Keeton-O'Connell Basic Protection Plan and Automobile Accident Reparations, 1968) and the Cotter Plan suggested by the insurance commissioner of Connecticut.[2] The basic concept of all these plans is that the automobile accident victim is entitled to recover for his economic losses, regardless of fault. This would include not only the automobile driver and his passengers, but also pedestrians as well. The only test for recovery would be whether or not the injured person sustained his injuries in an automobile accident. Borrowing from the workmen's compensation concept, the plans provided that there would be no recovery or payment for noneconomic losses, such as pain and suffering, disfigurement, or impairment to the future enjoyment of life.

1241   Benefits provided

The personal injury protection (PIP) plans suggest that the following benefits be paid: Economic Loss, consisting of (1) medical expense benefits; (2) income continuation benefits; (3) essential services benefits; (4) survivor benefits; and (5) funeral expenses.

1. *Medical expense benefits.* The general plan is that medical expenses means expenses for medical treatment, surgical treatment, dental treatment, professional nursing services, hospital services, rehabilitation services, prosthetic devices, ambulance services, medication and other reasonable and necessary expenses resulting from treatment prescribed by persons licensed to practice medicine and surgery; and dentistry. Some plans include treatment by a chiropractor and nonmedical remedial treatment rendered in accordance with a recognized religious method of healing.

Medical expense also includes hospital services consisting of: (1) the cost

---

[2] William R. Cotter, Commissioner, *A Program for Automobile Insurance and Accidents Benefits Reform* (Connecticut Insurance Department, 1969).

of a semiprivate room, based on rates customarily charged; (2) the cost of board, meals, and dietary services; (3) the cost of other hospital services, such as operating room, medicines, drugs, anesthetics, treatments with X ray, radium and other radioactive substances, laboratory tests, surgical dressings and supplies, and other medical care and treatment rendered by the hospital; (4) the cost of treatment by a physiotherapist; (5) the cost of medical supplies, such as prescribed drugs and medicines, blood and blood plasma, artificial limbs and eyes, surgical dressings, casts, splints, trusses, braces, crutches, rental of wheelchair, hospital bed or iron lung, and oxygen and rental of equipment for its administration.

2. *Income continuation benefits.* This is intended to pay for the economic loss suffered by the victim arising from his inability to work, and to compensate him for his loss of earnings. This would be recoverable regardless of whether his employer continued his salary or not.

3. *Essential services benefits.* Payment of this benefit is designed to pay for the necessary and reasonable expenses incurred for a substitute who would perform the essential services ordinarily performed by the injured person for himself and his family. This covers such things as cleaning, cooking, shopping and laundry. This type of payment usually comes into play where the wife, who has no income, is injured and the family requires someone to perform the services usually performed by her.

4. *Survivor benefits.* In the event of the death of an income producer as a result of injuries sustained in an accident which would entitle such person to income continuation benefits, the maximum provided for income continuation should be paid to the surviving spouse, or, if there is no surviving spouse, then to the surviving children, or to the estate of the deseased. In the case of the death of one performing essential services, the maximum amount provided will be paid to the person incurring the expense of providing such essential services.

5. *Funeral expenses.* These benefits consist of the payments of funeral, burial, and cremation expense. As in all other benefits, these amounts will be subject to a maximum amount.

1242   Insurance

The plans require that added coverage be provided in automobile liability policies, which will pay all of the PIP benefits to the named insured and members of his family residing in his household who sustain bodily injury as a result of an accident involving an automobile, to other persons sustaining bodily injury while occupying the insured automobile, or while using such automobile with the permission of the named insured and to pedestrians who sustain bodily injury caused by the named insured's automobile, or by being struck by an object propelled by or from such automobile. Some plans cover all motor vehicles, commercial and private, including motorcycles. Others restrict the operation of the plan to private passenger automobiles and exclude motorcycles. Under most of these plans, insurance is mandatory and the insured must provide it.

1243   Tort exemption

One of the objectives of all of these plans is to reduce litigation and to substitute in its place a sure method of recovery. Therefore, they exempt from tort liability all persons who are required to have PIP benefits insurance, with some exceptions. Thus, the injured person will recover the PIP benefits from his own insurance carrier and he is deprived of his common-law rights against the person responsible for his injury, and in its place the injured person is entitled to the immediate payment of benefits without regard to liability. The proponents of these plans argue that this plan is superior to the system of tort litigation with its attendant delays and the uncertainty of the outcome. This parallels the situation which obtained in the matter of workmen's compensation, wherein the common-law rights of employees against the master were abrogated and a system of periodic payments of compensation substituted therefor.

Unlike workmen's compensation the plans provide that in cases involving a certain amount of severity that the injured person may, at his option, assert his common-law rights. In such a cause of action the injured person may recover for such noneconomic losses as pain and suffering and future enjoyment of life. The cases in which the injured person retains his common-law rights are usually defined as those in which the medical treatment exceeds a certain sum (usually $500 or more), or the injury causes extensive temporary disability or disfigurement or permanent injury. Thus, if the results of the injury do not reach the "threshold" as set forth in the plan, the injured person is limited in his recovery to the PIP benefits and nothing more. If the injury goes over the threshold, then the injured person has the option of continuing to receive the PIP benefits or to bring action against the third party responsible for the injury. The PIP insurance carrier is entitled to subrogation against the carrier of the responsible party, but in most instances this right of recovery can be asserted only by arbitration.

It should be added that no plan has been suggested nor has any state legislated what could be considered a "true" no-fault system of automobile reparations. Such a plan would eliminate entirely all tort litigation arising out of automobile accidents and substitute in its place personal injury protection benefits alone. This would utilize the workmen's compensation approach and substitute one system of automobile reparations for another.

1244   Legislation

The legislatures of most states, as well as the federal government, have considered the enactment of "no-fault" statutes. Some have passed such laws and others have not. All no-fault statutes which have been passed are modifications of the plans which have been offered. They differ as to the extent of the benefits to be paid and as to the maximum liability for each of the scheduled benefits. For example, New Jersey mandates the payment of income continuation benefits at $100 per week subject to a maximum of $5,200. Michigan requires the payment of income continuation benefits of 85 percent of the injured person's earnings, subject to a maximum of $1,000 per month payable over a period of three years and also subject to a maximum of $36,000. Thus, the benefits to be paid will differ from state to state and it is to be expected that the amount of benefits may be reexamined by the legislatures and appropriate changes effected by amended legislation.

The "no-fault" legislation requiring PIP benefits are either (1) mandatory or (2) optional.

1. Mandatory. Under this form of legislation, the insurance carrier must provide the coverage set forth in the legislation and the insured must accept and pay a premium for it. The states are not uniform in setting forth the kind and types of automobiles which are affected by the legislation, nor are they in agreement as to the cases coming within the tort exemption. A list of the states having such legislation is shown in the accompanying table.

STATES HAVING MANDATORY NO-FAULT LEGISLATION

State and Statute	Vehicles Covered	Tort Exemption
Colorado Colo. Rev. Stat. Ann. Sec. 10–4–701	All except motorcycles	Damages for pain and suffering and bodily injury recoverable only if injury results in death, dismemberment, permanent disfigurement, permanent disability or a case in which medical and rehabilitative expenses are in excess of $500 or loss of uncompensated earnings and earning capacity for more than 52 weeks.
Connecticut Conn. Gen. Stat. Rev. Sec. 38–319	Private passenger cars only: Motorcycles excluded	Damages for pain and suffering recoverable only if allowable expenses exceed $400 or the injury consists of a fracture, permanent "significant" disfigurement, permanent loss of function, loss of a member, or death.
Delaware Del. Code Ann. Title 21, s. 2118	All automobiles	None.
Florida Fla. Stat. 627.730	Private passenger and pickups, panel, and utility vehicles not primarily used in business or occupation	Pain and suffering is recoverable only if the medical exceeds $1,000 or injury consists of disfigurement, serious fracture, loss of a member, permanent injury, permanent loss of body function, or death. Provision as to serious fracture held unconstitutional.
Georgia Ga. Code. Ann. 56–3401b	All except motorcycles	Pain and suffering recoverable only if injury results in death; a fractured bone, permanent disfigurement; permanent loss of bodily function; dismemberment; permanent partial or total loss of sight or hearing; medical expenses in excess of $500; or disability commencing within one year of the accident and rendering the individual unable to perform substantially all of the duties required by the person's usual occupation for at least ten consecutive days.

STATES HAVING MANDATORY NO-FAULT LEGISLATION (CONTINUED)

State and Statute	Vehicles Covered	Tort Exemption
Hawaii Hawaii Rev. Stat. 294–1	All	Damages recoverable only if injury results in death, significant permanent loss of a part or function of the body, permanent and serious disfigurement subjecting the insured to mental or emotional suffering, or if the amount paid or accrued exceeds the "medical rehabilitative limit" computed by the commissioner, or the maximum benefits are exhausted.
Kansas Kan. Stat. Ann. 40–3101	Private passenger cars only: Motorcycle owner may reject personal injury protection benefits	Pain and suffering recoverable only if injury results in permanent disfigurement; fracture to a weight-bearing bone, a compound, comminuted displaced or compressed fracture; loss of a body member, permanent injury within reasonable medical probability, permanent loss of a body function; death, or medical expenses in excess of $500.
Kentucky H.B. 314 (1974)	All motor vehicles, but motorcycle owner may reject personal injury protection benefits	Pain and suffering recovery only if injury results in: permanent disfigurement; a fracture to a weight-bearing bone, a compound, comminuted displaced or compressed fracture; loss of a body member; permanent injury within reasonable medical probability; permanent loss of bodily function; death; or medical expenses exceeding $1,000.
Maryland Md. Code Ann. Art. 48A, Sec. 539	All: As to motorcycles, benefits may be excluded	None
Massachusetts Mass. Ann. Laws, Ch. 90, 34A and Ch. 231, 60.	All except certain motor carriers	Pain and suffering recoverable only if medical exceeds $500 or injury causes death, dismemberment, disfigurement, loss of sight or hearing, or consists of a fracture. As to bodily injury recovery the defendant is exempt from liability to the extent of first-party benefits.
Michigan Mich. Comp. Laws Ann. 500.3101	All except motorcycles	General damages recoverable only if injured person suffered death, serious impairment of body function, or permanent serious disfigurement. Special damages recoverable for economic loss in excess of maximum benefits.
Minnesota Minn. Stat. Sec. 65B.41	All except motorcycles	Pain and suffering recoverable only if injury results in: permanent disfigurement; permanent injury; death; the injured person's inability to engage in substantially all of his usual and customary daily activities for 60 days or more; or medical expenses exceeding $2,000.

STATES HAVING MANDATORY NO-FAULT LEGISLATION (CONTINUED)

State and Statute	Vehicles Covered	Tort Exemption
Nevada Nev. Rev. Stat. 698.010	All except vehicles owned by persons under Medicare, motorcycles, or publicly owned vehicles	The third-party defendant has no liability except in cases involving: (1) uninsured owner; (2) dealer or repairer for defects; (3) intentional injury; (4) damage to property including a motor vehicle and contents; (5) injury to operator of or passenger on a motorcycle; (6) a person in the business of parking or storing motor vehicles; (7) damages for loss not recoverable as basic reparation benefits by reason of limitation on benefits; (8) damages for noneconomic detriment if medical benefits exceed $750 or if the accident causes death, chronic or permanent injury, permanent partial or permanent total disability, disfigurement, more than 180 days of inability to work, fracture of a major bone, dismemberment, or permanent loss of body function.
New Jersey N.J. Stat. Ann. 39: 6A–1	Private passenger cars only	Exemption applies to a person who has the right to receive benefits from use of the vehicle if the injury is confined to "soft tissue" and the medical is less than $200 exclusive of hospital expenses, X rays and other diagnostic expenses. No exemption in case of death, permanent "significant" disfigurement, permanent loss of any bodily function, or loss of a body member in whole or in part.
New York N.Y. Ins. Law 670	All except motorcycles	Pain and suffering recoverable only if injury results in death, dismemberment, "significant" disfigurement, compound or comminuted fracture, or permanent loss of use of a body organ, member, function or system; or if the medical expenses exceed $500.
Oregon Oreg. Rev. Stat. 743.800	Private passenger automobiles only: Motorcycles excluded	No tort exemption.
Pennsylvania H.B. 1973 (1974)	All except motorcycles	Pain and suffering recoverable only if injury results in death, serious and permanent injury, 60 days continuous physical or mental disability, cosmetic disfigurement which is permanent, irreparable, and severe, or medical expenses exceeding $750 exclusive of diagnostic X-ray and rehabilitation costs in excess of $100. The tortfeasor is also exempt from liability to the extent first-party benefits are payable or would be payable but for the deductions.

STATES HAVING MANDATORY NO-FAULT LEGISLATION (CONCLUDED)

State and Statute	Vehicles Covered	Tort Exemption
Puerto Rico P.R. Laws Ann. Ti. 9 Sec. 2051	All	Pain and suffering recoverable if in excess of $1,000. Tort-feasor is relieved of liability to the extent of no-fault benefits except where the damages exceed $2,000.
South Carolina S.B. 371	All: With respect to motorcycles first-party benefits may be excluded	No limitation on the recovery for pain and suffering or recovery for bodily injury, but the verdict shall be reduced by the expenses for economic losses previously recovered by the claimant from his insurer.
Utah	All except motorcycles	Pain and suffering recoverable only if injury results in death, dismemberment, fracture, permanent disability, permanent disfigurement, or if medical expenses exceed $500. Persons not receiving first-party benefits may recover.

In these states, where the claim comes within one of the exceptions to the tort exemption, the injured person is under no obligation to pursue his third-party remedy. He may continue to receive his first-party benefits. The reasons for this type of action may be that the claimant is satisfied with the benefits paid or to be paid, or he might feel that he would have some difficulty in establishing the liability of the third party. In any case, there is no way that the PIP benefits carrier can compel him to bring a third-party action.

2. Optional. In some states the legislation requires some form of no-fault benefits to be offered to the insured, which in most cases can be rejected by him. These states are:

State	*Statutory Provision*
Arkansas	Automobile liability policy covering a private passenger motor vehicle must include coverage for (1) medical up to $2,000; (2) 70 percent loss of income up to a maximum of $140 per week for 52 weeks, subject to an eight-day waiting period before benefits are to be paid; (3) substitute services for "non-income earners" up to a maximum of $70 per week for 52 weeks, also subject to an eight-day waiting period; (4) $5,000 for death. Insured may reject any provision or all of them.
New Hampshire	Policy covering a private passenger automobile shall, unless the insured person has equivalent coverage, include medical payments coverage for at least $1,000.
South Dakota	No policy shall be issued with respect to any automobile registered or principally garaged in the state unless coverage is made available for accidental death benefits of at least $10,000 for the named insured. Also indemnity of at least $60 per week after 14 days of disability for at least 52 weeks while the

State	Statutory Provision
	named insured is prevented from performing the usual duties of his regular occupation. Also medical payments coverage of at least $2,000 per person. If the injured person is not gainfully employed, the weekly indemnity is reduced by 50 percent. The insured may reject in writing any or all of these coverages.
Texas	The automobile liability policy shall provide personal injury protection coverage for payment to the named insured and members of his household and any authorized operator or passenger. The benefits shall include medical expenses up to $2,500 for each person and for loss of income and reimbursement of all expenses in the aggregate not exceeding $2,500 for each person. Benefits payable without regard to collateral source benefits. Coverage may be rejected.
Virginia	The liability insurer, at the request of the insured, shall provide medical coverage to the named insured, resident relatives while occupying any motor vehicle, and occupants of the insured vehicle up to $2,000 per person and for an employed person up to $100 per week for 52 weeks. Insurer must offer this coverage with premium notices and must indicate the approximate premium for it.
Wisconsin	Requires $1,000 medical payment coverage on all automobile liability insurance policies unless rejected by the insured.

1245   Subrogation under no-fault statutes

The general rule adopted in all states is that a personal tort, including personal injury actions, may not be assigned either in whole or in part. This rule can be amended by statute (cf. workmen's compensation law), which statute will set forth the nature of the permitted assignment and the extent of such permission. The no-fault statutes are no exception. Some laws permit an assignment of the injured person's cause of action to the PIP insurance carrier where benefits have been paid and set forth the circumstances under which such assignment may be enforced. Other statutes do not allow an assignment at all. The following states, having no-fault statutes, have provisions with regard to the subrogation rights, if any, of the PIP insurance carrier:

State	Subrogation or Assignment Provision
Colorado	Insurer may be reimbursed for its PIP payments if it sues the third party, but only for benefits paid in excess of $500. The automobile insurer's recovery against a commercial vehicle is not subject to the $500 threshold. The insurer may proceed under the Inter-Company Arbitration Plan, provided that the payment demanded is in excess of $500.
Connecticut	The PIP insurer may sue the third party for its payments, or, if the insured sues the third party, the PIP insurer is entitled to reimbursement for its payments out of the proceeds recovered by the insured.

State	*Subrogation or Assignment Provision*
Delaware	The PIP insurer may sue the third party in cases where it has paid PIP benefits.
Florida	The PIP insurer is subrogated to the rights of the insured if the insured has not sued the third party within one year after the last benefit payment. If the insured sues the third party, PIP insurer is entitled to reimbursement for its payments.
Georgia	An insurer providing first-party benefits shall have a right of action against an uninsured tort-feasor to the extent of such benefits. In the case of an insured tort-feasor, the PIP insurer must pursue its claim for reimbursement through the Inter-Company Arbitration Agreement.
Hawaii	Where the insured sues the third-party tort-feasor, the PIP insurer is entitled to reimbursement for its payments up to 50 percent of the benefits paid. The PIP insurer may submit its claim via the Inter-Company Arbitration Agreement.
Kansas	The PIP insurer has a right of action against the tort-feasor for reimbursement if the insured has failed to bring action within $1\frac{1}{2}$ years after the accident. The PIP insurer is entitled to reimbursement for its payments if the insured recovers from the third party. In addition, the PIP insurer may process its claim through the Inter-Company Arbitration Agreement.
Kentucky	The PIP insurer has a right to sue the third-party tort-feasor for reimbursement for the benefits paid. It likewise is entitled to reimbursement where the insured sues an unsecured tort-feasor. It may also process its claim under the Inter-Company Arbitration Agreement.
Maryland	No provision.
Massachusetts	The PIP insurer may sue the tort-feasor for reimbursement for the payments made. If the insured sues the tort-feasor and recovers, the insurer is entitled to reimbursement out of the recovery. Also, the insurer may submit its claim under the Inter-Company Arbitration Agreement.
Michigan	The PIP insurer is entitled to sue the third-party tort-feasor for the amount of the benefits paid. If the insured sues, then the insurer is entitled to reimbursement out of the recovery. In addition, the insurer is entitled to have recourse to the Inter-Company Arbitration Agreement.
Minnesota	The PIP insurer is entitled to reimbursement when the insured sues the third-party tort-feasor. The insurer also may submit its claim for reimbursement to arbitration under the Inter-Company Arbitration Agreement only if a commercial vehicle is involved.
Nevada	The PIP insurer may only submit its claim for reimbursement to arbitration under the Inter-Company Arbitration Agreement.
New Jersey	For accidents occurring prior to December 31, 1974, the PIP insurer may submit its claim to arbitration under the Inter-Company Arbitration Agreement. No subrogation is permitted with respect to accidents occurring after December 31, 1974.

State	Subrogation or Assignment Provision
New York	The PIP insurer is entitled to sue the tort-feasor if the insured has not begun action within two years after the accident. If the insured sues and recovers, the PIP insurer is entitled to reimbursement for its payments. The insurer also may submit its claim to arbitration under the Inter-Company Arbitration Agreement.
Oregon	The PIP insurer may sue the third-party tort-feasor for reimbursement for its payments. If the insured takes third-party action, the insurer is entitled to reimbursement for its payments out of the recovery. Also, the insurer may submit its claim to arbitration under the Inter-Company Arbitration Agreement.
Pennsylvania	The statute provides: "Insurer does not have and may not contract for a right of reimbursement or subrogation to the proceeds of a victim's claim for relief or a cause of action for noneconomic detriment except when the claim or cause of action is based on fault and the elements of damage compensated for by security for the payment of no-fault benefits in excess of minimum basic loss benefits required by law and the insurer has paid or is obligated to pay benefits in excess of the minimum basic loss benefits."
Puerto Rico	The Fund is entitled to recover from the tort-feasor when he has been convicted of causing intentional harm, or of driving while intoxicated, without a license, while committing a crime, or while participating in a race. If the insured recovers from the tort-feasor, the Fund is entitled to reimbursement for the benefits paid.
South Carolina	Statute prohibits subrogation or assignment of first-party benefits except (1) when the insurer has delivered to the person entitled to first-party benefits, a disclosure statement, setting forth that the first-party benefits are contractual obligations of the insurer and are entirely separate and distinct from any obligation which the insurer or other person may have because of the legal liability of any person and that the person receiving first-party benefits is not required and may not be required, to release or relinquish any rights which he may have arising out of the legal liability of any person in order to receive payment or settlement of the first-party benefits; and (2) when an interval of not less than three days have elapsed between the date (*a*) delivery of the disclosure statement or (*b*) the payment or settlement of the first-party benefits and the execution of the general release, covenant not to sue or similar instrument.
Utah	The PIP insurer may obtain reimbursement for its first-party payments through arbitration under the Inter-Company Arbitration Agreement.

Caveat. These "no-fault" automobile statutes are under constant reexamination and review by the various state legislatures. Therefore reliance should not be placed on this or any other analytical review of the statutes, but in each instance the claims representative should have reference to the latest legislative amendments. Also some states have no-fault statutes under consideration and may legislate on the same subject.

1246   Arbitration under no-fault statutes

Some statutes require that the PIP insurers submit their claims for reimbursement against the insurer of the tort-feasor to arbitration. In some states this is a mandatory requirement and provides the only means by which the PIP insurer may recover, and in other states it is an optional remedy which can be utilized or not as the PIP insurer sees fit. In order to comply with the requirements of the statutes, the insurance companies through their representatives, have subscribed to an intercompany arbitration agreement dealing with the subject of arbitration under no-fault statutes. The agreement is as follows:

AUTOMOBILE ACCIDENT REPARATIONS STATUTE
SUBROGATION ARBITRATION AGREEMENT

WHEREAS, the Committee on Insurance Arbitration representing the American Insurance Association, the American Mutual Alliance and the National Association of Independent Insurers and the signatories to the industry arbitration programs endorses the principles of arbitration for the purpose of resolving intercompany disputes arising from the pursuit of subrogation rights under automobile reparations statutes, and

WHEREAS, it is the object of companies which are now or may hereafter be signatories hereto to arbitrate disputes among themselves, the undersigned hereby accepts and binds itself to the following articles of agreement for inter-company arbitration:

ARTICLE FIRST

Signatory companies bind themselves to arbitrate all inter-company disputes arising from their pursuit of subrogation claims created by the payment of claims or benefits to insureds or qualified third parties under automobile accident reparations statutes; further, the compulsory jurisdiction of this agreement shall conform to the terms and provisions of the applicable statute giving subrogation rights.

ARTICLE SECOND

The monetary limits and extent of a signatory's claim shall be governed by the statute creating the subrogation rights.

ARTICLE THIRD

Where a subrogation claim under ARTICLE FIRST of this agreement, or a companion subrogation claim, are also under the compulsory jurisdiction of other industry agreements sponsored by the Committee on Insurance Arbitration, the jurisdiction of this Agreement is primary.

ARTICLE FOURTH

This agreement does not apply to any claim for recovery rights to which a company asserts a defense of lack of coverage on any grounds, unless specific written consent is obtained from the companies in interest.

ARTICLE FIFTH

Any determination as to whether a signatory is legally entitled to recovery from another signatory shall be made by an arbitration panel appointed under the authority of this Agreement.

ARTICLE SIXTH

The Committee on Insurance Arbitration representing the American Insurance Association, the American Mutual Alliance, the National Association of Independent Insurers and all signatories to the industry arbitration programs is authorized:

a. To make appropriate rules and regulations for the presentation and determination of controversies under this Agreement.

b. To select places where arbitration facilities are to be available, and adopt a policy for the selection and appointment of arbitration panels.

c. To make appropriate rules and regulations to apportion equitably among arbitrating companies the operating expenses of the arbitration program.

d. Except as to agreement mandated by statute, to authorize and approve as signatories to this Agreement such insurance carriers as may be invited to participate in the arbitration program and also to compel the withdrawal of any signatory for failure to conform with the Agreement or the rules and regulations issued thereunder.

ARTICLE SEVENTH

Arbitration Committees shall be appointed by the Committee on Insurance Arbitration from full-time salaried representatives of signatory companies and shall function in the following manner:

a. Members of Arbitration Committees shall be selected on the basis of their experience and qualifications, and they shall serve without compensation.

b. No arbitrator shall serve on a panel hearing a case in which his company is directly or indirectly interested.

c. The decision of the majority of an arbitration panel is final and binding upon the parties to the controversy without right of rehearing or appeal.

ARTICLE EIGHTH

Except as otherwise provided by statute, any signatory company may withdraw from this Agreement by notice in writing to the Committee on Insurance Arbitration. Such withdrawal shall be effective sixty days after receipt of such notice except as to cases then pending before arbitration panels. The effective date of withdrawal as to such pending cases shall be upon final settlement.

Comment.   This Agreement is designed to apply to all states having a mandatory or optional provision covering subrogation by arbitration, with the exception of Massachusetts, in which there is a special arbitration agreement.

1247   Arbitration rules under no-fault statutes

The Committee on Insurance Arbitration has compiled the following rules:

AUTOMOBILE ACCIDENT REPARATIONS STATUTE
SUBROGATION ARBITRATION RULES

The Rules hereinafter set forth are promulgated under the authority of Article Sixth of the Arbitration Agreement.

As a condition precedent to arbitration, local representatives of involved companies must make sincere efforts to settle controversies by direct negotiation.

GENERAL

1. The Arbitration Agreement shall be considered applicable to accidents, insured events, or losses under the jurisdiction of the automobile reparations statute giving subrogation rights to signatory companies for payments or benefits paid to insureds or third parties under said statute.

2. Home office and local representatives of signatory companies are entitled to copies of the Arbitration Agreement, the Arbitration Rules and the current list of Signatory Companies.
3. The Arbitration Agreement shall not be construed to create any causes of action or liabilities not existing in law or equity.
4. The Arbitration Agreement is applicable only to controversies involving insurance companies. The interest of parties other than insurance companies may not be arbitrated under the Agreement. The fact that such parties may be insureds of signatory companies does not alter this prohibition.
5. In arbitration proceedings and practice, the company which initiates the proceeding by filing a request for arbitration shall be known as the "applicant"; and the company or companies against which such controverted claim or issue was asserted shall be known as "respondent(s)."
6. Controversies between signatory companies and nonsignatory companies may be arbitrated provided:
   a. The Signatory company consents to jurisdiction.
   b. The Signatory company involved first obtains and files with the Arbitration Committee Secretary a duly executed agreement from the nonsignatory company consenting to the jurisdiction of the agreement and the binding effect of the award.
7. Any signatory company against whom a subrogation claim is being made shall promptly make known its identity.
8. Submission of a case to arbitration under the Agreement shall have the force and effect as to signatory companies with regards to the applicable Statute of Limitations as if litigation has been instituted.
9. Where the arbitrating signatory companies are also signatory to other industry arbitration programs sponsored by the Committee on Insurance Arbitration and the subrogation claim or companion subrogation claims are within the compulsory jurisdiction of these other agreements, the signatory companies waive their rights to proceed separately under the other programs and must include all claims arising out of the same accident, occurrence or insured event for disposition by an arbitration panel under this Agreement.
10. The hearing of a matter pending before an arbitration panel under this Agreement will be deferred because of pending claims or suits arising out of the same accident, occurrence or insured event, unless the involved companies waive such deferment in writing.
11. Where there are companion claims arising out of the same accident each of which would be, or is subject to, compulsory jurisdiction of this Agreement, only one filing is necessary to determine the issue of liability as to the drivers of the respective vehicles. A panel's decision on this issue is *re judicata* on the liability issue in all companion matters involving the same companies within the jurisdiction of this Agreement, except as to special defenses arising in the companion claim or suit.

ORGANIZATION

1. Signatory companies shall furnish the Committee on Insurance Arbitration on request, a list of names, titles and local addresses of all employees who are qualified to act as arbitrators.

2. The Chairman of the Arbitration Committee shall designate one disinterested member of said Committee to serve as a panel of arbitration in each case. However, three members will constitute a panel if requested by a controverting party in a specific case.

JURISDICTION

1. Compulsory arbitration under this Agreement applies to controversies arising out of accidents, insured events or occurrences within the state or jurisdiction of the statute giving rise to the subrogation claim. Controversies arising from accidents, insured events or occurrences outside the jurisdiction of the applicable statute cannot be submitted without the consent of the controverting companies.

FILING ASSESSMENTS

1. The Committee on Insurance Arbitration by resolution will prescribe the filing assessment for the use of local arbitration facilities.
2. The obligation for the prescribed filing fee assessment is incurred upon filing but payment by the applicant company to the Committee on Insurance Arbitration is deferred until the case is closed, either through hearing, settlement or withdrawal prior to hearing. The prescribed filing assessment shall also be paid in the same manner by a respondent company that files a counterclaim. There are no exceptions to a signatory company's obligation to pay the filing assessment.

PROCEDURE

1. An arbitration proceeding is commenced by the local representative of a signatory company filing an "Arbitration Notice" (three copies) with the Secretary of the local arbitration committee. At the same time three copies of the "Arbitration Notice" are to be submitted by the applicant directly to the local representative of the other involved signatory company. If there is more than one respondent company in a case the applicant shall so indicate on the original and all copies of the "Arbitration Notice" and send three copies thereof to each respondent company.
2. Notice by applicants shall set forth the following information:
   a. Names of applicant and respondent companies together with names and addresses of local representatives having supervision over the case in controversy.
   b. Name and address of respondent company's insured.
   c. Claim file numbers of applicant and respondent, if known.
   d. Date and place of alleged accident, loss or other insured event.
   e. Amount of company's claim payment and amount of any other expenses for recovery is requested.
   f. Certification that settlement efforts have been unsuccessful.
   g. Brief statement of allegation solely as to the issue in controversy.
   h. Signature of applicant's representative and date signed.
3. Answers filed by respondent shall set forth the following information:
   a. Supplement, if and as necessary, the information furnished by the applicant as to respondent company's name, local representative, address, name of insured, file number or kind of policy coverage.
   b. Whether there is an objection to arbitration. If so, the grounds on which the objection is based should be fully stated.

c. Brief statement of allegations as to the issue in controversy.

d. Signature of respondent's representative and date signed.

4. The respondent has thirty days after the applicant's filing in which to file a written answer. If a respondent fails to submit its answer within thirty days after applicant company files with a committee, it is presumed that the applicant's claim has been denied and the case is ready for hearing on the issues. Failure to file an answer will not operate to delay the arbitration hearing. However, if affirmative defenses are available to the respondent, and are not asserted by answer prior to notice of hearing, the applicant, on request, will be entitled to an adjournment to investigate the affirmative defenses.

5. The procedure set out in the preceding paragraphs of this section is also applicable to counterclaims. The "Arbitration Notice" should clearly indicate that it is submitted as a counterclaim and the original arbitration case to which it pertains shall be plainly identified. Unless a counterclaim is filed by a respondent and heard with the original arbitration case, the respondent is thereafter precluded from pursuing its claim against the adverse signatory company.

HEARINGS

1. When the secretary has received the essential facts and contentions from the controverting companies, the issue in the case shall be scheduled for a hearing by the Arbitration Panel at the earliest practical date.

2. Hearing date shall be determined by the Chairman of the Arbitration Panel, and one or more cases may be considered at any scheduled hearing.

3. Representatives of controverting parties shall be notified by the Secretary of the time and place of a scheduled hearing at least two weeks in advance of the hearing date.

4. Adjournments may be granted for cause by the Chairman of the Arbitration Committee or his designee.

5. Evidence which controverting parties desire to submit in support of their allegations shall be made available for examination by the arbitrators at the hearing. Such evidence may also be examined by the opposing parties at the hearing. If one of the controverting parties fails to produce evidence at a scheduled arbitration hearing, after due notice thereof, the arbitrators may at their discretion consider the information in the "Arbitration Notice" of such party and render a decision accordingly.

6. Procedure at Arbitration Panel Hearings shall be informal. Controverting parties are expected to present the facts of their respective cases in a brief, frank and direct manner.

7. The controverting parties shall submit for consideration to the arbitrators briefs of the law involved when requested by the arbitration panel hearing the case.

8. Controverting parties may present witnesses at an arbitration hearing, if considered necessary, after notice to the other interested party or parties sufficiently in advance of the hearing date to permit such other party or parties also to present witnesses if desired.

9. Controverting parties may, if they so desire, be represented at arbitration hearings by members of their staff or by any one employed or retained by them.

10. Documentary evidence submitted by controverting parties shall be left with the arbitrators for their scrutiny and consideration while reaching a decision.

11. If representatives of controverting parties attend an arbitration hearing, they must withdraw after presentation of their cases and may not be present while the arbitrators are considering their decision.

DECISIONS

1. Arbitration panels may, upon their own initiative, render a decision in favor of a respondent company without production of evidence by such respondent, if the Panel unanimously agrees following presentation of the applicant's evidence that such applicant has not made out a prima facie case.

2. The law of the locality in which the accident, insured event or loss occurred will control the decision on questions of liability. A finding as to the amount of damages in issue shall be based on the facts presented to the arbitrators.

3. The amount paid shall not be at issue unless pleaded specifically.

4. Decisions of the arbitrators shall be promptly rendered after consideration of the case, and the evidence submitted by the controverting parties shall be returned promptly.

5. The arbitrators shall prepare a written decision in each case, copies of which shall be distributed by the Secretary as follows: One copy will be retained by the arbitration panel secretary; one copy shall be furnished to each party involved in the arbitration, and the original shall be furnished to the Committee of Insurance Arbitration.

6. The decisions of the Arbitration Panel shall include the following minimum information:

   a. Date and place of hearing.

   b. Names of panel members.

   c. Names of applicant and respondent carriers and names of their respective insureds.

   d. Names of respective controverting party representatives, if any, attending the hearing.

   e. Brief description of the claim or controversy and amount involved therein.

   f. Name of controverting insurance carrier in whose favor an award is rendered and the amount thereof.

   g. Brief statement of the basis for the finding, such as lack of proof, contributory negligence, or other controlling principles of law.

   h. Signature of the arbitrator who prepared the decision.

7. Decisions of an arbitration panel shall be complied with as soon as possible. Any unwarranted delay on the part of the parties concerned should be reported to the Committee on Insurance Arbitration by the prevailing party.

* * * * *

The procedure contemplated by this Agreement is that the cases will be submitted on evidence consisting of the claim files of the applicant company and the respondents, together with any other documents which may have some probative value in the decision-making process. Ordinarily, witnesses are not presented before the arbitrator, but there is a provision in the agreement which permits this with the understanding that sufficient notice is given to the adverse party so that opposing witnesses may be presented.

The burden of proof is on the applicant company. If its file does not present a prima facie case of negligence, the decision must be in favor of the respondent. In the latter case no reference whatever is made to the respondent's file. Therefore, the claims representative for the applicant company must be satisfied that the file establishes a prima facie case of negligence on the part of the respondent's insured before application is made for arbitration.

1248   Claims administration under no-fault

Claim handling under no-fault represents something of a change in the normal approach to disposing of automobile bodily injury claims. Under no-fault the benefits are required to be paid by the automobile liability insurer covering the automobile which the injured was occupying at the time of the accident as well as pedestrians who sustain bodily injury caused by the automobile. The concept of the automobile liability carrier being liable for first-party benefits is not new. We have had medical payments coverage for some years which does require the payment of medical expenses incurred within one year. In addition, we have had workmen's compensation benefits prescribed for employees suffering injury while in the course of the employment. What is new is the requirement that the income continuation benefits, the essential services benefits, the survivor benefits, and the funeral expenses are payable as first-party claims by the automobile liability insurance carrier.

To recover any of these benefits, it must be established that the disability or death suffered by the claimant is causally related to the injury received in the automobile or by being struck by the automobile. When that is established, then the payments will continue only so long as the causally related disability continues. If the claimant is suffering from an unrelated condition, whether traumatic or not, which did not come about as a result of the accident, no benefits are payable.

Most states have provisions which exclude from the operation of the law intentional injuries, injuries due to intoxication, while under the influence of drugs, injuries sustained in the commission of a crime, avoiding arrest, stolen car or injuries received in a race or speed test. An analysis of the benefits to which a qualified claimant would be entitled is as follows:

1. *Medical expenses benefits.*   Under most statutes, the claimant is entitled to reimbursement for his medical expense incurred as a result of the accident. The amount is conditioned on the fact that it must be reasonable. What is reasonable and what is not is a question which imposes some difficulty. Some states have promulgated a medical fee schedule which will set forth the reasonable fees which may be charged in these cases. In other states, the question may be resolved by recourse to the usual charges made by the profession in the locality in which the medical treatment is rendered. In the

event of a dispute, the burden of proof will be on the claimant to establish that the charges claimed are reasonable. The amount of medical expense will be further limited by the maximum, if any, provided in the act.

The statute usually provides for reimbursement to the claimant for the amount of medical incurred. There is no relationship between the insurance carrier and the doctor rendering the treatment, and there is no obligation on the part of the carrier to guarantee the payment of medical or hospital bills. The doctor might, as is done in some workers' compensation cases, request that the insurance carrier authorize an operation and the hospital bills which will be incurred. The insurance carrier is under no obligation to do so.

In some states the amount of no-fault benefits are reduced by the collectible benefits under workers' compensation, disability benefits laws, and social security disability payments. In some cases the entire amount of the medical expense is collectible from these other sources, in which case no benefits are available under no-fault.

The insurance carrier is also granted the right to have periodic medical examinations to determine the reasonableness of the medical treatment that is being rendered.

In order to obtain the medical information from the attending physician, a medical authorization form should be obtained from the claimant. The usual medical authorization form may be used unless the state has other prescribed forms. The form could read as follows:

AUTHORIZATION FOR RELEASE OF HEALTH SERVICE OR
TREATMENT INFORMATION

This authorization or a photocopy thereof, will authorize you to furnish all information you may have regarding my condition while under your observation or treatment, including history obtained, X-ray and physical findings, diagnosis and prognosis. You are authorized to provide this information in accordance with the _____(state)_____ Automobile Reparations Act (no-fault law).

Name (print or type)   Date _____

Signature
(If a minor, parent or guardian
shall sign and indicate capacity
and relationship.)

Some states have regulations prescribing the forms to be used for medical reports. Others have not. Where no form has been created for this purpose, it would seem that the standard workers' compensation form with appropriate additions could be used. One such state form (New York) is shown below.

NEW YORK NO-FAULT MOTOR VEHICLE INSURANCE LAW
REPORT OF ATTENDING PHYSICIAN OR OTHER PROVIDER OF HEALTH SERVICE OR TREATMENT

Name of
[Insurance Company]

Date   [Our Policyholder]   Date of Accident   File Number

TO ASSIST US IN DETERMINING BENEFITS DUE UNDER THE NEW YORK
COMPREHENSIVE AUTO INSURANCE REPARATIONS ACT, THE ATTENDING
PHYSICIAN OR OTHER PROVIDER OF HEALTH SERVICE OR TREATMENT
MUST COMPLETE THIS REPORT AND RETURN IT DIRECTLY

TO: _____

CLAIM DEPARTMENT
(Claims Address and Phone No.)

1. Patient's Name and Address

2. Age   3. Sex   4. Occupation (If Known)

5. History of Occurrence as Described by Patient

6. Diagnosis and Concurrent Conditions

7. When did symptoms first appear?   8. When did patient first consult you for
Date: this condition? Date:

9. Has patient ever had same or similar condition?
Yes   No   If "Yes" state when and describe

10. Is condition solely a result of this accident?
Yes   No   If "No", Explain

11. Is condition due to injury or sickness arising out of patient's employment?
Yes   No

12. Will injury result in significant disfigurement or permanent disability?
Yes   No   Not determinable at this time   If "Yes", Describe

13. Was Patient Hospitalized?
Yes   No   Name and Address of Hospital

14. Patient was disabled (unable to work)   15. If still disabled the patient should be
From: Through: able to return to work on: (Date)

16. Report of Services

Date of Service	Place of Service	Description of Treatment or Health Service Rendered	Charges
			$
		TOTAL CHARGE TO DATE	$

17. Amount of total charges paid to date: $

---

18. Is patient still under your care for this condition?
    Yes   No   ESTIMATED   FUTURE   CHARGES $

19. May any health services be required for more than 1 year from date of accident?
    Probably Yes   Probably No

20. Estimate duration of future treatment:

| Date | Physician's Name (Print) | Physician's Signature | IRS/TIN Iden. No. |

| No. | Street | City or Town | State | Zip Code |

NOTE: IF YOU HAVE PREVIOUSLY SUBMITTED AN EARLIER REPORT ON
      THIS ACCIDENT, YOU NEED COMPLETE ONLY ITEM 1 AND NOTE ANY
      CHANGES FROM THE INFORMATION PREVIOUSLY FURNISHED.

In order for the claimant to be reimbursed for the medical, it must appear
that the treatment rendered was causally related to the automobile injury
received. If the treatment covers any other condition, it is not reimbursable.
This will be covered by the answer to question 10 on the medical form.
Question 11 covers the workers' compensation aspect of the claim. The answer
to question 12 will alert the claims representative as to the prospect of a claim
being made in tort against the third party.

   2. Income continuation benefits.   In order to recover for this benefit,
two elements must be present. There must be (1) medical proof of disability
and (2) evidence that the claimant did not in fact work earning a salary during
this period of time. The medical evidence can be in the form of the medical
report from the attending physician or a medical examination conducted by
the insurance carrier. In addition, there must be evidence from the claimant's
employer that he did not work. If either element is missing, there is no
recoverable claim for this benefit. In order to obtain the information from the
employer, it is customary to obtain an authorization from the claimant. Such
authorization might read as follows:

AUTHORIZATION FOR RELEASE OF WORK AND
OTHER INFORMATION

This authorization or photocopy thereof, will authorize you to furnish all information that you may have regarding my wages, salary or other loss while
employed by you. You are authorized to provide this information in accordance
with the _____(state)_____ Automobile Reparations Act (no-fault).

   Name (print or type)

        Signature
Social Security No. _____   Date _____

The authorization together with a letter requesting the work record of the claimant is then sent to the employer. The information usually required consists of answers to the following questions:

1. Employee's occupation:
2. Dates of employment: from: _____ to _____
3. Gross earnings during 52 week period prior to the accident:
   $_____
   Wages or salary as of the date of the accident:
   $_____ Hourly _____ Weekly _____ Monthly_____
4. Dates absent from work following the accident:
   from _____ to _____
5. Has employee filed a claim for benefits under any Worker's Compensation Law as a result of this accident?
   If "yes," name and address of worker's compensation Insurer:
6. Has employee received, or is he receiving or is he entitled to receive benefits under any Worker's Compensation Law as a result of this accident?
7. Is employee receiving, or is he entitled to receive any federal Social Security Disability benefits?

Date   Signed _____

Where the claimant is self-employed, statements can be obtained (where necessary) from his employees as well as making an examination of the books of account.

3. Essential services benefits. The payment of these benefits will be made only where there is medical proof of disability and not otherwise. If the claimant is not disabled and continues to incur these expenses, there is no obligation on the part of the insurer to pay them. In any event the amount of payment to be made under this benefit is limited to the amounts set forth in the statute, governed either by a time limit or a maximum dollar amount.

4. Survivor benefits and funeral expenses. When death of the income producer is caused by the accident under such circumstances which would have entitled him to income continuation benefits had he lived, the survivor benefits as set forth in the particular statute are paid, usually to the surviving spouse or children or the estate of the deceased. As to funeral expenses, some states have no provision whatsoever (Colorado and New York) and others require the payment of up to $2,000 (Delaware). Where there is a funeral benefit, the average amount is $1,000.

Worker's compensation deduction. Most states with the exception of Massachusetts provide that where the injured person is also entitled to worker's compensation, the compensation amount to which he is entitled will be deducted from the no-fault benefits. This would include disability compensation and also the medical expense. Some states also require that social security disability and public assistance benefits be deducted. In Massachusetts if the injured person is entitled to worker's compensation, he is not eligible for PIP benefits.

Payment and penalties. Most states require that payment of PIP benefits be made within 30 days after the filing of a proper proof of loss. Penalties of from 10 to 15 percent are assessed for late payments. The proof may be filed at any time after the injured person becomes entitled to some payment and further proofs may be submitted from time to time. Most states have forms which are utilized as a proof of loss or application for benefits. The New York form is shown below.

NEW YORK NO-FAULT MOTOR VEHICLE INSURANCE LAW
APPLICATION FOR BENEFITS

Name of
[Insurance Company]   [Self-Insurer]

Date   [Our Policyholder]   Date of Accident   File Number

TO ENABLE US TO DETERMINE IF YOU ARE ENTITLED TO BENEFITS UNDER THE NEW YORK COMPREHENSIVE AUTOMOBILE INSURANCE REPARATIONS ACT, PLEASE COMPLETE THIS FORM AND RETURN IT PROMPTLY.
IMPORTANT: 1. To be Eligible for Benefits you must Complete and Sign this Application.
2. You must also Sign any Attached Authorization(s).
3. Return Promptly with copies of any bills you have received to date.

To: _____
CLAIM DEPARTMENT

(Claims Address of Company and Phone No.)

Your Name   Phone Nos.   Home   Business

Your Address (No., Street, City or Town and   Date of Birth   Social Security No.
Zip Code)

Date and Time of Accident   Place of Accident (Street, City or Town and State)
  /   /   A.M.
              P.M.

Brief Description of Accident

....

....

....

At Time of Accident: Were you the driver of our [policyholder's] [car]*   Yes No
Were you a passenger in our [policyholder's] [car]†   Yes No
Were you a pedestrian?   Yes No
Were you a relative in our policyholder's household?   Yes No
If you have answered no to all of the above questions but believe you are entitled to benefits, please attach explanation.

As a Result of this Accident were you injured? Yes No ? If your answer is YES, complete the rest of this form. If NO, Sign here and return this form to us.

SIGNATURE: _____   Date: _____

Describe Your Injury

....

....

Were you treated by a Doctor or other person furnishing health services? Yes No	Name and Address of such **person** ....
If you were treated in a hospital, were you an In-patient? Out-patient?	Hospital's Name and Address ....

> YOU ARE ENTITLED TO RECEIVE HEALTH SERVICE BENEFITS WITHOUT ANY TIME LIMIT IF IT IS POSSIBLE TO DETERMINE DURING THE FIRST YEAR AFTER THE ACCIDENT THAT FURTHER HEALTH SERVICES MAY BE REQUIRED AFTER THE FIRST YEAR.

Amount of Health Bills to Date $	Will you have more health expenses? Yes No	At the time of your accident were you in the course of your employment? Yes No
Did you lose time from work? Yes No	If Yes, how much time?	What are your Average Weekly Earnings? $
If you lost time: Date disability from work began		Date you returned to work

Have you received, or are you eligible for benefits under Workmen's Compensation? Yes No	If Yes, Amount per week $	per **month** $
Have you received, or are you eligible for disability benefits under federal Social Security? Yes No	If Yes, Amount per week $	per month $

List Names and Addresses of your Employer and other Employers for one year **prior to** accident date and give occupation and dates of employment:

....
EMPLOYER AND ADDRESS   OCCUPATION   FROM   TO

....
EMPLOYER AND ADDRESS   OCCUPATION   FROM   TO

....
EMPLOYER AND ADDRESS   OCCUPATION   FROM   TO

As a result of your injury have you had any other expenses? Yes   No   If Yes, attach explanation and amounts of such expenses.

The applicant authorizes the insurer to submit any and all of these forms to **another** party or insurer if such is necessary to perfect its rights of recovery provided for under this act.

---

* Bracketed language to be used or omitted by insurer or self-insurer, as appropriate.
† Exact description of motor vehicle may be used.

1249   Settlement of claims and disputes

If the claim is not paid within 30 days after the submission of the proofs of loss and supporting papers, the claimant may bring action in contract under the policy, alleging that the insurer is guilty of a breach of its obligation to pay no-fault benefits. If a judgment is rendered the court will automatically add whatever penalties the law allows. In some states (cf. New York), the claimant has the option of bringing suit on the policy or submitting the dispute to arbitration conducted by the American Arbitration Association, with the claimant paying the $25 filing fee to the association and the insurer paying the arbitrator's fees, regardless of the outcome.

Where the claim is denied, the insurer can expect that some of the claimants will file a complaint with the Insurance Department of the state on the theory that the insurer has failed to meet the obligations of its contract.

1250   Third-party claims

Until the injured person has met the "threshold" fixed by the no-fault statute, he has no actionable claim against the third-party tort-feasor. However, when the insurer of the tort-feasor receives a report of accident, there is no reason why in serious cases that an investigation should not begin immediately and in most cases all the information can be supplied by the PIP carrier. From that point on, a decision can be made as to the quantum of investigation which will be required in order to meet the claim if it is made.

Even though the claimant has exceeded the threshold, there is nothing in the no-fault statutes which obligates him to begin suit against the tort-feasor. He can continue to receive and accept PIP benefits. The third-party carrier can, of course, expect a subrogation claim from the PIP carrier.

In serious cases, especially where the liability is clear, it can be expected that the existence of no-fault statutes will have some effect on jury verdicts. Since the jurors know that only serious cases can be brought to trial, the psychological effect on the jurors will be that if they find in favor of the plaintiff, they will be mentally prepared to bring in a large verdict.

Therefore, in appropriate cases there is no reason why the third-party insurer should not initiate settlement negotiations even before suit is started.

CHAPTER XIII

Federal jurisdiction and authority

1300   Historical development

Prior to the Revolutionary War, the King of England exercised all of the rights of sovereignty over the Thirteen American colonies. He appointed governors for each colony, each colony being a separate political subdivision from the others. By means of the Declaration of Independence, these separate 13 colonies each declared their independence of the English sovereign, and, with the successful termination of the war, became sovereignties in fact.

In order to successfully prosecute the war, the colonies were bound together by an alliance for that specific purpose. The terms of this alliance were fully set forth in a document called the Articles of Confederation.

As a result of the Revolutionary War, there came into existence 13 independent new nations, separate and distinct from each other. The war demonstrated the advantages of a united effort, and it was thought desirable that some method of alliance should be continued in order to provide a means of meeting the problems which were common to all 13 states. As a result, the 13 separate sovereignties entered into an agreement, forming a central federal government to which was delegated the entire responsibility in certain areas. Each separate sovereign state voluntarily transferred to this federal government certain rights and attributes of sovereignty. The agreement by which this union was accomplished is called the Constitution of the United States. The rights of sovereignty transferred to the federal government are fully set forth in that document, and any other rights not specifically delegated to the federal government by this agreement are still retained by the states.

1301   Federal judiciary

The Constitution provides that the judicial power of the United States shall be vested in one Supreme Court, and in such inferior courts as Congress may establish. By the Judiciary Act of 1789, Congress established federal district courts and circuit courts of appeals. Federal district courts were established throughout the country.

The Constitution defines the jurisdiction of the federal courts as follows:

The judicial power shall extend to all Cases, in Law and Equity, arising under this Constitution, the Laws of the United States, and Treaties made, or which shall be made, under their Authority;—to all Cases affecting Ambassadors, other public Ministers and Consuls;—to all Cases of Admiralty and maritime Jurisdiction;—to Controversies to which the United States shall be a Party;—to Controversies between two or more States;—between a State and Citizens of another State;—between Citizens of different States;—between Citizens of the same State claiming Lands under Grants of different States, and between a State, or the Citizens thereof, and foreign States, Citizens or Subjects.

The jurisdiction with which we are concerned most frequently is the jurisdiction with reference to controversies between citizens of different states. In that area, the present regulations passed by Congress limit this jurisdiction to cases involving $10,000 or more, exclusive of interest and costs. Therefore, to invoke federal jurisdiction at the present time, there must be diversity or citizenship between the plaintiff and the defendant, and the amount in controversy must be more than $10,000 exclusive of interest and costs. In absence of either of these elements, the federal courts do not have jurisdiction.

With reference to the other jurisdiction granted to the federal courts, there is no monetary limit whatsoever. This means that in all cases where the United States is a party the federal court has jurisdiction irrespective of amount. The same rule would hold true with respect to cases of admiralty and maritime jurisdiction.

The federal courts apply the common law and statutes of the state in which they sit or in which the cause of action arose. The federal courts apply the same law as is applied by the state courts and generally follow the decisions of the state courts as to the application of common-law rules.

Under this system, it is possible to find inconsistent decisions among the judgments of the various federal courts. The reason is that in each instance the court is applying the law of the state in which it is located or the law of the state which is applicable to the cause of action. Where the laws of the various states differ, so will the decisions of the federal courts.

The system likewise produces yet another problem. In some cases the federal court is called upon to interpret the law of the state, but the supreme court of the state has never passed on the question. Since the federal court must dispose of the litigation, it has to "guess" what the law of the state is. These cases frequently arise where the state legislature has passed a new statute and the federal court is required to interpret the statute even before the same type of litigation has been before the supreme court of the state. In any case, the supreme court of the state is not bound to follow the decision of the federal court and may come to the opposite conclusion. When the supreme court of the state has determined the law applicable, the federal courts interpreting the law of that state is bound to follow the latest decisions of the supreme court of the state.

This may be a little confusing, but our initial premise must be that the common law of the state is what the supreme court of that state says it is. The federal courts interpreting the state law must follow the decisions of the state supreme court. Where there are no reported cases from the supreme court of the state, the federal court may hazard a "guess" as to what the supreme court would decide if the question were presented to them. When the supreme court of the state finally decides the question, the federal courts will thereafter be bound to follow the decision, whether it agrees with their original "guess" or comes to an opposite conclusion.

Therefore, when a federal court decision is cited as the authority for the law of a particular state, it merely means that the decision represents the federal court's guess as to the applicable law of the state and it is subject to being confirmed or overruled by the state supreme court if and when a similar case is presented to that court.

1302   Treaties

The federal government has the power to make treaties with foreign nations. Treaties of the United States involve the pledged integrity of the nation and, in the event of a conflict, supersede even the constitution of the United States or the constitution of any state. The federal court has jurisdiction over any cases arising under treaties made by the United States.

1303   Preemptive statutes

The powers granted to Congress by the Constitution can be exercised only by legislation. Where Congress has not legislated in any particular area, the rule is that the states may exercise that power until it is displaced by Congressional legislation. Where Congress has legislated, the rule is that Congress has "preempted" the field, or occupied the area, and states thereafter cannot exercise the power. For example, Congress has passed the Federal Employers Liability Act which provides a remedy for personal injuries sustained by employees of interstate carriers by railroad. No state, therefore, can exercise that power with respect to interstate railroad employees. However, Congress has never legislated with respect to personal injuries sustained by other employees engaged in interstate commerce, such as interstate bus drivers and truck drivers. Therefore, as to this class of employee, the state may exercise jurisdiction and such employees come within the jurisdiction of state workmen's compensation laws.

Congress has exercised the powers granted to it by the Constitution in many fields. Under the interstate commerce power, Congress has regulated railroads, aircraft, pure food and drugs, television, and radio. The statutes passed by Congress are contained in the United States Code. This is a set of volumes numbered in sequence and published in annotated form. References, therefore, are made to the United States Code Annotated (abbreviated

USCA). Sections of the code are identified by the title or volume number, the name of the series (USCA), and followed by the section number. Therefore, 46 USCA 688 would refer to volume number 46, section 688.

1304   Federal Employers Liability Act

The Federal Employers Liability Act (abbreviated FELA) is found in 45 USCLA 51–60. The statute reads as follows:

Section 51. LIABILITY OF COMMON CARRIERS BY RAILROAD, IN INTERSTATE OR FOREIGN COMMERCE, FOR INJURIES TO EMPLOYEES FROM NEGLIGENCE, DEFINITION OF EMPLOYEES

Every common carrier by railroad while engaging in commerce between any of the several states or territories, or between the District of Columbia, or any of the states or territories and any foreign nation or nations, shall be liable in damages to any person suffering injury while he is employed by such carrier in such commerce, or, in the case of the death of such employee, to his or her personal representative, for the benefit of the surviving widow or husband and children of such employees; and, if none, then of such employee's parents; and if none, then of the next of kin dependent upon such employee, for such injury or death resulting in whole or in part from the negligence of any of the officers, agents, or employees of such carrier, or by reason of any defect or insufficiency, due to its negligence in its cars, engines, appliances, machinery, track, road bed, works, boats, wharves, or other equipment.

Any employee of a carrier, any part of whose duty as such employee shall be the furtherance of interstate or foreign . . . commerce, or shall, in any way directly or closely and substantially, affect such commerce as above set forth shall, for the purpose of this chapter, be considered as being employed by such carrier in such commerce and shall be considered as entitled to the benefits of this chapter.

Section 52. CARRIERS IN TERRITORIES OR OTHER POSSESSIONS OF THE UNITED STATES

Every common carrier by railroad in the territories, the District of Columbia, the Panama Canal Zone, or other possessions of the United States shall be liable in damages to any person suffering injury while he is employed by such carrier in any of said jurisdictions, or, in the case of the death of such employee, to his or her personal representative, for the benefit of surviving widow, or husband, and children of such employee; and if none, then of such employees' parents; and, if none, then of the next of kin dependent upon such employee for such injury or death resulting in whole or in part from the negligence of any of the officers, agents or employees of such carrier, or by reason of any defect or insufficiency, due to its negligence in its cars, engines, appliances, machinery, track, road bed, works, boats, wharves, or other equipment.

Section 53. CONTRIBUTORY NEGLIGENCE: DIMINUTION OF DAMAGES

In all actions hereafter brought against any such common carrier by railroad under or by virtue of any of the provisions of this chapter to recover damages for personal injuries to an employee, or where such injuries have resulted in his death, the fact that the employee may have been guilty of contributory negligence shall not bar a recovery, but the damages shall be diminished by the jury in proportion to the amount of negligence attributable to such employee; provided that no such employee who may be injured or killed shall be held to have been guilty of contributory negligence in any case where the violation by such common carrier of any statute enacted for the safety of employees contributed to the injury or death of such an employee.

Section 54. Assumption of Risks of Employment

That in any action brought against any common carrier under or by virtue of any of the provisions of this chapter to recover damages for injuries to, or the death of, any of its employees, such employee shall not be held to have assumed the risks of his employment in any case where such injury or death resulted in whole or in part from the negligence of any of the officers, agents, or employees of such carriers; and no employee shall be held to have assumed the risks of his employment in any case where the violation by such common carriers of any statute enacted for the safety of employees contributed to the injury or death of such employee.

Section 55. Contract, Rule, Regulation or Device Excepting from Liability; Set-Off

Any contract, rule, regulation or device whatsoever, the purpose or intent of which shall be to enable any common carrier to exempt itself from any liability created by this chapter, shall to that extent be void; provided, that in any action brought against any such common carrier under or by virtue of any of the provisions of this chapter, such common carrier may set off therein any sum it has contributed or paid to any insurance, relief benefit, or indemnity that may have been paid to the injured employee or to the person entitled thereto an account of the injury or death for which said action was brought.

Section 56. Actions; Limitation; Concurrent Jurisdiction of Courts; Removal of Case in State Court

No action shall be maintained under this chapter unless commenced within three years from the day that the cause of action accrued.

Under this chapter an action may be brought in a District Court of the United States, in the district of the residence of the defendant, or in which the cause of action arose, or in which the defendant shall be doing business at the time of commencing such action. The jurisdiction of the courts of the United States under this chapter shall be concurrent with that of the courts of the several states.

Section 57. Who Is Included in Term "Common Carrier"?

The term "Common Carrier" as used in this chapter shall include the receiver or receivers or other persons or corporations charged with the duty of the management and operation of the business of the common carrier.

Section 58. Duty or Liability of Common Carriers and the Rights of Employees under Other Acts Not Impaired

Nothing in this chapter shall be held to limit the duty or liability of common carriers or to impair the rights of their employees under any other act or acts of Congress.

Section 59. Survival of Right of Action of Person Injured

Any right of action given by this chapter to a person suffering injury shall survive to his or her personal representative, for the benefit of the surviving widow or husband and children of such employee, and, if none, then of such employee's parents; and, if none, then of the next of kin dependent upon such employee, but in such cases there shall be only one recovery for the same injury.

Section 60. PENALTY FOR SUPPRESSION OF VOLUNTARY INFORMATION INCIDENT TO ACCIDENT; SEPARABILITY CLAUSE

Any contract, rule, regulation, or device whatsoever, the purpose, intent, or effect of which shall be to prevent employees of any common carrier from furnishing voluntarily information to a person in interest as to the facts incident to the injury or death of any employee should be void, and whoever, by threat, intimidation, rule, order, contract, regulation, or device whatsoever, shall attempt to prevent any person from furnishing voluntarily such information to a person in interest, or whoever discharges or otherwise disciplines or attempts to discipline any employee for furnishing voluntarily such information to a person in interest, shall upon conviction thereof, be punished by a fine of not more than $1000 or imprisoned for not more than one year, or by both such fine and imprisonment, for each offense, provided that nothing herein contained shall be construed to void any contract, rule, or regulation with respect to any information contained in the files of the carrier or other privileged or confidential reports.

If any provision of this chapter is declared unconstitutional or the applicability thereof to any person or circumstances is held invalid, the validity of the remainder of the chapter and the application of such provision to other persons and circumstances shall not be affected thereby.

It should be emphasized that this statute refers only to employees of an interstate carrier by railroad. It does not refer to the employees of other employers, even though such other employers are engaged in the furtherance of interstate commerce by railroad. Thus it would not apply to persons employed by the Pullman Company, express companies, the United States Post Office, and independent truckmen who deliver freight to the railroad. Likewise, employees of contractors engaged in the construction or repair of railroad tracks, roadbed, signal devices, grade crossings or the inspection of railroad equipment, are not within this scope of the Fedeal Employers Liability Act. To qualify under the act, the employee must be actually employed by an interstate carrier by railroad and no other employer.

Some intrastate railroads connect with an interstate carrier by means of an interchange, and the cars hauled by the intrastate carrier ultimately find their way into interstate commerce. Where this condition exists, the intrastate railroad is held to be an interstate carrier and, as such, subject to the provision of this act.

1305   Federal Employees' Compensation Act

This act (5 USCA 751 *et seq.*) provides for a system of compensation for employees of the federal government who are injured in the course of employment. It is limited to civilian personnel only and does not refer to members of the armed services. The United States, as a self-insurer, meets its own obligations under the act. Therefore, the only contact with the act which the claimsman will have will be when he is representing a defendant whose negligence has caused an injury to a federal employee, which occurred in the course of the employee's employment. The applicable section of the act, with reference to third-party claims (5 USCA 776), reads as follows:

SUBROGATION OF THE UNITED STATES TO EMPLOYEE'S RIGHT OF ACTION; ASSIGNMENT BY EMPLOYEE; DISPOSITION OF MONEYS COLLECTED FROM PERSON LIABLE.

If an injury or death for which compensation is payable . . . is caused under circumstances creating a legal liability upon some person other than the United States to pay damages therefor, the Secretary (of Labor) may require the beneficiary to assign to the United States any right of action he may have to enforce such liability of such other person or any right which he may have to share in any money or other property received in satisfaction of such liability of such other person, or the Secretary may require said beneficiary to prosecute said action in his own name. Any employee who is required to appear as a party or witness in the prosecution of said action is, while so engaged, in an active duty status.

If the beneficiary shall refuse to make such assignment or to prosecute said action in his own name when required by the Secretary, he shall not be entitled to compensation . . .

The cause of action when assigned to the United States may be prosecuted or compromised by the Secretary, and if the Secretary realizes upon such cause of action, he shall apply the money or other property so received in the following manner: After deducting the amount of any compensation already paid to the beneficiary and the expense of such realization or collection, which sum shall be placed to the credit of the employee's compensation fund, the surplus, if any, shall be paid to the beneficiary and credited upon any future payments of compensation payable to him on account of the same injury.

The statute provides for the assignment of a personal injury cause of action to the United States. Where the cause of action has been assigned, settlement would have to be made with the party owning the cause of action, namely, the United States. If a settlement were made with the injured person, it would appear that a release of a cause of action, which had already been assigned, would not effectively bar the claim of the United States. Therefore, when dealing with a federal employee as an injured party, it should first be ascertained whether or not the claimant was in the course of his federal employment at the time of injury. If he was, the provisions of the statute are applicable and the question of assignment should be investigated. On the other hand, if the employee was not in the course of his employment at the time of the accident, then his position is exactly the same as any other injured person and dealings may be had with him directly.

1306   Federal Tort Claims Act

As a sovereign, the United States may not be sued for torts committed in the exercise of its governmental functions unless it consents to be sued. By passage of the Federal Tort Claims Act (abbreviated FTCA), 28 USCA 2671, the United States has waived its sovereign immunity in certain areas. The following is an outline of the pertinent sections of the act:

Waiver (sec. 2674) : The United States shall be liable, respecting the provisions of this title relating to tort claims, in the same manner and to the same extent as a private individual under like circumstances, but shall not be liable for interest prior to judgment or for punitive damages.

If, however, in any case wherein death was caused, the law of the place where the act or omission complained of occurred provides, or has been construed to provide, for damages only punitive in nature, the United States shall be liable for actual or compensatory damages, measured by the pecuniary injuries resulting from such death to the persons respectively, for whose benefit the action was brought, in lieu thereof.

Exceptions (sec. 2680) : The provisions of this chapter . . . shall not apply to

(a) Any claim based upon an act or omission of an employee of the Government, exercising due care, in the execution of a statute or regulation, whether or not such statute or regulation be valid, or based upon the exercise or performance or the failure to exercise or perform a discretionary function or duty on the part of a federal agency or an employee of the Government, whether or not the discretion involved be abused.

(b) Any claim arising out of the loss, miscarriage or negligent transmission of letters or postal matter.

(c) Any claim arising in respect of the assessment or collection of any tax or customs duty, or the detention of any goods or merchandise by any officer of customs or excise or any other law-enforcement officer.

(d) Any claim for damages caused by the imposition or establishment of a quarantine by the United States.

(e) Any claim arising out of assault, battery, false imprisonment, false arrest, malicious prosecution, abuse of process, libel, slander, misrepresentation, deceit, or interference with contract rights.

(f) Any claim for damages caused by the fiscal operations of the Treasury or by the regulation of the monetary system.

(g) Any claim arising out of the combatant activities of the military or naval forces, or the Coast Guard, during time of war.

(h) Any claim arising in a foreign country.

(i) Any claim arising from the activities of the Tennessee Valley Authority and any claim arising from the activities of the Panama Railroad Company.

(j) Any claim arising from the activities of the Panama Canal Company.

(k) Any claim arising from the activities of a Federal land bank, a Federal intermediate credit bank, or a bank for cooperatives.

Judgment as Bar (sec. 2676) : The judgment in an action . . . shall constitute a complete bar to any action by the claimant, by reason of the same subject matter, against the employee of the government whose act or omission gave rise to the claim.

Suits against Government Employees (sec. 2679) : . . .

(b) The remedy by suit against the United States . . . for damage to property or for personal injury including death, resulting from the operation by any employee of the Government of any motor vehicle while acting within the scope of his office or employment, shall hereafter be exclusive of any other civil action or proceeding by reason of the same subject matter against the employee or his estate whose act or omission gave rise to the claim.

(c) The Attorney General shall defend any civil action or proceeding brought in any court against any employee of the Government or his estate for any such damage or injury. The employee against whom such civil action or proceeding is brought shall deliver within such time after date of service or knowledge of service as determined by the Attorney General, all process served upon him or an attested true copy thereof to his immediate superior or to whomever was designated by the head of his department to receive such papers and such person shall promptly furnish the copies of the pleadings and process therein to the United States attorney for district embracing the place wherein the proceeding is brought, to the Attorney General and to the head of his employing Federal agency.

(d) Upon a certification by the Attorney General that the defendant employee was acting within the scope of his employment at the time of the incident out of which the suit arose, any such civil action or proceedings commenced in a state court shall be removed without bond at any time before trial by the Attorney General to the district court of the United States for the district or division embracing the place wherein it is pending and the proceedings deemed a tort action brought against the United States.

These paragraphs were added to section 2679 by Public Law 87:258 and became effective March 21, 1962. It is clear from the language of the statute that it refers to the operation of any motor vehicle (either privately or government owned) by a federal employee in the course of his employment. Where the employee carries insurance on his own automobile, a problem will arise as to the obligation of his insurance carrier where it is alleged that he was in the course of his federal employment at the time of the incident. If the Attorney General grants the certification under Paragraph (d), then the suit against the employee is deemed an action against the United States and the employee has no personal liability. On the other hand, if the employee contends that he was in the course of his employment and the Attorney General refuses the certification, then it would appear that there is some obligation on the part of the employee's insurance carrier, at least as to the matter of defense.

As to indemnification, in *Gustafson* v. *Peck* (216 Fed. Supp. 370), the court said: "These amendments . . . grant immunity from personal liability to Federal employees, which may arise out of their negligent operation of motor vehicles while in the scope of their Federal employment."

If this is a correct statement of the intent of the law, it would seem that since there is no liability imposed on the employee by law that the insurance carrier's promise of indemnification as far as the employee is concerned is not involved. The same thing would be true with respect to any other government employee who was a permissive user of the vehicle on government business. However, under the standard automobile policies, the "persons insured" are defined to include "any other person or organization legally responsible for the use of (1) an owned automobile, or (2) a non-owned automobile" under certain circumstances.

The United States has been held to be an additional insured under standard automobile policies where the employee was driving his own car in the course of his federal employment. While the statute does require that the United States assume responsibility for damages resulting from automobile accidents by employees driving their own or federally owned cars in the course of their employment to the exclusion of any action against the employee personally, an insurance policy issued to the employee on his own car so used also covers the liability of the United States as assumed by the statute since the United States was an "insured" under the policy definition which included "any other person or organization legally responsible for the use" of the automobile. [See *United States* v. *Myers*, 363 Fed. 2d 615; *Barker* v. *United States*, 233 Fed. Supp. 455; *Patterson* v. *United States*, 233 Fed. Supp. 447; *Government Employees Ins. Co.* v. *United States*, 349 Fed. 2d 83; cert. denied in 382 U.S. 1026.]

If it is the insurer's intent to exclude coverage for the United States, this can be accomplished by a specific agreement in the policy to that effect. See *Stephan* v. *Madison* (223 Fed. Supp. 256), wherein the court held that where the policy specifically excluded the United States as an insured, the insurer was not obligated to either defend or indemnify the United States, and further under the statute, action against the employee was precluded. Therefore, the employee's insurer could not be compelled either to defend the action or to pay any judgment which might be obtained.

Another question which is yet to be answered would arise where a state statute imposes the rule of liability on the owner of the vehicle where it is being used with his permission, express or implied, for the negligent acts of the permissive user. Under the federal statute, the suit against the employee operating the vehicle on government business is deemed an action against the United States, and the government employee so operating the vehicle has an immunity from personal liability, but the federal statute is silent as to any immunity for the owner of the vehicle. It would not seem to make any difference as to whether the owner of the vehicle was a government employee or not. The immunity runs only to the government employee who is operating the vehicle.

Another interesting problem which is posed by this legislation concerns the question of exoneration or subrogation. If the government employee, operating the vehicle on government business, is sued, and he does not report the claim or request the necessary certification from the Attorney General, but defends the case himself or is defended by his insurance carrier, and the judgment is satisfied, can he then bring suit against the United States in order to recover the costs of defense and the amount of the judgment which he paid? Would the failure of the employee to report the case or to request certification foreclose his right to indemnification? When the lawsuit was begun, would the failure of the employee to join the United States as a third-party defendant be fatal to his action for reimbursement?

From the standpoint of the claimsman, he should investigate and ascertain in all cases whether or not the employee was operating the vehicle on government business. If he was, then arrangements should be made to have the employee report the claim in accordance with the statute.

The statutory procedure for making a claim under the FTCA requires that the claim first be filed with the agency concerned within two years after it accrues, and requires that action be begun within six months after the final denial of the claim. The failure of the agency to make final disposition of the claim within six months after it is filed is deemed a final denial. The action is forever barred unless the time periods above noted are observed. The applicable sections of the statute are as follows:

Administrative Settlements (sec. 2672) :

(a) The head of each Federal agency or his designee, in accordance with regulations prescribed by the Attorney General, may consider, ascertain, adjust, determine, compromise, and settle any claim for money damages against the United States for injury or loss of property or personal injury or death caused by the negligent or wrongful act or omission of any employee of the agency while acting within the scope of his office or employment, under circumstances where the United States, if a private person, would be liable to the claimant in accordance with the law of the place where the act or omission occurred: *Provided,* That any award, compromise, or settlement in excess of $25,000 shall be effected only with the prior written approval of the Attorney General or his designee.

(b) Subject to the provisions of this title relating to civil actions on tort claims against the United States, any such award, compromise, settlement, or determination shall be final and conclusive on all officers of the Government, except when procured by means of fraud.

(c) Any award, compromise, or settlement in an amount of $2,500 or less made pursuant to this section shall be paid by the head of the Federal agency concerned out of appropriations available to that agency. Payment of any award, compromise, or settlement in an amount in excess of $2,500 made pursuant to this section or made by the Attorney General in any amount pursuant to section 2677 of this title shall be paid in a manner similar to judgments and compromises in like causes and appropriations or funds available for the payment of such judgments and compromises are hereby made available for the payment of awards, compromises, or settlements under this chapter.

The time for commencing action is set forth in Section 2401, which reads as follows:

(b) A tort claim against the United States shall be forever barred unless it is presented in writing to the appropriate Federal agency within two years after such claim accrues or unless action is begun within six months after the date of mailing, by certified or registered mail, of notice of final denial of the claim by the agency to which it was presented.

Just as immunity from liability is granted by the statute to government employees operating motor vehicles in the course of their federal employment, physicians, dentists, and medical personnel are likewise granted the same immunity. 38 USCA 4116 reads as follows:

(a) The remedy against the United States provided by sections 1346(b) and 2672 of title 28 for damages for personal injury, including death allegedly arising from malpractice or negligence of a physician, dentist, nurse, pharmacist, or paramedical (for example, medical and dental technicians, nursing assistants, and therapists) or other supporting personnel in furnishing medical care or treatment while in the exercise of his duties in or for the Department of Medicine and Surgery shall hereafter be exclusive of any other civil action or proceeding by reason of the same subject matter against such physician, dentist, nurse, pharmacist, or paramedical or other supporting personnel (or his estate) whose act or omission gave rise to such claim.

Therefore, under the present procedure, the claim must first be presented to the appropriate agency within the time period mentioned in the statute. Claims are filed by the use of a claim form which is available at all offices of federal agencies. (Standard Form No. 95; see Exhibit I below.) If the claim is denied, the claimant then may begin action against the United States by the service of process in the same manner as a private person. Suit, however, since the United States is a party, must be brought in the federal court. The failure of the gency to act on the claim within six months shall be deemed a denial of the claim and the claimant may also begin suit under those circumstances.

The term "federal agency" as used in the statute is defined in 28 USCA 2671 as follows:

As used in this chapter and sections 1346(b) and 2401(b) of this title, the term "Federal agency" includes the executive departments, the military departments, independent establishments of the United States, and corporations primarily acting as instrumentalities or agencies of the United States, but does not include any contractor with the United States.

Employee of the government includes officers or employees of any federal agency, members of the military and naval forces of the United States, and persons acting on behalf of a federal agency in an official capacity, temporarily or permanently in the service of the United States, whether with or without compensation.

Acting within the scope of his office or employment, in the case of a member of the military or naval forces of the United States, means acting in line of duty.

FTCA forms. The forms reproduced as Exhibit I and Exhibit II are used for the purpose of filing a claim against the United States and are filed with the agency against whom the claim is made.

1307 Insurance

In 1868, the Supreme Court of the United States decided that the business of insurance did not involve interstate commerce so as to come within federal jurisdiction (*Paul* v. *Virginia*, 231 U.S. 495). In 1944, the court reexamined the question in *United States* v. *Southeastern Underwriters Association* (64 S. Ct. 1171), in which it specifically reversed its earlier decision, holding that

EXHIBIT I

CLAIM FOR DAMAGE OR INJURY
(form 95)

Standard Form 95
Revised April 1961
Bureau of the Budget
Circular A-5 (Rev.)

SUBMIT TO:

CLAIM FOR DAMAGE OR INJURY
(Use additional sheets if necessary)

95—103

Use ink or typewriter.   See reverse side for instructions and additional information required.

1. NAME OF CLAIMANT *(Please print full name)*	2. AGE	3. MARITAL STATUS	8. AMOUNT OF CLAIM	
4. ADDRESS OF CLAIMANT *(Street, city, zone, State)*			PROPERTY DAMAGE	$
5. NAME AND ADDRESS OF SPOUSE, IF ANY				
6. PLACE OF ACCIDENT *(Give city or town and State; if outside city limits, indicate mileage or distance to nearest city or town)*			PERSONAL INJURY	$
7. DATE AND DAY OF ACCIDENT	TIME (A.M. or P.M.)		TOTAL	$

9. DESCRIPTION OF ACCIDENT--STATE BELOW, IN DETAIL, ALL KNOWN FACTS AND CIRCUMSTANCES ATTENDING THE DAMAGE OR INJURY, INDENTIFYING PERSONS AND PROPERTY INVOLVED AND THE CAUSE THEREOF

10.	PROPERTY DAMAGE	
NAME OF OWNER, IF OTHER THAN CLAIMANT	ADDRESS OF OWNER, IF OTHER THAN CLAIMANT	

BRIEFLY DESCRIBE KIND AND LOCATION OF PROPERTY AND NATURE AND EXTENT OF DAMAGE. SEE INSTRUCTIONS ON REVERSE SIDE FOR METHOD OF SUBSTANTIATING CLAIM

11.	PERSONAL INJURY

STATE NATURE AND EXTENT OF INJURY WHICH FORMS THE BASIS OF THIS CLAIM

12.		WITNESSES	
	NAMES		ADDRESSES

CRIMINAL PENALTY FOR PRESENTING FRAUDU-
LENT CLAIM OR MAKING FALSE STATEMENTS

Fine of not more than $10,000 or imprisonment for not more than 5 years or both.   *(See 62 Stat. 698, 749; 18 U.S.C. 287, 1001.)*

CIVIL PENALTY FOR PRESENTING
FRAUDULENT CLAIM

The claimant shall forfeit and pay to the United States the sum of $2,000, plus double the amount of damages sustained by the United States.   *(See R.S. §3490, 5438; 31 U.S.C 231.)*

13. *I DECLARE UNDER THE PENALTIES OF PERJURY THAT THE AMOUNT OF THIS CLAIM COVERS ONLY DAMAGES AND INJURIES CAUSED BY THE ACCIDENT ABOVE DESCRIBED. I AGREE TO ACCEPT SAID AMOUNT IN FULL SATISFACTION AND FINAL SETTLEMENT OF THIS CLAIM.*

SIGNATURE OF CLAIMANT

DATE OF CLAIM

NOTE: Signature used above should be used in all future correspondence.

EXHIBIT I (Continued)

NOTICE TO CLAIMANT

In order that your claim for damages may receive proper consideration you are requested to supply the information called for on both sides of this form. All material facts should be stated on this form, as it will be the basis of further action upon your claim. The instructions set forth below should be read carefully before the form is prepared.

INSTRUCTIONS

Claims for damage to or for loss or destruction of property, or for personal injury, must be signed by the owner of the property damaged or lost or the injured person. If, by reason of death, other disability or for reasons deemed satisfactory by the Government, the foregoing requirement cannot be fulfilled, the claim may be filed by a duly authorized agent or other legal representative, provided evidence satisfactory to the Government is submitted with said claim establishing authority to act.

The amount claimed should be substantiated by competent evidence as follows:

(a) In support of claim for personal injury or death, the claimant should submit a written report by the attending physician, showing the nature and extent of injury, the nature and extent of treatment, the degree of permanent disability, if any, the prognosis, and the period of hospitalization, or incapacitation, attaching itemized bills for medical, hospital, or burial expenses actually incurred.

(b) In support of claims for damage to property which has been or can be economically repaired, the claimant should submit at least two itemized signed statements or estimates by reliable, disinterested concerns, or, if payment has been made, the itemized signed receipts evidencing payment.

(c) In support of claims for damage to property which is not economically reparable, or if the property is lost or destroyed, the claimant should submit statements as to the original cost of the property, the date of purchase, and the value of the property, both before and after the accident. Such statements should be by disinterested competent persons, preferably reputable dealers or officials familiar with the type of property damaged, or by two or more competitive bidders, and should be certified as being just and correct.

Any further instructions or information necessary in the preparation of your claim will be furnished, upon request, by the office indicated at the top of the other side of this form.

INSTRUCTIONS REGARDING INSURANCE COVERAGE

In order that subrogation claims may be adjudicated, it is essential that the claimant provide the following information regarding the insurance coverage of his vehicle:

DO YOU CARRY COLLISION INSURANCE?	IF YES, GIVE NAME AND ADDRESS OF INSURANCE COMPANY AND POLICY NUMBER
☐ YES ☐ NO	

HAVE YOU FILED CLAIM ON YOUR INSURANCE CARRIER IN THIS INSTANCE, AND IF SO, IS IT FULL COVERAGE OR DEDUCTIBLE?	IF DEDUCTIBLE, STATE AMOUNT

IF SUCH CLAIM HAS BEEN FILED, WHAT ACTION HAS YOUR INSURER TAKEN, OR WHAT ACTION DOES IT PROPOSE TO TAKE WITH REFERENCE TO YOUR CLAIM? (*It is necessary that you ascertain these facts*)

DO YOU CARRY PUBLIC LIABILITY AND PROPERTY DAMAGE COVERAGE?	IF YES, GIVE NAME OF INSURANCE CARRIER
☐ YES ☐ NO	

SIGNATURE OF CLAIMANT

EXHIBIT II

Statement of Witness
(form 94)

File Reference:

This office has been advised that you witnessed an accident which occurred

It will be helpful if you will answer, as fully as possible, the questions on the back of this letter.

Your courtesy in complying with this request will be appreciated. An addressed envelope, which requires no postage, is enclosed for your convenience in replying.

Sincerely yours,

Encl.

U. S. GOVERNMENT PRINTING OFFICE 16—60708-8

(OVER)

EXHIBIT II (Continued)

Standard Form 94
Revised June 1953
Promulgated
by Bureau of the Budget
Circular A-5 (Rev.)

STATEMENT OF WITNESS

(Use additional sheets if necessary)

1. DID YOU SEE THE ACCIDENT?	2. WHEN DID IT HAPPEN? *(Time and date)*	3. WHERE DID IT HAPPEN *(Street location and city)*

4. TELL IN YOUR OWN WAY HOW THE ACCIDENT HAPPENED

5. WHERE WERE YOU WHEN THE ACCIDENT OCCURRED?

6. WAS ANYONE INJURED, AND IF SO, EXTENT OF INJURY IF KNOWN?

7. DESCRIBE THE APPARENT DAMAGE TO PRIVATE PROPERTY

8. DESCRIBE THE APPARENT DAMAGE TO GOVERNMENT PROPERTY

9. IN TRAFFIC CASES STATE APPROXIMATE SPEED *(Miles per hour)*	(a) GOVERNMENT VEHICLE	(b) OTHER VEHICLE

10. GIVE THE NAMES AND ADDRESSES OF ANY OTHER WITNESSES TO THE ACCIDENT

NAMES	ADDRESSES

11. DATE	SIGNATURE	
12. HOME ADDRESS		TELEPHONE NO.
13. BUSINESS ADDRESS		TELEPHONE NO.

14. INDICATE ON THE DIAGRAM BELOW WHAT HAPPENED:

1. Number Federal vehicle as 1—other vehicle as 2—additional vehicle as 3, and show direction of travel by arrow
   (Example: ⟶ ☐1 ⟩⟨ ☐2 ⟵)
2. Use solid line to show path before accident ⟶ ☐2
   Broken line after accident — — — ☐2

3. Show pedestrian by ⟶ O
4. Show railroad by ┼┼┼┼┼┼┼┼┼┼┼┼┼┼┼┼┼┼
5. Give names or numbers of streets or highways
6. Indicate north by arrow in this circle ◯

16—56709-2

the business of insurance was one which involved interstate commerce and therefore came within the area of federal regulation.

In 1945, Congress passed the McCarren-Ferguson Insurance Regulation Act (15 USCA 1011, *et seq.*), in which Congress declared its intent to allow the regulation of insurance to be retained by the states. The declaration of policy is contained in section 1011 and reads as follows:

Congress declares that the continued regulation and taxation by the several States of the business of insurance is in the public interest, and that silence on the part of the Congress shall not be construed to impose any barrier to the regulation or taxation of such business by the several States.

1308   The Warsaw Convention

This agreement between certain nations regulates and applies to all international transportation of persons, baggage, or goods performed by aircraft for hire. Its declared purpose is to unify rules for international air traffic and to facilitate such traffic. The United States is not a signatory to the convention, but has declared its acceptance and adherence to the provisions thereof, by a Declaration of Adherence, advised by the Senate and deposited at Warsaw on July 31, 1934. With Congressional implementation, it became effective for the United States on October 29, 1934. As far as the United States is concerned, the convention has the effect of a treaty.

The convention provides for a limitation of liability with respect to personal injury and death as well as property damage arising out of international flights between the nations subject to its terms. It provides that each passenger on such a flight (or in the case of death, his personal representative) shall receive provable damages from the airline carrier up to 125,000 gold francs, which would amount to about $25,000 in U.S. currency, in the case of ordinary negligence. The burden of proving freedom from negligence is placed upon the airline and the airline must pay up to the limitation without any proof on the part of the plaintiff of the airline's negligence or fault, unless the airline can prove that it and its servants were free from all fault. By a 1955 amendment (sec. 25A), the limitation was extended to include the servants and agents of the airline.

In the event that the passenger can establish an exceptional or gross degree of negligence on the part of the airline or its servants, the passenger may recover all provable damages without limitations. Article 25, Sec. (1) reads as follows:

The carrier shall not be entitled to avail himself of the provisions of this Convention which exclude or limit his liability, if the damage is caused by his willful misconduct or by such default on his part as in accordance with the law of the Court to which the case is submitted, is considered to be equivalent to willful misconduct.

In *Royal Dutch Airlines* (KLM) v. *Tuller* [292 Fed. 2d 775], the court defined willful misconduct as follows:

Willful misconduct is the intentional performance of an act with knowledge that the act will probably result in injury or damage, or . . . in some manner as to imply reckless disregard of the consequences of its performance; and likewise, it also means a failure to act in such circumstances.

With the increase in international flights and the rapid growth of airline travel, public dissatisfaction with the low limits of the Warsaw Convention became more and more evident, especially having in mind that American airlines are all privately owned as opposed to foreign airlines which are government owned and controlled. In 1955, the representatives of many of the countries who were signatories to the Warsaw Convention met at The Hague, and proposed by means of The Hague Protocol to increase the limits of the Convention to double its original limit, which would mean about $16,600 in U.S. currency. The United States never became a party to this protocol primarily because it opposed the inadequacy of the limit, taking the position that there should be no limit of liability whatsoever. Finally in November 1965, responding to public pressure, the United States filed its denunciation of the Warsaw Convention to be effective six months from that time or May 15, 1966. However, on May 13, 1966, the United States withdrew its denunciation in view of an agreement which was reached with the major airlines to increase the limitation to $75,000. This agreement was made with all of the major U.S. and foreign airlines, and applies to all international transportation by air which, according to the contract of carriage, includes a point in the United States as a point of origin, point of destination, or agreed stopping place. As to all other flights the limitations of the Warsaw Convention or The Hague Protocol, as the case may be, still apply. In *American Airlines* v. *Ulen* [186 Fed. 2d 529], an airplane crashed into a mountain. The flight was charted in violation of air regulations at less than 1,000 feet above the highest obstacle on the course intended to be flown. This was held to constitute willful misconduct within the terms of the Warsaw Convention.

The limitations of the Warsaw Convention apply only to international flights between signatory nations, or those who have declared their adherence to the provisions of the convention. The mere fact that the aircraft stops at intermediate points en route in countries which are not signatories will not affect the application of the limitation. The limitation, however, will not apply to an international passenger whose flight originated at the airport of one signatory and terminated in a nonsignatory country. Likewise, the limitation will not apply to domestic flights solely within the territorial limits of one signatory.

The applicability of the convention is determined by the contract of carriage entered into between the passenger and the airline. If the passenger has contracted for an international flight between signatories, the limitation applies from the moment the passenger begins his travel. This means that as soon as the passenger enters the aircraft, the airline is entitled to limitation. It makes no difference whether the aircraft has started its engines, or has moved from its receiving position.

For example, an international passenger entered the aircraft at La Guardia Field. The flight had not begun and the door to the aircraft was still open. The passenger left her seat and went to the door to wave to some friends. She did not observe that the stairway and platform had been removed from in front of the door, and, as a result, fell from the door of the aircraft to the ground. The limitation of the convention was held to be applicable to her case.

It is possible that in one aircraft individual passengers will have different relationships to the airline. For example, if an aircraft left New York for Mexico City, with intermediate stops en route, passengers flying between airports within the United States would not be subject to the limitations of the convention. As to passengers who entered the aircraft at some point in the United States with an ultimate destination in Mexico, a convention signatory, the convention limitations would apply irrespective of whether the accident occurred in the United States or Mexico. Their status as international passengers automatically made them subject to the Warsaw Convention.

The limitation applies only in favor of the airline, and then only when the passenger is in a travel status. If the international passenger is injured on the way to the airport, in the airport itself, or on premises in the airport maintained by the airline, the company furnishing transportation, the operator of the airport, and the airline, prior to the assumption of travel status, would not be entitled to limitation.

1309   Atomic Energy Act of 1954 (42 USCA 2011)

This act was passed in order to make radioactive isotopes available to private industry. Since the United States has ownership and control of all fissionable material, authority was delegated to the Atomic Energy Commission to issue general or specific licenses to private industry under which the particular company would receive and use by-product material, source material, or special nuclear material. In addition, the Atomic Energy Commission was directed to set up standards for protection against radiation to be observed by the licensees. The standards are found in volume 10 of the Code of Federal Regulations, part 20. The statute, 42 USCA 2210, prescribes the amount of insurance protection which must be available to the licensees, as well as setting up the amount of indemnification which will be provided by the United States as an excess insurer.

1310   Code of Federal Regulations

Congress has from time to time established various federal agencies and delegated to them, and to some of the executive departments, certain lawmaking power. Such agencies are authorized to make rules and regulations with reference to their particular responsibilities, and the rules thus made have the same force and effect of a law passed by Congress. The rules promulgated by these various agencies are collected in a series of volumes called the Code of Federal Regulations (abbreviated CFR) and the volumes are numbered consecutively in exactly the same way as any other series of law books. When reference is made to the code, the applicable volume number is cited first, then the code initials, and finally the section number. For example, section 250 of volume 21 of the code would be cited as 21 CFR 250.

A partial list of the agencies likely to be encountered by the claimsman, with the enabling act and the location of the rules formulated by the agencies, is as follows:

Agency	Enabling Act	Rules
Federal Aviation	Federal Aviation Act	14 CFR
Adm.	(49 USCA 1301–1342)	(Chaps. I–II)
Interstate Commerce	ICC Act	
Commission	(Railroads, 49 USCA 13;	49 CFR 125.9
	Motor Carriers, 49 USCA 304)	49 CFR 190
Food and Drug	Federal Foods, Drug,	21 CFR 1
Administration	and Cosmetic Act	
	(21 USCA 301)	
Department of Health,	Federal Food	21 CFR 121
and Human Services	Additives Act	
	(21 USCA 348)	
Department of Health,	Federal Hazardous	21 CFR 191
Education, and Welfare	Substances Labelling Act	
	(15 USCA 1261)	

Federal Aviation Act. This act created a federal aviation agency headed by an administrator who was empowered by a later act of Congress (49 USCA 1941) to promote the safety of flight of aircraft by prescribing such reasonable rules and regulations for the operation of aircraft as may be necessary. The civil air regulations thus promulgated do not determine legal liability, but they do impose duties and responsibilities which specify the standards of care which must be observed. Applying common-law principles, the courts have held that a failure to comply with the regulations is evidence of negligence. [*Lange* v. *Nelson-Ryan Flight Service, Inc.*, 259 Minn. 460, 108 N.W. 2d 428; *Sleezer* v. *Lang*, 170 Neb. 239; *Moody* v. *McDaniel* (Mississippi), 190 Fed. Supp. 24.]

Interstate Commerce Commission Act. This act created the Interstate Commerce Commission whose function it is to supervise the interstate transportation of passengers and freight by land and by water. The commission was also given the power to make rules and regulations governing such transportation. Among the numerous rules promulgated by the commission are those relating to safety of operation by the carriers. The Railroad Safety Rules are found in 49 CFR 125.9 *et seq.*, and the Motor Carrier Safety Regulations are contained in 49 CFR 190–197. Since the claimsman will frequently encounter accidents involving interstate motor carriers, he should be familiar with the following regulations:

Section 191.2 Minimum requirements (physical requirements for drivers). This section provides that no person shall drive, nor shall any motor carrier require or permit any person to drive, any motor vehicle unless such person possesses the following minimum qualifications.

a. Mental and physical condition:
   1. No loss of foot, leg, hand, or arm.
   2. No mental, nervous, organic, or functional disease likely to interfere with safe driving.
   3. No loss of fingers, impairment of use of foot, leg, fingers, hand, or arm, or other structural defect or limitation likely to interfere with safe driving.
b. Eyesight: 20/40 vision or better in each eye.
c. Hearing: 10/20 in the better ear for conversational tones without hearing aid.
d. Shall not be addicted to the use of narcotics or habit-forming drugs, or the excessive use of alcoholic beverages or liquors.

Section 191.3 Driving experience. Must have had not less than one year's experience in driving a motor vehicle throughout the four seasons.

Section 191.6 Minimum age. Twenty-one years, except that a person 18 or over may drive an interstate vehicle owned and controlled by a farmer.

Section 191.9 Periodic physical examination of driver. Driver must be examined every 36 months by a doctor of medicine or a doctor of osteopathy. To be satisfactory for continued driving, he must meet the minimum physical requirements of Section 191.2.

Section 191.10 Certificate of physical examination. Must be kept on file at the motor carrier's office, and the driver must have a copy thereof in his possession.

Section 191.11 Doctor's certificate. This rule sets forth the form and content of the doctor's certificate.

Section 191.13 Driver's past record. Requires that the motor carrier maintain records with respect to the driver's record and number of miles driven, including accidents, violations of traffic laws, etc., filed with driver's personnel records.

Section 192.4 Driving while ill or fatigued. Prohibited, except in an emergency, and then only to the nearest place of safety.

Section 195.4 Maximum driving time. Ten hours, excluding rest stops, in any 24-hour period. Also provides for eight consecutive hours of rest following the ten hours driving time.

Section 195.8 Driver's daily log. Requires that the driver maintain a daily log indicating his activity, driving time, territory, and so on. Form B.M.C. 59 is required for this purpose. A copy of the log must be maintained in the motor carrier's office for a period of three years. (Rule 203–207.)

Federal Food, Drug, and Cosmetic Act. This act regulates hundreds of commodities which move in interstate commerce, including all varieties of food stuffs and all types of drugs, together with cosmetics, as to their ingredients. Violation of the act is negligence per se. [*Orthopedic Equipment Co.* v. *Eutsler*, 276 Fed. 2d 455.]

Federal Food Additives Act.   This act gives authority to the Secretary of Health, and Human Services to regulate the ingredients which may be added to food to act as a preservative. It is his function to determine and regulate the safe products which can be added, and to prohibit the addition of any toxic substances. Since this act is an exercise of the interestate commerce power, the act and its regulations apply only to food products in interstate commerce.

Federal Hazardous Substances Labeling Act.   The act authorizes the Secretary of Health, Education, and Welfare to regulate household chemical products by requiring certain precautionary labeling. The purpose of the regulations is to safeguard the consumer against dangerous household products by placing a duty upon the manufacturer to adequately warn those who will probably come in contact with it as to the latent and inherent dangers of the product. The regulations set forth the manner of labeling and the requirement that the label contain first aid instructions and antidotes.

CHAPTER XIV

Law of admiralty

1400 Maritime jurisdiction of the United States

The United States Constitution, Article III, provides as follows:

Section I. The judicial Power of the United States, shall be vested in one supreme Court, and in such inferior Courts as the Congress may from time to time ordain and establish. . . .

Section II. The judicial Power shall extend . . . to all Cases of admiralty and maritime Jurisdiction. . . .

It should be noted that this is a direct grant of power given by the states to the Supreme Court. Immediately upon the ratification of the Constitution, the Court had the jurisdiction to hear and determine cases of admiralty and maritime jurisdiction. There was no requirement that Congress preempt the field by legislation, or was it necessary for Congress to take any action whatsoever in order to invest the Supreme Court with this power.

The first problem which confronted the new Supreme Court was the deter-

458

mination of the nature and extent of the jurisdiction. It reasoned that, since we had only recently been subject to English law, the framers of the Constitution intended to grant the Supreme Court the same admiralty and maritime jurisdiction exercised by the English courts.

In England the admiral was the officer charged with the responsibility of governing all maritime matters. This included not only the naval defense of the nation but the government and regulation of all shipping as well. He promulgated rules and regulations applicable to maritime matters. He set up courts for the purpose of determining maritime causes, civil and criminal, as well as controversies arising out of acts done upon or relating to the sea. These were called Courts of the Admiral, or Admiralty Courts, and they exercised jurisdiction over all maritime contracts, torts, injuries, or offenses. Strictly speaking, "admiralty" refers to the court and the jurisdiction it exercises rather than to the substantive law it applies.

Maritime law consists of the body of rules, precepts, and practices relating to maritime matters and, as such, is the substantive law applied by courts of admiralty. It is that system of law which particularly relates to commerce and navigation, to business transacted at sea, to navigation, to ships and shipping, to seamen, to the transportation of persons and property by sea, and to marine affairs generally. The system is somewhat related to the common law in the sense that it is not statutory but came into existence as a result of the decisions and judicial pronouncements of various admiralty courts. These commerce courts functioned in many countries on the European continent and the decisions are not uniform. Therefore, one of the first problems confronting the new Supreme Court was to decide exactly what rules of law should be applicable to maritime cases. In *The Lottawanna* case (21 Wall, 558), the court said:

> That we have a Maritime Law of our own, operative throughout the United States, cannot be doubted. The general system of a Maritime Law which was familiar to lawyers and statesmen of the country when the Constitution was adopted, was most certainly intended and referred to when it was declared in that instrument that the judicial power of the United States shall extend to all cases of admiralty and maritime jurisdiction.

Therefore in the initial stages the Supreme Court decided maritime cases on the basis of what it thought to be the general rules applicable at the time the Constitution was adopted. However, this approach did not mean that the United States was bound to follow any subsequent decisions of other courts or, as a matter of fact, to adopt any particular rules of law with respect to maritime cases. Since the constitutional grant of power was an absolute one, the Court took the position that it could adopt and reject such rules as it saw fit. In *The Western Maid* (257 U.S. 419), the Supreme Court, speaking through Mr. Justice Holmes, said:

> We must realize that however ancient may be the tradition of the maritime law, however diverse the sources from which it has been drawn, it derives its sole and only power in this country from its having been accepted and adopted by the

United States. There is no mystic overlaw to which even the United States must bow. When a case is said to be governed by foreign law or by general Maritime Law, that is only a short way of saying that for this purpose the sovereign power takes up a rule suggested from without and makes it part of its own rule.

Thus, American courts of admiralty are not in any way hindered by foreign rules of law, and preserve their independence by adopting that which they find to be acceptable and rejecting rules that are not.

The admiralty courts have likewise declared their independence of Congress. The courts take the position that under the constitutional grant of authority they alone have the right to determine the rules and regulations to be applied to maritime causes, and that there is nothing in the Constitution which gives Congress the right to legislate within the admiralty and maritime area. The courts regard laws passed by Congress merely as suggestions which the court may adopt or reject as it sees fit. In most instances the court has accepted new laws passed by Congress, but in each case has made it clear that it was adopting a new rule at the suggestion of Congress rather than following a mandate of the legislature.

This all may be very confusing to the student, especially having in mind that in all other situations courts are bound by the statutes passed by the legislature. It must be said that this admiralty area is unique in American law; it is the only situation where a court can decide whether or not it will follow the dictates of the legislature (Congress). The same judges, *not* sitting in admiralty, must follow the laws of the United States as passed by Congress; they have no discretion as to whether they will or will not follow the statutes passed by Congress in any other area. In admiralty, however, the same judges may exercise wide discretion as to what rule they will accept and what rule they will not, be such a rule passed by Congress or a foreign legislature.

1401   Judiciary Act of 1789

Under the Constitution, Congress may establish inferior federal courts. The Constitution says that the judicial power of the United States shall be vested in one Supreme Court and in such inferior courts as Congress may establish. It also states that the judicial powers shall extend to all cases of admiralty and maritime jurisdiction. Therefore, when Congress establishes an inferior federal court the constitutional provision immediately vests such federal court with admiralty and maritime jurisdiction. The Judiciary Act of 1789 set up the federal district courts and fixed the limitations of their jurisdiction. With respect to admiralty the Act reads as follows:

And be it further enacted, that the district courts . . . shall have exclusive original cognizance of all civil causes of admiralty and maritime jurisdiction . . . within their respective districts as well as upon the high seas; saving to suitors, in all cases, the right of a common law remedy, where the common law is competent to give it . . . and the trial of issues of fact, in the district courts, in all causes, except civil causes of admiralty and maritime jurisdiction, shall be by jury.

The federal courts and the Supreme Court have accepted the "saving to suitors" clause, which affords a common-law remedy, as a suggestion from Congress. Therefore, it is possible for a litigant in an appropriate case to have a choice between common-law or admiralty jurisdiction.

1402 Subject matter of maritime jurisdiction

Maritime jurisdiction refers to all transactions having to do with navigation and commerce on water. The mere fact that the transaction has some relationship to the water does not necessarily mean that the transaction is within the maritime jurisdiction. It must also have a direct relationship to navigation and commerce on water. For example, a contract to build a ship is nonmaritime. The rights of the parties under the contract are determined by land law as well as the liability of the shipbuilder to employees engaged in executing the contract. The reason for this is that the ship may never be finished, in which case it would never become an instrument of commerce. Until the ship is actually used or capable of being used for commerce on water, transactions concerning it, be they contract or tort, are not within the maritime jurisdiction. On the other hand, a contract to repair a ship which has already been used for commerce on water is a maritime contract. This is true even though the work to be performed is done in drydock located on land.

Illustrative of the fine line of distinction between maritime and nonmaritime is an old rule that damage done by a ship to a land structure is nonmaritime, whereas damage done by a land structure to a ship is maritime. For example, admiralty courts can deal with damage to a ship caused by a derrick located on a pier. If the ship's derrick caused damage to the pier, the damage was considered nonmaritime and not within admiralty jurisdiction. This rule which stood for many years was finally changed by Congress in 1948 and the present statutory rule (46 USCA 740) is as follows:

The admiralty and maritime jurisdiction of the United States shall extend to and include all cases of damage or injury, to person or property, caused by a vessel on navigable water, notwithstanding that such damage or injury be done or consummated on land. In any such case, suit may be brought in *rem* or in *personam* according to the principles of law and rules of practice obtaining in cases where the injury or damage has been done and consummated on navigable water.

With respect to employees and the rights they may have against their respective employers, the rule is that employees have the advantage of applicable maritime law in the case of injury, if the contract of hire is maritime in nature in the sense that it has a direct relationship to navigation and commerce on water. On the other hand, if the employee's contract of hire does not relate to navigation and commerce on water, his rights as against his employer are governed by state workmen's compensation laws and he has no admiralty right whatsoever as against his employer, even though his injury may have been sustained on navigable water.

For example, if an adjuster was a passenger on a ferryboat crossing the river and he sustained personal injuries as a result of the sinking of the ferryboat, his right as against his employer would be governed entirely by the workmen's compensation law of the state in which he is employed, and against his employer he would have no admiralty rights whatsoever. However a deckhand, employed in the same ferryboat and injured in the same transaction, would have a maritime remedy as against his employer. In the case of the adjuster, his contract was nonmaritime in nature and therefore he had no admiralty rights against his employer. The deckhand was employed under a maritime contract of hire, and since his work was maritime in nature he had admiralty rights against his employer.

A ship that has been withdrawn from navigation and is not being used as an instrument of commerce on water ceases to be subject to admiralty and maritime jurisdiction. For example, following World War II the U.S. government withdrew a large number of vessels from navigation and later utilized these vessels for the storage of surplus grain. It was held that the liability of the United States arising of this operation could not be determined by maritime law. The use to which the vessel was put had no direct connection between navigation and commerce on water and therefore was nonmaritime in character. The rights and liabilities of any parties arising as a consequence of such use of a vessel could be determined only in a common-law court by the application of common-law rules.

With respect to contracts of employment, the mere fact that an accident or injury occurred on navigable water is not sufficient to bring the employment within maritime jurisdiction. There must be a direct and not a remote relationship between the work being done and the navigation and commerce on water. Thus, masters and members of the crew of a vessel, longshoremen employed to load or unload a vessel, and artisans employed to repair a vessel already in navigation are within admiralty jurisdiction. On the other hand, a person employed as a watchman or custodian of a vessel withdrawn from navigation, a person engaged in preparing a vessel for the winter after it has been withdrawn from navigation, or one employed to prepare a vessel for navigation after it had been withdrawn are all outside the scope of admiralty jurisdiction. The theory is that the employment is too remote from navigation and commerce on water to involve admiralty jurisdiction.

Another illustration of the fine line which is drawn between maritime and nonmaritime occupations is a case of a seaman who is employed on a dredge boat, which boat is engaged in cutting a channel across land. It was held that this employment was nonmaritime for the reason that it has no direct connection between navigation and commerce on water. To be true, the channel when completed would be used for navigation and commerce, but until it is completed it could not be so used, and therefore employment in building it is nonmaritime in character.

The Admiralty Extension Act (46 USCA 740), as noted above is especially applicable in the case of oil spills and gives the owners of property on land which may have been damaged by the oil a cause of action in admiralty against the offending vessel. In order to impose liability on the vessel or the vessel owner, the plaintiff must identify the polluting vessel, proof of negligence or proof of some unseaworthy condition. For example, in *Salaky* v. *Atlas Tank Corp.* (208 Fed. 2d. 2d 174), 44 claimants brought action for damages to small boats moored in a yacht basin by oil pumped out of the ships' bilges. A recovery by the claimants was reversed when they were unable to identify the exact polluter.

On the other hand, *In re New Jersey Barging Corp.* (168 Fed. Supp. 925), an oil spill occurred when the pumpman of the barge of heating oil fell asleep and allowed the oil to overflow while the barge was discharging at a pier. The oil spill spread 1/4 mile north and south of the pier, extending out about 75 feet from the shore. The properties of some 155 beach front owners were affected. Recovery was allowed based on the out-of-pocket expenses sustained by each, and an added sum for inconvenience, discomfort, and annoyance. In addition, where proof was offered, other sums were allowed for the costs of cleaning, repainting, and reseeding, and decreases in property values.

Recoveries have been allowed for damage to small boats (*United States* v. *Ladd*, 193 Fed. 2d 929); shore structures (*Portland Tug & Barge Co.* v. *United States*, 90 Fed. Supp. 593); cables (*All American Cables & Radio* v. *The Dieppe*, 93 Fed. Supp. 923); and oyster beds (*Carr* v. *United States*, 136 Fed. Supp. 527).

1403   Area of maritime jurisdiction

The traditional area of maritime jurisdiction limited its application to the high seas and territorial waters within the ebb and flow of the tides. Territorial waters are defined as those waters encompassed within an area of one marine league of the shoreline of the country, the measurement being made from low-water mark (except in the case of small harbors and roadsteads, in which case the measurement would be made from the headlands of such bodies of water). A marine league is roughly three geographical land miles. The high seas refers to all other public waters beginning at the limit of territorial waters.

The United States has applied admiralty jurisdiction to inland lakes and waterways. This jurisdiction was originally suggested by an act of Congress in 1845. It reads as follows:

Be it enacted . . . that the District Courts of the United States shall have, possess, and exercise the same jurisdiction in matters of contract and tort, arising in, upon, or concerning steamboats and other vessels of 20 tons burden and upwards enrolled and licensed for the coasting trade, and at the time employed in business of commerce and navigation between ports and places in different states and territories upon the lakes and navigable waters connecting said lakes, as is now possessed and exercised by said courts in cases of the like steamboats and other vessels employed in navigation and commerce upon the high seas, or tidewaters, within the admiralty and maritime jurisdiction of the United States; and in all suits brought in such courts in all such matters of contract or tort, the remedies, and the forms of process, and the modes of proceeding, shall be the same as are or may be used by such courts in cases of admiralty and maritime jurisdiction; and the maritime law of the United States, so far as the same is or may be applicable thereto, shall constitute a rule of decision in such suits, in the same manner, and to the same extent, and with the same equities, as it now does in cases of admiralty and maritime jurisdiction; saving, however, to the parties the right of trial by jury of all facts put in issue in such suits where either shall require it; and saving also to the parties the right to a concurrent remedy at the common law, where it is competent to give it, and any concurrent remedy which may be given by the state laws, where such steamer or other vessel is employed in such business of commerce and navigation.

This means that federal admiralty jurisdiction will apply to any body of water which is used or capable of being used for navigation and commerce between different states or from one state to the open sea. Federal jurisdiction will not apply to any lake or other waterway entirely confined to one state, and this would be true irrespective of the size of the lake. To qualify for federal jurisdiction, the waterway must be a connecting link between ports of one state and those of another, or the ports of one state and the open sea.

It should also be noted that federal admiralty jurisdiction operates concurrently with common-law jurisdiction in these inland waterways, where the common law is competent to afford a remedy.

1404   General maritime law

The sources of maritime law are many and diverse. Some of the rules applicable today had their origins prior to the birth of Christ; some are unwritten and derive their validity from repetition; others came into existence as a result of codifications by various seafaring nations. Among the written sources of maritime law are the laws of Oléron, of Wisbuy, of the Hanse towns, and the marine ordinances of Louis XIV. The sum total of all of these rules, written and unwritten, is referred to as the general maritime law.

1405   Laws of Oléron

These laws were originally published at Oléron in Guienne in 1266. They are said to have been derived from ancient rules under the Rhodian law. They consist of 47 sections referring to commerce on water. With respect to the rights of seamen to wages, transportation, maintenance, and cure, Article VII reads as follows:

If it happens that sickness seizes on any one of the mariners, while in the service of the ship, the master ought to set him ashore, to provide lodgings and candlelight for him, and also to share him one of the ship-boys or hire a woman to attend him, and likewise to afford him such diet as is usual in the ship; that is to say, so much as he had on shipboard in his health, and nothing more, unless it pleased the master to allow it him; and if he will have better diet, the master shall not be bound to provide it for him, unless it be at the mariner's own cost and charges; and if the vessel be ready for her departure, she ought not to stay for the sick party—but if he recovers, he ought to have his full wages, deducting only such charges as the master has set for him. And if he dies, his wife or next of kin shall have it.

The intention of this article is to provide a means of protection for seamen who are taken ill during the course of the voyage. It should be noted that the only qualification for the imposition of this rule is that the seaman must fall sick while in the service of the ship. There is no requirement that there be any causal connection between the work of the seaman and the illness. The responsibility thus imposed upon the master is qualified only by Article VI, which excludes injuries or illnesses which are acquired because of the seamen's own misconduct. This article reads as follows:

If any of the mariners hired by the master of any vessel go out of the ship without his leave, and get themselves drunk, and thereby there happens contempt on their master, debates, or fighting or quarreling among themselves, whereby same happen to be wounded, in this case the master shall not be obliged to get them cured, or in anything to provide for them but may turn them and their accomplices out of the ship; and if they make words of it, they are bound to pay the master besides; but, if by the master's orders or command, any of the ship's company be in the service of the ship, and thereby happen to be wounded or otherwise hurt, in that case they shall be cured and provided for at the cost and charges of such ship.

As this section indicates, participants in a mutiny or general disobedience of orders are not entitled to maintenance and cure, whereas those of the crew who are injured in attempting to supress a mutiny or to ensure the obedience of orders are entitled to maintenance and cure.

1406　Wages, transportation, maintenance, and cure

Our admiralty courts have adopted the laws of Oléron insofar as they relate to seamen's right to wages, transportation, maintenance, and cure where the seaman falls sick in the service of the ship. These are rights which are contractual in the sense that they accrue to the seaman as a result of his contract of hire and are enforced against the ship in a contract action. They have no relationship whatsoever to any other rights which the seaman may have against the vessel or its owner arising from the unseaworthiness of the vessel or the negligence of the owner.

Wages refers to unearned wages to the end of the voyage, which are payable where the seaman falls sick or is injured in the service of the ship and is physically incapable of performing his usual duties. If he is found fit for duty before the voyage ends, then the liability for the payment of unearned wages ends as of that time. If, however, the illness continues beyond the end of the voyage, the liability of the vessel for the payment of unearned wages ends when the voyage terminates.

Transportation includes transportation back to the point of origin or to the end of the voyage, either in the ship to which the seaman is attached or another ship of comparable size and accommodations.

Maintenance includes food and quarters to the end of the voyage or to the point of origin either in the same ship or in a ship offering the same or similar accommodations, plus payments to cover maintenance during the period medical treatment might be required beyond the end of the voyage. The amount payable for maintenance and the period for which the obligation will continue can be modified or amended by contract. Usually, the terms and conditions are embodied within the union contracts. At the present time the rate for oceangoing vessels requires the payment of $12 per day for maintenance, such payments to continue while the seaman is under outpatient treatment at a marine hospital maintained by the U.S. Public Health Service, and until he is either cured or found by the doctors to have reached his maximum medical improvement. Where there is no agreement as to the value of maintenance the actual expenditures for board and lodging may be asserted in order to establish the value of the seaman's claim in this respect.

Cure actually means medical care—obviously, a complete cure cannot be accomplished in all cases. The term includes medical attention and other like services which extend beyond the end of the voyage and are required to either cure the condition or bring it to a point where it is pronounced permanent and incurable.

The medical treatment rendered in a marine hospital is provided by the U.S. government and the shipping companies are not required to make any payments in connection therewith. This is a form of subsidy given to shipping companies. The seaman, however, is not limited to treatment in a marine hospital and, after discharge, may seek the services of a private physician should the nature of his illness or injury so require. In the latter case, the shipping company would be liable to the treating physician for the value of his services.

It should be noted that where the seaman is a patient in the marine hospital his maintenance is provided for. Under those circumstances, in the absence of an agreement to the contrary, the vessel would not be required to pay for maintenance during the period of the seaman's confinement in the hospital. However, as soon as the seaman is discharged and becomes an outpatient, he is entitled to receive payment for maintenance.

As in the laws of Oléron, the only bar to a claim for maintenance and cure would come into existence if the seaman's illness or injury was due to his own misconduct or to his willful concealment of a known physical disability. His misconduct might consist of wrongful exposure to disease, injuries received as a consequence of a violation of orders, failure to obey orders, or from injuries received while participating in a mutiny. A seaman who is suffering from a disease prior to his contract of hire is bound to reveal the extent of his illness to the ship's owner. He impliedly warrants his own physical fitness to perform the duties ordinarily required of a seaman. If he is suffering from a known physical disease which he fails to disclose, and he later is taken ill as a consequence of this same disease, there is no liability on the part of the vessel for the payment of wages, transportation, maintenance and cure.

In *Writer* v. *The Richmond* (30 Fed. Cas. 718), the plaintiff insisted he was an able-bodied seaman, and shipped as such. On the voyage he died from a preexisting pulmonary disease which he had concealed from his employer. The court held that the man was "incompetent to perform the voyage for which he had shipped as an able-bodied seaman and it was a fraud on his part to have represented himself as such." The court held that merchants were not to be thus imposed upon by mariners being placed on board their vessels to die and thus give a foundation to claims. The court dismissed the claim.

Other cases seem to enunciate the rule that the seaman can be said to warrant his own fitness and must disclose material medical facts which might affect his ability to work. In *Lindquist* v. *Dilkes* (127 Fed. 2d 21), the court applied the analogy of representations used in accident and health cases, holding that the seaman's concealment of a material medical fact known to him would be sufficient cause to deny the right to maintenance and cure.

In *The Ben Flint* (3 Fed. Cas. 183), the court defines the rights of seamen in respect to maintenance and cure as follows:

A seaman who has received an injury or contracted a disease while in the service of the ship, is entitled to be cured or cared for at the expense of the ship. This right is an ingredient in the compensation to be paid to the seaman under the contract of shipment; and is enforced by award of additional wages.

This general rule is also applicable to seamen employed on the lakes and navigable rivers within the United States. The claim of a seaman to be cured at the expense of the ship is not forfeited because the hurt or sickness may have been incurred through his negligence unless something more than mere carelessness, consistent with good faith in the prompt discharge of duties, can be shown. To forfeit the claim, the disability of the seaman must be owing to vicious or unjustifiable conduct, such as gross negligence, operating in the nature of a fraud upon the owners, or a willful disobedience to orders, or persistent neglect of duty.

Where the period during which the shipowner is liable for maintenance and cure is known, in that the liability has terminated, or where the future period of maintenance and cure can be definitely ascertained, settlement can be made on a lump-sum basis either by a payment or by a judgment of the court. Either will effectively terminate the claim. Difficulty arises in cases where the right to maintenance and cure will continue for an indefinite period into the future, or for life. Attempts have been made to dispose of claims of this nature by means of the payment of a lump sum. In *Calmar S.S. Corp.* v. *Taylor* (303 U.S. 525), the court held that an award of a lump sum in anticipation of the continuing need for maintenance and cure for life or for an indefinite period was without support in judicial decisions.

The amount and character of medical care which will be required in the case of an affliction is well defined, but the time it will be required cannot be measured by reference to mortality tables or any other device with a reasonable degree of certainty. Moreover, courts recognize that in a marine hospital the seaman may be treated without expense, and an agreement to limit recovery to the expense of maintenance and cure on a lump-sum basis cannot be made by the seaman. Furthermore, the duty imposed, to safeguard the seaman from the danger of illness, and to protect him in case of illness from the consequences of his own improvidence, would hardly be performed by the payment of a lump sum to cover the cost of medical attention and maintenance during life. The seaman's recovery must, therefore, be measured in each case by the reasonable cost of that maintenance and cure to which he is entitled at the time of trial, including, in the discretion of the court, such an amount as may be needful in the immediate future for maintenance and cure of proper kind and quality and for a period which can be definitely ascertained. If the period cannot be ascertained, the liability of the shipowner is a continuing one, which requires that payments be made as they accrue. This liability cannot be extinguished by a payment of a lump sum.

As to the duration of maintenance and cure, the courts have refused to define with any degree of exactness the extent to which the liability of the owner of the vessel would attach. The courts took the position that each case presented a different problem and that the owner's liability for maintenance and cure following the end of the voyage should continue for a reasonable length of time. What was reasonable in one case might be unreasonable in another, and therefore the courts preferred to decide each case on its own merits.

This situation continued until 1939. At the general conference of The International Labor Organization at Geneva, a draft convention was submitted. This was ratified by the Senate and proclaimed by the President as effective for the United States on October 29, 1939 (54 Stat. 1693). The rule under Article 4, paragraph 1, provides:

The ship owner shall be liable to defray the expense of medical care and maintenance until the sick or injured person has been cured or until the sickness or incapacity has been declared of a permanent character.

Most of the union contracts at the present time contain provisions which are exactly the same as this rule. However, even in the absence of any contract whatsoever, the limitation is available to the shipowner.

Questions have been raised as to the liability of the shipowner for maintenance where the seaman is employed on a ferry boat or a tug, and whose trips are short enabling him to sleep ashore at home. In each case the courts have held that he is entitled to maintenance just as any other seaman. [See *Hudspeth* v. *Atlantic Gulf Stevedores, Inc.*, 266 Fed. Supp. 937.]

In *Weiss* v. *Central Railroad Company of New Jersey* (235 Fed. 2d 309), the plaintiff was employed as a ferry deckhand. During his period of employment, plaintiff slept at home and ate his meals there except for lunch. The court held that the plaintiff was a seaman entitled to the traditional rights to maintenance and cure. The court said:

But even if it be conceded that the plaintiff is a seaman for some purposes, it may still be argued that the right to maintenance and cure should be denied him because he did not lead the life traditionally peculiar to seamen, involving surrender of personal rights and liberties for a lengthy overseas voyage, exposure to peril, changes of climate, exhausting labor and the danger (were it not for maintenance and cure) of being forced to rely upon his own meager resources while sick and starving in a foreign port. We know of no authority, however, for holding that a seaman is not entitled to the traditional privileges of his status merely because his voyages are short, because he sleeps ashore, or for other reasons his lot is more pleasant than most of his brethren.

Other cases involving the same question in which the court found the shipowner liable for maintenance and cure include: *Creppel* v. *J. W. Banta Towing, Inc.* (202 Fed. Supp. 508) (captain of a tug who lived ashore); and *Ledet* v. *U.S. Oil of Louisiana, Inc.* (237 Fed. Supp. 183) (roughneck employed on a drilling barge used in the exploration and development of offshore oil fields).

1407 Marine hospitals

The U.S. government has relieved the shipowner from some of his liability for medical attention by creating the Marine Hospital Service. This service provides for hospital treatment for American seamen (and some foreign flag seamen) under certain circumstances. It is in the form of a subsidy to assist and encourage shipping in the United States, and was established by the same statute that established the U.S. Public Health Service. The sections involving seamen are found in Title 42, USCA, and are as follows:

Section 249. MEDICAL CARE AND TREATMENT OF SEAMEN AND CERTAIN OTHER PERSONS . . .

A. . . . The following persons shall be entitled in accordance with regulations to medical, surgical, and dental treatment and hospitalization without charge at hospitals and other stations of service.

1. Seamen employed on vessels of the United States, registered, enrolled and licensed under the Maritime Laws thereof, other than canal boats engaged in coasting trade.

2. Seamen employed on United States or foreign flag vessels as employees of the United States through the War Shipping Administration.

3. Seamen, not enlisted or commissioned in the military or naval establishment, who are employed on state school ships or vessels of the United States Government of more than five tons burden.

B. . . . When suitable accommodations are available, seamen on foreign flag vessels may be given medical, surgical, and dental treatment and hospitalization on application of the master, owner, or agent of the vessel at hospitals and other stations of the service at rates fixed by regulations. All expenses connected with such treatment, including burial, in the event of death, shall be paid by such master, owner, or agent. No such vessels shall be granted clearance until such expenses are paid or their payment appropriately guaranteed to the Collector of Customs.

The statute also provides (Section 251) that the Surgeon General may provide for making medical examinations of seamen for purposes of qualifying for certificates of service.

1408   Seamen defined

A seaman has been defined generally as a mariner or sailor whose occupation is to assist in the management and navigation or operation of ships at sea. The term was originally confined to persons who could "hand, reef, and steer." Changing conditions have enlarged the legal definition of the term so that now the word is not necessarily confined to those whose duties are solely in connection with the navigation of the vessel. It includes various and sundry other persons employed on or about the ship, even though these persons have no duties with respect to its navigation.

The general rule is that the term "seaman" includes all persons employed aboard the vessel for the purpose of providing or assisting in providing the service the ship ordinarily gives. For example, on a large oceangoing passenger vessel, a barber, tailor, cosmetician, storekeeper, laundress, musician, bartender, porter, telephone operator, and clerk would all be considered as seamen even though their duties have no relationship whatsoever to the navigation of the vessel. As seamen, these employees would be entitled to all of the rights of that class of employees, including the right to wages, transportation, maintenance, and cure. Conversely, employment in any of the categories mentioned aboard a tugboat or a barge would not make the individual a seaman for the reason that such vessels do not ordinarily provide service for passengers.

1409   Warranty of seaworthiness

The ship owes a warranty of seaworthiness to those working on board. This means that the warranty extends to seamen and all who do the work of seamen; longshoremen, stevedores, or ship repairers. This warranty does not extend to any others, such as passengers, visitors, or others legally on board the vessel.

It is an implied warranty arising out of the relationship between the ship and the person working thereon. The guarantee impliedly warrants not only the condition of the structure of the ship and its capacity to withstand the ordinary perils of the sea, it means also that it is properly loaded and the cargo is properly stowed; that is is provided with a competent master, a sufficient number of competent officers and seamen, and with the requisite appurtenances and equipment, such as ballast, cables, anchors, cordage, sails, food, water, fuel, lights, and other necessary or proper stores and implements for the voyage.

Should there be a breach of this warranty which results in personal injury to the seaman or the person doing the work of the seaman, there arises a cause of action for damages against the ship. This is a personal cause of action, arising out of a quasi-contractual relationship between the seamen or the person doing the work of the seaman and the vessel. The warranty of seaworthiness is considered part of the general maritime law of the United States.

The breach of warranty takes place in a situation where the seaman's injuries are due to the fact that the master is incompetent, the crew insufficient, or the appurtenances of the ship not in proper repair. If any of these situations occur and the seaman is injured because of it, there is a breach of warranty which would give rise to a cause of action against the vessel. It should be noted that the cause of action is not based on the negligence of the owner or the master of the vessel but on a showing that an unseaworthy condition was the cause of the injuries. It is, as noted, a quasi-contractual cause of action, and the contributory negligence of the seaman if any, is not a defense.

The warranty of seaworthiness is owed only when the vessel is in navigation. If the vessel has been withdrawn from navigation or stored for the winter, theoretically it is no longer an instrument of commerce on water, and therefore it is not subject to maritime law. This being so, with respect to such a vessel, there is no warranty of seaworthiness.

1410   Doctrine of transitory unseaworthiness

Under the warranty of seaworthiness, the vessel impliedly warrants that it is reasonably fit for a voyage at sea and its appurtenances as well as its crew are proper. Any failure to meet these requirements result in a breach of the warranty of seaworthiness. However, there are situations where the vessel might be considered temporarily unsafe because of conditions which are not foreseeable, which are unknown to the owner or master and which the owner or his agents could not reasonably correct.

For example, in *The Cookingham* v. *U.S.A.* (220 Fed. 2d 143), the injury was sustained by a fall caused by slipping on a blob of jello. The court held that the vessel owner or the master could not be charged with a breach of the warranty of seaworthiness and that the case rested solely on the required proof of the owner's negligence. Since the owner had no opportunity to know of the alleged unsafe condition and since he was not afforded an opportunity to correct it, the court held that there was no liability as a matter of law. In other cases, even those going to the U.S. Supreme Court, the holding has been that the question of seaworthiness was one of fact for the jury and not a question of law for the court. The imposition of this type of doctrine is almost entirely foreign to the line of cases which preceded it, and in view of the decision of the Supreme Court in *Mitchell* v. *Trawler Racer* (265 Fed. 2d 426), where a breach of warranty under exactly the same circumstances was held to be actionable, it would seem that the doctrine of transitory unseaworthiness is being abandoned and the vessel is being held strictly accountable for any breach of warranty of seaworthiness irrespective of whether the owner or master knew about the condition or not.

1411   The Jones Act

The Merchant Marine Act of 1920, generally referred to as the Jones Act, merely applied the same system and the same type of remedy granted to railroad employees (See paragraph 1304, Federal Employers Liability Act, above) to seamen. It also provides for the same type of remedy by the personal representative of the seaman should death ensue. The statute is found in 46 USCA 688 and provides as follows:

Any seaman who shall suffer personal injury in the course of his employment may, at his election, maintain an action for damages at law with the right of trial by jury, and in such action all statutes of the United States modifying or extending the common law right or remedy in cases of personal injury to railway employees shall apply; and in case of the death of any seaman as a result of any such personal injury, the personal representative of such seaman may maintain an action for damages at law with the right of trial by jury, and in such action all statutes of the United States conferring or regulating a right of action for death in the case of railway employees, shall be applicable. Jurisdiction in such actions shall be under the court of the district in which the defendant employer resides or in which his principal office is located.

This act gives the seaman an added remedy for personal injury. He still has his maritime law causes of action based on the breach of warranty of seaworthiness. The Jones Act provides for an action against the vessel owner in cases of negligence and it further provides that the seaman's contributory negligence is not a complete defense, but may be taken into account by the jury in reducing the amount of recovery. The remedies under the maritime law for unseaworthiness and those provided by the Jones Act are not mutually exclusive, in the sense that a seaman can bring an action wherein two counts are alleged: one, for the breach of the warranty of seaworthiness and, two, for the negligence of the vessel owner under the Jones Act. (In the case of death there would be no allowable recovery under maritime law and the seaman's action would be limited to the Jones Act, or, if it occurred on the high seas, under the Death on the High Seas by Wrongful Act statute.)

Unlike the warranty of seaworthiness, which the vessel makes to all persons employed on the vessel either as seamen or doing the work of seamen, the Jones Act specifically refers to seamen. This means that longshoremen or other maritime workers on the vessel do not come within the scope of the act; if the employee does not qualify as a seaman, he is not entitled to the benefits of the Jones Act.

The Jones Act applies to American seamen on American ships. Normally, it does not apply to foreign seamen employed on foreign flag vessels irrespective of whether the accident occurs within the territorial waters of the United States or not. The question then arises as to what happens when American-owned vessels have moved into foreign flag operations.

In *Bartholomew* v. *Universe* [263 Fed. 2d 437), a West Indian seaman, a resident of the United States who signed on a Liberian ship for a foreign voyage beginning at Baltimore and ending in New York, was injured within the territorial waters of the United States. The ship was owned and operated by a Liberian corporation and was flying the Liberian flag. However, the Liberian corporation was owned by a Panamanian corporation which, in turn, was owned by an American corporation. The circuit court of appeals held that the plaintiff was entitled to invoke the Jones Act against his employer on the theory that there was sufficient contact between the vessel, its ownership, the place of accident, and the place of the residence of the plaintiff to permit the application of American law to the case. The court used the term "substantial" contact, which it defines as being something between minimal and preponderant contacts.

In cases where the tort occurs in foreign waters, or the seaman involved is either a citizen or resident of the United States on a ship flying the American flag and with American ownership, the Jones Act would be applied since the law of the flag creates the fiction that a vessel flying an American flag is part of the United States wherever it is in operation.

1412 Death on the high seas by wrongful act

This act of Congress, as its name implies refers only to deaths which occur outside the territorial waters of the United States. As we have seen, territorial waters are defined as those waters within one marine league seaward from low-water mark. One marine league would be the equivalent of 3 land miles, so that the application of this statute would begin only when the vessel is beyond what is usually referred to as the 3-mile limit. It is found in 46 USCA 761–768. In defining the right of action, where and by whom brought, the act under Section 761 provides as follows:

Whenever the death of a person shall be caused by wrongful act, neglect, or default occurring on the high seas beyond a marine league from the shore of any State or the District of Columbia, or the Territories or Dependencies of the United States, the personal representative of the decedent may maintain a suit for damages in the District Courts of the United States, in admiralty, for the exclusive benefit of the decedent's wife, husband, parent, child, or dependent relatives against the vessel, person or corporation which would have been liable if death had not ensued.

Section 762 refers to the amount and apportionment of recovery, and states that the recovery shall be a fair and just compensation for the pecuniary loss sustained by the persons for whose benefit the action is brought. Section 763 sets forth the statute of limitations which is two years from the date of the wrongful act, neglect, or default unless during that period there has not been reasonable opportunity for securing jurisdiction of the vessel, person, or corporation sought to be charged, but after the expiration of such period of two years, the right of action given shall not be deemed to have lapsed until 90 days after reasonable opportunity to secure jurisdiction has been offered. Section 764 refers to the rights of action given by the laws of foreign countries, and section 765 refers to the death of a plaintiff in a pending action, indicating that such action shall not abate and may proceed in accordance with the provisions of the act.

Section 766 refers to contributory negligence and provides that suits under this act shall not fail because of the contributory negligence of the deceased, but that the court may take into consideration the degree of negligence attributable to the decedent and reduce recovery accordingly.

Section 767 refers to exceptions from the operation of the act and sets forth that the provisions of any state statute giving or regulating rights of action or remedies for death shall not be affected by the act. Nor shall the act apply to the Great Lakes or any waters within the territorial limits of any state or to any navigable waters in the Panama Canal Zone.

It should be noted from the language of the statute that this refers to any persons who sustains death on the high seas. This could include a crew member or seaman as well as a passenger. The act could conceivably apply to persons who are unlawfully on shipboard as well.

1413   Application of wrongful death statutes

In the case of a cause of action for wrongful death arising out of an event which occurs on a vessel, the applicable law will be determined by the status of the deceased with relation to the vessel as well as by whether the event took place in territorial waters or on the high seas.

As to seamen, if the wrongful death occurs within territorial waters there is only one cause of action available under the Jones Act. When a wrongful death occurs outside of the 3-mile limit, the deceased seaman's personal representative may elect whether he will bring action under the Jones Act or under the Death on the High Seas Act. As to seamen, these two acts of Congress overlap when it comes to a wrongful death which occurs outside of territorial waters. This does not mean that the personal representative of the deceased seaman can bring two separate actions, one under the Jones Act and one under the Death on the High Seas Act, and effect a double recovery. The personal representative is required to elect as to which of these two acts he will pursue.

Both acts have identical provisions, with one exception. The Death on the High Seas by Wrongful Act provision permits recovery on a pecuniary loss basis for the exclusive benefit of the decedent's wife, husband, parent, child, or the dependent relatives. Under the Jones Act, the action is by the personal representative and such recovery is solely for the benefit of the heirs at law. The classes of persons for whose benefit a wrongful death action may be brought under the High Seas Act is larger than the persons for whose benefit an action for wrongful death can be brought under the Jones Act.

For example, if the deceased seaman was survived by a wife and a child, recovery under the Jones Act would be for the sole benefit of the wife and child and to the exclusion of a parent or surviving dependent relatives. If the action were brought under the High Seas Act, the parent and dependent relatives would participate in the recovery, in addition to the wife and child. Therefore, as to deaths which occur outside territorial waters, we can expect that the action will be brought under one statute or the other, depending upon which one provides the greater benefits for the larger number of beneficiaries.

As to passengers, if the wrongful death occurs within territorial waters, the action for wrongful death can be brought only under the state wrongful death statute. As to wrongful deaths which occur outside of territorial waters, the Death on the High Seas Act would apply.

As to wrongful deaths involving longshoremen, we meet a rather curious situation. Longshoremen belong to that class of persons who are engaged in work traditionally done by seamen. As such they are entitled to the warranty of seaworthiness under the general maritime law. However, under general maritime law there is no recovery for death. The state wrongful death statutes provide for a remedy in cases where the wrongful death occurs as a consequence of the wrongful act, neglect, or default of another. Actions for wrongful deaths of longshoremen have been brought under state wrongful death statutes based on a claim of unseaworthiness. The courts which have considered this problem have decided that the breach of the warranty of unseaworthiness is a "wrongful act, neglect or default" and under those circumstances recoveries have been allowed. In admiralty, however, the longshoremen would not have a cause of action for wrongful death under the general maritime law. Should the longshoreman be killed outside of the 3-mile limit, the cause of action could then be brought under the Death on the High Seas Act.

1414   Responsibility to passengers for personal injuries

The vessel owner owes a high degree of care for the safety of a passenger. He is not, however, an insurer of the passenger's safety and is not liable solely because the passenger is injured. If the vessel owner has exercised a high degree of care, he has met the duty imposed upon him. On the other hand, to actions of this nature the maritime law traditionally applies the rule of comparative negligence. This means that contributory negligence will not defeat recovery but may be taken into account in order to reduce the amount of recovery.

In *Kermaiec* v. *Companie Générale Transatlantique* (79 Sup. Ct. 406), the Supreme Court held that a vessel owner owed a duty of reasonable care to all those on board for purposes not inimical to his legitimate interest. It held that a crew member's guest who is injured by a fall on a vessel stairway was entitled to recovery because of a defective canvas runner which had been tacked on to the companionway. The Supreme Court, in effect, held that the governing law was not the land law of the state of New York, where the injury occurred, but, since the plaintiff was injured aboard a ship in navigable waters, the maritime law. It held that contributory negligence was not a complete bar to recovery. It held that the maritime law imposes upon the shipowner a standard of care in the case of a crew member's guest higher than the duty owing to a licensee under the New York state law pertaining to land accidents.

1415   Maintenance and cure in actions for damages

The right to maintenance and cure is a contractual right which arises when the individual signs articles as a seaman. It is not influenced by the unseaworthiness of the ship or the negligence of the owner, but is an absolute right to which the seaman is entitled under his contract of employment, irrespective of any causes of action which may accrue to him under the general maritime law or the Jones Act. While there is no real clear-cut decisions on the point, the cases inferentially appear to hold that the right to maintenance and cure in a proper case would extend beyond the seaman's recovery of damages.

In *McCarthy* v. *American Eastern Corp.* (175 Fed. 2d 727), the court observed that when an injured seaman recovers full damages in an action for indemnity based on unseaworthiness and negligence in which he has claimed a loss of wages, including the value of board and lodging which form a part thereof, and medical expense, if any, he has thereby recovered maintenance and cure to which he is entitled up to the time of trial at least. But whether the recovery of full damages in an indemnity action could be regarded as involving a recovery of maintenance and cure for a period subsequent to the trial is a different question. In the *Calmar* case, previously cited, the Supreme Court held that the award of a lump sum in anticipation of the continuing need for maintenance and cure for life or for an indefinite future period is without support in law and erroneous. Therefore, a recovery of damages, which damages included as an item thereof an amount equivalent to the value of maintenance and cure for the rest of the plaintiff's life, would not relieve the shipowner of his obligation to provide maintenance and cure.

In a lower court decision, *John A. Roebling's Sons* v. *Erickson* (261 Fed. 986), the court held that a seaman in an action at law to recover damages for personal injury cannot be required to elect between recovery for maintenance, cure, and wages, to the end of the voyage to which he is entitled in any event, and a claim for indemnity. This would be true, irrespective of the fact that one of the elements of damage in his claim for indemnity would include loss of wages, medical expenses, and maintenance.

In the case where the seaman is injured ashore through the negligence of a third party, the owner is not relieved of his liability for maintenance and cure. In *Gomes* v. *Eastern Gas & Fuel Associates* [127 Fed. Supp. 435 (Massachusetts)], the court held that a seaman does not release the shipowner from responsibility in contract for maintenance and cure where the seaman recovers damages from an automobile driver whose negligence caused his injury while on his way back to the ship from shore leave. The court held that the shipowner is entitled only to a setoff of any part of the amount so received which could be considered as reimbursement for disability and medical expense against his responsibility to provide maintenance and cure.

1416   Seamen as wards of the admiralty

In order to fully understand the wardship theory, we must reexamine the history of maritime law. Seafaring nations derived their prosperity and economic status from trading and commerce on the water, and seamen naturally played an essential role in this system. Therefore, it became the policy of the maritime law to make seamen a privileged class of persons and to adopt rules for their protection. As we have seen, the seaman is entitled to maintenance and cure where he falls sick in the service of the ship. This is a form of liability without fault and its practical objectives are to restore the seaman to physical capacity for further work and in addition provide some inducement to those who would be available to enter such an occupation. This is a form of workmen's compensation, but the concept came into existence many centuries before compensation acts, as we know them today, were conceived. In addition, the seaman was given a cause of action against the vessel if his injury was caused by its unseaworthiness. This right has been extended by the Jones Act to include a cause of action based upon negligence and provides for a recovery not only in the case of personal injury but in the case of wrongful death as well.

The courts then added another element to the protection afforded seamen by announcing them to be "wards of the admiralty." This means that the court will protect the seaman to the same extent it protects infants, insane persons, idiots, and habitual drunkards, since in each of these classes the individual is under some disability and cannot properly act for himself. Our courts have adopted this rule. It was first enunciated by Justice Story in the case of *Harden* v. *Gordon* [11 Fed. Cas. 480, Case no 6,047 (1823)], in the following language:

They are emphatically wards of the Admiralty, and though not technically incapable of entering into a valid contract, they are treated in the same manner, as courts of equity are accustomed to treat young heirs, dealing with their expectancies, wards with their guardians and *cestui que* trusts with their trustees. . . . If there is any undue inequality in the terms, any disproportion in the bargain, any sacrifices on one side which are not compensated by extraordinary benefits on the other, the judicial interpretation of the transaction is that the bargain is unjust and unreasonable, that advantage has been taken of the situation of the weaker party and that *pro tanto* the bargain ought to be set aside as inequitable. . . . On every occasion, the court expects to be satisfied that the compensation for every material alteration is entirely adequate to the diminution of the right or privilege on the part of the seaman.

Ordinarily one who attacks the validity of a written release has the burden of sustaining his allegations by clear, precise, and credible evidence. A seaman in admiralty who attacks a release has no such burden. On the contrary, the burden of proof is the obligation of the party who seeks to sustain the release. A release executed by a seaman is subject to close scrutiny, and the one who claims that the seaman has signed away his rights to what in law is due him has the burden of sustaining the release as fairly made and fully comprehended by the seaman [*Garrett* v. *Moore-McCormick Co.*, 317 U.S. 239].

In *United States* v. *Johnson* (160 Fed. 2d 789), the seaman was treated by the U.S. Public Health Service and, upon his discharge, he settled his case with the shipowner. He made this settlement in reliance upon statements concerning his condition made to him by the U.S. Public Health Service that he had fully recovered. It developed that he had not fully recovered and the effects of his injury lasted much longer than was anticipated. The court invalidated the release because Johnson had been misled by the medical advice he received from the Public Health Service. It should be noted here that the medical statements on which the seaman relied were not made by the shipowner, nor was it claimed that the seaman was fraudulently induced to enter into the contract of release. In any event, the court held that advantage had been taken of the weaker party and that the release should be set aside and disregarded.

In *Hume* v. *Moore-McCormick Co.* (121 Fed. 2d 336), a release was set aside as being not conclusive where the seaman, who had been injured because of the shipowner's negligence, acting without a lawyer or other competent independent adviser, signed a release of all rights which expressly included injuries, illnesses, rights, and claims not mentioned or known to the seaman, as against the seaman's later recovery for tuberculosis not known to the seaman at the time executing the release.

Therefore, in all cases where the seaman is not represented by counsel, the court will look at two elements of the contract of release. These are whether or not the amount paid for the release is fair and equitable, and, second, whether or not the seaman had a full comprehension of all of the facts so as to understand that he was closing out his claim. The intelligence or education of the seaman are not considered; it makes no difference if the seaman has an engineering degree from a university—the rule is applied to him in all its vigor, just as it is to a seaman who cannot read or write.

On the other hand, where a seaman who signed a written release of all present and future claims for damages arising out of an accident on shipboard solely on the advice of his doctor, his lawyer cannot subsequently have the release set aside on the grounds of a mistake in his understanding of the nature of the release or his understanding of the nature and extent of injury.

Where the claimant is represented by counsel, there is no objection to the use of the ordinary printed general release. However, where settlement is made directly with the seaman, and he is not represented, the usual practice is to either take a detailed release or to prepare a special release for use in connection with the particular case. The reason for this is to have the release fully set forth all of the facts so that should there be a later claim by the seaman that he did not understand the nature of the instrument, the instrument will speak for itself in showing that all of the elements were called to his attention in simple and understandable language.

1417   Maritime law and the workmen's compensation acts

Enactment of workmen's compensation acts by the various states have created a problem of conflict of laws in their relationship with maritime law. The compensation laws abolished the common-law concept of negligence with relation to contracts of employment and substituted an obligation on the part of the employer to make compensation payments in every case where the accident arose out of and in the course of employment. The right to compensation thus became an element of the contract of employment. The questions immediately arose as to just what effect such laws would have with respect to persons within the jurisdiction of the maritime law. It became a most perplexing question, especially where no negligence was involved, because no recovery could be had under maritime law, whereas the compensation act provided for a liability without fault. Therefore, while the issue turned on the question of jurisdiction in many of these cases, as a practical matter the choice was one which involved a recovery of compensation or no recovery at all.

In order to fully understand the jurisdictional problem thus created, it is necessary to trace the history of the decisions, and the legislation which followed, down to the latest pronouncements of the Supreme Court, which are enunciative of the law as it exists today. In considering the question, we must divide persons injured in the maritime area into three classes:

1. Those whose contract of hire is maritime and who perform only maritime duties.
2. Those whose employment has no relationship whatsoever to any maritime activities but are injured in a maritime area.
3. Those whose contract of employment is partly maritime and partly non-maritime.

The first group includes seamen, masters, and members of the crews of vessels. These employees are traditionally within admiralty jurisdiction, and therefore since cases of admiralty and maritime jurisdiction have already been granted under the Constitution to the federal courts, it would be impossible for any state to legislate in this particular area. Therefore, state workmen's compensation acts are not applicable to seamen, irrespective of where the contract of hire was made.

This is also true where the accident occurs on land. In the following cases, seamen injured on shore in the service of the ship were entitled to recover under the Jones Act or the general maritime law, and the compensation law of the state had no applicaton: *O'Donnell* v. *Great Lakes Dredge & Dock Co.* (318 U.S. 36), *Occidental Indemnity Co.* v. *I.A.C.* (149 Pac. 2d 841), and *Marceau* v. *Great Lakes Transit* (146 Fed. 2d 4016).

The death of an employee of a river boat, who was killed when struck by a train while on land in the performance of instructions of his employer, was held not entitled to compensation under the state workmen's compensation law, the exclusive remedy being under the Jones Act [*Rudolph* v. *Industrial Marine Service*, 210 S.W. 2d 30 (Tennessee)].

As to employees whose contract of employment is not maritime and whose occupations bear no relationship to navigation and commerce on water, they are within the scope of the state workmen's compensation act even though the accident may occur on navigable water. The maritime law has no jurisdiction since the employment is nonmaritime. On the other hand, a maritime worker, not a member of the crew, who is injured on land[1] comes within the scope of the state compensation law.

A more difficult question arises when these maritime workers are injured while on navigable waters. In *Southern Pacific Co.* v. *Jensen* (244 U.S. 205), a claim was made under the New York Workmen's Compensation Act for the death of a longshoreman which occurred on a vessel then lying in navigable waters. The Supreme Court held the New York statute inapplicable, saying that any state legislation, to the extent that it deals with matters of possible admiralty jurisdiction, is invalid

. . . if it contravenes the essential purpose as expressed by an Act of Congress, or works material prejudice to the characteristic features of the General Maritime Law, or interferes with the proper harmony and uniformity of that law in its international and interstate relations.

The court held that the work of a longshoreman, in which the deceased was engaged, was maritime in nature, his employment was a maritime contract, the injuries which he received were likewise maritime, and the rights and liabilities of the parties in connection therewith were matters clearly within admiralty jurisdiction. Cases of admiralty in maritime jurisdiction are, by the terms of the U.S. Constitution, cognizable in the federal courts. Therefore, any legislation, be it a compensation law or other statute which purports to assume for the state jurisdiction over cases of this nature, conflicts with the Constitution and to that extent is invalid.

The court went on to say that it is essential that there be uniformity of law with respect to all matters subject to the general maritime law where such matters affect international and interstate relations. Any maritime employment which directly affects navigation and commerce on water, in its interstate or international relations, is not subject to state workmen's compensation acts; the sole remedy available is that granted by the maritime law.

1418   Local concern doctrine

The practical effect of the Jensen decision was to deprive thousands of maritime workers of a means of recovery for injury or death occurring on navigable waters because, in many cases, there were no grounds for recovery under maritime law. The workmen's compensation concept had been accepted by the people generally, and the courts were inclined to look with favor upon recoveries for personal injury or death which occurred in the course of employment. Therefore, the courts sought to discover some means by which workmen's compensation awards could be sustained in cases which occurred

---

[1] It should be pointed out that a pier or dock is considered in law an extension of the land, and therefore accidents which occur on a pier or dock are land accidents. For example, an employee of a watchman's service, injured through the shipowner's fault while on a pier watching cargo, came within the workmen's compensation act of the state and had no cause of action against the shipowner cognizable in admiralty. [*Isthmian S.S. Co.* v. *Olivari*, 202 Fed. 2d 492.]

on navigable waters. The courts seized upon the language of the opinion in the Jensen case that any maritime occupation which pertained to navigation and commerce on water was subject to maritime law because of the necessity for a uniform system dealing with such matters.

The courts reasoned that if the employment, although maritime in character, pertained to local matters having only an incidental relationship to navigation and commerce, that in such cases the rights, obligations, and liabilities of the parties, as between themselves, could be regulated by local rules which did not work material prejudice to the characteristic features of the general maritime law or interfere with its uniformity. This view was approved by the Supreme Court.

In *Teahan* v. *I.A.C.* (292 Pacific 120), the court laid down the following rules:

1. If an injury occurs on land, maritime law does not operate. (This decision was rendered prior to the enactment of the Longshoremen's and Harbor Workers' Act, and therefore the court did not take into account the matter of injuries occurring on a drydock.)
2. If it occurs on navigable waters, the jurisdiction of admiralty is *prima facie* exclusive.
3. If an injury occurs on navigable water and in the performance of a maritime contract, it is certainly within the exclusive jurisdiction of admiralty unless:
   a. The contract is merely of local concern.
   b. Its performance has no direct effect upon navigation or commerce.
   c. The application of the state law would not necessarily work material prejudice to any characteristic feature of the general maritime law or interfere with the proper harmony or informity of that law in its international or interstate relations.
4. State compensation laws, contractual in character, are applicable to maritime service on navigable waters when, and only when, the service is within the exceptions (*a*), (*b*), and (*c*) above.
5. If, however, the injury occurs on navigable waters but in the performance of a nonmaritime contract, it is at least *prima facie* local and within the operation of state laws.

The following employments have been held to be maritime, but of such a nature as to involve only local concern, with the result that the application of the state workmen's compensation act was held to be valid: *carpenter,* injured while working on a ship which has been launched but not yet completed [*Grant Smith Porter Ship Co.* v. *Rohde,* 257 U.S. 469]; *mechanic,* on a pleasure craft [*Klump* v. *Industrial Commission,* 29 N.E. 2d 627 (Ohio)]; *diver,* employed by a shipbuilding company to remove obstructions in the course of a river [*Miller's Indemnity Underwriters* v. *Braud,* 270 U.S. 59]; *longshoreman,* injured on land [*Smith & Son* v. *Taylor,* 276 U.S. 179]; *lumber inspector,* temporarily aboard a schooner checking cargo lumber [*Rosengrant* v. *Havard,* 273 U.S. 664]; *employee,* trying to launch a small boat [*Alaska Packers Association* v. *I.A.C.,* 276 U.S. 467] and *logging opera-*

tions employees [*Sultan Ry. & Timber Co.* v. *Department of Labor,* 277 U.S. 135]; and *dredgers,* engaged in digging new channels or improving the shore[2] [*Fuentes* v. *Gulf Coast & Dredging Co.,* 54 Fed. 2d 69; *United Dredging Co.* v. *Lindberg,* 18 Fed. 2d 453; *Kibadeux* v. *Standard Dredging Co.,* 81 Fed. 2d 670].

The following have been held not to be matters of local concern but cases in which the general maritime law is controlling and to which state laws cannot be constitutionally applied: *stevedores or longshoremen* injured on navigable waters [*Minnie* v. *Port Huron Terminal Co.,* 295 U.S. 647; *Employers Liability Assurance Corp.* v. *Cook,* 281 U.S. 233]; *repairmen* working on ships already in commission [*Baizley Iron Works* v. *Span,* 281 U.S. 222]; *operation of a ferryboat across the Mississippi River for transportation of all kinds of traffic* is a maritime business not of purely local nature, and hence a deckhand injured while engaged in such service cannot invoke the jurisdiction of a state court to recover compensation under the state law [*Swan* v. *Baton Rouge Transportation Co.,* 197 So. 191].

An interesting case is *American Red Cross* v. *Hinson* [122 S.W. 2d 433, (Tennessee)]. An employee of the American Red Cross, engaged as a rescue worker during a flood, was drowned when his boat overturned while crossing a navigable river. The point at which the accident occurred was some distance from the bank of the river, and was not covered with water except in flood times, so that the accident occurred on overflowed land and not on navigable water. The court held that since this was a land accident the widow's right to compensation was controlled by the state compensation act and not by any federal statute.

It should be emphasized that the foregoing rules of law refer only to vessels which are used or capable of being used for commerce on water. They do not refer to any other type of watercraft, regardless of size. Thus, the vessels of the U.S. Navy, including warships and auxiliary craft, are not used or capable of being used for commerce on water and are not subject to these rules of law.

1419   Longshoremen's and Harbor Workers' Compensation Act

The Jensen decision came at a time when the workmen's compensation concept had already been introduced and fully accepted not only by the courts but also by the public. The individual citizen found it hard to understand why the mere fact that the accident occurred on water would act to deprive the widow of a compensation remedy which she could have asserted had the accident occurred on the dock less than 20 feet away. The decision was therefore roundly criticized and the dissatisfaction found its way to the halls of Congress. Congress attempted, by means of legislation, to delegate to the states the power to legislate in this area and to make their compensation laws applicable to injuries which occurred on navigable waters. Congress made two

---

[2] A dredge digging up silt from the bottom and piping it on to the land for use as fill was held not to be engaged in a maritime occupation [*Melanson* v. *Bay State Dredging Co.,* 62 Fed. Supp. 482].

such attempts, and in each instance the Supreme Court struck down the legislation as an unlawful delegation of federal legislative powers to the states, and, in the last decision stated emphatically that since the power to legislate in the admiralty and maritime area was given to the United States by the Constitution, only Congress could act in that particular area, and any legislation which would return such power to the state was contrary to the Constitution and therefore invalid.

In 1927, some ten years after the Jensen decision, Congress finally passed the Longshoremen's and Harbor Workers' Compensation Act (33 USCA 901–950), providing for payments of compensation in respect to disability or death to an employee, but only if the disability or death results from an injury occurring upon the navigable waters of the United States (including any-drydock), and if recovery for disability or death through workmen's compensation proceedings may not be validly provided by state law. Excluded from the act are a master or member of the crew of any vessel, and any person engaged by the master to load or unload any small vessel under 18 tons net. Also in the excluded area is an officer or an employee of the United States, or any agency thereof, or of any state or foreign government, or of any political subdivision thereof.

To qualify for payment of compensation under this act, two elements must be present: (1) The accident must occur upon navigable waters of the United States (including any drydock), and (2) A recovery for disability or death through compensation proceedings may not be validly provided by state law.

The first element is not difficult. The specific language of the act refers to "injury occurring upon navigable waters." A dock is considered as an extension to the land, so that any injury occurring on the dock or pier does not occur on navigable waters and therefore is not within the scope of the act. The state compensation act, however, is applied within the state's territorial limits, and since the dock is part of the land and therefore part of the state, the state law may be validly applied to such an injury. If the injury occurs aboard a vessel lying in navigable waters, the Longshoremen's and Harbor Workers' Compensation Act will be applied to the exclusion of the state compensation act.

The application of the second element creates some difficulties. Generally most state compensation acts, either by their terms or by judicial interpretation, have an extraterritorial effect. This means that the provisions of the state act may be applied to accidents which occur outside the state itself. It is based upon the theory that the right to compensation arises as an element of the contract of hire. Therefore, if the contract of employment were made in state *A*, and the contract of employment contemplated service in state *A* and also in other areas, the injured employee may claim compensation under the compensation act of state *A*, irrespective of whether the accident occurs in another state or foreign country.

The application of this rule is limited to areas within which state *A* has never relinquished jurisdiction. By the Constitution of the United States, all states relinquished certain rights and privileges, as well as jurisdiction, in the area of admiralty and maritime cases. Therefore, if the contract of hire was maritime, and the employee was injured on navigable waters, the state act could not be validly applied. To such cases, the Longshoremen's and Harbor Workers' Compensation Act provided the exclusive remedy. However, the state did not relinquish jurisdiction to the federal government over cases in which the contract of hire was not maritime. Therefore, the courts reasoned that the cases to which the statute referred (where the state act could be validly applied) were cases outside what could be considered admiralty and maritime jurisdiction. All contracts of employment of a maritime nature, where the injury occurs on navigable waters, come within the scope of the Longshoremen's and Harbor Workers' Compensation Act. If the injury occurs on land, then the state act can be validly applied and the state compensation act provides the only remedy. Contracts of employment of a nonmaritime nature, even though the injury occurs on navigable waters, are not within the scope of admiralty jurisdiction, and therefore the state compensation act can be validly applied to cases of that nature.

A maritime contract is one which relates directly to transportation on water; for example, the loading and unloading of a commercial vessel is a maritime contract. The repair of a vessel used for transportation, and having already been used for that purpose, involves a maritime contract. On the other hand, the building of a vessel to be used as an instrument of commerce is *not* a maritime contract. The theory is that the vessel, until it is launched and in commission, is not used or capable of being used for transportation or commerce on water, or that work on the vessel may be abandoned before completion. Work on an uncompleted vessel, therefore, is not a maritime contract of employment. Similarly the dismantling of a vessel formerly used for commerce, but withdrawn from that purpose, is not a maritime contract.

Many employments contemplate some duties on navigable waters. These could include a truck driver who is required by his route to take a ferry boat in order to cross a river, lake, or any other body of water; moving picture actors, as well as cameramen, camera crew, director, and other employees engaged in filming a marine scene—as well as a carpenter assisting in the construction of a lighthouse. In all of these cases the state compensation act may be validly applied.

1420   The 1972 amendments

In 1972, Congress undertook a comprehensive review of the Longshoremen's and Harbor Workers' Compensation Act, and enacted revisions to many of the major sections of the act. In Section 903, Congress rescinded the requirement that the Longshoremen's and Harbor Workers' Compensation Act would be applicable only to cases where the state act could not be validly applied. It also extended the scope of the act to accidents on land. The revision of the section reads as follows:

Compensation shall be payable under this Chapter in respect of disability or death of an employee, but only if the disability or death results from an injury occurring upon navigable waters of the United States (including any adjoining pier, wharf, dry dock, terminal, building way, marine railway or other adjoining area customarily used by an employer in loading, unloading, repairing or building a vessel). No compensation shall be payable in respect of the disability or death of:

(1) A master or member of a crew of any vessel, or any person engaged by the master to load, unload or repair any small vessel under eighteen tons net; or

(2) An officer or employee of the United States or any agency thereof or of any state or foreign government, or any political subdivision thereof.

No compensation shall be payable if the injury was occasioned solely by the intoxication of the employee or by the willful intention of the employee to injure himself or another.

Prior to the passage of this amendment, the Supreme Court of the United States in *Callbeck* v. *Travelers Insurance Company* [370 U.S. 114 (1962)] held that the line of demarcation between federal and state jurisdiction was the water's edge. If the accident occurred on navigable waters and it involved a person engaged in maritime work, the federal jurisdiction was exclusive. If the accident occurred to the same worker on land, the state compensation act had exclusive jurisdiction.

In the *Callbeck* case a welder was fatally injured while working on an uncompleted barge which had been launched and was afloat. Apparently reversing its previous decisions creating a "twilight zone," the Supreme Court allowed a recovery under the Longshoremen's and Harbor Workers' Compensation Act, notwithstanding the nature of the employee's work. The court examined the congressional hearings which had taken place as a prelude to the enactment of the statute and concluded that Congress intended the federal act to cover all injuries sustained on navigable waters to an employee engaged in maritime employment. The 1972 amendment does not change this situation. What the amendment does change is the line of demarcation between state and federal jurisdiction, extending the federal jurisdiction to accidents on land suffered by employees engaged in maritime employment if the accident occurs on a wharf, pier, or other places on land which are normally used in connection with the loading and unloading of vessels. The report from the House Committee on Education and Labor is illustrative of the legislative intent and reads as follows:

The Committee believes that the compensation payable to a longshoreman or a ship repairman or builder should not depend on the fortuitous circumstances of whether the injury occurred on land or over water. Accordingly, the bill would amend the Act to provide coverage of longshoremen, harbor workers, ship repairmen, ship builders, ship breakers and other employees engaged in maritime employment (excluding masters and members of the crew of a vessel) if the injury occurred either upon the navigable waters of the United States or any adjoining pier, wharf, dry dock, terminal, building way, marine railway, or other area adjoining such navigable waters customarily used by an employer in loading, unloading, repairing or building a vessel. The intent of the Committee is to permit a uniform compensation system to apply to employees who would otherwise be covered by this Act for part of their activity. To take a typical example, cargo, whether in break bulk or containerized form, is typically unloaded from the ship and immediately transported to a storage or holding area on the prier, wharf or terminal adjoining navigable waters. The employees who perform this work would be covered under the bill for injuries sustained by them over navigable waters or on the adjoining land area.

The Committee made it clear that the intent of the bill was to cover only those engaged in a maritime occupation. The report is as follows:

The Committee does not intend to cover employees who are not engaged in loading, unloading, repairing or building a vessel, just because they are injured in an area adjoining navigable waters used for such activity. Thus, employees whose responsibility is only to pick up stored cargo for further transshipment would not be covered, nor would purely clerical employees whose jobs do not require them to participate in the loading or unloading of cargo. However, checkers, for example, who are directly involved in the loading and unloading functions are covered by the new amendment. Likewise, the Committee has no intention of extending coverage under the Act to individuals who are not employed by a person who is an employer, i.e., a person at least some of whose employees are engaged, in whole or in part, in some form of maritime employment. Thus, an individual employed by a person none of whose employees work in whole or in part on navigable waters is not covered even if injured on a pier adjoining navigable waters. (92d Congress, 2d Session, Report No. 92–1441, p. 10.)

The amendments also provide that the maximum compensation for disability shall not exceed 200 percent of the national average weekly wage, which is to be determined annually by the Secretary of Labor. The rate of compensation paid to the injured person is still 66 2/3 percent of his average weekly wage, subject, however, to this maximum.

Another innovation introduced by these amendments has to do with the rate of compensation paid in permanent disability and death cases. Ordinarily the amount of compensation payable weekly or monthly as the case may be is determined as of the date of the accident, and is payable over the period of time set forth in the statute—in most states for life with no consideration being given to the inflationary spiral or the increased costs of living. Under the new amendment the employees or their dependents, as the case may be, will receive annual increases based on the percentage increases in the national average weekly wage. The amendments also have included provisions to increase the benefits in cases of total disability permanent in nature and death where the accident occurred prior to the enactment of the amendments. As to the increases which are retroactive, half are paid out of the act's Special Fund and half will be paid by the federal government.

The provision with respect to the time for filing claims for compensation has been amended to newly provide that the time for filing claims shall be one year from the date of injury *or the last payment of compensation*. Medical treatment is not construed as tolling the expiration of the time period, as it is in some states. (cf. New Jersey.)

1421　Waiver of federal jurisdiction

A maritime employee may waive his rights under federal statutes, either (1) by conduct, or (2) by accepting alternate provisions set forth in the state law.

The federal judicial power extends to all cases of admiralty and maritime cognizance. Claims have been brought before state compensation commissions by injured seamen and others having a maritime contract. Assuming that neither party raises any plea to the jurisdiction of the state commission, then the problem to be decided is the legal significance of such conduct on the part of the claimant in making the claim, and the award and payment thereof.

In *Brassel* v. *Electric Welding Company* (145 N.E. 745), the facts indicated that the claimant, either in ignorance of his maritime rights or for other reasons, made a claim before the New York Workmen's Compensation Board. Various awards were made and paid and the case was closed by the compensation board by making of a final award and payment thereof by the employer. The claimant then brought an action against his employer based upon the employer's negligence, taking the position that the proceedings before the workmen's compensation board were void due to the lack of jurisdiction of that body over a maritime tort. In disposing of this contention, the court said:

We think the acceptance of the payments has destroyed the right of action. The question is not whether the award has the effect of a binding adjudication. We may assume that it is void, and that, at least while unpaid, it might have been set aside or disregarded. The question is whether a right of action has survived the collection of the award and the retention of the proceeds. The plaintiff made a claim under the statute and must be charged with knowledge of its provisions. The statute [Workmen's Compensation Act, sec. 11] provided that the liability of an employer thereunder shall be exclusive and in place of any other liability whatsoever on account of the injuries sustained by the employee. In the light of this provision, the employer, when it tendered payment of the award, affixed by implication the condition that the tender was made upon statutory terms. The employee, by accepting payment, signified his assent to the condition, and his willingness to receive the money upon the terms thereby imposed. The transaction thus resulted in accord and satisfaction. . . . Nor does the plaintiff help his case by crediting what he has received upon the damages to be recovered. By such a use of the money, payments made and accepted for one purpose are diverted to another. The defendant did not tender payment upon account of an unliquidated claim for damages to be enforced thereafter without prejudice, nor is there any other evidence that the plaintiff so understood the effect of the acceptance. The payment was in full.

Therefore, in a case such as this where a final award was granted and payment made and accepted by the claimant, the entire transaction amounted to an accord and satisfaction which extinguished the claimant's cause of action against the employer. Even though proceedings were had, the effect of the entire transaction was no different than a settlement. In a settlement some standard or method of evaluation can be agreed upon between the parties and final payment can be made based on those standards.

For example, if it is agreed between the claimant and the defendant that the measure of damage between the two will be twice the amount of the special damages, and if payment were made on those terms and a release executed, or, in the alternative, a written agreement entered into embodying these terms, the payment thereof would amount to a full satisfaction of the claim. The agreement as to the standard of measurement of damage would amount to an accord. When payment was made in connection with such an agreement and such payment did meet all of the terms of the agreement, then, in legal effect, this amounts to a satisfaction.

In the previous case, either in fact or by implication, the parties selected the provisions of the workmen's compensation law of the state of New York as being the yardstick by which the employer's liability to the claimant would be measured. Having participated in hearings and other proceedings directed toward the eventual consummation of this purpose, and having accepted a final payment in settlement of the entire claim, the court held that the agreement to receive the benefits of the act—in lieu of any other yardstick to measure the extent of liability—amounted to an accord. Payment under this agreement, in accordance with the terms, amounted to a full and complete satisfaction, extinguishing the claim.

The opposite result will be reached in a case where there has been a partial payment, either voluntary or as a consequence of an award and total payment has not yet been made. *Larczy* v. *Hogan & Sons* (146 N.E. 430), was such a situation. The court, in disposing of the contention that the agreement to receive compensation and the acceptance of partial payment thereof amounted to an accord and satisfaction, said:

We therefore have in this case an agreement which may or may not have resulted in an accord and under it part payment by the employer. Payment, and not an agreement, was to be the full and complete satisfaction. Payment has not been made. The Workmen's Compensation Law has no application to the case. The agreement as part of the procedure under that law was void, unless vitality can be preserved through it under common law rule governing contracts. . . . As an agreement for settlement at common law, the claim of the plaintiff would not be discharged or released until full and complete payment and execution. The agreement might have amounted to an accord but payment only would amount to a satisfaction. Until there was an accord and satisfaction of the claimant's claim by full and complete payment, the plaintiff was not barred from maintaining his action for negligence.

Therefore, where the employer has accepted a final award which has been paid to and accepted by the claimant, then the cause of action is extinguished, whereas only partial payment affords the employer no protection whatsoever. This is the state of the law as it exists today except insofar as it has been modified by state statutes permitting a waiver of federal jurisdiction. In the preceding example, the claimant has by his conduct indicated a desire to utilize a certain yardstick for the measurement of his damages. As has been seen, the claimant is not foreclosed from bringing an action for negligence because of a partial payment, even though he would have to credit the payment thus received to any future judgment recovered. Where the full payment has been made the cause of action has been extinguished. The employer thus is in a tenuous position during the period in which partial payments are being made and is not protected against future claims unless and until a final award has been made, paid, and accepted.

In order to afford some measure of protection to the employer in the case of partial payments, where there has been an accord, some states have enacted compensation legislation providing for a waiver of federal jurisdiction and for an irrevocable election by the claimant in advance of the final award. Illustrative of this type of statute is Section 113 of the New York State Workmen's Compensation Act. This deals not only with cases of admiralty jurisdiction but also with interstate commerce. The text of this statute is as follows:

The provisions of this chapter shall apply to employers and employees engaged in intrastate and also interstate foreign commerce, for whom a rule of liability or method of compensation has been or may be established by the Congress of the United States, only to the extent that their mutual connection with intrastate work may and shall be clearly separable and distinguishable from interstate or foreign commerce, provided that awards according to the provisions of this chapter may be made by the Board in respect of injuries subject to Admiralty or other Federal Laws in case the claimant, the employer and the insurance carrier waive their admiralty or interstate commerce rights and remedies, and the state insurance fund or other insurance carriers may assume liability for the payment of such awards under this chapter.

In *Heagney* v. *Brooklyn Eastern District Terminal* (190 Fed. 2d 976), the court held that Section 113 was valid and that the agreement of the parties to abide by the award, plus the payment of a substantial number of such awards, constituted a release or compromise of the rights of the parties under the federal acts. The courts, however, have uniformly held that the intention of all three parties, the employee, the employer, and the insurance carrier, to waive federal jurisdiction must clearly and unequivocally appear. In *Fitzgerald* v. *Harbor Lighterage Co.* (244 N.Y. 132), the court said:

Claimant, Employer, and insurance carrier must unite in forgoing their Admiralty remedies before the statute [113] will be operative. . . . we put aside the question whether waiver by the claimant . . . is sufficiently established by the election to file a claim, unaccompanied by an express disclaimer of Admiralty remedies. Even if this be assumed, the defendant is not helped unless the employer and insurance carrier by some definitive expression have renounced their remedies as well. We see no basis for finding that renunciation was effective when this action was begun. The employer paid provisional or interlocutory awards for temporary disability. It may have been moved to this course by charity or by indifference or by dislike of litigation. Its acquiescence would not have barred it from appearing at the final hearing and contesting the claim for sufficient cause including lack of jurisdiction. . . . In the setting of the context, it [113] imports a concurrent evidence of intention, having the force of an agreement to forego one set of remedies and abide by another. Until the intention is announced by all who must participate, a waiver by any one of them is inchoate and revocable.

The New Jersey Compensation Act creates a presumption of jurisdiction. The statute provides that the party shall be presumed to have elected compensation and every contract of hiring shall be presumed to have been made with reference to the statute. In *Erie Railroad* v. *Winfield* (244 U.S. 170), the court held that it was beyond the power of the state to interfere with the operation of the Federal Employers Liability Act by putting the carriers and their employees to an election between its provisions and those of a state statute, or imputing such an election to them by means of this statutory exemption. The court did not declare that it is beyond the power of the state to enact a statute conferring upon the employer, employee, and insurance carrier the privilege of compromising their disputes by submitting them to the state workmen's compensation board or to provide for a waiver of federal jurisdiction. The opinion indicates that a different result would have been reached had the parties actually agreed to forego their federal rights and remedies.

1422   Summary: Law applicable to personal injury and death

The following is a table of the compensation liability of the employer to various classes of employees. It must be emphasized that this table refers to only compensation liability and applies only to the relationship of employer and employee. The employer may be a vessel owner, or someone such as a stevedore or a ship repair company.

EMPLOYERS' RESPONSIBILITY TO EMPLOYEES

Type of Employee	State Comp. Act	L & H Act	Jones Act	Maintenance & Cure
Longshoreman				
Land accident	Yes	Yes	No	No
Vessel accident	No	Yes	No	No
Crew member				
Land accident	No	No	Yes	Yes
Vessel accident	No	No	Yes	Yes
Repairer or artisan				
Land accident	Yes	Yes	No	No
Vessel accident	No	Yes	No	No
Nonmaritime employee				
Land accident	Yes	No	No	No
Vessel accident	Yes	No	No	No

The following table is an analysis of the liability of the vessel owner to the members of the crew, employees of others, and passengers.

LIABILITY OF VESSEL

Status of Person	Jones Act	Warranty of Seaworthiness	Common Law
Longshoreman	No	No	Yes
Crew member	Yes	Yes	No
Repairer (not employed by vessel owner)	No	No	Yes
Passenger	No	No	Yes (High Degree of Care)
Nonmaritime employees (other than vessel owner's)	No	No	Yes

With respect to death cases, the following table will indicate the liability not only of the employer of the individual, if it be other than the vessel owner, but also the liability of the vessel.

DEATH CASES

Status	L & H Act	State Comp.	Gen. Mar. Law	State Wrong-ful Death (Terri-torial Waters)	Death on the High Seas Act (Outside Terri-torial Waters)	Jones Act
Longshoreman						
Liability of employer:						
Land accident	Yes	Yes	No	No	No	No
Vessel accident	Yes	No	No	No	No	No
Liability of vessel	No	No	No	Yes	Yes	Yes
Crew member	No	No	No	No	Yes	No
Passenger	No	No	No	Yes	Yes	No
Nonmaritime employee of vessel owner	No	Yes	No	No	No	No
Nonmaritime employee (other than vessel owner's) :						
Liability of employer	No	Yes	No	No	No	No
Liability of vessel	No	No	No	Yes	Yes	No

1423   Liability of the stevedore

The stevedore is the organization that contracts to work cargo on vessels and hires men to do the actual work. The longshoreman is the actual worker employed by the stevedore to handle cargo. The stevedore is charged with the responsibility of properly stowing and bracing the cargo and of doing his work in a workmanlike manner.

The earlier cases have held that since the longshoreman, in loading and unloading vessels, is doing the work which was traditionally done by seamen, the warranty of unseaworthiness on the part of the vessel owner extended to him. If the vessel was unseaworthy for any reason, and the longshoreman is injured as a consequence of such unseaworthiness, the longshoreman has a cause of action against the vessel. This was true even though the unseaworthy condition was created by the stevedore who is the longshoreman's employer. It made no difference who caused the unseaworthy condition; the only question was whether or not the vessel was unseaworthy and if so whether or not such unseaworthiness caused the injury.

Where the unseaworthy condition was created by the stevedore and the vessel was required to respond in damages to the longshoreman, the Supreme Court in *Ryan Stevedoring Co.* v. *Pan-Atlantic S. S. Corp.* (350 U.S. 124), held that the stevedore was liable to the vessel owner on the theory of indemnity, the concept being that the stevedore's contract contemplated that the work would be done in a satisfactory manner, and the creation of an unseaworthy condition was a breach of that contract obligation.

The 1972 amendments to the Longshoremen's and Harbor Workers' Act abrogated the Ryan doctrine as stated above, and substituted therefor the following provision under Section 905 (b):

In the event of injury to a person covered under this chapter caused by the negligence of a vessel, then such person, or anyone otherwise entitled to recover damages by reason thereof, may bring an action against such vessel as a third party in accordance with the provisions of Section 933 of this title and the employer shall not be liable to the vessel for such damages directly or indirectly and any agreements or warranties to the contrary shall be void. If such person was employed by the vessel to provide stevedoring services, no such action shall be permitted if the injury was caused by the negligence of the persons engaged in providing stevedoring services to the vessel. If such person was employed by the vessel to provide ship building or repair services, no such action shall be permitted if the injury was caused by the negligence of persons engaged in providing ship building or repair services to the vessel. The liability of the vessel under this subsection shall not be based upon the warranty of seaworthiness or a breach thereof at the time the injury occurred. The remedy provided in this subsection shall be exclusive of all other remedies against the vessel.

Thus, the liability of the vessel for an unseaworthy condition does not now extend to longshoremen or to those engaged by the vessel for ship repair or shipbuilding. The liability of the vessel is limited to negligence only.

1424   Jurisdiction of the continental shelf

The continental shelf is defined as submerged lands extending into the Gulf of Mexico. The Truman Proclamation stated the claim of the United States that the continental shelf consisted of an extension of the land mass of the United States and therefore the United States claimed ownership to all subsurface minerals. As to those submerged lands lying beneath navigable waters of the United States (within the 3-mile limit), the ownership, dominion, and jurisdiction of the United States had already been established by the Supreme

Court. The problem then arose as to the jurisdiction of the outer continental shelf, which consists of those submerged lands lying seaward and outside the area of lands beneath navigable waters. Congress has now legislated with respect to this area (43 USCA 1331, *et seq.*).

The statute (sec. 1333) declares the policy of the United States to be that the subsoil and seabed of the outer continental shelf appertain to the United States and are subject to its jurisdiction, control, and power of disposition. The statute further declares that the Constitution, laws, and civil and political jurisdiction of the United States are extended to the subsoil and seabed of the outer continental shelf and to all artificial islands and fixed structures which may be erected thereon for the purpose of exploring for, developing, removing, and transporting resources therefrom to the same extent as if the area were under exclusive federal jurisdiction within a state. The civil and criminal laws of each adjacent state are declared to be the law of the United States for that portion of the subsoil and seabed of the outer continental shelf which would be within the area of the state if its boundaries were extended seaward to the outer margin of the shelf. All such applicable laws shall be administered and enforced by the appropriate officers and courts of the United States.

The United States district courts shall have original jurisdiction of cases and controversies arising out of or in connection with any operations conducted on the outer continental shelf for the purpose of exploring, developing, removing, or transporting by pipeline the natural resources of the subsoil and seabed.

The act also applied the Longshoremen's and Harbor Workers' Compensation Act to operations on the shelf, excluding the master or member of a crew of any vessel, or an officer or employee of the United States or any agency thereof, or of any state or foreign government or of any political subdivision thereof. This means that employees on drilling platforms and other structures erected on the outer shelf are subject to the provisions of the Longshoremen's and Harbor Workers' Compensation Act to the exclusion of the workmen's compensation acts of the adjacent states or of those in which contracts of hire may have been made.

The act specifically authorizes the Coast Gurad to promulgate and enforce such reasonable regulations with regard to lights and other warning devices, safety equipment, and other matters relating to the promotion of safety of life and property on the islands and structures referred to in the act, and further authorizes the Coast Guard to mark for the protection of navigation any such island or structure whenever the owner has failed to mark the same in accordance with the regulations.

1425 Limitation of liability

The general rule is that the vessel owner is liable for the loss of a cargo due to the unseaworthiness of the vessel. The vessel owner is likewise held for a high degree of care for the safety of passengers. Another rule of admiralty is that once a vessel has left its home port, entire control is vested in the master, and his authority with respect to all matters involving the vessel is absolute. In the sailing days, voyages were of extremely long duration and it was quite possible for the master to permit the existence of an unseaworthy condition, which condition would be unknown to the owners and would exist without their approval. Because of the lack of communication, the owner could exercise no control over the vessel, but still was held responsible for an unseaworthy condition of which he had neither knowledge nor control.

England desired to encourage shipping. It was noted that there was a certain reluctance on the part of financiers to invest their money in ships over which they could not exercise control once they left port. Since liability was imposed upon the owners of the vessel for any losses caused by unseaworthiness, the vessel owner was entirely at the mercy of the master. Financiers were unwilling to risk their entire fortunes in such ventures.

Therefore, England adopted the rule that where a maritime casualty occurred through the unseaworthiness of the vessel, and the unseaworthiness of the vessel occurred without privity or knowledge on the part of the owner, the limit of liability to which the owner would be exposed would be an amount equivalent to the owner's interest in the vessel immediately following the catastrophe, plus the pending freight, if any. This limitation applied to all liability arising out of the catastrophe, that is, liability to another vessel, to its owners, its cargo owners, and its crew, as well as the liability of the vessel to its own passengers, crew members, and cargo owners. On the other hand, if the unseaworthiness of the vessel was caused by the owner, or if he had knowledge of it and failed to make the necessary correction or repairs, then he was deemed to be in privity with the situation and responsible for the entire consequences.

The United States adopted this rule and also included a rule with respect to loss by fire based on negligence. The United States Limited Liability Act (46 USCA, 182–188) reads as follows:

Loss by fire. No owner of any vessel shall be liable to answer for or make good to any person any loss or damage which may happen to any merchandise whatsoever, which shall be shipped, taken in, or put on board any such vessel by reason or by means of any fire happening on board the vessel, unless such fire is caused by the design or neglect of such owner.

Liability of owner not to exceed interest. The liability of the owner of any vessel for any embezzlement, loss, or destruction, by any person, or any property, goods, or merchandise shipped or put on board of such vessel, or for any loss, damage, or injury by collision or for any act, matter, or thing lost, damage or forfeiture, done, occasion or incurred, without the privity or knowledge of such owner or owners shall in no case exceed the amount or value of the interest of such owner in such vessel, and her freight then pending.

Apportionment of compensation. Whenever such embezzlement, loss, or destruction is suffered by several freighters or owners of goods, wares, merchandise, or any property whatsoever, on the same voyage, and the whole value of the vessel and her freight for the voyage is not sufficient to make compensation to each of them, they shall receive compensation from the owner of the vessel in proportion to their respective losses; and for that purpose the freighters and owners of the property and the owner of the vessel, or any of them, may take the appropriate proceedings in any court, for the purpose of apportioning the sum for which the owner of the vessel may be liable among the parties entitled thereto.

Under this system, the vessel is valued after the disaster as she reaches the final port of the voyage. When the ship sinks at sea, the liability is rendered to zero, or at most to the pending freight. All classes of claims rank together. However, following the *Moro Castle* disaster, Congress added to the Limited Liability Act a provision which obligated the owner to pay life and personal injury claims until his contribution reached $60 per ton of the ship's gross tonnage if the value of the vessel was insufficient to pay all of these claims. This additional fund of $60 per gross ton applies only to seagoing vessels and would not include barges, tugs, lighters, yachts, or pleasure craft of any description.[3]

1426   Limitation as applied to pleasure craft

A vessel has been defined as any watercraft used or capable of being used for transportation on water. The limitation of liability rules apply to all such vessels. Under this definition, pleasure boats would be included. The size of the vessel would have no influence on determining whether or not the particular craft comes within this definition, nor is it necessary that the watercraft have any means of self-propulsion. Since pleasure craft come within this definition of a vessel, the limitation of liability rules would apply to them as well as to commercial type vessels.

In the *Petition of Hocking* [158 Fed. Supp. 620 (New Jersey)], limitation was granted to the owner of a 21-foot motorboat, the value of which, following a collision, was $3,500, and in which claims were asserted totaling $305,-000. The boat was being operated by the owner's son at an excessive rate of speed, which would make the vessel unseaworthy. The court held that while the collision was principally due to the fault of the operator of the motorboat, driving at excessive speed under the circumstances and failing to maintain a proper lookout, since the unseaworthy condition occurred without privity or knowledge of the boat owner, the owner was entitled to limit his liability for any injury resulting from the collision of the value of his interest in the motorboat. It must be noted here that the owner was not present in the boat at the time of the collision nor was the boat in any way under his control.

In the *Petition of Robertson* (163 Fed. Supp. 242), limitation of liability was denied. The facts indicated that even though the vessel was being operated by a professional captain, the owner was on board at the time of collision and therefore presumptively had knowledge of or was privity to the unseaworthy condition of the vessel.

---

[3] For further legislation with respect to liability for damage to cargo, see Carriage of Goods by Sea Act (COGSA; 46 USCA 1300, *et seq.*).

In *Kuback* v. *The Pearl Jack* [79 Fed. Supp. 802 (Michigan); affirmed in 178 Fed. 2d 154], a Chris-Craft speedboat, operated in navigable waters of the Kalamazoo River and Lake Michigan as a duly licensed common carrier, was held to be a vessel within the meaning of the Limited Liability Act and entitled to limitation if the damage was caused without privity or knowledge on the part of the owner. The facts indicated, however, that the owner had knowledge of the unseaworthy condition of the vessel, and for that reason limitation was denied.

Conceivably, for the purpose of limitation, even rowboats could come within the definition of a vessel and could be the subject of a provision for limitation of liability. It is inconceivable that such a petition would be presented for the reason that the amount of damage that could be done by a rowboat would seem to be relatively small. However, as a matter of law, rowboats could come within the classification in spite of the fact that the Supreme Court in a 1905 decision inferred that rowboats were "beneath the dignity of the Admiralty Court" (The *Robert W. Parsons*, 191 U.S. 17).

1427   Liability of the operator of pleasure craft

The operator of a pleasure craft must exercise reasonable care for the safety of others, and he is answerable for his failure to do so, either in admiralty or at common law, at the election of the injured person. In admiralty, he is subject to the rules of navigation and must obey them but, even under the rules, his right-of-way is not absolute. It is conditioned by the general prudential rule, which requires that he avoid an accident if it is possible to do so, even if, by so doing, he violates a rule of navigation. At common law, he has the same duty of care to others, and his failure to observe this duty is negligence. He must maintain a proper lookout and avoid a collision whether he has the technical right-of-way or not. He must avoid a collision with bathers, swimmers, persons water-skiing, and those pursuing other sporting activities on the water.

As to other vessels, the navigational rules give a sailing vessel the preferential right-of-way. This is for reasons of necessity. A motorboat is more maneuverable and therefore has the greater opportunity to avoid a collision. However, a sailing vessel under power and not under sail has the same responsibilities as a motorboat.

Under certain circumstances, the owner of the pleasure craft may be entitled to limitation of liability (see Section 1426). Where such limitation has been granted to the owner, it does not absolve the operator from liability. The courts hold that the granting of limitation to the owner does nothing more than to fix the extent of the owner's responsibility. Payment by the owner merely releases his liability and bars any further action against him, but is without prejudice to the rights of the injured party to prosecute an action for damages against the operator [*Rautbord* v. *Ehman*, 197 Fed. 2d 323]

1428   Federal Boating Act

Recognizing the need for regulation resulting from the increase in privately owned pleasure boats operating on navigable waters of the United States, Congress passed the Federal Boating Act of 1958 (48 USCA 526, *et seq.*). The act refers to privately owned, undocumented domestic vessels, propelled by machinery of more than 10 hp., using the navigable waters of the United States, its territories, and the District of Columbia, and all such vessels owned in one of the states and using the high seas. The act provides that the owner must secure a registration number in the state in which it is principally used, in accordance with the state numbering system and approved by the Secretary of the Treasury.

In case of accident, the boat operator must render such assistance as may be practicable without serious danger to his own vessel and those on board, and he must identify himself and his vessel to persons injured or whose property is damaged. If the accident results in death or injury, or causes property damage in excess of $100, the operator is required to file a full description of the accident with the Secretary of the Treasury or the state.

Coast Guard officers may board any vessel required to be numbered under the act, require identification for those on board, examine the boat certificate, and examine the vessel for compliance with the Motorboat Act of 1940 (46 USCA 526, *et seq.*) and the applicable Rules of the Road. The act further empowers the Coast Guard to file boating accident reports as statistical information which are available as public records. Regulations with respect to reports of boating accidents as promulgated by the Coast Guard are found in 46 CFR 173. The Coast Guard form, designated CS 3865, is the boating accident report, which sets forth the details of an accident.

Regulations have also been made with respect to the recently formed St. Lawrence Seaway Development Corporation which require the reporting of all accidents on these navigable waters between the United States and Canada to the corporation. The regulations are found in 33 CFR 401.11.

The Federal Boating Act definition of a motorboat includes "every vessel propelled by machinery and not more than 65 feet in length, except tugboats and towboats propelled by steam." It also divides such boats into four classes, as follows:

A—less than 16 feet in length
1—16 feet or over but less than 26 feet
2—26 feet or over but less than 40 feet
3—40 feet or over and not more than 65 feet

The act prescribes the necessary running gear which must be used by motorboats of each class, as follows:

526 B—*Lights:* Every motorboat from sunset to sunrise shall carry and exhibit the following lights when under way, and during such time no other lights which may be mistaken for those prescribed shall be exhibited:

(a) Every motorboat of classes A and 1 should carry the following lights:

First: A bright white light aft to show all around the horizon. *Second:* A combined lantern in the fore part of the vessel and lower than the white light aft, showing green to the starboard and red to port, so fixed as to throw the light from right ahead to two points abaft the beam on their respective sides.

(b) Every motorboat of classes 2 and 3 shall carry the following lights:

First: A bright light in the fore part of the vessel as near the stem as practicable, so constructed as to show an unbroken light over the arc of the horizon of 20 points of the compass, so fixed as to throw the light ten points on each side of the vessel: namely, from right ahead to two points abaft the beam on either side.

Second: A bright white light aft to show all around the horizon and higher than the white light forward.

Third: On the starboard side, a green light so constructed as to show an unbroken light over an arc of the horizon of ten points of the compass, so fixed as to throw the light from right ahead to two points abaft the beam on the starboard side. On the port side, a red light so constructed as to show an unbroken light over an arc of the horizon of ten points of the compass, so fixed as to throw the light from right ahead to two points abaft the beam on the port side.

526 C—*Whistles or Other Sound Producing Appliances:* Every motorboat of class 1, 2 or 3 shall be provided with an efficient whistle or other sound producing mechanical appliance.

526 D—*Bells:* Every motorboat of class 2 and 3 shall be provided with an efficient bell.

1429   Rules of navigation

Since all kinds of watercraft move on water, there must be rules and regulations governing right-of-way and responsibilities of those in charge of watercraft in order to prevent collisions and other mishaps. As to the high seas, rules, called the International Rules, have been established by agreement between maritime nations. These rules were accepted by the United States in 1890 and enacted into law by Congress. They are found in "Navigation," Title 33 of the United States Code Annotated (USCA), beginning at Section 61.

Congress has also enacted Inland Rules, which apply to territorial waters as well as to all inland waterways of the United States. These rules are found in the same Title 33, beginning at Section 151. Congress enacted separate rules for the Great Lakes and their connecting and tributary waters, which are also found in the Title 33, beginning at Section 241. It was also found necessary to enact special rules for the Red River of the North and rivers emptying into the Gulf of Mexico. These begin at Section 301.

It must be emphasized that the rules enacted by Congress apply only to navigable waters of the United States, which consist only of those bodies of water which connect the ports of one state with the ports of another state or the open sea. As to bodies of water wholly within the territorial limits of one state, Congress has no jurisdiction, and therefore such states enact their own laws governing operation of watercraft on such waters.

The rules provide for safe navigation, and cover the actions that must be undertaken in the daytime, at night, in fog, and under extreme weather conditions. These have reference to signals, lights, horns, and other necessary gear. Likewise they cover the rules of the road and the signals necessary to advise other vessels of a change in course and other actions. All the rules, international and inland, are subject to the general prudential rule, which is Article 27 in both, and which reads as follows:

In obeying and construing these rules due regard shall be had to all dangers of navigation and collision, and to any special circumstances which may render a departure from the above rules necessary in order to avoid immediate danger.

A discussion of all of the rules is beyond the scope of this work, and the claimsman may have reference to the rules as set forth in the statute mentioned above. Some of the inland rules of the road are as follows:

1. When two vessels are approaching each other head-on, or nearly so, it will be the duty of each to pass on the port side of the other. Either vessel will give, as a signal of her intention, one short and distinct blast of her whistle, which the other vessel will answer promptly by a similar blast of her whistle. Thereupon the vessels will pass on the port side of each other. But if the courses of such vessels are so far on the starboard of each other as not to be considered as meeting head-on, either vessel shall immediately give two short and distinct blasts of her whistle, which the other vessel shall answer promptly by two similar blasts of her whistle, and they shall pass on the starboard side of each other.
2. A vessel going astern in sight of another vessel will indicate this fact by giving three short blasts of the whistle.
3. If, when two vessels are approaching each other, either vessel fails to understand the course or intention of the other, from any cause, the vessel in doubt immediately will give four or more short rapid blasts of the whistle or siren.
4. When a vessel is moving from a dock, and another vessel is likely to approach, one long blast will be given. After they have cleared the dock and are fully in sight, they will be governed by the steering and sailing rules.
5. Whenever a steam vessel is nearing a short bend or curve in the channel, where from the height of the banks or any other cause, a steam vessel approaching from the opposite direction cannot be seen for a distance of half a mile, such steam vessel, when she shall have arrived within half a mile of such curve or bend, shall give a signal by one long blast of the steam whistle, which signal shall be answered by a similar blast given by any approaching steam vessel that may be within hearing. Should such signal be so answered by a steam vessel upon the farther side of such bend, then the usual signals for meeting and passing shall immediately be given and answered; but, if the first alarm signal of such vessel be not answered, she is to consider the channel clear and govern herself accordingly.
6. When one vessel is overtaking another, the overtaking vessel must signify her intention of passing on the starboard side if the vessel ahead by giving one blast of her whistle. If the vessel ahead answers with one short blast of her whistle, then the overtaking vessel may direct her course to starboard. Similarly, two blasts of the whistle indicate the desire of the overtaking vessel to pass on the port side of the vessel ahead. If the vessel ahead answers with two short blasts of the whistle, then the overtaking vessel may direct her course to port. However, if the vessel ahead replies with four or more rapid, short blasts of the whistle, it signifies that the vessel ahead deems it unsafe for the overtaking

vessel to pass at that point, and the vessel astern must wait until receiving the signal to go ahead.

7. When two vessels are crossing and there is a risk of collision, the vessel which has the other on her port side has the right-of-way, and will hold her course and speed. The other vessel must keep out of the way by crossing astern of the vessel which is holding her course, or by slackening her speed, stopping, or reversing. If there is any misunderstanding by either party, it will be so indicated by blowing the danger signal of four or more short blasts of the whistle. If necessary, both vessels should be stopped or backed until signals for passing with safety are made and understood.

A vessel, which is being operated in violation of these rules is, in maritime law, unseaworthy. If the action be brought at common law, the violation of the rules would constitute negligence.

Sailing vessels approaching one another.   The inland rules with respect to sailing vessels on harbors and inland waters are found in 33 USCA 202, and read as follows:

Where two sailing vessels are approaching one another, so as to involve the risk of collision, one of them shall keep out of the way of the other, as follows, namely:

(a) A vessel which is running free shall keep out of the way of a vessel which is close-hauled;

(b) A vessel which is close-hauled on the port tack shall keep out of the way of the vessel which is close-hauled on the starboard tack;

(c) When both are running free, with the wind on different sides, the vessel with the wind on the port side shall keep out of the way of the other;

(d) When both are running free with the wind on the same side, the vessel which is to the windward shall keep out of the way of the vessel which is to the leeward;

(e) A vessel which has the wind aft shall keep out of the way of another vessel.

Close-hauled has been defined in admiralty law as the arrangement or trim of a vessel's sails when she endeavors to make progress in the nearest direction possible toward the point of the compass from which the wind blows [*Chadwick* v. *Packet Co.*, 6 El. 7 Bl. 771]. More simply stated, close-hauled means running *against* the wind as much as it is possible to do so, as opposed to "running free" which means sailing *with* the wind.

Sound signals in fog, etc.   The Pilot Rules, stated in 33 USCA 191, read as follows:

In fog, mist, falling snow, or heavy rainstorms, whether by day or night, signals shall be given as follows:

A steam vessel under way, except when towing other vessels or being towed, shall sound, at intervals of not more than one minute, on the whistle or siren, a prolonged blast.

A steam vessel, when towing other vessels, shall sound, at intervals of not more than one minute, on the whistle or siren, three blasts in succession, namely, one prolonged blast followed by two short blasts.

A vessel towed may give, at intervals of not more than one minute, on a fog horn, a signal of three blasts in succession, namely, one prolonged blast followed by two short blasts, and she shall not give any other.

A vessel when at anchor shall, at intervals of not more than one minute, ring the bell rapidly for about five seconds.

Speed of vessels in fog, etc. The rule with respect to the speed and navigation of the vessel under extreme weather conditions is as follows:

Every steam vessel shall, in a fog, mist, falling snow, or heavy rainstorms, go at a moderate speed, having careful regard to the existing circumstances and conditions.

A steam vessel hearing, apparently forward of her beam, the fog signal of a vessel the position of which is not ascertained shall, so far as the circumstances of the case admit, stop her engines, and then navigate with caution until the danger of collision is over.

So that reference may be had to all of the rules, either adopted by the United States or legislated by Congress, the following is a breakdown of the rules with references to their location: International rules for navigation at sea, 33 USCA 145–147d; harbors and inland waters, 33 USCA 151–232; Great Lakes and tributary waters, 33 USCA 241–295; and Red River of the North and rivers emptying into the Gulf of Mexico and tributaries, 33 USCA 301–356.

The rules are published in pamphlet form by the United States Coast Guard. The pamphlets, their description, and identifying Coast Guard designations are Rules of the Road—International-Inland, CG 169, Rules of the Road—Great Lakes, CG 172, and Rules of the Road—Western Rivers, CG 184.

The Secretary of the Army is charged with the general responsibility for the maintenance of inland waterways as well as for structures which extend from the land, either on the waterway itself, such as piers, docks, etc., as well as for structures which span the waterway, such as bridges and drawbridges. Under 33 USCA 499 he is empowered to make the rules with respect to the opening of drawbridges. The rules so made are found in 33 CFR 203.200 and read as follows:

When a vessel approaches within signalling distance of a bridge for passage, the master thereof shall signify his intention by three blasts of a whistle or horn. . . . The signal of the craft shall be immediately answered by the tender or operator of the bridge. If the draw is ready to be immediately opened, the answer shall be three blasts of a whistle or horn from the bridge. In case of delay in opening the draw, as is provided in this section, or as may be necessary by accident or other contingency, the signal from the vessel shall be answered by two long blasts of a whistle or horn from the bridge. In all cases where delay signals have been given, a signal of three blasts of a whistle or horn shall be given as soon as it is possible to open the draw.

Obstruction of navigable waters. The duties of the Secretary of the

Army with respect to obstruction to navigation, to floating timber, and to the marking and removal of sunken vessels are defined in 33 USCA 409:

It shall not be lawful to tie up or anchor vessels or other craft in navigable channels in such a manner as to prevent or obstruct the passage of other vessels or craft; or to voluntarily or carelessly sink, or permit or cause to be sunk vessels or other craft in navigable channels; or to float loose timber and logs or to float what is known as "sack rafts of timber and logs" in streams or channels actually navigated by steamboats, in such a manner as to obstruct, impede or endanger navigation. And whenever a vessel, raft or other craft is wrecked and sunk in a navigable channel accidentally or otherwise, it shall be the duty of the owner of such sunken craft to immediately mark it with a buoy or beacon during the day and a lighted lantern at night, and to maintain such marks until the sunken craft is removed or abandoned, and the neglect or failure of said owner so to do shall be unlawful; and it shall be the duty of the owner of the sunken craft to commence the immediate removal of the same, and to prosecute the removal diligently, and failure to do so shall be considered as an abandonment of such craft and subject to the removal by the United States.

This section forbidding vessels to anchor in navigable channels establishes a standard of care applicable in ordinary negligence actions for damages [*The Bohemian Club* 320 U.S. 462]. As to abandonment, the general maritime law established the rule that the owner of a craft sunk through no fault of the owner had the right to abandon her without any liability to those who might run into the wreck, and also that the owner was under no obligation to remove the wreck. The theory was that the owner had sustained enough loss by the loss of his ship, and should not be subject to any other and further liability in excess of that. This section does not change the rule except to set up certain standards which must be met either during salvage operations or the period prior to abandonment. The section does not attempt to change the general maritime law rule, but rather recognizes the owner's right to abandon the wreck. The following section (33 USCA 414) sets up the responsibilities of the Secretary of the Army with respect to the removal of obstructions to navigation:

Removal by Secretary of the Army of sunken craft generally: Whenever the navigation of any river, lake, harbor, sound, bay, canal or other navigable waters of the United States shall be obstructed or endangered by any sunken vessel, boat, watercraft, raft or other similar obstruction, and such obstruction has existed for a longer period of thirty days, or whenever the abandonment of such obstruction can be legally established in less space of time, the sunken vessel, boat, watercraft, raft or other obstruction shall be subject to be broken up, removed, sold, or otherwise disposed of by the Secretary of the Army at his discretion without liability to the owners of same; Provided, That in his discretion, the Secretary of the Army may cause reasonable notice of such obstruction of not less than thirty days . . . to be given by publication, addressed "to whom it may concern" in a newspaper nearest to the locality of the obstruction requiring the removal thereof. . . . Provided further, That any money received from the sale of any such wreck . . . shall be covered into the Treasury of the United States.

This section recognizes the right of abandonment by the owner and provides for a presumption of abandonment after 30 days [see *Orrell* v. *Wilmington Iron Works*, 89 Fed. Supp. 418]. Also, by the general maritime law, the owner of a vessel which is sunk, who does not intend to raise her and who does not raise her, is not responsible for damage caused to other vessels as a result of the other vessels running into her [*Thames Towboat Co.* v. *Fields*, 287 Fed. 155]. In the case of the *Petition of Highland Navigation Co.* (24 Fed. 2d 582), the court said:

> It is well settled that a shipowner whose vessel has been wrecked and sunk without his fault has a right to abandon it and that after abandonment, he is not under any obligation whatsoever to raise or remove it and is not personally liable for the expense of its removal.

The statute refers to the removal of sunken vessels which are obstructions to navigation in the sense that they are obstructing the channels of rivers and other bodies of water, and the statute provides for their removal by the Secretary of the Army, with the salvage money going to the United States Treasury, where such wrecks have been abandoned by the owner. It should be emphasized that the Secretary is obligated to remove only wrecks which are obstructions to navigation. If the wreck is not in a channel or obstructing navigation, the Secretary has neither the responsibility nor the authority to remove it. In some cases there are wrecks which impair some private use of part of the waterway but do not obstruct navigation, involving removal by the Secretary. The rule as to those wrecks is exactly the same as the rule under the general maritime law, which is that the owner has a right of abandonment and, once having abandoned the wreck, has no obligation to remove it.

For example, in one case a navigation company leased a city pier for wharfage for their excursion steamers. One of the steamers burned and sank next to the pier. The city demanded that the navigation company remove the wreck since the pier was useless in its present condition. The court held that company, having abandoned the wreck, was under no obligation to remove it [*Petition of Highland Navigation Co.*, 29 Fed. 2d 37]. In a similar case, a vessel sank beside a pier owned by New York City, and was abandoned by the owner. The owner refused to remove the wreck and the city sought to recover the expense to which it had been put in removing it. In denying the city's claim, the court said:

> The place where the said wreck was sunk was an arm of the sea and embraced a portion of the navigable waters of the state. It may be doubtful whether the defendants were under any obligation to remove said wreck. The current authority would seem to show that they were not (*Taylor* v. *Atlantic Mutual Ins. Co.*, 37 N.Y. 275).

It should be emphasized that these rules and cases refer to situations where the vessel sank through no fault of the owner. Where it sinks through the neglect, intent, or other fault of the owner, he is liable to anyone damaged by its presence.

The operator of a pleasure craft must observe and obey the applicable rules of navigation. Those under sail are subject to the pilot rules for sailing vessels; those under power are subject to the rules regulating steam vessels. The statute, 33 USCA 155, applies the following definitions for the purpose of determining the rules to which a vessel is subject:

. . . Every steam vessel which is under sail and not under steam is to be considered a sailing vessel, and every vessel under steam, whether under sail or not, is considered a steam vessel.

The word "steam vessel" shall include any vessel propelled by machinery.

A vessel is "under way" within the meaning of these rules when she is not at anchor, or made fast to the shore or aground.

1430   Glossary of nautical terms

Abaft. Toward the stern; aft.

Abeam. At right angles to the keel.

Aboard. In or on the vessel; off the beam or side of the vessel.

Abreast. Opposite to or bearing 90° from ahead.

Aft. At, near, or toward the stern; between the stern and the amidship section of a vessel.

Ahead. Forward of the bow.

Alongside. Beside a pier or another vessel.

Amidship(s). In the center of a vessel; halfway between stem and stern.

Anchor. An iron device shaped to grip the bottom and hold a vessel in place by the cable or line attached thereto.

Anchor light. White light visible all around the horizon; displayed by a ship at anchor.

Anchorage. Suitable place to anchor; a special place set aside for anchoring.

Astern. Signifying position, in the rear of or abaft the stern; as regards motion, the opposite of going ahead; backwards.

Athwart. At right angles to the center of the ship.

Auxiliary. An engine, other than the main propulsion unit, used to drive winches, pumps, generators, etc.

Backwash. Water thrown aft by the turning of the screw.

Ballast. Heavy weights such as iron, lead, stone, sand, or water, carried in the hold of a vessel to increase stability by lowering the center of gravity.

Beam. The maximum width of a vessel; the athwartship parts of the vessel's frame which supports the decks.

Bearing. The direction of any object expressed either in terms of degrees or compass points.

Berth. A vessel's place at anchor or at a dock.

Bight. Any part of a rope except the end; usually a loop in a rope.

Bilge. The curved part of a vessel's hull, where the sides and flat bottom meet inside the vessel.

Bilge water. Water accumulated in the bilge by seepage or leakage.

Bitts. A pair of vertical wooden or iron heads on board a vessel to which mooring or towing lines are made fast.

Blinker. A set of lights at the masthead or on the end of a yardarm connected to a telegraph key and used for sending flashing light signals, usually by International Morse Code.

Bollard. An upward wooden or iron post on a pier to which hawsers are secured.

Boom. A spar with special use, such as a cargo boom, the boom for a sail, etc.

Bow. The forward part of a vessel.

Bowline. A mooring or docking line leading from the bow of a vessel.

Bridge. The raised platform in the forward part of a vessel from which the vessel is navigated and controlled.

Broad on the bow. Bearing 45° from ahead; halfway between ahead and abeam.

Bulkhead. A partition separating compartments in a ship; corresponds to a wall in a building.

Buoy. A floating conical, cylindrical, or spar shaped object for marking channels, shoals, etc.

Cable. A chain or wire rope of great strength, used with an anchor or for towing.

Cable length. 100 fathoms or 600 feet.

Chock. A heavy wooden or metal fitting secured on a deck or pier and having jaws through which lines or cables may be passed; a block or wedge of wood or other material used to secure cargo in the holds so that it will not work loose.

Cleat. A fitting of wood or metal with two horns used for securing lines.

Coaming. The raised framework about deck openings, hatches and cockpits of open boats.

Compass. An instrument for determining bearings and courses indicating magnetic or true north and the vessel's heading.

Cordage. A general term for line of all kinds.

Davits. A set of cranes or radical arms on the gunwale of the ship, from which the lifeboats are suspended.

Dead ahead. Directly ahead, as on an extension of the keel line of the vessel.

Dock. Water area adjacent to or alongside a pier, quay or wharf.

Draft. The depth of water from the waterline to the vessel's keel.

Drift. The leeway of a vessel or the amount of set of a tide or current.

Fathom. A nautical unit of measure equaling 6 feet.

Fore and aft. Parallel to the ship's center line.

Forecastle. The upper deck forward of the foremast, and the compartments immediately below this deck.

Forward. At, near, or toward the bow.

Foul. Jammed; not clear.

Freeboard. The distance from the waterline to the top of the weather deck on the side. Sometimes refers to the whole out-of-water section of a vessel's side.

Gear. The general term for spars, ropes, blocks, and other equipment.

Green water. A large body of solid water taken aboard.

Gunwale.   The upper edge or rail of a vessel or a side of a boat.

Gypsy.   The drum of a windlass or winch around which line or cable is turned.

Harbor master.   The official in charge of the anchorage berths and harbor regulations of a port.

Hatch.   A large opening in the deck of a vessel through which the cargo is hoisted in and out and access is had to the hold; also called hatchway.

Hawser.   A heavy line 5 inches or more in circumference used for heavy work and towing.

Heave to.   To bring the vessel's head or stern into the wind or sea and hold her there by the use of rudder and engines.

Heave the lead.   To take soundings with a line and a lead.

Heaving line.   A small line thrown to a vessel or pier for passing larger lines.

Heel.   The lower end of a mast; to list over; a vessel turns on her heel when she turns in a short space.

Helm.   The apparatus by which the ship is steered, including the rudder, tiller, and wheel.

Hold.   The interior part of a vessel in which cargo is stowed.

Hull.   The body of a vessel, not including its masting, rigging, etc.

Inboard.   Toward the center line of the vessel.

Inland Rules.   The rules enacted by Congress governing the navigation of the inland waters of the United States.

International Rules.   The rules established by agreement between maritime nations governing navigation on the high seas.

Jury rig.   A term applied to temporary structures, such as masts, rudders, etc., used in an emergency.

Kedge.   A small anchor used to move a vessel. It is placed ahead or astern and the vessel is hauled up to it.

Keel.   A longitudinal beam or plate in the extreme bottom of a vessel from which the ribs and floors start.

Lash.   To tie or secure.

Lead line.   A line secure to the lead and marked to be used in soundings.

Lee.   Away from the direction of the wind.

Lighter.   A small vessel used for loading and discharging vessels at anchor.

Line.   A general term for a light rope.

List.   Inclination of a vessel to one side or the other because of excess weight or shifted cargo.

Log.   A record of the daily progress of a vessel and the events of a voyage; also a device for determining the speed of a vessel.

Logbook.   A book containing the official record of a ship's activities together with observations of weather conditions.

Long blast.   A whistle blast of at least 4 seconds duration.

Lubber line.   A vertical black or white line marked on the inner surface of the compass bowl parallel with the keel and indicating the vessel's head.

Main deck. The highest complete deck extending from stem to stern and from side to side.

Masthead light. A white running light carried on the foremast or in the fore part of a steam vessel under way.

Mooring. Securing a vessel to a pier or buoy; anchoring; the place where the vessel is moored.

Offshore wind. A wind blowing off the land.

On the bow. The bearing of an object from 0° to 45° from ahead.

On the quarter. The bearing of an object from 135° to 180° from ahead.

Out of trim. A ship carrying a list or down by the head or stern.

Outboard. Toward the sides of a vessel; entirely outside the vessel.

Part. To break, as a break in a cable or rope.

Pay out. To let out cable or ease off on a line.

Pier. A construction work running at an angle with the shore line, providing landing places for vessels on both sides.

Port. The left side of the vessel facing forward; an opening in a vessel's side; a harbor.

Propeller. A device often called a screw, which rotates under the water in the stern of a vessel to propel her. A propeller has a hub and from two to four radial blades.

Quarter. The portion of a vessel's sides near the stern.

Quay. A cargo-discharging wharf which is parallel with the basin or harbor edge and has water on both sides.

Range. Two or more objects in line to indicate a preferred course to steer; distance in yards from a vessel to the target.

Range lights. Lights at or near a lighthouse, passage or channel, set in a line to indicate the course of the channel.

Ribs. The frame of a vessel.

Ride. To lie at anchor.

Riding lights. Lights carried by a ship at anchor or moored.

Rigging. Fiber line or wire ropes securing masts, booms or sails.

Rudder. A flat vertical structure attached to the stern and connected with appropriate gear used to steer the vessel.

Rules of the Road. Regulations enacted to prevent collisions between vessels.

Salvage. To save a ship or cargo from danger; money paid for saving a ship or cargo.

Seaworthy. Capable of putting to sea and meeting usual sea conditions; it refers not only to the condition of the structure of the ship itself, but also means that it is properly laden, and provided with a competent master, a sufficient number of competent officers and seamen, and the requisite appurtenances and equipments, such as the ballast, cables and anchors, cordage and sails, food, water, fuel and lights, and other necessary or proper stores and implements for the voyage.

Secure. To make fast; safe; order given on completion of an operation.

Short blast. A whistle blast lasting about 1 second.

Slew. To yaw from side to side while at anchor or being towed.

Spar. A term applied to a pole serving as a mast, boom, gaff, bowsprit, etc. Spars are made of steel or wood.

Starboard. The right side of the vessel looking forward, indicated at night by a green light.

Stay. A rope of hemp or wire used to support a mast or spar in position.

Stern. The after part of a vessel.

Stern line. A mooring line leading from the stern of a vessel.

Sternway. Movement of a vessel in the direction of stern.

Stow. To put gear in its proper place.

Swell. Undulations of the sea having greater length than ordinary waves, usually caused by the wind of a distant storm.

Taut. Tight; without slack.

Tiller. A short piece of iron or wood fitting into the rudderhead, by which the rudder is turned.

Tow. To pull a vessel, barge, or other craft through the water by means of a line or cable; vessel or vessels being towed.

Trim. The difference in draft at the bow of a vessel from that at the stern.

Trough. The hollow between two waves; opposite of crest.

Ullage space. The unfilled part of a tank or container. Liquid at a certain level below this will roll around and affect the trim of the vessel.

Underway. Said of a vessel when not at anchor, not made fast to the shore, and not aground.

Veer. To pay out cable or line; to change the direction of a vessel in reference to the wind.

Waist. The middle part of a vessel, midway between the bow and the stern.

Warp. To move a vessel by line or by anchor.

Waterline. The line printed on the side of a vessel at the water's edge to indicate a proper trim.

Wharf. Installation for loading or discharging vessels; particularly a platform of timber, stone, or concrete against which vessels may be secured to load or discharge.

Winch. A hoisting engine secured to the deck used to haul lines or wire rope by turns around a horizontally turning drum.

Windward. In the direction from which the wind is blowing.

Yard. A spar attached at its center point to a mast running athwartship; used as a support for signal halyards or signal lights.

Yaw. To steer badly, zigzagging back and forth across an intended course.

CHAPTER XV

Law of evidence

1500   Nature of evidence

The trial of the lawsuit is a process which has for its objective the discovery of truth. The court and jury are the parties charged with the responsibility of performing this function. Since the court and jury have no means of investigating the case before them, they must rely upon data furnished by the interested parties. This data is called *evidence*. It consists of any species of proof, or probative matter, legally presented by the act of the parties and through the medium of witnesses, records, documents, and concrete objects. Both parties to the action present this data for the purpose of inducing belief in the minds of the court or jury of the validity of the claim asserted by the party producing the evidence.

There are generally three kinds of evidence: oral, documentary, and demonstrative.

Oral evidence consists of the testimony of witnesses testifying to the facts within their knowledge which are germane to the case. Oral evidence also includes the testimony of expert witnesses who express opinions the validity of which is dependent upon specialized knowledge and experience in the area in which the opinion is expressed.

Documentary evidence, as the name implies, consists of evidence in the form of books, papers, reports, public and private records.

Demonstrative evidence refers to matters of a visual nature; such as, photographs, motion pictures, scale models, X rays, moulages, as well as actual courtroom exhibitions of various scientific instruments such as a colorimeter, spectrograph, microscope, and X-ray shadow box. It could also include the offending instrumentality itself, such as a defective heater, motor, bottle, can, contaminated food, or an automobile.

The subject of evidence is of importance to the claimsman in that he must know what evidence is admissible, the kind and type of witnesses necessary in order to establish certain facts, as well as the inferences or presumptions which can be derived therefrom. All this is necessary so that the claimsman can determine the strength or weakness of the case which he has investigated.

1501   Admissibility of evidence

It was recognized early in the development of the law that there had to be some limitation with respect to the evidence that could be received in a given case. If this were not so, either side could prolong the trial indefinitely by producing an interminable procession of witnesses to testify to almost anything under the sun. In such a situation, the ends of justice would not be served. Therefore, as an initial premise, the courts decided that the only evidence which would be received would be evidence that was relevant, material, and competent. If the evidence did not contain these three qualities, the evidence was objectionable and was excluded.

Relevant evidence means such evidence that has a connection with the case. It must have some application or relation to the matter.

Material evidence is such evidence that goes to the substance of the matter in dispute and has a legitimate or effective influence or bearing on the decision in the case. It must tend to prove or disprove a fact which is in issue in the case.

Competent evidence refers to the source or the type of evidence offered. It means that the evidence must be by means of testimony of a person who had the ability to see, hear, or recall the event which is the subject matter of the law suit.

Some examples will probably be helpful in illustrating these three qualities. Let us suppose that there is a negligence action pending which arose as a result of an automobile accident. Evidence is offered that the driver of the offending vehicle was wearing a blue serge suit at the time of the accident. This fact would be relevant because it had some relation to the matter. If it were offered by a person who was in a position to see and to judge the type of clothing worn by the driver, the evidence would then be competent. However, the fact that the driver was wearing a blue serge suit would not in any way enable the court or the jury to determine the negligence of the driver.

The matter before the court for determination was whether or not the driver operated his car in a careless or negligent manner. The fact that he was wearing clothing of a certain color or texture would not in any way enable the court and jury to decide this question. Therefore, while the evidence did meet two of the requirements, relevancy and competency, the evidence is immaterial, and therefore objectionable.

Let us assume that there is a blind man who was present at an intersection where an accident occurred. He offers to testify as to exactly how the accident happened. His testimony might have some relation to the matter and his testimony could be material to the issue. However, a blind man who does not have the facility of sight is incompetent to testify as to the circumstances of the accident for the reason that, even though he was present at the time and place of the occurrence, he did not have the physical ability to observe the happening of the accident. His testimony is incompetent and inadmissible. He could testify to the sounds that he heard at the time that the accident occurred and to what was said by certain voices, but unless he had prior knowledge of the person speaking, he could not identify the person who spoke the words which he heard.

1502 Qualifications of witnesses

A witness is defined as a person who is possessed of knowledge of the matter pending before the court sufficient to enable him to testify concerning a specific matter. He is not disqualified from being a witness because of race, color, relationship to any of the parties, infancy, interest in the outcome of the litigation, mental derangement, conviction of a crime, or self-confessed moral turpitude. With the exception of race and color, all of the other matters mentioned, while not disqualifying the person from being a witness, can be taken into consideration by the jury in determining the weight to be given to his testimony.

Is the testimony of an infant six years of age to be given more, or less, consideration than opposing testimony given by an adult? Is the testimony of a person who had led a previous exemplary existence to be given more, or less, consideration than that of a person who has been convicted of a crime? What is the relative weight to be given to the testimony of a person with a mental disability as opposed to testimony by a person of sound and sane mind? These are questions which the jury will be called upon to decide. They decide the quality or believableness of the testimony rather than the qualification of the witness to testify.

A witness must be capable of expressing himself concerning the matter of his testimony so as to be understood by the judge and jury either directly or through interpretation by one who can understand him. The fact that a witness speaks a foreign tongue will not disqualify him. He may testify through an interpreter and if he is otherwise capable of adequately making himself understood in the foreign tongue, he can be a witness. The same thing would be true with respect to a person who is deaf or dumb, or both. This witness can testify through an interpreter who is capable of communicating with the witness by means of a sign language. An insane person, an idiot, or an infant may not be capable of making himself understood or expressing the circumstances in understandable terms. If this be the case, such a witness is not qualified to testify.

A witness is disqualified from testifying if he does not understand the nature of an oath, does not regard the taking of an oath as binding on his conscience, or does not understand the duty of a witness to tell the truth. The religious belief of a witness as such will not disqualify him, providing that the belief is one which recognizes the pains and punishments imposed in the hereafter for conduct on earth. Therefore, a witness who has such a belief presumptively will regard the sanctity of his oath and would be likely to tell the truth.

In most states, an atheist as well as a person who has conscientious scruples against taking an oath is prevented from testifying. The reasoning behind this view is that testimony given under oath is more likely to be truthful and honest than testimony that is not. Also, the testimony of a person who professes no religion at all and does not regard an oath as being binding on his conscience, or does not believe that he will be punished in the hereafter because of his actions on earth, is not worthy of belief. Some states have departed from the strict application of this rule and have permitted testimony by such witnesses provided the witness would recognize the duty to tell the truth and regard his testimony as being binding on his conscience. The taking of an oath in such cases has been waived. These states are in the minority.

1503   Presumptions and inferences

There are certain facts that the law will accept as true without any proof whatsoever. For example, it is presumed that everyone regulates his conduct in such a way so as to obey the law. In criminal cases, this is referred to as the presumption of innocence. Before any testimony whatsoever is offered to the court, the defendant, accused of the crime, is innocent. This may be overcome by the introduction of testimony that in truth and in fact the defendant is not innocent and did not regulate his conduct in accordance with the law, but actually followed a course contrary to the conduct expressly required by the law.

This same type of presumption applies to civil cases. A man is presumed to have driven his automobile in accordance with the statutes regulating its use; he is presumed to have utilized his property with due care and regard for the rights of his neighbors, and he is presumed to have kept his premises in proper repair. The same presumption applies in fatal cases, and the deceased is presumed to have obeyed the law and exercised due care.

These facts can be overcome only by evidence to show that the defendant did not operate his motor vehicle in accordance with the statute;

that he did not maintain his premises and use them with due regard for the rights of his neighbors, and that he did not keep his premises in the condition of repair which the law requires. The burden of proof is upon the person asserting that the defendant did not act in obedience to the law. These presumptions arise by operation of law and are rebuttable by the adverse party. This means that the presumptive fact may be shown to be incorrect by the testimony offered by the opposing party.

The proof of one basic fact may give rise to the assumption, as a matter of logic, that a second fact exists. For example, proof of possession gives rise to a presumption of ownership. Repairs to the premises gives rise to a presumption or inference that the person making such repairs has control of the property. These presumptions arise as a matter of common experience. Most of the time, property possessed by a person is owned by him. People do not make repairs on premises which they do not control nor repair premises they are not obligated to repair. The registration of a motor vehicle in the name of a person gives rise to a presumption that he is the owner. In order to prove ownership of a motor vehicle, therefore, mere proof of the fact that the motor vehicle is registered in the name of a certain person will be sufficient to establish ownership and, likewise, control. It would be unnecessary for the person seeking to establish ownership to ascertain where the owner bought the car, whether or not he paid cash for it, and to present the testimony of the automobile dealer plus the bill of sale and any other documents which accompanied the transaction. The mere fact that proof is offered of the registration of the motor vehicle will be sufficient to establish ownership.

In all these cases, the presumption is rebuttable and each can be overcome by specific testimony contradicting the presumed fact.

Where there is no evidence justifying a finding contrary to the presumed fact, the jury will be instructed that the presumed fact must be taken as true. If there is evidence justifying the finding contrary to the presumed fact, the jury then is at liberty to find the existence or nonexistence of the presumed fact upon all of the evidence exactly as if the presumption had never been in existence.

There is an additional presumption with respect to official records. Where official records of birth, marriage, divorce, and death are produced and identified by the official custodian thereof, there arises a presumption that the information contained in the official records is true, even though the custodian identifying the records has no specific knowledge with regard to the event set forth in the documents produced.

There is a presumption that a status once established is a continuing one. Proof that a man and a woman were married on a certain date is sufficient to raise the presumption that their status as married persons continued from that date forward. The presumption can be overcome only by evidence that the marriage has been terminated by death or divorce. Likewise, proof that an unsafe condition existed on a certain date will give rise to a presumption that the unsafe condition continued. This can be overcome by evidence that the condition was repaired or altered at a certain time, but in absence of such proof the presumption is that the unsafe condition once established was a continuing one and remained in existence.

For example, if it were shown that a dangerous or unsafe condition was present on a stairway on March 1, and an accident occurred wherein the plaintiff was injured as a consequence of the unsafe condition on March 30, proof that the condition existed on March 1 would give rise to the presumption that the unsafe condition continued to exist and was in existence on March 30, the day of the accident. Proof of repairs or alterations made between March 1 and March 30 could destroy the presumption.

In cases where the conduct of a deceased person is in issue, the presumption is that the deceased exercised due care. It makes no difference whether the action is one brought on account of the injuries suffered by the deceased under the survival statute, or for his wrongful death, or an action brought against his estate for his negligence in causing the injury of another person. The presumption is applied in all cases, irrespective of whether it grants an advantage to plaintiff or defendant. The presumption may be overcome by evidence to the contrary.

1504   Irrebuttable presumptions

The presumptions which we have considered in the preceding section may be overcome and destroyed by contrary evidence. There are some situations, however, in which, once the presumption is established, the court will not receive evidence in rebuttal. There is a common-law presumption that a child under the age of seven is incapable of negligence. Once the age of the child is established, a conclusive presumption arises that the child is not negligent. No evidence will be received to establish that the child's conduct was negligent in any way. The presumption is irrebuttable. The same type of presumption is found in the criminal law. A child of the age of seven and under is conclusively presumed to be incapable of committing any crime. Therefore, when the age of the child is established, the court will not receive any evidence of conduct on the part of the child which would be criminal if committed by an older person.

There is an irrebuttable presumption at common law that everyone knows the law. Therefore, ignorance of the law cannot be interposed as a defense to an action based upon a legal infraction. If a man drives his car at a speed of 60 miles per hour in a 25-mile zone, and an accident occurs as a consequence of his excessive speed, he will be charged with knowledge of the law which restricted the speed to 25 miles an hour whether he knew such law or not.

There are presumptions which are only partially rebuttable in the sense that they can be overcome by testimony or evidence in a very restricted area. Evidence that a man has been missing from his usual place of abode for more than seven years, plus evidence that he has not communicated with his wife, relatives, close friends, and people with whom he normally would maintain close contact, gives rise to a presumption of death. The presumption can be overcome only by evidence of someone who saw the man alive within the seven-year period. It cannot be overcome with any other evidence. Therefore, evidence of the man's age, state of health, life expectancy and similar matters will not destroy the presumption. In absence of direct evidence that the man was alive during the seven-year period, the presumption is irrebuttable.

At common law, a child conceived during a valid and subsisting marriage was conclusively presumed to be legitimate. This means that no testimony from either or both parents or others would be received to support a claim of illegitimacy. This is a rule of reason and common sense because the common-law court jealously guarded the rights of infants, incompetents, and others who were not in a position to adequately defend themselves. Obviously, if a claim of illegitimacy were sustained, the ultimate victim of such a decision would be the child himself.

Some states have modified the common law. Statutes have been passed which permit testimony of witnesses other than the parents to show non-access on the part of the husband for a period of one year prior to the birth of the child. Even in those states, neither parent is a competent witness, even though the parent could offer definite testimony as to the illegitimate origin of the child. This again is a rule of reason since the law recognizes the bitterness which sometimes attends the breakup or dissolution of a marriage. The law likewise recognizes the motives which might impel a parent to make a claim of illegitimacy or an admission concerning the origin of the child. Therefore, in the interest of the child, who is unable to adequately defend himself, the law still imposes the common-law restriction of incompetency upon both parents.

Illegitimacy, under the statutes, can be established by means of evidence that the husband was in foreign service, that his service in the foreign country was continuous for one year, and, further, that the wife never left the country during that period of one year. In such a case, illegitimacy of the child born can be established, but otherwise the presumption is irrebuttable.

1505 Res ipsa loquitur

Back in 1863, there was a case in which a barrel of flour rolled out of the second-story window of a warehouse and struck a passing pedestrian. The facts of the occurrence were produced in evidence but there was no proof of any specific act of negligence on the part of the warehouse owner. In sustaining a recovery for the plaintiff, the court said that the thing speaks for itself and that the circumstances of the accident were such that mere proof of the occurrence was sufficient to warrant an inference of negligence. The court in making the point that the thing speaks for itself, used the Latin equivalent, *res ipsa loquitur*. This has been repeated thousands of times since that case and now, a century later, we still have the phrase with us.

The court felt that this was the type of accident that normally would not have occurred had due care been exercised by the warehouseman. If there was an explanation for the occurrence, and if it did take place in spite of the exercise of due care, the defendant warehouseman was in the better position to explain how the accident occurred and that the exercise of due care could not have prevented it. This the defendant did not do, and in the absence of specific evidence as to the actual causation of the occurrence, proof by the plaintiff of the facts of the accident were sufficient to raise an inference of negligence on the part of the defendant.

The mere fact that an accident occurred does not compel the application of *res ipsa loquitur*. To invoke the doctrine, the following elements must be present:

1. The instrumentality which caused the accident must be in the exclusive control of the defendant.
2. The accident must be one which does not happen in the ordinary course of things if those who have control exercise proper care.
3. The accident must not have been due to any voluntary contribution (contributory negligence) on the part of the plaintiff.

This is a rule of circumstantial evidence for the benefit of the plaintiff and relieves him of the obligation of proving specific acts of negligence by the defendant. As a defense, the defendant must offer an explanation of the occurrence which will absolve him from responsibility. For example, if an automobile jumped the curb and struck a pedestrian on the sidewalk, *res ipsa* would compel the inference that the driver of the automobile was negligent. All three elements of the doctrine would be present. The instrumentality causing the accident was within the exclusive control of the driver. The accident is one which normally would not have occurred but for the negligence of the driver. Lastly, the pedestrian who was on the sidewalk, a place where he had a right to be, was not guilty of any contributory negligence. In the absence of any other evidence, the plaintiff pedestrian should prevail.

Suppose that the automobile driver was suffering from a latent heart condition of which he had no prior knowledge. While driving his automobile, he suffered a heart attack of such severity that he was unable to control the vehicle. The accident occurred while the driver was in the throes of this heart attack. Evidence of the heart attack, if believed by the jury, would overcome the presumption of *res ipsa loquitur* and would negate any conclusion that the accident occurred because of a lack of due care on the part of the automobile driver. Another possible explanation which also could be offered by the automobile driver would be evidence that his automobile was struck by another vehicle which forced it onto the sidewalk, the original impact between vehicles having occurred through no negligence on the part of the automobile driver.

Technical situations in which *res ipsa* has been applied include an action against the beauty shop proprietor for the loss of a patron's hair; action against an airline by a passenger for injuries sustained in an airplane crash; injuries sustained as a result of a collapsing counter stool in a hotel restaurant; injuries sustained when bricks or window panes fell from the defendant's premises; falling elevators; the collapse of structures; explosion of boilers; injuries to passengers for causes within the control of the railroad, such as derailment or defective equipment; and automobile accidents where the automobile ran into a stationary object.

A summarization of the doctrine of *res ipsa* most often quoted is found in *Scott* v. *London and St. Katherine Docks Company* [3 H & C 596 (1865)]. It reads as follows:

> There must be reasonable evidence of negligence; but where the thing is shown to be under the management of the defendant or his servants, and the accident is such as in the ordinary course of things does not happen if those who have the management use proper care, it affords reasonable evidence, in the absence of explanation by the defendant, that the accident arose from want of care.

In an action against the telephone company it was alleged that the plaintiff's hearing was injured by an explosive sound on the defendant's telephone line. The court applied the *res ipsa* doctrine, stressing the defendant's duty to control and prevent the passage of dangerous amounts of sound over its equipment. Likewise, in a case involving carbon monoxide poisoning of a bus passenger, the court applied *res ipsa* to the facts, pointing out the duty of the bus company to maintain its equipment so as to have regard for the safety of its passengers.

In *Plum* v. *Richmond* (233 N.Y. 285), the plaintiff, a passenger in the defendant's trolley car, was injured in a collision between the car and a motor truck. Testimony was given by the plaintiff as to the injury he sustained and the surrounding circumstances. Testimony was then given by the defendant, tending to explain the occurrence as happening without fault on its part. The court gave the following instructions to the jury, which was sustained on appeal with regard to the application of *res ipsa loquitur*.

> The management and control of the transportation of the passenger is wholly confided to the employees operating a car, and the passenger cannot be expected to account for a collision if one takes place. When such a collision takes place, there arises as a rule of evidence, a presumption of negligence upon the part of the carrier, which calls upon it for an explanation. I do not mean, in making this statement, that this rule of evidence shifts the burden of proof from the shoulders of the plaintiff onto the shoulders of the defendant, but only that the company, from the fact of the collision, if you find there was a collision, is called upon to make an explanation; and then it is for you to determine on the whole

case, on all the evidence, whether there is a preponderance of evidence in favor of the plaintiff's contention that there was negligence on the part of the defendant.

The following instructions were given in *Bischoff* v. *Newby's Tire Service* [333 Pac. 2d 44 (California)]:

It is only necessary for the plaintiff, in order to establish a prima facie case, to prove the fact of the accident and the injuries caused thereby. Having done this, he may rest, for the inference then arises that the accident occurred through the negligence of the defendant, and the burden of explaining that the defendant was not negligent is then cast upon him. In order to overcome this inference of negligence, the defendant must show that the accident was not caused by his negligence, or was the result of an inevitable casualty, or of some cause which human care and foresight could not prevent.

The rule of *res ipsa loquitur* is not merely a rule of evidence shifting the burden of going forward with proof, for inference of negligence under the rule does not disappear when met with substantial, credible evidence of due care. It remains in the case throughout, to be given consideration by the jury in weighing of the whole case.

I instruct you that such an inference of negligence is in itself sufficient to satisfy the burden placed upon the plaintiff to prove his case by a preponderance of the evidence.

You are instructed that the accident in this case is of such a character that it speaks for itself. Under the circumstances, the defendant will not be held blameless, except under a showing either of (1) a satisfactory explanation of the accident; that is, an affirmative showing of a definite cause for the accident, in which case no element of negligence on the part of the defendant inheres or (2) of such care in all possible respects as necessarily lead to the conclusion that the accident could not have happened from want of care, but must have been due to some unpreventable cause, although the exact cause is unknown. In the latter case, inasmuch as the process of reasoning is one of exclusion, it is satisfactory in the sense that it covers all causes which due care on the part of the defendant might have prevented.

Thus the application of the rule of *res ipsa* gives the plaintiff a legal advantage. It correspondingly places the defendant in the disadvantageous position of having to explain the details of the accident and to show that due care on the part of the defendant would not have prevented the accident from occurring. Its application has been justified, most often, on the theory that since the dangerous instrumentality causing the injury is in the control of the defendant, the defendant has greater access to the facts of the occurrence than the plaintiff.

1506   Identification of the defendant under *res ipsa*

One of the elements of the doctrine is that the offending instrumentality must be within the exclusive control of the defendant. The fact that the instrumentality was in the control of one of several defendants, without identifying which one, is not sufficient to establish a case under the doctrine. In *Wolf* v. *American Tract Society* [58 N.E. 31 (New York)], a brick fell from a building in the course of construction and injured a pedestrian. Many workmen, under the control of numerous contractors, were engaged in work on the building. It was held that the circumstances of the accident gave rise to a presumption that someone had been negligent, but not to a presumption that the owner of the building or a particular contractor had been guilty of negligence. The complaint was accordingly dismissed.

In *Sondler* v. *Garrison* (249 N.Y. 236), the plaintiff was standing on a public sidewalk near an elevated railway structure and, as the train was passing, was struck on the head by a metal object. The object was seen falling through the air, but whether it proceeded from the structure or the passing train was not observed. The object, identified and exhibited to the jury, was an iron door lock. Testimony was offered that the lock was similar to locks used on the inside of railway cars maintained by the defendant. But there was a failure of proof that the metal lock was possessed or controlled by the defendant and, so far as the proof showed, the lock may have been one which a passenger traveling on the train was carrying and had, accidentally or purposely, dropped from the car window.

Under those circumstances, the court refused to apply the doctrine of *res ipsa loquitur* and to hold the defendant liable. The element lacking in this case was control of the offending instrumentality. If proof could have been offered that there was a lock missing from one of the cars on the train which passed overhead, plus the evidence of a witness who saw the lock fall off and roll out of the train, then the missing element of *res ipsa* would have been established and a different result would have occurred.

1507   Constructive control under *res ipsa*

It frequently happens that a specific act of negligence occurs while the offending instrumentality is in the hands of the defendant, but the accident occurred after the defendant had relinquished possession. This situation usually arises in cases of defectively manufactured products. The doctrine of *res ipsa loquitur* has been applied to such cases and the requirement that the instrumentality causing the injury be under exclusive control of the defendant is overcome by one of several theories.

Some courts take the position that once the negligent act has occurred, the duty of the defendant is a continuing one and therefore, at least constructively or theoretically, the defendant has possession and control of the article until the defective condition is remedied, even though the defective article passes out of the possession of the defendant. Other cases merely hold that the requirement is met if it is shown that the negligent act occurred while the offending instrumentality was in the control of the defendant. In either of these cases the result is the same, and the doctrine of *res ipsa loquitur* is applied.

Illustrative of this type of situation would be a case where a manufacturer produced a loaf of bread with glass baked inside it, which bread was sold to the plaintiff in a sealed package. The *res ipsa* doctrine would be applied to any injury sustained by the plaintiff, even though this particular loaf of bread had passed from the possession of the manufacturer. Obviously, the manufacturer or packer of food products is charged with the knowledge that the item will be used for human consumption. Therefore, he must exercise a high degree of care to assure the purity of the product manufactured or prepared. The mere presence of deleterious substances in the product, glass in this case, would be sufficient to give rise to an inference that there was a failure on the part of the manufacturer to exercise the requisite amount of care.

The same principle has been applied to other than food products, such as defectively manufactured appliances which burst into flame upon use, explode, leak illuminating gas, or collapse when subjected to the use for which the appliance was intended. It is sufficient that the negligent act in the form of defective workmanship occurred while the product was in the possession of the defendant.

In order to sustain the burden of proof necessary, the plaintiff must eliminate any possible intervening cause of the accident. He must show that the product was handled with due care after it left the possession of the defendant. The plaintiff would have to show that the article was properly transported and handled with the requisite amount of care through all hands through which it passed, including the possession of the plaintiff. In order to have the advantage of the inference of negligence on the part of the manufacturer, the plaintiff would have to negative any possibility of the defect, whatever it was, as having been caused by someone other than the manufacturer.

For example, in *Evangelio* v. *Metropolitan Bottling Company* [158 N.E. 2d 342 (Massachusetts)], the facts indicated that the plaintiff-wife, while assisting her husband in the operation of his retail store, was injured by the explosion of a bottle of Pepsi Cola, manufactured and bottled by the defendant. While the plaintiff was in charge of the store, the defendant's employee deposited two cases of Pepsi Cola in the rear of the store, one on top of the other. About 15 minutes later, the plaintiff picked from the top case two bottles with her left hand and one bottle with her right, moving toward an icebox, 15 feet away. She placed the bottles in her left hand in the icebox and was likewise depositing the bottle held in her right when it exploded, injuring her hand, before any part of it touched any part of the icebox.

Thus, from the time the cases were delivered at the store until the accident, the plaintiff was alone in the store, and nothing had touched the bottles other than the indicated handling of them by the plaintiff. The court, in affirming a judgment for the plaintiff, held that an inference of negligence on the part of the defendant could have been drawn from the fact that the bottle exploded, coupled with proof that it was properly handled after it had left the defendant's control. The court observed that most of the courts which had considered this problem have permitted the trier of the fact to draw an inference that the explosion was caused by negligent conduct, leaving it to the defendant to explain why, in a given case, it was more probable that the explosion was the product of a cause for which the defendant was not responsible. Therefore, the court concluded that the plaintiff must prove more than the fact of the explosion to recover. Where the accident occurs after the defendant has surrendered control of the instrumentality involved, it is incumbent upon the plaintiff to show that the instrumentality had not been improperly handled by himself or intermediate handlers.

In *Bornstein* v. *Metropolitan Bottling Company* [139 Atl. 2d 404 (New Jersey)], the court, in upholding the recovery for injuries sustained in an exploding bottle case, stated that while exclusive control is the essence of *res ipsa loquitur*, the doctrine could be applied to the accident since the plaintiff had carried the burden of proving careful handling after the bottled beverage left the defendant's possession. To the same effect is *Ferrell* v. *Sikeston Coca-Cola Bottling Company* [320 S.W. 2d 292 (Missouri)], wherein it was held that the plaintiff's circumstantial evidence precluded third-party tampering and warranted the jury in finding that the explosion was not due to mistreatment or exposure to unusual temperature changes after the bottle passed from the defendant's control.

Similarly, in *Weggeman* v. *Seven-Up Bottling Company* [93 N.W. 2d 467 (Wisconsin)], the court approved the application of *res ipsa loquitur* on the theory that the bottler is required to put out a bottle strong enough to stand up under expectable rough handling with resulting nicks and abrasions by retailers, customers, and consumers.

Other cases in which the doctrine of *res ipsa loquitur* is applied to exploding bottle cases by state are as follows:

Alabama	*Florence Coca-Cola Bottling Co.* v. *Sullivan*, 65 So. 2d 169.
Arkansas	*Coca-Cola Bottling Co. of Fort Smith* v. *Fix*, 233 S.W. 2d 762;
	Dr. Pepper Bottling Co. of N.Y. v. *Whidden*, 296 S.W. 2d 432;
	Coca-Cola Bottling Co. v. *Jones*, 295 S.W. 2d 321.
California	*Escola* v. *Coca-Cola Bottling Co.*, 150 Pacific 2d 436;
	Zentz v. *Coca-Cola Bottling Co. of Fresno*, 247 Pacific 2d 344.
District of Columbia	*Canadian Canada Dry Ginger Ale Co.* v. *Jochum*, 43 Atl. 2d 42.
Florida	*Groves* v. *Florida Coca-Cola Bottling Co.*, 407 So. 2d 128.
Georgia	*Payne* v. *Rome Coca-Cola Bottling Co.*, 73 S.E. 1087.
Kansas	*Bradley* v. *Conway Springs Bottling Co.*, 108 Pac. 2d 601.
Louisiana	*Orpego* v. *Nehi Bottling Works*, 67 So. 2d 677.
Michigan	*Macres* v. *Coca-Cola Bottling Co.*, 287 N.W. 922;
	Pattison v. *Coca-Cola Bottling Co.*, 52 N.W. 2d 688.

Minnesota	*Johnson* v. *Coca-Cola Bottling Co.*, 51 N.W. 2d 573.
Missouri	*Stolle* v. *Anheuser-Busch, Inc.*, 271 S.W. 497;
	Ferrell v. *Sikeston Coca-Cola Bottling Co.* (above).
New Jersey	*MacPherson* v. *Canada Dry Ginger Ale, Inc.*, 29 Atl. 2d 868.
Ohio	*Fick* v. *Presner Brewing Co.*, 86 N.E. 2d 616.
Oklahoma	*Laughton Coca-Cola Bottling Co.* v. *Shaughnessy*, 216 Pac. 2d 579.
Tennessee	*Coca-Cola Bottling Works* v. *Crow*, 291 S.W. 2d 589.
Texas	*Honea* v. *Coca-Cola Bottling Co.*, 183 S.W. 2d 968.
Vermont	*Joly* v. *Coca-Cola Bottling Co.*, 55 Atl. 2d 181.
Wisconsin	*Zarling* v. *La Salle Coca-Cola Bottling Co.*, 87 N.W. 2d 263.
West Virginia	*Ferrell* v. *Royal Crown Bottling Co. of Charleston*, 109 S.E. 2d 489.

1508   Judicial notice

It is axiomatic that the law does not require that to be proven which is apparent to the court. To demand otherwise would be wasteful of time and contrary to common sense. It follows that there are numerous matters which the court would deem to be proven, either on its own initiative or whenever its attention is directed to them. This process by the court by which it dispenses with proof is called *judicial notice.*

The court will give judicial notice in matters of common and general knowledge, such as the time and the setting of the sun at a given place on a certain date, or the direction in which a river within the jurisdiction flows. Proof would not be required to establish that the United States is in North America, that North America is in the western hemisphere, or that the Atlantic Ocean is on the east coast and the Pacific Ocean on the west coast of the United States. These are matters of geographical certainty and it would be absurd for the court to demand proof thereof or to receive evidence to prove that any of these conditions did not exist. As to the existence of statutes, the court is required to give notice judicially to all statutes of general application in its jurisdiction, the federal statutes of general application, and the Constitution and treaties of the United States.

The court will give judicial notice to physical traits in that the height of an average man is less than 6 feet; that the average length of the body from the lower end of the spine to the top of the head is less than 36 inches; that the measurement varies little in adults, and the chief difference in the height of a man is in the length of his lower limbs. The court will also give judicial notice to matters of common knowledge with respect to the effect of certain things on the human body. For example, if the plaintiff testified that he was struck in the eye and that he later had a black eye, it would not be necessary for the plaintiff to produce medical evidence indicating in detail the exact physiological process which occurred following the blow in order to produce the black eye. On the other hand, the court would not take judicial notice of the remote and unusual effects of physical injury, such as cancer or tuberculosis, which would call for more than the average person's knowledge of cause and effect.

Generally speaking, therefore, the court will take judicial notice of facts which are within the knowledge of the average man as well as authoritative record books, such as Lloyd's Register of Ships, telephone directories, municipal directories, and the like. The court can inform itself with respect to the contents of volumes of this character by making reference to the book itself.

The following is a general list of specific matters which the courts will judicially notice:

1. Facts within the common knowledge of the average person.
2. Matters of governmental record and concern.
3. The course and laws of nature.
4. Qualities and properties of matter within the common knowledge of the average person.
5. Time, days, and dates of the calendar.
6. Scientific facts within the knowledge of the average person.
7. Geographical facts: location of principal rivers, boundaries, and municipalities.
8. Location of the 50 states and the boundaries of each, together with mountain ranges, lakes, and streams of national importance.
9. Historical facts concerning the nation as a whole and the state in which the court sits.
10. The United States census.
11. Mortality tables.

The court will likewise take judicial notice of physical facts produced in evidence which make it impossible for the alleged accident to have occurred. For example, it was shown that an archway was 9½ feet from the ground. It was alleged that the plaintiff, walking along the ground, struck his head against the archway, sustaining injuries. It is a matter of common knowledge that the average height of a man is 6 feet. Therefore, unless evidence were produced that the man was more than 9½ feet tall, it would have been impossible for this type of injury to have occurred. Therefore, to ask a jury to determine whether or not a man 6 feet tall could hit his head against an arch 9½ feet from the ground certainly would make a farce out of the legal process. Therefore, the court would take judicial notice of the impossibility and dismiss the claim. This type of reasoning is sometimes referred to as the doctrine of *incontrovertible physical facts*.

The court will take judicial notice of the common law and statutes of its own state, but not of municipal ordinances in the state; the latter must be alleged and proved as any other fact. As to the statute or common law of other states, the court will not take judicial notice thereof unless the law of the foreign state is alleged and proved as a fact. In the absence of proof, the court will presume that the common law of the foreign state is the same as its own.

1509   The hearsay rule

The rule is that evidence of any statement made out of court, no matter by whom, or who was present, or where it was made, if offered to prove the truth of what is contained in the statement, is hearsay and incompetent. A witness may testify only to information which he has of his own knowledge. He may not testify to what someone told him in order to establish the truth or falsity of the condition or event which is the subject matter of the statement. Any information he might have that came to him from a secondary source would not prove that a particular event happened or a particular set of facts were actually in existence at a specific time and place. As we all know from common experience, versions of a story become garbled when repeated. Therefore, any evidence which a witness could offer on this basis would be unreliable. In addition, since the witness is not testifying as to facts within his own knowledge, he could not be cross-examined in order to elicit further facts or to enlarge upon the facts which he has already given. The only question on which he could be examined would be the accuracy of his recollection of the statement which he heard.

An example of obvious hearsay would be where a witness offers to testify that his father was born at a certain time and at a certain place. It would have been physically impossible for the witness to have been present at the time of his father's birth. Any evidence which this witness might be prepared to give on this particular question must be based entirely upon what someone else told him. The witness could testify that a man purporting to be his father lived at a certain address and exercised the rights and prerogatives of a parent during a certain specific period since those facts are all within his actual knowledge. In addition, the statements made to him with respect to the time and place of his father's birth were not made under oath and could be unreliable and untrue. For these reasons, hearsay evidence is generally objectionable and excluded.

In slander cases, evidence by a witness of statements which he heard are admissible. This is not for the reason that the evidence tends to establish the truth of the statement made, or the truth of the facts or circumstances within the statement itself, but to establish that a statement was made. The basis of the cause of action for slander rests upon the oral publication of defamatory or untruthful statements concerning an individual. Therefore, the question before the court is whether or not the statement was in fact made, and not that the statement itself established the truth or falsity of an event or a fact. For example, if a witness testified that he heard A say to B that C is a thief, the witness' testimony is not hearsay evidence. It is evidence that the particular statement was made.

W testifies that X said, "I saw Jones strike Smith." If W's testimony is offered to prove only what X said, W's statement is not hearsay. However, if it is offered to prove either that X saw Jones strike Smith, or that Jones did strike Smith, the statement is a hearsay declaration and W's testimony is hearsay evidence.

For reasons of logic and sometimes for matters of pure necessity, the law permits certain evidence to be admitted as exceptions to the hearsay rule. The exceptions with which we are concerned are as follows:

1. *Res gestae* statements.
2. Declarations of pain and suffering.
3. Admissions against interest; plea of guilty at motor vehicle hearing.
4. Conviction in traffic court.
5. Conviction of prior crimes.
6. Testimony in prior proceedings.
7. Prior self-contradictory statements.
8. Book entries in the regular course of business.
9. Admissions by conduct.
10. Admissions by an agent.
11. Admissions by a joint tort-feasor.
12. Pedigree statements.

1510   Res gestae statements

One of the exceptions to the hearsay rule is the spontaneous utterance made during the happening of the event and made by the declarant as explanatory of the event. Included in this exception are things said, things written, things done simultaneously with the happening of the event before there has been an opportunity for reflection. Evidence is not limited to those things that are done by the parties to the action alone, but also things said, written, and done, even by a stranger. This evidence is admitted as a matter of necessity and the truth of the thing is based upon spontaneity. The statement must be simultaneous with the event and made before there was any opportunity for conscious, deliberate thought.

For example, if immediately after the accident between two automobiles the driver of one got out and stated "I was going too fast," or "My brakes would not function," or "I did not see your car," evidence by persons who heard these statements would be admissible against the person who made them. The reliability or truthfulness of the statement is based on the fact that it was made immediately after the event and is explanatory of the event.

Normally, to be a *res gestae* statement the utterance must be made simultaneously with the event or immediately thereafter. However, statements have been admitted in evidence where they were made by a person who was still under the nervous excitement of what he had seen. There is no specific rule as to the maximum period of time involved in such a situation. The evidence must show that the person is still under this nervous excitement and strain. An example is that of an individual who was knocked unconscious at the time of the accident and stayed in an unconscious state for several hours. Upon regaining consciousness, he made a statement. Obviously, he had no opportunity for reflection or fabrication. This is considered a *res gestae* statement.

The *res gestae* statement does not have to be made by a party to the action or event. Evidence is admissible if the court finds that the hearsay statement was made: (*a*) while the declarant was perceiving the event or condition which the statement narrates, or describes, or explains, or immediately thereafter; or (*b*) while the declarant was under the stress of a nervous excitement caused by his perception of the event or condition which the statement narrates or describes or explains.

For example, in an action by *P* against *D* for damages on account of an automobile collision at a street intersection, *W* offers to testify for *P*: "Just before we heard the crash, *X* said to me, 'That car (*D*'s) has driven through the red light without stopping.' " This is admissible.

In the same situation a police officer who reached the scene of the accident a few minutes after its occurrence offers to testify that immediately upon his arrival he heard *X* say to *W*: "That fool, this would never have happened if he hadn't driven through the red light." This is admissible in tending to prove that *D* drove through the red light if the court finds that *X* made this assertion while laboring under the excitement caused by seeing the event described.

1511   Declarations of pain and suffering

The usual manifestation of pain is by oral expression. Since such expression is solely within the control of the person manifesting it, only those expressions of pain made to others, which are involuntary, are admissible in evidence. This refers to evidence given by those who heard the declaration. The injured himself may testify to the pain he suffered as a fact, and upon this fact he may be cross-examined.

Declarations of pain and suffering can be admissible in evidence as a spontaneous utterance if made immediately after an accident occurred. This evidence is received on the same basis as other *res gestae* statements on the theory that it is made close to the happening of the event, without any opportunity for reflection and fabrication, and for that reason is bound to be truthful.

In only two situations are declarations of pain and suffering admissible in evidence. They are: (1) voluntary statements of pain communicated to a physician who was consulted for the purpose of treatment, which are admitted on the theory that such statements are motivated by an urge to be truthful; (2) voluntary statements of pain made by a person, since deceased, where the nature and cause of the injury are an issue, which statements are received on the theory that the necessity of the case demands it.

Where the patient is being examined by a physician employed by the defendant, statements as to the pain which he previously suffered are not admissible in evidence (as an exception to the hearsay rule) but declarations as to the patient's then existing state of mind, pain, and suffering, are admissible in evidence and the examining physician may so testify.

1512 Admissions against interest

An admission is any statement made, any act done, or any course of conduct pursued by which a party to the litigation has indicated a contrary attitude to the one which he is taking at the trial. Such prior contrary attitudes tend to throw suspicion on his claim at the trial and are used as independent evidence against him. Unlike the spontaneous utterance, an admission may be made at any time prior to the trial.

Declarations against interest are defined by the Model Code of Evidence as follows:

A declaration is against the interest of a declarant if the judge finds that the fact asserted in the declaration was at the time of the declaration so far contrary to the declarant's pecuniary or proprietary interest, or so far subjected him to civil or criminal liability or so far rendered invalid a claim by him against another, or created such a risk of making him an object of hatred, ridicule, or social disapproval in the community that a reasonable man in his position would not have made the declaration unless he believed it to be true.

The admission against interest does not necessarily have to be made by a party to the litigation. For example, in an action between P and D for damages for personal injuries, W offers to testify for D that X said, "I carelessly drove over P; I understand he is now suing D for the damage." This is an admission against the pecuniary interest of X and is therefore admissible in order to show that X was responsible for the accident and not D.

1513 Plea of guilty at a motor vehicle hearing

Should a party to the litigation allege that he was operating his motor vehicle within the traffic regulations, any action taken by him subsequent to the event, which would be inconsistent with his position, can be admissible in evidence against him. Such an act could consist of entering a plea of guilty to a charge of traffic violation arising out of the same event. Evidence of such a plea is received in evidence against him as an admission.

The courts recognize that in some cases one charged with a traffic violation will plead guilty, even though he believes himself innocent, in order to avoid the expenditure of time and money which would be involved if guilt were denied and the charge contested. However, the courts do allow evidence of the plea of guilty to be introduced and will allow the defendant to give his explanation and his reasons for so pleading. It is then for the jury to evaluate his testimony and decide whether the plea is entitled to any weight as an admission.

Where the defendant does not appear and plead in the traffic court, and merely suffers a forfeiture of his bail bond or a fine, this lack of action is not considered an admission and evidence thereof is not admissible. It is only where some action is taken by the person, which action is inconsistent with his position at the trial, that such evidence is admissible.

1514   Conviction in traffic court

Evidence of a conviction as a consequence of a motor vehicle hearing, wherein the defendant entered a plea of not guilty, cannot be received in evidence as an admission or for any other purpose. The fact that another court has made a decision with respect to one phase of the case is neither binding upon nor persuasive to the court before which the present action is being tried. It would be prejudicial to the defendant's chances of a fair trial before this court if any reference were made to an action taken by another court on the same or similar evidence.

From another point of view, evidence of conviction in traffic court is pure hearsay. The conclusion reached by the court on the traffic violation is likewise hearsay. In addition, if the traffic court conviction were given any weight whatsoever, the result would be that a superior court would be bound by the findings of a lower court of limited jurisdiction.

Some states have departed from this general rule and have by statute permitted evidence of a conviction in the traffic court to be received in evidence. In other states, only the conviction of a felony such as manslaughter, arson, and crimes of like quality can be received in evidence. Traffic violations, coming under the classification of minor offenses or misdemeanors, are not affected by this latter rule.

1515   Conviction of prior crimes

There are two phases to this subject. The first is the problem of the admissibility of evidence of the conviction of a crime arising out of the same subject matter as the pending action, such evidence being offered for the purpose of proving the liability of the defendant. The second phase of the problem refers to the admissibility of evidence of the conviction of a prior crime, totally unrelated to the action pending before the court, but offered for the purpose of affecting the credibility of any witness in the action, be he a party thereto or not.

As we have seen in the preceding paragraph, the majority view is that conviction of any crime arising out of the same event as the action pending before the court is not admissible for the purpose of establishing the liability of the defendant. Our courts have tenaciously adhered to this principle even though in many cases an inconsistent result was obtained.

For example, A is convicted of arson in the third degree. This crime consists of the intentional burning of his own building with intent to defraud or prejudice an insurer thereof. While serving his sentence A brings an action against his fire insurance company under a policy covering the building which he intentionally burned. The evidence of A's conviction of the crime is excluded. Under those circumstances, where the jury is ignorant of A's conviction, it is quite possible for the jury to bring in a verdict for A and against the fire insurance company. We then would have a situation where A is serving a sentence for arson, but is allowed to recover a money judgment as a consequence of his own criminal act. The inconsistency is immediately apparent. A has profited from the commission of his own crime, while at the same time being punished for it.

Public policy demands that there be no profit derived from the commission of a criminal act. Therefore, some states have enacted statutes modifying this rule and permitting evidence of such convictions to be received. Under the statutes, evidence of the conviction of the crime would be admissible in evidence whether the party so convicted testified or not. The statute permits the introduction of the evidence not to affect the party's credibility as a witness, but to prove the facts recited in the judgment of conviction.

When a party to a lawsuit puts any witness on the stand, including himself, he impliedly warrants that the witness is a truth-teller. Frequently the version as told by one witness will be entirely contradictory to the version given by another. The jury has the task of deciding which version is correct. In coming to this conclusion, the jury has an opportunity of observing the witness, noting his demeanor while on the stand as well as his cross-examination. In making their evaluation, the jury is entitled to know that the witness has been convicted of a crime involving moral turpitude, if such be the fact. Evidence of prior crimes which involve acts contrary to justice, honesty, modesty or good morals may be shown if the witness has in fact been convicted of committing them. A convicted thief is more likely to offer perjured testimony than a man who has no such record. In deciding the relative weight to be given to the testimony of witnesses, the fact that one witness is a convicted thief will weigh heavily against the jury's acceptance of his story.

To be admissible, the conviction must be a crime involving moral turpitude. In this category would come larceny, embezzlement, rape, murder, and adultery. Conviction of crimes not involving moral turpitude are not admissible. Suppose that a man was convicted of automobile homicide. This means that he operated his motor vehicle in a willful, wanton, and reckless manner. Evidence of such conviction would not in any way indicate that he was a person who was not to be believed. That he operated his motor vehicle in a culpably negligent manner does not in any way involve a moral issue, or is his conviction any indication of his character as an honest man. The same thing would be true if the witness were convicted of violating city ordinances by failing to remove the snow from his sidewalks or failing to keep his garbage cans covered. These matters likewise do not involve any moral issue and conviction of such crimes would not be received in evidence to affect his credibility.

It should be emphasized, however, that only evidence of a conviction may be received. If the witness was accused of a crime involving moral turpitude by indictment of the grand jury or an information filed by the district attorney, and was either acquitted after trial or the charges were dropped, evidence of these prior proceedings is not admissible for any purpose whatsoever.

1516   Testimony in prior proceedings

A witness' testimony in prior proceedings is not admissible in evidence unless the witness takes the stand in the subsequent proceedings. Then his prior testimony may be identified and used on cross-examination for the purpose of impeaching the witness and raising an issue as to his credibility, should his present testimony be contrary to his previous testimony on the same issue. This is permissible on the theory that the jury has a right to know whether or not he has testified under oath to a different version, and also a right to such testimony to help them decide whether they will believe him or not.

The prior testimony of a party to the action is always admissible in evidence, whether he testifies or not, as an admission against interest (see Section 1512).

1517   Prior self-contradictory statements

Oral statements made in public, which are inconsistent with the testimony offered by the witness, may be established by the testimony of other witnesses who were present at the time and place the statement was made. Limitation on this type of evidence is within the sound discretion of the court, and the extent to which the adverse party may go in introducing evidence along these lines is fixed by the court. The oral statements may include communications given to a police officer investigating the case at some time subsequent to the occurrence of an accident, or oral statements given to an insurance adjuster. Should the person who allegedly made the statements deny having made them, then a question of fact is presented to the jury. It will decide which witness is telling the truth and which is not.

Written statements verified by the witness carry much more weight and are documentary evidence of the statements made. Denial is more difficult. These could consist of written statements given to an insurance adjuster and signed by the witness, a motor vehicle report of the accident submitted to the state and signed by the witness, a written report of the accident signed by the witness and submitted to his insurance company, or a written statement or written claim for compensation for injuries arising out of the same accident. In this same category would be claims arising out of the same event for accident and health insurance, Blue Cross, Blue Shield, and other types of medical payment insurance coverage.

1518   Book entries in the regular course of business

A party to litigation may offer, under certain circumstances, the books kept and prepared by him or others as proof of the facts contained therein. If the books are prepared by the litigant, they are not only hearsay but also self-serving; whereas if they are prepared by another, they are purely hearsay. Nevertheless, for reasons of necessity, regular book entries have been admitted as exceptions to the hearsay rule upon the fulfillment of certain requirements to verify their accuracy.

Entries made in the regular course of business, prepared by record clerks and persons other than the litigants, are admissible. The preliminary proof required for the introduction of such books into evidence is as follows: it must appear that (a) the books are the regular books of entry; (b) the entries were made in the regular course of business at about the time of the transaction involved; (c) the person making the entry had personal knowledge of the transaction or was informed of it by one who had such knowledge and who was under a duty to communicate it to him.

Because of the difficulty in producing evidence of this character, especially where bookkeeping systems are intricate and where the turnover in help is large—with discharged employees having no inclination to be helpful even if they were able to remember something of a given transaction—many states have enacted statutes by means of which the mere identification of the books as the regular books of account of the corporation is sufficient to admit them into evidence.

1519   Admissions by conduct

Evidence of conduct on the part of one party which could be indicative of the fact that he himself felt that he had a poor case is admissible against him. Such an act might consist of an attempt to bribe a witness to give false testimony in his favor. Although collateral to the issues, it is competent as an admission by act and conduct that his case is weak and his evidence dishonest. It is not conclusive, even when believed by the jury, because the party may think that he has a poor case when in fact he has a good one. The evidence tends to discredit his witnesses and to cast some doubt upon his position. It is for the consideration of the jury, after ample opportunity for explanation and denial under proper instructions so as to prevent them from giving undue attention to the collateral matter to the detriment of the main issue.

Illustrative of this type of situation is the case of *Nowack* v. *Metropolitan Street Railway Co.* (166 N.Y. 433), decided in 1901. This was an action in tort to recover damages sustained by the plaintiff through the negligence of the defendant. The conflict in evidence was irreconcilable and several witnesses were called to sustain the theory of each party. One witness, Klein, was offered on behalf of the plaintiff, and on redirect examination he testified that he knew one Kaufmann, who had been to his house five or six times during the past week, the first time being on Saturday a week before. He was asked to state what Kaufmann said to him on that day. Objection to this question was sustained.

The witness was then withdrawn and Kaufmann, being put on the stand by the plaintiff, testified that he was employed by the defendant as an investigator; that his duties were "to see to the witnesses and take statements and to interview witnesses" (those who "expect" to be and "those who are" witnesses), and he had been acting in this case for the defendant. The plaintiff thereupon resumed examination of Mr. Klein and asked him to state the conversation he had with Kaufmann on the Saturday in question. Again the defendant's objection was sustained. The witness did testify that he had a conversation with Kaufmann on the occasion mentioned in reference to the testimony he was to give on the trial. He was asked these questions:

What conversation did he have with you in reference to the testimony you were to give on the trial of this action?

Did Harry Kaufmann make any offer to you of money or any other thing in reference to the testimony you were to give on the trial of this action?

Each of these questions was objected to by the defendant and the objections were sustained, the plaintiff excepting separately to each ruling.

On appeal, the decision in favor of the defendant was reversed and the court held that, whether authorized or not, the conduct of Kaufmann, if true, was binding on the defendant. The court said:

It is claimed, however, that such evidence is not admissible against the corporation without proof that some corporate act expressly authorizing an agent to tamper with witnesses. This is equivalent to claiming such evidence cannot be received against corporations at all, because in the nature of things, proof of express authority would be impossible. A corporation can act only through an agent and where a branch of its business, whether broad or narrow, is entrusted to an agent without any restriction, whatever he does which directly relates to that part of the corporate business and tends to promote it, is binding on the corporation. Under such circumstances, he has control of the method of action, and that which he does, whether morally right or wrong, within the general scope of the matter entrusted to him in legal effect is done by the corporation itself. Having authority to accomplish a certain result with no limitation as to the means to be employed, his acts, so far as they directly contribute to that result, even if unlawful, are corporate acts.

An analysis of the opinion indicates that Kaufmann was employed to "look up" and "see to" witnesses for the defendant so as to enable it to defeat the plaintiff's claim. He was to find witnesses, if possible, who would swear to such a state of facts as would prevent a recovery against the defendant. The method of doing this was left to his judgment and discretion. If he adopted a method not contemplated by the defendant, still it is responsible for what he did in the line of his employment to promote its interest. In order to promote its interest, he saw fit to use the power entrusted to him by trying to bribe witnesses for the plaintiff to testify falsely in favor of the defendant. He was to procure evidence, the method not being specified, and he tried to get it by an unlawful method.

The court held that the power of the corporation was entrusted to him with reference to this subject, to be used as he saw fit. His act related solely to that subject and was done by him as its agent wholly for its benefit. In concluding its opinion, the court said:

If this evidence would have been admissible against an individual defendant who had employed Kaufmann as he was employed, it is admissible against this corporate defendant. If an honest man by mistake employs a dishonest one to look up witnesses for him, and the latter through excess of zeal resorts to bribery, although it was never thought of by his employer, it is better for cleanliness and purity in the administration of justice, that the facts should be shown with the fullest opportunity for explanation than to exclude all evidence of the evil acts upon the ground that they were not authorized because authority may properly be inferred from the nature of the employment. In such a case all doubt should be resolved, if possible, in the interest of clean evidence and the exposure of foul practices.

In an action against a municipal corporation for damages caused by the construction and maintenance of a drain over the plaintiff's land, the plaintiff appeared at a hearing before the board of health and at that time stated that he would claim no damages. This conduct and statement were held to be inadmissible in evidence against the plaintiff in a later action for damages, the court holding that a statement that a person will claim no damages is not necessarily evidence that he has suffered no damages. An admission that he would claim no damages does not preclude him from later changing his mind. It may be rather an assertion of a wrong sustained, coupled with a statement that he would not seek redress for the wrong. In any event, the statement is not binding nor is it evidence that no damages were actually sustained.

1520   Admissions by an agent

Normally an agent has no authority to make any admissions which are binding on his principal. There is one exception, and that is where the agent makes an admission while he is acting within the scope of his agency and within the scope of his authority. For example, if an agent is driving his principal's motor vehicle, and after an accident has occurred, the agent admits that he was at fault, such an admission is binding on his principal.

An attorney, as agent for his client, has no authority to make any admissions on behalf of his client. However, an admission made by the attorney in open court, when such admissions are made as a necessary incident of the handling of the client's case, are binding on the client. The same situation is true here as in the agent driving the automobile. The admission was made as part and parcel of the agent's employment and was made within the scope of the agency.

1521   Admissions by a joint tort-feasor

Where two or more persons owe to another the same duty, and by their common neglect such other is injured, they are joint tort-feasors. Where the relationship of joint tort-feasors is established, an admission by one is binding on the others. It must be emphasized that an admission, to be binding on the others, must be made by a joint tort-feasor, and if the person occupies any other relationship the admission is not binding on the others.

The same rule would be applicable in the case of a conspiracy. Where the conspiracy is established, admissions made by any of the coconspirators is binding and admissible against the other coconspirators.

1522   Pedigree statements

This is one of the oldest exceptions to the hearsay rule in which merely genealogical, hearsay evidence is allowed as to the time of birth of a certain party, marriage, death, legitimacy, consanguinity generally (and the particular degrees thereof), and affinity. The reliability of such statements was recognized at an early date and the courts admitted them in evidence upon the principle that they are the "natural effusions of a party who must know the truth."

A pedigree statement consists of the evidence of a witness who heard a statement made by a declarant, now deceased, with reference to lineage, descent, and succession of families, or facts and dates of birth, marriage, and death. In addition, the statement was made prior to the inception of the litigation in which the evidence is offered. Usually what happens is that the oldest member of the family will make statements with regard to the relationships of the various members of the family with regard to each other. Because of his age, the declarant is perhaps the one in his family who has the greatest knowledge with regard to the family genealogical structure. As an additional safeguard, the statement must have been made prior to the beginning of the litigation in which the evidence is offered.

If, for instance, *A*'s parentage is an issue, the testimony of *B* that he heard *C*, now deceased, say that *A* was his son, is accepted as a statement of pedigree. It should be emphasized, however, that the statement must be positive. A negative statement is not a pedigree statement. For example, if *C*, now deceased, said that *A* was not his son, this statement would not constitute a pedigree statement and is not admissible.

Statements of this character are encountered in death cases where evidence is necessary with respect to whether or not the deceased was married, whether or not he left surviving issue, and whether a marriage was legal or bigamous.

1523   Privileged communications

There are certain classes of communications passing between persons who stand in a confidential of fiduciary relationship to each other, or who, on account of their relative situations are under a special duty of secrecy and fidelity, which communications the law will not permit to be divulged or inquired into, even in a court of justice and for the sake of public policy and the good order of society. Examples of such privileged relations are those of husband and wife, and attorney and client.

The holder of the privilege, or the person for whose benefit the secrecy is imposed, may waive the privilege and permit the other party to testify concerning matters in the privileged area. In most instances, the waiver must be made in open court and without qualification.

1524   Husband and wife

The general rule is that a husband or wife shall not be compelled, without the consent of the other (if living), to disclose a confidential communication made by one to the other during marriage. This rule is based on principles which are deemed important to preserve the marriage relation as one of full confidence and affection. Public welfare demands that domestic peace be placed above the necessities of a lawsuit or even a criminal proceeding.

This privilege is seldom involved in personal injury cases, and where it is, the privilege is waived by the holder when he presents the other marital partner as a witness in his behalf.

It is important to note that this privilege extends only to confidential communications between husband and wife which arise out of the marital relation. A wife or husband, as the case might be, is a competent witness as to all other evidence and may be compelled to testify in behalf of either party to the lawsuit. For example, the wife is a passenger in a vehicle driven by her husband. Husband sues for his personal injuries. The wife may be compelled to testify if called as a witness by either her husband or the defendant. Her knowledge of the facts of the accident is not knowledge gained as a consequence of the marital relation, and is not privileged.

1525   Attorney and client

The rule is that an attorney or counselor-at-law may not disclose a communication made by his client in the course of professional employment, or his advice thereon. And no employee of the lawyer—stenographer, clerk, or other person—is allowed to disclose any such communication. The rule is statutory in most states and in others it is considered to be a common-law rule.

The reason for the rule is a matter of necessity since expert legal advice, to be effective, can be given only by a consideration of all of the facts. Clients would be reluctant to make a full disclosure of all the facts if there was any possibility that the attorney could be compelled to testify against them. The client is the holder of the privilege and only the client may waive it.

The privilege is limited to situations where the relationship of attorney and client exists and where the communication is made as a result of such relationship. An attorney is competent and may be compelled to testify concerning other facts which were not gained from a confidential communication.

Obviously, if the relationship of attorney and client does not exist there can be no confidential communications, and an attorney, by reason of his profession, does not acquire a status that differs in any way from that of an ordinary witness. He is competent and compellable to testify to any matter other than a confidential communication made by a client to him in the course of his professional employment.

1526   Physician and patient

Necessity demands that if medical treatment is to be effective the physician must have all the facts leading up to the patient's present condition. This includes a personal history of previous illnesses, treatment, and exposures to disease, as well as information gained by a physical examination, treatment, reactions to medication, and diagnostic aids such as X rays, blood tests and similar tests, and exploratory operations. As to these matters, a privilege arises in favor of the patient. This privilege is also binding on all employees of the physician, secretary, stenographer, office nurse, X-ray technician, and physiotherapist. Likewise, the privilege binds registered nurses, technicians who make various physical tests, and the employees of a hospital or other medical institution in which the patient may be confined.

The privilege does not extend to examining physicians of an insurance company. There is no relationship of physician and patient in these situations, and as a result such a physician is competent and compellable to testify concerning the history received and his findings.

The patient, as the holder of the privilege, may waive the privilege and permit the doctor or registered nurse to testify to information thus obtained. In the case of death, this waiver can be given only by the personal representative of the deceased.

Privileged communications arising from the doctor-patient relationship consist of all communications made by the patient to the doctor relating to his physical condition, and, in addition, all information which the doctor obtained as a consequence of the examination and treatment of the patient. The doctor, of course, is at liberty to disclose information thus obtained to other doctors, or to a hospital, concurrently engaged in treating the same case. It should be emphasized that the privilege attaches only to communications made to the physician for the purpose of treatment or information gained as a consequence of examination and treatment.

As to communications which do not arise out of the relationship of doctor and patient, there is no privilege. Merely because the witness is a doctor does not disqualify him from testifying to other matters within his knowledge obtained from other sources. In personal injury cases, the plaintiff puts his physical condition in issue by his pleadings and by the presentation of witnesses as to the extent of his injuries. Under those circumstances, the privilege has been waived. The physician may be required to testify as to all communications received in connection with the treatment of the case as well as to submit any notes or memoranda that he may have made as to the progress of the patient.

The doctor and patient privilege did not exist at common law; it is the result of various statutes passed in different states, and they are variously interpreted. Some states go so far as to impose a legal liability upon the physician who discloses any information with regard to the patient's physical condition, whether in court or elsewhere. As a result, the medical profession is extremely hesitant to divulge medical information with respect to patients. Where a statute compels the physician to make reports, such as a workmen's compensation law, he must comply. As to other matters, the adjuster will find that the physician will rarely give any medical information without a specific written authorization signed by the patient. Since the patient is the holder of the privilege, only the patient may waive it. The doctor may not.

1527 Priest and penitent

This is another privilege which never existed at common law. It was never recognized, probably, because cases in which clergymen were called upon to testify to confidential communications (in the form of confessions and other information of like quality) were extremely rare. It is quite likely that the jury would develop a certain amount of antagonism toward the party who put a priest on the stand and sought to extract information from him that had been gained as a result of a confession. For that reason most attorneys would forego the evidence rather than risk the displeasure of the jury.

Today, the majority of states have enacted statutes providing for this very privilege. They define "priest" as a priest, clergyman, minister of the gospel, or other officer of a church or religious denomination or organization, who, in the course of its discipline or practice, is authorized or accustomed to hear, and has a duty to keep secret, penitential communications made by members of his church, denomination, or organization. "Penitent" means a member of the church, religious denomination, or organization who has made penitential communication to a priest thereof. The "penitential communication" usually means a confession of culpable conduct made secretly and in confidence by a penitent to a priest in the course of the discipline or practice of the church, religious denomination, or organization of which the penitent is a member. Statutes provide that the privilege is in favor of both the priest and the penitent. For the information to be admissible, both priest and penitent must waive the privilege. A waiver by one is not binding on the other.

1528 Deception tests

The so-called *lie-detector tests* are not admissible in evidence in civil cases. They are of no value in preparing a case for trial.

There are presently three types of lie-detector tests, as follows:

Systolic blood pressure test. The blood pressure of the individual is measured in much the same way as in an electrocardiogram. The principle on which this test is based is that an untrue answer to a question will cause a measureable increase in the subject's blood pressure.

Association-reaction test. The subject concentrates on a list of words that has been given to him, some of which may evoke a guilty sensation and indicate the subject's untruthfulness.

Respiratory test. This is based on the theory that the breathing of a subject varies perceptibly upon telling a falsehood.

People who specialize in giving these tests have recommended their use as a tool by the adjuster in his investigation. It is argued that in cases where there is sharp conflict between the versions given by the insured and the claimant, the adjuster could ascertain the amount of reliance that can be placed upon the insured's version by giving the insured one of these tests. This contention is of dubious value and could easily produce an irritating strain on the relations between the company and its insured. In addition, no company would seriously contend that the insured was in violation of the cooperation clause of his policy if he refused to submit to the test.

1529   Evidence of habit or disposition

The general rule is that evidence of habit is admissible whereas evidence of disposition is not. It is often difficult to distinguish between the two.

Evidence that A is a careful, cautious man, that he drives his car carefully, and is always careful crossing streets is evidence of disposition. This will not support a contention that A was careful and cautious in his actions when a particular incident took place. Evidence that A always stopped at a certain intersection, and made an observation in both directions before crossing, is evidence of habit and is admissible. It can be established by the testimony of one or more witnesses who will testify that they observed A on more than one occasion and that he followed the same pattern on each occasion. If an accident happened at that particular intersection, evidence of this sort would be persuasive of the fact that A was careful on that occasion—the evidence would not be persuasive that A acted with due care at any other place or under any other circumstances. It is possible that A would be careful and cautious when crossing this particular intersection and extremely careless crossing other intersections.

Evidence of this character is important only in death cases or in cases where the plaintiff has no memory of the occurrence. In both cases, the deceased or the injured person cannot testify that he exercised the degree of prudence which the law requires. Therefore scondary proof, in the form of evidence of habit, is admissible to supply the missing element.

The habit sought to be established does not necessarily have to be one of care and prudence. The defendant might introduce evidence of a careless habit which would be persuasive of contributory negligence and could be offered by way of explanation as to how the accident actually happened. Thus, evidence that A habitually became intoxicated every Saturday night and reeled home would be received in evidence to explain how an unwitnessed fall on the sidewalk on a Saturday night, with fatal results, could have occurred. Here again we have a specific instance and a habit of repetition as to one specific circumstance. That A was a drinking man and on occasions became intoxicated is evidence of disposition, but this type of evidence would not be admissible since it is too general to establish exactly what A's conduct could have been at a specific time and place.

1530   Subsequent precautions to prevent harm

Where an accident has occurred, the owner of the premises may make repairs or alterations in order to prevent a recurrence of the accident. He may adopt other means, such as the employment of watchmen or an increase in the number of watchmen. Evidence of these precautions to prevent future harm is not admissible against the owner to prove that his failure to take such precautions to prevent the previous accident was negligent. If such evidence were admissible, the owner would make alterations or repairs or plans to prevent future harm only at his peril. The policy of the law is to the contrary and it encourages the prevention of future accidents, especially where experience has indicated that some precautions are necessary.

While evidence of subsequent repairs or alterations is not admissible in order to establish the negligence of the owner, such evidence is admissible in order to show ownership and control of the premises, but then only when the owner denies such control. In absence of a denial of control, evidence of subsequent repairs is not admissible.

1531   Offers to compromise and similar conduct

The law encourages the compromise of disputed claims. It recognizes that very often a defendant will seek to avoid litigation and buy his peace by the payment of money—even though he does not believe himself to be responsible for the accident or the occurrence. Therefore evidence of offers to compromise (settlement negotiations as well as the plaintiff's demand in settlement) is excluded. Were it otherwise, the defendant would never be persuaded to make any offer of settlement, since to do so would be construed as an admission of liability. This would discourage compromises and prolong litigation.

Likewise, evidence that the defendant called a doctor for the injured plaintiff or took him to the hospital is not admissible as an admission of liability. Here again, the law encourages acts of human decency and compassion. Nor is the defendant penalized for acts of kindness to the injured person. Testimony that the defendant called on the injured person, sent flowers, fruit, or other gifts, paid for the doctor's services in rendering first aid, or paid all of the injured person's medical bills would not be received in evidence as an admission of liability. It is clear that the defendant may have been motivated by a charitable impulse, and his good deeds alone should not subject him to liability. The law recognizes this by excluding such evidence.

1532   Liability insurance

Evidence that the defendant was protected by a policy of liability insurance at the time of the accident is not admissible in proving the defendant was negligent. The mere fact that he had the foresight to purchase insurance does not support such an allegation, and the existence of such insurance does not imply a disregard of due care because a personal financial response in the case of an accident had been precluded.

The matter of liability insurance is likewise inadmissible in order to indicate the defendant's capacity to pay. The general rule is that any reference to liability insurance by the plaintiff is ground for a mistrial. The theory is that the defendant is not accorded a fair trial where the jury has knowledge of the fact that the defendant is insured. The jury certainly would be more likely to find against the defendant when they had knowledge that an insurance company and not the defendant would be required to respond in damages. Even in states where automobile liability insurance is compulsory, evidence of insurance is still excluded, although most juries will proceed on the assumption that there is insurance.

Some states have modified this rule of evidence by a statute which enables the plaintiff to join the insurance carrier as an additional defendant—or have provided for a direct action against the insurance carrier. In such states, the existence of insurance is admissible as a matter of statute; however, details of the coverage (such as the policy limits) are not admissible for any purpose.

1533 Photographs

Photographs are used to support the testimony of witnesses and to illustrate the existence of certain conditions. To be admissible there must be testimony either from the photographer or other witnesses that the photograph fairly and accurately represents the object or the place as it existed at the time of the accident. Thus, when the object of the photograph is to show the road conditions at the time of the accident, the sooner the photograph is taken after the accident the better. Clearly, if the accident occurred in the wintertime with snow on the ground, a photograph taken in the following summer would not accurately depict the circumstances and surrounding conditions at the time of the accident. Likewise, a photograph may be inadmissible if there has been a substantial change in the conditions since the accident. For example, if it is claimed that a field was so overgrown with weeds and other foliage that a stop sign was obscured, a photograph taken after the field had been cleared and mowed would not depict the circumstances under which the accident took place. It is within the court's discretion to admit photographs that have been taken in black and white and the negative has been retouched. Where the retouching does not distort or impair the picture's accuracy, such photographs have generally been admitted. Likewise, in the case of enlarged photographs, these have been generally admissible at the court's discretion.

1534 Motion pictures

The admissibility of motion pictures is also within the court's discretion. Motion pictures, when offered, must be relevant to the issue and where it is claimed that the pictures reveal activities on the part of the plaintiff, the pictures must be clear enough for the plaintiff to be identified in the pictures. The general foundation which must be submitted in order to offer motion pictures consists of the following:

1. Evidence of the circumstances surrounding the taking of the film, the

photographer's competence, the camera type, the lens type and lens adjustments, weather conditions, lighting, and camera speed.

2. Manner and circumstances surrounding the film's developing.
3. Evidence as to how the film was stored and how it was protected and also the projector speed and distance from the screen.
4. Testimony by a person present when the pictures were taken and that the pictures accurately depict the events as he or she saw them.

The fact that the motion picture film has been edited, spliced, or cut does not render the film inadmissible as long as the remaining film remains accurate. Where the photographer is unavailable, it is still possible to establish the admissibility of the pictures if there is a witness who was present at the time that the pictures were taken and can testify as to the type of camera used, the speed of the film, and the subject matter of the pictures.

1535 X rays

X rays present a peculiar problem. The only witness who can identify the person or object used to produce the X ray is the roentengenologist or the technician who took the X ray. No other witness, be he a physician or technician can testify with certainty as to the object depicted in the X rays. Therefore, for an X ray to be received in evidence, the person who took the X ray must testify to the following facts:

1. Identification of the subject matter and proof that the X ray is of the person, anatomical part, or the object lodged in the anatomy.
2. Absence of significant change in the subject and proof that the person X ray or his or her condition when the X ray was taken as at the time of the occurrence complained of.
3. Proof that the X ray machine was dependable and was properly operated when the picture was taken.
4. Proof that the operator was qualified.
5. Evidence as to how the X ray was taken.

X rays are not *pictures* even though the term is commonly used in referring to them. Actually, they consist of the shadow produced by placing the person or object between the X ray tube and the photographic material. Solids, such as bones, show up white whereas tissue shows up dark. In addition, it should be noted that the rays emitted by the X ray tube descend in umbrellalike fashion and the part where the tube is directly overhead will be sharp in contrast whereas other parts which are not directly under the tube will show some distortion. In other words, the greater the angle of the rays, the greater the distortion.

1536 Videotape

The federal courts and some states permit depositions to be taken in videotape. (See Fed. R. Civil Proc. 30 (b) 4.) The use of videotapes enables the jury to see the witness's demeanor and from this to determine whether the witness can be believed or not. This is most important where the witness is a party to the action.

Studies have been made as to whether the videotape is more effective when in color as opposed to black and white. The results have been inconclusive so that no recommendation can be made as to the use of either.

1537   Weight of evidence

In civil cases, the plaintiff, in order to prevail, must establish his claim by a preponderance of evidence; he must produce the greater weight of evidence, or evidence which is more credible and convincing. It must be evidence which, when fairly considered, produces the stronger impression, has the greater weight, and is more convincing than the evidence in opposition. Preponderance of evidence is not to be determined by the number of witnesses but by the greater weight of all evidence. This does not necessarily mean the greater number of witnesses, but that the opportunity for knowledge, the information possessed, and the manner of testifying determines the weight of testimony. The plaintiff will have sustained the burden of proof if his evidence outweighs that of the defendant. If the weight of evidence is equal on both sides, and since the plaintiff has the burden of proof, the defendant must prevail. And, if the defendant's evidence is more believable, the defendant likewise must win.

In criminal cases, the guilt of the accused must be established beyond a reasonable doubt. This is a much greater weight of evidence than the preponderance required in civil cases. "Beyond a reasonable doubt" means that the jury is entirely convinced and satisfied to a moral certainty. The phrase is the equivalent of clear, precise, and indubitable. If there is any reasonable question in the minds of the jury, they must acquit. The rule in the criminal law is that it is better that ten criminals escape punishment than one innocent man be convicted. It is for this reason that the prosecution must establish that the accused committed the crime, and the evidence must establish this beyond a reasonable doubt.

CHAPTER XVI

Liability insurance contracts

1600   General construction

Liability means responsibility recognized by law. In civil cases it refers to that which a person is bound or obligated in law or equity to do. Where there is a civil liability, a person may be compelled to do an act (specific performance), to refrain from doing an act (injunction), or to pay damages. The payment of damages is the response which the law obligates a person to make as satisfaction, compensation, or restitution for injuries to the person or property of others caused by his wrongful act, neglect, or default. He may also by contract assume the liability of others to so respond. Certain of these obligations to pay money damages can be the subject matter of insurance.

The vehicle by which this liability is assembled by an insurance company is the liability insurance contract. It is an agreement whereby the insurer, subject to the limitations and conditions of the agreement, promises to indemnify and save harmless the person, firm, or corporation insured from the obligation imposed by law or assumed by contract to respond in money damages for the injury to the person or property of others. Under this type of insurance contract, the promises of the insurer are twofold. The two general promises are *indemnification* and *defense*.

Indemnification.   The promise of the company is to indemnify or hold the insured harmless from all sums which he shall become legally obligated to pay as damages, arising out of the hazards covered, to the extent of the dollar limit expressed in the agreement. The limit may be expressed as a single limit per accident, as a double limit with an amount payable per person and a higher amount payable for the accident, or as a limit applicable to each accident, with an aggregate limit applicable to all accidents occurring during the policy period.

Defense. In addition to the applicable limits of liability, as set forth in the promise of indemnification, the company promises to defend any suit brought against the insured alleging injuries and seeking damages which are payable under the policy, and, in addition thereto, to pay all the costs of the defense, including all expenses incurred by the company and costs taxed against the insured. There is no dollar limitation applicable to this promise.

Two terms which are frequently used in referring to claims are *coverage* and *liability*. Coverage refers to the contractual obligation of the company to indemnify the insured in the area agreed upon and to the limit expressed in the policy contract. Liability refers to the legal responsibility of the policyholder to other persons or parties arising out of the accident or occurrence. Should there be no coverage, that is, no provision in the insuring agreements affording protection against the hazard involved in the accident, the insurance carrier is not obligated to indemnify the insured or defend him in any litigation, however great his responsibility may be in causing the injury.

For example, if the insurance carrier has issued a policy covering the liability imposed upon the insured arising out of the ownership or use of certain premises, the company would not afford protection to the insured for a liability arising out of an automobile accident which occurred away from the premises. In such a case there may be liability on the part of the insured, but there is no coverage under the policy.

On the other hand, there may be coverage but no liability on the part of the insured. The insurance carrier's responsibility to indemnify the insured is coextensive with that of the insured to the claimant, up to the limits of the policy, and where there is no responsibility imposed upon the insured by law there is no obligation on the part of the insurance carrier to make any payment, either by way of settlement or as a gift, even though the insured may feel morally obligated to assume some financial burden.

The liability insurance contracts are constructed in various forms, depending upon the hazards to be covered, and are tailored to meet the needs of the insurance buying public, premiums being calculated in proportion to the hazards assumed and the responsibility to which the insurer is exposed. The so-called package policies combine the liability insurance contract with other lines of insurance, such as the homeowners' policy. These policy forms are in constant process of revision and refinement, and in every case where there is any question regarding the coverage afforded, the claimsman must refer to the particular policy form which is the subject of the agreement between the insured and the company, as well as to all endorsements which enlarge or restrict the obligations assumed by the company.

Since it would be impossible (and perhaps serve no useful purpose) to cover and analyze all types of liability insurance contracts, this chapter will be devoted to the consideration of the basic format common to most of the liability forms, using as a model the automobile liability policy (with some reference to general liability forms) and citing some of the more important terms and conditions.

The pattern of every liability contract is generally the same, consisting of four main parts: the *declarations, insuring agreements, exclusions,* and *conditions.* To these may be added two additional sections: the *introductory statement,* which immediately precedes the insuring agreements and which consists of the agreement to insure between the insurance company and the insured, and the *signatory* clause at the end wherein the contract is signed by the persons having the authority to bind the insurance company.

1601 Declarations

The declarations are the representations of the insured concerning himself and the risk to be insured, and constitute the inducements which cause the company to enter into the insurance contract. If the representations are untrue, they will not form the basis of an action for rescission by the company unless they also are material to the risk. If they are untrue and are material to the risk or contract, the company, upon acquiring knowledge of their falsity, may either waive the material misrepresentation, or rescind the contract.

So that there can be no misunderstanding by the insured, all liability policies contain the following condition:

Declarations: by acceptance of this policy, the insured named in item 1 of the declarations agrees that the statements in the declarations are his agreements and representations, that this policy is issued in reliance upon the truth of such representations and this policy embodies all agreements existing between himself and the company or any of its agents relating to this insurance.

This condition is in the policy for a real purpose. It seeks to avoid a situation where the insured makes certain statements to the company's agent which are not included in the declarations. Normally, the knowledge of the agent is the knowledge of the company. With this condition added, it is made plain to the insured that the company will not be bound by any knowledge acquired by its agents which is not set forth in the declarations.

The situation most frequently encountered is one in which the insurance is taken out by one person for the benefit of another who is unable to secure insurance. For example, a minor child buys an automobile, either by the payment of cash or a conditional sales agreement signed by his father. Because of his minority, or because of his previous accident record, the child cannot obtain insurance. The car is registered in the name of the father, who applies for and is issued insurance, although the actual owner is the child and the insurance is taken out solely for the child's protection.

The representation by the father that he owns the vehicle is untrue and certainly material to the risk. When the insurance company obtains knowledge of the misrepresentation it can rescind its policy contract as of the date of issuance, of course, returning to the father the premium paid. This can be done even though the knowledge is acquired by the company after the occurrence of an accident.

In *Builders and Manufacturers Mutual Casualty Co.* v. *Paquette* (21 Fed.

Supp. 858), a son, whose driver's license had been suspended because of a conviction of reckless driving, bought automobiles and had them registered in his mother's name. His mother obtained liability insurance thereon, concealing the son's interest. The policies so issued were void since the policies required that the insured's (the mother's) interest be unconditional and sole ownership. [See also *Bowen* v. *Bernard*, 86 Fed. 2d 276; and *Maryland Casualty Co.* v. *Powers*, 113 Fed. Supp. 126.]

Another phase of the same situation is where the insured transfers the ownership of the automobile prior to renewing the insurance. In *Tyranauer* v. *Travelers Insurance Co.* (213 N.Y.S. 2d 475), the representation of the insured in the application that he was the sole owner of the automobile was held to be material and vital to the issuance of the policy, and the insurer was entitled to avoid the policy where the insured, prior to obtaining the renewal policy, transferred the ownership of the automobile. Were the insurance company to be unable to rescind such a policy, it would in effect be forced to accept as an insured anyone to whom the car might be transferred, irrespective of whether the company desired such an owner as an insured or not. It would be deprived of the right to select the persons to whom it would issue insurance. In *Savage* v. *Howard Insurance Co.* (52 N.Y. 502), the court said:

> An insurer is entitled to know who has title or an interest in the property proposed for insurance to the end that it may determine whether or not to enter into or continue a contract of insurance. Here it was willing to contract with the plaintiff as owner, but it does not follow that it would have been willing to do so with the new owner. The element is material to the risk.

1602   Insuring agreements and definitions

The insuring agreements and the definitions thereunder set forth the promises of the company and the obligations assumed. The insuring agreements state the promises in general terms and the definitions clarify, amend, enlarge, or modify the obligation so assumed. There are two general types of insuring agreements, those which assume only the obligations imposed upon the insured caused by accident, and those which eliminate the "caused by accident" requirement. The first type is said to be written on an accident basis, whereas the second is written on an occurrence basis.

1. *Accident basis.* The promises of the company in the insuring agreements read as follows:

> The *Blank* Insurance Company agrees with the insured, named in the declarations made a part hereof, in consideration of the payment of the premium and in reliance upon the statements in the declarations and subject to the terms of this policy:
>
> To pay on behalf of the insured all sums which the insured shall become legally obligated to pay as damages because of bodily injury, sickness or disease, including death at any time resulting therefrom, sustained by any person, caused by accident, and arising out of the hazards hereinafter defined.

The same agreement is made with respect to property damage in that the company promises to pay all sums which the insured shall become legally obligated to pay because of injury to or destruction of property, including the loss of use thereof, caused by accident and arising out of the hazards defined. The obligations assumed by the company refer only to claims for bodily injury and property damage, and are conditioned upon the presence of the following three elements. The claim must:

1. Involve the legal liability of the insured to pay money damages.
2. Be caused by accident.
3. Arise out of the hazards covered by the policy contract.

For the contract to be operative, all three elements must be present. If any one is absent, the claim does not come within the area of the contract.

Legal liability to pay damages.   The responsibility to pay money damages usually arises as a result of damage sustained by others as a result of a wrongful act, neglect, or default. The law will obligate the wrongdoer to compensate the injured victim by the payment of money which will reasonably repay him for the loss he has sustained. The insurance contract contains the promise of the insurer to pay all sums which the insured is obligated to pay as damages. The insurer does not assume the insured's responsibility to respond in respect to any other type of relief which the court may grant to the third party (such as an injunction) or is the insurer obligated to reimburse the insured for expense which he might incur in complying with the terms of the injunction or other similar court orders. The obligation assumed by the insurer has reference only to the insured's obligation to respond in money damages, and the promise is to pay these damages on behalf of the insured.

The legal liability of the insured is not established until there is a judgment of a court finding the insured legally responsible and awarding damages. The burden of proving the insured's responsibility is on the person asserting a claim. Should he be unsuccessful in establishing the responsibility of the insured, there is no legal liability and the promise of the insurer is not involved, whereas if the claim is established, the insurer will be obligated to keep its promise and to pay on behalf of the insured the amount awarded, subject to the limits of the policy.

The existence of the insurance policy will not in any way affect the rights of the parties insofar as it relates to their obligations to one another. It will not create rights which did not exist before the insurance was written nor will it relieve the insured of his obligations to respond in damages to the injured person where such an obligation exists. The insurance contract is merely an agreement between the insured and the insurer whereby the insurer promises to pay the amount which the insured would otherwise have to pay were it not for the insurance.

For example, if a wife were injured through the negligence of her husband, who is the insured, and if the accident happened in a state where the wife cannot assert an action in tort against her husband, the insurer has no obligation to make any payment in behalf of the insured since there could be no liability imposed on the husband. The insurer's responsibility comes into existence only where there is a legal liability on the part of the insured to pay damages.

The same result would obtain where the insured is a government body and the accident occurred as a result of the exercise of a governmental function. Since the insured is entitled to governmental immunity, the injured person could not assert a cause of action against the insured, and since the insured is not liable, the insurance carrier is not required to make any payment for and in behalf of the insured.

In both cases, the claimant could not recover from the insured, and the existence of the insurance policy did not alter the responsibilities of the parties to each other.

In another example, let us assume that the claimant recovered a judgment from the insured, and the insurer is in receivership and unable to meet its obligations. The insured is liable to the claimant and the insolvency of the insurer will not operate so as to relieve him of his responsibility to his judgment-creditor. On the other hand, the bankruptcy or insolvency of the insured will not relieve the insurer of its promise to pay in behalf of the insured. The condition of the policy reads as follows:

No action shall lie against the company unless, as a condition precedent thereto, the insured shall have fully complied with all the terms of this policy, nor shall an action lie under the Liability Coverage until the amount of the insured's obligation to pay shall have been finally determined either by judgment against the insured after actual trial or by written agreement of the insured, the claimant and the company.

Any person or organization or the legal representative thereof who has secured such judgment or written agreement shall thereafter be entitled to recover under this policy to the extent of the insurance afforded by this policy. No person or organization shall have any right under this policy to join the company as a party to any action against the insured to determine the insured's liability, nor shall the company be impleaded by the insured or his legal representative. Bankruptcy or insolvency of the insured or of the insured's estate shall not relieve the company of its obligations hereunder.

Under this condition, where the claimant has recovered a judgment after actual trial (as opposed to a confession of judgment by the insured or a default judgment) or by a written agreement to which the company is a party, the claimant may bring an action directly against the company for payment if the amount of the judgment or agreement is not paid, and the bankruptcy or insolvency of the insured will not operate to relieve the insurer. In any case, the condition does not give the claimant the right to bring action against the insurer, nor does it give the insured the right to implead the insurer in any action to determine the insured's liability. In some states that have a direct action statute (Louisiana), there is a provision for a direct action against the insurer, and in others (Wisconsin), the insurer may be made a party to the action. These actions may be taken because there is a statute of the state which authorizes it, but the policy itself does not give any party such a right.

Caused by accident. These words are not defined in the policy, with the exception that some policies enlarge the meaning with respect to the vicarious liability of the insured in cases of assault and battery. The provision reads: "Assault and battery shall be deemed an accident unless committed by or at the direction of the insured." This means that if the insured is held liable for the acts of his agent or employee who commits an assault and battery without his direction to do so, the company will pay on behalf of the insured all sums which he will be legally obligated to pay.

Since the words "caused by accident" are not defined in the policy, the courts of the various states have used various standards in applying them to factual situations. Some take the position that whether or not an injury is caused by accident is to be determined from the standpoint of the injured person and not from the will of the person responsible, while others exclude intentional acts of the insured from the scope of the coverage. For example, in *Sheehan* v. *Goriansky* [72 N.E. 2d 538 (Massachusetts)], a verdict was recovered against the insured based on "willful, wanton and reckless operation of the automobile." The insurer contended that this amounted to an intentional act of the insured, and that it was not "caused by accident" within the terms of the policy. The court held that the policy did cover, saying "A harm which is only constructively intentional does not, for that reason alone, fall outside of the category of an injury 'caused by accident' . . . we do not consider that there is any public policy against this interpretation."

As opposed to this conclusion, in *Basmajian* v. *Igo* [52 N.E. 2d 985 (Ohio)], the court held that willful conduct by the insured which caused an injury was not "caused by accident" so as to involve the coverage of the policy. In *Hartford Accident & Indemnity Co.* v. *Wolbarst* [57 Atl. 2d 151 (New Hampshire)], the policy used the terminology "accidentally sustained." The facts indicated that the insured deliberately struck the rear of the other car in which the injured was riding. The insurer contended that the injury was not "accidentally sustained." The court held that the purpose of the New Hampshire financial responsibility act, which was involved in the case, "is best served by construing the phrase 'accidentally sustained' to include any unfortunate occurrence causing injury or damage. Regardless of the mental state of the insured that precedes the injury or the damage suffered by the traveler, the suffering or the loss is the same."

In view of these interpretations (and there are many more), it is impossible to come to any conclusion other than that the decisions of the courts are not uniform, and no particular pattern can be offered as to how they will rule in future cases.

Where the insured's act is intentional and the damage inflicted is likewise intentional, the prevailing view taken by the courts is that the damage is not caused by accident. In *Kuckenberg* v. *Hartford Accident & Indemnity Co.* (226 Fed. 2d 225), the plaintiff was required to do a large amount of blasting during the construction of a highway. The blasting operation caused debris to slide down upon the tracks of the Southern Pacific Railroad, causing considerable damage. The plaintiff anticipated that damage would occur and took steps to avoid it, including the covering of the tracks with thick layers of dirt. In denying a recovery under the liability insurance policy, it was held that the damage inflicted "was the reasonably anticipated, ordinary and expected result" of the operation and was not caused by accident. In reaching this conclusion, the court said:

> It is true that the courts construing insurance contracts have differed in judgment whether the fact that the responsible cause is an intentional act and suffices in itself to preclude the resulting injury from being accidental damages . . . but, if, in addition to being intentional, the harmful conduct is reasonably calculated to cause substantial damage of the very sort that occurs, all courts seem to recognize that the damage is outside of the insured risk.

As to cases where the intention of the insured is not involved, the majority of the courts have been extremely liberal in their interpretation of the words "caused by accident." Most do not require that the cause be a single identifiable event but any factual situation wherein the average person would believe the resulting injury was caused by accident. For example, in *Commercial Casualty Insurance Co.* v. *Tri-State Tr. Co.* [1 So. 2d 221 (Mississippi)], the insured's bus suffered a mechanical breakdown and the passengers were forced to walk to their destination. One such passenger died as a result of pneumonia which followed his exposure during the walk. The court held that the passenger's death was caused by accident.

In *Cohen* v. *National Casualty Co.* [29 N.Y.S. 2d 999 (New York)], a general liability policy was involved. The facts were that coal gas permeated the claimant's apartment in a building owned by the insured, as a result of which the claimant was compelled to open windows, which created a draft and caused the claimant to catch cold and sustain a wry neck, or torticollis. The court held that the escape of coal gas, being something catastrophic or extraordinary, created a condition which was caused by accident within the terms of the policy and, further, that the illness suffered by the claimant constituted "bodily injuries" caused by accident. A recovery against the insurer was granted.

All bodily injuries are not caused by accident. In the broad sense, bodily injuries could include mental anguish caused by false arrest, malicious prosecution, willful detention or imprisonment, libel or slander, invasion of privacy, wrongful eviction, and wrongful entry. Such injuries are not covered under the liability policy where the insurer's obligations to pay is based on bodily injuries caused by accident. In each of the foregoing situations, the injuries are intentionally inflicted and therefore outside the scope of the insuring agreements.

Hazards covered by the policy contract.   It is clear from the contract that the agreement refers only to such liabilities of the insured as the company has contracted to insure. Such hazards are set forth in the declarations, are included by reference in the insuring agreements, and are subject to the definitions and exclusions of the policy.

2. *Occurrence basis.* The promises of the company in the insuring agreements, where the contract is written on an occurrence basis, are the same as those in policies written on an accident basis, with the exception that the words "caused by accident" are deleted and the limits of liability, as stated in the declarations, refer to a dollar limit per person and a limit per occurrence. The word "occurrence" is generally construed to mean any incident or event which happens without being designed or expected. Intentional acts for which the insured might have a responsibility are eliminated from the policy by excluding from coverage "bodily injuries and property damage caused intentionally by or at the direction of the insured."

The "definitions" are an important part of the policy. They modify, enlarge or limit the language of the insuring agreements and also limit or extend the hazards covered by the policy. For example, the insuring agreements of the autmobile policy obligate the company to pay on behalf of the insured all sums which the insured shall become legally obligated to pay as damages because of bodily injury and property damage "arising out of the ownership, maintenance or use of the owned automobile, or any nonowned automobile. . . ."

The definitions applicable to this portion of the insuring agreements are as follows:

Owned automobile means a private passenger, farm, or utility automobile or trailer owned by the named insured, and includes a temporary substitute automobile.

Temporary substitute automobile means any automobile or trailer not owned by the named insured but temporarily used as a substitute for the owned automobile or trailer, which is withdrawn from normal use because of its breakdown, repair, servicing, loss, or destruction.

Private passenger automobile means a four-wheel private passenger, station wagon, or jeep type automobile.

Farm automobile means an automobile of the truck type with a load capacity of 1,500 pounds or less, not used for business or commercial purposes other than farming.

Utility automobile means an automobile, other than a farm automobile, with a load capacity of 1,500 pounds or less of the pickup body, sedan delivery, or panel truck type, not used for business or commercial purposes.

Trailer means a trailer designed for use with a private passenger automobile, not used for business or commercial purposes, nor with other than a private passenger, farm, or utility automobile; or a farm wagon or farm equipment while used with a farm automobile.

These definitions all apply to the owned automobile and clarify the obligations assumed in the insuring agreement. For example, in *Phoenix Insurance* v. *Guthiel* (147 N.Y.S. 2d 341), the named insured sold the automobile prior to the accident but permitted his license plates to remain on it. The accident occurred when the automobile was being driven by the new owner. It was held that the automobile did not come within the definition of an owned automobile since it was not owned by the named insured at the time of the accident. The definition of a private passenger automobile as a four-wheel private passenger, station wagon, or jeep type of automobile excludes by its terms a three-wheel golf cart, a motorcycle and sidecar, and other similar vehicles.

The definitions with respect to the description of types of automobiles also apply to nonowned automobiles. *Nonowned automobile* means an automobile or trailer not owned by or furnished for the regular use of either the named insured or any relative other than as a temporary substitute automobile.

In excluding from the definition of nonowned automobiles covered by the policy of an automobile "furnished for the regular use of either the named insured or any relative," the plain purpose is to deny coverage for a company-owned vehicle which is furnished to the insured in connection with his business or a regular, as opposed to a single, use. In *Miller* v. *Farmers' Mutual Automobile Insurance Co.* [292 Pac. 2d 711 (Kansas)], an attorney employed in the adjutant general's office used one of four automobiles in a pool with 35 other employees in the office, although most of the time he used his own car for business purposes. It was held that the automobile under those circumstances was not furnished for his regular use and that the policy covered such use of a nonowned vehicle. (Other definitions affecting the insuring agreements will be considered in succeeding sections.)

1603   Policy period and limits

Under item 2 of the declarations, the policy period is shown by an inception date and a termination date. By its terms, the policy takes effect at 12:01 A.M. standard time, at the address of the named insured as stated, on the day shown as the inception date; it expires at 12:01 A.M. standard time on the termination date.

Ordinarily, the policy period does not present any problem when the accident occurs on a date between the two dates. Difficulty is encountered when the accident occurs on the inception date. While it is perfectly possible that a legitimate accident could have happened on the first day of the policy, this fact should be taken into consideration and some inquiry made as to when the policy was ordered and when it was actually issued, with special reference to whether or not it was ordered and issued after the accident happened. Usually the agent or the company date-stamps the order for insurance. This will indicate the date and time that the order for insurance was received. If this date and time is later in the day of inception than the time of the accident, there is no insurance coverage for the reason that at the time of the accident there was no policy of insurance in existence. Conversely, if the policy is a renewal of a previous policy, or if the insurance was ordered in advance of the inception date, the investigation would establish these facts, in which case there would be no question of coverage.

As to termination, the policy expires at 12:01 A.M. on the termination date. This means that the policy expires on the first minute of the last day, or one minute after midnight of the morning of the termination date. Where the accident occurs on the termination date, or the evening before, the time of accident becomes important in determining whether or not it occurred within the policy period, and especially important where the policy has not been renewed or the renewal has been replaced in another company. If the policy has been renewed in the same company, then the question of when the accident occurred becomes academic, and the only problem is to decide which policy will be charged with the claim.

The monetary limits of the amounts which the insurance carrier is obligated to pay as damages in behalf of the insured are set forth in the declarations and are incorporated by reference in the insuring agreements. These represent the extent of the insurer's financial promise with respect to indemnifying the insured. In the absence of special circumstances (see Section 1605, below) payments representing these amounts, when made by the insurance carrier, meet the entire promise of indemnity under the contract even though they do not extinguish the entire responsibility of the insured to the persons injured. While the company has assumed the payment of other expenses in addition to this promise of indemnity, the limits expressed in the declarations represent the maximum exposure of the company with respect to its promise of indemnification.

The agreement of the parties to the contract with respect to the financial limits may be expressed by provisions encompassing one of the following: *single limit, double limits, aggregate limit,* or *deductibles.*

Single limit. The policy may provide that a single amount shall be the maximum liability of the company with respect to any one accident or occurrence, irrespective of the number of injured persons involved. There is also a single limit expressed with regard to property damage.

Double limits. With regard to liability for bodily injury, the limit of liability may be expressed by two figures, one representing the maximum payable for each person injured, and the other the maximum payable for each accident or occurrence. There is also an additional provision that the claim for injury and the claim for loss of services arising out of the injury to one person is subject to the limit expressed for one person. A single limit is also usually expressed to cover the maximum payable in behalf of the insured for property damage, including the loss of use thereof.

Aggregate limit. Policies carrying an aggregate limit merely add another figure to the double-limit policy by providing one amount for the limit per person, one limit for each accident, and an aggregate limit which represents the total limit of the company's liability under the entire policy for the hazard to which the aggregate limit applies. For example, under the products liability and completed operations coverages, there is an aggregate limit expressed. When the company has paid claims which total the amount set forth in the aggregate limit, such payments extinguish the company's liability under that particular hazard under the policy, regardless of the policy period.

Deductibles. Some policies are written on a deductible basis, with the insured assuming liability for the first or deductible amount and the company assuming liability above the deductible amount. The company's liability does not become involved until the insured has paid or has agreed to pay its deductible, the amount of which will vary with the agreement of the parties. It may refer to each person and each accident, or it may refer to an amount for the entire policy with the insurer assuming responsibility only after the insured has paid claims to a certain amount.

A statement as to the meaning of the term "limit of liability" is found among the conditions in some policies and in the insuring agreements in others. In any case, the effect is the same. With respect to a double-limit situation, which is the most common, the provision usually reads as follows:

The limit of bodily injury liability stated in the Declarations as applicable to "each person" is the limit of the company's liability for all damages, including damages for care and loss of services, arising out of a bodily injury sustained by one person as a result of any one occurrence; the limit of such liability stated in the Declarations as applicable to "each occurrence" is, subject to the above provision respecting each person, the total limit of the company's liability for all such damages arising out of bodily injury sustained by two or more persons as a result of any one occurrence.

The limit of property damage liability stated in the Declarations as applicable to "each occurrence" is the total limit of the Company's liability for all damages arising out of injury to or destruction of all property of one or more persons or organizations, including the loss of use thereof, as a result of any one occurrence.

These provisions were taken from a liability policy providing for coverage on an occurrence basis. As to policies which offer coverage on an accident basis, the word *accident* is substituted for *occurrence* whenever it appears.

Some problems have arisen with respect to the application of the term "one accident," or "one occurrence," as the case may be. For example, in *Truck Insurance Exchange* v. *Rohde* (303 Pac. 2d 659), the facts indicated that the insured negligently crossed the center line of the highway and collided with the first of a group of three oncoming motorcycles, carrying five people, and traveling at a high rate of speed about 75 feet apart. The insured's car was spun so that it immediately collided with the second and then with the third motorcycle. The entire event took place in less than two seconds. All five people on the motorcycles were killed or seriously injured.

At the time of the accident the insured had a liability policy with limits of $20,000 for each person and $50,000 for each accident. Judgments in excess of $20,000 were entered against the insured in each of the five claims made against him. The insured contended that the transaction amounted to three distinct accidents; that each impact, however simultaneous, was a separate accident and that therefore the accident limit of $50,000 should be applied to each of the three accidents. The court held that the transaction amounted to one accident and that the $50,000 limitation applied to all claims which arose as a result of the collisions with all three motorcycles.

In *St. Paul Mercury Indemnity Co.* v. *Rutland* (225 Fed. 2d 689), a negligently operated truck collided with a train at a grade crossing causing derailment of some of the cars and damage to the roadbed of the railroad, to 16 freight cars owned by 14 different owners, and to cargo owned by various shippers. The truck owner had liability coverage for property damage with limits of $5,000 for each accident. A suit by the railroad was settled by the truck owner for $30,000. He thereafter brought suit against the insurer for the excess over $5,000, which the insurer had voluntarily paid. The insured contended that the policy was ambiguous as to the limit and that it should be viewed through the eyes of each party whose property was damaged. The theory was that the $5,000 limitation applied to each person whose property was damaged. In finding in favor of the insurance carrier's contention that the $5,000 limitation applied to the accident, irrespective of the number of owners of the damaged property, the court said:

It can hardly be denied that when ordinary people speak of an accident in the usual sense, they are referring to a single, sudden, unintentional occurrence. They normally use the word "accident" to describe the event, no matter how many persons are involved.

The court further held that the limitation of $5,000 for each accident, as set forth in the policy, did not constitute an ambiguity requiring judicial interpretation.

1604   Duty to defend

In addition to the promise of indemnity, the insurance carrier undertakes the following obligation:

The Company shall defend any suit alleging such bodily injury or property damage and seeking damages which are payable under the terms of this policy, even if any of the allegations of the suit are groundless, false or fraudulent.

The cases generally hold that the obligation to defend arises whenever the complaint filed by the injured party may potentially come within the coverage of the policy. The fact that the allegations are entirely untrue, or have no basis in fact, does not alter the obligation to defend.

In *Cadwallander* v. *New Amsterdam Casualty Co.* (152 Atl. 2d 484), the court said:

It is clear that where a claim potentially may become one which is within the scope of the policy, the insurance company's refusal to defend at the outset of the controversy is a decision it makes at its own peril. . . .

So long as the complaint filed by the injured party covered an injury which might fall within the coverage of the policy, the insurance company is obligated to defend. . . . When the complaint comprehends an injury which may be within the policy, we hold that the promise to defend includes it.

In determining whether or not there is an obligation to defend, the insurance company is required to regard all of the allegations of the complaint as being true. If the controversy then comes within the scope of the policy, there is a duty to defend. Should the insurance company refuse to defend where there is a duty to do so, it breaches its contract and the insured may recover from the company any damages which he may sustain because of the breach. Usually these will consist of the costs of the defense which the insured has been obligated to defray.

There is no monetary limit to defense costs which the insurance carrier has obligated itself to provide: there is a limit to the extent of the agreement to indemnity, but there is no such qualification with regard to the duty to defend. The cases uniformly hold that the insurance carrier is obligated to offer a proper defense irrespective of cost. It is conceivable that there will be cases where the costs of defense might equal or exceed the indemnification limit, but the carrier must provide the defense in any case. The carrier cannot pay the policy limit to the insured, or to the court, and thereby escape its obligation to defend. This duty exists separate and apart from the indemnification obligation.

Another phase of the duty to defend concerns cases where the policy limits have been exhausted by the payment of claims arising out of the same accident, and where there are still some other lawsuits pending. This is a rare situation and one which has not been before the courts of many states. The majority of the decided cases hold that the duty to defend ends when the policy limits are paid and that the insurance carrier has no duty to defend lawsuits then remaining. In *Lumbermen's Mutual Casualty Co.* v. *McCarthy* (8 Atl. 2d 750), the Supreme Court of New Hampshire held that where the insurer had satisfied a judgment against the insured, to the extent of the policy limit, it was not required to defend a remaining suit. The court observed that the insurer had agreed to defend "any suit coming within the terms of this policy seeking damages." The court, after construing all parts of the policy, said:

. . . The primary obligation imposed upon the insurer was to pay the insured's legal liability for damages on account of the contingencies specified, and that the other conditions were dependent thereon, and designed to implement that primary obligation.

. . . The policy obligates the insurer to pay the liability of the insured up to the policy limits, and, in addition thereto to pay those items of expense which it has definitely assumed. Until these duties of payment are fully performed, it also has the duty either to settle or to conduct the defense of actions against the insured. But, upon performance of its duties of payment, its duty to defend ceases to exist.
. . .

In *Liberty Mutual Insurance Co.* v. *Mead Corporation* [28 Auto Cas. 2d 1122 (CCH)], decided on May 9, 1963, the Supreme Court of Georgia was faced with the same problem. It cited the *McCarthy* case (above) with approval and concluded that the insurer's duty to defend ceased when its policy limits were exhausted by payment. In reviewing that phase of the case, the court said:

The facts as to this [the duty to defend] are recited in the insured's petition as follows: "Pursuant to the rights granted to the defendant insurer in said insurance policy, said insurer, with the consent of the insured, compromised and settled the claims for the death of two persons for a total of $160,000. Sixty thousand dollars of said settlement was contributed by the insured and $100,000 was contributed by the defendant insurer. It was agreed between the parties that the actions of each as alleged in this paragraph did not waive the rights of the parties under the remaining provisions of the insurance policy."

These allegations show that the insurer fulfilled its obligation under the policy. With the insured's consent and contribution, the insurer paid the full policy limit of liability in compromise and settlement of two of the claims and suits against its insured, thus defending with reference to "such insurance" as was afforded by the policy. Under our construction of the insurance contract nothing further was required.

Therefore, allegations of events which took place thereafter, namely, the insurer's withdrawal and refusal to defend the remaining claims and suits and the insured's incurrence of attorney's fees and expenses in defending them, constitute no basis for recovery of damages from the insurer. There is no allegation that the insured suffered any prejudice of its rights by the insurer's withdrawal; the only damage of which it complains is monetary.

Where the policy limits have been exhausted by payment, the claimsman will be confronted by one of the following situations:

1. Where the policy limits have been exhausted by the payment in one or more cases, and other cases are still pending, but no action has been commenced.
2. Where the policy limits have been exhausted by the payment of one or more cases and the insurer has already undertaken the defense of other pending cases.

The situation in 1 does not present any great problem; under the Mead decision there is no obligation to defend after the policy limits have been exhausted. Therefore, the company can return any further suit papers to the insured, disclaiming any obligation to defend.

A more difficult situation obtains in 2. The insurer can withdraw from cases only if the withdrawal can be accomplished without material prejudice to the insured. The insurer cannot merely refuse to defend, and do nothing. It must give the insured an opportunity to engage counsel and to arrange for a substitution of attorneys.

Where the policy limits have not been exhausted by payment, the duty to defend continues, even though the amount demanded in the complaint is in excess of the policy limits. The policyholder is insured up to the limit of the policy, and uninsured as to the excess. Therefore, as to the excess, the insured has the right to engage counsel and to participate in the defense. Whether or not he exercises this right is a matter of discretion with him. Should he decide not to engage counsel, the insurance carrier is obligated to defend the entire case, whereas if he does engage counsel the insurance carrier and its attorney will cooperate with his counsel although the primary obligation to defend the claim remains with the insurance carrier. However, in order to avoid any possible waiver or estoppel, where the *ad damnum* (prayer for damages) exceeds the policy limits, the insurance carrier usually puts the insured on notice of the fact that the damages claimed are in excess of his coverage and advises him of his right to employ counsel.

A letter typical of those usually sent to the insured under these circumstances reads as follows:

> This will acknowledge receipt of the summons and complaint in a suit against you in the captioned matter.
>
> We have referred the defense of the case to our attorneys, Jones & Smith, 123 Main Street, Anytown, Anystate, for the purpose of appearing in your behalf.
>
> The amount demanded in this suit is $150,000. The limit of liability under your insurance policy is $10,000. Therefore, if there is a verdict rendered against you in excess of $10,000, you will be personally liable for the excess. In view of the situation, you may wish to engage your personal counsel to protect yourself against a verdict in excess of the policy limits. You may be assured that both this office and the attorneys to whom the defense of this case has been assigned will cooperate fully with your personal counsel.
>
> Plaintiffs frequently sue for more than they expect to recover, and, therefore, if you do not desire to engage personal counsel, Jones & Smith will conduct the entire defense of the action under the terms of your insurance policy, and with no obligation on your part to assume any part of the legal expense.
>
> If you desire to discuss this matter personally with the attorneys, please feel free to do so.

This letter puts the insured on notice of the fact that the demand is in excess of the policy limits and calls attention to his responsibility and his right to be represented by counsel if he so desires. It likewise calls attention to the provisions of the policy and offers the entire defense in accordance with its terms.

Sometimes a complaint is received which demands not only general but punitive damages as well. Punitive damages are awarded in some cases where the defendant is guilty of some malicious or offensive conduct. The purpose of such damages is not to compensate the plaintiff to whom they are awarded but to punish the defendant for his conduct. The liability insurance policies are silent as to a definition of the damages which the insurance carrier is obligated to pay in behalf of the insured, but some courts have taken the position that, since the contract does not define damages, the payment for punitive damages is an obligation of the insurer. In the better reasoned opinions, other courts have taken the position that punitive damages are awarded as punishment to the defendant for what he has done and to prevent him from committing the same act again, holding that the purpose of punitive damages would be thwarted if an insurance carrier were required to pay them and thus absorb the defendant's punishment. Therefore, they hold that it would be against public policy to construe an insurance contract as contemplating the payment of punitive damages by the insurance carrier. Other courts have not passed on the subject at all, and the question may be regarded as being open in those jurisdictions.

In those states where punitive damages have been held to be outside the insurance contract, and in states where statutes have been enacted prohibiting coverage for punitive damages, the insurer has no obligation either to pay or defend the punitive damage count. Therefore in such jurisdictions the insurer must put the insured on notice of the fact that its policy does not cover punitive damages and that the insurer has no duty under the contract to defend the punitive damage count. The insurer must also notify the insured of his right to be represented by his personal counsel if he so desires. Such a letter might read:

This will acknowledge receipt of a summons and complaint in a suit against you in the captioned matter.

For the purpose of entering a defense in your behalf, we have referred the case to our attorneys, Jones & Smith, 123 Main Street, Anytown, Anystate.

Please note that an additional count in the complaint charges you with driving in a willful and wanton manner, and as a result demands judgment for punitive and exemplary damages in the sum of $20,000.

Since your policy of insurance does not provide coverage for punitive or exemplary damages so claimed, you may desire to engage personal counsel to protect yourself against the claim for such punitive or exemplary damages. Our attorneys will, of course, defend you in accordance with your policy of insurance as to the negligence phase of the case up to the limits of the policy.

It sometimes happens that the insured has purchased an excess liability policy which will provide for additional limits of liability over and above the limits provided by the primary policy. The primary policy insurer owes the same duty to the excess carrier as it does to the insured. It still has the duty of providing a defense, regardless of cost, but neither the insured nor the excess carrier has the right to control the defense. The excess carrier may engage counsel to cooperate in the defense of the case, but the right to control the litigation remains with the primary carrier. Where there is a dispute as to the trial preparation (such as depositions, and so on), the primary carrier has the right to settle the dispute since it has control of the litigation. Under no circumstances should the primary carrier permit either the insured or the excess carrier to engage the assigned defense counsel as their own since there would arise some questions of the representation of adverse interests.

1605   Duty to investigate and settle

This duty is governed by two provisions of the policy:

1. The company may make such investigation and settlement of any claim or suit as it deems expedient.

2. The insured shall not, except at his own cost, voluntarily make any payment, assume any obligation, or incur any expense other than for such immediate medical and surgical relief to others as shall be imperative at the time of accident.

The effect of these two provisions is to transfer to the insurance carrier the exclusive right to investigate and settle the claim as it deems expedient. Therefore, the decision as to the extent of the investigation, and whether or not the claim will be settled, belongs entirely to the insurance carrier.

As to the exercise of the duties of investigation and settlement by the insurance carrier, no problem is presented where the ultimate payment or verdict is within the policy limits. The insurer may be content with a very nominal investigation or no investigation at all, or it may overpay its cases or subject itself to an excessive verdict because of its failure to properly prepare its case. It is where the insured's interests are involved, and where the ultimate payment or verdict is in excess of the policy limits that the courts will scrutinize the activities of the inusrance carrier to determine whether or not it met its responsibilities to the insured in investigating and, if possible, settling the claim.

Failure of the insurer to meet these obligations, which results in a loss to the insured, will give rise to a cause of action on the part of the insured for breach of the contract of insurance. As one court defined the duties:

By asserting in the policy the right to handle all claims against the insured, including the right to make a binding settlement, the insurer assumes a fiduciary position towards the insured and becomes obligated to act in good faith and with due care in representing the interests of the insured. If the insurer is derelict in this duty, as where it negligently investigates the claim or unreasonably refuses an offer of settlement, it may be liable regardless of the limits of the policy for the entire amount of the judgment secured against the insured.

The majority of the courts, in evaluating the conduct of the insurance carrier to determine whether or not it has met its policy obligations, will utilize the good faith test in cases where the interests of the insured are involved. This does not mean that the insurer is obligated to settle every case where there is an opportunity to do so within the policy limits. It means that in making the decision to accept or reject the settlement it must take into consideration not only its own interests but the interests of the insured as well.

To understand the reasoning behind this view we must consider the claim from the standpoint of the insured. The insured reports the accident to the insurer as soon as practicable. He has, moreover, given up his right to investigate, settle, or litigate the claim, and if he attempts to do any of these things he violates the policy contract and will be without insurance. Therefore, he is powerless to intervene to protect his own possible liability in excess of the policy limits. Since the management of the entire claim is in the hands of the insurance carrier, the insured very often has no means whereby he can ascertain the possibility of a verdict in excess of his policy limits, and he must rely on the insurer to keep him informed of the status of the claim.

It is for these reasons that the courts place an obligation on the insurer to act in the utmost good faith in dealing with the claim so that the rights of the insured are not impaired. Some courts (in the minority) apply the negligence test to the insurer's conduct in that consideration is given whether or not the insurer exercised due care in the handling of the claim. The decisions which enunciate the negligence test were decided some time ago, and the trend in later cases seems to be that the good faith test should be applied. For our purposes, it is believed that the conduct of the insurer should be governed by the possibility of the application of the test of good faith. In *Radio Taxi Service, Inc.* v. *Lincoln Mutual Insurance Co.* (157 Atl. 2d 319), the New Jersey Supreme Court analyzed the problem and announced its adoption of the good faith test in the following language:

> The duty of the insurer to accept a proffered settlement which is within the available coverage has been expressed by the courts throughout the country in two forms. One group espouses the rule that the carrier must act in good faith in considering offers to compromise. The other group has adopted the negligence test, that is, the carrier is liable for the excess judgment if it fails to settle when a reasonable man with unlimited exposure in the exercise of due care would have settled. . . .
>
> These two tests of liability which have evolved from the cases are necessarily general, and at times the line of demarcation between them, as well as that between failure to exercise due care in investigation and breach of the duty to settle, is difficult to discern. For example, a failure to exercise due care in the investigation of a claim might well make it impossible to fashion a good faith evaluation of the case for settlement purposes. . . .
>
> Search for the just rule must be engaged in with an understanding that the purpose of insurance of this type is to protect the insured from liability within the limits of the coverage. And, in interpreting the policy, the courts cannot allow the insurer to frustrate that purpose by a selfish decision as to settlement, which exposes the insured to and results in a judgment beyond the specific monetary protection which his premium has purchased. But since our reports contain no definitive ruling on the basic issue involved, it seems advisable to announce the principle which gives fair and just recognition to the interests of both parties to the insurance contract. For that purpose, we hold that the obligation assumed by the insurer with respect to settlement is to exercise good faith in dealing with offers to compromise, having both its own and the insured's interests in mind. And it may be said also that a reasonably diligent effort must be made to ascertain the facts upon which a good faith judgment as to settlement can be formulated. . . .
>
> In considering cases such as this, and even though the fact does not affect the insurer's duty, it is not amiss to have in mind that the insured has purchased a specified amount of coverage for an agreed premium and more substantial monetary limits were available for relatively smaller additional premiums. . . .

It should be emphasized that the insurer has two basic duties to its insured. First, it must make an adequate investigation, and second, it must give the insured notice of the fact that the policy limits may be exceeded. Then, if a settlement can be made within the policy limits, the insurer is bound to act in good faith, with its own as well as the insured's interests in mind, in determining whether or not the settlement is to be accepted. Where an adequate investigation has been conducted and proper notice has been given to the insured, the cases involving possible settlement will fall into one of three categories:

1. Cases in which a settlement can be made within the policy limits.
2. Cases in which a settlement is possible over the policy limits and the insured is unwilling to contribute the excess.
3. Cases in which settlement is possible over the policy limits and the insured is willing to pay the excess.

1. *Settlement within policy limits.* Merely because the case can be settled within the policy limits does not obligate the insurer to settle even though subsequent events, in the form of a verdict in excess of the limits, result. The question of the insurance carrier's liability for the excess will turn on whether or not the insurance carrier exercised good faith in deciding whether or not to accept the settlement proposition. If the carrier had an adequate investigation, and the facts in its file indicated that the settlement offer should be rejected, then the rejection of the settlement opportunity will not expose the carrier to liability for the payment of the excess. In *Radio Taxi Service, Inc.* v. *Lincoln Mutual* (above), the court defined the insurer's duties this way:

The company, by the contract, reserved the right to control the settlement of claims. Such right is a necessity incident of the operation of its business. Because the insured is prohibited from interfering with this right, however, manifestly its exercise must be accompanied by considerations of good faith. A decision not to settle must be an honest one. It must result from the weighing of probability in a fair manner.

To be a good faith decision, it must be an honest and intelligent one in the light of the company's expertise in the field. Where reasonable and probable cause appears for rejecting a settlement offer and for defending the damage action, the good faith of the insurer will be vindicated. . . .

Liability to pay the excess of a verdict over the amount of the policy coverage does not depend upon the mere happening of the unexpected event. The Law does not expect an insurer to be gifted with the powers of divination or of accurate prophecy. The requirement is due care in the investigation and good faith in dealing with offers of settlement.

The ultimate question is not whether a verdict in excess of the policy limits should have been anticipated, but whether the insurer lacked good faith in deciding not to meet the settlement demand. Mere failure to settle within the policy limit when there was an opportunity to do so before or during trial is not evidence of bad faith. . . .

The fact that the policy limit was exceeded by the verdict, in the light of hindsight, may indicate a mistake of judgment. But such a mistake, when resulting from a decision made with good faith, regard for its own and the insured's interests, does not confer a cause of action on the insured for the excess. . . . Anyone familiar with the valuation of accident cases for settlement purposes, when acting either for the plaintiff or the defendant, is aware of the difficulties that beset the task. Those gifted with expertise in the field of judging issues of liability and extent of injury actually suffered by a plaintiff would probably be the first to admit that an informed judgment arrived at in good faith after reasonably diligent investigation represents the limit that should be demanded of human capacity.

It should be emphasized that the insurance carrier's file becomes important evidence in this type of case. It is utilized to show the extent of the investigation and the facts which prompted the insurance carrier to reject the settlement. Therefore, where such a possibility exists, the claimsman should give some thought to the fact that every report, memorandum, or other writing by him or others will come under the scrutiny of the court and jury. Therefore, care should be exercised so that all writings in the file clearly express the thoughts intended and cannot be construed as evidence of bad faith.

In *Moore* v. *Columbia Casualty Co.* (174 Fed. Supp. 566), the court's opinion set forth in detail an exchange of correspondence between the insured and the insurance carrier. The facts in the case indicated that a domestic, one Hilda Ruyle, complained that while the insured assisted her in moving a heavy chair he suddenly dropped his end of it with the result that she sustained a serious back injury. The insured sent the complaint to the insurance company and advised that it was the first notice he had received of the alleged accident, and that, in fact, no such accident had occurred. Even though he continued to maintain that no accident had occurred, he on two occasions requested the insurance company to settle the claim within the policy limits. The company refused, relying on his statement that no accident had occurred. On May 14, 1955, he wrote the company:

I wish to advise the Columbia Casualty Co. of New York by this letter that it is my desire that they negotiate a settlement of this case with the said Hilda Ruyle, since I am of the opinion that it could be settled for an amount well under the $10,000 limit of the policy.

If your company elects to try the case rather than make a settlement, please be advised that I will accept no responsibility for any judgment rendered against me in this case above the limits of the policy, and will hold the Columbia Casualty Company of New York, liable for any excess amount.

If the case goes to trial, I will of course, cooperate in every way in the defense of this claim.

On May 17, 1955, the company wrote him:

You state it is your opinion that this case could be settled for an amount well under the $10,000 limits of your policy. We have had no indication from the Plaintiff or her Counsel that they would be willing to compromise the litigation for any figure. There has been no settlement demand and Plaintiff's Counsel has made no overtures whatsoever to demonstrate that they might be willing to negotiate. If you have information which you have not disclosed, and which has caused you to conclude that the case can be settled within the policy limits, or that it should be settled, it is your duty to advise us without delay. Our Counsel reports that you have consistently taken the position that the Plaintiff is not telling the truth, and that the allegations in her complaint, with respect to the manner in which she claims to have been injured, are fabrications. This same position has been maintained in your conversations with me, and with other representatives of our Company. Under the circumstances, it seems quite inconsistent that you would "advise the Columbia Casualty Company of New York . . . that it is my desire that they negotiate a settlement of this case."

You are hereby notified that the Columbia Casualty Company has worked diligently in the investigation of this case, and that to date, that investigation has not disclosed anything to indicate that you were guilty of a negligent act of omission or commission which proximately caused the Plaintiff's injuries. We must, therefore, conclude that there is absolutely no basis for your position as outlined in your letter of May 14, 1955.

On May 25, 1955, Moore replied:

In reply to your letter of May 17, 1955, I wish to advise that I have not withheld information at any time from the Company or its representatives in regard to this claim. I know that the suit is groundless, and in my opinion the plaintiff is not entitled to recover in this case. The very weakness of the plaintiff's claim should indicate to any practicing attorney, that the case should be settled.

Your letter further asks for a reason why I desire the Company to negotiate a settlement of this case. I have been in the insurance business in Alton for over thirty-six years, and litigation against me personally definitely affects my Insurance Agency and volume of business. This suit also appears on every Abstract for real estate in which I have an interest and affects the title until the case is settled.

For the above reasons, we respectfully urge that an effort be made to negotiate a settlement.

The case was tried and resulted in a $35,000 judgment against Moore. Moore then brought an action to recover the excess. The district court found that the company had fully and completely performed each and every condition and obligation required by the policy, that it did not act unreasonably or arbitrarily toward its insured, and that neither the company nor its agents or employees were guilty of bad faith, fraud, or negligence. The mere fact that the insured demanded a settlement be made does not in and of itself support a claim for the excess.

The settlement of some of the claims arising out of an accident within the policy limits will not entirely insulate the insurance carrier from the complaint of bad faith and consequent liability for the excess verdict. For example, in *Brown* v. *U.S. Fidelity & Guaranty Co.* [314 Fed. 2d 675 (28 Auto Cas., CCH 2d 252], the facts indicated that Brown, the driver, and his friend Borowiak, his passenger, had visited several bars prior to the accident. Brown was driving his automobile south on New York's East River Drive when his car came in contact with the road divider, causing him to lose control, and the vehicle came to rest transversely upon the divider. A taxicab traveling in the opposite direction, driven by one Ruby and occupied by passengers Sacco and O'Dwyer, collided with the Brown automobile, jumped the divider, and turned over on the other side of the highway. Brown sustained minor injuries but all the others sustained serious injuries.

The insurance coverage had limits of 10/20. Judging from the opinion of the court, apparently the company felt that its limits were "gone" and did not conduct a detailed investigation. The company settled with Borowiak for $6,000 and with Ruby for $8,000, leaving a $6,000 balance of available insurance coverage for the other two claims. These cases, which involved the two passengers in the taxi, were tried and resulted in verdicts totaling $45,000, of which the driver Brown was personally responsible for $39,000. Action was then brought by Brown against the insurance carrier, charging that it had been guilty of bad faith in failing to conduct a thorough investigation and develop defenses against Borowiak and Ruby, with whom they settled.

As to Borowiak, the defense of assumption of risk might have been interposed in that he had accompanied the driver, Brown, on a round of taverns and therefore had knowledge of Brown's condition of insobriety when he entered the car. As to Ruby, the taxicab driver, there was a possible defense of contributory negligence. There was no allegation that the cases settled were overvalued or that the cases tried were not properly defended. The sole complaint of the plaintiff was that the company was guilty of bad faith.

In deciding that the issue of bad faith should have been submitted to the jury, the court said:

Although the defendant [insurance company] had a standing practice of investigating the possibility of contributory negligence on the part of claimants involved in automobile accidents, it failed to look into the possibility of Borowiak's contributory negligence stemming from his activities with young Brown on the evening of the accident. Nor did the company investigate the scene of the collision to determine the surface of the road, its curvature, the lighting, the possibility and significance of skidmarks. It is true that such an investigation might well have been rendered fruitless by the passage of time between the accident and the date the company was notified; but it could have secured an existing report of an investigation by the Police Accident Investigation Squad or obtained the minutes of a hearing before the New York State Motor Vehicle Bureau conducted shortly after the accident. The company did neither. . . .

This case differs from the usual case involving allegations of the insurer's bad faith. Ordinarily, the insurer is taken to task for obstinately refusing to reach a settlement at all, despite the availability of a reasonable offer from the injured party. Here, however, the insurer has participated, successfully, in settlement negotiations with two of the four claimants; it is the company's *overeager*[1] settlement of the claims in disregard of the possibility of the assured's resulting personal liability which, *inter alia*, is asserted as evidence of bad faith. We are well aware of the difficulties involved in appraising an insurer's conduct in reaching a purportedly unfair settlement rather than reaching no settlement at all. But the difference is not dispositive. In either case, the issue to be adjudicated will be whether the insurer's conduct reveals a bad-faith disregard of the assured's financial interest.

Crisci v. *Security Insurance Co. of New Haven* [426 Pac. 2d 173 (California)] demonstrates the power of the court to award damages for mental distress in addition to other damages where the insurer has failed to meet its duty of settlement. The facts of the case indicate that Mrs. Crisci, an immigrant widow of about 70 years, owned a building on which she secured a

---

1 Author's italics.

general liability policy with limits of $10,000. A Mrs. DiMare suffered physical injuries when a tread on a staircase gave way. She also suffered a very severe psychosis. There was a conflict of medical testimony as to the causal relationship between the psychosis and the accident. Mrs. Di Mare reduced her demand to $10,000 prior to trial. The insurer offered $3,000 taking the position that it could establish that the psychosis was not related to the accident. Other evidence indicates that the insurer refused a $9,000 demand to which Mrs. Crisci offered to contribute $2,500. The trial resulted in a verdict of $100,000 for Mrs. DiMare and $1,000 for her husband. The insurer then paid its policy limit of $10,000. A settlement was arranged with Mrs. Crisci whereby the DiMares received $22,000—the proceeds of the sale of Mrs. Crisci's building plus 40 percent of Mrs. Crisci's claim against the insurer.

In the present action, the court concluded that the insurer was liable for failing to settle the claim within the policy limits, and directed the payment of the excess over the policy limits. It also affirmed an award to Mrs. Crisci of $25,000 for mental suffering brought about by the insurer's refusal to settle.

While the insurer's duty to settle arises out of the contract of insurance, the court characterized the claim as sounding in tort so as to bring it within the tort rule that the injured party may recover for all damages caused, whether such damage could be anticipated or not. The court further pointed out that the decision should not be construed as opening the door to similar claims arising out of a breach of contract. The court said:

Recovery of damages for mental suffering in the instant case does not mean that in every case of breach of contract the injured party may recover such damages. Here the breach also constitutes a tort. Moreover, plaintiff did not seek by the contract involved here to obtain a commercial advantage but to protect herself against risks of accidental losses. Among the considerations in purchasing liability insurance, as insurers are well aware, is the peace of mind and security it will provide in the event of an accidental loss, and recovery of damages for mental suffering has been permitted for breach of contracts which directly concern the comfort, happiness or personal esteem of one of the parties.

The court undoubtedly was influenced by the dire circumstances of this case in which the plaintiff found herself. The change in her financial condition created a decline in her physical health, hysteria, and several suicide attempts. The court felt that the insurer who failed to settle a just claim should not escape scot-free from liability for a condition which its wrongful act—the failure to meet the duty of settlement—was the proximate cause. Obviously, this is an unusual case and the same circumstances will not be present in too many cases. However, it does stand for the proposition where mental distress can be established as being a result of the insurer's wrongful act, damages can and will be awarded.

Therefore, where a settlement can be made within the policy limits the company must exercise good faith in deciding whether it will accept or reject it. Good faith requires that the company have the advantage of an adequate investigation and that it make its decision considering the interests of the insured as well as its own. As one court put it: "The fairest method of balancing the interests is for the insurer to treat the claim as if it were alone liable for the entire amount." [*Bell* v. *Commercial Insurance Co.*, 280 Fed. 2d 514.]

2. Settlement over the policy limits; insured unwilling to contribute. In this situation there is no possibility of a settlement within the policy limits. If the demand always exceeds the policy limits, there is no duty on the part of the insurance carrier to attempt to influence the insured as to what course he should take, nor is the insurance carrier under any duty to recommend what the insured should do under the circumstances. The insurance carrier has met its duty if it conducts an adequate investigation, notifies the insured of the amount of the demand, and properly defends the case should litigation ensue. In situations such as this it is generally advisable to take a statement from the insured setting forth these facts so that there can be no question that notice of the excess demand was given, and, further, that the insured was given an opportunity to participate in a settlement if he was so disposed. The statement might read as follows:

On January 1, 1963, I was involved in an automobile accident with Joseph Green at Albany, New York. I understand that I am being sued for $150,000 and that the demand in settlement is in excess of my policy limit of $10,000.

I do not wish to contribute any money above my policy limit toward the settlement of this case, nor do I feel that my insurance company should make any settlement of the matter. I do not feel that I was at fault for the accident, and I stated to the police at the scene of the accident that it all was the fault of Mr. Joseph Green.

3. Settlement over the policy limits; insured willing to contribute. This situation poses the same problems as those encountered in 1 (above). With the insured willing to contribute the excess over the policy limits, settlement can be made within the policy limits. The same principles are applicable here as in situation 1, in that the insurer must make a good faith decision whether it will accept or reject the settlement. If it accepts, the case is settled. If the insurer rejects the settlement and the insured insists on making payment of the excess, he can arrange such a disposition of his interest through his own attorney by means of a covenant not to sue as to the excess over the amount of the policy limit. Most of the time, however, the plaintiff's counsel will not be interested in such a disposition since he usually insists on an entire settlement or none at all. In the latter case, the claim will have to be litigated, with the insurer taking the responsibility for an adverse result should the court find its decision not to settle was not in good faith.

1606 Supplementary payments

In addition to the applicable limits of liability under the indemnification promise of the company, the company also agrees to make certain payments contracted in connection with the happening of the accident or as a result thereof, and in connection with the defense of any suit brought against the insured. Under the automobile policy, these payments comprise four categories:

1. All expenses incurred by the company, all costs taxed against the insured in any such suit, and all interest on the entire amount of any judgment therein which accrues after entry of the judgment and before the company has paid or tendered or deposited in court that part of the judgment which does not exceed the limit of the company's liability thereon.

This provision has reference to the trial of the lawsuit wherein the company assumes all costs in connection therewith, those which it incurred itself and all costs taxed against the insured. In addition, the company agrees to pay the interest which accrues on the entire amount of the judgment after its entry, up until the time the company has paid, or tendered, or deposited its share of the judgment. This situation often comes about when there is a judgment in excess of the policy limits and the company decides to appeal. The company will assume all the costs of the appeal and, if unsuccessful, will also pay the interest on the entire judgment which as accrued during the pendency of the appeal until such time as it has paid its share of the judgment. Clearly, where the appeal took several years, this could be a sizable sum.

2. Premiums on appeal bonds required in any such suit, premiums on bonds to release attachments for an amount not in excess of the applicable limit of liability of this policy, and the cost of bail bonds required of the insured because of accident or traffice law violation arising out of the use of an automobile insured hereunder, not to exceed $100 per bail bond, but without any obligation to apply for or furnish any such bonds.

There is no limit as to the cost of appeal bonds required to be furnished in connection with the defense of a suit under the policy; the insurer must apply for, furnish such bonds, and pay the premium therefor. The insurer will pay the premiums on bonds to release attachments for an amount up to the limit of liability which is applicable to the case. If there is a property damage limit of $5,000, and a claim is made for property damage only, then the applicable limit of liability is $5,000 and the company would be liable for the premium of any bond required up to the face amount of $5,000—but no more.

On the other hand, if there was a claim for personal injury, and the limits of liability under the policy were $20,000, and there was an attachment, the company would be required to pay the premium on any bond to release the attachment, up to the face amount of $20,000, since this is the applicable limit of liability in the particular case. As to bail bonds, there is a limit of $100 for the premium regardless of the face amount of the bond required, and the company is under no obligation to apply for or furnish the bond. The obligation of the company is to pay the bail bond premium up to $100 and nothing more.

3. Expenses incurred by the insured for such immediate medical and surgical relief to others as shall be imperative at the time of an accident involving an automobile insured hereunder, and not due to war.

This merely refers to the insured's response to the demands of human decency and reimburses or pays in his behalf any sums for which he has become obligated for the immediate relief of others involved in the accident. It does not refer to any obligation to pay medical bills for services rendered some time after the accident; the payment here refers only to immediate relief as shall be imperative or absolutely necessary at the time of the accident. It might involve merely first-aid treatment—or an immediate surgical operation. The policy definition of war is declared and undeclared war, civil war, insurrection, rebellion or revolution, and any act or condition incident to the foregoing.

4. All reasonable expenses, other than loss of earnings, incurred by the insured at the company's request.

For the most part these expenses refer but are not limited to the preparation and trial of the lawsuit. The insured must cooperate with the insurance company and must attend all trials or hearings when requested to do so. If the trial is held some distance from the insured's home, the expenses described here could conceivably include his traveling expenses to and from the place of trial, his hotel and meal expenses, and any other expense which he might incur at the company's request. He is not entitled to reimbursement for loss of earnings of any kind.

1607   Insured defined

Liability insurance contracts not only afford insurance protection for the named insured but, according to their terms, the same or similar protection to others. This is accomplished by means of a specific agreement or addenda to the contract between the insured and the insurer, or through the terms of the standard policy forms themselves. Under the standard forms these additional insureds range from a very small group of people (in the case of general liability contracts) to the much larger group covered under the omnibus clause of the standard automobile policies. They may be designated by class, such as officers and directors of the insured corporation while acting in that capacity, or relatives of the named insured living in the same household, or they may be described by the circumstances, such as a person using the insured's vehicle with his permission. In any case, the persons insured, whether named or not, are entitled to all of the protection afforded by the insurance, irrespective of whether they paid any part of the premium. They are also subject to the conditions of the contract, and in order to take advantage of the insurance afforded must comply with all the terms and conditions of the contract.

Under the Comprehensive General Liability Policy, the definition of the insured is as follows:

The unqualified word "insured" includes the named insured and also includes any executive officer, director or stockholder thereof while acting within the scope of his duties as such, and any organization or proprietor with respect to real estate management for the named insured. If the name insured is a partnership, the unqualified word "insured" includes any partner therein but only with respect to his liability as such.

Under this definition it is clear that the intent of the contract is to offer insurance protection to a small number of persons. It covers the named insured, whether an individual, firm, or corporation, and will cover the named insured whether the liability sought to be imposed is vicarious, as a result of the acts of his agents or servants, or based on his own negligent act. A corporation is an artificial person created by statute which can act only through its agents. Therefore the only liability which could be imposed upon a corporation is vicarious, in the sense that all of its acts are done through agents alone. Certain of the corporation's employees or agents are defined as insureds: executive officers, directors, and stockholders acting within a certain scope of duties.

A partnership is an entity created by a contract between the partners. If the insured is a partnership, the individual partners are insureds, but only as to their liability as such. In all of these cases, whether the named insured is an individual, firm, or corporation, the employees or agents of the named insured, with the exceptions noted, are not additional insureds, and the policy affords them no protection with respect to their personal liability even though such liability is incurred in the course and scope of their employment as a result of acts calculated to further the interests of the employer or principal.

Under the omnibus clause (so-called because of the number of persons who qualify as insureds) of the family automobile liability policy, the definitions of the persons insured are divided into two sections, referring to owned and unowned automobiles.

Owned automobile. With respect to owned automobile, the following persons are insureds:

1. The named insured and any resident of the same household.
2. Any other person using such automobile with the permission of the named insured, providing his actual operation, or (if he is not operating) his other actual use thereof is within the scope of such permission.
3. Any other person or organization, but only with respect to his or its liability because of acts or omissions of an insured under (1) and (2) above.

1. *The named insured and any resident of the same household.* The named insured is defined in the policy to mean the individual named in item 1 of the declarations and includes his spouse if she is a resident of the same household. A household is defined as a family living together under the same

roof. Thus, in *Island* v. *Fireman's Fund* [172 Pac. 2d 520 (California), affirmed in 184 Pac. 2d 153], the court held that the son, while in the Armed Forces, was not a member of the named insured's household. It defined a member of the insured's household as one who dwells under the same roof as the insured. The household also consists of persons living together as a family. In *U.S. Fidelity & Guaranty* v. *Brann* [180 S.W. 2d 102 (Kentucky)], it was held that a delivery boy who occasionally slept and took meals at his employer's home was not a member of his employer's household.

2. *Person using the automobile with permission.* In the older policy forms (and in some still used) this provision contained the following language: "Any other person using such automobile, provided the actual use thereof is with the permission of the named insured." The decided cases are based on the above insuring agreement and definition, and it is an open question at this time as to the effect of the seemingly more restrictive language used in the newer policies.

To qualify as an insured under this provision, the person must be *using* the owned automobile and *have the permission* of the named insured. "Using" and "use" are not defined in the insurance contract except that "use" of the automobile is extended to include the loading and unloading thereof. The courts have construed "use" of the automobile to mean more than the mere operation of the vehicle, and while some have limited the use to the things for which an automobile is generally used, some construed the agreement to include any use to which the automobile may be put, whether such use is peculiar to the automobile or not. In an extreme case, for example, the insured was using the insured vehicle as a gun rest while on a hunting trip. Injury and death to another followed the negligent discharge of the gun. This was held to constitute "use" of the insured vehicle so as to bring the case within the coverage of the automobile policy. [*Fidelity & Casualty Co.* v. *Loth,* 271 Fed. 2d 500 (Ohio).]

In *Coletrain* v. *Coletrain* [23 Auto Cas. 2d 1364, CCH (South Carolina)], the claimant and her husband were alighting from a taxi and the husband negligently slammed the door on his wife's hand. In the wife's personal injury claim against her husband (permitted in South Carolina) the husband was held to be an additional insured, under the taxicab policy, since he was "using" the vehicle with the permission of the named insured.

Permission of the named insured may be express or implied, or it may be transmitted through an agent authorized to do so. Implied permission may arise from a course of dealing over a period of time where the permissive user, from the nature of the transaction, was not required to obtain specific permission for each use of the vehicle. Permission through an agent with authority might consist of permission given by an employee, or other agent, or by a permissive user where the initial permission contemplated use of the vehicle by others. (See Section 1608, below.)

3. *Any other person or organization.* Such other person or organization on whose business the owned automobile is being used is an additional in-

sured with respect to his vicarious liability arising out of use of the automobile. The insurance thus afforded is limited to use of the vehicle, either by the named insured, or a resident of his household, or a permissive user. Thus, if the named insured used his car on the business of his employer, and while so engaged an accident occurred as a result of which both the named insured as agent and his employer as principal were sued as co-defendants, the obligation imposed by this provision would require that the insurer defend and indemnify both.

Nonowned automobile.   With respect to a nonowned automobile, the following are insureds:

1. The named insured.
2. Any relative, but only with respect to a private passenger automobile or trailer, provided his actual operation or (if he is not operating) the other actual use thereof is with the permission, or reasonably believed to be with the permission of the owner, and is within the scope of such permission.
3. Any other person or organization not owning or hiring the automobile, but only with respect to his or its liability because of acts or omissions of an insured under 1 and 2 above.

1. *The named insured.*   When this "drive other cars" coverage was first introduced, there was considerable controversy as to whether or not the condition (permission of the owner) set forth in Section 2 also applied to the named insured. Some early cases, because of the alignment of the words, did hold that the named insured was covered whether he had the permission of the owner or not, and that the condition applied only to Section 2. However, by proper alignment of the paragraphs, it was made evident that the intention of the insurer was to have the condition applicable to the named insured as well. See *Bright* v. *Ohio Casualty Insurance Co.* [1971 Auto Cas. (CCH) 7039]; *State Farm Mut. Auto Ins. Co.* v. *Allstate Ins. Co.* [9 Cal. App. 3d 508 (88 Cal. Rptr. 246).

Under the present wording and alignment of the policy provisions, it has been held that the named insured is entitled to coverage when driving a nonowned vehicle, only when he has the permission (or reasonably believed to have the permission) of the owner, and then only when the nonowned vehicle is used within the scope of the owner's permission.

2. *Any relative.*   A relative has been defined as a relative of the named insured who is a resident of the same household. The insurance afforded as to a nonowned automobile should be compared with that afforded for the owned automobile. As to the owned automobile, any resident of the named insured's household is an insured. As to a nonowned automobile, only a relative who is a resident of the named insured's household is an insured, and then only when the nonowned vehicle is driven with the permission of the owner or when the insured reasonably believes he has such permission. This provision is in the contract to avoid providing coverage where the relative uses another's vehicle without permission, which in some instances may even amount to theft.

3. *Any person or organization.* This insurance is the same as that provided in the case of an owned vehicle with the exception that it does not apply to vehicles owned by the person or organization, or hired by him or it.

Severability of interests.   The policy provides:

The insurance afforded under Part I applies separately to each insured against whom claim is made or suit is brought, but the inclusion herein of more than one insured shall not operate to increase the limits of the company's liability.

This means that within the limits of the policy the liability of each person who qualifies as an insured is considered separately without reagard to other persons who may so qualify, or, to put it another way, the company will regard each claim made against each person insured as if the person insured were the only one insured under the policy.

For example, *A* is driving *B*'s car with *B*'s permission. *B* is a passenger in his own car and is injured through the negligent driving of *A*. *B* sues *A*. *A* is an additional insured under *B*'s policy, and the company is obligated to defend *A* in this suit and to indemnify him. It makes no difference in this situation that *B* is the named insured and, as such, is the person with whom the company entered into the insurance contract. The policy applies separately to each person insured, and the practical result here is the same as if *A* had purchased the policy and *B* was merely a personal injury claimant.

Let us assume the same facts but add to them that *A*'s negligent driving caused a collision with another vehicle, resulting in property damage to the other vehicle as well as bodily injuries to the passengers and driver. Assume further that *A* was driving the car on the business of *B*, and was therefore his agent. In addition to the suit brought by *B* against *A*, a suit is brought by the driver and passengers of the other car against both *A* and *B*. The company is bound to defend and indemnify *A* and *B* in the one suit and to indemnify *A* in the first suit.

Other insurance.   With respect to the automobile liability contract, the "Other Insurance" provision reads as follows:

If the insured has other insurance against a loss covered by Part I of this policy the company shall not be liable under this policy for a greater proportion of such loss than the applicable limit of liability stated in the declarations bears to the total applicable limit of liability of all valid and collectible insurance against such loss; provided, however, the insurance with respect to a temporary substitute automobile or non-owned automobile shall be excess over any other valid and collectible insurance.

This means that as to the owned automobile, any other insurance which the named insured may have available will be considered, and the automobile policy will participate pro rata in the payment of the claim.

For example, the named insured has a Comprehensive Personal Liability Policy covering his premises and an accident occurs on the premises as a result of the ownership, maintenance, or use of the insured automobile. Both the automobile insurer and the comprehensive liability insurer will share the loss on a pro rata basis. The same thing would be true if the named insured had two policies covering the owned vehicle. This could come about through inadvertence: the acquisition of a second car with insurance being purchased from another insurer, or the ownership of the second car by the spouse and insurance purchased from another insurer. Since the named insured and his spouse are defined as named insureds in the automobile policy, there would be two policies of insurance available on the two cars unless the insurance contract, by means of an endorsement, eliminated part of the coverage afforded. As to nonowned vehicles or temporary substitute vehicles, the general rule which the claimsman may follow is that the insurance follows the vehicle, that the specific insurance on the vehicle is primary, and all other insurance, with the exception of accidents occurring on the premises, is excess.

1608   Permissive use, automobile policies

In addition to the named insured under an automobile liability policy, a person "using" the automobile with the permission of the named insured is himself an insured and as such is entitled to all the insurance protection afforded by the policy. Whether or not such a person will qualify as an insured under the policy will depend upon the existence of two requirements, namely (1) actual permission to use the automobile and (2) use of the automobile within the scope of permission.

1. *Permission.*   The owner had the right to possession and use of the vehicle as being two of the attributes of ownership. He may surrender possession and retain to himself the right of use, such as would be the case where he parks the car in a parking lot or garage for storage purposes. The parking lot or the garage has the right of possession but no right of use, and if an employee of either should take and use the car for his own purposes, he is guilty of theft. He has unlawfully deprived the owner of the use of his car during the period of his conversion of the property to his own use. Such a person would not qualify as an insured under the terms of the policy, since the requirement of permission is entirely lacking.

The owner may give permission for limited use and the use of the automobile outside the limits of such permission would make any person so using the automobile guilty of theft or conversion. This situation might come about where the owner left his automobile in a garage for repairs. Clearly, the garageman would have the right to operate the automobile so as to move it from place to place in the garage and also to road test the car after the repairs had been completed. Both of these acts would be within the scope of the permission granted and the garageman would be a permissive user and, as such, an insured under the policy. On the other hand, if the garageman, or his employees, used the automobile for any other purpose, the person so using it would not be within the scope of the permission granted and therefore not an insured within the terms of the policy.

2. *Scope of permission.*   Where permission has been granted and the automobile is used for the purpose for which permission was granted and nothing else, then there is no problem as to the status of the user in relation to the insurance policy. It is where there has been a deviation from the area of permission that the courts are divided as to whether or not the user is or is not within the scope of permission while so deviating, so as to qualify as an insured under the policy. In determining this question, the court will apply one of the three following rules:

a. The liberal or so-called initial permission rule that if a person has permission to use the automobile in the first instance, any subsequent use while it remains in his possession, though not within the contemplation of the parties, is permissive use within the terms of the omnibus clause of the policy.
b. The moderate or *minor deviation* rule that the permittee is covered under the omnibus clause as an insured so long as his deviation from the permissive use is minor in nature.
c. The strict or *conversion* rule that any deviation from the time, place or purpose specified by the person granting permission is sufficient to take the permittee outside of the coverage of the omnibus clause.

(a) *The initial permission rule.* Illustrative of the liberality involved in the application of this rule is *Matita* v. *Nationwide Mutual Insurance Co.* (33 N.J. 488). In that case, the named insured gave a neighbor permission to use his car for the purpose of visiting her mother. After visiting her mother, the neighbor made a tour of the taverns and bars in the neighborhood of her mother's home, and while she was on her way home after this excursion, an accident occurred. Coverage was denied by the insurance carrier on the theory that her use of the automobile was outside the scope of permission. In deciding the case in favor of coverage and adversely to the contentions of the insurance carrier, the court said:

Accordingly, we hold that if a person is given permission to use the motor vehicle in the first instance, any subsequent use *short of theft or the like* while it remains in his possession, though not within the contemplation of the parties, is a permissive use within the terms of a standard omnibus clause of an insurance policy.

Thus, if *A* loans his car to *B* for the purpose of taking *B*'s children to school, and *B*, after transporting his children to school, drives to the grocery store to make a few purchases, he still would be within the scope of his permission. On the other hand, if *B*, after transporting his children to school, took the car on a 1,000-mile vacation trip, his use of the automobile would amount to "theft or the like." In the first case of minor deviation, *B* would come within the definition of a permissive user within the terms of the policy, and in the second case he would not.

Other cases stress the time element, and under this rule, hold that as long as the automobile is returned within a reasonable time after the initial permission is granted, regardless of the use to which the automobile has been put, the user is an insured under the omnibus clause. For example, in *Vezolles* v. *Home Indemnity Co.* [38 Fed. Supp. 455 (Kentucky); affirmed in 128 Fed. 2d 257], a young man named Ruemmele and his girl friend visited until 2:30 or 3:00 o'clock in the morning another young couple named Morton. When the party broke up, the Mortons allowed Ruemmele to use their car for the purpose of taking his girl friend home. The arrangement was that Ruemmele would return the car to the Morton's home at which time, the Mortons would drive him to his home. When Ruemmele arrived back at the Morton's home, the Mortons had retired and the house was locked. Since he could not arouse the Mortons, he took the car and drove to a cafe located about four blocks beyond the street on which he lived. At the cafe, he met another friend and they decided to take a ride before going home. While on that ride which took them even further away from the Morton home, they ran over a pedestrian. In holding that Ruemmele was a permissive user and entitled to the benefits of the Morton automobile liability policy, the court said:

The purpose of the omnibus clause was to extend the coverage beyond the limitations which would otherwise exist under the law of principal and agent. Its addition to the usual terms of liability insurance policies was for the purpose of increasing the advantages of the policy being purchased, to provide additional coverage, and to be used as a selling point in competition with standard policies. To give it a construction which is closely parallel to the existing law of principal and agent would ignore the evident purpose of its being made a part of the policy. In my opinion the purpose of the omnibus clause was to extend the liability insurance coverage to a person other than the owner who has possession and use of the car with the permission of the owner for a somewhat limited period of time, without arbitrary and definite restrictions as to just what could be or what could not be done with the car during that period of time. The time element during which the use is permitted by the owner is in my opinion the element to be stressed rather than the particular use to which the car is put, so long as the particular use does not vary materially from the contemplated or usual use of a car under similar conditions. The main purpose of the clause is to substitute the operator of the car for the owner of the car while the car is being operated with the permission of the owner.

The rule, however, contemplates that permission be granted in the first instance and that the use of the car is under the permission given. Merely because permission is given for use on one occasion does not mean that the permission can be deemed to include other occasions for which specific permission has not been given. For example in *U.S. Fidelity & Guaranty Co.* v. *Brann* [180 S.W. 2d 102 (Kentucky)], the insured, a grocer, asked his deliveryman to take the delivery truck on a Sunday morning and gather up a group of young men for a Sunday School class taught by the grocer. After completing the job, the deliveryman returned the truck to the garage but did not return the ignition key to the store. Later in the afternoon, the delivery-man took the truck and went joyriding with some friends, in the course of which he had an accident. The court held that his possession of the truck at the time and place of the accident did not originate from and therefore was in no sense a "deviation" from a permitted use. At the time he took possession of the truck without the knowledge of the owner, he had no permission whatever, express or implied, and as a result, he was not a permissive user and additional insured.

(b) *The minor deviation rule.*   This rule is the hardest to apply and the question posed is whether or not the deviation is a minor one. If it is a minor deviation, then there is coverage, whereas if it is a material one, there is no coverage. In spite of the difficulties attending the application of the rule, some 22 states at the present time have adopted it as the rule of decision in cases of this type. Each case will have to stand on its own facts, and where there is a dispute as to the facts, it will then become a jury question.

(c) *The conversion rule.*   This rule contemplates that permission must be given, but also that the use to which the automobile is put must be within the scope of the permission granted. If the use is outside of the area contemplated by the permission, then there is a conversion or theft of the use of the automobile and consequently the person in possession of the car is using it against the wishes of the owner. Therefore, he is not a permissive user within the contemplation of the insurance policy including permissive users within the definition of insured.

In some cases, the deviation from the permission consists of the use of the automobile by a second permittee with the permission of the first or original permittee. Whether or not the first permittee's act in allowing a second permittee to use the automobile is within the scope of the original permission will turn on the facts and circumstances attending the granting of the permission in the first instance. As to whether or not the first permittee has the authority of the owner to delegate his permission to others, the cases will fall into one of three general categories: (1) permission, express or implied to delegation; (2) permission silent as to delegation; and (3) delegation is expressly prohibited.

1. *Express or implied permission to delegate.*   Where the permission to delegate the use of the car to others is express and is within the contemplation of the owner, no problem is encountered. All of the use of the vehicle is within the scope of permission. Implied permission may be spelled out where the circumstances are such that the owner knew, or should have known, that delegation of the permission to others was involved, and his failure to prohibit such use by others amounted to consent. For example, in *Costanzo v. Pennsylvania Threshermen's Insurance Co.* (30 N.J. 262), permission was given by the insured to his son to use the insured automobile around a naval base where he was stationed and in traveling to and from his home. The court concluded that the permission granted included the authority to delegate the permission to others to operate the vehicle and that the operation of the vehicle by another sailor with the permission of the insured's son was within the scope of the owner's permission. Pointing out that the son was stationed at a place far distant from his home, that the father had another car and apparently did not require the use of the one loaned to his son, and that the father could reasonably expect that his son during the long journey to and from his home would on occasion share the driving with others, the court went on to say:

> While away from home, the son had the unsupervised control of the car for an extended period of time. He used it for social engagements and permitted others to drive it. Neither he nor his father testified that this was done contrary to the wishes of the father. We believe that the circumstances under which this car was entrusted to Sturgill, Jr. were such as to make it reasonable to say that the driving of the car while Sturgill, Jr. was riding therein was impliedly countenanced by Sturgill, Sr.

To the same effect was the case of *Brooks* v. *Delta Casualty Co.* [82 So. 2d 55 (Louisiana)]. The named insured gave his daughter permission to use his automobile on a business trip. He knew that the trip was a long one and that she would be accompanied by a friend. Where the daughter granted permission to the friend to drive the car, the court held that the permission of the named insured to the friend could be fairly implied from the circumstances of the initial permission granted, and that the driving of the car by the friend could reasonably be considered to be within the contemplation of the owner. In *Menn* v. *Mutual Auto Insurance Co.* [64 N.W. 2d 195 (Wisconsin)], it was held that where the insured granted permission to his son to use the automobile, and where he had knowledge that his son's school friends also drove the car, and he did not object, consent to such use by others could be fairly implied.

In *Utica Mutual Ins. Co.* v. *Rollaston* (246 Fed. 2d 105), an automobile service agency supplied its service manager with a car. His contract of employment required that he be furnished with "transportation without gasoline." It was held that if an insured automobile is left by the owner with someone for general use, and he in turn permits its use by another, such use by another is deemed to be with the permission of the owner. In *Robinson* v. *Fidelity & Casualty Co.* [57 S.E. 2d 93 (Virginia)], the insured left his car with his girl friend before going into service in the Marines. Nothing was said about lending it to anyone else; the insured merely said that he was leaving the car with her and did not want to come back and find it wrecked. It was held that the girl was more than a bailee. She had general authority over the use and oepration of the car during the insured's absence. She therefore stood in the place of the insured and could permit its use by others under appropriate circumstances.

2. Permission silent as to delegation. Where the original permission is given to the first permittee allowing unrestricted use of the vehicle, the cases generally hold that the first permittee has the implied authority of the owner to delegate the use of the vehicle to other persons, whether the use is for the benefit of the first permittee or is used for the personal purposes of the operator. The rationale of the cases is that by giving the first permittee complete dominion over the vehicle, the owner-insured clothes him with the same rights and authority to delegate the use of the vehicle that the owner-insured himself had.

Where the permission is not unrestricted but is limited to a particular purpose, a diffent rule will be applied. In *Aetna Casualty & Surety Co.* v. *DeMaison* [114 Fed. Supp. 106 (Pennsylvania)], the insured's son asked for and was granted permission to use his father's car to go to a theatre. Instead, he went to a tavern where he met a group of friends, and later it was decided that they would go to a diner. One of the friends, Mrs. DeMaison, drove the car from the tavern and was involved in an accident before they arrived at the diner. Coverage was denied to Mrs. DeMaison on the theory that she was not using the vehicle with the permission of the named insured. The court held that there was no express or implied permission given by the father for the use of the automobile to go to the tavern in the first place and that there was no permission express or implied given by the father to Mrs. DeMaison nor was there any express or implied permission given to the son to delegate his own permission to use the vehicle to Mrs. DeMaison or anyone else. In *Chase* v. *United States Fidelity & Guaranty Co.* [53 Atl. 2d 708 (Rhode Island)], the named insured, who had parked his automobile in a narrow alley among other cars, gave his keys to *A* in order that he, *A*, could remove his own vehicle. *A* accomplished this by having *B* drive the owner-insured's car into the street while *A* drove his car out of the alley. *B* then drove the car back into the alley and reparked it. Later that day *C* drove the insured automobile out into the street so as to allow the removal of another car parked in the alley. *C* was involved in an accident with another car while so doing. *C* testified that he had secured the keys from *B*. *C* contended that he was a permissive user on the theory that he had the implied permission of the owner since the owner had given the keys to *B* for the purpose of removing a car and the owner's failure to inquire about or ask for the return of his keys amounted to an implied permission to anyone to move the car whenever another car had to be removed. The court held that *B* was a permissive user and that *C* was not.

3. *Delegation expressly prohibited.* The general rule is that where the permission given expressly prohibits the use of the car by others, such others, whether using the car for the purpose for which permission was given, or for their own purposes, are not within the scope of permission and as such are not entitled to the insurance protection. Where an emergency arises and it becomes necessary for some other person to drive the car for the benefit of the first permittee, the question to be decided is whether or not such use of the vehicle is with the implied permission of the name insured, notwithstanding his express prohibition against the first permittee's allowing a third person to drive. The most common situation would be where the father gave his son permission to use the car with the express understanding that the son, and the son alone, would drive the car. The son becomes ill or passes out at a party and a third person uses the car to drive the son to his home. While so doing, the third person is involved in an accident. The question involves whether or not the third person has the implied permission of the named insured to so use the vehicle. If the third person acts as a volunteer without any permission from the first permittee, whether he is physically capable of giving permission or not, the courts generally hold that the third person is not a permissive user under the policy. In *Kadrmas* v. *Mudna* [107 N.W. 2d 346 (North Dakota)], the original permittee drank too much and he went to the parked automobile to sleep, asking that he be awakened when it was time to leave. A companion without waking him undertook to drive him home and was involved in an accident. The companion was not a permissive user and not covered by the omnibus clause of the policy. See also *Rosenbloom* v. *St. Paul Fire & Marine Ins. Co.* [214 Fed. Supp. 301 (New York)]. In *Adkins* v. *Inland Mut. Ins. Co.* [20 S.E. 2d 471 (West Virginia)], a companion undertook to drive the automobile home when the original permittee became too intoxicated to drive and passed out. While the original permittee may have been considered as having been given implied permission to the companion to drive, the court held that in absence of permission to use the car from the named insured, the companion was not within the terms of the policy. On the other hand, in *Aetna Life Ins. Co.* v. *Chandler* [193 Atl. 233 (New Hampshire)], the named insured, who did not drive, allowed a close friend to use the automobile for her own purposes, including driving to and from her place of employment in another city where she frequently remained overnight. One night she became ill and requested a third person to drive the car to another city to get some medicine for her. While so doing, the third person was involved in an accident. The court held that the third person was a permissive user and the use to which the automobile was being put was within the scope of the permission given by the named insured.

The decisions in other cases involve the question of whether or not there was in fact an emergency. In *Prisuda* v. *General Casualty Co.* [74 N.W. 2d 777 (Wisconsin)], the named insured expressly directed that no one but her son should drive the car. While on a trip, the son became tired and asked one of his companions to drive, and an accident occurred. The court held that this did not constitute an emergency, but if it did, then it was not of such a pressing nature that the named insured could not have been consulted as to her wishes. In any case, the companion was held to be outside of the coverage. To the same effect is *Lucas* v. *United States Fidelity & Guaranty Co.* [174 Atl. 712 (New Jersey)], in which the named insured's son, as the original permittee with general permission to drive the automobile, drove a friend and two girls to a tavern where they indulged in drinking. The son became dizzy and dazed and at his request the friend drove him to the insured's winter home and then drove the girls home. On this latter trip, an accident occurred in which both of the girls were injured. The court held that the friend was not a permissive user and in absence of express or implied permission from the named insured, he was outside the scope of the insurance coverage.

In *Bauer* v. *Hardware Mut. Casualty Co.* [108 N.W. 2d 271 (Wisconsin)], the named insured's daughter was given permission to use the automobile to go to a photographer to pick up some pictures. She was accompanied by a friend who rode along as a passenger. On arriving at the photographer's, she parked the automobile in a no parking zone with the motor running, leaving the friend in the car. Shortly thereafter, a police officer informed the friend that they could not park there and to get the car out of the zone. The friend tooted the horn but the driver merely waved to her from the photographer's shop. At the urging of the police officer, the friend undertook to drive the car away from its parked position and while so doing was involved in an accident. The court held that the case did not involve an emergency and since the permission given to the original permittee was for limited use, no permission from the named insured to the friend could be implied. The court also made the point that the original permittee did not give any permission to the friend.

1609　Loading and unloading

The loading and unloading of automobiles may involve not only automobile liability but general liability (premises) coverages as well. Under the automobile liability contract, the use of the automobile is defined to include the loading and unloading thereof. The words "loading and unloading" are not defined in the policy, and therefore the courts have been called upon to construe the meaning of the terms with reference to specific cases before them. In deciding the cases, the courts which have had occasion to pass on the question have applied either the Coming to Rest or Continuous Passage rule, or the Complete Operation rule.

1. *Coming to rest rule.* Under this rule, the operation of loading and unloading begins when the object is picked up in the vicinity of the automobile and in one continuous operation is placed on the automobile; the operation ends when the object is taken from the automobile and reaches the place of first deposit after being separated from the automobile. In other words, the unloading is complete when the object comes to rest either on the ground or sidewalk for the first time after being taken from the automobile. This rule has also been referred to as the Continuous Passage rule for the reason that the period covered by loading and unloading is measured from the time the article is picked up and placed on the automobile in one continuous passage until the article is first separated from the vehicle. This was the first rule enunciated by the courts, and it is still applied in some jurisdictions, although the majority of the courts who have considered the question currently apply the Complete Operation rule. Therefore, the Coming to Rest rule can be considered the rule of the minority at this time.

2. *Complete operation rule.* Under this rule, the loading operation begins when the articles are moved from their accustomed place of storage or from the place where they were being delivered to the automobile; the unloading process would not end until the articles reached the place of ultimate destination.

Because of the limited nature of its operation, the courts have experienced little difficulty in fixing the boundaries of the loading and unloading operation when applying the Coming To Rest rule. For example, in *Jackson* v. *Maryland Casualty Co.* (117 N.J.L. 401), the truck driver removed a roll of linoleum from the truck, placed it on a hand truck, and pushed the hand truck into the building. The linoleum rolled off and injured a pedestrian. The court held that the unloading operation ceased when the linoleum was removed from the truck and placed on the hand truck, and therefore the claim did not come within the automobile coverage. In *Franklin Co-op Creamery Association* v. *Employers' Liability Assurance Corp.* [273 N.W. 809 (Minnesota)], the court was confronted with the same type of unloading coverage under a teams liability policy. The facts were that the driver of a milk wagon stopped his horse and wagon, removed a basket of milk bottles, and entered a building to make a delivery. While in the course of delivering the milk, he negligently injured another person. The court held that the unloading operation ceased when he removed the basket of milk bottles from the wagon, and that at the time of the accident he was not within the insurance coverage.

The Complete Operations rule is clearly the more liberal and more difficult to apply. The courts have been struggling with it and have produced a mass of decisions which do not readily fit any particular pattern. It is possible in many cases to find the court deciding one case in one way and another, with almost identical facts, the other way. For example, in *Stammer* v. *Kitzmiller* [276 N.W. 629 (Wisconsin)], the truck driver had set a keg of beer on the sidewalk, had opened the cellar doors leading to the basement, had placed the keg in the basement, and was in the process of getting a receipt signed when a pedestrian fell over the open doors. The court held that the merchandise had come to rest at its ultimate destination and that "while the open hatchway may have been a convenience in the process of furthering the delivery of the goods, it was not included in the process of furthering the delivery of the goods, it was not included in the process of unloading." Thus the claim did not come within the coverage of the truck owner's automobile policy but did come within his general liability coverage.

However, in *Hardware Mutual Casualty Co.* v. *St. Paul Mercury Indemnity Co.* (58 N.W. 2d 646), the same court was confronted with almost identical facts which indicated that the truck driver double-parked and opened the hatch doors to the basement for the purpose of delivering a keg of beer. Another driver, who was boxed in by the double-parked truck, asked the driver to move it so that he could get out. While the truck driver was in the process of moving his truck, a pedestrian fell over the open doors and was injured. The unloading process had not yet begun and the keg of beer was still on the truck. Nevertheless, the Wisconsin court held that the accident arose out of the unloading of the truck and came within the automobile coverage.

In cases under this rule, the court is generally confronted with the question of when the operation starts and when it ends, or whether there was any loading or unloading at all. For example, in *Hartford A. & I. Co.* v. *Firemen's*

Fund [298 Fed. 2d 423 (7th Cir.)], a bottled gas deliveryman stopped at an address only to find that the tank was full but that the valve was in the off position. He turned the valve on and notified the houseowner that she did not need any gas, even though she had ordered it. He left the premises, and thereafter the house blew up due to the fact that he had turned a valve leading to an uncapped pipe. The court held that his action did not come within the process of unloading the vehicle for the reason that there was no unloading at all. Under the circumstances, the automobile carrier was relieved of responsibility under its policy.

In *Maryland Casualty Co.* v. *Tighe* [115 Fed. 2d 297 (9th Cir.)], the facts indicated that a vendor of vegetables was making a delivery to a restaurant. He had delivered one batch and bumped into a customer when he was hurrying back to his truck to get another load. The court held that he was engaged in the process of unloading the truck and therefore the automobile carrier had coverage.

In all of the foregoing cases, the question was solely whether or not the operation came within the loading and unloading operation, and only the negligence of the named insured was involved. Complications develop when there are two policies available for the same accident as to the named insured, but only one policy available to the other person involved. To illustrate, let us assume that the automobile is being loaded on the premises of the named insured by one of his employees. Through the negligence of the employee, a stranger is injured. Under the doctrine of *respondeat superior*, the named insured is liable for the negligence of his employee, but in this case the stranger sues both the employee and the named insured. The named insured has an automobile policy and a general liability policy.

As to the named insured, both policies cover him, and the "other insurance" provisions of both may come into play with the loss being distributed pro rata. As to the employee, he is not an insured under the general liability policy but is an additional insured under the automobile policy. Therefore the automobile insurer must defend and indemnify him. In addition, since the named insured's liability is vicarious, he has an action over against his employee to recover for any damage which he may sustain as a result of the employee's negligence. Therefore, in a case where matter is properly pleaded, the ultimate result will be that the automobile carrier is liable for the entire loss. For this result to obtain, the named insurer must assert his right of action against the employee, otherwise the loss will be distributed between the general liability carrier and the automobile carrier pro rata. [For a case where the employer failed to assert his action over against the employee, and where both carriers were held pro rata, see *Lamberti* v. *Anaco Equipment Co.*, 226 N.Y.S. 2d 70.]

The accident picture may be further complicated by a situation where the loading or unloading of the automobile or truck is being done on the premises of a customer and employees of the customer are assisting in the operation. (It should be again emphasized that any person using the vehicle with the permission of the named insured is an insured, and that "use" of the automobile includes the loading and unloading thereof.) The leading cases on this proposition are *Wagman* v. *American Fidelity & Casualty Co.* (108 N.Y.S. 2d 854; affirmed in 112 N.Y.S. 2d 662; also reported in 109 N.E. 2d 592), and *Bond Stores, Inc.* v. *American Fidelity & Casualty Co.* (133 N.Y.S. 2d 297), both cases having arisen out of the same event. Bond Stores were covered under a general liability policy which covered the named insurer but did not extend any coverage to its employees as insureds. A trucking concern was insured under an automobile liability insurance policy covering, as an insured, any person using the insured vehicle (including loading and unloading) with the permission of the named insured, and covering any person or organization legally responsible for such use. The truckman was employed to move some clothing from one of the Bond stores to another. Two of Bond's employees assisted in loading the truck, and Wagman, who was store manager, supervised the operation in counting the garments as they were loaded in the truck. When returning to the store, Wagman bumped into a pedestrian, causing her to fall to the sidewalk, as a result of which she sustained serious injuries.

In a declaratory judgment action brought against the automobile carrier of the truckman to determine whether Wagman had coverage under the automobile policy, the court held that he was an additional insured since he was engaged in loading the insured vehicle, and that such use was with the permission of the named insured. In the meantime, the pedestrian brought action against Bond Stores and Wagman. Bond Stores counterclaimed against Wagman as the person primarily liable. Judgment was rendered in the pedestrian's favor against Bond Stores and Wagman, and Bond Stores was given judgment on its counterclaim against Wagman.

The general liability carrier furnished certain funds (under a loan agreement) to Bond Stores, which funds were used to satisfy the judgment. Bond Stores then brought action against the automobile carrier for reimbursement for the judgment so satisfied, and the court granted summary judgment in favor of Bond. The practical result here was that the automobile carrier was ultimately responsible for the entire judgment since it was the only insurer of the negligent person, namely Wagman.

[For other cases involving this principle, see *Industrial Indemnity Co.* v. *General Ins. Co.*, 26 Cal. Rep. 568; *Pleasant Valley* v. *Cal-Farm Ins. Co.*, 298 Pac. 2d 109 (California); *Panhandle Gravel Co.* v. *Wilson*, 248 S.W. 2d 779 (Texas); *Pullen* v. *Employers' Liability Assurance Corp.*, 89 So. 2d 373 (Louisiana); *Maryland Casualty* v. *N.J. Manufacturers Casualty Co.*, 145 Atl. 2d 15 (New Jersey). For a discussion of the employee exclusion with relation to loading and unloading coverage, see Section 1610, below.]

1610   Exclusions

The exclusions form part of the insuring agreement and constitute the exceptions to the agreement by limiting, eliminating, or modifying the coverage provided. They may be amended, enlarged, or completely eliminated by agreement of the parties, which agreement may be expressed in an endorsement to the contract or by an addenda. The exclusions, however, are fully set forth in the contract itself, and in the absence of any endorsement clarify the coverage afforded by the policy. The exclusions differ in each contract, depending upon the intent of the parties and the insurance protection required by the type of policy. While it will be impractical and impossible to deal with all the exclusions of liability policies, we will use the Family Automobile Policy as a model and discuss the exclusions contained therein in order to provide an illustration of the effect which exclusions have upon the insuring agreements generally.

The Family Automobile Policy has ten exclusions, identified by letters from *a* to *j*. We will use the same designations. The policy does not apply under Part 1 (liability) to the following:

> *a*) to any automobile while used as a public or livery conveyance, but this exclusion does not apply to the named insured with respect to bodily injury or property damage which results from the named insured's occupancy of a non-owned automobile other than as operator thereof.

The intent of this *public livery exclusion* is to avoid affording coverage under this type of policy for a taxicab or other type of conveyance used indiscriminately in conveying the public without limitation to certain persons, or particular occasions, or without being governed by special terms. Where the passenger pays for the gas and oil on one or two occasions, or even pays a fee for one trip, does not make the vehicle one which is used as a public livery conveyance. The same thing is true with respect to a share-the-ride arrangement where the passenger pays a stated fee per week for transportation to work. The cases generally hold that the exclusion is inapplicable except in situations where the vehicle is held out to the public for hire.

> *b*) to bodily injury and property damage caused intentionally by or at direction of the insured.

This *intentional acts exclusion* refers to acts which can be directly attributable to the insured. It does not exclude acts of others which are intentional, but for which the insured is only vicariously liable. For example, if the insured's driver intentionally runs over a person, the insured would be vicariously liable if the driver were acting as an agent of the insured at the time of injury. The driver while driving the vehicle with the permission of the named insured would also be an insured. However, in this situation, applying the word *insured* to the driver, the injury was caused by the intentional act of this insured and therefore he would come within the exclusion. Therefore the named insured would not be affected by the exclusion in this instance, but rather the driver whose intentional act caused the injury.

> *c*) to bodily injury or property damage with respect to which an insured under this policy is also an insured under a nuclear energy liability policy issued by Nuclear Energy Liability Association, Mutual Atomic Energy Liability

Underwriters, or Nuclear Insurance Association of Canada, or would be an insured but for its termination upon exhaustion of its limit of liability.

As this *nuclear energy exclusion* makes clear, it is not the intent of the policy to cover any liability imposed because of the transportation of fissionable material or radioactive isotopes. The Atomic Energy Act of 1954 (see Section 1309, above) requires that certain insurance coverage be provided before such material is issued to private persons or corporations, such insurance being provided by the associations noted in the exclusion.

    d) to bodily injury or property damage arising out of the operation of farm machinery.

The policy covers farm automobiles under the definition of "owned automobile" and it is possible that farm equipment might be towed or transported by such an automobile. In such a case, there would be coverage under the policy, but where the equipment itself is being operated, either while being towed or transported, or while used on the premises, and the accident arises out of the operation of the equipment, such as due to a defect in its machinery, the accident is subject to this *farm machinery exclusion.*

    e) to bodily injury to any employee of the insured arising out of and in the course of (1) domestic employment by the insured, if benefits therefor are in whole or in part either payable or required to be provided under any workmen's compensation law, or (2) other employment by the injured.

The *employee exclusion* is one of the most controversial exclusions in the policy. The intent of (1), for example, is to exclude any domestic employees who come within the provisions of the workmen's compensation law. Since domestics are not covered in some of the compensation laws, it follows that the exclusion is intended to apply only to those who are so covered, and is not applicable to those who are not so covered.

As to all other employees, the intent is to exclude any liability which the insured may have to them, since they would come within the scope of the workmen's compensation law, and there is no contract here to cover the insured's workmen's compensation liability, which can be covered under an appropriate workmen's compensation policy. The controversy over this exclusion rages around what is meant by "insured." Where there is only one person involved who can qualify as an insured under the policy, there is no problem, but where a person qualifies as an additional insured, and an employee of the name insured is injured, the question is whether or not the exclusion is operative so as to deprive the additional insured of insurance protection. In other words, does the exclusion refer only to employees of the insured who is claiming the protection of the policy, or does it refer to an employee of any insured under the policy?

The problem arises most frequently in loading and unloading cases where another person or organization either assists in the operation or does it completely, thereby qualifying as an additional insured by reason of the fact that such person or organization is using the vehicle for the purpose of loading or unloading it. If the truck driver, who is an employee of the named insured, is injured in the operation, is the coverage afforded to the additional insured affected by the exclusion? Clearly, the truck driver is not the employee of the person claiming the insurance protection, and thus, for the purposes of the claim, there is no employer-employee relationship between the parties.

The courts are divided as to the answer to the problem, in spite of the severability of interests provision of the contract. Some courts (the majority) hold that the exclusion applies if the injured person is an employee of any person or organization insured under the policy, while others (the minority) hold that the exclusion applies only when there is an employer-employee relationship between the person claiming insurance protection and the person making the claim, irrespective of whether the person making the claim is an employee of any other who may also be classified as an insured under the policy. The underwriting intent of the insurance industry is in accordance with the latter, minority view. Thus, we have the surprising situation of the insurance industry wanting to afford the coverage and the majority of the courts opposing such coverage.

> *f*) to bodily injury to any fellow employee of the insured injured in the course of his employment, if such injury arises out of the use of an automobile in the business of his employer, but this exclusion does not apply to the named insured with respect to the injury sustained by any such fellow employee.

The *cross employee exclusion* avoids any compensation liability of an additional insured, such as the person or organization legally responsible for the use of the vehicle, but it is not intended nor does it exclude the liability of the named insured to his fellow employee where such liability is enforceable.

> *g*) to an owned automobile while used by any person while such person is employed or otherwise engaged in the automobile business, but this exclusion does not apply to the named insured, a resident of the same household as the named insured, a partnership in which the named insured or such resident is a partner, or any partner, agent, or employee of the named insured, such resident or partnership.

Automobile underwriters have felt for some time that the use of an automobile in the automobile business posed special hazards and exposed the company to liabilities beyond those encountered in other lines of endeavor. Therefore, the intent of the *automobile business exclusion* is to exclude such use of the owned automobile while it is in the hands of a mechanic, automobile dealer, service station, or garage for repairs, testing, or any other purpose. Where the named insured or a resident of his household is engaged in the automobile business, it is not intended to exclude such use by either one. In addition, where the insured or the resident is a partner in an automobile business partnership, coverage is likewise afforded to the named insured or resident and to any partner.

Whether the named insured or the resident is in the automobile business as an individual or as a partner, the coverage on the owned automobile also extends to an agent or employee of the named insured. Curiously enough, the exclusion does not by its terms refer to a corporation engaged in the automobile business. Therefore, if the insured or the resident is employed by a corporation so engaged, the coverage will apply only to the named insured or the resident and will not extend to the corporation or its employees or agents who may be using the owned automobile with the consent of the named insured.

> *h*) to a non-owned automobile while maintained or used by any person while such person is employed, or otherwise engaged in
>   1) the automobile business of the insured or of any other person or organization.
>   2) Any other business or occupation of the insured, but this exclusion (*h*) (2) does not apply to a private passenger automobile operated or occupied by the named insured or by his private chauffeur or domestic servant or a trailer used therewith or with an owned automobile.

The coverage afforded to the insured for the use of nonowned automobiles is gratuitous and is intended only to cover situations where there is little frequency and use, since nonowned automobiles furnished for the regular use of the insured are excluded. This is the *business exclusion for nonowned automobiles.* The same thing is true here as to business uses including use in the automobile business. Coverage is provided only for the use of a nonowned automobile when operated by or occupied by the insured or by his servants, or for the use of a trailer with an owned automobile. The plain purpose here is to exclude nonowned automobiles other than private passenger automobiles from the coverage. If this were not so, the insured could use a nonowned bus or truck and the use of such a vehicle would come within the insuring agreements. A private passenger automobile is defined in the policy so as to exclude such vehicles as a bus or truck.

> *i*) to injury to or destruction of (1) property owned or transported by the insured or (2) property rented to or in charge of the insured other than a residence or a private garage.

The *property in charge exclusion* is the automobile policy version of the general liability policy exclusion of property in the care, custody, and control of the insured. It refers to all property with the exception of a residence or garage rented to the insured. It should be noted that this exclusion refers to "the insured" and not the named insured, so that the exclusion applies under the severability of interests clause to the insured who is claiming coverage under the policy. The frequent example of the application of this exclusion comes about when the named insured allows another person to use the car and such other person damages the car through his own negligent operation. The person driving the car is an additional insured, and while he is liable to the named insured for the damage caused by his negligent driving, he has no coverage under the policy. This is for the reason that the property (in this case, the car) is in charge of the insured, who in this case is the person driving the owned vehicle with the permission of the named insured.

> *j)* to the ownership, maintenance, use, loading or unloading of an automobile ownership of which is acquired by the named insured during the policy period or any temporary substitute automobile therefor, if the named insured has purchased other automobile liability insurance applicable to such automobile for which a specific premium charge has been made.

The *newly acquired cars exclusion* ties in with the definition of "owned automobile" in the insuring agreements by means of which the company has agreed to insure newly acquired automobiles owned by the named insured on the date of the acquisition thereof, provided that the named insured notifies the company during the policy period or within 30 days after the date of acquisition of his election to make the policy and no other policy issued by the company applicable to such automobile. The exclusion merely prevents dual insurance where the insured has acquired ownership and insurance on the newly acquired vehicle and has not notified the company thereof or that he wishes to have the policy apply to the new vehicle.

In order to limit the liability coverage insofar as environmental claims are concerned, the general liability polices have included the following exclusion:

> This insurance does not apply:
>
> *k)* to bodily injury or property damage arising out of the discharge, dispersal, release or escape of smoke, vapors, soot, fumes, acids, alkalies, toxic chemicals, liquids or gases, waste materials, or other irritants, contaminants or pollutants into or upon land, the atmosphere, or any water course or body of water; but this exclusion does not apply if such discharge, dispersal, release, or escape is sudden and accidental.

This exclusion is designed to exclude damages resulting from an intentional pollution, whereas an accidental discharge of pollutants is within the scope of the coverage.

The courts have been almost unanimous in adopting the rule that the test of an "accident" is whether the actor intended the result of his actions or knew for a substantial certainty that such a result would ensue. Therefore, on the issue of insurance coverage, the question would be whether or not the insured knew or did not know about the release of chemicals into the air, water, or soil, but rather expected or intended that each of the plaintiffs to suffer bodily injury or property damage as a result of the purported conduct or nonfeasance.

The mere fact that the damages were incurred over a period of time does not make the event less accidental. See *Molton, Allen & Williams, Inc.* v. *St. Paul Fire and Marine Ins. Co.* (Alabama), 347 So. 2d 95.

The claims representative who is confronted with a case involving this exclusion will find the following cases helpful:

California	*Pepper Industries, Inc.* v. *Home Ins. Co.*, 134 Cal. Rptr. 904.
	(Pollution exclusion did not exclude the liability of the insured for dumping gasoline into the city sewer system and the resulting explosion.)
Indiana	*Barnett* v. *Security Ins. Group*, 425 N.E. 2d 201.
Louisiana	*Home Insurance Co.* v. *Deleglos*, 315 So. 2d 74.
Maine	*Travelers Insurance Co.* v. *Dingwell*, 414 Atl. 2d 220.
New Jersey	*Lansco* v. *Dept. of Environmental Protection*, 145 N.J. Super 435.
New York	*Niagara County* v. *Utica Mutual*, 439 N.Y.S. 2d 538 (Love Canal).
Ohio	*Grand River Lime Co.* v. *Ohio Casualty*, 289 N.E. 2d 300.
Oregon	*Sandblasting and Steam Cleaning Co.* v. *Baiden*, 632 Pac. 2d 1377.

All of the foregoing cases involve claims for pollution in which the insurance carrier has disclaimed coverage, and in which the insured brought an action asking for a judgment declaring the policy to be applicable to the particular facts and circumstances of the case. The majority of the cases were decided in favor of the insured, on the theory that the disposal of waste material constituted an "occurrence" as defined in the policy, regardless of whether the results of such disposal were gradual (where the exposure to the contaminants over a period of time produced illnesses) or immediate (where the exposure produced an injury immediately after exposure).

The claims were based on the insuring agreements which indemnified the insured against liability as a result of an "occurrence," which is defined in the policy as "an accident, including continuous or repeated exposure to conditions, which results in bodily injury or property damages neither expected nor intended from the standpoint of the insured." The insurers relied on the exclusion clause in the policy. However, the courts uniformly held that the language of the exclusion was ambiguous and therefore refused to apply it. Most of these cases arose because of the public awareness of the danger of dumping hazardous waste, the use of asbestos and the discharge of poisonous vapors into the atmosphere. For example, for years there was no awareness of the danger of using asbestos in buildings. It was widely used because of its fire resistant quality. It is only within the last 10 or 15 years that the medical profession called the public's attention to the hazards which accompany the use of asbestos. Obviously, the builders did not know of any health hazards which would result in the use of asbestos. Therefore, while the builders intentionally used asbestos in their buildings, the health hazards were unknown and unexpected. Under such circumstances, the liability insurance applied. Clearly, at the present time, the use of asbestos or any other hazardous material is known and the results expected. Therefore, the coverage would not apply.

To add to the present confusion, the federal government enacted the Resource Conservation Recovery Act. This refers to the treatment, storage, and disposal facilities, including generators retaining over 1,000 kilograms of hazardous wastes for more than 90 days. In all of these situations there must be insurance coverage of sudden and accidental occurrences as well as non-sudden (gradual) pollution. In order to provide the insurance required by the act, the Insurance Services Office recommended the following definition of a pollution incident:

Pollution incident means emission, discharge, release or escape of any solid, liquid, gases of thermal contaminants, irritants or pollutants directly from the insured site into or upon land, the atmosphere, or any water course or body of water, provided that such emission, discharge, or release or escape results in environmental damage. The entirety of any sudden or gradual emission, discharge, release or escape from an insured site shall be deemed one pollution incident.

The policy form is on a claims-made basis and also make available coverage for the cleanup costs of the pollution which emanates from the insured site.

As time passes, it is expected that there will be more and more attention paid to this problem, both from the standpoint of legislation as well as the insurance industry. Therefore, it is recommended that the claims representative who is confronted with problems of this sort keep abreast of developments in this area.

1611 Conditions

The conditions in the insurance contract serve generally as a limitation of the risk in that they impose duties upon the insured and describe the circumstances under which the contract shall be operative. The failure of the insured to comply with the duties and obligations imposed by the conditions constitutes a breach of the contract which can operate so as to release the insurance carrier from its contractual obligations.

One condition required of the insured is that upon the occurrence of an accident notification thereof be given to the insurance carrier in writing as soon as practicable. The reason for this requirement is that since the insurer has undertaken the duty of investigation, defense, and settlement (where indicated) it must have notice of the happening of the accident in order to complete its investigation, prepare its defense, or negotiate a settlement—as it deems expedient. The condition reads as follows:

Notice: In the event of an accident, occurrence or loss, written notice containing particulars sufficient to identify the insured and also reasonably obtainable information with respect to the time, place and circumstances thereof, and the names and addresses of the injured and of available witnesses, shall be given by or for the insured to the company or any of its authorized agents as soon as practicable.

In determining whether or not there has been a breach of this condition, the courts generally will take into account some or all of the following: (1) knowledge of the insured, (2) opportunity to give notice, and (3) prejudice to the insurer.

1. *Knowledge of the insured.* Clearly, the insured cannot report an accident or occurrence of which he has no knowledge. This is especially true where the suit which is brought is groundless, false, or fraudulent. Therefore, compliance with the requirement of notice is based upon knowledge of the occurrence by the insured. In general liability cases, it is sometimes alleged that an accident occurred on the insured's premises, and investigation will reveal that the insured had no knowledge of it—nor did any of his employees. The insured's first knowledge of the fact that an accident was alleged to have occurred was obtained when either he received an attorney's letter or was served with process in a lawsuit. If he transmits the information to the insurer as soon as it is received, he has given notice "as soon as practicable"—as soon as he was aware of the existence of the claim.

2. *Opportunity to give notice.* It is possible that the insured has knowledge of the claim but, because of a condition produced by the happening of the accident, he is physically incapable of giving the required notice or to have someone do it for him. For example, if the insured were involved in an automobile accident in which he himself sustained serious injuries, his failure to give notice may be excused for the period of time during which he was physically incapable of giving notice. If he were unconscious for a period of one month, no court would seriously suggest that he was required to give notice during that period of time. However, most courts require that when the insured has knowledge of the occurrence of an accident he must in cases where he himself is injured in the accident, give notice as soon as he is physically capable of doing so.

Where the insured has knowledge and opportunity, most courts hold that his failure to give notice within a reasonable time violates the condition and releases the insurer. In *Miller* v. *Zurich General Accident Co.* [115 Atl. 2d 597 (New Jersey)], the court held that where the insured had both knowledge of the accident and the physical capacity to give notice, a delay of three weeks in giving notice and failure to report the claim in writing constituted a breach of the condition. Where the insured has both knowledge and opportunity to give notice and fails to do so because he has no reason to believe that a claim will be made, some courts excuse the failure to give notice within a reasonable time after the event and hold that if he does report the accident as soon as he has knowledge that a claim is being asserted that he has then given notice "as soon as practicable."

For example, in a recent New Jersey case the insured's dog bit his neighbor's son. The insured was fully aware of the facts and cooperated with the board of health in having the dog tested for rabies. The neighbor told the insured that he did not regard his son's injuries as being serious and, because of their friendly relationship, that he did not expect to make any claim. Believing that no claim would be made, the insured did not report the accident to his insurance carrier. Subsequently, the neighbor had a change of heart and suit was instituted against the insured who promptly transmitted the suit papers to the insurer with a full explanation as to why the claim was not reported earlier. The court held that the insured had met the obligation imposed by the condition when he reported the accident as soon as he was aware that a claim was being made. It further held that the condition did not obligate the insured to report every trivial incident which might form the basis of a claim, especially where he had reason to believe that no claim was contemplated. This was an extreme case and it is doubtful if other courts when confronted with the same problem will reach the same conclusion.

3. *Prejudice to the insurer.* In deciding whether or not the insured has violated the condition by a delayed notice, some courts place their decisions on the basis of whether or not the delayed notice resulted in any prejudice to the insurer. If the insurer was not injured by the delay, was not hampered in its investigation, and could obtain the same information at the time the notice was given as would have been available had timely notice been given, the failure is excused and the notice is regarded as having been given "as soon as practicable." [See *St. Paul* v. *U.S. Fidelity & Guaranty Co.,* 105 S.W. 2d 14 (Missouri), where it was held that a delay in reporting of 18 months did not prejudice the rights of the insurer.] Even in these states, if the insurer can show that its rights were prejudiced by the delay, that it is hampered in its investigation and defense by the absence of physical evidence, such as skid marks and damage to the vehicles, failure to give notice "as soon as practicable" will not be excused.

With respect to claims asserted or suits brought, the same condition prescribes a more rigid requirement. It reads as follows:

If a claim is made or suit is brought against the insured, he shall **immediately** forward to the company every demand, notice, summons or other process received by him or his representative.

The reason for this condition, which requires *immediate* notice, is that since the company is required to investigate and defend the claim in behalf of the insured, it will be seriously hampered in its efforts if it does not have notice of any proceedings or claims made against the insured. This is especially true in the case of lawsuits which have been begun by the service of process on the insured. The failure of the insured to forward the suit papers immediately, or at least within a reasonable time, so as to permit the company to appear and answer within the required time, will produce a default in pleading to the detriment of the company. The condition is breached if the insured transmits an overdue process to the insurer.

The condition with respect to the assistance and cooperation of the insured, and which is common to all liability policies, reads as follows:

The insured shall cooperate with the company and, upon the company's request, attend hearings and trials and assist in making settlements, securing and giving evidence, obtaining the attendance of witnesses and in the conduct of any legal proceedings in connection with the subject matter of this insurance. The insured shall not, except at his own cost voluntarily make any payment, assume any obligation or incur any expense other than for such immediate medical and surgical relief to others as shall be imperative at the time of accident.

Thus the condition requires that the insured perform certain affirmative acts in assisting and cooperating with the company in the defense of the claim or suit.

As to the cooperation of the insured which is required with reference to the trial of the action, there is no particular problem involved. If he does not appear when notified so to do by the insurer, he has violated the condition. But the cooperation required by this condition means more than merely appearing in court when necessary. It includes the duty on the part of the insured to give the insurance carrier a truthful statement of all of the facts within his knowledge concerning the accident. If he makes statements which are untrue, and known to him to be untrue when they are made, he violates this condition.

In *Home Insurance Company* v. *Standard Accident* (167 Fed. 2d 919), the motorist, insured by Home, gave a statement to Home which exonerated him from liability. Later, after suit was brought, he changed his statement to one of liability on his part. In holding that the insured, by making an untruthful statement to the insurer, had breached the cooperation clause, the court said:

Truthfulness seems to be the keystone of the cooperative arch. The insured must tell his insurer the complete truth concerning the accident, and he must stick to his truthful version throughout the proceedings. He must not embarrass or cripple his insurer in its defense against the civil suit arising out of the accident by switching from one version to another. He must not blow hot and cold to suit his personal convenience. . . . The company is entitled, however, to an honest statement by the insured of the pertinent circumstances surrounding the accident. Lacking that, the company is deprived of an opportunity to negotiate a settlement, or to defend upon the solid ground of fact. Nothing is more dangerous than a client who falsifies the facts.

In another case, an automobile covered by the insurance policy was driven by the insured's 15-year-old son. Both the insured and his son gave written statements that the son had taken and driven the car without the insured's permission. In the action that followed, the insurer appeared for the insured and disclaimed as to the son. The insured and his son later stated that the son had been driving the car with the insured's permission. The insurer served notice disclaiming coverage because (1) there were contradictory statements made, and (2) the insured's lack of cooperation prejudiced the insurer in its handling of the claims and lawsuits arising out of the accident.

In deciding the case in favor of the insurer, the court stated that if the insured "failed to make a fair and truthful disclosure which would enable the insurer to determine whether there was a genuine defense, there was a breach of the condition of cooperation." The court further stated that if the first statement given to the insurer was true, and later the insured and his son gave false testimony to the aid of the plaintiffs in the negligence actions, "there was a cessation of the cooperation which was required by the contract." It should be emphasized that the insurer was not obligated to show which of the statements made by the insured was true and which one was not. The mere fact that contradictory statements were made establishes the breach of the condition of cooperation.

The same situation was also pinpointed in *Wright* v. *Farmers' Auto* [102 Pac. 2d 452 (California)], where the court made the following observation:

> If Seller's testimony on the witness stand was not the truth, he certainly was not cooperating. If it was the truth, he violated the cooperation clause of the policy by concealing the real facts from the insurer up to the moment he testified, thus causing the insurer to go to trial under an absolute misapprehension of what the facts were. That could not be other than prejudicial.

The condition also forbids the insured to assume any expense other than for such immediate medical and surgical relief to others as shall be imperative at the time of the accident. This part of the condition has been construed to mean that if the insured pays for the claimant's medical expense, or arranges for treatment by the insured's own doctor without expense to the claimant where immediate relief is not necessary, or where the insured expends money for the purpose of making gifts to the claimant, such as flowers, books, cigarettes, and other like items, the amounts so expended are not reimbursable under the policy. However, such actions on the part of the insured are not construed as admissions of liability and are not admissible in evidence in order to establish liability. The actions, therefore, are not prejudicial to the insurer, and do not constitute such a breach of the condition so as to relieve the insurer of its obligation. As stated, the insured is not entitled to be reimbursed for these expenditures even though the insured's actions were of assistance to the insurer in maintaining control of the claimant and in negotiating an attractive settlement. If the insured makes gifts of this character, he does so at his own expense, but he does not thereby lose any of his rights under the policy.

It is possible for one insured to breach a condition and another insured, under the same policy and in the same case, to comply with the contract. For example, in a Wisconsin case the named insured and an additional insured were codefendants. The named insured cooperated with the insurer and the additional insured failed to do so. The company appeared in the action for the named insured and disclaimed coverage as to the additional insured for lack of cooperation. The court sustained the insurer in this position [*Modl* v. *National Farmers*, 76 N.W. 2d 599]. In a Tennessee case, the court held that a statement given by the insured to the claimant, admitting liability, was a breach of the cooperation clause which relieved the insurer [*Pennsylvania Insurance Co.* v. *Horner*, 281 S.W. 2d 44]

1612   Breach of condition

Where a condition requires the performance of an affirmative act, or that a party refrain from doing another act, a violation of the obligations thus imposed will relieve the other party to the contract if he elects to be so relieved. On the other hand, he might waive the breach and treat the contract as operative in spite of the conduct of the other party. Where he decides to stand on the breach and disclaim any responsibility on his part to perform the contract because of it, he must give notice to the opposite party of his position. The same rules apply to the insurance contract. Where the insured has failed to meet the obligations imposed upon him by any one of the conditions, the insurer has the option of either waiving the breach and considering the contract as being operative, or to treat the contract as inoperative by reason of the breach. If the insurer decides on the latter course, it must give immediate notice to the insured of its position, and in some states it is also required to serve the same notice on the claimant, if he is known.

The reason for the notice requirement is that the insured, after reporting the accident, would have no reason to believe that the insurer was not going to perform the contract, and therefore the insured could take no steps to protect himself from a possible lawsuit arising out of the event. If the contract is operative, the insured has no right to investigate or defend since those rights are specifically delegated to the insurer by the contract. The purpose of notice is to inform the insured of the insurer's position and, further, to afford him an opportunity of taking whatever steps are necessary to protect himself. Notice is required even though the insured knows that he has breached the condition since, even in that case, he would have no knowledge of the company's position with regard to the claim.

Once the notice of disclaimer is served on the insured, the company has no further rights under the contract. It may not investigate or defend since these are rights granted to the insurer only by virtue of the contract and, having served notice that the contract is nonoperative as far as the particular claim is concerned, it then has no status with regard to it. Should the insurer continue with the investigation or appear and defend a lawsuit, the insured would have every reason to believe that the insurer had withdrawn its notice of disclaimer and that it intended to perform under the contract. Where a notice of disclaimer is served, the insurer's conduct from that point on must be consistent with the position that there is no insurance afforded under the contract. Contrary conduct could be construed as a waiver of the breach of condition and obligate the insurer to perform.

Where there has been a notice of disclaimer because of a breach of condition, it does not have the effect of cancelling the policy. The position is merely that the policy is not operative as to the particular case. The contract is still operative as to future accidents, under the conditions of the policy, until the termination date. The breach of the condition merely makes the contract inoperative as to one particular transaction, but it has no effect as to the contract itself and the continuing obligations of both parties thereunder.

1613   Declaratory judgments

Most of the states have laws that are patterned after the federal Declaratory Judgment Statute (28 USCA 400). Generally they provide that the courts of the state shall have the power to declare rights, status, and other legal relations, irrespective of whether or not further relief is or could be claimed. With respect to contracts, the statute reads as follows:

> A person interested under . . . a written contract or other writing constituting a contract . . . may have determined any question of construction or validity arising under the instrument . . . and obtain a declaration of rights, status or other legal relations thereunder.

The statute authorizes a cause of action for the purpose of declaring the rights of the parties under a contract. It has been utilized extensively by insurance carriers where there was some question as to the coverage or where it was claimed that a breach of contract had taken place. It has the advantage of giving the parties a ruling in advance of other litigation as to whether or not the policy contract covers the situation. It is also available to the insured if he chooses to bring the action.

From the standpoint of the courts, the statute has the advantage of reducing the number of litigated cases. If the action for declaratory relief is brought by the insurer, and the judgment rendered declares that the policy is in force, then the insurer would be bound by its contract and must perform its obligations. Thus there would be no necessity of further litigation on that point. On the other hand, if the judgment declared that the policy was not in force, then the insured could not successfully maintain a policy suit, and the statute has the additional advantage of affording a speedy determination. Most of the states have enacted procedural rules comparable to Rule 57 of the federal Rules of Civil Procedure, which states in part that "The court may order a speedy hearing of an action for a declaratory judgment and may advance it on the calendar."

To invoke the federal Declaratory Judgments Act, the usual elements of federal jurisdiction must be present. There must be (1) diversity of citizenship between the parties; (2) an actual controversy between the parties litigant; and (3) the amount involved must exceed the sum of $10,000, exclusive of interest and costs.

Diversity of citizenship means that the plaintiff and defendant must be citizens of different states. An insurance corporation is a citizen of the state under whose laws it was created. If the parties are not citizens of different states, the federal courts have no jurisdiction. [See *Pennsylvania Casualty Co.* v. *Thornton,* 61 Fed. Supp. 753 (Alabama).]

Actual controversy means exactly what it says. A party is not entitled to a declaratory judgment establishing a fact that is admitted. For example, if an action were brought against the *X* Insurance Co. for a judgment, declaring that the *X* Insurance Co. is an insurance corporation, which fact is admitted, it would not involve a controversy between the parties and would require a dismissal even though such a judgment might be used in some other action as a substitute for proof of this particular fact. There is no controversy.

Amount of controversy means that the amount involved must exceed the sum or value of $10,000, exclusive of interest and costs. If it does not involve that amount, the federal courts have no jurisdiction. Where an automobile liability policy is involved, as a general rule, the amount in controversy is the maximum amount for which the company could be held liable under the terms of the policy. [See *New Century Casualty Co.* v. *Chase,* 39 Fed. Supp. 768 (West Virginia).]

1614   Assignments

Any contract, except a contract for personal services, can be assigned unless the contract itself contains an agreement prohibiting assignment or transfer. Liability insurance policies have a provision that no assignment of interest shall bind the company until its consent is endorsed on the contract. The purpose of this condition is to provide the company with an opportunity to decide who it will insure and who it will not. If the company's consent were not required, it could be compelled to furnish insurance coverage to the assignee, irrespective of his financial solvency or past accident record. For example, if *A* sells his automobile to *B* and transfers his insurance policy to *B*, with *B* paying for the car and the balance of the premium on the policy, the assignment or transfer of the insurance would not be effective and binding on the insurance company until it consents to the substitution. It makes no difference that *B* paid the premium, even if he made the payment to the company or the company's agent, unless it could be shown that the company was aware of the attempted assignment and accepted the premium from *B* with that knowledge. In such a case it would be held that the company had waived the requirement of its consent and the required endorsement or, in the alternative, that its conduct amounted to an implied consent, and it is, as a result, estopped from denying the assignment.

Where the insured requests that an assignment be made and that the company consent to it, the company is under no obligation to do so; the company may consent or not, as it chooses. Furthermore, should the company refuse to assign the policy, it is under no duty of explanation nor are any rights created even if the company's decision refusing the assignment is based on whim or caprice.

In the event of the death of the named insured, most liability policies contain an agreement that the policy will automatically cover the legal representative of the named insured during the time the individual is so acting. The Family Automobile Policy offers some broad coverage in this respect, and the condition reads as follows:

. . . If, however, the insured named in Item 1 of the Declarations, or his spouse, if a resident of the same household, shall die, this policy shall cover (1) the survivor as the named insured, (2) his legal representative as named insured, but only while acting within the scope of his duties as such, (3) any person having proper temporary custody of an owned automobile, as an insured, until the appointment and qualification of such legal representative, and (4) under division 1 of Part II any person who was a relative at the time of such death.

1615   Statutory and required policies

All states and the federal government have recognized that common highway carriers of passengers (buses, taxicabs, and so on) and of freight expose the members of the public to increased risks of harm. Therefore, statutes have been passed regulating such carriers' use of the highways and requiring as a condition precedent to their licensing that certain insurance or security be furnished for the protection of the public with respect to bodily injury and property damage. The amount of the insurance or security will vary with the number of passengers carried or the size and capacity of the truck carriers. Where an insurance policy is offered as proof of the financial security required, it must contain an agreement by the insurance carrier that the policy will not be cancelled unless and until notice is given to the state or federal agency, usually 30 days prior to cancellation, the 30 days beginning to run from the date the notice is received.

In addition, the insurance policy must contain an agreement that no act of the insured will release the insurer while the policy is so certified to the state of federal agency. This means that where there is a breach of any condition of the policy, the insurance remains in force and the insurance carrier has waived in advance any right which it may ordinarily have had to disclaim for a breach of any condition of the contract. Clearly, the intent and purpose of the statute is to protect the public by having insurance available in the event of loss, and, if the insurer could avail itself of a policy breach, it would defeat the purpose of the legislation. The state agencies which usually supervise these matters are public utility commissions, and the federal agency which supervises and controls common carriers in interstate commerce is the Interstate Commerce Commission.

Under the financial responsibility laws of the states, where a policy is certified as proof of financial responsibility either by filing the policy or a certification that coverage exists (SR 22), the statutes require that the insurance carrier agree to the same conditions with regard to cancellation and the waiver of its right to disclaim for a policy breach. The amount of insurance required will vary from state to state, but the most common limits required are 10/20/5. To provide for a means of recoupment where the company could otherwise have disclaimed (but for the requirements of the statute), the Family Automobile Policy (as well as other automobile policies) contains the following agreement:

When this policy is certified as proof of financial responsibility for the future under the provisions of any motor vehicle financial responsibility law, such insurance as is afforded by this policy for bodily injury liability or for property damage liability shall comply with the provisions of such law to the extent of the coverage and limits of liability, but in no event in excess of the limits of liability stated in this policy. The insured agrees to reimburse the company for any payment made by the company which it would not have been obligated to make under the terms of this policy except for the agreement contained in this paragraph.

Therefore, if the insured breached one of the conditions of the policy, the insurer would still have to respond within the limits of the financial responsibility law, but where such payment would otherwise not have been required, the insured agrees to reimburse the company. Where there is a breach of the policy conditions, if limits are carried in excess of those required by the financial responsibility law, the breach automatically reduces the limits to those of the law and not those of the policy. The agreement is that the policy will conform to the law and that the insured will reimburse the company for any payment made because of the requirements of the law.

For example, if the insured carried 50/100/25 limits, and the policy is certified as proof of financial responsibility in a state requiring limits of 10/20/5, and the insured fails to cooperate with the insurer, the insurer could disclaim because of the insured's breach of the policy condition, but because the policy is certified under the financial responsibility law, the insurer has agreed that the policy will conform to the law. The insurer therefore would have to respond to the extent of 10/20/5 as required by the law, and could disclaim as to the excess.

In states having compulsory automobile liability insurance statutes, the owner of a motor vehicle must present proof of insurance, or his qualification as a self-insurer, before a license will be issued. These states usually require a certification and also an agreement from the insurer that, in the event of cancellation, notice will also be given to the state agency supervising the program. Failure of the insurer to give notice of cancellation to the state will prevent the insurer from effectively cancelling the policy, even though notice of cancellation is properly given to the insured.

In some states, as a means of enforcing their financial responsibility laws, it is required that the insured submit proof of existing insurance coverage with the minimum limits prescribed in the law in every case where a motor vehicle accident report is required to be filed. These cases usually involve bodily injury and property damage above a certain minimum amount. The form on which the insurance information is submitted is an SR 21, and it merely attests that there was insurance in force on the date of the accident within the limits required by law. The statutes differ as to how the insurance information is to be submitted, whether by the insured or by the insurance carrier. In absence of a filing of an SR 21, it will be presumed that the person filing the report is uninsured and is therefore subject to financial responsibility. This may mean that his license will be revoked unless he provides security for the payment of the damages which have already accrued from the present accident and also submits proof of future financial responsibility. Where the insurance carrier is required to file the SR 21, and fails to do so or delays the filing, the insured may be treated as uninsured by the state until the matter is cleared. This can produce an irritating situation between the insured and the company, and as a result most companies make the filing as promptly as possible.

1616   Uninsured motorist coverage, automobile policies

This coverage, titled Protection against Uninsured Motorists, is a first-party contract between the insured (as defined) and the company, and provides for the payment by the company to the insured of all sums which the insured or his legal representative shall be entitled to recover as damages from an uninsured motorist because of bodily injury. It is approved and written in all states except Alaska, Hawaii, Kansas, Maryland. It is written with statutory modifications in New York and Virginia.

The coverage is an insurance contract in itself, having insuring agreements, definitions, exclusions, and conditions, and it has no connection with the entire insurance contract of which it is a part except insofar as it incorporates by reference other parts of the policy as to definitions, limits and conditions, as well as applying recoveries in other coverages in reduction of the amount due, or providing that a recovery under its coverage shall reduce the company's obligation under the other agreements. It should be emphasized that this agreement does not provide insurance coverage for the uninsured vehicle, nor does it in any way create an obligation on the part of the company to the owner of the uninsured vehicle. The rights and obligations as between the insured and the owner or driver of the uninsured vehicle remain exactly the same as if the insurance was not in existence. A breakdown of the provisions of the coverage follows.

I. *Insuring agreements.*   The company undertakes the following obligation to the insured:

To pay all sums which the insured or his legal representative shall be legally entitled to recover as demages from the owner or operator of an uninsured automobile because of bodily injury, sickness or disease, including death resulting therefrom, hereinafter called "bodily injury," sustained by the insured, caused by accident and arising out of the ownership, maintenance or use of such uninsured automobile; provided, for the purposes of this coverage determination as to whether the insured or such representative is legally entitled to recover such damages, and, if so, the amount thereof, shall be made by agreement between the insured or such representative and the company, or, if they fail to agree, by arbitration.

The company's promise does not become binding and enforceable by the insured unless and until the insured has sustained a bodily injury by accident which gives rise to a possible cause of action against the owner or operator of an uninsured automobile. The insured must first establish that the possible cause of action is in fact against the owner or operator of the uninsured automobile. Unless the insured can do this, the coverage does not become operative, nor is the company obligated to arbitrate the question of whether the other vehicle with which the insured may be involved is or is not an uninsured vehicle. When the insured produces evidence that the other vehicle is uninsured within the definitions of the coverage, then the insurance carrier is obligated to arbitrate the question of liability, and the amount of damages, on the written demand of the insured. These two are the only issues which the parties, both the insurance carrier and the insured, are obligated by the contract to arbitrate.

There is an open question as to whether or not this agreement obligates the insurer to respond with respect to the amount which would be recoverable by the beneficiaries of the deceased in an action based on the wrongful death of the insured. One view is that since the agreement obligates the company to pay the amount which the insured or his legal representative may recover, the company's promise is limited to the damages which the insured sustained in his lifetime, and, in the case of death, damages which could be recovered by his legal representative. This would limit the subject matter of the insuring agreement to damages which the insured himself sustained, even though an action for their recovery could be brought after his death by his legal representative. Since the claim for wrongful death was not a cause of action which the insured owned in his lifetime, and is a cause of action created by statute for the benefit of and asserted by beneficiaries of the deceased person, it is not a cause of action which could be asserted by the insured himself, and therefore is not a cause of action which could be brought by the insured's legal representative but must be brought by the representative of the estate or the beneficiaries. The opposing view is that the words "including death resulting therefrom" are meaningless unless they provide for the damages recoverable by beneficiaries for the wrongful death of the insured. The question is an open one and it is to be anticipated there will be just as much disagreement among the courts in the future as to the meaning of the terms as there is at present among claimsmen.

The insuring agreements are qualified by the following provision:

No judgment against any person or organization alleged to be legally responsible for the bodily injury shall be conclusive, as between the insured and the company, of the issues of liability of such person or organization or of the amount of damages to which the insured is legally entitled unless such judgment is entered pursuant to an action prosecuted by the insured with the written consent of the company.

The purpose of this agreement is to protect the company from being bound by a judgment procured by collusion, confession, or default against the uninsured owner or driver on the issues of liability and the extent of damages.

The insuring agreements also provide for the limits of liability assumed by the agreement. The provision is as follows:

(a) The limit of liability for uninsured motorist coverage stated in the Declarations as applicable to "each person" is the limit of the company's liability for all damages, including damages for care or loss of services, because of bodily injury sustained by one person as a result of any one accident and, subject to the above provision respecting each person, the limit of liability stated in the Declarations as applicable to "each accident" is the total limit of the company's liability for all damages, including damages for care and loss of services, because of bodily injury sustained by two or more persons as a result of any one accident.

(b) Any amount payable under the terms of this Part because of bodily injury sustained in an accident by a person who is an insured under this Part shall be reduced by

(1) all sums paid on behalf of such bodily injury by or on behalf of (i) the owner or operator of the uninsured automobile and (ii) any other person or organization jointly or severally liable together with such owner or operator for such bodily injury including all sums paid under Coverage A, and

(2) the amount paid and the present value of all amounts payable on account of such bodily injury under any workmen's compensation law, disability benefits law or any similar law.

(c) Any payment made under this Part to or for any insured shall be applied in reduction of the amount of damages which he may be entitled to recover from any person insured under Coverage A.

(d) The company shall not be obligated to pay under this coverage that part of the damages which the insured may be entitled to recover from the owner or operator of an uninsured automobile which represents expenses for medical services paid or payable under Part II.

The intent of this agreement is to provide the same limits of coverage to this part of the policy as to the liability portion, but without any increase in the company's limits because of the existence of this insurance. Thus the provision is that any payments made under this coverage will be applied in the reduction of the limits applicable to the person's claim under Part I against any person who qualifies as an insured under that part of the insurance contract. Likewise, any payments made under Part I are applied in reducing the amounts for which the company may be liable under the uninsured motorist coverage. Payments made under the medical payments coverage are likewise applied in reducing the amounts payable under the uninsured motorist coverage.

In addition, it is agreed that the company will be entitled to credit for the payments made by others, such as the uninsured owner or driver, a person or organization jointly liable with either of them, as well as by workmen's compensation payments currently due or to become due in the future, and any such payments due under a disability benefits or similar law.

II. Definitions. The agreement incorporates by reference all the definitions of Part I, making them applicable to this coverage (except the definition of "insured"). The following definitions are included in the agreement: (1) insured; (2) insured automobile; (3) not an insured automobile; (4) uninsured automobile; (5) not an uninsured automobile; (6) hit-and-run automobile; (7) occupying; and (8) state.

1. *Insured.* The insured is defined as "(a) The named insured or any relative; (b) Any other person while occupying an insured automobile; (c) Any person, with respect to the damages he is entitled to recover because of

bodily injury to which this Part applies sustained by an insured under (*a*) or (*b*) above."

A relative is defined under Part I as a relative of the named insured who is a resident of the same household, and (*c*) covers any person who has a cause of action for care or loss of services arising out of the injuries of the persons insured under (*a*) and (*b*). The inclusion of more than one insured shall not increase the limits of liability, but the provisions of the policy shall apply separately to each insured. The provision reads: "The insurance afforded under Part IV applies separately to each insured, but the inclusion of more than one insured shall not operate to increase the limits of the company's liability."

2. *Insured automobile.*   The following come within the definition of insured automobile:

(*a*) An automobile described in the policy for which a specific premium charge indicates that coverage is afforded

(*b*) A private passenger, farm or utility automobile, ownership of which is acquired by the named insured during the policy period, provided (1) it replaces an insured automobile as defined in (*a*) above, or (2) the company insures under this coverage all private passenger, farm and utility automobiles owned by the named insured on the date of such acquisition and the named insured notifies the company during the policy period or within 30 days after the date of such acquisition of his election to make the Liability and Uninsured Motorist Coverages under this and no other policy applicable to such automobile,

(*c*) A temporary substitute automobile for an insured automobile as defined in (*a*) or (*b*) above, and

(*d*) A non-owned automobile while being operated by the named insured; and the term "insured automobile" includes a trailer while being used with an automobile described in (*a*), (*b*), (*c*), or (*d*) above.

The definitions of private passenger automobile, farm or utility automobile, temporary substitute automobile, and nonowned automobile are the same as those included in the definitions in part I of the policy.

3. *Not an insured automobile.*   The following are excluded from coverage as not coming within the definition of an insured automobile: (1) Any automobile or trailer owned by a resident of the same household as the named insured; (2) any automobile while used as a public or livery conveyance; and (3) any automobile while being used without the permission of the owner.

It is clear why the company would not wish to afford coverage in each of these instances. In (1) it should be noted that the word "resident" is used, whereas in the definition of insured "relative" is used. In this case the exclusion applies to any resident of the same household, whether a relative or not. Its purpose is to avoid affording insurance for any automobiles on the premises of the insured and not owned by him. This qualifies the prior definition of "insured automobile" which includes a nonowned automobile while being operated by the named insured. If the named insured should be operating an automobile owned by a resident of the same household, he would come within this exception.

As to (2), the company would not wish to enlarge its exposure by including the use of any automobile, whether owned or nonowned, while it is being used as a public or livery conveyance, (3) is clear in eliminating as an "insured automobile" any automobile being used without the permission of the owner. This would include the owned automobile while being driven without the permission of the named insured and any nonowned automobile while being so operated, even though such operation may be by the named insured.

4. *Uninsured automobile.* This term includes a trailer of any type and includes:

> (a) An automobile or trailer with respect to the ownership, maintenance or use of which there is, in at least the amounts specified by the financial responsibility law of the state in which the insured automobile is principally garaged, no bodily injury liability bond or insurance policy applicable at the time of the accident with respect to any person or organization legally responsible for the use of such automobile, or with respect to which there is a bodily injury liability bond or insurance policy applicable at the time of the accident but the company writing same denies coverage thereunder or
>
> (b) A hit and run automobile.

There are two parts to the definition under (a). A vehicle which does not carry insurance with the minimum limits prescribed by the state in which the *insured* vehicle is principally garaged is an uninsured vehicle for the purposes of coverage, whether it carries no insurance at all, or insurance which has limits below those prescribed by the financial responsibility law of the state in which the insured vehicle is principally garaged. It should be noted that the criteria applied in determining the question of whether or not the automobile is uninsured under the contract is not where the uninsured vehicle is registered, nor where the accident happens, but the state in which the insured automobile is principally garaged. The determination as to this phase of the provision is made as of the date of the accident.

The second phase of the definition refers to an automobile which carries sufficient liability insurance with reference to bodily injury, but, because of some condition occurring subsequently, the insurer denies or disclaims coverage. In such a case the automobile is considered as an uninsured automobile for the purposes of determining whether or not the coverage is operative. It should be noted that there is no reference as to whether or not there is any merit to the denial of coverage by the carrier of the adverse vehicle. If there is a denial of coverage, for the purposes of the uninsured motorist coverage, the automobile is an uninsured automobile whether there is any basis for the denial of coverage or not. If it should develop that the carrier for the adverse vehicle decides to withdraw its disclaimer and will admit coverage, and the coverage is sufficient to meet the criteria with respect to the financial responsibility law, the adverse automobile ceases to be an uninsured automobile as of that time and the uninsured motorist carrier can withdraw from the case since it then has no responsibility under the coverage.

5. *Not an uninsured automobile.*   The following, under the agreement, are not uninsured automobiles:

1) An insured automobile or an automobile furnished for the regular use of the named insured or a relative.

2) An automobile or trailer owned or operated by a self-insurer within the meaning of any motor vehicle financial responsibility law, motor carrier law or any similar law.

3) An automobile or trailer owned by the United States of America, Canada, a a state, a political subdivision of any such government or an agency of any of the foregoing.

4) A land motor vehicle or trailer if operated on rails or crawler-treads, or while located for use as a residence or premises and not as a vehicle.

5) A farm type tractor or equipment designed for use principally off public roads, except while actually upon public roads.

The intent of the coverage is to provide a means of recovery for the insured with respect to an accident caused by the negligence of a financially irresponsible motorist. These exceptions to the definition of an uninsured vehicle refer to vehicles owned by persons or organizations which are not financially irresponsible and can respond in damages, as well as to other types of vehicles which, in the ordinary sense, are not motor vehicles, such as motor-driven cars on rails and crawler tractors and farm machinery not on the public roads. Government-owned vehicles are for the most part uninsured in that there are no insurance policies applicable to their ownership, maintenance, and use; but the government, whether state or national, generally pursues a policy of self-insurance.

6. *Hit-and-run automobile.*   The agreement defines a hit-and-run automobile (considered for the purpose of coverage as an uninsured vehicle) as follows:

Hit and run automobile means an automobile which causes bodily injury to an insured arising out of physical contact of such automobile with the insured or with an automobile which the insured is occupying at the time of the accident, provided: (a) there cannot be ascertained the identity of either the operator or the owner of such "hit and run" automobile; (b) the insured or someone on his behalf shall have reported the accident within 24 hours to a police, peace or judicial officer or to the Commissioner of Motor Vehicles, and shall have filed with the company within 30 days thereafter a statement under oath that the insured or his legal representative has a cause or causes of action arising out of such accident for damages against a person or persons whose identity is unascertainable, and setting forth the facts in support thereof; and (c) at the company's request, the insured or his legal representative makes available for inspection the automobile which the insured was occupying at the time of the accident.

The first requirement under this definition is that there be physical contact between the hit-and-run automobile and the insured, or with the automobile which the insured is occupying at the time of the accident. If there is no such contact, then the hit-and-run automobile is not an uninsured automobile within the terms of the contract. For example, let us assume that the insured is occupying vehicle 1, which is stopped for a red light. Vehicle 2 stops immediately behind it. The hit-and-run automobile smashes into vehicle 2, forcing it into vehicle 1, as a result of which the insured sustains bodily injuries. Under these circumstances, since there is no physical contact between the hit-and-run automobile and the insured, or the automobile which he is occupying at the time of the accident, there is no coverage under this agreement.

The second requirement is that neither the owner nor the operator of the hit-and-run automobile can be ascertained and identified. If either can be identified, then the vehicle is not a hit-and-run automobile within the meaning of the coverage.

Because accidents of this type can be easily fabricated and because the company would have difficulty in establishing that the accident did not occur, the definition contains some rigid requirements as to reporting the accident to the police or other authority, reporting to the company within 30 days in the form of a statement under oath, setting forth the details of the cause of action against the hit-and-run owner or operator, and, in addition, permitting an inspection by the company of the vehicle which the insured was occupying at the time of the accident. The first two requirements reduce the period of time during which there can be reflection and fabrication, and, where the automobile occupied by the insured is involved, an inspection must be permitted to ascertain if there was any damage to the vehicle, the point of impact, and the estimate of the severity of the accident from the damage so sustained.

7. *Occupying.* Occupying means in, upon, entering into, or alighting from the automobile. (This definition modifies "occupying" in the preceding definitions.)

8. *State.* The word "state," as used in the agreement, includes the District of Columbia, a territory of possession of the United States, and a province of Canada.

III. Exclusions. Protection against uninsured motorists coverage does not apply

(a) to bodily injury to an insured while occupying an automobile (other than an insured automobile) owned by the named insured or a relative, or through being struck by such an automobile.

(b) to bodily injury to an insured with respect to which such insured, his legal representative or any person entitled to payment under this coverage shall, without the written consent of the company, make any settlement with any person or organization who may be legally liable therefor.

(c) so as to inure directly or indirectly to the benefit of any workmen's compensation or disability benefits carrier or any person or organization qualifying as a self-insurer under any workmen's compensation or disability benefits law or any similar law.

Exclusion (*a*) eliminates automobiles owned by the insured or any relative which are not within the coverage of the policy; (*b*) has to do with the preservation of the company's rights to reimbursement, as set forth in the conditions, and eliminates a situation where the insured could enter into a collusive, or an honest, settlement with the uninsured for an amount considerably less than the value of the claim, and then make a claim against the company for the balance. If such a situation were permitted, any rights to reimbursement which the company might have would be extinguished by the execution of the release by the insured. Therefore the exclusion requires that the written consent of the company to any settlement first be obtained before the act of the insured in settling the claim against any person or organization legally liable therefor.

It should be noted that the exclusion is not limited to the uninsured owner or operator; it refers to any person and could, conceivably, include settlement with an insured joint tort-feasor. Exclusion (*b*) refers to the right created by certain workmen's compensation and disability benefits laws on the part of the insurer to become subrogated to the rights of an injured person to whom benefits have been paid, and to prosecute the action against the person responsible in the name of the injured person, even though the real party in interest is the insurance carrier. The same exclusion applies to a person or organization who is a self-insurer and succeeds to the same rights as an insurance carrier under such laws.

IV. *Conditions.*   There are three conditions applicable to the agreement: (1) other insurance, (2) arbitration, and (3) trust agreement.

1. *Other insurance.*   In order to avoid a double recovery by an insured while occupying a nonowned automobile, the "other insurance" condition reads as follows:

With respect to bodily injury to an insured while occupying an automobile not owned by the named insured, the insurance under Part IV (Uninsured Motorist Coverage) shall apply only as excess insurance over any similar insurance available to such insured and applicable to such automobile as primary insurance, and this insurance shall then apply only in the amount by which the limit of liability for this coverage exceeds the applicable limit of liability of such other insurance.

This provision would come into operation where the named insured operated a nonowned automobile which, for the purposes of the coverage, would be an insured automobile while being so operated, and where the named insured or a passenger occupying the automobile are injured. If there was an uninsured operator or owner involved, and there was primary automobile insurance on the car (including uninsured motorist coverage), then the named insured's uninsured motorist coverage would apply to the named insured or the passenger insured only as excess over the primary insurance on the car, but excess only as to the amount which the named insured's coverage exceeded the primary coverage on the nonowned automobile.

For example, if the named insured had 5/10 limits on his uninsured motorist coverage and was involved in an accident with an uninsured while driving his neighbor's car with the neighbor's permission, and the neighbor had 10/20 limits on his uninsured motorist coverage, the named insured would be limited in his recovery to the 10/20 limits of the primary coverage. His own insurance would not be involved because of the "other insurance" condition. If the neighbor's limits of insurance were 5/10 and the named insured's insurance limits were 20/40, then the limits of liability of both companies to the named insured would be 20/40, with the primary carrier being liable for the first $5,000 and his own company liable for the second $15,000. If other insureds were involved, then the upper limits would come into operation.

This type of a policy provision is commonly referred to as an "excess—escape" clause. If the other insurance is less than that provided by the policy, then the insurer is liable for the difference between the other insurance limits and the limits of the uninsured motorist coverage. On the other hand, if the other insurance equals or exceeds the limits of the uninsured motorist coverage, then the insurer "escapes" and has no liability.

In order to reduce or eliminate the liability of the insurer, the underwriters have added the following condition to the uninsured motorist coverage:

Except as provided in the foregoing paragraph, if the insured has other similar insurance available to him and applicable to the accident, the damages shall be deemed not to exceed the higher of the applicable limits of liability of this insurance and such other insurance, and the Company shall not be liable for a greater proportion of any loss to which this coverage applies than the limit of liability hereunder bears to the sum of the applicable limits of liability of this insurance and such other insurance.

This condition is designed to prevent the "stacking," or adding together the uninsured motorist limits where the insured has coverage for two or more automobiles, either in one policy or separate policies. For example, in *New Hampshire Insurance Co.* v. *Bell*, 427 Atl. 2d 24 (New Hampshire), the insured was killed in an automobile accident caused by the negligence of an uninsured motorist. The policy covered not only the automobile that Bell was driving, but also two other automobiles as well. The uninsured motorist coverage had a limit of $20,000. The plaintiff contended that under the circumstances she was entitled to stack the uninsured motorist benefits for a total recovery of $60,000. The court held that the maximum recovery was limited to $20,000. See also *St. Paul Mercury Insurance Co.* v. *Andrews*, 321 N.W. 2d 483 (North Dakota), and *Goodville Mutual* v. *Borrer*, 275 S.E. 2d 625 (Virginia).

Conversely, the majority of the courts who have been faced with the problem have refused to apply the policy limitations where the *named insured* has uninsured coverage on two or more automobiles. Most of the decisions turn on the provisions of the state statute the decision being that if the legislature had intended that the limits could be reduced by a policy provision the legislature would have said so. In the absence of any authorization in the statute, the insurance carrier did not have the authority to reduce the limits set forth in the statute. Another argument that was used was the fact that the *named insured* had paid a premium for each of the automobiles insured and thus was entitled to coverage on each. It should be noted that in all of these cases the named insured sought to stack the policy limits with respect to the uninsured motorist coverage. Among the cases upholding the named insured's right to stack the limits are as follows:

Connecticut	*Nationwide* v. *Gode*, 446 Atl. 2d 1059.
Kansas	*Davis* v. *Hughes*, 622 Pac. 2d 641.
Minnesota	*VanTassel* v. *Horace Mann Mutual*, 207 N.W. 2d 348.
Missouri	*Cameron Mutual* v. *Madden*, 233 S.W. 2d 538.
Louisiana	*Fenasci* v. *Travelers*, 642 Fed. 2d 986.
Nebraska	*Eich* v. *State Farm Mutual*, 305 N.W. 2d 621.
New Mexico	*Lopez* v. *Foundation Res. Ins. Co*, 646 Pac. 2d 1230.
Rhode Island	*Tift* v. *Allstate*, 433 Atl. 2d 215.

On the other hand, where an "occupancy insured" such as a permissive user or an employee, seeks to stack the uninsured motorist limits, the courts have held that such an insured is subject to the provisions of the policy and may not stack the limits. See *Linderer* v. *Royal Globe*, 597 S.W. 2d 656 (Missouri).

a. Legislation. Some states have solved the problem of the stacking of limits on uninsured motorist coverage where the insured has covered two or more automobiles under a single policy or under separate policies. Unfortunately, the legislatures are not in agreement. The first group have enacted "anti-stacking" laws which provide that the insured is restricted in his recovery to the limit allocated to one automobile. Some statutes allow a recovery only as to the limit provided in the policy for the automobile involved in the accident, whereas others provide that the insured may recover up to the highest limit for any of the automobiles, assuming that the limits differ as to the automobile involved. In addition, where the insured is a pedestrian and is injured through the negligence of an uninsured motorist, his recovery is restricted to the limits provided for any one automobile. Among the states having such legislation are the following:

Arizona (20-259.01)	Indiana (27-7-5)
Connecticut (Ti. 18 3002)	North Dakota (26-02-42)
Deleware (Ti. 18 3902)	Ohio (3937.191)
Florida (627.4132)	Tennessee (56-7-1202)

Other state legislatures have been content to abide by the court interpretations of the policy and the existing statutes, but some may enact legislation to confirm the court decisions. For example the Wisconsin statute (Sec. 204.30) reads as follows:

The uninsured motorist bodily injury coverage limits provided in an automobile liability or motor vehicle liability policy shall not be reduced by the terms thereof to provide the insured with less protection than would be afforded him if he were injured by a motorist insured under an automobile liability or motor vehicle liability policy of insurance containing the limits provided in this subsection.

b. Caveat. Since this aspect of the uninsured motorist insurance is under scrutiny by the courts as well as the various legislatures, it is suggested that when the claims representative is confronted by this problem that he be familiar with the latest pronouncements of the courts as well as any statutory changes which may have taken place recently.

2. *Arbitration.* As set forth in the insured agreements, if the parties fail to agree on the issue of the liability of the uninsured owner or operator, or the amount of damages, or both, these issues may be settled by arbitration. The condition reads as follows:

If any person making claim hereunder and the company do not agree that such person is legally entitled to recover damages from the owner or operator of an uninsured automobile because of bodily injury to the insured or do not agree as to the amount of payment which may be owing under this Part, then, upon the written demand of either, the matter or matters upon which such person and the company do not agree shall be settled by arbitration in accordance with the rules of the American Arbitration Association, and judgment upon the award rendered by the arbitrators may be entered in any court having jurisdiction thereof. Such person and the company each agree to consider itself bound and to be bound by any award made by the arbitrators pursuant to this Part.

The American Arbitration Association has two plans for arbitrating disputes arising under insurance policies. The first is their usual commercial arbitration system which is applicable to all disputes, whether involving an insurance policy or any other business controversy. The other is the accident claims tribunal which is applicable to arbitration under uninsured motorist coverage and may be used only by those companies who are participating in an organized plan for the use of the American Arbitration Association services. Under this plan three insurance groups have underwritten the expense of setting up the staff and equipment for handling claims, and thus the plan may be used only by members of the three groups. These groups are the Association of Casualty and Surety Companies, the American Mutual Alliance, the National Association of Independent Insurers and some others. Arbitration is available to members of the groups at a cost of $50 for filing, and $50 for each additional day spent in arbitration. As to companies who are not participants in the accident claims tribunal plan, commercial arbitration is available at higher rates.

Under the accident claims tribunal system the arbitration is initiated by either the insurer's or insured's serving notice on the other party, demanding arbitration, and sending two copies of the notice (designated as a Demand for Arbitration) to the office of the American Arbitration Association. The party on whom the demand is served may file an answering statement within seven days. If he fails to do so it is presumed that he denies the claim.

The selection of the arbitrator is made by the association from a list of attorneys nominated by the various bar associations or generally selected in commercial arbitration cases. The rules of the tribunal provide that no attorney working for an insurance company or specializing in negligence cases may serve as an arbitrator on these cases. At the time of hearing either or both parties may be represented by counsel, although this is not a requirement.

There is no provision in the policy with respect to the fees to be paid for arbitration. Since the company did not obligate itself in that regard, the expenses of the arbitration proceeding are borne by the parties, each absorbing his own expense. The filing fee and expense of the arbitration itself are borne by the party filing the demand for arbitration.

While the policy provision obligates the parties to arbitrate on demand only two issues, liability of the uninsured and the amount of damages, they may by mutual agreement submit any other matters pertinent to the case to arbitration.

Some states, either by statute or by judicial decisions, do not recognize an agreement in an insurance policy to arbitrate claims occurring in the future as valid and enforceable (see Section 727, above) and therefore in those states neither party may enforce a demand for arbitration on the other in spite of the policy provision. However, there is no bar in those states to an agreement to arbitrate a dispute which is already in existence, and such an agreement, made after the event, is valid and enforceable.

3. *Trust agreement.* If a payment is made by the insurer under this coverage, it is agreed that the insurer has an interest in the recovery from the wrongdoer to the extent of its payment. In the absence of a statute, the common-law rule is that a personal injury claim may not be assigned either in whole or in part. Therefore, in order to provide a means of recovery for the company for the payment it has made, the agreement provides that while there can be no assignment of the personal injury cause of action, the insured will prosecute such an action at the company's request and at the company's expense and, if a recovery is had, the insured will hold the funds so received in trust for the company to the extent of the payment made. The agreement is as follows:

In the event of payment to any person under this Part:

(a) the company shall be entitled to the extent of such payment to the proceeds of any settlement or judgment that may result from the exercise of any rights of recovery of such person against any person or organization legally responsible for the bodily injury because of which such payment is made.

(b) such person shall hold in trust for the benefit of the company all rights of recovery which he shall have against such other person or organization because of the damages which are the subject of claim made under this Part;

(c) such person shall do whatever is proper to secure and shall do nothing after loss to prejudice such rights;

(d) if requested in writing by the company, such person shall take, through any representative designated by the company, such action as may be necessary or appropriate to recover such payment as damages from such other person or organization, such action to be taken in the name of such person; in the event of a recovery, the company shall be reimbursed out of such recovery for expenses, costs and attorney's fees incurred by it in connection therewith;

(e) such person shall execute and deliver to the company such instruments and papers as may be appropriate to secure the rights and obligations of such person and the company established by this provision.

While the rights and obligations of the parties are clearly set forth in the condition, in the event of a payment by the insurer some companies have felt it was good practice to enter into a written agreement with the insured at the time payment was made so that there would be no misunderstanding as to terms and conditions of the payment or the obligations undertaken by the insured by the acceptance of the payment.

The intent of the agreement is not to release the uninsured or any other defendant but merely to set forth the agreement of the parties with respect to the contractual obligations of both under the uninsured motorist coverage and to release the company from its contractual obligations by reciting that it has performed its obligations. The following is a form customarily used for this purpose:

RELEASE AND TRUST AGREEMENT
(For Injury and Death Caused by Uninsured Automobiles Only)

KNOW ALL MEN BY THESE PRESENTS:

That I, _____ *(Insured)* _____ of _____ *(Residence)* _____ for and in consideration of the payment of the sum of _____
($_____) Dollars to me paid by the _____ *(Insurance Company)* _____ the receipt of which is hereby acknowledged do hereby for myself, and for my heirs, executors, administrators and assigns, remise, release, acquit and forever discharge the said _____ *(Insurance Company)* _____ from any and all actions, claims, demands, costs, expenses, compensation, and any and all claims for damages instituted against the said _____ *(Insurance Company)* _____ under the Protection Against Uninsured Motorist Coverage forming a part of Policy No. _____ by me, or by any other person for the purpose of enforcing a claim for damages on account of injuries suffered by me as a result of an accident involving an uninsured vehicle, which occurred on or about _____ at or near _____
_____ meaning and intending hereby to release and discharge the said _____ *(Insurance Company)* _____ from only such contractual liability as it may have under the aforesaid Protection Against Uninsured Motorists Coverage.

I agree that the _____ *(Insurance Company)* _____ shall be entitled to the extent of such payment hereunder to the proceeds of any settlement or judgment that may result from the exercise of any rights or recovery by me against the owner or operator of the uninsured automobile involved in the accident causing the injury on account of which such payment is made.

I also agree in accordance with the terms of the aforesaid Protection Against Uninsured Motorists Coverage, to take through an attorney designated by the

_____(Insurance Company)_____ and at the sole expense of said Company, such action or actions as may be necessary or appropriate to recover from the owner, operator, persons or organizations responsible for the operation of the uninsured automobile causing the injury and the damage resulting therefrom; and furthermore, agree to hold any monies received as a result of settlement or judgment in Trust for said Company to be paid to said Company immediately upon the same coming into my hands, provided, however, that any sum received in excess of the amount paid by the Company, including legal expenses incurred by it in effecting the recovery, shall be retained by me.

Further, I agree to execute and deliver to the said _____
_____(Insurance Company)_____any and all papers and instruments that may be deemed necessary or appropriate to institute, prosecute, settle or compromise such actions or claims and to carry out the provisions and intent of the aforesaid Protection Against Uninsured Motorists Coverage.

IN WITNESS WHEREOF I have hereunto set my hand and seal at _____
_____(City and State)_____ this _____ day of _____ 19_____.

This is followed by the signature, with the address of the insured entering into the agreement, and either witnesses' signatures or a notary's certification.

In cases where an infant is the injured insured, the agreement is made with one of the parents of the infant (preferably the father). The form used in such cases is as follows:

PARENT'S RELEASE AND TRUST AGREEMENT
(For Injury and Death Caused by Uninsured Automobiles Only)

KNOW ALL MEN BY THESE PRESENTS:

That I _____(Name of Parent)_____ of _____(Residence)_____ individually, and as (*Father*) (*Mother*), next friend and natural guardian of my (*Son*) (*Daughter*), _____(Name of Infant)_____ of _____
_____(Residence of Infant)_____, for and in consideration of the payment of _____
_____ ($_____) Dollars to me in hand paid by the _____(Insurance Company)_____ the receipt of which is hereby acknowledged, do hereby for myself, and for my heirs, executors, administrators and assigns, and as (*Father*) (*Mother*), next friend and natural guardian of said (*Son*) (*Daughter*) remise, release, acquit and forever discharge the said _____(Insurance Company)_____ from any and all actions, causes of actions, claims, demands, damages, costs, expenses, compensation and any and all claims for damages, consequential or otherwise instituted against the said _____(Insurance Company)_____ under the Protection Against Uninsured Motorists Coverage forming part of Policy No. _____ by me, individually, or by me on behalf of said (*Son*) (*Daughter*) as (*Father*) (*Mother*), next friend and natural guardian or by any other persons for the purpose of enforcing a claim for damages, consequential or otherwise, on account of injury suffered by said (*Son*) (*Daughter*) as a result of an accident involving an Uninsured Vehicle, which occurred on or about _____ at or near _____ meaning and intending hereby to release and discharge the said _____(Insurance Company)_____ from such contractual liability as it may have under the aforesaid Protection Against Uninsured Motorists Coverage.

I agree that the _____(Insurance Company)_____ shall be entitled to the extent of such payment hereunder to the proceeds of any settlement or judgment that may result from the exercise of any rights of recovery by me, individually, or by me on behalf of said *(Son)* *(Daughter)* as *(his)* *(her)* *(Father)* *(Mother)*, next friend and natural guardian, or by any other persons, for and on said *(Son's)* *(Daughter's)* behalf, against the owner or operator of the uninsured automobile involved in the accident causing the injury and consequential damage on account of which such payment is made.

I also agree in accordance with the terms of the aforesaid Protection Against Uninsured Motorists Coverage to take through an attorney designated by the said _____(Insurance Company)_____, and at the sole expense of said Company, such action or actions as may be necessary or appropriate to recover from the owner, operator, persons or organizations responsible for the operation of the uninsured automobile causing the injury or damage resulting therefrom; and furthermore, I agree to hold any monies received by me, individually, or by me on behalf of my *(Son)* *(Daughter)* as *(his)* *(her)* *(Father)* *(Mother)*, next friend and natural guardian as a result of settlement or judgment in Trust for said Company to be paid to said Company immediately upon the same coming into my hands; providing, however, that any sum or sums received in excess of the amount paid by said Company, including legal expenses incurred by it in effecting the recovery, shall be retained by me.

Further, I agree to execute and deliver to _____(Insurance Company)_____ any and all papers and instruments that may be deemed necessary or appropriate to institute, prosecute, settle or compromise any action or claim and to carry out the provisions and intent of the aforesaid Protection Against Uninsured Motorists Coverage.

The usual signature clause follows at the end of the agreement, the same as that used in the preceding form.

Statutory uninsured motorist coverage. A number of states, in dealing with the problem of the uninsured and financially irresponsible motorist, have enacted statutes requiring either that the coverage be mandatory or that the coverage be offered to the insured, which he may accept or reject at his option. In addition, some states require that property damage coverage also be offered. When the coverage was first introduced, it was thought that a $10,000 limit would be adequate. Since that time, a number of states have increased the limit requirement, and some require that the uninsured motorist limits be the same as the bodily injury limits in the liability part of the policy. Also, some states permit the insured to purchase higher limits than those required by the state, but in no case higher than the bodily injury liability limits, except in Florida and Delaware where the insured may purchase limits up to 100/300. A list of the states having statutes with relation to the writing of uninsured motorist coverage with the limits required, whether or not property damage is included, and also whether or not the acceptance of the coverage is optional with the insured or mandatory is as follows:

State	Optional?	Statute	B.I. Limits	PD
Alabama	Yes	74 (62) (a)	10/20	No
Alaska	Yes	CA 146-L1966	10/20	No
Arizona	Yes	20-259.01	15/30	No
Arkansas	Yes	66-4004	15/30	No
California	Yes	11580-2	15/30	No
Colorado	Yes	10-4-319	15/30	No
Connecticut	No	P.A. 79-235	B.I. policy limits	No
Delaware	Yes	T18-3002	Insured may purchase limits up to 100/300	No
District of Columbia	No	35-2106	10/20	No
Florida	Yes	627.727	Insured may purchase limits up to 100/300	No
Georgia	Yes	56-407.1	10/20	5M
Hawaii	Yes	411-448	10/20	No
Idaho	Yes	41-2502	10/20	No
Illinois	No	143A-1	B.I. policy limits	No
Indiana	Yes	27-7-5	B.I. policy limits	Yes
Iowa	Yes	516 A-1	10/20	No
Kansas	Yes	40-284	B.I. policy limits	No
Kentucky	Yes	Ch 301, Sec 2	10/20	No
Louisiana	Yes	9-5604	B.I. policy limits	No
Maine	No	2902	B.I. policy limits	No
Massachusetts	No	1131		
Michigan	Applies no-fault benefits		10/20	No
Minnesota	No	Ch 408-1975	10/20	No
Mississippi	No	Ch 432	10/20	Yes
Missouri	No	379.203	10/20	No
Montana	Yes	33-23-201	25/50	No
Nebraska	Yes	60-509.2	10/20	No
Nevada	Yes	687B145	15/30	No
New Hampshire	Yes	268:15-a	25/50	Yes
New Jersey	No	17-28	15/30	Yes
New Mexico	Yes	66-5-301	15/30	Yes
New York	No	Sec. 167	10/20	No
North Carolina	Yes	20-279.21	25/50	Yes
North Dakota	No	26-02-42	25/50	No
Ohio	Yes	3957-183	Equal to B.I. limits	No
Oklahoma	Yes	36-3636	10/20	No
Oregon	No	743.789	15/30	No
Pennsylvania	No	40-2000	15/30	No
Rhode Island	Yes	27-7-2.1	25/50	Yes
South Carolina	No	56-9-831	15/30	Yes
South Dakota	No	58-11-9	B.I. policy limits	No
Tennessee	Yes	56-7-1202	10/20	No
Texas	Yes	5.06-1	10/20	Yes

State	Optional?	Statute	B.I. Limits	PD
Utah	Yes	41-12-21.1	20/40	No
Vermont	No	23.941	20/40	No
Virginia	No	38.1 381 6	B.I. policy limits	Yes
Washington	Yes	48.22.04	B.I. policy limits	Yes
West Virginia	No	33-6-31	20/40	No
Wisconsin	No	632.32-3	25/50	No
Wyoming	Yes	31-315.1,2	10/20	No

1617 Underinsured motorist coverage—automobile policies

The original purpose of the uninsured motorist coverage was to provide a means whereby an insured could recover damages up to the coverage limit caused by the negligence of an uninsured motorist or an unidentified hit-and-run driver, as well as by a motorist carrying insurance with an insolvent carrier. When the motorist carries insurance with a solvent carrier, regardless of the limits thereof, he is not an uninsured motorist and thus the uninsured motorist coverage is not applicable.

In a number of cases where the damages far exceeded the policy limits of the negligent motorist, it has been urged that the motorist was insured up to his limits but was uninsured as to the balance of the damages. The courts have uniformly held that the statutes and the policy provisions were clear and that there was no ambiguity for them to resolve. It was stated that while the statutes were clear, any change would have to come from the legislature. In other cases, the insured, who has sustained serious injuries, would be in a more advantageous position if he were involved with an uninsured motorist rather than a motorist who is insured but has low limits. For example, the insured has a $20,000 limit on his uninsured motorist coverage and he is injured through the negligence of an insured motorist, whose limits are $5,000. Under these circumstances, the insured would be limited in his recovery to the $5,000 available in insurance. Since the adverse motorist had insurance, he is not an uninsured motorist, and therefore the uninsured motorist coverage would not apply. If he had been an uninsured motorist, the insured could have recovered up to $20,000 under his uninsured motorist coverage.

To correct this situation, a number of states have required that underinsured motorist coverage be added to the usual uninsured motorist coverage. An underinsured motorist is defined as one whose liability limits for bodily injury are less than the limits provided for in the uninsured motorist coverage. In such a case, the limits of the uninsured motorist coverage are applied to the claim as excess insurance. In other words, the uninsured motorist limits are involved only where the claim is in excess of the insurance carried by the adverse motorist. If the claim or the damages are within the limits of the insurance carried, then the underinsured motorist coverage is not involved.

Likewise, if the insured settled his claim within the limits of the adverse motorist's coverage even though he is claiming additional damages, the underinsured motorist coverage would not be involved. Conversely, if the adverse motorist had bodily injury liability with limits which equaled or exceeded the uninsured motorist limits, he is not by definition an underinsured motorist. In most states, the purchase of underinsured motorist coverage is optional with the insured. If it was not purchased, it follows that the coverage is not involved regardless of the circumstances. See *Rogers* v. *Tennessee Farmers Insurance Co.,* 620 S.W. 2d 476.

The following states require that underinsured motorist coverage be offered:

Arizona	North Carolina
Connecticut	Ohio
Delaware	Oklahoma
Florida	Oregon
Illinois	South Carolina
Louisiana	South Dakota
Maine	Tennessee
Massachusetts	Texas
Minnesota	Vermont
Mississippi	Virginia
Nevada	Washington
New Hampshire	West Virginia
New Mexico	

Note that all states have not required this coverage, but it is possible that they may follow the others.

1618   Medical payments coverage

Under some liability insurance contracts medical payments coverage is available and may be purchased for an additional premium. Some of the contracts are:

1. Automobile Garage Liability
2. Automobile Liability
3. Comprehensive Personal Liability
4. Family Automobile
5. Farmers Comprehensive Personal Liability
6. Manufacturers' and Contractors' Liability
7. Owners', Landlords', and Tenants' Liability
8. Special Combination Automobile

In addition, there are special policies, approved by the insurance departments of the various states, in which the coverage is offered in package form.

Medical payments coverage is a separate and complete contract in itself. It is independent of and is not dependent upon the existence of any other part of the contract. Payments made under the coverage are applied in reduction of the liability of either the company (see Protection Against Uninsured Motorists, Limits of Liability (*d*) or the insured (see Section 2009, above). The insuring agreements are the same in each policy but differ as to the persons for whose benefit the contract is made and as to the hazards covered. The agreement generally reads as follows:

To pay all reasonable expenses incurred within one year from the date of accident for necessary medical, surgical and dental services, including prosthetic devices, and necessary ambulance, hospital, professional nursing and funeral services to or for each person who sustains bodily injury, sickness or disease, caused by accident and arising out of the hazards covered by the policy.

This is a direct contract with the named insured for the benefit of the insured (if he is so covered) and for the benefit of others who may sustain injury. It is a direct contractual obligation of the company, and the failure of the company to meet the obligation thus assumed is actionable against the company in an action of breach of contract. This action may be brought by the person who sustained bodily injuries by accident, whether such person was a party to the contract or not. Since this is a beneficiary contract as to others than the insured, who is a contracting party, the beneficiary succeeds to the same rights as he would have had had he been a party to the agreement. Generally, automobile policies include the named insured within the terms of the medical payments coverage, whereas the other policies do not.

For the company's obligations to come into existence, the bodily injury, sickness or disease must be (1) sustained by a person covered, (2) caused by accident, and (3) arise out of the hazards covered.

1. *Person covered.* Under automobile medical payments coverage, the insuring agreements include the insured as a person covered. The coverage is divided into two divisions:

Division 1. To or for the named insured and each relative who sustains bodily injury, sickness or disease, including death resulting therefrom, hereinafter called "bodily injury" caused by accident,

(a) while occupying the owned automobile.

(b) while occupying a non-owned automobile, but only if such person has, or reasonably believes he has, the permission to use the automobile and the use is within the scope of such permission, or,

(c) through being struck by an automobile or by a trailer of any type.

Division 2. To or for any person who sustains bodily injury, caused by accident, while occupying

(a) the owned automobile, while being used by the named insured, by any resident of the same household or by any person with the permission of the named insured; or

(b) a non-owned automobile, if the bodily injury results from

(1) its operation or occupancy by the named insured or its operation on his behalf by his private chauffeur or domestic servant, or

(2) its operation or occupancy by a relative, provided it is a private passenger automobile or trailer,

but only if such operator or occupant has, or reasonably believes he has, the permission of the owner to use the automobile and the use is within the scope of such
permission.

The persons for whose benefit the coverage is applied under liability policies other than automobile are those who sustain bodily injuries by accident
arising out of the hazards insured against, but they exclude the named insured
and any other person who qualifies as an insured under the liability part of
the policy. For example, the Comprehensive Personal Liability Policy contains
the following exclusion:

This policy does not apply under Coverage M (Medical Payments) to bodily
injury to (1) any insured within the meaning of parts (a) and (b) of insuring
agreement III (definition of insured) or (2) any person, other than a residence
employee, if such person is regularly residing on the premises including any part
rented to such person or to others, or is on the premises because of a business
conducted thereon, or is injured by an accident arising out of such business.

The intent here is to eliminate the named insured and all others who qualify as
insureds under the policy as well as those residing on the premises or conducting a business thereon.

The same underwriting intent is expressed in the Owners', Landlords', and
Tenants' Liability Policy, with the additional exclusion of services rendered
by the insured. Under that policy, the exclusion is as follows:

This policy does not apply under Coverage C (Medical Payments) to bodily
injury to or sickness, disease or death of (1) the named insured, any partner
therein, any tenant or other person regularly residing on premises owned by or
rented to the named insured, or any employee of such insured, tenant or other
person arising out of and in the course of his employment therewith, or (2) any
other tenant of such premises, or any employee of such other tenant arising out of
and in the course of his employment therewith, on that part of such premises
rented to such other tenant, or (3) any person arising out of and in the course of
his employment if benefits therefor are in whole or in part either payable or
required to be provided under any workmen's compensation law, or (4) any person
while engaged in maintenance, alteration, demolition or new construction operations for the named insured or for any lessee of the named insured or any lessor of
premises rented to the named insured, or (5) any person practicing, instructing or
participating in any physical training, sport, athletic activity or contest; . . . any
expense for services by the named insured, any employee thereof, or any person or
organization under contract to the named insured to provide such services.

The intention as expressed in the exclusion is to exclude all persons regularly living or conducting a business on the premises, and their employees,
and, in addition, the named insured, his employees who are under the compensation law, and those employed by him or the owner, if the premises are

leased to the named insured, or those employed by his tenants to make altera-tions in the premises. There is an additional exclusion with regard to services rendered by the insured, his employees, or a person or organization under contract to him to provide such services. This would come into operation where the insured is a member of the medical profession, operates a hospital or other business on the premises, or is a nurse or physiotherapist and renders treatment or other services in his professional capacity, or has the services performed by his employees or others obligated by contract to do so.

2. *Caused by accident.* It must be noted that even in those policies where the insuring agreements with respect to liability afford coverage on an occurrence basis, medical payments coverage is on an accident basis, and to qualify for the benefits of medical payments coverage the bodily injuries must be caused by accident. It is clear that where a person suffers a heart attack or the onset of an illness occurs while he is occupying an automobile or on the premises, he has not suffered a bodily injury caused by accident arising out of the hazards insured, but in very large areas the question of whether or not the bodily injury is caused by accident is not easy of solution.

For example, under the Comprehensive Personal Liability Policy, the named insured's children qualify as insureds and medical payments coverage applies to bodily injury caused by accident while away from the premises if caused by the activities of the insured. If the insured is playing baseball and hits a fly or four ball which injures either another player or a spectator, there is a problem as to whether or not the resulting bodily injury is caused by accident. The mere fact that an injury has been sustained does not in and of itself support a conclusion that the injury was caused by accident, even if the result was unexpected. The best that can be said in this area is that the claims representative must obtain all of the facts, and if the average person would regard the circumstances as constituting a bodily injury caused by accident, some consideration should be given to accepting the claim.

3. *Hazards covered.* The automobile medical payments restrict the hazard to bodily injury received while occupying an owned or, under some circumstances, an unowned automobile. Occupying is defined as meaning in or upon, or entering into or alighting from the automobile. Cases sometimes arise where the insured person is out of the automobile completely but is doing something in connection with the vehicle, such as changing a tire, when the accident occurs. In the few cases which have reached the courts, the holding has been that such insured persons were occupying the automobile within the meaning of the coverage. Where the insured person is completely away from the vehicle, although intending to return to it, such as going into a restaurant for food before continuing the journey, a bodily injury sustained during this period is not within the scope of the hazards covered.

Under the CPL policy, the liability of the company is limited to bodily injuries sustained while on the premises with the permission of the insured, or while elsewhere if such bodily injury arises out of the premises or the ways immediately adjoining, or out of the activities of an insured, or is sustained by a residence employee and arises out of and in the course of his employment by an insured, or is caused by an animal owned by or in the care of an insured. Under the OLT policy, the bodily injury, to come within medical payments coverage, must arise out of the ownership, maintenance, or use of the premises or operations necessary or incidental thereto.

The extent of the company's liability for the payment of medical services is set forth in the insuring agreement and is limited by the amounts in the limits of liability. Within such limits lies the obligation to make the medical payments provided for in the insuring agreements, provided they are (1) reasonable, (2) necessary, and (3) incurred within one year.

1. *Reasonable.* This has reference to the individual charges for the items of medical services rendered. If the amounts charged are the same as those prevalent in the community for similar services, then they are reasonable, but if the amount charged exceeds the average charges for similar services in the community where they were rendered, then the amounts are unreasonable and should be subject to adjustment. It is clear that what would be a reasonable charge in one community might be unreasonable in another, so that the determination of this question will be influenced by the place where the services are rendered.

2. *Necessary.* This question will be determined by reference to standard medical practice as to the treatment of the type of injury sustained, the frequency of treatment needed, and the kind and type of treatment to be rendered. The claimsman will be guided by his own medical examiner's opinion as to the amount of treatment needed, whether or not the case is being overtreated, and, if so, the number of treatments necessary as well as the frequency thereof.

3. *Incurred within one year.* The courts generally have held that medical treatment is "incurred" when the services are rendered, and because an injury is incurred or the need for treatment arises within one year does not mean that the company is obligated to provide or reimburse the insured for treatment rendered after one year from the date of the accident has elapsed.

For example, in *Czarnecki* v. *American Indemnity Co.* [29 Auto Cas. 2d 80 (CCH)], the plaintiff was injured on May 15, 1960, and was under continuous treatment from that date until considerably after May 15, 1961. She contended that her obligation to pay for the medical treatment was created at the time of the accident and that the company was obligated to reimburse her, up to the limit of the policy, whether the treatment extended beyond one year from the date of the accident or not. The court, pointing out that the parties to a contract could agree on any legal terms they wished, made the following observations:

> Since the policy provision is valid, the only question left for consideration is: What is the extent of the defendant's obligation? The answer is to be found in the language the parties have chosen to express their contract. . . . The language of the contract obligates the defendant to pay "expenses incurred within one year from the date of the accident." Plaintiff would rewrite the provision to read "pay

all expenses incurred because of accidental injuries;" but she stipulated defendant "has paid a total amount of $1,054.05 which amount is for all of the medical expenses of the appellant (plaintiff) incurred within one (1) year from the date of the accident except for the sum of $90.15." . . . The policy sued on insured the plaintiff for a term of one year, that is, from November 7, 1959 to November 7, 1960, but the expiration date of the policy did not terminate the defendant's liability for medical expenses incurred for accidental injuries sustained prior to November 7, 1960 until the expiration of one year from the date of the accident. Defendant is liable for $90.15, the unpaid balance of expenses incurred prior to May 16, 1961. It has admitted its liability for this sum. It is not, however, liable for any expenses incurred after May 15, 1961.

A troublesome problem arises where the insured has suffered a bodily injury resulting in a condition which can be corrected by surgery or dental replacements at any time, but, because of business or other commitments, the insured does not have the surgery or dental work done until a year after the date of the accident. There is no question but that if the insured had had the work done within the year the company would have been obligated to pay for it, but where the work is done more than one year after the accident the company is not obligated to make any payment. The insured might feel that the company has a moral obligation to pay for the services, but the plain engagement of the policy contract is that the company will pay for medical expenses incurred within one year and not thereafter.

The same reasoning would apply where the insured pays for the treatment in advance during the one-year period—under agreement with the physician that the payment will cover all the treatment to be rendered in the future. Since the company is obligated to pay for only such medical treatment as is actually rendered during the one-year period, the device of an advance payment will not serve to increase the extent of the contractual obligation.

Since there is a lack of definition in the policy contract as to what constitutes "necessary medical, surgical and dental services," and, more especially, what constitutes "funeral services," the claimsman will be confronted on occasions with items which appear to be unusual but could conceivably come within the assumed obligations of the company. Foremost among them undoubtedly will be claims based upon the services of chiropractors rendered in states where they are not licensed to practice medicine, as well as services rendered by Christian Science practitioners. Generally the companies, as a matter of policy, recognize these services in cases where the bills are reasonable.

Because the amounts involved in medical payment claims are small, and seldom reach the appellate courts, there is little case law to guide us as to unusual items. The following is a list of items, together with a notation, as to whether or not they will generally be allowed. The list is *not authoritative* and is not based on any case law, but is compiled on the basis of the opinions of some 20 companies as to whether they would or would not allow the items. Undoubtedly, there may be some differences of opinion among other companies, and some of the items could be considered controversial. The list is offered only as a sampling of the opinions of some claims representatives.

MEDICAL PAYMENTS

	Allow	Disallow
1. *Medical*		
a) Fee for examination, X rays, and reports to be used in pressing claim against tort-feasor		X
b) Services necessary and contracted for but not yet performed within one year from date of the accident		X
c) Taxicab fare from home to doctor's office to secure treatment or for examination		X
d) Additional medical expense when claimant is not satisfied with results obtained with first doctor so changes to another. No duplication of X rays, etc.	X	
e) Replacement or repair of prosthetic devices: eyeglasses, eyeballs, dentures, bridges, artificial limbs, hearing aids, etc.:		
1) When claimant sustained injury that necessitates prosthetic device not previously needed	X	
2) When claimant sustained injury and prosthetic device already in use was damaged		X
3) When claimant sustained no injury but prosthetic device already in use was damaged		X
f) Services of chiropractor	X	
g) Services of osteopath	X	
h) Services of psychologist	X	
i) Services of Christian Science practitioner	X	
j) Cost of hospital bed, equipment, or appliances purchased or rented for use at home:		
1) When claimant would have to be in hospital, if not rented	X	
2) When patient would not be confined in hospital, if not rented		X
2. *Surgical*		
a) Exploratory operations	X	
b) Operations that are found necessary after commencement of operation:		
1) Necessary because of original operation	X	
2) Not related to original operation		X
3. *Ambulance*		
a) Rental of private car from scene of accident when no ambulance is available	X	
b) Rental of private car in lieu of ambulance from hospital to home		X
c) Ambulance dispatched but never arrived, through no fault of the driver:		
1) When a second ambulance is called		X
2) When no other ambulance is called		X

4. *Hospital*

  a) Expenses while confined to a convalescent hospital   X

  b) Continuing expenses in hospital during convalescence after one year from date of accident, but necessary because of operation or treatment commenced within a one-year period   X

  c) Rental of TV, radio, and cost of newspapers, telephone calls, meals for visitors, etc.   X

5. *Professional Nursing*

  a) Services of practical nurse:

    1) Licensed and does nothing but nursing   X

    2) Not licensed and does other work besides nursing   X

  b) Cost of meals for professional nurse in hospital   X

  c) Allowance for meals and room for professional nurse in patient's home   X

  d) Services of housekeeper or baby-sitter while claimant is away from home, either in the hospital or to visit the doctor's office   X

6. *Funeral*

  a) Cost of burial plot   X

  b) Flowers sent by the family   X

  c) Headstone or marker   X

  d) Liner for grave, when required by law   X

  e) Liner for grave, when not required by law   X

  f) Donation to minister conducting service   X

  g) Fee paid singer when not furnished by the mortuary   X

  h) Cost of transporting body to another city for the burial   X

  i) Embalming expense when the body is moved to another city   X

  i) Acknowledgment cards   X

  k) Expenses of inserting notice of death in the newspaper   X

  l) Mourners' meals   X

  m) Rental of automobiles for use by relatives at funeral   X

  n) Cost of niche or crypt   X

  o) Opening and closing of the grave   X

Medical Payments Coverage is subject to the following condition, which is common to all liability policies affording such coverage:

MEDICAL REPORTS: PROOF AND PAYMENT OF CLAIM

As soon as practicable the injured person or someone on his behalf shall give to the company written proof of claim, under oath, if required, and shall, after each request from the company, execute authorization to enable the company to obtain medical reports and copies of records. The injured person shall submit to physical examination by physicians selected by the company when and as often as the company may reasonably require.

The company may pay the injured person or any person or organization rendering the services and such payments shall reduce the amount payable hereunder for such injury. Payment hereunder shall not constitute an admission of liability of any person or, except hereunder, the company.

By means of the exercise of the rights granted to the company under this condition, the claims representative can keep an accurate check on the medical treatment being rendered, the progress made, the records of the injury, and in addition may request as many physical examinations as the company may reasonably require, depending upon the nature of the injury and the kind of treatment being rendered. The exercise of these rights will also assist in the development of defenses to the medical payments claim where there is a question as to the relationship between the bodily injury and the treatment.

In the settlement of medical payments claims, some companies take a Medical Payments Proof of Loss from the injured person, wherein there is a statement as to the services rendered, the names of the physicians and others who rendered the services, and the amounts of the respective bills. There is also a statement that the company is authorized to pay certain bills direct to the doctor or hospital involved. This might be considered as surplusage since the company, under the terms of the contract, has the right to pay the doctor or hospital direct. However, with the statement or payment authorization signed by the injured person, it avoids a situation where the injured can claim that he had already paid the doctor or hospital and is entitled to reimbursement, and the doctor or hospital claims that the contrary is true—that they have not been paid at all. In addition, a Medical Expense Agreement is sometimes taken, especially where there is a possible liability claim, or doubt as to the validity of the claim, and a statement under oath is desirable. The agreement is usually printed on the reverse side of the Medical Payments Proof of Loss in the following form.

MEDICAL EXPENSE AGREEMENT

$_____   Date _____ 19_____

In consideration of the payment of medical expenses as described in the proof of loss appearing on the reverse side of this agreement, I hereby agree that:

1. The amount of such payment shall be applied toward the settlement of any claim, or the satisfaction of any judgment for damages entered on behalf of the said _____*(Name of Injured or Legal Representative)*_____ against any insured under the policy noted in the proof of loss because of bodily injury or death to which the liability coverage applies.

2. No medical expense has been paid or is payable to or on behalf of the injured person under the provisions of any (1) automobile or premises insurance affording benefits for medical expenses, (2) individual, blanket or group accident, disability or hospitalization insurance, (3) medical or surgical reimbursement plan, or (4) workmen's compensation or disability benefits law or any similar law.

3. I agree that _____*(Name of Insurance Company)*_____ shall be and is subrogated to all of my rights of recovery for the medical expenses paid to or on behalf of the injured person under the policy which I or anyone receiving such payment

may have against any person or organization. I further agree to execute and deliver instruments and papers and do whatever else is necessary to secure such rights. I have done nothing and shall do nothing to prejudice such rights.

4. I agree to hold in trust for the benefit of _____(Name of Insurance Company)_____ any and all funds coming into my hands to which it is entitled under this agreement.

Witness: _____

Signature

Since the contract itself measures the extent of the company's liability under the medical payments coverage, proof that the company has made the payments necessary to meet its agreement would seem to be all that is necessary to extinguish the claim. Therefore, the foregoing forms are of doubtful value except that they may have a place in the adjustment of claims where some unusual circumstances are present.

Under the conditions applicable to the coverage, the following refers to action on the contract:

No action shall lie against the company unless, as a condition precedent thereto, there shall have been full compliance with all the terms of this policy, nor until thirty days after the required proofs of claim have been filed with the company.

With respect to other insurance, the automobile policies have the following provision:

If there is other automobile medical payments insurance against a loss covered by Part II (medical payments) of this policy the company shall not be liable under this policy for a greater proportion of such loss than the applicable limit of liability of all valid and collectible automobile medical payments insurance, provided, however, the insurance with respect to a temporary substitute automobile or non-owned automobile shall be excess insurance over any other valid and collectible automobile medical payments insurance.

1619 Medical payments subrogation

The beneficiary of the medical payments portion of the liability contract is an insured, and, as such, is subject to all the terms and conditions of the policy. The liability policies which afford medical payments coverage contain the following applicable condition:

In the event of any payment under this policy, the company shall be subrogated to all of the insured's rights of recovery therefor against any person or organization and the insured shall execute and deliver instruments and papers and do whatever else is necessary to secure such rights. The insured shall do nothing after loss to prejudice such rights.

The purpose of this condition is to prevent the insured from collecting twice for the medical expense which he has incurred. Where the injury is caused by a third party (mostly in automobile cases), the insured would be entitled to claim as special damages the amount of the medical, surgical, and hospital expense. Even if the bills were paid under the medical payments coverage, they would be considered as payments from a collateral source and the defendant would not be entitled to credit for them, even though the ultimate result was that the insured was unjustly enriched.

Unfortunately, the condition contemplates the assignment of a portion of a personal injury claim. The common-law rule in most states is that a personal injury claim is personal to the injured person and may not be assignment in whole or in part. However, the proceeds of recovery from a personal injury cause of action may be assigned even before judgment is secured or payment made. The courts are not in agreement as to the interpretation of this provision and consideration must be given to the decided cases in each state to determine the view taken by the courts.

There are three factual situations to which the condition may be applied. They are (1) third-party recovery by the insured; (2) subrogation action by the medical payments carrier against the insured; and (3) subrogation action by the medical payments carrier against the third party.

1. *Third-party recovery.*   When the insured recovers from the third party, whether by settlement or judgment, one of the items of special damages will be his out-of-pocket medical, surgical, and hospital expense. Where no medical payments have been made, the insured sometimes thereafter makes a claim under the medical payments portion of the policy, seeking to recover the amount of the medical expense a second time. Under those circumstances it is clear that by settling or obtaining judgment, the insured has impaired the medical payments carrier's right of subrogation and thus has breached the condition. Since a condition defines the circumstances under which the contract shall be operative, the failure of the insured to meet the conditions will make the contract inoperative as to the particular claim. Defenses have been interposed that the condition contemplates the assignment of part of a personal injury claim, which in some common-law states cannot be assigned, and the insured could not validly make the assignment. The cases, however, recognize the insurance carrier's right of subrogation, holding either (*a*) a cause of action for personal injury can be assigned in part; or (*b*) even though the cause of action cannot be assigned, the medical payments subrogation clause merely impressed a lien in favor of the insurance carrier to the extent of its payments, or liability to pay, upon the proceeds of recovery obtained by the insured from the wrongdoer. Therefore, no matter which view the courts of a particular state take, the general conclusion is that where the insured has already recovered for his medical expense, he cannot thereafter collect a second time under the medical payments coverage.

In the following cases where the insured has already recovered from the tort-feasor, recoveries under the medical payments coverage have been denied.

Florida	*Despedes* v. *Prudence Mutual Casualty Co.*, 193 So. 2d 224, affirmed in 202 So. 2d 561.
Illinois	*Bernardi* v. *Home & Auto Ins. Co.*, 212 N.E. 2d 499.
Louisiana	*Washington* v. *Dairyland Ins. Co.*, 240 So. 2d 562.

New Jersey	*Busch* v. *Home Insurance Co.*, 234 Atl. 2d 250;
	Smith v. *Motor Club of America Ins. Co.*, 152 Atl. 2d 369.
New York	*Miller* v. *Liberty Mutual Fire Ins. Co.*, 264 N.Y.S. 2d 319.
Pennsylvania	*Demmery* v. *National Union Fire Ins. Co.*, 232 Atl. 2d 21.
Texas	*Foundation Reserve Ins. Co.* v. *Cody*, 458 S.W. 2d 214. (Construing a New Mexico insurance policy.)

In all of these cases, it would appear that the courts were impressed by the fact that the insured had already recovered his medical expense and was seeking an additional recovery to which he was not entitled.

2. *Action against the insured.* In cases where the medical payments carrier has paid all the medical and the insured thereafter recovers from the third party, either by settlement or judgment, it is clear that there has been a breach of condition and that the carrier's subrogation rights have been impaired. From the few cases involving this question, it would appear that the medical payments carrier is entitled to reimbursement for its payment from the insured. The carrier may urge that the insured has breached the contract by his recovery from the third party and therefore is required to return any benefits he has received under a contract which he breached, or that the recovery is impressed with a lien in favor of the carrier to the extent of the payments made.

3. *Action against the third party.* The question involved here is whether or not a stranger to the contract of insurance is bound to recognize the subrogation rights of the medical payments carrier, especially when it is on notice of such rights. The answer to the question will turn on whether or not under the law of the state a personal injury claim can be assigned in whole or in part. If the claim cannot be assigned, then the third party is not bound to recognize any right on the part of the medical payments carrier, whereas if a portion of the claim can be assigned, the third party must recognize the subrogation rights where it has been placed on notice thereof.

In the following cases the courts have held that the policy condition contemplates the assignment of a personal injury action and therefore recovery by the medical payments carrier have been denied even though the medical payments carrier put the third party on notice of its rights before any settlement was made:

Arizona	*Harleysville Mutual Insurance Co.* v. *Lea*, 410 Pac. 2d 495.
California	*Peller* v. *Liberty Mutual Fire Ins. Co.*, 34 Cal. Rptr. 41.
	Travelers Insurance Co. v. *Chumbley*, 394 S.W. 2d 418.
Missouri	*Forsthove* v. *Hardware Dealers Mutual Fire Insurance Co.*, 416 S.W. 2d 208.

In the following cases the courts have held that the clause does not constitute an assignment of an otherwise unassignable tort claim and allowed a recovery against the third party, holding that the concept of subrogation is distinct from that of an assignment. In each case the court found that subrogation is a creature of equity having for its purpose the ultimate discharge of a debt by the person who in equity and good conscience ought to pay it.

Nevada   *Davenport* v. *State Farm Mutual Automobile Insurance Co.*, 404 Pac. 2d 10.

Ohio   *Travelers Insurance Co.* v. *Lutz*, 210 N.E. 2d 755;
                Travelers Indemnity Co. v. *Godfrey*, 230 N.E. 2d 560.

West Virginia   *Travelers Indemnity Co.* v. *Rader*, 166 S.E. 2d 157.

In summary it may be said that where only the two parties to the insurance contract are involved, namely, the injured person and the medical payments carrier, the subrogation condition of the policy is given full effect. If the insured has settled with the third party before any payment of medical payments, the insured may not thereafter recover for his medical, surgical, and hospital expenses a second time. If medical payments have been made and there is a recovery from the third party without any knowledge or participation by the medical payments carrier, such carrier may recover from the insured the amount of the medical payments which it has made. In suits by the medical payments carrier against the third party, who was a stranger to the contract of insurance and not bound by its conditions, there are two schools of thought among the courts as to whether or not a recovery can be made. If the courts hold that the condition contemplates the assignment of an unassignable personal tort, no recovery can be had from the third party. On the other hand, if the courts hold that equitable principles are to be applied to the condition and the condition is not a mere assignment, a recovery by the medical payments carrier will be upheld. As one such court put it: "Subrogation serves to limit the chance of double recovery or windfall to the insured, and, when exercised, tends to place the primary liability upon the tortfeasor where it belongs." The court went on to say that: "So long as subrogation, as applied to this medical pay provision, serves to bar double recovery, it should be upheld."

CHAPTER XVII

Principles of investigation

1700   Nature of investigation

Unless the claimsman actually witnessed the accident or the occurrence, he will have no knowledge of the details of how it happened and will of necessity have to rely upon secondary sources of information as to the details of the event. The process by which these secondary sources are discovered and utilized is called investigation. It is a step-by-step inquiry into the facts, which has for its objective the development and accumulation of evidence upon which an informed judgment can be made as to the believable details of the event. It is a science in the sense that it follows a basic pattern or formula which, when correctly applied and accurately accomplished, will lead to the establishment of convincing evidence as a means of proof to support the final conclusion. The components of an investigation are (1) inquiry, (2) verification, and (3) comparison.

1. *Inquiry.*   Every claim will begin with some known facts. These come with the first notice of the occurrence, in the form of a report from the insured or a claim made directly to the company by the injured person. The inquiry is directed toward obtaining the required unknown facts. For example, the insured reports that he struck a parked car, that there was property damage

to the car, that the car was occupied at the time, and that there is a claim for both property damage and bodily injuries. The known facts are the insured's version of the accident and his understanding as to the claims which are being or will be asserted. This does not mean that the insured's version is a true account of what happened. Whether it is or it isn't will be the subject of further inquiry.

The unknown facts are the claimant's version of the accident, the extent of the property damage, the cost of repairs, the nature and extent of the bodily injuries, and the amount of the special damages in the form of medical bills, loss of earning capacity, and other out-of-pocket expenses. The inquiry may establish that the claimant's vehicle was *not* parked; that he was in the act of pulling out from a parked position into the insured's lane of travel when the accident occurred. It may also develop that the property damage was inconsequential and that there are no bodily injuries at all. In another case the insured may deny that any accident happened, or that he was stopped for a traffic light when he was struck in the rear by the other vehicle. The claimant says that the insured hit his parked vehicle or that the insured stopped short on the traveled highway where there was no traffic control whatever. Clearly, both of these versions cannot be correct, and the inquiry would be directed toward obtaining the unknown facts which will support one version or the other. This means that other witnesses, if any, must be contacted, a police blotter obtained, a copy of the motor vehicle report secured, and an examination made of the scene of the accident to establish the existence or nonexistence of traffic controls.

2. *Verification.* As the facts are obtained, they should be subjected to a checkup as to accuracy. This may be accomplished by obtaining statements from other witnesses who were present at the scene and saw the accident, by checking the police report, obtaining the motor vehicle report filed by the witness, and checking physical facts such as traffic controls, obstructions to vision, skid marks, gouges on the road, location of debris, and the like at the scene of the accident. In general liability cases, it would consist of an examination of the scene of the accident to determine the accuracy of statements as to hidden traps, absence of lighting, proper maintenance, or adequate warning of an unsafe condition.

The interest of the witness in the outcome of the claim should be taken into account in determining the weight that should be given his version and the extent of verification required. Such a witness often gives a statement which is colored by self-interest and a version of the accident which is most favorable to his recovery, placing responsibility for the occurrence on the shoulders of someone else.

This is especially true in automobile cases. The driver of the vehicle characteristically will give a version which exonerates himself. He will find some reason for the accident which involves lack of care on the part of the other driver or the pedestrian, as the case may be, and completely justifies his own actions. Verification in the form of a check of the statements he made to the police at the scene, statements he made in the presence of others (*res gestae* statements), and statements made in his motor vehicle report, as well as verification of the physical facts and an examination of the damage to the vehicles involved with respect to the point of impact, will establish the amount of reliance which should be placed upon his version.

The same treatment should be given to verification of the amount of the damages claimed, which will include damage to the vehicle, wages lost, the medical bills, the kind and quality of medical treatment received, the length of time under treatment, and the nature and extent of the injury. Damage to the vehicle can be verified by examination and an estimate of the cost of repairs. Wages can be verified by obtaining a copy of the payroll from his employer, an examination of his books if he is self-employed, or a check with his customers if he claims he was unable to perform work contracted for and not completed. As to the medical, this can be verified by hospital records, the records of the attending physician, X-ray reports, and by a physical examination of the claimant by the company doctor.

3. Comparison. During the investigation, comparison should be made between evidence as it is obtained, statements as they are made, facts as they are gathered, and the already known facts. This may establish the need for further information or further supporting facts. Since the objective of an investigation is to establish credible evidence, when contradictory "facts" appear an effort must be made to determine which are more believable and which are false and unsupportable, whether given by the insured or by the adverse party.

1701   Purpose of investigation

Whenever a claim is presented, the company must make a decision as to its disposition. Will it be accepted, rejected, or compromised? Investigation is the vehicle by means of which evidence is secured and preserved and upon which the answer to the question may be based. It is undertaken by an insurance company because of the right granted by the insurance contract and the duty correspondingly imposed. Investigation seeks to determine from the testimony of witnesses and the physical facts the answers to the questions of *who, what, where, when,* and *why*. These can be broken down as follows:

Who   The person involved.

What   What happened, or the elements of the claim and whether or not it is covered by the policy.

Where   Where the accident occurred and where the sources of information concerning it are.

When   The time when the investigation should be conducted (promptly) and the time and conditions (weather, etc.) surrounding the accident.

Why   Why the accident occurred and whether or not the proximate cause of the accident involves the insured's responsibility.

1702   Scope of investigation

In the investigation of insurance claims, there are three elements which must be covered: (1) coverage, (2) liability, and (3) damages.

1. *Coverage.* This refers to the insurance contract. For coverage to exist, there must be an accident or an occurrence which arises out of the hazards assumed by the insurance carrier within the period of time covered by the policy contract. If it does not, then there is no coverage. For example, if the insured reports that a social guest fell on his private sidewalk, and the insured carried a policy of liability insurance covering the hazards arising out of the ownership, maintenance, and use of an automobile, clearly there is no coverage applicable to the accident. Or there may be situations where the contract covers the accident or occurrence but, because of the insured's failure to comply with the terms and conditions of the policy, the insurance contract is inapplicable. This could come about because of the insured's failure to report the accident "as soon as practicable" or his failure to cooperate. In any case, investigation is required to establish the facts.

2. *Liability.* This refers to the merits of the claim against the insured. The problem concerns whether or not the insured was guilty of a negligent act of omission or commission, whether or not the claimant was guilty of contributory negligence, whether or not he assumed the risk of injury, and whether or not the claim is actionable because of the relationship of the parties. It amounts to establishing the existence of the legal responsibility, if any, of the insured, and the possibilities of a successful defense.

3. *Damages.* This refers to the amount of the loss sustained by the claimant, occasioned, it is claimed, by the accident or occurrence for which the insured is answerable. It may refer to bodily injuries, mental and physical distress, medical and hospital expenses, and the loss of earning capacity as a consequence thereof. Or it may refer to property damage and consequent loss of use. The claim might even be based upon damages sustained as a result of the loss of the services of the injured person. The function of investigation in these matters is to determine whether or not the damages were sustained as a proximate result of the accident, and if so, the reasonable value thereof.

Investigation may be made by (1) mail, (2) telephone, or (3) personal contact. The first two methods have their limitations and are used only in very small cases where there is no justification for incurring expense and where the essential information can be obtained by either method. Personal contact is the only method used on larger cases.

1703   Theory of defense

An investigation must have some direction, and the investigator must have some theory of what he is seeking to establish. The development of a theory of defense will point the way and will determine the course the investigation will take. When the first notice of the accident is received and reviewed, certain defenses will automatically suggest themselves to the experienced investigator, and his inquiry will be directed toward developing information and evidence which will support one or more of these defenses. As the investigation progresses, evidence may be obtained which will indicate that some of the theories cannot be supported and should be abandoned. Also, evidence may be uncovered which will suggest other and further defenses. The theory of defense merely suggests the areas to be investigated, but the investigation will determine whether or not the theory has any merit.

In determining whether the defense is tenable, the investigation will not ignore the unfavorable and concentrate on the favorable, but will contemplate an unbiased appraisal of all facts as they are developed. The theory will have to be sustained by the evidence, and the failure to find facts to support it will result in its abandonment.

The theories advanced can apply to one or all of the three elements of a claim, coverage, liability, or damages. On the coverage phase, can it be established that there is no policy coverage because the facts do not bring the case within the terms of the insurance contract? Did the insured fail to comply with the terms and conditions of the contract so as to relieve the insurer of its obligation? If the failure of the insured refers to lack of notice of the accident "as soon as practicable," did such failure result in material damage to the insurer so as to prejudice its rights with respect to the preparation of an adequate defense? If the defense is based on the failure of the insured to cooperate, the investigation must establish how and in what manner the insured so failed.

On the issue of liability it is usually alleged that the accident occurred through the negligence of the insured. To such an allegation the defense might be interposed that there was no act of commission or omission on the part of the insured, that the accident occurred through the sole neglect of the claimant, that the claimant's lack of care contributed to the happening of the accident, or that the accident was due to an act of God. It might also be urged that the claimant assumed the risk of injury or that the injury was sustained through an unavoidable accident. Investigation is the means through which evidence can be obtained to support these defenses.

On the issue of damages it might be established that the claimant has sustained no injury and consequently there are no damages, or that he has an injury which preexisted and was not aggravated by the accident, or that he has a condition which bears no causal relationship to the accident. It might also be urged that the amount of damages is inflated and does not represent the reasonable value of the items claimed. An investigation and verification of these same items will resolve the question of reasonableness.

Having decided the possible theories of defense available, the investigator must next consider the various available means of establishing the defense. The testimony of "fact witnesses," witnesses who either saw the accident or have some particular knowledge of the event, would include the ambulance doctor, ambulance driver, or police officer called to the scene. Secondary witnesses in the form of the doctor who treated the injuries, the mechanic who repaired the vehicle, witnesses who heard *res gestae* statements, evidence of admissions against interest, evidence from official documents, and newspaper items all comprise a secondary area of inquiry. A third area includes expert witnesses called upon by the investigator himself: a medical specialist to testify to the relationship between the injury and the claimant's present condition, an engineer, a chemist, or an accountant. We will consider the mechanics of gathering and preserving these types of evidence in the succeeding paragraphs.

1704   Stages of investigation

Investigation may be divided into three phases: (1) the preliminary or inquiry stage, (2) the settlement stage, and (3) the trial preparation stage.

1. *The preliminary stage.* This consists of an adequate inquiry to develop an understandable factual picture of what occurred and the exact amount of the damages sustained. The objective is to establish sufficient believable evidence upon which a reasonable conclusion can be based as to the classification within which the claim will fall. Should it be accepted, rejected, or compromised? Clearly, the amount of inquiry required will vary depending upon the extent of the known facts at the outset, the seriousness of the claim, and whether or not there are conflicting versions of the event. In any case, the inquiry must be of sufficient scope to justify a conclusion that the insured's responsibility for the happening of the accident is either apparent (accept), nonexistent (reject), or questionable (compromise).

2. *The settlement stage.* This refers to carrying out the plan of action determined by the first stage. If the claim is to be rejected, but is being actively pressed, the denial of liability should be communicated to the claimant as promptly as it is possible to do so. If it is a case to be accepted or compromised, this may be accomplished immediately after the termination of the first stage if the injuries are in the healing stage, or completely healed, and the amount of the special damages is known. In cases where the claimant is still under treatment and the outcome is unknown, the settlement may not be possible until a period of time has elapsed. During this time the investigator should keep the claimant under control and make the settlement at the earliest opportunity.

3. *The trial preparation stage.* Strictly speaking, this is not part of the investigation but it does involve the investigator's responsibility. It refers to cases which are not disposed of during the settlement stage, or cases which have been rejected and which the claimant seeks to litigate. The investigator will be guided in this phase by the instructions of the company attorney and will complete whatever further investigation is outlined by him. It might be noted in passing that the investigator should always have the possibility of litigation in his mind while completing the first two stages. There is no guarantee that all cases can be settled on a reasonable basis or that a claim once rejected will not be made the subject of later litigation. Therefore the investigator, in gathering the evidence, should acquire and preserve it in such form that it can be used as evidence in the event of trial.

1705   Plan of investigation

When an assignment is received, the investigator must determine the known facts from the accident report or other information submitted and decide what unknown facts are needed in order to decide the type of handling required. He must also decide the order in which the evidence will be obtained. It is clear that he cannot see all witnesses and gather all the evidence at one and the same time. Generally, the rule is that critical evidence should be secured as promptly as possible. Critical evidence is evidence which is available now but may not be available after the passage of time.

For example, if the point of impact in an automobile case is important, time will obliterate skid marks, gouges, and other marks in the roadway, and the damage to the cars will be repaired. Therefore, if pictures are needed to establish the existence of these things, they must be taken immediately, and evidence by witnesses, identifying the marks made by each car, must be secured before their memory of the details fades. The same thing would be true of a products case, or a case where there is a claim of an unsafe condition on the premises. The defective product should be secured as soon as possible and tests made, or the premises must be examined for defects and photographs taken of the place of accident under conditions as nearly similar to the circumstances of the accident as possible. In each instance, the passage of time will handicap the investigation, and may make the evidence unobtainable.

Another example of critical evidence is the statement of the adverse driver and the personal injury claimant. In the initial stages, it may be possible to get statements from all participants in the accident. After they have retained counsel, no direct contact can be made with them. Where there is more than one personal injury claimant, generally the most seriously injured should be seen first, and the others in order of the seriousness of their injuries.

Another factor which brings the injured party or parties within the realm of critical evidence is the fact that part of the investigation will refer to the injuries sustained, the treatment rendered, and the diagnosis made. Since doctors and hospitals are reluctant to release medical information without an authorization from the patient, medical authorizations can be obtained from the injured party at the time of the first contact. Later it may be too late, especially if the information is refused or the injured person is represented by counsel. Therefore, contact with the injured person will result in securing two things: his version of the accident and the subsequent medical treatment he received, and the authorization to obtain detailed medical information from the doctor and the hospital where the treatment was rendered.

Less critical but equally important is the evidence of other fact witnesses who saw the accident, or some part of it, but who are not interested in the result since they were not involved. Such witnesses should receive the same priority as that given to parties to the event. Secondary fact witnesses who can contribute to the delineation of the event are the police officer who investigated the case, the tow truck driver who towed the wrecked automobiles away, and the ambulance doctor and ambulance driver. All of these can testify to the scene of the accident when they arrived, the condition of the injured parties, the location of the cars when they came to rest, skid marks, gouges in the roadway, debris on the road, blood, glass, etc., and its relationship to the center line. These witnesses are given less priority than the others, but there is always the possibility of the opposing side getting its statements first. Therefore, while the gathering of critical evidence will occupy the investigator's initial efforts, it is important to contact these secondary witnesses as soon as possible after the happening of the accident.

The plan of investigation might include attendance at the coroner's inquest in death cases, attendance at traffic court hearings, or the securing of school reports, weather reports, the adverse driver's license (and record of whether the license required the wearing of glasses, and whether there have been any refusals, suspensions, or revocations of the license), as well as securing the official documents referring to the event, such as the police report, motor vehicle accident reports, and, if a public utility is involved, reports to the government authority. This latter would include reports to the public service commission by bus and trolley companies, and electric light and power companies, reports to the CAB by airlines, and reports to the hack bureau by taxicab companies.

The plan of investigation must include the area of inquiry. The investigator must decide which facets require inquiry and which elements can be conceded without more than cursory inquiry. He must also decide how far the inquiry will go in any given area. For example, in the ordinary automobile collision the inquiry would be limited to the events immediately preceding the accident, the accident itself, and whatever subsequent events have a bearing on the cause of the accident and the injuries sustained as a result thereof. If it develops that either the insured driver or the adverse driver has been accused of driving under the influence of intoxicants, then the inquiry will have to go further back than the events immediately preceding the accidents; it will have to trace the movements of the driver from the bar or place where he got his first drink right up to the time of the accident, ascertaining how much liquor was consumed and over what period of time. Thus the inquiry in one case would be limited to the accident and its surrounding circumstances, whereas in the second the inquiry must take in a larger area.

Hazardous products. In cases involving these products, a certain amount of investigation is required to determine the theory of defense, if there is one. In many of these cases, the public is exposed over a period of time and the first manifestation of a disease does not occur immediately but over a period of years. For example, asbestosis is an incurable lung condition which is caused by the inhalation of asbestos fibers over a period of years and the diagnosis is not made until the patient has been exposed for a long period of time. The result is fatal. The same thing is true with regard to the ingestion of some drugs. The results are not apparent until the drug has been taken over a long period of time.

In making an investigation, the areas of inquiry include: (1) coverage; (2) liability; and (3) possible additional defendants.

1. Coverage. The first inquiry must be directed to the insured's records to determine when the manufacture of the deleterious material began and when it was released to the general public or discharged into a waste disposal area. If the release began after the termination of the insurer's policy, there would be no coverage applicable. On the other hand, if the same insurer was on the risk during the period when the hazardous material was first released and still on the risk when the claims were made, the insurer's coverage would be involved. If the release produced effects which were unintended or unexpected, the transaction could be considered as an "occurrence" within the terms of the Standard Comprehensive General Liability policy (CGL), which is the type of coverage purchased by industries engaged in high-risk products. For example, in *Pepper Industries, Inc.* v. *Home Insurance Co.*, 134 Cal. Rptr. 904, the insured dumped 5,000 gallons of gasoline into the city's sewer system and an explosive resulted. The court held that this was an "occurrence" within the terms of the insurance coverage, regardless of the fact that the insured was aware of the risk of explosion which was involved.

A more difficult problem arises when there are one or more insurers on the risk during the period of exposure with another on the risk at the time of the first manifestation of injury or disease. The court then would have the problem of deciding which insurer was liable under its policy for the injury or damage. The courts have been struggling with this problem for quite some time. The decisions are not in agreement, some courts holding that the insurer on the risk at the first manifestation of the condition is liable, whereas others take the position that all insurers who were on the risk during the period of exposure are jointly liable. Thus, we have decisions based on the (a) "Manifestation Theory" or (b) "The Exposure Theory," as follows:

a. Manifestation Theory. This theory was first announced in a case involving the liability of the manufacturer of DES, which the plaintiff ingested. The court held that the insurer on the risk at the time that the cervical cancer was discovered was liable. The case is *American Motorists Insurance Co.* v. *E. R. Squibb & Sons, Inc.*, 406 N.Y.S. 2d 658. DES (diethylstilbestrol), a synthetic estrogen, was advertised as preventing miscarriages. In holding the insurer liable, the court pointed out that "coverage is predicated not on the act which might give rise to ultimate liability, but upon the result.'

See also *Michigan Chemical Corp* v. *Travelers Indemnity Co.*, 530 Fed. Supp. 147, in which the court held that the insurer on the risk at the time that the damage was discovered rather than at the time of delivery of the toxin, was liable. In a more recent case (1982), the court impliedly adopted the manifestation theory. See *Eagle-Pitcher Industries, Inc.* v. *Liberty Mutual Insurance Co.*, 523 Fed. Supp. 110, affirmed in 682 Fed. 2d 12 (1st Cir., Mass.). Here, the circuit court defined "manifestation" as being the time when the disease is manifest "when it becomes reasonably capable of medical diagnosis" rather than the date of the actual diagnosis. This case involved over 5,000 asbestos-related injuries.

It should be noted that in a number of Workers' Compensation Statutes, the occupational disease section provides that in such cases the date of disability is regarded as the "date of the accident" in determining the insurer who is liable.

b. The Exposure Theory. In determining the liability of the insurers of a particular risk, the courts have held that all insurers who were on the risk during the period of exposure were jointly liable. For example, in *Insurance Company of North America* v. *Forty-Eight Insulations, Inc.* (633 Fed. 2d 1212, affirmed on rehearing 657 Fed. 2d 814, certiorari denied in 454 U.S. 1109), involved the liability of the defendant from the manufacturer of products containing asbestos during the period from 1923 to 1970. During this period of time the defendant was insured by the following insurers: Insurance Company of North America (October 31, 1955 to October 31, 1972); Affiliated FM Insurance Co. (October 31, 1972 to January 10, 1975); Illinois National Insurance Co. (January 10, 1975 to January 12, 1976); Travelers Indemnity Co. (January 12, 1976 to November 8, 1976); and Liberty Mutual Insurance Co. (November 8, 1976 to the time of the lawsuit). The Michigan District Court adopted the exposure theory holding that all insurers were jointly liable. Since there was no evidence of insurance prior to 1955, the Forty-Eight was deemed to be a self-insurer.

The exposure theory was also advanced in *Porter* v. *American Optical Corp.* (641 Fed. 2d 1128, certiorari denied in 454 U.S. 1109). In that case suit was brought against the manufacturer of respiratory masks at an asbestos cement products plant. The court held that the principles applicable to the asbestos plant applied equally to the manufacturer of respiratory masks which were alleged to be defective. In *Keene Corp.* v. *Insurance Company of North America* (667 Fed. 2d 1034, certiorari denied in 455 U.S. 1007), the lower court held that the liability should be apportioned among those insurers on the risk at the time of exposure. The exposure theory was further advanced in the case of *Borel* v. *Fibreboard Paper Products Corp. et al.*, (493 Fed. 2d 1076). In that case the plaintiff brought suit against a number of manufacturers who had supplied insulation materials with which he worked for a period of some 33 years. He contracted asbestosis and mesothelioma as a result of his exposure. The manufacturers failed to warn him of the dangers of handling the material. The District Court (Eastern District of Texas) found in favor of the plaintiff against all defendants. This verdict was affirmed on appeal to the Circuit Court of Appeals (5th District). The U.S. Supreme Court refused certiorari.

It should be emphasized that the liability of the insuer is limited only to periods of exposure. If there was no exposure during a particular insurer's policy period, the insurer is entitled to disclaim and refuse coverage.

2. Liability. The investigation should include an inquiry as to the kind and nature of the product which is alleged to have been deleterious, either to human beings, animals, or the environment. The claimant must be able to allege the nature of the product, now the exposure was created as well as establishing that there was causal relationship between the alleged exposure and the subsequent medical condition. The investigation should be directed toward ascertaining these facts as well as the lack of them in a particular case.

In addition, the investigation should include the insurance history of the insured, the insurers involved, and the policy period in each case. Where the exposure theory is advanced, all insurers should be put on notice by the insured.

It should be emphasized that liability is imposed upon the manufacturer or creator of the dangerous substance because of the exposure to others which the process may make. If the process does not create any exposure, then there is no liability. For example, a manufacturer of pesticides sells the product to exterminators and the exterminator fails to follow the instructions for safe use as prepared by the manufacturer, then it would appear that the manufacturer is insulated from liability. The same thing would be true in the case of cleaning solutions, especially those containing benzol. The user must follow the manufacturer's instructions as to the safe use of the product.

3. Possible additional defendants. The investigation should also include others who may have contributed to the exposure, and while in some cases the manufacturer or creator of the hazard may be insulated from liability, there are situations where such additional defendants may be jointly liable. The prime example is the Love Canal situation where several defendants are involved. The history of Love Canal goes back almost 100 years. In 1892, William T. Love started to construct a canal between the upper and lower levels of the Niagara River in order to develop a means of creating hydroelectric power. The project was abandoned in the latter part of the 1890s, and there remained only a partially dug canal in the southeast corner of the city of Niagara Falls. There was no housing in the area and children used to travel to the site and use it as a swimming hole. In the 1920s the canal became a disposal site for many chemical companies, including the Hooker Chemical and Plastics Co. Subsequently, the land was sold to developers in the 1950s and the land was covered over with earth, houses were built, and a school opened. On August 2, 1978, the New York Health Commissioner declared that a health emergency existed in the Love Canal area, recommending that families with pregnant women near the canal temporarily move from the area as soon as possible, and that the residents avoid using their basements. Within months, the two elemenary schools were closed and the state agencies purchased hundreds of residential homes. Over 600 lawsuits were instituted against Hooker Chemical, the city of Niagara Falls, the Niagara Falls Board of Education and the county of Niagara. The insurers of the defendants disclaimed liability. However, in *Niagara County* v. *Utica Mutual Insurance Co.* (427 N.Y.S. 2d 171), the lower court held the pollution exclusion on which the insurer relied did not apply, holding in favor of the plaintiff. This decision was unanimously affirmed by the Appellate Division (439 N.Y.S. 2d 538). The court said:

The complaints in the underlying actions, besides charging the various defendants collectively with dumping and abandoning chemicals, waste products, etc., further allege that Niagara County was negligent in failing to warn and safeguard its citizens or enforce health regulations, failing to remove chemicals and the planitiffs from the Love Canal area and wrongfully conveying property in the area without notice of the infirmities contained and in violation of ordinances and regulations.

This situation illustrates that there can be more than one defendant involved in a particular incident. Therefore, the plan of investigation must include all possible defendants. The same type of inquiry should be made with respect to injuries. If the injured person was in normal health at the time of the accident, then the inquiry with respect to injuries would be limited to the period following the date of accident. However, if the claimant was suffering from some preexisting injury or disease, then the inquiry would have to develop the nature of the preexisting disability and whether such disability had any influence upon the injury sustained, and also, if the claimant was the adverse driver, whether or not that disability had any influence on the causation of the accident.

In creating the plan of investigation, due regard should be had for the theories of defense and the necessary legal elements needed to establish it. In gathering the evidence the investigator will determine the presence or absence of the facts necessary to make the defense available. He will also consider other and further defenses should the inquiry reveal that the elements are present. In a word, the plain of investigation should be flexible, contemplating the abandonment of certain theories of defense when inquiry shows they are untenable, and adopting other defenses if the inquiry indicates their existence.

A general plan of investigation, where the insurance coverage is in order, will consist of all or some of the following elements in this sequence:

1. Critical Evidence
   a) Statement of the adverse driver (if an auto case)
   b) Statement of the claimant (or claimants in the order of the severity of the injuries)
   c) Photograph of the scene of the accident, showing skid marks and other evidence of the accident
   d) Examination and photographs of the vehicles themselves showing the damage and point of impact
   e) The product itself or the instrumentality causing the injury
2. Fact Evidence
   a) Statements of disinterested witnesses
   b) Statement of the insured, his driver, or employee having knowledge of the accident, the instrumentality causing it, or the part of the premises in which the accident is alleged to have occurred

    c) Negative statements from persons who were in a position to have seen the accident or have some knowledge of its occurrence, but who deny having such knowledge

3. Official Reports
    a) Police report
    b) State motor vehicle reports filed by the parties to the accident
    c) Fire department reports
    d) Reports of state motor vehicle inspectors
    e) Traffic court proceedings
    f) Arraignment in magistrate's court
    g) Death certificates
    h) Autopsy reports
    i) Coroner's inquest transcript
    j) Birth and marriage certificates
    k) Weather reports
    l) School records
    m) Certified copies of court records showing prior convictions of crimes
    n) Hack bureau reports (if a taxicab is involved)
    o) C.A.B. reports (aircraft)
    p) I.C.C. reports (interstate truckers)
    q) Coast Guard reports (boats)

4. Unofficial Reports
    a) Newspaper accounts

5. Medical Reports
    a) Hospital records
    b) Attending physician's report and records
    c) Medical or hospital reports covering preexisting injury or disease

6. Documentary Evidence
    a) Deeds of ownership of land
    b) Leases
    c) Contracts and agreements, especially contracts for construction, alteration and repair, as well as hold harmless agreements

7. Visual Evidence
    a) Diagrams or sketches of the scene of accident
    b) Engineering plats
    c) X rays
    d) Photographs

8. Verification Evidence
    a) Employer's records to show wage loss
    b) Index bureau reports
    c) Workmen's compensation claims made by injured, arising out of the same accident

9. Expert Evidence
    a) Report of company medical examiner
    b) Automobile inspector or appraiser
    c) Engineer or chemist
    d) Actuaries
    e) Handwriting expert

In states requiring the renewal of operators' licenses on an annual basis, investigators have found it to be advantageous to obtain a photostat of the claimant's application for this license whether he was driving a car at the time of the accident or not. If he was the driver, the license might reveal that it was issued on a conditional basis, requiring that he wear glasses at all times when driving, or that it has been revoked or suspended. More importantly, however, most applications require an answer relative to the applicant's physical condition and whether or not there has been any change in it during the past year. The question usually reads "Have you suffered any physical or mental injury during the past 12 months?" If the application is made after the accident and it is claimed that there were severe physical injuries suffered, a negative answer on the application could be used in evidence to controvert such a claim.

1706   Witnesses

A witness is defined as a person who testifies as to what he has seen, heard, or otherwise observed. This definition includes the parties to the accident as well as others who have acquired some knowledge of the facts. The witness may testify to the facts which he has acquired through the use of one or more of his five senses. What the witness saw, heard, smelled, felt, or tasted can be the subject of testimony.

An expert witness is one who is skilled in some art, science, profession, or business, which skill or knowledge is not common to his fellowmen and which has come to such person by reason of special study and experience in such art, science, profession, or business. Such witnesses may testify to opinions or conclusions drawn from the facts presented because their special training qualifies them to do so. For example, a physician may testify to his opinion as to whether or not a certain injury or disease was caused by a certain accident (causal relation). He may also testify as to what, in his opinion, the future course of the injury or disease will be (prognosis). He may testify to what X-ray studies reveal and what diagnosis can be drawn from a physical examination using X-ray and other diagnostic tests. An ordinary witness is confined in his testimony to the facts within his knowledge and usually may not testify to his opinion, judgment, or conclusion except within a very limited area. He may be allowed to express his opinion as to

1. The speed of moving objects.
2. His own intention of doing or omitting to do an act.
3. The excited or emotional state of another person.
4. The drunk or sober condition of another person.
5. The value of objects or services with which he is familiar (value of parts and services by garageman).
6. Identity of a person by his appearance or voice (telephone conversations, for example), provided that he is familiar with the appearance or voice of the person.

7. Handwriting, provided that he is familiar with the person's handwriting.
8. Color of an object, provided that he has the facility of sight and is not color-blind.
9. Character and reputation of another person, providing that the witness is familiar with both by actual knowledge and experience.

The last item may require some clarification. Let us assume that a person is employed to operate a derrick. His incompetence to do so may be established by testimony as to his lack of skill (character), his reputation as a "killer" among the employees working on the job, and as to specific instances of where his lack of competence caused other accidents.

1707 Classification of witnesses

Witnesses may be classified generally as friendly or unfriendly. A friendly witness is one who cooperates and gives assistance to the investigator, whereas an unfriendly witness is one who does not. The friendly witness may not necessarily support the defense, but he is one who makes his evidence accessible to the investigator and freely cooperates in giving all the information which he has. He may be a close friend of the insured, but he may feel compelled to testify to a version of the accident which is directly opposed to the interests of the insured. Therefore, while he is a friendly witness in the sense that his attitude is cooperative, he is an adverse witness and his testimony may be used as evidence by the opposing side.

The unfriendly witness may acquire his noncooperative attitude because of his reluctance to "get mixed up" in the case or aversion to testifying in court. His version of the accident may be favorable to the insured. In that sense he would be classified as an unfriendly but supporting witness. On the other hand, the claimant may be a friendly witness by exhibiting a cooperative spirit, but his interests are adverse to those of the insured, and he will usually give a version of the occurrence which is unfavorable to the insured and favorable to himself.

A hostile witness is more than unfriendly and adverse. He is one who exhibits definite bias or prejudice against the insured, which has no basis in fact. His motivation may be an aversion to certain races, nationalities, occupations, or positions of affluence. He may be opposed to all persons who own and drive automobiles because he does not own or drive one himself, or he may be opposed to all persons of wealth because he has never been able to acquire any wealth himself. Whatever the motivation, the hostile witness is of little benefit to either side. It is important for the investigator to recognize his hostility and, if possible, tie him down to a statement which will clearly indicate his hostility.

Therefore, as to attitude, we can classify witnesses as friendly or unfriendly, as to subject matter as adverse or supporting, and those exhibiting bias or prejudice as hostile. Witnesses may also be classified as to information which consists of (1) preaccident details, (2) accident details, or (3) postaccident details.

1. *Preaccident details.*   Where there is a question as to a party's physical condition or sobriety immediately preceding the accident, the testimony of a physician as to the man's physical condition or the testimony of witnesses who saw the man drinking at a bar for a long period of time immediately prior to the accident will supply preaccident details. The same thing would be true of a witness who can testify that a matter of seconds before the accident happened the claimant passed him at a high rate of speed, or that the claimant was driving in such an erratic manner that the car was weaving from side to side and just avoided hitting several other cars before the accident occurred.

2. *Accident details.*   The witness may have seen the entire accident, or only part of it. He may have been a pedestrian waiting to cross the street, paying attention to traffic, and he may have seen two cars collide; or he may have been following a man down the stairs and have seen him slip and fall down the entire stairway. On the other hand, he may have been attracted to look at the scene of an accident by the noise of the impact and have seen one car turning over or skidding to a stop; or he may have seen a man falling down the stairs. In the last two cases, the witness could not testify as to causation or the details of the negligent act, if any, which contributed to the happening of the accident.

3. *Postaccident details.*   When an ambulance is called, attendants, doctor, or driver, may be able to testify as to the positions of the cars and the injured persons as well as to admissions against interest which may have been made by any of the parties. The driver of a wrecker called to tow away the damaged vehicles might be able to supply information as to the location of the cars after the accident and their condition with respect to brakes, lights, horn, and tires. He could also testify with respect to admissions against interest made by either driver or other party to the accident. While witnesses of this kind cannot supply information as to the actual event, their evidence will contribute to the jury's understanding of the accident.

Witnesses are also classified as to their interest or relationship to the event. A party to the accident is interested in the outcome of litigation arising from the event. His wife or relatives are likewise interested in the outcome if only for the reason that they would like to see their relative recover, and for that reason they are more sympathetic to his side of the case. The same thing is true as to the passengers; they may feel a compulsion to help him in his suit. However, if they have been injured they have their own interests to consider. In any event, all of these witnesses are interested witnesses, who have an interest, either close or remote, in the outcome of the litigation.

Disinterested witnesses are those who have no interest in either party and no interest in the outcome of the litigation, who merely testify to the facts as they know them. Juries are more likely to rely on the evidence given by disinterested witnesses since there is no compelling reason why they should falsify any facts—and for the further reason that they do not stand to lose or gain by the outcome of the case. Therefore, juries are persuaded to believe that their testimony is honest and not motivated by any considerations of self-interest. The best type of evidence that an investigator can locate is the disinterested witness who will support his side of the case.

1708 Finding the witness

Before the evidence of a witness is available he must be identified and located. The insurance investigator begins with the report of the insured, who is an interested witness, and the name of the claimant, who is likewise an interested witness. In some cases, the insured has been able to supply the names of other witnesses, who may be his friends, or of disinterested people he had the presence of mind to identify. In many cases, however, the investigator will have to use his own devices for the identification and location of witnesses other than the parties to the claim.

There are several sources available to locate or identify disinterested witnesses. The police report (blotter) may contain the names and addresses of witnesses. The newspaper account may give some names, or the reporter who wrote the account may have interviewed some witnesses at the scene. In automobile cases, the tow truck operator, who is usually located near the scene of the accident, may have some names of witnesses. The motor vehicle report filed by the adverse party may also contain the names of witnesses.

Lastly, but not least important, is the neighborhood canvass. In this quest for witnesses, the investigator will call at all the homes or apartment houses in the vicinity of the accident and ask each person in each house whether or not he saw the accident. This is a painstaking and painfully slow process, but it has been known to produce remarkable results. Another use of this method requires that the investigator be at the scene of the accident at exactly the same time the accident occurred. He may then question people on the street, especially tradesmen, milkmen, postmen, meters readers, and salesmen, as to whether or not they saw the accident or know anyone who did. Often the occurrence of an accident, especially a serious one, precipitates considerable neighborhood discussion, and while the person the investigator meets may not have seen the accident, if he lives in the neighborhood the chances are that he knows someone who did. Tradesmen, such as store owners, are usually the best source of this type of information.

The sooner the neighborhood canvass is undertaken the better. As a rule, people are more willing to talk about an accident for a short time after it occurs. When they have repeated the story innumerable times they become tired of it and are less willing to discuss it. Also, memories fade with the passage of time, and while the storekeeper may for a short time remember who saw the accident, he is likely to put it out of his mind, and an inquiry long after the accident will not be productive. Likewise, the witness himself, if located, will not have the fresh recollection he once had of all of the details.

1709 Interviewing the witness

Any consideration of this problem must begin with the concept that the witness is under no legal compulsion to grant an interview, discuss the case, or give a statement. When a lawsuit is brought, the witness may be compelled to testify and give evidence, but prior to suit there are no legal means available to the investigator to force the witness to even discuss the case and his relation to it. This applies to all witnesses, interested or disinterested, the claimant and even the insured. In the latter case, the refusal of the insured to make a statement at the request of his insurance carrier will constitute a policy violation which will relieve the insurance carrier of its obligations under the contract, but nevertheless the insured, at his peril, may assert his right to refuse an interview.

The claimant as a rule invites the interview with the investigator on the theory that the interview will result in some kind of a settlement, and in any case the claimant is anxious to find out exactly what position the insurance carrier will maintain in reference to his claim. Interested witnesses of other types who desire to aid one party or the other will usually welcome the opportunity to assist the cause of the party in which they have an interest. As to disinterested witnesses, there is no method of forecasting what their attitudes might be, and the chances are about even that the witness may be unfriendly and uncooperative, or friendly and cooperative. The chances of finding the witness to be cooperative are better if the investigator seeks the interview early in the case or as soon after the accident as possible. Witnesses invariably are willing to talk about an event which just happened, and are likely to become annoyed when someone calls on them to discuss something which happened months ago. In addition, the investigator might be confronted with a situation where the witness states that he has already given one statement to the other side and is unwilling to go through the same thing again. While most witnesses are honest, psychologically they are more likely to support the cause of the party who interviews them first than the cause of the second party. Therefore, the sooner a witness is interviewed, the greater are the chances of a successful result.

Since the interview is for the purpose of obtaining information, the investigator should plan in advance the exact information which he expects to obtain. While he will not know what information the witness may have, he will consider the possible theories of defense, the elements needed to establish them, and the information he has already received from others. He will then evolve the plan of the interview, certain that he has considered all the elements which must be discussed. Reinterviews are mostly unsatisfactory, and therefore the investigator should proceed as if the present interview is the only one he will be able to get. The plan must exhaust all the information the witness has. This is especially necessary when the witness is the claimant. He may be represented by counsel when the investigator calls on him the next time, in which case no further statement can be obtained.

Properly timing the interview can sometimes be as important as the interview itself. The witness should not be interviewed when he is emotionally upset, fatigued, or ill. Likewise, the investigator should not insist upon conducting the interview when the witness has company or household tasks which require his entire attention. The investigator should arrange to return at a more convenient time, when the witness can devote his entire time and attention to the interview. Aside from the discourtesy involved, the investigator will not conduct a successful interview if it is held under adverse circumstances—if the witness is the mother of four small children and, at the time of the call, has her hands full feeding the children. It is clear that her attention will be focused on the task of feeding the children, and it necessarily follows that an interview under those circumstances will not be productive. Therefore, the investigator should bow out and arrange to come back when the children are asleep or the mother is not occupied in attending to them.

There are two schools of thought as to whether or not an appointment should be made. The first school holds that no advance appointment should be made; the witness should be taken by surprise. Thus the witness has no opportunity for reflection and fabrication, and the interview is more likely to produce the true facts. The other school feels that since the interview should be conducted at the convenience of the witness the courteous thing to do would be to make an appointment whenever it is possible to do so. This has the advantage of saving the investigator's time as well as creating an impression of fair and courteous dealing.

It has been the writer's experience that there is more to be gained by following the second procedure and making appointments for interviews. If the witness is going to tell a fabricated story, he will do so whether an appointment is made or not. It is therefore submitted that the most successful results will be obtained when the interview is conducted at the convenience of the witness and by an advance appointment, if this is at all possible.

Some witnesses can be interviewed at their place of business, others cannot. It depends upon the nature of the business, the position of the witness, and whether he can devote any time to a personal matter during business hours. It is best to inquire before calling at the place of business. When in doubt, see the witness at his home.

The interview itself will break down into four general phases: (1) Introduction and identification, (2) Discussion, (3) Summarization, and (4) Termination.

Introduction and identification. The interview should begin by the investigator introducing himself, stating the person or persons he represents, and giving a brief statement of the purpose of his visit and why he feels the witness can be of assistance. He can comment on the weather, some current event, or some hobby that he can see that the witness has, and other matters of a general nature. This is calculated to put the witness at ease and is, in reality, a "get acquainted" phase. The investigator should avoid any and all controversial issues, especially religion and politics.

If he is asked if he represents an insurance company, he should freely admit that he does, but that he is investigating the case for and in behalf of the insured. He should not interview the witness under a pretext that he is representing the other side; that he is a police officer, a post office inspector, or an agent of the F.B.I. or the Secret Service. Not only is such action morally wrong, but such impersonation is a crime punishable by fine or imprisonment. In addition, if the statement of the witness is of any value, he will be needed to testify if the case comes to trial. The investigator will experience extreme difficulty gaining the confidence and cooperation of a witness who has been interviewed under a subterfuge.

Discussion.   As soon as the witness is at ease, the investigator will begin a discussion of the event. Just when to break off the introduction and begin the discussion will depend upon the circumstances. When interviewing a witness at his place of business, it is essential the discussion take place as soon as possible so that the introduction phase will be comparatively short. In another case, the witness may be a farmer who insists that the investigator see his farm or his new equipment. In that case the introduction phase will be extended. In any case, the investigator will exercise his judgment as to when the discussion of the case is to begin.

In discussing what the witness saw, the investigator will ask some questions merely to give the discussion some direction and purpose. He will not argue with the conclusions expressed nor will he attempt to persuade the witness to change his version of the accident. The investigator is somewhat like a newspaper reporter in the sense that he is there to get the story of the witness and not to change it. An attempt to persuade a witness to testify falsely, whether for a consideration or not, is a criminal act and is punishable. The investigator therefore should avoid making any suggestions as to how the accident happened but should merely get the facts from the witness as he (the witness) believes them to be. The investigator can be sure that the witness will probably tell the same story should he be called upon to testify, and for that reason he should take into consideration not only the favorable facts but also the facts which are damaging. A fair appraisal of the witness' evidence must include both.

During the discussion, the investigator will bring out his pad and pen so that some of the facts can be noted and a rough sketch made of the scene of the accident. This is especially helpful in automobile cases since the witness will be able to describe what he saw with reference to the diagram. If the witness can and will draw the diagram himself, so much the better. When the interview is over, the investigator will have him either initial or sign the sketch which he made.

Summarization.   After the investigator has the story in outline and has covered all the points, he will proceed to summarize the witness' version by compiling a statement. This will be given to the witness to read and he will be asked to make any corrections or additions which may be appropriate.

Termination.   If the witness is not the insured or the claimant, then after the statement is signed, the investigator will leave as soon as possible without imposing on the witness' time any further. Should the witness ask for a copy of the statement he signed, the investigator should give him one but should ask the witness to acknowledge that he received a copy of the statement by adding to the original statement a sentence acknowledging the copy and signing it. If the witness is the claimant, the investigator should also obtain signed forms authorizing him to obtain medical and hospital records. In some areas, the doctors and the hospitals will accept photostatic copies of the medical authorization, in which case one copy from the claimant will be sufficient. In other areas, both the doctors and the hospitals demand originals, in which case the investigator must be careful to obtain a sufficient number of signed copies to meet the demand. It is important to bear in mind that this may be the only opportunity that the investigator has to obtain the medical authorizations. The claimant may be represented by counsel at the time of the next call and, although counsel will eventually supply the medical authorizations, it will save considerable time and trouble if the investigator will obtain them at the time of the first interview.

Group interviews should be avoided. The investigator will obtain the best results by interviewing witnesses one at a time, either alone or with not more than two other persons present. Where two witnesses are involved it is better to interview them separately rather than in the presence of each other. The investigator should desire the exact story of the witness and not one which is influenced by what some other witness says he saw at the same time.

1710   The signed statement

The purpose of the signed statement is to preserve the evidence. It is the record of the story told by the witness and signed by him to attest to its authenticity. It can be used by the witness before trial in order to refresh his recollection of the past event. Should he testify to a different version, the statement can be used to discredit him.

Some witnesses shy away from the word "statement" since it seems to have some legal import. Some investigators find it is more satisfactory to refer to it as a "report" and to avoid the word "statement" entirely. The legal effect is the same whether the document is referred to as a statement, report, or an account.

The statement should be reflective of the witness and the language used should be near to his ordinary language. The investigator should not attempt to translate what a witness says into good English when the witness habitually uses bad grammar. It should be borne in mind that at some future time the statement may be offered in evidence in a court proceeding and the jury might find it hard to believe that a witness whose exposure to literature is confined to comic books could make a statement in the language of a business executive. If the statement contains language similar to that which the witness has used when testifying, it will be more believable. Let us consider two examples of a statement taken from a maintenance worker on the night shift of a factory. The first example is:

John Smith and myself are permitted, beginning at 11:30 P.M. and ending at 11:45 P.M. to go outside of the factory for the purpose of having a smoke. This is in the nature of a break in our routine and is a privilege afforded to us for the reason that due to the fire regulations, we are forbidden to smoke within the confines of the building. While we were thus engaged, we saw a black Buick sedan come down the hill in front of the factory at an extremely high rate of speed and crash into a parked Ford on the north side of the highway. The Ford was unoccupied.

The second example is:

Me and Jack were having a smoke. We ain't allowed to smoke in the factory so we take a smoke outside by the road. We seen a black Buick come down the hill like a bat outta hell and smash into a Ford parked on the other side of the street. There weren't nobody in the Ford.

The second example is more reflective of the witness, and even though the English is poor and the grammar bad, a jury would be more inclined to believe that a maintenance worker made the second statement rather than the first.

It is always best to have the witness estimate speed and distance. In the two examples above, the writer purposely made the same mistake in each. In the first, it was said that the Buick came down the hill "at an extremely high rate of speed" and in the second "like a bat outta hell." Neither of these statements tells us what the witness means as to the actual speed, whether or not it was in excess of the speed limit or excessive under the driving conditions. It would have been better to say that the car was being driven at a high rate of speed, approximately 75 miles per hour in a 50-mile zone, and to state how the witness could estimate the speed, either because he has driven many years himself, worked as a traffic officer, or the like. Distance likewise should have been covered. How far from the point of impact were the witnesses? How far from the crest of the hill was the Ford parked? For what distance did the driver have an unobstructed view of the road ahead? The distance should be estimated in feet, and terms like "near," "short distance," or "long distance" should be avoided.

The statement must be taken in ink or indelible pencil, or be typewritten. It should be done all in one paragraph so that there are no blank spaces— permitting a later claim that words or sentences were added. Likewise, there should be no blank lines, each page should be initialed at the bottom by the witness, and his signature should appear at the end. If corrections are made the witness should place his initials next to the correction so that there will be no question but that he was aware of and approved the corrections. As a matter of fact, some investigators purposely make mistakes in the statement so as to make corrections with the witness' approval and initial. Then if the witness should deny that he gave a statement, say that the statement is not a true account of what he told the investigator, or that he did not read it but merely signed it, the corrections made at his request will belie such testimony.

It is also good practice to continue a sentence from one page to another, since this is further evidence of the fact that no pages have been substituted for the original. Legal language is to be avoided and the investigator should not use such terms as tort-feasor, tort, negligence, or contributory negligence.

While some witnesses may know what they mean, the jury often does not. Therefore, the use of such terminology detracts rather than adds to the believableness of the statement. A simple statement in ordinary language which describes exactly what happened and how it happened is the best form to follow.

The signature of the witness is placed at the end of the statement, and there should be no blank spaces between the last written words and the signature. The best method of securing the signature is to have the witness write: "I have read the above and it is true," followed by his signature. If the statement consists of more than one page (and most of them do), the witness should place his initials or his signature at the bottom of each page, and on the last page the language above may be used, or "I have read the above four-page report and it is true." If these methods are not practical because the witness does not write well or is reluctant to write any more than his name, the following form can be used:

Have you read the above four-page report?   _____
Is it true and correct?   _____

Signature

The witness can answer the questions in the affirmative in the space provided and sign his name beneath. The first question should be on the line immediately below the last line of the statement and there should be no blank lines between the questions, or between the questions and the signature.

If it should be necessary to use the statement during the trial for the purpose of showing the witness has testified to something contrary to the statement, witnesses frequently will try to avoid the statement by saying they signed the paper but did not know what it was, or that they merely wrote their names at the end because the investigator told them to do so, or that they did not read the statement but answered the questions "yes" because they were told it was necessary. Therefore the first method, having the witness write the sentence that he has read the report and it is true, is the best method, and the second method, although used in cases where the first method cannot be used, is definitely inferior and affords the witness an opportunity to deny that the statement is his own.

The signature of the witness should be witnessed by someone who was present at the time the signature was made. The person witnessing the signature does not have to know what is in the statement, and his witnessing the signature is merely evidence of the fact that he saw the document signed and nothing more. If no one else is available the investigator can witness the signature even though, in the case of a dispute as to whether or not the statement was actually signed, the investigator is a less-desirable witness than someone who is not an interested party. Where the statement is witnessed by a member of the family or a friend, it is best to have him include his home address, if other than that of the person giving the statement, so that he can be located when the case comes to trial.

At the top of the first page of the statement the investigator should note the date, time, and place the statement was taken. Since the investigator will take many statements in the course of his work, he will not have an independent recollection as to where and when he took a particular statement. The inclusion of the time, place, date, and circumstances will jog his memory and he will be able to testify, if necessary, exactly when, where, and under what circumstances the statement was taken.

1711   Statements: Form and substance

The statement should be the story of the event as told by the witness. It should, as in a newspaper account, answer the questions of who, what, when, where, and why, and it should proceed, in natural sequence, with the steps leading up to the happening of the event. It should first identify the informant, the place where the event took place, how the witness came to be there, what the witness saw happen, the talk the witness heard at the time of or immediately after the event, the observations made by the witness of the scene of the accident, and the injuries. So that the statement will have the required continuity, it can be divided into five main divisions: (1) identification, (2) foundation, (3) accident, (4) injuries, and (5) additional facts or additional witnesses. In applying these divisions to the statement, we will consider how they are to be used in connection with automobile, general liability, and workmen's compensation claims.

Automobile

1. *Identification.* The beginning of the statement should identify the witness as to name, address and occupation. If the witness is disinterested, the investigator will probably need to locate him if the case comes to trial. Therefore, it is best to get as much information as possible so as to be able to locate him when the time arrives; names and addresses of close relatives and his employer, as well as the names of clubs or fraternal organizations to which he belongs. If the witness is an injured party, in addition to the name and address of his employer the statement should contain an expression of his income, how long he has worked for the employer, whether the employment is steady or seasonal, piece or time work, and so on. The statement might read as follows:

My name is John T. Jones and I am 25 years of age, residing at 42 John Street, Brooklyn, N.Y. (Telephone 676–7328) with my wife, Mary, and my two minor children, Joan, aged 6, and John, Jr., aged 3. My nearest relative is my sister, Dorothey Jones Maguire, who lives at 55 Fargo Street, Jersey City, N.J. I am employed by the Brooklyn Edison Company at their plant at 234 Flatbush Avenue, Brooklyn, N.Y., as an electrician's helper. My foreman's name is Pete Smith.

Many other matters of identification could be included, such as social security number and driver's or chauffeur's license. If the witness was the driver involved in an automobile accident, his driver's license number, whether or not it was revoked or suspended at the time of the accident or any prior time, should be included. If the statement is taken while the witness is in a hospital, a sentence to the effect that he is not under opiates or narcotics should be included. This can be substantiated by a short report from the nurse on duty or the attending physician.

2. *Foundation.*   Before going into the happening of the accident the statement should describe the surrounding conditions, the site of the event, date, time of day, weather, etc. In an automobile case the foundation might read as follows:

U.S. Highway #1 runs in a general northerly and southerly direction, and is approximately 44 feet wide, or four lanes of traffic. It is of concrete construction and there is a painted yellow center line. State Road 119 intersects Highway #1 at right angles and is approximately 18 feet in width. It is of blacktop construction and the traffic lines are separated by a painted white line.

On October 20th, 1963, at about 5:00 P.M. I was driving my 1959 Ford sedan in a southerly direction on U.S. Highway #1 at about 50 m.p.h. The weather was clear and the road was dry. It was about dusk and I had my headlights on low beam. Riding with me at the time was James Smith, who was sitting in the right front seat and in the rear seat was Joe Green and Pete Brown.

At this point the statement should cover where the witness had been previously and why he was on the road: returning from work, from a party or tavern, or just out for a ride, as the case may be. If there was any drinking, the statement should cover the movements of the witness from the time he started drinking up to the time of the accident, showing just how many drinks were consumed and over what period of time. Also at this point other pertinent information such as permissive use, agency, ownership of the vehicle, etc., should be inserted if applicable. If the weather was rainy or snowy, then reference to the operation of the windshield wipers (whether or not they were working) and any impairment to visibility should be noted.

3. *Accident.*   After conditions and surrounding circumstances, the statement should cover the happening of the accident. In an automobile case, this would include the travel prior to impact, the impact, and where both vehicles came to rest. For example:

While so driving my car in the west lane of U.S. Highway #1 and while approximately 300 feet north of the intersection of State Road 119, I saw for the first time a 1958 Chevrolet being driven in an easterly direction about 200 feet west of the center of the intersection and travelling at about 35 m.p.h. I took my foot off the gas and assumed that the other car would stop for the stop sign.

The narrative should follow from this point of first observation toward the point of impact. Such details as the sounding of the horn, application of brakes, and any deviation from the path of travel by either vehicle should be covered. The narrative should continue to trace the paths of travel of both vehicles to the point of impact, which would be the point on the street where the vehicles first came in contact with each other, and also describe the point of contact with respect to the parts of the vehicles which came in contact with each other. For example:

The left front fender of the Chevrolet struck the right front door of my automobile at a point about 9 feet east of the west edge of U.S. Highway #1 and approximately 12 feet to the south of the center line of State Road 119.

It is extremely important in many cases to fix the exact point of impact since the issue of negligence may turn on the place of impact with relation to the position of the cars on the road. Therefore, locating the exact point by the use of two intersecting axes, as in the example above, will pinpoint the exact spot where the impact took place. Such directions as the "center of the intersection" or "near the west shoulder of the road" should be avoided since they do not convey any idea of exactly where the point of impact was. It should again be emphasized that the statement may be used as evidence at the trial of the case, and it is the task of the investigator to tie up the details in such a way as to make them understandable to others and not subject to variation by the witness should he be called upon to testify.

The next point to be covered in the accident description is where the vehicles came to rest. The failure to trace the paths of the vehicles from the point of impact to the points of rest has lost many a lawsuit. The paths should be shown by describing the direction the car was facing with a two-directional orientation of one of the wheels of the vehicle. For example:

My Ford came to rest facing in a general southeasterly direction with the right rear wheel at the east edge of the pavement and approximately 75 feet south of the center line of State Road 119. The Chevrolet came to rest facing south with both left wheels on about the center line of U.S. Highway #1 and the rear end of the automobile approximately 30 feet south of the center line of State Road 119.

Skid marks left by either of the vehicles should be described and should be located by direction of travel, length, origin, and termination of the skid.

If anything was said by any of the parties involved it should be recorded in the statement. The accurate relating of the first words spoken by any such party is admissible in evidence as an exception to the hearsay rule on the theory that since they are said spontaneously and under the stress of the accident, there is no possibility of reflection and fabrication. Therefore they are part of the *res gestae* and descriptive of the facts of the accident.

4. *Injuries.*   Where the witness is not the injured person it will be helpful to secure a layman's description of the injuries, including any bleeding and other outward manifestations of injury which can be observed by the average person. If the witness heard the injured person make any complaints regarding his injuries, these remarks should be noted. In addition, there should be some information as to whether or not the injured person received treatment

at the scene, how he left the scene (whether by ambulance, private car, or other means), together with information as to whether he was able to walk or required assistance.

Where the claimant is the witness whose statement is taken, a clear description of his injuries, in his own words, is essential. It should accurately locate and describe the type of injuries sustained and should state that there were no other injuries except those described. This latter becomes very important if the claimant later asserts a claim for other and further injuries, which he will say he forgot to mention because the statement-taker failed to inquire about them. Whenever possible the statement should eliminate injury to the head, neck, and back by negative statements of fact. Where head injuries are involved the statement should, if possible, rule out the matter of unconsciousness by a sentence that the claimant did not at any time lose consciousness, or that he was dazed only for a matter of seconds. It should also negative the clinical signs of skull fracture by a sentence that there was no bleeding from the nose, mouth, and ears.

The claimant's statement should also cover all prior injuries and conditions which have any bearing whatsoever on the accident. Prior accidents should be covered and a statement as to the injuries sustained in each included. If the claimant is suffering from or under treatment for any disease, such as diabetes or tuberculosis, the statement should indicate that fact, together with information as to whether or not the claimant was under treatment at the time of the accident and, if so, the name and address of the physician rendering the treatment.

The topic of injuries should also include information as to the treatment received up to the date of the statement, such as where and when first aid was given and by whom, and what treatment has been received since that time, whether given by a hospital, physician, nurse, or whether consisting simply of home remedies. It should include whether or not the claimant was confined to bed and for what period of time and, if the claimant is still disabled, some information as to his activities should be covered: whether he merely sat in the sun, went swimming, golfing, bowling, etc. These bits of information may prove important later.

When taking a statement regarding the injuries, whether from the claimant or any other witness, those occupying both vehicles who were not injured, or showed no outward signs of being injured, or said that they were not injured, should be noted.

5. *Additional facts or additional witnesses.* Very often the investigator will find that additional facts not covered in the foundation play a material part in the fixing of responsibility. Therefore, he should include at this point such additional facts as may be required: the width and construction of the shoulders of the highway, traffic warning signs, traffic control signs, and traffic controls, as well as a description of all buildings or foliage on the sides of the road which might constitute an obstruction to the view of either driver.

If the witness knows the names of others who were at the scene of the accident, the names and addresses should be noted, whether or not the witness knows they saw the accident. The mere fact that they were observed at the scene of the accident is indicative that they may have some knowledge of it, even if only an observation as to the position of the cars after the accident occurred. Having the names and addresses will open up other and further avenues of investigation which may be explored.

General Liability

The same format is used in taking statements on general liability claims, such as the usual slip and fall cases, either on sidewalks, premises, or buildings open to the public. The identification paragraph is the same as that used in the automobile claim, and the same as the paragraph relating to injuries. The other sections of the statement will differ from the automobile statement, and we will consider those paragraphs in which there are differences.

Foundation. This should cover the claimant's (or witness') entrance to the premises, why he (or she) was there, the weather (if a factor), and where the person was going. For example:

On October 28th, 1963, at about 11:00 A.M., I entered the north entrance of the store operated by R. H. Gimbel & Co. where I intended to purchase some housewares on the second floor. It was raining at the time and there was water on the floor that had been tracked in by many customers. I was wearing low-heeled shoes with leather soles and heels.

This description establishes the claimant's status as a business invitee and sets forth the time and the circumstances under which she entered the premises.

From this point, the investigator should trace the claimant's travel to the point of the accident. For example:

I proceeded to walk in a generally southerly direction down the main aisle to the ascending escalator.

The statement should show the claimant's itinerary for the day, where she had been, where she intended to go, whether or not she was carrying packages, whether or not she was in a hurry or under any emotional stress due to later appointments. A person under a special stress of circumstances generally is more accident-prone.

Accident. A complete description of the accident, how it happened, what caused it, and who came to the claimant's assistance, should follow:

When I was two feet north of the entrance to the ascending escalator, my attention was attracted to a display of women's wear. I remember placing my right hand on the right moving rail and I think I attempted to enter the escalator by putting my left foot on the moving tread. My left foot was suddenly jerked from under me and I fell in a sitting position on the moving treads.

At this point the claimant should describe the place of accident. Invariably, the investigator will find that the claimant's observation of the surroundings is not good even though he or she has visited the premises numerous times. The person usually will not recall essential facts about the area. This point should therefore be incorporated in the statement:

I don't remember if the floor was of wood or tile construction. I don't remember if the treads were covered by rubber or metal although I have been a customer at Gimbel's for many years.

The next item to be covered is an accurate description of the thing or things the witness claims caused the accident. The description should be the witness' own words concerning the walk, road, flooring, steps, elevator, or ramp, together with their condition. Lighting conditions, including the location of the lights and their effectiveness, as well as the condition of the handrails, rubber mats, or the amount of wax or oil on linoleum, wood, or tile flooring, should also be covered. Any signs or warning devices should be noted. With regard to ramps or steps, the level or grade, height of risers, and width and kind of tread are necessary facts. A description of any defects in these objects, or foreign substances thereon, which it is claimed caused or contributed to the accident, should be noted.

The next point is the matter of assistance. Usually the first person to assist the injured after the accident is an eyewitness to its occurrence. The investigator should get the names of all persons who in any way assisted the injured person, and these persons should be interviewed and their statements taken as to the occurrence and what was said. Every effort should be made to ascertain from the claimant and the witnesses the exact words spoken by the claimant after the accident.

Spontaneous utterances (*res gestae*) are admissible in evidence if made so near in point of time to the accident to be explanatory of it. A mere narrative of past events is not so admissible. The usual explanation of a person under such embarrassing circumstances as a fall in a public place makes it clear that he was contributorily negligent in not looking where he was going, ignoring warning signs, or momentarily forgetting that he was at the head of a stairway or a similar dangerous place. The words spoken might also be indicative of the presence of some systemic disease which caused vertigo, a fainting spell, or some other similar condition.

Additional facts. The place of the accident must be established with certainty in the claimant's statement. If it occurred outside a private dwelling, the statement should pinpoint whether the fall took place on the premises, such as on the private driveway or walk, or on the public sidewalk. If it is a multiple dwelling, information should be obtained which will place the accident either on the premises, sidewalk, or common stairway (under the control of the landlord), or in the tenant's apartment, or on the public street or sidewalk. If it occurred in a store, the status of the injured should be established by indicating exactly why he or she was in the store—either as an invitee, licensee, or trespasser—and it is likewise important to show exactly where and in what department the accident occurred. Very often it will be found that portions of the store are leased to others, that the store owner retains control only of main aisles and passageways, elevators, and stairways, and that the lessee has control of a specified area. Therefore the question of responsibility will turn on who has control of the premises where the accident occurred and who was responsible for the maintenance. In statements from the owner or lessee, the statement should cover the control of the area and should include by reference the terms of the lease, hold harmless agreements, and any other written documents referring to the duty of maintenance and repair of the site of the accident.

In all cases where the claimant's statement is taken an inquiry should be made and recorded as to whether or not the claimant was in the course of employment when the accident occurred. If the claimant was on an errand for his employer or driving an automobile in connection with his work, then the inquiry should cover whether or not a compensation claim has been made or contemplated, whether or not any compensation has been paid and accepted (if so, how much), and the name of the insurance company which made the payment. Clearly, where the claimant is a housewife who is not employed or a claimant who is unemployed, this inquiry is unnecessary.

WORKMEN'S COMPENSATION

In workmen's compensation cases the measure of the employer's responsibility is governed by the workmen's compensation law, and the test of liability is not negligence but whether or not the accident arose out of and in the course of employment. In spite of this difference, statements taken from the injured claimant, eyewitnesses, or witnesses to any material fact follow the same format as other statements, with additional information being sought as to items peculiar to workmen's compensation. The statement from an injured claimant should cover the following information.

Identification. This paragraph will be the same as in other statements from an injured claimant in that it will give his name, age, address, and the names of his wife and children (if any) with the ages of the children. In states where the number of dependents is a factor in determining the compensation rate, or where the injury is so serious that there is a possibility of a fatality, it will be necessary to expand this phase of the statement to include his own past marital history and that of his wife. In the ordinary case, the marriage under consideration was the first marriage for both, and in that case a statement that "My wife and I were married in South Bend, Indiana by Reverend Jones of the First Presbyterian Church on May 1, 1942. Neither of us had been married before" will cover the situation.

Where a common-law relationship is alleged or where either or both of the parties to the marriage have been married before, it will be necessary to cover when and where the common-law relationship was initiated, where they have lived since that time, whether there was any break in the continuity of the relationship, and why. Where there has been a previous marriage it will be necessary to get all the information as to when and where it took place and whether it was terminated by death or divorce, with the date and place of death of the previous spouse or in the case of divorce, the court in which it was obtained and the date of the decree—or the fact that no divorce was obtained.

Foundation. This phase of the statement is concerned with the status of the injured as an employee, his job and the amount of remuneration received, whether in actual cash, in other advantages, or both. To qualify for the benefits of the compensation law the claimant must be an employee and his employment must be one covered by the law—not in one of the excluded classes such as domestic servants, farm laborers, casual employees, and independent contractors.

It should cover the contract of hire and the amount of the salary paid. Salary includes not only the actual money received but any additional advantages, and the statement should indicate whether or not the claimant reported the additional advantages on his income tax. This is particularly important in those occupations where the bulk of the remuneration comes from sources other than the employer, such as tips to waiters. The statement might read as follows:

I am employed by the ABC Company as a butcher and deliveryman, at a salary of $5 per hour for an eight-hour day, five days per week. I receive time-and-a-half for overtime and I have been averaging $250 per week. I also receive a Sunday roast once a week, which is valued at $10 and we also share the vegetables which are unsold at the end of the week. I estimate the value of the vegetables at $6 per week. I did not report the latter two items on my income tax.

Where tips are involved, the statement should show the weekly average of salary and tips. Again, inquiry should be made as to the amount reported on his income tax return.

In states where compensation is based upon the average weekly wage over a period of time, it is best to include in the statement the period of time the claimant was employed since these state laws provide for alternative methods of computing the average weekly wage where the injured person has not been employed for the average period prescribed in the act.

Accident. The statement should show exactly when the accident occurred, exactly what the claimant was doing at the time of the accident, and whether it was caused by the claimant's action or whether other persons were involved. If others were involved, they should be identified by name and by employer. For example:

On September 25, 1976, at about 3:00 P.M., I was driving my employer's panel truck to the Ace Plumbing Supply Co. at 3rd Av. and 1st Street. While traveling south on 3rd Avenue, I stopped for a red light at the intersection of

5th Street. I was stopped for about 3 seconds when the truck was struck in the rear by a Chevrolet, driven by Joseph Green, of 123 Brown St., Anytown, Anystate, and owned by the Black Sales Co., of 100 Brown Street, Anytown, Anystate. Mr. Green told me that his brakes wouldn't work and that's the reason he hit me. He said he was going to call on White's Drug Store at 3rd Avenue and 2nd Street. At the time of the accident, I was on a direct route to the plumbing supply house and I had not stopped at any time since leaving my employer's plant, except to stop one block from the plant to get a pack of cigarettes.

In cases where an occupational disease is alleged, most states hold that the date of the accident is the date of disability for the purpose of reckoning the time for filing the claim and for coverage purposes. Therefore, it is important to go into detail as to how the condition first came to the attention of the claimant and when for the first time he was unable to work, even though his work record is intermittent. For example:

I am employed by the ABC Restaurant as a dishwasher and have been so employed for the past five years. On March 1, 1976, we started to use a new detergent, called "Soapine" and on March 3rd, 1976, I noticed that both my hands were red and sore. I continued to work until March 5th, 1976, when my hands broke out in blisters and I couldn't work with them. I stayed home on March 5th and 6th, and returned to work on March 7th, 1976. I wore rubber gloves and my hands seemed to get better, but on September 15th, 1976, the same condition returned only worse. I stopped work on September 15th, 1976, and I haven't been able to work since.

In describing the accident, the claimant may use terminology which is peculiar to his particular industry. These should be defined and explained in the statement. For example, an oil well worker may refer to a "monkey board," "Christmas tree," or a "cat line." Also, where the claimant refers to another individual as the "pusher," it should be explained that he is the assistant foreman.

Injuries.   A detailed description of the claimant's complaints and symptoms is an integral part of the compensation statement. It should contain an exact description of the part of the body which was injured, whether or not any other part of the body was affected and whether or not he had ever been similarly injured before. Where the effects of the injury are not immediate, a description of when and how the pain or other symptom manifested itself is important. For example:

I lift heavy boxes as part of my work. I have been doing this for over 3 years. On September 1, 1976, I lifted a real heavy box with two other men. They let go and I had the full weight on me. It strained my arms a little, but I continued working. I did not feel a pain in any other part of my body. On the evening of September 5, 1976, when I was taking a bath at home, I noticed a large lump in the lower left side of my abdomen. It pained when I squeezed it. I went to Dr. Smith, 25 Orange Avenue, Anytown, Anystate, and he told me that I had a hernia and that I would have to be operated on. I never had a hernia or rupture before, and I guess that I got it when I lifted that heavy box on September 1,

1976. Until I noticed the lump on September 5, 1976, I felt fine and I did my work just as I always did.

The extent of the medical treatment rendered up to the time of the statement should be covered in detail. First, it should show whether or not the physician was authorized by the employer or whether he is the claimant's family doctor. The date of the first treatment should be noted as well as the actual treatment rendered. Second, the dates of the subsequent treatments should be shown, together with information as to the type of treatment, whether the doctor or nurse rendered the treatment, or whether the claimant treated himself with the doctor's equipment. If X rays were taken the name of the physician, together with the part or parts of the body X rayed and how many views (if the claimant remembers), should all be incorporated in the statement. All of this information will be helpful in determining whether or not the doctor is in a position to render an opinion as to causal relationship and, if nothing else, will be helpful in evaluating the medical bill when it is received. For example:

I did not ask my employer for a doctor, but went to my family doctor, Dr. Joseph Green, 123 Main Street, Anytown, Anystate. He first treated me on October 4, 1975, when he examined my back and put some adhesive tape all around my back and chest. He did not take an X ray, nor did he give me any shots with a needle. He also put me under a baking lamp. He told me to come back the next day, but I didn't feel well so I didn't go. I called the doctor on Sunday, October 6, 1975, but his office told me that he didn't have office hours on Sunday. I next saw the doctor on Monday, October 7, 1975. He put me under the baking lamp again. He told me to come back every day that week, which I did. I did not see the doctor again until two weeks later. During this time either the nurse put me under the lamp or I did it myself because I knew what to do. I did not get any treatment on Wednesdays or Sundays because the office is closed on those days. I next saw the doctor on October 21, 1975 and he took the tape off my back and told me to continue with the lamp treatments until I felt better. I continued to get the lamp treatments until November 1, 1975 when I felt better and I quit going. During this time I only saw the doctor three times, October 4, 7, and 21.

The claimant's work record should be shown, indicating when he discontinued work due to the injury and when he returned to work, and whether he returned on a partial or full-time basis, or whether he was able to work but that there was no work for him.

Another part of the inquiry into the injuries concerns the matter of prior accidents and previous injuries. We should record the dates of prior accidents, the injuries sustained, whether or not the previous disability was continuing up to the time of our accident, and the names and addresses of all physicians, hospitals, or others who rendered treatment. Also recorded should be whether or not settlements, either compensation or other, were made, and the name and address of the person, firm, or corporation responsible for the payment.

Additional facts or additional witnesses. Where the accident is caused by a third party, the statement should show whether or not a claim has been made or is contemplated against the third party. In most states, the claimant has the option of claiming compensation or making a claim against the third party (if there is one), and in some states he may do both. In any event, the statement should contain information as to the name and address of the third party, whether a settlement has been made (and if so how much), or whether or not there is a claim for compensation.

The statement should show the names of any witnesses as well as the name of the claimant's superior to whom he reported the accident. When and to whom the report of the accident was made should be set forth.

In summary it should be said that a statement worth taking is worth taking well, and the document should exhaust the knowledge of the witness as far as the subject matter is concerned. Checklists of items to be covered are available and useful, but the most important ingredient in statement taking is the curiosity, imagination, and resourcefulness of the investigator.

1712   Statements taken in hospitals

When an injured claimant is a patient in a hospital and in a condition to receive visitors, a statement may be taken. So that the statement cannot later be denied on the theory that the patient was under opiates or drugs, and therefore unable to know or understand what he was saying or doing, it is best to obtain a statement from the attending physician or the nurse on duty that the patient was not under the influence of drugs at the time that the claimant's statement was taken. This can be done by means of a separate statement (indicating the date and the time) or by a sentence or two added to the original statement under the claimant's signature:

Mr. (Miss or Mrs.) _____ read this report and signed it as being true and correct. He (or she) was alert and not under the influence of any drugs or other medication.

_____ M.D. (or R.N.)

When the claimant is hospitalized and is not in a condition to receive visitors, it is clear that the investigator will not be able to see him until his condition improves. It is best to then contact the claimant's family, identify himself as the investigator for the other party, and arrange for an appointment to see the claimant as soon as his condition will permit. This will have the effect of maintaining control of the case and will, perhaps, give the investigator an opportunity of making a settlement if such is in order. While the investigator is continuing with his task of contacting other witnesses and completing his investigation, he should keep in touch with the claimant's family and the hospital so that he will be able to interview the claimant at the earliest possible moment.

One of the easiest ways to lose control of the case is to make the initial contact and then fail to follow up at appropriate intervals, even though the claimant's family promised to communicate when the time for interview arrived. In most cases, the members of the claimant's family are permitted to see him and will naturally communicate to him the information concerning the initial contact and the investigator's desire to see him. This creates in the claimant's mind a desire to see the investigator and hear what he has to say. If the investigator does not make the contact with the claimant within a short time, he will have lost the opportunity of securing the claimant's statement. If a period of time elapses and no contact is made with the claimant, he is likely to conclude that the investigator either has lost interest in the case or does not now have any intention of discussing settlement. It is then that the claimant will make his move by retaining an attorney.

Some states have statutes which make it unlawful for either an investigator or the claimant's own attorney to interview him while he is in a hospital within a prescribed period (usually the first 15 days after admission) without his written consent. Typical of such statutes is Section 270-b of the Penal Law of New York:

It shall be unlawful for any person to enter a hospital for the purpose of negotiating a settlement or obtaining a general release or statement, written or oral, from any person confined in said hospital or sanitarium as a patient, with reference to any personal injuries for which said person is confined in said hospital or sanitarium within fifteen days after the injuries were sustained unless at least five days prior to the obtaining or procuring of such general release or statement, such injured party has signified in writing his willingness that such general release or statement be given. This section shall not apply to any release or statement obtained by or in behalf of the attorney of the person confined in said hospital or sanitarium.

This section makes it a crime for the investigator to enter the hospital for the purpose of taking a statement, written or oral, within the first 15 days following the accident unless he has 5 days prior thereto obtained the consent in writing of the injured person. Where there is a statute similar to this, the investigator still will want to make his presence known to the claimant. He can contact the claimant's family and explain that he cannot interview the claimant within the first 15 days unless the claimant consents to the interview. He can give the family a letter, addressed to the claimant, explaining the situation, together with a consent form which the claimant can sign and return to him. They could be mailed to the claimant, but the procedure is more impressive if the investigator contacts the family and has them deliver the letters. The letter can read as follows:

Date _____

Dear Mr. Brown:

I am making an investigation in behalf of Mr. Joseph Green in regard to the accident in which you were recently injured. I should be glad to talk with you in reference to this matter.

However, under the provisions of Section 270–b of the Penal Law of the State of New York, I am not permitted to enter the hospital to see you within the first fifteen days after the accident except by your written request.

If you desire to see me, please sign the attached request and return it to me. In accordance with the law, I will call upon you five days after the letter is returned.

Very truly yours,

_____

Some investigators prefer to quote the entire section of the law at the bottom of the letter in order to promote greater understanding on the part of the claimant. The request form usually reads as follows:

Date _____

REQUEST TO:
John Smith
420 Main Street
Anytown, Anystate
Dear Sir:

In accordance with Section 270–b of the Penal Law, I hereby request you to call on me for all or any of the purposes set forth therein, at the Anytown City Hospital.

Very truly yours,

_____

1713   Statements: Serious injury and death claims

In cases involving serious injury which might result in death and in death claims, it is necessary to investigate the persons dependent upon the injured person for support and their relationship toward him. First, the investigator should know when and where the injured was married if he leaves surviving a widow or a possible widow. For a marriage to be legal, both parties must have been free from any legal disability and free to marry. If either had a spouse living it was no marriage at all, and, as to the spouse under the disability of a previous marriage, it is a bigamous marriage. If the first marriage was terminated by divorce, then the person is free to remarry and has the legal right to do so. However, the divorce must be granted by a court having jurisdiction of the parties. As to children, it must be shown that they are natural or adopted children to whom the deceased owed a duty of support. The wrongful death statutes of the various states define the persons for whose benefit an action may be brought. Therefore, the investigator must determine whether the claimed dependents come within the classes of persons defined in the statute. The same thing is true with reference to workmen's compensation cases in that the compensation act defines the dependents for whose benefit compensation will be paid.

From the standpoint of investigation, where there is a fatality, or a possibility of a fatality, the following information should be obtained:

1. Date and place of marriage if there is one, together with information as to whether or not either spouse had been married before, and if so, the date

and place of the previous marriage and whether or not it was terminated by death or divorce.

2. If there was a previous marriage, the nature of its termination should be ascertained, if by death, then the place and date of death of the previous spouse, or, if by divorce, the name of the court and the date when the marriage was dissolved. If the person does not have the latter information, then the name and address of the attorney who handled the matter will be helpful in checking out the divorce.

3. A copy of the marriage certificate should be obtained, and birth certificates for all of the children.

4. If the wife survived, a statement should be obtained as to whether or not she is pregnant.

5. The investigation should show the names and ages of the children, including children by a previous marriage and other possible dependents.

6. Finally, the investigation should show the extent of the support provided to the dependents including children of prior marriages.

1714 Statements of illiterates

The mere fact that a witness cannot read and write does not disqualify him as a witness, nor do these facts preclude the possibility of getting an adequate statement from him. The statement can be recorded in exactly the same way as any other statement, but when it comes to the matter of verification and signature, it is best to have a disinterested witness present who can read the statement to the witness. Then the investigator will sign the witness' name, leaving a space between the first and last name. Above this space write "His" and below the space write "Mark." Then have the witness place an X in the blank space. Then add a statement for the disinterested witness to sign to the effect that he read the statement to the witness; that the witness acknowledged it to be true and correct, and that he made his mark to so signify. Some investigators have the witness place his right thumbprint just below his X. This can be accomplished by using a stamp pad or a fountain pen rubbed over the witness' thumb.

1715 Statements through interpreters

A witness is not disqualified because he speaks a foreign language and does not understand English. A statement can be taken through an interpreter who is qualified to speak the language of the witness as well as English. The witness can sign the statement after it is read to him in his language by the interpreter. Then a statement should be added, by the interpreter, that he read the statement to the witness in the Italian (German, Swedish, etc.) language; that the witness then acknowledged it true and correct, and signed it to so signify. Have the interpreter sign this statement and record his address. It may happen that the statement will be offered in evidence and the evidence of the interpreter will be necessary to identify it as the statement taken from the witness.

1716   Statements of persons with a physical or mental disability

Statements can be taken from persons with a physical or mental disability, and the nature of the disability will determine the procedure to be followed. If the disability is such that it does not in any way impair the facilities of the witness to hear, understand, and read the statement, then the usual procedure may be utilized. On the other hand, if the disability impairs such facility, other methods must be used. If the witness is blind he obviously cannot read the statement and acknowledge it to be true and correct, and the procedure used in the case of a person speaking a foreign language is followed.

A disinterested witness should be present, and when the statement is completed this witness should read the statement to the blind person and guide him in the signing of the instrument. Then a short statement should be added stating that the witness read the statement to the blind person, that the blind person acknowledged it to be true and correct, and that he (the blind person) signed the statement to so signify. The witness should sign this addenda with his name and address so that he can be located if needed to prove and identify the statement.

A person who is a deaf-mute usually uses a type of sign language for the purpose of communication. If possible, the investigator should obtain the services of an "interpreter" who can use the same type of sign language. This will facilitate the taking of the statement and will provide the investigator with a witness who can testify to the statement and the circumstances under which it was taken. He should witness the signature on the statement (along with his address so that he can be located if needed). However, if an interpreter is not available, a statement can be obtained by writing out the questions and having the deaf and dumb witness write the answers and incorporating the information into statement form. Since such a person can usually read, he can acknowledge the truth of the statement in the usual way. This latter is a time-consuming method and it is recommended that an interpreter be secured if it is at all possible.

A person who is suffering from a mental disability is not disqualified from testifying as a witness provided that he has strength of mind enough to recall and describe past events. A statement can be taken and the evidence admitted even though the witness is an inmate of an insane asylum. In most cases, it will be necessary to obtain a statement from the attending physician that the patient's mental illness is such that it does not interfere with his ability to recall past events. In any case, a person with a mental disability is not necessarily disqualified as a witness, but the nature of the disability from which he is suffering will undoubtedly be taken into account by the jury in determining the weight that should be given his testimony. Such witnesses are not the best evidence and are to be avoided if it is possible to establish the same facts through other means.

1717   Statements of children

Children are not disqualified from appearing as witnesses merely because of age. If they are old enough to know the difference between right and wrong, and it is made to appear that they believe in the pains and punishments of the hereafter for telling a lie, they may testify. The weight which will be given to their testimony will depend upon their ability to recall and describe past events.

Statements can be taken from children irrespective of age, but some distinction will have to be made between those of tender years and teenagers. As to children in their teens, who are able to read and write, statements can be taken in the same manner as those taken from an adult. As to those of tender years, it is good practice to take these statements in the presence of one or both parents so that there can be no allegation that unfair advantage was taken of the child. When the statement is signed by the child, the parents should sign an appended statement that they were present during the time the statement was taken and that the story told by their child was accurately recorded. If the child cannot read and write, then the parents can sign the statement and attest that it is a truthful recording of what the child had to say about the accident.

1718   Negative statements

It sometimes happens that a person who was in a position to have seen the accident denies having seen it. This is especially true of persons who were employed at or near the scene of the accident. Under such circumstances the investigator should take a short statement from the person stating that he was otherwise occupied at the time of the accident and he did not see it occur. Such a statement will destroy the witness and if he should testify to the contrary he can be confronted by his statement taken within a short time after the accident in which he denies having seen anything.

For example, if an accident occurred at an intersection where there is a gasoline station, the chances are that the employees would have witnessed the accident. If one such employee states that he did not see the accident because he was lubricating a car, or was in the back of the station getting some oil, a short statement to that effect will protect the investigator's file.

Taking the negative statement may seem to be a waste of time, but many a case has been won solely because the statement was taken and the witness forgot all about it and tried to testify that he had seen the accident, or, in the alternative, the witness did see the accident but the opposing side could not use him for fear of being confronted with the statement. On the other hand, the experienced investigator can recount instances where he failed to get a negative statement only to find the witness testifying for the other side at the time of trial. Therefore, when the investigator is faced with a witness who could have seen the accident because of his presence at the scene, he should take a negative statement. The time devoted to obtaining the negative statement is time well spent.

An honest man who did not see the accident will have no hesitancy in giving a negative statement, if only to extricate himself from any involvement in the case. However, where the witness denies any knowledge of the accident but refuses to give a negative statement, then some consideration should be given to the possibility that he may have seen the accident and will testify for the other side. This fact should be taken into account when appraising the strengths and weaknesses of the case.

1719   Multiple statements

Normally, multiple or group statements are unsatisfactory. They should be avoided and separate statements should be taken from each person if such is possible. It sometimes happens that no one in a group saw the accident and all are willing to give a group statement to that effect, but, because of the nature of their business or the pressure of time, cannot devote time and attention to the statement. Under those circumstances a statement can be prepared to the following effect:

Date _____

We, the undersigned, are employees of the ABC gasoline station located on the corner of Main and First Sts., Anytown, Anystate, and we are all on duty on September 20, 1976, at 8 P.M. when an accident occurred on Main Street in front of the station. None of us saw the accident nor do we know how the accident happened or who was at fault.

> John Jones
> Pete Smith
> Joe Brown

This procedure is not recommended and should be used only when separate statements cannot be obtained.

1720   Court reporter statements

Statements of witnesses may be taken by means of questions and answers recorded by a stenographer or court reporter. If the reporter is a notary, the witness may be sworn and his testimony may be taken in affidavit or deposition form. On the other hand, the questions and answers may be transcribed and submitted to the witness for his certification by having him sign a statement attesting to the fact that the transcript faithfully records his statement. Where only the information is required and there is no likelihood of a dispute as to whether the statement is his actual testimony, a mere transcription will usually suffice.

There are two approaches which can be made to the witness with respect to the taking of a statement by a reporter. One school believes that the statement can be taken by means of questions and answers without any reference in the record that there is a reporter or that everything said is being recorded. The other school feels that the record should show the witness knew that it was being taken down in shorthand and that no attempt was made to take advantage of him. The proper procedure to be followed would seem to depend upon the purpose for which the statement is being taken. If it is taken with a certain amount of solemnity, and will be used for impeachment if the witness should, for any reason, give testimony at the trial in variance with the statement, then the record should be clear that there was no attempt to entrap the witness and that the statement was given freely with full knowledge that it was being taken down verbatim by the reporter.

This type of situation might come about where a person claiming insurance under a liability policy is giving his statement as to his relationship with the named insured and the details of the occurrence. Other situations might include statements from a joint tort-feasor, an injured claimant in a hospital, and, more importantly, a disinterested witness. Where it is decided that the record should show the circumstances and the knowledge of the witness regarding the stenographic record, the investigator can have the record show his identity and announce his purpose in asking the questions. The foundation might be as follows:

Q. You understand that my name is John Jones?

Q. You understand that I am representing Mr. William Green and that I am investigating an automobile accident in which Mr. Green was involved?

Q. This gentleman is Mr. Joseph Smith. You understand that he is a court reporter and that he is taking down everything that we both say?

Q. I am going to ask you about an accident which happened last night on the highway in which Mrs. Betty Brown was killed. You know that?

Q. The questions that I am about to ask you are solely for the purpose of finding out what you know about the accident; you understand that?

Here the investigator has introduced himself, made a disclosure of the party he represents, introduced the court reporter, and established that the reporter is there to record everything that is said. This negatives any claim that the witness did not know who the investigator was, or whom he represented, or that the witness was not aware that the reporter was present taking down the exact words which were spoken.

Where a statement is taken from a disinterested witness, it is good practice to include some reference to the witness' motives for giving the statement and to negative any idea that the witness received a gift or other inducement for giving the detailed statement. The final questions might be framed as follows:

Q. For the record, did I promise you anything, a reward of any kind whatsoever for answering these questions?

Q. They are answered freely without any influence one way or the other, were they not?

No matter which approach the investigator uses, since the objective of the reporter statement is to get as much information from the witness as possible, the investigator should frame his questions so as to get the maximum response from the witness. He should avoid leading questions and he should avoid testifying for the witness. For example, he should *not* ask questions similar to the following:

Q. Did you see the Chevrolet traveling at a high rate of speed?
Q. Did you see it crash into the rear of Mr. Green's car?
Q. Did you see it skid for over 25 feet before the impact?

These questions call for a yes or no answer so that, in effect, the investigator is giving the statement and putting his words in the witness' mouth.

To get the maximum response from the witness, the questions should be as short as possible and should give the witness an ample area to give his version of what he saw. For example, the questions could follow this form:

Q. Did you see the accident?
Q. Tell us what you saw.
Q. How fast was Mr. Green's car going?
Q. How fast was the other car going?

These questions give the witness an opportunity of telling what he saw without any suggestion from the investigator. The questions as to speed are used merely to direct the witness to one of the items concerning which information is sought. In this way, the witness does the testifying and the investigator gives him an opportunity to do so.

1721   Recorded statements

Some investigators advocate the use of certain types of dictating/recording equipment in order to obtain sound reproduction of the voice of the witness telling his story, thus saving the time that a longhand statement would take, and in order to eliminate any possibility of misunderstanding as to what the witness said. It is claimed that the actual voice of the witness reproduced in court is more effective than the written statement since it shows the inflections of the witness' voice and the emphasis which is given to certain words. The equipment to be used may produce the recording on a belt, disk, or tape. Since identification of the record is important, the usual method is to have the witness sign or initial each recording with a special pencil or other device so that it can be identified when produced in court as the record made and authenticated by the witness.

When the equipment is set up, a foundation will have to be laid as to the time and circumstances under which the recording was made, and, more importantly, that it was made with the knowledge and consent of the witness. The opening statement of the investigator might take the following form:

This is Mr. John Jones speaking. I am interviewing Mr. Peter Smith at his home at 450 Main Street, Anytown, Anystate, at approximately 10:30 A.M. Do I have your permission to record this interview, Mr. Smith?

Some investigators find it helpful, as part of the foundation, to include some reference to the surroundings so that there can be no question but that the interview took place in the witness' home. This could take the following form:

Mr. Smith, you have a very attractive home. I particularly like the green wallpaper in this living room. Did you select it yourself?

I see some very excellent pictures of you taken on a fishing trip. Is fishing one of your hobbies?

Such questions are calculated to put the witness at ease but also establish the exact location of the interview.

The same rules, with respect to court reporter statements, are applicable to the recorded statement. The investigator should get as much of the witness' voice as possible and his questions to the witness should be short and only give direction to the interview. When interruptions occur (if there aren't too many) it is good practice to keep the equipment running, and the investigator can note the interruption by saying "Mr. Smith has just left the room to answer the door." By keeping the equipment operating, the record will have more weight as evidence of a recording of the entire interview. Where it is necessary to use a second belt (or disk or tape), the investigator can say, "Mr. Smith, we are going to have to continue our interview on belt number two."

At the conclusion of the narrative, it is best to ask a general question which will give the witness an opportunity to give an unrestricted answer. The question could be: "Mr. Smith, do you have any other information concerning this accident and the people involved which you would like to add?" Some investigators find it helpful to ask as a final question: "Mr. Smith, has everything you have told me concerning this accident been true and correct to the best of your knowledge and belief?" Others use a form of attestation: "Mr. Smith, do you swear that the foregoing answers given by you are the truth, the whole truth and nothing but the truth, so help you God?"

At the conclusion of the interview the investigator should thank the witness for his cooperation and time. This may or may not be on the recording, but in any case the investigator should avoid terminating the interview too abruptly so as to give the witness the impression that the investigator has no further interest in him now that the recording has been made.

As to the admissibility of a recorded statement, the courts are in general agreement that it can be admitted if there is a proper foundation laid as a preliminary to the offer. This includes evidence that the recording machine was capable of recording voices clearly, that the operator of the device was competent in its use, that the recording is identified, that there have been no additions, deletions, or changes, and that the recording was preserved in such a way as to preclude any tampering. Evidence will also have to show the identity of the speakers and that the recording was made with the knowledge and consent of the witness, voluntarily and without any coercion. In *United States v. McKeever* (169 Fed. Supp. 426), the court said:

Current advances in the technology of electronics and sound recordings make inevitable their increased use to obtain and preserve evidence possessing genuine probative values. Courts should deal with this class of evidence in a manner that will make available to litigants the benefits of this scientific development. Safeguards against fraud and other abuses are provided by judicial insistence that a proper foundation for such proof be laid.

Recorded statements taken by telephone are likewise admissible in evidence provided proper foundation is laid for the submission of such evidence.

While there can be no question but that the majority of the courts will admit recorded statements into evidence under proper circumstances, there is a problem as to the weight which the jury will give such evidence in its evaluation. Many jurors have seen television shows were recordings have been "doctored" so that a person "says" something entirely different from his original spoken statement. Therefore, even though there is evidence that the recording has not been changed, it is difficult to predict what the reaction of the jury will be. Where the witness is uneducated, there is also the risk of the jury's concluding that unfair advantage had been taken of the witness and rejecting the evidence of the recorded statement.

1722   Evaluation of witnesses

Since the investigator usually will be the only person who sees the witnesses prior to the inception of a lawsuit, it is important that the file reflect the overall impression which the witness will create should he be called upon to testify. If his evidence is favorable, the kind and type of witness he will make will determine the amount of reliance which can be placed on his evidence. If his evidence is unfavorable, the problem to be resolved will have to do with a decision as to how damaging his testimony will be. So that an informed appraisal can be made of the evidence, the file should contain a general evaluation of the witness as to (1) appearance, (2) education, (3) characteristics, and (4) general impression.

1. *Appearance.*   This has reference to the eye appeal, or the lack of it, the appearance of the witness will project. The description should contemplate whether he is tall or short, thin or fat, gray-haired or bald, and whether he normally is well or poorly dressed. His facial characteristics should be noted, such as facial scarring, skin disease, or other similar conditions which detract from his appearance. Does he wear glasses, and if so, are the lenses thick or thin? Extreme magnification might create some doubt in the minds of the jury as to whether the witness saw the accident clearly. Any other appliance or prosthesis which may be worn should be noted, especially a hearing aid. Where the witness is a driver of a car, whether the insured vehicle or another, the file should show the age of the driver and any physical condition which might have some effect upon his ability to drive carefully and fully control the vehicle: such as the absence of a hand, arm, foot, leg, or eye, even though he has an "adequate" replacement in the form of a glass eye.

2. *Education.*   The person reviewing the file may be able to come to

some conclusion on this point by referring to the occupation of the witness. However, it is not uncommon to find a college student or graduate driving a truck or performing other types of manual labor, possibly on a temporary basis. In any case, it is best to comment on the education of the witness as well as his ability to understand and use the English language. If he is a foreigner and talks with an accent, some comment should be made as to whether he can express himself well enough to be understood in English, or whether his testimony will have to be taken through an interpreter.

3. Characteristics. These can be the most important parts of the evaluation process; and the investigator should observe and analyze the demonstrated characteristics of the witness: when he first contacts him, throughout the taking of his statement, and during any subsequent contacts the investigator may have. For the most part, the investigator will base his conclusions on the actions of the witness and the responses received while the statement is being taken. Is he talkative or timid, nervous and excitable or relaxed, opinionated and obstinate or open-minded, and finally, does he have any speech defect, a tendency to stutter or lisp, or does he speak distinctly?

4. General impression. The investigator should record the general impression the witness made on him. Did the witness tell a convincing, believable story of the event? Did the story check out with the physical facts as well as with the statements of others? Finally, does the investigator himself believe him? In discussion of the case, did the witness ask to be paid for his testimony?

1723 Physical facts

A physical fact is one having actual existence as distinguished from a mere conception of the mind; it is visible, audible, or palpable, such as the scene of an accident, the sound of the impact, or the skid marks laid down by one of the vehicles. The scene of the accident includes all of the details which have any bearing on the happening of the event, such as the place near an escalator where the claimant fell, including the advertising displays which may have had some influence in distracting the claimant, and the offending device be it an elevator, escalator, or obstruction in the aisle.

In automobile cases, the physical facts of the scene will include the position of the streets, their width, and physical construction, the obstructions to vision of the drivers such as buildings, shrubbery, trees, advertising signs; traffic controls such as warning signs, stop signs, traffic lights; the location of landmarks such as fire hydrants, telephone poles, fire alarm boxes, etc. The physical facts of the accident would include skid marks, debris or blood on the highway, the position of the cars at impact, the position where each came to rest, and the damage to the vehicles themselves as indicating the point of impact. The audible physical facts can be described only by those who heard them, but the other physical facts can be established by photographs and diagrams.

1724   Photographs

Photographs of the scene of the accident should depict the place of accident under the same conditions as when the accident happened. This means that the sooner the photographs are taken the better. Difficulties may arise if an interval of time has elapsed, especially where there has been a change in the surrounding conditions, such as new construction, changes in weather, or where shrubbery or trees have been removed. While photographs taken after changes have taken place are not entirely valueless, nevertheless they are subject to objection that they do not faithfully represent the scene as it was at the time of the accident, and testimony must be presented to show the changes.

If obstructions to vision are alleged (in a case where high grass obscured a traffic control sign), a photograph taken showing the grass in the same condition as it was at the time of the accident will be of significant value. But if the investigator allows some time to pass, he may find that the grass has been cut so that the sign is no longer obscured; a photograph taken after this has happened is not as effective as one taken before the grass was cut. The same is true of old buildings or new construction. Time is of the essence, and the sooner a needed photograph is taken the better. If physical marks of the accident are important, it is clear that gouges in the highway and skid marks become obliterated with time, and even if some of the marks remain it will be difficult, if not impossible, to identify them as the result of the particular accident.

Photographs also play an important part in general liability claims, especially where there is a claim of insufficient lighting or dangerous construction, or where premises are being altered by new construction. Photographs can show the conditions at the time of the accident, location of the lighting fixtures with relation to the place of accident, and the presence of handrails, barricades, warning signs, and other items which have some bearing on the issue of negligence or contributory negligence. As in automobile cases, where the condition is subject to change (new construction, etc.), the photograph must be taken as soon after the accident as possible and must reproduce the conditions which were in existence at the time of the accident as nearly as possible. Where the condition will not change and the insured does not contemplate any alterations, photographs may be taken at any time, but even in those cases, if photographs are needed the best rule to follow is that the sooner they are taken the better.

In automobile cases, a practice has grown in some areas whereby professional photographers obtain information as to the occurrence of a serious accident and take pictures of the scene, the position of the cars, etc. The pictures are for sale and can be bought by either or both sides. When the pictures are purchased the purchaser usually insists on having both the prints and the negatives, together with the assurance of the photographer that no other prints have been run off. It sometimes happens that this latter statement is untrue; that other prints have been sold to the opposing side. Therefore, in cases such as this, the investigator should proceed on the assumption that the other side has seen or is in possession of prints.

1725   Diagrams

A diagram is a flat sketch of the scene of the accident and the activity that took place. It can be used to depict the scene of the accident together with the location and relationship of fixed objects, or to locate damage to objects, or to locate injuries and scarring sustained by the injured person. The type of diagram which the investigator will draw most frequently will be the scene of the accident or, in automobile cases, the scene plus the activity which occurred. Certain symbols are commonly used to represent objects and vehicles, and are usually made with a template or stencil, available in most stationary stores. The illustrated symbols are only a partial list of those used.

The diagram is made to explain, orient, or clarify the file so that it will reflect the occurrence of the accident and the surrounding circumstances. It is a visual aid to the investigator in transmitting to the file a picture of exactly what happened. Also where photographs have been taken, either by the investigator or by a professional photographer, it is helpful if the position of the camera for each photograph is tied in on the diagram. This leads to a better understanding of the photographs and eliminates the need for further identification of them.

Diagrams are used most frequently in automobile cases. The minimum requirements of such a diagram are that it show the

1. Direction of the cars involved.
2. Course of the cars immediately prior to impact.
3. Obstructions to the view of either driver.
4. Grade of the street.
5. Traffic controls.
6. Position of the cars at impact.
7. Position of the cars when they came to rest.

Skid marks, center lines, and gouges or debris on the highway can be located and depicted, as well as the locations of utility poles and intersecting rights-of-way, such as railroad crossings, bridges, and overpasses.

The diagram is always made with the compass direction North at the top of the page, and the best diagram is drawn to scale, especially where distances are factors in the defense. Two such diagrams, one to scale and one not to scale, are shown.

When taking a statement it is sometimes helpful to have the witness draw a rough diagram of the intersection or place where the accident happened—and answer the investigator's questions as to the relative positions of the cars at impact and when they came to rest by utilizing the diagram. Witnesses often become confused as to directions and the corners of an intersection can be easily identified if they are marked as NW, NE, SW, and SE. After the statement is taken, it is good practice to have the witness identify the diagram

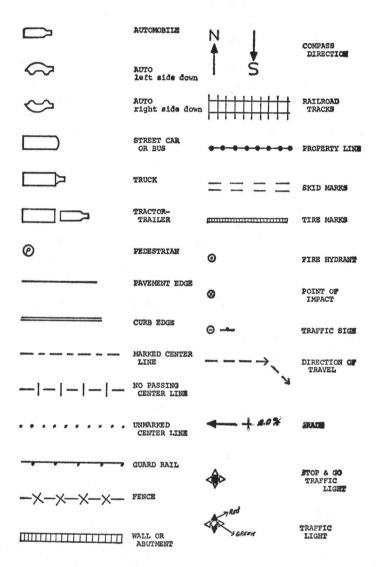

made by him with a statement thereon together with his signature. Then, if he testifies, he can be given the diagram, together with his statement, to refresh his recollection.

1726   Verification

Verification is the process by which the investigator tests the accuracy or reliability of the evidence he has gathered. He will take each statement and decide whether it is corroborated or discredited by the statements of others.

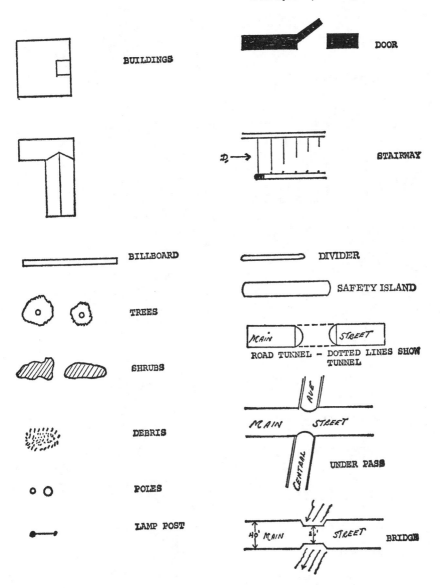

He will determine whether a statement is contrary to reports made by the same witness to the police (police blotter) or the state motor vehicle bureau, or contrary to admissions made at the scene of the accident (*res gestae*), or contrary to admissions against interest made after the event. He will also test the statement with the physical facts. Can he establish that the point of impact is where the witness says it occurred? Do the tire marks, skid marks, and debris support the witness on this point?

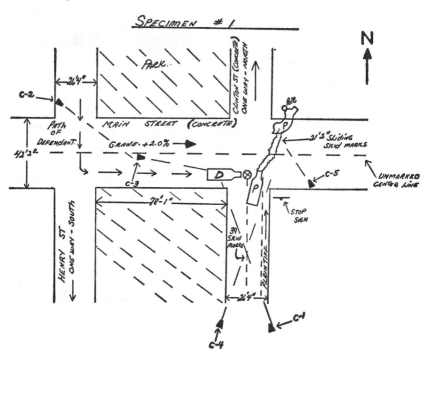

SPECIMEN #1

Legend: 1 inch = 30 feet

[P] PLAINTIFF

[D] DEFENDANT

WEATHER: CLEAR

TRAFFIC: LIGHT

DATE OF ACCIDENT: 9-22-60 @ 3 P.M.

▶ CAMERA	
C-1 - Photo #1	
C-2- " #2	
C-3- " #3	
C-4- " #4	
C-5- " #5	

Where the witness is friendly and favorable it is sometimes important to take him to the scene of the accident so that he can point out various landmarks and actually measure distances. It will be found that most people are poor judges of time and distance, and what the witness believes to be 250 feet (a favorite number) will actually turn out to be 75 feet. The witness is not to be discredited because he is a poor judge, but if he actually steps off the distance he will be able not only to testify more accurately but can say he verified

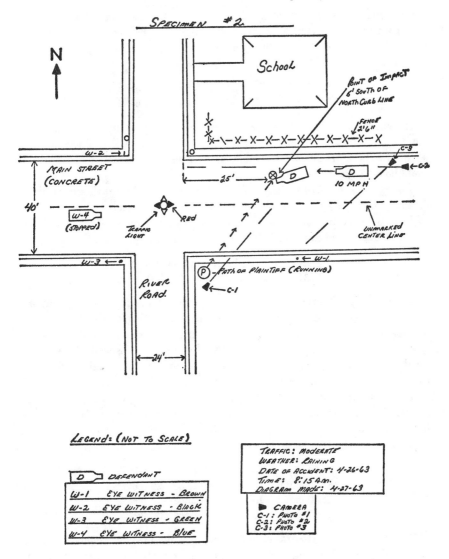

SPECIMEN #2.

N

School

POINT OF IMPACT
5' SOUTH OF
NORTH CURB LINE

FENCE
2'6"

C-3

MAIN STREET
(CONCRETE)

W-2 →

25'

D

D

10 MPH

← C-2

40'

W-4
(STOPPED)

TRAFFIC
LIGHT

Red

UNMARKED
CENTER LINE

W-3 ←

RIVER
ROAD

• ← W-1

P - PATH OF PLAINTIFF (RUNNING)

C-1

24'

LEGEND: (NOT TO SCALE)

D	DEFENDANT

W-1	EYE WITNESS - BROWN
W-2	EYE WITNESS - BLACK
W-3	EYE WITNESS - GREEN
W-4	EYE WITNESS - BLUE

TRAFFIC: MODERATE
WEATHER: RAINING
DATE OF ACCIDENT: 4-26-63
TIME: 8:15 A.m.
DIAGRAM MADE: 4-27-63

◗ CAMERA
C-1: PHOTO #1
C-2: PHOTO #2
C-3: PHOTO #3

his estimate of the distance after the accident happened. Or if he says it took him 10 seconds to go a certain distance at a certain speed, speed charts may prove him to be inaccurate, but a test at the scene of the accident may put him straight and make him a more reliable witness.

There are a number of shorthand methods by which the adjuster can make an approximate determination concerning the physical facts involved in an automobile accident. These can be used when an approximation is needed and time does not allow the use of more complicated and more accurate methods. These methods are as follows.

Feet per second.   A close approximation of the number of feet per second traveled by a vehicle at any given speed can be made by multiplying the number 1.5 (or 1½) by the speed of the vehicle in miles per hour. For example:

At 30 m.p.h. : 1.5 × 30   45 feet per second
At 60 m.p.h. : 1.5 × 60   90 feet per second

The exact speed in feet per second can be arrived at by multiplying the number 1.47 (feet per second at 1 m.p.h.) by the speed of the vehicle in miles per hour. Therefore 30 m.p.h. would be 44.1 feet per second and 60 m.p.h. would be 88.2 feet per second.

Emergency braking distance.   To determine the maximum braking distance for a passenger vehicle in good mechanical condition over a dry, level, hard-surfaced road, take one-half of the first number of the speed (in miles per hour) and multiply it by the speed in miles per hour. For example:

At 30 m.p.h. : 1.5 × 30   45 feet
At 60 m.p.h. :   3 × 60   180 feet

If the vehicle is traveling downgrade, the braking distance increases by the same percentage as the grade. If the vehicle is traveling uphill, the braking distance would decrease by the same percentage as the grade. It should be noted that braking distances vary as does the square of speed. Thus if the speed is doubled the braking distance is four times greater and if the speed is tripled the braking distance increases nine times.

Reaction time and distance.   It is generally accepted that it takes the average driver three-quarters of one second to react to danger. To determine the number of feet the vehicle will travel during this reaction time, the formula of 11 feet for each 10 miles an hour of speed can be used. For example:

At 10 m.p.h. : Reaction Distance   11 feet
At 20 m.p.h. : Reaction Distance   22 feet
At 30 m.p.h. : Reaction Distance   33 feet
At 60 m.p.h. : Reaction Distance   66 feet

Overall stopping distance.   This includes the braking distance plus the reaction distance. The point of reaction can be established by measuring the reaction distance back from the first tire skid mark. It should be noted that there are two lags between the forcible application of brakes and the appearance of skid marks on the road surface. First, the wheels do not lock until there has been sufficient heat created between the brake band and the drum. Second, the well-defined skid mark does not appear on the road surface until sufficient heat has been created by the sliding tire and the road surface to melt the asphalt or bitumin in the composition of the tire. The combined distance of these two lags approximates the wheel base of the vehicle. A fairly accurate chart of stopping distances with good brakes, good pavement and a level roadbed is as follows:

Speed (*in miles per hour*)	Distance Traveled during Thinking Time (*in feet*)	Distance Traveled after Brakes Applied (*in feet*)	Total Distance Traveled after Seeing Danger (*in feet*)
20 22	21	43
30 33	46	79
40 44	82	126
50 55	128	183
60 66	185	251
70 77	251	328

Deceleration time element.   The maximum emergency braking dis-. tances noted above are based on the vehicle's loss of velocity of approximately 22 feet per second, a coefficient of friction (or drag factor) of 0.665g, "g" representing the pull of gravity at sea level, namely 32.2. Therefore, the time factor in an emergency braking case can be calculated by dividing the number of feet per second the vehicle was traveling at the time of driver reaction by the number 22. For example:

At 30 m.p.h. : 44 feet per second ÷ 22   2 seconds
At 60 m.p.h. : 88 feet per second ÷ 22   4 seconds

To establish the overall stopping time three-quarters of a second reaction time must be added to the above figures.

Pedestrian speed.   It is sometimes important to determine the walking speed of a pedestrian. The average gait of both males and females is the same —about 4 feet per second. The female takes a shorter step, usually about two steps per second while the average male will take about one and three-quarter steps per second.

The figures developed as a result of these formulae can be used to test the possibility or impossibility of a version of the accident when it comes to time and distance. For example, suppose a witness made the following statement:

When I came to the intersection, going north, I slowed down to 20 m.p.h. I saw another car about 250 feet away, traveling east, at about 60 m.p.h. I thought I had plenty of leeway so I proceeded to make a left turn, intending to travel west, when suddenly my car was struck at the left front fender by the right front of the other car. My front wheels had not yet reached the center line.

While the actual statement would have more detail, the accident could not have happened under the facts as given. If we assume that the claimant was traveling at 20 m.p.h., and didn't increase his speed, he would be traveling at the rate of 29 feet per second. If the other car was 250 feet away and traveling at 60 m.p.h., he would be going at the rate of 88 feet per second. Since he had to travel 250 feet to get to the intersection, this would take him approximately 3 seconds. In 3 seconds the claimant would have traveled 87 feet—more than enough to make his left turn. Therefore, on the basis of these facts, it is clear that the claimant would have cleared the intersection before the other car got there and the accident could not have happened. Clearly, if the figures are inaccurate, this conclusion is inaccurate. If this was the statement of a favorable, friendly witness, it might be well to take him to the scene and recheck the distances. If the oncoming car was 50 feet away, rather than 250 as stated, an entirely different picture would be presented.

1727   Verification by experts

An expert is a skillful or experienced person who, because of education and training, has acquired special knowledge with respect to some particular art, science, trade, or profession not possessed by ordinary persons. Included within this definition would be a physician, surgeon, chemist, engineer, college professor, police officer with special training in accident reconstruction, or a mechanic. Within the limits of their respective specialties, any one of these experts can examine evidence and express an opinion which will guide the investigator. In most cases, the opinion will corroborate or refute the statement of a witness as to the happening of the accident, its causation, the speed of the vehicles, the point of impact, whether or not a substance is deleterious, and whether or not a medical condition could be caused by the trauma described by the witness. The expert will assist the investigator in determining what evidence is believable and what is not.

The services of an expert can be utilized in any one of three ways. The opinion can be elicited as a result of (1) a hypothetical question, (2) an examination or test of an object, and (3) an examination of the scene of the accident and measurements or tests made at the site.

Hypothetical question.   This consists of submitting the evidence to the expert in the form of assumed facts and requiring an answer as to whether or not certain conclusions can be reached on the basis of the evidence. For example, let us assume that the investigator has a claimant who says he was involved in an accident in which he twisted his back. He did not think anything of it for a period of time, continued to do his usual work (which involved manual labor), but about 30 days later felt an excruciating pain in his neck and, upon consulting a physician, an X ray was taken which indicated a compression fracture of one of the cervical vertebrae, all of which he claims was due to the accident. The investigator will immediately want to know whether it is possible for a man to sustain such a fracture and have no immediate manifestation thereof, to continue to do manual labor for a period of 30 days without discomfort, and to experience the pain for the first time after that interval of time. In a case such as this, the investigator would submit the question to a surgeon specializing in orthopedics, with all of the facts obtainable and, if possible, the original X-ray plates, and will ask for an opinion as to whether or not there could be any relationship between the accident as described and the resultant injury.

In another case, let us assume a claim that, while being used, a can of lead paint exploded and started a fire. The story sounds impossible, particularly where the claimant insists there are no other facts. The opinion of an expert would confirm the impossibility of this version, but would also point out circumstances under which the accident could have happened: if the paint were subjected to extreme heat, let us say. This latter opinion gives the investigator a lead as to the information he should seek in contradicting the alleged version of the accident.

Examination or test of an object.   In the last illustration, let us assume the particular can of paint is available and can be identified as the one which exploded and burned. It could be submitted to an expert chemist to determine, by examination, what caused the can to explode and whether there is any evidence that it was exposed to extreme heat. In products cases where it is claimed that a certain item was the offending cause of an injury, the item (or a similar item) can be subjected to a chemical analysis to determine its ingredients and an opinion can be expressed as to whether or not such ingredients could cause the condition of which the claimant complains.

For example, a claimant maintains he was made ill by eating a cake from the local bakery and that the illness was caused by some unwholesome ingredient in the cake. An analysis of the cake by a chemist will determine the truth or falsity of this claim. If possible, the remaining parts of the cake should be obtained and analyzed. If not possible, the same type of cake, baked at the same time as the other cake and made from the same batch or mixture, should be subjected to analysis.

It is important that the investigator be able to establish that the object subjected to analysis is the same as or similar to the product used by the claimant. When the case comes to trial, one of the issues will be whether or not the analysis refers to the particular object or product involved in the case. The expert will be asked to identify the source from which he obtained the tested sample. Therefore it is best to have the chemist get the sample from the claimant directly or to have the baker deliver the sample to the chemist.

In the first case, the chemist can testify that he received the sample from the hands of the claimant himself, and, in the second, the baker can testify that the sample came from the same batch. The investigator should not handle the sample because he will then have to testify when and where he received it and that there was no substitution or change while it was in his hands. The element of insurance might be brought out when he is asked about his interest in the case and whom he represented in the investigation.

The object does not necessarily have to be examined in the expert's own office or laboratory; it can be examined while in the possession of the claimant or of someone else. In each case, however, it is essential that the object be identified as the one involved in the accident. If the identification is lacking or insufficient, it may be fatal to the admissibility of the expert testimony.

For example, a mechanic is sent to the garage where a damaged vehicle is located. He examines the vehicle and expresses an opinion as to the point of impact, based on the damage he observed. The adverse party introduces testimony of the garage owner who says the mechanic examined a car in his garage, that the car examined was the same make and model as the one involved in the accident, but that it was not the car at all. The mechanic never asked the garageman to identify the car involved in the accident, and therefore the mechanic examined the wrong car.

Examination of scene and tests at site.   An engineer can make an examination of the scene of the accident, prepare plats of the area, note the marks of the accident (gouges, skid marks, debris, etc.), and express an opinion as to where the accident took place with reference to the center line, the speed of the vehicles as evidenced by the damage caused, and where each came to rest. He could also make tests by using the car involved in the accident, or one of similar make and model, to determine braking distance, roadability, control, and any other factors which may have been involved in the causation of the accident.

Identification is important in this case as well as in others. A witness, either an eyewitness or a police officer who investigated the case immediately after the accident, must identify the marks on the roadway as being the results of the accident, since roadway marks cannot be connected with the accident unless there is identification. Clearly, if the evidence on which the expert relies cannot be established as being involved in the accident, the expert's opinion is based upon an untenable premise. The scene of the accident can easily be identified by the evidence of others as to the names of the streets and the fixed objects thereon: buildings, traffic signs, fire hydrants, fire alarm boxes, and so on.

In a case where it is claimed a person contracted a disease, such as silicosis, from the inhalation of dust containing silica or other deleterious substance, the investigator will want to know whether or not there is any such substance in the atmosphere where the person worked or visited. This can be accomplished by having an engineer make dust counts of the air, identifying the dust as to kind, size, and quantity, and expressing an opinion as to whether or not the dust particles can be inhaled. Identification will consist of the testimony of a witness that the test was conducted in the place where the claimant worked and under conditions which were the same or similar to those to which the claimant was exposed.

The investigator is frequently confronted with a case where it is alleged that a customer in a store slipped and fell because of an excessive amount of wax on the floor. The contention will be that wax was applied to linoleum or asphalt tile, creating an extremely slippery and unsafe condition. The fact of the matter is that the manufacturers of floor wax, especially the type used by commercial establishments, have mixed a nonskid substance in the wax and a floor treated with this wax is less slippery than it is in an unwaxed condition; the nonskid substance increases the coefficient of friction.

The investigator will have to overcome the general notion that the more wax that is applied, the more dangerous and slippery the floor becomes. To do this he will require the testimony of an expert who has examined the floor and subjected it to friction tests under circumstances similar to the conditions under which the accident is alleged to have occurred. To set the scene for the test, he will have an eyewitness present who can identify the place of the accident and can testify that the floor appeared to be in the same condition it was at the time of the accident. In addition, the maintenance man who applied the wax prior to the accident should be present to participate in the test.

Normally the test is run in three or four stages. First, the floor will be tested in its present condition. Second, the maintenance man will prepare the floor in exactly the same way he prepared it prior to the accident, usually by the application of some solvent or of soap and water. When this has dried, the floor should be subjected to a second friction test. Thirdly, the maintenance man should apply the wax in the same way he did prior to the accident, and another friction test made. Fourthly, if a buffer was used to bring out the sheen, another test should be made after the maintenance man uses the buffer. The results of these tests usually will be that the floor, without wax, offers the least skid resistance, and is actually less slippery immediately after the wax is applied, offering more skid resistance. Buffing will have no effect on friction resistance.

In addition, the investigator should know the ingredients of the wax used, information which can be obtained from the manufacturer or from a wax expert. In most cases, the manufacturer, interested in selling his product, will be most cooperative in assisting the investigator resist the claim. The manufacturer also may be legally vulnerable on the basis of a breach of warranty should the wax prove to be of unmerchantable quality or not in conformity with the conditions of an express warranty.

1728   Verification by medical examination

The claims of disability and the necessity for medical treatment can be verified by having the claimant examined by the company physician. The examining physician will verify the history of the accident, and the claimant's past medical history and present condition. He will express an opinion on the causal relationship between the claimant's present condition and the alleged accident, and an opinion as to whether or not the claimant is disabled from working, temporarily, partially, or permanently, whether any further treatment is indicated, and, if so, for how long a period.

Prior to litigation the claimant is not required by law to submit to a medical examination. He may and usually does so, however, because he realizes that the examination is a necessary part of the investigation which he hopes will lead to a settlement. The same considerations will motivate the claimant's attorney when he represents the injured person. However, the investigator should recognize that during the period the claimant is under the treatment of his own physician, the only evidence of his physical condition, and disability, will be that of the attending physician. In the absence of an examination by the company's physician, the company will have no evidence to contradict the testimony of the attending physician. Therefore, prior to litigation, the claimant or his attorney sometimes promise an examination but the claimant fails to appear. This is one of the earmarks of a possible buildup of the disability issue and, where it is recognized, the investigator should consider an activity check, either through a neighborhood survey, surveillance, or motion pictures, as the necessity of the case demands. (See Section 1729, below.)

Where the claim is in litigation, the defendant is entitled to at least one physical examination as part of the discovery or disclosure proceedings. This is a matter of right, and if the claimant refuses, he can be compelled to submit to the examination by means of a court order. In some states, the defendant is entitled not only to an examination when the case is in the preliminary stages but also to a final examination at least 10 days prior to the trial date.

Where it is conceded that the claimant has fully recovered, and this is supported by his own statement or a certification from his doctor, there would be little point in conducting an examination; the company is sufficiently protected against any further claims by either of these statements. If a further claim is made, then the company can consider the advisability of an examination. Where it is conceded that the claimant has recovered and does not require further medical treatment, but that he has sustained some permanency, then an examination may be indicated to determine whether there is any permanent condition, and if so the extent of it.

When it is decided that a medical examination is indicated and necessary, the following factors should receive consideration: (1) the time of examination, (2) extent of examination, (3) selection of the medical examiner, and (4) the report of examination.

1. *Time of examination.*   The first decision is the time the examination should take place. Should it be conducted immediately or be deferred to some future date, and, if so, how long should it be deferred? It is elementary that the examination should obtain information as to the claimant's physical condition. Therefore, it should take place at a time and under such circumstances as will produce the maximum information. If it is known that the claimant is in a plaster cast or in the hospital, either in traction or recovering from an operation, an immediate examination would not be revealing since the examining physician would not be permitted to remove the cast, take the claimant out of traction, or remove the bandages to examine the operative area. The examining physican could examine the X rays, hospital records, and operative report, but since these records are available any time, their immediate examination is not necessary. Therefore in these cases, it is best to defer the examination.

As to cases where examination can be made, the answer to when it should be made will depend upon what the claimsman desires to accomplish by having it. Where there is some question as to the extent of an injury, the earlier the examination is conducted the better, since it is essential that the company have a complete picture of the injury, its extent, and potential. Also, where there is a question as to the amount of treatment required, an immediate examination can act as a deterrent to overtreatment and extended disability. It should be emphasized again that in the absence of verification of the claimant's injury and the need for medical treatment, the statements of the attending physician stand as the only evidence on these two points. In every case, there will be an interval between the date of the accident and the examination. As to that interval, reliance will have to be placed on the report of the attending physician because no other medical evidence is available. The longer this interval is, the longer the claimant will have uncontrovertible proof of disability and of the necessity for medical treatment. Because of these considerations, an early examination is a definite requirement where the matter of disability or of the necessity for medical treatment is an issue.

Where the claimsman is satisfied that the case is in good hands, and that there is no tendency on the part of the attending physician to overtreat, there would be reason to defer the examination until the treatment is concluded in order to have the examination show the final result and whether or not there is any permanent condition present.

The claimsman is not always restricted to having only one examination in each case. It may well be that arrangements can be made for a preliminary examination and for a final examination at a later date. Where this is evident, it might have some influence on the claimsman's thinking as to the time of the first examination.

2. Extent of the examination. This will vary with the type of case and the objective to be accomplished. In every case, whether the examination is made by a specialist or a general practitioner, and irrespective of the objective, the claimsman should see that the examiner is given all the information in the file as to the causation of the injury, the exact injuries claimed, whether or not the claimant was hospitalized, the type of treatment or operation performed, whether or not X rays were taken, and the result thereof. If a copy of the hospital record has been obtained or a certificate received from the attending physician, the examiner should be furnished with a copy.

If X rays were taken, arrangements should be made with the attending physician to make the original plates available to the examiner. In appropriate cases, the examiner should be authorized to take X rays himself, especially where the originals were positive and some time has elapsed since they were taken. In this way, he can give an up-to-date opinion as to the progress of the healing process. Also, where X rays are unsatisfactory, either because they were improperly taken or misinterpreted because of some defect in the plate (artefact), the examiner should have comparative X rays in order to reach a definite conclusion. Usually, the authorization for taking X rays is not given on a blanket basis, but each case is considered in light of its own particular facts and the need for new X rays, and the examiner is required to solicit authorization in each case where he feels there is a need for new plates. The giving of a blanket authorization not only increases the cost of the examinations, but the X rays may frequently disclose other conditions, not being claimed, as additional results of the accident. Thus, when the X rays are produced, an additional claim may be advanced. Authorization for X rays is not given unless some purpose useful to the defense can be achieved, but in any case where there are X rays the examiner should see the original plates rather than rely on the findings of another physician as to what they disclose.

The same criteria apply to other tests, such as blood tests, electrocardiograms, basal metabolism tests, encephalograms, and myelograms. They are authorized if they will serve some purpose in producing a more complete examination or in uncovering some condition, unrelated to the accident, which may be used as a defense on the theory that the condition and not the accident is the cause of the claimant's disability.

The examination is not necessarily restricted to the findings of one physician. There can be more than one doctor participating, especially in cases where there is a multiplicity of injuries, each coming within a different specialty. For example, if the claimant is suffering from a fractured skull and he claims some eye complications such as diplopia (double vision), it might be necessary to have him examined by an eye specialist in addition to the general examination. The extent and number of the specialists, who will be called in on the case, will in each instance depend upon the particular facts of the case and the objective to be achieved.

3. *Selection of the medical examiner.*   Many doctors, otherwise competent, make poor witnesses in court. They may be inarticulate or may have a gruff and uncompromising personality or other defects which may influence the jury unfavorably. The first requisites include a pleasing personality, the ability of expression, and the facility for expressing technical medical terms in layman's language.

The examiner must have medical knowledge sufficient to make an accurate appraisal of the injuries, the need for treatment, and the prognosis for future recovery. He must report his findings accurately and must not be inclined toward optimism, or to minimizing the injury, merely because he is examining for the defendant. Nothing is more frustrating to the claimsman than to rely on an overly optimistic report which cannot be supported by facts or testimony at the time of trial. The examiner should be capable of reporting the injuries as he finds them, whether such findings are favorable to the defendant or not. An accurate estimate of the potential of the case cannot be made when the medical report is misleading, and in some cases an attractive settlement possibility will be turned down because of an inaccurate medical report.

The same considerations should influence the selection of a specialist who is needed in certain situations, but his qualifications also should be such that they are not open to attack by adversaries. He should have hospital connections in his particular specialty and be able to support his position as a specialist by showing education and experience beyond that held by the ordinary general practitioner.

4. Report of examination. The medical report should be addressed TO WHOM IT MAY CONCERN, or some similar designation, and never addressed to the company or to the claimsman. The reason is that the report may have to be offered in evidence, and if it is addressed to the company or the claimsman, the form of the address will reveal the existence of insurance. Concealment of the existence of insurance may give the defendant a doubtful advantage, however, especially where the defendant is a large corporation or where state law requires the carrying of liability insurance. In any case, it is good practice to follow this procedure because it is difficult to predict the cases in which insurance may become an important issue, and by following this precautionary procedure the risks of revealing the existence of insurance are reduced.

A satisfactory medical report will contain, as a minimum, these five items: (1) history, (2) findings, (3) causal relationship, (4) prognosis, and (5) opinion.

History. The examiner should elicit as complete a statement as possible from the claimant as to how the accident occurred, what parts of his body were injured, what pain he suffered, when he experienced the first manifestation of pain—whether simultaneously with the accident or some time thereafter—whether or not he was unconscious, when and from whom he received his first medical treatment, and the number and kinds of treatment he has received since that time. If the history differs in any way from the information supplied by the company as to the causation of the injury, the examiner should make some effort to reconcile the differences if it is possible to do so. Inquiry should also be made as to X rays and other diagnostic aids which may have been used, as to information developed, and as to when and by whom the tests were performed. The information thus gained might assist in the further investigation as well as bring to light any questions which may exist as to the medical treatment. Some attorneys are aware of this practice involving the taking of a complete history, and insist that all examinations be made at their offices and in their presence. This limits the examiner's opportunity to explore the history thoroughly, but he is entitled to inquire how the claimed injuries were acquired and what treatment was rendered up to the time of the examination.

Findings. The actual results of the examination should be detailed, setting forth the claimant's complaints and stating whether or not they are substantiated by any objective signs. The report should indicate what tests were made by the examiner and the claimant's reaction to each.

Causal relationship. The examiner should state whether or not all the injuries complained of could be the result of the accident as described to injuries complained of could be the result of the accident as decribed to him in the history, whether there is any evidence of preexisting injury or disease, and if so, whether or not in his opinion this condition was aggravated by the accident.

Prognosis. The examiner should state whether the claimant has fully recovered or whether further medical treatment is required. If the claimant is still disabled, some estimate of future disability should be made, and if further treatment is necessary, an estimate of the period of time needed, together with the nature and the frequency of such treatment, should be included. He should also comment as to whether or not the injuries will produce a permanent condition, and if so, the nature and extent of the permanency. If it consists of a restriction in motion of any member, he should express the loss of use in terms of a percentage as compared with normal motion. Where facial scarring is involved, the report should contain a description of the scar as it now exists and an opinion as to whether it will improve by bleaching out with the passage of time, and if so, the residual result which can be expected. If plastic surgery will improve the condition, he should express an opinion as to the possible result, the nature and extent of the surgery, and the approximate cost.

Opinion. The examiner should give his opinion as to the treatment already rendered, whether or not it was indicated or effective, and his recommendations as to further treatment, if necessary, whether of the same or of a different type. Where permanency is involved, he should give his opinion as to what the permanent condition means to the claimant in relation to his ability to continue with his usual work and in relation to his future enjoyment of life, if the latter is involved.

1729   Verification of disability

Disability can be verified or denied by obtaining evidence of the physical activity of the claimant. This can be secured by one or more of the following methods: (1) neighborhood check, (2) surveillance, and (3) motion pictures.

Neighborhood check. The claimant's activities can be checked through interviews with neighbors, storekeepers, milkmen, postmen, newspaper delivery boys, and others in the neighborhood. Inquiry should develop exactly what physical activity has been observed, such as engaging in sports, doing yard work, making repairs, sweeping the sidewalk, doing the marketing, washing the car, and other activities which involve physical exertion. Where positive information is obtainable it should be made the subject of a signed statement. If the informant knows that the claimant has been working, an effort should be made to find out where and the kind and type of work.

Surveillance. This consists of the observation by the investigator of the claimant's activities. It might mean that the claimant's home will have to be kept under observation for long periods of time, or it might mean that the surveillance should take place at different hours on different days. The objective is to observe the claimant and to ascertain exactly what physical activity he is capable of doing and to what extent. Where positive information is developed, statements can be taken from others who made the same observation.

Surveillance may also reveal that the claimant is working even though there is a denial that he is capable of so doing. This is usually ascertained by observing the claimant leave at the same time each day and return at the same time each evening. Trailing him to his place of business will establish his business activity and further investigation at that point, through the employer, will establish the date of his return to work and the regularity of his attendance.

Difficulties arise when the claimant is working at more than one location, and sometimes it is necessary to keep him under surveillance for a period of time in order to establish that fact. In any case, the period of the surveillance will have to depend upon the particular facts of the case and whether or not prefessional persons are engaged for the task will likewise so depend.

Motion pictures. These are usually taken to establish the claimant's physical ability to perform work. If he is working around the house, making major repairs, or painting, pictures of him engaged in such activity can be used to controvert any claims that the injuries are such that the claimant is unable to perform any physical labor.

The motion pictures are usually taken without the claimant's knowledge, and for that reason cannot be taken very close to the scene of the activity. Telephoto lenses are used and the position of the camera is some distance from the claimant. In spite of these difficulties, the picture must clearly identify the claimant as the person engaging in the activity. If the pictures fail to do this, they may not be admissible in evidence. Therefore, for the most part, motion pictures used in connection with the trial of cases are usually taken by professionally trained persons who make a specialty of doing this type of work. There is no reason, however, why they could not be taken by a staff investigator of equal competence.

1730   Verification through the index bureau

The claims bureau of the American Insurance Association maintains an index bureau for the purpose of accumulating records of bodily injury claims and of making this information available to its subscribers. The information is received by the index bureau by the submission on each case of an information sheet, containing the data on each bodily injury claim as it is made. When these information sheets are received the bureau checks each case with its records, and if there is a previous record of the claimant information is returned to the subscriber indicating the details of the previous claim or claims, giving the injuries claimed, the date of the accident, the company involved, the company file number, and the type of claim. If further information is desired the subscriber can contact the other company for more details.

The index bureau is nationwide in its operation and therefore, even though the claimant is a transient, information as to prior claims is available.

1731   Comparison

Throughout the investigation, comparison is a continuing process. As each new fact is developed it should be compared with what is already known or alleged. As conflicts appear an effort should be made to reconcile them or, where contrary facts appear, to ascertain which of the two facts are more believable and conform more closely to the physical facts. This very often may change the direction of the investigation and impose a further requirement of inquiry and verification.

When the investigator has exhausted every means of ascertaining the facts, he may still wind up with two conflicting, contrary versions. His report should show both versions, the verification which was made of each, and the supporting evidence in connection with them. He should give a fair evaluation of the evidence he has gathered and should comment on the strengths and weaknesses of each version. He should not fall into the trap of regarding favorable evidence as truthful and unfavorable evidence and unbelievable. He must give his opinion based on his estimate of the evidence and the reliability of the testimony of the witnesses, whether they support his theory of defense or not.

CHAPTER XVIII

Medical aspects

1800   Medical knowledge in relation to personal injury claims

In the evaluation and settlement of personal injury claims, the objective is to measure the extent of the injury in terms of money. To accomplish this, the claimsman must have a working knowledge of anatomy and the effects of an injury upon the human body. Clearly, he is not expected to have the knowledge of a medical practitioner, but he must have some familiarity with conditions caused by accidents, and what these conditions mean in terms of causation, treatment, pain and suffering, as well as disability, both temporary and permanent. The following pages are intended to give only a small view of the subject with reference to the more common terms and the more frequently recurring types of injury.

Medical knowledge is an ever-expanding subject in the claimsman's portfolio of information. As cases are handled he is confronted with medical reports from the claimant's physician, reports from specialists, and is guided by the examinations and reports made by his own examining physician. To properly understand and evaluate this medical information he must know and understand all the terminology used, how and why certain tests are made, and the significance of the conclusions expressed. To understand the terms, reference must constantly be had to a medical dictionary, and in matters involving complicated injuries consultation with the examining physician will be helpful in acquiring an understanding of the medical factors involved in the claim.

When it comes to the settlement of personal injury claims, the claimsman is a purchaser. He is buying the cause of action which accrued to the claimant as a result of the accident. One of the items in this purchase is the physical and mental distress suffered by the claimant. The claimsman must know the details of this distress, its extent, its effect upon the claimant in terms of pain and disability, as well as the treatment that is required to cure or relieve it. The buying of a commodity of this kind is no different from any other type of bargain and sale. The buyer usually insists upon examining the subject of the sale, either personally or by having an expert make the examination for him. The buyer then decides whether he will make the purchase, depending upon whether he feels the price is reasonable. Similarly, in the purchase of personal injury claims, the claimsman must know the nature of the article that is being bought before he can determine whether or not the price is reasonable and whether or not he should make the purchase.

In making this determination an adequate and detailed description of the injury is the primary step. If the physician reports that the claimant has sustained "an injury to the back" or a "traumatic condition of the spine," the description is inadequate. Both of these terms could mean various types of fractures of the spine, a sprain of the muscles, or a contusion in the area of the back. They could also refer to a herniation of the disc, a spondylolisthesis, a spondylitis, or a spina bifida. The value of the case and the action to be taken by the claimsman will depend upon which of these terms actually describes the injury. Some of the terms are indicative of a serious injury and others refer to congenital conditions not caused by an accident, and rarely aggravated by one.

In medical reports there are certain descriptive words which are used generally to pinpoint the exact area of injury. Anatomists have divided the body by means of an imaginary line, running from the head downward at the center of the body, called the median line. The medial aspect of any bone or organ is that part which is nearest the median line. The other side of the bone or organ away from the median line is called the outer or external aspect. Lateral refers to the side, anterior to the front and posterior to the rear. In classifying X ray views, a side view is referred to as a lateral view. One taken from front to back is called an anterior-posterior view.

Dorsal refers to the back. For example, the dorsal surface of the hand is the back of the hand, as distinguished from the palm, which is referred to as the palmar surface. The largest muscle of the back is called the latissimus dorsi which, literally translated, means "largest of the back." The bones of the arms and legs are divided into thirds for anatomical purposes. In locating a fracture or other bone condition, the report will refer to the upper third of the femur, or the middle third, or the lower third.

Muscles are described by the number of "ceps" or heads which they have. For example the biceps muscle (arm) is one with two heads. The quadriceps muscle (thigh) is one with four heads.

1801   Causation

Obviously, in order to recover for an injury the claimant must sustain the injury as a result of the accident. He may be suffering from some preexisting condition which bears no relationship to the accident, in which case he should not recover. He may have a preexisting condition which has been aggravated by the accident, in which case, theoretically at least, he should recover for the period of aggravation, and his disability should cease at the termination of that time. Unfortunately, a line as fine as this cannot be drawn, and the condition never returns to its former state. In such cases the defendant might be responsible for the entire condition.

In other situations, the claimant may have a systemic or chronic condition which delays his recovery. A prime example of this is a claimant with a 4+ Wassermann, one suffering from tertiary syphilis. Syphilis is a bloodstream disease which, in the case of injury, retards and sometimes bars full recovery. The responsibility of the defendant encompasses the entire period of disability even though, in the case of a normal person, recovery would be much more rapid. Again, the defendant would not be responsible for the cure of the syphilitic condition but would have to bear the cost of whatever treatment was required to cure the accidental injury, even though some of the treatment might be directed toward the control and care of the syphilis.[1]

In all cases, where the defendant is alleged to be responsible, there must be a definite chain of causation leading from the accident to the ultimate injury claimed. For example, if a claimant sustained contusions and lacerations of the right hand, one would hardly assume any responsibility for a bunion on his right foot which allegedly began to pain right after the accident. However, if as a result of the laceration of the hand an infection in the hand and arm, or a lymphangitis of the arm developed, then there would be a direct chain of causation and the defendant would be responsible for the entire condition.

In determining whether or not there is this chain of causation, our examining doctor must have all the facts. These include the history (the facts of the accident), hospital records, reports of attending physicians, X rays, and laboratory tests. Medical diagnosis depends upon a review of all the facts and examination of the patient with special reference to objective and subjective symptoms. Objective symptoms are those that can be seen or verified by the use of X ray or other diagnostic tools. Subjective are the complaints made by the patient. The latter, of course, can easily be fabricated. In some cases, there is an interval between the trauma and the first physical manifestation of the injury or disease. It is important to cover this point in the claimant's statement, exactly indicating when he for the first time experienced any discomfort in the area. Generally, the rule is that the longer the interval of time between

---

[1] It might be added that you will seldom find the word "syphilis" on a hospital record; a synonym, "lues," is used primarily because it is relatively unknown to the public. The adjective is leutic, meaning the same thing as syphilitic. The various Kings Louis of France, were afflicted with hereditary syphilis and the disease became known as "Louis' Disease," later contracted to Lues Disease. Hence the term.

the trauma and the onset of symptoms, the less the likelihood of any relationship between the two.

Therefore, when a case is referred to our examining doctor, he should have the benefit of all the previous medical information that you have obtained. This will consist of hospital records, X rays (if not the plates, at least a copy of the findings), past medical history, reports of doctors treating such past conditions, a concise but complete statement of how the accident occurred, the injuries complained of, the symptoms claimed (both subjective and objective), and the kind and type of disability claimed. The more information and factual data the doctor has, the more accurate will be his opinion on disability and causal relationship.

Certain injuries are so definite that they can be demonstrated by clinical examination or diagnosed by the use of X rays and other means. Head and back injuries pose a particular diagnostic problem and it is in this area that most fraudulent or malingering claims will be found.

1802   Trauma

This is the medical word you will meet more frequently than any other. It means a blow or wound. There are internal and external traumas. An internal trauma is caused within the body by one organ exerting pressure on another. External trauma refers, as the name implies, to a blow or pressure from outside. Any condition which comes about as a result of a blow is said to be traumatic in origin. It is used to differentiate, as to origin, conditions which could be spontaneous (chronic) and those caused by external force.

1803   Etiology

The etiology of a condition refers to the causes of disease, both direct and predisposing, and their mode of operation. It does not refer specifically to the cause of the condition but generally to the causes of similar conditions, the usual progress, and the usual termination. The terminology is used in discussing a particular case with a doctor with reference to the usual cause and progress of the condition.

1804   X Rays

Contrary to the popular belief, X rays are not pictures in the sense that they are mirrorlike reflections. The X ray is made by placing an object between the plate and the X-ray tube, and the shadow cast by the object is developed on the plate. X rays (or Roentgen rays) are produced by this tube, which emits the rays in an umbrellalike fashion. As a result, the object directly beneath the tube will be in sharp focus whereas the parts of the object not under the center will show up on the plate with a certain amount of distortion. The greater the angle of the ray, the greater the distortion.

It was originally discovered that the outline of bones only would be seen on the X ray plate; other organs would not. The problem then was to provide ways and means of making other organs radioopaque for diagnostic purposes. This was solved by introducing radioopaque material into the organ. For example, barium is introduced orally into the body and will outline the stomach and the gastrointestinal system. The use of lipiodol and other dyes has been introduced by injection into the body and will outline intervertebral discs and the course of the spinal fluid.

An X ray plate is said to be negative when it demonstrates no abnormal condition, and positive when it outlines a fracture or other condition. In the skull, because of the number of bones crossing each other, a diagnosis of fracture of certain of these bones is sometimes difficult to make because (we must again bear in mind) the image produced on the plate is a shadow. Therefore, it is possible for the claimant to actually sustain a fracture of the base of the skull which is not demonstrable by X ray.

Usually, more than one view of the condition is made by X ray. These views are produced by placing the object at different angles to the X ray tube. As noted above, a lateral view is a side view and an anterior-posterior is one taken from front to back.

1805　Diagnostic tests

There are other means of diagnosis available in addition to X rays. Listed below, with their definitions and use, are some of the tests most frequently encountered in claim work.

Bone conduction. Testing the hearing threshold by placing a tuning fork or audiometer oscillator directly against the mastoid process.

Electrocardiogram (EKG). A graphic record made by an electrocardiograph of the electric potential differences due to the heat action, taken from body surfaces. A typical normal record shows P, Q, R, S, T, and U waves. The P wave is due to excitation of the atria, Q, R, and S waves to the excitation of the ventricles; the T wave to repolarization of the ventricles. The U wave is a diastolic wave; used in the diagnosis of patients with heart disease.

Encephalogram (X ray of the brain). It is made radioopaque by the removal of the cerebrospinal fluid and by air or oxygen replacement.

Kahn. A microscopic flocculation test for syphilis; similar to Kline Test.

Kolmer. A complement-fixation test for syphilis. See also Wassermann.

Patch test. An allergy test in which material is applied to intact skin surface to demonstrate tissue sensitivity.

Snellen. Test for central vision in which the subject stands a certain distance from a standard chart and reads letters on the chart. Results are calculated by the ability of the subject to read letters of different sizes. Results are expressed by figures: 20/20 is the normal degree of visual acuity.

Wassermann. A complement-fixation test for syphilis.

Weber. A hearing test in which the vibrations from a tuning fork placed on the forehead of a normal person are referred to the midline and heard equally in both ears. In unilateral middle-ear deafness, the sound is heard in the diseased ear.

1806   Diagnostic signs

In medical reports we will note references to signs, which in the general sense are physical manifestations of disease or injury. The most frequent in our work are as follows:

Babinski.   A sign for injuries to the corticospinal tract in which the response to plantar reflex shows dorsiflexion of the great toe with plantar flexion and fanning of other toes.

McBurney's.   A sign for early acute appendicitis in which the area of maximum tenderness is over McBurney's point of the abdomen.

Lasegue.   A sign of sciatic nerve disease where elevation of the extended lower extremity produces pain in the nerve trunk. Superficial lesions or simple functional ailments of an organ increase, whereas organic disease decreases the reflexes.

Romberg.   A sign for tabes dorsalis (a disease referring to the spinal cord), in which the patient cannot maintain equilibrium when standing with feet together and eyes closed.

1807   Anatomy

1. *Skeleton.*   The skeleton is a bony framework which supports the soft parts of the human body. It is composed of a number of separate bones of varying size and use.

2. *Cranium and face.*   These are the two major divisions of the skull. The cranium refers to the part of the skull that contains the brain, its membranes, and vessels. The cranium is made up of the occipital (rear of head), frontal (forehead), sphenoid (base of skull), and ethmoid (back of the nose).

The face is composed of 14 bones consisting of two nasal, two lacrimal, two zygomatic (zygoma), two palate, two inferior turbinate bones, two maxillas, the vomer, and the mandible. The principal bones are the nasal bones, which form the bridge of the nose; the superior maxilla, two bones which form the upper jaw; the inferior maxilla (or mandible), which forms the lower jaw, and the malar bones which form the cheek.

The bones of the ear are commonly referred to as the anvil, stirrup, and hammer. The medical names for these bones are incus (anvil), stapes (stirrup), and malleus (hammer).

3. *Spinal column.*   The spine is a flexible column composed of irregularly shaped bones called vertebrae. There are 24 of these vertebrae in the spinal column proper. They are classified as cervical, dorsal, and lumbar. There are seven cervical vertebrae, which are located in the neck. Immediately below the cervical vertebrae are the 12 dorsal vertebrae. They extend from the base of the neck vertebrae to the small of the back. Next are the five lumbar vertebrae. The vertebrae in each section are numbered starting at the top and are so designated. For example, the first cervical vertebrae is the topmost vertebrae of the cervical region and its designation is abbreviated to C-1. Likewise, if reference is made to the fourth lumbar vertebrae, this might be designated as L-4.

Each vertebra is made up of two parts, a solid segment in the front and a hollow segment or arch in the back, the latter being formed by two pedicles and two laminas. The solid parts of the vertebrae are one beneath the other, and the hollow parts accommodate the spinal cord. Between each vertebra are intervertebral discs of cartilage which act as shock absorbers between the bones and permit the spine to have movement.

In addition to the vertebrae mentioned are the five sacral (the sacrum) and four coccygeal (the coccyx) bones.

4. *The thoracic cage.* The chest, or thorax, includes the ribs, the 12 dorsal vertebrae, and the sternum. These bones form a sort of cage which protects the viscera. The viscera in this area consists of the heart and the lungs.

The sternum (breastbone) is in front and the first seven pairs of ribs are attached to it by cartilages which permit movement and allow the chest to expand in breathing. The upper three pair of the lower five pair of ribs are connected to the cartilages, but the lower two pair are not attached at all in the front, and are therefore called "floating" ribs. All 12 pair of ribs are attached to the spine in the back.

5. *Clavicle and scapula.* The upper arms are joined to the body by the shoulders. Each shoulder is formed by two bones, the clavicle, or collarbone, in front, and the scapula, or shoulder blade, in the back. The inner end of each clavicle is attached to the sternum and the outer end attaches to the scapula.

6. *Pelvis.* The pelvic cavity is a strong bony ring between the lower end of the spine and the lower limbs. It is formed by the two innominate bones (ilium, ischium, and pubic bone) and the sacrum and coccyx. (The three parts of the two innominate bones fuse or unite in adulthood and form the os innominata (the unnamed bone). This os innominata is connected with the sacrum and the fifth lumbar vertebra, forming the sacroilia joint.

7. *Upper extremities.* These consist of the arm, forearm, and hand. The arm contains one bone, the humerus. The forearm is formed by two bones, the radius and ulna. The ulna is longer than the radius, and it forms part of the elbow joint.

The hand is made up of the carpus, metacarpus, and phalanges. The carpus (wrist) has eight bones arranged in two rows of four each. There are five metacarpals, forming the back of the hand and extending from the wrist to the fingers. The bones in the fingers are called phalanges. They are designated as proximal (closest to the hand), middle, and distal or terminal (furthest from the hand).

8. *Lower extremities.* The thigh, leg, and foot comprise the lower extremities. The thigh has one bone, the femur. The leg is formed by the tibia and fibula. The tibia is the larger of the two and is located on the front side of the leg. (Note the similarity between the bony structure of the arm and the leg.)

The foot, like the hand, has three parts: the tarsus, metatarsus, and the phalanges. There are seven bones in the tarsus, which includes the os calcis (or oscalcis) or heel bone. There are five metatarsal bones. As in the fingers, the toe bones are called phalanges (singular is phalanx).

The patella (kneecap) is part of the knee.

9. *Joints.* A joint is formed by the articulation of junction of two or more bones. The joint is made up of smooth surfaces, one at the end of each bone, lined with a thin layer of cartilage and covered by a layer of cells which supply lubricating fluid so as to prevent friction.

In some joints there are small enclosed pads called bursae, containing fluid in which the joint moves. These include the olecranon bursa (elbow), sub-deltoid (shoulder), and prepatella (knee).

Ligaments are bands of flexible connective tissue which bind the articular surfaces of the bones together, forming a joint.

10. *The muscular system.* Beneath the skin are masses of tissue which have specific anatomical functions. These are contractile organs affecting the movements of various organs and parts of the body. Mechanically, the muscles operate by contracting and relaxing. The muscles moving the arms, legs, and other bones of the body are attached to the bones by tendons and bring about motion by pulling the bone into a new position. Other muscles provide for the movements of the internal organs. These are the heart muscle, muscles in the walls of the digestive tract, and those in the walls of various tubular structures such as blood vessels, glandular ducts, bronchi, and the ureter. These muscles influence the flow of blood into an organ, the flow of air into the lungs, and the passage of food through the alimentary canal. Muscles are controlled by the central nervous system, which is composed of the brain and its intercommunicating mechanism, the spinal cord. Muscle movements are of two kinds: voluntary (striated), subject to the will of the brain, and involuntary (unstriated), not subject to the will of the brain, such as the beating of the heart muscle.

11. *The nervous system.* The nerve center is the brain. It controls two systems of nerves, the cerebrospinal and the sympathetic systems. The cerebrospinal system includes the brain and the spinal cord with its various branches. The sympathetic system includes cords which run down each side of the body from the base of the skull to a point in front of the coccyx. This system supplies nerve energy to the internal organs and blood vessels, and ultimately communicates with the cerebrospinal system.

The spinal cord is the connecting link between the brain and the various parts of the body, functioning not unlike an electrical wiring system by transmitting the impulses or stimuli which originate in the brain. Any damage to the cord, or interference with the transmission system, which destroys or impairs its communication function will result in partial or complete malfunction of the organs from the point of damage downward. In cases of extreme damage, there will be partial or complete paralysis.

The spinal cord connects with the brain and is contained in the bony arches of the spinal vertebrae. The brain itself is contained in the brain cavity of the skull and consists of two hemispheres. The hemispheres are connected with the spinal cord by means of the medulla oblongata. There is a nexus, or binding together, and a crossing at the base of the skull so that the left hemisphere controls the right side of the body and the right hemisphere the left. Any brain damage to the left hemisphere might produce paralysis of the right side of the body.

The nerves of the cerebrospinal system have a motor function. They are the energizers of muscle action and provide voluntary control for starting, accelerating, or stopping bodily movement. The sympathetic nerves have a sensory function. They control the five senses and bring impulses received from without to the cerebrospinal system.

12. *The circulatory system.* The food which is passed from the small intestine to the bloodstream must be conveyed and deposited in cells all over the body. This is accomplished by various parts of the circulatory system, which is a closed system of tubes into which a pump (the heart) is sealed. Leading from the heart are large blood vessels, called arteries, which progressively subdivide into smaller and smaller vessels. The smallest of these vessels, almost microscopic in size, are called capillaries. These unite with each other, forming larger and larger vessels, and the largest vessels resulting from this union are the veins, which lead back to the heart.

The heart is continually pumping blood around this circuit, arteries to capillaries to veins, and back to the heart. From the capillaries a watery solution, called tissue fluid, is brought to the cells. This contains the nutrients, carried by the blood, which feed the tissue cells. Some tissue fluid returns directly to the blood through the capillary walls and the rest filters into small tubes called the lymph vessels. These merge with one another, creating larger and larger vessels, and the largest empty into the veins. This is called the lymphatic system and is regarded as an accessory part of the circulatory system.

One means of determining whether the circulatory system is functioning normally is by a measurement of the blood pressure. Blood pressure refers to the pressure exerted in the arterial system and is measured in millimeters by a column of mercury. Systolic pressure is the top limit reached at the end of the contraction of the heart. Diastolic pressure is the lowest pressure in the arteries when the chambers of the heart are dilated and the heart is in the diastolic phase (between beats). In recording pressure two figures thus are given, the first or upper figure beating the systolic pressure and the second or lower representing diastolic. Normal blood pressure is 120 over 80. Normal heart beat rate or pulse is 72 at rest. Any marked difference from these figures indicates an abnormal condition.

1808   Fractures

One of the most frequent injuries with which we are confronted are fractures of bones. A fracture is defined as a break in the normal continuity of the bone. Fractures are classified as follows:

1. *Simple fracture.*   A simple fracture occurs when a bone is broken into only two parts. If the break is straight across, it is described as transverse; if it is on a slant, it is called oblique.

2. *Compound fracture.*   Where either or both of the pieces of the fractured bone pierce the skin, the fracture is compound.

3. *Comminuted.*   A comminuted fracture is one where there is a splintering or fragmentation of the bone.

4. *Compound comminuted.*   A fracture causing splintering of the bone, which pierces the outer skin.

5. *Compression.*   One in which two opposite surfaces of the bone are driven together, usually found in fractures of the vertebrae of the spine.

6. *Contra-coup.*   A fracture of the skull caused by transmitted violence to the cranial vault, causing a break at a point distant from, and usually opposite, the point of trauma.

7. *Greenstick.*   An incomplete fracture of a long bone, seen in children. The bone is bent, but splintered only on the convex side.

8. *Colles fracture.*   A fracture of the distal end of the radius, characterized by dorsal displacement of the distal fragment and radial and dorsal deviation of the wrist and hand.

9. Depressed.   A fracture of the skull in which the fractured part is depressed below the normal level.

10. Impacted.   A fracture in which the harder cortical bone of one fragment has been driven into the softer cancellous bone of another fragment.

11. Incomplete.   A fracture which does not extend through the entire bone.

12. Multiple.   Two or more fractures occurring in the same or different bones.

13. Pathologic.   One which occurs at the site of a local disease in a bone (such as carcinoma) without external violence.

14. Pott's fracture.   Fracture of the inferior tibiofibular joint, usually associated with a splitting off of the tip of the medial malleous, rupture of the tibial collateral ligament, and outward displacement of the foot.

15. Sprain fracture.   A sprain, usually of the ankle joint, complicated by a fracture or chipping of the bone.

16. Stellate.   One in which there are numerous fissures radiating from the central point of injury ("starlike").

Treatment of fractures.   The correction of a fracture consists of replacing the bones in their normal positions and keeping them in that position, without any movement, until healing takes place. The correction of the position of the bones is called a reduction of the fracture. This can be accomplished by a closed reduction, which means that the bones are placed in position by manipulation. An open reduction is a surgical procedure whereby the fracture site is exposed by incision and the bone fragments are manually placed into position. Frequently, the fragments cannot be held in position without the use of surgical nails, plates, or screws, which are inserted.

Most fractures can be immobilized by the application of a plaster cast or by strapping with adhesive tape. More serious fractures frequently require the application of traction, which keeps the bones in place by the use of weights and pulleys.

The first stage in healing or "union" of a fracture is one of blood clot formation between the bone ends. The next stage is the formation of fibrous tissues at the fracture site. Bone-forming cells next make their appearance and these convert the fibrous tissue into bone. This new bone at the fracture site is referred to as callus. This callus bridges the fracture completely. Where there is an inadequate callus formation, the condition is referred to as a "non-union" or an ununited fracture. Treatment of this complication might consist of grafting bone to the fracture site for the stimulation of bone growth.

Ordinarily fractures of the shaft of the long bones are not serious and seldom result in any permanency—except fractures of the shaft of the bones of the leg, femur, tibia, and fibula where there is a complete fracture with the fragments overriding each other. Such fractures can result in a bone loss and a consequent shortening of the leg. Fractures of the bones in a joint will cause some restriction of motion in the joint and will require treatment to restore normal motion, the result depending on the nature of the fracture and the age of the patient. In older persons, full restoration of normal motion is the exception rather than the rule, and in most cases there is a residual restriction which is permanent.

1809   Head injuries

The head is a complex mechanism. The bony structure consists of two parts, the braincase or cranium, and the face, with upper (maxilla) and lower (mandible) jaws. Each of these two parts is the enlarged end of one of the main tubes of the body, the alimentary tube and the neural tube. The functions of the alimentary tube are well known to all. Suffice it is to say that its purpose is to introduce food into the body. The head end of the tube consists of the mouth and throat into which the food is first introduced, masticated, and swallowed. The end of the neural tube is the brain, which creates impulses which are transmitted to the muscular part of the body through the spinal cord and the nervous system. These impulses activate the muscles. The brain also has special senses, seeing, hearing, and smelling, which it translates through the spinal cord to the nervous system. Finally, the brain controls the involuntary muscular movements of some parts of the body, such as the beating of the heart, respiration, and digestion.

Injuries in which there is a direct blow or trauma to the head may be trivial or serious, usually depending upon whether the brain is affected or not. In all cases a detailed investigation of the medical history of the claimant is essential, together with a description of the cuts, bruises, or swellings of the head which followed the trauma, and mention of any bleeding from the ears, nose, or mouth. These latter signs are usually symptomatic of a possible skull fracture. A period of unconsciousness following the injury is usually indicative of a brain concussion. If the period is of short duration, then the damage to the brain is inconsequential. Unconsciousness over a long period of time is indicative of a more serious condition, usually of a severe contusion of the brain.

What happens in the latter case is that a portion of the brain swells and in some cases impairs its function to the extent that it loses control over other parts of the body. An impairment or paralysis of the vocal chords, vision, or movements is an indication of this brain condition. The swelling will usually subside in about six to eight weeks, and the claimant will gradually return to normal. If after this period of time, there is no improvement, then it can be concluded that the claimant has sustained more than a mere contusion and the condition may be due to a massive hemorrhage or a laceration of the brain, which generally require surgery. Even after surgery, these conditions can produce some permanent impairment of speech, vision, or movement.

Where it is alleged that the claimant has sustained a contusion of the brain or a shaking up of that organ producing some concussion—whether the claimant was unconscious or not—claims are frequently made for some residual condition called a "post concussion syndrome." This term merely describes a group of symptoms following a concussion or contusion of the brain. They are subjective complaints and consist of headaches and dizziness. Since there is no method whereby the existence of these conditions can be verified, the complaints are easy to claim and can be simulated.

It is sometimes claimed that an injury to the head either caused or produced epilepsy. Therefore, it seems appropriate to consider the condition in some detail. Epilepsy is a symptom and not a disease, just as headache, fever, chills, or dizziness are symptoms. The cause is unknown and the condition is regarded as idiopathic, or of unknown origin. Where there is a definite cause, the condition is diagnosed not as epilepsy but by the actual terms, a depressed fracture of the skull, alcoholic epilepsy, etc.

The mechanics of epilepsy consist of a massive disturbance in the transmission of impulses from the brain to the other parts of the body. For some unknown reason, the brain suddenly transmits maximum impulses to all parts of the body under its control, resulting in confusion not only to the motor mechanism but also to the sensory and mental centers. Epilepsy is classified by the extent of the symptoms produced by these disturbances. The classifications are (1) grand mal, (2) petit mal, and (3) Jacksonian.

Grand mal. The impulses emitted by the brain are of such proportions that they result in a massive convulsion which extends to the sensory and mental centers, producing confusion and unconsciousness. The second stage is the exhaustion of the nervous system, and the attack is completed by an almost total cessation of function. When this passes, the patient will return to consciousness without any recollection of what happened.

Petit mal. In this type, attacks are of short duration, consisting particularly of momentary unconsciousness. There is little or no motor convulsion.

Jacksonian. In the preceding two forms of epilepsy, the patient has no advance warning of the onset. In the Jacksonian type, there is some warning. The mechanism is the same as in grand mal, but the impulse starts in some limited portion of the brain with muscular contraction in some distant part of the body. Contraction then spreads to other parts of the body, in exact order, through the extension of the disturbance within the brain. This gradual onset of symptoms is called the "march" of Jacksonian epilepsy.

The authorities all seem to agree that trauma or a brain concussion from blows on the head rarely lead to epilepsy. The mechanical situation is that the brain itself must be seriously affected and anything short of a brain laceration, produced by a fracture of the skull in which a bone fragment pierces the brain, will not produce the classic symptoms of epilepsy.

1810   Spinal or back injuries

Fractures of the vertebrae of the spine can be serious or trivial, depending upon the portion of the bone affected. If the fracture involves one of the spinous processes, such as the transverse process or one of the pedicles, it is not serious and will involve only the bone and the muscular attachments. A fracture of the neural arch or the vertebral body is usually serious since damage to the spinal cord may follow such a fracture. Impacted fractures of the vertebrae, where one vertebra is crushed against another, may have some effect on weight-bearing.

Sprain of the muscles of the sacroiliac region (referring to the area of the sacrum and the ilium), or a sprain of the muscles of the sacroiliac joint, are quite common, especially in workmen's compensation cases. They usually come about as a consequence of lifting heavy weights. The period of disability following such an injury differs with severity according to the individual's age and muscular structure.

A subluxation is an incomplete dislocation or sprain of a joint; when vertebrae are out of alignment as a result of injury, this term is used.

Treatment of mild fractures and sprains of the back consists of immobilization by means of bed rest, or in more serious fractures by application of strapping (adhesive tape), plaster cast, or traction.

1811   Traumatic neurosis

This covers a situation where, as the result of trauma, it is claimed the individual has undergone mental and emotional conflicts which cannot be faced. Usually these conflicts are apprehensive in form with the claimant developing an unreasonable fear of the thing that caused the accident, an automobile, or a machine used in his job. Another type is schizophrenia, usually referred to as a change of personality. Actually, it is a psychosis characterized by unpredictable behavior, and sometimes terminates in mental regression and total withdrawal from reality.

Many individuals are predisposed to these neuroses by their environment and mental makeup, but an accident may be a precipitating cause. If the accident aggravated the condition, this would make the insured liable for the entire condition. When claim of this type arises, a neurologist should be consulted and should examine the case for you at the earliest possible moment.

1812   Disc injuries

Claims of this type are frequent. They involve a claim that the intervertebral disc was injured in such a way as to rupture or herniate the nucleous pulposis. The nucleous pulposis is located in the center of the disc. The most common cause is lifting heavy objects. Other causes include a sudden twisting of the back (see "whiplash," below). When this condition is diagnosed, either by a lumbar puncture or X ray, an operation is necessary for a cure.

1813   Whiplash

Often claims will be made for whiplash injury to the spine. The claim, usually arising from rear-end-hit cases, is that the force or impact caused the person's spine to go through a forward and backward motion similar to the cracking of a whip. Patently, this is not a diagnosis of the injury but more a description of how the injury was acquired. The result might be a ruptured disc, contusion of the cord, strain of the muscles, or a fracture of the vertebrae.

When faced with claims of this sort, the adjuster should insist on a specific diagnosis.

1814   Hernia

A hernia is a protrusion of any organ through an abnormal opening in the wall of the containing cavity. It commonly refers to a rupture of the wall of the abdomen although, strictly speaking, there are other types of hernia. The condition, normally congenital, is most frequently encountered in workmen's compensation cases. The claim is one of aggravation of a pre-existing condition. There are four common types of hernia. (1) inguinal, in the groin, and either direct or indirect. In the direct hernia, the hernia passes directly through the abdominal wall. The indirect (or incomplete direct) hernia is one that does not protrude beyond the inguinal canal. Even more common herniae types are the (2) umbilical, at the naval, (3) ventral, through the forward wall of the abdomen, and (4) femoral, in the region of the thigh where the femoral artery passes through a ring; protrusion may occur through this ring and the lump will appear on the inner side of the thigh.

Strangulation occurs when the herniated organ is so pinched that it cannot function properly. This condition usually requires immediate surgery. The inner surface of the organ is covered by a thin structure called the peritoneum. When the organ protrudes it carries with it a portion of this structure, which forms a sac. Old sacs are thicker than new ones and a careful examination of the sac at the time of operation may permit the surgeon to estimate the age of the condition. Therefore, in compensation cases where the sole issue is causal relationship, the earlier the operation is performed, the more accurate this estimate will be.

1815   Arthritis

Generally this disease, which means an inflammation of a joint, is either chronic or infectious. There are many types of the condition, but the chronic type most frequently encountered in claim work is the hypertrophic (degenerative, osteoarthritis). Its cause is unknown, but when an arthritic individual is subject to severe strain or trauma, his recovery will be much less rapid.

Other types include atrophic (rheumatoid, proliferative) arthritis, usually a result of heredity, body type, or focal infection, and gout or gouty arthritis, usually a systemic disease secondary to improper protein metabolism, and infectious due to organisms such as staphylococcus or streptococcus.

1816   Inflammatory Diseases

The following diseases of this type are frequently met in claim work:

Neuritis. Inflammation of the nerve trunk or one of its branches; usually toxic in origin and can be considered occupational only in instances where the claimant is exposed to toxic substances. It is not the result of trauma.

Myositis. Inflammation of a muscle or groups of muscles due to overuse, fatigue, or infection. It is not caused by trauma.

Tenosynovitis and *tendonitis.* Inflammation of the tendon or tendon sheath. These conditions can be either spontaneous or traumatic in origin.

Bursitis. Inflammation of the bursal sac. It can arise by reason of direct trauma, or occur spontaneously. The most common types involve the subdeltoid (shoulder), olecranon (elbow), and the prepatella (knee). Prepatella bursitis is popularly referred to as "housemaid's knee."

Osteomyelitis. An infectious inflammatory process of the bone. It may occur spontaneously but is most frequently encountered in a direct infection, as in compound fractures.

Periostitis. Inflammation of the bone covering (periosteum) is usually due to infection. There is a noninfectious type, however, in which direct trauma may activate a reaction of the periosteal tissues.

Phlebitis. Inflammation of a vein. There are two general types: thrombophlebitis, in which a blood clot of infectious origin causes the condition, and phlebothrombosis, in which there is no infection. Usually chronic in origin although it is possible, especially in injuries to the lower extremities, for trauma to play a part in causing or activating the condition.

Cellulitis. Infection and inflammation of the skin and subcutaneous tissue. The port of entry of the bacteria is a break in the skin surface.

Lymphangitis. Inflammation of lymph channels secondary to a localized infection.

Lymphadenitis. Inflammation of the lymph gland, secondary to local infection.

1817 Common injuries

Abrasions, scratches; *Contusions,* bruises; *Incisions,* cuts of the skin; *Lacerations,* tears of the skin; *Sprains,* strains; *Burns* (there are six degrees): *first degree,* pierce outer skin; *second degree,* extend to dermis; *third degree,* extend into the dermis; *fourth degree,* extend into subcutaneous tissue; *fifth degree,* extend into muscle; *sixth degree,* extend into bone; *Dislocation,* out of joint; and *Amputations,* removals.

1818 Lengths of disability

Skull (uncomplicated fracture)	4–8 weeks
Cervical Spine (fracture or dislocation)	4–6 months
Dorsal Spine (compression fracture)	3–5 months
Fractures (uncomplicated)	
Clavicle	10–12 weeks
Humerus	3–4 months
Elbow	6–10 months
Head of radius	3–5 months
Colles	3–5 months
Olecranon	3–5 months
Forearm (one bone)	3–5 months
(both bones)	6–10 months
Carpal	3–6 months

Metacarpal	6–10 weeks
Finger	6–10 weeks
Toe	8–12 weeks
Os Calcis	4–6 months
Hernia	6–8 weeks
	(following surgery)
Ruptured Disc	4–6 months
Amputations	
Finger	6–8 weeks
Major amputations	
(arm or leg)	4–6 months
Stump Revision	3–6 weeks

1819   The eye

The eye is the organ of vision. It occupies the anterior part of the orbit and is nearly spherical in shape. It is covered by three concentric coats: (1) the sclera and cornea, (2) the choroid, ciliary body, and iris, and (3) the retina.

The *sclera* is the white portion and outer coat of the eye, except in the area covered by the cornea. It contains blood vessels and serves for attachment of the muscles which move the eye.

The *choroid* is the second coat. It covers the inner surface of the sclera and its anatomical function is to serve as the principal medium for nourishment of the eyeball. It contains many blood vessels for this purpose.

The *retina* is the innermost coat. It is a light-receptive layer and the terminal expansion of the optic nerve. The structures of the eye permit the passage of light, and the parts of the eye are constructed like a camera in that there is a combination of lenses and accommodating mechanisms so as to produce a clear image on the retina, which in turn transmits the image through the optic nerve to the sight area of the brain.

The first mechanism to deal with light as it enters the eye is the iris. This is the colored portion of the eyeball, with a hole in the center called the pupil. Its function is similar to that of the lens-opening in a camera in that it regulates the amount of light allowed to enter the eye, prevents the introduction of excess light, and increases vision in darkness by increasing the opening. The second mechanism is the lens which operates exactly as the lens of a camera. It is operated by the tiny ciliary muscles which are designed so that they can relax the tension which the suspensory ligament holding the lens normally maintains. The ciliary muscles cause the lens to bulge so as to increase magnification. This muscular action permits us to see close objects in more minute detail. A simple diagram of the functional parts of the eye accompanies this chapter.

Where there is any interference with the transmission of light through the eye, a distorted image is produced on the retina. Thus, if any of the functions of the iris or the lens are disturbed, either due to injury or to lack of function due to age, a hazy image will be produced on the retina. If the retina itself becomes detached from the optic nerve completely, then there is no transmission of the image to the brain. Where there is a disturbance in the functions of the auxiliary mechanisms, the lens and the iris, usually these defects can be corrected by wearing glasses.

The claimsman will encounter the word "vision" in many reports. Standing alone, it usually refers to central vision, or the ability of a person to see an object by focusing his eyes directly at it. Peripheral vision refers to side vision, or the sight of other objects in the same field as the object on which the eyes are focusing. Binocular vision refers to the image produced by both eyes working together. Thus if one eye is stronger, or introduces more light than the other, then the image transmitted to the brain by both eyes is distorted. This can be corrected by the use of proper glasses.

Visual acuity is the measurement of the actual vision in each eye, tested separately. The test is made by the use of a chart of letters, called a Snellen chart. A normal person 20 feet from the chart will be able to read the size and type of letters on the chart that one with perfect vision could read. Such vision is expressed as 20/20, meaning that the test was made at 20 feet and that the line read was the top or "20" line. Let us assume that the person could not read the top line but could read a line which a normal person could read while sitting 30 feet away. The visual acuity then would be expressed as 20/30, meaning that the patient, sitting 20 feet from the chart, could read only the line, which a normal person could read at 30 feet. This same type of

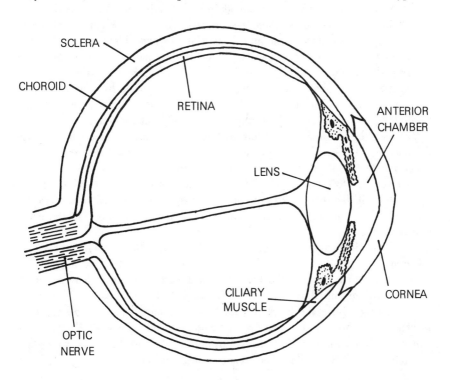

measurement applies to other results from the use of the chart. Thus, if the visual acuity is said to be 20/200, this means that the patient, sitting 20 feet from the chart, could read only the line which a normal person could read at 200 feet. Eye reports also use abbreviations to designate the eye involved. OD or O-D to the right eye; OS or O-S means the left eye.

1820   The heart

The heart is a pear-shaped muscular organ, situated between the lungs and protected by the sternum (breastbone) and the ribs in front, and the fifth, sixth, seventh, and eighth thoracic vertebrae in the back. Its function is to act as a pump for the blood, circulating it through the lungs and to all parts of the body.

Internally, it is composed of four chambers, the right auricle and right ventricle on one side, and the left auricle and left ventricle on the other. The two sides of the heart are completely separated from each other. The function of the right auricle and right ventricle is to receive the blood from all parts of the body, with the exception of the lungs, and to pump it through the pulmonary artery into the lungs. The blood is received in the right auricle through two large veins called the superior and inferior vena cavae. When the right auricle, which occupies the upper right quarter of the heart, becomes filled, it contracts and forces the blood into the right ventricle below. The ventricle then contracts forcing the blood into the pulmonary artery.

To prevent the return of the blood into the right auricle, a heart valve, called the tricuspid, closes when the ventricle contracts. When the ventricle is completely empty, the pulmonary valve at the exit closes, preventing the return of the blood to the heart. The blood is then passed through the lungs where it discharges waste products in the form of carbon dioxide and picks up oxygen. The blood then is returned to the left auricle by four large pulmonary veins and forced into the left ventricle, which contracts and pumps it into the aorta, which distributes the blood throughout the body.

Between the left auricle and left ventricle is the mitral valve which closes the opening between them to prevent a return flow of blood into the auricle. When the ventricle is empty, the aortic valve closes and the blood is prevented from returning to the ventricle. The blood then is circulated throughout the body where it deposits the oxygen and picks up waste. It then returns to the right auricle of the heart via the superior and inferior cavae, and the cycle begins again.

The heart is enclosed in a sac, called the pericardium. Its inner layer is adherent to the outside of the heart, and it contains a fluid which acts as a lubricant which permits the heart to contract freely. An inflammation of the pericardium caused by infection or disease is called pericarditis.

The lining within the heart is called the endocardium. It is a very thin layer of cells similar to the inner layer of other blood vessels, such as arteries and veins. Inflammation of the endocardium is called endocarditis, which the physicians tell us is due almost entirely to infectious bacteria.

The heart muscle is called the myocardium. It differs from other muscles of the body in that it requires little or no activation from the brain, originating its contractions within itself. It does, however, respond to stimuli from other parts of the body, such as increased rate of contraction due to exercise, the need for increased blood supply after eating, or a condition requiring blood supply brought on by a tumor or disease. Physicians tell us that because of the automatic action of the heart muscle, an injury to the brain or any part of the central nervous system seldom produces any heart condition. The heart muscle can be inflamed, usually due to chronic conditions and seldom due to injury. The inflammation is called myocarditis.

The consensus of medical opinion is that the heart cannot be injured by accident except in cases where there is a penetrating wound into the heart itself. Medical opinion also takes the position that it is possible to aggravate a previously diseased heart in cases where the accident produces a strain on the circulatory system or where an infection produces microorganisms which gain entrance to the bloodstream.

When there is a defect in the valves of the heart, the blood will leak backward through the defective valve and the result might be that there is insufficient blood supply for the body's needs. Nature seeks to compensate for defects of this sort, and the heart muscle and the heart will increase in size in order to pump enough blood for the bodily needs. If the heart can continue the normal blood supply through this means, the individual is said to have a compensated heart. However, if the defect is so serious that the heart in spite of the increase in size cannot fully supply the need for blood, the patient is said to have a decompensated heart. He will suffer from shortness of breath upon exertion, and there will be a bluish tinge to his skin or mucous membranes. While it is sometimes claimed that an injury will aggravate a decompensated heart, physicians tell us this is seldom the case, since even a strain on the circulation seldom produces any further damage to the heart if it is of short duration.

1821 The blood

The majority of the cells of the body have no means of nourishment from the outside and are supplied with food solely by the blood. Also these cells have no means of distributing their own products, if any (hormones), nor a means of disposing of waste, usually in the form of carbon dioxide. The circulating blood is utilized for these purposes. It follows that where the blood is incapable of reaching a cell because of some breakdown in the arterial system, due to injury, chronic disease, or infection, the cell will die. This mortification or death of a part of the body is called gangrene.

The blood itself is a watery fluid which contains many cells. These cells are distinguished as red blood cells, called erythrocytes, and white blood cells, called leukocytes. These cells and some cell fragments called platelets are referred to as formed elements. The liquid portion of the blood is the plasma.

Red blood cells.   The majority of the formed elements of the blood are the red blood cells, or erythrocytes. In one cubic millimeter of blood there are about 5 million red blood cells. The principal function of the red blood cell is to act as a carrier of oxygen and to assist in carrying carbon dioxide. In this task the cell utilizes one of its important chemical elements, the red pigment called hemoglobin, which combines with the oxygen and acts as its carrier in the red blood cell. Arterial blood is bright red whereas venous blood is dark red. This is due to the fact that arterial blood contains oxygen and the hemoglobin, combined with the oxygen, produces the bright red color, whereas hemoglobin without oxygen shows up as a dark red.

The life cycle of a red blood cell is estimated at from 10 to 30 days, but since the count remains constant it is clear that there is a continual process of replacement. New red blood cells are produced primarily by the red bone marrow. When there is a marked reduction in the number of red blood cells, due to injury, loss of blood, or a failure on the part of the body to manufacture sufficient replacements, the person is suffering from anemia. Decreased red blood count means there is a lack of oxygen in the blood, that the cells of the body do not receive the oxygen needed, and thus there is a decrease in bodily efficiency.

White blood cells.   The white blood cells, or leukocytes, are fewer in number than the red cells; there are about 5,000 to 9,000 white blood cells in one cubic millimeter of blood. The leukocytes are of several varieties and are classified into several subgroups. For our purposes we will make only one division, between mononuclear and polynuclear cells, or leukocytes with one nucleus and those with many nuclei. A condition of the blood wherein there is a large increase in the number of large mononuclear leukocytes (also called monocytes) is referred to as mononucleosis.

Polynuclear leukocytes have the property of being able to reach sites of infection, whether within the bloodstream or outside. They engulf and digest infectious organisms and injured or dead tissue cells. Many of them are destroyed in this process and the destroyed leukocytes and the debris of dead cells constitute pus, which is characteristic of infection.

Plasma.   The liquid portion of the blood is the plasma, constituting about 55 percent of the whole blood. Plasma is composed mainly of water in which are dissolved hormones of the endocrine glands and other substances needed for the maintenance of the cells. The plasma also picks up the waste products of the cells for elimination through the kidneys.

Coagulation of the blood.   All of us who have had a laceration of the skin are familiar with the process by which a scab is formed at the site of the wound. This clotting process is produced by a change of fibrinogen, a substance in the plasma, from a liquid state to a solid state. When clotting takes place, tiny threads of fibrin, the solid part of the fibrinogen, interlace to form a net in which the blood cells and plasma become enmeshed. This produces a red, jellylike mass, which is recognized as a clot. As the clot shrinks and dries, a yellow liquid collects above it and is pressed out. This is called serum.

Thrombosis and embolism.   Blood does not usually clot within the body, but sometimes the wall of a blood vessel becomes weakened, due to injury or some systemic condition, and clots form at the site of the lesion. This is a protective mechanism of the body since the formation of clots might prevent further damage to the wall of the vessel or prevent the rupture of the wall and an ensuing escape of blood into the area, which is called a hemorrhage. Such a clot is called a thrombus. When it increases in size, so as to interfere with the normal flow of blood within the vessel, or to plug up the vessel completely, the condition is thrombosis. The complete plugging up of the blood vessel is referred to as an occlusion of the blood vessel. Sometimes a clot breaks away and is carried by the blood throughout the body until it reaches a smaller vessel through which it cannot pass. It then sets up an occlusion, or plugging of that vessel. Any foreign substance in the bloodstream, be it a clot as described, or an air bubble or oil globule, is called an embolus. The resultant condition, where the substance occludes the blood vessel, is called embolism. The cells which do not receive food because of the complete cessation of the blood flow die and the area of dead cells so produced is referred to as an infarct.

In some cases the embolus plugs up a small artery or capillary and the blood pressure behind the plug builds up to the point where the wall of the blood vessel gives way and the blood floods the area. The results of this condition can be extremely serious and can cause death. Mechanically, this is what occurs when a person is said to have suffered a "stroke." An embolus plugs up a blood vessel in the brain and the walls of the blood vessel give way with the result that the blood hemorrhages into the surrounding area, impairing the function of the flooded area.

The outward manifestations of the condition will depend upon the area of the brain which is affected. If the area controls the patient's vocal cords, his speech will be affected by a paralysis of those cords. If the area controls muscular movements of one side of the body, we can expect to find a paralysis of the muscles of that side as a result. Should the blood be absorbed and the area of the brain return to something approaching normal function, the paralysis will subside proportionately to the healing in the brain. In any case, the outward manifestation will be indicative of the condition which has arisen within the brain. Other areas beside the brain where this situation can occur include the lungs and the coronary artery, which is part of the aorta.

These conditions can come about as a result of a chronic condition as well as traumatic injury. Where an injury is alleged, it becomes important to establish when, for the first time after the injury, the first manifestation of the condition appeared. The general rule is that the longer the interval of time between the injury and the onset of the first symptoms, the less evidence there is that the injury was the precipitating cause.

1822   Blood grouping and transfusions

In analyzing blood, scientists have discovered that the red blood cells contain a substance called an antigen and the serum contains antibodies. A group of antigens is called an agglutinogen. Two distinct agglutinogens were discovered which were labeled *A* and *B*. Examination and analysis disclosed that all human blood contains one, both, or none of these agglutinogens. Thus a person whose blood contains only agglutinogen *A* was typed as A, *B* as type B, and the person whose blood contained neither was type O. Those with both *A* and *B* agglutinogens were typed as AB.

It was also found that a person having one agglutinogen had a corresponding antibody, so that the person having the agglutinogen *A* in his red blood cells has an antibody or agglutinin anti-*B* in his serum. The antibody or agglutinin is so called because of its reaction to the agglutinogen. Thus, agglutinogen *A* is compatible with antibody or agglutinin anti-*B* and there is no reaction, but if agglutinogen *B* is added, the reaction of the agglutinin anti-*B* will be to cause a clumping of the cells of antinogen *B* with resulting serious effects. A person with agglutinogen *B* has the agglutinin anti-*A*. The O type has neither agglutinogen *A* nor *B*, but both anti-*A* and anti-*B* agglutinins. Later it was recognized that some persons had both agglutinogen *A* and agglutinogen *B*, but such a person had neither agglutinin anti-*A* nor anti-*B*.

Therefore, when transfusions are performed it becomes essential that the correct type of blood be infused. As long as the blood is of the same type and is compatible, no serious results can be anticipated. To guard against the possibility of error, hospitals not only type the blood of the patient and that of the donor, but also take a blood sample from each and combine them, noting the reaction, if any, under a microscope. If there is any agglutination, then the donor's blood is not used. This is called cross-typing.

Rh factor.   It was found that the foregoing analysis and blood grouping was not entirely sufficient in that there were cases where the proper type blood was transfused but where agglutination took place. It was later discovered that some persons would react to an antibody created in the serum of rabbits injected with the blood of the rhesus monkey. A person who would react to this serum, called anti-Rh serum, had an Rh agglutinogen in his red blood cells. (The Rh designation came from the name of the monkey, rhesus.) An individual whose red blood cells were not agglutinated by the serum did not possess the Rh agglutinogen. The former were classified as Rh positive and the latter as Rh negative.

Individuals in the Rh positive group have been divided into subgroups depending upon the blood reaction to the anti-Rh serum. These are Rh' (Rh prime) and Rh'' (Rh double prime). Presently anti-Rh' and anti-Rh'' serum has been developed so that reaction can be ascertained more easily. Also the anti-Rh_0 serum has been developed and is utilized before a person can be definitely typed as Rh negative.

Hr factors. It is known that persons who are Rh negative have factors, or agglutinogens, called Hr factors. These are divided into subgroups similar to the Rh typing, being known as Hr_o, Hr', and Hr''. Unfortunately, antiserum containing anti-Hr agglutinin cannot be produced by animals other than humans, and therefore the availability of the antiserum for testing purposes is limited. However, medical opinion is that the Hr factor is not so important as the other types of classification and that Hr incompatible blood does not produce the same sensitivity as other types of incompatible blood.

1823 Compressed-air disease

This disease is found where the patient has been exposed to increased air pressure outside his body. This may be while he is at work or at play. It is found where the patient is engaged in deep-sea diving, scuba diving, caisson work under pressure, and coffer dam work. It comes about when air bubbles form in the bloodstream following too rapid a reduction in the outside pressure. These air bubbles, or air emboli, cause symptoms of headache, dizziness, fainting spells and, in severe cases, paralysis and death. The disease is also called the "bends," the "chokes," or caisson disease. Since the symptoms are similar to conditions produced by other diseases, the claimsman will require expert advice from a qualified physician in handling claims of this type.

1824 Dust and fiber diseases

The inhalation of deleterious dust and fiber particles over a period of years can and does produce certain serious conditions. The particles involved are infinitismal and usually cannot be seen with the naked eye, and are of such size that they are almost weightless being suspended in the air for certain periods of time. These diseases are as follows:

1. Silicosis. This condition comes about as a result of the inhalation of silica over a period of years. The silica particles lodge in the lungs and are absorbed by the dust cells (macrophages) ultimately destroying them. The dust cells clump and form a fibrosis which ultimately collapses the lung. There is no known cure for this condition. The condition comes about as a result of mining and drilling of siliceous rock and is usually found in mining operations where the process is conducted in a small space. It is believed that the wearing of respiratory masks and the use of water in the drills (Kelly trap) will reduce the risk.

2. Anthracosis. Similar to silicosis, caused by the inhalation of anthracite particles or other particles containing silicon dioxide and carbon. (Also referred to as black lung disease.)

3. Asbestosis. Caused by the inhalation of asbestos fibers over a long period of time. This condition comes about not only because of the handling or use of asbestos related products, but can also be caused by the inhalation of the fibers in any confined space where asbestos is part of the building. The asbestos fibers constitute a carcinogen (cancer causing) substance where some form of cancer is the ultimate result, such as mesothelioma, which is the common form found in asbestos workers. As others who have been exposed to asbestos fibers, the incidence of gastrointestinal cancers is quite high.

1825   Hematoma

A hematoma is a blood clot which finds its way into a small space in the body and becomes enclosed in a capsule, or encapsulated. It is caused by an injury to a blood vessel wherein blood clots are formed and are discharged into a small space. Hematomas may form on the surface of the skin where they resemble a blister with bloody fluid and are referred to by laymen as "blood blisters." They may also form in the subcutaneous layers of the skin, the belly of a muscle, and in many other spaces within the body. Hematomas represent the most serious condition when they are located either above or within the layers of matter covering the brain and the spinal cord, where they exert pressure. The more severe the pressure, the more serious the condition will be.

The brain and the spinal cord are covered by three membranes, called collectively, the meninges, which constitute three different layers. The outer membrane is the dura mater, usually referred to as the dura. The middle membrane is the arachnoid membrane, and the inner layer is the pia mater, or the pial membrane. A hematoma which occurs above the dura and exerts its pressure from that point is referred to as an epidural hematoma. One which is formed in the space between the dura and the arachnoid membrane is referred to as a subdural hematoma. Bleeding into the space between the arachnoid and the pia mater does not produce a hematoma but will cause a bloody spinal fluid.

1826   Infection

Infection is the result of the implanting of the seeds of disease in the body. These seeds of disease may be bacterial in origin or may be the result of a fungus. The microorganisms, either fungus or bacteria, gain entry to the body usually through a wound or by ingestion. They settle in a certain place and feed on the surrounding tissue.

As they grow they give off certain growth products which are called ptomaines. These may or may not be poisonous or harmful. If they are non-poisonous, they will not produce disease or infection, and in some cases they aid in the body processes. If the ptomaine is poisonous, it is called a toxin. As a defense to this toxin, the body produces a substance called an antitoxin. This will not destroy the toxin but it will, if produced in sufficient quantity, combine with the toxin and either make it harmless or reduce its virulent effect.

White blood cells are the destructive agents as far as bacteria are concerned. They devour, destroy, and carry away the bacteria. The cells utilized for this purpose are called phagocytes, and the process by which they destroy bacteria is called phagocytosis. This process is a battle for survival between the phagocytes and the bacteria, and in many cases the outcome will depend upon numbers. If there is more bacteria than the phagocytes can devour and carry away, the outcome of the disease may have serious consequences, even resulting in the death of the patient.

Incubation period. The incubation period in infection is defined as the period of time within which the first manifestation of the disease becomes apparent after the entry of the infecting agent. The period is usually relatively short, in most cases about 3–5 days, so that if there is a wound which it is claimed was the port of entry of the bacteria, the first symptoms of infection should be present within the period mentioned. If the symptoms present themselves at a later time, it is generally agreed by the medical profession that the bacteria did not enter the body at the time of the wound but gained entrance at a later time and perhaps through other means.

1827   Blood tests for intoxication

Intoxication is the condition which is produced by the presence of alcohol in the brain. It is characterized by a lack of coordination, a reduction in reflex action, and, in extreme cases, complete insensibility. The extent to which coordination, mental response, and reflex action is impaired will depend upon the quantity of alcohol which reaches the brain: the greater the amount of alcohol, the greater the reaction. Mechanically, what occurs is that ingested alcohol is absorbed by the blood from the stomach. The blood carries it to all parts of the body, including the brain. Since alcohol is a sedative it reduces the activity of the brain not only as to its control over the motor senses of the body but also sensory reflexes and mental responses to the stimulation normally produced by apprehension.

Medical standards. Medically, intoxication is classified by the objective signs which are observable by an examination of the patient's activity. These are:

1. *Acute Intoxication.* This follows the drinking of a considerable amount of liquor at once. Profound insensibility follows rapidly with stentorious breathing, purplish face, frothing at the mouth, weak pulse and increasing coma. While this form is unusual, when it does happen, immediate measures are necessary to save the patient's life.
2. *Subacute Intoxication.* This is the usual drunkenness. It can be mild or of serious nature. The mild form is usually found in persons who merely drink for the exhilaration which alcohol gives them, and who discontinue their drinking before they lose control of their faculties. The serious type refers to persons who drink until they are stupefied.
3. *Mild Intoxication.* This causes some increase in the circulation and stimulates the nervous system. In some cases, it upsets the digestive apparatus.

Legal standards. All statutes prohibit the driving of a motor vehicle while "in an intoxicated condition," "in a drunken or partly drunken condition," or "while under the influence of liquor." In considering the problem of law enforcement, the medical profession was called upon to assist in supplying scientific information. It was reasoned that the most accurate test of the amount of alcohol in the brain would be a test of the brain itself. Unfortunately, this is not possible except in the case of death. Tests, however, indicated that there was very little variation (about $\frac{1}{100}$th of 1 percent) between the alcohol content of the blood as compared to that of the brain. Therefore, based on the medical findings and its own tests, the National Safety Council promulgated standards of alcohol within the body with recommendations as to the ability to drive referable to each level. These are based upon the alcohol concentration within the blood and are as follows:

0.05%	Able to drive; should not be prosecuted. (Equivalent of two ounces of whiskey or two bottles of beer.)
0.15 or less	Should not drive.
0.15 or over	Definitely drunk. (Equivalent of 6–7 ounces of whiskey or 6–7 bottles of beer.)
0.2	Dizzy and delirious.
0.3	Dazed and dejected.
0.4	Dead drunk.
0.5	Dead.

These standards have been generally accepted by the courts, and in some states they are part of the motor vehicle statute.[2]

1828   Other intoxication tests

Other tests which are utilized for determining intoxication are tests of the urine, spinal fluid, and, if a sufficient sampling can be obtained, the sputum. Since there is a direct relationship between these fluids and the blood, it is claimed that by test and mathematical computation a conclusion as to the alcoholic content of the blood can be drawn.

Air or breath tests are made by the use of one of the various machines designed for that purpose, such as the Drunkometer, the Alcometer, the Intoximeter, and the Breathalyzer. The advantage of these machines is that a properly trained layman can take the sample and make an analysis, whereas in the other tests, including the blood, the sample usually must be taken by a physician and in all cases the analysis must be made by a fully qualified technician.

1829   Intoxication tests as evidence

When the result of an intoxication test is offered in evidence it must be shown that the test was conducted under the above circumstances and within

---

[2] While the standards were created for the purpose of determining the ability of a person to drive a motor vehicle, it would appear that they could also be used as the basis for any defense involving the physical ability of a person to exercise care for his own safety and for the safety of others.

a short period of time after the accident so as to be indicative of the patient's condition at the time of the accident. If the sample is taken by one person and analyzed by another, the evidence must show how the sample was preserved, how it was labeled, and any possibility that the sample tested was taken from anyone other than the patient must be excluded. Clearly, unless it can be established with certainty that the sample came from the patient, the patient cannot be bound by the result of the test.

In addition, evidence must exclude the possibility of any change in the patient's condition from the time of the accident to the time of the test. For example, if following the accident the patient was given a few shots of whiskey, a test would show the result of all the alcohol consumed, both before and after the accident. It is estimated by the medical profession that one ounce of whiskey or one bottle of beer will produce about 0.02 percent alcohol within the blood. Where the patient has had some whiskey after the accident, and the amount thereof can be established with certainty, the test can be factored by a percentage reduction to cover the after-acquired alcohol. Unfortunately, evidence of this kind is seldom available.

1830   Osteology chart: Skeleton

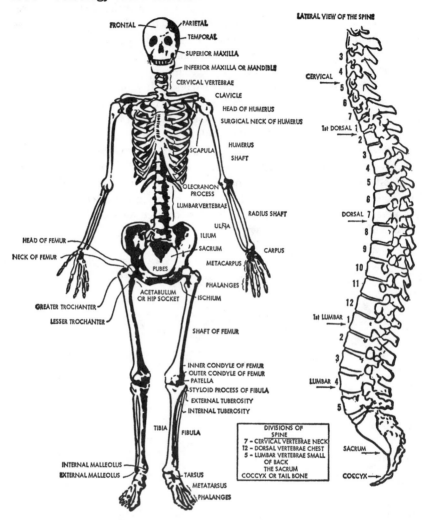

1831 Osteology chart: Hands and feet

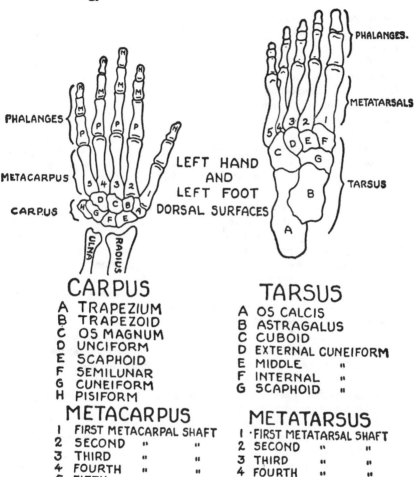

PHALANGES.

METATARSALS

PHALANGES

METACARPUS

CARPUS

TARSUS

LEFT HAND
AND
LEFT FOOT
DORSAL SURFACES

ULNA

RADIUS

CARPUS
A TRAPEZIUM
B TRAPEZOID
C OS MAGNUM
D UNCIFORM
E SCAPHOID
F SEMILUNAR
G CUNEIFORM
H PISIFORM

TARSUS
A OS CALCIS
B ASTRAGALUS
C CUBOID
D EXTERNAL CUNEIFORM
E MIDDLE "
F INTERNAL "
G SCAPHOID "

METACARPUS
1 FIRST METACARPAL SHAFT
2 SECOND " "
3 THIRD " "
4 FOURTH " "
5 FIFTH " "

METATARSUS
1 FIRST METATARSAL SHAFT
2 SECOND " "
3 THIRD " "
4 FOURTH " "
5 FIFTH " "

PHALANGES
P PROXIMAL
M MIDDLE
N DISTAL

1832   Common medical terms

Abduction.   Withdrawal of a part from the axis of the body or of an extremity. In ophthalmology, the turning of the eyes outward from the central position by the lateral rectus muscles.

Abrasion.   A spot of denuded skin, mucous membrane, or superficial epithelium by rubbing or scraping.

Abscess.   Localized collection of pus in any part of the body.

Acetylsalicylate.   Aspirin.

Acuity.   Sharpness, clearness, keenness, or distinctness; as of vision.

Acute.   Sharp, severe. Not chronic.

Adduction.   Any movement whereby one part or limb is brought toward another, or toward the median line of the body. In ophthalmology, the turning of the eyes inward from the central position, through contraction of the medial rectus muscle.

Adhesion.   Abnormal union of an organ or part to another.

Agglutinin.   An antibody occurring in a normal or immune serum, which when added to a suspension of its homologous particulate antigen causes the antigen elements to adhere to one another causing clumps. This action takes place when incompatible blood is introduced into the blood serum.

Allergy.   Altered reaction capacity to a specific substance.

Analgesia.   Insensibility to pain without loss of consciousness.

Anemia.   Loss of normal balance between productive and destructive blood processes due to diminution of the normal blood volume.

Anesthesia.   Loss of sensation. The most common types are *block anesthesia,* produced by injecting an anesthetic solution into the nerve trunks supplying the operative field, and *inhalation anesthesia,* produced by the inhalation of anesthetic vapors.

Angina pectoris.   Pain of psychosomatic origin characterized by a sense of oppression and severe constriction about the chest.

Angioma.   A tumor composed of blood or lymphatic vessels.

Anthrax.   An acute infectious disease of cattle and of sheep, transmissible to man.

Antitoxin.   A substance elaborated in the body, capable of neutralizing a given toxin or poison.

Aorta.   The large vessel arising from the left ventricle of the heart, which distributes by its branches arterial blood to every part of the body.

Arteriosclerosis.   Abnormal thickening or hardening of the arterial walls resulting from chronic inflammation.

Artery.   A vessel carrying blood from the heart.

Arthritis.   Inflammation of a joint.

Atrophy.   The wasting away of a muscle or a vital organ.

Audiometer.   An instrument for measuring the acuity and range of hearing.

Balkan frame.   An overhead quadrilateral frame supported by uprights fastened to the bed; used to suspend immobilized fractured limbs and to apply continuous traction by weights and pulleys.

Bel.   A unit frequently used to measure the intensity of sound, commonly the intensity above the normal threshold of hearing. A *decibel* is one-tenth of a bel.

Benign.   Not endangering the health and life; not malignant, innocent; applied to certain tumors.

Biceps.   A muscle having two heads.

Block.   To obstruct the path of sensory impressions by injections of an anesthetic agent in the nerve trunks in the area of a surgical operation.

Blood.   The fluid tissue which circulates through the heart, arteries, capillaries, and veins, and which supplies oxygen and food to the other tissues of the body, and removes from them carbon dioxide and waste products of metabolism. It is made up of plasma and cellular elements. The latter consists of red cells, white cells, and blood platelets. One cu. mm. of normal blood contains about 6,000 white and 5,000,000 red cells. The bright red color of arterial blood is due to oxyhemoglobin of the red cells and the darker red of venous blood to reduced hemoglobin or the methenoglobin. The total amount of blood is equal to $\frac{1}{12}$ of body weight. Healthy blood contains about 78 percent water and 22 percent solids.

Blood groups.   In the human, there are four classifications of blood, depending upon agglutinogens in the red cells, and agglutinins in the serum which lead to hemolysis or agglutination (clumping) when incompatible bloods are mixed, as in a transfusion. These groups are classified as O, A, B, and AB.

Brain.   That part of the central nervous system contained in the cranial cavity, consisting of the cerebrum, cerebellum, pons, and medulla oblongata.

Bursa.   A small sac interposed between parts that move on one another.

Callus.   An area of hardened or thickened skin, seen usually in the palm or sole. New growth of incompletely organized bony tissue surrounding the bone ends in fractures, which is a part of the reparative process.

Calor.   Heat; one of the classic signs of inflammation; calor (heat), tumor (swelling), rubor (redness), and dolor (pain).

Calcaneus.   The heel bone.

Capillary.   A minute blood vessel; one of a network connecting the smallest arteries and veins.

Carcinoma.   An epithelial tumor, which is malignant; cancer. Another form of cancer is called sarcoma.

Cardiac.   Relating to the heart; a person with a heart lesion.

Cardiogram.   A record of the heart's pulsation taken through the chest wall.

Carotid.   The principal large artery on each side of the neck.

Carpal.   Pertaining to the wrist or carpus.

Carpus.   The wrist, consisting of eight bones.

Cartilage.   Gristle; a white semiopaque, nonvascular connective tissue composed of a matrix containing nucleated cells which lie in cavities or lacunas of the matrix.

Causalgia.   The burning pain that is sometimes present in injuries of the nerves.

Cecum.   The large blind pouch or cul-de-sac in which the large intestine begins. It is the connecting link between the small and the large intestines. Also spelled secum or caecum.

Cerebellum.   The inferior part of the brain, lying below the cerebrum and above the pons and medulla, consisting of two lateral lobes and a middle lobe.

Cerebrum.   The chief portion of the brain, occupying the whole upper part of the cranium and consisting of the right and left hemispheres. It is the seat of consciousness and thought.

Chiropractic. A system of therapeutics based on the theory that disease is caused by the abnormal function of the nervous system. Attempts to restore normal function are made through manipulation and treatment of the structures of the body, especially those of the spinal column.

Chronic. Long continued, of long duration; as opposed to acute.

Cicatrix. A scar.

Clavicle. A bone of the shoulder girdle articulating medially with the sternum and laterally with the acromion of the scapula; the collarbone.

Clonus. A series of movements characterized by alternate contractions and relaxations; a clonic spasm. Involuntary reflex; irregular contraction of muscles when suddenly put upon stretch. According to the part affected, the phenomenon is referred to as ankle-clonus, wrist-clonus, etc.

Coccyx. The last bone of the spinal column, formed by the union of four rudimentary vertebrae. Some anatomists claim that this bone is a degeneration of the bones which constituted a tail, when man was in a primary state.

Coma. Unconsciousness from which the patient cannot be aroused. It may be due to ingested poison, such as opiates or alcohol; to poison developed in the body, as in uremia or overwhelming toxemias; to profound disturbances of the acid-base balance as in diabetic acidosis; or to brain injury, trauma, apoplexy, or tumor.

Comminuted. In fractures, a bone so fractured that it is shattered in several places.

Compatibility. Congruity; the power of a medicine or substance in a medicine to mix with another without deleterious chemical change or loss of therapeutic power.

Concussion. Shock; a severe shaking or jarring of a part and a condition of lowered functional activity of an organ due to shock.

Concussion of the brain. A condition produced by a fall or blow on the head and evidenced by unconsciousness, feeble pulse, cold skin, and pallor. Residual symptoms following concussions are referred to as post concussion syndrome, and consist principally of headaches and dizziness.

Conduction. The passage or transfer of electrons, heat, or sound waves through suitable media, or of nerve or muscle impulses through those tissues.

Conjunctiva. The mucous membrane covering the interior portion of the globe of the eye, reflected upon the lids, and extending to their edges.

Contraction. Shortening, especially of the fibers of the muscle tissue.

Cord. Any stringlike body; spinal cord is that part of the central nervous system contained within the vertebral canal and extending from the medulla oblongata at the level of the foramen magnum to the filum terminals at the level of the first or second lumbar vertebra.

Cornea. The transparent interior portion of the eyeball, its area occupying about ⅙ of the circumference of the globe.

Cyst. A sac, with a distinct wall, containing fluid or other matter. It may be a normal or pathologic structure.

Cystoscope. An instrument used in the diagnosis and treatment of lesions of the bladder, ureter, and kidney.

Deafness. Loss, lack, or impairment of the sense of hearing. It may be due to disease of the external auditory canal, the middle ear, the internal ear, or the auditory nerve and brain.

Debridement.   In surgery, removal of foreign material or devitalized tissue from a wound.

Deltoid.   Triangular, shaped like the Greek *delta*. Refers to the deltoid ligament of the ankle joint and the large triangular shaped muscle covering the shoulder joint.

Dementia.   Deterioration or loss of intellectual faculties, the reasoning power, the will, and memory; characterized by confusion, disorientation, apathy, and stupor of varying degrees.

Derma.   The layer of skin between the epidermis and the subcutaneous tissue.

Dermatitis.   Inflammation of the skin.

Diagnosis.   The act of determining the nature of a disease or disability.

Diplopia.   Double vision; one object being seen as two.

Disk (or disc).   A circular platelike organ or structure. Intervertebral disks are disks of fibrocartilage between the adjacent surfaces of the bodies of the vertebrae.

Dislocation.   The displacement of one or more bones of a joint or of any organ from its original position.

Duodenum.   The first part of the intestine, beginning at the pylorus. It is 8 to 10 inches long and is the most fixed part of the small intestine.

Dura mater.   The fibrous membrane forming the outermost covering of the brain and spinal cord.

Ecchymosis.   An extravasation of blood into the subcutaneous tissues, marked by a purple discoloration of the skin; black and blue mark.

Electrocardiogram.   (Abbreviated EKG.) A graphic record of the electric potential differences due to the actions of the heart, taken from the body surfaces. A typical record shows P, Q, R, S, T, and U waves. The P wave is due to the exitation of the atria; Q, R, and S through exitation of the ventricles; T to repolarization of the ventricles; U is a diastolic wave of unknown origin.

Embolus.   Any foreign matter in the bloodstream. It may be a blood clot, air, cancer, or other tissue cells, fat, cardiac vegetations, a clump of bacteria, or a foreign body such as a needle or bullet which gains entrance to the individual's body and is carried by the bloodstream until it lodges in an artery and obstructs it, causing embolism.

Encephalogram.   X ray of the brain following removal of the cerebrospinal fluid by lumbar or cisternal puncture, and its replacement by air or oxygen.

Ethmoid.   A bone of the base of the skull perforated for the olfactory nerve and forming the upper bony nose.

Fetus.   The unborn offspring of man from the end of the third month until birth.

Fluoroscope.   The instrument used for examining the form and motion of internal structures of the body by means of roentgen rays (X rays). The image or shadow is projected on a fluorescent screen.

Fracture.   A breaking of a bone or cartilage.

Fusion.   The process of melting; the act of uniting or cohering, as in spinal fusion where there is a union of two or more vertebrae caused by surgical means for the purpose of immobilizing the spinal column. Used in the treatment of spinal deformities, tuberculosis of the spine, or severe arthritis of the spine.

Gangrene. Mortification or death of a part due to failure of the blood supply because of a disease or injury.

Gynecology. The science of the disease of women.

Heart. A hollow muscular organ, whose function is to pump blood through the vessels. It is enveloped by the pericardium and consists of two symmetrical halves, a right atrium and ventricle and a left atrium and ventricle.

Hematoma. A localized extravasation of blood which soon clots to form a solid mass and readily becomes encapsulated by a tissue; a blood blister.

Hemoglobin. The respiratory pigment of the red blood cells; abbreviated hb.

Hernia. The abnormal protrusion of an organ or part through the containing wall of its cavity beyond its normal confines. The term usually applies to the abdominal cavity and implies the existence of a covering or sac. Also called a rupture.

History. The account obtained from a patient as to his health, past, and present, and the symptoms of his disease or injury.

Hyoid. A bone between the root of the tongue and the larynx.

Hypertension. Excessive tension, usually synonymous with high blood pressure.

Hypertrophy. An increase in the size of an organ, independent of natural growth, due to enlargement or multiplication of its constituent cells.

Hypotension. Diminished or abnormal tension, usually synonymous with low blood pressure.

Ilium. The superior broad portion of the hip bone.

Impaction. A condition in which a fragment of bone is firmly driven into another fragment of bone so that neither can move against the other.

Incision. A cut or wound of the body tissue, usually named as to location, such as an abdominal incision.

Incompatible. Incapable of being used or put together because of resulting chemical change or antagonistic qualities; used in describing two drugs or two types of blood.

Induration. The hardening of a tissue or part.

Infection. Contamination of a wound; implanting a disease from without by the intrusion of bacteria into the wound.

Inflammation. The reaction of tissues to injury.

Inguinal. Pertaining to the groin.

Insanity. A loose term for any mental disorder or derangement.

Jaw. Either bone of the oral skeleton; the upper jaw is formed by the maxilla and the lower by the mandible.

Jerk. A sudden, spasmodic movement; a term often applied to certain reflexes, such as the knee-jerk.

Joint. The articulation or coming together of two or more bones.

Jugular. Pertaining to the neck above the clavicle; as the jugular vein.

Keratitis. Inflammation of the cornea of the eye.

Kyphosis. Angular curvature of the spine; hunchback or humpback.

Laminectomy. An operation for the removal of the vertebral arches.

Larynx. The organ of voice situated between the trachea and the base of the tongue.

Leukemia. A disease of the blood-forming organs, characterized by uncontrolled proliferation of the leukocytes; cancer of the white blood cells.

Leukocyte. White blood cell.

Ligament. A band of flexible, tough, dense white fibrous tissue, connecting particular ends of bones and sometimes enveloping them in a capsule.

Malignant. Virulent, threatening life, as in malignant tumors; cancer.

Malingerer. One who feigns illness, injury, or disability for the purpose of obtaining a reward.

Medial. Internal; through the body.

Medulla. Marrow; anything resembling marrow in structure or in its relation to other parts, as in the medulla oblongata, which is the lower end of the brain stem, extending from the spinal cord opposite the foramen magnum to the pons.

Meningitis. Inflammation of the membranes of the brain or cord.

Metabolism. The phenomena of synthesizing foodstuffs into complex tissue elements; assimilation of food.

Myelitis. Inflammation of the spinal cord or inflammation of the bone marrow.

Myelogram. A radiograph or X ray of the spinal column after the injection of a contrast medium.

Myositis. Inflammation of a muscle.

Nebula. A faint, grayish opacity (a spot impervious to light) of the cornea.

Necrosis. The pathologic death of a cell or group of living cells in contact with living cells.

Nephritis. Inflammation of the kidney.

Nephrosis. Any degeneration of the kidney without signs of inflammation.

Nervous system. The entire nervous apparatus of the body, including the brain, brain stem, spinal cord, cranial and peripheral nerves and ganglions.

Neuralgia. Severe paroxysmal pain along the course of a nerve, not associated with demonstrable structural changes in the nerve.

Neuritis. Inflammation of a nerve.

Neuroma. A tumor on a nerve.

Neuropsychiatry. The branch of medical science dealing with both nervous and mental diseases.

Neurosis. A disorder of the psyche or psychic functions. It is characterized by emotional instability, irritability, apprehension, and a sense of utter fatigue.

Neurotic. Pertaining to or affected with a neurosis.

Noxious. Harmful; poisonous or deleterious.

Nystigmus. An oscillatory movement of the eyeballs. It may be congenital or due to intercranial disease, such as meningitis or multiple sclerosis.

Obliteration. The complete removal of a part by disease or surgical operation.

Obstetrics. The branch of medicine dealing with women during pregnancy, labor and childbirth.

Occiput. The back part of the head.

Occlusion. A closing or complete obstruction of a blood vessel; as a coronary occlusion, which is a complete closure of the artery which supplies the blood to the heart muscle.

Opacity. The condition of being impervious to light, an opaque spot; as opacity of the cornea or lens.

Ophthalmia. Inflammation of the eye.

Ophthalmology. The science of the anatomy, physiology, and diseases of the eye.

Opiate. A preparation of opium; a substance which brings on rest, inaction, and dulls the feelings.

Orbit. The bony cavity that contains the eye and which is formed by the frontal, sphenoid, ethmoid, nasal, lacrimal, maxillary and palatal bones.

Os. A bone.

Osteitis. Inflammation of a bone.

Osteochronditis. An inflammation involving both bone and cartilage.

Osteopathy. The school of healing which teaches that the body is a vital mechanical organism whose structural and functional integrity are coordinate and interdependent, the malfunction of either constituting disease. Its major effort in treatment is by manipulation, but surgery is also included.

Osteomyelitis. Inflammation of the marrow of a bone.

Otology. The science of the ear; its anatomy, functions, and diseases.

Otorhinology. The study of diseases of the ears and nose.

Palate. The roof of the mouth.

Palliative. Relieving or alleviating suffering; any drug which relieves or soothes the symptoms of disease without curing it.

Palsy. A synonym for paralysis, used to designate certain types.

Paralysis. Loss of muscle function or of sensation, caused by injury to the nervous system or by the destruction of neurons.

Paranoia. A psychosis characterized by well-systemized delusions of persecution and hallucinations.

Parietal. A bone of the skull.

Pathology. That branch of the biological medical science which deals with the nature of disease through the study of its causes, its processes, and its effects.

Pediatrics. A branch of medicine dealing with children's diseases.

Pelvis. The bony frame formed by two innominate bones and the sacrum and coccyx.

Periarthritis. Inflammation of the tissues around a joint.

Pericardium. The membranous sac enveloping the heart.

Periosteum. The fibrous membrance surrounding a bone.

Periostitis. Inflammation of the periosteum, usually caused by trauma or infection.

Peritoneum. The serous membrane lining the interior of the abdominal cavity.

Peritonitis. Inflammation of the peritoneum.

Pes planus. Flatfoot.

Phalanx. One of the bones of fingers or toes.

Phlebitis. Inflammation of a vein.

Plastic. Formative; concerned with building up tissues, restoring lost parts, repairing or rectifying malformations or defects, as in plastic surgery.

Pleura. The serous membrane enveloping the lung.

Pneumonoconiosis. Inflammation of the lung caused by the inhalation of dust, as in silicosis.

Pneumothorax. The presence of air or gas in the pleural cavity; may occur from penetrating wounds of the chest, by rupture of an abscess, or by a cavity in the lung.

Podiatry. Treatment of disorders of the feet, chiropody.

Poliomyelitis. Inflammation of the gray matter of the spinal cord.

Pons. A process or bridge of tissue, connecting two parts of an organ.

Postmortem. An examination of the body after death; an autopsy.

Prognosis. A prediction of the duration, course, and termination of a disease, based on all the information available and knowledge of how the disease or injury usually terminates.

Psyche. The mind as a functional entity, serving to adjust the total organism to the needs or demands of the environment.

Psychology. The science which studies the functions of the mind, such as sensation, perception, memory, thought, and generally its relation to environment.

Psychosis. A specialized mental disorder, especially one without demonstrable organic disease.

Psychosomatic. Of or pertaining to the mind and body together, as in affections with an emotional background, having both mental and bodily components; a science which emphasizes the interdependence of mind and the physical or somatic functions.

Pylorus. The circular opening of the stomach into the duodenum.

Quadriceps. Four headed; the large extensory muscle of the thigh.

Radiograph. An X ray.

Radiologist. A physician specializing in the use of roentgen or radium rays in the diagnosis and treatment of disease.

Radius. The outer of the two bones of the forearm. The other bone is the ulna.

Rale. An abnormal sound arising from within the lungs.

Ramus. A branch, especially of a vein, artery, or nerve. Also a slender process of bone projecting like a branch from a large bone.

Reflex. An involuntary, invariable adaptive response to a stimulus.

Refraction. The act or process of correcting errors in eye function.

Regeneration. The new growth or repair of structures or tissues lost by disease or injury.

Regurgitation. A back flow of blood through a defective heart valve.

Retina. The light-receptive layer and terminal expansion of the optic nerve of the eye.

Retractor. A surgical instrument used to hold back the edges of a wound to give access to deeper parts.

Rheumatism. A general term indicating diseases of a muscle, tendon, joint, bone, or nerve, resulting in discomfort or disability.

Rhinology. The science of the anatomy, functions, and diseases of the nose.

Rib. One of the 24 long, flat, curved bones, forming the wall of the thorax.

Roentgenology. The branch of medical science which deals with diagnostic and therapeutic application of roentgen rays; also called radiology or X ray.

Rupture. A forcible tearing of a part; hernia.

Sacroiliac. Pertaining to the sacrum and the ilium, a joint formed at the junction of both of these bones.

Sacrospinalis. A large muscle arising from the posterior aspect of the sacrum and inserted above on the spine and ribs.

Sacrum. A curved triangular bone composed of five united vertebrae, situated between the last lumbar vertebra and the coccyx.

Schizophrenia. A psychosis characterized by inappropriate mood, unpredictable behavior, and disintegration; frequently terminates in mental regression or total withdrawal from reality into phantasies; sometimes called "split personality."

Sciatica. A disease characterized by neurologic pain along the course of the sciatic nerve, caused by injury to or inflammation of the nerve.

Sclerosis. Hardening, especially of a part by the overgrowth of fibrous tissue; applied particularly to hardening of the arteries and veins.

Shock. Sudden vital depression due to injury or emotion; state of physical collapse.

Spondylitis. Inflammation of one or more vertebra.

Sprain. A wrenching of a joint, producing a stretching or laceration of the ligaments.

Subdeltoid. Beneath the deltoid muscle, as a subdeltoid bursa.

Subluxation. A partial dislocation or sprain.

Tachycardia. Excessive rapidity of the heart's action.

Tendon. The fibrous cord which connects a muscle with bone.

Tendovaginitis. Inflammation of a tendon and its sheath; tenosynovitis.

Tenovaginitis. Inflammation of the sheath of a tendon.

Tetanus. An infectious disease, usually fatal, characterized by spasm of voluntary muscles, intense exaggeration of reflex activity, and convulsions. It is due to the toxin developed by the tetanus bacillus. Since the bacillus can grow only in the absence of oxygen, the character of a wound is important, the most dangerous being puncture, penetrating, and crushing injuries; commonly referred to as "lockjaw."

Therapeutics. The branch of medical science dealing with the treatment of disease. The course of treatment is called therapy.

Thrombus. A clot of blood formed within the heart or blood vessel due to slowing circulation or alteration in the blood vessel walls; the latter could be due to external trauma.

Thrombosis. The formation of a plug or clot in a blood vessel; contrast with embolism where the clot moves in the bloodstream. Thrombosis is a localized condition.

Transverse. Crosswise; at right angles to the longitudinal axis of the body.

Trauma. A wound or injury.

Trichinosis. A disease produced by the ingestion of pork containing trichinella spiralis.

Truss. Any mechanical apparatus for preventing the reoccurrence of a hernia protrusion which has been reduced.

Tularemia. An infectious disease transmitted to man by the handling of infected rabbits or other rodents.

Tumor. A swelling; specifically, a new growth of cells. It is progressive and of unknown origin, and in malignant form is called cancer.

Ulna. The bone on the inner side of the forearm, articulating with the humerus and the head of the radius above, and with the radius below.

Undulant fever. Brucellosis; a remittent febrile disease caused by infection with bacteria. In man, it is transmitted from infected cows, goats, or pigs. In cows, it is called Bang's disease.

Vaccine. Any organism used for preventive inoculation against a specific disease.

Vas. A vessel.

Vascular. Consisting of, pertaining to, or provided with vessels.

Vein. A blood vessel, carrying blood from the tissues to the heart.

Virus. A general term for the poison of an infectious disease.

Zygoma. The arch formed by the union of the zygomatic process of the temporal bone and the malar bone; the cheek bone.

1833   Medical combining forms

Many medical terms are made up by adding prefixes or suffixes, or by combining two or three terms to describe a part of the body, a surgical procedure, or a condition. For example, the heart is called the *cardium*. The prefix *myo* means muscle. Thus *myocardium* is the heart muscle. The suffix *itis* means inflammation. Therefore, the term *myocarditis* means an inflammation of the heart muscle. The following is a list of the more common combining forms.

Prefixes

A- *or* ***an-***   From, without; ***asepsis,*** without infection.

A- *or* ***ab-***   Away, lack of; ***abnormal,*** departing from normal.

Acr-   Pertaining to an extremity; ***acroagnosis,*** absence of sense perception in a limb.

Ad-   To or toward, near; ***adrenal,*** near the kidney.

Aden-   Pertaining to a gland; ***adenocellulitis,*** inflammation of a gland.

Ambi-   Both; ***ambiocularity,*** ability to use both eyes equally well.

Anti-   Against; ***anticoagulant,*** opposed to or preventing coagulation.

Auto-   By or for one's self; ***autoinfection,*** infection by organism produced within the body.

Bi-   Two, twice, double; ***biceps,*** a muscle having two heads.

Bio-   Pertaining to life; ***biology,*** the science of life.

Bleph-   Pertaining to eyelids; ***blepharitis,*** inflammation of the eyelids.

Brady-   Slow; ***bradypraxia,*** slow or retarded physical movement.

Cardi-   Pertaining to the heart; ***cardiogram,*** a record of the heart's pulsation.

Cephal-   Pertaining to the head; ***cephalad,*** toward the head.

Cheil-   Pertaining to the lips; ***cheilitis,*** inflammation of the lips.

Chole-   Pertaining to bile; ***cholecyst,*** the gall bladder.

Chondr-   Pertaining to cartilage; ***chondroblast,*** a cartilage-forming cell.

Circum-   Around, about, on all sides; ***circumarticular,*** around a joint.

Cleid- *or* ***cleido-***   Denoting the clavicle; ***cleidomastoid,*** pertaining to the clavicle and the mastoid process.

Contra-   Against, in opposition; ***contraception,*** prevention of conception.

Cost- or costo-   Pertaining to a rib; **costochondral,** pertaining to the ribs and their cartilage.

Counter-   Against; **counteraction,** action of a drug opposed to that of some other drug.

Crani-   Pertaining to the skull; **craniometer,** a caliper used for measuring the skull.

Cyst- or cysto-   Pertaining to any fluid-containing sac; **cystography,** an X ray of the urinary bladder.

Cyt- or cyto-   Pertaining to a cell; **cytology,** the division of biology which deals with cells.

Dacry-   A tear; denoting relation to tears or the lacrimal apparatus; **dacryoadenitis,** inflammation of the lacrimal or tear gland.

Derm- or dermat-   Relating to the skin; **dermatitis,** inflammation of the skin.

Di-   Twice or double; **diplopia,** double vision.

Dis-   Apart, separation; **discission,** torn apart.

Dys-   Difficult, painful; **dysentery,** painful colon due to inflammation.

Ecto-   Outside, on the outer side; **ectogenous,** capable of growth outside the body, usually refers to bacteria.

En-   In; **encapsulated,** enclosed in a capsule.

Encephal-   Pertaining to the brain; **encephalitis,** inflammation of the brain.

End- or endo-   Within; **endothelium,** cells lining the heart.

Enter-   Referring to intestine; **enterocentesis,** surgical puncture of the intestine.

Epi-   Above, over, on the outside; **epidermis,** the outermost layer of the skin.

Erythro-   Red; **erythrocyte,** a red blood cell.

Ex-   From, off, out of; **excision,** the cutting out of a part of the body.

Exo-   Outside, out of; **exocrine,** applying to glands which deliver their secretion to the outside of the body, such as sweat glands; opposite of **endocrine,** which refers to glands which deliver their secretion inside the body.

Extra-   Outside of; **extracapsular,** outside the capsular ligament of a joint.

Fibro- or fibr-   Containing fibers, fibrous tissue; **fibrocarcinoma,** a cancerous tumor with fibrous elements.

Fluo-   Containing fluorine; **fluoridation,** the addition of fluorides to water.

Fronto-   Denoting anterior or forward position, or expressing a relation with the forehead or frontal bone; **frontonasal,** pertaining to the forehead and the nasal bones.

Galact-   Milk or milky fluid; **galactoid,** resembling milk.

Gastr-   Referring to the stomach; **gastrectasis,** dilation of the stomach.

Genito-   Referring to the genitals; **genitourinary,** referring to the genetalia and urinary organs or functions.

Gluco-   Signifying glucose; **gluconeogenesis,** the formation of glucose by the liver.

Glyco-   Sweet, signifying sugar; **glycogenesis,** the formation of sugar in the liver.

Gnatho- *or* **gnath-**   Referring to the jaw; **gnathalgia,** pain in the jaw.

Gynec-   Referring to woman; **gynecology,** the science of the diseases of women.

Heli- *or* **helio-**   Pertaining to the sun; **heliophobe,** one who is sensitive to the sun's rays.

Hem- *or* **haem-**

Hema- *or* **hemo-**   Of or pertaining to the blood; **hemothorax,** an accumulation of blood in the thorax.

Hemato- *or* **haemato-**   Of or pertaining to the blood; **hematoma,** a focalized clotting of blood, forming a tumor.

Hemi-   Half, or one side; **hemiplegia,** paralysis of one side of the body.

Heter- *or* **hetero-**   Other than usual, different; **heteroplasty,** the operation of grafting parts taken from another species or individual.

Homo-   The same, like; **homoplasty,** surgery using grafts taken from another individual of the same species.

Hydro-   Signifying water or fluid; **hydrocele,** an accumulation of water in the sac of the testis.

Hyper-   Abnormally excessive; **hyperglycemia,** excess of glucose or sugar in the blood.

Hypo-   Deficiency or lack; **hypoglycemia,** a low level of glucose or sugar in the blood.

Ilio-   Pertaining to the ilium or superior portion of the hipbone; **iliofemoral,** relating to the ilium and the femur.

Infra-   Below or beneath; **infracardiac,** situated below or beneath the heart.

In-   Not; **innominate,** not named, as in the os inominata or unnamed bone.

Inter-   Between or among; **interatrial,** between the atria and the heart.

Intra-   Within; **intracranial,** within the skull.

Isch- *or* **ischo-**   Suppression, stoppage; **ischuria,** suppression or retention of urine.

Iso-   Similarity, sameness; **isochromatic,** having the same color throughout.

Ken- *or* **keno-**   Empty; **kenophobia,** fear of large empty spaces.

Kerat- *or* **kerato-**   Referring to the cornea of the eye; **keratitis,** inflammation of the cornea.

Kilo-   One thousand; **kilogram,** 1,000 grams.

Leuk- *or* **leuko-**   White, colorless; **leukocyte,** a white blood cell.

Lip- *or* **lipo-**   Fat or fatty; **lipemia,** the presence of fatty substances in the blood.

Lith- *or* **litho-**   Stone; **lithonephritis,** inflammation of the kidney due to the presence of a stone or calculus.

Macro-   Abnormally large; **macrocyte,** a giant red blood cell.

Mal-   Ill, bad; **malaise,** general feeling of illness.

Meg-   Great, extended; **megacardia,** a large heart.

Mer- *or* **mero-**   Part or partial; **meropia,** partial blindness.

Mesa *or* **meso-**   Middle; **mesarteritis,** inflammation of the middle coat of an artery.

Met- *or* **meta-**   Change or transformation; **metastasis,** transfer of disease from a primary focus to a distant one through blood vessels or lymph channels.

Micro-   Small; **micrognathia,** abnormal smallness of the jaw.

Mio-   Smaller, less, decrease or contraction; **miosis,** decrease in the size of the pupil of the eye.

Mono-   One; **mononucleosis,** an imbalance in the blood caused by the increase in monocytes (uninuclear leukocytes), or white blood cells with a single nucleus.

Myc- *or* **myco-**   Fungus; **mycosis,** an infection caused by fungus.

Myo-   Muscle; **myositis,** inflammation of a muscle.

Neo-   New or recent; **neoplasm,** a new growth or formation.

Nephr-   Pertaining to the kidney; **nephroma,** a malignant tumor of the kidney.

Neur-   Referring to a nerve; **neuroanatomy,** the anatomy of the nervous system.

Odont-   Teeth, a tooth; **odontopathy,** any disease of the teeth.

Oleo-   Oil; **oleotherapy,** the treatment of disease by the administration of oils.

Olig-   Deficiency, lack; **oligemia,** deficiency in the volume of blood.

Onych-   A nail, resembling a nail; **onychoclasis,** the breaking of a nail.

Ophthalm-   Referring to the eye; **ophthalmorrhea,** a watery discharge from the eye.

Orth-   Straight, normal; **orthodontist,** a dental practitioner specializing in the straightening or normal alignment of teeth.

Oste-   Bone; **osteochondritis,** inflammation involving both bone and cartilage.

Ot-   The ear; **otitis,** inflammation of the ear.

Pan-   All; **panarteritis,** inflammation of all the coats of an artery.

Ped-   Children; **pediatrics,** the branch of medicine dealing with diseases of children.

Ped- *or* **Pod-**   Foot; **pedopathy,** a disease of the foot: **podalgia,** pain in the foot.

Per-   Excessively; **peracidity,** excessive acidity.

Peri-   Around; **periosteum,** a fibrous membrane around a bone.

Pneum- *or* **pneumon-**   Pertaining to the lung; **pneumocentesis,** puncture of a lung: **pneumonoconiosis,** inflammation of the lung caused by the inhalation of dust.

Polio-   Gray; **poliomyetitis,** inflammation of the gray substance of the spinal cord.

Poly-   Many, excessive; **polycystic,** containing many cysts.

Post-   After; **postconvulsive,** coming on after a convulsion.

Pre-   Before, in front of; **precordia,** the area of the chest in front of the heart.

Pro-   Before; **prognosis,** a forecast as to the duration, course and termination of a disease.

Pseud- False; *pseudoanemia,* false anemia, pallor, and whiteness of color without any blood changes to support the diagnosis.

Psych- Pertaining to the mind; *psychiatry,* treatment of the diseases of the mind.

Py- Referring to pus; *pyocyst,* a cyst containing pus.

Pyel- Pertaining to the pelvis of the kidney; *pyelonephritis,* inflammation of the kidney and its pelvis.

Quadri- Four; *quadriceps,* a muscle having four heads.

Rach- Pertaining to the spine; *rachiocampsis,* curvature of the spine.

Rhin- Referring to the nose; *rhinologist,* a physician specializing in conditions of the nose.

Sacro- Pertaining to the sacrum; *sacroiliac,* pertaining to the sacrum and the ilium.

Salping- Pertaining to the auditory tube or the uterine tube; *salpingitis,* inflammation of the uterine tube: *salpingocatheterism,* catheterization of an auditory tube.

Schisto- or schizo- Split; *schistoglossia,* a split or cleft tongue: *schizophrenia,* a split personality.

Sclero- Hard; *sclerocataracta,* a hard cataract.

Septic- Poison; *septicemia,* a poisoned condition of the blood.

Spondyl- Of or pertaining to the vertebra; *spondylitis,* inflammation of a vertebra.

Supra- Above; *suprapatella,* above the patella.

Syn- With or together; *syndrome,* a group of symptoms which when considered together compromise a disease or lesion.

Tachy- Swift, fast; *tachycardia,* fast beating of the heart.

Thermo- Heat; *thermomassage,* massage with the application of heat.

Tox- or toxic- Poison; *toxicology,* the science of the nature and effect of poisons.

Trich- Hair; *tricholith,* a calcified hairball in the stomach or intestines.

Uni- One; *unicellular,* composed of only one cell.

Ur- or uro- Pertaining to urine; *urology,* the scientific study of urine.

Vaso- Pertaining to blood vessels; *vasoconstriction,* constriction of blood vessels.

Vita- Life; *vitamin,* an organic compound required to maintain life in animals, including man.

Xanth- or Xantho- Yellow; *xanthochromia,* a yellowish discoloration of the skin.

Xer- Dry; *xeromycteria,* the lack of moisture in the nasal passages.

Suffixes

-asthenia. Weakness; *neurasthenia,* weakness of the nerve centers.

-algia. Pain; *cardialgia,* pain in the heart.

-asis or -osis. Increase above normal; *leukocytosis,* an abnormal increase in the leukocyte count.

-blast.   A formative cell; **myeloblast,** a bone-marrow cell.

-cele.   A chamber; **hydrocele,** the accumulation of water in a sac or chamber.

-clysis.   Injection; **hypodermoclysis,** injection under the skin.

-cyte.   Cell; **leukocyte,** a white blood cell.

-ectasis.   Dilation; **angiectasis,** abnormal dilation of a blood vessel.

-ectomy.   Excision, removal; **appendectomy,** excision or removal of the appendix.

-emia.   Blood; **septicemia,** poison in the blood.

-esthesia.   Relating to sensation; **anesthesia,** lack of sensation.

-genic.   Producing; **pyogenic,** producing pus.

-iatrics.   Pertaining to the practice of medicine; **pediatrics,** science of medicine dealing with children's diseases.

-itis.   Inflammation; **appendicitis,** inflammation of the appendix.

-logy.   Science of; **pathology,** science of disease.

-lysis.   Losing, destruction; **hemolysis,** destruction of the red blood cells.

-malacia.   Softening; **osteomalacia,** softening of a bone.

-oma.   Tumor; **neuroma,** a tumor on a nerve.

-osis.   Diseased condition; **tuberculosis,** a diseased condition caused by the tubercle bacillus.

-ostomy.   Creation of an opening; **gastrostomy,** the creation of an artificial opening into the stomach through the skin for artificial feeding.

-otomy.   Surgical incision into or through; **herniotomy,** a surgical incision through the neck of the sac for the relief of an irreducible hernia.

-pathy.   Disease of; **myopathy,** a disease of a muscle.

-penia.   Lack of; **leukopenia,** lack of white blood cells.

-pexy.   A surgical fixation; **gastropexy,** a fixation of a prolapsed stomach by suturing it to the abdominal wall or other structure.

-phagia.   Eating; **polyphagia,** excessive intake of food.

-phage or -phag.   An eater; **phagocyte,** a cell having the function of digesting foreign matter and other particles harmful to the body.

-phasia.   Speech; **alphasia,** loss of the power of speech.

-phobia.   Fear; **claustrophobia,** fear of being in a confined place.

-plasty.   Denoting a plastic or molding operation; **hernioplasty,** a plastic operation for the radical cure of a hernia.

-poiesis.   Making, forming; **hematopoiesis,** forming blood.

-pnea.   Breathing; **dyspnea,** difficult or labored breathing.

-ptosis.   Falling; **enteroptosis,** falling of an intestine.

-rhythmia.   Rhythm; **arrhythmia,** a disturbance in the rhythm of the heart.

-rrhagia.   Flowing; **otorrhagia,** a hemorrhage, or discharge of blood from the ear.

-rrhapy.   Suture of; **herniorrhaphy,** a hernia operation which includes sewing.

-rrhea. Discharge; ***otorrhea,*** discharge from the ear.

-rrhexis. Rupture; ***cardiorrhexis,*** rupture of the heart.

-sthenia. Pertaining to strength or the lack of it; ***neurasthenia,*** weakness or exhaustion of the nerve centers.

-taxia. Arrangement or coordination; ***ataxia,*** incoordination of muscular action.

-trophia *or* **-trophy.** Nourishment; ***atrophy,*** a wasting or reduction in size of an organ or cell due to lack of nourishment.

-uria. Pertaining to urine; ***polyuria,*** the passage of an excessive amount of urine.

1834 Common medical abbreviations

When writing orders for medication, either on hospital records or a prescription order, physicians use certain abbreviations of Latin words for purposes of brevity and to make the order unintelligible to the average layman. The orders will convey to the nurse or the pharmacist the amount of the medication to be compounded, its mixture, and the form in which it is to be given. In addition, there will be orders as to the dosage and the interval of time between doses. In the hospital the nurse follows the orders and gives the medication as directed.

The pharmacist will be directed to write the instructions as to dosage on the label of the prescription. For example, the instructions to the pharmacist might read: *Sig 1 tab tid a. c.* With the elimination of the abbreviations it would read in Latin: Signa: 1 tabella ter in die ante cibum. Translated into English, the direction would read: Write: 1 lozenge (tablet) three times daily before meals.

The following is a partial list of the more common abbreviations used by physicians, compiled in the hope that the claimsman will find it of value in interpreting hospital and physicians' records with respect to medical orders and the medication given.

Abbreviations	*Latin*	*English Equivalent*
aa	ana	of each
a.c.	ante cibum	before meals
p.c.	post cibum	after meals
ad lib.	ad libitum	freely
agit.	agita	shake
ant.	ante	before
aq.	aqua	water
aq. bull.	aqua bulliens	boiling water
aq. dest.	aqua destillata	distilled water
aq. ferv.	aqua fervens	warm water
bib.	bibe	drink
b.i.d.	bis in die	twice daily
b.	bis	twice
cap.	capiat	let him take
caps.	capsula	a capsule
cera	cera	wax

cib.	cibus	food
coch.	cochleare	a spoonful
coch. amp.	cochleare amplum	a tablespoonful
coch. mag.	cochleare magnum	large spoonful (½ oz.)
coch. med.	cochleare medium	dessertspoonful (¼ oz.)
coch. parv.	cochleare parvum	teaspoonful (⅛ oz.)
collyr.	collyrium	eyewash
collun.	collunarium	a nose wash
collut.	collutorium	a mouth wash
comp.	compositus	compound
conf.	confectio	candy
confricamentum	confricamentum	liniment
cong.	congius	a gallon
contra	contra	against
cor	cor	heart
cordis	cordis	heart
d.	da	give
dec.	decanta	pour off
de d. in d.	de diem in diem	from day to day
det.	detur	let be given
dil.	dilutus	dilute
dim.	dimidius	one-half
d. t d No. IV	dentur tales doses No. IV	give four such doses
emp.	emplastrum	a plaster
enem.	enema	an enema
ft.	fiat	make
fiat pulvis in chartulas XII divenda	same	make 12 powders
filt.	filtra	filter
flav.	flavus	yellow
fol.	folium	a leaf
f. pil. XII	fiant pilulae XII	make 12 pills
gr.	grana	grains
gtt.	gutta, guttae	drop or drops
H.	hora	hour
haust.	haustus	a drink
h. d.	hora decubitus	at bedtime
h. s. or h. som.	hora somni	just before sleep
in d.	in die	daily
lac	lac	milk
liq.	liquor	a solution
m.	misce	mix
mag.	magnus	large
noct.	nocte	at night
non rep.	non repetatur	do not repeat
O.	octarius	a pint
octavus	octavus	one-eighth
octo	octo	eight
O. D.	oculus dexter	the right eye
O. L.	oculus laevus	the left eye
ol.	oleum	oil
omn. bih.	omni bihora	every 2 hours
omn. hor.	omni hora	every hour
omn. 2 hor.	omni 2 hora	every 2 hours
omn. man.	omni mane	every morning
omn. noct.	omni nocte	every night
omn. quadr. hor.	omni quadrante horae	every 15 minutes
O. S.	oculus sinister	the left eye
p. ac.	partes aequales	equal parts

parvulus	parvulus	an infant
placebo	placebo	sugar pill
pocul.	poculum	a cup
pot.	potus	a drink
prand.	prandium	dinner
p. r. n.	pro re nata	as occasion arises
pulv.	pulvis	powder
qq. hor.	quaque hora	every hour
q. 2 h.	quaque 2 hora	every 2 hours
q. i. d.	quater in die	4 times a day
q. l.	quantum libet	as much as desired
rec.	recens	fresh
rub.	ruber	red
Sig.	signa	write, label
sine	sine	without
s. o. s.	si opus sit	if necessary
stat.	statim	immediately
S.V.R.	spiritus vini rectificatus	rectified spirit of alcohol
tab.	tabella	a lozenge
t.d.	ter die	3 times a day
t.i.d.	ter in die	3 times a day
tinct. (tr.)	tinctura	tincture
ut dict.	ut dictum	as directed

CHAPTER XIX

Public records

1900   Admissibility of public records

In the course of investigation public records can very often be utilized as a means of proving the existence of a fact, establishing admissions against interest made by one of the parties, and also providing a source of information upon which further investigation can be based.

Public records when properly identified by the custodian thereof are usually admissible in evidence where there is no statutory restriction of such use. The custodian of the record does not necessarily have to be the maker thereof, and records of this sort come within the exception to the hearsay rule in much the same manner as do business entries in books of account kept in the regular course of business. Police records covering an automobile accident are particularly helpful, and in those states where such records are not available an interview with the police officer who investigated the case will often give you the same information.

A partial list of public records, their extent, availability, and sources from which they are obtained follows.

1901   Motor vehicle accident reports

Privileged reports. The Uniform Act (regulating the operation of vehicles on highways), adopted in many states requires the filing of an accident report, without prejudice to the individual making it and solely for the confidential use of the bureau of motor vehicles. The written report is by statute privileged and not admissible in or to be used in a civil

742

action arising out of the facts upon which the report is based. Therefore, reports under this type of statute are not available to us in the investigation of claims arising therefrom.

This statute has been adopted in Illinois, Iowa, Kansas, Mississippi, and Utah, and with modifications in Arkansas, Colorado, Delaware, Indiana, Louisiana, Maine, Michigan, Minnesota, Nebraska, New Mexico, North Carolina, North Dakota, Ohio, Oregon, Pennsylvania, South Carolina, South Dakota, Virginia, and Washington.

Nonprivileged reports. Some states take the opposite view. New York requires the filing of a written report with the commissioner of motor vehicles within 48 hours where any person is killed or injured, or where damage to the property of any one person exceeds $100. Copies of these reports are kept on file for a period of three years after the accident and are available to interested persons upon the payment of a fee. Such reports are admissible in evidence as admissions.

1902   Intoxication tests

New York and Delaware have statutes which provide that $5/100$ to $15/100$ percent of alcohol by weight in the blood of a person is *relevant* evidence of being under the influence of intoxicants, and that over $15/100$ percent is prima facie evidence of intoxication. Where the results of a blood test are desired by an adverse party, and the information is not privileged by statute, the chemist who made the test, together with the result thereof, is subject to subpoena. The statute provides that the result of the test must be made available to the person tested upon his request. Such records are admissible in evidence by the person tested as public documents and by the adverse party (as an exception to the hearsay rule) as an admission against interest.

1903   Police records

Police reports are normally available upon request or by offer of a stipulated fee. In states where the record can be reached only by subpoena, the investigating officer may be interviewed and, if cooperative, his conclusions reported to the file. If the officer was not a witness the report is usually based on hearsay and some physical facts.

1904   Traffic court hearings

Minutes of traffic court proceedings (if a court of record) are available upon the payment of the requisite fee, usually based upon a price per page. If possible, in a case warranting such treatment, the adjuster should be present at the time of hearing and make notes of the testimony, the witnesses produced, and the verdict. From these notes a determination may be made as to whether or not the expense of ordering the minutes is justified. The adjuster will also have an opportunity to observe the witnesses on the stand and to evaluate them as to appearance, credibility, and knowledge of the accident.

1905   Weather reports

Weather information for a particular date and locality may be obtained from the nearest weather bureau office or from the Superintendent of Documents, Washington, D.C. Hourly precipitation, meteorological, and other data may also be obtained for a slight charge. These reports are admissible in evidence, most states having specific statutes dealing with their admissibility. When certified by the government meteorologist they constitute prima facie evidence of the facts and circumstances stated therein.

1906   Autopsy reports

Many states, counties, and municipalities require that an autopsy be performed where the deceased person was not under the care of a physician, or was not so attended within the 24-hour period immediately preceding his demise. Such autopsies are mandatory and the consent of the next of kin is not required. These reports may be obtained upon payment of the requisite fee from the appropriate medical examiner's office.

1907   Public service commission accident reports

In most states a public service law provides that all proceedings of the commission and all documents and records in its possession shall be public records. However, in some states there is a distinction between accident reports filed by railroad and omnibus companies and those filed by gas and electric corporations.

In New York, for example, a railroad or an omnibus company is required to give immediate notice to the public service commission of any accidents of a serious nature. However, the law does provide that such notice shall not be admitted as evidence or used for any purpose against such common carrier or railroad corporation giving such notice in any suit or accident for damages growing out of any matter mentioned in said notice.

Gas and electric companies are also required to make reports of accidents to the public service commission, but no such restriction applies to these accident reports, and application may be made for a certified copy of the company's report of accident. It may be offered in evidence.

1908   Civil aeronautics reports

In every accident involving a commercial airline, there are at least three possible defendants. The airline who owned and operated the plane may be held for negligent operation; the United States may be sued because commercial carriers are subject to various governmental regulations at or near the control towers and in landing and taking off; or the manufacturer may be involved because of negligence in servicing or designing the plane, or the negligent failure to reveal a condition discovered on subsequent investigation and not corrected.

The Civil Aeronautics Board, created by the Federal Aviation Act of 1958, is required under that statute to assume the following duties in the case of accident (49 USCA 144):

A. It shall be the duty of the Board (2) to investigate such accidents and report the facts, conditions, and circumstances relating to each accident and the probable cause thereof: . . . (4) make such reports public in such form and manner as may be deemed by it to be in the public interest.

In furtherance of this duty the board may conduct accident investigation hearings, the objective of which is to determine the probable cause, and to prepare recommendations for safety in the future to prevent the occurrence of similar accidents.

All factual information contained in an accident investigation report, and supporting papers, may be obtained from the C.A.B.'s regional or Washington office upon the request of any person at any stage of the accident investigation, except that the board shall not make available that portion of the file containing any opinion, suggestion, or recommendation of any employee of the Civil Aeronautics Administration when acting on behalf of the board. The regulation governing disclosure applies whether or not an action for wrongful death is involved and whether or not the United States is a party to the suit. The Federal Aviation Act of 1958 provides as follows:

. . . That no part of any report or reports of the Board relating to any accident, or the investigation thereof, shall be admitted as evidence or used in any suit or action for damages growing out of any matter mentioned in such report or reports.

While the report itself may not be admitted in evidence, it can be used for purposes of cross-examination and impeachment, and in addition the C.A.B. investigator's factual report, exclusive of opinions, could be admissible as a past recollection recorded in connection with his deposition.

1909 Federal income tax returns

Federal income tax returns of individuals, while matters of public record, are open to public inspection only upon the order of the President and under rules and regulations prescribed by the Secretary of the Treasury and approved by the President. The rules approved provide that the return of an individual shall be open to inspection by the individual for whom the return was made, or by the duly constituted attorney in fact of that person. However, in court proceedings where the plaintiff's income is in issue, the courts have generally compelled the plaintiff to obtain copies of his income tax return at the expense of the defendant when proper application was made for such a procedure. Also, as adjusters, there is no reason why we could not ask to see the claimant's copy of the return, obtaining all the information necessary from that source and making a copy or photostat if necessary.

1910   Veterans Administration records

All files, records, reports, and other papers and documents pertaining to any claim under any of the laws administered by the Veterans Administration are confidential and privileged and no disclosure thereof can be made except as follows:

1. To a claimant or his duly authorized agent or representative as to matters concerning himself alone when, in the judgment of the administrator, such disclosure would not be injurious to the physical or mental health of the claimant.

Veterans Administration regulations provide that an authorization can be executed by the veteran; it should be dated, addressed to the Veterans Administration, contain the name and address of the person about whom information is to be released, and the purpose for which it is to be used. The authorization should be signed by the veteran. A convenient form is available at the Veterans Administration for this purpose, but its use is for convenience only and is not required.

1911   Selective service records

The present regulations provide that information contained in the records of a registrant's file may be disclosed, or furnished to, or examined by the registrant or any person having written authority signed by the registrant.

Dependency information in the selective service files is expressly made nonconfidential. The regulations provide that the fact that dependency has been claimed, and the names and addresses of the claimed dependents, shall not be confidential and may be disclosed or furnished.

1912   Social security

These records by statute are made confidential and may be disclosed only to the individual involved—or after his death to a surviving relative or representative of the individual's estate. Under certain circumstances, the information may be released to an employer or former employer of an individual as to the individual's social security account number, or as to the coverage of services rendered by him for the employer, or as to any information originally supplied by the employer. Disclosure of the records may be made to others only upon written authorization by the claimant or his duly authorized representative.

Therefore, it would seem that if social security records are important in our investigation of the case, they can be secured when the request is accompanied by written authorization. This regulation, however, does not apply to medical information which, under the present regulations, can be disclosed only to the individual's physician or to a medical institution at which he is a patient.

1913   Unemployment compensation records

In most states, where an injury is responsible for the initial disability, in order to qualify for unemployment compensation, the applicant must show that he is physically capable and available for work. This eliminates those who are receiving or claiming workmen's compensation benefits. The applicant shows his physical capacity by means of a physician's certificate that the disability occasioned by the accident has terminated. Records of the unemployment compensation board are public records and in most states they can be inspected. In all states they can be reached for production in court by a *subpoena duces tecum.*

1914   Workmen's compensation records

In states having a workmen's compensation board or similar body, the claims filed, heard, and determined are public records, and as such are available for inspection in accordance with the rules of the compensation authority. They can be reached by a *subpoena duces tecum* and may be offered in evidence in the trial of a claim against a third party. Where the claimant has elected to proceed against the third party and to defer his claim for compensation, it will be found that the state file contains very little information beyond the employee's claim and his election. The compensation insurance carrier's file will be more complete since they will accumulate the medical reports even where the claimant is not actively seeking compensation. In some cases the compensation carrier will be cooperative and will make its file available. Where inspection of the file is refused, the file still can be reached in the event of trial by means of a *subpoena duces tecum.*

1915   Vital statistics: Birth, marriage, death

Vital statistics are public records and can be inspected by anyone complying with the rules of the custodian thereof. Usually when such information is required, a photostatic copy of the records (duly authenticated) is necessary. The bureau having custody of the records will make a charge for the search of its records and for the certified copy. To facilitate the search the investigator should supply the custodian with the date of the birth, marriage, or death concerning which information is requested. If the date is unknown, the custodian usually makes a charge for each year that is searched.

1916   Court records: Divorce or prior proceedings

Court records are public records and may be inspected in accordance with the rules of the court. While a case is pending the records are usually in the custody of the clerk of the court and may be inspected through his office. When the case has been closed the papers are filed in the archives of the court or in the clerk's vault, where they may be located and inspected. Certified copies of papers are available upon the payment of the requisite fee.

Where information is required with respect to a divorce, or to prior proceedings of any kind, the investigator will have to know the court in which these proceedings were held and, if possible, the approximate date. In addition, the court usually assigns a docket or index number to the case and files it under that number. Therefore, if the investigator can ascertain the case number he will be able to locate the file much more readily.

1917   Interstate Commerce Commission records

The rules of the Interstate Commerce Commission require motor carriers subject to its jurisdiction to report to it all accidents involving personal injury or death, as well as those involving property damage to the extent of $250 or more. Such reports, however, are for the information of the commission and are not open to public inspection (49 CFR 194.1 & 194.2). Therefore the reports are confidential and may not be reached. However, under 49 CFR 194.3, the motor carrier is required to keep an accident register at its principal place of business. These records are subject to subpoena, or may be inspected if the carrier decides to make them available.

CHAPTER XX

Claims evaluation

2000   Purpose and scope of claims evaluation

The purpose of claims evaluation is to determine the company's position and attitude with respect to each individual claim. It consists of an objective appraisal of all of the elements of the claim, an estimate of the maximum dollar value of the company's exposure, and a decision as to whether or not it would be to the company's advantage to make any payment in settlement, and if so, the maximum settlement amount. Evaluation contemplates a consideration of all of the facets of the claim which have an influence on its value. These include, among other things, the facts and circumstances of the accident, the applicable law, the nature and extent of the injuries, the measure of damages applicable to the claim, the damages claimed, the provable damages (both tangible and intangible items), and the defenses available.

The maximum settlement amount, or the settlement value of the case, is based on the degree of danger to the company which the claim presents. It represents the amount that the company is willing to pay rather than risk the uncertainties of the trial and the possibility of an adverse verdict. It contemplates the consideration of the estimate of the company's maximum exposure, the possibilities of a plaintiff's verdict, the difficulties which will confront the plaintiff in proving his case, the possibilities of a successful defense, the difficulties (if any) of producing evidence of a defense, and imponderables such as the personalities of the parties and the effect they will have on the jury, and the ability and past performance of the plaintiff's counsel.

Some claimsmen fix the settlement valuation by first calculating the amount (if anything) the company would have to pay if the verdict of the jury was the best possible result obtainable on the basis of the facts of the case, and second by calculating the amount of the verdict on the basis of the worst possible result. An amount between the two extremes would represent the settlement value. Just how near the top figure the settlement value would come would depend upon the degree of the danger posed by the facts of the case. If the danger is minimal, then the settlement figure would approximate the amount of the best possible result, or a little more, whereas if the danger were great a higher settlement figure would be required.

No matter what system the claimsman uses in making these estimates, all claimsmen will agree that no proper determination of the value of an individual case can be made without considering the case on the basis of its own particular facts. There are some areas which are common to most cases which will be discussed in the succeeding paragraphs. These will include the measure of damages, the items considered in settlement valuation, as well as the formula appraisals of value as used by our adversaries.

2001   Nature of damages

Damages are defined as the pecuniary compensation or indemnity which may be recovered by any person who has suffered loss, detriment, or injury, whether to his person or property, through the unlawful act or omission or negligence of another. Compensation means that the amounts so awarded are intended to reasonably repay the injured person for the loss which he has suffered and to place him in the same or an equivalent position to that which he occupied prior to the event.

The amount to be awarded is a question of fact for the jury to decide. The court will instruct the jury as to the matters which it may take into account in computing the amount of the damages, but the actual amount to be awarded is left to the discretion of the jury. Should the jury fail to follow the court's instructions, or if the amount of the verdict is against the weight of evidence, or if the amount of the verdict is so low or so excessive so that it "shocks the conscience of the Court," the court may, on its own motion or upon motion made by either party, set the verdict aside, dismiss the claim, or grant a new trial.

Damages for breach of contract involving property rights are not difficult to determine. The jury will be instructed to take into consideration the advantages which would have accrued to the injured party had there been no breach, less his obligations under the contract. The difference will be his damages. For example, A agrees to sell and B agrees to buy a certain lot for $5,000. On the due date A refuses to sell. B can procure a similar lot in the same area for $6,000. B's damage will be $1,000, or the difference between the sale price of the first lot and the price B is required to pay for a similar lot. On the same facts, if B can obtain a similar lot for $5,000 or less, and he has suffered no other loss due to A's breach, then B has suffered no damages.

Suppose A, an adjuster, makes an agreement with B to settle B's claim for $500. A breaches the contract by refusing payment, after B has submitted a release. If B elects to sue on the contract, his measure of damages will be the amount which he would have obtained had there been no breach, or $500.

In personal injury cases, compensatory damages serve the same purpose. Consideration is given to the position of the injured person prior to the event and his condition after the event has occurred. His items of damage will consist of the losses he has suffered up to the time of trial and, if the effects of the injury are continuing, the losses he will suffer in the future. Suppose A sustained injuries in an automobile accident caused by the negligence of B. A's injuries consist of a strain of the muscles of the cervical region of the neck. A is unable to work for two weeks and loses $200 in salary. His medical bills total $150.

To reasonably compensate A for his injuries, consideration should be given to the actual out-of-pocket expenses he has incurred; namely, the loss of salary and the cost of the medical services, and also such amount as the jury may award for his pain (if there was any), discomfort, and inconvenience. Thus, by such an award of damages, A is now in a position comparable to that which he occupied prior to the happening of the accident.

The same principles are applicable to property damage cases. For example, A's automobile is damaged by the negligence of B. It will cost $400 to repair the automobile and to restore it to its condition prior to the accident. A's damages are $400. This payment will compensate A for the loss he has suffered. It makes no difference whether A uses the money to have the repairs made on his automobile or for any other purpose. A is entitled to the money since he has suffered the loss. B's only obligation is the payment of the money. B is under no obligation to repair A's automobile or to pay the person who repairs it. B's sole obligation is to pay A the money damages, and when that is done A's claim against B is extinguished.

2002 Special and general damages

Compensatory damages are divided into special and general damages. Special damages, for the purposes of this discussion, are those specific items which are represented by actual out-of-pocket expenses, such as past and future loss of salary or other income, past and future medical, surgical, hospital, and nursing services, money expended to minimize the loss, funeral expenses in death cases, and repair bills for damaged property.

General damages are those which do not require a specific showing of a monetary loss, but are such losses which can be inferred from the evidence of injury. These include, among other things, damages for pain and suffering, loss of use or loss by amputation of a member (hand, arm, leg, eye, etc.), total or partial loss of vision, and the effect of facial or bodily scarring on the injured person's future enjoyment of life, as well as the value of the loss of ability to bear children.

2003   Duty of the claimant to establish damages

The defendant is responsible for all damages proximately caused by his tortious act. Since the burden of proof is always placed upon the shoulders of the person asserting the claim, the plaintiff must establish exactly what damages he claims he sustained, as well as to show a direct chain of causation running from the event to the injury or loss sustained. His evidence with respect to damages must clearly demonstrate the actual damages claimed. The jury is not required to imagine or speculate, and the failure of the plaintiff to produce evidence establishing his damages with certainty will result in a dismissal of his claim.

For example, in *Deutsch* v. *Connecticut Co.* [119 Atl. 281 (Connecticut)], a contributorily negligent plaintiff was run over by the defendant's trolley car and further injured when the motorman negligently backed the trolley car over him. As to the first injury, the plaintiff could not recover due to his contributory negligence. As to the second injury, the defendant was liable. The plaintiff established all of his injuries, but failed to produce evidence as to the injuries which were sustained as a result of the second impact alone. Since he failed to establish the exact damage caused by the impact for which the defendant was liable, he did not meet the burden of proof required. Recovery was denied. There was no evidence on which the jury could base a conclusion as to the value of the claim, since it had no information as to the extent of the injury caused by the defendant's negligence.

From this and other cases the courts have developed the *rule of certainty* as to damages. The rule of certainty requires that the plaintiff establish his exact damages without recourse to speculation or conjecture. The failure to establish damages with certainty requires a dismissal of the cause of action. However, cases which involve continuing medical treatment or continuing disability beyond the date of the trial pose special problems. It would be impossible for the plaintiff to establish such projected losses with certainty until the losses had actually been incurred. Therefore, in those cases involving projected losses, and those cases alone, the courts have relaxed the rule of certainty to the extent that the plaintiff will sustain the burden of proof if he can establish future losses with a reasonable degree of certainty. This means that the plaintiff's proof must be clear and convincing in establishing that the future losses will be sustained, and, further, the actual value of such losses. As to losses already sustained, the rule of certainty is applied.

The rule of subtraction is a corollary of the rule of certainty and is applied in all cases where the defendant is either not liable for the entire damage or is entitled to some reduction as a result of credits, deductions, or salvage. As part of the plaintiff's burden of proof he must establish the amount that should be deducted from the total loss. If he fails to show the amount of the deduction, he has not established his exact damage and may not recover at all. For example, suppose that A's automobile has been damaged by the negligence of B. The automobile is a total loss in the sense that the cost of repairs will exceed the value of the car before the accident. To establish his damages, A must show the value of the automobile prior to the accident, and must also show the amount that should be deducted from that figure because of the junk value of the salvage. If A fails to establish the value of the salvage, or that the salvage has no value, he has failed to establish his exact damages and may not recover.

Where a plaintiff is salaried and the effect of the injury is such that he is unable to work for a period of time, evidence of his medical disability and the fact that he was employed and did not work will meet the requirements of certainty. Where the plaintiff seeks damages for a lost opportunity, he is faced with some difficulty in the way of proof. He must establish with certainty that the opportunity actually existed, that his condition was such that he could not take advantage of it, and, most importantly, that he would have profited by taking it and the exact extent of the profit. In most cases of this type the proof will fall short of the legal requirements. Speculative testimony as to the possibilities of profit will not be sufficient. In other cases, where the plaintiff's income is derived from a business in which he has a monetary investment, the legal requirements are that he must show the amount of income that is derived from his services as opposed to that portion which represents interest on his investment.

In addition to showing the exact damages, the plaintiff must establish that the damages were sustained as a proximate result of the defendant's act. Where medical testimony is offered it must establish that the plaintiff's injuries were caused by the tortious act of the defendant. The plaintiff must show with certainty that there is a chain of causation running from the defendant's act to the condition from which the plaintiff is suffering. The medical testimony so offered must have some foundation in medical fact or experience. For example, if the injured person sustained severe lacerations and later developed a virulent infection even though all medical precautions were undertaken, the defendant's liability would extend not only to the lacerations but to the infection as well. It can be established with medical certainty that lacerations can become infected even though preventative measures are undertaken.

The rule of proximate cause has been applied to cases where the defendant is responsible for the original injury but where the injury has been aggravated by the malpractice of a physician, selected by the injured with due care. In such a case, the defendant and the physician are joint tort-feasors as to the injuries caused by the malpractice. The defendant's tortious act is the proximate cause of the entire injury and the malpractice of the physician is within the foreseeable orbit of danger. The malpractice is not an intervening cause which will reduce the defendant's liability or absolve him from his responsibility to respond in damages. The injured may, at his election, hold either the defendant, or the doctor, or both, for the injuries he sustained as a result of the malpractice. Clearly, the physician is not responsible for the original injury. His liability is confined to the damages occasioned by his malpractice and no more.

The rule of proximate cause has also been applied to cases where the plaintiff suffered such excruciating pain that he was driven to suicide. If it can be established with medical certainty that the motivation for the suicide was the result of the injury suffered, a recovery will be allowed. The suicide would not be considered to be an intervening cause.

2004   Duty of the claimant to mitigate damages

The plaintiff may not recover for any damages which occur as a result of his own lack of care after the happening of the accident. For example, in property damage cases the plaintiff must exercise reasonable care in protecting the property from further damage from the weather or the actions of others. He may not abandon a damaged vehicle at the place of accident and expect to hold the defendant responsible for all of the damage to the vehicle, including that caused by the weather, or the action of vandals, when reasonable care would have required the removal of the vehicle to a garage or other safe place.

In another case, let us assume that *A*'s roof is damaged by the negligence of *B*. *A* is under the duty to make emergency repairs so as to protect his other property from weather damage. *B*'s liability is limited to the damage to the roof, and then only to such damage as was caused by his negligent act. If *A* fails to make the repairs, emergency or otherwise, and the roof is further damaged, as well as other property, *A* then would have the additional burden of showing the exact damage caused by *B*'s negligence. He could only accomplish this by showing the entire damage and showing the amount that should be deducted from the total damage because of his own lack of reasonable care.

In personal injury cases, the injured is bound to act in good faith and to resort to such means and adopt such measures as are reasonably within his reach to cure and restore himself. He cannot neglect his injury and seek to hold the defendant responsible for the entire result. If he should choose a physician who is otherwise qualified, but whose neglect of the case amounts to malpractice, he is not charged with a lack of reasonable care. The possibility that the attending physician might fail to exercise the proper care is a foreseeable consequence of the original tort-feasor's negligent act, and for that reason the malpractice is not charged against the injured person. As to the malpractice, both the tort-feasor and the physician are jointly and severally liable, occupying the legal position of joint tort-feasors. The defendant, however, is not liable for the aggravation of the injury or additional pain and suffering that is attributable to

1. The failure of the injured person to secure timely medical treatment.
2. The failure of the injured person to follow the advice or instructions of the attending physician.
3. The failure of the injured person to exercise reasonable care in the selection of the physician or surgeon.
4. The intervention of any factors that are not the natural, direct, and proximate consequences of the tort.

The rule is that the tort-feasor is not liable for the avoidable consequences of the injury brought about by the plaintiff's failure to exercise reasonable care, and in addition there must be an unbroken chain of causation running from the negligent act to the injuries claimed, without any intervening factors.

Because of this duty of reasonable care which is imposed upon the plaintiff, the defendant is liable for the expenses incurred and the property loss or personal injuries sustained by the plaintiff in a reasonable effort to minimize the damages. These would include expenses for medical services, damage to clothing or other property as a result of an effort to extinguish a fire, or personal injuries sustained while attempting to remove or rescue people from a burning building or vehicle, or attempting to salvage valuable property endangered by the accident. These expenses are recoverable even though the attempt is unsuccessful, or proves to be unnecessary, or aggravates rather than reduces the loss. The test is whether or not the incurring of the expense or the exposure to injury was reasonable under the circumstances attending the event. If the effort was a reasonable one under the circumstances, the expense or damages for the injury are recoverable. If the effort was unreasonable or foolhardy, there is no recovery. Reasonableness is a question of fact to be decided by the jury.

Thus if the plaintiff, believing he may have sustained a broken bone, has an X ray taken, the tort-feasor is liable for the cost of the X ray even though it shows no bone pathology. The expense of an X ray under those circumstances is reasonable and justified for the reason that the injured would be guilty of neglect if he failed to make use of this diagnostic aid to ascertain the extent of his injury and to determine the needed treatment. The injured could not know in advance that the X ray would be negative. Therefore, the expense is justified and recoverable even though subsequent facts indicate that it was unnecessary.

In a case where a surgical operation is indicated and, in the opinion of the physicians, will cure the plaintiff's condition, the plaintiff must submit to it if it does not involve any great risk. If he fails to do so, he is neglectful of his own physical condition and may not recover of the defendant any damages which are sustained as a result. On the other hand, if the evidence shows that the operation will involve great risk, and there is no guarantee of a successful result, the jury can (and usually will) find that the plaintiff is justified in his refusal to submit to the operation and that such refusal does not amount to neglect. The defendant is not liable for the avoidable consequences of the injury. If the operation will avoid further disability, the defendant is not responsible for the disability occasioned by the plaintiff's failure to take advantage of the operation. In such a case there must be convincing evidence that the operation will actually cure or reduce the disability and will not expose the plaintiff to an unreasonable risk.

In a situation involving property, the value of the property will have some influence upon whether or not the effort to save it is reasonable. If *A* negligently sets fire to *B*'s building, *B* might be justified in exposing himself to the risk of injury in attempting to salvage a valuable painting from the building. He would not be justified in making the same effort to retrieve his lunch. In the case of the painting, *A* would be liable for *B*'s injuries, even though the salvage attempt was unsuccessful. In the case of *B*'s lunch, *A* would not be liable for *B*'s injuries under any circumstances.

2005   Effect of a religious belief on mitigation

The religious belief of the plaintiff does not excuse him from the duty of exercising reasonable care to cure himself by using all medical means available. A problem is presented in cases involving Christian Scientists (and others) who hold to the same belief that all human injuries, ailments, diseases, pain, and suffering have no real existence, but are merely false beliefs, illusions, or "errors" of the mind which can be erased by pointing the way to "truth." In a word, these are beliefs in faith healing in that healing the mind by faith is considered to be all the treatment that is necessary. Since there is no proof that can be adduced that this belief has any basis in fact, the same rules are applicable to those who hold these beliefs as are applied to others. If the injured person allows an unreasonable period of time to elapse between the injury and the application for medical treatment, he has not exercised the reasonable care which the law requires. This failure is regarded as an intervening cause of the injury, so as to either bar the entire claim for damages or to materially reduce it. The injury so aggravated by the failure to secure timely medical treatment is an avoidable consequence of the original injury, for which the defendant is not liable. The religious belief of the plaintiff, however honestly held, will not exonerate him from the charge of neglect.

As to infants, the rule is not strictly applied. The courts recognize that infants are subject to the authority and guidance of their parents, and that where the parents are neglectful, even because of a religious belief, their negligence should not be imputed to the infant. In *Lange* v. *Holt* [159 Atl. 575 (Connecticut)], an eight-year-old girl was injured through the negligence of the defendant. Her parents were Christian Scientists, and she received no proper medical treatment for a period of some 25 days, although she had the services of a Christian Science practitioner during that time. The defendant contended that her injuries were aggravated by the lack of medical attention, and further that such neglect was the proximate cause of the permanent injury which she suffered. In overruling this defense, the court said:

> The test of conduct on the part of the plaintiff in promoting a recovery from injuries suffered is one of reasonable care, and cannot be made to depend on the idiosyncrasies of personal belief, no matter how honestly held. . . . A child of eight years is necessarily dependent upon her parents in regard to the steps to be taken to bring about a recovery from an injury, and, if she herself is not guilty of negligence, or improper conduct, the failure of the parents to take proper steps to that end, by a parity of reasoning, cannot be such a cause of any portion of the injuries as will defeat a recovery for all the results of the defendant's wrongdoing.

This case enunciates a rule of expediency. Both the defendant and the child's parents were negligent. An eight-year-old child could have no knowledge of what medical or other treatment was needed, and even if she did she would have no means of securing the treatment. Since the child cannot sue her own parents in tort, the court felt that someone should be charged with the responsibility for the child's injury. The original injury was caused by the defendant's negligence, so that recovery should be had from that source for the entire results of the injury and the lack of medical treatment. The opinion does not exonerate the parents from responsibility, but it does hold that the negligence of the parents cannot be imputed to the infant under these circumstances.

2006 Single recovery principle

Our common-law system requires a single lump-sum recovery for all damages caused by negligence. This does not present any great problem when all of the items of damage have accrued prior to the trial date. The damages are known and capable of ascertainment and proof. The difficulty arises when the effects of the injury are continuing and some of the damages sought must be based upon a projection of losses to be sustained in the future. The failure of the plaintiff to seek sufficient damages, or the failure of the court to award enough money to take care of future losses will not give rise to a further cause of action to recover the deficiency. On the other hand, if the projection is inaccurate or the injuries prove to be less serious than was believed at the time of trial, there are no means available to the tort-feasor whereby he can recover the excess. Once there has been a determination of the amount of recovery, whether adequate or not, it terminates the cause of action, with the exception of the right of either party to appeal within the time limited for such action.

2007 Measure of damages: Property damage

The various state courts are in agreement that the amount to be awarded to the injured party for his property damage is the amount that will reasonably compensate him for the loss suffered. They are not in agreement as to how this is to be accomplished. There are three different rules. Each court has adopted one of the following rules, and will allow damages based on

1. The diminution in value. Evidence of the cost of repairs is admissible as some proof of this diminution.
2. The cost of repairs as the measure of damages, except where the repair costs exceed the value of the article before the damage. In the latter case, the value of the article is the measure of damages.
3. Either of the above rules, the damages being the difference in value of the article before and after the damage, or, at the plaintiff's election, the reasonable cost of repair, or restoration where possible, with due allowance for any difference between the original value and the value after repairs.

In the majority of cases, the application of these rules will produce the same result since the available proof of damage will be restricted to the cost of repairs. Where there is evidence that the repaired article has suffered a diminution from the preaccident value, the application of the first rule will allow a greater recovery than the second. Also, it should be noted that where the cost of repairs exceeds the diminution in value, the second rule will allow a greater recovery than the first, the test being the relationship between the preaccident value and the cost of repairs rather than the relationship of the diminution in value and the cost of repairs.

The third rule, which is recommended by the American Law Institute (Restatement, Law of Torts, sec. 928), combines the better features of both rules and is being generally adopted by the courts. Under this rule, the difference in value is taken into account. This includes not only the diminution in the value of the repaired article, but an increase in value as well. In the latter case, the rule of subtraction would apply, and the amount of the increased value would be applied in diminishing the amount of damages recoverable.

Market value.   The value referred to in these rules is the exchange or market value. Such value is the amount that the owner would have to pay in order to replace it with property of the same kind and quality. It does not include the sentimental value or the value of the emotional distress caused by its loss (except in an unusual situation where the clothing of a person is destroyed and he suffers humiliation because of the lack of it). In all other cases, where the article is replaceable, the damages are limited to the replacement value.

Market value will differ as to the status of the owner in relation to it. Thus, if the owner is a consumer the market value as to him would be the retail price. If he is a retailer, the value would be the wholesale price. And if he is the manufacturer, the value would be his selling price.

Articles having no market value.   An item may have special value to the owner but no exchange or market value. Such items might include a family heirloom, a portrait of a deceased ancestor, or merely photographs of members of the family. The damages recoverable will be the special value to the owner, as determined by the jury, with due consideration being given to the original cost, its age, and condition. Where the property consists of a work product of the owner, such as a manuscript, records of experiments, or case studies, the value thereof will be computed on the basis of the value of the time, labor, and effort which will be required to reproduce it.

The value of an old building is not determined solely by its replacement cost or the original cost less depreciation or obsolescence. In some cases, old buildings cannot be replaced for the reason that there are no artisans available who are capable of doing the type of work necessary to reproduce it. In such cases, the value can be established by showing the use to which the building was put immediately prior to its loss, its rental value, and the present character of the neighborhood, as well as the price that a prospective purchaser would be willing to pay for the property. Of necessity, experts would be required in order to establish this type of valuation.

Loss of use.   This terminology is used by the courts to denote an element of damage arising from the injury to or destruction of certain species of tangible personal property. The term arose with the development of the law of personal property and while there are similar damages which may be sustained as a result of the damage to real property, the courts have never applied the term to real property. Consideration will be given to (1) personal property, and (2) real property.

1. *Personal property.*   Loss of use is most frequently involved in cases of damage to motor vehicles, although there is no reason why the same principles could not be applied equally to other types of machinery used for commercial purposes, such as printing presses, computers, punch presses, etc. Loss of use does not refer to or is not an element of damage considered in connection with the injury to or destruction of all types of personal property. For example, annual crops are personal property. In the case of the destruction of the crop, the damages will consist of the value of the crop destroyed or damaged, and even though the owner may have planned to use the crop to feed his family and its destruction may have frustrated that purpose, there is no recovery per se for that type of damage. The payment for the crop will cover the entire damage. Likewise, loss of use is not an element of damage in the case of damage to intangible personal property, such as the damage to an economic advantage, such as the goodwill of a business, or the impairment of an action at law.

As to tangible personal property, where the article can be repaired, most courts will allow a recovery for damages for loss of use for the period of time reasonably required to make such repairs, provided that the plaintiff can establish that damages, in fact, were sustained. Where the article is a total loss, in that the article is either completely destroyed or the cost of repairs exceeds its preaccident value, and recovery is based on the value of the article prior to the accident, most courts will not allow damages for loss of use.

Some courts, such as Arkansas, do not allow damages for loss of use under any circumstances [*Kane* v. *Carper*, 177 S.W. 2d 41]; others, such as Colorado, allow damages only for the loss of a business use [*Hunter* v. *Quaintance*, 168 Pac. 918]; and still others, such as New York, do not allow damages for loss of use where the general claim is based upon a diminution of value [*Johnson* v. *Scholz*, 93 N.Y.S. 2d 334]. The majority view, however, is to permit recovery in all the cases as noted in the first paragraph.

The amount claimed for loss of use is subject to the rule of certainty in that the plaintiff must establish with certainty his exact loss. Where there has been some inconvenience but no actual monetary loss, the plaintiff will encounter some difficulty by way of proof. For example, where *A* has been deprived of the use of his automobile during the repair period, and he uses public transportation, he has sustained no provable monetary loss. The value of his inconvenience is speculative. He cannot produce evidence which will measure this inconvenience in terms of money. Should he use the vehicle for a business purpose, he could show the amount of the profit he has lost, the amount of earnings that he has been forced to forego, or if the vehicle is a commercial one, he could show the amount of earnings reasonably expected from such use. Where he actually rents a substitute vehicle, the cost of the rental during the reasonable period of repair would be the measure of damages for loss of use.

Claims for loss of use are also subject to the rule of subtraction. If a substitute vehicle is rented and the lessor provides the gas and oil, the measure of damages would be the cost of the rental less the cost of gas and oil. If the vehicle had not been damaged, the owner would have had to pay for the gas and oil. Therefore, the cost of gas and oil does not represent any part of his damage caused by the accident and for that reason is not a recoverable item.

2. *Real property.*   Any wrongful intrusion on to the lands of another is a trespass and where damages are incurred the owner has a cause of action against the intruder to recover his loss, whether it be for permanent or temporary damage to his use of the property. The rule in real property is that the owner is entitled to the enjoyment of his land and the "rents, issues are profits" arising therefrom. Any wrongful intrusion which deprives the owner of any of these is actionable and the value of each is an element of damage. Real property includes not only the land, but the structures thereon permanently affixed to the land, plus the perennial crops—trees, bushes, grass, etc., which are not planted annually—and in addition any other conditions on the land, whether man-made or natural, such as lakes, streams, drainage ditches, roads, fences, and swimming pools.

As has been said, the owner's enjoyment of his real property includes, among other things, the rights to rents, issues, and profits. Rents do not need definition, but it does mean the net rents, and would not be the gross receipts from the rental of the property since there are usually other expenses to be paid, such as taxes, assessments, and the normal repairs to the property, which are the responsibility of the owner, whether there was a wrongful intrusion or not. Issues refers to growing things on the land, such as trees, etc., and the owner is entitled to the enjoyment of these things whether he planted them or not, or whether they just grew over the years. Profits usually refer to the benefit, advantage or pecuniary gain accruing to the owner or the occupant of the land from its actual use. This might seem to overlap the matter of rents and issues, but it is a catch-all phrase used to cover anything that was possibly not covered by the prior terms. The question then will arise is for how long a period of time will the loss of rents, issues, and profits be taken into account. In the case of a structure which can be replaced, the period of time would be measured by the length of time reasonably required to make the replacement or repairs.

An interest in real property can consist of something less than complete ownership. The most common example of this is where the owner divests himself of the use of all or part of the property for a term of years by lease, with the right of reversion to him at the expiration of the term of the lease. In this sense, the tenant is the "owner" of the realty which is the subject matter of the lease for the period of time limited in the lease. Therefore, any damage suffered by him as a result of the impairment of his right of use is recoverable by him. Where the damage is not only to the tenant's occupancy but also permanently damages the realty, then the adjuster will have two claimants with whom to deal. He will settle with the tenant for the interference with his occupancy and he will settle with the owner for the damage to his reversionary interest.

The right to engage in business is a property right, and any damage to it can be classified as property damage. An impairment of this right which results in the loss of profits as a consequence of damage to the premises or the property on which the business is conducted is actionable and the loss of profits is an item of damage. The period of time during which this loss of profits is measurable may be the period of time necessary to repair the building, or the period of time needed to move the business to another location, depending on the circumstances.

Other allowable expenses.   Money expended to prevent further damage to the article is also recoverable. These items could include towing charges or temporary repairs to a building. In addition, in some jurisdictions interest is allowed from the time of the accident to the time of payment on either the diminution of value or the cost of repairs.

Settlement value.   In cases involving a repairable article the settlement value is usually the reasonable cost of repairs. No allowance is made for loss of use with respect to motor vehicles unless (1) there is a business use involved and (2) there is an actual money loss due to the rental of a substitute vehicle, or a provable loss of profit due to the lack of it. Mere discomfort or inconvenience caused by the lack of the car is not an item considered in a settlement valuation. In Arkansas, where the courts do not allow any recovery for loss of use, no loss of use is considered under any circumstances.

With respect to damage to property other than a motor vehicle, such as damage to a business building, a home, a store, or a display window, the same tests are used in determining whether or not a loss of use claim will be recognized. Loss of use is not considered unless (1) the property is used for business and (2) an actual business loss can be established. Mere inconvenience during a period of repaid with respect to a private dwelling is not considered as an item of damage. However, where the repairs are of such a nature as to make it impossible for the owner to occupy the premises and he is required to incur expense in living elsewhere or conducting his business elsewhere during the repair period, such expenses as are reasonable are usually recoverable.

With respect to a completely destroyed article, or one in which the repairs will exceed the preaccident value, settlement value is usually based on the market value of the article prior to the accident, less the junk value of the salvage. No damages for loss of use are considered, nor is any consideration given to the matter of interest on the cost of repairs or diminution of value. In all cases, charges for towing or temporary repairs are given some consideration. If the expenses for these items is reasonable under the circumstances, they are allowable, even in the case of a total loss.

2008   Measure of damages: Personal injury

As in other claims for damages arising from the tortious act of another, the injured is entitled to recover reasonable compensation for his injuries, past, present, and future, caused by the tort. Reasonable compensation means an award of money that will repair and restore the injured to his preaccident condition, and should be an amount commensurate with the extent of the injury. It is clear that in many cases the payment of money will not place the injured person in a position equivalent to his physical condition prior to injury. The payment, therefore, is to compensate the plaintiff for the pain or deterioration of the body which he has suffered and is likely to suffer in the future.

The amount is not what a person would suffer the same injury for since this type of transaction is not a bargain and sale. The injured certainly had no opportunity to decide whether he would suffer the injury or not. His damages consist of the amount that the jury, in its discretion, decides will reasonably represent in money the value of the injuries suffered. The jury award is decided on the basis of the evidence of injury and follows the instructions of the court. The elements which the court will instruct the jury to take into consideration when deciding the question of damages are (1) out-of-pocket expenses, (2) loss of earning capacity, and (3) mental and physical distress. In appropriate cases, the jury has been instructed to take into account additional elements—such as the effect of a disfiguring scar or of the inability to bear children—upon the chances of marriage in the case of a girl or a young woman.

It is to be noted that the first two items are tangible in the sense that their value can be ascertained with certainty, and for that reason the rule of certainty is applied; the injured must establish his exact loss. The third item is a matter of speculation. The value of the injured's mental or physical distress is left to the discretion of the jury, and the injured's proof of this particular item is not subject to the rule of certainty. He must, however, produce evidence of injury and testimony as to the pain or suffering that he has endured or will continue to endure. Let us consider in detail exactly what each of these elements include.

1. *Out-of-pocket expenses.* These involve expenditures which the injured was compelled to make solely because of the injury. In most cases, they will consist largely of medical, surgical, hospital, and nursing costs. The injured is entitled to recover the reasonable value of such services, and in most states he must establish that the amounts which he claims represent not only the amount which he paid, but also that the amount so paid is the reasonable value of the services rendered. He will also have to establish that the services so rendered were made necessary, solely as a result of the injury.

If the injury is a continuing one, the injured is entitled not only to the medical expense incurred up to the time of trial, but also to the reasonable value of medical services which will be required in the future. He must establish the need for future medical attention by offering expert medical testimony as to these facts.

Other out-of-pocket expenses could include the hiring of a housekeeper, a practical nurse, or even the expense of a trip necessary for convalescence. These are allowable items if it can be shown that the necessity for the expense is causally related to the injury. Thus any expenses which would not have been incurred but for the injury are recoverable if the amount is reasonable.

2. *Loss of earning capacity.* Where the injuries are such that the injured person has been totally or partially deprived of his earning capacity, damages are allowed for such disability. It makes no difference whether the injured is unemployed, on vacation, or so financially situated that he does not have to work at all. Damages are nevertheless recoverable for his loss of earning capacity.

Where the injured is employed at the time of injury, proof of his loss of earning capacity is a comparatively easy matter. Evidence of his earnings on the job, plus medical proof of disability for the period he was away from work, will establish this item. Difficulty is encountered when the injured is unemployed at the time of injury, whether due to economic conditions in his line of work, his aversion to work of any kind, or his financial situation which does not make work a necessity. Under proper instructions of the court, the jury will be allowed to determine the amount that he would have been able to earn during his period of incapacity. They will take into account his age, education, work habits, his skill, and the general condition of the labor market. In the case of a housewife who ordinarily does not work, the measure of her loss of earning capacity could be the amount paid to a baby-sitter or house-keeper.

Where the injured is in business for himself, his earning capacity will be measured by the value of his services and not by the total profit he derived from the business. The profit obtained from a business is usually due to the services rendered by the owner, the return on the capital invested, as well as profit realized from the work of others. In presenting evidence of his loss of earning capacity, he is subject to the rule of certainty and must establish the exact value of his earning capacity. He must show the exact amount that must be subtracted from the total profit, as representing the value of the factors other than his own work. This can be accomplished by showing the profit made before his injury as compared to the profit made during his period of in-capacity, or, if the profit remains constant and a substitute was hired to do his work, then the amounts paid to the substitute could be utilized as evidence of the value of his loss of earning capacity.

In some rare cases, evidence may be available that, immediately prior to the accident, the injured's earnings were below his actual earning capacity. If such be the case, the jury may, with appropriate instructions from the court, determine what his earning capacity is, based on what he could earn and not necessarily on what he was earning at the time of the accident. While the jury is not bound to conclude that his earning capacity is measured by his prior earnings, the injured is confronted with a problem of proof. He will have to show why he was willing to accept less than his earning capacity and, further, that he could have earned more in another job, and why he did not take the other job. Juries are not ready to accept evidence of this sort and it is unlikely that they would go along with the injured unless the proof is clear and con-vincing.

Where the loss of earning capacity continues up to the time of trial and is likely to continue beyond that time, damages for loss of future earning capacity are recoverable. Clearly, the injured cannot establish such a loss with certainty. He must, however, establish the loss with a reasonable degree of certainty. This will require the testimony of experts as to the length of time the incapacity will continue, whether for the duration of the injured's work life or a shorter period of time. In addition, the injured will have to establish with a reasonable degree of certainty exactly what his earning capacity will be during the projected period of disability. In some occupations the ability to earn diminishes with advancing age, so that the burden is on the injured to establish with a reasonable degree of certainty what his future earnings will be, subtracting whatever amounts the future changes in his earnings will require. The defendant is entitled to the reduction, and the injured's failure to establish the amount to be subtracted could result in a failure of the requi-site amount of proof necessary to sustain an award. Conversely, where the injured's earnings could reasonably be expected to increase in the future, the injured is entitled to recover on the basis of anticipated earnings, so that any increase must be taken into consideration if sufficient evidence of such increases is offered.

As to the evidence required to establish the loss of future earning capacity, the injured must show (1) that his disability will continue beyond the date of trial and for how long thereafter, and (2) the effect that such disability will have on his earning capacity. To meet the first requirement expert testimony, in the form of medical proof, must be submitted. The physician must testify as to the nature of the disability and the prognosis for future recovery, if any, and in addition must testify as to the extent that the disability affects his earning capacity. Having once established disability, the injured must show that he had an earning capacity prior to the accident, the effect of his disability on his earning capacity, and the present value of the dollar loss which he has suffered. Earning capacity prior to the accident is established in the same way it would be if the disability was merely temporary. As to the projected future loss, the average weekly or yearly loss must be established. This may be shown by evidence of the average earnings of a similar person, and evidence that the injured was either above average, average, or below average as to future earning capacity. When the average earnings are established, then the testimony of an actuary must be offered to show the work-life of the injured and the present value of the projected loss of earning capacity. We say "present value" for the reason that the judgment will be rendered on the trial date and the defendant will be required to pay for future losses as of that date. Since payment is actually made in advance, the defendant is entitled to a discount for the advance payment.

In computing the value of loss of earning capacity, the injured's take-home pay is used as the basis, not his gross earnings. This is for the reason that the Internal Revenue Code of 1954 (sec. 104a), lists as an exemption from gross income "The amount of any damages received (whether by suit or agreement) on account of personal injuries or sickness."

Therefore the actual earnings after taxes will measure the net loss and, since the recovery is not subject to tax, an award based on take-home pay will reimburse the injured for what he has actually lost. If gross wages were used, then the injured would recover in tax-free damages an amount on which he would have had to pay taxes if he received it in salary or other income. Therefore, the use of a gross wage figure would result in the injured recovering more than he lost.

While a plaintiff who has recovered for the loss of his earnings on a pre-tax basis is placed in a better position than the one he occupied prior to the accident, the majority of the courts follow the rule that net earnings before taxes are the proper measure of damages for loss or impairment of earning capacity. There are several reasons given for this conclusion. First, some courts felt that the inclusion of the deduction of income tax would be "too conjectural," in the sense that the jury would have to calculate the amount of the tax together with the deductions to which the plaintiff was entitled, and also they would be required to guess just what taxes would be imposed in the future together with whatever increases or decreases the legislature would see fit to allow. [*Stokes* v. *United States*, 144 Fed. 2d 82.] Second, some courts felt that the congressional intent was to benefit injured persons by exonerating them from paying taxes on bodily injury awards, and to reduce the award by consideration of the tax advantages would be to frustrate the congressional intent. [*Hall* v. *Chicago & North Western Ry.*, 125 N.E. 2d 77.] Third, some courts utilized the collateral source rule, holding that the tax exemption was a benefit derived from a collateral source and not from the defendant, and as a result the defendant was not entitled to credit therefor. [*Mitchell* v. *Emblade* 298 Pac. 2d 1034 (Arizona).] Other cases denying the defendant credit for the income taxes and giving various reasons for such conclusions are: *Cunningham* v. *Rederiet Vindeggen* (333 Fed. 2d 308); *Highshew* v. *Kushto* [134 N.E. 2d 555 (Indiana)]; *McWeeney* v. *New York, N. H. & H. R. R.* (282 Fed. 2d 34, cert. denied, 364 U.S. 870); *Pfister* v. *City of Cleveland* (113 N.E. 2d 366); and *Hudson* v. *Lazarus* (217 Fed. 2d 344, cert. denied 364 U.S. 870).

Not all of the courts have passed on this question, but, as noted, the majority who have considered it, have decided in favor of the injured person. However, regardless of whether the question has or has not been submitted to the courts in a particular jurisdiction, it would appear that for settlement purposes only the net income or the take-home pay should be the basis for the computation of loss of earning capacity.

Both out-of-pocket expenses and loss of earning capacity are tangible items in the sense that they are pecuniary losses amenable to actual proof. They are referred to as "special damages" since they can be so measured and represent actual money losses sustained by the injured person.

3. Mental and physical distress.   This item of general damages is often referred to as "pain and suffering," "discomfort," or "inconvenience," depending upon the degree of pain accompanying the injury. It is a nonpecuniary loss in the sense that the injured has incurred no monetary deprivation because of it. It is, however, compensatory since it is designed to reimburse or repay the injured for the pain which he suffered. Distress of this nature has no exchange value in the market, nor is there any guide or standard which can be used to measure it. It is a question of fact which is submitted to the sound discretion of the jury, under appropriate instructions from the court. The jury thus is the final arbiter as to the valuation of this item in terms of dollars.

The injured is entitled to compensation for the mental and physical distress that he has experienced up to the time of trial, and if the condition is such that it will cause pain into the future, the amount of compensation will contemplate such future suffering. In establishing such damages, the injured will have to show by medical testimony that the pain will continue, and for how long, as well as whether or not the discomfort will abate in intensity, remain constant, or increase in intensity with the passage of time. Where the discomfort will persist for the rest of the injured's life, mortality tables may be utilized to establish his life expectancy.

2009 Collateral source rule

The general rule is that the tort-feasor is answerable for all of the damages sustained as a result of his wrongful act. However it frequently happens that the injured, because of the accident, receives benefits in the form of medical payments or accident and health disability payments. These come to him from a collateral source, other than the tort-feasor, usually because of some insurance policies for which he paid the premium. Since the tort-feasor had nothing to do with these benefits, he is not entitled to reduce his liability because of the collateral source benefits received by the injured. In a word, the injured party can recover more than once for the same item.

It also happens that in some cases the injured's employer will continue the payment of salary during the period of disability, so that the injured actually sustained no wage loss. The money so paid is not earned income and represents merely a gift from the employer. The tort-feasor is not entitled to credit for the money so paid, since it came to the injured from a collateral source.

With respect to medical payments coverage, the question arises as to whether or not the claimant, who has received reimbursement for his medical bills under the defendant's insurance coverage, can claim reimbursement for the same bills in a subsequent tort action against the defendant. The problem is whether or not the medical payments insurance is a "collateral source" so as to permit a double recovery. In the cases decided up to the present time, some courts have held that medical payments received under the defendant's insurance coverage are not collateral source payments and that a double recovery will not be permitted. The question is apparently open in most of the states, but the decisions already made seem to be persuasive of the conclusion that should be reached.

In *Tart* v. *Register* [125 S.E. 2d 754 (North Carolina)], the Supreme Court decided that it was unconscionable to permit a passenger in a motor vehicle to collect under the medical payments coverage and again in an action for damages from the same company. In *Gunter* v. *Lord* (140 So. 2d 11), the Louisiana Supreme Court reached the same conclusion. It felt that the payments for medical were received from the same source and, whether the payment was made as a result of a contract or a tort action, the claimant was entitled to only one recovery for the item. The court said:

> The result follows, when the instrument (the policy) is viewed as a whole . . . that it was not contemplated that an injured person should collect his medical expenses twice, i.e., that having already been paid such expenses at the instance of the insured by the insurance company following the accident, that he should again be awarded the same medical expenses as an incident of the tort action. His damages, in that respect, have been repaired.

In *Dodds* v. *Bucknum* (344 Pac. 2d 25), a California district court of appeal made the point that if the defendant had paid the medical expenses out of his own pocket, there would be no question but that the plaintiff could not collect them again. The court could see no difference between a cash payment by the defendant direct and a cash payment made by the defendant to an insurance company who became obligated thereby to make the payment. The court said:

> It can make no difference either in principle or in justice that defendant did not pay these bills out of his own pocket but that the source of such payments was insurance purchased by the defendant with his own funds for such an eventuality. It would indeed be strange if a wrongdoer who had foresight enough to cover himself with insurance, and thus in fact cause the payment of any doctor and hospital bills which his wrongful act may make necessary, should be penalized, whereas the person who does not similarly provide a fund for such contingencies should obtain the benefit if, perchance, at the time of the injury or thereafter he has the cash with which to pay such expenses. It should therefore logically follow that if a wrongdoer provides a source or fund out of which the injured party's special damages are paid prior to trial the recovery of the plaintiff is diminished to that extent.

A similar conclusion was reached in *Yarrington* v. *Thornburg* [205 Atl. 2d 1 (Delaware)], and *Adams* v. *Turner* [238 Fed. Supp. 643 (District of Columbia)].

Workmen's compensation payments are not subject to the collateral source rule. This is for the reason that under most compensation statutes the claimant has an election either to take compensation, proceed against the third-party tort-feasor, or do both. In the case of the acceptance of compensation payments or the payment of medical, the insurance carrier making such payments is usually subrogated to the rights of the claimant or has a lien on the proceeds of recovery to the extent of the payments made. Therefore, such payments do not represent benefits received from a collateral source, independent of the defendant, since in most states the compensation carrier either has a lien on the claimant's cause of action or, in the alternative, is subrogated to all of the claimant's rights against the defendant. In states where there is no right of lien or of subrogation, compensation recovered might be subject to the collateral source rule.

2010   Time of valuation

The general rule is that the damages sustained by the plaintiff are determined as of the date of the trial. Thus everything that occurs between the time of the accident or event will be taken into account, whether it increases or diminishes the amount of damages sustained. For example, if *A* suffers what seems to be a trivial injury through the negligence of *B*, but as a consequence of the malpractice of his physician, selected with due care, *A* suffers an aggravation of the condition, *A* is entitled to recover damages from *B* for all of his injuries, including those caused by the physician's malpractice. Similarly, if *A* sustained a slight laceration and, through no neglect on *A*'s part the wound became infected, *A* would be entitled to recover not only for the laceration but for the infection as well. On the other hand, if *A* recovered a judgment against *B* for $500, which was satisfied, *A* would not be entitled to recover any further damages which he might sustain as a result of the original injury even though the harmful effects of the injury were not manifest and were unknown at the time of trial.

For another example, let us assume that *A* is injured through the negligence of *B*, and *A* recovers a judgment against *B* for $1,500. *B* appeals from the judgment on the grounds that it is excessive, since *A* sustained only a trivial injury which required only three treatments from the doctor. The judgment is reversed and the case is sent back for a new trial. In the meantime it is discovered that the trivial injury has aggravated a latent bone disease and, as a result, *A* has been hospitalized and has submitted to several operations. When the case is retried some two years after the original verdict, *A* introduces evidence of the entire injury proximately caused by *B*'s negligence and the jury brings in a verdict to $10,000. Under the circumstances this latter award, based on the evidence submitted, may not be excessive since the facts now support a greater verdict than before. The claim is valued as of the trial date, so when the case is set down for a new trial it is as if there never had been a trial. *A* is not limited to proving only the facts as they existed at the time of the previous trial. Since this is a new trial he can introduce evidence of his injury and the damage suffered up to the date of this new trial.

Suppose *A* libels *B* by publishing an untrue statement concerning *B*'s presence in a gambling house at the time of a raid. *B* is president of the local bank and this statement threatens his position and that of the bank. *A* publishes a retraction, acknowledging the error and stating that *B* was not present in the gambling house. Evidence of the retraction is admissible for the purpose of diminishing the damages to which *B* would otherwise be entitled.

Again, suppose *A* is injured through the negligence of *B* and the injuries are of such a permanent nature that *A* will never work again. *A* is 30 years of age, his life expectancy is over 35 years, and his work-life expectancy is about 29 years. The case is tried and the verdict is based on these figures. Subsequently, *A* outlives the expectancy and dies at the age of 105. He obtained no payment for the years following the age of 75. *A* is not entitled to any further recovery.

Let us assume the same facts as above, but that two weeks after the judgment is paid *A* is killed in an automobile accident. *B* is not entitled to recover from *A*'s estate for the obvious overpayment. The rule is that the claim is valued as of the date of trial and subsequent events, after the satisfaction of the judgment, have no influence whatsoever.

Let us again assume the same facts as above, but that *A* is killed in an automobile accident two weeks before trial. The measure of damages then would be limited to the actual losses suffered between the date of the accident for which *B* is responsible and the date of *A*'s death. This again is for the reason that the rule requires that the claim be valued as of the date of the trial. The mere fact that the injuries were so severe that A would have been incapacitated for the rest of his life, had he lived, is not taken into account in valuing the amount of his recovery.

In property damage cases where the damage is measured by the value of the article at the time of its destruction, or the time the plaintiff was deprived of its use, the plaintiff is usually entitled to recover the value of the article as it was at sometime prior to the trial, ordinarily the time of the accident.

2011   Effect of a preexisting physical disability

The law does not require that the innocent victim, who suffers personal injuries because of the negligence of another, be in perfect health in order to recover. The law recognizes the existence of disease and residual disability caused by prior injuries, as well as the infirmities of age. The presence of any of these conditions does not relieve the tort-feasor of his responsibility to respond in damages. He is answerable for all the injuries proximately caused by his negligent act. The fact that a person in perfect health would have sustained little disability is not taken into account in reducing the tort-feasor's liability where the injury superimposed upon a preexisting infirmity, disability, or disease produces a serious condition. The tort-feasor is answerable for whatever injuries are produced, irrespective of whether a preexisting condition contributes to the injury or not. In a word, the tort-feasor takes his victim as he finds him, and he is responsible for all disability causally related to the injury. Therefore, theoretically, the tort-feasor is answerable for all the effects of the injury, and where a preexisting condition is aggravated, this responsibility attaches to the aggravation. When the effects of the aggravation have ceased, and the injured is in the same condition as he was prior to the accident, the defendant's responsibility is at an end.

For example, let us assume that prior to the accident A was suffering from tertiary syphilis. A is injured through the negligence of B and sustains deep lacerations which, because of his syphilitic condition, require extensive treatment and produce a long period of disability. In addition, because of the prior condition, arsenic treatments are necessary in order to heal the lacerations. B is liable for the treatment and the period of disability even though, had A been a normally healthy person, the disability would have been of shorter duration and arsenic treatments would not have been necessary. It should be noted that B is not responsible for the cure of A's syphilis but is answerable for all the effects of the injury, including whatever treatment is necessary to restore A to the same physical condition as he was prior to injury.

In the preceding example it will be noted that it was possible to entirely disassociate the two conditions and to measure the disability and medical expense necessitated by the injury. Where the two conditions cannot be separated, the plaintiff is faced with a problem of proof. He is confronted by the rule of certainty and must establish the exact extent of the injury caused by the accident and the expense occasioned thereby.

Suppose that A is suffering from a progressive arthritis of the spine, for which he is under treatment, prior to the accident. A suffers an injury to the spine which, it is claimed, aggravated the arthritic condition and accelerated its disabling effects. In this case the condition is progressive, and even if the accident had not occurred A's condition would have deteriorated with the passage of time. A must establish with certainty the exact injury which he sustained in the accident and must also produce evidence of the losses which he sustained as a result. It is clear that A's condition will never return to the state in which it was prior to accident. Therefore A must resort to medical testimony to show the pain and suffering he experienced as a result of the accident, the increase in medical treatment required after the accident, the difference, if any, between the treatment rendered before the accident and that rendered thereafter, together with the increased costs of the treatment, if any.

In addition, if A were employed prior to the accident and after the accident could not work, the change in his earning capacity could be offered as some evidence of the effects of the injury. However, A is also faced with the rule of subtraction since it is evident that his condition is not a stationary one and would possibly have prevented him from doing any work at some point in the future. A then would have to show the prognosis of his condition prior to injury, and the present prognosis with the injury. The difference would be the extent of the tort-feasor's liability.

Suppose A is blind in one eye. Through the negligence of B, A loses the sight of his good eye and is now completely blind. B is answerable for A's blindness, and the extent of his liability is not mitigated by the fact that A's previous condition contributed to the final result. Absent the accident and A would not have been blind. Therefore, the accident is responsible for A's condition of blindness.

2012   Loss of consortium

At common law the relationship of the wife to her husband was that of a very superior servant to the master. Any tortious act of a third person (including negligent personal injury) which interfered with the relationship and deprived the master (husband) of the services to which he was entitled gave rise to a cause of action by the master (husband) against the wrongdoer for the damages which he sustained as a consequence of the loss of such services. It should be pointed out that this is an independent cause of action which accrues to the husband because of the damages which he himself has suffered, and for which only he may recover. Under our present statutes, the wife may recover for her personal injuries, but the settlement or judgment recovered by the wife will not extinguish the husband's cause of action for loss of services. The death of the wife will not abate the husband's cause of action, but it will limit his recovery to the damages which he has sustained up to the time of her death. In the case of divorce or separation after the tort has been committed, the husband's right to the services of his wife would be limited to the period of time measured from the date of the accident up until the date of the divorce or separation.

Consortium consists of (1) sex, (2) society, and (3) services. Any injury to the wife which deprives the husband of one or more of these elements will support the husband's cause of action.

Sex refers to the marital relation of sexual intercourse and, since this item does not have a market or exchange value, the amount to be awarded is left to the discretion of the jury under instructions from the court. They may take into consideration the age and physical capacity of both husband and wife in determining the amount to be awarded.

Society refers to companionship. Again this is an item which has no market or exchange value. The jury will decide its value. They may take into account the conditions of the home life of the husband prior to the injury and the changes that have occurred as a result of the wife's injury. If there was no home life to speak of, then there would be at the most a minimal loss. This might be evidenced by the fact that the wife spent very little time at home, consorted with other men, and generally neglected her housewifely duties. In such a case the companionship lost by the husband would be practically nil.

Services refer to the wife's services as a housewife. This loss could be demonstrated by the employment of a housekeeper or baby-sitter to accomplish the tasks normally undertaken by the wife. The cost of such a substitute would be the measure of damages. As to services rendered to others, as where the wife is gainfully employed, the husband has no interest. The wife's earnings are her own and, therefore, any loss of earning capacity which she might sustain must be recovered in her own action.

For the husband to have a cause of action for loss of services there must be a relationship of husband and wife at the time of the occurrence of the tort. The relationship must be a legal one. Where two people are living together as husband and wife in a state which does not recognize such a relationship as a common-law marriage, the "husband" does not have a cause of action for loss of services even though he has sustained a loss. The same situation would obtain where there was a bigamous marriage. Since a bigamous marriage is legally no marriage at all, the so-called husband would not be entitled to recover. In a case where both parties were engaged at the time of the accident and subsequently married, the husband did not have that status at the time of the tort and, therefore, has no cause of action. To sustain a cause of action for loss of services there must be a legal relationship of husband and wife at the time of the commission of the tort. If such a relationship is not in existence, the husband has no cause of action.

Defenses. The husband's action is based upon the liability of the tortfeasor to his wife. Therefore as an element of his case the husband must assert a tort cause of action based on the facts of the accident. Defenses such as contributory negligence, assumption of risk, or the statute of limitations, which could be asserted as defenses to the action by the wife, are likewise available as defenses to the husband's action. In addition, any defenses which the defendant may have against the husband personally may be asserted. For example, *H* and *W* are husband and wife. *H* is driving the automobile in which *W* is a passenger. An accident occurs in which the cars of *H* and *X* collide. The accident is due to the joint negligence of both drivers. *H*'s contributory negligence in most states is not imputed to *W*. *W* may recover. To *H*'s cause of action for loss of services, *X* can set up *H*'s contributory negligence as a defense, with the result that *H* cannot recover. In states subscribing to the community purpose doctrine, the result would be that neither *H* nor *W* could recover.

As part of his marital obligation the husband is responsible for the medical and other care needed by his wife. In personal injury cases, where the wife is injured, this obligation continues. Therefore, the husband has a cause of action against the tort-feasor for the money expended for the care of his wife. This item of damage is in addition to his claim for loss of consortium. Some few states have abandoned the theory of loss of consortium and have limited the husband's recovery only to the money expended for medical care of his wife. Most others still recognize the husband's claim for loss of consortium and make awards accordingly.

The common law never recognized a similar claim on the part of the wife for the loss of her husband's services. Therefore, when the husband was injured only one cause of action arose, the claim of the husband. Some few courts have modified the common-law rule and have recognized such a right on the part of the wife. (See Section 603, above.)

2013 Loss of services of infants

At common law unemancipated children were considered to have about the same status as that of the wife with relation to the husband and father. They were superior servants and the father was entitled not only to the services they rendered for him personally, but was also entitled to their earnings. The father was obligated to care for his child and to provide medical and other necessary care in the case of illness or injury. Where injury has been caused by the negligence of a third party, the father has an independent cause of action for the value of the loss of the child's services, as well as for the reasonable value of the medical and other care which were required as a result of the injury.

The mother of the injured child does not have this same cause of action unless the child is illegitimate, or she is a widow, or has custody of the child under a court order due to its abandonment by the father. Only in the latter three instances can the mother assert the claim for loss of the child's services.

At one time it is clear that children were economic assets. They could be sent to work at an early age and their earnings contributed to the family purse. The early common-law courts evolved the "wage-profit" formula which in essence provided that the loss sustained by the father was the amount of the child's wages, less the costs of feeding and housing him.

Fortunately, this situation does not obtain in this modern day. Children are not sent out to work at an early age, and, because of the costs of education and upbringing, children very definitely are liabilities rather than assets. Therefore, it is only in rare cases that any allowance is made for the value of the child's services. Medical and other expenses are regularly allowed and are recovered by the child's father or mother, as the case may be.

2014   Effect of illegitimacy

In Roman law an illegitimate child was characterized as a *filius nullius* (son of no one). The only natural relative that such a child would have was his mother. This concept is applied to this very day. The child inherits only from his mother and, conversely, the mother is the child's sole heir. In case of injury only the mother has a cause of action for the loss of the child's services and for his medical expenses. This is true even though the paternity of the child has been established through filial proceedings and the putative father is under a court order to contribute to the child's support. These proceedings do not give the putative father any of the rights of parenthood, nor do they legitimatize the origin of the child.

2015   Effect of divorce or separation

A final decree of divorce terminates the marriage as of the date of the decree. The divorced husband has no further rights to consortium or the services of his divorced wife. Where the wife is divorced prior to the injury, no right of action accrues to the divorced husband for loss of services or the recovery for her medical expenses, even though the award of alimony obligates him to pay for her medical expenses. Where the divorce occurs after the accident, the husband would have a cause of action for the loss of consortium from the date of the accident up to the time they both separated.

The same situation would obtain in the case of a separation. Where both husband and wife are living apart, whether by agreement or court decree, the husband is not entitled to the services of his wife. In the event of an injury to the wife, the husband has sustained no damage, and therefore does not have an actionable claim.

2016   Personal injury claims evaluation: Tangible items

The first step in the determination of the settlement value of a case, or the amount which it would be to the advantage of the company to pay in settlement, involves an estimate of the possible jury verdict in the event of trial. The estimate is based on a comparison of the applicable measure of damages to the facts of the claim, the proof which can be offered in support of each item of damage claimed, and the anticipated jury reaction to the evidence offered. The applicable measure of damages in personal injury cases consists of both tangible and intangible items. The tangible items are the out-of-pocket expenses which are susceptible of definite proof, such as the medical, surgical, and hospital expenses incurred, and the loss of earning capacity. The intangible items include mental and physical distress.

The initial attention is directed to the tangible items. All of the details of the items claimed must first be obtained. These include detailed medical, surgical, or hospital bills showing the dates of the treatment; the kind and type and charge for each treatment, together with an itemization of the claimed loss of earning capacity; the period of time during which total incapacity is claimed; as well as the period of time during which it is claimed that the incapacity was partial, and the extent of the partial disability. Each item then can be evaluated as to its reasonableness by subjecting it to all three of the following tests: (1) necessity, (2) duration, and (3) verification.

(As an initial example, let us apply the tests to the claimed items of medical expense. The procedure would be as follows:)

1. *Necessity*.   First, the exact medical diagnosis must be obtained. This can be secured from the attending physician by means of a medical report or a medical certificate. The diagnosis must be medically descriptive of the injuries sustained and not merely descriptive of the manner of causation. For example, a "whiplash type of injury" is not a medical diagnosis and is not descriptive of the injury sustained. It refers only to the manner of causation. Second, the standard medical practice with respect to the treatment of the injury must be ascertained. This includes the method of treatment, the frequency, and the usual anticipated result. This information can be obtained by reference to standard medical textbooks or can be obtained from the company's examining physician. Third, a comparison can be made between the standard medical practice and the treatment rendered as evidenced by the itemized bills submitted. A determination can be made as to whether standard medical practice was followed, whether treatment was rendered with the frequency which such practice demanded, and whether the case was overtreated or undertreated.

2. *Duration*.   While it is true that no two cases are alike, there is a certain pattern which is applicable to the course of treatment which each condition will require. For the most part, recovery usually follows within the accepted period of time unless there are complications (which will have to be considered in the cases where they occur). A medical examination by the company physician during the period of treatment will be a helpful guide in deciding whether or not the treatment followed the usual pattern of frequency and duration, and whether the case was overtreated.

3. *Verification*.   There are several means of verification available. Where an inquiry has been made into the medical treatment at the time the claimant's statement was taken, the actual bill can be compared with the statement made by the claimant as to the treatment rendered, the dates of the treatment, whether house or office calls were made, and the type of treatment rendered up to the date of the statement. If there is any discrepancy between the two, the claimsman is immediately put on inquiry as to the validity of the other charges made. In the case of a lawsuit, the claimant can be questioned either by deposition or interrogatory as to the exact details of the medical treatment. He will usually be prepared to testify to the general course of treatment received and the total amount which he expended for the treatment, but if he is questioned as to exactly what treatment he received on a week-to-week basis, what was done at the occasion of each treatment, and whether or not the doctor rendered all of the treatment himself or if it was rendered by a nurse, some surprising answers may be obtained.

Where there is a charge for transportation to and from the doctor's office, such as taxi fares, the receipts for such charges should be obtained and the dates compared with the dates of treatment. If the dates do not coincide with the dates of treatment on the bill, and treatment was allegedly rendered on dates for which no transportation is claimed, the claimsman is put on notice of the possibility of the medical bill being padded. On the other hand, if no treatment was rendered on the dates of any of the taxi receipts, it is clear that the transportation furnished on those dates had no reference to the medical treatment of the case. Where the claimant has been hospitalized, the nurses' notes will indicate the date and the time of the doctor's visits.

Finally, recourse may be had to the doctor's own records. He may voluntarily permit an examination of his records, or it may be necessary to take his deposition in order to obtain them. An examination of the records may show that some or all of the treatment was rendered for conditions entirely unassociated with the injury, or that the dates of the entries on the records do not coincide with the dates of treatment on the bill. If it is known from the investigation that the claimant was out of town, on vacation, or in jail, a check of the dates of treatment should reflect that no treatment was rendered during these periods of time.

To explain more fully, let us examine the two bills illustrated by Examples 1 and 2 and apply the first test of reasonableness, necessity. Neither bill meets the test of necessity. In Example 1, the standard medical practice is merely to examine, diagnose, and recommend either a truss or an operation. There is no known medical treatment of a conservative nature that will cure or relieve a hernia in the inguinal region. Therefore, even if the treatment were rendered, the value of this bill is the reasonable value of the first treatment and, at most, one subsequent office visit for the purpose of determining whether or not the recommended truss was properly fitted.

For the purpose of further examination, let us assume that the condition treated in Example 1 required treatment for a period of time. Most doctors do not have office hours on Wednesdays and Sundays, unless there is a coming holiday. By reference to this bill it will be noted that Wednesdays are excluded

EXAMPLE 1

STATEMENT OF DOCTOR ___ Joseph Green

NAME OF PHYSICIAN

Name of Injured ___ Guisseppe Di Angelo ___ Age 30 Date of Injury June 3 , 19 84

Name of Employer ___ Blank Construction Co.

First Aid Rendered by ___ Joseph Green, M.D. Subsequent Aid by ___

CODE: O—office. V—house visit. H—hospital visit. N—night visit. X—X-ray. S—operation.

Month	1	2	3	4	5	6	7	8	9	10	11	12	13	14	15	16	17	18	19	20	21	22	23	24	25	26	27	28	29	30	31
June				F	V	V	V			0	0	0		0	0	0		0	0	0		0	0	0	0	0	0	0		0	
July	0	0	0		0	0																									

Total Cost First Aid Treatment ___ $ 35 00

Office Visits 21 @ $ 15.00 each 315 00

Home Visits 4 @ $ 20.00 each 80 00

Hospital Visits ___ @ $ ___ each ___

Night Visits ___ @ $ ___ each ___

Operations ___ @ $ ___ each ___

X-Rays ___ @ $ ___ each ___

Other Charges must be itemized and explained fully ___

Total Expense for Medical Aid ___ $ 430 00

DIAGNOSIS LEFT INGUINAL HERNIA

Explain in detail special treatment, if any, giving reasons for same and of what they consisted ___

TRUSS

Describe Treatment ___ BAKING AND MASSAGE

Result ___ IMPROVED

Patient refused treatment on ___, 19___.

Is patient capable of doing same work as before injury? NO If not, why? HERNIA

Patient pronounced able to resume work as of July 8 19 84 Patient discharged as cured on ___ 19 ___

Any permanent injury? Describe fully ___ Hernia – Operation necessary for cure

Dated at New City (CITY) , New York (STATE) ,this 8th day of July , 19 84

(Signed) Joseph Green M.D.

(LOCAL ADDRESS)

from the office visits except during the last week in June (Wednesdays are June 5, 12, 19, and 26). Sundays are likewise excluded (Sundays are June 2, 9, 16, 23 and 30). Therefore, the matter of consecutive daily treatment on other days is open to some question. The bill also has a charge for June 31. June has only 30 days.

In Example 2, the diagnosis is a fracture of the right clavicle. The standard medical practice is merely to immobilize the patient's arm by means of a splint and to check the case once a week for about four weeks. Since the clavicle is not a movable bone, no baking and massage will be needed to restore motion or to promote callus. Also, a patient with a fractured clavicle is ambulatory, and under such circumstances there does not appear to be any necessity for

EXAMPLE 2

STATEMENT
OF DOCTOR __JOSEPH GREEN__

Name of
Injured   __JOHN SMITH__   NAME OF PHYSICIAN

Age __24__   Date of
Injury __10/2__ , 19 __84__

Name of
Employer __CHARLES BROWN__

First Aid
Rendered by __JOSEPH GREEN, M.D.__   Subsequent
Aid by_____

CODE: O—office. V—house visit. H—hospital visit. N—night visit. X—X-ray. S—operation.

Month	1	2	3	4	5	6	7	8	9	10	11	12	13	14	15	16	17	18	19	20	21	22	23	24	25	26	27	28	29	30	31
OCTOBER	F	V	V		V		V		V		V			O		O		O		O					O			O			

Total Cost First Aid Treatment____ 25 ____ $. 25
Office Visits ___7___ @ $ _30_ each   210
Home Visits ___6___ @ $ _40_ each   240
Hospital Visits _____ @ $ ___ each
Night Visits _____ @ $ ___ each
Operations _____ @ $ ___ each
X-Rays __10/2, 4, 10, 30__ @ $ _75_ each   300
Other Charges must be itemized and explained fully__

Total Expense for Medical Aid_____ $ 775

DIAGNOSIS___ FRACTURE RIGHT CLAVICLE

Explain in detail special treatment, if any, giving reasons
for same and of what they consisted_____

Describe
Treatment_____ BAKING AND MASSAGE

Result_____ IMPROVED

Patient refused treatment on _____ , 19___ .

Is patient capable of doing same work as before injury?__YES__ If not, why?_____

Patient pronounced able to resume work as of ___10/31___ 19_84_ Patient discharged as cured on___10/28___ 19___

Any permanent injury? Describe fully _____

Dated at_____ NEWARK _____ , __N.J.__ ,this __3rd__ day of ___NOVEMBER___ , 19 _84_
       (CITY)   (STATE)

(Signed)_____ JOSEPH GREEN _____ M.D.

(LOCAL ADDRESS)

house visits. The number of X rays seems out of proportion to the injury. While a fractured clavicle can be demonstrated clinically, the usual practice is to take an X ray to verify the fracture and to rule out any further bony pathology. It might be argued that a second X ray was necessary in order to be certain of the position of the bone after the arm was immobilized. In any case, two X rays would seem to be the maximum allowable in this particular case.

For Example 3, let us assume the following "bill" is submitted:

John Smith, M.D.

Services rendered	*William Green*	
Diagnosis:	*Whiplash injury to the spine*	
Date of Injury:	*January 2, 1975*	
First Aid	*January 2nd*	$45.00
Strapping	*January 3rd*	30.00
House Visits:	*January 3, 4, 5, 6, 8, 9, 10, 11,*	
	12, 13, 15, 16, 17, 18, 19, 22,	
	23, 24, 25, 26, 29, 30, 31.	
	February 1, 2, 5, 6.	
	27 @ $25.00	1215.00
Office Visits:	*February 7, 8, 9, 10, 12, 13,*	
	15, 16, 19, 20, 21, 23, 26, 27, 28, 29.	
	March 1, 2, 3, 5, 6, 8, 9, 12, 13,	
	15, 16.	
	27 @ $25.00	675.00
	Total	$3,198.00

In analyzing this bill, the first consideration is the matter of diagnosis. There is no such medical diagnosis as "whiplash injury to the spine." It probably tells us the manner of causation, but it is not indicative of exactly what injuries were sustained. It could mean an impacted fracture of a vertebra, a fracture of a transverse process, contusion of the spinal cord, a herniation of the nucleus pulposes, or merely a strain of the muscles of the back. In addition, the bill does not reflect exactly what treatment was rendered, except for the strapping on January 3. The frequency of the treatment appears to be out of line, especially when we check the dates of the treatment and the fact that no treatment was rendered on Sundays during the entire period. In addition, there is a charge for strapping on January 3 and also a charge for a house visit. There is a charge for February 29—in 1975 there was no Feb. 29. Finally, the bill is added incorrectly, the correct total being $1,965.

In its present form, the bill cannot be approved. Further information is needed as to diagnosis, the kind of treatment rendered, and an explanation for the daily treatments with the exception of Sundays. The reasonableness of the individual charges likewise is open to some question, especially the charge for first aid and strapping. As to the charges for house and office visits, we should ascertain the prevailing rate in the community in which the treatment was rendered. In some states, the medical society has a minimum fee schedule, and in others there is a fee schedule applicable to workmen's compensation cases. Both of these should be utilized by the claimsman as a guide, if they are available.

Loss of earning capacity. We can use the same criteria in deciding the claim for loss of wages or loss of earning capacity.

Necessity. Merely because the claimant takes a vacation, does not have a job, or does not have a desire to work will not alone support the claim for loss of earning capacity. There must be medical proof of disability in the form of a medical report which will indicate the condition, the disability caused by the condition (whether temporary or partial), and the duration of the disability. To recover for loss of earning capacity, two elements must be established; first, that there actually was a loss of earning capacity, and second, that the loss of earning capacity was caused by the injury. The lack of either of these elements will defeat the claim.

Duration.   The period of time during which it is claimed that there was a loss of earning capacity must be supported by medical proof of disability during the entire period. This means that not only must there be a medical report but that the doctor rendering the medical report must be capable of actually knowing that there was incapacity and was not merely expressing an opinion.

For example, let us assume that the claimant was injured on June 1 and was treated by a doctor on June 2. This is the only medical treatment received. Let us further assume that the claim is for two months' disability running from June 1 to July 30. The claimant presents a report from the doctor that his disability, as a result of the accident, extended to July 30. Such a report could not support the period of disability. The doctor saw the case only once and his knowledge of the claimant's condition is limited to the condition as it existed on June 2. Any opinion he may express as to how long the claimant was disabled after that date is entirely speculative and is not based on actual knowledge.

In settling such a case the most that could be allowed would be an approximate one-week disability. It could be said that the doctor could predict that period of disability from the one treatment and examination. Anything beyond that would be pure guesswork. It is also obvious that the claimant's condition could not have been serious or he would have required more than one treatment.

Conversely, let us assume that the claimant received medical treatment during the entire two-month period, and that such treatment was necessary, but that the claimant went back to work two weeks after the accident. The medical report from the physician indicated a total disability during all of the treatment. The loss of earning capacity is limited to the period during which the claimant did not have any earning capacity, the two-week period. After that time his earnings were unimpaired and therefore there was no demonstrable loss of earning capacity, even though medically he would have been justified in not working.

Verification.   The claimant's physical condition can be verified by medical examinations by the company physician. The loss of earning capacity can be verified by the claimant's employer, by a copy of the claimant's payroll record (by the books of his business if he is self-employed), as well as by a check with his customers as to exactly what work he did or was capable of doing during the period of alleged incapacity.

2017 Personal injury evaluation: Intangible items

These items refer to physical and mental distress. They are intangibles in the sense that they are not measurable by any mathematical standards and are subject only to a limited form of verification. When these items are submitted the jury will hear the claimant's evidence as to the intensity and duration of the discomfort and inconvenience which he suffered, usually supported by the testimony of the attending physician or a specialist testifying in the claimant's behalf. In appropriate cases, this evidence may be controverted by the evidence of the defendant's examining physician. The jury verdict will represent the reaction of the community in which the case is tried as to the value of these items. Where the verdict is rendered in a lump sum, it would be a comparatively easy matter to subtract the provable special damages from the verdict amount in order to ascertain the amount allowed by the jury from physical or mental distress. When the claimsman is required to evaluate these items, he will use the same criteria: (1) intensity, (2) duration, and (3) community reaction.

1. *Intensity*.   Consideration of this aspect begins with the claimant's description of the severity of the discomfort or inconvenience he suffered and the effect that it had on his normal activities, as well as the discomfort, if any, associated with the kind and type of treatment which he received. The complaints will be compared with the diagnosis, the available medical information from the claimant's doctor, and the report of the company's examining physician. The latter report should indicate the complaints which were made at the time of examination, the history of the claimant's distress, and also the physician's opinion as to whether or not it is medically possible for the injury to have produced the discomfort of which the claimant complains. A conclusion will be reached as to whether the claimant has honestly stated the extent of the discomfort or has overstated it.

2. *Duration*.   The duration of the distress can be checked by the claimant's medical information, the medical bills submitted in support of the medical out-of-pocket expenses, and by the examining physician's report. For example, if it is claimed that the distress was such that the claimant could not even leave the house, the medical bill might show office visits and contradict this assertion. Also, the activity checks made of the claimant during his alleged disability might reveal that he engaged in strenuous recreational activities. In substance, the claim of the duration of distress will be compared with the available information so as to verify or deny the extent of it.

3. *Community reaction*.   Having established the intensity or the distress, and the duration of it, the claimsman will apply his experience—as well as his knowledge of the amounts awarded by the jury in prior cases—and will value the distress accordingly. Clearly, community reaction to this aspect of the case will differ from community to community, some placing a higher valuation than others. Past experience as to jury awards is one of the guides to this valuation. The claimsman will utilize his own experience and may also have the benefit of some reporting service or contacts with local practicing attorneys in order to keep his experience up to date. No general rule can be enunciated as to which communities will be within the "high verdict" area and which will not. While the income level of the community may have some influence on jury awards, there is no substitute for current and up-to-date experience.

Our adversaries like to refer to mental and physical distress as "pain and suffering" on the theory that the psychological impact of that terminology will produce a greater valuation. Clearly, every injury does not cause pain and suffering. There may be discomfort, either severe or slight, or there may be mere inconvenience with no pain or discomfort of any kind. For example, if a man cuts his finger he will have to suffer the inconvenience of wearing a bandage, which will be somewhat of a nuisance for a period of time, but it could not be seriously urged that he experienced any pain and suffering. In another case, the claimant might have some discomfort for a period of time and, as the injury improves, suffer no discomfort but be inconvenienced by a bandage or a strapping.

Therefore, when confronted with claims for pain and suffering, the claimsman should use the more descriptive terms of discomfort or inconvenience, whichever more appropriately describes the distress. This may have a desirable effect on the claimant or his attorney from a psychological standpoint in that it may reduce the demand somewhat in demonstrating that the characterization of the slight discomfort or inconvenience as "pain and suffering" is ridiculous.

2018   Formula methods of evaluation

Numerous formula methods of evaluation have made appearances from time to time. Most of them were created by the fertile imagination of various plaintiff's counsel and were conceived solely for the purpose of inducing the insurance companies to place higher settlement values on their cases. The use of some formula method was urged as a justification for the demand which, usually, was more than the case was worth.

The formula methods have one common ingredient. They are founded on one or more arbitrary assumptions which have no basis either in law or in fact. As a result, they do not produce figures which represent a fair and realistic settlement valuation, nor do they produce figures which approximate the verdicts. Therefore, formula methods have not received general acceptance by the insurance industry.

There are apparently three schools of thought among the companies on this subject. Some are unalterably opposed to the use of any formula evaluations whatsoever; first, because they are unsound, and second, because the use and acceptance of formula methods of any kind would lend support to the program of the plaintiff's attorneys, which advocates their use. Others will value their cases by their own methods and will accept and utilize the formula method only where it produces a lower valuation. Still others utilize a formula method of some kind in the majority of their cases. In any event, no matter which view is taken by the company he represents, the adjuster should be familiar with the more common methods of formula evaluation, their basic assumptions, and their inherent weaknesses. He will be confronted by demands which are based on them and should be prepared to meet the arguments which are urged in their support.

2019   The "three times the medical" formula

In seeking some means of placing a dollar value on the item of physical and mental distress, some lawyers reasoned that there must be some relationship between the amount of the medical treatment that was rendered and the distress the claimant endured. It was reasoned that the more medical treatment required, the greater was the amount of the claimant's distress. They felt that a fair recompense for the claimant's distress would be an amount equal to twice the amount paid for the medical treatment. It is also argued that the medical bill is a reflection of the discomfort suffered: the higher the bill the greater the discomfort.

The two basic assumptions along this line are that the amount of the medical bill measures the discomfort, and that the community response as to the value of the discomfort is an amount equal to twice the medical bill. No evidence can be adduced that either one of these assumptions is valid. Nevertheless, while recognition must be given to the inherent weakness of the reasoning which created it, the formula did produce settlement figures that were acceptable to both parties, and for that reason the formula was and still is used extensively as the basis for settlement negotiations.

In applying the formula to specific instances, let us assume that the medical bill was $100. The value of his discomfort would be $200, or a total of $300 for both items. For a more convenient method of figuring, the parties usually take the medical bill figure and multiply it by 3 in order to produce the value of both items. Let us further assume that X rays were taken at a cost of $50 and that the doctor required some other tests, such as a basal metabolism, blood, Wassermann, or culture test of some kind at a cost of $25. The claimant was disabled for a period of three weeks, during which he suffered a loss of earning capacity (salary) of $225, representing a weekly wage of $75. The formula evaluation of the case would work out as follows:

Medical treatment	$100.00
Distress	200.00
X rays	50.00
Tests	25.00
Wages	225.00
Total value	$600.00

Some attorneys have modified the formula and have based their demands on "three times the medical specials," which would include all of the medical expense whether incurred for treatment, examinations, or tests. There is some question as to whether or not the period and amount of treatment can be used as a measure of the claimant's distress, but certainly the number of X rays and other diagnostic tests can have no relationship whatsoever to the extent of the distress. This did not prevent the making of demands on that basis and, where the insurance carrier was agreeable, a settlement on this basis would be made. Using our original case, the result would be:

Medical	$175.00
Distress	350.00
Wages	225.00
Total value	$750.00

Thus, by the simple expedient of lumping all the medical together, the settlement valuation has been increased by $150. Clearly, if more X rays were taken or more tests were made, whether either is necessary or not, the total would go that much higher.

A further modification in the original formula comes about where the demand is based on "three times the specials," rather than limiting the basic figure to the medical or the medical treatment. As in the tests made, there is no real relationship between the amount of salary or wages earned and the claimant's distress. Following this method, the following result is produced:

Medical total	$ 175.00
Wages	225.00
	$ 400.00
	× 3
Total value	$1,200.00

Thus, by changing the concept of the formula to "three times the specials" we have changed the original valuation of $600 to $1,200—for the same case. Further analysis will reveal that in the first instance, the value of the distress was fixed at $200, but the last method of computation produces a distress valuation of $800—in a case involving only three weeks' disability. Comparing the amount claimed for distress with the claimant's take-home pay of $75 per week, the distress comes to an average of $266.67 per week, or 3½ times his salary.

In presenting the variations of the formula, we have used the same figures. Where the case has been overtreated medically, or the medical bills are based on exorbitant rates per visit, and where more X rays and other diagnostic tests are used than is necessary, it is clear that higher valuations will be produced.

A further variation of the formula concerns a change in the multiplier from 3 to 4, 5, and even 10. This is usually justified on the theory that the multiplier of 3 refers to low-verdict areas, and also contemplates a case where there is a full recovery with no residuals. Where the case is to be tried in a high-verdict area, or where there is some small permanent disability or facial scarring, a higher multiplier is utilized either to cover the verdict differential or the permanent condition.

2020   The unit of time formula

This is an approach to the valuation of intangible items which is used exclusively by plaintiff's counsel. It begins with an arbitrary value being placed on the plaintiff's discomfort on a unit of time basis, so much per hour, day, week, or month. This unit value is multiplied by the number of hours, days, weeks, or months during which the discomfort continued. In cases where medical evidence indicated that the discomfort would continue beyond the date of evaluation or trial, projections are made to cover the future duration of the discomfort, and the same figures are applied to the anticipated discomfort to be suffered in the future, whether it be for a short period or for the remainder of the claimant's life.

As an illustration of the application of this formula, let us assume that we have a case in which the discomfort allegedly covered a period of 6 months and the arbitrary figure of 25¢ per hour is claimed as the reasonable value of the discomfort suffered. The plaintiff's attorney will concede that the claimant slept 8 hours a day and was therefore insensible to pain during that time. Therefore, the claim will be based only on the actual pain suffered, or 16 hours per day. The computation would be as follows:

> 16 hours @ 25¢ .... = $4.00 per day
> 6 months .... = 180 days
> Value of discomfort .... = $720.00

The attorney will then argue that this figure only compensates the claimant for his discomfort and does not take into consideration the value of the enjoyment of life of which the claimant has been deprived during his disability. The claimant likes to swim, bowl, fish, or engage in other sports, but, because of his disability, was deprived of these pleasures. These items are arbitrarily valued at $3 per day, or $540, which, when added to the previous discomfort claim of $720, now makes the claim $1,260.

As a further item, the attorney could argue that the claimant was unable to perform his usual marital functions and that the loss of this ability during his disability, plus the humiliation and embarrassment, should have a value of at least another $2 per day, or $360, making the total $1,620. While other items could be and often are added to those already considered, the illustration will sufficiently set forth the form and substance of the procedure.

Plaintiff's attorneys have also used this type of evaluation in statements to the jury in summation, implemented by the use of a blackboard on which the figures are placed. While some courts have permitted such arguments, there is a growing tendency on the part of the majority to whom the question has been presented to reject them. [For a discussion of this problem in which the court rejected the use of unit of time evaluations in summation, see *Botta* v. *Brunner*, 138 Atl. 2d 713 (New Jersey); *Henne* v. *Balick*, 146 Atl. 2d 394

(Delaware) ; and *Certified T.V. & Appliance Co.* v. *Harrington,* 109 S.E. 2d (Virginia).]

The weakness of this formula approach is the same as we find in the others. There is no logical basis for the arbitrary assumptions of the values on which it is based. As one court analyzed it:

> The absurdity of a mathematical formula is demonstrated by applying it to its logical conclusion. If a day may be used as a unit-of-time in measuring pain and suffering, there is no logical reason why an hour or a minute or a second could not be used, or perhaps even a heart beat, since we live from heart beat to heart beat. If one cent were used for each second of pain, this would amount to $3.60 per hour, to $86.40 per twenty-four hour day, and to $31,536 per year. The absurdity of such a result must be apparent, yet a penny a second for pain and suffering might not sound unreasonable. The principle is the same, whether one uses a second, an hour or a day as the basic unit-of-time, because to the unit-of-time used one must assign some money value which has no foundation in the evidence. . . . [*Affett* v. *Milwaukee & Suburban Transit Corp.,* 106 N.W. 2d 274 (Wisconsin).]

2021   The three values formula

This formula seeks to measure mental and physical distress by dividing it into three time periods, and setting an arbitrary weekly valuation to be applied to each. The formula recognizes that the claimant will suffer pain for a period of time following the accident, and this period of time is measured by his period of total disability. As he recovers, he will be able to do some work, or will have a partial disability. During this period his pain will have subsided, but he will be suffering some discomfort. The last period consists of the time after he has returned to work, but during which he is still under treatment, so that he is put to some inconvenience in undergoing continued treatment. The values placed on these three classes of distress could be:

```
Pain (total disability period) ............... $100 per week
Discomfort (partial disability) ...............   75  "    "
Inconvenience (no disability) ...............     35  "    "
```

Proponents of this type of formula evaluation claim that these figures will produce the maximum distress valuation, but that lesser figures should be used where there are other factors—such as earnings of the claimant, his station in life, and the area in which the cause of action will be tried—which might require a reduction in the arbitrary amounts allocated to each class, but that the differences between the valuation of each class should remain the same. For example, pain might be valued at $75 per week, discomfort at $50 per week, and inconvenience at $25 per week.

To illustrate further, let us assume that the claimant was injured Jan. 9, 1980. He was totally disabled from work from that date until Feb. 18, 1980, at which time he returned to light work on a reduced salary basis. From Fez. 18 until March 11, partial disability continued, and he returned to his regular work at the end of that time. He did, however, require further medical treatment until March 22, at which time he was discharged as completely cured. The computation of the value of distress might be:

Pain	1/9–2/18	5 and 5⁄7 wk. @ $100	$571.43
Discomfort	2/18–3/11	3 wk. @ $75	225.00
Inconvenience	3/11–3/22	1 and 5⁄7 wk. @ $35	60.00
		Total	$856.43

This is claimed to give a median or average value of the claimant's distress, or a rounded off formula valuation of $850.

It sometimes happens that the claimant is able to do light work, as far as his physical condition is concerned, but, because of his lack of education, the unavailability of light work, or his aversion to work in general, he does not actually return to work. In such cases, the formula relies on the attending physician's estimate of the date on which he was able to do light work and the date on which he was able to return to his full duties. These dates, verified by the company's examining physician, are used in exactly the same manner as would be the case if the claimant had actually returned to work.

While the theory of this formula emphasizes the changing nature of the intensity of the distress, it suffers from the same weaknesses present in other mathematical computations in that it is based upon arbitrary assumptions for the weekly values of each class of distress. There is no evidence that the values so estimated are reflective of the community response to the distress suffered. Some companies have used this method successfully, especially as a vehicle for settling claims directly with the claimant or for reducing demands in cases where the claimant is represented by counsel. In appropriate cases, higher values can be allocated to the three types of distress.

2022   Factors increasing settlement valuation

In some cases there are additional factors which increase the possibilities of a large verdict and, as a result, will increase the amount which it would be to the company's advantage to pay in settlement rather than to risk the trial of the case. Among the factors are

1. Applicable law.
2. Nature of the offending instrumentality.
3. Locality of the accident.
4. Horror factor.
5. Personal and physical characteristics of the insured.
6. Character of defense witnesses.
7. Employment of an attorney.
8. Place of trial.

1. *Applicable law.* Where the facts give the claimant the advantage of the application of strict or absolute liability against the insured, or where the claimant has the benefit of a presumption of *res ipsa loquitur,* the applicable law favors the claimant and the case will involve a jury question. Since the burden of proof which the claimant must sustain is light, and the burden of explanation or defense is heavy, the claim poses a greater degress of danger to the company, and the claimsman will be persuaded to pay more in settlement than in the average case.

2. *Nature of the offending instrumentality.* Where the offending instrumentality is one which exposes the community or the claimant to an increased degree of peril because of its intrinsic nature, juries are apt to bring in larger verdicts. Such instrumentalities might consist of poisons, acids, explosives, and wild animals. Included in this area also would be instrumentalities which are not in themselves dangerous, but because of their poor maintenance expose people to greater danger, such as poorly maintained premises in such dilapidated condition that they expose those entering them to additional risk of injury, or motor vehicles whose brakes, lights, and steering apparatus are not properly functional, and which are driven with the knowledge of the defective conditions.

Some juries have a natural aversion to taxicabs, motorcycles, and sports cars, and where any of these is involved, such fact may be persuasive of the necessity of a higher settlement valuation.

3. *Locality of the accident.* This is a factor where the accident occurs at or near an old folks' home, children's playground, school, hospital, or congested area. The negligent operation of the vehicle in those areas will have an influence on value.

4. *Horror factor.* This is present when the act which caused the injury is reprehensible in nature or where the effects of the injury are such that the claimant presents a bizarre, grotesque, or gruesome appearance because of facial or head scarring, the enucleation of an eye, the amputation of a prominent member, such as a hand, foot, arm, or leg, as well as a mental condition which completely removes him from the world of reality. To illustrate the effect of this factor arising from the reprehensible nature of the act causing the injury, let us take two cases, both of which resulted in the death of a nine-month-old baby.

In the first case, the baby is held in its mother's lap while riding in an automobile. The defendant, a middle-aged schoolteacher, is driving her car in the opposite direction at a speed of approximately 25 m.p.h. The road is covered with snow and, in spite of her precautions, the schoolteacher loses control of the car and it sideswipes the vehicle in which the baby is riding. The baby falls from his mother's lap and sustains a fractured skull from which death ensues. The schoolteacher is technically chargeable with negligence in failing to keep her car under control and, while the claim is actionable, there is no horror factor and no increased valuation is indicated.

In contrast to that case, let us assume that the nine-month-old baby is placed in a carriage and wheeled by his mother onto the front lawn. It is a beautiful summer day and the child is sleeping peacefully out in the sun. A truck comes down the street at a high rate of speed. The driver has a bottle of beer in one hand, and his other arm is around his girl friend who is riding with him. The truck goes out of control and runs onto the lawn and over the child, causing its death. The facts, as related by eyewitnesses, will indicate that the huge wheels passed completely over the baby's body, crushing it beyond recognition. There was a closed-casket funeral.

Both cases had the same result: the death of a nine-month-old baby, but the second case, which involved the horror factor because of the manner in which the accident was caused, will bring a much higher valuation at the hands of a jury than will the first.

5. *Personal and physical characteristics of the insured.* This factor is involved when the insured is likely to be a substandard witness because of age, appearance, language, or reputation. Jurors generally regard young drivers (especially teen-agers) as being irresponsible with respect to the operation of a motor vehicle. Older drivers are viewed as having impairments as to sight, reflexes, and response as to the apprehension and avoidance of the dangers of the highway. An insured whose appearance indicates a physical impairment, such as the absence of an arm or a leg, the wearing of extremely thick eyeglasses or the use of a hearing aid, will incline the jury to the belief that the physical impairment contributed to the causation of the accident. His ability to use language to describe the event, his recall of the details of the event, as well as the appearance of sincerity, will all be taken into account. If any of these attributes are lacking—the language halting, rambling, and incoherent, or the recall of the past event hazy, or the appearance of sincerity is questionable—the insured is a less-than-desirable witness. Likewise his reputation of wealth, where the claimant is a poor man, can count heavily against him.

6. *Character of defense witnesses.* Evaluation of the defense witnesses may disclose that they have an interest in the outcome of the lawsuit, are friends of the insured, have poor appearances, lack the ability to testify clearly, give the appearance of dishonesty, or have criminal records. If any of these conditions are present, the amount of reliance which can be placed upon them to establish the defense will be open to question.

7. *Employment of an attorney.* Where some settlement negotiations have been conducted with the claimant, the appearance of an attorney in the case may influence the amount which will be required to settle the case. The attorney usually charges a contingent fee, based on one-third to one-half of the recovery. It stands to reason that if the claimant's demand is $1,000, the case will have to bring $1,500 in settlement for him to net that amount after the attorney's fee is paid. Just how far the claimsman will be induced to go over the amount of his original settlement valuation will depend on the other factors of the case, the defenses available, the ability of the claimant's attorney and whether he is a trial man or a "settler," and how near the trial date the settlement negotiations are held.

8. *Place of trial.* If the case is to be tried in a court of inferior jurisdiction, such as a municipal or justice of the peace court, where the proceedings are presided over only by a judge, the general trend is to allow a recovery. Upper court cases tried in high-verdict areas likewise offer an inducement to increase the valuation.

2023   Factors decreasing settlement valuation

Among the factors which, if present, will decrease the amount that the company should be induced to pay in settlement are the

1. Applicable law favoring the defendant.
2. Personal and physical characteristics of the claimant.
3. Credibility of the claimant's witnesses.
4. Responsibility of a codefendant.
5. Attorney's lack of control of the claimant.

1. *Applicable law favoring the defendant.* This factor applies where the claimant is chargeable with contributory negligence or assumption of risk, or where, because of the facts of the event, the claimant will have difficulty in establishing the negligence of the defendant.

2. *Personal and physical characteristics of the claimant.* As opposed to the appearance of the insured, the claimant's appearance may be such that he does not inspire belief, has poor recall of the event, is hesitant in answering questions, or has some speech defect which makes him difficult to understand. As in the case of the insured, the presence of a physical defect unrelated to the accident, such as the absence of an arm, leg, or eye, as well as a defect in sight or hearing (as evidenced by extreme magnification in eyeglass lenses or the wearing of a hearing aid), might well justify a belief on the part of the jury that these defects had some part in the causation of the accident.

3. *Credibility of claimant's witnesses.* If the claimsman has reason to know that the claimant's witnesses will create a poor impression as to the believableness of their testimony because of their interest in the outcome because of bias, prejudice, or relationship to the claimant, or because of a record of convictions of crimes involving moral turpitude, the value of these witnesses to the claimant may be discounted accordingly. Included in the claimant's witnesses would be the claimant himself, and his testimony and credibility should be subject to the same criteria.

4. *Responsibility of a codefendant.* Where the insured is one of two or more joint tort-feasors, his liability is joint or individual. Where the other tort-feasor, or tort-feasors, as the case might be, are codefendants, or where they can be brought in by the insured as such, it is clear that the responsibility for the claimant's damage is divided among them. The claimsman will weigh the degree of danger posed by the case and will evaluate the probabilities of his insured being exonerated and the others held liable. If the chances of his insured are good, the claimsman may offer to make a small contribution to the settlement, if one is agreed upon, but will not actively engage in settlement negotiations. If the probabilities of a successful defense for his insured are remote, he will engage in carrying on the negotiations, either alone or in concert with the representatives of the other defendants.

If the case is settled, he will insist on some participation from the other defendants, or at least a contribution toward the amount paid. If participation or a contribution is refused, consideration will be given to disposition of the case by means of a covenant not to sue. In any case, the presence of one or more codefendants should reduce the amount that the company would be induced to pay in settlement.

5. *Attorney's lack of control of the claimant.* This is an intangible element but can sometimes be an important factor in reducing the amount of settlement. The claimsman will usually know something about the claimant's background and occupation. Where the claimant is a migratory worker, a hobo, or a person who does not stay in any one place for any appreciable period of time, the attorney may have some difficulty in having him present in court at the time of trial. This is especially true where the attorney has made some financial advances to the claimant. Clearly, the attorney will not be able to establish his case without his client, and his anxiety to settle may be motivated by a desire to close the case before his client takes off for places unknown. With this problem confronting him, the attorney will usually settle for an amount less than the sum which would be required if this factor did not exist.

2024   Measure of damages: Permanent disability

When a disability is said to be permanent it means that the injuries are such that the claimant will never recover from them. The effects of the injury are fixed, stationary, and not subject to change. If the disability is of such a nature that it will improve with treatment or the passage of time, it has not reached a permanent stage. If it improves to the extent that there is a full recovery, then the disability is not permanent at all but merely temporary. If the improvement will not result in a full recovery, then the improved condition, when it reaches a stationary stage, is the permanent injury and is measured and evaluated as of that time.

Cases involving permanent disability may be divided into two classes: those which involve only minor disabilities, such as restrictions of motion of a finger or a toe joint, or minor amputations such as a part of a phalanx of a finger or toe (neither of which have any effect on the claimant's earning capacity), and those which involve major restrictions, such as limited motion in a hip joint, complete stiffness of a knee joint, or amputations of major members, such as a hand, foot, arm, and leg, loss of sight of an eye or of hearing of either one or both ears, which affect not only the claimant's earning capacity but also his future enjoyment of life.

As to both classes of cases, the jury will decide the amount which will reasonably compensate the claimant for the injury. In the first class, they will determine what the permanency is worth, having in mind their own experience, and the extent to which they believe the injury will inconvenience the claimant. They will hear evidence of the damage from the claimant as to how the injury affects him, what he can do and what he cannot do because of it. They will hear the testimony of his physician as to his appraisal of the permanency and how it will affect the claimant. In addition they may hear the defendant's examining physician (if his testimony is offered), as to his view of the disability and how it will or will not restrict the claimant's activity. On the basis of the evidence, the jury will fix the amount of reasonable compensation, usually an arbitrary figure, which when added to the other provable items will constitute the verdict.

In the second class of cases, the evidence will show the exact loss of earning capacity up to the time of trial and the effect that the permanency will have on the claimant's earning capacity. This might be for a measurable period of time or for the rest of the claimant's work-life. The evidence of future disability must establish the disability with a reasonable degree of certainty. In addition, where the permanent injury interferes with the claimant's future enjoyment of life, such as continuous pain, or the loss of the ability to engage in sports of various kinds, to drive an automobile, etc., the jury may fix an additional amount which will compensate him for these lifelong losses.

Thus we have two measurements applicable to the case. First, the loss of earning capacity is measured by the period of time that a man of the claimant's age and occupation would be able to continue working. Second, the loss of enjoyment or the suffering of pain would be measured by the number of years that a man of the claimant's age would be expected to live. Clearly, the life expectancy would exceed the work-life expectancy.

Since there is no way of predicting with absolute certainty how long a particular individual will continue working, or how long the individual will live, evidence in the form of tables or other evidence which will show the average expectancy of a large number of persons is admissible for the purpose of assisting the jury in arriving at its verdict. The jury may accept the tables, or reject them, or use any means it desires in reaching a verdict. In any case, they are not bound by the figures produced by the tables or by the testimony of the witness who offers them. The evidence is admissible, but whether the jury utilizes the tables or not is a decision which is within their province to make. In the absence of other evidence, however, they usually accept the tabular figures.

Expectancy tables measure only average expectancies, whether of life or work, of average persons. If there are any unusual circumstances applicable to the claimant which would place him in a class either above or below the average, the jury will take these factors into account. Factors which would place the claimant in a below-average category are:

1. *State of health.*   Presence of disease or injury: past medical history of illness.
2. *Heredity.*   Longevity of ancestors; history of hereditary disease in parents.

3. *Occupation.* Average life, or work-life of a person similarly employed with special reference to the hazards to which persons in that occupation are particularly exposed.

4. *Habits.* Addiction to alcohol or habit-forming drugs; excessive smoking.

The jury may hear evidence on any of these points and may find that such factors have an influence on the average figures. The award will be made according to their findings. In investigating cases of this character it is important for the claimsman to thoroughly explore the possibilities that one or more of these elements may be present in the case.

In any case, the measure of damages in permanent disability claims will be the projected value of the claimant's loss of earning capacity and the projected value of his distress, if the evidence shows that such distress will continue for the rest of his life. His loss of earning capacity will be measured by his work-life expectancy, that is, the number of years that a man of his age would be able to work, and his distress will be measured by his life expectancy since the distress will continue until death.

2025 Life expectancy

There is evidence in history of the need for information as to the number of years the average man would be expected to live. The first indication for this need goes back as far as the year 2 A.D. in the time of the Roman Empire. The paymaster was required to have sufficient money on hand to pay the troops, and, since communication was poor, he had to estimate the amount of money that would be needed over a period of years. To do this, he had to calculate the number of soldiers who would be alive to collect their pay and the number who would die before payment was due. Some crude attempts, based on past performance, were made. Although none of the tables thus calculated have survived to the present time, the paymaster was an officer called an *actuarius,* and it from that title that we derive our present terminology, referring to the mathematician who calculates projections from expectancy tables as an actuary, and referring to the tables themselves as actuarial tables.

The earliest recorded evidence of the application of this actuarial science to insurance came into prominence in England in 1762 with the incorporation of a life insurance organization called the Equitable Society for the Assurance of Life and Survivorship. To establish probable cost figures and to promulgate the premium to be charged, this organization first used tables compiled by two mathematicians. The tables, however, proved completely inadequate because they were based upon figures developed during the year 1740, the year of the Great Plague. Since the figures were computed by measuring lives during a period of unusually high mortality, the premiums thus calculated were exorbitant and not actuarially sound.

A subsequent measurement was undertaken and the now famous Northampton tables were the result. These tables were based on the bills of mortality kept in the parish of All Saints, a town in the north of England, for the years from 1755 to 1780. Although compiled almost two centuries ago, the table is still in use as a base for insurance calculations and is accepted in the courts.

The Northampton table was followed by the Carlisle table, which measured lives during the period from 1780 to 1787. The sampling involved studies of the population of the parishes of Saint Mary and Saint Cuthbert, Carlisle, England. During the period of calculation the population of these two parishes ran between 7,677 and 8,677. In spite of this small sampling, the Carlisle table has received wide acceptance and is still utilized as some evidence of life expectancy, both in this country and in England.

NORTHAMPTON TABLE

Age	Expectancy	Age	Expectancy	Age	Expectancy
0	25.18	33	26.72	65	10.88
1	32.74	34	26.20	66	10.42
2	37.29	35	25.68	67	9.96
3	39.55	36	25.16	68	9.50
4	40.58	37	24.64	69	9.05
5	40.84	38	24.12	70	8.60
6	41.07	39	23.60	71	8.17
7	41.03	40	23.08	72	7.74
8	40.79	41	22.56	73	7.33
9	40.36	42	22.04	74	6.92
10	39.78	43	21.54	75	6.54
11	39.14	44	21.03	76	6.18
12	38.49	45	20.52	77	5.83
13	37.83	46	20.02	78	5.48
14	37.17	47	19.51	79	5.11
15	36.51	48	19.00	80	4.75
16	35.85	49	18.49	81	4.41
17	35.20	50	17.99	82	4.09
18	34.38	51	17.50	83	3.80
19	33.99	52	17.02	84	3.58
20	33.43	53	16.54	85	3.37
21	32.90	54	16.06	86	3.19
22	31.39	55	15.58	87	3.01
23	31.88	56	15.10	88	2.86
24	31.36	57	14.63	89	2.66
25	30.85	58	14.15	90	2.41
26	30.33	59	13.68	91	2.09
27	29.82	60	13.21	92	1.75
28	29.30	61	12.75	93	1.37
29	28.79	62	12.28	94	1.05
30	28.27	63	11.81	95	.75
31	27.76	64	11.35	96	.50
32	27.24				

From the time of the Carlisle table to the present time, a number of mortality tables have been compiled. Among them is a table of life expectancy published by Professor Edward Wigglesworth of Harvard University in 1789. This study was restricted to selected groups of the general population of Massachusetts and New Hampshire, and, since the study did not include all groups, it has not been accepted as representative of the average expectancy of life, even in the area under consideration. In addition, the experience figures of various life insurance companies have been available for years. These figures are subject to the same objection in that they are based upon mortality among a selected group; namely, insured lives only. Since life insurance is

CARLISLE TABLE

Age	Expectancy	Age	Expectancy	Age	Expectancy
1	38.72	35	31.00	68	10.23
2	44.68	36	30.32	69	9.70
3	47.55	37	29.64	70	9.18
4	49.82	38	28.96	71	8.65
5	50.76	39	28.28	72	8.16
6	51.25	40	27.61	73	7.72
7	51.17	41	26.97	74	7.33
8	50.80	42	26.34	75	7.01
9	50.24	43	25.71	76	6.69
10	49.57	44	25.09	77	6.40
11	48.82	45	24.46	78	6.12
12	48.04	46	23.82	79	5.80
13	47.27	47	23.17	80	5.51
14	46.51	48	22.50	81	5.21
15	45.75	49	21.81	82	4.93
16	45.00	50	21.11	83	4.65
17	44.27	51	20.39	84	4.39
18	43.57	52	19.68	85	4.12
19	42.87	53	18.97	86	3.90
20	42.17	54	18.28	87	3.71
21	41.46	55	17.58	88	3.59
22	40.75	56	16.89	89	3.47
23	40.04	57	16.21	90	3.28
24	39.31	58	15.55	91	3.26
25	38.59	59	14.92	92	3.37
26	37.14	60	14.34	93	3.48
27	36.41	61	13.82	94	3.53
28	35.69	62	13.31	95	3.53
29	35.00	63	12.81	96	3.46
30	34.34	64	12.30	97	3.28
31	33.68	65	11.79	98	3.07
32	33.03	66	11.27	99	2.77
33	32.36	67	10.75	100	2.28
34	31.68				

restricted to those who are capable of meeting the health standards of the life insurance company, the experience figures are not conclusive as evidence of the average length of life that could be expected of an average group. The figures show the probable duration of life of a healthy person capable of obtaining life insurance, and nothing more. Therefore, life insurance mortality tables based upon the average life expectancies of policyholders are not ordinarily admissible as evidence of average life expectancy.

The U.S. government entered the life table field in 1936 and compiled the U.S. Life Tables from the census figures developed between the years from 1900 to 1930. These tables are used extensively as evidence of life expectancy and are referred to as the U.S. Life Tables, or, more generally, the American Table of Mortality.

The general impression today is that life expectancy is greater now than it ever was in the past, but a comparison of the tables will reveal that this is not entirely a true statement. Arbitrarily taking the ages of 21 and 45, the

AMERICAN TABLE OF MORTALITY

Age	Expectancy	Age	Expectancy	Age	Expectancy
10	48.72	39	28.90	68	9.47
11	48.09	40	28.18	69	8.97
12	47.45	41	27.45	70	8.48
13	46.80	42	26.72	71	8.00
14	46.16	43	25.99	72	7.55
15	45.51	44	25.27	73	7.11
16	44.85	45	24.54	74	6.68
17	44.19	46	23.81	75	6.27
18	43.53	47	23.08	76	5.88
19	42.87	48	22.35	77	5.49
20	42.20	49	21.63	78	5.11
21	41.53	50	20.91	79	4.75
22	40.85	51	20.20	80	43.9
23	40.17	52	19.49	81	4.05
24	39.49	53	18.79	82	3.71
25	38.81	54	18.09	83	3.39
26	38.12	55	17.40	84	3.08
27	37.43	56	16.72	85	2.77
28	36.73	57	16.05	86	2.47
29	36.03	58	15.39	87	2.18
30	35.33	59	14.74	88	1.91
31	34.63	60	14.10	89	1.66
32	33.92	61	13.47	90	1.42
33	33.21	62	12.86	91	1.19
34	32.50	63	12.26	92	.98
35	31.78	64	11.67	93	.80
36	31.07	65	11.10	94	.64
37	30.35	66	10.54	95	.50
38	29.63	67	10.00		

following comparison of the three tables will demonstrate the spread of expectancies:

Tables	Age 21	Age 45
Northampton	32.90	20.52
Carlisle	41.46	24.46
American Table of Mortality	41.53	24.54

2026   Work-life expectancy

It is obvious that the average man does not work until the day he dies. He may be prevented from continuing with his usual occupation because of the infirmities of age, retirement, or other contingencies. Where it is necessary to estimate the working life of an individual who has suffered either permanent disability or death, we would expect to find that the period of life remaining which could be devoted to actual work would be considerably less than the same individual's life expectancy. In this area, there are few guides. The most accurate tables are called the Smith tables, and they were compiled by the Railroad Retirement Board for the purpose of developing figures to insure the solvency of various railroad retirement funds. While the figures are restricted to experience of railroad employees, they have some validity due to the fact that all railroad employees were included in the study; that is, clerks, stenographers, and ticket agents, as well as employees actually engaged in operating the rolling stock.

2027   Present value of future damages

The plaintiff will recover damages which are payable as of the time of trial. As to losses which have been sustained prior to trial, the recovery will be based upon the reimbursement due to the plaintiff, but as to losses which will occur in the future, and which losses have not as yet been incurred, the verdict will be based upon projections as to the extent of the loss as it occurs. Clearly, the defendant is being required to pay the plaintiff now for expenses or losses to be sustained in the future. Since payment is being made in advance, before the loss has occurred, the defendant is entitled to an interest discount on the amount so paid. In other words, if the plaintiff will suffer a loss of earning capacity of $20 per week for the rest of his work-life, the loss would be incurred at the end of each week of his work life. If his work-life is 20 years, then the payment required now should be the present value of $20 per week for 20 years. Clearly, this is not $1,040 per year times 20 years because the defendant would lose the interest that would be earned by that money had he retained it and paid the plaintiff $20 each week as the loss was incurred. The rate of discount or interest to which the defendant will be entitled is based on on the American Table of Mortality, with an interest discount of 5 percent, regarded as the average return.

Another way of illustrating the problem is to compare it with the situation of a bank advancing mortgage money. The amount which the bank advances is comparable to the defendant's payment. This amount is the equivalent of the money to be paid back over the period of years, or, in the case of the defendant, the payment is the equivalent of the losses that will be suffered over a period of years. Therefore, the award for future losses will be based

SMITH-GRIFFIN RAILROAD EMPLOYEES WORK-LIFE
EXPECTANCY TABLE

Exact Age in Years	Number Living and at Work	Number Withdrawing from Work (before Next Exact Age) because of			Expectancy in Years of Life at Work
		Death	Disability	Retire- ment	
18	1,318.040	2,054	2,397	0	40.11
19	1,313,589	2,126	2,467	0	39.24
20	1,308,996	2,171	2,550	0	38.38
21	1,304,275	2,241	2,606	0	37.51
22	1,299,428	2,311	2,687	0	36.65
23	1,294,430	2,392	2,742	0	35.79
24	1,289,296	2,498	2,795	0	34.93
25	1,284,003	2,617	2,873	0	34.07
26	1,278,513	2,733	2,925	0	33.22
27	1,272,855	2,873	2,975	0	32.36
28	1,267,007	2,999	2,999	0	31.51
29	1,261,009	3,136	2,997	0	30.66
30	1,254,876	3,271	3,008	0	29.81
31	1,248,597	3,417	3,018	0	28.95
32	1,242,162	3,561	3,026	0	28.10
33	1,235,575	3,727	3,047	0	27.25
34	1,228,801	3,903	3,080	0	26.40
35	1,221,818	4,100	3,111	0	25.54
36	1,214,607	4,330	3,152	0	24.69
37	1,207,125	4,581	3,205	0	23.84
38	1,199,339	4,851	3,279	0	22.99
39	1,191,209	5,139	3,376	0	22.15
40	1,182,694	5,480	3,469	0	21.30
41	1,173,745	5,836	3,582	0	20.46
42	1,164,327	6,254	3,693	0	19.62
43	1,154,380	6,696	3,891	0	18.79
44	1,143,793	7,193	4,173	0	17.96
45	1,132,427	7,719	4,458	0	17.13
46	1,120,250	8,294	4,933	0	16.31
47	1,107,023	8,878	5,490	0	15.50
48	1,092,655	9,512	6,103	0	14.70
49	1,077,040	10,178	6,753	0	13.91

SMITH-GRIFFIN RAILROAD EMPLOYEES WORK-LIFE
EXPECTANCY TABLE (continued)

Exact Age in Years	Number Living and at Work	Number Withdrawing from Work (before Next Exact Age) because of			Expectancy in Years of Life at Work
		Death	Disability	Retire-ment	
50	1,066,109	10,859	7,519	0	13.12
51	1,041,731	11,599	8,391	0	12.34
52	1,021,741	12,347	9,394	0	11.57
53	1,000,000	13,131	10,381	0	10.81
54	976,488	13,930	11,488	0	10.06
55	951,070	14,736	12,853	0	9.32
56	923,481	15,538	14,485	0	8.58
57	893,458	16,305	16,456	0	7.85
58	860,697	17,006	18,916	0	7.13
59	824,775	17,656	20,559	0	6.42
60	786,560	18,060	21,237	15,329	5.71
61	731,934	18,279	21,090	10,677	5.10
62	681,888	18,435	20,527	13,239	4.44
63	629,687	18,397	19,520	18,304	3.76
64	573,466	18,073	18,078	24,960	3.08
65	512,355	14,517	0	206,323	2.39
66	291,515	10,097	0	60,033	2.82
67	221,385	8,267	0	47,683	2.56
68	165,435	6,608	0	38,803	2.56
69	120,024	5,018	0	34,539	1.92
70	80,467	3,163	0	40,344	1.62
71	36,960	1,722	0	13,284	1.94
72	21,954	1,105	0	7,872	1.92
73	12,977	706	0	4,641	1.90
74	7,630	449	0	2,721	1.87
75	4,460	284	0	1,586	1.85
76	2,590	179	0	917	1.83
77	1,494	112	0	528	1.80
78	854	69	0	300	1.78
79	485	42	0	169	1.75
80	274	26	0	95	1.70
81	153	16	0	53	1.66
82	84	9	0	29	1.61
83	46	6	0	16	1.52
84	24	3	0	8	1.46
85	13	2	0	5	1.27
86	6	1	0	2	1.17
87	3	1	0	1	0.83
88	1	0	0	1	0.50

upon the present value of the losses to be sustained in the future. Expectancy tables will tell us how long the claimant will live or be able to continue to work. Present value tables take into consideration the expectancy figures and project them to a present figure at a discount rate. A present value table, based on the American Table of Mortaility, with an interest discount of 5 percent, accompanies the text.

The table gives the present value of $1 per year payable until death. By the use of it we can readily determine present value of the claim. For example, let us assume that we have a claimant, aged 51, who has sustained a permanent injury that will cause him to suffer pain for the rest of his life. The value of the pain is estimated at $20 per week. According to the American Table of Mortality, his life expectancy is 20.20 years. Twenty dollars per week amounts to $1,040 per year. If we did not consider any discount, we would multiply $1,040 by 20.20 years, and the result would be $21,008. Using the present value table at the discount rate of 5 percent our figures would be:

Present value of $1 per year at age 51 .... $ 11.41594
Yearly payment .... × 1040
Present or commuted value $11,872.58

From this example it can be seen that there is a substantial difference between the value without any discount, and the same amount subject to a discount figure.

In using these tables, the age figure to be taken will be the claimant's age as of his nearest birthday. If he is 22 years and 8 months at the time of computation, then the figures which should be used are those applicable to age 23, his nearest birthday. If he is 22 years and 4 months old at the time of computation, then the figures for age 22 should be used.

To return to our example, let us add one more fact. Let us assume that our claimant is suffering from a preexisting condition, namely cancer, which in the opinion of our physician will reduce his life expectancy about one third. With all the other figures remaining the same, the following is the recommended method for taking into account the reduction in life expectancy.

Present value of $1 per year at age 51 .... $ 11.41594
Minus reduction (one-third) .... − 3.80531

                                                    7.61063
Yearly payment .... × 1040
Present or commuted value .... $ 7,915.05

The same principles apply to discounting claims based on the loss of future earning capacity. The loss will be measured by the claimant's work-life expectancy.

MORTALITY TABLE

(American experience table, interest at 5 percent)

Age	Annuity or Present Value of $1 Due at the End of Each Year during the Life of a Person of Specified Age	Age	Annuity or Present Value of $1 Due at the End of Each Year during the Life of a Person of Specified Age
10	16.50475	53	10.90499
11	16.46076	54	10.64036
12	16.41469	55	10.37017
13	16.36642	56	10.09472
14	16.31581	57	9.81450
15	16.26274	58	9.52988
16	16.20722	59	9.24127
17	16.14896	60	8.94928
18	16.08779	61	8.65445
19	16.02372	62	8.35742
20	15.95658	63	8.05876
21	15.88620	64	7.75900
22	15.81257	65	7.45885
23	15.73552	66	7.15921
24	15.65484	67	6.86074
25	15.57033	68	6.56420
26	15.48176	69	6.27048
27	15.38910	70	5.98022
28	15.29210	71	5.69422
29	15.19051	72	5.41286
30	15.08425	73	5.13592
31	14.97307	74	4.86279
32	14.85666	75	4.59264
33	14.73492	76	4.32477
34	14.60774	77	4.05856
35	14.47479	78	3.79392
36	14.33572	79	3.53109
37	14.19057	80	3.27017
38	14.03897	81	3.01349
39	13.88092	82	2.76062
40	13.71604	83	2.51052
41	13.54430	84	2.26066
42	13.36528	85	2.00986
43	13.17891	86	1.76061
44	12.98494	87	1.51750
45	12.78344	88	1.28611
46	12.57414	89	1.06704
47	12.35728	90	0.85453
48	12.13275	91	0.64497
49	11.90076	92	0.44851
50	11.66175	93	0.28761
51	11.41594	94	0.13605
52	11.16361		

MONTHLY ANNUITIES FOR THE DURATION OF
LIFE AT WORK

(present value of $1 per month while at work, at 5 percent)

Age	Work Expectancy (years)	Present Value	Age	Work Expectancy (years)	Present Value
18	40.11	$202.20	54	10.06	$91.40
19	39.24	200.73	55	9.32	86.11
20	38.38	199.21	56	8.58	80.67
21	37.51	197.64	57	7.85	75.08
22	36.65	196.00	58	7.13	69.34
23	35.79	194.29	59	6.42	63.45
24	34.93	192.52	60	5.71	57.30
25	34.07	190.68	61	5.10	51.96
26	33.22	188.78	62	4.44	45.86
27	32.36	186.80	63	3.76	39.39
28	31.51	184.74	64	3.08	32.57
29	30.66	182.60	65	2.39	25.32
30	29.81	180.36	66	2.82	30.07
31	28.95	178.03	67	2.56	27.47
32	28.10	175.59	68	2.26	24.37
33	27.25	173.05	69	1.92	20.81
34	26.40	170.39	70	1.62	17.48
35	25.54	167.63	71	1.94	20.88
36	24.69	164.75	72	1.92	20.69
37	23.84	161.74	73	1.90	20.50
38	22.99	158.62	74	1.87	20.58
39	22.15	155.38	75	1.85	20.05
40	21.30	152.00	76	1.83	19.81
41	20.46	148.50	77	1.80	19.54
42	19.62	144.86	78	1.78	19.29
43	18.79	141.09	79	1.75	19.00
44	17.96	137.19	80	1.70	18.59
45	17.13	133.16	81	1.66	18.11
46	16.31	129.00	82	1.61	17.62
47	15.50	124.73	83	1.52	16.74
48	14.70	120.34	84	1.46	16.12
49	13.91	115.83	85	1.27	14.08
50	13.12	111.19	86	1.17	13.03
51	12.34	106.43	87	.83	9.31
52	11.57	101.55	88	.50	5.50
53	10.81	96.55			

As an example, let us assume that the claimant, aged 46, sustained an injury that will result in the diminution of his earning capacity of $80 per month. The computation would be as follows:

Present value of $1 per month at age 46	$ 129.00
Reduced earning capacity	× 80.00
Present or commuted value	$ 10,320

Under the single recovery rule the award would cover all the damage, that already suffered and future losses. Therefore, let us add some facts to the foregoing example so as to reflect the full recovery. Assume that the case is tried or settled two years after the accident. To that date, the claimant has medical bills in the sum of $2,675, provable loss of earning capacity covering total disability of 40 weeks at $100 per week, and 64 weeks of partial loss of earning capacity of $20 per week; in addition, his future loss of earning capacity is estimated at $80 per month. The valuation then would cover the following items:

Medical	$ 2,675.00
Total disability	4,000.00
Partial disability	1,280.00
Future disability	10,320.00
Total value	$18,275.00

Let us add another fact. Let us assume that the claimant will suffer pain for the rest of his life because of the injury, and that the value of the pain is estimated at $10 per week. The pain will have no relationship to his work-life, but will continue for the rest of his life whether he works or not. Therefore we must go to the life expectancy tables for our figures. At age 46 the value of $1 paid annually is $12.57414. Ten dollars per week is $520 per year. Therefore the computation of the value of this item is:

Present value of $1 at age 46	$ 12.57414
Annual payment	× 520.00
Present or commuted value	$ 6,538.55

The rule is that where there is an item of loss, which loss will continue only for the period of the claimant's work-life, such as a loss of earning capacity, the tables to be used are the Work-Life Expectancy tables. Where the item of loss will continue for the claimant's life, such as pain and suffering, medical expense, or whatever, the table to be used is the Life Expectancy Discount table.

When we are dealing with a matter concerning work-life expectancy, we are frequently confronted with a case where the claimant's earning capacity at the time of the accident is at a peak and where, because of his occupation, his ability to earn will diminish with advancing age. This is especially true where the occupation involves physical labor. In such cases it is necessary to establish the claimant's average wage for the period of his remaining work-life.

For example let us assume that the claimant is 46 years of age and is employed as a day-laborer. Investigation discloses that laborers of his class usually work at full wages, averaging $100 weekly, until they reach age 52, at which time they work as watchmen, earning $50 per week. At age 46 the claimant's work-life is 16.31 years. Assuming that he could work, he would have earned $5,200 per year for 6 years, and for the balance of the time, or 10.31 years, his average would have been $2,600 per year. Therefore his total wages would have been $59,006. This amount, divided by 16.31, will develop his average yearly wage, or $3,617.84. Therefore, to calculate the value of this claimant's work-life expectancy, we would use his average yearly earnings as the base on which the value is computed and not the earnings which he enjoyed at the time of the accident.

In cases where the claimant's wages are expected to increase over the period of his work-life, the same procedure may be followed. It is necessary to establish the average wages to be earned each year and, using the average, apply the present value tables to that figure.

2028   Measure of damages: Survival claims

At common law the death of either plaintiff or defendant ended the litigation; to use legal terminology, the action "abated" with the death of either party. Legislation has changed the rule, and at the present time when either party to the litigation dies, the action may be brought or continued by or against the personal representative of the deceased. When the injured person dies, whether as a result of the accident or not, whatever cause of action he had against a tort-feasor during his lifetime may be brought by his personal representative. For the cause of action to survive to the personal representative, it must have been such a cause of action as could have been asserted by the deceased had he lived. If the deceased settled the case during his lifetime, or the statute of limitations had run against the claim, the deceased could not have asserted the claim had he lived. Therefore in those two cases there was no cause of action to survive, since the deceased did not have a cause of action which could be asserted at the time of his death. The test is whether or not the deceased could have asserted the claim at the time of his death. If he could, then the action survives; otherwise it does not.

The survival statute merely allows the personal representative to take the place of the deceased and to perform whatever acts the deceased could have performed with relation to the case if death had not intervened. It does not give the personal representative any greater rights than the deceased himself had; it does not alter the burden of proof nor does it in any way affect the running of the statute of limitations. The personal representative must sustain the burden of proof, producing evidence of liability, as well as evidence of damages, just as the deceased would have had to do if he brought the action himself. The statute of limitations will continue to run against the case just as if the deceased had lived. For example, let us assume that the deceased passed away one year, 11 months, and 29 days after the accident, and that the statute of limitations on personal injury cases is two years. The personal representative has exactly one day within which to bring the action. The statute will run two years after the accident, whether the injured died or not.

The measure of damages is exactly the same as any other personal injury case, with the exception that the loss of earning capacity would be measured by the period from the date of the accident to the date of death, and the out-of-pocket expenses would be limited to those expenses incurred by the deceased during his lifetime. The obligation to pay for his funeral expenses was not incurred during the deceased's lifetime, and therefore this is not an item of damages. It should be emphasized that the action brought by the personal representative is exactly the same action that the deceased could have brought had he lived. The personal representative is a substitute for the deceased, and whatever the deceased could have recovered had he been alive can be recovered by the personal representative—and nothing more. If the deceased was alive, he could not have recovered for his funeral expense; neither can the personal representative in the absence of a statutory provision that permits this item to be included. The items of damage, then, are the out-of-pocket expenses, loss of earning capacity, and physical and mental distress incurred or suffered by the deceased during his lifetime.

Survival claims can be divided into three classes, according to the cause of death:

1. Death from causes other than the accident;
2. Instantaneous death caused by the accident; and
3. Death due to the accident after a period of time.

1. *Death from causes other than the accident.* Death may have occurred after the deceased had completely recovered from the effects of the accident, or may have occurred while the deceased was still under treatment, or still suffering disability as a result of the accident. In either case the measure of damages is the same; namely, the expenses incurred and the distress suffered up to the time of death. In the second case, where the deceased, had he lived, might have suffered for years from the effects of the injury, the result is exactly the same. The fact that he might have so suffered is not an element of damage to be considered; the only measure is the suffering actually sustained and no more.

2. *Instantaneous death.* If death occurred instantly, or simultaneously with the happening of the accident, it is clear that the deceased has sustained no out-of-pocket expenses, no loss of earning capacity, and has suffered no distress; therefore the claim has no value. It must be emphasized that this conclusion relates to instantaneous death only, and if the deceased survived the accident, even for a matter of seconds, the case is not one of instantaneous death and must be considered under the third division.

3. *Death due to the accident after a period of time.* Death may occur seconds, minutes, weeks, or years after the happening of the accident. We
use exactly the same measurement in all cases when it comes to damages. Let
us assume that the claimant died 60 seconds after the happening of the accident, and that his survival for that period of time can be established. He has
sustained little or no out-of-pocket expenses, but he may have been conscious
during that minute and experienced severe physical distress. If he was unconscious during that minute, then he suffered no physical distress. The damages
would be measured in such a case by the period of conscious pain and suffering, and if there was no conscious pain and suffering the case has little or no
value. The same criteria would be applied to all other cases in this class. If
the deceased survived for a longer period of time but did not regain consciousness at any time after the accident and before death, there is no basis for a
claim for conscious physical distress. But other items, such as out-of-pocket
expenses and loss of earning capacity, must be taken into account.

Some states have combined the survival action with an action for wrongful
death where there is a relationship between the two. The majority of the states,
however, have statutes which completely disassociate the two causes of action.
In any case, it is possible to have an action brought under the survival statute,
and none under the wrongful death statute, for the reason that death was not
the result of the accident. On the other hand, where the deceased survived for
any period of time and then died as a result of the accident, there are two
causes of action: one for the damages which the deceased sustained during his
lifetime, and the other for damages for wrongful death.

2029   Measure of damages: Wrongful death

The cause of action for wrongful death did not exist at common law. It is
a cause of action created by legislative enactment and, therefore, we must look
to the statute itself to determine the measure of damages and the persons for
whose benefit such damages may be sought. The first of these statutes was
enacted in England in 1846 as the Fatal Accidents Act, more generally known
as Lord Campbell's Act. The purpose of the act was to provide a means
whereby the bereaved family of the accident victim could recover a sum of
money which would be the equivalent of what they would have received from
the victim had he lived. The family of the victim was frequently left destitute,
and it was to relieve this situation that the act was passed.

No recovery was provided for the mental anguish and bereavement suffered
by the members of the family. The measure of damages was based entirely
upon the pecuniary loss suffered by each member of the family. This does not
mean that damages are measured by the total future income that the deceased
would have enjoyed had he lived, but by that portion of his income which
could reasonably be expected to have been contributed to the family members.
For example, a single man earning $100 per week regularly sent his mother
$35 per week for her support. In the case of his death the mother's pecuniary
loss would be $35 per week for the balance of *her* life. The obligation assumed

by the son would continue only as long as his mother lived and would end with her death.

The loss of society, companionship, sex (in the case of a surviving husband or wife), love, and affection does not represent a pecuniary loss, however great the loss might be. For that reason these items are not taken into account. On the other hand, the loss of guidance and advice (spiritual and otherwise) is a pecuniary loss in the sense that such guidance and advice can be secured from other sources at a monetary cost.

All of the American states have wrongful death statutes. The great majority have enacted Lord Campbell's Act type statutes by providing for a recovery based upon the deceased's future contributions. Others have introduced variations of the original act, and still others provide for an entirely different measure of damages. Some states provide for a maximum limit of recovery whereas others leave the amount of the award to the discretion of the jury with no limit whatsoever. The claimsman must be familiar with the wrongful death statute of his state and thoroughly understand the measure of damages. He must also keep abreast of legislative amendments to the statute, something especially important at this time for the reason that legislative attention is continually occupied with suggested changes.

While it is beyond the scope of this work to analyze the various statutes in detail, wrongful death statutes generally will fall into one of four classifications: (1) punitive statutes, (2) damages based on loss to the estate, (3) damages based on contributions, and (4) combined death and survival statutes.

1. *Punitive statutes.* Some of the earlier wrongful death statutes provided assessment of damages by way of punishment for causing the death of a human being, with no regard to the loss suffered by the survivors. The trend has been away from this notion, and today only two states award damages on this basis: Massachusetts (by statute) and Alabama (by judicial interpretation). The Massachusetts statute reads in part as follows:

. . . For death of a person, exercising due care and not in one's employ, by negligence or wilful, wanton or reckless acts of one's self or servants, recovery may be had of not less than $5,000 or more than $50,000, according to the culpability of the defendants in the case.

This means that the amount of damages recoverable, subect to the monetary limitations set forth, is based upon the degree of negligence or "culpability" of the defendants. The greater the negligence, the greater the award; or the more wrongful the act, the greater the punishment to be inflicted.

The Alabama statute provides for the recovery of "such damages as the jury may assess" with no limitation as to the amount of recovery. The courts of that state have construed the statutory language to mean that damages should be proportioned to the degree of culpability. [See *Brown* v. *Southeastern Greyhound Lines*, 51 So. 2d 524.]

2. *Damages based on loss to the estate.* Among states that have this type of statute there are three distinctly different approaches to the measurement of damages, each state using one of the three. These measurements are:

1. *Net loss to the estate.*   The net earnings of the deceased, after subtracting the amount which he would have spent on himself for food, clothing, shelter, and entertainment, are reduced to present value.

2. *Gross loss to the estate.*   Damages are based on the earnings of the deceased over the period of his work-life, without any deduction for expenditures by the deceased. This would provide a greater recovery than if the actual loss sustained by the estate is reduced to present value.

3. *Accumulation.*   Damages are based on what the deceased would have earned and saved during his work-life (plus interest thereon), the damages being established by his past performance as to the percentage of his earnings which were actually saved. This measurement offers the least recovery for the death of the breadwinner who expends most or all of his salary to sustain the family. The amount here is likewise reduced to present value.

Where there are survivors, and damages are based on the net loss to the estate, the result will be practically the same as would be the case where a Lord Campbell's Act type of statute was involved. In the two other situations, the amount of the recovery would differ considerably in that the second would provide for a greater recovery, and the third considerably less. In any case, where there are no survivors, this fact would not in any way alter the amount of the recovery under this type of statute whereas, under a Lord Campbell's Act type, there would be no pecuniary loss if there were no survivors, and there would be no recovery. Under this type of statute funeral expenses, since they represent a loss to the estate, are recoverable.

3. *Damages based on contributions.*   The great majority of the states have enacted statutes of this type. They closely parallel Lord Campbell's Act, and provide for a recovery based on the probable future contributions to the beneficiaries by the deceased. Clearly, the length of the deceased's work-life, his net income, and the life expectancy of each beneficiary will all have an influence on the value of the claim. For example, if a beneficiary should die prior to the trial, the period of the deceased's possible contributions to that beneficiary would be limited to the beneficiary's lifetime, or the period from the date of the deceased's death to the date of the beneficiary's death. Also, where the beneficiary is much younger than the deceased, it is clear that contributions by the deceased would continue only so long as he was able to earn. Therefore, the value of such a claim would be measured by the deceased's work-life. Where the beneficiary is older than the deceased, and the life expectancy of the beneficiary is less than the deceased's work-life, the recovery is measured by the life expectancy of the beneficiary rather than by the work-life of the deceased.

Since the recovery is measured solely by the pecuniary loss suffered by the beneficiaries, damages are limited to that measurement and no other. Funeral expenses are ordinarily not included (unless specifically provided for by the statute), nor is there any recovery for mental anguish or bereavement, or loss of society, companionship, love, and affection, since none of these represent a pecuniary loss. Some states regard the loss of the advice, help, instruction, and guidance which reasonably could have been expected to have been received by the beneficiaries from the deceased as a pecuniary loss and allow damages for such losses. The theory is that if the beneficiaries sought such advice and guidance from other sources, it could be obtained by the payment of fees for such services. Among the states which have adopted this view are California [*Munro* v. *Pacific Coast Railroad*, 24 Pac. 303], Idaho [*Butler* v. *Townsend*, 298 Pac. 375], Utah [*Evans* v. *Oregon Railroad*, 108 Pac. 638], Washington [*Pearson* v. *Picht*, 52 Pac. 2d 314], and Wyoming [*Coliseum Motor Co.* v. *Hester*, 3 Pac. 2d 105].

Wrongful death claims based on the death of a child present a particularly troublesome problem. In the distant past, a child was an economic asset since he could be set to work at a very early age, and, at common law, the wages of the child were (and still are) the property of the father (the mother would have no claim unless she was a widow, had been deserted by the father, or the child was illegitimate). The older cases refer to the wage-profit formula in evaluating claims for the death of a child, basing the recovery on the wages earned or expected to be earned by the child, less the anticipated costs of raising the child. The damages thus produced were limited to the period of the child's minority since the father had no right to the child's wages when the child came of age. In some rare cases, where the facts indicated that the father was an invalid or was suffering from an incurable disease, damages have been allowed beyond the age of majority on the theory that the child would recognize an obligation to continue to make contributions to the family. In absence of such special circumstances, however, damages in such cases are limited to the period measured by the child's minority.

The situation is quite different at the present time. The costs of raising and educating a child usually far exceed any possible profit which the father might receive from the child's work. As a matter of fact, in the majority of families—in the absence of special circumstances—the father seldom receives any part of the child's earnings. In spite of these facts, evidence is offered of the child's possible earnings. Such evidence is highly speculative, but substantial awards have been made by juries who were undoubtedly swayed by the mental anguish and bereavement of the parents rather than the actual pecuniary loss.

Some states have approached the problem more honestly by providing a remedy in the wrongful death statute for mental anguish and bereavement of parents caused by the death of a minor child. The Florida Wrongful Death statute (Section 768.03) provides that the recovery in the case of the death of a minor child may be for the loss of the child's services and "such sum for the mental pain and suffering of the parents as the jury may assess." As in other states, the action is brought by the father, if living, or by the mother.

4. Combined death and survival statutes. Some statutes provide for one cause of action to recover for the damages sustained by the deceased before death and for the damage caused by the death itself. These statutes avoid some of the complications which arise where there are separate survival and wrongful death statutes, disposing of all claims arising out of the accident and death in the one action.

In all of these statutes the measure of damages is not affected by the fact that the survivors or the estate are the beneficiaries of life insurance policies carried by the deceased; the amounts so recovered are not allowed in mitigation of the damages. While the cases do not so state, it would seem that tacit recognition is being given to the collateral source rule in that recoveries from a collateral source do not diminish the tort-feasor's liability to respond in damages.

2030   Settlement valuation: Wrongful death

It is clear that because of the variations between the wrongful death statutes the method of establishing the settlement value will depend upon the provisions of the statute. Under punitive type statutes it is practically impossible to anticipate, with any degree of accuracy, the amount of the jury verdict. Suffice it to say that consideration must be given to the facts of the accident, the tort-feasor's conduct, and the degree of fault charged against the tort-feasor. Clearly, the presence or absence of the horror factor will influence the verdict. As a guide, the claimsman can refer to verdicts in similar cases in the same area. While the outcome of other cases will not be conclusive—in the sense that juries cannot always be expected to follow the same verdict pattern—they will be persuasive of the jury thinking in the particular area in which the case is to be tried.

Where the measure of damages depends upon the income or contributions of the deceased, the value of these cases can be estimated by the use of the appropriate present value tables. To do this, however, the most important element to be established is the net income of the deceased, whether or not it will increase or decrease during the period of his work-life, and the portion of the income which must be devoted to the deceased's subsistence. Again it should be emphasized that the net income is the deceased's take-home pay and not his gross wages. In cases involving the net loss to the estate, or contributions, it becomes important to ascertain his probable personal expenses; that is, the amount he normally would expend for his own food, clothing, shelter, and entertainment. The net income, less this amount, will be the net loss to the estate, or the amount which is available for contributions. It is clear that if the amount needed for personal expenses either equals or exceeds the net income, there is no loss to the estate or no money available for contributions, even if such are claimed.

We will consider a number of cases, with respect to the computation of estimated damages, where the recovery is based on the loss to the estate and where it is based on the deceased's contributions to his beneficiaries. The figures in all of the following examples do not contemplate any limitation as to the amount recoverable under the statute. If there is a maximum limit provided, and the computations exceed that amount, the limit of the statute will be controlling.

Damages based on loss to the estate.   Under this classification, there are the three approaches to the measurement of damages: net loss to the estate, gross loss to the estate, or accumulations. Let us assume that the deceased is

40 years of age at the time of his death. His take-home pay is $400 per month; his personal expenses are $250 per month, and he is able to save and accumulate $25 per month. Further assume that his wages will remain constant for the remainder of his work-life and that there is no anticipated change in income, either increasing or decreasing it. According to the Monthly Annuity for the Duration of Life at Work table, the present value of $1 per month, discounted at 5 percent, at age 40, is $152. And according to these figures, the computations of the value in each category is as follows.

Net Loss to the Estate

Net income per month	$ 400.00
Personal expenses	250.00
Net loss	$ 150.00
Present value $1 per month	× 152.00
Present value	$22,800.00

Gross Loss to the Estate

Net income per month	$ 400.00
Present value $1 per month	× 152.00
Present value	$60,800.00

Accumulations

Savings per month	$ 25.00
Present value $1 per month	× 152.00
Present value	$ 3,800.00

In all of these cases, accuracy in the determination of the basic figures is essential. For example let us assume that, instead of a net income of $400 per month, investigation would have revealed that the deceased was employed on a time and overtime basis; that his income did not remain constant for the entire year and, over the period of one year (taking into consideration the slack season), his average income was $350—not $400. The difference would affect the present value figures in the first two categories considerably in that the net loss to the estate would be $15,200 as compared to $22,800, and the gross loss figure would be $53,200 as compared to $60,800. The difference in income would have no effect on the computation based on accumulations unless the comparison between the deceased's personal expenses and his net income demonstrated the impossibility of any savings whatsoever, or indicated that the amount of saving must have been something less than claimed. In any event, it cannot be overemphasized that accuracy in the establishment of the basic figures is extremely important.

Damages based on contributions. In computing present value which is based on contributions, we will have to consider the age of the beneficiary and his life expectancy, and the age of the deceased and his work-life expectancy. If the beneficiary is older than the deceased, the obligation of contribution would continue only during the lifetime of the beneficiary, which in many cases is shorter than the work-life expectancy of the deceased. On the other hand, where the life expectancy of the beneficiary is greater than the deceased's work-life, the obligation to make contributions would continue only so long as the deceased was capable of producing an income. In addition, the health of the beneficiary might have an effect upon his life expectancy in reducing it to below the average expectancy. The same would be true of the health of the deceased. If at the time of the accident he was suffering from some condition which would reduce his work-life expectancy, this fact must be taken into consideration.

The amount of the contributions must be accurately verified. This can be done by examining canceled checks, past income tax returns, allocations of salary made to dependents, as well as books of account, paid bills, and other documents of similar nature. Also, the income of the deceased will sometimes furnish a clue as to whether or not the contributions were in fact made. If his income was such that all of it was needed to sustain himself, this would leave little room for contributions of anything but a very small payment. For example, if the deceased earned $100 per week, and his personal expenses were $90 per week, it is clear that the most that could be available for contributions to others would be $10 per week, or less. Any claim for contributions of more than $10 would be untenable and, undoubtedly, untrue. Examples 1, 2, 3, 4, and 5 illustrate the use of the tables with reference to computing valuations in respect to damages based on contributions.

EXAMPLE 1

PROBLEM: Evaluation, one older beneficiary.
CLAIM: Wrongful death.
LAW: Compensatory damages to beneficiaries; no limit.
DECEASED: Age 38, unmarried, good health prior to accident.
CLAIMANT: Dependent mother, age 66.
HEALTH OF DEPENDENT: Excellent.
LIABILITY: Clear.
WAGES: Take-home pay $125 per week.
CONTRIBUTION: $35 per week to mother.

VALUATION (Commutation Rate 5%)

With the mother as the sole dependent, her loss as a result of the accident is the loss of contributions from her son for the rest of her life. Therefore, since the son will outlive his mother, the measure of damages would be the present value of $35 per week ($1,820 annually) for the mother's life expectancy.

Present value $1 per year (at age 66)* .... $	7.15921
Annual payment	× 1820
Present commuted value .... $	13,029.76

* Mortality Present Value table.

The difference between the commuted value and the noncommuted value can be demonstrated by the following figures:

Life expectancy at age 66	10.54
Annual payment	× $1820.00
Noncommuted value .... $	19,182.80
Commuted value (5%)	13,029.76
Interest credit .... $	6,153.04

EXAMPLE 2

PROBLEM: Evaluation, two older beneficiaries.
CLAIM: (Same facts as No. 1.)
CLAIMANTS: Mother, age 66; father, age 69.
HEALTH OF BENEFICIARIES: Excellent.
CONTRIBUTIONS: $35 weekly to both.
ASSUMPTION: Contribution equal to both parents.

VALUATION (*Commutation Rate 5%*)

Loss is measured by the lives of both mother and father. Annual payment of $1,820 is divided equally, $910 to each.

Mother's Claim
Present value $1 per year at age 66 .... $ 7.15921
Annual payment ....   × 910

Present commuted value .... $ 6,514.88

Father's Claim
Present value $1 per year at age 69 .... $ 6.27048
Annual payment ....   × 910

Present commuted value .... $ 5,706.13
Commuted value of both claims $12,221.01

EXAMPLE 3

PROBLEM: Evaluation, one older beneficiary in poor health.
CLAIM: (Same as No. 1.)
CLAIMANT: Mother, age 66.
HEALTH OF BENEFICIARY: Poor; suffering from cancer which, in the doctor's opinion, reduces her life expectancy by one-third.
LIABILITY: Clear.
WAGES: $35 per week, or $1,820 annually.

VALUATION (*Commutation Rate 5%*)

Present value $1 per year at age 66 .... $ 7.15921
One-third reduction a/c poor health 2.38640

                                                       4.77281
Annual payment ....   × $1820

Present commuted value .... $ 8,686.51

The method followed here was to take one-third of the present value figure for persons of average health (⅓ of $7.15921) and subtract it from the same average health figure to give us the present value figure for a person in poor health, whose life expectancy has been reduced by one-third.

EXAMPLE 4

PROBLEM: Evaluation, one younger beneficiary.
CLAIM: Wrongful death.
LAW: Compensatory damages; no limit.
DECEASED: Mechanic, regularly employed, age 38; married, no children, no previous health impairment.
CLAIMANT: Wife, age 25.
HEALTH OF BENEFICIARY: Excellent.
LIABILITY: Clear.
WAGES: Take-home pay, $125 per week.
CONTRIBUTION: Cost of maintenance of deceased (lunches, clothing, rent, transportation to and from work, and entertainment) computed at $75 per week; wife's portion of earnings, $50 per week.

VALUATION (*Commutation Rate 5%*)

The wife's life expectancy at age 25 is 38.81 years. This is greater than the deceased's work-life expectancy of 22.99 years. Since the deceased's obligation is limited to the years during which he can produce income, the valuation will be based on the deceased's work-life expectancy.

Present value $1 per month at age 38* .... $ 158.62
Monthly contribution ($50 × 4) ....   × 200

Present commuted value $31,724.00

* Monthly Annuities Life at Work table.

EXAMPLE 5

PROBLEM: Evaluation, one younger and one older beneficiary.
CLAIM: Wrongful death.
LAW: Compensatory damages; no limit.
DECEASED: Mechanic, regularly employed, age 38; married, no children, no previous health impairment.
CLAIMANT: Wife, age 25, and mother, age 70.
HEALTH OF BENEFICIARIES: Excellent.
LIABILITY: Clear.
WAGES: Take-home pay, $125 per week.
CONTRIBUTIONS: To mother, $15 per week; to wife, $45 per week; personal expenses of deceased, $65 per week.

VALUATION (*Commutation Rate 5%*)

Mother's Claim
Present value $1 per year at age 70* .... $ 5.98022
Annual payment ($15 × 52) ....   × 780

Commuted value .... $ 4,664.57

Wife's Claim
Present value $1 per month at age 38† .... $ 158.62
Monthly payment ($45 × 4) ....   × 180

Commuted value $28,551.60

* Mortality Present Value table.
† Monthly Annuities Life at Work table.

The utilization of these present value tables is not mandatory as far as the jury is concerned, and the claimsman is not obligated to base his settlement values or estimated values thereon. They are included here merely to serve as a guide to estimated values and for use in connection with reducing settlement demands. In any case, the claimsman will be guided by the specific facts of each case and by his experience and judgment in arriving at a settlement figure.

CHAPTER XXI

Settlement negotiations and termination

2100 Nature and purpose of settlement

Settlement is the process by which parties having disputed matters between them reach an agreement as to what is due from one to the other. It contemplates a willingness on the part of each to forego his legal remedy and perform his part of the bargain if a satisfactory arrangement can be reached. In liability claims, a settlement usually involves the payment of money to the claimant as consideration for his forebearance of the right to assert a cause of action against the insured. It is evidenced by the execution of a document, either a release or a covenant not to sue, plus an act by the opposing party, consisting of the transfer of the money to the claimant. To be an executed and binding settlement, both acts must be completed. While either act is yet to be done, the contract of settlement is executory and is subject to avoidance by the party who has performed.

For example, if the claimant signs a release and the money is not paid within a reasonable time, the claimant may consider the contract as breached. He may seek to enforce the contract by suing the insurance carrier for damages for breach of contract, the damages being the amount which he would have received under the agreement. On the other hand, he may consider that, since the contract has been breached, it is no longer binding, and assert his cause of action against the insured as if no contract of settlement had been made.

The claimsman will utilize the process of settlement as a means of terminating those cases which qualify for that type of treatment. He may be able to make the determination as to settlement immediately or it may be necessary for him to conduct some investigation to reach such a conclusion. In any case, he will have to be persuaded that the claim involves a possible responsibility on the part of the insured and that the claimant has sustained provable damages. He will reject claims which do not involve any responsibility on the part of the insured, as well as claims in which there is a responsibility but in which the claimant has sustained no damages which are susceptible of proof.

2101   Burden of proof

In determining the cases which qualify for settlement, consideration will be given to the facts and whether or not the claimant can meet the burden of proof which the law imposes upon him. To recover, the claimant must cross the "bridge of proof" from accident to verdict. He must be able to establish certain points, and to defend against the issue of contributory negligence. This "bridge" may be illustrated as follows:

$$
\text{ACCIDENT} \left\{ \begin{array}{l} \text{Negligence} \\ \text{of the} \\ \text{Defendant} \end{array} \right\} \left\{ \begin{array}{l} \text{Proximate} \\ \text{Cause} \end{array} \right\} \left\{ \begin{array}{l} \text{Freedom} \\ \text{from} \\ \text{Contributory} \\ \text{Negligence} \end{array} \right\} \left\{ \begin{array}{l} \text{Damages} \end{array} \right\} \text{VERDICT}
$$

The claimant must prove that the defendant was negligent, that the defendant's negligence was the proximate cause of the accident, and that the damages were sustained as a result of the accident. In addition, he mut be prepared to go forward with the evidence and rebut any evidence that is offered that his own negligence contributed in any degree to the causation of the accident. The law requires that the claimant establish his case by a preponderance of evidence. This means that he must produce evidence which, when fairly considered, produces the stronger impression, has the greater weight, and is more convincing as to its truth than the evidence in opposition. It does not mean the greater number of witnesses, but it does mean that the testimony of witnesses will be weighed by the opportunity for knowledge, the information possessed, and the manner of testifying.

The claimant (or plaintiff) is not entitled to have his claim submitted to the jury until he has made out a prima facie, or basic case. This means that he must establish all the elements of the claim and offer proof of the existence of all the necessary parts of his cause of action. Should he fail to establish one of the required items, his cause of action will fail and there is nothing for the jury to consider. For example, if the claimant proves that the defendant was negligent but fails to prove that such negligence was the proximate cause of the accident, he has not established one of the necessary elements of his cause of action, and it must fail. If he proves his damages, and that they were proximately caused by the accident, but fails to prove the negligence of the defendant, his claim will likewise fail.

Where the plaintiff has produced evidence proving the existence of the basic elements of his case, he is entitled to have the case submitted to and considered by the jury, even though there is strong believable evidence produced by the defendant tending to contradict the plaintiff's proof. Where there is a conflict of evidence on any point, it is the jury's duty to decide the matter as a question of fact and to indicate by its verdict in whose favor the question has been decided. For example, if it is alleged that the defendant was operating his vehicle at a speed of 50 m.p.h. in a 25 m.p.h. zone (an act of negligence), and that the defendant's excessive speed was the proximate cause of the accident, as against the defendant's contention that he was going 20 m.p.h. and that the accident occurred solely through the negligence of the plaintiff, a verdict by the jury for the plaintiff is an indication that they decided they believed the plaintiff's evidence of speed and proximate cause and did not believe that of the defendant.

In some cases, the plaintiff will have the benefit of a rule of evidence which will make his burden of proof somewhat easier. For example, where the dangerous instrumentality doctrine is involved, mere proof of the possession of the dangerous instrumentality by the defendant and the ensuing accident will be sufficient to make out a prima facie case of negligence. Where the *res ipsa loquitur* rule can be invoked, mere proof by the plaintiff of the basic elements of the rule will establish the negligence of the defendant. In any case, it should be emphasized that the burden of proof still remains with the plaintiff and he must establish his claim even though the application of some rules may aid or assist him in meeting his obligation of proof.

2102 Qualifications for settlement

The settlement process is undertaken only where both parties to the controversy are willing to resolve their disputes by that means. In insurance claims the plaintiff is always willing to employ the settlement process. He has made a claim for a specific amount and if the amount is paid to him, his demands have been met and there would be no reason why he should proceed to litigation. He might be willing to forego litigation and accept something less than his demand where payment will be made immediately. On the defense side, the insurance carrier is always interested in the disposition of its claims, but whether or not it is willing to make a payment or engage in settlement negotiation will depend upon the particular facts of each case.

It is the claimsman's duty, therefore, to determine at the earliest possible moment the cases which qualify for settlement discussion and those which do not. At the same time, he will make a determination in the qualified cases just how far the company will be willing to go in meeting the claimant's demands. He will consider the facts of the case and will apply rules regarding burden of proof to the situation. Cases thus subjected to examination will fall into one of three classifications: (1) clear liability, (2) doubtful liability, or (3) no liability.

Clear liability.   Where the responsibility of the insured defendant can be established and there is no defense available, the claim is regarded as one of clear liability. If a reasonable settlement can be agreed upon, these cases should be settled promptly. For example, if the insured hits a properly parked car and causes property damage to the parked vehicle, the insured's responsibility is clear and there is no defense available. The claimant is entitled to recover the reasonable value of the damage thus inflicted. The same thing would be true as to personal injuries if the car was occupied at the time of the accident and the occupants thereof sustained injury.

Doubtful liability.   There will be cases where the claimant can make out a prima facie case, and therefore be entitled to submit the case to the jury, but where defenses also can be asserted, which, if believed by the jury, would require a defendant's verdict. These cases usually should be compromised, the extent of the compromise depending upon the strengths and weaknesses of the claimant's case as opposed to the strengths and weaknesses of the defense.

No liability.   In cases where the claimsman is convinced that the claimant cannot make out a prima facie case, or where the investigation reveals that the accident was caused solely by the negligence of a third party, there is no liability and these cases should be rejected. For example, let us assume that the insured was properly and legally parked and the claimant's vehicle ran into it. Certainly there is no responsibility on the part of the insured, and the claimant would not be able to establish any negligence. Therefore, the claimant would not be able to establish the first element of a cause of action against the insured. If a claim is made by the claimant for the damage to his vehicle it should be resisted.

2103   Nuisance settlements

When a claim is reported, the insurance company must create a file, establish a reserve thereon, and enter the file and other information in its records. In the course of development the file is ultimately closed, either by payment or by the passage of time where no claim is asserted. Cases which qualify for settlement treatment are usually disposed of by that method, or are brought to trial by the claimant and disposed of by that means. In between these two classes of claims are those which have no merit, but which are being actively pressed by the claimant or his attorney, either by continuous demands for settlement or by the filing of a suit. The insurance company cannot close such a file while the claim is pending, and therefore it must expend clerical time, maintain its records, and include the claim in its open-file inventory for a variety of purposes. Since the insurance industry is a business, it is cost-conscious and will, like any other business, attempt to reduce costs where possible. In the early days of the casualty industry, some companies felt that it was desirable to dispose of these nonmeritorious claims by a small payment in order to avoid the nuisance of keeping them open with its attendant burdens of record-keeping. For that reason nominal payments were made in order to close the files. Thus the terms "nuisance claims" and "nuisance value" were introduced into insurance terminology.

The insurance companies are divided in their approach to the handling of these claims. Some still follow the practice and feel they come out better in the final analysis by making the payment and buying a release for an amount which will be commensurate with what it would cost them to maintain the file and defend the lawsuit. The opponents of this view take the position that payment of these claims is a surrender to legal blackmail and, further, that payment of the claims will encourage the bringing of other and further claims of similar variety. They feel that claims should be disposed of strictly on merits and that no payment should be made unless the facts justify it. The handling of this type of claim will depend upon the company policy and likewise the extent of the payment to be made will also so depend.

Both sides, incidentally, agree that the terms "nuisance" and "nuisance value" have no place in insurance parlance and should not be used. Therefore they discourage the use of the terms.

2104   Classification of claims as to liability

Claims arising in areas of absolute liability, such as impurities in food, inherently dangerous operations, dangerous instrumentalities, and cases in which absolute liability is created by statute, come within the clear liability category. In addition, most companies regard the following situations, arising in automobile claims, as coming within the clear liability definition:

1. Pedestrian knockdown where the pedestrian is on the crosswalk, or, if a controlled intersection, crossing with the green light in his favor.
2. Defendant's car, out of control, mounts the sidewalk, knocking down one or more pedestrians, or causes property damage.
3. Rear-end hit, where defendant's car strikes the rear of the plaintiff's car, which is properly parked, or legally stopped on the highway, without any contributory negligence on the part of the plaintiff.
4. Wrong turns cases in which the defendant makes a right or a left turn from the wrong lane in the face of following traffic.
5. Pull-out cases where the defendant's car pulls out from the curb and strikes the plaintiff's car without any contributory negligence on the part of the plaintiff.
6. Unattended vehicle parked by the defendant on an incline rolls downhill without any interference by a third party.
7. Defendant driving from private driveway on to highway strikes pedestrian

or cars on the highway. This is regarded as clear liability whether the defendant is backing out or driving ahead.

These claims should be settled as promptly and as economically as possible.

Cases of doubtful liability usually qualify for a compromise settlement, but the amount the defendant should be willing to pay will vary with the facts of the particular case and the seriousness of the injury. If a compromise cannot be effected, most of these cases will have to be tried rather than settled for the full demand. Cases in this category are as follows:

1. Uncontrolled intersection cases where there is a question of fact as to which car entered the intersection first.
2. Controlled intersection cases where each driver claims the light was in his favor.
3. Where defendant made a left turn in the face of oncoming traffic and the plaintiff had an opportunity to stop and failed to do so.
4. Dart-out cases of an infant crossing the street not at the crosswalk but between two parked cars.
5. Passing on the right cases where plaintiff's vehicle, traveling in the same direction, passes on the right rather than the left, and where there are circumstances which may justify such action.

Examples of cases of no liability, which do not qualify for any settlement consideration whatsoever, irrespective of the seriousness of the inury, are as follows:

1. Injuries to trespassers, other than infants, caused by a defective condition of the premises, or by any cause other than the intentional act of the owner to injure them.
2. Injury to licensees occurring in a part of the premises outside the licensed area.
3. Rear-end hit where the defendant's car was properly parked or legally stopped on the highway and was hit in the rear.
4. Wrong turns where the plaintiff made a left turn in the face of oncoming traffic and the defendant had no opportunity to stop.
5. Stop sign cases where plaintiff's car went through a stop sign without regard to traffic moving in either direction.
6. Private driveway accidents where plaintiff's car came out of a private driveway or private road in the path of the defendant.
7. Dart-out cases involving an adult with no negligence on the part of the automobile operator.

It must be emphasized that the foregoing categorizations of case facts are offered solely for the purpose of providing examples. Each case handled by the claimsman should be viewed in the light of its own particular facts and its merits determined on the basis of the available evidence. It is possible that the same type of case will fall into the same category as is set forth in the foregoing list, but it is just as possible that, with the addition of one fact or another, the case will not be so classified. Therefore, if the listing is to be used at all, the conclusion reached must be conditioned by (1) additional facts, (2) experience in the particular category, and (3) company policy with respect to the particular type of claim.

1. *Additional facts.* The categories listed are limited to the particular facts presented and no others. If there is an additional fact, it may move the case from one category to another. For example, in the clear liability category, under Example 2, we say that where the defendant's car, out of control, mounts the sidewalk and injures a pedestrian, the case should be settled as one of clear liability. However, if we add one fact, that the defendant driver sustained an unpredictable heart attack (which caused him to lose control), or if it can be established that another car struck the defendant's vehicle (causing it to go out of control), the case is not in the clear liability category at all.

In the doubtful liability category we refer to a dart-out case involving an infant crossing the street. This presupposes that the driver was driving within the speed limit and has his car under reasonable control. If we add the fact that the accident occurred at night, that the driver was exceeding the speed limit and had no lights, or that he was knowingly driving with faulty brakes and made no effort to stop, the case could easily be classified as clear rather than doubtful liability.

2. *Experience.* This has to do with the results obtained in cases in the particular community where the case will ultimately be tried. In some localities juries are prone to apply the right-of-way rule strictly with respect to intersections and find in favor of the driver in the favored position every time. This would definitely affect the claimsman's estimate of the case and might well move the situation set forth in Example 1 from the doubtful to the clear liability category.

3. *Company policy.* Some companies have adopted a firm policy of either resistance or settlement with respect to particular kinds of claims. The policy may be dictated by the company's experience or by other reasons. In any case, company policy obviously would take precedence.

As the claimsman's experience broadens he will recognize over and over again that each case must stand on its own particular facts, and it will be seldom that any two cases are exactly alike. The foregoing list may be helpful in establishing some suggested guide lines, but the ultimate decision as to the merits of any case must be made on the basis of the particular facts.

2105   Relationship of injury to settlement

The nature and extent of the injury will have some influence upon the question of settlement. If the injuries are serious and of a permanent nature, or if there is a death claim involved where there are minor children, a sympathetic element may be introduced into the trial of the case. In those cases settlement consideration should also contemplate the possible jury reaction, and the amount estimated for settlement should be increased to cover these elements. Just how far the claimsman should be willing to go will be dictated by the eye appeal of the injury or the dependents involved. Experience gained from past cases, as well as current jury awards in similar cases, is the only guide that can be utilized. Since each case will have to stand on its own particular facts, the only possible guide that can be given in advance is a breakdown of the various types of cases and the general treatment which they should receive:

1. *No liability and minor injury.*   This claim clearly should not be settled and if no claim is pressed, no action is required. If the claim is being pressed, on completion of the investigation there should be a prompt denial to the claimant with an explanation as to why the claim will not be paid.

2. *No liability and serious injury.*   The treatment of this case will depend upon the facts and the severity of the injury. In some cases, because of the facts of the accident, there may be a possibility of a loss of some vital evidence or the possibility of being unable to produce a disinterested witness upon whom the defendant's case depends. In others there may be extremely high costs of defense, together with a pathetic picture presented by the claimant. In such cases, a compromise settlement may be indicated. In cases where these elements are not present, even though the injury is severe, no settlement should be considered.

3. *Doubtful liability and minor injury.*   If the claimant is seriously pressing the claim settlement should be consummated on the basis of the cost of trial and no more. Where the claimant is not seriously pressing the claim, no action is indicated and it may be that the claim will be forgotten. In the latter case, if the claimant should later actively press his claim, then settlement treatment of the basis of the cost of trial may be considered.

4. *Doubtful liability and serious injury.*   Claims in this category definitely require settlement on a compromise basis. The amount paid in settlement will depend upon the nature and the extent of the injury, and the figure should contemplate the impact of the sympathetic elements of the case on the jury.

5. *Clear liability regardless of injury.*   These cases should be investigated promptly, and, as soon as a definite determination is made as to liability and injury, efforts should be made to effect as economical a settlement as can be made commensurate with a fair and reasonable valuation.

2106   Liens

A lien is a charge, security, or encumbrance upon property. In liability insurance claims it is a charge that can be asserted against the property of the claimant (the settlement money) by another person because of some services rendered in connection with the claim. Liens arise either at common law or are created by statute. For example, at common law when an attorney is engaged, he has a lien on the client's cause of action for the payment of his fee. Therefore, if there is a settlement of the client's cause of action, the attorney may assert his right of lien against the settlement money. In all cases, the person paying the money must recognize the lien if he is on notice of its existence. Where the insurance carrier is on notice of the employment of an attorney, usually in the form of a letter from the attorney advising of his employment, the insurance carrier is bound to recognize that lien unless the attorney releases the lien or the lien is satisfied.

Should the insurance carrier pay over the money to the claimant, the attorney may sue the company for his fee. In order to avoid any problems, insurance carriers always add the name of the attorney as an additional payee on the settlement draft, so that the draft would be payable to "John Jones and Henry Brown, his attorney." Thus the draft, in order to be negotiated, would require the endorsements of both payees. The endorsement by the attorney is evidence that his lien has been satisfied. However, it sometimes happens that the claimant engages one attorney and, because of some dissatisfaction with his work, discharges him and engages another. In such a case, in the absence of a notice from the first attorney either that his lien has been satisfied or that he is claiming no lien, the practice is to include the names of both attorneys as additional payees. In order to negotiate the draft, the claimant will need the endorsements of both attorneys and the liens can be satisfied at that time. If the insurance carrier is not on notice of the employment of the attorney at the time the settlement is made and the money paid, it has no obligation to recognize the lien.

Some states have passed statutes which create a lien in favor of hospitals or doctors who have rendered treatment for an injury caused by the negligence of a third party. These laws usually provide for notice in the form of a direct notification to the tort-feasor, or, where the name or address of the tort-feasor is unknown, the statute will usually provide for constructive notice in the form of a filing of the lien with some public official, such as the county clerk, county registrar, or similar officer. The statutes provide that where notification is given, either directly or constructively, the physician or hospital has a lien on the proceeds of the claimant's recovery which must be recognized by the insurance carrier paying the money. Failure to recognize the lien, where notice has been given, will subject the insurance carrier to liability to the physician or hospital for the amount of the bill. This type of lien is referred to as a statutory lien, whereas the attorney's lien existed at common law and is referred to as a common-law lien.

Most workmen's compensation laws provide that where the claimant was injured in the course of employment because of the negligence of a third party, the claimant has the right to claim compensation, or proceed against the third party, or both. In case compensation is paid, the insurance carrier or the employer who made the payments is given a lien on the proceeds of the claimant's recovery from the third party to the extent of the compensation and medical paid. Just as in any other lien, the third party is not bound to recognize the lien unless and until he has notice of its existence.

It should be emphasized that the liens of the hospital, physician, and compensation insurance carrier exist solely because they are granted by a statute. If there is no state statute creating the line, then it has no existence in that state. On the other hand, the attorney's lien is a common-law lien and is in existence in all states. Therefore, the claimsman must be familiar with the laws respecting liens in all the states in which he operates.

It may happen that there is more than one lien involved in a specific case and a question may arise as to which lien has the priority. The rule is that the lien which is prior in time is prior in right. Since the attorney's lien attaches to the cause of action, it comes into existence prior to any other liens which attach to the proceeds of recovery. The cause of action existed before the recovery, and therefore the attorney's lien came into existence before any other. As to the liens which attach to the recovery, the lien filed first by the giving of actual or constructive notice is prior in right to liens filed subsequently.

It should be pointed out that the existence of the lien does not in any way operate so as to divest the claimant of his cause of action nor does it give the lienholder the right to pursue the action against the tort-feasor. All the lien does is give the lienholder a claim against the claimant's money, which is in the hands of a third-party tort-feasor. If the tort-feasor has no money belonging to the claimant, there are no funds against which a lien or claim may be asserted. For example, if the attorney or a doctor has a lien, notice of which has been given to the tort-feasor, unless there is a settlement or verdict in favor of the claimant, there is no money in the hands of the tort-feasor belonging to the claimant against which the lien may attach. If there is no settlement, or the case is tried to verdict and no recovery is allowed, there likewise is no money in the hands of the tort-feasor against which the line may attach. On the other hand, if the claimant has a valid cause of action but for reasons best known to himself he prefers not to bring the action, the lienholder is in the same position as if the verdict were for the defendant. He has no cause of action against the tort-feasor nor can he compel the claimant to bring the action. Therefore, the exercise of the rights given to the lienholder is entirely dependent upon a recovery or settlement.

If there is a recovery by the claimant, either by settlement or verdict, and the tort-feasor is on notice of a lien, he is bound to recognize it and liable to the lienholder if he fails to do so. For example, in one of the earliest reported cases on this subject, the defendant had notice of the employment of an attorney by the claimant, and therefore was on notice that the attorney had a lien on the claimant's cause of action. They settled the case directly with the claimant without the consent of the attorney and without any recognition of the attorney's lien. The attorney sued both the defendant and the claimant for his fees. The cause of action against the claimant was based on the charges for services rendered, and the cause against the defendant was based on the damages sustained by the attorney as a consequence of the defendant's failure to recognize his lien.

It developed that the claimant had received the money, and spent it all, and, since he was now insolvent, there was no possibility of recovery from that source. The defendant contended that the lien attached only to the money which was paid and, since the money had already been disbursed, they had no funds in their possession against which a lien could attach. The court held that as soon as the settlement was agreed upon, the defendants had money in their possession against which the line did attach. When the defendants paid the money to the claimant, they did so at their peril, since they were already on notice of the attorney's lien. The defendant could not defeat the attorney's lien by paying the money to the claimant. Judgment was entered for the attorney for the amount of his lien [*Fenwick* v. *Mitchell*, 70 N.Y.S. 667].

2107   Satisfaction of liens

Where a settlement is made or a verdict rendered for the plaintiff, a lien, properly asserted by notice to the defendant, can be extinguished only by payment or release by the lienholder. As to cases in which a verdict is rendered, there is no problem as far as the claimsman is concerned. He will issue the draft in payment of the judgment with the claimant and all lienholders named as payees. Under those circumstances, it is no part of the claimsman's duty to either investigate or decide the merits of the lien, whether it is reasonable or not, or whether the claimant has any defenses which may be available against the lienholder. The claimsman has met his only duty when he recognizes the lien by naming the lienholder as one of the payees. This is true even though the total amount of the liens exceeds the judgment.

The division of the draft is not a matter which is of any concern to the claimsman. It may happen that the claimant will request that the original draft be canceled and one issued to him alone, or that separate drafts be issued to himself and each lienholder. The claimsman is under no duty to thus accommodate the claimant and may do so only when he has definite proof of the amount of each lien. If for any reason, the information which the claimsman has in reference to the amount of the lien is inaccurate, and the amount of the lien is greater than the amount provided for by the separate draft, the company is liable to the lienholder for the excess. Therefore the better practice is to issue one draft and let the claimant work his problem out himself with the aid and assistance of his attorney.

Where a settlement is being made and where the amount of the settlement is adequate to meet the claims of the lienholders as well as the claimant, the same treatment should be given. Again, it is of no concern to the claimsman whether or not the amounts of the liens are reasonable. However, where a compromise settlement is being negotiated, the existence of liens may present obstacles, especially where the payments of the liens in full will leave little or nothing for the claimant. In such a case it might be to the advantage of the claimsman, in working out the settlement, to attempt to secure an agreement from the lienholders to release their respective liens for an amount less than the full lien. It should be emphasized again that the lienholder never has a cause of action directly against the tort-feasor arising out of the accident. The lienholder's rights against the tort-feasor come into existence only when there is a settlement or verdict. In a compromise settlement case, especially where the liability is doubtful, the lienholder is interested in seeing a settlement made. If the case is tried and the verdict is in favor of the defendant, it is possible that the lienholder may never get any money. Therefore, in compromise cases, it is very often to the lienholder's advantage to reduce the amount of his claim so as to assure the settlement, rather than to insist on the full amount and to run the risk of getting nothing.

Clearly, the financial status of the claimant will have some influence on the lienholder's decision, as will the nature of the claim and the possibilities of a defendant's verdict. To illustrate, let us assume that the claimant is a laborer who is married and has four children. He has sustained a rather serious injury which necessitated hospitalization over an extended period of time. The hospital bill is $3,000, a lien has been properly filed, and the tort-feasor is on notice of its existence. The liability, however, is extremely doubtful, and it is only because of the seriousness of the claimant's injuries and the outside chance that the sympathy of the jury might persuade them to bring in a verdict for the plaintiff that the insurance carrier is induced to consider the matter of settlement at all.

The insurance carrier is willing to pay a top figure of $3,500 for a full release, including the hospital lien. The claimant will not settle for $500, which is all that would be left after the hospital lien is satisfied, but will settle if he can be guaranteed a payment of $2,000 net. In such a case, the claimsman will discuss the matter with the hospital and if he can secure a commitment from them that they will release their lien for the payment of $1,500, the case can then be settled on the claimant's terms.

It is clear in this case that the only hope of recovery that the hospital has is based on a recovery by the claimant. If the claimant does not recover, the hospital will get nothing from the alleged tort-feasor and will be relegated to the claimant for whatever it can get from him. In this case, the claimant is clearly insolvent so that the prospects of the hospital collecting anything from him are not very bright. The hospital then has the choice of getting $1,500 certain, or taking their chances as to what the future developments of the case will be.

It should also be pointed out that the claimant is under no obligation to press his claim, in which case the hospital's lien is worthless. The hospital cannot compel him to press the claim and therefore, in the case illustrated, the hospital has more to gain by agreeing to the settlement of its lien and much to lose if it refuses. In a good many of these cases, the claimsman will have to patiently work with both parties, especially where the lienholder will release his claim for a certain amount and the claimant is unwilling to settle for the balance. In most instances the differences can be worked out and the settlement ultimately consummated.

The status of the lienholder or his relationship to the claimant does not alter the claim handling procedure. The same approach should be made if the lienholder is a physician, a surgeon, or the claimant's attorney. They are all subject to the same claim treatment. In the case of the claimant's attorney, the attorney will seldom suggest anything as drastic as a revision in his fee. However, there is nothing unethical or illegal about suggesting to him that the acceptance of a lesser fee than the one agreed upon can be one of the means of settling the claim. The claimsman can estimate that in most cases where the case is subject to a contingent fee the usual percentage is 33⅓ percent. In some larger cities (New York, for example), some lawyers insist on a contingent fee of 50 percent.

2108   Assignment and subrogation

An assignment is the transfer of property, real or personal, to another. The person making the assignment is called the assignor and the person to whom it is made is the assignee. Any type of property can be the subject of assignment, including a cause of action against a third party. There is one exception to this rule: personal injury actions may not be assigned, in whole or in part. Property damage actions on the other hand may be assigned. The common-law rule applicable to personal injury causes of action has been modified in certain areas (workmen's compensation, for example) by statute. In the absence of statute, personal injury causes of action may not be assigned since the common law felt that the cause of action was personal to the owner thereof. In property damage actions, which have been assigned, the third party is not bound by the assignment until he has notice of it. In absence of such notice, the tort-feasor has every right to assume that the property damage claimant still owns the cause of action and may deal with him with perfect safety. However, when the assignment has been served on the tort-feasor, he has actual knowledge that the property damage claimant no longer owns the cause of action, and he must deal with the new owner. As to the assignee, the same defenses which were available against the original property damage claimant may be interposed against the claim of the assignee.

Subrogation technically means the substitution of one party for another with reference to a lawful claim, demand, or right. It arises by operation of either law or equity. An assignment is a voluntary act of the owner of a right whereby he transfers that right to another. Subrogation is the transfer which the law compels him to make because of the circumstances. Under most compensation laws, for example, where the injury is caused by a third party and the employee claims compensation, the compensation insurance carrier is substituted for the claimant for the purpose of bringing suit against the third party after a specific period of time if the claimant fails to do so. This is subrogation and comes about by operation of law when the period of time expressed in the statute has passed. No act, voluntary or otherwise, is required by the claimant. The cause of action passes to the compensation carrier in accordance with the provisions of the statute and the compensation carrier may assert the rights formerly held by the claimant. The failure of the claimant to assert his rights within the time provided for in the statute has the effect of transferring the cause of action to the compensation carrier. Nothing further is necessary.

In equity, subrogation is regarded as a legal fiction through which a person, not as a volunteer but because of some obligation (as in an insurance contract), pays the debt of another and is substituted to all the rights and remedies available to the creditor, who has been paid. The debt is treated, in equity, as still existing for his benefit. Therefore, where a collision carrier has paid for damage to the insured's vehicle caused by the negligence of a third party, the collision carrier is the owner of the cause of action for damages to the vehicle as against the negligent third party and not the owner of the vehicle, whose loss it has paid.

2109   Subrogation by the United States

There are a number of situations where the U.S. government is required by law to render medical and hospital services to various classes of persons. These classes include members of the armed services, veterans who received treatment at Veterans Administration hospitals, seamen who are treated by the Public Health Service in marine hospitals, officers of the Public Health Service, officers and enlisted personnel of the Coast Guard, as well as military and naval cadets attending service academies. As to members of the Armed Forces, the obligation to furnish medical and hospital care extends not only to injuries or diseases occurring while in the course of duty, but also to injuries sustained while on authorized leave or furlough which are not sustained because of misconduct. Where any of these classes of persons is injured because of a tortious act of a third person, the question whether the United States could assert a claim against the third party for the value of the medical services rendered was an open one until legislation was finally enacted by Congress and approved by the President on September 25, 1962. The legislation (42 USCA 2651–2653) affects all classes of persons noted above, with the exception of seamen treated in marine hospitals (see Section 1407, above) and veterans treated for a service-connected disability. The exception with regard to veterans applies only to service-connected disabilities but it does not apply to treatment rendered in the Veterans Administration hospitals to veterans with a nonservice-connected disability. The statute (76 Stat. 593–594) is as follows:

An act to provide for the recovery from tortiously liable third persons of the cost of hospital and medical care and treatment furnished by the United States.

Be it enacted by the Senate and House of Representatives of the United States of America in Congress assembled, that (a) in any case in which the United States is authorized or required by law to furnish hospital, medical, surgical, or dental care and treatment (including prostheses and medical appliances) to a person who is injured or suffers a disease, after the effective date of this Act, under circumstances creating a tort liability upon some third person (other than or in addition to the United States and except employers of seamen treated under the provisions of section 322 of the Act of July 1, 1944 (58 Stat. 696), as amended (32 U.S.C. 249) to pay damages therefor, the United States shall have a right to recover from said third person the reasonable value of the care and treatment so furnished or to be furnished and shall, as to this right be subrogated to any right or claim that the injured or diseased person, his guardian, personal representative, estate, dependents, or survivors has against such third person to the extent of the reasonable value of the care and treatment so furnished or to be furnished. The head of the department or agency of the United States furnishing such care or treatment may also require the injured or diseased person, his guardian, personal representative, estate, dependents, or survivors, as appropriate, to assign his claim or cause of action against the third person to the extent of that right or claim.

(b) The United States may, to enforce such right, (1) intervene or join in any action or proceeding brought by the injured or diseased person, his guardian, personal representative, estate, dependents, or survivors, against the third person who is liable for the injury or disease; or (2) if such action or proceeding is not commenced within six months after the first day in which care and treatment is furnished by the United States in connection with the injury or disease involved, institute and prosecute legal proceedings against the third person who is liable for the injury or disease, in a State or Federal court, either alone (in its own name or in the name of the injured person, his guardian, personal representative, estate, dependents, or survivors) or in conjunction with the injured or diseased person, his guardian, personal representative, estate, dependents, or survivors.

(c) The provisions of this section shall not apply with respect to hospital, medical, surgical, or dental care and treatment (including prostheses and medical appliances) furnished by the Veterans Administration to an eligible veteran for a service-connected disability under the provisions of chapter 17 of title 38, United States Code.

Sec. 2(a) The President may prescribe regulations to carry out this act, including regulations with respect to the determination and establishment of the reasonable value of the hospital, medical, surgical, or dental care and treatment (including prostheses and medical appliances) furnished or to be furnished.

(b) To the extent prescribed by regulations under subsection (a), the head of the department or agency of the United States concerned may (1) compromise, or settle and execute a release of, any claim which the United States has by virtue of the right established by section 1; or (2) waive any such claim, in whole or in part, for the convenience of the Government, or if he determines that collection would result in undue hardship upon the person who suffered the injury or disease resulting in care or treatment described by section 1.

(c) No action taken by the United States in connection with the rights afforded under this legislation shall operate to deny to the injured person the recovery for that portion of his damage not covered hereunder.

Sec. 3. This Act does not limit or repeal any other provision of law providing for recovery by the United States of the cost of care and treatment described in section 1.

Sec. 4. This Act becomes effective on the first day of the fourth month following the month in which enacted.

Approved September 25, 1962

This statute creates a cause of action on behalf of the United States to recover for the reasonable value of the medical services rendered where the United States is required by law to render such service as against a negligent third party. Under the statute, the right of the injured person is transferred or subrogated to the United States insofar as it relates to the medical treatment rendered. In addition, the United States may intervene in any legal proceeding as a party plaintiff, and if the injured person does not commence any legal proceeding within six months of the rendering of the first treatment, the United States may bring an action in its own name to recover for the reasonable value of the medical or hospital services rendered. This is not a lien statute. The United States owns a claim for medical services immediately upon the rendering of the first treatment. Therefore, if the claimant were to execute a release of his claim after treatment has been rendered, such release will not be binding on the United States since the claimant cannot release a claim which he does not own, a claim which is owned by the United States.

The right of the United States to recover is not, as would be the case in a lien statute, dependent upon the recovery by the claimant. Likewise, there is no provision requiring that the United States give notice to the responsible third party. It would seem that any settlement of cases in the category covered by the statute would be at the tort-feasor's peril and, if there was medical treatment rendered by the United States, that the release given by the claimant would not extinguish the right of the United States to recover, whether the tort-feasor was aware of the fact that treatment was rendered or not. Where the claim is released by the claimant prior to the rendition of treatment by the United States, it would seem that, under the statute, the United States would acquire no right against the tort-feasor. The statute provides for a transfer of the claimant's right against the third party insofar as it relates to the United States. If the claim has already been released, then the claimant has no right remaining and cannot transfer anything to the United States.

By virtue of a statute, the President of the United States issued Executive Order 11060 on November 7, 1962, which reads as follows:

PRESCRIBING CERTAIN REGULATIONS AND DELEGATING TO THE ATTORNEY GENERAL CERTAIN AUTHORITY OF THE PRESIDENT TO PRESCRIBE OTHER REGULATIONS RELATING TO THE RECOVERY FROM TORTIOUSLY LIABLE THIRD PERSONS OF THE COST OF HOSPITAL AND MEDICAL CARE AND TREATMENT FURNISHED BY THE UNITED STATES.

Under and by virtue of the authority vested in me by Title 3 of the United States Code by Section 2(a) of the Act of September 25, 1962 (Public Law 87–693), it is hereby ordered as follows:

SECTION 1. The Director of the Bureau of the Budget shall, for the purposes of the Act of September 25, 1962, from time to time, determine and establish rates that represent the reasonable value of hospital, medical, surgical, or dental care and treatment (including prostheses and medical appliances) furnished or to be furnished.

SECTION 2. Except as provided in Section 1 of this order, the Attorney General shall prescribe regulations to carry out the purposes of the Act of September 25, 1962.

By reference to the statute, it will be noted that the head of the department or agency furnishing medical care may require the injured person to assign his claim for medical services to the United States. This apparently is a discretionary duty, and the assignment would not seem to have any legal significance. The assignment form which has been prescribed for this use is as follows:

POWER OF ATTORNEY AND ASSIGNMENT

For a valuable consideration I hereby assign to the United States of America to the extent authorized or required by 76 Stat. 593, 42 U.S.C., Sections 2651–2653, all claims, demands, entitlements, judgments, administrative awards, and the proceeds thereof, and all causes of action which I now have, and which I may have hereafter for hospital, medical, surgical, or dental care and treatment (including prostheses and medical appliances).

I hereby irrevocably appoint the Attorney General of the United States or his designee, my attorneys-in-fact in the premises, to do all acts, matters and things deemed necessary or desirable by any such authorized person, with full power and authority in my name, but at the cost, risk and charge, and for the sole benefit of the United States of America to sue for, or compromise, and to recover and receive all or part of the amount hereby assigned; and irrespective of assignment, to collect and disburse such funds in my behalf; and to give releases for the same; but no such action shall limit or prejudice my right to recover for my own benefit all sums in excess of those amounts representing the reasonable value of said care and treatment, or other sums to which I may be entitled.

Dated this   day of   19

_____
(Signature of assignor)

FB Form 1627–R (Temp)
1 Feb 63 (JA)

2110   Psychology of settlement

When a claimant sustains an accident resulting in a personal injury, he has been exposed to a new, and in some cases, a frightening experience. The more serious the injuries are, the greater the mental as well as physical impact. He will have had time to reconstruct the accident, to relive the events, and, more importantly, he will develop a mental certainty as to the part that the negligent act of omission or commission by the insured played in the causation of the event. He is likely to have some financial worries as to how bills will be met and about the cost of his medical expenses. He will have had to forego a number of planned pleasures because of his physical condition, and he will have suffered some pain, discomfort, or inconvenience because of his injuries.

All these items he will blame on the person he believes to have been responsible for the accident. The adjuster who calls on him for the purpose of discussing settlement represents the wrongdoer, or the cause of all his troubles. The adjuster is part of the opposition and, as such, is regarded as the claimant's opponent. In addition, he may have a suspicion that all insurance companies exist solely for the purpose of defrauding people and that those who work for such organizations are not entirely honest. These are the obstacles which the adjuster must overcome before he can get down to the business of disposing of the claim by settlement.

The psychology of salesmanship is applicable to the settlement problem.

The adjuster is in a sense a salesman, attempting to offer ideas rather than merchandise and to secure the claimant's acceptance of them. The commodities for sale, then, are courtesy, service, sympathy, understanding, and, at the proper time, money. The salesman has the advantage of the adjuster since he can handpick his prospects. The adjuster has no privilege of selection, and the prospective purchasers with whom he deals are the people who are involved in his cases. These include not only the injured claimant, but also the insured and the members of the various profession with whom the insurance carrier must deal. Nevertheless the psychological factors which influence salesmanship apply equally to the matter of settling claims. These factors are:

1. Establishment of friendly relations.
2. Appreciation of the claimant's position and feelings.
3. Agreement on noncontroversial issues.
4. Attention to the claimant's views.
5. Sales argument.
6. Solution by settlement.

1. *Establishment of friendly relations.* How this can be accomplished will depend largely upon the personality of the adjuster and the claimant with whom he is dealing. As a general rule, if the adjuster can find some common ground, such as a hobby in which they are both interested or a subject in which the claimant is something of an expert and concerning which he is willing to talk—or even the weather, these can be used as an opening gambit to friendly relations. Some adjusters avoid talking about the accident, except to express their sympathy for the claimant's injuries, for at least the first 30 minutes of the interview. This time will have to be varied, depending on the claimant's condition and his willingness to engage in such talk.

Also, to establish the proper climate for this factor, an appointment should be made in advance and the adjuster should not insist on beginning the interview if the claimant has company or is about to sit down to a meal. The adjuster under those circumstances should postpone his interview until another time which is more convenient to the claimant. In any event, the consideration of the adjuster for the claimant and the establishment of some common ground of discussion, aside from the accident itself, will all contribute to the establishment of friendly relations.

2. *Appreciation of the claimant's position.* This factor should be invoked from the beginning. The adjuster should express his sympathy for the claimant's condition. Since no one is happy to see a person injured in an accident, the expression of sympathy is the response to a human emotion. Merely because sympathy is expressed does not necessarily mean that liability is admitted, nor that a large settlement payment is about to be made. The claimant will automatically regard the adjuster as representative of an insurance company which is opposed to his recovery of money. The adjuster should admit that he represents a business organization but should also point out that this does not preclude him from understanding the feelings of others and from having the normal human emotions. The adjuster will demonstrate by his conversation that he has analyzed the claimant's side of the case, understands the claimant's fears, his uncertainty as to the future, and, most of all, his problem. In developing this factor, the adjuster will not disparage the claimant's case but will dwell on the strengths of his position.

For example, the adjuster will *not* say "You have sustained a very serious injury, *but* there is no liability," or "The X rays show a fracture, *but* it is only a slight crack." In both of these statements, the adjuster has disparaged the claimant's case and has aroused antagonism. The adjuster should say "You have sustained a very serious injury and I can appreciate the pain you have suffered," or "The X rays show a fracture, and I can understand how uncomfortable the plaster cast must be, especially in this hot weather." Each adjuster will fit this factor to his own personality, but the general idea is to make the claimant realize that the adjuster does understand his problem and his side of the case.

Where the injury is slight, the adjuster can stress this fact in his conversation. He can point out to the claimant how lucky he is that the injuries sustained were not more serious. For example, he can say "I'm glad that you didn't have a broken bone; you should be well on the road to complete recovery in no time," or "I'm glad that, if you had to be injured, the bone has only a slight crack." In this approach the result is to minimize the effects of the claimant's injury, but it also shows an appreciation of the claimant's position, especially with respect to what might have happened.

3. Agreement on noncontroversial issues. If it becomes necessary to discuss the details of the accident and the injuries, the adjuster should begin by covering those details which are admitted, such as that the claimant was a passenger in the other car, that it was a very dark night, that it was raining, and that it took an ambulance over an hour to reach the scene. As the accident is outlined, the adjuster will present the story with scrupulous fairness, showing first the evidence in favor of the claimant's version of the case and then presenting the statements of other witnesses which are to the contrary. But throughout the discussion, the adjuster will stress the fact that he, the adjuster, was not present at the time and place of accident, and must, as a matter of necessity, depend upon what others say they have seen and heard. The adjuster will strive for a pattern of agreement on the part of the claimant so that the claimant will see the case through the eyes of the adjuster, who is endeavoring to weigh the evidence as fairly as he can. The claimant will begin to admit that certain things look bad for him and certain other things look good for him. He will see the adjuster as a person who emphasizes the points on which both can agree and who has the additional burden of fairly evaluating the points of disagreement.

Just how much evidence should be revealed, whether the names of witnesses should be mentioned, or whether a witness' statement will be referred to without identifying him as all matters which must be decided as a matter of the adjuster's judgment, having in mind the kind and type of person with whom he is dealing, whether or not the adjuster feels there is an attorney in the background, and whether or not the adjuster feels the case will ultimately wind up in litigation.

In many cases, it will not be necessary to go over the facts of the accident; the conversation can be led immediately into the matter of settlement and discussion of the accident details can either be avoided or limited to small points. Some claimsmen feel that a discussion of the accident details should be avoided unless it is absolutely necessary to discuss them. The thinking is that a discussion of the details is bound to provoke some controversy and should be avoided where it is possible to get into the settlement discussion without it.

4. *Attention to the claimant's views.*   Sometimes in the course of the discussion, a claimant will want to get certain gripes off his chest. It may consist of his opinion of the insured, based on the failure of the insured to call on him or to inquire about his injuries, or it may be that he dislikes what the insured said to him at the time of the accident or statements which the insured made about him after the accident which have come to his attention. When this occurs, the adjustor should let the claimant talk himself out. Many times the things which the claimant has on his mind don't seem so serious (even to him) when they are put into words. The adjuster should let the claimant have the floor and should not interrupt except for an occasional short comment. If the claimant goes into a real tirade, or is getting into an emotional upset, the adjuster should seek an appropriate break in the conversation to terminate the interview, making an appointment to resume the discussion at a more convenient time.

Cases in which the claimant excites himself into an emotional outburst are rare, but the adjuster should be watchful of signs which indicate that the claimant is losing control of himself, and when that happens the interview should be terminated as quickly as is tactfully possible. In most cases, the claimant will feel better after he has had an opportunity to air his grievances to someone other than his immediate family, and subconsciously he will appreciate the attention which the adjuster has given to his views.

5. *Sales argument.*   The adjuster has already outlined the case, indicated his appreciation of the claimant's problem, called attention to the points on which both can agree, and outlined the strengths and weaknesses of the case from both sides. At this point he will slant the discussion toward the insurance carrier's side of the case, the business reasons why insurance carriers settle some cases and litigate others, what the advantages are that accrue to the company when cases are settled promptly, and how both parties benefit from a prompt and fair disposition of the case. In presenting these ideas, the adjuster will use some of the things that the claimant has said and build on the claimant's view so that the claimant will adopt most of the things which the adjuster says as being based on his own concepts.

6. *Solution by settlement.*   Having considered all the factors, the claimant's problem, the insurance carrier's problem, the views of the claimant, and the facts of the case, the adjuster must solve the entire problem. What is the best way for these differences and agreements to be resolved? The adjuster offers the solution by way of a reasonable and fair settlement. The settlement will take care of the claimant's entire problem, his loss of earning capacity, his medical and hospital bills, his pain and suffering, and all other expenses and recoverable items related to the accident. In a word, the settlement is a "package deal" which takes care of everything, or, in the alternative, will be a package which will take care of the bulk of the expenses and give the claimant a recovery so that he can meet at least some of the debts which have been incurred.

The application of these factors is calculated to influence the claimant in the direction of settlement. Just how much time and attention will be paid to each factor will depend upon the seriousness of the injuries and, more importantly, upon the seriousness of the liability. Where liability is weak, there is no justification for the expenditure of the same time and trouble which would be necessary in a case where liability is clear. As to these matters the judgment of the adjuster will determine the specific treatment which is to be given to the particular case. In a word, the greater the necessity of settlement from the company's standpoint, the greater should be the application of the psychological factors.

2111 The settlement interview

Settlements can be consummated by mail, telephone, or personal interview. Small cases usually qualify for disposition by one of the first two methods. A request can be made by mail or telephone for the bills incurred, either for medical treatment or property damage as the case may be; the case can be discussed by telephone, and a settlement agreed upon; or an offer of a settlement at a specific amount can be made by mail. A variation of the latter procedure could include sending the claimant a release form draft, endorsement of which will constitute a release. Small claims are those which involve $100 or less. Company policy may dictate a larger or a smaller amount as the breaking point between which claims can be handled by mail or telephone and those which require a personal contact with the claimant.

Where a personal settlement interview is desirable, there are three elements which require consideration: (1) timing, (2) preparation, and (3) climate.

Timing. The settlement interview should take place as soon after the happening of the accident as possible, at a time when the claimant is willing and able to discuss settlement. The adjuster should not attempt to force the claimant into a settlement discussion when it is clear that the claimant wants to wait until some future date. The adjuster can endeavor to persuade the claimant that the time for settlement has arrived, but if the claimant is adamant in his refusal to discuss the subject, arrangements should be made for it to take place at some future time.

For example, let us assume that the claimant says he is not ready to discuss settlement until he has had a final examination from his doctor, which is to take place within the next 10 days. The adjuster may attempt to persuade the claimant that the best judge of his physical condition is himself, and that if he feels all right there isn't much more the doctor can tell him. If the claimant is amenable to this argument, then the discussion can be had. Otherwise, if he insists that he will not settle the case until he sees his physician for a final examination, there is no point in even opening the discussion.

Should the adjuster insist on discussing settlement, and make an offer, it is obvious that, under the circumstances, the case will not be settled. However, one of two things may happen. The claimant will consult his physician as to the adequacy of the amount offered. The doctor might advise him that the amount is much too low and recommend a considerably higher figure or the employment of an attorney. The fact that the doctor doesn't know anything about settlement values will not prevent him from expressing an opinion. On the other hand, the physician may feel that the claimant's physical condition does not support the offer made and will counsel the claimant to see if he can get a little more, but in any case settle on the adjuster's terms. Then the doctor will give a report which will not justify the offer made by the adjuster. In either case, the adjuster has nothing to gain by insisting on making an offer. The practical effect will be to get the doctor into the discussion (if only indirectly), as the controlling influence as to whether or not the case will be settled.

The same principle would apply to fatal cases. After the accident, the adjuster should call and express his sympathy to the dependents, but he should not talk settlement until they are mentally ready to sit down and discuss financial matters. The worst thing that the adjuster could do would be to try to discuss settlement while the dependents are in the state of bereavement. Not only will the attempt be fruitless, but the adjuster will project himself as a callous individual, devoid of human feelings, who is interested only in his business and nothing else. This will be a tremendous obstacle to overcome when the time for actual settlement arrives. Occasionally, there will be a case where the dependents are interested and willing to talk settlement even before the funeral has taken place. If such indication is made, there is no reason why the settlement discussion cannot be had immediately. But this is the exception rather than the rule.

Preparation.   For the discussion to result in a settlement, both parties must be prepared to consummate the settlement. This means that the claimant should have all of his bills in itemized form, if necessary, and any other data which is needed, such as a certificate from his physician or an estimate of the damage to his property. The adjuster should have completed a sufficient inquiry into the facts so as to know whether or not his insured was entirely responsible for the accident or partly chargeable with the injury. He should know just how far his company will want to go in meeting the claimant's demands and the limits of his authority to bind the company to a settlement.

Climate.   This is an extremely important element. The settlement discussion should take place under the best possible circumstances with only the adjuster and the claimant present, or with the addition of his wife or near relative. The more people present and participating, the more difficult the interview will be. Therefore, even though there has been an appointment in advance, if the adjuster calls on the claimant and finds he is entertaining company or has a group of people at his home, the adjuster should postpone

the settlement interview until a more convenient time. Nothing is more discon-
certing than to have the claimant's attention continually diverted by others or
to have others who are not concerned in the case participate in the discussion.

Therefore, even though the claimant insists that the presence of company
will not interfere with the discussion, it is better to delay the interview until
the circumstances are more conducive to a successful conclusion. If the adjuster should even begin the discussion, he may find himself in a situation
where he cannot graciously terminate it. Therefore, it is better to recognize a
situation in the beginning and take the trouble to make another settlement call
rather than attempt to proceed under adverse circumstances.

A settlement discussion does not have to be concluded at the first meeting.
If company should arrive, or the claimant's children come home from school,
and it is obvious that the claimant cannot devote his entire attention to the
subject, the adjuster should suggest that the discussion be postponed until a
more convenient time. This may be the very next day, but in any case, the
adjuster will find he will attain a more satisfactory result if the discussion is
had under favorable circumstances and in a climate where both he and the
claimant can proceed without interruption.

2112   First-call settlements

In some cases, it is possible to dispose of a claim by settlement when the
initial contact is made. If the adjuster has sufficient information as to liability,
such a settlement should be made on the first call. These settlements not only
save considerable time for the adjuster but also save the company the expense
of maintaining the file. Therefore, first-call settlements should be made wherever possible.

One word of caution should be added, however. If the adjuster has not
completed enough of an inquiry to be reasonably certain of the responsibility
of the insured, and if the claimant looks for a "fast settlement" for an amount
which seems to be much less than the obvious value of the injuries as claimed,
the adjuster should not be stampeded into making a settlement. Signs such as
these point to a possible fraudulent claim, and further inquiry must be made
before liability is assumed. Other danger signs are ridiculously low demands
on a "take it or leave it" basis with the implication that if the demand is not
met at that moment, the claimant will engage counsel in the morning.

It is difficult to set a rule as to when the opportunity for a first-call
settlement should not be grasped. Suffice it to say that if there is anything in
the case—the claimant's anxiety to conclude the case or a lack of sufficient
information as to liability—which raises a doubt in the adjuster's mind as to
the good faith of the claim, he should decide in favor of further inquiry rather
than quick settlement. In other cases, first-call settlements should be encouraged.

2113   Control of the claimant

Control of the claimant means that no attorney has been retained and that
the adjuster is in control of the situation insofar as a settlement discussion

with the claimant is concerned. When the claimant retains an attorney, the adjuster has lost control of the case. In most cases first-call settlements cannot be made, some because the claimant is still hospitalized or under treatment and others because the results of the injury as to permanency or temporary disability are unknown. If the adjuster is to maintain control of the case, he must make an immediate contact with the claimant, even though this first contact cannot possibly produce a settlement, and he must arrange for frequent call-backs to check the claimant's progress. When the time for settlement arrives, the adjuster will be able to discuss settlement with the claimant and not with an attorney.

Generally, cases in the hands of attorneys cost more to settle than those in which the settlement is made with the claimant direct. For the most part, attorneys in personal injury cases work on a contingent fee basis, the fee being a percentage (usually one third) of the amount recovered. Therefore in a case where the claimant wants to net $600 for himself, the company would have to settle with the attorney for a much larger sum. If we assume that the fee will be one third of the recovery, then only by payment of $900 would the claimant receive the $600 he is seeking. If the company is willing to meet the claimant's demand it is clear that, from the company's point of view, it would be better to deal with the claimant direct than through an attorney. The objective of claimant control is to maintain an open line of communication with the claimant so that when the time for settlement arrives it can be consummated directly with the claimant.

If control is to be established it must begin with an immediate contact with the claimant. It must be continued by return calls until settlement time. Just how much of an interval can elapse between calls will depend on the nature of the case, the disposition of the claimant, and the adjuster's own judgment. To plan a course of claimant control we must place ourselves in the position of the claimant. Here is a person who has sustained an injury. It is a new experience. He suffers pain, but more than that he wonders how he is going to pay for all the expense. He wonders if there is any insurance available, and how much. Will it be sufficient to cover the losses he is sustaining? Perhaps he has been told that the person responsible for the accident has insurance, but he has never seen the policy. He wonders if there is one.

If no one contacts him during this period he will assume that either there is no insurance or that the insurance company is not interested in his case. In either event he will retain an attorney to protect his interests. However if, during this time, an adjuster from the insurance company calls on him, expresses his sympathy, inquires about his progress, assures him that the company is interested in him and at the proper time would like the opportunity of discussing the settlement of the case with him, and then continues to call and express interest in his recovery, he may be willing to see what the company has to offer by way of settlement before he retains an attorney.

The adjuster will not advise him against the employment of an attorney. He will, however, point out that attorneys do not work for nothing and that it might be to his interest to wait and see whether or not the case can be settled to his satisfaction without the employment of an attorney, in which case he would have no attorney's fee to pay. He can always retain counsel, and if not satisfied with the company's offer can retain counsel then.

Another method of maintaining control of the case is through an immediate contact with the attending physician. A telephone call to the doctor, advising him that the adjuster has seen his patient, and telling him that in the event of settlement, which appears favorable at this time, the adjuster will try to see that the doctor's bill is protected, will very often make the doctor feel he has a real part in the case and all the more willing to cooperate with the adjuster. This is good psychology since no one wants to be ignored.

In many cases, the adjuster will merely ask the doctor for a report and tell him nothing about the case, nor will he show any interest in the doctor's bill. Under those circumstances nobody could blame the doctor if he feels left out and does not care to cooperate with the adjuster in settling the case even when asked to do so in the later stages. Cooperation of the doctor can be a very valuable asset and should be cultivated. The doctor is much closer to his patient than an adjuster ever will be; the patient develops the habit of listening to his doctor in medical matters affecting his health, and will continue that habit when the doctor talks about the settlement of the case. If his bill is to be protected, then his own interest is involved in the case.

2114   Settlement negotiations

In all cases involving the possible responsibility of the insured there is a settlement value. This value is an amount that would be to the advantage of the claimant to accept and to the company's advantage to pay. Settlement negotiations are the means by which both parties seek to arrive at a figure which is agreeable to each. There is a certain amount of "horse trading" in this process, with the claimant seeking to get as much as he can for his injuries and the adjuster seeking to make a settlement at a reasonable figure, saving as much as he can for the company. There is no reason why this situation should be a secret and if the claimant maintains that the adjuster is seeking the low-dollar settlement for his company, it should be freely admitted, while calling attention to the fact that the adjuster does not blame the claimant for trying to get as much as he can for the injury.

Before entering into settlement negotiations the adjuster will consider the relative bargaining positions of the parties, the advantages which the facts of the case give to the insurance company, and the disadvantages which will accrue if the case is not settled. He will consider the possibilities of the claimant's recovery, the possible amount of recovery, and the probability of a defense verdict. He will consider at least the one bargaining advantage which the insurance company has in all cases: that they can call the turn as to whether or not the case will be settled. They control the money, and if they decide not to go along with the claimant's settlement demand, no settlement can be made. There is nothing the claimant can do to force a payment at that moment. He can force a payment only by bringing the case to trial and obtaining a verdict. Then he may be faced with the possibility of an appeal, if the facts so warrant. During the period of time from the demand to the verdict, there is no way that the claimant or his attorney can compel the company to disburse any funds. The company alone can decide whether it is to its advantage to pay some money in settlement before verdict or to make the claimant prove his case before any money is paid.

Whether dealing with the claimant or his attorney, the policy limits should not be discussed. They have no bearing on the issue of liability or the amount of damages which may be claimed for an injury. There has been a growing demand by claimants' attorneys for this information, and, as a matter of fact, some states permit discovery of the policy limits as part of the pretrial practice. Even if this be the case, the attorney or the claimant is not entitled to the information until a lawsuit has been filed and proper demand made on the defendant for it. In negotiations for settlement it should have no place and should not even be discussed. If a request is made for the information, it should be politely declined.

Where the policy limits are minimal and the injuries severe, the company may feel that a disclosure of its policy limits will facilitate the settlement. This probably will come about in a case where the only source of recovery is the insurance policy, with the insured unable to respond to a judgment in excess of the limits. Unless the company is prepared to pay the major portion of its policy limits, they should not be disclosed. If the company is willing, for example, to pay $7,500 where the limits are $10,000, then disclosure of the limits may be helpful in inducing a settlement. But if the limits are $10,000 and the company is unwilling to pay more than $3,500 or $5,000, the disclosure of the policy limits will not normally be to the company's advantage.

In any case, however, where disclosure of the policy limits is made, the information must be accurate. It is considered sharp practice for a company or its adjuster to deliberately falsify the information and to state that the limits are less than they are. Should such a thing be done, and the opposing side become aware of it, a complaint to the state insurance department might place the company in an embarrassing position. If the policy limits are disclosed, the disclosure must be accurate.

While the case is in the negotiation stage, some attorneys will seek to obtain a disclosure of the policy limits indirectly. They will tell the adjuster that if the policy limits are $5,000 they will accept $3,500 in settlement, but if the policy limits are $10,000 they will accept $7,500 in settlement. If the adjuster then offers $3,500 he is tacitly admitting that the policy limits are $5,000. When the attorney tries to use this method, the adjuster should insist that the policy limits have no relationship to the matter of settlement and that he will only accept a demand with no strings attached to it. He should carefully record all such conversations in the file, with the time and the date of the discussion, as well as the circumstances under which it took place, such as by telephone or by personal contact.

The objective of settlement negotiations is to make a contract. The contract will come into existence through the usual preliminary steps of an offer from one side and acceptance by the other. In these cases there will be consideration moving from each party to the other. The defendant will pay a certain sum of money to the claimant in return for which the claimant will forego his right to sue. As evidence of his agreement to forego his legal rights, the claimant will execute a document, or contract, which we call a release.

In cases where there are other parties alleged to be jointly responsible, the claimant may wish to retain his rights against such other joint tort-feasors and merely to release one defendant. In such a case, and in some states, the use of a covenant not to sue will accomplish this result. The claimant by means of that document does not relinquish his claim, but he does promise not to sue the defendant in consideration of the payment of money.

2115   The offer

The offer, as one of the elements in the formation of a contract, may be made by either party. It must be definite in its terms and is, in effect, a proposal to make a contract. The person to whom the offer is made may, by acceptance, create a binding contract. The offeror cannot make a binding contract and there is nothing that he can do after having made the offer to bring the contract into existence. Therefore, the person making the offer is at this stage in a less-favorable position than the offeree. The offeree can bring a contract into existence by acceptance; the offeror cannot. A counteroffer is construed as a rejection of the original offer and terminates it. The counteroffer then becomes the only offer and the person to whom it is made can create a contract by acceptance.

In insurance terminology we refer to "offer" and "demand" to distinguish between an offer made by the company and an offer made by the claimant or his attorney. They are both offers, and although we refer to the claimant's offer as a demand, the legal significance is the same. The insurance carrier's acceptance of the demand will create a contract.

There is no limit to the number of offers or demands that may be made, and each offer or demand will cancel the one previously made. For example, if the adjuster offers $250, and the claimant demands $1,000, there are two offers and no acceptance. The $1,000 demand is a counteroffer and therefore a rejection of the adjuster's offer of $250. The legal situation, then, is that there is outstanding an offer to settle for $1,000, and nothing more. Should the adjuster offer $500, it is a rejection of the claimant's offer to settle for $1,000 since it is a counteroffer. The claimant's demand or offer to settle for $1,000 has been rejected by the adjuster's counteroffer of $500. As in the previous situation, the rejection of an offer terminates it.

Some attorneys like to proceed on the assumption that once an offer is made the company is bound by it, and that a counterproposal, in the form of a demand, does not release the company from its obligation to pay its original offer if it is accepted. This is not a true statement of the law. The law is, as has been stated, that a counteroffer is a rejection and terminates the offer. If the attorney makes a counteroffer and it is not accepted by the company, then there is no offer open. Then the attorney will accept, or try to accept, the company's original offer. This so-called acceptance is, legally, another offer which the company can accept or reject as it sees fit. For example, if the company offers $500 and the attorney demands $750, the offer of $500 has been terminated by rejection and there is an offer of $750 from the attorney. When the demand of $750 is rejected, the attorney then will say that he accepts the offer of $500. Clearly, he cannot accept an offer which is not in existence, so that his "acceptance" will be construed in law as an offer to settle for $500, and nothing more. If the company does not accept this new offer there is no contract; there is only an offer to settle.

2116   When to make an offer

There are two schools of thought among claimsmen and text writers as to whether or not the adjuster should make the initial offer. One school advocates the making of the first offer by the adjuster on the theory that if the claimant has a much larger figure in mind, the offer of a much smaller amount will condition his thinking and lower his demands without subjecting him to the necessity of exposing his thinking as to value. In a word, he will not ask as much as he originally had in mind if he hears an offer which is much lower. On the other hand, the fact that the offer is so disproportionate to the figure the claimant had in mind might drive the claimant to an attorney and terminate the possibility of a settlement directly with the claimant. It can be argued that in such a case the adjuster has lost nothing because if the claimant's valuation was so high that it would be impossible to meet it, no settlment with the claimant could be consummated. In this way the problem of bringing the claimant into the area of a reasonable figure would be transferred to the attorney. The attorney would recognize the impossibility of the claimant's demand and will endeavor to bring the claimant's thinking as to value within reasonable and attainable limits. Thus the attorney will be indirectly accomplishing exactly what the adjuster would do in reducing the demand.

The arguments against this course of dealing are impressive. When the adjuster makes the first offer he gives the claimant a bargaining advantage. The claimant will know exactly what the adjuster has in mind as to the amount he is willing to pay. The claimant will have disclosed no information as to his position. The adjuster will not know whether his figure is too high or too low, from the claimant's standpoint. It is just as likely that the adjuster's offer will be more than the claimant had in mind as it is that the offer is considerably less. Therefore, the adjuster runs the risk of either overpaying the case or of losing the case to an attorney because his figure is regarded as too niggardly. He won't know in advance how his offer will be received. In making the first offer the adjuster is taking a calculated risk, one which, in the usual case, is unnecessary.

Most claimsmen subscribe to the second school. They feel the better procedure is to find out from the claimant exactly what his thinking is as to value. He can point out the out-of-pocket expenses and suggest that the claimant give him some idea of what he thinks a reasonable settlement should be. If the claimant expresses a figure, then the adjuster can decide whether to make an offer or not, depending upon the amount of the claimant's demand and whether it is within reasonable limits or not.

Often the claimant will answer the question by asking another. He will inquire as to what the adjuster usually pays in cases of this kind. The adjuster can then state that he is willing to pay the out-of-pocket expenses and can then make a list of them. He can work this out on a piece of paper and ask the claimant what he thinks of that figure. The claimant might accept the figures, or he might say that he should receive something more. He will be asked to identify, in dollars, exactly what is meant by "something more."

Ultimately, the adjuster will wind up with a settlement demand. He can pay it or he can endeavor to work it down to within what he considers reasonable limits. He can accomplish this by means of a lower, or trading, offer and, as the claimant comes down in his demand, can raise his original offer.

2117   When not to make an offer

The general rule is that an offer should not be made unless the amount of the offer is such that there is a possibility of the case being settled at or near the amount offered. If the amount of the demand is so high that any offer the adjuster might be able to make will seem ridiculously small, no offer should be made. The task of the adjuster will be to reduce the demand before making any offer. If he cannot reduce the demand there is no reason to make an offer which will not settle the case.

For example, let us assume that the adjuster's estimate of the value of the case in settlement is $750, and the claimant demands $5,000. Even if the adjuster offers his top figure, it is clear that it will not settle the case. If the claimant is serious in his demand, an offer of $750 will only upset him, and may have the effect of terminating the negotiations at that point. If the claimant is not serious, but is making the demand on the off-chance that the adjuster might pay it, and if that doesn't happen willing to take considerably less, an offer of $750 at that point cannot be accepted. It would be the unusual claimant who would admit that his demand was facetious. Most would attempt to justify the $5,000 demand. In any case, the claimant could not accept $750 in the face of his demand without making some admissions and "losing face."

Therefore, the procedure to follow would be to work on the demand and get it reduced, by easy stages if necessary. This can be accomplished by having the claimant state the basis for his demand, and again going back to the special damages and pointing out that the claimant would have difficulty in justifying the demand. The suggestion might be made that a reasonable demand would receive much more favorable consideration by the company. When the demand is reduced to somewhere near $1,000, or even $1,500, the adjuster can make a trading offer of $500, which he can increase to $750 if and when the demand is reduced to meet the offer. An offer of $750 in the face of a demand of $5,000 will never be accepted and should not be offered until the demand is reduced as noted in this example. If the demand is never reduced from $5,000, no offer should be made unless the company is willing to make an offer of something over $2,500.

2118   Negotiations with attorneys

The adjuster should bear in mind that in dealing with an attorney he is dealing with a limited agent, one who normally has no authority to settle the claim without specific authorization from his client. Therefore any negotiations are subject to the approval of the client, and no offer of settlement can be accepted without having been submitted to the client. Since the attorney is charged with some knowledge of the value of the claim, there is no reason why he should not be asked to make his demands known. The adjuster should not, in any case, make the first or initial offer. Once the attorney has made a demand, usually considerably more than he expects to get, the adjuster may make a counteroffer. This offer can only be accepted by the client, and the attorney's agreement that the case is settled for that figure is still subject to the wishes of his client.

Some attorneys will use this limited agent relationship as a vehicle for getting an increase in the offer. What sometimes happens is that the attorney agrees that the offer is fair and that he will submit it to his client. He assures the adjuster that the client will accept it. However, he later calls the adjuster and tells him that he could not get his client to accept the offer. He will go to great lengths as to the arguments he advanced to the client, that his client is a stubborn mule, but that he was finally able to get the client to agree upon another figure, larger than the offer but not too far above it. If the adjuster believes the story he can increase the offer to meet the new demand, provided the facts in the file justify an increase. On the other hand, if the attorney's case is weak, the adjuster can stand on his original offer and refuse any increase. In most cases, the original offer will ultimately be accepted.

A variation of the same type of procedure is where the attorney makes a demand, let us say of $2,000. After some discussion the adjuster offers $500. The attorney will say that he must submit the offer to his client but is quite sure the client will not accept it. He will inquire of the adjuster as to whether or not the adjuster would be willing to pay $1,000, provided he can get his client to accept it. If the adjuster answers this inquiry in the affirmative, he has increased his offer to $1,000, whether he meant to do so or not. If the case follows the usual course what will happen will be that the attorney will come back and say he couldn't get the client to agree to $1,000, but that he was successful in securing the client's approval of a $1,500 figure. Since the difference between the offer and the demand is only $500, the adjuster should not let such a small difference stand in the way of a settlement.

By such a simple device, the attorney has obtained an increase in the offer to $1,000 and has placed the adjuster in a position where a demand of $1,500 does not seem too far out of line. The adjuster should meet the attorney's inquiry whether a payment of $1,000 would be made, if he can get his client to accept it, by stating that the offer is $500. It will remain open for a reasonable period of time. If it is not accepted, then the attorney has no offer. If the client wishes to make a demand of $1,000, the adjuster will consider it but cannot guarantee that the company will accept it. As far as the adjuster is concerned, the offer is $500 and no more.

In dealing with attorneys the adjuster should consider the strengths and weaknesses not only of his own case but also that of the attorney. As in the case of the claimant, there is no way the attorney can compel the company to settle the case. This can come only as the result of an agreement, and the adjuster is the one who can decide if the case will be settled or not. The adjuster should also recognize that most plaintiffs' counsels handle these cases on a contingent fee basis, which means that the attorney will not receive a fee until some money is recovered by the client, by settlement or verdict. The attorney cannot spend money that is represented by open files in his office. Therefore he has a pecuniary interest in the disposition of his files, and cannot collect a fee until there is a recovery.

Some attorneys are settlers and never try a case; if they have a case of sufficient severity they will turn it over to trial counsel for trial. Where the case is forwarded to another attorney, the attorney of record loses part of his fee. Therefore, the adjuster should recognize the attorneys in his area who are of the settling type, and those who are capable of bringing a case to trial. The settlers will ultimately abandon small cases in which no settlement can be made. They will forward the larger cases. The usual arrangement between counsel is that the trial counsel receives as his fee 25 percent of the recovery. If the original attorney has a contingent fee arrangement of $33\frac{1}{3}$ percent it is clear, in a forwarded case, that his fee is reduced to $8\frac{1}{3}$ percent. Figures of this sort should have some place in the adjuster's valuation of the case and should influence his case handling.

2119   Increasing offers

The general rule is that an offer should not be increased unless there is a corresponding decrease in the demand. The reason is that an increase under those circumstances would serve no useful purpose and will impede the settlement negotiations rather than advance them. For example, if the demand is $1,000 and the adjuster offers $500, an increase in the offer to $600, without any action by the claimant, will immediately create the impression in the claimant's mind that the $500 was not a serious offer. He will stand on his $1,000 demand until such time as he is sure that the adjuster has reached his top figure. If the adjuster then raises his offer to $700, the claimant is sure the first offer of $500 was hardly serious since he has received a $200 advance without making any move himself. The increase in the offer only made the claimant suspicious of the adjuster's motives in offering that sum in the first place.

What should happen in such a case is that the adjuster should stand on the $500 offer until the claimant reduces his demand. When there is a reduction in the demand, then and only then should the adjuster even consider an increase in the offer. How much of an increase should be made will depend upon the circumstances—and the ultimate figure the adjuster has in mind as the top settlement value. If the claimant comes down $100, reducing the demand to $900, the adjuster does not have to increase the offer by the same amount. He can increase the offer to $550, or, if the circumstances dictate, increase the offer by the same amount. In no case should the increase in the offer be more than the decrease in the demand.

The mere fact that there has been a decrease in the demand does not necessarily require that the adjuster increase the offer. He can stand on his offer and attempt to force another and further decrease in the demand before making any move at all. Just what technique the adjuster will use will depend upon his judgment and the circumstances of the case, in the sense of just how dangerous the adjuster thinks the case is. If it is a case of clear liability, the adjuster will be justified in being more liberal in his increases; if it is a case of doubtful liability the adjuster may make small increases in the offer, or none at all.

2120   Matching offers technique

This procedure is used by many attorneys and claimsmen, and can be used in dealing with the claimant as well. It consists of matching the decrease with a corresponding increase, and is based on the horse trader's principle that "if we come down a little, you'll come up a little." At the start the adjuster has a final settlement figure in mind. He will not make an offer until the demand is exactly one and one-half times the amount of the settlement figure he has in mind. Then he will offer one third ($\frac{1}{3}$) of the demand (which is one and one-half times the settlement figure). No matter what the amount of the increase or decrease, if they are matched by exactly the same amount, the adjuster will reach his ultimate figure.

For example, if the adjuster's settlement figure is $1,500 he should not make an offer until the demand is $2,250. At that point he will offer $750. From these figures it can be readily seen that if the claimant (or the attorney) and the adjuster make equal moves, the ultimate figure will be $1,500. If we use $250 as the amount of increase and decrease, the claimant would be at $2,000 when the adjuster is at $1,000. On the next move the claimant would be at $1,750 and the adjuster at $1,250. The next move will bring the figure to $1,500, the ultimate objective.

The duration of the procedure will differ, depending upon the type of person with whom the adjuster is dealing and upon the amount of increase and decrease. In some cases, the matter can be completed in a matter of days and in others it may be a matter of days and weeks between offer, counteroffer, demand, and counterdemand.

2121   Creating a problem for the claimant or his attorney

Every claimsman can recall at least one case involving serious injuries in which substantial offers of settlement were made and the offers were refused.

The case went to trial and resulted in a verdict for the defendant. The result may have produced some amusement among the claim department personnel, but to the claimant it was a tragedy, and to his attorney an embarrassing nightmare. Not only has he lost a fee but he must explain to a seriously injured client why there was no recovery and, more importantly, why he recommended the refusal of the offer (if he did) or why he did not insist that the offer be accepted. No matter what the explanation is, the claimant will blame the attorney for the result and for the fact that he received no money for his injury.

The writer can recall an automobile passenger case in which the claimant was severely injured in a two-car collision. The injuries were such that the 30-year-old claimant would never work again. He sued both drivers. Prior to trial he released his own driver, giving a covenant not to sue for $5,000. The demand was finally reduced to $75,000. We had $50,000 coverage and were willing to pay our policy limits, but the insured refused to contribute anything and the case proceeded to trial. The plaintiff's counsel had somehow discovered the policy limits, but at no time did the demand come within those limits. The jury returned a verdict for the defendant. The covenant not to sue was definitely a tactical error and our defense was based on the fact that the accident was due solely to the negligence of the other driver, who was not in court and who was not then a defendant. From the attorney's standpoint, he not only gambled his own fee on the outcome of the trial but had also gambled the claimant's future. Just how he explained the result to the claimant is a part of the story that has never been told.

In both of these cases, the attorney would not have been faced with a problem if a ridiculous offer had been made. But where a realistic offer is made, the attorney is faced with the problem of whether to accept it or to take his chances with the trial. The burden of proof is always on the claimant, and if he fails to meet it there could be a directed verdict (where a prima facie case is not made out) or an adverse verdict from the jury. The problem then comes down to whether he wants to exchange certainty, which the acceptance of the offer will give, for the uncertainty which is the ingredient found in all lawsuits.

In our automobile passenger case, the attorney could have had a settlement of $50,000. He chose to risk the uncertainty of a lawsuit in an effort to recover more. The decision clearly was his to make, together with his client. It was an extremely difficult decision not only because of the amount of money involved, but also because of the difference that the recovery of money, as opposed to no recovery at all, would mean to the claimant. If we had offered some ridiculous sum, such $1,000, the attorney and his client would have had no problem. The $1,000 would hardly take care of the claimant's future needs and would not even approach the out-of-pocket expenses incurred up to the time of trial. Therefore the offer of $1,000 would not merit one moment's consideration.

The point of all this is that an offer should be calculated to settle the case. It must be one which will merit consideration, and in serious cases (and in some not so serious), a realistic offer will create a problem for the claimant and his attorney who, in most cases, will accept the offer rather than risk the uncertainties of trial. The attorneys who represent plaintiffs are fully aware of these possibilities, which should also influence the adjuster in his handling of these matters.

2122   Mary Carter agreements

In a lawsuit involving two or more co-defendants, it sometimes happens that one of the co-defendants will execute a guarantee agreement with the plaintiff whereby the settling defendant will guarantee that the plaintiff will receive a certain amount of money, regardless of the outcome of the lawsuit. If the verdict equals or exceeds the amount of money agreed upon, the plaintiff agrees to satisfy the judgment from the other defendants and the settling defendant will pay nothing. If the verdict is less than the amount agreed upon, the settling defendant will pay the difference between the agreed amount and the verdict. The agreement further provides that the existence of the agreement will not be revealed except by order of the court.

One of the earliest cases involving the elements of a guarantee agreement was the California case of *Pellett* v. *Sonotone,* 160 P. 2d 783 (1945). In that case, the plaintiff purchased a hearing aid from the defendant Sonotone through one of its salesman, Brown. A mold had to be made of the plaintiff's ear and Brown arranged with the defendant, Compton, a dentist to do the work. Compton prepared the plaster cast of the plaintiff's ear, but failed to remove all of the plaster. As a result the plaintiff's ear was injured and the plaintiff sued Brown, Sonotone, and Compton.

Compton entered into an agreement with the plaintiff which called for a payment by Compton of $5 regardless of the outcome of the suit and a $10 payment if there was a verdict in the plaintiff's favor. The agreement was not filed or revealed to the other defendants. Compton was to remain in the case throughout the trial. Plaintiff appealed from a directed verdict.

The existence of the agreement was revealed in the second trial, and thus the question before the court was whether or not this agreement constituted a release. The court held that it did not and was more in the nature of a covenant not to sue than anything else. There was a vigorous dissent and Justice Traynor characterized the arrangement as a "collusive proceeding" with "immoral consideration." It was argued that the plaintiff should be bound by his agreement with Compton and should not be permitted to pursue a separate cause against Sonotone and its salesman for the same negligent acts from which Compton was released.

In 1967, the Florida Appellate Court decided the case of *Booth* v. *Mary Carter Paint Co.,* 202 So. 2d 8. The heirs of the decedent Elsie Booth brought action against the Willoughby Trucking Company and the Mary Carter Paint Company as a result of a two-truck and one-auto accident which resulted in Mrs. Booth's death. Prior to trial, the defendant, Willoughby, and the plaintiffs entered into an agreement whereby Willoughby's exposure would be limited to $12,500. If the verdict exceeded $37,500 the plaintiff would satisfy the verdict against Mary Carter only. If the verdict was less than $37,500, the satisfaction of judgment would be against Mary Carter, but Willoughby agreed to pay up to $12,500 to make the recovery total $37,500. Finally, if there was a defense verdict, Willoughby agreed to pay the full $12,500. It was further agreed that the agreement would not be revealed to the other defendants, except by order of the court. Willoughby continued as a defendant and neither the court nor the jury was informed of the existence of the agreement. After a plaintiff's verdict of $15,000, Mary Carter sought a setoff on the theory that the agreement constituted a release by one of the tort-feasors. The court denied the motion and this was affirmed on appeal.

In a later Florida case, *Bill Currie Ford* v. *Cash* 252 So. 2d 407 (1971), the court upheld the validity of the Mary Carter agreement, and, in addition, held that the nonsettling defendant could not introduce the agreement on the theory that such an admission would prejudice the settling defendant. Other Florida cases have held that the Mary Carter agreement was not against public policy and upheld the lower court's refusal to hold the agreement to be void. See *Ward* v. *Ochoa*, 284 So. 2d 385 and *Maule Indus. Inc.* v. *Rountree*, 284 So. 2d 389. In the latter case, the court did hold that the agreement was subject to discovery. Other states which have considered the Mary Carter agreements include the following: Arizona, California, and Nevada.

1. Arizona. In *City of Glendale* v. *Bradshaw*, 16 Ariz. App. 348, the case involved a one-car accident resulting in injuries to a passenger. The plaintiff sued the driver and the City of Glendale. An agreement was made between the plaintiff and driver under which the driver would pay the plaintiff $50,000, in the event of a defense verdict or a verdict against the driver only, but to pay nothing if the verdict was against the city or both defendants. The jury returned a verdict of $280,000, against both defendants. The agreement was revealed to the nonsettling defendant and the trial judge at the trial. The court held that the agreement was valid and did not constitute a fraud on the nonsettling defendant. See also *City of Tucson* v. *Gallagher*, 493 P. 2d 1197, and *Hemet Dodge* v. *Gryder*, 534 P. 2d 454.

2. California. In *Pellett* v. *Sonotone*, previously noted above, while the court sustained the guarantee agreement, the dissenting opinion did criticize the lack of disclosure by the settling defendant of the existence of the agreement. However, since that case, the California legislature has given its approval to the use of the guarantee agreement, by enacting a statute with the provision that the existence of the agreement be disclosed to the court and to the nonsettling defendant. See Title XI, Code of Civil Procedure, Sec. 877.5. See also *Pease* v. *Beech Aircraft Corporation*, 113 Cal. Rptr. 416; and *River Garden Farms, Inc.* v. *Superior Court*, 103 Cal. Rptr. 498.

3. Nevada. Thus far, Nevada is the only state which questions the validity of the guarantee agreement. The court reached the conclusion by some circuitous reasoning that the agreement was void as against public policy. In

Lum v. Stinnett, 488 P. 2d 347, there was a medical malpractice suit brought against three doctors, namely Romero, the family physician, Greene, the hospital resident, and Lum, the radiologist. During the trial the family physician, Romero, and the hospital resident, Greene, entered into an agreement with the plaintiff calling for a guarantee of $20,000, and in the event of a verdict of $20,000 or more against Lum and the other defendants, the plaintiff would execute against Lum alone. The plaintiff also agreed to vigorously prosecute the case against Dr. Lum and would not settle for less than $20,000. It developed that the authors of the agreement were the insurance carriers for Romero and Greene. The court held that the interference by parties who were strangers to the action constituted champerty and maintenance. The opinion defined maintenance as intermeddling by a person *without interest in a suit,* by assisting either party with money or otherwise to prosecute or defend it. Thus, the interference in the suit by parties who had no interest in it was against public policy and required the court to reverse the lower court and grant a new trial. In addition, there was a more cogent argument in support of the court's decision is that the agreement required the settling defendant's attorney to participate in the litigation as a defense counsel when he actually was interested in enhancing the plaintiff's recovery.

Clearly, the insurance carriers were interested parties and would gain or lose by the outcome of the litigation. Therefore, it is difficult to understand the court's reasoning that they had no interest in the suit.

Several jurisdictions have cited the *Lum* case, but have refused to adopt its reasoning with the exception of the North Dakota court in *Degman* v. *Beyman*, 200 N.W. 2d 134. The latter case involved a loan receipt agreement and the court cited the *Lum* case with approval, adopting the reasoning thereof.

Loan Receipt Agreements

Another facet of the guarantee agreement is the loan receipt agreement, wherein the settling defendant provided that plaintiff with an interest-free loan with the undersanding that in the event of a verdict against one or both defendants, the plaintiff would execute against the nonsettling defendant and would reimburse the settling defendant out of the proceeds. The difference between this type of agreement and the guarantee agreements is that an actual payment of money was made, whereas in the guarantee there was only a promise to pay certain monies conditioned upon the outcome of the lawsuit. Some courts have held that the loan receipt agreement was in violation of the rule against contribution among joint tort-feasors and was construed as a covenant not to sue, allowing a *pro tanto* reduction of the judgment against the nonsettling defendant. See *Bolton* v. *Zeigler*, 111 Fed. Supp. 516 (Federal Court of the northern district of Iowa).

On the other hand, in *Northern Indiana Public Service Co. (NIPSCO)* v. *Otis,* 250 N.E. 2d 378, the plaintiff was injured in a gas explosion and he sued the gas company and the installing contractor, Dehner. NIPSCO granted the plaintiff an interest-free loan of $50,000, to be repaid out of the verdict, if any obtained against Dehner. In the case of a verdict against both defendants, the plaintiff agreed to execute against Dehner. However, in the case of a verdict against NIPSCO alone, NIPSCO would be liable in excess of the $50,000 loaned. The court accepted the fact that the agreement was an attempt to evade the Indiana rule against contribution between joint tort-feasors. The court felt that the policy of the law favoring settlements took precedence over the existing rule against contributions among joint tort-feasors. The agreement did not settle the case because there was a lengthy trial and appeal in prospect. In *American Transport Company* v. *Central Indiana Railway*, 264 N.E. 2d 64, the Indiana Supreme Court, citing the *NIPSCO* decision stressed the desirability of loan receipt agreements as far as the damaged party was concerned in that substantial sums could be placed at the injured party's disposal immediately rather than after prolonged litigation, during which time the plaintiff's situation may change due to unavailability of witnesses, death of witnesses, and so on. In 1973, the Illinois Supreme Court followed the *NIPSCO* decision in upholding the loan receipt as valid in spite of the fact that it did violate the rule of no contribution between joint tort-feasors in *Reese* v. *Chicago, Burlington & Quinn Railway*, 303 N.E. 2d 382.

However, the more recent decisions seem to reject the loan receipt principle in that generally it violates the rule of no contribution between joint tort-feasors. See *Biven* v. *Charlie's Hobby Shop*, 500 S.W. 2d 597 (Kentucky) ; *Cullen* v. *Atchison, Topeka & Santa Fe*, 507 Pac. 2d 353 (Kansas) ; and *Monjay* v. *Evergreen, School District*, 537 Pac. 2d 825 (Washington).

Thus there is a certain amount of confusion among the courts as to the validity of the loan agreements. Therefore, it is suggesed if this device is contemplated that advice of counsel be obtained by the claims representative before proceeding. In determining whether or not the loan agreement should be used, consideration should be given to the following: the present state of the law regarding loan agreements in the state in which the contract is to be executed; whether or not the courts of that state will uphold the validity of loan agreements; agreement as to the lender-defendant's maximum liability; the method of repayment; the possibilities of repayment; and last but not least the exposure of the lender and his co-defendants. If it is determined that the possibilities of repayment are not very great, the possible settlement of the claim by means of a covenant not to sue should be considered.

2123　Form of agreement

The form of the loan agreement will vary according to the circumstances, the promise of repayment and the maximum liability to which the lender will be exposed. As to the guarantee agreement (Mary Carter), there should be inserted in the agreement a paragraph setting forth the negligence of the other defendants and exonerating the settling defendant from liability. This paragraph is inserted so as to create some reluctance on the part of other defendant to offer the agreement in evidence, since in some cases the paragraph might be likely to influence the jury. The agreement usually contains a promise on the part of the plaintiff that the existence of the agreement will not be disclosed except upon the order of the court. In some states the disclosure of the agreement is mandatory so that the plaintiff cannot be held to the promise. Otherwise, the plaintiff is bound not to disclose the existence of the agreement except when ordered by the court to do so.

While the conditions of the guarantee agreement might vary with the circumstances, the following is a typical Mary Carter agreement.

JOHN DOE AND RICHARD ROE, CO-DEFENDANTS

WHEREAS, the undersigned counsel of record for the plaintiffs and the undersigned counsel of record for John Doe desire to resolve amicably between them the extent of the liability, exposure or possible contribution of the defendant, John Doe.

[Here a paragraph should be inserted setting forth the negligence of the other defendant (Richard Roe) and exonerating John Doe, the settling defendant, from any responsibility for the causation of the accident.]

NOW, THEREFORE, the parties hereto agree as follows:

1. The maximum liability, exposure or financial contribution of John Doe shall be $10,000. [For the purposes of this form, we have chosen the sum of $10,000. The amount could be any agreed upon amount.]

2. Such liability, exposure or financial contribution of the defendant John Doe shall abate to the extent that the plaintiffs are able to effect collection from the other defendant or his insurance carrier, as provided herein.

3. The purpose of this agreement is to guarantee the plaintiffs a recovery of at least $10,000 and to decrease the exposure of the defendant, John Doe. It is the intention of the parties hereto that this agreement shall be construed as a conditional agreement between them as to financial responsibility only and it shall in no way constitute or be construed to constitute a release, settlement, admission of liability, or otherwise, and shall have no effect upon the trial of the case as to liability or the extent of damages, nor shall said agreement be revealed to the jury trying the said case.

The plaintiffs agree that in the event of a verdict against Richard Roe and his insurance carrier only or a joint verdict against defendants, Richard Roe and John Doe, the plaintiffs will first collect said judgment against Richard Roe and his insurance carrier. If the plaintiffs effect collection of $10,000 or more from Richard Roe and his insurance carrier upon any such judgment, plaintiffs agree to execute a full and complete release of all liability to defendant, John Doe, without any payment by the latter.

Plaintiffs agree that in the event of a verdict in favor of defendant, Richard Roe, and his insurance carrier, and against defendant, John Doe, the latter will be furnished a full release and satisfaction upon payment of $10,000, regardless of said judgment amount.

Another type of agreement is as follows:

Plaintiffs and defendant, John Doe, agree that in the event a verdict is rendered in favor of Richard Roe, his insurance carrier, and John Doe, the latter agrees to pay the sum of $10,000 for a release.

Plaintiffs and defendant, John Doe, agree that should the trial result in a verdict against all defendants or Richard Roe and his insurance carrier only, the plaintiffs will first collect said judgment against Richard Roe and his insurance carrier. Should said judgment be less than $10,000, defendant, John Doe, agrees to pay to the plaintiffs a sum representing the difference between $10,000 and the total amount collected from Richard Roe and his insurance carrier for which he shall be furnished with a full release and satisfaction by the plaintiffs.

In the event that Richard Roe or his insurance carrier appeals any judgment against either of them, defendant, John Doe, shall not be responsible for any payment under this agreement until final determination of all issues of such appeal and any new trial which may result therefrom.

No costs or interest shall be paid by defendant, John Doe, in addition to any sum he shall be obligated to pay hereunder. However, he must pay any obligated sum within 15 days from the date his obligation is determined.

In the event that the plaintiffs settle their lawsuit of claims prior to verdict with the defendant, Richard Roe, for $10,000 or more, the plaintiff will furnish to the defendant, John Doe, a full and complete release of all liability without payment by him. In the event that the plaintiffs settle their claim with the defendant, Richard Roe, prior to verdict, for a sum less than $10,000, the defendant, John Doe, agrees to pay to the plaintiffs herein the sum of $6,000 for which the plaintiffs shall furnish him a complete release. Settlement between the plaintiffs and Richard Roe after verdict shall not affect the terms hereof.

The defendant, John Doe, will continue to act as an active defendant in the active defense of this litigation until all questions of liability and damages are resolved between the plaintiffs and other defendants.

The contents of this agreement shall be furnished to no one unless so ordered by the court.

2124 Order of settlement

Where two or more claimants are injured the order of contact, for the purposes of control, will be the most seriously injured first, the next most seriously injured second, and so on down to the claimant who is the least seriously injured. The theory is that if it is impossible to control all the claimants, the next best thing is to control the serious cases, if possible. When it comes to settlement, the best method will consist of settling all the personal injury claims at one and the same time. If this cannot be done, and it is possible to do so, the most seriously injured claimant should receive the first settlement consideration. The reason is that once one claim is settled, the other claimants will regard the settlement as an admission of liability even though, as a matter of law, it is not. Therefore, the remaining claimants may be more difficult to deal with and may make excessive demands. If there are to be excessive demands, it is better to receive them in the cases which are the less dangerous. Therefore, if at all possible, the settlement in the first case should be with the most seriously injured person.

Obviously this cannot be a hard and fast rule, and circumstances will alter the procedure. Where there are three claimants, and two have completely recovered, and the seriously injured claimant is still under treatment with the outcome in doubt, it will be extremely difficult to hold the claimants who have recovered in line until the third claimant recovers sufficiently to discuss settlement. In such a situation, the adjuster might properly decide to settle the less seriously injured cases rather than run the risk of losing the claimants to an attorney because of the delay in settling.

In any case, personal injury cases should take precedence over property damage claims. Group settlement discussions should be avoided and the adjuster should not discuss settlement with more than one claimant at one and the same time. The best climate for a settlement discussion is with the claimant alone.

In cases involving both property damage and personal injury claims, there has emerged a rule that no property damage claim will be settled until all the personal injury claims have been closed. These cases are generally automobile claims where two cars are involved. The adverse driver is anxious to get his car repaired and wants to settle his property damage claim promptly. If there were injured passengers in the adverse vehicle, they will regard the settlement of the property damage as an admission of liability, since the defense of contributory negligence is available against the adverse driver and would not be available against them. Therefore, since the weakest claim was settled, they will feel that there should be no question about their right to recover for their injury—this is the reason for the rule.

In addition, if the adverse driver is anxious to get his claim settled, he will be of assistance to the adjuster in disposing of the claims of his passengers. If he knows he cannot receive any settlement consideration until all the personal injury claims are settled, he will have a personal interest in seeing that they are settled. In cases where the injuries are minimal, he will sometimes assist the adjuster in securing nominal releases from his passengers.

Where both cars are moving at the time of the accident, and passengers in either vehicle are injured, actions may be brought by the passengers against both drivers as joint tort-feasors. If both are insured, usually the insurance carriers get together and settle with the passengers, securing duplicate releases. The companies may participate in the settlement payment on an equal basis, or it may be that the facts are more strongly in favor of one as against the other and that the carrier will not be persuaded to participate in the settlement on any basis, or merely make a small contribution to the settlement in order to secure a release. In any case, where the first insurance carrier settles the property damage claim, the insurance carrier for the property damage claimant considers this to be evidence of the weakness of the other carrier's case and refuses to either participate or contribute to the settlement on any basis. Therefore, where there is another carrier involved, or a possibility of holding the other driver for part of the settlement, there is a definite advantage in refusing to settle the property damage until all the claims are settled.

Where there are two cars involved, and the property damage involves property owned by a third party, such as road signs, fences, traffic control barriers, telephone poles, and buildings, the same considerations would govern the settlement as where settlement of the property damage was made with the adverse driver. The settlement would be construed by others as an admission of liability and might make the settlement of other claims more difficult. Where there is only one car involved it would appear that settlement of property damage claims of this nature would not affect the settlement of other cases, and for that reason such claims can be settled at once.

All companies do not subscribe to this line of thinking. Some feel that where multiple claims are involved it is best to settle the claims as quickly as possible, whether small or large, or whether involving property damage or not. They feel that there is an advantage to be gained by settling as many claims as possible and that the severity factor should not determine the order of settlement. The advantages of this approach are: (1) The smaller cases are easy to settle and can be disposed of in a short space of time after the accident; (2) It minimizes the problem of keeping claimants under control in that the settlement of the smaller cases tends to keep the more serious cases under control; (3) It keeps the demands on the smaller cases within reasonable limits, which might not be the case if one of the more serious claims was settled for a large amount; and (4) It keeps the demands in the more serious claims at a lower figure because of the small amounts paid in the other cases.

Where the injuries involved in the claim are of such severity that the demands will equal or exceed the policy limits, and the case is one for settlement, it would appear that the second approach might afford a better chance of disposing of the cases within the policy limits than would the first.

Some insurance commissioners have condemned the practice of deferring the settlement of property damage claims where there are outstanding bodily injury claims in cases of clear liability. Therefore, the adjuster should be familiar with the rulings of the insurance department on this subject and be guided accordingly. In cases of doubtful liability it would appear that the rule of settlement could be followed. In clear liability cases, no matter what the attitude of the insurance department might be, the application of the rule would seem to afford the insurance carrier little advantage.

2125 Releases

A release is a contract whereby the person executing the instrument (the releasor) gives up a right, claim, or privilege to the person against whom it might have been demanded or enforced (the releasee). To be a binding contract, it must be supported by a valuable consideration. The consideration passing from the release to the releasor in our cases is the payment of a sum of money, and the consideration passing from the releasor to the releasee is the extinguishment of the releasor's right to bring legal action to enforce his claim.

The contract of release is executed, or completed, when both parties have performed their respective obligations thereunder; namely, where the claimant has relinquished his right and as evidence thereof has signed the release, and the company has performed its obligation by making the payment of the money recited as the consideration. When both these things have happened the release is a binding contract and may be interposed as a defense to any later action which the claimant might bring against the releasee. In the absence of fraud or other special circumstances, an executed release is a complete defense to any action which the claimant might seek to enforce against the releasee arising out of the same accident.

The contract of release is executory, or incomplete, when one party has performed his obligation and the other has not. Under such circumstances the nonperforming party usually has a reasonable time to perform. What would constitute a reasonable time will depend upon the circumstances. In liability insurance cases, where the claimant has signed the release, he is entitled to the money at once. He may agree to some delay, perhaps a day or two, but since he is entitled to the money at the time of signing the instrument, he may refuse the tender of the money if it is made at any other time. On the other hand, he may accept it and, having accepted it, he ratifies the contract and waives any breach which may have arisen because of the company's failure to pay the consideration at the time the release was signed.

Where one party has performed and the other has not, the performing party has an election of one of two remedies. He may regard the contract as breached and sue the other party for damages for breach of contract. This is an action on the contract, and the measure of damages will be the amount which he would have received if the contract had not been breached. In the other remedy, the performing party may also regard the contract as breached but that the breach by the opposite party has the effect of canceling the contract, thereby relieving the performing party from any obligations thereunder and permitting him to pursue any other remedies which may be available.

For example, the adjuster agrees to settle a personal injury claim for $500 and the claimant signs a release for that amount. The adjuster promises to deliver the draft to the claimant within a few days. He does not do so. The claimant can sue the release on the contract, and the measure of his damages will be the amount he would have received had the contract been performed by the releasee, namely $500. Or the claimant may exercise his other option and regard the contract as a nullity because of the nonperformance by the releasee. The claimant may bring a tort action for personal injury as if no contract of release had ever been made. The executory contract of release, which was not performed by the releasee, will not be a defense to the cause of action for personal injuries. The measure of the claimant's damages in this case will be based on the usual special damages and general damages for discomfort and inconvenience. The amount recovered may exceed $500 or it may be less. In any case, the release and the agreed consideration of $500 will not have any influence on the verdict, nor may evidence thereof be received by the court.

We may also consider a third situation. The claimant signs the release without receiving payment. One week later the adjuster tends a draft to the claimant for the amount of the consideration. The claimant within his legal rights to do so, refuses the draft. The contract then remains an executory contract and the claimant may exercise either option as to his future course of action. It is clear, however, that the claimant would bring an action for personal injuries since he could have enforced the contract by merely accepting the draft. He still has the option and could, if he changed his mind, bring action for breach of contract.

2126   Effect of a release

Generally, an executed contract of release extinguishes any cause of action that the releasor may have against the releasee. It generally does not release any claim that the releasor may have against anyone else other than the person named as the releasee. Therefore, the adjuster should be careful to include as releasees the names of all persons who qualify as insureds under the liability policy.

For example, let us assume that A, the named insured under an automobile policy, gives B permission to use the vehicle. B is involved in an accident while using the vehicle. When taking a release from the injured party, the adjuster should name as the releasees both A and B. A is the named insured and as such is entitled to the protection of the policy. B is likewise an insured under the policy and entitled to its protection. If B was acting as the agent of A at the time of the accident, A could be liable under the doctrine of *respondeat superior*. If B was not the agent of A, and this fact could be established, then A would have no common-law liability. If it were alleged that B was acting as agent of A, the company might have a problem of proof. It certainly would be in a better position if it could interpose a release running to both A and B as a defense than to defend on the theory of no agency.

Also, some states have changed the common-law rule so as to make the owner of the automobile liable where the vehicle is being used with his permission, express or implied, irrespective of whether there is an agency relationship or not. It is for these and other reasons that the adjuster should include as releasees the names of all persons who could possibly qualify as insureds under the policy.

Where there are joint tort-feasors involved, the common-law rule is that the release of one of several joint tort-feasors releases all. For this rule to be applied, it must be emphasized that the person released must occupy the position of a joint tort-feasor with relation to the other parties. If he does not, even though a release is given, the rule is not applicable. For example in an automobile case, A is stopped for a traffic light. B stops behind him. C negligently strikes the stopped car of B and forces it into the stopped car of A, causing damage. The proximate cause of the accident clearly is the negligence of *C*. *B* was not guilty of any negligent act whatsoever. Because of his dislike of litigation, *B* settles with *A* for $100 and *A* executes a release to *B* for that amount. *A* later sues *C*. The release to *B* did not extinguish *C*'s liability. *B* was not a joint tort-feasor, and therefore the rule has no application.

The releasor can release only the claim which he has against the releasee. If he has assigned his claim, in whole or in part, he can release only that part of the claim which he still owns. Personal injury claims may not be assigned, so we are concerned only with claims of property damage which can be assigned. If a property damage claim is assigned in whole or in part, and the tort-feasor has notice of the assignment, he must recognize the assignment, and a release from the original claimant or owner of the property damage cause of action will not protect the tort-feasor from the claim of the assignee. If the tort-feasor has no notice of the assignment, he may deal with the claimant directly, and even though there has been an assignment of the cause of action, the failure of the assignee to give notice of the assignment where knowledge of the assignment did not reach the tort-feasor from any other source is fatal to the assignee's cause of action.

We will encounter this situation most frequently in connection with claims for property damage to automobiles which are covered by collision policies. If the collision carrier pays for its portion of the property damage loss, and the insurer of the tort-feasor has notice or knowledge of such payment, any settlement with the property damage claimant must be made in contemplation of the subrogation right of the collision carrier, and the release given by the property damage claimant will release only that portion of the claim which has not been assigned or subrogated to the collision carrier. On the other hand, if the insurer of the tort-feasor has no notice or knowledge of the payment by the collision carrier and the assignment to it, a release given by the property damage claimant will extinguish the entire claim.

It is true that the collision policy obligates the insured to protect the rights of the insurance carrier with regard to subrogation and to do nothing to prejudice its rights against the wrongdoer. Where there is no knowledge or notice on the part of the wrongdoer or his insurer of the payment by the collision carrier, they are under no duty to respect the assignment. Should a release be given by the property damage claimant (the insured under the collision policy) to the wrongdoer, it will effectively extinguish the claim and foreclose the rights of his collision carrier. In such a situation the collision carrier would have a cause of action against its insured for restitution of the money it paid, but the wrongdoer would neither be a party to such action nor responsible for any payment required. To repeat, where the wrongdoer or his insurance carrier has notice or knowledge of a right of subrogation or assignment, they are bound to respect the rights of the subrogee or assignee, and any settlement with the former owner of the cause of action is made with the property damage claimant by the wrongdoer or his insurance carrier at their peril. The release will extinguish only the rights which the property damage claimant still possesses. If the wrongdoer or his insurance carrier have no notice or knowledge of a right of subrogation or an assignment, and make a settlement with the claimant, such settlement effectively extinguishes all claims.

Where the wrongdoer or his insurance carrier has knowledge or notice of a subrogation right on the part of the collision carrier, they may still make a settlement with the property damage to cover his deductible and also his personal injuries, if any. Such a settlement would not extinguish the rights of the subrogee or assignee, but a release given by the claimant will effectively extinguish any rights or claims which he might have against the wrongdoer. A release can be given by the claimant, which will not prejudice the rights of his collision carrier, by adding to the release: "It is understood and agreed that this release does not prejudice the subrogation claim of my collision insurance carrier above my \$_____ deductible." The inclusion of this paragraph, or one of similar wording, will enable the claimant to settle his claim without violating his insurance contract with the collision carrier.

2127   Execution of the release

Printed release forms are used by all insurance carriers. All the adjuster has to do is to fill in the blank spaces properly and obtain the signature or signatures of the claimant or claimants. In accordance with the agreement with the American Bar Association, filling in the blank spaces on a release prepared by the legal department of the insurance carrier does not constitute the practice of law. [See "Statement of Principles on Respective Rights and Duties of Lawyers and Laymen" in *The Business of Adjusting Insurance Claims,* para. 5 (g).]

The printed general release forms are so worded that they can be used either in the singular or plural, depending upon whether the release is being executed by one person or more than one. In some cases it may be desirable to take a special form of release because of special circumstances. These special release forms should be prepared by the company's legal department or attorney.

The general release form has a blank space where the name or names of the persons released can be inserted. It is important that the adjuster include the names of every person (or firm, or corporation) entitled to the insurance protection of the policy so that the release will discharge and release any and all claims against them. It does not matter that the possibility of a claim against any of them is remote or unidentifiable. If they are entitled to the protection of the policy as additional insureds and they are concerned in the accident, however remotely, they should be named as releasees.

The release should be signed by the releasor, and the releasor's acknowledgment should be taken by a notary if possible. In small cases, the releasor's signature, witnessed by another person who saw him sign it, will be acceptable. If no one else is present the adjuster may sign as a witness. The reason for all this is that if it should become necessary at a later date to prove the release, one taken before a notary will be the easiest to prove—should the claimant deny he executed the instrument. Where his signature has been witnessed by another person it is best to obtain the address of such person, so that if it should become necessary to prove the release the witness can be easily located. Where the adjuster signs the release he, likewise, can be used as a witness to the event. However his testimony is not as effective as that of a notary or a disinterested witness.

The rule followed by most companies is that where the claim involves a substantial payment, or where the injuries are such that the results of the treatment are unknown, or where there is any possibility of future litigation because of a recurrence or aggravation of the condition, or for any other cause, the release should be notarized. In all other cases witnesses who saw the release signed, or the adjuster, are acceptable as witnesses to the document.

Since a release may have to be offered in evidence, the name of the insurance carrier should never appear as a releasee (except in Louisiana and Wisconsin where state statutes permit an action against the insurer), either alone or in connection with an action against the insured. Likewise there should be no notations made on the document, such as a company date stamp or comments of the supervisor, and there should be no alterations or erasures. If the adjuster has made a mistake in spelling, or any other error, it is better to use another form, rather than to correct the form by a strikeover or an erasure.

2128   Releases by individuals

The release by an individual should be signed by the releasor signing his name in full, his first name, middle initial, and last name. If he has no middle initial or normally signs his name by the use of his initials only, then it is acceptable to have him omit the middle initial (which he does not have) or to use his initials only. The reason it is better to have him sign his full name is that it makes identification easier to prove against a denial of the execution of the document. Married women must sign the releases with their given names, such as Mary Jones and not Mrs. John Jones. If for any reason it is necessary to identify her as a married person, and to have her release not only a claim which she has personally but also one which she owns as a result of her relationship to her husband, the release should show as the releasor, "Mary Jones, Individually, and as the wife of John Jones." This release should then be signed merely "Mary Jones."

The printed release forms recite that the releasor is over the age of 21 or of legal age. If there is any doubt in the adjuster's mind whether or not the releasor is of legal age, he should make inquiry and, if necessary, have the releasor present some proof of age. If the release is presented to the adjuster by the releasor's attorney, it is not necessary for him to make this inquiry. He can rely on the presenting of the release by the attorney as including a warranty that the release is legally executed.

Where the wife is injured, all states recognize the husband's cause of action for loss of consortium. Therefore, when a claim is settled with a married woman it is necessary that both husband and wife join in the release so that both causes of action may be extinguished at one and the same time. The wife can release her claim for her injury but not her husband's claim for the loss of her services and the medical expenses which she incurred and for which he alone is responsible. A release by the wife alone will then only release one part of the claim. A release from husband and wife should read "We, Mary Jones and John Jones, husband and wife," or "We, Mary Jones and John Jones, living together as husband and wife." The release should be signed by both.

If a release were taken only from the married woman herself, it will release only her claim, and it is possible that the husband would bring an action for loss of services and medical expenses. Therefore, as we have noted above, the release must be taken from both. But there are cases in which this is not possible because the injured claims that one of the three following situations exist:

1. She is either divorced or separated from her husband.
2. Her husband is serving in the Armed Forces.
3. Her husband is absent from home on business but is expected to return.

1. *Divorced or separated.* An absolute divorce terminates the marriage and ends any marital rights which either party may have. Therefore where there has been an absolute divorce the divorced husband has no further right to his wife's services nor is he responsible for her medical attention. He, therefore, has no cause of action for loss of consortium in the event of her injury. Where the adjuster is dealing with a divorced woman he should note the fact of her divorce, and when and where it was obtained, in her statement. Then after settlement, if a claim is made by the former husband, the record of divorce can be readily located. These cases can be settled with the divorced woman as if she were single, which she legally is.

In the case of separation, called a limited divorce in some states, the same situation will prevail. Where the parties are separated, either by agreement or by a court decree, the husband has no further right to her services nor is he responsible for her medical expenses. In such cases the woman usually has a copy of the separation agreement or the decree which can be examined, or she can tell the adjuster the name and address of her attorney who will have a copy of the papers. In case of doubt, or an overabundance of caution, the adjuster can check these things out. In any event, these cases can be settled with the claimant, and a release from her alone will extinguish the entire claim.

2. *Husband in the Armed Forces.* Where the husband enters the service he usually, on recommendation of his attorney or the armed force itself, provides his wife with a power of attorney, enabling her to transact the family business in his absence. Under this power of attorney she can release the husband's claim. It is best for the adjuster to make a copy of the power of attorney for the file. When this is done, the claim can be settled and the release signed by the wife alone. The releasor will be shown as "Mary Jones, for myself, and for and behalf of my husband, John Jones, by virtue of the power invested in me by the power of attorney, dated _____ 19__ executed by my husband, John Jones."

3. Husband absent.   Handling this situation will require the exercise of judgment. The safest procedure would be to maintain control of the injured wife until the husband returns and the claim can be discharged by a settlement with both. If the adjuster is anxious to settle the case, and feels that he will lose it to an attorney if payment is not made, then he may take an individual release from the wife and leave a joint release with her to be executed by both her husband and herself. It is clear that in following this method the adjuster is taking a calculated risk that the husband will refuse to sign the release, but in most cases he will do so. Upon the execution of the individual release by the wife, payment should be made. Most people will feel that, since the adjuster has shown his good faith in making the payment, they are morally bound to execute the documents he requests.

Where the husband is injured, some states recognize a cause of action by the wife for loss of consortium and follow the Hitaffer rule [*Hitaffer* v. *Argonne Products*, 183 Fed. 2d 811]. Other states have considered the question and have rejected the rule, and still others have not considered the question at all. If there is any doubt in the adjuster's mind, or if the state in which the accident occurred has not passed on the question, it is recommended that a joint release be obtained. In such a case, the releasors should be described as "We, John Jones and Mary Jones, husband and wife," or "We, Mary Jones, as wife of John Jones, and John Jones, individually . . ." In either case, the intent is plain that the claim being released is that of John Jones and any claim that Mary Jones may have as the wife of John Jones.

It sometimes happens that both the husband and wife are injured in the same accident and it is necessary to settle the personal injury claims of both. A joint release should be taken because, in the case of the wife, in all states, the husband has a cause of action for the loss of consortium in addition to the wife's claim for personal injury. In the case of the husband's injury, in some states only he has a cause of action, and in others the wife has an additional claim for loss of consortium. The joint release should show the releasors to be, "We, Mary Jones, individually and as wife of John Jones, and John Jones, individually, and as husband of Mary Jones . . ." This wording would take care of a situation where there are claims for loss of consortium on the part of each for the injury to the other.

Where the state has considered the Hitaffer rule and rejected it, the releasors can be described as, "We, Mary Jones and John Jones, individually, and as husband of Mary Jones . . ." Here the wording covers the individual claims of both Mary and John, and also releases only John Jones's claim for loss of consortium.

In all cases where the individual or individuals sign the release in other than an individual capacity, the signature should be followed by the same description as appears in the release itself. For example, in the preceding case Mary Jones would simply sign as "Mary Jones," since she is releasing only her individual claim and the release is given by her only in her individual capacity. John Jones would sign the release with his name, followed by a description of the capacity in which he is signing, namely "John Jones, individually and as husband of Mary Jones."

Some individuals operate their private businesses under a trade name, even though it is entirely owned by one person. Where it is advisable to settle a property damage or other claim involving the business, it is sometimes advisable to indicate on the release that the claim being discharged covers not only the claim by the individual but the claim of the business itself. Therefore, the releasor will be named as "John Jones, individually and as owner of the Colonial Cleaners," and his signature on the release will be followed by the same descriptive words. A variation of this could be used by having the releasor described as the Colonial Cleaners, and the release could be signed "Colonial Cleaners, by John Jones, sole owner." This type of handling refers only to businesses solely owned by one individual. It does not refer to partnerships or corporations, even though all of the stock of the corporation is owned by the individual and his family.

2129   Releases by or in behalf of infants

An infant is a person who has not attained full legal age. In most states, this age is 21 years, and 18 in others. The infant attains his full legal age on the day before his 21st, or 18th, birthday, as the case may be, and from that day forward can execute a complete and binding release even though the accident may have occurred during his minority. In some states, where the infant is legally married, both the husband and wife are considered *sui juris* and capable of doing legal acts in their own behalf. With this exception, the infant during minority is under a legal disability and cannot give an effective legal release as far as claims for personal injury and property damage are concerned. In some states, a contract made by a minor, under these circumstances, is considered voidable at the option of the minor, while others regard the minor's contract as totally void. Therefore, in either case, a release given by the minor would afford the defendant little or no protection.

At common law, the father was entitled to the wages and services of an unemancipated minor child. He was likewise responsible for the support and maintenance of the child. This latter responsibility includes such medical attention as the child might require, whether as the result of an accident or otherwise. Where there has been an accident resulting in personal injuries to the minor child, the father has lost the services of the child and, in addition, has had to assume the responsibility for medical expenses and other items needed for the care of the child's injury. At common law, and today, the father has an independent cause of action for the loss of services of the infant. Therefore, when settling cases involving injuries to a minor, there are two causes of action which must be extinguished: first, the claim by the minor for his injuries, including pain and suffering and permanency, if any, and second, the claim for medical expense and loss of services by the father.

Since the minor is under a legal disability and cannot act for himself, someone of legal age must act for him. As to the father's claim, the father himself can give a binding release. In cases involving small settlements a practice has grown whereby a release is taken from the father to cover both claims. The father as the releasor will be described as "We, John Jones, a minor, by Thomas Jones, individually and as father and next friend of said John Jones." The release then will be signed only by the father, with the same descriptive words following his signature, "Individually and as father and next friend of John Jones, a minor." This will effectively release the claim of the father for the loss of the infant's services. It will not effectively extinguish the claim of the minor for his injury. The procedure is used only on small cases where it is unlikely that any further claim will be made for or in behalf of the minor child. While it does not have any binding force legally, it is used nevertheless for psychological reasons, and in most cases, barring any un-anticipated physical complication as far as the minor is concerned, no further claim will be made. It should not be used in major cases or those where there are possibilities of future premanency or recurrences of the injury. Such cases should be settled only by means of a court-approved settlement or a friendly suit, which ever the local practice dictates.

Since the release taken under these circumstances is not binding, it is customary to take a "no injury" statement from the father in addition to the release. This statement will indicate that the infant has fully recovered from the effects of the injury, has returned to his normal school activity or normal play activity, and that he exhibited no evidence of the injury at the time the statement was taken. Also included should be the fact either that no medical treatment was required or that it consisted of several treatments and that the treatment has been concluded. A medical certificate or report from the attending physician might also be secured, indicating the trivial nature of the condition and that the patient was discharged as cured with no residual defects.

It is well to reemphasize that this procedure will not result in a binding release of the infant's claim, but will effectively extinguish the father's cause of action for loss of services. Therefore most companies restrict the use of this procedure to cases involving the payment of $100 or less on the theory that cases of that size do not justify the expense of a court-approved settlement. There is a calculated risk that the case may result in a further claim, but the amount involved, plus the "no injury" statement and the medical certificate, reduce the risk to the minimum.

It is to be noted that at common law, the father was the head of the family and the one to whom the cause of action for loss of services accrues. Where the minor's mother is a widow, she then is the head of the household and succeeds to the rights which the father had. In such cases, the same treatment can be accorded, with the mother substituted for the father in the release. The same thing is true if the mother is divorced and has custody of the minor. She is the one who is then entitled to the minor's services and can enforce the cause of action.

In the case of adopted children, the "father" has the same rights and obligations as if the children were his natural issue. The natural father of the adopted children has no rights whatsoever.

In the case of an illegitimate child, the mother is the only parent recognized by the law. She alone is entitled to the services of the child and has the obligation of providing medical treatment and maintenance for him. She then is the one who can bring the action for medical expense and loss of services. This is true even though the putative father is furnishing support for the child under a court order to do so.

An emancipated child is one who has been freed from the power and authority of the family. This usually comes about by means of an agreement between the child and his parents (father) that the child, able to care for himself, may go out from his home and make his own living, receive his own wages, and spend them as he pleases. The result is that the parent has made an entire surrender of the care, custody, and earnings of the child, as well as a complete renunciation of his parental duties. In most states, the marriage of a child with the parent's consent, if the marriage is sanctioned by law, is construed to be a complete emancipation. Since the parent no longer has any obligation to care for the child and no right to the services and earnings of an emancipated child, in the case of injury to the child, the parent has no cause of action for either the medical expense or for the loss of the child's services.

While the emancipation of the child divests the parents of their interests, the fact of emancipation does not give the infant legal status to contract. His contracts are still subject to the disabilities of infancy, and may be avoided or disaffirmed by the infant. Therefore, the settlement of a personal injury claim with an emancipated infant is subject to the same procedure which would be followed in connection with a settlement with any infant.

2130 Indemnifying releases by the parents

Where a minor has sustained relatively trivial injuries, instead of following the procedure outlined in the preceding paragraph, some companies use a special form of release and indemnifying agreement. This agreement purports to release the claim of the parent for care and loss of services, and also the minor's claim for injuries, but in addition it contains an agreement by the parent that in the case of a claim by the minor, he (the parent) will indemnify the releasee from any loss so sustained. This type of agreement reads as follows:

Whereas on or about the 1st day of November, 1975, an accident occurred at or near Main and Mulberry Streets, Anytown, Anystate, resulting in bodily injury to John Jones, Jr., a minor 10 years of age, and Whereas, the undersigned parents and natural guardians of said minor, parties of the first part, have made a claim upon Joseph Smith, party of the second part, for money compensation for such injury, asserting that the said party of the second part is legally liable for said accident and injury, which said legal liability the said party of the second part expressly denies.

Now, THEREFORE, the said parties of the first part do hereby acknowledge receipt of the sum of Twenty-Five and no/100 ($25.00) dollars, in hand paid by the said party of the second part, and in consideration thereof, in full accord and satisfaction of such disputed claim, the said parties of the first part, acting for said minor and in their own right, do hereby remise, release and forever discharge the said party of the second part, his heirs, successors, administrators and assigns and all other persons, firms or corporations who are or might be liable, from any and all actions, causes of action, claims and demands, for, upon or by reason of any damage, loss, suffering or injury to person and/or property, whether developed or undeveloped, which heretofore has been or which hereafter may be sustained by the said minor and/or by the said parties of the first part including all claims for loss of services and expenses in consequence of such accident and injury.

AND FURTHERMORE, the said parties of the first part do hereby expressly stipulate and agree, in consideration of the aforesaid payment, to indemnify and hold forever harmless the said party of the second part against loss from any further claims, demands or actions that may hereafter, or at any time, be made or brought against the said party of the second part by said minor, or by any one on behalf of said minor or the party of the first part for the purpose of enforcing a further claim for damages on account of the injuries sustained in consequence of the aforesaid accident.

It is understood and agreed that the parties of the first part rely wholly upon their own judgment, belief and knowledge of the nature, extent and duration of said injuries and that no representations or statements regarding said injuries or regarding any other matters made by the party of the second part or by any person or persons representing him or them or by any physician or surgeon by him or them employed has influenced the first parties to any extent whatever in making this release.

All agreements and understandings between the parties hereto are embodied and expressed herein and the terms of this release are contractual and not a mere recital.

IN WITNESS WHEREOF, we have hereunto set our hands and seals this 20th day of November, 1975.

> /s/ Mary Jones
>   (Mother)
> /s/ John Jones
>   (Father)

Signed, Sealed and delivered
in the presence of
Mary Smith
20 Main Street, Anytown, Anystate
Peter Smith
20 Main Street, Anytown, Anystate

This type of agreement is intended to be a general release of both the parent's and the infant's claims and, in addition, contains an affirmative agreement by the parent to indemnify and hold harmless the defendant against all loss occasioned by any action subsequently brought by or on behalf of the infant. It is generally agreed that while the parent cannot effectively release the infant's claim by this means, he can release his own claim. The legal effect of the indemnity agreement is open to question. It has not been considered in many cases.

In *Valdimer* v. *Mount Vernon Hebrew Camps* (195 N.Y.S. 2d 24), the infant sustained injuries at a summer camp operated by the defendant. The parent negotiated a settlement and signed the parent's release and indemnity agreement. In an action brought by the parent individually and as guardian *ad litem* of the infant, the granting of a motion to strike from the answer a counterclaim against the parent, based on the indemnity agreement, raised the issue of the validity of the agreement. The court held that the agreement was void since it was against public policy.

The court observed that "to uphold such agreements would effectively frustrate the purpose of requiring judicial approval (of infants' settlements), since a parent who has placed himself in the position of an indemnitor will be a dubious champion of his infant child's rights." The court further characterized the transaction as one in which "the indemnitor and the indemnitee have attempted to circumvent a procedure designed for the safety of the child, a procedure established on the theory that no one but a court can bind an infant to a contract settling a claim for the negligent infliction of personal injuries." [See also *Loesch* v. *Vassiliades*, 17 N.J. Super 306; and *Ohio Casualty Co.* v. *Mallison*, 354 Pac. 2d 800 (Oregon).]

In other states, the question is apparently still an open one at this time and it is doubtful as to the view that will be taken. The courts could conceivably follow the decision in the New York case and hold the indemnity agreement to be contrary to public policy and void, or they could hold that the indemnity agreement is valid since it binds only the parent and does not affect the rights of the infant.

2131 Guardianship proceedings and friendly suits

While the procedure used for settling infants' claims differs from state to state, the fundamental principle is the same. An infant's claim can be effectively released only by means of a court-approved settlement. The matter is submitted to the court in accordance with the rules of court of the state, and they might take the form of a guardianship proceeding or a friendly suit. In either case, both sides are usually represented by counsel. The court will be advised of the details of the settlement and will decide whether or not it is in the best interests of the infant that the settlement be made.

If the court decides against the acceptance of the settlement, the application will be denied, whereas if the court approves of the settlement, it will issue a judgment or order approving the settlement and the amount. Frequently, where large amounts are involved, the court will include in the order the person to whom the amount is to be paid and how the money is to be handled for the benefit of the infant. This sometimes takes the form of payment to a trustee who is ordered to invest the money for the infant and to disburse the funds only upon further order of the court. The defendant is bound to make the payment in accordance with the terms of the order to the person or persons designated therein.

2132   Nominal or no consideration releases

Where a person has been involved in an accident, he is a potential personal injury claimant even though he denies having sustained any injury. In such cases, some companies follow the practice of taking a release from such a possible claimant, reciting as consideration a nominal amount, such at $1 or $5, or reciting that the release is being given for no consideration at all. Such releases have no legal effect whatsoever and are taken for psychological reasons. The theory is that possible future claims are not likely to be pressed if the claimant persists in a belief that the claim has been released. There is, of course, the calculated risk that if anything of a serious nature develops, the claimant will seek legal advice and possibly make a claim. If that happens, the release will not afford the defendant very much protection, and in most cases the release will not be pleaded as a defense. Since this is a rare situation, it would seem that the nominal or no consideration release has a place in the handling of claims and, in an appropriate case, should be utilized.

2133   Releases by partnerships or corporations

A partnership is a joint business enterprise by two or more persons. It is created by a contract called a partnership agreement. Each partner, acting within the scope of the partnership business, is the agent of the other partners. Therefore where a release is required of a partnership, the instrument may be signed by any one of the partners and is binding on the partnership as a whole and upon each other partner individually. As a general rule, no one other than a partner has the authority to execute a release, so that in these matters the adjuster must be certain that he is taking a release from one of the partners. He should not be satisfied with a document signed by any other person, even if he alleges that he is the manager of the partnership enterprise. The partner signing the release will sign his name under the firm name as a partner. The releasor in the instrument will be the name of the partnership, whether it consists of the names of the partners or is a fictitious name. For example, if the partnership name is *Jones & Smith,* the releasor's name will be given as "Jones & Smith, a partnership," and the release will be signed "Jones & Smith, by John Jones, partner." Where the partnership uses a fictitious name, the same form may be used, such as "J & S Auto Parts, a partnership," and the release signed "J & S Auto Parts, by John Jones, partner."

A corporation is an artificial person, created by law, which can function only through agents. It is created by compliance with the corporation law of the state in which it is located. This compliance usually consists of the filing of the articles of incorporation and the payment of a fee to the secretary of state.

A corporation and only a corporation can use the designation "Inc." after the corporate name. The corporation is managed by a board of directors who may delegate certain duties of management to various officers and other officials.

Among these duties which can be delegated is the power to release claims which the corporation may have against others, and the power to execute the necessary documents as evidence thereof. When this power is delegated, there must be action by the board of directors and the action must be entered on the minutes of the directors' meeting. Therefore, when the adjuster takes a release from a corporation he must take it from the officer of the corporation who has the power to release claims and the power to execute the document. The releasor will be the corporation and the document will be signed by the corporate name, plus the name of the officer executing the document.

For example, the releasor in the body of the release will be the *ABC Corporation,* and the document will be signed "ABC Corporation, by John Jones, Secretary." The officer then will affix the corporate seal. Since all releases by a corporation must be notarized, the notary's jurat will read as follows:

On the 15th day of November, 1976, before me came John Jones, to me known, who, being by me duly sworn, did depose and say that he resides at 124 Main Street, in the city of Anytown, County of Anycounty, State of Anystate, that he is the Secretary of the ABC Corporation, the corporation described in, and which executed the foregoing instrument; that he knows the seal of the said corporation; that the seal affixed to said instrument is such corporate seal; that it was so affixed by order of the Board of Directors of said corporation and that he signed his name thereto by like order.

2134 Settlements: Survival and wrongful death

The survival statutes refer to the claim which the deceased had at the time of his death. It consists of the special damages which he sustained, together with compensation for conscious pain and suffering. The action for these damages is maintainable by the personal representative of the deceased. The personal representative can be one who was appointed by the deceased in his lifetime, such as the executor under his last will and testament, or if no such appointment has been made, the personal representative can be one who qualified as the administrator of the estate of the deceased and received such appointment from the surrogate's court. This latter court is designated in some states as a probate court, or a court of the ordinary, etc. In any case, it is the court which has jurisdiction over decedents' estates.

The personal representative is the person with whom the adjuster will settle, if settlement is indicated, and the settlement so made will be for the benefit of the heirs at law. Technically, the adjuster has only to deal with the personal representative and he is not concerned with the manner in which the proceeds of the settlement are distributed to the heirs. As a practical matter, the adjuster will be dealing with the heirs at law, and the settlement agreed upon will be one that they approve, and the personal representative will merely go through the legal motions which are necessary to close out the case. In the majority of cases, the adjuster will be confronted with a situation where the victim died intestate (without a will) and will be dealing with the heirs directly. The settlement will be agreed upon, and then one of the heirs will qualify as the personal representative of the deceased, and the settlement will be concluded with him. This requires a simple legal procedure in the probate court, but the proposed representative must be represented by counsel.

In some cases, the adjuster will agree that as part of the settlement the company will either provide counsel or pay for the reasonable counsel fees in connection with this proceeding. Where the heirs are represented by counsel, the adjuster should not make any agreement with respect to counsel fees unless it is to the company's advantage to do so. In the latter case, the adjuster will be dealing only with counsel, and the matter of attorney's fees is normally not a subject of settlement discussion. In an appropriate case, the adjuster could agree to add something to the settlement figure to take care of the attorney's fee, but in no case should the adjuster agree to pay the counsel fee to the attorney for the heirs directly. The reason behind this procedure is that the attorney cannot serve adverse interests. If he is representing one party, and is paid by the adverse party, there may be some question of ethics involved; but more importantly, the settlement may be opened to attack should the heirs ever seek to set it aside.

In a survival action, the measure of damages will be the amounts which the deceased could have recovered from the defendant had he lived. This would include his out-of-pocket expenses, such as medical, hospital, and surgical bills, property damage, loss of earning capacity, and, in addition, the value of his conscious pain and suffering. These damages will be measured by the deceased's lifetime and will not include any expenses which were incurred after his death, such as funeral expenses, etc. To put it another way, the cause of action here is one which the deceased could have brought had he lived, and, therefore, the recovery is limited only to those items which the deceased could have claimed and no others. He never had a claim for his funeral expenses during his lifetime since those expenses were not incurred. Therefore, as to the items which can be claimed in a survival action, if the deceased could have recovered for them had he lived, they are recoverable; otherwise they are not.

In a survival action it should be emphasized that the cause of the deceased's death has no bearing on the existence of the cause of action. The survival action may be maintained if the deceased had a cause of action at his death. If he dies from causes other than the injury, the action still may be maintained. However, if the deceased did not have a cause of action at his death, then there is no action which can survive. This might come about where the deceased released the claim during his lifetime, or the case was tried and resulted in a verdict which was satisfied or a verdict for the defendant, or the claim was barred by the trolling for the statute of limitations. The survival action does not arise unless the deceased had a cause of action which he could have maintained at the time of his death.

The same defenses which could have been interposed against the deceased can be interposed against the personal representative in the survival action. These include contributory negligence, assumption of risk, unavoidable accident, act of God, etc. Also, the personal representative is bound by the statute of limitations in exactly the same way as the deceased, so that the survival action must be brought within the period of limitation applicable to the original cause of action.

For example, let us assume that the statute of limitations for personal injury is two years. One year, 11 months, and 29 days after the accident, the claimant dies. No action has been begun during the two-year period. In such a case, the personal representative has only one day left within which to bring the survival action. If he fails to do so, the action is barred by the running of the statute. On the other hand, if the deceased had started an action during his lifetime and prior to the running of the statute, the survival action is not barred, irrespective of when the claimant died, since the personal representative may be substituted for the plaintiff in the pending action and the case can then proceed to trial in its usual course.

Therefore, the personal representative succeeds only to the rights which the deceased himself had, and if the deceased had released the claim during his lifetime there would be no action which he could have brought had he lived, and therefore there was no claim to survive to the personal representative. Also, all defenses which were available against the deceased, had he lived, are available against his personal representative. All the survival statute does is transfer any cause of action which the decreased may have had at his death to his personal representative, who may prosecute the action in the place and stead of the deceased. The statute does not in any way enlarge the cause of action and extend the statute of limitations. The statute of limitations applicable to the cause of action is binding on the personal representative just as it was on the deceased, and it makes no difference if the statute ran during the period between the date of death and the appointment of the personal representative.

Again, it should be emphasized that the intent of the statute is merely to transfer the rights of the deceased to his personal representative and to permit the personal representative to bring the action in the place of the deceased. The cause of the deceased's death has no bearing on the existence of the survival action. The test is whether or not the deceased had an actionable claim at the time of his death.

Where the adjuster is dealing with the heirs directly, there is no reason why a settlement cannot be made, even where the state law requires the appointment of an administrator of the estate. If the heirs can agree on the person (usually one of their number) who will qualify as administrator or executor (if so named in the deceased's will), the adjuster can settle the case then, taking from the proposed administrator a release, signed by him as administrator, and to show his good faith the adjuster can turn over a draft to the administrator for the amount recited as the consideration in the release. The draft will be drawn to the order of the administrator and not to him personally.

For example, if the proposed administrator was John Jones, the draft would be drawn to the order of "John Jones, as Administrator of the Estate of Henry Jones, Deceased." This draft must be endorsed as drawn and John Jones cannot cash it until he can establish that he is the administrator. Therefore all John Jones has to do to be able to secure the money is to qualify as the administrator and dispose of the money in accordance with the order of the surrogate. The adjuster has no concern with respect to the distribution of the money. He is only concerned with obtaining a binding release. When the person qualifies as the administrator, the settlement is approved, and the draft properly cashed, the adjuster's task is at an end.

In some states, a settlement can be made with the heirs at law directly, without any reference to a personal representative. Where this procedure is permissible, it is suggested that the final papers be prepared by counsel.

In the survival action, we are concerned only with the claim which a decreased had in his lifetime and the procedure required by the statute in order to recover for the deceased's claim. The survival action is a modification of the common-law rule that a man's cause of action for personal injuries dies with him, and merely permits the action to continue with the personal representative taking the place of the deceased.

Where the death of the deceased is caused by the wrongful act of the defendant, the deceased himself never owned a cause of action for his own wrongful death, and, both at common law and under our law today, since such a cause of action does not exist, it does not survive to the personal representative of the deceased. Therefore any action for wrongful death is separate and distinct from any claim that the decreased might have had during his lifetime, and the survival statutes have no relationship whatsoever to that cause of action.

At common law, there was no recovery by the persons who sustained damages as a result of the wrongful death of another person upon whom they were dependent for support or from whom they could reasonably expect to receive some gifts during his lifetime and to receive a final gift in the form of a testamentary bequest at the time of his death. At common law, these persons were considered strangers to the cause of action arising from the accident, since they were not directly involved, and, from the defendant's standpoint, he owed no duty of care to persons who were not even present at the time and place of the accident. Therefore, when the English Parliament passed the Fatal Accidents Act (usually referred to as Lord Campbell's Act), they created a new cause of action which never existed before. It gave to persons who sustained a pecuniary loss due to the wrongful death of the decedent a right of recovery to the extent of the loss which they had suffered because of the death of their benefactor. This cause of action was created solely by the statute, solely for the benefit of the persons defined in the statute, and has no relationship to any other cause of action which the deceased may have had during his lifetime, which cause of action may have been asserted under the survival statutes by the deceased's representative.

The action for wrongful death is another and further action, owned by the persons for whose benefit the statute was passed, and the settlement of a cause of action which survived the deceased's death will have no influence one way or the other on the existence or the prosecution of the action for wrongful death. Nor is the existence of the wrongful death action dependent upon whether or not the survival action is brought. It could happen that the deceased had a cause of action at his death, and his personal representative either never brought the action, or permitted the statute of limitations to run against it. In neither case would the cause of action for wrongful death be affected in any way.

The action for wrongful death exists solely because of the statute and is for the benefit only of those persons who are defined in the statute. For the cause of action to exist, it must meet the requirements of the statute. While more state statutes vary as to the amount of damages recoverable and as to the basis of recovery, whether it be pecuniary loss or degree of culpability, there is some agreement as to the basic criteria which must be met before the cause of action comes into existence. These qualifications usually are as follows:

When the death of a person is caused by the wrongful act, neglect, or default, such as would, if death had not ensued, have entitled the person injured to maintain an action for damages resulting from the injury, the person who would have been liable in damages for the injury, if death had not ensued, shall be liable in an action for damages, notwithstanding the death of the person injured . . .

Before the wrongful death action can come into existence, two elements must be present: (1) liability, and (2) a maintainable cause of action for personal injury by the deceased at the time of his death.

Liability.   The accident and the death must have been caused by the "wrongful act, neglect or default" of the person sought to be charged, committed under circumstances which would have permitted the deceased to maintain an action for personal injuries had he lived. This means that the circumstances must create a responsibility on the part of the defendant, and that the same criteria for judging the deceased's personal injury action if he had lived would be applied to the wrongful death claim. If the deceased could not have recovered because of his contributory negligence, assumption of risk, or because the accident was not due to the wrongful act, neglect, or default of the defendant, then the wrongful death action must fail.

A maintainable cause of action.   If for any reason, at the time of the deceased's death, he could not have maintained a cause of action for personal injury, then there is no wrongful death action maintainable. For example, if the deceased during his lifetime released the claim, then he did not have a cause of action at the time of his death and would not have been entitled to maintain an action for personal injuries had he lived. In that case, the requirements of the statute could not be met. If the deceased had brought a cause of action against the defendant, and the case resulted in a judgment for the defendant, or a judgment for the plaintiff which had been satisfied, he would not have been entitled to maintain a cause of action for personal injuries at the time of his death and, likewise, the requirements of the statute could not be met. The same thing would be true if the statute of limitations had run against the claim before the deceased's death. Therefore, the test as to whether or not the second requirement of the statute can be met is whether or not the deceased could have maintained an action for personal injuries if death had not ensued. If he could have done so, then the statute has been met. If he could not, there is no cause of action for wrongful death.

When the first two requirements are met, the action may be brought, but it may be brought only within the time limited in the statute and in the manner which the statute prescribes. The general provision is similar to the following:

Every action . . . shall be brought in the name of the administrator ad prosequendum of the decedent . . . except where the decedent dies testate and his will is probated, in which event the executor named in the will . . . shall bring the action. Every action . . . shall be commenced within two years after the death of the decedent and not thereafter.

This section of the statute provides for the method of bringing the action in the name of the administrator *ad prosequendum* or the executor named in the will. While it is true that either of these persons is merely a nominal plaintiff, the fact remains that no other person may bring the action. In addition, the action is barred if the action is not begun within two years after the death of the decedent.

It should be noted that the statute has no reference whatsoever to the date of the accident. If the action is brought within two years of the date of the death of the decedent, it is timely. It should be emphasized, however, that the first two requirements must be met even before the action is maintainable. This means that there must have been a cause of action, based on the negligence of the defendant, which the deceased could have asserted if death had not ensued. If those two elements are present, the action may be brought by the administrator *ad prosequendum* or the executor, but such action must be brought within two years of the death of the decedent.

While the action is brought by a nominal plaintiff, namely the administrator or executor, it is brought for the benefit of certain persons. The statute may name the persons and their relationship to the deceased, or it may designate the beneficiaries of the action by reference to the state laws of descent and distribution. The following is the latter type:

The amount recovered in proceedings under this chapter shall be for the exclusive benefit of the persons entitled to take any intestate personal property of the decedent in the proportions in which they are entitled to take the same.

This means that the beneficiaries of the action are the same persons who would be entitled to take the deceased's personal property if he had died without a will. Reference then would have to be had to the state statutes to determine who these people are, but it should be emphasized that the statute is a modification of the common law and is construed only by a strict interpretation of its language. The persons for whose benefit the action was created are those mentioned in the statute or those included by reference to other statutes, but no others.

Most of the statutes which are patterned after Lord Campbell's Act base the measure of damages on the pecuniary loss sustained by the persons for whose benefit the action may be brought. Therefore, the identity of such persons and the extent of their pecuniary loss will determine the settlement or verdict value. The adjuster will have to be familiar with the applicable wrongful death statute in all these cases, as well as the persons for whose benefit the action may be brought and the measure of their damages. Merely because a person has sustained a pecuniary loss through the death of the decedent is not enough to create a cause of action in his favor. He must also be within the class of persons for whom the statute created the cause of action.

For example, the statute may identify the beneficiaries by reference to the laws of descent and distribution, as was the situation in the statute above quoted. In such laws the usual provision is that a surviving wife will take all of the deceased's personal property. If there is a surviving wife and child or children, the wife will be entitled to one third and the child or children two thirds of the personal property. Where either of these two situations obtain, the beneficiaries are limited to the wife, or the wife and child or children, to the exclusion of any other relatives, even though such relatives actually did sustain some pecuniary loss by reason of the death.

Another example: if a decedent left a surviving wife, she would be the only beneficiary, and even though he supported his parents or his brothers and sisters, none of them would have a cause of action even though they had sustained a pecuniary loss. The same would be true of an illegitimate child. Unless the decedent was the mother, the illegitimate child would not be entitled to any part of the personal property of its intestate father, even though the father was under a court order to support the illegitimate child. The child has unquestionably sustained a pecuniary loss, but the statute does not create a cause of action for his benefit.

When the adjuster has reached the point where he feels that settlement discussions are in order, he must be certain that the persons with whom he is dealing are those for whose benefit a recovery can be had. For example, if the beneficiaries are the wife and the child of the deceased, he must be certain that she is a legitimate wife—that she did not attain that title by means of a bigamous marriage or a so-called common-law marriage contracted in and carried on in a jurisdiction which does not recognize common-law marriages as legal. The same would be true as to the child; he must secure copies of the birth certificate and the marriage certificate. Also, where there is a bigamous marriage, the usual pattern is that some other collateral relative will seek a settlement and will supply the information that the so-called "wife" is not a legitimate wife at all. In most cases, however, a copy of the marriage certificate and the widow's statement that neither she nor her husband had been married before is sufficient—in the absence of any other information which may be voluntarily supplied by others.

The settlement can be made with the beneficiary and a draft may be made payable to whoever will qualify as the administrator in return for a release. The draft will be drawn to the order of the administrator and the release will be signed by him (or her) as administrator. The draft cannot be cashed if it is properly drawn to the administrator until that person qualifies. When that happens, another release can be signed, if it is needed.

For example, if we assume that the adjuster is dealing with Mary Jones, the widow of John Jones, he can explain to her that she must qualify as administratrix *ad prosequendum* of the estate. She will sign the release in such capacity, and the adjuster, in order to show good faith, will draw a draft to "Mary Jones, Administratrix of the Estate of John Jones, Deceased."

2135   Settlements by joint tort-feasors

It frequently happens that the insured is one of two or more joint tort-feasors, all of whom are responsible for the accident. If the representatives of all the joint tort-feasors are in agreement that the case should be settled and the amount needed in settlement will be shared equally, then one adjuster can handle the settlement for the entire group and, if the case is settled, will obtain a copy of the release for all defendants. The releasees will include the names of all joint tort-feasors. In such a situation it is best to have one adjuster speak for the group rather than to have all tort-feasors represented at the settlement conference, but if it cannot be avoided there can be a conference at which all representatives are in attendance.

Unfortunately, where there are joint tort-feasors, they seldom agree as to the extent of their liability and, as a consequence, one feels that the others should pay the major portion of the settlement with a small contribution from him. He may be motivated by the fact that he has low-policy limits (which are never disclosed) or that his investigation indicates a possibility that his insured will not be involved. In any case, each claim must stand on its own facts, and the attitude taken by the adjuster will depend on the extent of his exposure, whether it be on the issue of liability or the matter of low-policy limits.

2136   Covenants not to sue

It sometimes happens in a case where there are joint tort-feasors that one will be willing to settle his share of the case and the other will not. If the claimant is willing to settle with the one, with the understanding that the settlement will not prejudice his rights against the other tort-feasor, this can be accomplished by the use of the covenant not to sue. Should the claimant give a release to one of several joint tort-feasors, the general rule is that he has released the entire claim, and, in most states, the release of one releases all. Therefore, a release cannot be used. Instead, the covenant not to sue can be utilized. It is an agreement that the claimant will not sue the tort-feasor with whom the agreement is made. The cause of action against all the joint tort-feasors remains unchanged. The claimant has merely agreed with one of them that he, the claimant, will not sue him. Such an agreement usually reads as follows:

> FOR AND IN CONSIDERATION of the payment of the sum of Five Hundred Dollars ($500.00), receipt of which is hereby acknowledged, the undersigned, his heirs, administrators, executors and assigns hereby expressly covenants and agrees forever to refrain from bringing suit or proceeding at law or in equity against JOHN JONES, his agents or assigns, either severally or jointly with any other person, on account of, or in any way growing out of, any and all known and unknown personal injuries and property damage resulting or to result from an accident that occurred on or about the 15th day of November, 1963, at or near First and Main Streets, Anytown, Anystate.
>
> It is understood and agreed that this payment is the compromise of a doubtful and disputed claim, and is not to be construed to be an admission of liability on the part of JOHN JONES, by whom liability is expressly denied.
>
> It is further understood that this is a covenant not to sue as to the above mentioned parties and not a release.

In legal effect this instrument does not release the claim, even against John Jones. It does agree that the claimant will not sue John Jones on account of the accident and nothing more. Should the claimant sue John Jones on his claim, John Jones could counterclaim for breach of contract. The amount recoverable on the counterclaim would be exactly the same amount that could be recovered on the claim.

2137   The releasee

Normally the release should run to the insured as the releasee. Since the insurance company is not a party to the accident or occurrence, the name of the company should not appear on the release. In two states, Louisiana and Wisconsin, the insurance carrier can be named as a defendant in cases in litigation. Prior to litigation, a release running to the insured will effectively protect the insurance company. If the company is a named defendant and the lawsuit is settled, then the company should be included as a releasee.

Where more than one of the insureds is involved in the accident, even remotely, it is best to add the names as releases. For example, if A is driving B's car (with B's permission on A's business) when the accident happened, it is best to have the release run to both A and B.

2138   Open-end releases

It sometimes happens that the claimant is reluctant to settle his claim for fear that some medical condition may develop and he may have some further medical expense. If he settles the case, obviously he would have to absorb this expense himself. In order to terminate such a case, some companies utilize the open-end release by means of which payment is made for the known items of damage and as an additional consideration for the release, the releasee agrees to pay for reasonable medical expenses incurred within one year from the date of accident, provided that the treatment is rendered by a legally licensed physician or a legally constituted hospital. The form utilized for this purpose is designated as a "Medical Expense Agreement." The usual form is as follows:

FOR AND IN CONSIDERATION OF the payment to me/us of the sum of _____
_____ dollars (\$_____) and in further consideration of the promise to pay the following additional reasonable and necessary medical expenses incurred by me/us within one year from an occurrence on _____
_____ at or near _____ and directly resulting therefrom but only to the extent of my/our proportionate share of the statutory bodily injury financial/safety responsibility limits of \$_____
per person and \$_____ per occurrence, which amount shall be reduced by the payment received herewith.
Hospitals _____
Doctors _____
all of whom are expressly authorized to give to the bearer any information acquired by them while attending me/us in a professional capacity. I/we, being of lawful age, have released and discharged, and by these presents do for myself/ourselves, my/our heirs, executors, administrators and assigns, release, acquit and forever discharge the promisor(s) _____
and any and all other persons, firms, corporations of and from any and all actions, causes of actions, claims, demands, damages, costs, loss of service, expenses, compensation, and all consequential damage on account of, or in any way growing out of, any and all known and unknown personal injuries and death and property damage resulting or to result from the accident or occurrence above described.

Thus, by the use of this method of termination, not only does the company effectively close the case, but in the case of future complications, the intent of the agreement is to limit the recovery for future medical expense to the period of one year from the date of the accident or occurrence. Therefore, if the claimant required medical attention any time during the one-year period, the company or the insured would be liable for such expenses as were incurred during the one-year period and no more, this, even though the medical treatment continued beyond the year. On the other hand, if the necessity for medical treatment did not occur until after the one-year period had passed, there would be no liability for any payment.

2139   Advance payments

For many years the insurance companies followed a system whereby no payment, partial or otherwise, would be made of any claim unless it was in full settlement of the claim. It was made only in return for a general release extinguishing the claim. Such a system may have had its merits, but it did create an adversary relationship between the injured person and the company and, in addition, in serious injury cases it did have an adverse effect upon the injured person's rehabilitation. Therefore, in recent years many of the companies have adopted a system whereby in appropriate cases payments would be made to the injured person or his doctor and hospital as the need accrued with the understanding that the payments thus advanced would be credited to the insured or the insurer in the event of a settlement or judgment.

Advance payments are usually made for one or more of the following items:

1. Property damage sustained.
2. Medical bills as incurred.
3. Hospital bills as incurred.
4. Usual take-home pay or an amount which will be needed for current living expense.

Payments for these items as noted will be made periodically as required. When initiated, these payments will continue during the period of the injured person's disability and medical treatment and will continue even though the injured person subsequently retains an attorney.

Some companies require a receipt for each and every advance payment made. Since a receipt might read as follows:

RECEIPT FOR ADVANCE PAYMENT
(This is not a release)

This is to acknowledge receipt of $＿＿＿＿＿＿ paid on behalf of ＿＿＿＿＿＿
＿＿＿＿＿＿＿＿＿＿＿＿＿＿＿ to be credited to the total amount of any final settlement or judgment in my/our favor for alleged damages resulting from an accident on ＿＿＿＿＿＿＿＿ 19＿＿ at ＿＿＿＿＿＿＿＿＿＿＿.
I/We authorize the above sum to be distributed at follows: ＿＿＿＿＿＿＿＿

Date ＿＿＿＿＿＿

＿＿＿＿＿＿＿＿＿＿＿＿＿
Claimant

＿＿＿＿＿＿＿＿＿＿＿＿＿
Spouse

＿＿＿＿＿＿＿＿＿＿＿
Witness

＿＿＿＿＿＿＿＿＿＿＿
Witness

The majority of the companies merely make an oral agreement with the injured person which is confirmed by letter with respect to the kind and type of advance payments which will be made and when such payments will be made. This is usually confirmed by letter. When payments are made, the release form of endorsement common on most claim drafts is deleted and appropriate wording is inserted either on the face of the draft or on the reverse side explaining the payment, such as the following:

Advance allowance for hospital expenses from November 1st to November 30th, 1975.

Advance allowance for payment of Dr. Jones' bill for services rendered to date.

Reimbursement for salary loss from November 1st to November 30th, 1975.

Payment of repair costs to 1974 Chevrolet automobile.

If an attorney is employed by the injured person, and an advance payment agreement has been made, most companies will continue the advance payments through the attorney. Usually, a letter will be addressed to the attorney advising him of the fact that advance payments have been made and that they will continue so long as the claimant is disabled. Of course, the company could take the position that the employment of an attorney ends the advance payment procedure, but the company has more to gain by continuing the procedure.

Where the advance payment procedure is continued, the attorney has the problem of determining what his fee is to be. Surely, he cannot expect the client to pay a percentage of the money which has already been paid voluntarily as part of his fee. It would seem that his fee would be restricted to the amount that the attorney has been able to obtain through his efforts. However, this is a matter between the attorney and his client in which the claimsman can have no interest.

Advance payments as an admission.   Under the rules of evidence followed in most states, advance payments are not admissible in evidence on the question of liability nor is the fact that such payment has been made construed as an admission. Some states have adopted the Uniform Rules of Evidence (Section 52) which provides as follows:

(1) Evidence that a person has, in compromise or from humanitarian motives, furnished or promised to furnish money, or any other thing, act or service to another who has sustained or claimed to have sustained loss or damage, is inadmissible to prove his liability for the loss or damage or any part of it.

Even in states which have not as yet adopted the Uniform Rules of Evidence it is extremely doubtful that evidence of advance payments would be admissible. Certainly a voluntary payment made by a third party (the insurance company) would not be binding on the insured defendant. In the absence of a special agreement, the insurance company is not the agent of the insured for the purpose of admitting liability. Therefore the action of the insurance company could not be admitted in evidence to establish the liability of the insured.

Selection of advance payment cases.   All cases do not qualify for advance payment treatment. The use of this technique is usually restricted to cases involving clear liability and moderate to severe injuries. In doubtful liability cases, each case will have to be judged on its own merits and a decision made as to the pospects of successfully defending the claim.

Each company using the advance payment system has devised its own program for its utilization and the cases to which it will be applied. Some apply it to cases of minimum severity and others limit its use to severe injuries only and then only in clear liability cases.

Advance payments and the policy limits.   In considering the use of advance payments, the company must at all times be aware of the possible consequences to the insured. In a case where the policy limits are high and the prospects of any verdict approaching that figure, there is normally no problem. It is where the policy limits are low and the injuries severe that a question arises. The company has undertaken to indemnify and defend the insured up to the limits of the policy. If the company has undertaken advance payments and the amount paid reaches the policy limits, the problem arises as to the responsibility of the company to defend a subsequent lawsuit. In ordinary cases when the policy limits have been exhausted, there is no further obligation on the part of the company to defend or to assume the costs of defense. Therefore, if the advance payment technique is to be used in such cases, it can be adopted only where the insured is in agreement with the procedure. If the insured will not agree, the system cannot be used. The insured has every right to expect that the insurance company will meet all the terms of the insurance contract. There is nothing in the insurance contract that would permit advance payments to be made at the expense of the insured. Therefore, if the policy limits have been exhausted by means of advance payments, the insured may institute an action on the policy with a possible successful result.

Advance payment credit.   The understanding between the injured person and the company is that the company will be entitled to credit for all payments made in advance against any future settlement or judgment with respect to the claim. Where there is a settlement, no particular problem is encountered, since no final settlement will be made unless credit is given for the advance payments made. When the case proceeds to judgment, and credit for the payments made is thereafter sought, the question arises as to whether or not the fact of the advance payments should be offered in evidence by the defendant so that it might have some influence on the amount which the jury will award. In *Edwards* v. *Passarelli Bros.* [221 N.E. 2d 708 (Ohio)], the insurance carrier advanced $1,574.25 prior to the trial. The jury award was $10,000. The defendant paid the amount of the judgment and costs in full less the advance payments of $1,574.25. The defendant then sought a satisfaction of judgment on motion, basing its contention on the receipt for advance payments which the claimant had signed. On appeal, the court said:

. . . In essence, plaintiff is attempting to recover $11,574.25 from a $10,000.00 judgment.

Here plaintiff has received $1,574.25 from defendant's insurer and has signed a receipt therefor. The receipt is clear and unambiguous. It states that a certain sum has been paid on behalf of a named person for alleged damages resulting from a certain accident and that such sum is to be credited to any final settlement or judgment won by the receiver of such certain sum. These terms are self-explanatory. Should there be no final settlement or judgment, nothing remains to be done, and the receiver of such sum has benefitted by that amount. However, should a final settlement occur between the parties, or should the issue proceed through the courts to final judgment, then a sum equal to the advance payment is to be credited to such final settlement or judgment.

At the outset, we note that the very terms of the "Receipt for Advance Payment" create no right in defendant or his insurer until the existence of "any final settlement or judgment." This being so, defendant or his insurer has no existing right until the occurrence of such an event, and the provisions of the counterclaim statute, Section 2309.16, Revised Code, prohibits defendant from asserting any such right not already in existence at the time of trial of this cause. In short, defendant could not assert a right to credit for advance payments at the trial of this cause because prior to final judgment therein no such right existed. Thus, plaintiff's argument that the principle of res judicata controls defendant's attempt to obtain credit for advance payments has no application to the case at hand. Further, we note both that the insertion of such extraneous insurance matters would interfere with the trial and rules of evidence and that the terms of the agreement demonstrate that credit is to be applied to the judgment and not deducted from the verdict to arrive at the judgment. In view of this, defendant's only recourse is to assert his right to credit for advance payments after final judgment is rendered.

The court recognized that it would be a distinct advantage to the plaintiff if the defendant were required to introduce evidence of the advance payment agreement, whether it be in writing or the result of letters sent to the claimant. The jury no doubt would be influenced by the fact that an insurance company had voluntarily made the payments which would be taken into account in determining the issue of liability. In addition, the fact of insurance would be in evidence. Having in mind that the claimant had already received a certain amount of money, the jury might be persuaded to award a larger amount which would be over and above that which the plaintiff had already received. Obviously, if the jury is not aware of the fact that the claimant had already received the advance payments, they are more likely to determine the issue of damages on the merits.

Advance payments and the statute of limitations.   In some cases the running of the statute of limitations may complicate the system of advance payments. This is especially true in states which have a one-year statute, such as California and Connecticut, applicable to bodily injury claims. Clearly, if advance payments are continued up to and perhaps beyond the date the statute ran, the insurance company could be accused of misleading the claimant and lulling him into a false sense of security. This would in some cases enable to the claimant to allege that the insurance company has waived the running of the statute, especially in cases where some payments were made after the statute ran against the case. Thus, the insurer has the option of either (1) waiving the running of the statute or (2) putting the claimant on notice that the statute is about to run.

1. Waive the statute. Payments can be continued until the claimant has recovered and then if needed a final settlement can be made. The continuation of the payments would seem to waive the running of the statute. The danger here is that if a final settlement is not made to the satisfaction of the claimant, there is always the possibility of litigation, and this after the statute of limitations has tolled.

2. Put the claimant on notice. Even though advance payments are being made and the date of the tolling of the statute is approaching, the insurer can put the claimant on notice by letter advising him that within a certain period of time (usually 30–60 days) a final settlement must be made. If this is not done, the insurer will no longer be responsible for further payments of any kind. In some cases this notice will result in immediate litigation and in others a final settlement might be consummated.

As to the approach to be taken, the decision will have to be made on the merits of the case, the possibility of litigation and the prospects for a final settlement on an equitable basis.

A few states require that where advance payments are being made that the insurer notify the claimant in writing of the date on which the statute of limitations will run. In the absence of such notice, the statute will not be tolled. For example the California statute (Insurance Code, Sec. 11583) reads as follows:

Any person, including any insurer, who makes such an advance or partial payment, shall at the time of beginning payment, notify the recipient thereof in writing of the statute of limitations applicable to the cause of action for such injury or death, including any time limitations within which claims are required to be made against the state or any public entity. Failure to provide such written notice shall operate to toll any applicable statute of limitations or time limitations from the time of such advance or partial payment until such written notice is actually given.

Similar statutes are found in Delaware (Title 10, Sec. 4318), Massachusetts (Chap. 231, Section 140B, as amended 140C), New Hampshire (Chap. 508–B, as added by Chap. 456, Laws of 1971), and Oregon (Chap. 331, Laws of 1971).

Payments to others. It sometimes happens that it will be to the company's advantage to pay the medical and hospital bills direct to the doctor or hospital. This is especially necessary in states where there are lien laws favoring either the hospital or doctor or both. Agreement can be made with the claimant that such a payment be made after he has submitted an unpaid bill. In transmitting the payment, it is suggested that a letter be addressed to the payee with a copy to the claimant which would read as follows:

We are pleased to enclose our draft/check in the sum of $\$$_____ in payment of your bill covering services rendered from _____ to _____ and consisting of the following:

Hospitalization, operating room, x rays, etc.

This payment is being made direct to you at the request of _____
_____ .
(Claimant's name)

When payment is made in this fashion the claimsman will find that the payee will be more than cooperative in furnishing authorized medical information and hospital records.

2140   Settlement without release

In an effort to increase the number of first-call settlements, some companies follow the technique of a settlement without release in small cases (usually under $1,000) where the amount of the claimant's damage is low and has already been ascertained. No release or receipt is required and the case is paid with the understanding that if the claimant should incur any further expense in connection with the accident the company will be glad to consider it. This is sometimes referred to as a "walk-away" settlement. The claimant has received his full damages and there would be no reason to make any further claim unless other injuries or other expense is sustained. Generally, if the entire amount of the claim is ascertainable the entire procedure can be concluded with one call, either in person or even by telephone. Such cases will eliminate the necessity for call-backs and ultimately will save the company a certain amount of claim expense.

If the entire amount is not ascertainable on the first call, the advance payment technique can be used with respect to the known damage and an agreement reached that the company will pay the reasonable amount of the outstanding items.

CHAPTER XXII

Trial preparation and litigation

2200   Trial preparation generally

Trial preparation begins with the original investigation. In a case which qualifies for investigation, the claimsman has no way of anticipating whether the case will be settled or whether it will result in litigation. Therefore he will investigate the claim as if it were being prepared for trial. He will evaluate the witnesses, including the claimant and the insured. He will arrange with all favorable witnesses some means of communicating with them so that, should their presence be required at the trial, he will be able to reach them easily. This might in some cases consist of obtaining the names and addresses of relatives who will alway know where they are, the name and address of the union to which they belong, or the name and address of some close friend who will always be in touch with them.

The defense of the case will be based on the investigation, and any other evidence which is required will be obtained under the direction and guidance of counsel. The successful defense of the case will depend upon the accuracy and completeness of the claimsman's work. The case is usually won or lost long before it ever reaches the courtroom. It is won because of the investigation and the claimsman's painstaking efforts in developing the true facts and supporting them by evidence. It is lost because of the lack of investigation or the lack of accurate information. Defense counsel represents the vehicle through which the claimsman's work product is presented to the court and jury. When a case is won, the real victor is the claimsman who investigated and prepared the case for trial.

2201   The summons

A lawsuit is begun by the service of a process called a summons. It is a writ issued by the clerk of the court and directed to the sheriff or other proper officer, requiring him to notify the person named that an action has been commenced against him in the court from which the writ issues, and to appear on a day named to answer the complaint in such action. The purpose of the summons is twofold. The court does not have jurisdiction of the defendant unless and until the summons is served upon him within the jurisdictional limits of the court. Its second purpose is to notify the defendant of the action.

Since most states follow the Federal Rules of Procedure, we will use those rules in discussing the service of process and the time limitations within which they must be served. If your state does not utilize the federal rules, it will be necessary to check your own code of civil procedure to determine if there are any differences. Under the federal rules, the summons must be served by a sheriff or other proper officer on the individual, other than an infant or an incompetent person, by delivering a copy of the summons and complaint to him personally or by leaving copies thereof at his dwelling, house, or usual place of abode with some person of suitable age and discretion then residing therein, or by delivering a copy of the summons and of the complaint to an agent authorized by appointment or by law to receive the service of process.

Service upon an infant or an incompetent person is made by serving the summons and complaint in the manner prescribed by the law of the state in which the service is made. Some states provide for the appointment of a guardian for the minor or incompetent, and then service on the guardian by the sheriff.

Service on a domestic or foreign corporation or upon a partnership or other unincorporated association, which is subject to suit under a common name, is made by delivering a copy of the summons and of the complaint to an officer, a managing or general agent, or to any other agent authorized by appointment or by law to receive service of process, and, if the agent is one authorized by statute to receive service (such as the director of motor vehicles in automobile substituted service cases), and the statute so requires, by also mailing a copy to the defendant.

The form of the summons is practically the same in every state, with some very minor differences. So that the claimsman may be familiar with this process, the form of summons used in the federal district courts has been reproduced:

UNITED STATES DISTRICT COURT
FOR THE
SOUTHERN DISTRICT OF NEW YORK

Civil Action, File No. ⎯⎯⎯⎯⎯

John Doe ⎤
Plaintiff   ⎥
  vs.   ⎬ **Summons**
Richard Roe ⎥
Defendant ⎦

To The Above Named Defendant:

You are hereby summoned and required to serve upon James Brown, plaintiff's attorney, whose address is 144 Main Street, City of Moneola, New York, an answer to the complaint which is herewith served upon you, within 20 days after service of this summons upon you, exclusive of the day of service. If you fail to do so, judgment by default will be taken against you for the relief demanded in the complaint.

Joseph Green
Clerk of Court

Seal of U.S. District Court
Dated: ⎯⎯⎯⎯⎯⎯⎯⎯ 1976

2202   The complaint

The federal rules and those of most states require that the complaint be served with the summons. In others, the summons may be served without the complaint, which is served within 20 days after the defendant appears. The complaint is sometimes referred to in different jurisdictions as the Narrative, or Narr, or the Declaration. In any case the complaint, by whatever name it is called, is merely a statement of the plaintiff's claim, setting forth the material facts on which the plaintiff depends in supporting his demand. Its purpose is to inform the defendant of the nature of the action against him and the amount of the damages (*ad damnum*) claimed. Where the action is brought in courts of special or limited jurisdiction, facts must be alleged in order to support the jurisdiction of the court.

For example, federal district courts do not have jurisdiction in actions between individuals unless there is a diversity of citizenship (plaintiff and defendant are citizens of different states) and the amount in controversy exceeds $10,000, exclusive of interest and costs. Therefore, the complaint will allege both of these facts for jurisdictional purposes. In the first of the two accompanying complaints (a simple pedestrian knockdown case which does not require much information to set forth the cause of action), these facts are alleged in paragraph 1. The second complaint alleges that the plaintiff sustained injuries as a consequence of slipping on snow and ice.

UNITED STATES DISTRICT COURT

FOR THE

SOUTHERN DISTRICT OF NEW YORK

Civil Action, File No. _____

John Doe
Plaintiff
vs.
Richard Roe
Defendant

COMPLAINT

1. Plaintiff is a citizen of the State of New Jersey and defendant is a citizen of the State of New York. The matter in controversy exceeds, exclusive of interest and costs, the sum of ten thousand dollars.
2. On May 1, 1976, on a public highway called William Street in the City of New York, New York, the defendant negligently drove a motor vehicle against plaintiff who was then crossing said highway.
3. As a result, plaintiff was thrown down and had his leg broken and was otherwise injured, was prevented from transacting his business, suffered great pain of body and mind, and incurred expenses for medical attention and hospitalization in the sum of three thousand dollars.

   Wherefore, plaintiff demands judgment against defendant in the sum of twenty-five thousand dollars and costs.

> James Brown
> Attorney for Plaintiff
> Office and Post Office Address
> 144 Main Street
> Mineola, New York

UNITED STATES DISTRICT COURT

FOR THE

SOUTHERN DISTRICT OF NEW YORK

[Title of Action]

1. [Allegation of jurisdiction]
2. Plaintiff is a tenant of the defendant and resides in an apartment house project known as "Kent Village." Kent Village consists of various separate units connected by interior sidewalks, which are owned and maintained by the defendant for the use of their tenants and guests.
3. On May 1, 1976, plaintiff, after shopping in the American Store on the property of the defendant, was pushing her baby stroller over an interior walkway owned and maintained by the defendant. This walkway was the most direct route to the apartment occupied by her. The walkway was covered by a heavy coating of slippery ice, which has been on the walkway for a lengthy period of time and which defendant had negligently failed to remove or failed to treat in such a manner as to make the same safe for pedestrians.
4. As a result of defendant's negligence, plaintiff in traversing this walkway, slipped on the ice and fell to the ground.
5. As a result, plaintiff's coccyx bone and lower sacrum were seriously and permanently injured, and she was otherwise injured. Plaintiff was, and will be, prevented from carrying on her duties as a housewife, suffered great pain

of mind and body, and incurred medical attention and hospitalization in the sum of $5,000.00. Wherefor, plaintiff demands judgment against defendant in the sum of $25,000.00 and costs.

2203 Duties of the insured receiving process

All liability policies contain the following condition with respect to the action which must be taken by the insured when process is served on him:

If claim is made or suit is brought against the insured, he shall *immediately*[1] forward to the company every demand, notice, summons or other process received by him or his representative.

The purpose of this condition is to give the company adequate opportunity to perform its obligations under the policy contract. Since the company is obligated to defend any suit or other proceeding brought against the insured arising out of the hazards insured against, it is apparent that the company must have the process which was served in time to appear and answer or to take whatever other legal proceedings are appropriate. Therefore, the company has included in its contract, as a condition of its responsibility, that the insured must forward the process to the company immediately. This does not mean that the insured will satisfy the condition by merely notifying the company of the suit. It means that the actual process served must be forwarded to the company at once. Failure on the part of the insured to comply strictly with this condition will release the company from its obligations under the contract.

There has been considerable litigation over what "immediately" means in connection with this contract. Most companies construe it to mean that if the process is received in time to appear and answer within the 20 days, or whatever period of time is applicable, the insured has met the obligation of forwarding the process to the company immediately.

2204 Duties of the claimsman receiving process

When the summons and complaint is received by the company, whether delivered by the insured personally, or by mail, or by the insured's agent, the claimsman's first duty is to ascertain the date and the manner of service. The date on the summons merely indicates the date on which the clerk issued the process, not when it was served—the sheriff may have had the process in his office for a week before service was effected. The insured can advise of the actual date he received it and whether or not it was served on him personally (and if not, upon whom it was served). When the date of service has been ascertained, the defendant has 20 days, exclusive of the day of service, within which to appear and answer. If he fails to take this action within the time limits, the plaintiff may apply for and receive a judgment by default. This latter situation is to be avoided. It not only means that increased legal

---

[1] Author's italics.

fees are going to be incurred, but also that the plaintiff has gained a bargaining advantage if the case is one for settlement. In some states, it is extremely difficult to set aside a default judgment without conclusive evidence of a meritorious defense being offered in support of the application. In others it is not so serious, but in any case it calls for more legal work than would be necessary if the case were handled expeditiously.

If the case is one for trial, then the papers should be transmitted to defense counsel as soon as possible. The more time he has to prepare his anwer and consider the defenses available, the better. It is recommended that where this situation obtains, the papers should be transmitted to counsel the same day as they are received. In any case, where the process is received within the 20-day period, defense counsel must have them in time to appear and answer before the 20 days expires.

In some cases the process is served while settlement negotiations are in progress. If the case can be settled before the 20 days have gone by, then the action can be discontinued by the plaintiff and the company will have incurred no legal expense whatsoever. Where this situation obtains, the claimsman must keep a close diary on the case, and if settlement is not consummated he should see to it that the process is transmitted to defense counsel in time for him to appear and answer within the 20-day period.

2205   Stipulation to extend time for answer or otherwise plead

Where settlement negotiations are in progress and there seems to be some possibility of reaching an agreement, the plaintiff's counsel is just as anxious as the claimsman to dispose of the case by settlement. Under the circumstances, he will probably agree to extend the 20 days for an additional period of time. In most jurisdictions this can be done by a stipulation, which the plaintiff's attorney will draw and send to the company, or merely by a letter on the attorney's stationery, extending the time within which the defendant must appear and answer. The claimsman will have to be familiar with the rules of court in his particular jurisdiction as to the periods of time which can be the subject of extensions. Local defense counsel should be consulted as to the procedures to be followed in these matters.

In any case, the use of the extension of time is helpful in reducing legal costs, and if a case can be settled, even with an extension of time, the plaintiff can discontinue the cause of action and the company will have incurred no legal fees whatever.

2206   Tender of an overdue process

When the insured forwards a process to the company which has been served more than 20 days before he forwards it, he has breached the policy condition. Should the company accept the process with knowledge of the breach of condition, such action might constitute a waiver of the breach. Therefore, when the claimsman acquires knowledge that the process was not forwarded within time, he must immediately return the process to the insured and notify the insured that the company does not regard itself as bound by the insurance contract because of the insured's breach of condition. If the claimsman has that knowledge at the time the process is received, he must refuse to accept it if it is tendered personally by the insured, or he must return it to the insured immediately, calling attention to the breach of condition. He cannot retain the process beyond the time when he acquires knowledge of the breach of condition.

When the process is received by mail and there is no information accompanying it to inform the company as to when and upon whom it was served, the claimsman has a reasonable time to investigate and ascertain when it was served. If he finds that it was served more than 20 days before it was forwarded or received by the company, at that moment, he must return it to the insured and notify the insured of the company's election to stand on the breach of condition. If the claimsman accepts the process and does not immediately investigate as to the date of service, but retains the process for a period of time, only to find out later that the process was overdue at the time it was received, he will be held to have waived the breach. He only has a reasonable time, from the time the process is received, within which to ascertain whether or not there has been a breach of condition. If he fails to investigate, he will be charged with the knowledge that he would have acquired had he made a timely investigation. Retaining the process with knowledge of the breach of condition could constitute a waiver.

2207   The answer

The answer is a pleading served on the plaintiff by which the defendant endeavors to resist the plaintiff's demand by an allegation of facts, either denying the allegations of the plaintiff's complaint or confessing them and alleging new matters in avoidance, which the defendant alleges should prevent recovery on the facts alleged by the plaintiff. The complaint is the statement of the claim by the claimant, and the answer is the statement of the defendant's defense. The answer may deny some allegations of the complaint and may admit others. As to the allegations admitted, the plaintiff does not have to offer proof.

For example, in the pedestrian knockdown complaint (cited above) the defendant could admit the first part of paragraph 1, where the plaintiff alleges the diversity of citizenship between plaintiff and defendant, and could deny that the controversy exceeds $10,000 exclusive of interest and costs. His answer would read "The defendant admits the allegations of paragraph 1, except that he denies that the matter in controversy exceeds the amount of ten thousand dollars exclusive of interest and costs." Then the plaintiff would not be required to offer any proof of the diversity of citizenship between plaintiff and defendant, since this is admitted, but he would have to sustain the burden of proof that the matter in controversy exceeds the amount of $10,000 exclusive of interest and costs.

The rule of pleading is that any allegation of the plaintiff's complaint that is not denied is deemed admitted. Therefore, if the answer was silent as to the allegations of paragraph 1, the plaintiff's allegations are admitted and no proof of the allegation is required.

New matter may be alleged in the answer as an affirmative defense. Let us assume that the claimsman has settled the case and taken a release in return for the payment. Later a suit is brought, and the complaint does not mention anything about the release or the settlement. The answer would set up as an affirmative defense the allegation that the claim had been released.

It is no part of the claimsman's duty to prepare pleadings or to supervise the work of defense counsel in that phase of the work. Pleadings and other legal proceedings must be handled by counsel, and the claimsman must be guided by counsel as to what is required in that regard. However, this does not preclude the claimsman from having some familiarity with the general objective of pleadings and the purposes they serve.

The complaint is a statement of the claimant's cause of action and is served to give notice to the defendant of the claim that is being made against him. The answer is a statement of the defendant's defense, and gives notice to the plaintiff of the allegations which he must prove and the allegations which are admitted and do not require proof. All this adds up to a determination by both sides as to what evidence will have to be offered when the case comes to trial. The court will not be required to consider matters which are admitted, so that pleadings serve the purpose of eliminating issues insofar as the trial of the case is concerned.

2208   Provisional remedies: Attachment

There are certain provisional remedies or steps which can be taken in advance of trial in order to provide for some security for the plaintiff, so that if a judgment is obtained there will be some property or other thing of value to which the plaintiff can have recourse in order to satisfy his judgment. The remedy which can be chosen will depend on the nature of the action and the relief sought by the plaintiff. Among the remedies which can be utilized to secure the plaintiff against loss while the action is pending are injunction, appointment of a receiver, attachment, or arrest. In liability claims, since the relief demanded is the payment of money, the plaintiff may use the remedies of attachment of the defendant's property located within the jurisdiction of the court, or the civil arrest of the defendant himself. The purpose of the attachment is to prevent the defendant from disposing of his property or removing it from the jurisdiction of the court, and the purpose of arrest is to confine the defendant's person to the jurisdiction of the court. The latter, in essence, is an attachment of the defendant's person in the same manner as property is attached. All this is calculated to secure the plaintiff's claim and to assure a recovery if a judgment is obtained.

Attachment is the process of seizing property by virtue of a judicial order and taking it into legal custody so that it may be applied to the defendant's debt to the plaintiff when such is established. The court order is directed to the sheriff and he is commanded to seize certain property of the defendant and to hold it in custody until further order of the court. Before the court will issue the order, the plaintiff must furnish a bond which will secure the defendant against loss in case the plaintiff is unsuccessful in his suit. When the property is attached or taken into legal custody by the sheriff, and the defendant wishes the return of the property, he may apply to the court which issued the order for a release of the attachment and the substitution of the property with a bond of good and sufficient surety for an amount equivalent to the value of the property in custody. If the court grants the application, the sheriff is directed to return the property and the bond is substituted for the property.

Under the liability insurance contracts, the supplementary payments provision obligates the company to pay all premiums on bonds to release attachments for an amount not in excess of the applicable limit of liability of the policy, but without any obligation to apply for or furnish any such bonds. Some policies limit the amount of the premium to $100 or $250. Where the property of the insured has been attached, the insured will have to apply for an order releasing the attachment and will have to offer a bond in substitution for the property. The insurance carrier has no obligation with respect to this proceeding, and its only obligation is to pay for the premium on the bond secured by the insured up to the limit of liability of the policy applicable to the case, or to reimburse the insured for the premium paid by him.

For example, if the insured has an automobile policy with limits of 10/20 for bodily injury and $5,000 property damage, and the complaint alleges a cause of action for property damage, the applicable limit of the company's liability in such a case would be the property damage limit of $5,000, and it would be liable for the payment of premium for the release of attachment bond only to the extent of the premium required to post a bond up to $5,000. The bodily injury limits are not involved and the applicable limit of liability in this case would be the property damage limit. If, under the same circumstances, there was a claim for bodily injuries in addition to the property damage, then the bodily injury limits would be involved as well as the property damage. Then the obligation on the part of the company to pay the premium on the bond would be governed by the total of the bodily injury and the property damage limits.

2209 Provisional remedies: Arrest

Arrest is the attachment of the person of the defendant rather than his property. It is granted in the same way as the order of attachment, that is, by application to the court for an order directed to the sheriff to take the defendant into custody so that he can answer the plaintiff's demand against him. In states following the common-law pleading, this result is obtained by issuing a writ called a *capias* and the securing of a writ called a *capias ad respondendum*, which commands the sheriff to take the defendant into custody and to produce his body before the court on a certain day to satisfy the demands of the plaintiff.

In either case, the defendant is deprived of his liberty until the case is tried and satisfaction is given, or he is released by court order, with a bond being substituted as security for his person. This form of proceeding is rarely used in our liability insurance claims, but it is available to the plaintiff and it is possible for the claimsman to be confronted with the situation.

The obligation of the company is the same as in an attachment of the insured's property: it has the obligation of paying the premium on the bond, required up to the applicable limit of liability of the policy, without any obligation to apply for or furnish the bond. The securing of the order of release, and the bond, must be undertaken by the insured, and the company is under no legal or contractual obligation to do any more than pay the premium its policy contract requires it to do.

2210   Discovery proceedings

Any party to an action may take the testimony of any person, including a party, by deposition upon oral examination or written interrogatories, for the purpose of discovery or for use as evidence in the action, or for both purposes. When the action has been commenced, the deposition may be taken without the leave of the court and the attendance of witnesses can be compelled by the use of subpoena.

These, of course, are matters handled by counsel. The importance of the proceedings to the claimsman is that he can be present at the time and place that the oral depositions are taken, whether they be the depositions of the plaintiff, defendant, or other witnesses. Since these proceedings are in advance, the claimsman will have an opportunity to check the truth or falsity of the statements made under oath, and also be able to observe the claimant and ascertain the type of witness he will make at the time of trial. He also will be able to observe his own insured and determine the kind of witness he will make.

Oral depositions consist of taking the witness' testimony under oath, before a notary or other person authorized to administer oaths, and with a question and answer record being taken by a court reporter. Interrogatories on the other hand, consist of the submission of written questions to the witness and the return of them with the answers. This procedure is usually used where the oral deposition is deemed unnecessary, either because of the cost factor or because written interrogatories will serve the same purpose. It is clear that the taking of oral depositions is a costly undertaking in that the party demanding the depositions must defray the costs, which will include the services of the reporter and the transcription of the testimony taken. If the same result can be obtained by the use of written interrogatories, which are served on the adverse party by mail and returned by the same means, such procedure is less costly. An illustration of a written interrogatory used in a personal injury action by the defendant has been inserted.

CAPTION

The defendant demands of the plaintiff the following particulars in accordance with the cause of action set forth in the complaint.

1. Full name, address, and place of birth.
2. Date, approximate time and condition of weather at the time of accident.
3. Detailed description of the nature, extent, and duration of any and all injuries.
4. Detailed description of injury or condition claimed to be permanent together with all present complaints.
5. If confined to hospital, state name and address of same, date of admission and discharge therefrom.
6. If X rays were taken, state the name and address of the place where they were taken, the name and address of the person who took them, the date on which each were taken, and what is disclosed.
7. If treated by doctors, state name and present address of each doctor, the dates and places where treatments were received and the date of last treatment.
8. If still being treated, the name of and address of each doctor rendering treatment, when and how often treatment is received, and the nature thereof.
9. If a previous injury, disease, illness, or condition is claimed to have been aggravated, accelerated, or exacerbated, specify in detail the nature of each and the name and present address of each doctor, if any, who rendered treatment for said condition.
10. If employed at the time of accident, state:
    a. Name and address of the employer.
    b. Position held and nature of work performed.
    c. Average weekly wages for the past year.
    d. Period of time lost from employment, giving dates.
    e. Amount of wages lost, if any.
11. If other loss of income, profit or earnings is claimed:
    a. State total amount of said loss.
    b. Give complete detailed computations of said loss.
    c. State nature and source of loss of such income, profit, and earnings, and the date of deprivation thereof.
12. If there has been a return to employment or occupation, state:
    a. Name and address of present employer.
    b. Position held and nature of work performed.
    c. Present weekly wage, earnings, income or profit.
13. Itemize in complete detail any and all monies expended or expenses incurred for hospitals, doctors, nurses, X rays, medicines, care and appliances and state name and address of each payee and the amount paid or owed each payee.
14. Itemize any and all other losses or expenses incurred not otherwise set forth.
15. State the names and addresses of all persons who have knowledge of any relevant facts relating to the case.
16. State names and addresses of any and all proposed expert witnesses.

It can be seen that the answers, either to the depositions or the interrogatories, will open many avenues of investigation to the claimsman. They will also disclose the extent of the injuries claimed and the special damages. Specific questions can be designed for special cases and can be added to the interrogatories or asked at the time the deposition is taken. In most states, the witness, either by deposition or interrogatory, may be examined regarding any matter, not privileged, which is relevant to the subject matter in the pending action, whether it relates to the claim or defense of the examining party or to the claim or defense of any other party, including the existence, description, nature, custody, condition, and location of any books, documents or other tangible things, and the identity and location of persons having knowledge of relevant facts. A party may require the adverse party to disclose the names and addresses of proposed expert witnesses on whom he will rely. Discovery may not reach the work product of the attorney for either party and any communications passing between attorney and client.

In most states the disclosure of the fact that the defendant is insured is grounds for a mistrial. It is an immaterial fact and, if introduced by the plaintiff, might deprive the defendant of a fair trial in that the jury would not give adequate consideration to the defense on the theory that the defendant was not going to have to pay the claim anyway. However, in some states, the rules of discovery permit an inquiry and disclosure of insurance, and the limits thereof, even though such evidence is not admissible in the trial of the case. The rationale of this procedure is that where the plaintiff knows exactly the extent of the insurance coverage, there is a greater likelihood of settlement than where the plaintiff is in the dark and cannot know that his demand is in excess of the policy limits. In any event, the following is typical of the rule:

In an action for personal injury or property damage arising out of negligence, a party may require any other to disclose the policy limits of his liability or property damage insurance. Such disclosed matter shall not be introduced in evidence, but shall be used solely for the purpose of enabling the party to evaluate the advisability of making or accepting an offer of settlement. (New Jersey Rules of Court, R.R. 4:16–2)

Discovery proceedings include medical examinations of the claimant, and the defendant may compel the plaintiff to submit to a medical examination which may include the taking of X rays, blood samples, and other tests where appropriate. These are all matters of evidence to which the defendant is entitled prior to trial.

2211   Motions

A motion is an application to the court for a ruling or for an order, made by counsel. There are a number of kinds of motions, depending upon the ruling sought. They may be made in advance of trial, during, or after trial. In advance of trial, the defendant may make a motion to compel the plaintiff to answer interrogatories—where the plaintiff has failed or neglected to do so when the proper demand was made. If the motion is granted, the court will issue an order directed to the plaintiff to answer the interrogatories. During the trial, the attorney for the defendant may move to dismiss the complaint, and if this motion is granted it ends the trial right at that point; the court will direct a verdict for the defendant. After trial, the defendant may move for a new trial on the grounds that the verdict is against the weight of evidence or that the amount is excessive so as to shock the conscience of the court. If any of these motions are granted the verdict will be set aside and a new trial ordered. (These are merely examples of motions which can—and must—be made by counsel.)

2212 Subpoenas

A subpoena (Latin *sub*, under; *poena*, penalty) is a process to cause a witness to appear and give testimony, commanding him to lay aside all pretenses and excuses, and to appear before a court or magistrate, named therein at a time therein mentioned, to testify. It is a writ issued either by the clerk of the court, or the attorney as an officer of the court, directed to the witness. It is served on him personally, either by the sheriff or other officer so authorized, or, in some jurisdictions, by any person over the age of 21. The process will also state on its face that for failure to attend and testify, the person will be held in contempt and subject to penalties. In addition, a fee must be tendered to the witness covering his expenses in coming to and going from the court. This amount is usually fixed by the court in an amount for all cases, with additional mileage being allowed where the witness has to travel some distance.

A straight subpoena merely calls for the presence of the witness and nothing more. Where the witness is required to bring with him and produce books of account, records or other items, documentary or otherwise, a process called a *subpoena duces tecum* is utilized. This process commands the witness, who has in his possession or control some document or paper or other thing which is pertinent to the issues of a pending controversy, to produce it at the trial. The most common use of this type of process is used to obtain the production of hospital records of the claimant by serving the custodian of the records and having him appear and identify the records. It is also used to compel the attending physician to appear and bring with him all office records, records of tests, X-ray plates, and other information in his possession relating to the treatment of the patient.

2213 *Habeas corpus ad testificandum*

Although a witness is in jail or the state prison, he can still be called upon to testify. Whether or not the party calling him would want to rely on his testimony, especially when he is serving a sentence resulting from the conviction of some heinous crime, or one involving moral turpitude, is a tactical matter to be decided by the party or his attorney. If it should be deemed necessary to produce such a witness it can be done, but only at great expense and through a rather cumbersome procedure. Application must be made to the court for a writ of *habeas corpus ad testificandum,* which is directed to the warden of the prison to bring up the prisoner so that he may give evidence at the trial.

Before the court will grant the writ, however, the party applying must guarantee the expenses of producing the prisoner. These usually consist of the traveling expenses and meals of the prisoner and the guard or marshal who must accompany the prisoner. If the prisoner is needed more than a portion of a day, the expense of his lodging in the local jail and the hotel expense of the guard must also be guaranteed. Therefore, the production of a prisoner as a witness is not without considerable expense, and consideration should be given to the value of his testimony as opposed to the cost of producing him.

2214   Functions of the judge and jury

The fundamental principle is that the judge decides the law and the jury determines the facts. For example, the judge decides the applicable law in a situation where the defendant had been operating his motor vehicle in excess of the speed limit, and that damages should be awarded if the defendant was in fact speeding and his excessive speed was the proximate cause of the accident. The defendant contends that he was going 20 m.p.h. in a 25 m.p.h. zone and that the proximate cause of the accident was the plaintiff's negligence in failing to take reasonable precautions for his own safety. The plaintiff contends that the defendant was going 50 m.p.h. in a 25 m.p.h. zone and that the proximate cause of the accident was the defendant's excessive speed.

It is clear that both of these contentions cannot coexist; one has to be right and one has to be wrong. The jury will decide which contention it will believe. If it believes the defendant, and so finds, the judge will instruct them to bring in a verdict for the defendant. Conversely, if it believes the plaintiff, the verdict will go the other way.

The jury, therefore, has two questions of fact to decide. The first is the speed of the defendant. If they find that the speed of the defendant exceeded the speed limit, then they have to decide, from the facts, if the excessive speed was the proximate cause of the accident. The judge will decide, as a matter of law, what evidence is admissible and what is not. He will exclude evidence which is offered and which he decides is not admissible.

The most frequent question of fact which is submitted to the jury is the application of the reasonably prudent man standard to a set of circumstances. The evidence will indicate certain facts. As to disputed facts the jury will decide the ones that it will believe. Having decided the believable facts, it will then decide whether or not such conduct approximated what the reasonably prudent man would do under the same or similar circumstances. The law of the situation, as given to the jury by the judge, would be that if the defendant's conduct was the same as that of a reasonably prudent man, then the defendant would not be guilty of negligence, whereas if it did not, the defendant could be charged with negligence.

2215   Waiver of a jury

The Constitution of the United States (Seventh Amendment) respecting the right to a trial by jury in civil cases, reads as follows:

In suits at common law, where the value in controversy shall exceed twenty dollars, the right of trial by jury shall be preserved, and no fact tried by a jury, shall be otherwise re-examined in any Court of the United States than according to the rules of the common law.

Therefore either litigant, plaintiff, or defendant, is entitled to a trial by jury of his cause of action if the amount in controversy exceeds twenty dollars. The rules of court in most states require that the litigant who desires a jury trial make a demand for a jury in his suit papers. If he fails to do so, the right to a jury trial is waived, in which case the judge sits as both judge and jury, deciding both questions of fact and questions of law. However, if either party demands a jury, the case is tried by a jury irrespective of the desires of the opposing side.

2216   Selection of the jury

Jurors are selected from a panel and are usually questioned by the attorneys for each side. This is called the *voir dire:* "to speak the truth." It refers to this preliminary examination which is made of the prospective jurors, either by the court or by the counsel for each side. The purpose of the examination is to determine their fitness to serve as jurors, and the questions are intended to bring out whether or not they have any interest whatsoever in the case, are related to any of the litigants or witnesses (or counsel for either side), and whether or not they have any knowledge of the case or have formed an opinion as to its merits. The questions are likewise used to elicit any mental reservations that the prospective juror may have as to his ability to render a true verdict under the facts of the case. Some attorneys like to use questions similar to the following:

The plaintiff claims that he was injured through the negligence of the defendant, Mr. John Jones. Unless he proves to your satisfaction by a preponderance of evidence that Mr. Jones was in fact negligent, will you be guided by the law which requires that you bring in a verdict for the defendant, Mr. Jones?

If the plaintiff proves negligence on the part of the defendant, John Jones, and that it was the proximate cause of the injuries of which he complains, but if the evidence shows that the plaintiff's own lack of reasonable care for his own safety contributed to the cause of his injuries, will you, as required by the law, bring in a verdict for the defendant, John Jones? Will this be your verdict, as required by the law, even if the plaintiff's negligence contributed only in the slightest degree to the causing of the accident?

Either party may challenge a juror. This means that he objects to the person serving as a juror in the case. Challenges or objections to prospective jurors are of two kinds, peremptory and for cause. In a peremptory challenge, the party making the objection is not required to give any reason whatsoever for the objection. Since the use of this challenge could delay the trial, in civil cases most jurisdictions limit either side to six peremptory challenges. When the party has used up his six challenges, he may not challenge peremptorily thereafter. Challenges for cause are unlimited. They refer to prospective jurors who are related to either party, have an interest in the outcome of the case, or are employed by either party. Such persons are challenged for cause since it is clear that they could not render a fair verdict under the circumstances.

2217   Opening statements

After the jury has been selected and sworn, both sides are required to make opening statements. These serve as an introduction for the jury as to the nature of the case and the evidence which will be presented. Since the plaintiff has the burden of proof, he will open the case by making a statement as to the claims he alleges and the evidence he will produce. Then the defendant makes his opening statement, admitting whatever facts he will not controvert and outlining his theory of defense, as well as the evidence he will produce to support it. The rules of court of most states define opening statements as follows:

(a) The plaintiff must concisely state his claim and briefly may state his evidence to sustain it.

(b) The defendant must then briefly state his defense and briefly may state his evidence in support of it.

It should be noted that neither side is *bound* to state the evidence on which he relies, but, as a practical matter, attorneys seldom forego the opportunity to acquaint the jury with the facts they intend to prove. Most attorneys feel that this gives the jury the "feel" of the case and makes the evidence more understandable as it is presented.

2218   The trial

The plaintiff introduces his evidence first. Witnesses are sworn and testify on direct examination by the plaintiff's attorney. Each is then cross-examined by the defense. Physical exhibits, such as plats, photographs, diagrams, X-ray plates, etc., are identified and offered in evidence. At the close of his evidence, the plaintiff rests.

The evidence offered by the plaintiff must establish the allegations of the complaint. He has the burden of persuasion as to the existence of the facts on which he relies, including the fact of the damages suffered and the monetary value thereof. In negligence claims the plaintiff must establish:

1. A wrongful act or omission on the part of the defendant.
2. The wrongful act or omission was the proximate cause of the injury to the plaintiff.
3. Damages as a result thereof.

The sum total of these three requirements constitute a prima facie case. The failure of the plaintiff to establish all three requirements, or a prima facie case, will compel a dismissal of the action since the plaintiff will not have sustained the burden of proof which the law requires. The defendant does not have to prove anything. The law does not require that he produce any evidence or testify in his own behalf. The law *does* require the plaintiff to meet the burden of proof.

At the close of the plaintiff's case, the defendant may, at his option, introduce evidence in contradiction of the plaintiff's evidence, as well as evidence sustaining any affirmative defenses which may have been interposed. For example, in most jurisdictions contributory negligence of the plaintiff is a defense to be alleged and proved by the defense. The defendant may establish this fact by evidence or by the cross-examination of the plaintiff. The same thing is true with respect to assumption of risk as a defense. The statute of limitations is also an affirmative defense as well as the fact that the claim has been released. These may be alleged and proved by the defendant.

Where the defendant offers evidence, the plaintiff is permitted to introduce rebuttal evidence, contradicting the defendant's evidence. He may recall his prior witnesses in order to accomplish this. If rebuttal evidence is offered, the defendant likewise has an opportunity to offer further evidence in contradiction to the rebuttal evidence. If no rebuttal evidence is offered, once both sides have rested there is no further right, by either party, to introduce further evidence. It should be emphasized that when the plaintiff introduces rebuttal evidence, he is limited to only such evidence as will contradict the defendant's case. He cannot introduce new evidence for any other purpose. If the plaintiff does not introduce rebuttal evidence, the defendant has no further right to introduce evidence once the defense has rested.

At the close of both the plaintiff's case and the defendant's case, there are certain motions or requests for rulings which may be made to the court, relating to a dismissal of the complaint, a directed verdict, or a mistrial. Each side is then given an opportunity to sum up in an effort to persuade the jury as to the merits of their respective cases.

2219   The court's charge

When both sides have rested, the court will outline to the jury the questions which it must decide and will instruct them as to how they are to do it. For example, if there is a sharp conflict as to any of the facts of the accident, with witnesses testifying to different versions, the jury will have to decide which version it will believe. The charge might be as follows:

You may take into consideration with respect to the credibility of the various witnesses produced, their demeanor on the witness stand, their interest in the outcome of the case, the vagaries of the human mind in its attempt to recall past matters, the opportunities of the witness to see and hear what may have taken place, and the likelihood of their making particular note, or recalling particular details. You may then accept the credible and reject the incredible.

A charge with respect to the presumption of due care and the plaintiff's duty to prove his allegations by a preponderance of evidence might be as follows:

The Court has advised you that negligence is never presumed, and that the presumption of the law is that everyone discharges the duties which the law imposes. In other words, the law presumes that everyone does what, in law, he should do. Because of this presumption, the person making a claim has the burden of proving the truth of the alleged facts upon which he bases his claim. In this case, therefore, the burden rests upon the plaintiff, John Doe, to prove by a preponderance of the evidence that the defendant, Richard Roe, was negligent as he charges in his complaint; and if, under the law and evidence, he proves to your satisfaction that the defendant, Richard Roe was negligent, then in addition thereto, the plaintiff must prove by a preponderance of the evidence that such negligence was the proximate cause of the injury of which the plaintiff, John Doe, complains.

Another charge, covering the same area of presumption, negligence, and proximate cause, might be as follows:

The fact of the happening of the occurrence in question in this case raises no presumption of negligence, nor does the injury to the plaintiff, John Doe, raise any presumption that either the plaintiff, John Doe, or the defendant, Richard Roe, was negligent at the time and place in question. What the plaintiff affirmatively alleges, unless admitted by the defendant, the plaintiff must prove by a preponderance of the evidence.

The plaintiff, John Doe, must not only prove by a preponderance of the evidence that the defendant was negligent, but he must also prove by a preponderance of the evidence that such negligence was the proximate cause of the injury of which he complains, and also that he sustained damages. If the plaintiff, John Doe, fails to prove any of these by a preponderance of the evidence, your verdict must be for the defendant, Richard Roe.

Where a clear exposition of the meaning of proximate cause is needed, the charge on that question might be as follows:

Members of the Jury, before you can return a verdict in favor of the plaintiff, you must find that the negligence of the defendant, Richard Roe, was the proximate cause of the damages alleged by the plaintiff, John Doe. If you find that the negligence of Richard Roe was a remote cause and not the proximate cause for said damage, then your verdict must be for the defendant, Richard Roe.

"Proximate cause" means the nearest cause, not necessarily nearest in point of time or space, but nearest in causation; the direct cause without which the damage would not have occurred. The proximate cause is that which in a natural and continuous sequence of events, unbroken by any new cause, produces a result, and without which the damage would not have occurred. If John Doe has failed to prove that the negligence of the defendant, Richard Roe, was the proximate cause of the damages claimed by the plaintiff, John Doe, your verdict must be for the defendant, Richard Roe.

A charge with respect to the question of contributory negligence might be as follows:

As a matter of law, if you find that the plaintiff, John Doe, was guilty of negligence, even in the slightest degree, directly causing, or directly contributing to cause the injuries and damage of which he complains, then your verdict must be for the defendant, Richard Roe. This is true even though you find that the defendant, Richard Roe, was also guilty of negligence.

2220   The verdict

After the charge the jury retires to its deliberations. This takes place in the jury room, where they are completely alone, and each juror acts independently and voluntarily in forming his conclusions. Votes are taken by the foreman of the jury at intervals to determine if they are in agreement. When an agreement is reached they return to the court and deliver their decision. This is called their verdict. The word is of Latin derivation, meaning "To speak the truth." In some jurisdictions the verdict must be unanimous: all the jurors must agree. In others, a 5/6th verdict is acceptable: which means that if 10 of the 12 jurors agree the agreement of the 10 will be the verdict of the jury. When the jury fails to agree it is called a "hung" jury. At the discretion of the court, such a jury may be discharged and a new trial ordered.

2221   Motions after verdict

After verdict, either side may make a motion to set the verdict aside or for judgment notwithstanding the verdict. Usually the basis of the motion is that the verdict is against the weight of evidence, excessive, or contrary to the evidence. The motion may be granted, or denied, in the discretion of the court.

The general rule is that the court will deny the motion unless the verdict is so inadequate, or excessive, or so contrary to the evidence that it "shocks the conscience" of the court. Merely because the amount awarded is less than the plaintiff demanded, or in excess of what the defendant thinks it should have been, is not enough. The verdict must be so far out of proportion to the evidence that the court itself will term it inadequate, or excessive, as the case may be. If the motion is granted, the court may then grant a new trial.

2222   *Additur* and *remittitur*

Where a motion has been made to set aside the verdict and grant a new trial, the court may, as we have seen in the preceding paragraph, grant a new trial. In an effort to reduce litigation and encourage settlement, sometimes the court will recommend either an increase or a decrease in the verdict and, if acceptable to the adverse party, will enter a verdict by consent for the new amount, and deny the motion.

For example, if the verdict for the plaintiff was $500, and a motion was made to set aside the verdict as inadequate, and the court felt that the case

was worth $1,500, the court might give the defendant an opportunity of set-
tling the case for $1,500 before deciding the motion. The court will usually
phrase its decision by saying that if the defendant will agree to an *additur*
of $1,000, making the verdict $1,500, it will deny the motion and enter a verdict for $1,500. If the defendant does not agree to the *additur*, the motion
will be granted.

The converse is true where the verdict is excessive. The plaintiff will be
given an opportunity to accept a lesser amount than that awarded by the jury.
A reduction in the amount of the verdict is called a *remittitur*. For example,
if the verdict was $2,500 in a case where the court felt that the maximum
value was $1,500, the court will advise the plaintiff that unless he accepts a
remittitur of $1,000, making the verdict $1,500, it will grant the motion and
set the verdict aside. If the plaintiff accepts the *remittitur*, a verdict is entered
for $1,500. If the plaintiff refuses to reduce the verdict, the court will set the
verdict aside and grant a new trial.

2223   Responsibilities of the claimsman with respect to litigation

Every claim in litigation can be settled by the simple expedient of paying
the plaintiff what he wants in settlement. It is the claimsman's duty to decide
how far the company should go in meeting the demand of the plaintiff. He
will determine which cases will be tried and which will be settled, either prior
to or during trial. He will weigh the evidence he has gathered and will estimate the evidence which the plaintiff has or is available to him. He will obtain the opinion of counsel as soon as the case goes into litigation and will
compare counsel's opinion with his own as to the possibilities of a successful
defense, the possibilities of a lesser verdict than the plaintiff's demand, as
well as the possibilities of an adverse verdict.

While it is counsel's responsibility to recommend, the final decision as to
trial or settlement rests with the claimsman. If he decides that it is a case to
try, and it eventually comes to trial, the claimsman will keep in touch with
the progress of the case, the evidence offered by the plaintiff, and the recommendations of counsel at the close of the plaintiff's case, and will take advantage of a settlement opportunity even during the trial if it is to the advantage of the company to do so. In major cases, it is not uncommon for the
claimsman to sit at the counsel table during the trial, so that if the evidence
is against the defense a settlement can be arranged before submitting the case
to the jury. In any case, it is the claimsman's duty to make the final decision
as to whether the case is to be submitted or settled.

2224   Responsibilities of the claimsman with respect to
     trial preparation

Generally the responsibilities of the claimsman in this respect is to place
in the hands of defense counsel a fully investigated case and to see that the
witnesses upon whom he will rely are available to testify at the time and
place of trial. This will undoubtedly mean that they will all have to be recon-

tacted, and in some cases relocated. He will, in addition, conduct such additional investigation as is recommended by counsel.

When the date of trial is reached the claimsman will arrange for the presence of the witnesses when needed, arranging for their transportation and their reimbursement for the time they have lost in appearing at the trial. He will also serve subpoenas when necessary and, in general, see that counsel is provided with all the evidence that it is possible to produce in support of the defenses which are being urged.

CHAPTER XXIII

Employers' liability and workmen's compensation

2300 Common-law duties of the employer

The common law applied tort concepts to the relationship of master and servant. The servant, or employee, was entitled to the safety of his person while in the course and scope of his employment, just as he would be at any other time. Since the fact of employment exposed the employee to special risks of injury that were not present at other times, the employer owed the employee a higher degree of care relating to the employee's safety. To meet the degree of care required by the common law, the employer was obligated to assume the following duties:

1. To provide the employee with a safe place to work.
2. To provide the employee with competent fellow servants.
3. To provide the employee with the proper tools with which to perform the work.
4. To warn the employee of any inherent dangers in the process of the work, which were not open and apparent.
5. To make reasonable rules for the safe performance of the work.

The failure of the employer to meet any one of these obligations constitutes negligence. Should that negligence be the proximate cause of the employee's injury, the employer is answerable in damages. As in all tort causes of action, the burden of proof is on the shoulders of the party asserting the claim, which means that the employee must establish all the elements of his claim. He must prove the duty owed by the employer, the failure to meet that duty, and that the injuries he sustained were proximately caused by his employer's failure to perform. The rules of certainty and subtraction, as well as the single recovery principle, are applicable.

2301   Common-law defenses of the employer

To the employee's cause of action, the employer has the following defenses:

1. Contributory negligence.
2. Negligence of a fellow servant.
3. Assumption of risk.

Contributory negligence.   As in any other tort cause of action based on negligence, the contributory negligence of the employee will defeat recovery. If the employee's negligence contributed to the happening of the accident in any degree, the employer is relieved of responsibility.

Negligence of a fellow servant.   If the accident is caused by the negligence of an otherwise competent fellow servant, the employer is not answerable for the injuries. This defense should be contrasted with the employer's duty to provide competent fellow servants. If the employer exercised care in the selection of the fellow servants, he has met the duty thus imposed upon him. *Care* in this instance consists of a reasonable examination of the fellow servant's work, and a reasonable inquiry as to the prospective employee's qualifications and past record of employment.

It is clear that the extent of the inquiry will vary in accordance with the type of work involved and the duties to be assumed by the employee. If the employer did not make any inquiry where one was required, or conducted an insufficient inquiry, or failed to observe the employee's work habits while on the job, then he has not exercised reasonable care and he will be answerable. Therefore, if the fellow employee is incompetent and that fact was known to the employer, or by the exercise of reasonable care the employer should have been known, then the employer has failed in his duty and can not take advantage of this defense.

Assumption of risk.   Where the risk of injury inherent in the process in which the employee is engaged is one which is open and apparent to the employee, even before he began his employment, the employee will have assumed the risk and the employer is not responsible for the injuries suffered as a result of the exposure. The same elements which comprise the defense in ordinary tort situations are applicable to the relationship of employer and employee. These elements are (1) knowledge of the risk by the employee, and (2) voluntary exposure to the risk.

Where the risk is open and apparent, the employee will be charged with the knowledge of its dangers. A voluntary exposure to such a risk will absolve the employer from liability. Where the risk is not open and apparent to the average individual, there are two situations which may arise. If the employer meets his common-law duty of giving an adequate warning of the dangers, then the assumption of the risk of injury is construed to be done with knowledge of the dangers and, consequently, gives rise to the defense. Where the employer fails in his common-law duty and does not warn the employee of the danger (which is not open and apparent), the defense of assumption or risk will not be available for the reason that there was no voluntary exposure to a known risk. It is only where the employee voluntarily exposes himself to a risk known to him that the defense will lie.

2302   Statutory modifications: Workmen's compensation laws[1]

The common-law system worked quite well when industrial processes were simple and injuries few. The employee could adequately protect himself against injury, and for that reason the number of cases in which recoveries were had exceeded the number of cases in which no recovery was allowed. As high-speed machinery was introduced into industry, huge buildings erected, and more extensive engineering projects undertaken, these changes brought with them increased hazards and risks of injury to the employee. Accidental injuries increased. More importantly, the number of cases in which recoveries were even possible decreased, with the result that in the majority of industrial accident cases there was no recovery at all. This condition created a serious social problem. The injured workers and their families had to have some means of support, and since the common law denied them a recovery, they had to turn to public charity in order to survive. As the injuries became more numerous, the burden on public charity became so heavy that in the highly industrialized states the state legislatures were confronted with the problem of materially increasing the appropriation for public charity—which would mean increased taxation to the individual citizen, or seeking some other means of providing financial assistance to injured workers and their families.

---

[1] To bridge the gender gap, some states have reentitled the statute to "Workers' Compensation Law."

A workmen's compensation system had been adopted in Germany in the 1880's, and had already been adopted in England. Under this system, the employer was obligated to take care of the injured worker, or, in the case of death, his family, and public charity was not involved. It was suggested that this type of solution would avoid the necessity of an increase in taxation and would place the burden of caring for the victims of industrial accidents upon industry itself. The measure of liability based on the negligence of the employer would be scrapped in favor of a system which provided for a recovery if the accident arose out of and in the course of employment, irrespective of whether the employer was negligent or not.

The proponents of the compensation system argued that the cost of compensating the victims of industrial accidents was an item which should be added to the price of the product, whatever it was, and that this cost should be allocated to the ultimate consumer and not borne by public charity. The opponents of the system argued that the plan deprived the employer of his property without due process of law in that a contributorily negligent claimant could recover from his employer for the injury, even in cases where the employer was not negligent.

Neither argument went to the heart of the problem which confronted the legislatures. They were faced with a choice between increasing the charitable appropriation or adopting a workmen's compensation system. They chose the latter. Since the problem was more acute in the highly industrialized states, we find these were among the first to embrace workmen's compensation. However, as time passed, other states gradually adopted the system so that today we have a workmen's compensation system operative in all our states.

The workmen's compensation concept not only changed the measure of the employer's liability but also modified the means and type of recovery. The single recovery rule was abandoned, and there was substituted a procedure whereby the employer's responsibility could be extinguished only by periodic payments of compensation benefits, payable in the same manner as wages, plus the payment of the employee's medical, surgical, and hospital expense. The period of time during which these payments are to continue depends upon the period of disability suffered by the claimant. The amount of the weekly benefit provided is based on the claimant's wages at the time of the injury, wages earned during a prior period to the date of the accident. Some states base the average weekly wage on the earnings of the claimant over the period of one year prior to the accident, while others base the weekly wage on lesser periods.

Payments in the case of death are likewise made on a periodic basis as a substitute for the wages which the deceased would have earned had he lived. The period of time during which such payments will continue is set forth in the state statute. Some states require that the payments be continued to the widow until she dies or remarries, and payments to the children until they reach the age of 18. Other states have a maximum period of time during which these benefits are paid, usually measured by a certain number of weeks.

Where permanent disability is involved, each state statute sets out a sched-

ule of payments which are made periodically to cover the diminution in earning capacity resulting from the permanent condition. Some states also provide for an award where facial, head, or bodily disfigurement is sustained,
the theory being that scarring or other disfigurement has a definite influence
on the injured's future earning capacity.

The workmen's compensation concept is based entirely on earning capacity. There is no recovery for property damage, discomfort, inconvenience,
or pain and suffering. The underlying theory is to place the injured person
in the same position, economically, as he would have been in had the accident never occurred. Therefore, the workmen's compensation system deprived
the employer of his common-law defenses and obligated him to respond in
accordance with the terms of the compensation act. But the employee was
also deprived of his right to claim damages for pain and suffering, the value
of a lost opportunity, and property damage.

2303   Types of compensation laws

Compensation statutes are divided into two types: elective and compulsory. Under the elective type of statute the employer and the employee may
elect to accept, or reject, the compensation act. In the absence of a specific
rejection of the act, both parties are presumed to have accepted it. Should
the employer reject the act, the statute usually provides that he is deprived of
one or more of his common-law defenses to actions brought by employees.
This serves as an inducement to the employer to accept rather than reject the
act.

Under a compulsory type statute, all employments defined as hazardous in
the act come within the compensation act, and there is no right of election
on the part of either the employer or the employee. The employer is obligated
to post security to cover his compensation liability. This might be in the form
of an insurance policy, a deposit of security with the state, or insurance in
a state insurance fund, where such is provided for in the statute. Failure to
obtain the necessary security will expose the employer to penalties.

2304   Employments covered

Since the original compensation laws were directed toward meeting a social problem, the only industries which were affected were those whose operations were hazardous. Other industries which did not expose the employees
to any great danger, and who contributed little to the creation of the social
problem, were eliminated from the compensation laws. The definition of
what constitutes a hazardous employment (and what does not) is contained
in the particular compensation statute—there is no real uniformity among
the states. However, most laws eliminate domestic servants and farm laborers
from the operation of the statute. Some states permit the voluntary acceptance
of the act by the employments not covered, and require that notice of such
election be brought to the attention of the employees. Should an employee

reject the act under those circumstances, his rights are the same as if the employer had not voluntarily elected to come under the act.

Hazardous employment may be defined by a specific listing of all such employments or may be included by some definition either referring generally to the processes required to come under, the act or to the number of employees.

While the original compensation acts affected only a small number of employments, the general trend at the present time is to expand the number of employers subject to the act so that today there are very few employments which are not affected by it.

As to employments not subject to the compensation act, the rights and liabilities of the parties, both employer and employee, remain the same as they were at common law. Since the compensation act is "in derogation of" (or contrary to) the common law, it is strictly construed. Therefore, where the employment is not specifically within the terms of the compensation act, the courts hold that the common-law rights and remedies still remain and are not affected by the compensation legislation.

2305   Compensation as an exclusive remedy

Where the employer has complied with the requirements of the compensation statute, the employee may claim compensation only, this being his sole and exclusive remedy. Since the compensation law has deprived him of his common-law cause of action, the right to compensation has been substituted, and irrespective of whether the accident was caused by the negligence of the employer, the only claim the employee can make is one for compensation. There usually is a provision in the statute to this effect, reading as follows:

The liability of an employer . . . shall be exclusive and in place of any other liability whatsoever to such employee, his personal representatives, husband, parents, dependents, or next of kin, or anyone otherwise entitled to recover damages, at common law or otherwise on account of injury or death . . .

Where the employer has failed to comply with the statute by securing workmen's compensation insurance or otherwise providing for the required security, he is deprived of the protection afforded by the preceding section, and in most states penalties, in the form of the restoration of the employee's common-law rights, are imposed—without restoration of some of the employer's common-law defenses. The following is a typical statute:

. . . Except that if the employer fail to secure the payment of compensation for his injured employees and their dependents . . . an injured employee, or his legal representative in case death results from the injury, may, at his option, elect to claim compensation under this Chapter, or to maintain an action in the courts for damages on account of such injury; and in such action it shall not be necessary to plead or prove freedom from contributory negligence, nor may the defendant plead as a defense that the injury was caused by the negligence of a fellow servant nor that the employee assumed the risk of his employment, nor that the injury was due to the contributory negligence of the employee.

Therefore, where the employer has failed to comply with the compensation act he is not only deprived of the protection of the act as to its being the employee's only remedy, but in case the employee elects to bring an action for damages based on the negligence of the employer, the employer is deprived of the defenses of contributory negligence, assumption of risk, and the negligence of a fellow servant. Under the circumstances the employee need only establish the negligence of the employer in order to recover.

In some states, suits for damages are permitted even where the employer has complied with the law, but where there are some aggravating circumstances. For example, under the Texas compensation law (art. 8306, sec. 5), a suit for damages is permitted if the employer's willful or gross negligence causes the death of an employee. Under the Kentucky compensation law (secs. 342.015, 342.170, and 342.340), suits for damages are permitted if a minor is willfully and knowingly employed in violation of the law, or if the injury is due to the deliberate intention of the employer. Even in these states, compensation is the exclusive remedy available to the employee in the absence of the special circumstances set forth in the statute.

2306   Security for workmen's compensation

The states are divided on the issue of how the payment of compensation is to be assured. Some take the position that it is an insurable item and that private insurance, written by a stock, mutual, or reciprocal insurance organization, or self-insurance by the deposit of the requisite security with the insurance department of the state, is all that is needed. Others feel that, since this is a social matter, it should not be a business transaction, such as a contract of private insurance, and that the entire program should be supervised and controlled by the state. In those states, there is a state-managed insurance fund with which all employers subject to the act are compelled to insure. Still other states provide a state-managed insurance fund, in competition with private insurance. In these latter states, the compulsory nature of their acts made this necessary since, if the employer is compelled to carry insurance, there must be some means by which he can obtain it, especially if private insurance carriers refuse to carry the risk.

Therefore as to the security for the payment of compensation, the states can be divided into three classes:

1. Private insurance or self-insurance only.
2. Monopolistic state-managed insurance only.
3. State-managed insurance, private, and self-insurance.

Private insurance or self-insurance only.   The situation obtains in the majority of states. As to self-insurance, it can be accomplished only by the deposit of securities with the state compensation board or the insurance commissioner. Because of this requirement (as a general rule) only large corporations are able to comply. Private insurance is obtainable, and in some cases, the insurance industry has provided a means, through pool arrangements and assigned risks, whereby private insurance can be obtained even though the risk involves serious hazards.

Monopolistic state-managed insurance only. Under this system, insurance must be obtained from the state fund. All employers are charged a premium, based either on a rate of the payroll or on the number of man-hours worked per month. Nevada, North Dakota, Ohio, Oregon, Washington, West Virginia, and Wyoming have this system. (In West Virginia self-insurance is permitted with the filing of a bond or the deposit of securities with the commission.)

State-managed, private, and self-insurance. In some states, there is a state insurance fund which writes workmen's compensation insurance in competition with private self-insurance. These states are Arizona, California, Colorado, Idaho, Maryland, Montana, New York, Oklahoma, Pennsylvania, and Utah.

2307 Administration of compensation laws

The majority of the compensation statutes have created a quasi-judicial body, variously called a workmen's compensation board or an industrial accident commission. It is the function of these bodies to supervise the administration of the law and to hear and determine disputes which arise under it. Usually the decision of the board is conclusive as to questions of fact and an appeal will lie to the courts only on questions of law. One exception to this rule is Texas, where the statute provides that an appeal may be taken from the determination of the board to the district court where the case will be tried *de novo* (a second time) before the court and jury.

In five states, the administration of the compensation law is exercised by the courts. In these five states—Alabama, Louisiana, New Mexico, Tennessee, and Wyoming—the actual supervision of the insurance companies (if any) operating within the state and writing workmen's compensation insurance is done by the superintendent of insurance or the labor commissioner. The courts merely hear and determine claims for compensation and issue judgments in exactly the same way as they would in any other type of case, except that the decision can order the continuance of the payment of compensation beyond the date of trial.

2308 Employee defined

Compensation laws refer only to persons who are employees, and do not affect in any way other relationships. The definition of an employee within the meaning of the particular compensation act is usually contained in the act itself. There is a wide variance among the states as to the kind and type of employee which the particular compensation is intended to cover A general definition, which would be applicable in all states, is contained in *Young* v. *Demos* [28 S.E. 2d 891 (Georgia)]. It reads as follows:

Generally, when a person for whom services are performed has the right to control and direct the individual who performs the services not only as to the result to be accomplished by the work, but also as to the details and the means by which the result is accomplished, the individual subject to direction is an employee.

It should be noted that under this definition, the question of whether or not a person is an employee turns on the matter of control and direction as to the means and methods of accomplishing the work. If the employer has the right of direction as to these two items, then there is a contract of employment. On the other hand, if the individual represents the employer only as to the result to be accomplished, and the employer has no control over the methods and means of accomplishing the work, the individual is an independent contractor and is not an employee.

In *Johnson* v. *Ashville Hosiery Co.*, (153 S.E. 591), the court defined an independent contractor as

One who exercises an independent employment and contracts to do a piece of work according to his own judgment and methods, and without being subject to his employer except as to the results of the work, and who has the right to employ and to direct the action of the workmen, independently of such employer and freed from any superior authority in him to say how the specified work shall be done, or what the laborers shall do as it progresses.

The most common type of an independent contract is found where a store owner or factory owner contracts with an electrician to do a specific job of wiring or putting in lights. The electrician will use his own methods, his own tools, and his own employees if needed. In addition, he will fix his own hours of employment and will be responsible to the store owner only as to a satisfactory result within the time fixed by the contract. The mere fact that the store owner might interfere by making suggestions or changing the specifications of the contract while it is in progress will not alter the nature of the relationship; the electrician is still an independent contractor.

Nor will the method of payment change the relationship. The usual contract calls for the payment of a specific sum for the work, but a contract whereby the store owner pays the contractor on a time rather than a lump-sum basis does not change the nature of the transaction into a contract of employment. On the other hand, if the store or factory owner employs an electrician as part of his labor force on a regular basis, fixing the hours of his employment and directing the methods and means of doing the work, then the electrician is an employee. Generally the questions to be asked are

1. Does the employer have the right to direct the methods and means of doing the work?
2. Does the employer furnish the tools and other material with which to do the work?
3. Does the employer fix the hours of employment?

If the answers to these questions are in the affirmative, the relationship is that of employer and employee, with the result that the compensation law is operative. On the other hand, if the answers are in the negative, then there is an independent contractor relationship in which the compensation law is not involved.

With respect to the example given above, the answer to the question of an independent contract is comparatively simple, but problems frequently arise as to the status of individuals such as newspaper delivery boys, caddies, baby-sitters, and boys doing household or yard work chores. In the case of the newspaper delivery boy, he is not under the control of the newspaper. Usually he pays for his papers and collects his money from his customers. The newspaper has no control over when and where he delivers the newspapers. The only concern of the newspaper is that it receives payment for the papers sold to the boy. Since the boy pays for the newspapers as he gets them, he can dispose of them in any manner he sees fit, even to the extent of giving them away if he is so minded. He is, therefore, an independent contractor, but some states have defined such employment as coming within the compensation law and making the newspaper liable for the payment of compensation in the case of an injury occurring in the course of delivering newspapers.

In some states, caddies have been held to be the employees of the country club and not the employees of the individual members, in spite of the fact that the only recompense received by the caddy was paid by the persons who had engaged his services and no salary or other remuneration was paid by the club. Baby-sitters have been held to be independent contractors, and in some states, the compensation statute specifically excludes them. For example, the New York statute (sec. 2, subd. 4) defines an employee as follows:

> Employee means a person engaged in one of the occupations enumerated . . . or who is in the service of an employer whose principal business is that of carrying on or conducting a hazardous employment upon the premises or at the plant, or in the course of employment away from the plant of his employer; "employee" shall also mean for the purposes of this chapter civil defense volunteers who are personnel of volunteer agencies sponsored or authorized by a local office under regulations of the civil defense commission . . . and for the purposes of this chapter only a newspaper carrier boy under the age of eighteen years . . . and shall not include farm laborers or domestic servants except as provided in Section 3 of this chapter, and except where the employer has elected to bring such employees under the law by securing compensation. . . . The term "employee" shall not include baby sitters . . . or minors fourteen years of age or over engaged in casual employment consisting of yard work and household chores in and about a one-family owner-occupied residence or the premises of a non-profit, noncommercial organization, not involving the use of power-driven machinery.

In states applying the strict common-law principles, a wife cannot be an employee of her husband, even though she is occupied in his business and he pays her a salary just as he does other employees, pays social security taxes, and withholds income tax. The theory is that at common law the husband was entitled to the services of his wife as a matter of right, and merely because he chooses to pay her for what he is legally entitled to receive does not change her status from that of a superior servant to an employee. This rule will apply only where the husband is engaged in business on his own account as an individual. If he is employed by a corporation, even though he holds the majority of the stock, the wife owes no duty to the corporation, which legally exists separate and apart from her husband, and therefore, she can be an employee of the corporation. The same thing is true, where the husband is a member of a partnership. She can qualify as an employee of the partnership.

Most states exclude casual employees from the operation of the compensation law. A casual employee is one who is engaged for a specific task not in the usual course of the trade, business, occupation, or profession of the employer. For example, a physician employs a painter to paint his office. The physician supplies the paint, brushes, ladders, and other needs, and pays the painter on an hourly basis, fixing the hours of employment. The painter is a casual employee. He was engaged for the specific task of painting the office. This task is not in the usual course of the profession of the physician, although having the office painted does have some influence on his business. The painter is an employee in that all the incidents of employment are present.

A volunteer is not an employee, no matter how necessary the service is that he renders. For example, a factory is on fire and the custodian of the building asks a bystander for assistance in putting out the fire. The bystander does not by assisting the custodian become an employee of the factory so as to entitle him to compensation in the event of injury.

A partner cannot be an employee of the partnership of which he is one of the members. Since the employer in such a case would be the partnership, a partner is one of the owners thereof. The partner is liable jointly with the other partners and individually for the debts of the partnership and conversely is entitled to a share of the profits of the partnership. Therefore he is one of several employers. If he were to be considered as an employee, he would be partly employed by himself. Under the circumstances, for the purposes of workmen's compensation, he is not an employee and not within the scope of the act.

An officer of a corporation, if employed in a working capacity by the corporation, can be an employee. However, where the so-called employee is the sole stockholder of the corporation, most states will hold that he is not an employee. Since he controls the corporation and in effect is the corporation, he cannot make a contract with himself. Therefore, there is no contract of employment.

2309   Employer defined

The compensation acts have their own definition of an employer for the purposes of the act. The definition will set forth the types of employers who are subject to the requirements of the act and who are entitled to the protection which the act will give. It will be found that each statute has its own definition, which is largely influenced by the employments which the legislature wanted to bring within the act. For example, the New York act defines an employer as follows:

Employer means a person, partnership, association, corporation, and the legal representatives of a deceased employer, or the receiver or trustee of a person, partnership, association or corporation, having one or more persons in employment, including the state, a municipal corporation, fire district, or other political subdivision of the state, and every authority or commission heretofore or hereafter continued or created by public authorities law. . . .

This definition in the New York act is modified further by the definition of employment:

Employment includes employment in a trade, business or occupation carried on by the employer for pecuniary gain, or in connection therewith, except where the employee elects to bring his employes within the provisions of this chapter . . . and except employment as a domestic worker . . . and except where a town elects to have the provisions of this chapter apply to the town superintendent of highways. Employment shall also include, in connection with the civil defense effort and for the purposes of this chapter the service of a civil defense volunteer in authorized activities of a volunteer agency sponsored by or authorized by a local office as defined in a state defense emergency act. . . .

Therefore, taking the two sections together, an employer is one who employs the services of another in a business carried on for pecuniary gain. This would exclude churches and charities operated on a nonprofit basis. In any case, recourse should be had to the specific language of the applicable statute when seeking to determine the employers who are subject to the act.

2310   Multiple employers

It is possible for an employee to be employed by more than one employer at one and the same time. For example, a salesman is employed by a tobacco company and a dress house, and is required to make trips throughout the territory calling on the trade. When he is traveling from one city to the other, he is furthering the interests of both employers. If he should be injured while so traveling, both employers would be equally liable for his compensation benefits. If he was injured while going to or calling on a local tobacco store, the tobacco company would be solely responsible for his compensation.

The test as to which employer is to be responsible will turn on the answer to the question of which interest he was serving at the time of the accident. If both interests were being served, as in the case of his traveling from one city to another, both are liable for compensation, whereas if he was performing a specific task for one or the other, the one whose interests were being served is the one liable for his compensation. It should be emphasized that this situation obtains only where the salesman is an employee of both.

If he is an independent contractor, or if he is an employee of one and not the other, then these rules will not apply.

If he is an independent contractor, then there is no contract of employment whatsoever and the compensation act will not apply to the situation at all. If he is the employee of one and not the other, the question then would be whether or not his injury occurred in the course of his employment. For example, if he was employed by the tobacco company and not the dress house, and he was injured while calling on a dress store, as to the tobacco company, the injury did not occur in the course of his employment, and therefore there would be no liability for the payment of compensation by the tobacco company. Since he was not an employee of the dress house, the compensation law would not apply to the relationship.

2311   Special and general employers

It sometimes happens that an employee is "loaned" by one employer to another, with the employee remaining on the payroll of his original employer. Such a situation involves the doctrine of special and general employers. The regular employer is the employee's general employer and the employer to whom he is loaned is called the special employer. If such an employee should be injured while working for the special employer, the general rule in most states is that either the general employer or the special employer or both are responsible for the employee's compensation. The responsibility question is usually decided by making an award for the compensation against both employers equally. It should be emphasized that this doctrine is applicable only to the situation which is outlined above. If the employee terminates his employment with one company and is hired by another, the doctrine of special and general employer is not involved. It is involved only where the employee remains on the payroll of the general employer and is loaned to the special employer.

It might be added parenthetically that while the employee is performing services for the special employer and under his direction, the employee is the agent of the special employer only and the general employer, although answerable for the employee's compensation, is not answerable to others under the doctrine of *respondeat superior* since the agency relationship between the general employer and the employee is suspended during the period of the employee's employment by the special employer.

2312   Illegal employment

The labor laws of most states set up the conditions under which minors and women may be employed. As an example, such laws usually provide that it is illegal to employ a minor on a power-driven machine with moving parts. If a minor is so employed and an injury results, the compensation statute provides for a penalty either in the form of increased compensation or gives the injured minor the option of accepting compensation or bringing an action against the employer with the employer deprived of all of his common-law defenses. The same thing applies to the employment of women where the statute provides for the kind and type of work which they may be employed to do and the hours during which such employment may be undertaken. If there is a violation of the labor law, which violation results in an injury to a woman, then the same penalties are usually imposed.

As to employments which are themselves illegal, such as the operation of a bookmaking establishment, the selling of policy slips, or the operation of a "speakeasy," the compensation law does not apply, and employees of such establishments are without a compensation remedy in the case of injury.

2313   Notice of injury

The first step the claimant must take in making his claim for compensation consists of giving notice to his employer of the occurrence of the accident. Notice may be given to the employer, or the supervisor, or someone in a managerial position. Notice to a fellow servant will not suffice. Notice must be given within a certain period of time (usually 30 days) set forth in the statute. The failure of the claimant to give notice of injury is excused where

1. The employer had actual notice of the occurrence of the accident, or,
2. The failure to give notice did not prejudice the employer's rights.

Where the employer actually witnessed the accident, or where the employer had knowledge of the accident communicated to him by other employees or the claimant's supervisor, notice by the claimant would serve no useful purpose and would be surplusage. The requirement of notice is the vehicle by which the employer obtains knowledge of the accident, and where he already has the knowledge, the requirement has been met.

Where the claimant has failed to give notice within the period required by the statute, and the employer can obtain as much information when he received knowledge of the accident he could have obtained if notice had been given within the statutory period, then the employer has not been prejudiced by the delay. On the other hand, if the delay does hamper the employer in his investigation, and the passage of time makes it impossible to obtain verification of the details of the accident, then the employer has been prejudiced, and the failure to give notice will not be excused.

Therefore, to assert the failure of the claimant to give notice as a defense to his claim, it must be established that the employer did not have knowledge or receive notice within the statutory period, and also that the employer was prejudiced by the lack of notice or knowledge. Unless both of these elements can be proven, the defense will fail.

2314   Employer's first report of injury

States having administrative agencies supervising the operation of the compensation law require that the employer file with the agency a first report of injury on a form prescribed by the agency within a certain number of days after the employer acquires knowledge of the occurrence of the accident. The law prescribes certain penalties in the form of a fine should the employer fail to meet this requirement. What usually happens when the employer is insured is that he will send the report of accident to the insurance carrier and will assume that they will take care of it. It then becomes the duty of the claimsman to see that the report is properly filed, making a copy for his own file and entering on the file the date that the report was filed with the agency.

Unless the statute has a provision to the contrary, the employer's first report of injury is treated as an admission against the interest of the employer. For example, if the employer files a report which sets forth the details of an accident, and he later testifies that no such accident occurred, or that he had no knowledge whatsoever as to whether an accident occurred or not, the report of injury filed by him which sets forth the details of an accident will weigh heavily against him, and will raise some question as to his credibility. He cannot file a report that an accident happened and then deny the truth of the statement made. Therefore, if there is any question as to the occurrence of the accident, the claimsman should see to it that no admissions are made on the first report and that the report contains only information that the employer has of his own knowledge and is not based on hearsay information. Where there is such a doubt, the details of the accident as relayed to the employer can be given but should be prefaced by the words "It is alleged that" or "The injured alleges that." The date of accident is given as the "date of the alleged accident." Where these phrases are used, the employer has admitted nothing and is merely reporting what he heard and nothing more.

Where the defense of the failure of the claimant to give notice of the injury is urged, the claimsman should be certain that the employer did not report an accident within the statutory period. For example, if the period within which notice must be given is 30 days, and the employer denies having any knowledge or notice during that period of time, a report of accident filed by the employer within the 30-day period will belie his statement that he had no knowledge or notice of the accident within the statutory period.

2315   Employee's claim for compensation

The compensation laws have their own statute of limitations and they prescribe the time within which an action must be brought or a claim must be filed. Failure to file a claim within the statutory period (usually one year) will bar the claim. This operates in exactly the same way as the statute of limitations does in the case of actions brought in the courts. The claim for compensation form is prescribed by the administrative agency and must be filed with them. Compensation laws give recognition to the principle that there must be some point in time at which the defendant can be certain that claims will not be brought against him, and therefore the requirement that the claim be filed or an action begun within a certain period of time. After the time has passed, the claim still remains but the law makes it unenforceable. The running of the statute has nothing to do with the merits of the claim, but when the statute has run without any action on the part of the claimant, the claim, meritorious or not, is barred and cannot thereafter be asserted.

2316   Measure of liability

The compensation law modified the common-law liability of the employer to the employee by substituting an entirely new measure of responsibility. The employer is liable to the employee for all the benefits of the compensation law if the employee sustains an accident arising out of and in the course of employment. To qualify for compensation benefits, the employee's claim must meet three tests:

1. He must sustain an accident.
2. The accident must arise out of the employment.
3. The accident must have occurred in the course of the employment.

1. *Accident.* The courts have been called upon to construe the word "accident" on countless occasions and in a variety of circumstances. They have been asked to decide what the word means in connection with insurance policies, such as liability, and accident, and health, and in connection with what the legislature meant by the term when applied to compensation cases. Of all the constructions given by the courts, the most liberal has been applied to compensation. It has been defined as a befalling; an event which takes place without one's foresight or expectation; an undesigned, sudden, and unexpected event.

The application of these definitions to factual situations is not without its difficulties. We can at the outset rule out any intentional acts on the part of the injured that are calculated to injure himself as being nonaccidental. However, the intention to injure one's self must be clear and unequivocable. Merely because the act of the injured person is ill-advised, or even stupid, is not evidence of an intentional self-injury. For example, in the absence of any other facts, if a man drops a heavy object on his foot, grasps a piece of red hot steel with his bare hands, or puts his hand into a moving machine, he has sustained an accident within the meaning of the compensation act. These acts may be characterized as foolhardy but certainly not intentional.

The sudden, unexpected event which constitutes an accident must be a sudden and tangible happening of a traumatic nature, producing an immediate and prompt result and occurring from without. The accident must have happened at a specific time and at a specific place. It must have been produced by conditions outside the body, which conditions are peculiar to the employment.

For example, in *Carter* v. *International Detrola Corp.* (43 N.W. 2d 890), it was claimed that the claimant's excessive use of the scelenus anticus muscle, which resulted in his disability, was an accident within the meaning of the compensation act. The court held that the claimant's disability did not result from an accidental injury or a fortuitous event and that, if it was to be compensable at all, it must be "a disability which is due to causes and conditions which are characteristic of and peculiar to the business of the employer." The court held that "muscle use is common to most other employments and the act does not permit compensation for injuries caused by this alone."

Unusual conditions of the employment may expose the employee to a risk of injury, and where these conditions produce a deleterious effect on the body, the resulting condition is regarded as accidentally sustained. For example, heat prostration is an accidental injury if the employment exposes the employee to the risk of such an injury. Those who suffer prostration while working in a blast furnace, or those whose employment exposes them to the sun's rays on a hot day, can qualify as being victims of an accidental injury. The exposure, however, must be greater than the exposure of the general public. If the employee is merely subject to weather conditions which are the same as those endured by the general public, then heat prostration would not be considered as an accidental injury. It is only where the employment increases the risk of heat prostration because of the conditions peculiar to the employment that the resulting heat prostration is considered as an accident.

The same reasoning is applied to other conditions which produce harmful physical conditions of the body, such as freezing, or overheating, and sudden chilling. If the condition to which the employee is exposed is the same as that to which the general public is exposed, then there is no accidental injury, but where the special hazard of the employment exposes the employee to a greater risk than that of the general public, then the resulting condition of the employee is an accident.

The question of whether the event constitutes an accident is decided from the standpoint of the injured person. For example, a fellow employee intentionally drops a heavy object on the claimant's head, or throws an object at him; as to the claimant, he has sustained an accidental injury. As to the fellow employee, the injury was intentional. The claimant is entitled to compensation under those circumstances. The same reasoning is applied to cases of assault by either a fellow employee or anyone else. The claimant, as the innocent victim, has sustained an accident even though the person assaulting him intended to produce a physical injury.

An accident is not always the result of a physical impact. It can come about as a result of a mental injury. For example, in *Klimas* v. *Trans-Caribbean Airways* (10 N.Y. 2d 209), the court held that "undue anxiety," strain, and mental stress are frequently more devastating than physical injury, and therefore, where it was claimed that the employee's death because of a heart attack was induced by emotional stress without physical strain or contact, the facts supported the conclusion that the deceased had sustained an accident within the meaning of the compensation act. The facts indicated that the deceased was the director of maintenance for the airline. One of his employer's planes having been grounded by the C.A.A., he was blamed for the damage. Threats of loss of employment, the high cost of repairs, and delay in repairs brought on great emotional stress, climaxed by a fatal heart attack. There was substantial medical testimony connecting the heart attack to the emotional stress. In finding that the deceased had sustained an accident, the court observed that "Whether a particular event was an industrial accident is to be determined, not by any legal definition, but by the common-sense viewpoint of the average man."

There are various shades of opinion among the courts of the various states as to what constitutes an accident. In some cases, this is due to the particular wording of the compensation statute, some referring to accidents, others to personal injuries, and still others to accidental injuries. Where marginal or doubtful situations arise, it is recommended that recourse be had to the decided cases of the applicable jurisdiction.

2. *Arising out of the employment.* This is the second requisite which must be established. The most often-quoted definition was formulated by the Supreme Court of Massachusetts in 1913 in the *McNichol's* case (102 N.E. 697). The court said:

The injury arises out of the employment when there is apparent to the rational mind upon consideration of all the circumstances a causal connection between the conditions under which the work is required to be performed and the resulting injury. Under this test if the injury can be seen to have followed as a natural incident of the work and to have been contemplated by a reasonable person familiar with the whole situation as a result of the exposure occasioned by the nature of the employment, then it arises out of the employment, but it excludes an injury which cannot be throughly traced to the employment as a contributing proximate cause and which comes from a hazard to which the workman would have been equally exposed apart from the employment. The causative danger must be peculiar to the work and not common to the neighborhood. It must be incidental to the character of the business and not independent of the relation of master and servant. It need not have been foreseen or expected but after the event, it must appear to have had its origin in a risk connected with the employment and to have flowed from that source as a rational consequence.

The words "arising out of the employment" refer to the origin or the cause of the injury. The accident, to be compensable, must arise out of some risk reasonably incidental to the employment. The employee must be doing something that he was employed to do and the accident must have occurred while he was so occupied.

Where the employee is employed at a fixed location with certain specified duties at that location, the question of the relationship of his duties to the cause of an accident is easy to determine. He is entitled to an ingress and an egress from the premises, so that once he is on the employer's premises and going to his area of work, he is in the scope of his employment; and an accident occurring while he is so occupied is considered as arising out of the employment. In addition, the employer must contemplate certain personal acts, such as answering a call of nature, as being within the scope of the employment. However, where the employee is employed to do a job at a fixed location, he is not within the scope of his employment when he is preparing to come to work or on his way to the employer's premises.

For example, if he should cut himself while shaving in the morning, and he is required to appear for work clean-shaven, he is not within the scope of his employment while so doing. The same reasoning applies to his travel from his home to the place of work, where the employer does not furnish the transportation. Where the employer furnishes the transportation, the employee is then within the scope of his employment while being so transported, since the risk of injury while being transported by the employer is one of the risks of the employment. This type of situation refers solely to cases where the employer supplies the transportation as part of the contract of hire and does not refer to an isolated transaction where the employer or one of the managing personnel drives an employee to work.

This same employee goes out to lunch or out for a coffee break. He is entitled to an egress and a ingress from the premises, and while on the premises, whether going or returning, is within the scope of his employment. But once he is outside the premises, the risks of injury are personal, and should he be injured during that period, the accident does not arise out of the employment. It makes no difference that the employer granted a lunch period or a coffee break.

In other cases, the employer may have a lunchroom where the employee may eat, either bringing his own food or purchasing the food from the employer, or the employer may permit the employee to eat his lunch at his workbench. If the employee is injured during any of these periods, the question of whether the accident arose out of the employment will depend upon whether the risk was one to which his employment exposed him or one which was entirely personal.

For example, if the employee brought his own lunch and was eating it at his workbench and the ceiling fell on him, the accident occurred as a result of a risk to which his employment exposed him. On the other hand, if while eating his own lunch he swallowed a chicken bone, or the food contained a deleterious substance which made him ill, the risk of injury was not one to which the employment exposed him but a personal risk having no relationship whatsoever to his employment. Should the employer either sell or provide the food for lunch and such food contained some harmful substance which made the employee ill, then the accident would arise out of the employment since this risk was one created by the employment.

Cases in which the employee is not employed at a fixed place but is required to travel from place to place present some difficulty. The general rule is that if the employee is furthering the interests of the employer at the time the travel was being performed, then he is within the scope of his employment, otherwise he is not. For example, where the employee is hired to call on customers, whether from a prepared list or at random, as long as he is engaged in calling on customers he is within the scope of his employment. But if he deviates from that task to perform some personal mission, he is not within the scope of his employment. He is back within the scope of his employment when he returns to the task of calling on customers. In *Barber* v. *Harvey & Eddy Co.* [193 N.E. 433 (New York)], the court held that the death of a traveling salesman in an auto collision while he was proceeding to a lunch cart before finally departing for another city on business did not arise out of his employment.

Where traveling employees are required to be away over night, and the employer does not designate the place where they are to stay, or does not provide a place for them, even though the employer does defray the cost of meals and hotel, they are not in the scope of their employment while eating, sleeping, or occupying a hotel room. For example, in *Johnson* v. *Smith* [188 N.E. 140 (New York)], the employee contracted typhoid fever while eating in a restaurant in another town to which he had been sent to sell goods. It was held that the accident did not arise out of the employment, even though all expenses of such journeys were borne by the employer, since the employee exercised his own discretion as to where he would eat. A salesman injured while taking a bath in the hotel, or walking down the stairway, or through the lobby is not within the scope of his employment, even though the employer paid the hotel bill.

Where the employer designates a specific place where the employee must stay, then if the employee is injured because of any unsafe condition of the premises, even though not actually working at the time, the accident arises out of the employment. The reasoning is that the employee must stay at the place selected by the employer and no other, the exposure to any risk connected with the place is an exposure of the employment. On the other hand, even if the employer designates the place to stay and the employee is injured not because of any defect in the premises but because of some personal matter, such as shaving or taking a bath, the accident would not arise out of the employment for the reason that such an accident could occur whether the employer provided the place to stay or not.

Where the employee is required to live on the premises of his employment, or where he is on call 24 hours a day and the employer provides accommodations, the same rule applies. If the accident is due to the premises and not some personal act, the accident arises out of the employment. For example, a chef was required to sleep on the premises and was subject to call at all hours. The premises were destroyed by fire and the chef suffered fatal burns. It was held that the accident arose out of the employment since the employment exposed him to the risk of injury by fire. [See *Giliotti* v. *Hoffman Catering Co.*, 246 N.Y. 279.]

On the other hand, if the cause of the accident is a personal matter, even though it occurs on the premises, the accident does not arise out of the employment. In *Pisko* v. *Mintz* (262 N.Y. 176), the claimant, a janitor required to sleep on the premises, was burned by a fire caused by a lighted cigarette while he was smoking in bed. It was held that his injuries did not arise out of the employment.

It sometimes happens that the employee is going on a personal errand and the employer asks him to do some trifling task for him at the same time. If the employee is injured while serving this dual purpose, the question arises as to whether the accident occurred in the scope of his employment. The answer to the question will turn on whether the employee would have gone on the errand irrespective of the employer's business or, in the alternative, would not have gone on the errand if the personal matter had been dropped.

For example, a plumber, hearing that his helper was going to a nearby town on a personal errand, asked him to do some trifling tasks while there. The tasks assigned would not have justified the trip, but as long as the employee was going there anyway the employer asked that these tasks be done. The employee was killed while driving on the highway while returning from the nearby town. The question thus was presented as to whether or not the accident arose out of the employment.

In *Marks* v. *Gray* (251 N.Y. 90), the court held that the accident did not arise out of the employment for the reason that the primary motivation for the trip was the personal matter and not the business of the employer. The court said:

> . . . If, however, the work has had no part in creating the necessity for travel; if the journey would have gone forward though the business errand had been dropped, and would have been cancelled upon the failure of the private purpose though the business was undone, the travel is personal, and personal the risk.

3. *In the course of employment.* An injury or an accident befalls a man in the course of his employment if it occurs within a time during which he is employed at a place he may reasonably be during that time. The words "arising out of the employment" refer to the origin of the cause of the injury, whereas "course of employment" refers to the time, place, and circumstances under which the injury took place. To be compensable, the accident must meet the test not only of arising out of the employment, but it must be suffered in the course of employment as well.

For example, during the period of work two men get into a heated argument as to how the work should be done. On the way home, the argument continues, to the point where one of the men assaults the other, causing personal injuries. The accident arose out of the employment in the sense that the cause of the argument originated in the employment, but the accident did not occur in the course of the employment, since neither man was working at the time and neither was at the place of employment.

In *Lampert* v. *Simons* (235 N.Y. 311), a department head continued to work during a strike of employees. He was assaulted by a striker on his way to work. It was held that the assault or accident did not occur in the course of employment. In that case, the accident might have met the test as arising out of the employment, but since it did not happen during the time and at the place of employment, it did not occur in the course of the employment.

As another example, let us assume that during the hours of work, the employee uses the employer's equipment to make a toy for his own son, and while so doing suffers an injury. The accident occurred in the course of the employment in the sense that it occurred during the hours of work and on the employer's premises, but the work was not done in the furtherance of the employer's interest but for a purpose personal to the employee. Therefore, the accident did not arise out of the employment, even though it did occur in the course of it. The accident is therefore not compensable.

2317   Injury defined

An injury, or personal injury, to come within the scope of the compensation act, consists of violence to the physical structure of the body and such disease or infection as may naturally or unavoidably result therefrom, caused by a single incident. This excludes systemic conditions from within the body and refers to violence to the body from without. Since the injury is confined to the physical structure of the body, it would by its terms exclude damage to property. Therefore, damage to clothing, damage to a wooden leg, false teeth, or a glass eye are not within the scope of the definition of injury and are excluded as recoverable items.

The injury must come from a single incident and not a series of incidents. For example, if an employee is subjected to an unusual strain in lifting a specific weight at a specific time, the injury caused by the strain is within the definition. On the other hand, if the employee claims to have a back sprain which came upon him gradually and he cannot point to any single incident which caused the condition, the condition is not the result of an accident or an injury within this definition.

Claims are frequently made for conditions which were acquired over a period of time either from constant use of some part of the body or from a series of exposures to the same precipitating cause. These are all noncompensable. For example, a claimant acquired a felon on his hand from the constant use of a screwdriver, a machine operator sustained callous formations on his hands from the constant use of the machine, or a carpenter sustained prepatella bursitis (water on the knee) from constant kneeling. These do not qualify as accidental injuries within the terms of most compensation acts.

2318   Aggravation of a preexisting disability

The general rule is that industry takes the employee as it finds him, and if he is suffering from a preexisting disability which is aggravated by injury, the employer is obligated to cure and relieve him just as if there was no preexisting disability. This obligation must be assumed even though the same injury to a relatively healthy employee would have produced only a minor injury or no injury at all. Knowledge on the part of the employer of the existing disability is not a necessary element of the employer's responsibility. Whether the employer knew about the previous condition or not, he is liable for the compensation and medical benefits which accrue to the employee as a result of the injury superimposed upon the preexisting condition.

Theoretically, the employer is only required to place the employee back in the same condition as he was prior to the accident; he is not required to entirely cure the preexisting condition. Therefore, the employer is responsible only for the aggravation, and when the results of the aggravation have ceased, the employer's responsibility is at an end. Unfortunately, in most cases the condition and the aggravation cannot be separated—or the claimant's physical condition never returns to its original status and, as a result, the employer winds up being responsible for the entire condition.

For example, if the employee has a preexisting bone condition such as osteomyelitis, and he suffers an accident which involves direct trauma to the bone, aggravating the infectious condition, the employer will be responsible for the treatment of the osteomyelitis and the disability occasioned thereby, until the osteomyelitis returns to a quiescent condition. Since this is highly unlikely, the employer will really have to cure the condition before he will be relieved of liability. Or if an employee suffering from a systemic condition, such as syphilis or diabetes, sustains an injury resulting in deep lacerations, the employer may find himself in a position where he will have to assume the responsibility for medical treatment directed toward a cure, or at least the control, of the syphilis or diabetes.

Because of this possible liability, many employers insist on having a preemployment physical examination prior to hiring an employee. In this way prior conditions are detected before employment, and if the condition is such that a second injury will expose the employer to an increased liability, such employees are not engaged. In other cases, where the preexisting condition does not so expose the employer, the preemployment physical examination establishes the existence of such conditions and can be utilized in defending claims that the condition was acquired through the employment. This usually happens in hernia cases, where the preemployment physical reveals the existence of a hernia prior to employment. If it is later claimed that the work produced the hernia, the preemployment physical will disprove the claim.

2319   Occupational diseases

An occupational disease is one which results from the nature of the employment, and by nature is meant not those conditions brought about by the failure of the employer to furnish a safe place to work, but conditions to which all employees of a class are subject, and which produce the disease as a natural incident of a particular occupation, and attach to that occupation a hazard which distinguishes it from the usual run of occupations and is in excess of the hazard attending employment in general (*Goldberg* v. *Marcy*, 276 N.Y. 313). It is a disease that is peculiar to the occupation and not common to the general public.

The original compensation laws referred only to accidents occurring in the scope of employment and did not contain any provision as to occupational diseases. Therefore, since the law modified the common law as to accidents, the claimant was limited to his compensation remedy in such cases, but since the law did not apply to occupational diseases, the common-law rights and liabilities of both employer and employee remained. Later compensation laws were amended by adding a provision with respect to occupational diseases. These amendments named the diseases covered, and in some laws, the particular process from which the disease could arise, was also named. This meant that the claimant had to be suffering from one of the diseases listed and that the disease must have been suffered in the particular process named in the act. If the claimant did not acquire one of the diseases covered in the processes named, he was not covered under the compensation act and was relegated to his common-law rights as far as recovery was concerned. The process of amending the compensation laws has continued and more and more diseases have been added, with some states covering any and all occupational diseases while others still retain a limited listing of the diseases covered.

The addition of occupational diseases to the compensation statute brought with it problems which were not encountered in cases resulting from accident. Where the claimant has been continuously employed by the same employer and exposed to a disease hazard right up to the date on which he is disabled, there is no particular problem. However, where the employee was exposed to the disease while working for more than one employer, and the medical testimony indicates that the disease was contracted over the entire period of exposure, the problem then arises as to which employer is responsible for the payment of compensation.

Each state has dealt with this problem either by statutory enactment or by judicial interpretation. The solution in some states consists of holding the last employer responsible for the compensation, with the others going scot-free, while in other states there is an apportionment between all the employers on a pro rata basis, depending on the length of the claimant's exposure during his employment with each. For example, if the claimant worked six months for one employer, and a year each for two other employers, and in each case was exposed to the same hazard, then the compensation would be apportioned by holding the first employer for one-fifth of the compensation and medical benefits, with the other two being held two-fifths each.

The second problem encountered in occupational diseases is where the date of disablement takes place sometime after the last injurious exposure. The statutes have dealt with the problem by providing that the case is compensable only where the date of disablement comes within 12 months after the last injurious exposure and not otherwise. This means that if the last exposure was more than 12 months prior to disablement the claimant cannot recover. Some states limit the time even further by making it 6 months instead of 12 months. With the average case of disease, the limitation of 6 to 12 months works out quite well in the sense that most of the diseases will manifest themselves during that period following the last exposure.

However, with exposures to dust diseases, such as silicosis, asbestosis, anthracosis, the insidious nature of the disease is such that it will not manifest itself until years after the last exposure. Therefore, the states have found it necessary to enact special legislation with respect to these dust diseases and to provide for a longer period of limitation than is applied to other diseases. In addition, we now find ourselves confronted with radiation exposures which act in exactly the same way as the dust diseases in that the effect of the exposure is not manifest until years later. As of this writing, the states in which radiation exposures have been reported, have considered or have passed legislation extending the period of limitation in the cases of radiation exposures.

Of special concern to the claimsman is the matter of insurance coverage. The workmen's compensation policy will cover the liability of the employer during the policy period. If there are several insurance carriers who covered the employer during the period of the claimant's exposure, the problem arises as to which of them is liable for the compensation. The states have met this problem by either holding the carrier who was on the risk at the time of the claimant's disablement solely liable, or by apportioning the liability among all the carriers, this by special legislation. In addition, some states have provided for the creation of a special fund for the purpose of paying compensation on dust disease cases after the carrier has assumed a certain amount of the payment. Recourse must be had to the specific statute as to the existence and the extent of the liability assumed by these special funds.

2320   Evidence and proof

Theoretically under the compensation acts, the claimant must establish his claim, but in many jurisdictions he has the benefit of presumptions which make his proof less difficult and in practical effect shift the burden of proof from the claimant to the employer. Therefore, the employer must disprove the claim which is asserted by the claimant, who has the benefit of the presumptions.

The presumptions in favor of the claimant are assumed in the absence of substantial evidence to the contrary. Under the statute it is usually presumed that:

1. The claim comes within the provisions of the compensation law.
2. Sufficient notice thereof was given.
3. The injury was not occasioned by the willful intention of the injured employee to bring about the injury or death of himself, or of another.
4. The injury did not result solely from the intoxication of the injured employee while on duty.
5. The contents of medical and surgical reports introduced in evidence by the claimant for compensation shall constitute prima facie evidence of fact as to the matter contained therein.

The uncontradicted testimony of the claimant as to the happening of an accident or of his exposure to conditions which precipitated an occupational disease will establish a prima facie case. It is then up to the employer to present evidence in contradiction, and if he fails to do so, the claimant will prevail. This is especially burdensome in cases of unwitnessed accidents, and the only possibility of producing contrary evidence will lie in the direction of contradictory statements made by the claimant, the history of accident given by the claimant to his doctor, or to the admitting intern if he was hospitalized. If the claim involved a motor vehicle, then the accident report filed by the claimant might be enlightening. If he carries accident and health insurance and makes a claim therefor (even though such policies usually exclude compensation cases) the records of the A & H carrier could possibly indicate some contradictory statements. In addition, evidence could be produced of some physical facts which would make the happening of the accident as described by the claimant impossible.

In death cases where the accident which caused the death was unwitnessed, the physical facts will be enough to establish the presumptions; that is, if the deceased was found at a place where he was required to be as a result of his employment, and the cause of death could be reasonably related to his occupation.

Most statutes provide that the compensation board is not bound by the common law, statutory rules of evidence, or formal rules of procedure. This means that hearsay evidence, which would not be admissible in the usual common-law action, can be admitted in evidence in compensation claims. This would include declarations of a deceased employee made to others concerning the occurrence of an accident in which he or some other employee was involved. Generally, the various compensation boards hold that hearsay evidence must be corroborated either by the testimony of others or by the circumstances under which the accident occurred.

For example, if a deceased employee told his wife that he hit his head on a ceiling beam while walking through the factory, evidence that the ceiling beam was more than 10 feet from the floor surface would negative the deceased's declaration as to the causation of the accident, whereas if the ceiling beam was 5 feet from the floor, the deceased's statement would be corroborated by the physical facts. In the first instance, the accident could not have happened in the manner as described in the deceased's declaration, whereas in the second instance the declaration is supported by the physical facts.

2321   Causal relationship between accident and injury

The presumptions aid the claimant in establishing that an accident took place. There is no presumption that the physical disability from which the claimant may be suffering was caused by the accident. The relationship between the trauma caused by the accident and the claimant's physical disability must be established by medical evidence. Lacking proof that the accident caused the physical injury, the claimant cannot prevail.

For example, suppose the claimant says that he felt a pain in his back while lifting a heavy weight. His testimony, plus the presumptions, establishes that he has sustained a compensable accident. If the doctor should find that the claimant had a series of boils on his back, and no other injury, the doctor would say that there was no evidence of injury but evidence of a systemic or chronic condition which bore no relationship to the history of accident as related by the claimant. Proof of causal relationship between the accident and the injury suffered would be lacking and the claimant could not prevail. On the other hand, if the doctor found evidence of a strain of the muscles of the back, muscle spasm, and a restriction in the motions of the back, he could reasonably conclude that these conditions came about as a consequence of the lifting.

Claims involving inguinal herniae are frequently made. The history given is that the employee lifted a heavy weight and while so doing felt a sharp pain in the lower quadrant (left or right) of the abdomen. With such a history, it is quite possible that the intra-abdominal pressure engendered by the lift could have caused the hernia. However, if the physician's examination revealed some gross pathology in the form of a thickened sac, or that a truss had been worn on that side for some time, it would be clear to the physician that the hernia antedated the accident. Then, the proof of causal relationship between the accident and the resulting condition would be lacking. In some cases, it is impossible to tell the age of the hernia without performing an operation. When the operation is done, the operating surgeon can tell by the pathology presented as to whether the hernia has existed for a period of time or whether it is of recent origin.

In some cases, the claimsman may find that there was causal relationship between the accident and the injury, that after a period of disability the claimant's traumatic condition entirely cleared up, but that the claimant was still disabled because of some other unrelated condition. The liability of the employer is limited to the injury caused by the accident and the disability resulting therefrom, but is not liable for disability caused by some other chronic condition not the result of the accident.

In such a case, the defense would be a partial one, in that the employer would admit the period of disability caused by the accident but would deny the period of disability caused by another condition. For example, let us assume that the claimant injured his back, which responded to treatment. When the back injury had subsided, the claimant did not return to work because it was found that he was suffering from a carcinoma of the stomach (cancer) which disabled him from working. The employer's responsibility would be limited to the disability caused by the back condition, and, if it could be shown that the disability of the back had ended, the employer would have no responsibility for the claimant's further disability.

2322   Disposition of disputed claims

The underlying philosophy of the compensation laws is that compensation benefits are a substitute for wages and should be paid in the same manner and at the same time as wages. Where a claim is disputed, no compensation is paid until the dispute is resolved. Therefore, the laws usually provide for a prompt and speedy hearing before the industrial accident board, or similar body, at which time a decision will be made either affirming or denying the employee's right to compensation. Adjournments are grudgingly granted, and in some states, where the employer or insurance carrier requests an adjournment, penalties are imposed. The reason for this is that during the time the matter remains in dispute, the employee is not receiving any compensation, and a delay in the payment of a meritorious claim defeats the purpose and intent of the law. From the claimsman's standpoint, this means that where a defense is being asserted the evidence on which the defense is based must be in existence and available at the time of hearing.

The hearing is conducted in a summary fashion, and, as we have seen, the board is not bound by the rules of evidence. However, as in every adversary proceeding, the person making the claim must establish it by a preponderance of evidence. Since the employee has the benefit of the presumptions, his own testimony as to the occurrence of the accident, if compensable, plus the presumptions, will establish a prima facie case in his favor. To overcome the presumptions the employer must present substantial evidence to the contrary, so that where the claimant testifies to an accident arising out of and in the course of employment, the employer, to sustain his defense, must present substantial evidence to the contrary. The practical effect of the application of these rules will be, in most cases, the transfer of the burden of proof from the employee to the employer.

The hearing officer or the board, as the case may be, performs the functions of both judge and jury. Questions of fact are decided (a jury function) and the law is applied to the facts so determined (the judge's function). The employer may appeal from the decision to a reviewing court, which will consider only errors of law and will not review questions of fact. However, where there is no evidence to support the finding of fact, or where the finding of fact is so contrary to the weight of the evidence that it constitutes an error of law, the court can decide as a matter of law that the fact question was improperly decided, and reverse the decision. In some of the earlier cases, the reviewing court announcd a rule of decision called the "scintilla"[1] rule. In applying this rule to appeals by the employer from awards made in favor of the employee, the reviewing courts held that if there was a scintilla of evidence in favor of the employee, they were bound to find in his favor. Some boards took this to mean that they should decide the cases before them on the same basis, and that if there is a mere scintilla of evidence in favor of the claimant, the award must be in his favor. The word scintilla is seldom used today, and the words "substantial evidence" or "credible evidence" have taken its place.

In any case, reference will have to be had to the latest decisions of the industrial accident board to ascertain whether or not they are applying the scintilla rule, irrespective of the nomenclature employed. For example, in a recent case there was a conflict in the medical evidence. A general practitioner testified in favor of the employee that there was causal relationship between the accident and the claimant's resulting medical condition. On behalf of the employer, two specialists in internal medicine testified that the employee's condition had no relationship whatsoever to his employment. The reviewing court refused to disturb the findings of fact in favor of the employee, stating that it was not for the court to say whether the testimony of specialists in internal medicine was entitled to greater weight than that of a general practitioner, and that the testimony of the general practitioner amounted to "substantial evidence" which supported the award [*Cline* v. *Dept. of Labor and Industries,* 313 Pac. 2d 687 (Washington)].

2323   Defenses to compensation claims

The defenses to compensation claims fall into four main divisions: (1) accident, (2) notice, (3) causal relation, and (4) limitation.

1. *Accident.* This defense goes to the heart of the claim and is interposed in opposition to the claim where (1) the claimant did not sustain an accident, or (2) the accident did not occur in the course of employment, or (3) the accident did not arise out of the employment. Some states hold, either by statute or decision, that an accident does not arise out of the employment if it occurs due to a violation of orders or safety regulations enforced by the employer.

This latter qualification is very important. The mere fact that there is an order or a safety regulation in force is not enough. It must be shown that the regulations or orders are enforced by the employer. For example, most factories have rules that machines must be operated with a hand guard in position. This slows up the work and many employees, especially those on

---

[1] "Scintilla" is a metaphorical expression to describe a very insignificant or trifling item or particle of evidence. It was borrowed from an old common-law rule to the effect that if there is any evidence at all in a case, even a mere scintilla, tending to support a material issue, the case cannot be taken from the jury, but the question must be submitted and decided by them.

a piecework basis, will habitually neglect to have the guard in position. If this is the case, and the employer does not enforce the safety regulation by discharging those who disobey it when he knows of their disobedience, the employer will have waived the enforcement of the regulation, and an injury occurring because of the lack of the safety guard will be compensable. The disobedience of the regulation was concurred in by the employer and therefore he cannot use it as a defense. On the other hand, if the safety regulation is strictly enforced, any injury due to a violation thereof will not be compensable.

Either by statute or decision, most states bar a recovery where the claimant's injury was occasioned by his own willful intent to injure himself or another. As to a self-inflicted injury, the evidence must be clear as to the employee's intent, and mere carelessness will not be clear evidence of the intention to injure oneself. Where the employee attempts to commit suicide, and makes statements evidencing such an intent, then there is evidence of a self-inflicted injury. In cases where the employee's injury comes about as a result of his willful intention to injure another, his injuries are not compensable. Therefore, in cases of assault by one employee upon another, the aggressor can never recover. As to the employee assaulted, if the assault arises out of and in the course of employment, he may recover. If the assault does not meet the test of arising out of and in the course of employment, then even the person assaulted may not recover.

For example, A and B are employed at the same plant. A asks B to loan him $10. B refuses and remarks that A is a poor credit risk who never pays his debts. A hits B with a hammer, and B retaliates by kicking A in the stomach. Both have sustained injuries. Neither can recover compensation. As to A, his injuries came about as a consequence of his willful intention to injure another, to wit, B. As to B, the accident did occur in the course of the employment, in the sense that it happened during working hours, but it arose out of a personal matter entirely unrelated to the employment, and for that reason did not arise out of the employment.

In a second situation, A complains to B that he, B, is working too slowly. B calls A a slave driver. Incensed by this remark, A hits B, and B retaliates in kind. As to A, he is the aggressor and cannot recover compensation. His injuries were caused by his willful intention to injure another. As to B, he can recover compensation. The accident occurred in the course of the employment, and since the argument had to do with the manner of doing the work, the accident also arose out of the employment.

In a third situation, let us assume that both A and B are walking home. A complains that B is a slowpoke in his work. B calls A a slave driver. A assaults B and B retaliates. Neither can recover compensation: A because he is the aggressor, and B because the accident did not occur in the course of the employment. The accident did arise out of the employment, in the sense that the cause of the argument was the manner in which the work was to be done, but B had finished his work for the day and was on his own time.

The accident did not occur in the course of his employment but in the course of his travel from work.

In investigating cases involving assault, it is sometimes difficult to determine who is the aggressor, particularly if the aggressor is the foreman, the son of the owner, or an officer of the corporation, since the other employees may be reluctant to talk to the investigator about the incident. Sometimes tact and diplomacy will accomplish the desired result, and in other cases threats of subpoena and testimony under oath will get the necessary facts. In any case, the claimsman should not attempt to decide the merits of either claim unless and until he is certain that he has the true facts. If he does not, he runs the risk of making a voluntary payment to the aggressor and later having to make a payment to the other party, when he is liable only to one. In doubtful cases, both claims should be contested and the compensation authority should be called upon to decide which of the two is entitled to recovery.

An assault connotes a willful intention to injure, but there are cases where there is no such intention but where an injury nevertheless results. Usually these cases are the result of horseplay outside the scope of the employment. Where one employee plays a practical joke on another and the victim of the joke is injured, even though he took no part in the horseplay, the injured person is entitled to compensation. On the other hand, if both are engaged in horseplay, such as boxing or wrestling, and one is injured, the usual decision is that the injured person is not entitled to compensation.

The statute denies compensation to an employee if the injury is due solely to the employee's intoxication while on duty. This is a difficult defense to sustain. The employer must show that the employee was intoxicated at the time of the accident. He must also show that the accident would not have happened but for the intoxication of the employee. If the accident would have occurred whether the employee was intoxicated or not, the claim is compensable. Both elements must be present before the defense will be sustained.

2. Notice.   The Compensation statute provides that the employee give the employer written notice of the happening of the accident within a certain period of time after its occurrence, usually 30 days, and within 90 days after disablement in the case of occupational diseases. Failure to give written notice is excused either on the ground that for some sufficient reason notice could not be given (usually the severity of the injury), on the ground that the employer or his or its agents in charge of the business in the place where the accident occurred (or having immediate supervision of the employee to whom the accident happened) had knowledge of the accident or death, or that the employer has not been prejudiced by the failure to give notice. Where notice could have been given and the employer is prejudiced by the failure to receive such notice because he or it has no knowledge of the accident, the failure to give notice will be a bar to the claim for compensation.

Therefore, for the employee's failure to give notice to be a defense, it must be established (1) that notice could have been given, (2) that the employer and his or its managing agents had no knowledge of the occurrence of the accident, and (3) that the employer was prejudiced by the failure to give notice. Unless the employer can establish all three of these elements, the defense will not be sustained.

3. *Causal relation.* For a compensation recovery to be allowed, the accident must be the competent producing cause of the injuries from which the claimant is suffering. If the condition came about because of any other cause, the resulting period or disability is not compensable.

4. *Limitation.* The compensation statute provides for the filing of a claim for compensation with the compensation authority, that is, the industrial accident board, or the workmen's compensation board, or whatever designation is given to such authority in the state. This must be filed within the statutory period (usually one year), a requirement in addition to the obligation to give notice to the employer. It is comparable to the statute of limitations in other types of cases, and the failure to assert a claim by filing the claim for compensation with the proper authority within the time limited bars the claim.

Some jurisdictions, however, provide for a waiver by the employer if the employer fails to assert the defense at the first hearing at which all parties in interest are present. This parallels the defense of the statute of limitations in negligence and other cases in that the failure to assert the running of the statute as an affirmative defense will constitute a waiver of the defense.

2324   Compensation benefits generally

Compensation benefits consist of periodic payments paid in the same manner as wages in order to reasonably reimburse the claimant for the wages lost, plus the payment for medical, surgical, hospital, nursing services, and other medical services as the nature of the injury and the process of recovery may require. The statute will set forth the weekly amount to be paid which will reasonably reimburse the claimant for wages lost. This is subject to a maximum and a minimum and is based on a percentage of the claimant's average weekly wages. The percentage runs from 55 to 80 percent, with the majority of states fixing the percentage at $66\frac{2}{3}$ percent.

The payment of compensation is designed to repay the claimant for any loss of wages which he may sustain as a result of an industrial accident. The loss of his wages may be total in that he has lost his entire salary, or partial in that he is capable of doing only a smaller job which does not pay as much as his regular work. In any case the compensation is payable in order to reimburse him for any loss of wages he has suffered.

The disability suffered by the claimant may be either temporary, which means that there will be an ultimate recovery, or it may be permanent, which would mean that he would never recover from the condition. Therefore, compensation payments are classified as to whether the disability for which payment is made is total or partial, and whether it is temporary or permanent.

The compensation law sets forth the amount to be paid and the manner of payment in each of four classifications, based on the considerations of disability. These are (1) temporary-total, (2) temporary-partial, (3) permanent-partial, and (4) permanent-total.

1. *Temporary-total.* This refers to payments of compensation to an employee who is totally disabled or incapable of doing any work, for a temporary period of time, with ultimate recovery anticipated.

2. *Temporary-partial.* This refers to payments made where the employee is capable of doing some work, but not his full duty, and he suffers some wage loss as a result thereof, the period of which is only temporary in the sense that full recovery is anticipated.

3. *Permanent-partial.* Where the claimant has suffered an injury from which he will not recover, but which only partially affects his earning capacity, the payments are classified as permanent-partial. An example of this type of disability is where the claimant has suffered an amputation of a finger, toe, arm, leg, foot, or a permanent diminution in either hearing or vision.

4. *Permanent-total.* As the name implies, this refers to a case where the claimant is totally disabled or is incapable of doing any work whatsoever, and the condition is such that the claimant will never recover. Some statutes provide that where the claimant has suffered the loss of both hands, both arms, both legs, or is permanently blind in both eyes, that any one of these injuries will constitute permanent total disability.

In addition to these classes of disability, some statutes provide for payments for serious facial or head disfigurement, or cosmetic defects, and some go beyond the face and head and provide for compensation for any bodily disfigurement. The theory of these payments is that they will repay the claimant for any loss which he may sustain in the employment market because of the existence of scarring or other disfigurement which would make him a less-desirable employee.

2325   Average weekly wages

The compensation rate payable is based on the average weekly wage in most states. What constitutes the "average weekly wage" is defined in the compensation law. In most instances, it does not mean the wages the claimant received during the week immediately preceding the accident. The definition usually refers to the average earnings over a period of time, some states limiting the period to 13 weeks immediately preceding the accident, and others taking into consideration the employee's earnings over the period of one year. The only way that such earnings can be established is by the securing of the employee's actual payroll from the employer. This should be secured on a payday-to-payday basis and should be itemized so as to be an exact copy of the entries made in the employee's pay account.

Where the employee has not been employed for a sufficient period of time to meet the requirements of the statute as to average wages, the statute usually provides for an alternative method of determining the figure, usually the payroll of a similar worker employed for the statutory period.

Where the employee has more than one job for more than one employer, some difficulty will be encountered. The statute will provide that the average wages shall be the wages earned in the employment in which he was working at the time of the accident. If all of the jobs the claimant had were in the same or a similar line of work, then all of his earnings will be taken into account in calculating the average weekly wage. Where the jobs are not the same or similar, then the usual ruling is that only the wages earned in the same or similar employment will be considered.

For example, a man is employed on a part-time basis as a janitor of an apartment house, and he is also employed as a tailor. Clearly these occupations are not the same or similar. If he should be injured while on his janitor job, then only his earnings as a janitor will be taken into account in fixing the average weekly wage, even though he also lost his wages as a tailor. Therefore, it is important to carefully check the provisions of the statute as to what constitutes average weekly wage.

In computing the average weekly wage, advantages received by the claimant other than the payment of salary must be taken into account. The most common type of employee in this category is the waiter or bellhop, the major portion of whose remuneration is derived from tips. The amount of the tips per week will have to be ascertained and computed. This can be done by the claimant's own estimate, together with the amount which he reported on his income tax return, as well as estimates from fellow employees and the employer. Where the advantage consists of something other than money, as room and board, meals, and the like, the value of these items is part of the employee's salary and must be ascertained and included in the calculation. In the case of a janitor, as in the previous illustration, the usual employment agreement provides for a small monthly payment of money together with the free rental of an apartment and free gas and electricity. His wages therefore would consist of the monthly payment plus the value of the apartment, the gas, and electricity.

The fact that the employee is on a commission arrangement, or is paid on a time basis for only those hours which are worked, will not mitigate against a proper calculation of his earnings. The employer's payroll will provide the proper basis.

2326 Waiting period

Most statutes (except Oregon) provide that no compensation shall be paid during the waiting period, which consists of a certain number of days following the accident, unless the disability continues beyond a certain period of time. These periods differ in each state and range from a minimum of two to a maximum of seven days, the majority of the laws providing for a seven-day waiting period. Payment of compensation for the waiting period is provided only in those cases where the disability exceeds a certain number of days. For example, Alabama provides for a 7-day waiting period, retroactive after 28 days. This means that if the claimant has a disability of 28 days or more, he will be paid for the waiting period, which is the first seven days following the accident. If he is disabled for 27 days or less he will not receive payment for the waiting period.

The waiting period refers only to the payment of compensation; medical benefits are provided from the time of injury. The claimant is entitled to medical benefits, whether he is disabled or not, provided that the medical treatment is necessary as a result of the accident. The claimsman will find that the great majority of his compensation cases do not result in a disability beyond the waiting period, and that these cases can be disposed of by the payment of the medical bills alone.

2327   Compensation for temporary-total disability

The statute provides for the payment of compensation at a rate fixed as a percentage of the average weekly wage, subject to a maximum weekly amount as specified in the law. It is payable each week, after the waiting period has passed, during which the claimant is disabled and unable to work at all. This means that not only must the claimant be unable to work or absent from work, but also the period of time must be supported by medical evidence in the form of a physician's report that he is unable to work. The two factors must be present: the claimant is not working and his disability is established by medical proof. If either factor is lacking, no compensation is payable. If the doctor says that the claimant is unable to work, but he actually does work at the same salary as he earned before the accident, no compensation is payable after the date of his return to work. On the other hand, if the claimant says he cannot work and does not do so, and the doctor says that he is able to work, likewise no compensation is due and payable.

The payment of compensation has no relationship to the liability for the payment of medical. It is quite possible that the claimant is able to work, or does continue to work, but does require medical treatment on account of his injuries. The fact that there is no compensation due for the period, or the fact that the period of disability is being contested, will not affect the claimant's right to receive medical attention.

2328   Compensation for temporary-partial disability

Compensation for this type of disability is payable in the same manner and under the same circumstances as the payment of temporary-total. To qualify for payment the claimant must be partially disabled, that is, able to do some of his work but not all, and this disability must be supported by medical evidence. The weekly rate of compensation is a percentage (usually two thirds) of the difference between his average weekly wages and his present earnings. If the doctor certifies that the claimant is partially disabled, but the claimant does not return to any form of work, either because he refuses to do so or because there is no light work which he is capable of doing available, his earning capacity can be established by evidence of the kind and type of work which his physical condition will permit him to do, and the average earnings received in such an occupation.

For example, let us assume that the claimant's average weekly wage was $100. He is partially disabled, and the doctor certifies that he could do the work of a watchman. The average earnings of a watchman is $55 per week. Therefore the claimant would be entitled to two thirds of the difference between $55 and $100 per week, or two thirds of $45 per week.

It is in the area of partial disability that the failure of the claimsman to establish accurately the average weekly wage will be costly. For example, if the employee claims a weekly wage of $150 and the maximum temporary total compensation is $50, based on a percentage of 66⅔, it might be said that there would be no point in securing a payroll since even if the employee's earnings were less than $150 he would still be entitled to $50 temporary-total compensation if he earned a minimum of $75. Therefore, some claimsmen would waive the payroll and make no investigation as to the actual earnings.

However, let us assume that if the payroll had been checked it would have revealed that the employee had an average weekly wage of $120. As to temporary-total compensation, he would still be entitled to the maximum of $50, but if he returned to work at reduced earnings of $100, he would be entitled to two thirds of the difference between his average weekly wage and his reduced earnings. If it were conceded that his average weekly wage was $150, he would be entitled to two thirds of $50 as partial compensation per week. But if the payroll were introduced in evidence and it showed $120 per week, he would be entitled to only two thirds of $20. Consequently, payrolls and the establishing of an accurate average weekly wage are important items in the calculation of partial disability rates.

2329 Compensation for permanent-partial disability

Permanent-partial disability means that the employee has suffered a permanent injury from which he will not recover, but that he is not totally disabled as a result; he can do some work. He may be able to do his old job, but the permanent injury usually will reduce his efficiency and in general will affect his future competitive position in the labor market. For example, if the employee has suffered an amputation of his left index finger, he may be able to continue with his work as a carpenter or electrician, but his future employability will not be as desirable as a person who has sustained no injury.

It should be emphasized that compensation is designed solely to pay for the effect of the injury on the employee's earning capacity only. There is no recovery for the damage which the employee may sustain socially or as to his future enjoyment of life. The injury is tested only by the effect which it will have on the employee's ability to earn. Compensation for permanent-partial disability is paid in accordance with the provisions of the particular statute. Most statutes divide the injuries involved in this class of disability into two groups: (1) schedule injuries and (2) nonschedule injuries.

Schedule injuries.   With few exceptions, most compensation laws provide that where there has been a permanent injury to certain members of the body, or the loss of vision, total or partial, and loss of hearing, either total or partial, the amount of compensation to be paid to the employee can be fixed arbitrarily, without reference to the actual influence which the injury has on the employee's earning capacity.

Included in the law is a listing or schedule, noting the amounts to be paid for each injured member. The amount to be paid is measured by a number of weeks during which compensation will be paid, irrespective of whether the employee works or not. This compensation is designed to pay for the permanent disability only. For example, the New York schedule:

Member Lost	Number of Weeks Compensation
Arm	312
Leg	288
Hand	244
Foot	205
Eye	160
Thumb	75
First finger	46
Great toe	38
Second finger	30
Third finger	25
Toe, other than great toe	16
Fourth finger	15

In addition, compensation for the complete loss of the hearing in one ear is 60 weeks, and for complete loss of hearing in both ears 150 weeks.

The rules for applying these figures to specific injuries are as follows:

Phalanges.   Compensation for the loss of more than one phalange of a digit shall be the same as the loss of the entire digit. Compensation for the loss of the first phalange shall be one-half of the compensation for the loss of the entire digit. For example, if the employee lost by amputation, the first phalange of the index finger (to the first joint), he would be entitled to 23 weeks, or one-half of the amount payable for the entire finger. If he lost by amputation the first two phalanges, or the first phalange and part of the second, he would be entitled to 46 weeks, or compensation for the entire finger.

Amputated Arm or Leg.   Compensation for an arm or leg, if amputated at or above the wrist or ankle, shall be for the proportionate loss of the arm or leg. For example, if the employee's hand were amputated at the wrist, and the loss were limited to the hand, he would receive 244 weeks. Under this provision, the loss would be considered on the basis of the arm, or 312 weeks, so that he might receive as much as 90% of the arm, which would be 90% of 312 weeks, or 280.8 weeks.

Binocular Vision. Compensation for loss of binocular vision, or for the loss of 80% or more of an eye shall be the same as for the loss of the eye.

Two or More Digits. Compensation for loss or loss of use of two or more digits, or one or more phalanges of two or more digits, of a hand or foot, may be proportioned to the loss of use of the hand or foot occasioned thereby, but shall not exceed the compensation for the loss of a hand or foot.

Total Loss of Use. Compensation for permanent loss of use of a member shall be the same as for the loss of the member. For example, the member does not have to be amputated. It can be so permanently restricted so as to have no motion whatsoever, in which case the compensation would be the same as if it were lost by severance.

Partial Loss, or Partial Loss of Use. Compensation for permanent partial loss or loss of use of a member may be the proportionate loss or loss of use of the member. For example, if an employee sustains a fracture of two of the metacarpal bones and he has a permanent loss of use of the hand as a result, the amount of compensation will be based on the percentage loss proportioned to the loss of a hand. If his hand is impaired by a restriction of motion and the loss of some grasping power to the extent of 25% of the normal function of the hand, he would be entitled to receive 25% of 244 weeks, or 61 weeks compensation.

There is a difference in the state laws as to whether compensation for permanent-partial disability is to be paid at the same rate as temporary-total disability. Some have a lesser rate payable for this class of disability, but in the majority the rate of compensation is the same.

There is also a variance as to whether or not this compensation is to be paid in addition to temporary-total compensation, or is to be paid in lieu of all other compensation. In states where it is payable in addition to temporary-total disability, the problem is comparatively simple. When temporary-total disability ceases, a determination can be made as to the amount of permanent compensation which is due, and arrangements can be made for its payment. Where the employee has sustained a loss by amputation, the estimate of the permanent disability can be made almost at once, since the X rays will show the amount of the bone loss, and the compensation can be readily computed.

In cases of loss of use, the permanent restriction of motion cannot be ascertained right after treatment has ended, and the claimant will have to use the member for a period of time before the actual residual restriction can be estimated. Most doctors agree that in cases of restriction of motion, the earliest date on which an accurate estimate can be made is about six months after the termination of treatment. Therefore, in those cases there will be a period of time which will have to elapse before final settlement can be made. However, when the amount is agreed upon, the permanent compensation should start as of the date of the termination of temporary total disability.

For example, if the temporary total disability ceased as of January 1, 1976, and compensation was suspended as of that date, and the final estimate of the permanent disability was made on June 1, 1976, there would be about 21 weeks between January 1 and June 1. If the permanent compensation amounted to 21 weeks or less, it would be all due and payable at the time of settlement, whereas if the claimant had 50 weeks compensation due, he would receive 21 weeks to the date of settlement, and compensation weekly until the total of 50 weeks was paid.

Where permanent-partial compensation is in lieu of all other compensation, then the number of weeks paid for temporary-total disability is included in the total number of weeks due. For example, using the New York schedule, if the employee received 10 weeks temporary-total compensation, and his schedule loss amounted to 50 percent of the index finger, he would be entitled to 23 weeks (50 percent of 46 weeks) for the entire injury. Since he has already been paid 10 weeks compensation, he is entitled to receive an additional 13 weeks compensation, so that he winds up with 23 weeks compensation for the entire injury.

Under this type of system it is immediately apparent that there is some possibility that the claimant will not be adequately compensated in cases where the temporary-total disability and the treatment is prolonged. For example, if in the foregoing case the claimant's treatment was extensive and his temporary-total disability amounted to 40 weeks, then, if temporary-total disability were paid, he would receive nothing for permanent partial, or, if the entire injury were to be measured by the permanent disability schedule, he would receive only 23 weeks and nothing for the balance of his disability. To take care of this possibility, the law establishes what is to be the normal healing period for each member, and if the disability exceeds that healing period, any disability in excess of the normal healing period is added to the compensation due. The New York healing period schedule is as follows:

Member	Normal Healing Period (in weeks)
Arm	32
Leg	40
Hand	32
Foot	32
Ear	25
Eye	20
Thumb	24
First finger	18
Great toe	12
Second finger	12
Third finger	8
Fourth finger	8
Toe, other than great toe	8

Temporary-total disability in excess of these figures is considered to be a protracted healing period and is awarded in addition to the other compensation. For example, to return to the previous case, the claimant had 40 weeks temporary-total and a permanent disability of 50 percent of the first, or index finger. Since the disability in excess of 18 weeks is considered as a protracted healing period, he would be entitled to 22 weeks compensation for the protracted healing period. For his permanent-partial compensation, including temporary-total, he would be entitled to 23 weeks. Therefore, the total award would be for 45 weeks compensation.

Some states schedule all injuries, those to members (as above) and those to other parts of the body, estimating the permanency on the basis of the relationship of the injury to the body as a whole. If a man has a back injury which impairs his working capacity to the extent of 20 percent, the finding is that he has sustained a permanent disability of 20 percent of the body as a whole. Using the amount of compensation which would be due if the man had sustained permanent total disability, the award is for 20 percent of that amount. For example, if the amount payable for permanent-total disability is 400 weeks, then with a 20 percent disability he would be entitled to receive 80 weeks compensation, or 20 percent of 400 weeks.

Nonschedule injuries. States that do not estimate on the basis of the body as a whole compensate permanent injuries, other than those covered by the schedule, on the basis of actual loss of earning capacity, awarding compensation in the same manner and by the same computation as temporary-partial compensation. This would be a percentage of the difference between the employee's earning before the accident and his present earnings. Such compensation would have to be continued during the continuance of the disability. In most states, cases in this category can be compromised by the payment of a lump sum. If this is possible, the claimsman should recognize such cases early and make arrangements to settle them out as early as possible. To obtain the best results, in the case of a male employee, the settlement should be made before the case is two years old, and in the case of a female employee, if disability exists at the end of one year, settlement should be considered. This does not mean that the claimsman should wait for these periods of time. The earlier he recognizes the potential danger of the case, the sooner he can get his settlement negotiations under way.

2330 Compensation for permanent-total disability

Strictly speaking, permanent-total disability means that the employee is totally disabled and unable to do any work, and that this condition is such that it will continue for the rest of his life. It is so interpreted in the majority of states. Some states, however, hold that an employee can be permanently and totally disabled on each different job which he holds, and therefore entitled to an award in each occupation. These are the states where the period of permanent-total compensation is limited, and it seems to be a rule of expediency rather than substance.

Most laws provide that certain injuries, without any proof whatsoever, shall be conclusively presumed to involve permanent total disability. These conditions are usually the loss of both arms or both feet, both hands, both legs, both eyes, or any two of these conditions.

The laws differ as to the period during which permanent-total compensation will be paid, some providing for payment for the rest of the employee's lifetime and others limiting the period to a certain specified number of weeks from the date of injury. It can be argued that payment for life is too long in the sense that compensation, being a substitute for wages, should continue only for the balance of the employee's work life and not his entire life. On the other hand, laws which limit the compensation to a specific period frequently provide for too short a period. In any case, the law represents the will of the people of the particular state as expressed by its legislature.

2331   Medical benefits

In addition to the payment of compensation, all laws provide for the rendering of medical service to the injured employee. The extent and the circumstances under which the medical treatment is to be rendered differ state by state. While most of the states (36) provide for unlimited medical, hospital, and surgical treatment, some limit the liability for medical either by a limitation of time or a dollar amount. Some require the furnishing of prostheses, such as artificial hands, arms, legs, glass eyes, eyeglasses, and the like, while others do not. Some laws provide for the payment of full medical in the case of accidental injuries and limit the amount of medical for occupational diseases.

As to circumstances, the majority of the states provide that the employer is required to furnish medical attention to the employee, and if he fails to do so upon the demand of the employee, then the employee may seek medical attention at the expense of the employer. In a minority of the states the injured employee may select his own physician in accordance with whatever rules the statute provides. Some statutes require that the physicians rendering treatment in compensation cases, who are selected by the employee, be specially licensed as to the kind and types of cases they can handle.

Where the statute provides that the employer shall furnish the medical attention, the insurance carriers have found it to advantage to supply the employers with a panel of physicians who can be called upon to render such treatment. Since the insurance carrier has a certain amount of expertise in the selection of competent practitioners, such an arrangement works out quite well. It is to the advantage of the insurance carrier to provide the best medical attention obtainable for the reason that the longer the employee is disabled, the larger will be the amount of compensation due. Therefore, if only for self-serving reasons, the insurance carrier has a definite interest in seeing to it that the employee is well and properly treated and, in addition, obtains a satisfactory result.

In states where the medical treatment is limited either by a time period or a dollar amount, the insurance carrier is often faced with the problem of deciding whether it will assume the responsibility for medical treatment be-

lated from annuity tables which contemplate such factors as the life expectancy of the dependents, as well as the possibility of the remarriage of the widow. The figures are discounted at the statutory rate of interest, as set forth in the compensation act. In New York, the present commutation rate applicable to future payments of compensation is $3\frac{1}{2}$ percent.

2333 Compensation: When payable

The intent and design of the compensation statutes generally is that compensation is a substitute for wages and should be paid in the same manner and at the same time as wages. This means that where the right to compensation is uncontested the injured employee will receive a compensation payment at the end of each week of compensable disability. As to the first payment, this is complicated to some extent by the waiting period, which is deducted from the disability period. For example, in a state where the waiting period is 7 days the claimant would not be entitled to compensation for the first 7 days of disability, but he would be entitled to a payment of one week's compensation at the end of 14 days of disability. Therefore, the first payment of compensation is due and payable on the 14th day. In states having a 3-day waiting period, the first week's compensation would be due on the 10th day of disability. After the first payment, if disability continues, a compensation payment must be made each week until the disability terminates.

It should be emphasized that the time when compensation is due and payable is computed from the first day of disability and not from the date of the accident. In many cases, disability begins immediately after the accident, and in most states, if the accident occurs before half a day's work has been completed, the date of disability is the same as the date of the accident. If the accident occurs after more than half a day's work has been completed, the date of disability is the next day. For example, if a man works from 9 A.M. to 5 P.M., and is injured at 10 A.M. on December 2, then disability begins December 2. However, if he is injured at 2 P.M., having completed more than half a day's work, disability then would begin December 3.

In some cases the employee does not stop work immediately after the accident but tries to work with his injury. Disability then would begin on the first day that he is unable to work. If the accident occurred on December 2 and the employee finished out the week, working until December 6, but was unable to work thereafter, the date that disability began would be computed as December 7.

The days of disability do not have to be consecutive. For example let us assume an accident on December 2, where the employee was injured at 10 A.M. He immediately stops work, but returns to work on December 5. He works the 5th and 6th but is unable to work thereafter. Disability began on December 2. He has suffered three days of disability between December 2, the date of the accident, and December 5, the date of his first return to work. These days are the 2nd, 3rd, and 4th. Disability began again on December 6.

If the state has a seven-day waiting period, such period would end on

December 9, and one week from that date the first payment of compensation would be due. If the state has a three-day waiting period, then one week from December 6, or December 13, would be the date on which the first payment of compensation would be due.

In other words, for computing the date on which compensation is due, the payment is due when the employee has sustained a disability of one week beyond the waiting period, irrespective of whether the days of disability are consecutive or intermittent.

2334   Computation of the compensation period

Most states require that compensation be paid on a seven-day basis, irrespective of the number of days per week which the injured employee regularly works. This influences the amount of the payment only when fractional parts of the week are paid. If a claimant worked on a five-day week, and is entitled to two days' compensation, he would receive two sevenths of the weekly compensation rate. Holidays and Sundays are included. For example: the employee was a five-day worker and the medical proof of disability extended to December 9, a Monday. Assume that he has been paid compensation up to and including December 5, a Thursday. He would be entitled to three days' compensation covering December 6, 7, and 8, or three sevenths of the weekly compensation rate. Under this seven-day system he would be so entitled, even though he normally would not work on Saturday, the 7th, and Sunday, the 8th.

In a minority of states the computation of time is based on the number of days worked, eliminating the days normally not worked. Therefore if a five-day worker was entitled to one day's compensation, he would receive one fifth of the weekly compensation rate. Therefore, in the foregoing example, the employee would be entitled to only one day's compensation, namely for Dec. 6. Since he did not normally work on Saturday and Sunday, these would be excluded from the computation. For the purposes of computing compensation periods, holidays are always considered as working days and are included in the computation.

2335   Compensation: How payable

The objective of the compensation laws is to provide a means whereby payments of compensation are made and received when due, and, where payments are not made, to provide a speedy, effective method of disposing of any controversies which may arise. Since most injured workers cannot survive very long when deprived of their regular wages, therefore the effectiveness of any compensation law can be judged only by whether or not the injured workman receives his compensation payment when he needs it the most —and that is when it is due. In uncontested cases there are two general methods of making payment: the *agreement system,* to which the majority of the states subscribe, and the *direct payment system.*

Under the agreement system the employer (or his insurance carrier) and the injured employee enter into an agreement as to the payment of compensation, the date of disability, and the rate of compensation to be paid. If the case is of a minor nature, the first agreement may embody the entire settlement of the claim. This agreement is subject to the approval of the agency administering the compensation law. In most states, compensation must be paid as soon as the agreement is made, and if for any reason the agreement is inadequate or contrary to the law, the agency will require that it be amended to comply with the provisions of the statute. In a few states, compensation may not be paid until the agreement is approved. After agreement, when compensation is to be suspended, the statutes usually provide for the execution of a further agreement to discontinue the payment or for a final settlement receipt.

Under the direct payment system the employer or the insurance carrier begins the payment of compensation without any agreement from the injured employee, such payments being subject to the approval of the administrative agency. Notice of the payment of compensation is required by the filing of certain forms with the agency, evidencing the date of accident, the date of disability, and the rate of compensation. When compensation is discontinued, another form must be filed with the agency indicating the amount of compensation paid, the period covered by the payments, and the reason why compensation is being discontinued.

In contested cases, the laws vary as to how the controversy is brought before the administrative agency. Some states require that the employer or his insurance carrier file a notice of controversy which will automatically bring the case on for hearing; others require no action whatsoever on the part of the insurance carrier or employer, and bring the cases on for hearing only where a claim is asserted by the injured employee.

In states where the compensation law is administered by the courts, the claim must be initiated by the claimant who brings an action to recover compensation by the service of process on the employer and the insurance carrier, who are required to appear and answer in just the same manner as any other type of lawsuit. The judgment rendered can determine the entire case and can be reduced to a lump sum, or the court can determine the rights and liabilities of the parties up to the date of the trial without prejudice to the claimant's right to bring another and further action for future disability, either temporary or permanent.

In states where the compensation law is administered by an administrative agency, each agency has promulgated its own forms for the employer's first report, supplemental reports (indicating return to work), surgeon's report, as well as the agreement forms and other types of forms used. To an insurance carrier this difference in format state by state for practically the same thing posed an onerous printing and supply problem. In order to assist the carriers the International Association of Industrial Accident Boards and Commissions, an organization composed of the administrative agencies of the United States and Canada, suggested to their members the use of standard forms approved by the organization. These forms bear the designation *SF 1, SF 2*, etc., to indicate that they are standard forms, and they bear the notation that they are approved by the I.A.I.A.B.C. Some states have adopted the use of these forms and some have not, but the project is continuing and it is hoped that as further forms are developed they will be adopted by the various states to the end that we may have some uniformity among the states, if only in the area of forms.

2336 Penalties

Under the various compensation laws there are certain penalties for the failure of the insurance carrier to function within the requirements of the law. These penalties are not uniform nor are they imposed to the same extent. For example, some states impose a penalty for the late payment of compensation, for the failure to pay an award of the administrative agency within a certain period of time, or for the failure to file the necessary forms within the time limit provided in the statute. In states where the courts administer the law, the courts frequently apply the vexatious litigation statute to compensation claims and add a percentage penalty to the judgment. This statute, found mostly in the South and West, was originally enacted to reduce litigation between policyholders and the insurance carriers, and provides that where the policyholder is forced to sue the insurance carrier in order to compel the payment of insurance, and the judgment is against the insurance carrier, a penalty is added to the judgment on the theory that the insurance carrier should have paid the claim without forcing the policyholder to litigate. In compensation cases, the courts have taken the position that the claimant is an insured or at least a beneficiary of an insurance policy, and if he is forced to litigate in order to obtain that which the policy should have paid voluntarily, the vexatious litigation penalty will be added.

Where a minor is employed in violation of the labor law, and is injured, some states provide for a penalty by way of increased compensation. In some states this penalty is assessed solely against the employer and in others the entire assessment is made against the insurance carrier. Other penalties include an increased award for the failure of the employer to furnish safety appliances, and for violations of the hours of work.

The claimsman should carefully review the penalties imposed by the compensation law of his jurisdiction and avoid exposure to such penalties insofar as it is within his power to do so.

2337 Second injury fund

Because of the responsibilities placed upon the employer by the compensation laws, employers as a group were reluctant to employ any person with a preexisting disability. Therefore the employment of handicapped persons exposed the employer to a much greater risk of liability than would be the case if the employee were not suffering from any condition whatsoever. To further protect themselves against the possibility of hiring a person with a disability, many employers insisted upon preemployment examinations by their own physicians before any contract of hire was made. It would be a rare instance indeed to find an employer who would hire an individual who was blind in one eye and thus subject himself to a possible liability for permanent total disability if the person lost the sight of his good eye.

Generally, handicapped persons were more or less in an unemployable position, and finally the legislatures of the various states came to a point where they had to do something about it. They first of all declared the public policy of the state to be that every person who works for a living is entitled to a reasonable opportunity to maintain his independence and self-respect through self-support, even after he has been physically handicapped by injury or disease. They then created a second injury fund, the purpose of which was to pay for the compensation awarded over and above the amount which normally would have been awarded against the employer for the injury but for the handicapped condition.

For example, if in our eye case the claimant was blind in one eye and lost the sight of the other, he would be permanently and totally disabled. If the claimant had been physically perfect prior to the accident, and he sustained an injury causing the loss of one eye, the liability of the employer would be limited to the loss of one eye. Because of his preexisting disability, however, the loss of his good eye made him a permanent total disability rather than a permanent partial one. The second injury fund relieved the employer of his excess liability because of the claimant's previous handicap with the result that the claimant would receive the same award of permanent total disability, but the employer would pay only for the loss of the eye, and the remainder of the compensation due to the claimant would be paid by the second injury fund.

The plan placed the handicapped person in the same position as any other with respect to the liability of the employer for the payment of compensation, and the purpose of the legislature was to accomplish just that. There would be no reason why the employer should not employ a handicapped person since the employer's compensation liability would be no greater because of the employee's physical disability.

The fund is usually maintained by the compensation authority and its solvency is usually guaranteed by a tax on insurance premiums, or a tax on the compensation awarded, or some similar plan.

2338 Employee's claim against a third party

Compensation laws are dispositive of the rights and remedies of the employee as against his employer. They are, as we have seen, modifications of the common law and, unless the law specifically changes other rights which the employee may have against others, his common-law rights remain as to those others. For example, if the employee were on an errand for his employer and was struck by an automobile operated by some third party, the mere fact that the employee was in the course of his employment would have no influence on his cause of action against the negligent motorist. The employee is not limited to his remedy under the workmen's compensation law since the law does not in any way affect his common-law right of action against anyone except his employer.

The compensation laws generally recognize that the employee's common-law rights are still enforceable against a third party, and provide that where the injury is caused by a third party the employee may proceed against the third party, or may elect to claim compensation from his employer. Most compensation acts provide that the employee may do both; that is collect compensation from his employer and also proceed against the third party.

In any case where the employer has paid compensation, the employer has a claim against the third party. Where the claimant may also proceed against the third party, and the employer has paid compensation, the law usually provides that the employer shall have a lien on the proceeds of recovery to the extent of the compensation and medical benefits paid. In order to perfect the lien, however, the employer must put the third party on notice of its existence. As a matter of procedure, the insurance carrier usually puts the third party on notice at the same time that any payment, either of compensation or medical, is made. The notice may be by letter by either registered or certified mail, and can read as follows:

We are the compensation insurance carrier for the Jones Company, whose employee, John Smith, was injured on April 15, 1964, at Main and First Streets, under circumstances which involve your responsibility.

This is to advise you that we will hold you responsible for any payments of compensation or medical benefits which we are called upon to make because of this accident.

This puts the third party on notice of the fact that there is a compensation carrier involved and also that the claimant was in the course of his employment at the time of injury. If desired, the letter can also set forth the amount of compensation and medical benefits which have been assumed at the time the letter was written. The failure of the employer to put the third party on notice of his lien may result in the loss of the lien.

Should the third party settle with the claimant without extinguishing the lien of the employer, the question of whether or not the third party is also answerable to the employer will turn on whether the third party had notice or knowledge of the lien, either actual or constructive. Where a notice has been given, then the third party has actual notice and he makes the settlement at his peril; the employer may still assert his lien and recover. Where no notice has been given or received prior to the settlement, the question then would be whether or not the third party knew of the existence of the lien or, by the exercise of reasonable diligence, could have discovered the existence of the lien.

For example, if the claimant were merely walking across the street when he was struck by the third party's automobile and no inquiry was made and no information given as to whether the claimant was working or not at the time of the accident, the third party would have no way of knowing that the claimant was collecting or had collected compensation payments, and, under the facts, there was nothing which should have put the third party on inquiry as to the compensation feature. On the other hand, if the employee was driving a truck owned by his employer with his employer's advertising on the sides of it, and it contained a commodity in which the employer dealt, and the employee was injured by a collision between the truck and another vehicle, the third party would have every reason to inquire as to whether the employee was working at the time of the accident or not.

If the third party fails to inquire, he is charged with the knowledge which he would have received had he done so. The difference between the two cases is that in the first case there were no indicia of employment and no facts which would put the third party on inquiry as to employment, whereas in the second there was every likelihood that the claimant was in the course of his employment because of the surrounding circumstances.

Where the employee has a possible claim against a third party and where he elects to accept compensation and forego this third-party remedy, the compensation statute usually provides that if the employee does not begin his action against the third party within a certain period of time, usually six months or one year from the date of the accident, the cause of action is automatically subrogated to the employer. This is a transfer of a personal injury cause of action from one person to another and is statutory in its origin. At common law, a personal injury cause of action could not be assigned or transferred, either in whole or in part, so that the compensation statute in this regard is a modification of the common-law rule. The compensation statute usually provides that where the claim is subrogated the employer may bring the action against the third party, either in his own name or in the name of the claimant, and if there is a recovery of more than the compensation and medical benefits paid after deduction of the costs of trial, the excess is to be turned over to the claimant or divided between the employer and the employee, with the employee receiving the larger share.

As to whether or not a fellow servant could be considered a third party where the injury is caused by his negligence, the laws vary. The majority permit the employee to bring an action against a "third party not in the same employ." Under those statutes, no cause of action can arise against a fellow employee, whereas under other statutes an action against a fellow employee is permissible.

Under statutes which exclude actions against fellow servants it must be emphasized that the relationship of fellow employees must be present at the time of the accident. Merely because a person is a fellow employee of another, this fact in and of itself will not operate to exonerate that person from all responsibility. The relationship of fellow employees must be present at the time of the accident, otherwise the tort-feasor is answerable just the same as any other wrongdoer.

For example, let us assume that *A* and *B* are fellow employees. *A* is on vacation. *B* is working. *A* negligently knocks *B* down with his automobile while *B* is on an errand for his employer. The accident did not arise out of the fellow servant relationship and *B* has a cause of action against *A*, notwithstanding the statutory prohibition against actions against fellow employees. Technically, *A* was not in the same employ at the time of the accident. The same thing would be true if *B* was working and *A* was driving home in his own car from the place of business. Conversely, if both *A* and *B* were on the premises of the employer when the accident occurred, then the relationship would be that of fellow employees. If *A* and *B* both were driving their cars out of the employer's parking lot when a collision occurred due to *A*'s negligence, *B* would not have a cause of action against *A* since the accident arose out of the relationship of fellow servants. Both employees are in the course of employment while they are on the premises and are covered during their egress therefrom, but only while they are still on the premises. Here, both *A* and *B* were still on the premises of the employer. The accident arose out of the employment and their status as to each other was that of fellow employee.

Where neither of the fellow employees are working when the accident occurs, then the compensation law has no application and the common-law rights and remedies are the same as if there was no compensation law at all. If on a Sunday *A* and *B*, driving their own cars for pleasure, collide with each other, the mere fact that, under business circumstances, they are fellow employees has no application to the rights of either against the other.

The same principles apply to the employer. Where the accident arises out of the relationship of employer and employee, the employee's sole and exclusive remedy is under the compensation law, but where the accident occurs when neither is occupying the status of employer and employee, the compensation law has no application. In such a case, the common-law rights of the employee are the same as would be the rights of any other person and, conversely, the employer could have a cause of action against the employee. For example, if the employer were driving his car on a Sunday for his own pleasure, and he collided with the automobile driven by his employee, the rights and liabilities of the parties are the same as if the relationship of employer and employee was not in existence. If the employer was negligent, the employee would have a cause of action against him and, conversely, if the employee were the negligent party, the employer could maintain an action against him for damages.

Under the compensation statute, there is a further provision with reference to the application of the claimant's recovery from the third party and the claimant's right to deficiency compensation where the recovery from the third party is less than the compensation provided for in the statute. The effect of this provision can best be illustrated by a specific example. Let us suppose that the compensation value of the employee's claim is $8,000 due to a schedule loss of use of a member or a part of a member. He brings action against the third party and recovers $5,000. Had he merely elected to accept compensation, he would have received $8,000. Therefore, the compensation law provides that he is entitled to recover the difference by way of deficiency compensation from his employer, so that the third party would pay the judgment of $5,000 and the employer would be liable for the difference between the amount recovered and the compensation due under the act, $3,000.

In this situation, the claimant would have to assume the costs of trial and his own attorney's fees so that, while the judgment is $5,000, if the attorney were employed on a contingent fee basis at 33⅓ percent, even eliminating other disbursements, the claimant would receive as a net recovery $5,000, less one third, or $3,333.33. The question then is whether the claimant is charged with the entire amount of the recovery as against the compensation liability, or only the net recovery to him after the payment of costs and attorney's fees. Some statutes charge him with the entire recovery, while others charge only his net recovery against the compensation liability of the employer. The answer may be found only in the particular statute involved, and if there is no specific provision as to recovery, then the claimant is charged with the entire judgment amount.

Where the employee's claim against the third party is settled, whether during the trial or prior thereto, some statutes provide that the claimant's right to deficiency compensation is barred unless the settlement is made with the consent of the employer, or, if he is insured, of the insurance carrier. Where the settlement amount is in excess of the possible compensation liability, no problem is presented. Whether or not the claimant obtains the consent of the employer (or carrier) will not make any difference because there is no possibility of any deficiency being due. Competent attorneys, however, insist on obtaining the carriers' consent anyway, since there is always the possibility that the claimant may suffer some future disability arising out of the injury. By obtaining the consent of the carrier, the claimant's rights to future compensation, if any, are not impaired.

Where the contemplated settlement is less than the compensation provided for in the act, and the carrier's consent is requested, the insurance carrier is confronted with a problem. If it consents to the settlement it will at least have the advantage of being able to reduce its liability by the amount of the settlement. On the other hand, if it does not consent to the settlement, and the case goes to trial and results in a defendant's verdict, then it will have to pay the entire amount of the compensation with no offset or reduction whatever.

There is also a third possibility, and that is that the claimant may settle the case anyway without the consent of the carrier, in which case there would be no liability for the payment of deficiency compensation.

In any case, the decision of the insurance carrier as to whether it will or will not give its consent to the settlement must be dependent upon the facts of the case and the carrier's own estimate of the possibilities of a higher verdict as well as the possibilities of a verdict for the defendant. If the prospects of a higher verdict are good, then the carrier will refuse its consent, whereas if the prospects are doubtful, the carrier can consent to the settlement, or participate in the future discussions to the extent of trying to induce a higher settlement figure before giving its ultimate consent.

2339   Claim by third party against employer

It sometimes happens that because of the existence of a hold harmless agreement or of a tort liability, after the injured employee has recovered from the third party, the third party may assert an action against the employer. Where the employer has given the third party a hold harmless agreement, the employer is required to reimburse the third party for any payment it has been called upon to make on account of injuries to the employer's employees. The failure of the employer to respond to this contractual obligation will give rise to a cause of action by the third party against the employer based on the contract.

The possible tort liability of the employer to the third party is a bit more complicated and can best be illustrated by an actual case. In *Westchester Gas Co.* v. *Westchester Small Estates Corp.* [15 N.E. 2d 567 (New York)], the facts indicated that the defendant was engaged in constructing a housing development and in the course of this work negligently broke the gas main, which it repaired. The defendant employed a watchman who, after making his rounds, usually slept in one of the houses under construction. One morning he was found dead as a result of the inhalation of illuminating gas. His dependents brought suit against the gas company, alleging negligent maintenance of its gas lines and equipment, and recovered a substantial judgment. After satisfying the judgment, the gas company brought suit against the contractor on the theory that the contractor's negligence in breaking the gas main and improperly repairing it created the gas company's liability to the deceased's dependents.

The defendant contended that the gas company was an assignee or subrogee of the deceased's dependents and, as such, succeeded to no greater rights than those owned by dependents themselves. Since the only cause of action which could be asserted by the dependents against the employer-contractor was under the compensation law, the exclusive remedy, the gas company was relegated to that means of recovery, if any recovery were to be allowed at all. The court rejected this theory and held that the gas company was bringing the action in its own right and not as an assignee or subrogee of the dependents, and that the cause of action arose out of the breach of an independent duty which the contractor owed to the gas company, which consisted of the proper repair of the gas main which it fractured. The fact that the gas company was held liable to the dependents for its failure to maintain its equipment in a proper manner did not detract from the fact that the proximate cause of the gas company's liability was the negligence of the contractor. The gas company therefore was allowed to recover from the contractor.

Therefore, there is always a possibility of a recovery by the third party as against the employer where the employer's negligence is the proximate cause of the injury, even though the claimant himself would have no cause of action based on negligence against the employer.[2]

---

[2] See also *Dole* v. *Dow Chemical Co.* [282 N.E. 2d 288 (New York)].

2340   Extraterritoriality

Under all compensation laws, either by statutory enactment or judicial interpretation, where the contract of hire is made within the state and where the employee does some work within the state, the compensation act of the state can be applied to accidents which occur outside of the state, whether in the United States or in a foreign country. The underlying theory is that where a contract of hire is made within the state for work to be done in the state, the right of the employee to compensation under the law of the state of hire is an incident of the contract of hire. Therefore, no matter where the accident occurs, the right to compensation in the state of hire is a contractual right which the injured employee may assert.

Where the contract of hire is made in one state for work to be performed exclusively outside the state, the parties impliedly contemplate the compensation law of the state where the services are to be performed as an incident of the contract rather than the state where the contract of hire is made. Therefore, where there are services to be performed in the state where the contract of hire is made, the parties impliedly include the right to compensation in that state as an incident of the contract of employment, whereas, if the contract of hire contemplates only services to be performed exclusively outside the state of hire, the state of hire has no jurisdiction and the parties impliedly intended that the compensation law of the state where the services are to be rendered be an incident of the contract.

Some states limit the extraterritorial effect of their compensation laws by applying their laws only to accidents which occur within a certain time period after the employee leaves the state. Texas fixes one year, and Colorado, Nevada, New Mexico, Pennsylvania, Utah, and Wyoming fix six months as the time within which their laws will be operative and not thereafter, the time period being measured from the date that the employee leaves the state. Delaware provides that the law will be applied only during a period of 90 days after the employee leaves the state. In applying these time periods, the time is not cumulative and the period applies to each time the employee leaves the state.

For example, if the employee leaves the state and works outside the state for five months and then does one day's work in the state and leaves again, the time period as expressed in the law begins to run all over again. If the state is one which provides for a six-month period, the state law would be operative for six months from the date that the employee left the state the second time. The five months' prior absence would have no influence on the latter time period.

2341   Conflicts of compensation laws

When an employee sustains a compensable injury within the state, it is clear that the state where the accident occurred may assume jurisdiction. Where the employee is hired in another state and does some work in that state, as well as in the state in which the injury occurred, the extraterritorial provisions of the state of hire may be applicable. Where this occurs the employee has an election as to whether he will claim compensation in one state or the other. He cannot make claims in both states and thus effect a double recovery.

Usually, when the claimant is fully informed, he will elect to make his claim in the state which affords him the greater recovery. The rate of the weekly compensation and the limits of liability under the two compensation laws will ordinarily induce him to claim under the more liberal statute. If he recovers under the more liberal statute, generally there is no particular problem involved, but a problem does arise where he has already made a claim, and recovered in the less liberal state, and then discovers that he could have obtained a greater recovery in the other state. The question to be decided is whether he can then make a claim in the second state for the difference or whether the recovery of an award in the first state will preclude him from making any further claim.

The general rule governing matters of this kind is found in Section 403 of the Restatement on Conflict of Laws, which reads as follows:

Award already had under the Workmen's Compensation Act of another state will not bar a proceeding under an applicable act, unless the act where the award was made was designed to preclude the recovery of an award under any other act, but the amount paid under the prior award in one state will be credited on the second award.

This conclusion was reached as a consequence of two decisions (detailed below) of the Supreme Court of the United States.

In *Magnolia* v. *Hunt* (320 U.S. 430), the plaintiff Hunt was hired in Texas, did some work for his employer in Texas, and was injured in Louisiana. He filed his claim for compensation in Texas and recovered the full benefits for his injury. The Texas compensation act specifically invests the decisions of the Industrial Accident Board and the district courts with the status of a judgment of a court of law, and further provides that if the compensation claim is pursued to judgment, such judgment shall be exclusive. The plaintiff Hunt later discovered that he could have obtained a greater recovery had he asserted his claim in Louisiana. He then brought action in Louisiana, which was opposed by the employer on the ground that since the Texas award was exclusive, he had no further remedy which could be asserted and, further, that since the award in Texas had proceeded to judgment, Louisiana was bound to give it full faith and credit. Therefore the matter was *res judicata* and Louisiana was without jurisdiction. The Supreme Court agreed with the employer's position and vacated the Louisiana judgment which Hunt had obtained.

The second case was *Industrial Commission of Wisconsin* v. *McCartin* (330 U.S. 622). The facts indicated that McCartin was employed by an Illinois corporation and was hired in Illinois, but was injured in Wisconsin. He filed a claim for compensation before the Illinois Compensation Commission and an award was made, which award was paid by his employer. As part and parcel of the award there was a reservatory provision that the award was intended to be conclusive only as to the employee's rights against the employer in Illinois, and that any rights which the employee might have against his employer in Wisconsin were specifically reserved. He then filed a claim in Wisconsin and the Wisconsin commission made an award, giving appropriate credit to the employer for the payments made in Illinois. An appeal was taken to the Supreme Court of the United States, the employer contending that the *Hunt* case precluded another and further action in another state after an award had been made and the payment made.

The Court held that the *Hunt* case was limited to its own special facts where the award was intended to be "final and conclusive of all of the employee's rights against the employer," and that it had no application to the facts in this case. In deciding that the Wisconsin award should be upheld, the Court called attention to the reserve provision in the Illinois award which was a clear indication that the Illinois award was not intended to be a final and conclusive adjudication of all of the rights of the employee against his employer. The Court went further and stated that even without the reserve provision, since the Illinois statute did not preclude a second action in Wisconsin, the claimant's rights against his employer in Wisconsin were preserved to him and were not extinguished by the Illinois award.

The cases can be distinguished in that the Texas statute provided for an exclusive remedy and precluded another and further action elsewhere, whereas the Illinois statute did not bar an action in another state. When Mr. Hunt elected to bring his action in Texas, he chose an exclusive remedy. When Mr. McCartin brought his claim in Illinois, he did not choose an exclusive remedy since the Illinois act did not bar an action elsewhere. [See also *Industrial Indemnity Exchange* v. *Industrial Accident Commission*, 182 Pac. 2d 309 (California), where compensation payments made under a Utah award were credited against an award made by the California commission, even though the Utah award was a final award under the Utah act. Utah, like Illinois, did not include in its compensation act any provision which would bar another and further action in another state.]

The conflict of laws involved in the jurisdiction of the state as opposed to the federal government has been discussed in a preceding chapter, Admiralty, Section 1417 and following.

2342 Nonoccupational disability benefits laws

Some states (not all) have enacted legislation which compels the employer to enter into an accident and health insurance plan, by means of which the employee is compensated for disability sustained as a result of accidents or illnesses which do not occur in the course and scope of employment. The premiums for this insurance are paid jointly by the employer and employee. Payments of these benefits are made by the insurance carrier issuing the insurance coverage, and the administration of the law is usually under the direction of the labor authority. The laws are variously titled as disability benefits laws or unemployment disability compensation laws. While they are administered by the Department of Labor, they have no connection with nor are they part of the compensation system. They require a payment of a certain number of weeks at a specific rate of benefit.

The only area in which the disability benefits carrier and the compensation carrier will meet is where a claim has been made for a compensable accident and the compensation carrier opposes the claim on the ground that the accident did not arise out of and in the course of employment. Under those circumstances, the disability benefits carrier is obligated to pay disability benefits to the claimant, but the disability benefits law gives the carrier a lien on any compensation benefits recovered under the compensation law to the extent of the disability benefits paid. In other words, where there is such a contest the disability benefits carrier is obligated by law to make the payments. If the compensation carrier is sustained in its contentions, then that ends the situation and the claim properly belongs to the disability benefits carrier, whereas, if the compensation carrier is not sustained, then the case properly belongs to the compensation carrier, and the disability benefits carrier has no liability. However, since the disability benefits carrier has made some payments, the law creates a lien in favor of the disability benefits carrier on the compensation awarded against the compensation carrier.

2343   Unemployment insurance law

All states and the federal government have laws dealing with the payment of benefits to those who are able and willing to work but who are unemployed because of their failure to find a job. There is no connection whatever between these claims and a claim for workmen's compensation. A person who is claiming compensation for disability caused by an industrial accident cannot qualify as being able and willing to work, and therefore he would not be entitled to unemployment insurance benefits. It does happen on some occasions that the compensation claimant will attempt to make such a claim at the same time that he is asserting a claim for compensation. The evidence which he uses to support his claim for unemployment insurance can be utilized in opposing his claim for compensation. If he is able to work, he is not entitled to workmen's compensation, and if he is not able to work because of an injury or illness, he is not entitled to unemployment insurance benefits. He cannot make one claim to one agency and a contrary claim to another if a proper investigation is conducted which will reveal the facts.

Federal Social Security Act.   In 1956, the Social Security Act was amended to provide benefits for total and permanent disability for those 50 years of age and over, irrespective of the cause of the disability. Where the claimant was entitled to workmen's compensation, the social security benefits were reduced by the amount receievd for compensation. In 1958, the deduction of the workmen's compensation benefits was eliminated, and in 1960, the age limitation of 50 or over was removed, so that at the present time all qualified persons, irrespective of age, may collect social security benefits for permanent and total disability without any deduction of workmen's compensation benefits in cases where they are payable.

While the payment of the social security benefits does not affect the liability of the compensation insurance carrier, it does provide the claimant with a greater incentive to prolong his disability, which would not be the case if he did not have this additional income. For example, if a disabled employee with a wife and two dependents was earning $400 per month prior to the accident, he would be entitled to $254 in social security benefits. If the compensation weekly rate was $50 he would receive $200 in compensation, and his total income would be $454 per month. If he was able to do any work, and actually did so, he would lose the social security payment, and his compensation rate would be reduced. Therefore, as long as he can establish total disability, and can support his claim with a medical report that the condition is permanent, he will continue to collect more money while disabled than he would get if he were earning his full wages.

In other cases, the employer provides benefit plans whereby the injured employee receives certain payments for disability. Most of these plans exclude claims for disability where compensation benefits are recoverable, but others do not make any distinction. In the latter cases, the compensation insurance carrier is confronted with the same situation which obtains where social security disability payments are involved. In both cases, since it is to the claimant's financial advantage to prolong his disability as long as possible, detailed investigations must be undertaken to verify the actual fact of disability. The investigation will be concerned with activity checks of the claimant at various times and a complete medical investigation into his condition.

2344   The workmen's compensation and employers' liability policy

This policy is designed to indemnify the employer against all liability which might be imposed because of accidents and occupational diseases which might be sustained by his employees in the course and scope of their employment. Since the compensation laws do not always include within their scope all employees or all occupational diseases, it is possible for some common-law rights to remain in existence. It is for that reason that the policy covers both phases of the employer's possible responsibility to his employees, namely the liability imposed by the workmen's compensation law and any common-law liability which might still remain. Therefore, the insuring agreements are in two parts, one dealing with the obligations of the insured employer under the compensation law and the other with his common-law liability, if any.

Coverage *A* of the insuring agreements refers to the insurance afforded to meet the employer's responsibility under the applicable compensation law, and reads as follows:

The company agrees with the insured, named in the declarations made a part hereof, in consideration of the payment of the premium, and in reliance upon the statements in the declarations and subject to the limits of liability, exclusions, conditions, and other terms of this policy:

Coverage A: To pay promptly when due all compensation and other benefits required by the workmen's compensation law.

"Workmen's compensation law," as used in the insuring agreement quoted, is defined under Item III to mean the following:

The unqualified term "workmen's compensation law" means the workmen's compensation law and the occupational disease law of a state designated in Item III of the declarations, but does not include those provisions of any such law which provide non-occupational disability benefits.

Therefore, under the policy, the company assumes the compensation liability of the employer in the state or states designated in Item III of the declarations. This is the extent of the insurance carrier's obligation. It does not extend to states not designated in the declarations no matter what the circumstances of the injury are.

For example, let us assume that New York is the only state designated in the declarations. An employee is injured while working in New Jersey and files a claim under the New Jersey compensation act. The insurance carrier has no coverage for the state of New Jersey and therefore has no obligation to either defend the claim or to pay any awards which may be made by the New Jersey compensation commission. New York's statute has been construed to have extraterritorial effect, and if the same employee, injured in New Jersey, were to make a claim under the New York workmen's compensation act the insurance carrier would have coverage and would be obligated to defend and pay the claim. The reason is that the insurance carrier contracted to assume all of the insured's obligations under the compensation law of New York and, whatever the circumstances, if there is an obligation under the New York act the insurance carrier must indemnify the employer.

However, if a claim is made under any other law in any other state not designated under Item III of the declarations, there is no coverage. Many large corporations are insured for compensation in one state by one insurance carrier and in another state by another insurance carrier. The obligations of each carrier will be determined by the state or states designated in their policies. The situation thus created by the policy contracts will sometimes produce a rather peculiar result. For example, if an employer was insured for compensation in Pennsylvania by insurance carrier X, and insured for compensation in the state of New York by insurance carrier Y, and the employer sent one of his New York employees to Pennsylvania to do some work, and such employee was injured in that state, the question of which insurance carrier would have to respond in compensation would depend upon the state in which the injured employee asserted his claim.

If he filed a claim under the Pennsylvania act, insurance carrier X would have to pay the claim, whereas if he filed his claim in New York, then insurance carrier Y would have the coverage. The fact that the accident occurred in Pennsylvania would not give carrier Y a cause of action in subrogation against carrier X, nor would the fact that the employee was a New York employee give carrier X a right of reimbursement from carrier Y.

To further complicate the situation, let us assume that the claimant received a final award in Pennsylvania which was paid by carrier X, and assume further that he filed another claim in New York. Carrier Y would be obligated to defend the New York action, and if a further award were made under the New York act, carrier Y would be obliged to pay it. Carrier Y would get credit for the payments made in Pennsylvania. Carrier X still could not recover its payments from Y in spite of the credit received under the New York award.

It sometimes happens that an employer operates from more than one location within one state and is insured by a different insurance carrier at each location. To further complicate the situation, the compensation act provides that the compensation insurance carrier assumes all of the compensation obligations of the employer. To take care of this situation and to avoid overlapping coverages, the policy contains the following exclusion:

This policy does not apply (a) to operations conducted at or from any workplace not described in item 1 or 4 of the declarations if the insured has, under the workmen's compensation law, other insurance for such operations or is a qualified self-insurer therefor.

Two factors must be present from the exclusion to operate. First, the location must be one which is not described in item 1 or 4 of the declarations, and secondly, the employer must have insurance for that location or qualify as a self-insurer therefor. If the employer has no insurance for the location, which is not described in the declarations, since the law obligates the carrier to assume all of the compensation obligations of the insured, the policy will cover the undescribed location. If the employer has insurance, then the policy does not afford coverage. If it should happen that the location is one described in the declarations and the employer also obtained other insurance for that location, there are then two policies of insurance applicable to the location and both insurance carriers are equally liable for the payment of claims arising therefrom.

As can be noted, there is no limit of liability expressed in the insuring agreement except that the company assumes the obligation of the insured under the workmen's compensation law. Therefore the limit of the company's liability will be coextensive with the provisions of the applicable compensation law, and, in addition, the compensation law is made part of the policy contract by reference under condition 8, which reads as follows:

All of the provisions of the workmen's compensation law shall be and remain a part of this policy as fully and completely as if written herein, so far as they apply to compensation and other benefits provided by this policy, and to special taxes, payments into security or other special funds, and assessments required of or levied against compensation insurance carriers under such law.

This means that the compensation law is part of the policy. It does not mean the compensation law as it existed at the inception of the policy, but the compensation law as it exists. Therefore, any legislative changes in the law immediately become part of the policy contract, even though such changes were not even contemplated at the time the policy contract was made. For example, if the compensation rate in the state was $40 at the inception of the policy, and six months later the legislature increased the compensation rate to $75 the obligation of the insurance carrier would be to pay the $75 compensation rate on and after the date of the increase. At all times, the responsibility of the compensation carrier is coextensive with the provisions of the compensation law, and this without any endorsements or amendments to the policy itself.

The insuring agreement with respect to the common law liability of the insured, if any, is contained in the following paragraph:

Coverage B, Employers' Liability: To pay on behalf of the insured all sums which the insured shall become legally obligated to pay as damages because of bodily injury by accident or disease, including death at any time resulting therefrom, sustained in the United States of America, its territories or possessions, or Canada, by any employee of the insured arising out of and in the course of his employment by the insured either in operations in a state designated in Item 3 of the declarations or in operations necessary or incidental thereto.

It should be noted that the territorial limits of the policy refer to the United States and Canada, which would include within the terms the territorial waters of each, or 3 land miles seaward from low water mark. Therefore, if there is any liability under maritime law on the part of the employer to his employee for an accident occurring within the 3-mile limit of either country, the policy affords coverage. It should be noted that the coverage is limited to the United States and Canada and does not in any way involve Mexico or any other country. The coverage was designed to covert tort liability, and since the situs of the tort is determinative of the jurisdiction, there is no problem with respect to extraterritoriality as we find it under the compensation acts. This liability coverage is limited by the following exclusions:

This policy does not apply (c) under coverage B to liability assumed by the insured under any contract or agreement: (d) under coverage B, (1) to punitive or exemplary damages on account of bodily injury to or death of any employee employed in violation of law, or (2) with respect to any employee employed in violation of law with the knowledge or acquiescence of the insured or any executive officer thereof; (e) under coverage B, to bodily injury by disease unless prior to thirty-six months after the end of the policy period written claim is made or suit is brought against the insured for damages because of such injury or death resulting therefrom; (f) under coverage B, to any obligation for which the insured or any carrier as his insurer may be held liable under the workmen's compensation law or occupational disease law of a state designated in Item 3 of the declarations, any other workmen's compensation or occupational disease law, any unemployment compensation or disability benefits law, or under any similar law.

These exclusions spell out the intent of the contract to eliminate from its scope all obligations under any workmen's compensation law and other laws and all damages imposed because of the employment of an employee in violation of the law, whether such damages be punitive or compensatory, as well as a limitation with respect to occupational diseases. It excludes from its terms any obligation assumed by the insured under any contract or agreement.

Under coverage B, consideration is also given to claims by third persons against the insured, which claims arise out of the injury to or death of an employee of the insured (See Section 2339, above). Condition 9 of the policy covers this liability and reads as follows:

Limits of Liability, Coverage B. The word "damages" because of bodily injury by accident or disease, including death at any time resulting therefrom in coverage B include damages for care and loss of services and damages for which the insured is liable by reason of suits or claims brought against the insured by others to recover the damages obtained from such others because of such bodily injury sustained by employees of the insured arising out of and in the course of employment.

This covers only the tort liability of the insured and does not cover any liability assumed under any contract or agreement. Therefore, if the insured is held liable because of a hold harmless agreement to which he was a party, the coverage is not applicable.

Limits of liability.   With respect to coverage A, there is no limit of liability expressed in the contract except that the company's liability will be coextensive with that of the insured under the applicable compensation law. Therefore, the liability of the company would not exceed the maximum payments under the compensation law. As to coverage B, the limits of liability are expressed in the declarations.

Voluntary compensation.   In some states where there are classes of employees not within the coverage of the act, the employer may, with their consent, bring them within the terms of the act. The employer evidences his voluntary acceptance of the terms of the act by securing a workmen's compensation policy and giving notice to his employees by means of a notice conspicuously posted on the premises, or by actual notice. The employee's acceptance of the act is presumed in the absence of a notice from him to the employer that he does not accept the act and wants to retain his common-law rights.

Where the employer has secured workmen's compensation insurance and he fails to give notice to the employee of that fact, the employee, when he does receive notice, may then elect whether to accept the compensation act or to retain his common-law rights. This situation usually arises where there has been an accident and the employee learns for the first time that the employer has voluntarily accepted the compensation act. The employee then has the right of election and may enforce his common-law rights, rejecting the employer's acceptance of the act, or he may ratify the employer's acceptance and claim compensation benefits. Where the employee has notice of the employer's election and he fails to object, and an accident happens subsequently, the employee is limited to his recovery under the act and has no other remedy.

Voluntary compensation endorsement.   As to employees who are subject to federal jurisdiction, such as employees of an interstate carrier, or seamen, neither employer nor employee may confer jurisdiction on the state compensation authority. Both are still subject to the federal jurisdiction, and recovery may be had only under the Federal Employers' Liability Act, the Jones Act, or other maritime law. Where employers' liability coverage is provided, it will come within the terms of coverage B.

Under these federal statutes the liability of the employer is based on negligence, and the claims may be settled by means of a release without any recourse to court procedure. Where there is no negligence on the part of the employer, no recovery may be had. In order to provide a recovery for their employees, employers of such employees sometimes purchase additional insurance coverage in the form of a voluntary compensation endorsement, which is added to the workmen's compensation and employers' liability policy. Under this additional agreement, the insurer agrees to offer the injured employee, or in the case of death his dependents, an amount of money which will be equivalent to the compensation value of the case under the compensation law of a state mentioned in the agreement in return for a release of all claims.

In other words, the insurer is obligated to make a offer of the compensation value of the case, irrespective of negligence, in return for a general release. If the claimant rejects the offer, then there is no further responsibility on the part of the insurer under the endorsement, the case will be handled from that point on as if there was no endorsement to the coverage and the claimant has no further rights thereunder. In addition, the filing of any suit or other proceeding to recover on the claim is deemed a rejection of the compensation offer, whether one was made or not. The insurer agrees to make an offer of settlement using the compensation law of the state agreed upon between the employer and the insurer as the measure of damages, irrespective of the liability of the employer in return for the execution of a general release by the claimant. Once the offer is made, accepted and payment is made, or the offer is rejected, the insurer's obligation under the agreement is at an end, and the case then will be dealt with as if there was no voluntary compensation endorsement.

2345   Statement of principles: Workmen's compensation

The following statement of principles was issued by the American Insurance Association on behalf of their member companies:

STATEMENT OF PRINCIPLES OF INSURANCE CLAIMS MANAGEMENT
AND PRACTICE IN THE FIELD OF WORKMEN'S COMPENSATION

The Workmen's Compensation System was adopted in this country to provide certain, prompt and adequate benefits to employees injured in industry, or their dependents. Insurance is not only an important, but a necessary part of this system, because without some guarantee of ability to pay on the part of all employers, the remedy provided would often be empty and fruitless.

Insurance claims representatives, because of their daily contact with both employers and employees, hold a position of especial responsibility in this system. It is by their actions that the whole Insurance Industry is judged. The companies which they represent have recognized constantly the responsibility of discharging the obligations provided by the Workmen's Compensation Laws, promptly, efficiently and in complete accordance with their spirit. Failure so to function is detrimental to the whole insurance business.

Despite the difficulties of operating under present day conditions, and in order to attain maximum efficiency it is important to make certain that existing claim practices measure up fully to the high standards which the Insurance Industry has set.

In appreciation of the foregoing, the companies comprising the membership of the American Insurance Association here restate and reaffirm their traditional policies, which must be followed by all who are responsible for the payment of Workmen's Compensation claims:

FIRST, all legitimate claims should be paid promptly and fully. In order to accomplish this, an immediate investigation of the facts and coverage should be made upon receipt of notice of injury. As far as possible, all questions should be covered thoroughly in first interviews. If any doubt exists as to the amount due, the claimant should be paid the sum which, in the judgment of the claims representative, fairly represents the value of the claim, subject to whatever subsequent adjustment may be found necessary. It should always be remembered that receipt of a compensation check on the day it is due is of great importance to the claimant.

SECOND, a frank and friendly attitude should be adopted towards all claimants. If there is any question of compensability, he should be told of the insurer's position at the earliest possible moment.

THIRD, the best medical and surgical attention possible should be provided in those states whose laws permit the carriers to select the physicians and surgeons. The insurer's objective and that of the injured man are identical in this respect. By receiving the best medical care, the worker, in the average case, will be rehabilitated and returned to full earning capacity more promptly. The physician should never feel that he must "favor" the carrier in order to retain its business.

FOURTH, only when necessary should cases go to hearings. Full use of informal conferences, where possible, should be made. Only real issues should be raised. Adjournments should be avoided and cases fully prepared before hearings. Appeals should be taken only when reasonable grounds exist—not simply because of disappointment.

FIFTH, payments should be made directly to beneficiaries. They should be made through the employer only when that method will expedite receipt of payment, or be more convenient to the injured man or his dependents. After payment of compensation is started, following an agreement or award, it should not be discontinued because of change of status of disability, except when otherwise provided by law, until the injured party is so advised, or returns to work.

SIXTH, employers should be given every assistance in obtaining an adequate understanding of the proper operation of the Workmen's Compensation System. The necessity for promptly reporting the occurrence of injuries should be impressed upon them by agent or broker, working in close cooperation with the Claim Department. It should be explained, when necessary, why certain claims may have to be contested and why, in other instances, payment must be made. Employers should not be advised that the employment of handicapped workers, for tasks they are fitted to perform, is undesirable.

SEVENTH, there should be complete cooperation with the agencies administering the Workmen's Compensation Laws. Personal contact with them should be established and periodical conferences held to learn at first hand of any possible complaints or criticisms. Full compliance with the provisions of the Workmen's Compensation Laws must be observed. The high level on which the business of Insurance is conducted should be apparent through the fair dealing and efficiency of its representatives.

EIGHTH, dishonest claims should be fought. It is a duty the carrier owes to its policyholders, honest claimants and itself. But intent to defraud should be clear before it is concluded that the claimant is dishonest.

NINTH, the great and exacting responsibilities of insurance companies in the proper, economical and efficient administration of Workmen's Compensation Laws must be freely accepted by those engaged in claims management. Through their actions, they should continue to demonstrate the ability of insurance companies to retain the confidence of employers, employees, compensation administrators and the public as a whole. The insurance business, thus conducted on a high level of social awareness and motivated by the complete appreciation of its responsibilities, will stand the test of scrutiny from all other points of view.

Glossary of legal and insurance terms

Ab initio. From the beginning.

Accident. An undesigned, unexpected, or sudden result. Some insurance policies define accident, or *accidental means*, in the contract itself. Where that condition exists, the wording of the contract will govern the meaning contemplated by the parties, and not the dictionary definition.

Accountable. Subject to pay, responsible, liable.

Accretion. The act of growing; usually applied to the gradual accumulation of land by natural causes, as out of a sea or river.

Acknowledgment. Formal declaration before an authorized official by a person who executed (signed) an instrument that it is his free act and deed.

Acquisition cost. The cost to an insurance company of securing business. This would consist of commissions paid to agents and brokers, and other related expenses.

Act of God. An act occasioned exclusively by the violence of nature with no interference or concurrence by any human agency.

Action. The legal demand of one's right to recover from another person or party made before a court; a lawsuit.

Action ex contractu. Action for breach of a promise set forth in a contract, express or implied.

Action ex delicto. An action arising out of a breach of duty; action in tort.

Actual authority. In the law of agency, such authority as a principal intentionally confers on the agent, or intentionally (or by want of ordinary care) allows the agent to believe himself to possess; includes both express and implied authority.

Actual cash value. The fair or reasonable cash price for which the property could be sold in the market in the ordinary course of business and not at a forced sale; the price it will bring in a fair market after reasonable efforts to find a purchaser who will give the highest price. It is the greatest amount the insured can recover in practically all policies indemnifying for damage to property, except in states where valued policy laws are in effect.

Additur. The power of a trial court to assess damages or to increase the amount of an inadequate award made by a jury verdict, as a condition for denial of a motion for a new trial; with consent of defendant, whether or not plaintiff consents to such action.

Administrator. In the usual sense of the word, a person to whom letters of administration, that is an authority to administer the estate of a deceased person, have been granted by the proper court; a representative of limited authority whose duties are to collect assets of the estate, pay its debts, and distribute the residue to those entitled. He resembles an executor, who is a representative appointed by the will of the deceased. The administrator is appointed by the court and not by the deceased and therefore has to give security for the due administration of the estate by entering into a bond with sureties, called the *administration bond*.

Admissions. Confessions, concessions, or voluntary acknowledgments made by a party of the existence of certain facts.

Affiant. The person who makes and subscribes an *affidavit.*

Affidavit. A written or printed declaration or statement of fact, made voluntarily and confirmed by the oath or affirmation of the party making it, and taken before an officer having authority to administer such oath.

Affirmative warranty. Affirms existence of a fact at the time policy is entered into. A *promissory warranty* requires that something be done or not done after the policy has taken effect.

Agency. Includes every relation in which one person acts for or represents another by the latter's authority; where one person acts for another either in the relationship of principal and agent, master and servant, or employer-proprietor and independent contractor.

Agent, general. One employed in his capacity as a professional man or master of an art or trade, or one to whom the principal confides his whole business or all transactions or functions of a designated class; one empowered to transact all business of a principal at any particular time or any particular place.

Agent, local. One appointed to act as the representative of a corporation and transact its business generally (or business of a particular character, at a given place or within a defined district).

Agent, special. One employed to conduct a particular transaction or piece of business for his principal, or authorized to perform a specified act. In the insurance business, special agents are field representatives of the company whose duty is to stimulate business for their company throughout the territory to which they are assigned. They have the power to appoint agents, and may also withdraw their company from an agency.

Ambiguity. Doubtfulness or doubleness of meaning, duplicity, or indistinctness or uncertainty of meaning of an expression used in a written instrument.

Answer. A pleading by which the defendant in a suit at law endeavors to resist the plaintiff's demand by an allegation of facts, either denying allegations of the plaintiff's complaint, or confessing them, and alleging new matter in avoidance, which defendant alleges should prevent recovery.

Appeal. The right of a party, who has received an adverse decision, to take the case to a higher court for review.

Application. The preliminary request, declaration, or statement made by a party applying for an insurance policy.

Arbitration. The submission for determination of disputed matter to private unofficial persons selected in a manner provided by law or by agreement.

Arising out of and in the course of employment. Workmen's compensation acts provide for compensating an employee whose injury arises out of and in the course of employment, and these words describe an injury directly and naturally resulting in a risk reasonably incident to the employment. They mean that there might be some causal connection between the conditions under which the employee worked and the injury which he received. *Arising out of employment* refers to the origin of the cause of the injury, while *course of employment* refers to the time, place, and circumstances under which the injury occurred.

Arraign. In criminal practice, to bring a prisoner to the bar of the court to answer the matter charged against him either in an indictment or information.

It consists of calling the prisoner by name, reading the charges against him, demanding of him whether he is guilty or not guilty, and entering his plea.

Assault. An intentional, unlawful offer of corporal injury to another by force, or force unlawfully directed toward the person of another, under such circumstances as create well-founded fear of imminent peril, coupled with apparent present ability to execute the attempt. *Battery* consists of the actual execution of the act offered in an assault. Hence, the placing of the victim in fear (*assault*) and the actual infliction of the injury (*battery*) constitute what is commonly referred to as *assault* and *battery*.

Assign. To make over or set over to another. The person doing the act is called the *assignor* and the person to whom the cause of action or other property is assigned is called the *assignee*.

Assured. A person who has been insured by some insurance company or underwriter against losses or perils mentioned in the policy of insurance.

Attachment. A remedy ancillary to an action by which the plaintiff is enabled to acquire a lien upon the property or effects of the defendant for satisfaction of a judgment which the plaintiff may obtain. The purpose is to take the defendant's property into legal custody so that it may be applied on the defendant's debt to the plaintiff when the debt is established.

Attest. To bear witness to; to bear witness to a fact; to affirm it to be true or genuine; to act as a witness to; to certify; to make solemn declaration in words or writing to support a fact.

Attorney. In the most general sense denotes an agent or substitute, or one appointed and authorized to act in the place or stead of another.

Attorney-at-law. An advocate, counsel or official agent employed in preparing, managing, and trying cases in the courts. An officer, in a court of justice, who is employed by a party in a cause to manage it for him.

Attorney-in-fact. A private attorney authorized by another to act in his place and stead, either for some particular purpose, or for the transaction of business in general, not of a legal character. This authority is conferred by an instrument in writing called a *letter of attorney* or, more commonly, a *power of attorney*.

Attorney's lien. The right of an attorney-at-law to hold or retain in his possession the money or property of a client until his proper charges have been adjusted and paid. Also a lien on funds in court payable to the client, or on a judgment, decree, or award recovered through the exertions of the attorney, and for the enforcement of which he must involve the equitable aid of the court.

Audit. In insurance, an examination of the insured's books and payroll records for the purpose of determining the premium due. This is especially true in workmen's compensation and manufacturers' and contractors' public liability policies, where the amount of the premium is based upon the insured's actual payroll records.

Award. The decision or determination rendered by arbitrators, commissioners, or other private or extrajudicial deciders upon a controversy submitted to them. Under workmen's compensation acts, the term may signify a decision or determination of the Industrial Board or some equivalent body.

Bad faith. Generally implying or involving actual or constructive fraud, or a design to mislead or deceive another, or a neglect or refusal to fulfill some duty or some contractual obligation; not prompted by an honest mistake as to one's rights or duties, but by some interested or sinister motive. It differs from the negative idea of *negligence* in that it contemplates a state of mind affirmatively operating with a furtive design or some motive of interest or ill will. See *good faith.*

Bail.   To procure the release of a person from legal custody by undertaking that he shall appear at the time and place designated and submit himself to the judgment of the court.

Bailee.   One who has possession of property belonging to another. He may be a bailee for the benefit of the bailor, his own benefit, or for their mutual benefit.

Bailment.   A delivery of goods or personal property by one person to another in trust for the execution of a special object upon or in relation to such goods, beneficial either to the bailor or bailee or both, and upon a contract expressed or implied to perform the trust and carry out such object, and thereupon redeliver the goods to the bailor, or otherwise dispose of the same in conformity with the purpose of the trust.

Battery.   Any unlawful beating or other wrongful physical violence or constraint inflicted upon a human being without his consent.

Benficiary.   One for whose benefit a contract is made; the person to whom a policy of insurance is payable.

Bill of lading.   The written evidence of a contract for carriage and delivery of goods sent by sea or land transportation; receipt given by the carrier for the merchandise and must be surrendered before the goods will be delivered.

Binder.   Memorandum of an agreement for insurance which gives temporary protection, pending investigation of the risk and issuance of a formal policy; a verbal contract of insurance, temporary in nature, but binding on both parties.

Breach of contract.   Failure, without legal excuse, to perform any promise which forms the whole or part of a contract.

Broker.   An agent employed to make bargains and contracts for a compensation. In insurance, an individual or organization which acts as the representative of the insured in writing insurance contracts; an insurance specialist, under no obligation to place policy contracts with any one company, whose only duty is to secure the best possible coverage for his clients at the lowest possible rates. A broker's actions are not binding on any specific insurance company, and his acts are those of the insured.

Burden of proof.   In the law of evidence, the necessity or duty of affirmatively proving a fact or facts in dispute on an issue raised between the parties in a cause.

Burglary.   The breaking and entering of the house of another in the nighttime with intent to commit a felony therein, whether the felony be actually committed or not.

C.I.F.   These letters in contracts of sale indicate (as does *C.F.I.* or *CF&I*) that the price fixed covers the cost of goods, insurance, and freight.

C.O.D.   *Collect on Delivery.* These letters import the carrier's liability to return to the consignor either the goods or the charges. The carrier accepts a check instead of cash at its own peril.

Cancellation.   Abandonment of a contract. In insurance, termination of a contract before its expiration by either the insured or the company. The notice of cancellation and methods by which it can be effected are usually set forth in the insurance contract.

Carlisle tables. Life annuity tables, compiled at Carlisle, England, about 1780 and still used by actuaries as one of the bases for estimating life expectancy.

Carriage. The act of carrying, or a contract for the transportation of persons or goods. The contract of carriage is for the conveyance of property, persons, or messages from one place to another.

Carrier. One undertaking to transport persons or property. Carriers are either common or private. Common carriers are those who hold themselves out or undertake to carry persons or goods of all persons indifferently, who may apply for passage, so long as there is room and there is no legal excuse for refusal. Private carriers transport or undertake to transport in a particular instance for hire or reward. The term also refers to the insurance carrier, or insurer.

Casual employment. Employment at uncertain times or irregular intervals; casual and not in the usual course of trade, business, occupation, or profession of the employer; for a short time and for limited and temporary purpose.

Casualty. Accident; event due to sudden, unexpected or unusual cause; event not to be foreseen or guarded against; misfortune or mishap.

Caveat emptor. *Let the buyer beware.* This maxim summarizes the rule that a purchaser must examine, judge, and test for himself.

Certiorari. The name of a writ of review or inquiry; an appellate proceeding for reexamination of the action of an inferior tribunal, or an auxiliary process to enable an appellate court to obtain further information in a pending cause.

Chattel. An article or personal property; any species of property not amounting to a freehold or fee in land. *Chattels* is more comprehensive than *goods* as it includes animate as well as inanimate property.

Chiropractor. One professing a system of manipulation which aims to cure disease by the mechanical restoration of displaced or subluxated bones, especially the vertebrae, to their relation.

Claim. The right, real or alleged, of an individual or corporation to recover for a loss which may come within an insured's policy contract.

Claimant. One who claims or asserts a right, demand, or claim.

Classification of risks. A term used in insurance with reference to the nature and situation of articles insured and to the occupation and business of the applicant.

Client. A person who employs or retains an attorney, or counsellor, to appear for him in the courts, advise, assist, and defend him in legal proceedings, and to act for him in any legal business.

Code. A collection, compendium, or revision of laws.

Coinsurance. A relative division of risk between insurer and insured, depending upon the relative amount of the policy and the actual value of the property insured, and taking effect only when the actual loss is partial and less than the amount of the policy, the insurer being liable to the extent of the policy for a loss equal to or in excess of that amount.

Collusion. An agreement between two or more persons to defraud a third person of his rights by the forms of law, or to obtain an object forbidden by law. It implies the existence of fraud of some kind, the employment of fraudulent means, or of lawful means for the accomplishment of an unlawful purpose.

Commission. The recompense or reward of an agent, factor, broker, or bailee, when same is calculated as a percentage on the amount of his transactions or the profit to the principal. In insurance this refers to a certain percentage of the premiums given to the agent as compensation for his work in selling and servicing the policy.

Common law. Distinguished from law created by the enactment of legislatures, common law comprises the body of those principles and rules of action, relating to the government and security of persons and property, which derive their authority solely from usages and customs of immemorial antiquity, or from the judgments and decrees of the courts recognizing, affirming, and enforcing such usages and customs.

Common-law marriage. One not solemnized in the ordinary way but created by an agreement to marry, followed by cohabitation.

Commotion. A *civil commotion* is an insurrection of the people for general purposes (though it may not amount to *rebellion,* where there is usurped power) which occasions a serious and prolonged disturbance and infraction of civil order, but not attaining the status of war or an armed insurrection. Term refers to political disorders, not to an economic disturbance.

Comparative negligence. That doctrine in the law of negligence by which the negligence of the party is compared in degrees of slight, ordinary, or gross, and a recovery permitted, notwithstanding the contributory negligence of the plaintiff, when the negligence of the plaintiff is slight and that of the defendant gross; but refused when the plaintiff has been guilty of a want of ordinary care, thereby contributing to his injury; or when the negligence of the defendant is only ordinary or slight when compared with the contributory negligence of the plaintiff.

Where negligence of both parties is concurrent and contributes to injury, recovery is not barred under such doctrines, but the plaintiff's damages are diminished proportionately, provided his fault is less than the defendant and that, by the exercise of ordinary care, he could not have avoided the consequences of the defendant's negligence after it was or should have been apparent.

Complaint. In civil practice in states having a code of civil procedure, the complaint is the first initiatory proceeding on the part of the plaintiff in a civil action; it corresponds to a declaration of narrative in common-law practice.

Compulsory insurance. Any form of insurance which is required of all members of a class by the state. For example, in Massachusetts and New York, automobile liability insurance is compulsory for all owners of automobiles. Likewise, the carrying of workmen's compensation insurance is compulsory in many states.

Concurrent insurance. Where two or more insurance policies cover the same interest, or identical property; overlapping insurance.

Condition. A clause in a contract or agreement which may suspend, rescind, or modify the principal obligation; conditions may be *positive* (requiring that a specified event shall happen or an act be done), *restrictive,* or *negative* (the latter imposing an obligation not to do a particular thing).

Conservator. A guardian, protector, preserver; a person appointed by the court to take care of the person and the estate of an incapable person, such as an infant, idiot, or other incompetent.

Consideration. In the law of contracts, an inducement to a contract. The cause, motive, or price, are impelling influences which induce a contracting party to enter into a contract.

Consignee. One to whom a *consignment* is made; the person to whom goods are shipped or otherwise transmitted; the one to whom the carrier may lawfully make delivery in accordance with its contract of carriage.

Constructive loss. Sometimes referred to as *constructive total loss.* Loss resulting from such injuries to property, without its destruction, as render it valueless to the insured or prevent its restoration to the original condition except at a cost exceeding its value.

Contempt. Willful disregard or disobedience of a public authority.

Contempt of court. Any act calculated to embarrass, hinder, or obstruct the court in the administration of justice, or lessen its authority or dignity; committed by a person who does any act in willful prevention of its authority, or tending to impede or frustrate the administration or dignity of justice; or by one who, being under the court's authority as a party to a proceeding therein, willfully disobeys its lawful orders or fails to comply with an undertaking which he has given.

Continuity rider. A clause attached to a surety bond, assuming the liability for certain or all losses which may have occurred during the term of a previous bond, which have not as yet been discovered.

Contractual liability. Liability assumed under any contract or agreement, express or implied. Such liability is excluded in automobile liability policies and, with certain exceptions, most other liability policies unless there is a specific agreement on the part of the company to assume such liability.

Conversion. Unauthorized assumption and exercise of the right of ownership over goods or personal chattels belonging to another, to the alteration of their condition or the exclusion of the owner's rights; any unauthorized act which deprives an owner of his property permanently or for an indefinite period of time.

Coroner's inquest. An inquisition or examination into the causes and circumstances of any death happening by violence or under suspicious conditions within his territory; held by the coroner with the assistance of a jury.

Corporation. An artificial person or legal entity created by or under the authority of the laws of a state, consisting of an association of numerous individuals; regarded in law as having a personality and existence distinct from that of its several members, and which is, by the same authority, vested with the capacity of continuous succession, irrespective of changes in its membership, either in perpetuity or for a limited term of years, and of acting as a unit or single individual in matters relating to the common purpose of the association, within the scope of the powers and authority conferred upon such bodies by law.

Costs. A pecuniary allowance made to the successful party (and recoverable from the losing party) for his expenses in prosecuting or defending the suit or a distinct proceeding within a suit.

Covenant not to sue. An agreement by one who had a right of action at the time of making it against another person, by which he agrees not to sue to enforce such right of action.

Daily report. A summary of all the essential facts with reference to a risk on which a policy has been issued, which the agent sends to the company after writing the policy; usually takes the form of a carbon copy of the face or declaration of the policy and is submitted to the company at the close of each day of business. For that reason policy copies in the possession of the company are sometimes referred to as *Dailies.*

Damages.   A pecuniary compensation or indemnity which may be recovered in the courts by any person who has suffered loss, detriment, or injury, whether to his person, property, or rights through the unlawful act or negligence of another.

Declaration.   A statement by the applicant or the insured with regard to the circumstances of the risk. Technically the declarations are the statements made by the insured as to the existence of certain facts on which the insurance company relied in entering into the contract. A declaration by the insured, if untrue, may release the insurance company from its obligation.

Defendant.   The person defending or denying; the party against whom relief or recovery is sought in an action or suit.

Delictum.   A delict, tort, wrong, injury, or offense. *Actions ex delicto* are founded on a tort, as distinguished from *actions on contract;* culpability; blameworthiness, or legal delinquency.

Dependent.   One who derives support from another, not merely persons who derive a benefit from the earnings of the deceased; one who depends on or is sustained by another, or who relies on another for support.

Diagnosis.   Medical term meaning the discovery of the source of the patient's illness, or the determination of the nature of his disease from a study of its symptoms; the art or act of recognizing the presence of disease from its symptoms and deciding as to its character; also the decision reached for determination of type or condition through case or specimen study, or conclusion arrived at through critical perception or scrutiny. A *clinical diagnosis* is one made by means of physical measure, such as palpation and inspection.

Disclaimer.   The refutation or renunciation of a claim or power vested in a person and formerly alleged to be his. In insurance law, a denial by the insurance carrier that the policy of insurance covers the circumstances claimed by the insured.

Discovery.   The disclosure by the defendant of facts, titles, documents, and other things which are in his exclusive knowledge or possession, and which are necessary to a party seeking the discovery as part of a cause of action pending or to be brought in another court, or as evidence of his right or title in such proceeding. More particularly it refers to legal practice where facts within the knowledge of the adverse party may be demanded as a part of the preliminary proceedings to the lawsuit.

Earned premium.   The amount at any time during the life of the policy which would compensate the company for the protection furnished for the expired portion of the policy term. Since insurance premiums are paid in advance, the premium is not earned until all of the protection required by the policy has actually been afforded to the insured. Therefore, the entire premium would not be earned until the expiration date of the policy. However, during the life of the policy, as time passes, the amount of premium advanced commensurate with the period of time for which protection has been afforded then becomes earned premium. The balance of the premium is referred to as *unearned premium.*

Embezzlement.   The fraudulent appropriation of property or money by clerk, agent, trustee, public officer, or other person acting in a fiduciary character.

Embracery.   In criminal law, the attempt to influence a jury corruptly by promises, persuasions, entreaties, entertainments, and the like.

Emergency.   A sudden unexpected happening, an unforeseen occurrence or condition; a perplexing contingency or complication of circumstances; a sudden or unexpected occasion for action.

Emergency employment doctrine.   A regularly employed servant possesses implied authority to engage an assistant to aid in performance of a task, including an emergency situation, when it is necessary to obtain such assistance.

Endorsement.   A supplementary agreement attached to an insurance policy for the purpose of changing its conditions or altering its coverage.

Et al.   An abbreviation of *et alii,* and others; the singular is *et alius*

Ex gratia   As a matter of grace, favor, or indulgence; gratuitous; applied to anything accorded as a favor, as distinguished from what might be demanded as a matter of right.

Ex parte.   In behalf or on the application of one party only.

Excess insurance.   The amount of insurance which is available only when this amount exceeds a certain figure. The risk of the initial loss or damage, so excluded in the excess policy, may be carried by the insured himself or insured by another policy which gives primary or specific protection. Excess insurance applies only to the amount of money involved over and above the initial sum retained by the insured or his primary insurance carrier.

Expectancy of life.   In life annuities, the number of years a person of a given age may, upon any quality of chance, expect to enjoy.

Experience.   Applied to insurance, the loss record of an insured, or a class of coverage over a period of years.

Experience rate.   A special rate for casualty insurance available to an insured because of satisfactory past insurance; this rate is a deviation from the manual rate.

Express.   Clear, definite, explicit, unmistakable; manifested by direct and appropriate language; distinguished from that which is inferred from conduct.

Extraordinary repairs.   Within the meaning of a lease, made necessary by some unusual or unforeseen occurrence which does not destroy the building but merely renders it less suited to the use for which it was intended.

Extraterritoriality.   Operation of laws upon persons, rights, or jural relations existing beyond the physical limits of an enacting state.

Falsus in uno, falsus in omnibus.   *False in one thing, false in everything.* Doctrine means that if testimony of a witness on a material issue is willfully false and given with intent to deceive, the jury may disregard all of the witness' testimony.

Family automobile doctrine.   Also referred to as the family car or the family purpose doctrine: that one who owns and maintains an automobile for the general use of his household makes use of the automobile for such purpose as a part of his business, so that any member using the automobile for those purposes (under general authority to do so) becomes his representative, for whose negligence he is responsible. It is an extension of the *respondeat superior* principle to the operation of the family automobile.

The person upon whom it is sought to fasten liability under this doctrine must own, provide, or maintain an automobile for the general use, pleasure, and convenience of the family. Liability under the doctrine is not confined to the owner or driver; it depends upon control and use. A widow, wife, or mother may be liable as well as a husband or father.

To bring a case within the doctrine, it must be shown that the automobile was, in fact, a family pleasure automobile. However, an automobile purchased and used for business purposes may come within the doctrine where it is also used for family pleasure.

Fellow servant.   One who serves and is controlled by the same master; also those engaged in the same common pursuit under the same general control; those who derive authority in compensation from the same common source and are engaged in the same general business, though in different grades or departments.

Fellow servant rule.   Rule that a master is not liable for injuries to a servant caused by the negligence of a fellow servant engaged in the same general business and where the master has exercised due care in the selection of servants.

Fidelity bond.   A contract of fidelity insurance; a guarantee of personal honesty of the officer furnishing indemnity against his defaultation or negligence; a form of insurance or suretyship which protects a party against loss from the dishonesty of his employees.

Fiduciary.   A person or corporation having the duty created by his undertaking to act primarily for another's benefit in matters connected with such undertaking, or an agent handling the business of another when the business which he transacts or the money or property which he handles is not his own or for his own benefit, but for the benefit of another person to whom he stands in a relation implying and necessitating great confidence and trust on the one part and a high degree of good faith on the other.

Financial responsibility law.   A statute requiring motorists to furnish evidence of ability to pay damages either before or after an accident has occurred.

Flat cancellation.   Termination of an insurance policy without any refund of premium by the company or without any payment of earned premium by the insured; cancellation as of the inception date.

Fleet policy.   An insurance contract covering a number of automobiles specifically designated, or providing automatic coverage of all automobiles owned by the insured on a reporting or payroll basis; a device utilized to obtain a lower premium.

Forgery.   False making or material altering, with intent to defraud, of any writing which, if genuine, might be of legal efficacy or the foundation of a legal liability; the signing of a name of another with an attempt to imitate the handwriting for the purpose of obtaining money or other property.

Friendly suit.   In casualty insurance, a suit brought by the guardian of an infant or incompetent against the defendant solely for the purpose of having the court enter judgment for the amount agreed upon as a settlement in advance.

Gift.   A voluntary transfer of personal property without consideration. Essential requisites of a gift, or capacity of the donor: intention of donor to make a gift, completed delivery to or for the donee, and acceptance of the gift by the donee.

Good faith.   Honesty of intention and freedom from knowledge of circumstances which ought to put the holder upon inquiry; an honest intention to abstain from taking any conscious advantage of another, even through technicalities of law, together with absence of all information, notice, or benefit or belief of facts which render the transaction unconscionable.

Goods.   Every species of personal property.

Guardian.   A person lawfully invested with the power and charged with the duty of taking care, and managing the property and rights, of another person, who for some peculiarity of status or defect of age, understanding, or self-control is considered incapable of administering his own affairs.

Hazard.   In insurance law, the risk, danger, or probability that the event insured against may happen; varies with the circumstances of the particular case.

Hearsay.   Evidence proceeding not from the personal knowledge of the witness; mere repetition of what he has heard others say.

Imputed negligence.   Not directly attributable to the person himself, but the negligence of a person in privity with him, and with whose fault he is chargeable.

Increase in hazard.   In insurance, a change in the circumstances of a risk, making a loss more probable.

Independent contractor.   One who, exercising an independent employment, contracts to do a piece of work according to his own methods and without being subject to the control of his employer, except as to the result of the work.

Inevitable accident.   An accident is inevitable, so as to preclude recovery on the ground of negligence, if the person by whom it occurs neither has, nor is legally bound to have, sufficient power to avoid it or to prevent its injuring another.

Inherently dangerous.   Danger inhering in an instrumentality or condition at all times so as to require special precautions to prevent injury; not the danger arising from mere casual or collateral negligence of others.

Injunction.   A judicial process operating in personam and requiring the person to whom it is directed to do, or refrain from doing, a particular thing.

Insurable interest.   An interest as will make the loss of the property of pecuniary damage to the insured. Every interest in property, or any relation thereto or liability in respect thereof, of such nature that a contemplated peril might directly damnify the insured, is an insurable interest.

Insurance.   A contract whereby, for a stipulated consideration, one party undertakes to compensate the other for loss on a specified subject by specified perils.

Interstate commerce.   Traffic, intercourse, commercial trading, or transportation of persons or property between or among the several states of the Union, or from or between points in one state and points in another state, or commerce between two states or between places lying in different states.

Intrastate commerce.   Commerce within the confines of one state only.

Ipso facto.   *By the fact itself.*

Joint and several.   A liability is said to be joint and several where the creditor may sue one or more of the parties to such liability separately, or all of them together, at his option.

Joint control.   A practice in fiduciary bonds whereby trust assets may be handled only upon the signature and consent of both the principal and the surety.

Judgment.   The official and authentic decision of a court of justice upon the respective rights and claims of the parties to an action or suit therein litigated and submitted to its determination.

Judgment creditor.   One who has obtained a judgment against his debtor, under which he can enforce execution; the owner of an unsatisfied judgment.

Judgment debtor. A person against whom judgment has been recovered, and which remains unsatisfied.

Judicial notice. The act by which a court, in conducting a trial or framing its decision, will, of its own motion and without the production of evidence, recognize the existence and truth of certain facts having a bearing on the controversy at bar, which, from their nature are not properly the subject of testimony, or which are universally regarded as established by common notoriety.

Larceny. Felonious stealing, taking and carrying, leaving, riding, or driving away another's personality with intent to convert it or deprive the owner thereof. Larceny is the fraudulent taking and carrying away of a thing, without claim or right, with the intention of converting it to a use other than that of the owner, and without his consent.

Latent defect. A hidden defect; a defect in an article known to the seller but not to the purchaser, and not discoverable by means of observation.

Lease. Any agreement which gives rise to the relationship of landlord and tenant; contract for exclusive possession of lands for a determinate period.

Legal representative. In its broadest sense, one who stands in place of and represents the interests of another; usually refers to *executors* or *administrators*.

Legally liable. Liable under law, as interpreted by the courts; liability imposed by law or liability which the law fixed by contract.

Liability. Any legally enforceable obligation; most commonly used in a pecuniary sense. In insurance terminology an important distinction is made between *liability imposed by law*, which means an obligation forced upon a person because of his acts or omissions, and the broader term *legal liability* which embraces all pecuniary obligations, including liability assumed by contract. With certain exceptions, most liability insurance policies protect merely against liability imposed by law and exclude any liability assumed by contract.

Malice. The intentional doing of a wrongful act, without just cause or excuse, with an intent to inflict an injury, or under such circumstances that the law will imply an evil intent.

Malpractice. Any professional misconduct, unreasonable lack of skill or fidelity in professional or fiduciary duties; evil practice, or illegal or immoral conduct.

Manual rates. Insurance costs for a particular phase of the business, as published in the pertinent manual. These rates are usually fixed by a rating bureau, and all members of the bureau must write the insurance at the rate set forth in the manual, or under rules appertaining thereto. Discounts from manual rates are sometimes allowed because of favorable loss experience.

Merchantability. This means that the article sold shall be of the general kind described and reasonably fit for the general purpose for which it shall have been sold. Where the article sold is ordinarily used in but one way, its fitness for use in that particular way is impliedly warranted.

Misrepresentation. An untrue statement of fact, an incorrect or false representation, a statement made to deceive and mislead.

Narr. Common abbreviation of *narration,* a declaration in an action; one of the common-law names for a plaintiff's count or declaration, being a narrative of the facts on which he relies; the *complaint.*

Navigable in fact. Streams or lakes are navigable in fact when they are used or susceptible of being used in their natural and ordinary condition as highways for commerce over which trade and travel are or may be conducted in the customary modes of trade and travel on water.

Navigable waters of the U.S.   Waters are *navigable waters of the United States* when by themselves, or by uniting with other waters, they form a continued highway over which commerce is or may be carried on with other states or foreign countries in the customary modes.

Nuisance.   That which annoys and disturbs one in possession of his property, rendering its ordinary use or occupation physically uncomfortable to him; everything that endangers life or health, gives offense to senses, violates the laws of decency, or obstructs reasonable and compatible use of property. This class of wrongs derives from the unreasonable, unwarrantable, or unlawful use by a person of his own property, either real or personal, or from his own improper lawful personal conduct, working an obstruction of or injury to the right of another or of the public, and producing such material annoyance, inconvenience, discomfort, or hurt, that the law will presume resulting damage.

Oath.   An affirmation of the truth of a statement which renders one willfully asserting untrue statements punishable for perjury.

Obligation.   Any enforceable duty assumed by or imposed upon a person, firm, or corporation. An obligation or debt may exist by reason of a judgment as well as an express contract.

Obligee.   The person in favor of whom some obligation is contracted, whether such obligation be to pay money, or to do, or not do something; the party to whom a bond is given.

Obligor.   The person who has engaged to perform some obligation; one who makes a bond.

Occupancy.   In insurance contracts, refers to the type and character of the use of property; in a burglary policy implies actual use of the house as a dwelling place, not absolutely continuous but as a place of usual return.

Occupational disease.   Disease gradually contracted in usual and ordinary course of employment, because of and incidental thereto.

Ocean marine insurance.   As commonly used, applies to any form of marine coverage while the subject of the insurance is on water: "wet marine." Contrary to popular belief, insurance on ships and cargo on inland lakes and rivers also comes under the general classification of ocean marine insurance. *Inland marine insurance* properly refers to any risk *not* on water assumed by a marine insurance company, such as personal property floaters and the like.

Omnibus clause.   A provision in the automobile liability policy which extends coverage to any person, firm, or corporation legally responsible for the operation of the insured automobile, and to any person operating the car with the consent of the named insured.

Opinion evidence.   Evidence of what the witness thinks, believes, or infers in regard to facts in dispute; distinguished from his personal knowledge of the facts themselves.

Order.   In legal practice, every direction of a court or judge made or entered in writing and not included in a judgment; an application for an order is a *motion.*

Ordinary care.   That degree of caution which the ordinary person of reasonable prudence would use under any given set of circumstances.

Ostensible agency.   An implied or presumptive agency which exists where one, either intentionally or from want of ordinary care, induces another to believe that a third person is his agent though he has never, in fact, employed him. Strictly speaking, it is no agency at all, but is in reality based entirely upon *estoppel.*

Ostensible authority.   Such authority as a principal, intentionally or by want of ordinary care, causes or allows a third person to believe the agent possesses.

Ostensible partner.   One whose name appears to the world as such, though he has no interest in the firm.

Osteopathy.   A method or system of treating various diseases of the human body (without the use of drugs) by manipulation applied to various nerve centers, rubbing, pulling, kneading parts of the body, flexing and manipulating the limbs, and the mechanical readjustment of any bones, muscles, or ligaments not in the normal position, with a view to removing the cause of disorder and aiding the restorative force of nature in cases where the trouble originated in misplacement of the parts, irregular nerve action, or defective circulation.

Parol evidence.   Oral or verbal evidence, that which is given by word of mouth; the ordinary kind of evidence that is given by witnesses in court.

Parol evidence rule.   When parties put their agreement in writing under this rule, all previous oral agreements merge in the writing and a contract, as then written, cannot be modified or changed by parol evidence in the absence of a plea of mistake or fraud in the preparation of the writing. But the rule does not forbid a resort to parol evidence that is not inconsistent with the matters stated in the writing. Under this rule, parol or extrinsic evidence is not admissible to add to, subtract or vary from, or contradict judicial or official records or documents, or written instruments which dispose of property or are contractual in nature, and which are valid, complete, unambiguous, and unaffected by accident or mistake.

Parties.   The persons who take part in the performance of any act, or who are directly interested in any affair, contract, or conveyance, or who are actively concerned in the prosecution and defense of any legal proceeding.

Partnership.   A voluntary contract between two or more competent persons to place their money, effects, labor, and skill, or some or all of them, in lawful commerce or business with the understanding that there shall be a proportional sharing of the profits and losses.

Payroll audit.   An examination of the insured's accounts by a representative of the insurer to determine the premium due on a payroll, receipts, or other unit basis.

Penalty.   The sum of money which the obligor of a bond undertakes to pay in the event of his omitting to perform or carry out the terms imposed upon him by the conditions of the bond.

Peremptory.   Imperative, absolute, conclusive, positive, not admitting of question, delay, or reconsideration.

Perjury.   In criminal law, the willful assertion to a matter of fact, opinion, belief, or knowledge made by a witness in a judicial proceeding as part of his evidence, either upon oath or in any form allowed by law to be substituted for an oath, whether such evidence is given in open court, or in an affidavit, or otherwise, such assertion being material to the issue or point of inquiry, and known to such witness to be false.

Plaintiff.   The person who brings an action; the party who complains or sues in a personal action and is so named on the record.

Possession. The detention and control, or manual or ideal custody of anything for one's use and enjoyment, either as owner or proprietor of a qualified right in it, and either held personally or by another who exercises it in one's place and name. Possession does not necessarily connote ownership.

Postmortem. After death. A term generally applied to an autopsy or examination of a dead body to ascertain the cause of death; also the inquisition for that purpose by the coroner.

Power of attorney. An instrument authorizing another to act as one's agent or attorney; a letter of attorney.

Precedent. Adjudged case or decision of a court of justice, considered as furnishing an example or authority for an identical or similar case afterwards arising on a similar question of law.

Premium. The sum paid or agreed to be paid by an insured to the underwriter as the consideration for the insurance.

Preponderance. Greater weight of evidence, or evidence which is more credible and convincing.

Prima facie. *At first sight.* On the first appearance, on the face of it, so far as can be judged from the first disclosure.

Prima facie case. Such as will suffice until contradicted and overcome by other evidence; a case which has proceeded upon sufficient proof to that stage where it will support a finding, if evidence contrary to it is disregarded.

Principal. The employer or constitutor of an agent who gives authority to an agent or attorney to do some act for him; one who, being competent *sui juris* to do any act for his own benefit or on his own account, confides it to another person to do for him.

Privity of contract. That relationship or connection which exists between two or more contracting parties. It is essential to the maintenance of an action on any contract that there should subsist a privity between the plaintiff and defendant in respect to the matter sued on.

Probate. The act or process of proving a will.

Probate bond. Bond required by law to be given to the probate court or judge as incidental to proceedings in such courts, such as the bonds of executors, administrators, and guardians.

Probative. In the law of evidence, having the effect of proof, tending to prove, or actually proving.

Probative facts. In the law of evidence, facts which actually have the effect of proving facts sought; evidenciary facts; matters of evidence required to prove ultimate facts.

Proper lookout. Duty imposed on a motorist, requiring him to use care, prudence, watchfulness, and attention of an ordinarily prudent person under the same or similar circumstances.

Proximate. Immediate, nearest, direct, next in order; in its legal sense, closest in causal connection.

Proximate cause. That which in a natural and continuous sequence, unbroken by any efficient intervening cause, produces the injury, and without which the result would not have occurred.

Rate. In insurance, the agreed factor in determining an insurance premium.

Reasonable certainty rule. Permits recovery of damages only for such future suffering as is reasonably certain to result from the injury received. To authorize recovery under such rule for common injury, permanency of injury must be shown with reasonable certainty, which is not mere conjecture, or likelihood, or even a probability of such injury.

Reckless disregard of the rights of others. As used in automobile guest law, the voluntary doing by a motorist of an improper or wrongful act, or, with knowledge of existing conditions, the voluntary refraining from doing a proper or prudent act when such act, or failure to act, evinces entire abandonment of care; needless indifference to results which may follow and the reckless taking of chances, but without intent that any accident occur.

Reckless driving. Operation of an automobile with a reckless disregard of possible consequences and indifference to others' rights.

Reinsurance. A contract by which an insurer procures a third person to insure him against loss or liability by reason of the original insurance; a contract that one insurer makes with another to protect the latter from a risk already assumed. It binds the reinsurer to pay to the reinsured the whole loss sustained, in respect to the subject of the insurance, to the extent to which he is reinsured.

Release. Relinquishment, concession, or giving up of a right, claim, or privilege by the person in whom it exists, or to whom it accrues, to the person against whom it might have been demanded or enforced.

Relevancy. Applicability to the issue joined; that quality of evidence which renders it properly applicable in determining the truth and falsity of the matters in issue between the parties to a suit.

Remote cause. In the law of negligence, with respect to injury or accident, a cause which would not, according to the experience of mankind, lead to the event which happened; where the effect is uncertain, vague, or indeterminate, and does not follow necessarily.

Representation. A statement, express or implied, made by one contracting party to the other before or at the time of making the contract in regard to some past or existing fact, circumstance, or state of facts pertinent to the contract, which is influential in bringing about the agreement; an allegation of any facts by the applicant to the insurer, or vice versa, preliminary to making the contract and directly bearing upon it, having a plain and evident tendency to induce the making of the policy.

The statements may or may not be in writing and may be either express or by obvious implication. In relation to the contract of insurance, there is an important distinction between a representation and a *warranty*. The former, which precedes the contract of insurance and is no part of it, need be only materially true; the latter is a part of the contract and must be exactly and literally fulfilled or else the contract is broken and inoperative.

Reputation. Estimation in which one is held, the character or general opinion, good or bad, imputed to or held of a person by those of the community in which he resides.

Res adjudicata. A common but indefensible misspelling of *res judicata*. The latter term designates a point, question, or subject matter which was in controversy or dispute and has been authoritatively and finally settled by the decision of a court. Such issuable fact, once legally determined, is conclusive between the parties in the same action or subsequent proceeding.

Res gestae. *Things done.* Those circumstances which are the automatic and undesigned incidents of a particular litigated act and which may be separated from the act by a more or less appreciable lapse of time, and which are admissible when illustrative of such act; the whole of the transaction under investigation and every part of it.

Res gestae is an exception to the hearsay rule; it renders acts and declarations, which constitute a part of the things done and said, admissible in evidence even though they would otherwise come within the rule excluding hearsay evidence or self-serving declarations. The rule is extended to include not only declarations by the parties to the suit but, under certain circumstances, statements made by bystanders and strangers.

Res ipsa loquitur.   *The thing speaks for itself.* Rebuttable presumption that the defendant was negligent; the presumption arises upon proof that the instrumentality causing the injury was in the defendant's exclusive control, and that the accident is one which ordinarily does not happen in the absence of negligence.

Rescind.   To abrogate, annul, avoid, or cancel a contract; particularly, nullifying a contract by the act of a party; not merely to terminate the contract and release the parties from further obligation to each other, but to abrogate it from the beginning and restore the parties to the positions they would have occupied had no contract been made.

Respondeat superior.   *Let the master answer.* A master is liable in certain cases for the wrongful acts of his servant, being principal for his agents. The doctrine does not apply where the injury occurs while the servant is acting outside the legitimate scope of his authority.

Slander.   The speaking of base and defamatory words tending to prejudice another in his reputation, office, trade, business, or means of livelihood.

Oral defamation.   The speaking of faults and malicious words concerning another, whereby injury results to his reputation.

An essential element of slander is that slanderous words be spoken in the presence of someone other than the person being slandered; publication is always a material and issuable fact in action for slander. Hence, an oral defamation, heard only by one who does not understand the language in which it is spoken, is not slander.

Libel and slander are both methods of defamation; the former being expressed by print, writing, pictures, or signs; the latter by oral expressions.

Subpoena.   A process to cause a witness to appear and give testimony, commanding him to lay aside all pretenses and excuses and appear before a court or magistrate therein named at a time therein mentioned to testify for the party named under a penalty therein mentioned.

Subpoena duces tecum.   A process by which the court, at the instances of a suitor, commands a witness, who has or controls some document or paper pertinent to the issues of a pending controversy, to produce it at the trial.

Subrogation.   The substitution of one person in the place of another with reference to a lawful claim, demand, or right, so that he who is substituted succeeds to the rights of the other in relation to the debt or claim, and its rights, remedies, or securities.

Substituted service.   Service of process upon a defendant in any manner authorized by statute—other than personal service within the jurisdiction—as by publication, by mailing a copy to his last known address, or by personal service in another state.

Surety.   One who undertakes to pay more or do any other act in the event that his principal fails therein; one bound with his principal for the payment of a sum of money, or performance of some duty or promise, who is entitled to be indemnified by someone who ought to have paid or performed, if payment or performance be enforced against him.

Trap.   A device, as a pitfall, snare, or machine that shuts suddenly as with a spring, for taking game and other animal. Hence, any device or contrivance by which one may be caught unaware. The doctrine of trap as a grounds for recovery by trespassers is rested upon the theory that the owner expected trespassers and prepared an injury.

Trespasser.   One who enters the premises of another without invitation or permission, expressed or implied, but merely for his own convenience or out of curiosity; unlawful entry upon the land of another.

Unilateral.   One-sided, having relation to only one of two or more persons or things.

Unilateral Mistake.   Mistake or misunderstanding as to the terms or effects of a contract, made or entertained by one of the parties but not by the other.

Verdict.   The formal decision or finding made by a jury impaneled and sworn for the trial of a cause, and reported to the court upon the matters or questions duly submitted to them upon trial.

Verify.   To confirm or substantiate by oath. When used in a statute it ordinarily imports a verity attested by the sanctity of an oath; frequently used interchangeably with *swear*.

Waiver.   The intentional or voluntary relinquishment of a known right; renunciation, repudiation, abandonment, or surrender of some claim, right, or privilege, or of the opportunity to take advantage of some defect, irregularity, or wrong.

In insurance law, the doctrine is that if the insurer, with knowledge of facts which would bar existing primary liability, recognizes such primary liability by treating the policy as enforced, the insurer will not thereafter be allowed to plead such facts to avoid its primary liability.

Willful (or wanton) misconduct.   Failure to exercise ordinary care to prevent injury to a person who is actually known or reasonably expected to be within range of a dangerous act.

Index

This book has been set in 10 and 9 point Bodoni Book, leaded 2 points. Chapter numbers are 11 point News Gothic Bold and chapter titles are 14 point News Gothic Bold. The size of the type page is 27 by 46½ picas.